lonely p

Western USA

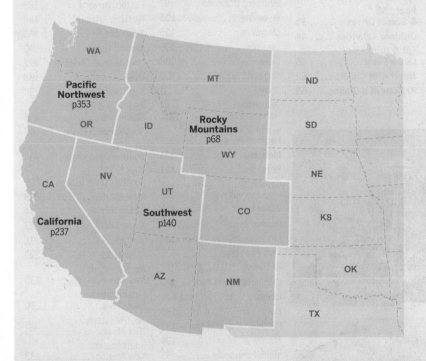

WA

Pacific
Northwest
p353

MT

ND

OR

ID

Rocky
Mountains
p68

SD

WY

NV

NE

CA

UT

California
p237

Southwest
p140

CO

KS

AZ

NM

OK

TX

Hugh McNaughtan, Brett Atkinson, Loren Bell, Greg Benchwick,
Andrew Bender, Sara Benson, Alison Bing, Cristian Bonetto,
Celeste Brash, Jade Bremner, Nate Cavalieri, Michael Grosberg,
Ashley Harrell, Carolyn McCarthy, Becky Ohlsen, Christopher Pitts,
Liza Prado, Josephine Quintero, Andrea Schulte-Peevers,
Helena Smith, John A Vlahides, Benedict Walker, Clifton Wilkinson

PLAN YOUR TRIP

SEATTLE P357

XUANLU WANG / SHUTTERSTOCK ©

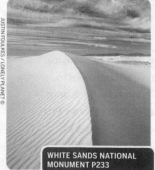

WHITE SANDS NATIONAL
MONUMENT P233

JUSTIN FOULKES / LONELY PLANET ©

ON THE ROAD

Contents

Welcome to Western USA

Landscapes and legends draw adventurers to the West, where a good day includes locavore dining, vineyard wine-sipping, Native American history and outdoor adventure.

Great Outdoors

When it comes to scenery in the West, the hyperbole is usually on point. Awesome. Epic. But what gives it extra punch? The sounds of adventure – woosh! splash! clink! – rippling across the landscape. Surfers, kayakers and beachcombers flock to the Western coastline, which stretches from sunny San Diego to the bluffs of central California and on to the rocky, moody beaches of Oregon and Washington. Red rocks, plunging gorges and prickly-pear deserts lure hikers and cyclists to the Southwest and the Grand Canyon. Meanwhile, the Rockies offer some of the world's best skiing and snowboarding.

Regional Food & Wine

Fish tacos in San Diego, Sonoran dogs in Tucson, trout and bison in the Rockies, green and red chiles in New Mexico and wild salmon in the Pacific Northwest. Regional specialties are as diverse as the landscapes. One commonality? Chefs and consumers alike are focusing on fresh and locally grown food, a locavore trend that started in the West. A movement that's also been embraced by wine producers, who are increasingly implementing organic and biodynamic growing principles. And speaking of winemaking, Napa and Sonoma now share the spotlight with Washington, Oregon and central California.

Urban Allure

Western cities have distinct personalities. In California there's the 'hey-bro' friendliness of San Diego, the Hollywood flash of Los Angeles and silicon-meets-bohemian in San Francisco. Further north in Seattle, cutting-edge joins homegrown, often over a cup of joe. Rootsy vibes and outdoor fun pair in Denver, while patio preening and spa pampering give Phoenix a strangely compelling spoiled-girl vibe. Artsy, historic Santa Fe is a world unto itself. And then there's Vegas, a glitzy neon playground where you can get hitched in the Elvis Chapel, spend your honeymoon in Paris and then bet the mortgage.

Hands-on History

Museums? Save 'em for later. First you'll want to climb a wooden ladder into a cliff dwelling, poke around the ruins of a Pony Express station, or simply join the congregation inside a 1700s Spanish mission. What else is there to explore in the West? Crumbling forts and trading posts. Abandoned ghost towns. Adobe pueblos. A former Titan Missile silo and the town that didn't exist – that's where the A-bomb was designed. Wander historic sites like these for up-close and evocative links to the region's rich, multilayered past.

Why I Love Western USA

By Christopher Pitts, Writer

Like so many people, I first fell in love with the West on a road trip. I remember the exact moment: sitting next to a campfire in Colorado and gazing up at the stars, which were so bright and thickly scattered that I could finally imagine them stretching into infinity. Everything else that followed lived up to that moment: the surrealistic desert landscapes, the coyotes and bison roaming beneath big cobalt skies, the wild and untamed Pacific Coast and, of course, those majestic national parks. All reasons why I finally chose to make the West my home.

For more about our writers, see p480

Above: Rocky Mountain National Park (p84)

Western USA

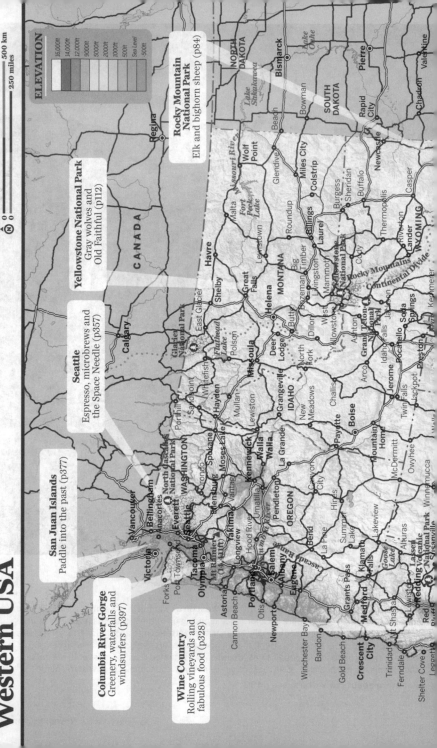

San Juan Islands
Paddle into the past (p377)

Seattle
Espresso, microbrews and
the Space Needle (p357)

Yellowstone National Park
Gray wolves and
Old Faithful (p112)

**Rocky Mountain
National Park**
Elk and bighorn sheep (p84)

Columbia River Gorge
Greenery, waterfalls and
windsurfers (p397)

Wine Country
Rolling vineyards and
fabulous food (p328)

ELEVATION

16,000ft
14,000ft
12,000ft
9000ft
5000ft
2000ft
1000ft
500ft
Sea Level
-500ft

N↑
0
0   250 miles
0   500 km

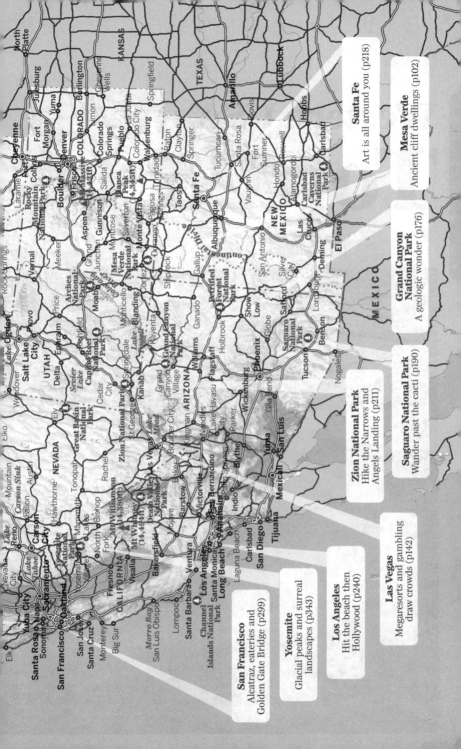

Santa Fe
Art is all around you (p218)

Mesa Verde
Ancient cliff dwellings (p102)

Grand Canyon National Park
A geologic wonder (p176)

Saguaro National Park
Wander past the cacti (p190)

Zion National Park
Hike the Narrows and Angels Landing (p211)

Las Vegas
Megaresorts and gambling draw crowds (p142)

Los Angeles
Hit the beach then Hollywood (p240)

Yosemite
Glacial peaks and surreal landscapes (p343)

San Francisco
Alcatraz, eateries and Golden Gate Bridge (p299)

Western USA's
Top 25

Yellowstone National Park

1 What makes the world's first national park (p112) so enduring? Geologic wonders for one thing, from geysers and fluorescent hot springs to fumaroles and bubbling mud pots. Then there's the wildlife: grizzlies, black bears, wolf packs, elk, bison and moose, roaming across some 3500 sq miles of wilderness. Pitch a tent in Yellowstone's own Grand Canyon, admire the Upper and Lower Falls, wait for Old Faithful to blow and hike through the primeval, fuming landscape for a real taste of what is truly the Wild West. Grand Prismatic Spring (p113)

San Francisco

2 Change is afoot in this boom-and-bust city, currently enjoying a very high-profile boom. Amid the growth, the fog and the clatter of old-fashioned trams, the diverse neighborhoods of San Francisco (p299) invite long days of wandering, with great indie shops, fabulous restaurants and bohemian nightlife. Highlights include peering into Alcatraz, strolling across the Golden Gate and dining inside the Ferry Building. And you must take at least one ride on the trolley. How cool is San Francisco? Trust us – turn that first corner to a stunning waterfront view, and you'll be hooked.

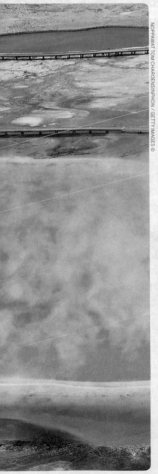

NOPPAWAT TOM CHAROENSINPHON / GETTY IMAGES ©

GAGAN KAUSHAL / 500PX ©

Grand Canyon National Park

3 The sheer immensity of the canyon (p176) is what grabs you at first – a two-billion-year-old rip across the landscape. But it's Mother Nature's artistic touches, from sun-dappled ridges and crimson buttes to lush oases and a ribbon-like river, that hold your attention and demand your return. To explore the canyon, take your pick of adventures: hiking, biking, rafting or mule riding. Or simply grab a seat along the Rim Trail and watch the earth change colors before you.

Los Angeles

4 A perpetual influx of dreamers, go-getters and hustlers gives this sprawling coastal city (p240) an energetic buzz. Learn the tricks of movie-making during a studio tour. Bliss out to acoustically perfect symphony sounds in the Walt Disney Concert Hall. Wander gardens and galleries at the hilltop Getty Museum. And stargazing? Take in the big picture at the revamped Griffith Observatory or look for stylish, earthbound 'stars' at the Grove. Ready for your close-up, darling?

Coastal Highways

5 A drive along America's stunning western coastline is road tripping at its finest. In California, Hwy 1 – also called the Pacific Coast Highway (p37) – Hwy 101 and I-5 pass dizzying sea cliffs, idiosyncratic beach towns and a few major cities: laid-back San Diego, rocker LA and beatnik San Francisco. North of the redwoods, Hwy 101 swoops into Oregon for windswept capes and rocky tide pools. Cross the Columbia River into Washington for wet-and-wild Olympic National Park. Bixby Creek Bridge (p294)

The Deserts

6 The saguaro cactus is one of the West's most enduring symbols. It's a hardy survivor in a landscape both harsh and unforgiving, but also strangely beautiful. Five deserts stretch across the Southwest and California, each with its own distinct climate. Each is also home to an amazing array of well-adapted reptiles, mammals and plants. This thriving diversity makes a stroll through the desert a wondrous, one-of-a-kind experience – try it at Saguaro National Park (p190).

JARED ROPELATO / SHUTTERSTOCK ©

California Wine Country

7 The Golden State is home to more than 100 wine regions. The rolling vineyards of Napa (p328), Sonoma and the Russian River Valley lure travelers north from San Francisco. Sample a world-class Cab in chichi Napa, enjoy a picnic in laid-back Sonoma, or cap off an outdoor adventure with a complex Pinot Noir near the Russian River. Further south, day trippers head to the lovely vineyards clustered east of Santa Barbara, a bucolic area made famous by the 2004 wine-centric movie *Sideways*.

Santa Fe & Taos

8 Santa Fe (p218) is an old city with a young soul. On Friday nights, art lovers flock to Canyon Rd to gab with artists, sip wine and explore more than 80 galleries. Art and history partner up in style within the city's consortium of museums, and the food and the shopping are first rate too. With that turquoise sky as a backdrop, the experience is darn near sublime. Artists also converge in adobe Taos, where the vibe is quirkier, with ski bums, off-the-grid Earth-shippers and a few celebs keeping things offbeat.

Native American History & Culture

9 The Southwest is home to a fascinating array of Native American sites. To learn about America's earliest inhabitants, climb into the ancient clifftop homes of Ancestral Puebloans at Mesa Verde National Park (pictured; p102) in Colorado. For living cultures, visit the modern-day Pueblo of Taos, or Arizona's Navajo and Hopi nations. As you'll discover here and in regional museums, many designs have religious significance.

Seattle

10 A cutting-edge Pacific Rim city with an uncanny habit of turning locally hatched ideas into global brands, Seattle (p357) has earned its place in the pantheon of 'great' US metropolises with a world-renowned music scene, a mercurial coffee culture and a penchant for internet-driven innovation. But, while Seattle's trendsetters rush to unearth the next big thing, city traditionalists guard its soul with distinct urban neighborhoods, a home-grown food culture and what is arguably the nation's finest public market, Pike Place (pictured).

Yosemite National Park

11 Meander through wildflower-strewn meadows in valleys carved by rivers and glaciers, whose hard, endless work makes everything look simply colossal here (p343). Thunderous waterfalls tumble over sheer cliffs, climbers scale the enormous granite walls, while hikers walk beneath ancient groves of giant sequoias, the planet's biggest trees. Even the subalpine meadows of Tuolumne are magnificently vast. For the most sublime views, perch at Glacier Point on a full-moon night or drive the high country's dizzying Tioga Rd in summer.

Rocky Mountain National Park

12 From behind the line of RVs growling along Trail Ridge Rd, Rocky Mountain National Park (p84) can feel a bit overrun. But with hiking boots laced and the trail unfurling beneath your feet, the park's majestic, untamed splendor becomes unforgettably personal. From epic ascents along the Longs Peak Trail and the Continental Divide to family-friendly romps to Calypso Falls, there's a vista for every ability and ambition.

San Juan Islands

13 Go back in time by hopping on a ferry to the San Juan Islands (p377), a low-key archipelago north of Puget Sound between Washington and Vancouver Island. Of the more than 450 'islands' (most are only rocky promontories), only about 60 are inhabited and just four are regularly served by ferries. Nature is the main influence here and each island has its own personality, both geographic and cultural. What can you do here? Start with cycling, kayaking and spotting orcas – then just sit back and relax.

Las Vegas

14 Just when you think you've got a handle on the West – majestic, sublime, soul-nourishing – here comes Vegas (p142) shaking her thing like a showgirl looking for trouble. Beneath the neon lights of the Strip, she puts on a dazzling show: dancing fountains, a spewing volcano, the Eiffel Tower. But she saves her most dangerous charms for the gambling dens trying to separate you from your money. Step away if you can for fine restaurants, Cirque du Soleil, Slotzilla and the Mob Museum.

Zion & Bryce Canyon National Parks

15 Towering red cliffs hide graceful waterfalls, narrow slot canyons and hanging gardens in Zion National Park (p211). This lush wonderland lies in the shadow of Angels Landing, the lofty terminus of one of the great North American day hikes.Photographers should scoot north to Bryce Canyon National Park, where pastel colored rock spires shimmer like trees in a magical forest of stone – a hypnotic, Tolkienesque place.

ANNA GORIN / GETTY IMAGES ©

Columbia River Gorge

16 Carved by the mighty Columbia as the Cascade Range was uplifted, the Columbia River Gorge (p397) is a geological marvel. With Washington State on its north side and Oregon on its south, the state-dividing gorge offers countless waterfalls and spectacular hikes, as well as an agricultural bounty of apples, pears and cherries. If you're into windsurfing or kiteboarding, head to the sporty town of Hood River, ground zero for these extreme sports. Whether you're a hiker, an apple lover or an adrenaline junkie, the gorge delivers. Multnomah Falls (p397)

Moab

17 Moab (p205) is the mountain-biking capital of the world, where the desert slickrock surrounding the town makes a perfect 'sticky' surface for knobbly tires. Challenging trails ascend steep bluffs, twist through forests and slam over 4WD roads into the wilds of canyon country. And you'll surely redefine adventure after ripping down 8000ft from Burro Pass through alpine streams, aspen groves, juniper scrub and desert slickrock along the Whole Enchilada. There's a reason why some Moab hotels have showers for bikes. One trip and you'll be hooked.

Portland

18 It's easy to brag about PDX, but no one will hassle you for it – after all, everyone loves this city (p385). It's as friendly as a big town, and home to a mix of students, artists, cyclists, hipsters, young families, old hippies, eco-freaks and everything in between. It has great food, music and culture aplenty, plus it's as sustainable as you can get. Come visit, but be careful – like everyone else, you might just want to move here.

Theme Parks

19 California is theme-park heaven, bringing Hollywood movie magic, Disney and roller coasters galore. Universal Studios Hollywood (p258) features movie-themed action rides and the Wizarding World of Harry Potter. Disneyland Park (p265) and neighboring Disney California Adventure are SoCal's most visited tourist attraction: beloved cartoon characters waltz arm in arm down Main Street, U.S.A., and fireworks explode over Sleeping Beauty Castle. Knott's Berry Farm (p266) was SoCal's original theme park. Top: The Simpsons Ride, Universal Studios

Monument Valley & Canyon de Chelly

20 'May I walk in beauty' is the final line of a famous Navajo prayer. Beauty takes many forms on the Navajos' sprawling reservation, but makes its most famous appearance at Monument Valley (p185), an otherworldly cluster of rugged buttes and stubborn towers. Beauty swoops in on the wings of birds at Canyon de Chelly, where farmers till the land near age-old cliff dwellings.

Route 66

21 As you step up to the counter at the Snow Cap Drive-In at Seligman, Arizona, you know a prank is coming – a squirt of fake mustard, perhaps, or ridiculously incorrect change. Though it's all a bit hokey, you'd be disappointed if the owner forgot to 'get you.' It's these kitschy, down-home touches that make the Mother Road (p35) so memorable. Begging burros, the Wigwam Motel, the neon signs of Tucumcari (pictured) – and a squirt of fake mustard beats a mass-consumption McBurger every time.

Snow Sports

22 The softest, lightest snow you'll ever ski combined with outrageous scenery and every type of terrain imaginable: Western resorts are some of the best in the world. Aspen (p92), Vail and Jackson Hole may sound like playgrounds for the rich and famous, but shredders and ski bums have always found a way to keep it real. Launch off a cornice, slalom through trees, grind in a terrain park or faceplant repeatedly while learning to snowboard: one thing's certain, you'll end the day with a snow-encrusted smile.

Glacier National Park

23 Yep, the rumors are true. The namesake attractions at Glacier National Park (p128) are melting away. There were 150 glaciers in the area in 1850; today there are 26. But even without the giant ice cubes, Montana's sprawling national park is worthy of an in-depth visit. Road warriors can maneuver the thrilling 50-mile Going-to-the-Sun Road; wildlife-watchers can scan for elk, wolves and grizzly (but hopefully not too close); and hikers have 700 miles of trails, trees and flora – including mosses, mushrooms and wildflowers – to explore.

Flagstaff

24 Another thing the West does well? Mountain towns. Where outdoorsy types drop in from the trail and the slopes to swap stories and savor the microbrews. Many of the best double as gateways to the country's finest national parks. One favorite? Flagstaff (p172), which sits ruggedly on the Colorado Plateau in northern Arizona. Highlights include a thriving ale trail, innovative farm-to-table eateries, an observatory and Route 66's awesome Museum Club. And we almost forgot to mention the Grand Canyon, just 80 miles north.

Microbreweries

25 Microbreweries are a specialty of the West, and you'll find at least one good one in outdoorsy towns from Missoula to Moab. Though usually closely identified with their home towns, these popular watering holes share a few commonalities: boisterous beer sippers, deep-flavored brews with locally inspired names, and cavernous tap rooms that smell of hops, sweat and adventure. Hiking, biking or climbing near Boulder? Celebrate post-adventure with one of the 30 beers on tap at Avery (p83).

Need to Know

For more information, see Survival Guide (p445)

Currency
US dollar ($)

Language
English

Visas
Visitors from Canada, the UK, Australia, New Zealand, Japan and many EU countries don't need visas for less than 90-day stays. Other nations, see https://travel.state.gov.

Money
ATMs widely available. Credit cards normally required for hotel reservations and car rentals.

Cell Phones
GSM multiband models will work in the USA. If you have an unlocked phone, you can find prepaid SIM cards fairly easily.

Time
The 11 states follow either Mountain Standard Time (GMT/UTC minus seven hours) or Pacific Standard Time (GMT/UTC minus eight hours).

When to Go

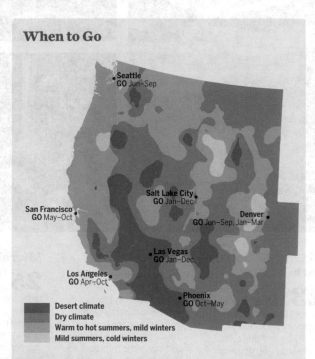

Seattle
GO Jun–Sep

Salt Lake City
GO Jan–Dec

San Francisco
GO May–Oct

Denver
GO Jun–Sep, Jan–Mar

Las Vegas
GO Jan–Dec

Los Angeles
GO Apr–Oct

Phoenix
GO Oct–May

- Desert climate
- Dry climate
- Warm to hot summers, mild winters
- Mild summers, cold winters

High Season
(Jun–Aug; Sep–Apr)

➡ Summer temperatures soar well above 100°F (38°C) and national parks are at maximum capacity.

➡ In winter hit the slopes in the mountains; giddy-up at southern Arizona dude ranches.

Shoulder (Apr & May; Sep & Oct)

➡ Clouds may blanket the southern coast (May and June).

➡ Mountain towns shut down in spring.

➡ A good time to visit national parks, with milder temperatures.

➡ Blooming spring flowers; fiery autumn colors.

Low Season
(Nov–Mar)

➡ Accommodation rates drop by the coast.

➡ Dark, wintery days, with snowfall in the mountains and heavier rains.

Websites

National Park Service (www.nps.gov) Information on national parks and monuments.

Recreation.gov (www.recreation.gov) Camping reservations on federally managed lands.

Lonely Planet (www.lonelyplanet.com/usa) Destination info, bookings and forums.

Roadside America (www.roadsideamerica.com) Find offbeat tourist attractions.

Important Numbers

To call any regular number, dial the area code, followed by the seven-digit number.

USA country code	☑1
International access code	☑011
Emergency	☑911
National Sexual Assault Hotline	☑800-656-4673
Directory assistance	☑411
Statewide road conditions	☑511

Exchange Rates

Australia	A$1	$0.74
Canada	C$1	$0.73
China	Y10	$1.45
Europe	€1	$1.09
Japan	¥100	$0.88
Mexico	MXN10	$0.53
New Zealand	NZ$1	$0.69
UK	£1	$1.29

For current exchange rates, see www.xe.com.

Daily Costs
Budget: Less than $100

➡ Campgrounds and hostel dorms: $10–45

➡ Free activities (beach, park concerts): $0

➡ Food at farmers markets, taquerias, food trucks: $6–12

➡ Bus, subway: $0–5

Midrange: $100–250

➡ Mom-and-pop motels, low-priced chains: $50–125

➡ Museums, national and state parks: $5–25

➡ Diners, good local restaurants: $10–35

➡ Economy car rental per day: from $20

Top End: More than $250

➡ B&Bs, boutique hotels, resorts: from $175

➡ Meal in top restaurant, excluding drinks: $30–100

➡ Hiring a guide; going to a show: from $100

➡ SUV or convertible rental per day: from $70

Opening Hours

Opening hours vary throughout the year, with many attractions and visitor centers open longer hours in high season. We've provided high-season hours.

Banks 8:30am–4:30pm Monday to Thursday, to 5:30pm Friday (some 9am–noon Saturday)

Bars 5pm–midnight Sunday to Thursday, to 2am Friday and Saturday

Cafes 7:30am–8pm

Restaurants 11am–2:30pm and 5pm–9pm; many Utah restaurants are closed on Sunday

Stores 10am–6pm Monday to Saturday, noon–5pm Sunday

Arriving in Western USA

Denver International Airport The easiest way to get from DIA to downtown is the train ($9, 35 minutes, every 15 minutes). The AB bus runs to Boulder ($9, 82 minutes, hourly). Shuttles run to all the major ski resorts.

Los Angeles International Airport Taxis cost about $47 to downtown; door-to-door shuttles from $17 for shared ride; free Shuttle G to Metro Green Line Aviation Station and free Shuttle C to the Metro Bus Center; FlyAway bus to downtown LA is $9.75.

Seattle-Tacoma International Airport Light-rail trains run regularly from the 4th floor of the parking garage to downtown ($3, 30 minutes, frequent); shuttle buses stop on the 3rd floor of the airport garage and cost from $18 one way; taxis cost from $42 to downtown (25 minutes).

Getting Around

Car The best option for travelers who leave urban areas to explore national parks and more remote areas. Drive on the right.

Train Amtrak can be slow due to frequent delays, but trains are a convenient option for travel along the Pacific Coast. Cross-country routes to Chicago run from the San Francisco area and Los Angeles.

Bus Cheaper and slower than trains; can be a good option for travel to cities not serviced by Amtrak.

For much more on **getting around**, see p460

If You Like...

Geology

Grand Canyon A 277-mile river cuts through two-billion-year-old rocks, whose geological secrets are revealed within a mile-high stack. (p176)

Yellowstone National Park Explosive geysers, rainbow-colored thermal pools and a supervolcano base – this 3472-sq-mile national park puts on a dazzling show. (p112)

Arches National Park Drive, hike or bike past sandstone arches, windows, fins and a precariously balanced rock. (p207)

White Sands National Monument Ripples of chalk-white dunes mesmerize photographers and sand sledders alike. (p233)

Carlsbad Caverns National Park Descend to the 1800ft-long Big Room – a veritable underground cathedral concealed in a massive cave system. (p22)

Chiricahua National Monument A rugged wonderland of rock chiseled by rain and wind into pinnacles, bridges and balanced rocks. (p193)

Volcanoes The earth's shifting crust formed powerful volcanoes in Washington. Hike around Mt Rainier or visit Mt St Helens to learn about its mighty 1980 eruption. (p383)

Dinosaur National Monument Touch a 150-million-year-old fossil at one of the largest dinosaur fossil beds in North America. (p204)

Old West Sites

The Southwest, particularly Arizona and New Mexico, is your best bet if you want to walk in the footsteps of cowboys and gunslingers at sites within a day's drive of each other.

Lincoln Historic Site Billy the Kid's old stomping – and shooting – grounds during the Lincoln County War. (p235)

Tombstone Famous for the gunfight at the OK Corral, this dusty town is also home to Boot Hill Graveyard and the Bird Cage Theater. (p192)

Whiskey Row A block of Victorian-era saloons in downtown Prescott has survived fires, filmmakers and tourists. (p170)

Pony Express Stations Rte 50 across Nevada, known as the Loneliest Road, traces the route of the Pony Express. (p160)

Virginia City Site of the Comstock Lode silver strike, this hard-charging mining town gained notoriety in Mark Twain's semi-autobiographical book *Roughing It.* (p159)

Durango & Silverton Narrow Gauge Railroad Channel the Old West on the steam-driven train that's chugged between Durango and Silverton for 125 years. (p103)

Film & TV Locations

Los Angeles Hollywood was born here, and iconic celluloid sites beckon from Mulholland Dr to Malibu. (p240)

Monument Valley Stride John Wayne tall beneath the iconic red monoliths that starred in seven of the Duke's Westerns. (p185)

Las Vegas Bad boys and their hijinks brought Sin City back to the big screen in *Ocean's Eleven* and *The Hangover.* (p142)

Moab The directors of *Thelma & Louise* and *127 Hours* shot their most dramatic scenes in nearby parks. (p205)

Albuquerque The backdrop for the TV series *Better Call Saul* and hit predecessor *Breaking Bad.* (p214)

Kanab From *Stagecoach* to *Planet of the Apes*, Kanab has been a Hollywood favorite since the 1930s. (p211)

Top: Arches National Park (p207), Utah

Bottom: Venice Beach (p253), Los Angeles

Fabulous Food

San Francisco Temptations await: real-deal taquerias and trattorias, top-notch Vietnamese, magnificent farmers markets and trailblazing chefs. (p299)

Chez Panisse Chef Alice Waters revolutionized California cuisine in the '70s with seasonal Bay Area locavorian cooking. (p327)

Santa Fe The best Southwestern flavors are found in the chile-laced New Mexican capital. (p218)

Las Vegas Great food is never a gamble in Sin City, with famous chefs and flavor-rich world cuisine. (p142)

Food Trucks LA sparked the mobile gourmet revolution, but the food-truck craze also thrives, well, everywhere. (p319)

Green Chiles Roasted, stewed and slathered over enchiladas and cheeseburgers. Celebrate them at the Hatch Chile Festival. (p104)

Emerging Wine Regions

Verde Valley Wine Country Home to an up-and-coming Arizona wine trail that winds through Cottonwood, Jerome and Cornville. (p173)

Willamette Valley Outside Portland, OR, this fertile region produces some of the tastiest Pinot Noir on the planet. (p395)

Walla Walla Washington's hot wine-growing region, with its namesake town as a very pretty centerpiece. (p384)

Santa Barbara Wine Country Large-scale winemaking since the 1980s, and the climate is perfect for Pinots near the coast and further inland. (p290)

Hiking

Grand Canyon Rim to Rim Earn bragging rights on this classic 17-mile trek. (p177)

Red Rock Country Hike to vortexes in Sedona, hoodoos in Bryce Canyon, and slender spans in Arches and Canyonlands National Parks. (p211)

Rocky Mountain National Park Longs Peak gets all the buzz, but there are summits, waterfalls, glacial lakes and trails galore. (p84)

Wonderland Trail Circumnavigate Mt Rainier's lofty peak – it's 93 miles of spectacular nature. (p382)

Maroon Bells There's a reason Aspen's breathtaking alpine backdrop has become the quintessential Colorado photograph. (p92)

Zion National Park Slot canyons, hanging gardens and lofty scrambles make this stunner an unmissable destination. (p211)

Highline Trail A natural high in Glacier National Park, passing bighorn sheep, mountain wildflowers and snowcapped peaks, with a side-hike to glacier views. (p128)

National Parks

Few things are as quintessentially American as the national parks, and the crown jewels are scattered across the West.

Yellowstone The nation's first park is a stunner: lakes, waterfalls, mountains, wildlife galore and a cauldron of geysers and springs. (p112)

Grand Canyon Two billion years of geological history? Yeah, yeah, that's cool, but have you seen that view? (p176)

Grand Teton Grazing bison, prowling grizzlies and snowcapped dagger peaks erupting from the valley floor. (p117)

Yosemite Flanked by El Capitan and Half Dome, Yosemite Valley is indeed cathedral-like, but the lush Sierra Nevada backcountry will have you singing hallelujah, too. (p343)

Southern Utah There's too much red-rock goodness in Utah to narrow it down to one fave. Arches, Canyonlands, Bryce, Zion, Escalante – see 'em all! (p207)

Great Sand Dunes You can rub your eyes all you like, this massive sea of sand is no mirage. It's also one of the quietest places in the US. (p63)

Weird Stuff

Route 66 This two-lane ode to Americana is dotted with wacky roadside attractions. (p35)

Burning Man Festival A temporary city in the Nevada desert hosts a week of self-expression, gifting and blowing sand. (p161)

Roswell Did a UFO crash outside Roswell, NM, in 1947? The truth is out there. (p236)

Seattle's Public Sculptures In Fremont, look for a car-eating troll, a human-faced dog, and folks waiting, and waiting, for the train. (p362)

Venice Boardwalk Gawk at the human zoo, which includes chainsaw-jugglers, medical marijuana 'clinicians' and Speedo-clad snake-charmers. (p253)

Mini Time Machine Museum of Miniatures The exhibits get small – very small – at this whimsical museum in Tucson. (p190)

Museums

Getty Center & Getty Villa Art museums as beautiful as their ocean views in west LA and Malibu. (p251)

Los Angeles County Museum of Art More than 150,000 works of art spanning the ages and crossing all borders. (p250)

California Academy of Sciences SF's natural-history museum breathes 'green' in its eco-certified design, with a four-story rainforest and living roof. (p315)

Meow Wolf Just one of Santa Fe's fabulous cultural treasures, but definitely the most far out. (p218)

Heard Museum Highlights the history and culture of Southwestern tribes. (p161)

Museum of Pop Culture Enjoy a little fantasy, a little sci-fi and a lot of rock and roll at this Seattle museum. (p359)

Native American History & Culture

Mesa Verde National Park Climb to cliff dwellings that housed Ancestral Puebloans more than 700 years ago. (p102)

Indian Pueblo Cultural Center Essential introduction to New Mexico's 19 Pueblos. (p214)

Taos Pueblo Tour the best example of original Pueblo architecture, still occupied today. (p228)

Museum of Indian Arts & Culture Excellent overview of the origins and history of all the Native peoples living in the Southwest. (p221)

Little Bighorn Battlefield National Monument Native American battlefields where General George Custer made his

Durango & Silverton Narrow Gauge Railroad (p103), Colorado

famous 'last stand' against the Lakota Sioux. (p125)

Chaco Canyon The enigmatic remains of what was once the cultural hub of the Four Corners, some 1000 years ago. (p230)

Petroglyph National Monument One of many sites at which to ponder ancient petroglyphs, with some 23,000 examples. (p215)

Wheelwright Museum of the American Indian Sublime collection of Navajo, Zuni and Hopi jewelry. (p218)

Spas & Resorts

Ojo Caliente Minerals Springs Resort & Spa Premier hot springs retreat at this 145-year-old resort in northern New Mexico. (p226)

Riverbend Hot Springs Soak in hot springs beside the Rio Grande, where pools bubble with soothing, hydro-healing warmth. (p231)

Phoenix & Scottsdale Honeymooners, families, golfers – there's a resort for every type of traveler within a few miles of Camelback Rd. (p161)

Las Vegas Mandalay Bay, Cosmopolitan and other top hotels offer lavish resort amenities. (p142)

Sheraton Wild Horse Pass Resort & Spa On the Gila Indian Reservation, this resort embraces its Native American heritage with style. (p165)

Month by Month

January

Skiers and snowboarders descend on lofty ski resorts. Palm Springs and the southern deserts welcome travelers seeking warmer climes and saguaro-dotted landscapes.

☆ Rose Parade

This famous New Year's Day parade of flower-festooned floats, marching bands and prancing equestrians draws about 700,000 spectators to Pasadena, CA, before the Rose Bowl college football game. (p256)

☆ Sundance Film Festival

Park City, UT, unfurls the red carpet for indie filmmakers, actors and moviegoers who flock to the mountain town in late January for a week of cutting-edge films. (p201)

☆ National Cowboy Poetry Gathering

Wranglers and ropers gather in Elvo, NV, for a week of poetry readings and folklore performances (www.nationalcowboy poetrygathering.org). Started in 1985, this event has inspired cowboy poetry readings across the region.

February

It's the height of ski season, but there are plenty of distractions for those not racing down the slopes – low-desert wildflowers bloom, whales migrate off the California coast, and dude ranches saddle up in southern Arizona.

☆ Carnival in Colorado

Mardi Gras meets the mountains in Breckenridge (www.gobreck.com), where folks celebrate with a street party, live jazz and, well, fire dancers.

☆ Oregon Shakespeare Festival

In Ashland, tens of thousands of theater fans party with the Bard at this nine-month festival (that's right!), which kicks off in February and features world-class plays and Elizabethan drama. (p408)

☆ Tucson Gem & Mineral Show

At the largest mineral and gem show in the US, held the second full weekend in February, about 250 dealers sell jewelry, fossils, crafts and lots of rocks. Lecture seminars and a silent auction round out the weekend. (p188)

March

Ah spring, when a young man's fancy turns to thoughts of...beer! Jet skis! Parties! March is spring-break season, when hordes of college students converge on Arizona's lakes. Families ski or visit parks in warmer climes.

☆ Spring Whale-Watching Week

Gray whales migrate along the Pacific Coast. Around Oregon's Depoe Bay, it's semi-organized, with docents and special viewpoints. The northward migration happens through June.

☆ Spring Training

Major-league baseball fans head to southern Arizona in March and early April for the preseason Cactus League (www.cactusleague.com), when some of the best pro teams play ball in Phoenix and Tucson.

☆ McDowell Mountain Music Festival

This nonprofit Phoenix music fest (http://mmmf.com) pulls in big names – think Beck, the Avett Brothers and Trombone Shorty – and donates the proceeds to local charities. Also a good spot to check out up-and-coming local bands.

April

Wildflowers bloom in California's high deserts while migrating birds swoop into nature preserves in southern Arizona. For ski resorts, it's the end of the season, meaning slightly lower room prices.

☆ Coachella Music & Arts Festival

Indie rock bands, cult DJs, superstar rappers and pop divas converge outside Palm Springs for this musical extravaganza (www.coachella.com), now held on two consecutive long weekends in mid-April.

☆ Gathering of Nations

More than 3000 Native American dancers and singers from the US and Canada compete in this powwow in late April in Albuquerque, NM. There's also an Indian market with more than 800 artists and craftspeople. (p215)

May

A great time to visit most national parks. With children still in school, the masses don't show until Memorial Day weekend, the last weekend of the month.

🎊 Cinco de Mayo

Celebrate the victory of Mexican forces over the French army at the Battle of Puebla on May 5, 1862, with margaritas, music and merriment. Denver (www.cincodemayodenver.com), Los Angeles and San Diego (www.cincodemayooldtown.com) do it in style.

🏃 Bay to Breakers

Tens of thousands run costumed, naked and/or clutching beer from Embarcadero to Ocean Beach in San Francisco on the third Sunday in May. The race dates from 1912. (p311)

🎊 Boulder Creek Festival

Start the summer in the Rockies on Memorial Day weekend with food, drink, music, a rubber duck race and glorious sunshine. It closes with Bolder Boulder, a 10km race celebrated (and run) with all kinds of wacky merriment accompanying it. (p82)

☆ Sasquatch! Music Festival

Indie music fans converge on the outdoor Gorge Amphitheater in George, WA, near the Columbia River Gorge, for live music on Memorial Day weekend (www.sasquatchfestival.com).

June

High season begins for most of the West. Rugged passes are open, rivers are overflowing with snowmelt and mountain wildflowers are blooming. There may be gray fog (June gloom) over southern California beaches.

🎊 Pride Month

California's LGBTQ pride celebrations occur throughout June, with costumed parades, coming-out parties, live music and more. The biggest, bawdiest celebrations are in Los Angeles (lapride.org) and San Francisco. (p311)

☆ Telluride Bluegrass Festival

In mid-June, join 'Festivarians' for four days of camping and the high lonesome sounds of bluegrass in the mountain-flanked beauty of Telluride, CO. (p99)

☆ Electric Daisy Carnival

The world's largest EDM (electronic dance music) fest, the Electric Daisy Carnival (www.electricdaisycarnival.com) is a nonstop three-night party with DJs, carnival rides, art installations and performers at the Las Vegas Motor Speedway.

July

Vacationers head to beaches, theme parks, mountain resorts, and state and national parks. Broiling desert parks are best avoided.

🎆 Independence Day

Across the West, communities celebrate America's birth with rodeos, music festivals, barbecues, parades and fireworks on July 4.

☆ Aspen Music Festival

From early July to mid-August, top-tier classical performers put on spectacular shows while students from orchestras led by sought-after conductors bring street corners to life with smaller groups (www.aspenmusicfestival.com).

🍷 Oregon Brewers Festival

During this fun beer festival in Portland, about 85,000 microbrew lovers eat, drink and whoop it up on the banks of the Willamette River. Held the last full weekend in July. (p390)

🎆 Comic-Con International

'Nerd Prom' is the alt-nation's biggest annual convention of comic-book geeks, sci-fi and animation lovers, and pop-culture memorabilia collectors (www.comic-con.org). It takes over San Diego in mid-July.

☆ Cheyenne Frontier Days

Celebrate the American cowboy with roping, riding and a parade at this 115-year-old Wyoming rodeo. (p106)

August

Learn about Native American culture at art fairs, markets and ceremonial gatherings across the Southwest. Rodeos are popular in the West.

◉ Santa Fe Indian Market

Santa Fe's most famous festival is held the third week of August on the historic plaza where more than 1100 artists from about 220 tribes and Pueblos exhibit. (p220)

🎆 Old Spanish Days Fiesta

A celebration of early rancho culture with parades, a rodeo, crafts exhibits and shows in Santa Barbara (www.oldspanishdays-fiesta.org) in early August.

✖ Hatch Chile Festival

On Labor Day weekend, join green chile lovers in Hatch, NM, for a parade, a mariachi competition and numerous chile-eating contests.

◉ Perseids

Peaking in mid-August, these annual meteor showers are the best time to catch shooting stars with your naked eye or a digital camera. Try darksky.org for info. For optimal viewing, head into the southern deserts.

September

Summer's last hurrah is the Labor Day holiday weekend. It's a particularly nice time to visit the Pacific Northwest, where nights are cool and days are reliably sunny. Fall colors begin to appear in the Rockies.

🎆 Burning Man

Outdoor celebration of self-expression known for elaborate art displays, an easygoing barter system, blowing sand and the final burning of the man. This temporary city rises in the Nevada desert the week before Labor Day. (p161)

🍷 Great American Beer Festival

This three-day celebration of beer, held in Denver in late September or early October, is so popular it always sells out in advance, with 700 US breweries getting in on the sudsy action. More than 3500 beers available. (p71)

☆ Bumbershoot

In early September, Seattle's biggest arts and cultural event hosts hundreds of musicians, artists, comedians, writers and theater troupes on various stages. (p364)

🎆 Santa Fe Festival & Burning of Zozobra

The original Burning Man (Old Man Gloom) – torched every September since 1924 – is the highlight of this 10-day fiesta. (p220)

October

Shimmering aspens lure road-trippers to Colorado and northern New Mexico for the annual fall show. Watch for ghouls, ghosts and hard-partying maniacs as Halloween, on October 31, approaches.

✈ International Balloon Fiesta

Look to the skies in early October for the world's biggest gathering of hot-air balloons in Albuquerque, NM. (p215)

✈ Halloween Carnivals

Hundreds of thousands of costumed revelers come out to play in LA's West Hollywood LGBTQ neighborhood for all-day partying, dancing, kids' activities and live entertainment (www.weho.org/visitors/events-in-the-city/halloween-carnaval).

☆ Litquake

Author readings, discussions and literary events, such as the legendary pub crawl in San Francisco (www.litquake.org), in mid-October.

◉ Sedona Arts Festival

This fine-art show (www.sedonaartsfestival.org) overflows with jewelry, ceramics, glass and sculptures in early October when 125 artists exhibit their works at Sedona's Red Rock High School.

November

Temperatures drop across the West. Most coastal areas, deserts and parks are less busy, with the exception of the Thanksgiving holiday. Ski season begins.

✈ Día de los Muertos

Mexican communities honor dead ancestors on November 2 with costumed parades, sugar skulls, graveyard picnics, candlelight processions and fabulous altars.

♉ Wine Country Thanksgiving

More than 160 wineries in the Willamette Valley (www.willamettewines.com) open their doors to the public for three days in late November.

⚡ Yellowstone Ski Festival

This Thanksgiving week celebration at West Yellowstone (www.skirunbikemt.com/yellowstone-ski-festival.html) is a great time for ski buffs and newcomers alike. Highlights include ski clinics and races. Nordic skiing kicks off around this time too.

December

'Tis the season for nativity scenes, holiday light shows and other celebrations of Christmas. The merriment continues through New Year's Eve. Expect crowds and higher prices at ski resorts.

✈ Holiday Light Displays

Communities decorate boats, parks and shopping malls with twinkling lights. In California, watch colorful boat parades in Newport Beach and San Diego, or check out displays in LA's Griffith Park Zoo. The Desert Botanical Gardens are aglow in Phoenix, as is the Tlaquepaque Arts & Crafts Village in Sedona.

✈ Snow Daze

Vail, CO, marks the opening of the mountain with a week-long festival (www.vail.com/events) featuring an expo village, parties and plenty of big-name live performances.

Itineraries

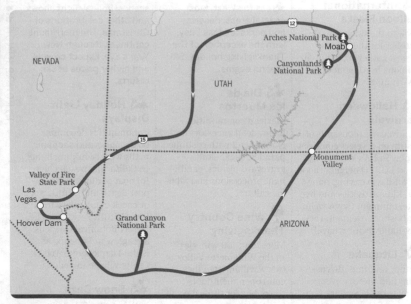

 2 WEEKS Best of the Southwest

Cameras get a workout on this tour, which spotlights the most iconic sites in the Southwest. You'll loop past the region's most famous city, its biggest canyon and its most breathtaking red-rock scenery.

Start in **Las Vegas** and spend a few days traveling the world on the Strip. Partied out? Swoop east past **Hoover Dam**, then say hello to the **Grand Canyon**. Spend two days exploring America's most famous park. For a once-in-a-lifetime experience, descend from the South Rim into the chasm on a mule and spend the night at Phantom Ranch on the canyon floor. From the Grand Canyon head northeast to **Monument Valley**, with scenery straight out of a Hollywood Western, and then to the national parks in Utah's southeast corner – they're some of the most visually stunning in the country. Hike the shape-shifting canyons of **Canyonlands National Park**, mountain bike slickrock outside **Moab**, or take a photo of Balanced Rock in **Arches National Park**. Drive west along a spectacular stretch of pavement, Hwy 12, until it hooks up with I-15. Swing south for a sunset meditation at **Valley of Fire State Park**, before heading back to Las Vegas.

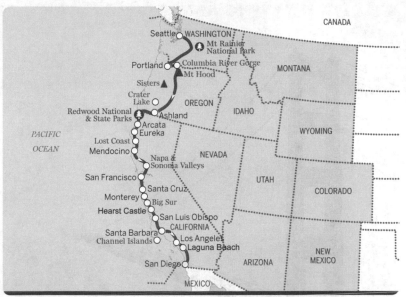

Winding Down the West Coast

Hug a tree, surf a wave and taste the fresh deliciousness of West Coast fare on this nature-lover's trip, which ribbons from Seattle to San Diego.

Kick off with fresh-roasted coffee in java-loving **Seattle** and check out the city's sprawling food markets, microbreweries and waterfront. Heading south, visit **Mt Rainier National Park**, where superb hiking trails and relaxing inns nestle beneath the snow-covered peak. Continue to the cutting-edge city of **Portland**, known for its sprawling parks, eco-minded residents and progressive urbanism – plus food carts, coffeehouse culture and great nightlife. Wonder at waterfalls and indulge in fresh roadside produce with a scenic drive east along the **Columbia River Gorge**, then turn south to get to **Mt Hood** for winter skiing or summer hiking. Further adventures await at the **Sisters**, a trio of 10,000ft peaks, and the striking blue waters of **Crater Lake**. Catch a Shakespearian play in sunny **Ashland**, then trade the mountains for the foggy coast. Enter California via Hwy 199 and stroll through the magnificent old-growth forests in **Redwood National and State Parks**.

Hug the coast as it meanders south through funky **Arcata** and seaside **Eureka**, lose yourself on the **Lost Coast**, and catch Hwy 1 through quaint **Mendocino**, where the scenic headlands and rugged shoreline make a wander mandatory. For wine tasting with a photogenic backdrop, travel inland to the rolling vineyards of the **Napa and Sonoma Valleys**, then continue south to romantically hilly **San Francisco**. Return to scenic Hwy 1 through surf-loving **Santa Cruz**, stately bayfront **Monterey** and beatnik-flavored **Big Sur**. In no time, you'll reach the surreal **Hearst Castle** and laid-back, collegiate **San Luis Obispo**. Roll into Mediterranean-esque **Santa Barbara** for shopping and wine tasting then hop aboard a ferry in Ventura to the wildlife-rich **Channel Islands**. The pull from **Los Angeles** is strong. Go ahead – indulge your Hollywood fantasies then stroll the rugged hills of Griffith Park, followed by a cruise through LA's palm-lined neighborhoods. After racking up a few sins in the City of Angels, move south to wander the bluffs of **Laguna Beach** then cruise into picture-perfect **San Diego**.

JOHN ELK III / GETTY IMAGES ©

Top: Golden Gate Bridge (p309), San Francisco

Bottom: Folk dancers, Albuquerque (p214)

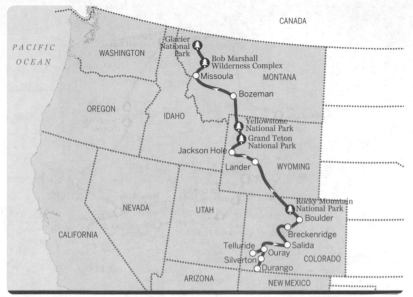

3 WEEKS Rocky Mountain High

Pack your bathing suit, mountain bike and hiking boots for this high-altitude cruise atop the Continental Divide; it's big skies, big peaks and big wildlife the whole way.

Spend your first two days enjoying craft beers and singletrack mountain-biking trails in **Durango**, a fine mountain town. From here, take the Million Dollar Hwy (Hwy 550) north through the San Juan Mountains, sightseeing in **Silverton** and dipping into hot springs in **Ouray**. Take a side trip to **Telluride** for a festival – there's one almost every weekend in summer. From Montrose, drive east on Hwy 50 to the Arkansas River Valley and white-water rafting through Brown's Canyon National Monument in **Salida**. Hwy 24 continues past Colorado's tallest peaks; finish your first week in style with an overnight stay in historic **Breckenridge**.

Enjoy tubing, happy hour and people-watching in funky **Boulder** then twist up to **Rocky Mountain National Park** to hike and horseback ride. While here, drive the thrilling Trail Ridge Rd up above the treeline. Continue north on I-25. In Wyoming, take I-80 west to Hwy 287; follow this highway to **Lander** for rock climbing.

Continue north to **Jackson Hole**, another fun gateway town. Anchored by a central park surrounded by chic stores and cowboy bars, it's a good place to relax, indulge in a gourmet meal or spend the night before rafting the Snake River. From here, it's an easy glide north into **Grand Teton National Park**, a scenic spot for a lazy lake day and bison photo-ops. Next up is mighty **Yellowstone National Park**, where geysers, bears and hiking are highlights.

Start your last week with a drive on the gorgeous Beartooth Hwy, following it into Montana then hooking onto I-90 west to **Bozeman** and **Missoula**; both are good places to stock up before the final push. Serious wilderness awaits in the **Bob Marshall Wilderness Complex**, while **Glacier National Park** is a place to visit now – there are still some 26 glaciers hanging tight, but they may not be there for long. Scan for wildlife on a hike, then end with a drive on the stunning Going-to-the-Sun Road.

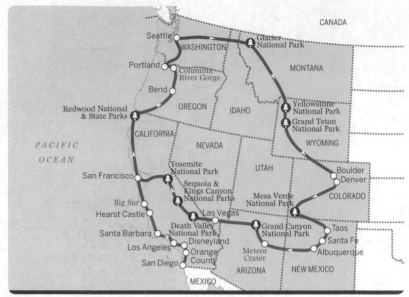

4 WEEKS Western US Grand Tour

This lasso loop corrals the best of the West as it rolls north along the California coast, cruises through the lush landscapes of the Pacific Northwest, the alpine towns of the Rockies and the glowing red-rock beauty of the Southwest, with a final swing back into California for a hit-parade tour of the state's national parks.

From sunny **San Diego**, follow Hwy 1 north through the surf-loving coastal villages of **Orange County**, detouring to **Disneyland** before driving into shiny **Los Angeles**. Continue up the coast on scenic Hwy 1, stopping to shop and sample wine in glossy **Santa Barbara**. Gawk at gawdy **Hearst Castle** then continue north through woodsy **Big Sur**. Dine and shop then wander through Alcatraz in bohemian **San Francisco**. Return to Hwy 1 for the quirky towns dotting the northern California coast.

View the big trees in **Redwood National and State Parks** and continue into Oregon, taking time for outdoor fun in **Bend**. Soak in the greenery while traveling west along the **Columbia River Gorge**, then spend a few days savoring brews and views in **Portland**. Zip up the Space Needle in **Seattle** and drive east into wide-open Montana, heading for the outdoor wonders of **Glacier National Park**. Continue south into **Yellowstone National Park** where Old Faithful blasts regularly beside its namesake lodge, and sightseers brake for buffalo. Swoosh below majestic peaks in **Grand Teton National Park** before swinging southeast through Wyoming's vast cowboy plains.

In Colorado, breathe deep in outdoorsy **Boulder** then uncover current hot spots in burgeoning **Denver**. The mining towns of central Colorado are next, followed by **Mesa Verde National Park**. Just south in New Mexico, artist meccas **Taos** and **Santa Fe** are fab stops for one-of-a-kind gifts. Slurp green chile in **Albuquerque** and follow Route 66 west into Arizona, stopping at **Meteor Crater** before detouring north for **Grand Canyon National Park**. Continue west to **Las Vegas**, then drive into central California for **Death Valley National Park**, and **Sequoia & Kings Canyon National Parks**, concluding with **Yosemite National Park**. Complete the loop with a glass of Californian wine in **San Francisco**.

Plan Your Trip
Route 66 & Scenic Drives

Underground minerals drew prospectors and adventurers to the West in the 19th and 20th centuries. Today, the allure is in the above-ground treasures: the stunning drives. From desert backroads to coastal highways to mountain-hugging thrill rides to the iconic Mother Road, the West is chock-full of picturesque byways and backroads.

Route 66

A wigwam motel. A meteor crater. Begging burros. And a solar-powered Ferris wheel overlooking the Pacific Ocean. Hmm, looks like 'Get your kitsch on Route 66' might be a better slogan for the scrubby stretch of Mother Road running through California, Arizona and New Mexico. It's a bit off the beaten path, but folks along the way will be very glad you're here.

Why Go

History, scenery and the open road. This alluring combination is what makes a Route 66 road trip so enjoyable. Navigators should note that I-40 and Route 66 overlap through much of New Mexico and Arizona.

In New Mexico, the neon signs of Tucumcari are a fun-loving welcome to the West. They also set the mood for adventure – the right mood to have before dropping into the scuba-ready **Blue Hole** (☏575-472-3763; http://santarosabluehole.com; 1085 Blue Hole Rd; parking $5; ⊙8am-8pm) in Santa Rosa. Fuel up on lip-smacking green chile stew at Frontier (p35) in Albuquerque then grab a snooze at the 1937-built **El Rancho motel** (☏505-863-9311; www.elranchohotel.com; 1000 E Hwy 66; r $98-116, motel r $54-74; [P][🖥][❄]) – John Wayne slept here! – in Gallup.

Road-Trip Necessities

Top Tips

A prepared road-tripper is a happy road-tripper, especially in the West, with its lonely roads and unpredictable weather.

Pack a spare tire and a tool kit (eg jack, jumper cables, ice scraper), as well as emergency equipment; consider buying a roadside safety kit.

Bring good maps, especially if you're touring away from highways; don't depend on GPS units or phones as they may not work in remote areas.

Carry extra water. You may need it if the car breaks down in the desert. Fill up the tank regularly; gas stations can be few and far between.

Always carry your driver's license and proof of insurance.

Best Roadside Dining

Hell's Backbone Grill (p210), Highway 12, Boulder, UT

Asylum Restaurant (p170), Highway 89/89A, Jerome, AZ

Scenic Drives

0 ▬▬▬▬▬▬ 1000 km
0 ▬▬▬▬▬▬ 500 miles

PACIFIC
OCEAN

WA

MT

OR

ID

WY

NV   UT

CA

CO

AZ

NM

1 Route 66
2 Pacific Coast Highway
3 Highway 89/89A
4 Million Dollar Highway
5 Beartooth Highway
6 Highway 12
7 High Road to Taos
8 Going-to-the-Sun Road
9 Historic Columbia
      River Highway

In Arizona, swoop off the highway for a grand drive through Petrified Forest National Park (p186). First up? Sweeping views of the Painted Desert. Trade panoramas for close-up views in the southern section of the park, where fossilized 225-million-year-old logs are clustered beside the main park road. You can snooze in a concrete tipi in Holbrook, west of the park. Next stop is the 'Take It Easy' town of Winslow where there's a girl, my Lord, in a flatbed Ford... Snap a photo of the famous corner then savor a spectacular dinner in the Turquoise Room at La Posada Hotel. Meteor Crater (p188), east of Flagstaff, is a mighty big hole in the ground – and a good place to slow down and catch your breath. From here, Route 66 parallels the train tracks into energetic Flagstaff, passing the wonderful **Museum Club** (☑928-526-9434; www.themuseumclub.com; 3404 E Rte 66; ⊙11am-2am), a cabin-like roadhouse where everyone's having fun or is about to. Next up is Williams, a railroad town lined with courtyard motels and brimming with small-town charm.

Seligman is a quirky little village that greets travelers with retro motels, a roadkill cafe and a squirt of fake mustard at the Snow Cap Drive-In (p188). Burma Shave signs share funny advice on the way to

Grand Canyon Caverns, where you'll be lured 21 stories underground for a tour or possibly an overnight stay. From here, highlights include an eclectic general store in Hackberry, the **Route 66 museum** (☑928-753-9889; www.gokingman.com; 120 W Andy Devine Ave; adult/senior/child 12yr & under $4/3/free; ⊙9am-5pm, last entry at 4pm) in Kingman and hay-loving burros in Oatman.

Things stay sun-baked in California the road swoops into the Mojave Desert and passes ghost towns heralded by lonesome railroad markers. In Victorville, the Brian Burger comes with a spicy kick at **Emma Jean's Holland Burger Café** (www.hollandburger.com). The vibe kicks up in stylish Pasadena before the road's final push to the Pacific. At the Santa Monica Pier (p252), hop on the solar-powered Ferris wheel and soak up a panoramic sunset view.

When to Go

The best time to travel Route 66 is from May to September, when the weather is warm and you'll be able to take advantage of more outdoor activities.

The Route

This journey starts in Tucumcari, NM, then continues west through Arizona and

California, roughly paralleling I-40 all the way to Barstow, CA. After Barstow, Route 66 south passes through San Bernardino on the I-15 before cutting west and heading into Pasadena. Follow I-110 to Santa Monica Blvd west to seaside Santa Monica.

Time & Mileage

Time: You might be able to do this trip in two or three days if you rush, but plan for six and enjoy the drive.

Mileage: About 1250 miles, depending on segments driven.

Pacific Coast Highway

Slip on your sunglasses, roll down the window and crank up your favorite song. The highways connecting Canada and Mexico on the West Coast were made for driving, and the ridiculously scenic Pacific Coast Hwy (PCH) is the king of them all.

Why Go

This epic West Coast journey, which rolls through California, Oregon and Washington, takes in cosmopolitan cities, surf towns and charming coastal enclaves ripe for exploration. For many travelers, the biggest draw is the magnificent scenery: wild and remote beaches, cliff-top views overlooking crashing waves, rolling hills, and lush forests thick with redwoods and eucalyptus trees. But the route is not loved only for its looks. It's also got personality, offering beside-the-highway adventures for surfers, kayakers, scuba divers and hikers.

Highlights? Let's start with the cities. Coastal highways connect the dots between some of the West Coast's most striking municipalities, starting with surf-loving San Diego in Southern California and moving north through glitzy Los Angeles and techie San Francisco. Way up north, take a worthwhile detour to alternative-minded Seattle.

If you want to bypass urban areas, it's easy to stick to the places in between. In southern California, PCH rolls past the almost-too-perfect beaches of California's Orange County ('the OC') and Santa Barbara (the 'American Riviera'). Further north, Hwy 1 passes wacky Santa Cruz, a university town and surfers' paradise, then redwood forests along the Big Sur coast and north of Mendocino. Hwy 1 cruises past the sand dunes, seaside resorts and fishing villages of coastal Oregon; and finally, the wild lands of Washington's Olympic Peninsula, with its primeval rainforest and bucolic San Juan Islands, served by coastal ferries.

When to Go

There's no bad time of year to drive the route, although northern climes will be rainier and snowier during winter. Peak travel season is June through August, which isn't always the best time as many stretches of the coast are socked in by fog during early summer (locals call it 'June Gloom'). The shoulder seasons before Memorial Day (April and May) and after Labor Day (September and October) can be ideal, with sunny days, cool nights and fewer crowds.

The Route

Highways stretch nearly 1500 miles from border to border – that is, from Tijuana, Mexico, to British Columbia, Canada. In California, the coastal route jumps between

THE HISTORY OF ROUTE 66

Launched in 1926, Route 66 would ultimately stretch from Chicago to Los Angeles, linking a ribbon of small towns and country byways as it rolled across eight states. The road gained notoriety during the Great Depression, when migrant farmers followed it west from the Dust Bowl across the Great Plains. Its nickname, 'The Mother Road', first appeared in *The Grapes of Wrath*, John Steinbeck's novel about the era. Things got a little more fun after WWII, when newfound prosperity prompted Americans to get behind the wheel and explore. Nat King Cole recorded 'Get Your Kicks on Route 66' in 1946, which added to the road's allure. But just as things got going, the Feds rolled out the interstate system, which eventually caused the Mother Road's demise. The very last town on Route 66 to be bypassed by an interstate was Arizona's Williams, in 1984.

I-5, Hwy 101 and Hwy 1 (when in doubt, just hug the coast) before committing to Hwy 101 in Oregon and Washington.

Time & Mileage

Time: No stopping? Give yourself four days because traffic and two-lane roads will slow you down; to fully enjoy the sights, allow 10 to 14 days.

Mileage: About 1500 miles.

Highway 89/89A: Wickenburg to Oak Creek Canyon

Hwy 89 and its sidekick Hwy 89A cross some of the most scenic and distinct regions in Arizona. The route described here travels north over the Weaver and Mingus mountains before rolling into Sedona and Oak Creek Canyon.

Why Go

This is our favorite drive in Arizona. It may not be the prettiest or the wildest, but there's a palpable sense of the Old West infusing the trip, like you've slipped through the swinging doors of history. But the route's not stuck in the 19th century – far from it. Weekend art walks, a burgeoning wine trail, stylish indie-owned shops and restaurants all add 21st-century sparkle.

For those interested in cowboy history, Wickenburg and its dude ranches are a good place to spend some time. Hwy 89 leaves town via Hwy 93 and soon tackles the Weaver Mountains, climbing 2500ft in 4 miles. The road levels out at mountain-topping Yarnell, site of a devastating fire in the summer of 2013, then passes grassy buttes and grazing cattle in the Peeples Valley. From here, one highlight is Prescott's infamous Whiskey Row, home of the historic Palace Saloon (p170). Thumb Butte is a hard-to-miss landmark west of downtown, and you'll pass the unusual boulders of Granite Dells on your way out of town.

Follow Hwy 89A to Jerome and hold on tight. This serpentine section of road brooks no distraction, clinging tight to the side of Mingus Mountain. If you dare, glance east for stunning views of the Verde Valley. The zigzagging reaches epic proportions in Jerome, a former mining town

cleaved into the side of Cleopatra Hill. Pull over for art galleries, tasting rooms, quirky inns and an unusually high number of ghosts. Stand over a 1910ft-deep mining shaft at Audrey Headframe Park (p170) then visit the mining museum at Jerome State Historic Park (p170) next door.

Hwy 89A drops through Clarkdale, on its way to Old Town Cottonwood. On the way to Sedona, detour to wineries on Page Springs Rd or loop into town via the Cathedral Rock (p171), passing Red Rock Loop Rd. Sedona is made for rejuvenation. It's a pretty place to commune with a vortex, dine on a fine meal or shop for art and Navajo rugs. This trip ends with a cannonball into Oak Creek Canyon where the namesake creek sparkles with riparian lushness.

When to Go

This route is best traveled in spring, summer and fall to avoid winter snow – although you might see a few flakes in the mountains in April! In the dead of summer, you won't want to linger in low-lying, toasty Wickenburg.

The Route

From Wickenburg, follow Hwy 93 to Hwy 89 then drive north to Prescott. North of town, pick up Hwy 89A, following it to Sedona.

Time & Mileage

Time: This route can be driven in a half-day, but we recommend two to three days for maximum enjoyment.

Mileage: 134 miles.

Million Dollar Highway

Stretching between Ouray and Silverton in southern Colorado is one of the most gorgeous alpine drives in the US. Part of the 236-mile San Juan Skyway, this section of US 550 is known as the Million Dollar Hwy because the road, they say, is filled with ore.

Why Go

Twenty-five miles of smooth, buttery pavement twists over three mountain passes, serving up views of Victorian homes, snow-capped peaks, mineshaft headframes and a gorge lined with rock. But the allure isn't just the beauty; part of the thrill is the driving. Hairpin turns, occasional rock slides and narrow, mountain-hugging pavement flips this route from a Sunday-afternoon drive to a NASCAR-worthy adventure.

Charming Ouray sits at nearly 7800ft, surrounded by lofty peaks. It also fronts the Uncompahgre Gorge, a steep, rocky canyon famous for its ice climbing. While here, take a hike or soak in the town's hot springs. From Ouray, the Million Dollar Hwy – completed in 1884 after three years of construction – hugs the side of the gorge, twisting past old mines that pock the mountainsides. Stay vigilant for the masochistic, spandex-clad cyclists pumping over the passes on the ribbon-thin road. In Silverton, step away from the car and enjoy the aspen-covered mountains or watch the steam-powered Durango & Silverton Narrow Gauge Railroad (p103) chug into town.

When to Go

Summer is the best time to visit. In winter, the highest pass sometimes closes and at other times you may need chains. You might even see snow on the ground in summer, though it likely won't be on the road.

The Route

From Ouray, follow Hwy 550 south to Silverton.

Time & Mileage

Time: The drive can be done in a few hours, but give yourself a day to see the sights.

Mileage: 25 miles.

MILLION DOLLAR HIGHWAY DETOUR

The drive between Ouray and Telluride is 50 miles – if you take the paved route. If you're feeling adventurous and have a 4WD (don't try it otherwise), consider the unpaved 16-mile road over Imogene Pass. On this old mining road you'll cross streams, alpine meadows and one of the state's highest passes. You'll also pass an old mine. We should mention one thing: this 'short cut' takes three hours. Still game?

Beartooth Highway

Depending on who's talking, the sky-high Beartooth Hwy is either the best way to get to Yellowstone, the most exciting motorcycle ride in the West or the most scenic highway in America. Not bad choices.

Why Go

Sometimes you just want to find a place so beautiful that it'll make you pull over, leave your car, beat your chest (or shake out your hair) and yell 'Yeah!' In the West, that place is the Beartooth Hwy.

From Red Lodge, Montana, this adventurous drive ascends Rock Creek Canyon's glaciated valley via a series of spaghetti-loop switchbacks, gaining an amazing 5000ft in elevation in just a few miles. Pull off at Rock Creek Vista Point Overlook for a short, wheelchair-accessible walk to superb views. The road continues up onto the high plateau, past 'Mae West Curve' and into Wyoming.

Twin Lakes has views of the cirque as well as the ski lift that carries the daring to an extreme spring ski run. After a series of switchbacks, look northwest for the Hellroaring Plateau and the jagged Bears Tooth (11,612ft). The route, flanked by alpine tundra, crests at the Beartooth Pass West Summit, the highest point at 10,947ft. Fifteen-foot snowbanks may linger here as late as June (sometimes even July).

After passing more lakes, the road descends past Beartooth Butte, a huge lump of the sedimentary rock that once covered the Beartooths. The highway drops to several excellent fishing areas on the Clark's Fork, then re-enters Montana, reaching Cooke City via Colter Pass (8066ft). The northeast entrance of Yellowstone is 4 miles from Cooke City.

When to Go

To add some hiking to your driving, visit in August. That's when the weather is typically the best for outdoor adventure.

The Route

From Red Lodge, follow Hwy 212 west – crossing into and out of Wyoming – to Cooke City, MT.

MARK READ / LONELY PLANET ©

Top: Columbia River
Highway (p43), Oregon

Bottom: Death Valley
National Park (p286),
California

Time & Mileage

Time: It's hard to zip along the twisty Beartooth Hwy; allow at least an afternoon or morning to drive it.

Mileage: 68 miles.

Highway 12

Arguably Utah's most diverse and stunning route, Hwy 12 winds through a remote and rugged canyon land, linking several national and state parks – and several fantastic restaurants – in the state's red-rock center.

Why Go

With crimson canyons, sprawling deserts, thick forests and lofty peaks calling out for exploration, Hwy 12 in remote southern Utah works well for adventurous explorers. The trip kicks off at Bryce Canyon National Park where the eye-catching gold-and-crimson spires set the stage for the color-infused journey to come.

Traveling east, the first highlight is **Kodachrome Basin State Park** (☑435-679-8562; www.stateparks.utah.gov; off Cottonwood Canyon Rd; day use per vehicle $8; ☺day use 6am-10pm), home to petrified geysers and dozens of red, pink and white sandstone chimneys – some nearly 170ft tall. Pass through tiny Escalante and then, 8 miles down the road, pull over for the view at Head of the Rocks Overlook, atop the Aquarius Plateau. From here you'll lord it over giant mesas, towering domes, deep canyons and undulating slickrock, all unfurling in an explosion of color.

The adjacent Grand Staircase-Escalante National Monument (p210) is the largest park in the Southwest at nearly 1.9 million acres. The Lower Calf Creek Recreation Area, inside the park and beside Hwy 12, holds a picnic area and a pleasant campground. It's also the start of a popular 6-mile round-trip hike to the impressive 126ft Lower Calf Creek Falls. The razor-thin Hogback Ridge, between Escalante and Boulder, is pretty stunning, too.

The best section of the drive? Many consider it to be the switchbacks and petrified sand dunes between Boulder and Torrey. But it's not just about the views. In Boulder, treat your taste buds to a locally sourced meal at Hell's Backbone Grill (p35), followed by homemade pie at the Burr Trail Grill & Outpost (p210), or enjoy a flavor-packed Southwestern dish at Cafe Diablo (p209) further north in Torrey.

When to Go

For the best weather and driving conditions – especially over 11,000ft Boulder Mountain – drive Hwy 12 between May and October.

The Route

From US Hwy 89 in Utah, follow Hwy 12 east to Bryce Canyon National Park. The road takes a northerly turn at Kodachrome Basin State Park then continues to Torrey.

Time & Mileage

Time: Although the route could be driven in a few hours, two to three days will allow for a bit of exploration.

Mileage: 124 miles.

High Road to Taos

This picturesque byway in northern New Mexico links Santa Fe with Taos, rippling through a series of adobe villages and mountain-flanked vistas in and around the Truchas Peaks.

Why Go

Santa Fe and Taos are well-known artists' communities, lovely places brimming with galleries, studios and museums. Two cities this stunning should be linked by an aesthetically pleasing byway, and the mountainous High Road to Taos obliges.

From Santa Fe follow Hwy 84/285 north. Exit onto Hwy 503 toward Nambe, where you can hike to waterfalls or simply meditate by the namesake lake. From here, the road leads north to picturesque Chimayo. Abandoned crutches line the wall in El Santuario de Chimayó (p227), also known as 'The Lourdes of America.' In 1816 this two-towered adobe chapel was built over a spot said to have miraculous healing powers. Take some time to wander through the community, and admire the fine weaving and woodcarving in family-run galleries.

Near Truchas, a village of galleries and century-old adobes, you'll find the **High**

Road Marketplace (☎505-689-2689; 1642 Hwy 76; ⊙10am-5pm, to 4pm winter). This cooperative that on SR 676 sells a variety of artworks by local artists. Up Hwy 76, original paintings and carvings remain in good condition inside the **Church of San José de Gracia** (☎505-351-4360; Hwy 76, Las Trampas; ⊙by appointment, call ahead), considered one of the finest surviving 18th-century churches in the USA. Next is Picuris Pueblo, once one of the most powerful pueblos in the region. This ride ends at Penasco, a gateway to the Pecos Wilderness, and also home to the engagingly experimental **Penasco Theatre** (☎575-587-2726; www.penascotheatre.org; 15046 Hwy 75). From here, follow Hwys 75 and 518 into Taos.

When to Go

The high season is summer, but spring can be a nice time to see blooming flowers. Fall presents a show of colorful leaves. With mountains on the route, winter is not the best time to visit.

The Route

From Santa Fe, take Hwy 84/285 west to Pojoaque and turn right on Hwy 503, toward Nambe. From Hwy 503, take Hwy 76 to Hwy 75, then drive into Taos on Hwy 518.

Time & Mileage

Time: Without stopping, this drive should take about half a day, but give yourself a full day if you want to shop and explore.

Mileage: 85 miles.

GOING-TO-THE-SUN ROAD: A LEGEND & A LANDMARK

Going-to-the-Sun Road was named after Going-to-the-Sun Mountain. According to legend – or a story concocted in the 1880s – a deity of the Blackfeet Tribe once taught tribal members to hunt. After the lesson, he left an image of himself on the mountain as inspiration before he ascended to the sun. Today, the road is a National Historic Landmark and a National Civil Engineering Landmark, the only road in the country to hold both designations.

Going-to-the-Sun Road

A strong contender for the most spectacular drive in America, the 53-mile Going-to-the-Sun Road is the only paved road through Glacier National Park in Montana.

Why Go

Glaciers! Grizzlies! A mountain-hugging marvel of modern engineering! Yep, the Going-to-the-Sun Road inspires superlatives and exclamation points. But the accolades are deserved. The road, completed in 1933, crosses a ruggedly beautiful alpine landscape, twisting and turning over a lofty Continental Divide that's usually blanketed in snow.

From the park's west entrance, the road skirts the shimmering Lake McDonald. Ahead, the looming Garden Wall forms the 9000ft spine of the Continental Divide and separates the west side of the park from the east side. The road crosses the divide at Logan Pass (6880ft). From here, the 7.6-mile Highline Trail (one way) traces the park's mountainous backbone, with views of glaciated valleys, sawtooth peaks, wildflowers and wildlife. And the wildlife you might see? Mountain goats. Bighorn sheep. Moose. Maybe even a grizzly bear or an elusive wolverine. After Logan Pass, the road passes Jackson Glacier Overlook, where you can bear witness to one of the park's melting monoliths. Experts say that at current global temperatures, all of the park's glaciers will be gone by 2030, so now is the time to visit.

When to Go

This snow-attracting route opens late and closes early. It's typically drivable between mid-June and mid-September. In 2011, due to an unusually heavy snowpack, the road didn't completely open until July 13.

The Route

From the west entrance of Glacier National Park, follow the Going-to-the-Sun Road east to St Mary.

Time & Mileage

Time: It varies depending on conditions, but plan to spend at least a half-day on the drive.

Mileage: 53 miles.

MORE SCENIC DRIVES

••

Hungry for more road trips? Here are a few more good ones.

Turquoise Trail, NM This back route between Tijeras, near Albuquerque, and Santa Fe, was a major trade route for several thousand years. Today it rolls past art galleries, shops (with turquoise jewelry) and a mining museum. From I-40, follow Hwy 14 north to I-25. Also see www.turquoisetrail.org.

Apache Trail, AZ This isn't your grandmother's Sunday-afternoon drive – unless your grandmother likes 45 miles of rabid road. From Apache Junction east of Phoenix, follow Hwy 88 past a kid-friendly ghost town, the wildflowers of Lost Dutchman State Park and three Salt River lakes. In the middle of it all? A snarling dirt section that drops more than 1000ft in less than 3 miles. Hold tight!

The Loneliest Road Hwy 50 slices across the white-hot belly of Nevada, stretching east from Fallon to Great Basin National Park and the Utah state line. This remote highway unfurls past a singing sand dune, Pony Express stations, and mining towns. A burger at Middlegate Station is a tasty pit stop.

Eastern Sierra Scenic Byway, CA From Topaz Lake, follow Hwy 395 south along the eastern flank of the mighty Sierra Nevada, ending at Little Lake. The region holds 14,000ft peaks, ice-blue lakes, pine forests, desert basins and hot springs.

Historic Columbia River Highway

Lush foliage and trailblazing history are highlights on US 30, a carefully planned byway that ribbons alongside the Columbia River Gorge east of Portland, Oregon.

Why Go

Look, there's a waterfall. And another waterfall. And another. Just how many waterfalls can one scenic highway hold? Quite a few if that road is the Historic Columbia River Hwy. The original route – completed in 1922 – connected Portland to The Dalles. The first paved road in the Pacific Northwest, it was carefully planned and built with the pleasure of driving in mind rather than speed. Viewpoints were carefully selected, and stone walls and arching bridges stylishly complement the gorgeous scenery.

Also notable is the history. Lewis and Clark traveled this route as they pushed toward the Pacific Ocean in 1805. Fifty years later, Oregon Trail pioneers ended their cross-country trek with a harrowing final push through the gorge's treacherous waters. Today, although sections of the original byway have been closed, or replaced by US 84, much of US 30 is still open for driving and some closed portions can be traversed by hiking or cycling.

One roadside highlight is the Portland Women's Forum Park, which provides one of the best views of the gorge. Just east the 1916 Vista House, honoring the Oregon Trail pioneers, holds a visitor center. It's perched on Crown Point, a good viewpoint that also marks the western edge of the gorge. And those gushing cascades? For oohs and ahhs, don't miss Multnomah Falls, Oregon's tallest waterfall at 642ft.

When to Go

Waterfalls are at their peak February to May, while summer is great for hiking.

The Route

To reach the historic highway, take exit 17, 28 or 35 off I-84 east of Portland. The western section of the original highway ends at Multnomah Falls. From here hop onto I-84 and continue east to exit 69 at Mosier where you can return to Hwy 30.

Time & Mileage

Time: One day.

Mileage: 100 miles.

Plan Your Trip
Outdoor Activities

Whether you're a couch potato, a weekend warrior or an ironman (or maiden), the West has an outdoor activity for you. The best part? A stunning landscape as your backdrop. Scan for hummingbirds, paddle rapids, ride through epic powder, surf curling waves or hike into the world's most famous canyon.

Best Outdoors

Ultimate Outdoor Experiences

Rafting the Colorado River through the Grand Canyon, AZ

Hiking to the summit of Half Dome, Yosemite National Park, CA

Cycling in Maroon Bells, Aspen, CO

Rock climbing in Joshua Tree National Park, CA

Scrambling to Angels Landing, Zion National Park, UT

Skiing in Vail, CO

Mountain biking in Moab, UT

Kayaking the San Juan Islands, WA

Hot springs in Ojo Caliente, NM

Glacier spotting in Glacier National Park, MT

Best Wildlife-Watching

Bears in Glacier National Park, MT

Elk, bison and gray wolves in Yellowstone National Park, WY

Birds in Patagonia-Sonoita Creek Preserve, AZ

Whales and dolphins in Monterey Bay, CA

Camping

Campers are absolutely spoiled for choice in the West. Pitch a tent beside alpine lakes and streams in Colorado, sleep under saguaro cacti in southern Arizona or snooze on gorgeous strands of California sand.

Campground Types & Amenities

Primitive or dispersed camping May have fire pits, but otherwise don't expect any amenities or even official sites; always free and possible in national forests (USFS) and on Bureau of Land Management (BLM) land.

Backcountry sites The most peaceful and only available to backpackers on public land. Permits and reservations may be required.

Developed campgrounds Typically found in state and national parks, with more amenities, including (sometimes) drinking water, toilets, picnic tables, barbecue grills and occasionally hot showers and a coin-op laundry.

RV (recreational vehicle) hookups and dump stations Available at many privately owned campgrounds, but only a few public-land campgrounds.

Private campgrounds Cater mainly to RVers and offer hot showers, swimming pools, wi-fi and family camping cabins; tent sites may be few and uninviting.

Rates & Reservations

Many public and private campgrounds accept reservations for all or some of their sites, while a few are strictly first-come, first-served. Overnight rates range from free for the most primitive campsites to $50 or more for pull-through RV sites with full hookups.

These agencies let you search for campground locations and amenities; check availability and reserve campsites online:

Recreation.gov (www.recreation.gov) Camping and cabin reservations for national parks, national forests, BLM land.

ReserveAmerica (www.reserveamerica.com) Reservations for state parks, regional parks and some private campgrounds across North America. See website for phone numbers by state.

Kampgrounds of America (http://koa.com) National chain of reliable but more expensive private campgrounds offering full facilities, particularly for RVs.

Hiking & Trekking

Good hiking trails are abundant in the West. Fitness is a priority throughout the region, and most metropolitan areas have at least one large park with trails. National parks and monuments are ideal for both short and long hikes. If you're hankering for nights in the wilderness beneath star-filled skies, however, plan on securing a backcountry permit in advance, especially in places like the Grand Canyon – spaces may be limited during summer.

Hiking Resources

Wilderness Survival, by Gregory Davenport, is easily the best book on surviving nearly every contingency. Useful websites:

American Hiking Society (www.americanhiking. org) Links to local hiking clubs and 'volunteer vacations' building trails.

Backpacker (www.backpacker.com) Premier national magazine for backpackers, from novices to experts.

SummitPost (www.summitpost.org) Routes, forums and trail descriptions for peaks and rock climbing.

Fees & Wilderness Permits

➡ State parks typically charge a daily entrance fee of $5 to $15; there's often a reduced fee, or no charge, if you walk or bike into these parks.

➡ National park entry averages $10 to $30 per vehicle for seven consecutive days; some national parks are free. Check the national park website for dates for Free Entrance Days (www. nps.gov/findapark/feefreeparks.htm).

➡ For unlimited admission to national parks, national forests and other federal recreation lands for one year, buy an 'America the Beautiful' pass ($80).

➡ Often required for overnight backpackers and extended day hikes, wilderness permits are issued at ranger stations and park visitor centers. Daily quotas may be in effect during peak periods (usually late spring through early fall).

➡ Some wilderness permits may be reserved ahead of time, and very popular trails (eg Half Dome, Mt Whitney) may sell out several months in advance.

➡ To hike in the forest surrounding Sedona, AZ, you'll need to buy a Red Rock Pass ($5 per day, $15 per week). National park interagency passes are accepted in lieu of the Red Rock Pass.

Bicycling

The popularity of cycling is growing by the day in the US, with cities adding more cycle lanes and becoming more bike-friendly. An increasing number of greenways traverse urban areas and the countryside. You'll find diehard enthusiasts in every town, and numerous outfitters offer guided trips for all levels and durations.

Many states offer social multiday rides, such as **Ride the Rockies** (www. ridetherockies.com) in Colorado. For a fee, you can join the peloton on a scenic, well-supported route; your gear is ferried ahead to that night's camping spot.

In Colorado, Aspen is a top cycling spot. Another standout ride is Arizona's **Mt Lemmon** (www.fs.usda.gov/main/coronado), a thigh-zinging, 28-mile climb from the Sonoran Desert floor to the 9157ft summit. You can also rent bikes on the South Rim of the Grand Canyon at Grand Canyon National Park (p179). Ride to Hermit's Rest on the park's Hermit Rd and the

ever-lengthening **Greenway Trail** (www.
nps.gov/grca/planyourvisit/bicycling.htm).

Top Cycling Towns

San Francisco, CA A pedal over the Golden Gate
Bridge lands you in the stunningly beautiful, and
stunningly hilly, Marin Headlands.

Boulder, CO Outdoors-loving town with loads of
great biking paths, including the Boulder Creek
Trail and Marshall Mesa mountain biking.

Portland, OR A trove of great cycling (on- and
off-road) in the Pacific Northwest.

Surfing

The best surf in the continental USA
breaks off the coast of California. There
are loads of options – from the funky and
low-key **Santa Cruz** to San Francisco's
Ocean Beach – a tough spot to learn! – or
bohemian **Bolinas**, 30 miles north. South,
you'll find strong swells and Santa Ana
winds in **San Diego**, **La Jolla**, **Malibu**
and **Santa Barbara**, all of which sport
warmer waters, fewer sharks of the great
white variety and a saucy SoCal beach
scene; the best conditions are from September to November. Along the coast
of Oregon and Washington are miles of
crowd-free beaches and pockets of surfing
communities.

Top California Surfing Spots

Huntington Beach (aka Surf City, USA)
is the quintessential surf capital, with
perpetual sun and a 'perfect' break, particularly during winter when the winds
are calm.

Huntington Beach, Orange County (www.
huntingtonbeachca.gov; ⊙5am-10pm; P) Surfer
central is a great place to take in the scene – and
some lessons.

Oceanside Beach, Oceanside One of SoCal's
prettiest beaches boasts one of the world's most
consistent surf breaks in summer. It's a family-
friendly spot.

Rincon, Santa Barbara Arguably one of the
planet's top surfing spots; nearly every major
surf champion on the globe has taken Rincon for
a ride.

Steamer Lane and Pleasure Point, Santa Cruz
There are 11 world-class breaks, including the
point breaks over rock bottoms, at these two
sweet spots.

Swami's, Encinitas Located below Seacliff Roadside Park, this popular surfing beach has multiple
breaks guaranteeing you some fantastic waves.

Surfing Resources

Surfline (www.surfline.com) Browse the comprehensive atlas, live webcams and surf reports for
the lowdown from San Diego to Maverick's.

Surfer (www.surfermag.com) Orange County–
based magazine website with travel reports, gear
reviews, newsy blogs and videos.

Surfrider (www.surfrider.org) Enlightened surfers
can join up with this nonprofit organization, which
aims to protect the coastal environment.

White-Water Rafting

There's no shortage of scenic and spectacular rafting in the West. In California,
both the **Tuolumne** and **American
Rivers** surge with moderate to extreme
rapids, while in Idaho the Middle Fork
of the Salmon River (p134) has it all:
abundant wildlife, thrilling rapids, a rich
history, waterfalls and hot springs. The
North Fork of the Owyhee – which
snakes from the high plateau of southwest
Oregon to the rangelands of Idaho – is
rightfully popular and features towering
hoodoos. In Salida, Colorado, **Brown's
Canyon National Monument** stakes a
claim as one of the most popular stretches
of white water in the country. North of
Moab, UT, look for wildlife on an easy
float on the **Colorado River** or ramp it
up several notches with a thrilling romp
through class V rapids and the red rocks
of Canyonlands National Park (p207).

To book a spot on the Colorado River
through the Grand Canyon, the quintessential river trip, make reservations at
least a year in advance. And if you're not
after white-knuckle rapids, fret not – many
rivers have sections suitable for peaceful
float trips or inner-tube drifts that you can
enjoy with a cold beer in hand.

WESTERN US NATIONAL PARKS

PARK	FEATURES	ACTIVITIES	BEST TIME
Arches	more than 2000 sandstone arches	scenic drives, day hikes	spring, fall
Bryce Canyon	brilliantly colored, eroded hoodoos	day & backcountry hikes, horseback riding	spring-fall
Canyonlands	epic Southwestern canyons, mesas & buttes	scenic viewpoints, backcountry hikes, white-water rafting	spring, fall
Carlsbad Caverns	extensive cave system; free-tail bat colony	cave tours, backcountry hikes	spring-fall
Death Valley	hot, dramatic desert & unique ecology	scenic drives, day hikes	spring
Glacier	impressive glaciated landscape; mountain goats	day & backcountry hikes, scenic drives	summer
Grand Canyon	spectacular 277-mile-long, 1-mile-deep river canyon	day & backcountry hikes, mule trips, river running	spring-fall
Grand Teton	towering granite peaks; moose, bison, wolves	day & backcountry hikes, rock climbing, fishing	summer-fall
Mesa Verde	preserved Ancestral Puebloan cliff dwellings, historic sites, mesas & canyons	short hikes	spring-fall
Olympic	temperate rainforests, alpine meadows, Mt Olympus	day & backcountry hikes	spring-fall
Petrified Forest	fossilized trees, petroglyphs, Painted Desert scenery	day hikes	year-round
Redwood	virgin redwood forest, world's tallest trees; elk	day & backcountry hikes	spring-fall
Rocky Mountain	stunning peaks, alpine tundra, the Continental Divide; elk, bighorn sheep, moose, beavers	day & backcountry hikes, cross-country skiing	summer-winter
Saguaro	giant saguaro cactus, desert scenery	day & backcountry hikes	fall-spring
Sequoia & Kings Canyon	sequoia redwood groves, granite canyon	day & backcountry hikes, cross-country skiing	summer-fall
Yellowstone	geysers & geothermal pools, impressive canyon; prolific wildlife	day & backcountry hikes, cycling, cross-country skiing	year-round
Yosemite	sheer granite-walled valley, waterfalls, alpine meadows	day & backcountry hikes, rock climbing, skiing	year-round
Zion	immense red-rock canyon, Virgin River	day & backcountry hikes, canyoneering	fall-spring

SKREIDZELEU / SHUTTERSTOCK ©

Top: The Narrows, Zion National Park (p211), Utah

Bottom: Grand Canyon National Park (p176), Arizona

Kayaking & Canoeing

For exploring flatwater (no rapids or surf), opt for a kayak or canoe. For big lakes and the sea coast use a sea kayak. Be aware that kayaks are not always suitable for carrying bulky gear.

For scenic sea kayaking, you can push into the surf just about anywhere off the California coast. Popular spots include **La Jolla** as well as the coastal state parks just north of **Santa Barbara**. In the Pacific Northwest, you can enjoy world-class kayaking in and around the **San Juan Islands**, the **Olympic Peninsula** and **Puget Sound**. There's a full-moon paddle in Sausalito's **Richardson Bay**, CA. Sea-kayak rentals average $32 to $40 for two hours. Reputable outfitters will make sure you're aware of the tide schedule and wind conditions of your proposed route.

White-water kayaking is also popular wherever there's rafting. In the Pacific Northwest, where water tumbles down from the ice-capped volcanoes, look for bald eagles on the **Upper Sgakit River** or slip through remote wilderness canyons on the **Klickitat River**. Close to Portland, try the **Clackamas** and the **North Santiam**. For urban white-water kayaking, you can't beat Colorado. Look for white-water parks in **Salida** and **Boulder**.

Kayaking & Canoeing Resources

American Canoe Association (www.american canoe.org) Organization supporting and providing information about canoeing and kayaking.

American Whitewater (www.americanwhitewater .org) Advocacy group for responsible recreation works to preserve America's wild rivers.

PLAN YOUR TRIP OUTDOOR ACTIVITIES

TOP TRAILS IN THE WEST

Ask 10 people for their top trail recommendations throughout the West and no two answers will be alike. The country is so varied and distances so enormous, there's little consensus. That said, you can't go wrong with the following all-star sampler.

South Kaibab/North Kaibab Trail, Grand Canyon, AZ (p179) A multiday cross-canyon tramp down to the Colorado River and back up to the rim.

Chasm Lake, Rocky Mountain National Park, CO (p84) The exposed climb to the summit of Longs Peak (14,259ft) is not recommended for casual hikers, but if you're in good shape, the 8.4-mile round-trip to Chasm Lake is equally amazing.

Angels Landing, Zion National Park, UT (p211) After a heart-pounding scramble over a narrow, precipice-flanked strip of rock, the reward is a sweeping view of Zion Canyon. It's a 5.4-mile round-trip hike.

Mt Washburn Trail, Yellowstone National Park, WY (p115) From Dunraven Pass, this wildflower-lined trail climbs 3 miles to expansive views from the summit of Mt Washburn (10,243ft). Look for bighorn sheep.

Pacific Crest Trail (PCT; ☏916-285-1846; www.pcta.org) Follows the spines of the Cascades and Sierra Nevada, traipsing 2650 miles from Canada to Mexico, passing through six of North America's seven ecozones.

Half Dome, Yosemite National Park, CA (p344) Scary and strenuous, but the Yosemite Valley views and sense of accomplishment are worth it. Park permit required.

Enchanted Valley Trail, Olympic National Park, WA (p372) Magnificent mountain views, roaming wildlife and lush rainforests – all on a 13-mile out-and-back trail.

Great Northern Traverse, Glacier National Park, MT (p128) A 58-mile haul that cuts through the heart of grizzly country and crosses the Continental Divide.

The Big Loop, Chiricahua National Monument, AZ (p193) A 9.5-mile hike along several trails that wind past an 'army' of wondrous rock pillars in southeastern Arizona once used as a hideout by Apache warriors.

Tahoe Rim Trail, Lake Tahoe, CA (p351) This 165-mile all-purpose trail circumnavigates the lake from high above, affording glistening Sierra views.

Canoe & Kayak (www.canoekayak.com) Special-interest magazine for paddlers.

Kayak Online (www.kayakonline.com) Advice for buying gear and helpful links to kayaking manufacturers, schools and associations.

Skiing & Other Winter Sports

Skiing, snowboarding, snowshoeing, cross-country hut trips, backcountry snowcat tours, World Cup races, 22ft superpipes and ski mountaineering competitions: the West has some of the best snow – and most fun – in the world. The ski season typically runs from December to mid-April, though some resorts have longer seasons. In summer, many resorts offer mountain biking, hiking and adventure parks courtesy of chair lifts. Ski and snowboard packages (including airfares, hotels and lift tickets) are easy to find through resorts, travel agencies and online travel booking sites; these packages are often your best bet if your main goal is to ski.

Wherever you go, it won't come cheap. Find the best deals by purchasing multiday tickets – or better yet, a season pass – heading to lesser-known 'sibling' resorts, like **Alpine Meadows** (www.squawalpine.com) near Lake Tahoe, or checking out mountains that cater to locals, including Ski Santa Fe (p219) and Colorado's **Wolf Creek** (www.wolfcreekski.com).

Top 10 Ski Resorts

Vail, CO (p90) The largest (and most expensive) resort in Colorado, with legendary back bowls that have to be skied to be believed.

Aspen, CO (p92) It doesn't matter if you're a celebrity or a lifelong ski bum, Aspen's four mountains live up to the hype.

Park City and Canyons, UT (p201) These two Utah resorts combine for over 7000 acres of bliss and light, fluffy powder.

Jackson Hole, WY (p109) The expert's choice, with some of the steepest terrain in the US.

MAD FOR MOUNTAIN BIKING

Mountain-biking enthusiasts will find trail nirvana in Crested Butte and Salida, CO; Moab, UT; Bend, OR; Ketchum, ID; and Marin, CA, the latter being where Gary Fisher and Co bunny-hopped the sport forward by careening down the rocky flanks of Mt Tamalpais on home-rigged bikes. For info about trails and trips, check out the MTB Project (www.mtbproject.com) and BikePacking (www.bikepacking.com); the latter is especially good for long-distance hauls on epics like the Colorado Trail and Arizona Trail. Great destinations include the following:

Kokopelli Trail, UT One of the premier bikepacking trails in the Southwest stretches 142 miles on a variety of terrain between Fruita, CO, and Moab, UT.

Monarch Crest, CO (p94) Extreme 20- to 35-mile adventure along the Continental Divide with fabulous high-altitude views. Near Salida.

Sun Top Loop, WA A 22-mile ride with challenging climbs and superb views of Mt Rainier and surrounding peaks on the western slopes of Washington's Cascade Mountains.

Downieville Downhill, CA (www.downievilleclassic.com) Not for the faint of heart, this piney trail, located near its namesake Sierra foothill town in Tahoe National Forest, skirts river-hugging cliffs, passes through old-growth forest and drops 4200ft in under 14 miles.

McKenzie River Trail, Willamette National Forest, OR Twenty-five miles of blissful single-track winding through deep forests and volcanic formations. The town of McKenzie is about 50 miles east of Eugene.

Whole Enchilada, UT Stitches together four incredible Moab trails, with over 26 miles of riding and 7000ft of vertical drop from alpine forests all the way down onto the legendary slickrock.

Top: White-water rafting (p46) the Salmon River, Idaho

Bottom: Skiing in the Wasatch Mountains (p198), Utah

ERIK ISAKSON / GETTY IMAGES ©

Salt Lake City, UT (p199) Does Utah have the best skiing? Brighton, Alta, Solitude, Snowbird and 500in of powder annually say yes.

Telluride, CO (p99) Over 4400ft of vertical, 2000 acres of terrain, 300in of snow and gulp-worthy views.

Lake Tahoe, CA (p351) Has a dozen resorts to play in, including Heavenly and Squaw Valley.

Taos, NM (p227) New ownership and expansions on- and off-mountain are keeping the Taos steeps in the mix.

Silverton, CO (p101) Top pick for the hardcore – there's no resort or fur-coat-wearing poseurs here, just a yurt and mind-blowing extreme terrain.

Big Sky, MT (p122) No attitude and no lift lines, just big-time skiing from the top of Lone Peak through 5800 acres of terrain.

Cross-Country Skiing & Snowshoeing

Most downhill ski resorts have cross-country (Nordic) ski trails. In winter, popular areas of national parks, national forests and city parks often have cross-country ski and snowshoe trails, and ice-skating rinks.

You'll find superb trail networks for Nordic skiers and snowshoers in California's **Royal Gorge**, North America's largest Nordic ski area, and Washington's sublime and crowd-free **Methow Valley**. Backcountry passionistas will be happily rewarded throughout the **Sierra Nevada**, with its many ski-in huts. There are 60 miles of trails around five ski-in huts in the **San Juan Mountains** (www.sanjuanhuts. com) in Colorado; the 10th Mountain Division Association (www.huts.org) manages more than 30 backcountry huts in the central Rockies. The **South Rim of the Grand Canyon** and the surrounding **Kaibab National Forest** are pretty spots for winter exploring.

Ski & Snowboard Resources

Cross-Country Ski Areas Association (www. xcski.org) Comprehensive information and gear guides for cross-country skiing and snowshoeing across North America.

Cross Country Skier (www.crosscountryskier. com) Magazine with Nordic-skiing news stories and destination articles.

Liftopia (www.liftopia.com) Shop for discount lift tickets.

Open Snow (https://opensnow.com) Get your daily powder report and forecast here.

Powder (www.powder.com) Online version of *Powder* magazine for skiers.

Ski (www.skimag.com) Online versions of *Ski* magazine.

SnoCountry Mountain Reports (www.snocountry.com) Snow reports for North America, plus events, news and resort links.

WHALE-WATCHING

Gray and humpback whales have the longest migrations of any mammal in the world – more than 5000 miles from the Arctic to Mexico, and back again. In the Pacific Northwest, most pass through from November to February (southbound) and March to June (northbound). Gray whales can be spotted off the California coast from December to April, while blue, humpback and sperm whales pass by in summer and fall. Bring binoculars! Top spots include the following:

Depoe Bay and Newport, OR (p405) Good whale-watching infrastructure; tour boats.

Puget Sound and San Juan Islands, WA (p377) Resident pods of orca.

Point Reyes Lighthouse, CA (p326) Gray whales pass by in December and January.

Monterey, CA (p295) Whales can be spotted year-round.

Channel Islands National Park, CA (p288) Take a cruise or peer through the telescope at the visitor center tower.

Cabrillo National Monument, CA (p275) The best place in San Diego to watch the gray-whale migration from January to March.

AND LET'S NOT FORGET...

ACTIVITY	WHERE?	WHAT?	MORE INFORMATION
Horseback riding	Southern Arizona dude ranches, AZ	Old West country (most ranches close in summer due to the heat)	www.azdra.com
	Grand Canyon South Rim, AZ	low-key trips through Kaibab National Forest; campfire rides	www.apachestables.com
	Santa Fe, NM	kids' rides; sunset rides	www.bishopslodge.com
	Telluride, CO	all-season rides in the hills	www.ridewithroudy.com
	Durango, CO	day rides and overnight camping in Weminiuche Wilderness	www.vallecitolakeoutfitter.com
	Yosemite National Park, CA	rides in Yosemite Valley, Tuolumne Meadows & near Wawona	www.yosemitepark.com
	Florence, OR	romantic beach rides	www.oregonhorsebackriding.com
Diving	Blue Hole near Santa Rosa, NM	81ft-deep artesian well; blue water leads into a 131ft-long submerged cavern	www.santarosanm.org
	La Jolla Underwater Park, CA	beginner-friendly; snorkelers enjoy nearby La Jolla Cove	www.sandiego.gov/lifeguards/beaches
	Channel Islands National Park, CA	kelp forests, sea caves off coastal islands	www.nps.gov/chis
	Point Lobos State Reserve, CA	fantastic shore diving; shallow reefs, caves, sea lions, seals, otters	www.pointlobos.org
	Puget Sound, WA	clear water, diverse marine life (including giant octopus!)	www.underwatersports.com
Hot-air ballooning	Sedona, AZ	float above red-rock country; picnic with bubbly	www.northernlightballoon.com
	Napa Wine Country, CA	colorful balloons float over vineyards	www.balloonrides.com; www.napavalleyballoons.com
	Albuquerque, NM	Albuquerque's box winds make this a prime ballooning destination.	http://discoverballoons.com

Rock Climbing & Canyoneering

In California, rock hounds test their mettle on the big walls, granite domes and boulders of world-class **Yosemite National Park**, where the climbing season lasts from April to October. Climbers also flock to **Joshua Tree National Park**, an otherworldly shrine in southern California's sun-scorched desert. There, amid craggy monoliths and the country's oldest trees, they make their pilgrimage on 8000 routes, tackling sheer vertical, sharp edges and bountiful cracks. For beginners, outdoor outfitters at both parks offer guided climbs and instruction.

Outside **Zion National Park** in Utah, canyoneering classes teach the fine art of going down: rappelling off sheer sandstone cliffs into mysterious slot canyons. Some of the more intense routes are done in wetsuits, down the flanks of waterfalls and through ice-cold pools.

For ice climbing, try Ouray Ice Park (p98) in Ouray, off the Million Dollar Hwy in southwest Colorado. Inside a narrow slot canyon, 200ft walls and waterfalls are frozen in thick sheets.

Other great climbing spots:

Grand Teton National Park, WY Good for climbers of all levels: beginners can take basic climbing courses and the more experienced can join two-day expeditions up to the top of Grand Teton itself; a 13,770ft peak with majestic views.

Smith Rock, OR Sport-climbing mecca in central Oregon, with the country's first 5.14 route.

City of Rocks National Reserve, ID More than 500 routes up wind-scoured granite pinnacles 60 stories tall.

Red River Gorge, KY The most popular sport climbing area in the US is buried deep in the Appalachian Mountains.

Bishop, CA This sleepy town in the Eastern Sierra is the gateway to excellent climbing in the nearby Owens River Gorge and Buttermilk Hills.

Red Rock Canyon, NV Ten miles west of Las Vegas is some of the world's finest sandstone climbing.

Indian Creek, UT Perfect multipitch sandstone cracks near Moab.

Devil's Tower, WY The 80-story butte of *Close Encounters of the Third Kind* fame is on every serious climber's bucket list.

Eldorado Canyon, CO More than 1000 superb granite multipitch climbs, right outside Boulder.

Flatirons, CO Not the best climbing in Boulder, but you can't miss the appeal of these 1000ft sandstone slabs.

Climbing & Canyoneering Resources

American Canyoneering Association (www.canyoneering.net) An online canyon database with links to courses, local climbing groups and more.

Climbing (www.climbing.com) Cutting-edge rock-climbing news and information since 1970.

CUSA (www.canyoneeringusa.com) Incredible online guide to Utah's canyoneering routes.

Rock & Ice (www.rockandice.com) The US' premiere climbing magazine.

SuperTopo (www.supertopo.com) One-stop shop for rock-climbing guidebooks, downloadable topo maps and route descriptions.

Plan Your Trip
Eat & Drink Like a Local

Food served in the western part of the United States can't be slotted into one neat category because regional specialties abound – and they can be very distinct. Half the fun of any trip is digging into a dish that has cultural and agricultural ties to a region, from green chile enchiladas in New Mexico to grilled salmon in the Pacific Northwest to San Diego's delicious fish tacos to sizzling steaks in Arizona.

Staples & Specialties

Breakfast

Morning meals in the West, as in the rest of the country, are big business. From a hearty serving of biscuits and gravy at a cowboy diner to a quick Egg McMuffin at the McDonald's drive-thru window or lavish Sunday brunches, Americans love their eggs and bacon, their waffles and hash browns, and their big glasses of orange juice. Most of all, they love that seemingly inalienable American right: a steaming cup of morning coffee with unlimited refills.

Lunch

After a mid-morning coffee break, an American worker's lunch hour (or half-hour these days) affords only a sandwich, quick burger or hearty salad. The formal 'business lunch' is more common in big cities like Los Angeles, where food is not necessarily as important as the conversation.

Dinner

Americans settle in to a more substantial weeknight dinner, usually early in the evening, which, given the workload of

Eating Basics
Dos & Don'ts

Tip 15% of the total bill for standard service; tip 20% (or more) for excellent service.

It's customary to place your napkin on your lap.

Avoid putting your elbows on the table.

Wait until everyone is served to begin eating.

In formal situations, diners customarily wait to eat until the host has lifted a fork.

Must-Try Regional Specialties

Fish tacos (San Diego, CA)

Frito pie (NM)

Green chile cheeseburgers (NM)

Navajo tacos (northeastern AZ)

Sonoran dogs (Tucson, AZ)

Rocky Mountain oysters (CO)

FARMLAND, WILD FOODS & FISH

The diverse geography and climate – a mild, damp coastal region with sunny summers and arid farmland in the east – foster all types of farm-grown produce. Farmers grow plenty of fruit, from melons, grapes, apples and pears to strawberries, cherries and blueberries. Veggies thrive here too: potatoes, lentils, corn, asparagus and Walla Walla sweet onions, all of which feed local and overseas populations.

Many wild foods thrive, especially in the damper regions, such as the Coast Range. Foragers seek the same foods once gathered by local Native American tribes – year-round wild mushrooms, as well as summertime fruits and berries.

With hundreds of miles of coastline and an impressive system of rivers, Northwesterners have access to plenty of fresh seafood. Depending on the season, specialties include razor clams, mussels, prawns, albacore tuna, Dungeness crab and sturgeon. Salmon remains one of the region's most recognized foods, whether it's smoked or grilled, or in salads, quiches and sushi.

so many two-career families, might be takeout (eg pizza or Chinese food) or pre-packaged meals cooked in a microwave. Desserts tend toward ice cream, pies and cakes. Some families still cook a traditional Sunday-night dinner, when relatives and friends gather for a big feast, or grill outside and go picnicking on weekends.

Quick Eats

Eating a hot dog from a street cart or a taco from a roadside food truck is a convenient, and increasingly tasty, option in downtown business districts. Don't worry about health risks – these vendors are usually supervised by the local health department. Fast-food restaurants with drive-thru windows are ubiquitous, and you'll usually find at least one beside a major highway exit. At festivals and county fairs, pick from cotton candy, corn dogs, candy apples, funnel cakes, chocolate-covered frozen bananas and plenty of tasty regional specialties. Farmers markets and natural food markets often have more wholesome prepared foods.

California

Owing to its vastness and variety of microclimates, California is truly America's cornucopia for fruits and vegetables, and a gateway to myriad Asian markets. The state's natural resources are overwhelming, with wild salmon, Dungeness crab and oysters from the ocean; robust produce year-round; and artisanal products such as cheese, bread, olive oil, wine and chocolate.

Starting in the 1970s and '80s, star chefs such as Alice Waters and Wolfgang Puck pioneered 'California cuisine' by incorporating the best local ingredients into simple yet delectable preparations. The influx of Asian immigrants, especially after the Vietnam War, enriched the state's urban food cultures with Chinatowns, Koreatowns and Japantowns, along with huge enclaves of Mexican Americans who maintain their own culinary traditions across the state. Global fusion restaurants are another hallmark of California's cuisine scene.

North Coast & The Sierras

San Francisco hippies went back to the land in the 1970s for a more self-sufficient lifestyle, reviving traditions of making breads and cheeses from scratch and growing their own everything (note: farms from Mendocino to Humboldt are serious about No Trespassing signs). Hippie-homesteaders were early adopters of pesticide-free farming, and innovated hearty, organic cuisine that was health-minded yet satisfied the munchies.

On the North Coast, you can taste the influence of wild-crafted Ohlone and Miwok cuisine. In addition to fishing, hunting game and making bread from acorn flour, these Native Northern Californians also tended orchards and carefully cultivated foods along the coast. With such attentive stewardship, nature has been kind to this landscape, yielding bonanzas of wildflower honey and blackberries.

Alongside traditional shellfish collection, sustainable caviar and oyster farms have sprung up along the coast. Fearless foragers have identified every edible plant, from Sierra's wood sorrel to Mendocino sea vegetables, though key spots for wild mushrooms remain closely guarded local secrets.

San Francisco Bay Area

Based on 2010 census data, San Francisco has nearly 40 restaurants per 10,000 households – the highest number per household in the US. Hundreds of licensed food trucks crisscross the city.

Some city novelties have had extraordinary staying power, including ever-popular *cioppino* (Dungeness crab stew), chocolate bars invented by the Ghirardelli family, and sourdough bread, with original gold-rush-era mother dough still yielding local loaves with that distinctive tang. Dim sum is Cantonese for what's known in Mandarin as *xiao che* (small eats). It's served at *yum cha* (trolley-serviced meals), and there are dozens of places in San Francisco where you'll call it lunch.

Mexican, French and Italian food remain perennial local favorites, along with more recent SF ethnic food crazes: *izakaya* (Japanese bars serving small plates), Korean tacos, *banh mi* (Vietnamese sandwiches featuring marinated meats and pickled vegetables on baguettes) and *alfajores* (Arabic-Argentine crème-filled shortbread cookies).

SoCal

Los Angeles has long been known for its big-name chefs and celebrity restaurant owners. Robert H Cobb, owner of Hollywood's Brown Derby Restaurant, is remembered as the namesake of the Cobb salad (lettuce, tomato, egg, chicken, bacon and Roquefort). Wolfgang Puck launched the celebrity-chef trend with the Sunset Strip's star-spangled Spago in 1982.

For authentic ethnic food in Los Angeles, head to Koreatown for flavor-bursting *kalbi* (marinated barbecued beef short ribs), East LA for tacos *al pastor* (marinated, fried pork), and Little Tokyo for ramen noodles made fresh daily.

Further south, surfers cruise Hwy 1 beach towns from Laguna Beach to La Jolla in search of the ultimate wave and

---

BREAKFAST BURRITOS

There is one Mexican-inspired meal that has been mastered in the West: the breakfast burrito. It's served in diners and delis in Colorado, in coffee shops in Arizona and beach-bum breakfast joints in California. In many ways, it is the perfect breakfast – cheap (usually under $6), packed with protein (eggs, cheese, beans), fresh veggies (or is avocado a fruit?), hot salsa (is that a vegetable?) and rolled to go in paper and foil. Peel it open like a banana and inhale the savory steam.

---

quick-but-hearty eats like breakfast burritos and fish tacos. And everybody stops for a date shake at Ruby's Crystal Cove Shake Shack south of Newport Beach.

Pacific Northwest

The late James Beard (1903–85), an American chef, food writer and Oregon native, believed foods prepared simply, without too many ingredients or complicated cooking techniques, allowed their natural flavors to shine. This philosophy has greatly influenced modern Northwest cuisine. Pacific Northwesterners don't like to think of their food as trendy or fussy, but at the same time, they love to be considered innovative, especially when it comes to 'green,' hyper-conscious eating.

The Southwest

Moderation is not a virtue when it comes to food in Arizona, New Mexico, Utah, southern Colorado and Las Vegas. These gastronomic wonderlands don't have time for the timid. Sonoran hot dogs, green chili cheeseburgers, huevos rancheros, juicy slabs of steaks and endless buffets – take your Instagram photo then dig in and dine happy.

Two ethnic groups define Southwestern food culture: the Spanish and the Mexicans, who controlled territories from Texas to California until well into the

Top: Baja fish tacos

Bottom: Wine tasting in Walla Walla (p384)

INTI ST CLAIR / GETTY IMAGES ©

19th century. While there is little actual Spanish food today, the Spanish brought cattle to Mexico, which the Mexicans adapted to their own corn-and-chili-based gastronomy to make tacos, tortillas, enchiladas, burritos, *chimichangas* (deep-fried burritos) and other dishes made of corn or flour pancakes filled with everything from chopped meat and poultry to beans. In Arizona and New Mexico, a few Native American dishes are served on reservations and at tribal festivals. Steaks and barbecue are always favorites on Southwestern menus, and beer is the drink of choice for dinner and a night out.

For a cosmopolitan foodie scene, visit Las Vegas, where top chefs from New York City, LA and even Paris sprout satellite restaurants.

Mexican & New Mexican Food

Mexican food is often hot and spicy. If you're sensitive, test the heat of your salsa before dousing your meal. In Arizona, Mexican food is of the Sonoran type, with specialties such as *carne seca* (dried beef). Meals are usually served with refried beans, rice and flour or corn tortillas; chiles are relatively mild. Tucsonans refer to their city as the 'Mexican food capital of the universe,' which, although hotly contested by a few other places, carries a ring of truth. Colorado restaurants serve Mexican food, but they don't insist on any accolades for it.

New Mexico's food is distinct from, but reminiscent of, Mexican food. Pinto beans are served whole instead of refried; *posole* (a corn stew) may replace rice. Chiles aren't used so much as a condiment (like salsa) but more as an essential ingredient in almost every dish. *Carne adobada* (marinated pork chunks) is a specialty.

If a menu includes red or green chile dishes and sauces, it probably serves New Mexican–style dishes. The state is famous for its chile-enhanced Mexican standards. The town of Hatch, New Mexico, is particularly known for its green chiles. For both red and green chile on your dish, order it Christmas-style

STEAK & POTATOES

Have a hankerin' for a juicy hunk of beef with a salad, baked potato and beans? Look no further than the ranch-filled Southwest, home to intimate chophouses, family-friendly steak restaurants and trail-ride cookouts. In Utah, the large Mormon population influences culinary options. Here, good, old-fashioned American food like chicken, steak, potatoes, vegetables, homemade pies and ice cream prevail.

Native American Food

Modern Native American cuisine bears little resemblance to that eaten before the Spanish conquest, but it is distinct from Southwestern cuisine. Navajo and Indian tacos – fried bread usually topped with beans, meat, tomatoes, chili and lettuce – are the most readily available. Chewy *horno* bread is baked in the beehive-shaped outdoor adobe ovens *(hornos)* using remnant heat from a fire built inside the oven, then cleared out before cooking.

Most other Native American cooking is game-based and usually involves squash and locally harvested ingredients like berries and piñon nuts. Though becoming better known, it can be difficult to find. Your best bets are festival food stands, powwows, rodeos, Pueblo feast days and casino restaurants.

In the Southwest there is a new trend in upscale restaurants with a modern take on Native American food, using native ingredients like blue corn, wild mushrooms and venison in contemporary gourmet preparations.

Vegetarians & Vegans

Most metro eateries offer at least one vegetarian dish, although very few are dedicated solely to meatless menus. These days, fortunately, almost every larger town has a natural-food grocer. You may go wanting in smaller towns in the hinterlands, and in those cases your best bet is pulling together a picnic from the local grocery store.

FAVORITE VEGETARIAN EATERIES
•••••••••••••••••••••••••••••••••••

Green New American Vegetarian (p165), Phoenix, AZ

Lovin' Spoonfuls (p189), Tucson, AZ

Macy's (p174), Flagstaff, AZ

Greens (p319), San Francisco, CA

City O' City (Map p76; ☑303-831-6443; www.cityocitydenver.com; 206 E 13th Ave; mains $9-14; ⊙7am-2am; ☑; 🚌0, 6, 10, 16) ☞, Denver, CO

Leaf (☑303-442-1485; www.leafveg etarianrestaurant.com; 2010 16th St; mains $13-18; ⊙11:30am-9pm Mon-Thu, 11:30am-10pm Fri, 10am-10pm Sat, 10am-9pm Sun; ☑; 🚌204) ☞, Boulder, CO

One potential pitfall in the Southwest? Traditional Southwestern cuisine uses lard in beans, tamales *sopaipillas* (deep-fried puff pastry) and flour (but not corn) tortillas. Be sure to ask – even the most authentic places have a pot of pintos simmering for vegetarians.

Drinks

Work-hard, play-hard Americans are far from teetotalers. About 56% of Americans drink alcohol monthly.

Beer

Craft & Local Beer

Microbrewery and craft-beer production has sky-rocketed in the US over the last 10 years. Craft beer sales now account for 12.2% of the domestic beer market. The term microbrew is used broadly, and tends to include beer produced by large, well-established brands such as Sam Adams and Sierra Nevada. According to the Brewers Association, however, a true craft brewery must produce no more than six million barrels annually. It must also be independently owned and the beer made with traditional ingredients.

In recent years it's become possible to 'drink local' all over the West as microbreweries pop up in urban centers, small towns and unexpected places. They're particularly popular in gateway communities outside national parks, including Moab, Flagstaff and Durango.

Wine

There are more than 8700 wineries in the US, and 2010 marked the first year that the US consumed more wine than France. To the raised eyebrows of European winemakers, who used to regard Californian wines as second class, many American wines are now even (gulp!) winning prestigious international awards. In fact, the nation is the world's fourth-largest producer of wine, behind Italy, France and Spain.

Wine isn't cheap in the US, but it's possible to procure a perfectly drinkable bottle of American wine at a liquor or wine shop for around $12.

Wine Regions

Today almost 90% of US wine comes from California, and Oregon and Washington wines have achieved international status.

Without a doubt, the country's hotbed of wine tourism is in Northern California, just outside of the Bay Area in the Napa and Sonoma Valleys. As other areas – Oregon's Willamette Valley, California's Central Coast and Arizona's Patagonia region – have evolved as wine destinations, they have spawned an entire industry of bed-and-breakfast tourism that goes hand in hand with the quest to find the perfect Pinot Noir.

There are many excellent 'New World' wines that have flourished in the rich American soil. The most popular white varietals made in the US are Chardonnay and Sauvignon Blanc; best-selling reds include Cabernet Sauvignon, Merlot, Pinot Noir and Zinfandel.

Margaritas

In the Southwest it's all about the tequila. Margaritas are the alcoholic drink of choice, and synonymous with this region, especially in heavily Hispanic New Mexico, Arizona and southwestern Colorado. Margaritas vary in taste depending on the quality of the ingredients used, but all are made from tequila, a citrus liquor (Grand Marnier, Triple Sec or Cointreau) and either freshly squeezed lime or premixed Sweet & Sour.

BEER GOES LOCAL

In outdoorsy communities across the West, the neighborhood microbrewery is the unofficial community center – the place to unwind, swap trail stories, commune with friends and savor seasonal brews. Here are a few of our favorites:

Beaver Street Brewery (928-779-0079; www.beaverstreetbrewery.com; 11 S Beaver St; 11am-11pm Sun-Thu, to midnight Fri & Sat) Flagstaff, AZ

OHSO Brewery & Distillery (Map p166; 602-955-0358; www.ohsobrewery.com; 4900 E Indian School Rd; 11am-midnight Mon-Thu, 11am-1:30am Fri, 9am-1:30am Sat, 9am-midnight Sun;) Phoenix, AZ

Black Shirt Brewing Co (p75) Denver, CO

Mountain Sun (p83) Boulder, CO

Steamworks Brewing (970-259-9200; www.steamworksbrewing.com; 801 E 2nd Ave; 11am-midnight Mon-Thu, to 2am Fri-Sun) Durango, CO

Squatters Pub Brewery (www.squatters.com; 147 W Broadway; dishes $10-22; 11am-midnight Mon-Thu, to 1am Fri, 10am-1am Sat, 10am-midnight Sun), Salt Lake City, UT

Snake River Brewing Co (p111) Jackson, WY

North Coast Brewing Company (707-964-2739; www.northcoastbrewing.com; 455 N Main St; mains $17-25; restaurant 4-10pm Sun-Thu, to 11pm Fri & Sat, bar from 2pm daily;) Fort Bragg, CA

Ecliptic Brewing (p393) Portland, OR

Fremont Brewing Company (p367) Seattle, WA

Margaritas are either served frozen, on the rocks (over ice) or straight up. Most people order them with salt. Traditional margaritas are lime flavored, but also come in a rainbow of other flavors – they're best ordered frozen.

Coffee

America runs on caffeine, and the coffee craze has only intensified in the last 25 years. Blame it on Starbucks. The world's biggest coffee chain was born amid the Northwest's progressive coffee culture in 1971, when Starbucks opened its first location across from Pike Place Market in Seattle.

The idea, to offer a variety of roasted beans from around the world in a comfortable cafe, helped fill the American coffee mug with more refined, complicated (and expensive) drinks compared to the ubiquitous Folgers and diner cups of joe. By the early 1990s, specialty coffee houses were springing up across the country.

Independent coffee shops support a coffee-house culture that encourages lingering; think free wi-fi and comfortable seating. That said, when using free cafe wi-fi, remember: order something every hour, don't leave laptops unattended, and deal with interruptions graciously.

VINTAGE COCKTAILS

Across the US, it's become decidedly cool to party like it's 1929 by drinking retro cocktails from the days of Prohibition, when alcohol was illegal to consume. While Prohibition isn't likely to be reinstated, you'll find plenty of bars where the spirit of the Roaring Twenties and the illicit 1930s lives on. Inspired by vintage recipes featuring spirits and elixirs, these cocktails, complete with ingredients like small-batch liqueurs, whipped egg whites, hand-chipped ice and fresh fruit, are lovingly concocted by nattily dressed bartenders who regard their profession as something between an art and a craft.

Plan Your Trip
Travel with Children

The West is a top choice for adventure-loving families, with superb attractions for all ages: amusement parks, zoos, science museums, unique campsites, hikes in wilderness reserves, boogie-board surfing at the beach and bike rides through scenic forests. Most national and state parks offer kid-focused programs.

Best Regions for Children

Grand Canyon & Southern Arizona

Hike into the Grand Canyon, splash in Oak Creek and ponder the saguaro cacti outside Tucson. Water parks, dude ranches and ghost towns should also keep kids entertained.

Los Angeles & Southern California

See celebrity handprints in Hollywood, ogle the La Brea tar pits, take a studio tour in Burbank and hit the beach in Santa Monica or San Diego. Theme parks galore.

Colorado

The whole state is like a giant playground: museums and water parks in Denver, zip lines and horseback rides in the Rockies, rafting near Buena Vista and Salida, exploring cliff houses in Mesa Verde and ski resorts everywhere.

Utah

Red-rock fun park for older kids who enjoy the outdoors: slickrock mountain biking, slot canyon adventures and a bevy of unbelievable fantasy-worthy landscapes.

Western USA for Children

To find family-oriented sights and activities, accommodations, restaurants and entertainment in our coverage, just look for the child-friendly icon (🖼).

Dining

The US restaurant industry seems built on family-style service: children are not just accepted almost everywhere, they are usually encouraged by special children's menus with smaller portions and lower prices. In some restaurants children under a certain age even eat for free. Restaurants usually provide high chairs and booster seats. Some may also offer crayons and puzzles.

Restaurants without a children's menu don't necessarily discourage kids, though higher-end restaurants might; however, even at the nicer places, if you arrive early, you can usually eat without too much stress. You can ask if the kitchen will make a smaller order of a dish (check the price), or if they will split a normal-size main dish between two plates for the kids.

Accommodations

Motels and hotels typically have rooms with two beds, which are ideal for families.

Some also have roll-away beds or cribs that can be brought into the room for an extra charge (these are usually portable cribs, which may not work for all children). Many hotels have adjoining doors between rooms. Some offer 'kids stay free' programs, for children up to 12 or sometimes 18 years old. Many B&Bs don't allow children; ask when reserving. Most resorts are kid friendly and many offer children's programs, but ask when booking, as a few cater only to adults.

Babysitting

Resort hotels may have on-call babysitting services; otherwise, ask the front-desk staff or concierge to help you make arrangements. Always check that babysitters are licensed and bonded, and ask what they charge per hour per child, whether there's a minimum fee, and if they charge extra for transportation or meals. Most tourist bureaus list local resources for child care, plus recreation facilities, medical services and so on.

Discounts

Child concessions often apply for tours, admission fees and transport, with some discounts as high as 50% off the adult rate. However, the definition of 'child' can vary from under 12 to under 16 years. Some sights also have discount rates for families. Most attractions give free admission to children under two years.

Children's Highlights

Outdoor Adventure

Yellowstone National Park, WY (p112) Watch powerful geysers, spy on wildlife and take magnificent hikes.

Grand Canyon National Park, AZ (p176) Gaze across one of the earth's great wonders, followed by a hike, a ranger talk and biking.

Olympic National Park, WA (p372) Explore the wild and pristine wilderness of one of the world's few temperate rainforests.

Zion National Park, UT (p211) Free shuttles, river access, rock scrambling and all levels of hikes.

Oak Creek Canyon, AZ (p171) Swoosh over red rocks at Slide Rock State Park in Arizona.

Moab, UT (p205) Mountain biking, rafting, petroglyphs and rock climbing make this a great destination for teens.

San Diego, CA (p269) Boogie boarding and tide pools on superb, laid-back beaches.

Great Sand Dunes National Park, CO (☑719-378-6399; www.nps.gov/grsa; 11999 Hwy 150; adult/child $3/free; ☉visitor center 8:30am-5pm Jun-Aug, 9am-4:30pm Sep-May) An ankle-deep stream flowing through giant sand dunes – younger kids will spend hours here.

Theme Parks

Disneyland, CA (p265) It's the attention to detail that amazes most at Mickey Mouse's enchantingly imagined Disneyland, in the middle of Orange County.

Legoland, CA (☑760-918-5346; www.legoland.com/california; 1 Legoland Dr; adult/child 3-12yr from $95/89; ☉hours vary, at least 10am-5pm year-round; ℗⚐) Younger kids will get a kick out of the Lego-built statues and low-key rides scattered across this amusement park in Carlsbad.

Universal Studios, CA (p258) Hollywood-movie-themed action rides, special-effects shows and a studio back-lot tram tour in Los Angeles.

Epic Discovery, CO (☑970-496-4910; www.epicdiscovery.com; day pass Ultimate/Little Explorer $94/54; ☉10am-6pm Jun-Aug, Fri-Sun only Sep; ⚐) Eco-themed adventure park in Vail and Breckenridge.

Aquariums & Zoos

Arizona-Sonora Desert Museum, AZ (p187) Coyotes, cacti and docent demonstrations are highlights at this indoor-outdoor repository of flora and fauna in Tucson.

Monterey Bay Aquarium, CA (p295) Observe denizens of the deep next door to the California central coast's biggest marine sanctuary.

Aquarium of the Pacific, CA (p254) High-tech aquarium at Long Beach houses critters whose homes range from balmy Baja California to the chilly north Pacific; there's also a shark lagoon.

San Diego Zoo, CA (p271) This sprawling zoo is home to creatures great and small, with more than 3700 animals.

Rainy-Day Activities

LA Museums, CA See stars (the real ones) at LA's Griffith Observatory (p249), dinosaur bones at the Natural History Museum of Los Angeles (p248) and the Page Museum (p250) at the La Brea Tar Pits, then get hands-on at the amusing California Science Center (p247).

SF Museums, CA San Francisco's Bay Area is a mind-bending classroom for kids, especially at the interactive Exploratorium (p299) and eco-friendly California Academy of Science (p315).

Pacific Science Center, WA (p364) Fascinating, hands-on exhibits at this center in Seattle, plus an IMAX theater, planetarium and laser shows.

New Mexico Museum of Natural History & Science, NM (p214) Check out the Age of Super-giants in Albuquerque.

Denver Museum of Nature & Science, CO (p71) From space to local Ice Age fossils, with an IMAX and planetarium for good measure.

Mini Time Machine Museum of Miniatures, AZ (p190) You may not get many rainy days in Tucson, but when the monsoon season arrives this museum of tiny but intricate houses and scenes is a mesmerizing place to explore.

Planning

Consider the weather and the crowds when planning a Western USA family getaway. The peak travel season is from June to August, when schools are out and the weather is at its warmest. Expect high prices and abundant crowds – meaning long lines at amusement and water parks, fully booked resort areas, and heavy traffic on the roads; reserve well in advance for popular destinations. The same holds true for winter resorts (eg the Rockies, Lake Tahoe) during the high season (January to March).

What to Pack

➡ Bring lots of sunscreen, especially if you'll be spending time outside.

➡ For hiking, you'll need a front baby carrier (for children under 12 months old) or a backpack (for children up to about four years old) with a built-

in shade top. These can be purchased or rented from outfitters throughout the region.

➡ Older kids need sturdy shoes and water sandals for playing in streams.

➡ To minimize concerns about bed configurations, it's a good idea to bring a portable crib for infants and sleeping bags for older children.

➡ Towels, for playing in water between destinations.

➡ Rain gear.

➡ A snuggly fleece or heavy sweater (even in summer, desert nights can be cold).

➡ Sun hats (especially if you are camping).

➡ Bug repellent.

Resources

Travel with Children For all-round information and advice, check out Lonely Planet's guide.

Undercover Tourist (www.undercovertourist. com) Discounted tickets and more at the big theme parks.

Find Your Park (https://findyourpark.com) Great way to research which national parks to visit.

Trekaroo (www.trekaroo.com) Reviews, ideas and itineraries for families.

Family Vacation (www.familyvacationcritic.com) Trip ideas and packages sorted by age, destination and style.

Tracks & Trails (http://tracks-trails.com) Squeezing everyone into an RV? Check out this handy planner.

Kids.gov The eclectic, enormous national resource, where you can download songs and activities and follow links to kid-focused information.

Regions at a Glance

What image springs to mind when someone mentions the West? A saguaro cactus, or maybe the Grand Canyon? Either would be accurate – for Arizona. But the West holds so much more. Sun-kissed beaches in California. Lush forests in the Pacific Northwest. Epic singletrack trails in the Rockies. Crimson buttes and crumbly hoodoos in Utah. There's a landscape for every mood and adventure.

Cultural travelers can explore Native American sites in Arizona and New Mexico. You'll find upscale shopping, fine dining and big-city bustle in Los Angeles, Phoenix, San Francisco, Denver and Seattle. Are you a history buff? Visit Mesa Verde in Colorado, Spanish missions in California or Old West towns just about everywhere. Ready to let loose? Two words: Las Vegas.

Rocky Mountains

Outdoor Adventure
Western Culture
Landscapes

Rugged Fun

Adrenaline junkie? Hit the Rockies, a world-class skiing, hiking, climbing and cycling destination. Everyone is welcome, with hundreds of races and group rides, and an incredible infrastructure of parks, trails and backcountry huts.

Modern Cowboys

Once sporting Stetson cowboy hats and prairie dresses, today's freedom-loving Rocky folk are more often spotted in lycra, with a mountain bike hitched nearby, sipping a microbrew or latte at a sunny outdoor cafe. Hard playing and slow living still rule.

Alpine Wonderland

The snow-covered Rocky Mountains are pure majesty. With chiseled peaks, clear rivers and mountain lions, bears, bison and wolves in the backyard, the Rockies contain some of the world's most famous parks, and bucketloads of clean mountain air.

p68

Southwest

Natural Scenery
Native Culture
Food

Red-Rock Country
The Southwest is famous for the jaw-dropping Grand Canyon, the dramatic red buttes of Monument Valley, the crimson arches of Moab and the fiery buttes of Sedona – just a few of the many geographic wonders in and around the spectacular national parks and forests.

Pueblos & Reservations
Visiting the Hopi and Navajo Nations or one of the 19 New Mexico Pueblos is a fine introduction to America's first inhabitants. This is your best bet for appreciating, and purchasing, crafts made by Native American people.

Good Eats
Try chile-smothered chicken enchiladas in New Mexico, a messy Sonoran hotdog in Tucson or grilled trout in Utah. In Vegas, stretch your fat pants and your budget at one of the extravagant buffets. For gourmands, off-the-Strip restaurants offer the most intriguing epicurean experiences.

p140

California

Beaches
Outdoors
Food & Wine

Gorgeous Shores
With more than 800 miles of coastline, California rules the sands: you'll find rugged, pristine beaches in the north and people-packed beauties in the south, with great surfing, sea kayaking or beach-walking all along the coast.

Romping Room
Ride the snow-covered slopes, raft on white-water rivers, kayak beside coastal islands, hike past waterfalls and climb boulders in the desert. The problem isn't choice in California, it's finding enough time to do it all.

King's Table
Fertile fields, talented chefs and an insatiable appetite for the new make California a major culinary destination. Browse local food markets, sample Pinot and Chardonnay beside lush vineyards, and dine on farm-to-table fare.

p237

Pacific Northwest

Cycling
Food & Wine
National Parks

Pedal Power
Bicycle on paved, rolling roads in the tranquil San Juan Islands, cruise the bluff-dotted Oregon coast along Hwy 101 or pedal the streets of Portland, a city that embraces two-wheeled travel with loads of bike lanes, costumed theme rides and handcrafted bike shows.

Locavores & Oenophiles
No longer 'up and coming,' the food scene has arrived and smudged up its apron in the Pacific Northwest. In Portland and Seattle, chefs blend fish caught in local waters with vegetables harvested in the Eden-like valleys surrounding the Columbia River. Washington's wine is second only to California's.

Classic Playgrounds
The Northwest has four national parks, including three classics dating from the turn of the 20th century – Olympic, Mount Rainier and Crater Lake. The newest is North Cascades, established in 1968.

p353

On the Road

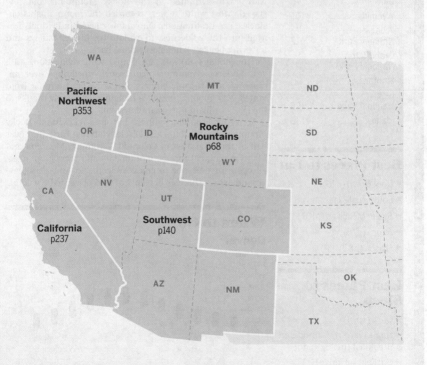

Rocky Mountains

Best Places to Eat

➡ Root Down (p75)

➡ Loula's (p127)

➡ Sweet Melissa's (p107)

➡ Acorn (p75)

➡ Frasca (p83)

Best Places to Sleep

➡ Curtis (p74)

➡ Nagle Warren Mansion Bed & Breakfast (p106)

➡ Old Faithful Inn (p117)

➡ Crawford Hotel (p74)

➡ Chautauqua Lodge & Cottages (p82)

➡ Wort Hotel (p110)

Why Go?

Adventure has always defined the United States' backbone. Native tribes hunted in the Rocky Mountains, but few stayed. Most white settlers regarded the mountains as obstacles, not destinations. Only a few rugged individuals forayed into the wilderness to explore the hidden valleys and towering peaks – some never came back.

True, today's Rockies are dotted with civilization. And, yes, modern adventurers plan casual expeditions over microbrews and organic burgers. But these lands are far from tamed. Vast mountain ranges remain wild, largely thanks to the USA's brilliant public lands system.

You're likely familiar with the big ones: Yellowstone, Rocky Mountain, Grand Teton and Glacier National Parks, but over half of the total area of Colorado, Wyoming, Montana and Idaho is national forests, monuments and recreation areas, all open for everyone to enjoy. Welcome to America's playground, where there's still plenty of wild places to be wild in.

When to Go

Denver

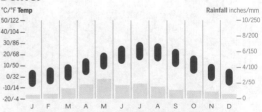

Jun–Aug Long days of sunshine for biking, hiking, farmers markets and summer festivals.

Sep & Oct Fall foliage coincides with terrific lodging deals and far fewer crowds.

Jan–Mar Snow-dusted peaks, powdery slopes and deluxe après-ski parties.

History

When French trappers and Spaniards 'discovered' the Rocky Mountains in the late 18th century, they found the area was already home to several tribes of Native Americans, including the Nez Percé, the Shoshone, the Crow, the Lakota and the Ute. This fact did not slow the European conquest, and countries began claiming, defending, buying and selling what they called 'unclaimed' territory.

A young US government purchased all lands east of the Continental Divide from France in the 1803 Louisiana Purchase. Shortly thereafter it dispatched Meriwether Lewis and William Clark to survey the area and see exactly what they had bought. Their epic survey covered nearly 8000 miles in two-and-a-half years, and tales of what they found urged on other adventurers, setting migration in motion.

Wagon trains voyaged to the Rockies and beyond right into the 20th century, only temporarily slowed by the completion of the Transcontinental Railroad across southern Wyoming in the late 1860s.

To accommodate settlers, the US purged the western frontier of the Spanish, British and, in a truly shameful era, most of the Native American population. The government signed endless treaties to defuse Native American objections to increasing settlement, but always reneged and shunted tribes onto smaller reservations. Gold-miners' incursions into Native American territory in Montana and the building of US Army forts along the Bozeman Trail ignited a series of wars with the Lakota, Cheyenne, Arapaho and others.

Gold and silver mania preceded Colorado's entry to statehood in 1876. Statehood soon followed for Montana (1889), Wyoming (1890) and Idaho (1890). Mining, grazing and timber played major roles in regional economic development, sparking growth in financial and industrial support. The miners, white farmers and ranchers controlled power in the late 19th century, but the boom-and-bust cycles of their industries coupled with unsustainable resource management took their toll on the landscape.

When the economy thrived post-WWII, national parks started attracting vacationers, and a heightened conservation movement flourished. Tourism became a leading industry in all four states, with the military a close second (particularly in Colorado).

Political shifts in recent years have placed many of the Rocky Mountain region's protected areas in jeopardy. Special interest groups continually lobby for increased resource extraction and development on federal lands, which may cut off access for the public.

Land & Climate

Extending from British Columbia, Canada, to northern New Mexico, the Rocky Mountains are North America's longest chain of mountains. Over 100 separate ranges make up the Rockies and most uplifted during the Laramide orogeny, when a chunk of oceanic crust took a shallow dive under the continental plate bumping along just under the surface of the earth. This movement forced the Rockies upwards, sideways and in some cases on top of itself – like at the Lewis Overthrust Fault in Glacier National Park where older rock, miles thick, was pushed some 50 miles (80km) across the top of younger rock. Over time, glaciers and erosion have worn the peaks down to their present form, revealing rock layers that betray their long and chaotic past.

The spring is largely a muddy time as the snow melts and deciduous trees begin to bud. It generally doesn't feel 'summery' in many regions of the mountains until late June. During the brief summer months (typically July through September) all the plants must get on with the business of reproduction at once, and high alpine meadows glow with the colors of the rainbow. All the humans must get on with the business of recreating during this time, too, and trails are flooded with bikers and backpackers – particularly in much of Colorado.

It can snow any time of year in the Rockies, though typically the first flurries fly in early October as the aspen leaves blanket the hillsides with shimmering gold. The days are warm, nights are cool and most of the crowds have gone back to school. This is possibly the best time to visit (but don't tell anyone).

ℹ Getting There & Around

Denver has the only major international airport (p80) in the Rocky Mountains area. Both Denver and Colorado Springs offer flights on smaller planes to Jackson, WY; Boise, ID; Bozeman, MT; Aspen, CO; and other destinations. Salt Lake City, UT, may be more convenient to destinations in the west and north regions.

Two Amtrak (www.amtrak.com) train routes pass through the region. *California Zephyr*, traveling daily between Emeryville, CA, and Chicago, IL, has six stops in Colorado, including Denver, Fraser-Winter Park, Glenwood Springs and Grand Junction. *Empire Builder* runs daily from Seattle,

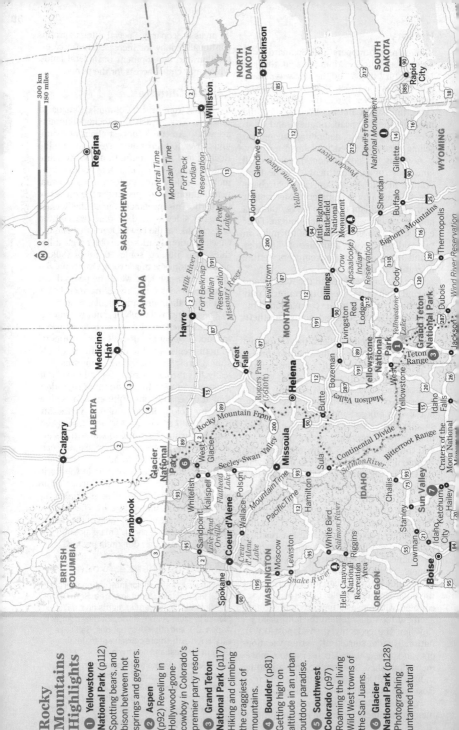

Rocky Mountains Highlights

1 Yellowstone National Park (p112) Spotting bears, and bison between hot springs and geysers.

2 Aspen (p92) Reveling in Hollywood-gone-cowboy in Colorado's premier party resort.

3 Grand Teton National Park (p117) Hiking and climbing the craggiest of mountains.

4 Boulder (p81) Getting high on altitude in an urban outdoor paradise.

5 Southwest Colorado (p97) Roaming the living Wild West towns of the San Juans.

6 Glacier National Park (p128) Photographing untamed natural

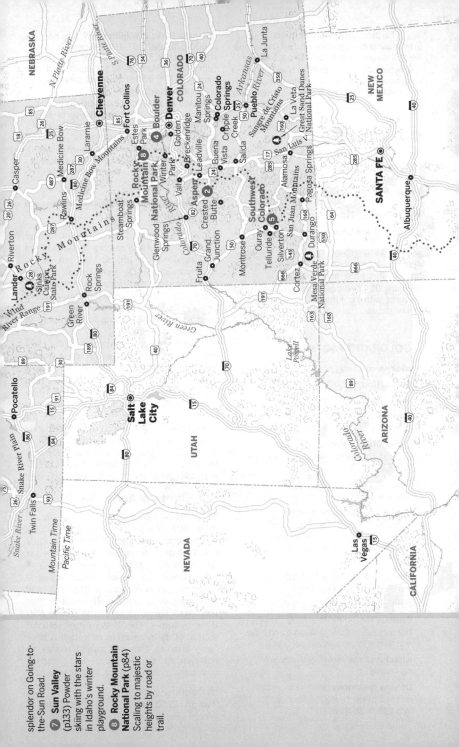

splendor on Going-to-the-Sun Road.

7 Sun Valley (p133) Powder skiing with the stars in Idaho's winter playground.

8 Rocky Mountain National Park (p84) Scaling to majestic heights by road or trail.

WA, or Portland, OR, to Chicago, IL, with 12 stops in Montana (including Whitefish, East Glacier and West Glacier) and one stop in Idaho at Sandpoint.

Greyhound (📞214-849-8100; www.greyhound. com) travels some parts of the Rocky Mountains, but to really get out and explore you'll need a car.

COLORADO

Spectacular vistas, endless powder runs and mountain towns with echoes of the Old West – Colorado is a place that has long beckoned people to adventure.

ℹ Information

Bureau of Land Management Colorado (BLM; 📞800-877-8339, 303-239-3600; www.co.blm. gov; 2850 Youngfield St, Lakewood; ⊗8:30am-4pm Mon-Fri; 🚌28) Provides information on historic sites, trails, and more.

Camping USA (www.camping-usa.com) A great resource, with more than 12,000 campgrounds in its database.

COLORADO FACTS

Nickname Centennial State

Population 5,500,000

Area 104,185 sq miles

Capital City Denver (population 693,100)

Other Cities Boulder (population 97,385), Colorado Springs (population 445,830)

Sales tax 2.9% state tax, plus individual city taxes

Birthplace of Ute tribal leader ChiefOuray (1833–80); South Park creator Trey Parker (b 1969); actor Amy Adams (b 1974); climber Tommy Caldwell (b1978)

Peaks over 14,000ft 53, 54 or 58 (depending on who's counting)

Politics Swing state

Famous for Sunny days (300 per year), the highest-altitude vineyards and longest ski run in the continental USA

Kitschiest souvenir Deer-hoof bottle-opener

Driving distances Denver to Vail 100 miles, Boulder to Rocky Mountain National Park 38 miles

---

Colorado Parks & Wildlife (CPW; Map p76; 📞800-678-2267, 303-470-1144; www.cpw. state.co.us; 1313 Sherman St, Denver; ⊗8am-5pm Mon-Fri) Manages 42 state parks and more than 300 wildlife areas; handles reservations for campgrounds.

Colorado Road & Traffic Conditions (📞511; www.codot.gov; ⊗24hr) Provides up-to-date information on Colorado highway and traffic conditions, including cycling maps.

Colorado Travel & Tourism Authority (📞800-265-6723; www.colorado.com) Offers detailed information on sights, activities and more throughout the state.

Denver

As an urban center, Denver has come a long way. Sure you'll still catch a Stetson or two walking down the 16th St Mall, but the Intermountain West's cosmopolitan capital now delights in a growing culinary and arts scene, plus plenty of brewpubs, great parks and cycling trails, and close proximity to spectacular hiking, skiing and camping in the Rocky Mountains.

Thanks to a re-urbanization of the city's central core, Denver now has name-worthy neighborhoods with flavors that are all their own – River North (RiNo) for hipster bars and eye-catching street art, Lower Highlands (LoHi) and South Broadway for great eateries and live music, Cherry Creek for glam, Lower Downtown (LoDo) for upscale restaurants and cocktail lounges as well as the Golden Triangle and Santa Fe for arts, theater and museums. In all, there's a neighborhood and a vibe for just about anybody.

◎ Sights & Activities

⭐**Denver Art Museum** MUSEUM
(DAM; Map p76; 📞ticket sales 720-865-5000; www.denverartmuseum.org; 100 W 14th Ave; adult/child $13/free, 1st Sat of month free; ⊗10am-5pm Tue-Thu, Sat & Sun, to 8pm Fri; 🅿🚻; 🚌0, 52) 🚲
DAM is home to one of the largest Native American art collections in the USA, and puts on special multimedia exhibits that vary from treasures of British art to *Star Wars* costumes. The Western American Art section of the permanent collection is justifiably famous. This isn't an old, stodgy art museum, and the best part is diving into the interactive exhibits, which kids love.

⭐**Confluence Park** PARK
(Map p76; 2200 15th St; 🚻; 🚌10, 28, 32, 44) 🚲
Where Cherry Creek and South Platte Riv-

er meet is the nexus and plexus of Denver's sunshine-loving culture. It's a good place for an afternoon picnic, and there's a short white-water park for kayakers and tubers. Families also enjoy a small beach and shallow water areas for playing.

★ **Clyfford Still Museum** MUSEUM
(Map p76; ☑720-354-4880; www.clyffordstillmuseum.org; 1250 Bannock St; adult/child $10/free; ⊙10am-5pm Tue-Thu, Sat & Sun, to 8pm Fri; ☐0, 52) Dedicated exclusively to the work and legacy of 20th-century American abstract expressionist Clyfford Still, this fascinating museum's collection includes over 2400 pieces – 95% of his work – by the powerful and narcissistic master of bold. In his will, Still insisted that his body of work only be exhibited in a singular space, so Denver built him a museum. Free tours are offered throughout the week; check the website for dates and times.

History Colorado Center MUSEUM
(Map p76; ☑303-447-8679; www.historycoloradocenter.org; 1200 Broadway; adult/child $12/8; ⊙10am-5pm; P⏏; ☐0, 10) Discover Colorado's frontier roots and high-tech modern triumphs at this sharp, smart and charming museum. There are plenty of interactive exhibits, including a Jules Verne–esque 'Time Machine' that you push across a giant map of Colorado to explore seminal moments in the Centennial State's history. Periodically, story times for toddlers and low-sensory morning sessions are offered before the museum opens.

★ **Blair-Caldwell African American Museum** MUSEUM
(Map p76; ☑720-865-2401; https://history.denverlibrary.org/blair; 2401 Welton St, 3rd fl; ⊙noon-8pm Mon & Wed, 10am-6pm Tue, Thu & Fri, 9am-5pm Sat; P⏏; ☐43, ☐D) FREE Tucked into the 3rd floor of a public library, this multimedia museum provides an excellent overview of the history of African Americans in the Rocky Mountain region – from their migration and settlement to their discrimination and achievements. Exhibits on Wellington Webb, Denver's first African American mayor, as well as Five Points, Denver's historically black neighborhood, are particularly interesting.

Denver Museum of Nature & Science MUSEUM
(DMNS; ☑303-370-6000; www.dmns.org; 2001 Colorado Blvd; museum adult/child $17/12, IMAX $10/8, Planetarium $5/4; ⊙9am-5pm; P⏏; ☐20, 32, 40) The Denver Museum of Nature & Science is a classic natural-science museum with excellent temporary exhibits on topics like the biomechanics of bugs, Pompeii and mythical creatures. Permanent exhibits are equally engaging and include those cool panoramas we all loved as kids. The **IMAX theater** and **Gates Planetarium** are especially fun. Located on the eastern edge of City Park.

⭐ **Festivals & Events**

First Friday CULTURAL
(www.rivernorthart.com) FREE On the first Friday of every month, Denverites come out for an art stroll, cruising galleries for free wine and fun conversations in the Santa Fe and RiNo Arts Districts. The event typically runs from 6pm to 10pm.

Five Points Jazz Festival MUSIC
(www.artsandvenuesdenver.com; Welton St; ⊙May; ⏏; ☐12, 28, 43, ☐D) FREE This one-day jazz fest celebrates the historically African American neighborhood of Five Points, which was once home to several jazz clubs. Over 50 bands perform on stages set up on Welton St. Several kid-friendly activities – instrument making, drum circles, face painting – are offered, making it a fun event for all. Held the third Saturday of May.

Great American Beer Festival BEER
(☑303-447-0816; www.greatamericanbeerfestival.com; 700 14th St; $85; ⊙Sep or Oct; ☐1, 8, 19, 48, ☐D, F, H) Colorado has more microbreweries per capita than any other US state, and this hugely popular festival sells out in advance. More than 500 breweries are represented, from the big players to home enthusiasts.

🛏 **Sleeping**

★ **Hostel Fish** HOSTEL $
(Map p76; ☑303-954-0962; www.hostelfish.com; 1217 20th St; dm/r from $53/185; ✳⏴; ☐38) This swanked-out hostel is an oasis for budget travelers. Stylish, modern and squeaky clean, dorms have themes – Aspen, Graffiti, Vintage Biker – and sleep five to 10 people in bunks. Mattresses are thick, duvets plush and each guest gets a locker and individual charging station. A common kitchen and pub crawls make it easy to make new friends.

Mile High Guest House HOSTEL $
(☑720-531-2898; www.milehighguesthouse.com; 1445 High St; dm $38, r with shared bath $82; ⏴; ☐15) A gorgeous old Denver mansion makes for a cool hostel, and a welcome addition to Denver's budget lodging options. Large

parlor rooms serve as dorms, outfitted with bunk beds (but no lockers, oddly). Private rooms with shared bathrooms are also available, and the friendly staff help organize group outings, like pub crawls, art walks and backyard BBQs. Convenient bus-friendly location.

★ Queen Anne Bed & Breakfast Inn
B&B $$

(Map p76; ☏303-296-6666; www.queenanne bnb.com; 2147 Tremont Pl; r/ste from $160/230; ▣☺✳☎; ▣28, 32) ✎ Soft chamber music wafting through public areas, fresh flowers, manicured gardens and evening wine tastings create a romantic ambience at this eco-conscious B&B in two late-1800s Victorian homes. Featuring period antiques, private hot tubs and exquisite hand-painted murals, each room has its own personality.

★ Crawford Hotel
HOTEL $$$

(Map p76; ☏855-362-5098; www.thecrawfordhotel. com; 1701 Wynkoop St, Union Station; r $349-469,

ste $589-709; ✳☎☎; ▣55L, 72L,120L, FF2, ▣A, B, C, E, W) Set in the historic Union Station (p80), the Crawford Hotel is an example of Denver's amazing transformation. Rooms are luxurious and artful, with high ceilings and throwbacks like the art-deco headboards and clawfoot tubs. Service is impeccable, and the station's bar, the Terminal, is a fun hangout. Steps away, there's light-rail service to Denver International Airport (p80).

Curtis
HOTEL $$$

(Map p76; ☏303-571-0300; www.thecurtis.com; 1405 Curtis St; r $269-449; ☺✳@☎; ▣9, 10, 15, 20, 28, 32, 38, 43, 44) The Curtis is like stepping into a doo-bop Warhol wonderland: 13 themed floors, each devoted to a different genre of American pop culture. Rooms are spacious and very mod. Attention to detail – either through the service or the decor – is paramount at the Curtis, a one-of-a-kind hotel in the heart of downtown Denver.

ROCKY MOUNTAINS IN ...

Two Weeks

Start your Rocky Mountain odyssey in the **Denver** area. Go tubing, vintage-clothes shopping or biking in outdoor-mad, boho **Boulder**, then soak up the liberal rays eavesdropping at a sidewalk cafe. Enjoy the vistas of the **Rocky Mountain National Park** before heading west on I-70 to play in the mountains around **Breckenridge**, which also has some of the best beginner slopes in Colorado. Go to ski and mountain-bike mecca **Steamboat Springs** before crossing the border into Wyoming.

Get a taste of prairie-town life in **Laramie**, then stop in **Lander**, rock-climbing destination extraordinaire. Continue north to chic Jackson and the majestic **Grand Teton National Park** before hitting iconic **Yellowstone National Park**. Save at least three days for exploring this geyser-packed wonderland.

Cross the state line into 'big sky country' and slowly make your way northwest through **Montana**, stopping in funky **Bozeman** and lively **Missoula** before visiting **Flathead Lake**. Wrap up your trip in Idaho, exploring Basque culture in up-and-coming **Boise**.

One Month

With a month on your hands, you can really delve into the region's off-the-beaten-path treasures. Follow the two-week itinerary, but dip southwest in **Colorado** – a developing wine region – before visiting **Wyoming**. Ride the 4WD trails around **Ouray**. Be sure to visit **Mesa Verde National Park** and its ancient cliff dwellings.

In **Montana**, you'll want to visit **Glacier National Park** before the glaciers disappear altogether. In Idaho, spend more time playing in **Sun Valley** and be sure to explore the shops, pubs and yummy organic restaurants in delightful little **Ketchum**. With a one-month trip, you also have time to drive along a few of Idaho's fantastically remote scenic byways. Make sure you cruise Hwy 75 from **Sun Valley** north to **Stanley**. Situated on the wide banks of the **Salmon River**, this stunning mountain hamlet is completely surrounded by national forestland and wilderness areas. Stanley is also blessed with world-class trout fishing and mild to wild rafting.

Take Hwy 21 (the **Ponderosa Pine Scenic Byway**) from Stanley to **Boise**. This scenic drive takes you through miles of dense ponderosa forests and past some excellent, solitary riverside camping spots – some of which come with their own natural hot-springs pools.

★ **Art – a Hotel**   BOUTIQUE HOTEL **$$$**
(Map p76; ☑303-572-8000; www.thearthotel. com; 1201 Broadway; r $305-348, ste $382-518; P❖@🛜🐾; 🚌0, 6, 10, 52) As the name suggests, this hotel has intriguing artwork in the guest rooms and common areas, befitting its location, just around the corner from the Denver Art Museum (p70). Rooms are sizable and modern, and the large patio with fire pits and great views is perfect for happy-hour cocktails. The location close to downtown restaurants and attractions, could hardly be better.

✗ Eating

Denver's food scene is booming, with new restaurants, cafes and food trucks seemingly opening every month. Downtown offers the greatest depth and variety in Denver, though strollable neighborhoods like LoHi, RiNo, South Broadway, Uptown and Five Points hold some of Denver's best eateries. Check out www.5280.com for new eats.

★ **Denver Central Market**   FOOD HALL **$**
(Map p76; 2669 Larimer St; ⊙8am-9pm Sun-Thu, to 10pm Fri & Sat; 🚌44, 48) Set in a repurposed warehouse, this gourmet market place wows with its style and breadth of options. Eat a bowl of handmade pasta or an artisanal sandwich; consider a wood-fired pizza or street tacos. Or just grab a cocktail at the bar, and wander between the fruit stand and chocolatier. Patrons eat at communal tables or on the street-side patio.

★ **Civic Center Eats**   FOOD TRUCK **$**
(Map p76; ☑303-861-4633; www.civiccentercon servancy.org; cnr Broadway & Colfax Ave, Civic Center Park; mains $5-10; ⊙11am-2pm Tue-Thu May-Oct; 👫👶; 🚌0, 9, 10, 52) When the weather gets warm, head to **Civic Center Park** for lunch. There are heaps of food trucks – everything from BBQ and pizza to sushi and Indian – roll into the park and serve up hearty meals. Tables are set up, live bands play, office workers picnic on the grass. It's Denver at its best.

★ **Hop Alley**   CHINESE **$$**
(Map p76; ☑720-379-8340; www.hopalleydenver. com; 3500 Larimer St; mains $10-25; ⊙5:30-10:30pm Mon-Sat; 🐾; 🚌12, 44) Hop Alley was a slur used for Denver's hardscrabble Chinatown in the 1880s, until a race riot and anti-Chinese legislation scattered the community. The moniker was reclaimed for this small bustling restaurant located in (what else?) a former soy sauce plant. Come for authentic yet inventive Chinese dishes, and equally creative cocktails, named after the signs of the Chinese zodiac.

★ **Acorn**   AMERICAN **$$$**
(☑720-542-3721; www.denveracorn.com; 3350 Brighton Blvd, The Source; ⊙11:30am-10pm Mon-Sat, 5:30-10pm Sun; P🅿️🐾; 🚌12, 20, 48) The oak-fired oven and grill are the shining stars of this superb restaurant, where small plates of innovative and shareable eats make up meals. The menu changes seasonally but dishes like crispy fried pickles, oak-grilled broccolini and smoked-pork posole are hits. If dinner is too pricey, consider a midday meal (2:30pm to 5:30pm) – the menu is limited but more affordable.

★ **Rioja**   MODERN AMERICAN **$$$**
(Map p76; ☑303-820-2282; www.riojadenver.com; 1431 Larimer St; mains $19-39; ⊙11:30am-2:30pm Wed-Fri, 10am-2:30pm Sat & Sun, 5-10pm daily; 🐾; 🚌10, 28, 32, 38, 44) This is one of Denver's most innovative restaurants. Smart, busy and upscale, yet relaxed and casual – just like Colorado – Rioja features modern cuisine inspired by Italian and Spanish traditions and powered by modern culinary flavors.

★ **Root Down**   MODERN AMERICAN **$$$**
(Map p76; ☑303-993-4200; www.rootdowndenver. com; 1600 W 33rd Ave; small plates $8-19, mains $14-35; ⊙5-10pm Sun-Thu, 5-11pm Fri & Sat, 11am-2pm Fri, 10am-2:30pm Sat & Sun; 🐾; 🚌19, 52) 🌿 In a converted gas station, chef Justin Cucci has undertaken one of the city's most ambitious culinary concepts, marrying sustainable 'field-to-fork' practices, high-concept culinary fusions and a low-impact, energy-efficient ethos. The menu changes seasonally, but consider yourself lucky if it includes the sweet-potato falafel or lamb sliders. Vegetarian, vegan, raw and gluten-free diets very welcome.

🍸 Drinking & Nightlife

Denver's top nightlife districts include Uptown for gay bars and a young professional crowd, LoDo for loud sports bars and heavy drinking, RiNo for hipsters, LoHi for an eclectic mix, and South Broadway and Colfax for Old School wannabes.

★ **Black Shirt Brewing Co**   BREWERY
(☑303-993-2799; www.blackshirtbrewingco.com; 3719 Walnut St; ⊙11am-10pm Sun-Thu, to midnight Fri & Sat; 🐾; 🚌12, 44, 🚆A) Artisanal brewers create the all-red-ale menu at the popular BSB; ales take anywhere from two months

ROCKY MOUNTAINS DENVER

Denver

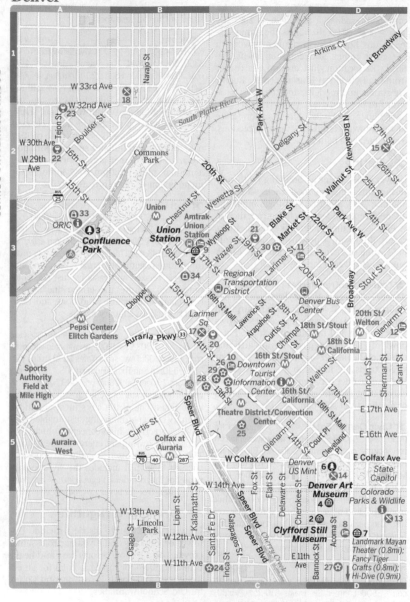

to three years to brew. So careful are they with the handcrafted beers, the brewers developed lopsided glasses to showcase the aromas. Live music is part of the culture here, as is good food. A kitchen offers brick-oven pizzas and gourmet salads.

★ **Williams & Graham** COCKTAIL BAR
(Map p76; ☐303-997-8886; www.williamsandgraham.com; 3160 Tejon St; ☺5pm-1am; ☐32,44) Denver's top speakeasy looks like an old Western bookstore, but ask for a seat and the cashier pushes a wall of books and leads you

Map

Acorn (0.4mi)

Blake St
Walnut St
Larimer St
32nd St
31st St
30th St
29th St
28th St

Tracks (84yd);
Black Shirt
Brewing Co
(0.2mi)

⊗ 16   36th Ave

35th Ave

Bruce
Randolph Ave

33rd Ave

Martin Luther
King Blvd

E 31st Ave

30th St/
Ⓜ Downing

Downing St

Curtis
Park

Lawrence St
Curtis St
Champa St
Stout St

Welton St

Ⓜ 27th St/
Welton

California St

E 26th Ave

E 25th Ave

E 24th Ave

E 23rd Ave

E 22nd Ave

Ⓜ 25th St/
Welton

⊞ 1
Blair-Caldwell African
American Museum

Tremont Pl

E 20th Ave

E 19th Ave

E 18th Ave

Park Ave

Clarkson St
Emerson St
Ogden St
Downing St

BUS
⑦⓪ ④⓪ ②⑧⑦

⊛ 32   E Colfax Ave

Mile High Guest
House (0.3mi);
Bluebird Theater (1mi);
Denver Museum of
Nature & Science (2mi);
Denver International
✈ (26mi)

Logan St
Pennsylvania St
Pearl St
Washington St

E 14th Ave

E 13th Ave

E 12th Ave

E 11th Ave

Corona St
Downing St
Marion St
Lafayette St
Humboldt St

0 — 500 m
0 — 0.25 miles

Denver

⊙ Top Sights
1	Blair-Caldwell African American Museum	E3
2	Clyfford Still Museum	D6
3	Confluence Park	A3
4	Denver Art Museum	D6
5	Union Station	B3

⊚ Sights
| 6 | Civic Center Park | D5 |
| 7 | History Colorado Center | D6 |

🛏 Sleeping
8	Art – a Hotel	D6
9	Crawford Hotel	B3
10	Curtis	C4
11	Hostel Fish	C3
12	Queen Anne Bed & Breakfast Inn	D4

⊗ Eating
13	City O' City	D6
14	Civic Center Eats	D5
15	Denver Central Market	D2
16	Hop Alley	F1
17	Rioja	B4
18	Root Down	B1

🍷 Drinking & Nightlife
19	Crema Coffee House	E2
20	Crú	C4
21	Falling Rock Tap House	C3
22	Linger	A2
23	Williams & Graham	A2

🎭 Entertainment
24	Colorado Ballet	C6
25	Colorado Convention Center	C5
26	Colorado Symphony Orchestra	C4
27	Curious Theatre	D6
28	Denver Center for the Performing Arts	B4
29	Denver Performing Arts Complex	C4
30	El Chapultepec	C3
31	Ellie Caulkins Opera House	C4
32	Ogden Theatre	F5
	Opera Colorado	(see 31)

🛍 Shopping
| 33 | REI | A3 |
| 34 | Tattered Cover Bookstore | B3 |

deeper into the era. Polished wood, gleaming brass features, antique lamps, tin ceilings and mixologists in aprons await. Cocktails are creative and artfully prepared – almost too beautiful to drink. Almost.

★ **Crema Coffee House**　　　CAFE
(Map p76; ☏720-284-9648; www.cremacoffeehouse.net; 2862 Larimer St; ⊗7am-5pm; 🐾; 🚌44) Noah Price, a clothing-design-er-turned-coffee-impresario, takes his job seriously, selecting, brewing and pouring

Denver's absolute-best coffee. The espresso and French-pressed are complete perfection, but it's the oatmeal latte, delicately infused ice teas and spectacularly eclectic menu – Moroccan meatballs to peanut-butter and jelly sandwiches with goat's cheese – that put this place over the top.

Linger
LOUNGE

(Map p76; ✆303-993-3120; www.lingerdenver.com; 2030 W 30th Ave; ☺11:30am-2:30pm & 4-10pm Tue-Thu, to 11pm Fri, 10am-2:30pm & 4-11pm Sat, 10am-2:30pm Sun; 🚌28, 32, 44) This rambling LoHi complex sits in the former Olinger mortuary. Come nighttime, they black out the 'O' and it just becomes Linger. There's an interesting menu, but most people come for the tony feel and light-up-the-night rooftop bar, which has great views of downtown Denver and even a replica of the RV made famous by the Bill Murray smash *Stripes*.

Falling Rock Tap House
BAR

(Map p76; ✆303-293-8338; www.fallingrock taphouse.com; 1919 Blake St; ☺11am-2am; 🚌0, 15, 20) High fives and hollers punctuate the scene when the Rockies triumph and beer drinkers file in to forget an afternoon of drinking Coors at the ball park. There are – count 'em – 80-plus beers on tap and the bottle list has almost 150. With all the local favorites, this is *the* place to drink beer downtown.

Crú
WINE BAR

(Map p76; ✆303-893-9463; www.cruawine bar.com; 1442 Larimer St; glass of wine $10-27; ☺2pm-midnight Mon-Thu, noon-2am Fri & Sat, 10:30am-3pm Sun; 🚌10, 28, 32, 38, 44) This classy Larimer Sq wine bar is decked out in wine labels and glassware, with dim lighting and gentle music. It looks so bespoke it's surprising to learn it's a chain (Dallas, Austin). Come for happy hour (4pm to 6:30pm Monday to Friday) when flights of wine are $3 off and light fare includes mussels and goat's cheese beignets.

☆ Entertainment

Denver is bursting with entertainment options. There's live music and theater practically everywhere, from intimate jazz clubs to the amazing multitheater Denver Center for the Performing Arts. Denver is a four-sport town (one of few in the country) and also has professional soccer and lacrosse. Add to that comedy, movies, dance and yearly festivals and there's truly something for everyone.

★ Denver Performing Arts Complex
PERFORMING ARTS

(Map p76; ✆720-865-4220; www.artscomplex.com; cnr 14th & Champa Sts; 🚌9, 15, 28, 32, 38, 43, 44) This massive complex – one of the largest of its kind – occupies four city blocks, and houses 10 major venues, including the historic **Ellie Caulkins Opera House** and the Boettcher Concert Hall. It's also home to the **Colorado Ballet** (✆303-837-8888; www.colo radoballet.org; 1075 Santa Fe Dr; ☺box office 9am-5pm Mon-Fri; 🚻; 🚌1, 9), **Denver Center for the Performing Arts** (✆303-893-4100; www. denvercenter.org; 1101 13th St; ☺box office 10am-6pm Mon-Sat & 1hr before each show; 🚻; 🚌9, 15, 28, 32, 38, 43, 44), **Opera Colorado** (✆303-468-2030; www.operacolorado.org; ☺box office 10am-5pm Mon-Fri; 🚻; 🚌9, 15, 28, 32, 38, 43, 44) and the Colorado Symphony Orchestra. Not sure what you want to do tonight? Come here.

★ Curious Theatre
THEATER

(Map p76; ✆303-623-0524; www.curioustheatre. org; 1080 Acoma St; tickets from $18; ☺box office 2-7pm Tue-Sat; 🚌0, 6, 52) 'No guts, no story' is the tagline of this award-winning theater company, set in a converted church. Plays pack a punch with thought-provoking stories that take on social justice issues. Think race, immigration, sexuality. Stay for talk backs at the end of each show, when actors engage with the audience about everything from the plot to the set.

★ El Chapultepec
JAZZ

(Map p76; ✆303-295-9126; www.thepeclodo. com; 1962 Market St; ☺7am-1am, music from 9pm; 🚌38) This smoky, old-school jazz joint attracts a diverse mix of people. Since it opened in 1951, Frank Sinatra, Tony Bennett and Ella Fitzgerald have played here, as have Jagger and Richards. Local jazz bands take the tiny stage nightly, but you never know who might drop by.

Hi-Dive
LIVE MUSIC

(✆303-733-0230; www.hi-dive.com; 7 S Broadway; 🚌0) Local rock heroes and touring indie bands light up the stage at the Hi-Dive, a venue at the heart of Denver's local music scene. During big shows it gets deafeningly loud, cheek-to-jowl with hipsters and humid as an armpit. In other words, perfection.

Ogden Theatre
LIVE MUSIC

(Map p76; ✆303-832-1874; www.ogdentheatre.com; 935 E Colfax Ave; ☺box office 10am-2pm Sat, 1hr before doors open show days; 🚌15) One of Denver's best live-music venues, the Ogden Theatre has a checkered past. Built in 1917, it was derelict for many years and might have been bulldozed in the early 1990s, but it's now listed on the National Register of Historic Places. Bands such as Edward Sharpe & the Magnetic Zeros and Lady Gaga have played here.

Colorado Symphony
Orchestra   CLASSICAL MUSIC
(CSO; Map p76; ☑303-623-7876; www.colorado symphony.org; 1000 14th St, Boettcher Concert Hall; ⊘box office 10am-6pm Mon-Fri, noon-6pm Sat; ☑; ☐9, 15, 28, 32, 38, 43, 44) The Boettcher Concert Hall in the Denver Performing Arts Complex is home to this renowned symphony orchestra. The orchestra performs an annual 21-week Masterworks season, as well as concerts aimed at a broader audience – think live performances of movie scores during the screening of films.

Bluebird Theater   LIVE MUSIC
(☑303-377-1666; www.bluebirdtheater.net; 3317 E Colfax Ave; ☑; ☐15) This medium-sized theater is general admission standing room and has terrific sound and clear sight lines from the balcony. The venue often offers the last chance to catch bands – Denver faves the Lumineers and Devotchka both headlined here – on their way up to the big time.

Landmark Mayan Theater   CINEMA
(☑303-744-6799; www.landmarktheatres.com; 110 Broadway; ☑; ☐0) Even without the fancy sound system and enormous screen, this is the best place in Denver to take in a film. The 1930s movie palace is a romantic, historic gem and – bonus! – it serves beer.

🛍 Shopping

★**Tattered Cover Bookstore**   BOOKS
(Map p76; ☑303-436-1070; www.tatteredcover.com; 1628 16th St; ⊘6:30am-9pm Mon-Fri, 9am-9pm Sat, 10am-6pm Sun; 🛜☑; ☐10, 19, 28, 32, 44, MallRide) There are plenty of places to curl up with a book in Denver's beloved independent bookstore. Bursting with new and used books, it has a good stock of regional travel guides and nonfiction titles dedicated to the Western states and Western folklore. There's a second smaller location on Colfax near City Park.

★**REI**   SPORTS & OUTDOORS
(Recreational Equipment Incorporated; Map p76; ☑303-756-3100; www.rei.com; 1416 Platte St; ⊘9am-9pm Mon-Sat, to 7pm Sun; ☑; ☐10, 28, 32, 44) The flagship store of this outdoor-equipment super supplier is an essential stop if you are heading to the mountains or

OFF THE BEATEN TRACK

LIVE AT RED ROCKS!
....
Set between 400ft-high red sandstone rocks 15 miles southwest of Denver is **Red Rocks Park & Amphitheatre** (☑303-697-4939; www.redrocksonline. com; 18300 W Alameda Pkwy; ⊘5am-11pm; ☑). Acoustics are so good many artists record live albums here. The 9000-seat theater offers stunning views and draws big-name bands all summer. To see your favorite singer go to work on the stage is to witness a performance in one of the most exceptional music venues in the world. For many, it's reason enough for a trip to Colorado.

just cruising through Confluence. In addition to top gear for camping, cycling, climbing and skiing, it has a rental department, maps and the Pinnacle, a 47ft-high indoor structure of simulated red sandstone for climbing and rappelling.

★**Fancy Tiger Crafts**   ARTS & CRAFTS
(☑303-733-3855; www.fancytigercrafts.com; 59 Broadway; ⊘10am-7pm Mon & Wed-Sat, to 9pm Tue, 11am-6pm Sun; ☑; ☐0) So you dig crochet and quilting? You knit a mean sweater and have a few too many tattoos? Welcome to Fancy Tiger Crafts, a sophisticated remodel of granny's yarn barn that's ground zero for Denver's crafty hipsters. There are classes in the back (including ones by Jessica, 'mistress of patchwork') and a rad selection of fabric, yarn and books.

ⓘ Information

The Tourist Information Center website (www. denver.org) has great information about events.
DIA Information Booth (☑303-317-0629; www. visitdenver.com; Denver International Airport; ⊘hours vary; 🛜☑; ☐A) Tourist and airport information is available at this booth on the east end of Denver International Airport's central hall.
ORIC (Outdoor Recreation Information Center; Map p76; ☑REI main line 303-756-3100; www. oriconline.org; 1416 Platte St; ⊘hours vary; 🛜; ☐10, 28, 32, 44) Inside REI, this information desk is a must for those looking to get out of town for outdoor adventure. It has maps and expert information on trip planning and safety. The desk is staffed by volunteers, so hours vary wildly, but arriving on a weekend afternoon is a good bet.
Downtown Tourist Information Center (Map p76; ☑303-892-1505; www.denver.org; 1575

WORTH A TRIP

BEST DAY HIKES & RIDES FROM DENVER

There are literally hundreds of day hikes within an hour of Denver.

Jefferson County Open Space Parks (www.jeffco.us/openspace) Jefferson County runs along most of the western edge of Denver, and its open spaces are the best around.

Golden Gate Canyon State Park (☑303-582-3707; www.cpw.state.co.us; 92 Crawford Gulch Rd; entrance $7, camping $20-26; ☺5am-10pm; ⛺🚴) Located halfway between Golden and Nederland, this massive 12,000-acre park has plenty of hiking trails and rockclimbing.

Staunton State Park (☑303-816-0912; www.parks.state.co.us/parks; 12102 S Elk Creek Rd; ☺7am-9pm; ⛺🚴) Colorado's newest state park sits on a historic ranch site 40 miles west of Denver. Ranging in elevation from 8100ft to 10,000ft, it has a rich variety of landscapes – from grassy meadows to dramatic granite cliffs.

Waterton Canyon (☑303-634-3745; www.denverwater.org/recreation/watertoncanyon; 11300 Waterton Rd; ☺30min before dawn-30min after dusk; ⛺) South of Denver, just west of Chatfield Reservoir, this pretty canyon has an easy 6.5-mile trail to the Strontia Springs Dam.

Pike National Forest (☑303-275-5610, campsite reservations only 877-444-6777; www.fs.usda.gov; 19316 Goddard Ranch Ct; ☺8am-4:30pm Mon-Fri; ⛺) Start exploring this large national forest by picking up information available at the South Platte Ranger Station, about 5 miles from Morrison.

Buffalo Creek Mountain Bike Area (www.frmbp.org; 18268 S Buffalo Creek Rd, Pine; ☺7am-7pm; ⛺) If you're into singletrack mountain biking, this area has about 40 miles of bike trails, including the sections of the Colorado Trail that permit bikes.

California St; ☺9am-6pm Mon-Fri, 9am-5pm Sat, 10am-2pm Sun May-Oct, 9am-5pm Mon-Fri, 9am-2pm Sat, 10am-2pm Sun Nov-Apr; 🚌9, 15, 20, MallRide, 🚊D, F, H) When you get to town, make for the largest and most central information center, located just off the 16th St Mall. You can load up on brochures, browse online travel pages and get solid information from knowledgeable staffers.

ℹ Getting There & Away

Denver International Airport (DIA; ☑303-342-2000; www.flydenver.com; 8500 Peña Blvd; ☺24hr; 🛜⛺; 🚊A) is a major air hub and one of the country's busiest facilities. In all, DIA has 53 sq miles of land, making it the biggest airport in the country by area. The facility has an automated subway that links the terminal to three concourses (Concourse C is almost 1 mile from the terminal). Give yourself a little extra time to find your way around.

Greyhound offers frequent buses on routes along the Front Range and on transcontinental routes. All buses stop at the **Denver Bus Center** (Map p76; ☑303-293-6555; 1055 19th St; ☺6am-midnight; 🛜; 🚌8, 48).

The **Colorado Mountain Express** (CME; ☑800-525-6363; www.coloradomountainexpress.com; 8500 Peña Blvd, Denver International Airport; 🛜⛺; 🚊A) has shuttle services from Denver International Airport (DIA), downtown Denver or Morrison to Summit County, including Breckenridge

and Keystone (adult/child $66/35, 2½ hours) and Vail (adult/child $84/44, three hours).

Amtrak (☑800-872-7245; www.amtrak.com; 1701 Wynkoop St, Union Station; 🚌55L, 72L,120L, FF2, 🚊A, B, C, E, W) runs the *California Zephyr* train service daily between Chicago ($121-325, 19 hours) and San Francisco ($144-446, 33 hours) stopping in Denver's gorgeously renovated **Union Station** (Map p76; ☑303-592-6712; www.unionstationindenver.com; 1701 Wynkoop St; 🅿; 🚌55L, 72L,120L, FF2, 🚊A, B, C, E, W).

ℹ Getting Around

TO/FROM THE AIRPORT
An **RTD** (☑303-299-6000; www.rtd-denver.com; per ride $2.60-4.50, day pass $5.20-9; ⛺) light-rail transports people from DIA to downtown Denver (Line A; $9, 45 minutes), servicing Denver suburbs along the way.

BICYCLE
You can get all the information you need on cycling in Denver from Bike Denver (www.bikedenver.org) and City of Denver (www.denvergov.org), both of which have downloadable bike maps for the city.
B-Cycle (☑303-825-3325; www.denverbcycle.com; 1-day membership $9; ☺5am-midnight; ⛺) This bike-share company has more than 80 stations throughout Denver. The daily rate includes unlimited rides as long as they're under 30 minutes.

CAR & MOTORCYCLE

Street parking can be a pain, but there is a slew of pay garages in downtown and LoDo. Nearly all the major car-rental agencies have counters at Denver International Airport, though only a few have offices in downtown Denver.

Enterprise Rent-A-Car (☑303-293-8644; www.enterprise.com; 2255 Broadway; ⊙7am-7pm Mon-Fri, 8am-4pm Sat & Sun; ☐44, 48) is an international car-rental agency with several offices in the Denver metro area.

PUBLIC TRANSPORTATION

Regional Transportation District (RTD; Map p76; ☑303-299-6000; www.rtd-denver.com; 1600 Blake St; ☐10, 19, 28, 32, 44, MallRide) provides public transportation throughout the Denver and Boulder area (local/regional fares $2.60/4.50). The website has schedules, routes, fares and a trip planner.

TAXI

Two major taxi companies offer door-to-door service in Denver:

Metro Taxi (☑303-333-3333; www.metrotaxi denver.com; ⊙24hr)

Yellow Cab (☑303-777-7777; www.denveryel lowcab.com; ⊙24hr)

Boulder

Twenty-five square miles surrounded by reality. That's the joke about Boulder that never goes away. The weather is perfect, the surroundings – stone Flatirons, gurgling creek, ponderosa trails and manicured college campus – beg idylling. And the populace – fit do-gooders with the beta on the best fair-trade coffee and hoppiest home brew – seals the stereotype.

Boulder's mad love of the outdoors was officially legislated in 1967, when it became the first US city to tax itself specifically to preserve open space. Thanks to such vision, people (and dogs) enjoy a number of city parks and open spaces while packs of cyclists whip up and down the Boulder Creek corridor.

For travelers looking for an outdoorsy holiday with the cultural outlets of an urban oasis – gourmet restaurants, lively bars, concerts and theater – Boulder is where it's at.

◎ Sights & Activities

Few towns have this combination of nature and culture. Whether you're climbing the Flatirons (p82), cycling up **Flagstaff** (☑303-441-3440; www.bouldercolorado.gov; Flagstaff Summit Rd; P♿), roaming Pearl St (p83) or patrolling CU's campus, there are plenty of sights and activities to keep you and the family smiling. Most sites are fairly centrally located, along W Pearl St or on the Hill, where you'll also find the university.

★**Chautauqua Park**   PARK
(☑303-442-3282; www.chautauqua.com; 900 Baseline Rd; ☐HOP 2) This historic landmark park is the gateway to Boulder's most magnificent slab of open space adjoining the iconic Flatirons, and its wide, lush lawn attracts picnicking families, sunbathers, Frisbee folk and students from nearby CU. It also gets copious hikers, climbers and trail runners. It's a popular site so parking can be a hassle. During the summer of 2017, the City of Boulder piloted a free shuttle to several lots around the city to ease the congestion. Check the website for updates.

★**Dairy Arts Center**   ARTS CENTER
(☑303-440-7826; www.thedairy.org; 2590 Walnut St; prices vary; P♿; ☐HOP) A historic milk-processing-factory-turned-arts-center, the Dairy is one of Boulder's top cultural hubs. Recently renovated, it's a state-of-the-art facility with three stages, four gallery spaces and a 60-seat cinema. There's always something going on – from lectures and plays to modern dance and art exhibits. There's a small cafe and bar on-site too.

★**Boulder Creek**   WATER SPORTS
(♿) An all-time favorite Boulder summer ritual is to tube down Boulder Creek. Most people put in at **Eben G Fine Park** (Boulder Canyon Dr; P♿☼; ☐205, N) and float as far as 30th St, or even 55th St. Be sure to check the water volume, especially early in the season; anything over 200 cu feet per second can be a real rodeo. Rent tubes at **White Water Tube** (☑720-239-2179; www.white watertubing.com; 2709 Spruce St; rental per day tube $16-21, kayak $45-50, paddleboard $35; ⊙10am-6pm May-Sep; ♿; ☐205, BOLT, HOP) or **Lolita's Market** (☑303-443-8329; www.face book.com/lolitasmarket; 800 Pearl St; tube hire $10; ⊙market 24hr; ♿; ☐HOP).

Eldorado Canyon State Park   OUTDOORS
(☑303-494-3943; www.cpw.state.co.us; 9 Kneale Rd, Eldorado Springs; $8; ⊙dawn-dusk, visitor center 9am-5pm) Among the country's best rock-climbing areas, Eldorado has Class 5.5 to 5.12 climbs. Suitable for all visitors, a dozen miles of hiking trails also link up to Chautauqua Park. A public pool (summer only) offers chilly swims in the canyon's famous spring water. Located 5 miles southwest of town.

★Local Table Tours FOOD & DRINK
(☎303-909-5747; www.localtabletours.com; tours $35-70; ⏲hours vary) Go behind the scenes with one of these fun downtown walking tours presenting a smattering of great local cuisine and inside knowledge on food and wine or coffee and chocolate. The tours also highlight locally owned businesses with regional or sustainable food sources. The cocktail crawl is a hit.

★ Festivals & Events

Bolder Boulder SPORTS
(☎303-444-7223; www.bolderboulder.com; adult/child from $70/55; ⏲Memorial Day; 👪; 🚌209, STAMPEDE) With over 50,000 runners and pros mingling with costumed racers, live bands and sideline merrymakers, this may be the most fun 10km run in the US, ending at Folsom Field, CU's football stadium.

Boulder Creek Festival MUSIC, FOOD
(☎303-449-3137; www.bceproductions.com; Canyon Blvd, Central Park; ⏲May; 👪; 🚌203, 204, 225, AB, B, DASH, DD, DM, GS, SKIP) FREE Billed as the kick-off to summer and capped with the Bolder Boulder, this summer festival is massive. Over 10 event areas feature more than 30 live entertainers and 500 vendors plus a whole carnival ride zone. There's food and drink, entertainment and sunshine. What's not to love?

🛏 Sleeping

★Chautauqua Lodge & Cottages HISTORIC HOTEL $$
(☎303-952-1611; www.chautauqua.com; 900 Baseline Rd; r from $103, cottages $196-303; 🅿🚭❄📶🐾; 🚌HOP 2) Adjoining beautiful hiking trails to the **Flatirons** (900 Baseline Rd, Chautauqua Park; 🚌HOP 2) and in a leafy neighborhood inside Chautauqua Park (p81), this is our top Boulder pick. It has contemporary rooms and one- to three-bedroom cottages with porches and patchwork-quilt beds. It's perfect for families and pets. All have full kitchens, though the wraparound porch of the Chautauqua Dining Hall is a local favorite for breakfast.

★Boulder Adventure Lodge HOTEL $$
(A-Lodge; ☎303-444-0882; www.a-lodge.com; 91 Fourmile Canyon Dr; r from $159; 🅿🚭❄📶🏊; 🚌N) You've come to Boulder to get outdoors, so why not stay nearer the action? Located a short distance from town, the A-Lodge has hiking, biking, climbing and fishing right from the property. Rooms are simple but well-appointed, ranging from dorms to suites. There's a pool, fire pit and more, generating a warm esprit de corps among guests and staff alike.

★St Julien Hotel & Spa HOTEL $$$
(☎720-406-9696, reservations 877-303-0900; www.stjulien.com; 900 Walnut St; r/ste from $400/650; 🅿❄@📶🏊; 🚌205, HOP, SKIP) In the heart of downtown, Boulder's finest four-star option is modern and refined, with photographs of local scenery and cork walls that warm the ambience. With fabulous views of the Flatirons, the back patio hosts live world music, jazz concerts and popular Latin dance parties. Rooms are spacious and plush. The on-site spa is considered one of the best around.

🍴 Eating

★Rayback Collective FOOD TRUCK $
(☎303-214-2127; www.therayback.com; 2775 Valmont Rd; mains $6-12; ⏲11am-10pm Mon-Fri, to 11pm Sat, to 9pm Sun; 🌿👪🐾; 🚌205, BOLT) A plumbing-supplies warehouse turned urban oasis, Rayback is a snapshot of Boulder. A place to feel community. A huge outdoor space with fire pit and lawn games. A lounge with cozy chairs and live music. A bar serving up Colorado brews. A food truck park with loads of good eats. Young or old, even furry friends, are welcome here.

★Rincón Argentino ARGENTINE $
(☎303-442-4133; www.rinconargentinoboulder.com; 2525 Arapahoe Ave; mains $4-13; ⏲11am-8pm Mon-Thu, to 9pm Fri & Sat; 👪; 🚌JUMP) Don't be turned off by the shopping plaza setting: Rincón packs a wallop of authentic Argentina. It bakes fresh empanadas – savory, small turnovers filled with spiced meat, or mozzarella and basil – which are perfect with a glass of malbec. It also offers *milanesas*-breaded beef cutlet sandwiches and gourds of yerba maté, a high-octane coffee alternative.

★Oak at Fourteenth MODERN AMERICAN $$
(☎303-444-3622; www.oakatfourteenth.com; 1400 Pearl St; mains $13-30; ⏲11:30am-10pm Mon-Sat, 5:30-10pm Sun; 🚌205, 206) Zesty and innovative, locally owned Oak manufactures top-notch cocktails and tasty small plates for stylish diners. Standouts include the grilled bacon-wrapped pork tenderloin and cucumber sashimi drizzled with passion fruit. Portions at this farm-to-table eatery are minimal – when it's this scrumptious you notice. Waiters advise well. The only downside:

it tends to be noisy, so save your intimate confessions.

★ Brasserie Ten Ten
BISTRO $$

(☏303-998-1010; www.brasserietenten.com; 1011 Walnut St; mains $15-27; ⊙11am-10pm Mon-Thu, 11am-11pm Fri, 9am-11pm Sat, 9am-9pm Sun; ☐203, 204, 225, AB, B) A go-to place for both students and professors, this sunny French bistro has a refined menu and an elegant atmosphere – think fresh flowers, marble high tops and polished brass. Sure, it's fancy, but not too uppity to offer killer happy-hour deals on crepes, sliders, mussels and beer. Don't miss the truffle fries.

Salt
MODERN AMERICAN $$

(☏303-444-7258; www.saltthebistro.com; 1047 Pearl St; mains $15-30; ⊙11am-9pm Mon-Thu, 11am-11pm Fri & Sat, 10am-9pm Sun; ☀; ☐208, HOP, SKIP) While farm-to-table is ubiquitous in Boulder, this is one spot that delivers and surpasses expectations. The handmade fettuccine with snap peas, radicchio and herb cream is a feverish delight. But Salt also knows meat: local and grass-fed, basted, braised and slow roasted to utter perfection. When in doubt, ask – the waiters really know their stuff.

★ Frasca
ITALIAN $$$

(☏303-442-6966; www.frascafoodandwine.com; 1738 Pearl St; mains $35, tasting menus $50-115; ⊙5:30-9:30pm Mon-Thu, to 10:30pm Fri, 5-10:30pm Sat; ☀; ☐HOP, 204) Deemed Boulder's finest by many (the wine service earned a James Beard award), Frasca has an impeccable kitchen and only the freshest farm-to-table ingredients. Rotating dishes range from earthy braised pork to housemade gnocchi and grilled quail served with leeks and wilted pea shoots. Reserve days, even weeks in advance. Mondays offer 'bargain' $50 tasting menus with suggested wine pairings.

🍷 Drinking & Entertainment

★ Mountain Sun
BREWERY

(☏303-546-0886; www.mountainsunpub.com; 1535 Pearl St; ⊙11am-1am; ☀; ☐HOP, 205, 206) Boulder's favorite brewery cheerfully serves a smorgasbord of fine brews and packs in everyone from yuppies to hippies. Best of all is its community atmosphere. The pub grub, especially the burgers and chili, is delicious and it's fully family friendly, with board games and kids' meals. There's often live bluegrass and reggae on Sunday, Monday and Wednesday nights. Cash only.

Avery Brewing Company
BREWERY

(☏303-440-4324; www.averybrewing.com; 4910 Nautilus Ct; ⊙3-11pm Mon, 11am-11pm Tue-Sun; ☐205) For craft breweries, how big is too big? Avery pushes the limit, with its imposing two-story building, complete with gift shop selling hats and tees. But the 1st-floor patio and tap room are lively and fun, while upstairs has a quieter restaurant feel. One thing's for sure: the beer's outstanding, from Apricot Sour to a devilish Mephistopheles Stout. Guided tours available.

Located about 6 miles northeast of downtown.

Boulder Dushanbe Teahouse
TEAHOUSE

(☏303-442-4993; www.boulderteahouse.com; 1770 13th St; mains $8-24; ⊙8am-9pm; ☀; ☐203, 204, 205, 206, 208, 225, DASH, JUMP, SKIP) It's impossible to find better ambience than at this incredible Tajik teahouse, a gift from Dushanbe, Boulder's sister city. The elaborate carvings and paintings were reassembled over an eight-year period on the edge of **Central Park**. It's too bad the fusion fare is so lackluster, but it's very worth coming here for a pot of tea.

eTown Hall
LIVE MUSIC

(☏303-443-8696; www.etown.org; 1535 Spruce St; from $25; ⊙hours vary; ☐HOP) Beautiful, brand-new and solar-powered, this repurposed church is the home of the eTown radio show (heard on National Public Radio). The show features rising and well-known artists and you can get in on it by attending a live taping in its 200-seat theater. Tapings run two hours starting at 7pm, and are typically held on weeknights.

🛍 Shopping

★ Pearl Street Mall
AREA

(Pearl St, btwn 9th & 15th Sts; ☀☻; ☐205, 206, 208, HOP, SKIP) The highlight of downtown Boulder is the Pearl Street Mall, a vibrant pedestrian zone filled with kids' climbing boulders and splash fountains, bars, galleries and restaurants. Street performers often come out in force on weekends.

★ Boulder Book Store
BOOKS

(☏303-447-2074; www.boulderbookstore.net; 1107 Pearl St; ⊙10am-10pm Mon-Sat, to 9pm Sun; 🛜☀; ☐208, HOP, SKIP) Boulder's favorite indie bookstore has a huge travel section downstairs, along with all the hottest new fiction and nonfiction. Check the visiting-authors lineup posted at the entry and on its website.

★**Common Threads** CLOTHING
(☑303-449-5431; www.shopcommonthreads.
com; 2707 Spruce St; ☺10am-6pm Mon, Tue &
Thu-Sat, to 7pm Wed; ☐205, BOLT, HOP) Vintage
shopping at its most haute couture, this
fun place is where to go for secondhand
Choos and Prada purses. Prices are higher
than at your run-of-the-mill vintage shop,
but clothes, shoes and bags are always in
good condition, and the designer clothing is
guaranteed authentic. Offers fun classes on
clothes altering and innovating.

❶ Information

Boulder Visitor Center (☑303-442-2911;
www.bouldercoloradousa.com; 2440 Pearl St;
☺8:30am-5pm Mon-Fri; ☐HOP) Set in the
Boulder Chamber of Commerce, this visitor
center offers basic information, maps and tips
on nearby hiking trails and other activities.
There's a more accessible **tourist information
kiosk** (☑303-417-1365; cnr Pearl & 13th Sts;
☺10am-8pm; ☐208, HOP, SKIP) on the Pearl
St Mall in front of the courthouse.
Boulder Ranger District (☑303-541-2500;
2140 Yarmouth Ave; ☺8:30am-4:30pm Mon-
Fri; ☐204) This US Forest Service outpost
provides information on the national forests
that surround the Rocky Mountain National
Park, including campgrounds and trails that
cross between the two.

❶ Getting There & Around

Located just 45 miles from Boulder, Denver
International Airport (p80) is the main entry
point for travelers arriving by air.
Green Ride (☑303-997-0238; http://greenride
boulder.com; 4800 Baseline Rd, D110; 1-way $28-
38) Serving Boulder and its satellite suburbs, this
Denver International Airport shuttle is cheap and
convenient ($28 to $38), working on an hourly
schedule (3:25am to 11:25pm). The cheapest
service leaves from the depot. Additional travelers in groups are discounted.
SuperShuttle (☑303-444-0808; www.
supershuttle.com; 1-way from $84) Provides a
private van service to the airport (from $84).
The base fare includes up to three people; each
additional person costs $25. Unless you have
loads of luggage, parties of four or more are
better served by a taxi.
RTD (p80) buses travel to Denver, Denver International Airport, Nederland and within Boulder. **Boulder Transit Center** (☑303-299-6000;
www.rtd-denver.com; 1800 14th St; ☐204, 205,
208, N, DASH, HOP, JUMP, SKIP) is a good place
to pick up maps of the area's bus system, and
offers free public parking on weekends.

Most streets have dedicated bike lanes and the
Boulder Creek Bike Path (🚲) is a must-ride commuter corridor. There are plenty of places to get
your hands on a rental. With rental cruisers stationed all over the city, **Boulder B-Cycle** (☑303-
532-4412; www.boulder.bcycle.com; 24hr rental
$8; ☺office 9am-5pm Mon-Fri, 10am-3pm Sat) is
a popular citywide program of hourly or daily bike
rentals, but riders must sign up online first. The
downtown area is also pleasantly walkable.

Northern Mountains

With one foot on either side of the continental divide and behemoths of granite in every
direction, Colorado's Northern Mountains offer out-of-this-world alpine adventures, laid-
back skiing, kick-butt hiking and biking, and
plenty of rivers to raft, fish and float.

Rocky Mountain National Park

This **park** (www.nps.gov/romo; vehicle 1/7 days
$20/30, motorcycle, foot & bicycle 1/7 days $10/15,
annual passes $60) is a place of natural spec-
tacle on every scale: from hulking granite
formations, many taller than 12,000ft, some
over 130 million years old, to the delicate
yellow burst of the glacier lily, one of the
dozen alpine wildflowers that explode in
short, colorful life at the edge of receding
snowfields for a few days every spring.

Though it doesn't rank among the largest
national parks in the USA (it's only 265,000
acres), it's rightly among the most popular,
hosting four million visitors every year.

This is a place of natural spectacle on
every scale: from hulking granite formations, many taller than 12,000ft, some over

---

BOULDER COUNTY FARMERS MARKET

This **market** (☑303-910-2236; www.
boulderfarmers.org; 13th St, btwn Canyon
Blvd & Arapahoe Ave; ☺8am-2pm Sat Apr-
Nov, 4-8pm Wed May-Oct; 🚲♿🐕; ☐203,
204, 205, 206, 208, 225, DASH, JUMP, SKIP)
is a massive spring and summer sprawl
of colorful, mostly organic local food.
Find flowers and herbs, as well as brain-
sized mushrooms, delicate squash
blossoms, crusty pretzels, vegan dips,
grass-fed beef, raw granola and yogurt.
Prepared food booths offer all sorts of
international taste treats. Live music is
as standard as the family picnics in the
park along Boulder Creek.

130 million years old, to the delicate yellow burst of the glacier lily, one of the dozen alpine wildflowers that explode in short, colorful life at the edge of receding snowfields for a few days every spring.

And though it tops many travelers' itineraries and can get maddeningly crowded, the park has miles of less-beaten paths and the backcountry is a little-explored nature-lovers' wonderland. Excellent hiking trails crisscross alpine fields, skirt the edge of isolated high-altitude lakes and bring travelers to the wild, untamed heart of the Rockies.

◉ Sights & Activities

With over 300 miles of trail, traversing all aspects of its diverse terrain, the park is suited to every hiking ability. Those with the kids in tow might consider the easy hikes in the **Wild Basin** to Calypso Falls, or to Gem Lake in the **Lumpy Ridge** area, while those with unlimited ambition, strong legs and enough trail mix will be lured by the challenge of summiting **Longs Peak**. Regardless, it's best to spend at least one night at 7000ft to 8000ft prior to setting out to allow your body to adjust to the elevation. Before July, many trails are snowbound and high water runoff makes passage difficult. In the winter, avalanches are a hazard.

★ **Moraine Park Museum**   MUSEUM
(☑970-586-1206; Bear Lake Rd; ☺9am-4:30pm Jun-Oct; ⊛) **FREE** Built by the Civilian Conservation Corps in 1923 and once the park's proud visitors lodge, this building has been renovated in recent years to host exhibits on geology, glaciers and wildlife. Kids will like the interactive exhibits and half-mile nature trail out the door.

🛏 Sleeping

Glacier Basin Campground   CAMPGROUND $
(☑877-444-6777; www.recreation.gov; off Bear Lake Rd; RV & tent sites summer $26) This developed campground is surrounded by evergreens, offering plenty of sun and shade. It also sports a large area for group camping and accommodates RVs. It is served by the shuttle buses on Bear Lake Rd throughout the summer. Make reservations through the website.

Aspenglen Campground   CAMPGROUND $
(☑877-444-6777; www.recreation.gov; State Hwy 34; summer tent & RV sites $26) With only 54 sites, this is the smallest of the park's reservable camping grounds. There are many tent-only sites, including some walk-ins, and

a limited number of trailers are allowed. This is the quietest campground in the park while still being highly accessible (5 miles west of Estes Park on US 34). Make reservations through the website.

Moraine Park Campground   CAMPGROUND $
(☑877-444-6777; www.recreation.gov; off Bear Lake Rd; summer tent & RV sites $26, winter $18) In the middle of a stand of ponderosa pine forest off Bear Lake Rd, this is the biggest of the park's campgrounds, approximately 2.5 miles south of the Beaver Meadows Visitor Center and with 245 sites. The walk-in, tent-only sites in the D Loop are recommended if you want quiet. Make reservations through the website.

Olive Ridge Campground   CAMPGROUND $
(☑303-541-2500; www.recreation.gov; State Hwy 7; tent sites $26; ☺mid-May–Nov) This well-kept USFS campground has access to four trailheads: St Vrain Mountain, Wild Basin, Longs Peak and Twin Sisters. In the summer it can get full; sites are first-come, first-served.

ℹ Information

For private vehicles, the park entrance fee is $20 for one day and $30 for seven. Annual passes are $60. Individuals entering the park on foot, bicycle, motorcycle or bus pay $10 each for one day and $15 for seven.

Backcounty permits ($26 for a group of up to seven people for seven days) are required for overnight stays in the 260 designated backcountry camping sites in the park. A bear box to store your food in is required if you are staying overnight in the backcountry between May and October (established campsites already have them).

Alpine Visitor Center (www.nps.gov/romo; Fall River Pass; ☺10:30am-4:30pm late May–mid-Jun, 9am-5pm late Jun-early Sep, 10:30am-4:30pm early Sep–mid-Oct; ⊛)

Beaver Meadows Visitor Center (☑970-586-1206; www.nps.gov/romo; US Hwy 36; ☺8am-9pm late Jun–late Aug, to 4:30pm or 5pm rest of year; ⊛)

Kawuneeche Visitor Center (☑970-627-3471; 16018 US Hwy 34; ☺8am-6pm last week May–Labor Day, to 5pm Labor Day–Sep, to 4:30pm Oct-May; ⊛)

ℹ Getting There & Away

Trail Ridge Rd (US 34) is the only east–west route through the park; the US 34 eastern approach from I-25 and Loveland follows the Big Thompson River Canyon. The most direct route from Boulder follows US 36 through Lyons

ROCKY MOUNTAINS NORTHERN MOUNTAINS

to the east entrances. Another approach from the south, mountainous Hwy 7, passes by **Enos Mills Cabin** (☑970-586-4706; www.enosmills. com; 6760 Hwy 7; $20; ☺11am-4pm Tue & Wed summer, by appointment only; 🖝) and provides access to campsites and trailheads on the east side of the divide. Winter closure of US 34 through the park makes access to the park's west side dependent on US 40 at Granby.

There are two entrance stations on the east side: **Fall River** (US 34) and **Beaver Meadows** (US 36). The **Grand Lake Entrance Station** (US 34) is the only entry on the west side. Year-round access is available through Kawuneeche Valley along the Colorado River headwaters to **Timber Creek Campground** (Trail Ridge Rd, US Hwy 34; tent & RV sites $26). The main centers of visitor activity on the park's east side are the Alpine Visitor Center (p85), high on Trail Ridge Rd, and Bear Lake Rd, which leads to campgrounds, trailheads and the Moraine Park Museum (p85).

North of Estes Park, Devils Gulch Rd leads to several hiking trails. Further out on Devils Gulch Rd, you pass through the village of Glen Haven to reach the trailhead entry to the park along the North Fork of the Big Thompson River.

ⓘ Getting Around

A majority of visitors enter the park in their own cars, using the long and winding Trail Ridge Rd (US 34) to cross the Continental Divide. There are options for those without wheels, however. In summer a free shuttle bus operates from the **Estes Park Visitor Center** (☑970-577-9900; www.visitestespark.com; 500 Big Thompson Ave; ☺9am-8pm daily Jun-Aug, 8am-5pm Mon-Fri, 9am-5pm Sat & 10am-4pm Sun Sep-May) multiple times daily, bringing hikers to a park-and-ride location where you can pick up other shuttles. The year-round option leaves the Glacier Basin parking area and heads to Bear Lake, in the park's lower elevations. During the summer peak, a second shuttle operates between Moraine Park campground and the Glacier Basin parking area. The second shuttle runs on weekends only from mid-August through September.

Estes Park

Estes Park is just seconds from one of the US's most popular national parks. The town itself is a jib-jab of T-shirt shops and ice-cream parlors, sidewalks jammed with tourists and streets plugged with RVs. But when the sun reflects just right off Lake Estes, or you spend an afternoon with a lazy coffee on the riverwalk, you might just find a little piece of zen.

🏃 Activities

★**Colorado Mountain School**   CLIMBING
(☑800-836-4008;   https://coloradomountain school.com; 341 Moraine Ave; half-day guided climbs per person from $125) Simply put, there's no better resource for climbers in Colorado – this outfit is the largest climbing operator in the region, has the most expert guides and is the only organization allowed to operate within Rocky Mountain National Park. It has a clutch of classes taught by world-class instructors.

🛏 Sleeping

Be warned: lodgings fill up very fast during the peak July and August period, when prices are sky high.

Estes Park KOA   CAMPGROUND $
(☑970-586-2888, 800-562-1887; www.estespark koa.com; 2051 Big Thompson Ave; tent sites $27-33, RV sites $38-48, cabins from $75; 🛜) With so much excellent camping just up the road in Rocky Mountain National Park, it's hard to see the allure of this roadside RV-oriented camping spot. But for those in need of a staging day before a big adventure, the proximity to town is appealing.

★**YMCA of the Rockies –
Estes Park Center**   RESORT $$
(☑888-613-9622; www.ymcarockies.org; 2515 Tunnel Rd; r & d from $109, cabins from $129; 🅿🐾❄🛜🏊) Estes Park Center is not your typical YMCA boarding house. Instead it's a favorite vacation spot with families, boasting upmarket motel-style accommodations and cabins set on hundreds of acres of high alpine terrain. Choose from roomy cabins that sleep up to 10 or motel-style rooms for singles or doubles. Both are simple and practical.

Stanley Hotel   HOTEL $$
(☑970-577-4000; www.stanleyhotel.com; 333 Wonderview Ave; r from $200; 🅿🛜🐾🏊) The white Georgian Colonial Revival hotel stands in brilliant contrast to the towering peaks of Rocky Mountain National Park that frame the skyline. A favorite local retreat, this best-in-class hotel served as the inspiration for Stephen King's famous cult novel *The Shining*. Rooms are decorated to retain some of the Old West feel while still ensuring all the creature comforts.

Black Canyon   LODGE $$$
(☑800-897-3730; www.blackcanyoninn.com; 800 MacGregor Ave; 1-/2-/3-bed r from $150/199/399;

P♿❄🐾) A fine place to splurge, this lovely, secluded 14-acre property offers luxury suites and a 'rustic' log cabin (which comes with a Jacuzzi). The rooms are dressed out with stone fireplaces, dark wood and woven tapestries in rich dark colors.

✖ Eating

Self-caterers will make out best by stocking up at the local **Safeway supermarket** (🖉970-586-4447; 451 E Wonderview Ave; ⊙9am-7pm Mon-Fri, to 6pm Sat, 10am-4pm Sun; P♿) on the way into town to picnic at **Bond Park** (E Elkhorn Ave) or in one of the national park picnic spots up the road.

Ed's Cantina & Grill   MEXICAN $
(🖉970-586-2919; www.edscantina.com; 390 E Elkhorn Ave; mains $9-12; ⊙11am-late Mon-Fri, 8am-10pm Sat & Sun; 🖢) With an outdoor patio right on the river, Ed's is a great place to kick back with a margarita. Serving Mexican and American staples, the restaurant is in a retro woodsy space with leather booth seating and bold primary colors.

**Smokin' Dave's BBQ
& Tap House**   BARBECUE $$
(🖉866-674-2793;   www.smokindavesbbqand
taphouse.com; 820 Moraine Ave; mains $8-20; ⊙11am-9pm Sun-Thu, to 10pm Fri & Sat; 🖢) Half-assed BBQ joints are all too common in Colorado's mountain towns, but Dave's, situated in a spare dining room, fully delivers. The buffalo ribs and pulled pork come dressed in a slightly sweet, smoky, tangy sauce and the sweet potato fries are crisply fried. Also excellent? The long, well-selected beer list.

❶ Getting There & Away

Estes Park Shuttle (🖉970-586-5151; www.estesparkshuttle.com; one-way/round-trip $45/85) This shuttle service connects Denver's airport to Estes Park about four times a day. The trip takes two hours.

Steamboat Springs

Sitting on the edge of the Western Slope, Steamboat Springs is an idyllic ski town that's unpretentious, direct, laid-back and just about as Colorado-friendly as you can get.

The ski area here is one of the best in the West, offering terrific skiing for the whole family. Summer is almost as popular as winter, with hiking, backpacking, white-water rafting, mountain biking and a host of other outdoor activities.

🏃 Activities

Steamboat Mountain Resort   SNOW SPORTS
(🖉ticket office 970-871-5252; www.steamboat.com; lift tickets adult/child $120/$75; ⊙ticket office 8am-5pm) The stats of the Steamboat Ski Area speak volumes for the town's claim as 'Ski Town, USA' – 165 trails, 3668ft vertical and nearly 3000 acres. With excellent powder and trails for all levels, this is the main draw for winter visitors and some of the best skiing in the US. In summer, check out the **Steamboat Bike Park** (www.steamboat.com; Steamboat Mountain Resort; $25; ⊙gondola rides 8:30am-4:30pm Jun 10–Aug 28).

★ Strawberry Park Hot Springs   HOT SPRINGS
(🖉970-879-0342;   www.strawberryhotsprings.com; 44200 County Rd; per day adult/child $15/8; ⊙10am-10:30pm Sun-Thu, to midnight Fri & Sat; 🖢) 🖉 Steamboat's favorite hot springs are actually outside the city limits, and offer great back-to-basics relaxation. The natural pools sit lovingly beside a river. After dark it is adults only and clothing optional (though most people wear swimsuits these days); you'll want a headlamp if you are visiting at this time. On weekends, expect a 15 to 45 minute wait to park.

Orange Peel Bikes   CYCLING
(🖉970-879-2957; www.orangepeelbikes.com; 1136 Yampa St; bike rental per day $20-65; ⊙10am-6pm Mon-Fri, to 5pm Sat; 🖢) In a funky old building at the end of Yampa, this is perfectly situated for renting a bike to ride the trails crisscrossing Howelsen Hill. A staff of serious riders and mechanics can offer tons of information about local trails, including maps. This is the coolest bike shop in town, hands down.

Bucking Rainbow Outfitters   RAFTING, FISHING
(🖉970-879-8747; www.buckingrainbow.com; 730 Lincoln Ave; inner tubes $18, rafting $50-100, fishing $150-500) This excellent outfitter has fly-fishing, rafting, outdoor apparel and the area's best fly shop, but it's most renowned for its rafting trips on the Yampa and beyond. Rafting trips run from half-day to full-day excursions. Two-hour in-town fly-fishing trips start at $155 per person. It has a tube shack that runs shuttles from Sunpies Bistro on Yampa St.

Old Town Hot Springs   HOT SPRINGS
(🖉970-879-1828;   www.oldtownhotsprings.org; 136 Lincoln Ave; adult/child $18/11, waterslide $7; ⊙5:30am-10pm Mon-Fri, 7am-9pm Sat, 8am-9pm Sun; 🖢) Smack dab in the center of town,

the water here is warmer than most other springs in the area. Known by the Utes as the 'medicine springs,' the mineral waters here are said to have special healing powers. Because there's a 230ft waterslide, a climbing wall and plenty of shallow areas, this is your best family-friendly hot springs in town.

🛏 Sleeping & Eating

★ **Vista Verde Guest Ranch**   RANCH $$$
(📞 800-526-7433; www.vistaverde.com; 31100 Seedhouse Rd; per week per person from $2700; ❄️📶)
Simply put, this is the most luxurious of Colorado's top-end guest ranches. Here, you spend the day riding with expert staff, the evening around the fire in an elegantly appointed lodge, and the night in high-thread-count sheets. If you have the means, this is it.

Rex's American Bar & Grill   AMERICAN $
(📞 970-870-0438; www.rexsgrill.com; 3190 S Lincoln Ave; mains $11-15; ⊘ 7am-11pm; 🅿️ 🍴) Grassfed steaks, elk sausage, bison burgers and other carnivorous delights are the ticket at this place, and they're so good that you'll have to forgive the restaurant's location – attached to the Holiday Inn. By serving until 11pm, it's also the latest dinner you can have in town.

Laundry   AMERICAN $$
(📞 970-870-0681;   www.thelaundryrestaurant.com; 127 11th St; small plates $10-16, large plates $35-38; ⊘ 4:30pm-2am) This new-generation Steamboat eatery has some of the best food in town. You'll love creative takes on comfort food, charcuterie boards, big steaks, barbecue, creative presentations and pickled everything. Budget-busters will love sharing small plates – which all go a long way.

ℹ Information

Steamboat Springs Visitor Center (📞 970-879-0880; www.steamboat-chamber.com; 125 Anglers Dr; ⊘ 8am-5pm Mon-Fri, 10am-3pm Sat) This visitor center, facing Sundance Plaza, has a wealth of local information, and its website is also excellent for planning.
USFS Hahns Peak Ranger Office (📞 970-879-1870; www.fs.usda.gov; 925 Weiss Dr; ⊘ 8am-5pm Mon-Sat) Rangers staff this office offering permits and information about surrounding national forests, including Mount Zirkel Wilderness, as well as information on hiking, mountain biking, fishing and other activities in the area.

ℹ Getting There & Away

Greyhound Terminal (📞 800-231-2222; www.greyhound.com; 1505 Lincoln Ave) Greyhound's

US 40 service between Denver and Salt Lake City stops here, about half a mile west of town.
Storm Mountain Express (📞 877-844-8787; www.stormmountainexpress.com) This shuttle service runs to Yampa Valley Regional Airport ($38 one-way) and beyond, though trips to DIA and Vail get very pricey.

Central Colorado

Colorado's central mountains are well known for their plethora of world-class ski resorts, sky-high hikes and snow-melt rivers. To the southeast are Colorado Springs and Pikes Peak, which anchor the southern Front Range.

Winter Park

Located less than two hours from Denver, unpretentious Winter Park Resort is a favorite with Front Rangers, who drive here to ski fresh tracks each weekend. Beginners can frolic on miles of powdery groomers while experts test their skills on Mary Jane's world-class bumps.

The congenial town is a wonderful base for year-round romping. Most services are found either in the ski village, which is actually south of Winter Park proper, or strung along US 40 (the main drag), which is where you'll find the visitor center. Follow Hwy 40 and you'll get to Fraser – essentially the same town – then Tabernash, and eventually the back of Rocky Mountain National Park.

In addition to downhill and cross-country skiing, Winter Park has some 600 miles of mountain biking trails for all levels. The paved 5.5-mile **Fraser River Trail** runs through the valley from the ski resort to Fraser, connecting to different trail systems. Pick up trail maps at the **visitor center** (📞 970-726-4118; www.winterpark-info.com; 78841 Hwy 40; ⊘ 9am-5pm). You can even bike in winter, too – it's known as fatbiking.

🛏 Sleeping & Eating

There are two first-come, first-served USFS campgrounds off Hwy 40 on the way into Winter Park: **Robber's Roost** (Hwy 40; tent & RV sites $20; ⊘ mid-Jun–Aug; 🐕), which has no water, 5 miles from town, and **Idlewild** (Hwy 40; tent & RV sites $20; ⊘ late May–Sep; 🐕), 1 mile from town. There's also plenty of free dispersed camping in the surrounding national forest.

★ **Devil's Thumb Ranch** LODGE $$$
(☑800-933-4339; www.devilsthumbranch.com; 3530 County Rd 83; bunkhouse $119-149, lodge r from $270, cabins from $450; ❉🅿🛜🐾❉) ✐ The classiest digs in the Winter Park area, this high-altitude ranch is a fantastic base for year-round **activities** (☑970-726-8231; trail passes adult/child $22/10, horseback riding $95-175; 🐾). Accommodations are plush, but not out of reach. The self-service bunkhouse has the cheapest rates, while the cowboy-chic lodge is a must for a romantic weekend escape. Cabins are a good bet for groups or for more privacy.

★ **Pepe Osaka's Fish Taco** JAPANESE $
(☑970-726-7159; www.pepeosakas.com; 78707 US Hwy 40; 2 tacos $13-15; ⊗4-9pm daily plus noon-3pm Sat & Sun) You like sushi. You like fish tacos. And as it turns out, you love sushi tacos, because…why not? At this almost-but-not-quite Nikkei eatery (that's Japanese-Peruvian cuisine if you haven't been keeping up), dig in to some outstandingly spicy tuna tacos, ahi *poke* ceviche tacos and blackened mahi-mahi *al pastor* tacos. All served with delish fried plantains and margaritas.

Breckenridge & Around

Set at the foot of the marvelous Tenmile Range, Breck is a sweetly surviving mining town with a vibrant historic district. The down-to-earth vibe is a refreshing change from Colorado's glitzier resorts, and the family-friendly ski runs and gold-nugget history make it Summit County's most atmospheric destination.

◉ Sights & Activities

Thanks to its endless peaks and adventure opportunities, Breckenridge is easily the highlight of Summit County. Ski groomed runs and high-alpine bowls, snowshoe cross-country, ascend 14,000ft summits, race over miles of mountain-biking trails, go white-water rafting or fish the Blue River.

★ **Barney Ford Museum** MUSEUM
(www.breckheritage.com; 111 E Washington Ave; suggested donation $5; ⊗11am-3pm Tue-Sun, hours vary seasonally) **FREE** Barney Ford was an escaped slave who became a prominent entrepreneur and Colorado civil-rights pioneer, and made two stops in Breckenridge (where he ran a 24-hour chopstand serving delicacies such as oysters) over the course of his incredibly rich, tragic and triumphant

life. He also owned a restaurant and hotel in Denver. The museum is set in his old home, where he lived from 1882 to 1890.

★ **Breckenridge Ski Area** SNOW SPORTS
(☑800-789-7669; www.breckenridge.com; lift ticket adult/child $171/111; ⊗8:30am-4pm Nov–mid-Apr; 🐾) Breckenridge spans five mountains, covering 2900 acres and featuring some of the best beginner and intermediate terrain in the state, as well as plenty of exhilarating high-alpine runs and hike-to bowls. There are also four terrain parks and a super pipe.

✵ Festivals & Events

Ullr Fest CULTURAL
(www.gobreck.com; ⊗Jan) The Ullr Fest celebrates the Norse god of winter, with a wild parade and four-day festival featuring a fatbike race, a town-wide talent show and a bonfire.

**International Snow
Sculpture Championship** ART
(www.gobreck.com; ⊗Jan-Feb) The International Snow Sculpture Championship begins in mid-January and lasts for three weeks. It starts with Technical Week, when the snow blocks are made, proceeds with Sculpting Week, when the sculptures are created and then judged by the public, and concludes with Viewing Week, when the sculptures decorate the River Walk.

⌾ Sleeping

★ **Bivvi Hostel** HOSTEL $
(☑970-423-6553; www.thebivvi.com; 9511 Hwy 9; dm winter/summer from $85/29; 🅿🛜) A modern hostel with a log-cabin vibe, the Bivvi wins points for style, friendliness and affordability. The four- to six-person dorm rooms come with private lockers, en suites and complimentary breakfast; chill out in the funky common room or out on the gorgeous deck, equipped with a gas grill and hot tub. Private rooms are also available.

★ **Abbett Placer Inn** B&B $$
(☑970-453-6489; www.abbettplacer.com; 205 S French St; r winter/summer from $179/129; 🅿❉@🛜) This violet house has five large rooms decked out with wood furnishings, iPod docks and fluffy robes. It's very low-key. Warm and welcoming hosts cook big breakfasts, and guests can enjoy an outdoor Jacuzzi deck and use of a common kitchenette. The top-floor room has massive views of the peaks from a private terrace. Check-in is from 4pm to 7pm.

✕ Eating & Drinking

★Breckenridge Distillery AMERICAN $$
(📞970-547-9759; www.breckenridgedistillery.com; 1925 Airport Rd; small plates $10-18; ⊙4-9pm Tue-Sat) Served in a big-city-cool dining space, the eclectic menu at this **distillery** (⊙11am-9pm Tue-Sat, to 6pm Sun & Mon) follows the delightful whims of former DC chef Daniel O'Brien, jumping from the sublime *cacio e pepe* (Roman spaghetti and cheese) to chicken-liver profiteroles to dates and mars-capone without missing a beat. It's mostly small plates, perfect for sharing over the top-notch cocktails.

★Crown CAFE
(📞970-453-6022; www.thecrownbreckenridge. com; 215 S Main St; ⊙7:30am-8pm; 🛜) Breck's living room might as well be at the Crown, a buzzing cafe-cum-social hub. Grab a mug of Silver Canyon coffee and a sandwich or salad, and catch up on all the latest gossip.

Broken Compass Brewing BREWERY
(📞970-368-2772; www.brokencompassbrewing. com; 68 Continental Ct; ⊙11:30am-11pm) Set in an industrial complex at the north end of Airport Road, the Broken Compass is gen-erally regarded as the best brewery in Breck-enridge. Fill up with a pint of their Coconut Porter or Chili Pepper Pale and sink back with a couple of friends in the old chairlift. They run a shuttle every two hours between the brewery and town.

ⓘ Information

Visitor Center (📞877-864-0868; www.go breck.com; 203 S Main St; ⊙9am-6pm; 🛜) Along with a host of maps and brochures, this center has a pleasant riverside museum that delves into Breck's gold-mining past.

ⓘ Getting There & Away

Breckenridge is 80 miles west of Denver via I-70 exit 203, then Hwy 9 south. **Summit Stage** (📞970-668-0999; www.summitstage. com), Summit County's free bus service, links Breckenridge with Keystone and A-Basin in winter (Swan Mountain Flyer) and with Frisco year-round.

Vail

Blessed with peaks, graced with blue skies and fresh powder, carved by rivers and groomed with ski slopes and bike trails, Vail is the ultimate Colorado playground. The real draw has always been Vail Mountain, a hulking, domed mass of snow-driven eupho-ria that offers more terrain than anywhere else in the US: 1500 acres of downhill slopes on the north face and 3500 acres of back-bowl bliss.

Factor in Vail's gourmet offerings, well-coiffed clientele and pretty young pow-der-fueled staff and you have an adrena-line-addled yuppie utopia.

◉ Sights & Activities

The draw to Vail is no secret. It's the endless outdoor activities in both winter and sum-mer that make this resort so attractive. Do remember that the mud season (mid-April through May, plus November) holds little attraction for visitors – you can't ski, but you can't really get up into the mountains to hike around either.

★Vail Mountain SNOW SPORTS
(📞970-754-8245; www.vail.com; lift ticket adult/child $189/130; ⊙9am-4pm Nov–mid-Apr; 🚡) Vail Mountain is our favorite in Colorado, with 5289 skiable acres, 195 trails, three ter-rain parks and (ahem) the highest lift-ticket prices on the continent. If you're a Colora-do ski virgin, it's worth experiencing your first time here – especially on a bluebird fresh-powder day. Multiday tickets are good at three other resorts (Beaver Creek, Breck and Keystone).

Vail to Breckenridge Bike Path CYCLING
(www.summitbiking.org) This paved, car-free bike path stretches 8.7 miles from East Vail to the top of Vail Pass (elevation gain 1831ft), before descending 14 miles into Frisco (it's 9 miles more if you go all the way to Breck-enridge). If you're only interested in the downhill, hop on a shuttle from **Bike Valet** (📞970-476-7770; www.bikevalet.net; 616 W Lions-head Cir; bike rental per day from $50; ⊙9am-6pm; 🚡) and enjoy the ride back to Vail.

🛏 Sleeping

Gore Creek Campground CAMPGROUND $
(📞877-444-6777; www.recreation.gov; Bighorn Rd; tent sites $22; ⊙mid-May–Sep; 🐾) This camp-ground at the end of Bighorn Rd has 19 tent sites with picnic tables and fire grates nestled in the woods by Gore Creek. There is excellent fishing near here – try the Slate Creek or Deluge Lake trails; the latter leads to a fish-packed lake. The campground is 6 miles east of Vail Village via exit 180 (East Vail) off I-70.

Austria Haus HOTEL **$$$**
(☎866-921-4050; www.austriahaushotel.com; 242 E Meadow Dr; r winter/summer from $500/280; P⚟❄🛜💺) One of Vail's longest-running properties, the Austria Haus offers both hotel rooms and condos (more information at www.austriahausclub.com), so make sure you're clear on what you're signing up for. In the charming details such as wood-framed doorways, Berber carpet and marble baths make for a pleasant stay. Fuel up at the generous breakfast spread in the morning.

★ **Sebastian Hotel** HOTEL **$$$**
(☎800-354-6908; www.thesebastianvail.com; 16 Vail Rd; r winter/summer from $800/300; P⚟❄🛜💺🐾) Deluxe and modern, this sophisticated hotel showcases tasteful contemporary art and an impressive list of amenities, including a mountainside ski valet, luxury spa and 'adventure concierge.' Room rates dip in the summer, the perfect time to enjoy the tapas bar and spectacular pool area, with hot tubs frothing and spilling over like champagne.

✕ Eating & Drinking

★ **Westside Cafe** DINER **$**
(☎970-476-7890; www.westsidecafe.net; 2211 N Frontage Rd; mains $9-16; ⊙7am-3pm Mon-Wed, to 10pm Thu-Sun; 🛜👶) Set in a West Vail strip mall, the Westside is a local institution. It does terrific all-day-breakfast skillets – like the 'My Big Fat Greek Skillet' with scrambled eggs, gyro, red onion, tomato and feta served with warm pita – along with all the usual high-cal offerings you need before or after a day on the slopes. Also has a grab-and-go counter.

bōl AMERICAN **$$**
(☎970-476-5300; www.bolvail.com; 141 E Meadow Dr; mains $18-27; ⊙2pm-1am; 🛜🍴) Half hip eatery, half space-age bowling alley, bōl is the most unusual hangout in Vail. You can go bowling in the back ($105 to $300 per hour!), but it's the eclectic menu that's the real draw: creations range from lamb lollipops and blue corn–crusted chile rellenos to duck-confit gnocchi.

★ **Game Creek Restaurant** AMERICAN **$$$**
(☎970-754-4275; www.gamecreekvail.com; Game Creek Bowl; 3-/4-course meal $99/109; ⊙5:30-9pm Tue-Sat Dec-Apr, 5:30-8:30pm Thu-Sat & 11am-2pm Sun late Jun–Aug; 🍴👶) This gourmet destination is nestled high in the spectacular Game Creek Bowl. Take the Eagle Bahn Gondola to Eagle's Nest and staff

---

CLIMBING YOUR FIRST FOURTEENER
....
Known as Colorado's easiest fourteener, **Quandary Peak** (www.14ers.com; County Rd 851) is the state's 15th highest peak at 14,265ft. Though you'll see plenty of dogs and children, 'easiest' may be misleading – the summit remains 3 grueling miles from the trailhead.

It's 6 miles round-trip, taking roughly between seven and eight hours. To get here, take Hwy 9 south from Breckenridge toward Hoosier Pass. Make a right on County Rd 850 and turn right again onto 851. Drive 1.1 miles to the unmarked trailhead. Park parallel on the fire road. Go between June and September.

---

will shuttle you (via snowcat in the winter) to their lodge-style restaurant, which serves an American-French menu with stars like wild boar, elk tenderloin and succulent leg of lamb. Reserve.

★ **Sweet Basil** AMERICAN **$$$**
(☎970-476-0125; www.sweetbasilvail.com; 193 Gore Creek Dr; mains lunch $18-22, dinner $27-48; ⊙11:30am-2:30pm & 6pm-late) 🍃 In business since 1977, Sweet Basil remains one of Vail's top restaurants. The menu changes seasonally, but the eclectic American fare, which usually includes favorites such as Colorado lamb and seared Rocky Mountain trout, is consistently innovative and excellent. The ambience is also fantastic. Reserve.

ⓘ Information

Vail Visitor Center (☎970-477-3522; www.vailgov.com; 241 S Frontage Rd; ⊙8:30am-5:30pm winter, to 8pm summer; 🛜) Provides maps, last-minute lodging deals and activities and town information. It's located next to the Transportation Center. The larger **Lionshead welcome center** is located at the entrance to the parking garage.

ⓘ Getting There & Around

Eagle County Airport (☎970-328-2680; www.flyvail.com; 217 Eldon Wilson Dr, Gypsum) This airport is 35 miles west of Vail and has services to destinations across the country (many of which fly through Denver) and rental-car counters.

Colorado Mountain Express Shuttles to/from Denver International Airport ($92, three hours) and Eagle County Airport ($51, 40 minutes). All buses arrive and depart from the Vail Transportation Center.

Eagle County Regional Transportation Authority (www.eaglecounty.us; per ride $4, to Leadville $7) ECO buses offer affordable transport to Beaver Creek, Minturn and even Leadville. Buses run from roughly 5am to 11pm; check the website for the exact schedule. Buses leave from the **Vail Transportation Center** (☑ 970-476-5137; 241 S Frontage Rd).

Vail Transit (☑ 970-477-3456; www.vailgov. com; ⊙ 6:30am-1:30am) Loops through all the Vail resort areas – West Vail (both North and South), Vail Village, Lionshead and East Vail, as well as Ford Park and Sandstone. Most buses have bike and ski racks and all are free.

Aspen

Here's a unique town, unlike anyplace else in the American West. It's a cocktail of cowboy grit, Euro panache, Hollywood glam, Ivy League brains, fresh powder, live music and lots of money. It's the kind of place where no matter the season you can bring on a head rush in countless ways.

⊙ Sights & Activities

★ **Aspen Center for Environmental Studies**   OUTDOORS
(ACES; ☑ 970-925-5756; www.aspennature.org; 100 Puppy Smith St, Hallam Lake; ⊙ 9am-5pm Mon-Fri; 🚼) **FREE** The Aspen Center for Environmental Studies is a 25-acre wildlife sanctuary that hugs the Roaring Fork River and miles of hiking trails in the Hunter Creek Valley. With a mission to advance environmental conservation, the center's naturalists provide free guided hikes and snowshoe tours, raptor demonstrations (eagles and owls are among the residents) and special programs for youngsters.

★ **Aspen Snowmass Ski Resort**   SNOW SPORTS
(☑ 800-525-6200; www.aspensnowmass.com; 4-mountain lift ticket adult/child $164/105; ⊙ 9am-4pm Dec–mid-Apr; 🚼) OK, the top winter activity here is pretty much a given: the pursuit of powder, and lots of it. The Aspen Skiing Company runs the area's four resorts – **Snowmass** (☑ 970-923-0560; ⊙ late Nov–mid Apr; 🚼), best all-around choice, with the most terrain and vertical; **Aspen** (☑ 970-925-1220; 601 E Dean St; ⊙ late Nov–mid-Apr), intermediate/expert; the **Highlands** (☑ 970-920-7009; Prospector Rd; ⊙ Dec–early Apr), expert; and **Buttermilk** (☑ 970-925-1220; Hwy

82; ⊙ Dec–Mar; 🚼), beginner/terrain parks – which are spread out through the valley and connected by free shuttles.

★ **Maroon Bells**   HIKING, SKIING
If you have but one day to enjoy a slice of pristine wilderness, spend it in the shadow of Colorado's most iconic mountains: the pyramid-shaped twins of **North Maroon Peak** (14,014ft) and **South Maroon Peak** (14,156ft). Eleven miles southwest of Aspen, it all starts on the shores of **Maroon Lake**, an absolutely stunning spot backed by the towering, striated summits.

Aspen Art Museum   MUSEUM
(☑ 970-925-8050; www.aspenartmuseum.org; 637 E Hyman Ave; ⊙ 10am-6pm Tue-Sun) **FREE** Opening in 2014, the art museum's striking new building features a warm, lattice-like exterior designed by Pritzker Prize winner Shigeru Ban, and contains three floors of gallery space. There's no permanent collection, just edgy, innovative contemporary exhibitions featuring paintings, mixed media, sculpture, video installations and photography by artists such as Mamma Andersson, Mark Manders and Susan Philipsz. Art lovers will not leave disappointed. Head up to the roof for views and a bite to eat at the cool cafe.

🛏 Sleeping

★ **Difficult Campground**   CAMPGROUND $
(☑ 877-444-6777; www.recreation.gov; Hwy 82; tent & RV sites $24-26; ⊙ mid-May–Sep; 🐾) The largest campground in the Aspen area, Difficult is one of four sites at the foot of Independence Pass and the only one that takes reservations. Located 5 miles west of town, it also has the lowest altitude (8000ft). Higher up are three smaller campgrounds: **Weller**, **Lincoln Gulch** and **Lost Man**. Water is available, but no electrical hookups for RVs.

Annabelle Inn   HOTEL $$
(☑ 877-266-2466; www.annabelleinn.com; 232 W Main St; r winter/summer from $249/200; 🅿 ❄ @ 🛜) Personable and unpretentious, the cute and quirky Annabelle Inn resembles an old-school European-style ski lodge in a central location. Rooms are cozy without being too cute, and come with flat-screen TVs and warm duvets. We enjoyed the after-dark ski-video screenings from the upper-deck hot tub (one of two on the property); a good breakfast is included.

★ **Limelight Hotel** HOTEL $$$
(☑855-925-3025; www.limelighthotel.com; 355 S Monarch St; r winter/summer from $500/250; ⓟ🅿🛜🟰🛜) Sleek and trendy, the Limelight's brick-and-glass modernism reflects Aspen's vibe. Rooms are spacious, with stylish accoutrements: granite washbasins, leather headboards and mountain views from the balconies and rooftop terraces. Additional perks include shuttles that run to all the slopes and a fab breakfast.

✖ Eating & Drinking

Justice Snow's AMERICAN $$
(☑970-429-8192; www.justicesnows.com; 328 E Hyman Ave; mains lunch $12-18, dinner $17-26; ⊙11am-2am Mon-Fri, 9am-2am Sat & Sun; 🛜🅿) 🍴 Located in the historic **Wheeler Opera House** (☑970-920-5770; www.aspenshowtix.com; 320 E Hyman Ave; ⊙box office noon-5pm Mon-Fri), Justice Snow's is a retro-fitted old saloon that marries antique wooden furnishings with a deft modern touch. Although nominally a bar – the speakeasy cocktails are the soul of the place – the affordable and locally sourced menu (a $12 gourmet burger – in Aspen!) is what keeps the locals coming back.

★ **Pyramid Bistro** CAFE $$
(☑970-925-5338; www.pyramidbistro.com; 221 E Main St; mains lunch $12-18, dinner $19-29; ⊙11:30am-9:30pm; 🅿) 🍴 Set on the top floor of **Explore Booksellers** (☑970-925-5336; www.explorebooksellers.com; 221 E Main St; ⊙10am-9pm; 🛜), this gourmet veggie cafe serves up some delightful creations, including sweet-potato gnocchi with goat's cheese, red-lentil sliders and quinoa salad with avocado, goji berries and sesame vinaigrette. Definitely Aspen's top choice for health-conscious fare.

★ **Matsuhisa** JAPANESE $$$
(☑970-544-6628; www.matsuhisarestaurants.com; 303 E Main St; mains $29-42, 2 pieces sushi $8-12; ⊙5:30pm-close) The original Colorado link in Matsuhisa Nobu's iconic global chain that now wraps around the world, this converted house is more intimate than its Vail sibling and still turns out spectacular dishes such as miso black cod, Chilean sea bass with truffle, and flavorful uni (sea urchin) shooters.

Aspen Brewing Co BREWERY
(☑970-920-2739; www.aspenbrewingcompany.com; 304 E Hopkins Ave; ⊙noon-late; 🛜) With five signature flavors and a sun-soaked bal-cony facing the mountain, this is definitely the place to unwind after a hard day's play. Brews range from the flavorful This Year's Blonde and high-altitude Independence Pass Ale (its IPA) to the mellower Conundrum Red Ale and the chocolatey Pyramid Peak Porter.

Woody Creek Tavern PUB
(☑970-923-4585; www.woodycreektavern.com; 2 Woody Creek Plaza, 2858 Upper River Rd; ⊙11am-10pm) Enjoying a 100% agave tequila and fresh-lime margarita at the late, great gonzo journalist Hunter S Thompson's favorite watering hole is well worth the 8-mile drive – or **Rio Grande Trail** (www.riograndetrail.com; Puppy Smith St) bike ride – from Aspen. The walls at this rustic funky tavern, a local haunt since 1980, are plastered with newspaper clippings, photos of customers and paraphernalia.

ℹ Information

Aspen-Sopris Ranger District (☑970-925-3445; www.fs.usda.gov/whiteriver; 806 W Hallam St; ⊙8am-4:30pm Mon-Fri) The USFS Aspen-Sopris Ranger District operates about 20 campgrounds and covers Roaring Fork Valley and from Independence Pass to Glenwood Springs, including the Maroon Bells Wilderness. Come here for maps and hiking tips.

Aspen Visitor Center (☑970-925-1940; www.aspenchamber.org; 425 Rio Grande Pl; ⊙8:30am-5pm Mon-Fri) Located across from Rio Grande Park.

Cooper Street Kiosk (cnr E Cooper Ave & S Galena St; ⊙10am-6pm) Maps, brochures and magazines.

ℹ Getting There & Around

Aspen-Pitkin County Airport (☑970-920-5380; www.aspenairport.com; 233 E Airport Rd; 🛜) Four miles northwest of Aspen on Hwy 82, this spry airport has direct year-round flights from Denver, as well as seasonal flights direct to eight US cities, including Los Angeles and Chicago. Several car-rental agencies operate here. A free bus runs to and from the airport, departing every 10 to 15 minutes.

Colorado Mountain Express (☑800-525-6363; www.coloradomountainexpress.com; adult/child to DIA $120/61.50; 🛜) Runs frequent shuttles to/from the Denver International Airport (four hours).

Roaring Fork Transportation Authority (RFTA; ☑970-925-8484; www.rfta.com; 430 E Durant Ave, Aspen; ⊙6:15am-2:15am; 🛜) RFTA buses connect Aspen with the Highlands, Snowmass and Buttermilk via free shuttles, while the **VelociRFTA** serves the down-valley towns of Basalt ($4, 25 minutes), Carbondale ($6, 45 minutes) and Glenwood Springs ($7, one hour).

Salida

Blessed with one of the state's largest historic districts, Salida is not only an inviting spot to explore, it also has an unbeatable location, with the Arkansas River on one side and the intersection of two large mountain ranges on the other. The plan of attack here is to hike, bike or raft during the day, then come back to town to refuel with grilled buffalo ribs and a cold IPA at night.

🏃 Activities

Both bikers and hikers should note that some big-time trails – the **Continental Divide** (www.continentaldividetrail.org), the **Colorado Trail** (www.coloradotrail.org) and the **Rainbow Trail** – are within spitting distance of town. If you don't want to sweat it, a **gondola** (☑719-539-4091; www.monarchcrest. net; adult/child $10/5; ☺8:30am-5:30pm mid-May–mid-Sep) can haul you from Monarch Pass nearly 1000ft up to the top of the ridge.

★ **Absolute Bikes**   CYCLING
(☑719-539-9295; www.absolutebikes.com; 330 W Sackett Ave; bike rental per day $15-100, tours from $90; ☺9am-6pm; 🚲) The go-to place for bike enthusiasts, offering maps, gear, advice, rentals (cruisers and mountain bikes) and, most importantly, shuttles to the trailhead. Check out the great selection of guided rides, from St Elmo ghost town to the Monarch Crest.

★ **Monarch Crest Trail**   MOUNTAIN BIKING
One of the most famous rides in all of Colorado, the Monarch Crest is an extreme 20- to 35-mile adventure. It starts off at Monarch Pass (11,312ft), follows the exposed ridge 12 miles to Marshall Pass and then either cuts down to Poncha Springs on an old railroad grade or hooks onto the Rainbow Trail. A classic ride with fabulous high-altitude views.

Arkansas River Tours   RAFTING
(☑800-321-4352; www.arkansasrivertours.com; 19487 Hwy 50; half-/full-day adult $59/109, child $49/99; ☺May-Aug; 🚲) This outfit runs from Brown's Canyon downstream, specializing in Royal Gorge trips. They have an office in Cotopaxi, 23 miles east of Salida.

🛏 Sleeping

Salida has a good hostel and hotel in town, along with a smattering of generic motels on the outskirts. The **Arkansas Headwaters Recreation Area** (☑719-539-7289; http://cpw. state.co.us; 307 W Sackett Ave; ☺8am-5pm, closed noon-1pm Sat & Sun) operates six campgrounds (bring your own water) along the river, including **Hecla Junction** (☑719-539-7289; http://coloradostateparks.reserveamerica.com; Hwy 285, Mile 135; tent & RV sites $18, plus daily pass $7; 🅰). Another top campground is **Monarch Park** (☑877-444-6777; www.recreation.gov; off Hwy 50; tent & RV sites $18; ☺Jun-Sep; 🅰), up by the pass, near the hiking and biking along the Monarch Crest and Rainbow Trails.

★ **Simple Lodge & Hostel**   HOSTEL $
(☑719-650-7381; www.simplelodge.com; 224 E 1st St; dm/d/q $24/60/84; 🅿@🛜🅰) If only Colorado had more spots like this. Run by the super-friendly Mel and Justin, this hostel is simple but stylish, with a fully stocked kitchen and a comfy communal area that feels just like home. It's a popular stopover for touring cyclists following the coast-to-coast Rte 50 – you're likely to meet some interesting folks here.

🍽 Eating

Fritz   TAPAS $
(☑719-539-0364; 113 East Sackett St; tapas $5-10, mains $10-15.50; ☺11am-9pm; 🛜) This fun and funky riverside watering hole serves up clever American-style tapas: think three-cheese mac with bacon, fries and truffle aioli, seared ahi wontons, and brie ciabatta with date jam. It also does a mean grass-fed beef burger and other salads and sandwiches. Good selection of local beers on tap.

★ **Amícas**   PIZZA $$
(☑719-539-5219; www.amicassalida.com; 127 F St; pizzas & paninis $6.90-13; ☺11am-9pm Mon-Wed, 7am-9pm Thu-Sun; 🚲🅰) Thin-crust wood-fired pizzas, panini, housemade lasagna and five microbrews on tap? Amícas can do no wrong. This high-ceilinged, laid-back hangout is the perfect spot to replenish all those calories you burned off during the day. Savor a Michelangelo (pesto, sausage and goat cheese) or Vesuvio (artichoke hearts, sun-dried tomatoes, roasted peppers) alongside a cool glass of Headwaters IPA.

ℹ Information

Salida Chamber of Commerce (☑719-539-2068; www.nowthisiscolorado.com; 406 W Rainbow Blvd; ☺9am-5pm Mon-Fri) General tourist info.

USFS Ranger Office (☑719-539-3591; www. fs.usda.gov; 5575 Cleora Rd; ☺8am-4:30pm Mon-Fri) Located east of town off Hwy 50, with camping and trail info for the Sawatch and northern Sangre de Cristo Ranges.

❶ Getting There & Away

Located at the 'exit' of the Arkansas River Valley, Salida occupies a prime location at the crossroads of Hwys 285 and 50. Indeed, this used to be a railroad hub, and you'll likely spot an abandoned line or two while exploring the area. Gunnison, Colorado Springs, the Great Sand Dunes and Summit County are all within one to two hours' drive, provided you have your own car.

Colorado Springs

One of the nation's first destination resorts, Colorado Springs is now the state's second-largest city. Its natural beauty and pleasant climate attract visitors from around the globe, who come to ascend majestic Pikes Peak and admire the exquisite sandstone spires of the Garden of the Gods.

Recently, the Springs has come of its own as a year-round adventure and leisure tourism destination, with a bunch of new family-focused attractions adding to the appeal of the Front Range and its existing cache of sights, from the excellent fine-arts museum to the historic Air Force Academy and an up-and-coming restaurant scene.

◉ Sights & Activities

★**Pikes Peak**   MOUNTAIN
(☑719-385-7325; www.springsgov.com; highway per adult/child $12/5; ☺7:30am-8pm Jun-Aug, to 5pm Sep, 9am-3pm Oct-May; Ⓟ) Pikes Peak (14,110ft) may not be the tallest of Colorado's 54 14ers, but it's certainly the most famous. The Ute originally called it the Mountain of the Sun, an apt description for this majestic peak, which crowns the southern Front Range. Rising 7400ft straight up from the plains, over half a million visitors climb it every year.

★**Garden of the Gods**   PARK
(www.gardenofgods.com; 1805 N 30th St; ☺5am-11pm May-Oct, to 9pm Nov-Apr; Ⓟ) **FREE** This gorgeous vein of red sandstone (about 290 million years old) appears elsewhere along Colorado's Front Range, but the exquisitely thin cathedral spires and mountain backdrop of the Garden of the Gods are particularly striking. Explore the network of paved and unpaved trails, enjoy a picnic and watch climbers test their nerve on the sometimes flaky rock.

★**Colorado Springs Fine Arts Center**   MUSEUM
(FAC; ☑719-634-5583; www.csfineartscenter.org; 30 W Dale St; adult/student $12/5; ☺10am-5pm Tue-Sun; Ⓟ) Fully renovated in 2007, this expansive museum and 400-seat theater originally opened in 1936. The museum's collection is surprisingly sophisticated, with some terrific Latin American art and photography, and great rotating exhibits that draw from the 23,000 pieces in its permanent collection.

Colorado Springs Pioneers Museum   MUSEUM
(☑719-385-5990; www.cspm.org; 215 S Tejon St; ☺10am-5pm Tue-Sat; Ⓟ) **FREE** Colorado Springs' municipal museum is set in the old El Paso County Courthouse, built in 1903. The collection and exhibition of some 60,000 pieces sums up the region's history. Particularly good is the Native American collection, which features hundreds of items from the Ute, Cheyenne and Arapaho Nations.

US Air Force Academy   SCHOOL
(☑719-333-2025; www.usafa.af.mil; I-25, exit 156B; ☺visitor center 9am-5pm; Ⓟ) **FREE** A visit to this campus, one of the highest-profile military academies in the country, offers a limited but nonetheless fascinating look into the lives of an elite group of cadets. The visitor center provides general background on the academy; from here you can walk over to the dramatic chapel (1963) or embark on a driving tour of the expansive grounds.

🛏 Sleeping

Mining Exchange   HOTEL $$
(☑719-323-2000; www.wyndham.com; 8 S Nevada Ave; r from $149; Ⓟ❈🛜) Opened in 2012 and set in the former turn-of-the-century bank where Cripple Creek prospectors traded in their gold for cash (check out the vault door in the lobby), the Mining Exchange takes the prize for Colorado Spring's most stylish hotel. Twelve-foot-high ceilings, exposed brick walls and leather furnishings make for an inviting, contemporary feel.

★**Broadmoor**   RESORT $$$
(☑855-634-7711; www.broadmoor.com; 1 Lake Ave; r from $295; Ⓟ❈🛜🏊🐕) One of the top five-star resorts in the US, the 744-room Broadmoor sits in a picture-perfect location against the blue-green slopes of Cheyenne Mountain. Everything here is exquisite: acres of lush grounds and a lake,

a glimmering pool, world-class golf, myriad bars and restaurants, an incredible spa and ubercomfortable guest rooms (which, it must be said, are of the 'grandmother' school of design).

★ **Garden of the Gods Resort** RESORT $$$
(☑719-632-5541; www.gardenofthegodsclub.com; 3320 Mesa Rd; d/ste from $309/459; P❋✿☎) Under new management, with ongoing expansion, and having just completed the renovation of all its luxury hotel rooms and suites and the construction of an enormous day-spa facility, the resort wing of the Garden of the Gods Club is giving the competition (known for its historic elegance) a run for its old-money.

✗ Eating & Drinking

Shuga's CAFE $
(☑719-328-1412; www.shugas.com; 702 S Cascade Ave; dishes $8-9; ⊘11am-midnight; ☎) If you thought Colorado Springs couldn't be hip, stroll to Shuga's, a Southern-style cafe with a knack for knockout espresso drinks and hot cocktails. Cuter than a button, this little white house is decked out in paper cranes and red vinyl chairs; there's also patio seating. The food – brie BLT on rosemary toast, Brazilian coconut shrimp soup – comforts and delights. Don't miss vintage-movie Saturdays.

★ **Pizzeria Rustica** PIZZA $$
(☑719-632-8121; www.pizzeriarustica.com; 2527 W Colorado Ave; pizzas $12-24; ⊘noon-9pm Tue-Sun; ☑✚) Wood-fired pizzas, locally sourced ingredients and a historic Old Colorado City locale make this bustling pizza joint the place to make a beeline for when you have a craving for pie. Its popularity means that it's always smart to make dinner reservations when possible.

★ **Uchenna** ETHIOPIAN $$
(☑719-634-5070; www.uchennaalive.com; 2501 W Colorado Ave, Suite 105; mains $12-22; ⊘noon-2pm & 5-8pm Tue-Sun; P☑✚) Chef Maya learned her recipes from her mother before she moved to America, and you'll love the homely cooking and family-friendly vibe at this authentic Ethiopian restaurant. Go for well-spiced meat or veg options and mop everything up with the spongy injera.

★ **Marigold** FRENCH $$
(☑719-599-4776; www.marigoldcafeandbakery.com; 4605 Centennial Blvd; mains lunch $8-13, din-

ner $11-24; ⊘bistro 11am-2:30pm & 5-9pm, bakery 8am-9pm Mon-Sat) Way out by the Garden of the Gods is this buzzy French bistro and bakery that's easy on both the palate and the wallet. Feast on delicacies such as snapper Marseillaise, garlic-and-rosemary rotisserie chicken, and gourmet salads and pizzas, and be sure to leave room for the double (and triple!) chocolate mousse cake or the lemon tarts.

★ **Blue Star** MODERN AMERICAN $$$
(☑719-632-1086; www.thebluestar.net; 1645 S Tejon St; mains $21-38; ⊘3pm-midnight; P☑) One of Colorado Springs' most popular gourmet eateries, the Blue Star is in the gentrifying Ivywild neighborhood just south of downtown. The menu at this landmark spot changes regularly, but always involves fresh fish, top-cut steak and inventive chicken dishes, flavored with Mediterranean and Pacific Rim rubs and spices.

Bristol Brewing Co BREWERY
(☑719-633-2555; www.bristolbrewing.com; 1604 S Cascade Ave; ⊘11am-10pm; ☎) Although a bit out of the way in southern Colorado Springs, this brewery – which in 2013 spearheaded a community market center in the shuttered Ivywild Elementary School – is worth seeking out for its Laughing Lab ale and pub grub from the owner of the gourmet Blue Star.

❶ Information

Colorado Springs Convention and Visitors Bureau (☑719-635-7506; www.visitcos.com; 515 S Cascade Ave; ⊘8:30am-5pm; ☎) A well-stocked resource for all things Southern Colorado.

❶ Getting There & Around

A smart alternative to Denver, **Colorado Springs Airport** (COS; ☑719-550-1900; www.flycos.com; 7770 Milton E Proby Pkwy; ☎) is served principally by United and Delta, with flights to 11 major cities around the country. There is no public transportation into town, however, so you'll have to rent a car or take a cab, about $35 with **Yellow Cab** (☑719-777-7777; www.yccos.com).

Up to six **Greyhound** (☑800-231-2222; www.greyhound.com) buses a day ply the route between Colorado Springs and Denver (from $10, 90 minutes), departing from the **Colorado Springs Downtown Transit Terminal** (☑719-385-7433; 127 E Kiowa St; ⊘8am-5pm Mon-Fri).

Reliable **Mountain Metropolitan Transit** (☑719-385-7433; www.coloradosprings.gov/department/91; per trip $1.75, day pass $4) buses serve the entire Pikes Peak area.

Southern Colorado

Home to the dramatic San Juan and Sangre de Cristo mountain ranges, Colorado's bottom half is just as pretty as its top.

Crested Butte

Powder-bound Crested Butte has retained its rural character better than most Colorado ski resorts. Ringed by three wilderness areas, this remote former mining village is counted among Colorado's best ski resorts (some say the best). The old town center features beautifully preserved Victorian-era buildings refitted with hip shops and businesses. Two-wheel traffic matches the laid-back, happy attitude.

In winter, the scene centers on Mt Crested Butte, the conical ski mountain emerging from the valley floor. But come summer, these rolling hills become the state wildflower capital (according to the Colorado State Senate), and many mountain bikers' fave for sweet alpine singletrack.

◉ Sights & Activities

★**Crested Butte**
Center for the Arts ARTS CENTER
(☑970-349-7487; www.crestedbuttearts.org; 606 6th St; prices vary; ☺10am-6pm; P⊛) With a magnificent recent expansion, the arts center hosts shifting exhibitions of local artists and a stellar schedule of live music and performance pieces. There's always something lively and interesting happening here.

★**Crested Butte Mountain Resort** SKIING
(☑970-349-2222; www.skicb.com; 12 Snowmass Rd; lift ticket adult/child $111/100; ⊛) One of Colorado's best, Crested Butte is known for open tree skiing, deep powder and few crowds. Catering mostly to intermediates and experts, the resort sits 2 miles north of the town at the base of Mt Crested Butte. Surrounded by forests, rugged peaks, and the West Elk, Raggeds and Maroon Bells-Snowmass Wilderness Areas, the scenery is breathtaking.

Alpineer MOUNTAIN BIKING
(☑970-349-5210; www.alpineer.com; 419 6th St; bike rental per day $25-75) Serves the mountain-biking mecca with maps, information and rentals. There's a great selection of men's and women's clothing. It also rents out skis and hiking and camping equipment.

🛏 Sleeping

Crested Butte International Hostel HOSTEL $
(☑970-349-0588, toll-free 888-389-0588; www.crestedbuttehostel.com; 615 Teocalli Ave; dm $37, r $104-115; ☎) For the privacy of a hotel with the lively ambience of a hostel, grab a room here, one of Colorado's nicest hostels. The best private rooms have their own baths. Dorm bunks come with reading lamps and lockable drawers, and the communal area has a stone fireplace and comfortable couches. Rates vary with the season, with winter being high season.

Inn at Crested Butte BOUTIQUE HOTEL $$
(☑970-349-2111, toll-free 877-343-211; www.innatcrestedbutte.com; 510 Whiterock Ave; d $199-249; P⊛☎) This refurbished boutique hotel offers intimate lodgings in stylish and luxurious surrounds. With just a handful of rooms, some opening onto a balcony with views over Mt Crested Butte, and all decked out with antiques, flat-screen TVs, coffee-makers and minibars, this is one of Crested Butte's nicest vacation addresses.

★**Ruby of Crested Butte** B&B $$$
(☑800-390-1338; www.therubyofcrestedbutte.com; 624 Gothic Ave; d $149-299, ste $199-499; P⊜⊛☎☎) Thoughtfully outfitted, down to the bowls of jellybeans and nuts in the stylish communal lounge. Rooms are brilliant, with heated floors, flat-screen TVs with DVD players and DVD selections, iPod docks and deluxe linens. There's also a Jacuzzi, a library, a ski-gear drying room and use of retro townie bikes. Hosts help with dinner reservations and other services.

🍴 Eating & Drinking

★**Secret Stash** PIZZA $$
(☑970-349-6245; www.thesecretstash.com; 303 Elk Ave; mains $12-18; ☺8am-late; ☑⊛) With phenomenal food, the funky-casual Stash is adored by locals, who also dig the original cocktails. The sprawling space was once a general store, but now is outfitted with teahouse seating and tapestries. The house specialty is pizza; its Notorious Fig (with prosciutto, fresh figs and truffle oil) won the World Pizza Championship. Start with the salt-and-pepper fries.

Soupçon FRENCH $$$
(☑970-349-5448; www.soupcon-cb.com; 127 Elk Ave; mains $39-47; ☺6-10:30pm) 🍴 Specializing in seduction, this petite French bistro occupies a characterful old mining cabin with

WORTH A TRIP

RAFTING THE ARKANSAS RIVER

Running from Leadville down the eastern flank of Buena Vista, through Browns Canyon National Monument, and then rocketing through the spectacular Royal Gorge at class V speeds, the Arkansas River is the most diverse, the longest and arguably the wildest river in the state. Brace yourself for yet another icy splash swamping the raft as you plunge into a roaring set of big waves, or surrender to the power of the current as your shouting, thoroughly drenched crew unintentionally spins backwards around a monster boulder. Is this fun? You bet! See p94 for tours.

just a few tables. Chef Jason has worked with big NYC names and keeps it fresh with changing menus of local meat and organic produce. Reserve ahead.

★ **Montanya** BAR
(www.montanyarum.com; 212 Elk Ave; snacks $3-12; ☺11am-9pm) The Montanya distillery receives wide acclaim for its high-quality rums. Its basiltini, made with basil-infused rum, fresh grapefruit and lime, will have you levitating. There are also tours, free tastings and worthy mocktails.

ⓘ Information

The **Visitor Center** (☎970-349-6438; www.crestedbuttechamber.com; 601 Elk Ave; ☺9am-5pm) is just past the entrance to town on the main road and stocks loads of brochures and maps.

ⓘ Getting There & Away

Crested Butte is about four hours' drive from Denver, and about 3½ hours from Colorado Springs. Head for Gunnison on US 50 and from there head north for about 30 minutes to Crested Butte on Hwy 135.

Ouray

With gorgeous icefalls draping the box canyon and soothing hot springs dotting the valley floor, Ouray (you-ray) is privileged, even for Colorado. For ice climbers, it's a world-class destination, but hikers and 4WD fans can also appreciate its rugged and sometimes stunning charms. The town is a well-preserved quarter-mile mining village sandwiched between imposing peaks.

✦ Activities

★ **Million Dollar Highway** SCENIC DRIVE
The whole of US Hwy 550 has been called the Million Dollar Hwy (p39), but more properly it's the amazing stretch south of Ouray through the Uncompahgre Gorge up to Red Mountain Pass at 11,018ft. The alpine scenery is truly awesome and driving south towards Silverton positions drivers on the outside edge of the skinny, winding road, a heartbeat away from free-fall.

★ **Ouray Hot Springs** HOT SPRINGS
(☎970-325-7073; www.ourayhotsprings.com; 1200 Main St; adult/child $18/12; ☺10am-10pm Jun-Aug, noon-9pm Mon-Fri & 11am-9pm Sat & Sun Sep-May; ⊞) For a healing soak or kiddish fun, try the recently renovated historic Ouray Hot Springs. The natural springwater is crystal-clear and free of the sulphur smells plaguing other hot springs. There's a lap pool, water slides, a climbing wall overhanging a splash pool and prime soaking areas (100°F to 106°F). The complex also offers a gym and massage service.

Ouray Ice Park CLIMBING
(☎970-325-4061; www.ourayicepark.com; County Rd 361; ☺7am-5pm mid-Dec–Mar; ⊞) **FREE**
Enthusiasts from around the globe come to ice climb at the world's first public ice park, spanning a 2-mile stretch of the Uncompahgre Gorge. The sublime (if chilly) experience offers something for all skill levels. Get instruction through a local guide service.

✹ Festivals & Events

Ouray Ice Festival CULTURAL
(☎970-325-4288; www.ourayicefestival.com; donation for evening events; ☺Jan; ⊞) The Ouray Ice Festival features four days of climbing competitions, dinners, slide shows and clinics. There's even a climbing wall set up for kids. You can watch the competitions for free, but various evening events require a donation to the ice park. Once inside, you'll get free brews from popular Colorado microbrewer New Belgium.

🛏 Sleeping & Eating

Amphitheater Forest Service Campground CAMPGROUND **$**
(☎877-444-6777; www.recreation.gov; US Hwy 550; tent sites $20; ☺Jun-Aug) With great tent sites under the trees, this high-altitude campground is a score. On holiday weekends, a three-night minimum applies. South of town on Hwy 550, take a signposted left-hand turn.

★ **Wiesbaden**   HOTEL $$
(☑970-325-4347; www.wiesbadenhotsprings.com; 625 5th St; r $132-347; ☻🐾🛜🖵) Quirky, quaint and new age, Wiesbaden even boasts a natural indoor vapor cave, which, in another era, was frequented by Chief Ouray. Rooms with quilted bedcovers are cozy and romantic, but the sunlit suite with a natural rock wall tops all. In the morning, guests roam in thick robes, drinking the free organic coffee or tea, post-soak, or awaiting massages.

Box Canyon Lodge & Hot Springs   LODGE $$
(☑800-327-5080, 970-325-4981; www.boxcan yonouray.com; 45 3rd Ave; r $189; 🛜) 🅿 It's not every hotel that offers geothermal heating, not to mention pineboard rooms that are spacious and fresh, and spring-fed barrel hot tubs – perfect for a romantic stargazing soak. With good hospitality that includes free apples and bottled water, it's popular, so book ahead.

Bon Ton Restaurant   FRENCH, ITALIAN $$$
(☑970-325-4419; www.bontonrestaurant.com; 426 Main St; mains $16-40; ⊙5:30-11pm Thu-Mon, brunch 9:30am-12:30pm Sat & Sun; 🅙) Bon Ton has been serving supper for a century in a beautiful room under the historic St Elmo Hotel. The French-Italian menu includes specialties like roast duck in cherry peppercorn sauce and tortellini with bacon and shallots. The wine list is extensive and the champagne brunch comes recommended.

ⓘ Information

Ouray Visitors Center (☑970-325-4746, 800-228-1876; www.ouraycolorado.com; 1230 Main St; ⊙9am-6pm Mon-Sat, 10am-4pm Sun; 🛜)

ⓘ Getting There & Away

Ouray is on Hwy 550, 70 miles north of Durango, 24 miles north of Silverton and 37 miles south of Montrose. There are no bus services in the area and private transportation is necessary.

Telluride

Surrounded on three sides by mastodon peaks, exclusive Telluride is quite literally cut off from the hubbub of the outside world. Once a rough mining town, today it's dirtbag-meets-diva – mixing the few who can afford the real estate with those scratching out a slope-side living for the sport of it. The town center still has palpable old-time charm, though locals often villainize the recently developed Mountain Village,

whose ready-made attractions have a touch of Vegas. Yet idealism remains the Telluride mantra. Shreds of paradise persist with the town's free box – where you can swap unwanted items (across from the post office) – the freedom of luxuriant powder days and the bonhomie of its infamous festivals.

⊙ Sights & Activities

You don't have to be a skier to appreciate Telluride, but loving the outdoors is a must. The town is surrounded by epic alpine scenery. Ajax Peak, a glacial headwall, rises up behind the village to form the end of the U-shaped valley. To the right (or south) on Ajax Peak, Colorado's highest waterfall, Bridal Veil Falls, cascades 365ft down; a switchback trail leads to a restored Victorian powerhouse atop the falls. To the south, Mt Wilson reaches 14,246ft among a group of rugged peaks that form the Lizard Head Wilderness Area.

Telluride Ski Resort   SNOW SPORTS
(☑970-728-7533, 888-288-7360; www.tellu rideskiresort.com; 565 Mountain Village Blvd; adult/ child full-day lift ticket $124/73) Known for its steep and deep terrain – with plunging runs and deep powder at the best times, Telluride is a real skier's mountain, but dilettantes love the gorgeous San Juan mountain views and the social town atmosphere. Covering three distinct areas, the resort is served by 16 lifts. Much of the terrain is for advanced and intermediate skiers, but there's still ample choice for beginners.

★ **Ashley Boling**   HISTORY
(☑970-728-6639, cell 970-798-4065; per person $20; ⊙by appointment) Local Ashley Boling has been giving engaging historical walking tours of Telluride for over 20 years. They last over an hour and are offered year-round. Rates are for a minimum of four participants, but he'll cut a reasonable deal for two or more. By reservation.

🎊 Festivals & Events

Telluride Bluegrass Festival   MUSIC
(☑800-624-2422; www.planetbluegrass.com; 4-day pass $235; ⊙late Jun) This festival attracts thousands for a weekend of top-notch rollicking alfresco bluegrass. Stalls sell all sorts of food and local microbrews to keep you happy, and acts continue well into the night. Camping out for the four-day festival is very popular. Check out the website for more info.

★ **Mountainfilm**   FILM
(www.mountainfilm.org; ⊙ May) An excellent four-day screening of outdoor adventure and environmental films, with gallery exhibits and talks, held on Memorial Day weekend. Events (some free) are held throughout Telluride and Mountain Village.

⌷ Sleeping

Aside from camping, there's no cheap lodging in Telluride. If staying in the summer or winter peak seasons, or during one of the city's festivals, you'll pay dearly. Off-season rates drop quite a bit, sometimes up to 30%. If you're coming during festival time, contact the festival organizers directly about camping.

★ **Telluride Town Park
Campground**   CAMPGROUND $
(✍ 970-728-2173; 500 E Colorado Ave; campsite with/without vehicle space $28/17; ⊙ mid-May–mid-Oct; ☎ ⛆) Right in the center of town, this convenient creekside campground has 43 campsites, along with showers, swimming and tennis. Sites are all on a first-come, first-served basis, unless it is festival time (consult ahead with festival organizers). Fancy some nightlife with your camping? Why not.

New Sheridan Hotel   HOTEL $$
(✍ 800-200-1891, 970-728-4351; www.newsheridan.com; 231 W Colorado Ave; d from $223; ⊜ ☎) Elegant and understated, this historic brick hotel (erected in 1895) provides a lovely base camp for exploring Telluride. High-ceilinged rooms feature crisp linens and snug flannel throws. Check out the hot-tub deck with mountain views. In the bull's eye of downtown, the location is perfect, but some rooms are small for the price.

Inn at Lost Creek   BOUTIQUE HOTEL $$$
(✍ 970-728-5678; www.innatlostcreek.com; 119 Lost Creek Lane, Mountain Village; r $275-500; ⊜ ☎) This lush boutique-style hotel in Mountain Village knows cozy. At the bottom of Telluride's main lift, it's also very convenient. Service is personalized, and impeccable rooms have alpine hardwoods, Southwestern designs and molded tin. There are also two rooftop spas. Check the website for packages.

✘ Eating & Drinking

Meals and even groceries can be pricey in Telluride, so check out the food carts and the taco truck on Colorado Ave, with picnic table seating, for quick fixes. There's more good times to be had in Telluride than the rest of southern Colorado combined. Bring your wallet; those drinks aren't free or even close. Live bands liven it up.

Tacos del Gnar   MEXICAN $
(✍ 970-728-7938; www.gnarlytacos.com; 123 S Oak St; mains $7-14; ⊙ noon-9pm Tue-Sat) The second outlet of a no-nonsense taco shop that puts flavor ahead of frills. Its fusion-style tacos, borrowing from Korean BBQ and Asian flavors, will make your tastebuds sing. Do it.

Oak   BARBECUE $$
(The New Fat Alley; ✍ 970-728-3985; www.oaksteluride.com; 250 San Juan Ave, base of chair 8; mains $11-23; ⊙ 11am-10pm; ⛆) You can pick something off the chalkboard or just take what the other guy has his face in – a cheap and messy delight. Go for the pulled-pork sandwich with coleslaw on top. Do it right by siding it with a bowl of crispy sweet-potato fries. The beer specials are outrageous.

★ **Chop House**   MODERN AMERICAN $$$
(✍ 970-728-4531; www.newsheridan.com; 231 W Colorado Ave, New Sheridan Hotel; mains $26-62; ⊙ 5pm-2am) With superb service and a chic decor of embroidered velvet benches, this is an easy pick for an intimate dinner. Start with a cheese plate, but from there the menu gets Western with exquisite elk shortloin and ravioli with tomato relish and local sheep-milk ricotta. Top it off with a flourless dark chocolate cake in fresh caramel sauce.

New Sheridan Bar   BAR
(✍ 970-728-3911; www.newsheridan.com; 231 W Colorado Ave, New Sheridan Hotel; ⊙ 5pm-2am) It's rush hour for beautiful people, though in low season you'll find real local flavor and opinions. In summertime, beeline for the breezy rooftop. Old bullet holes in the wall testify to the plucky survival of the bar itself, even as the adjoining hotel sold off chandeliers and antiques to pay the heating bills when mining fortunes waned.

☆ Entertainment

Fly Me to the Moon Saloon   LIVE MUSIC
(✍ 970-728-6666; 132 E Colorado Ave; ⊙ 3pm-2am) Let your hair down and kick up your heels to the tunes of live bands at this saloon, the best place in Telluride to party hard.

Sheridan Opera House THEATER
(☑970-728-4539; www.sheridanoperahouse.com; 110 N Oak St; 🎭) This historic venue has a burlesque charm and is always the center of Telluride's cultural life. It hosts the Telluride Repertory Theater, and frequently has special performances for children.

❶ Information

Telluride Visitor Center (☑888-353-5473, 970-728-3041; www.telluride.com; 230 W Colorado Ave; ⊙10am-5pm winter, to 7pm summer)

❶ Getting There & Around

In ski season **Montrose Regional Airport** (☑970-249-3203; www.montroseairport.com; 2100 Airport Rd), 65 miles north, has direct flights to and from Denver (on United), Houston, Phoenix and inland cities on the east coast.

Commuter aircraft serve the mesa-top **Telluride Airport** (☑970-778-5051; www.telluride airport.com; 1500 Last Dollar Rd), 5 miles east of town – weather permitting. At other times, planes fly into Montrose.

The **Galloping Goose** (☑970-728-5700; www.telluride-co.gov; ⊙7am-9pm) has routes downtown and to nearby communities. The **Telluride Express** (☑970-728-6000; www.tellurideexpress.com; to Montrose adult/child $53/31) shuttles from town to Telluride Airport, Mountain Village or Montrose airport; call to arrange pickup

---

Silverton

Ringed by snowy peaks and steeped in the sooty tales of a tawdry mining town, Silverton would seem more at home in Alaska than the Lower 48. But here it is. For those into snowmobiling, biking, fly-fishing or just basking in some very high-altitude sunshine, Silverton delivers.

It's a two-street town, but only one is paved. Greene St is where you'll find most businesses (think homemade jerky, fudge and feather art). Still unpaved, notorious Blair St – renamed Empire – runs parallel to Greene. During the silver rush, Blair St was home to thriving brothels and boozing establishments.

🏃 Activities

★Silverton Railroad Depot RAIL
(☑970-387-5416, toll-free 877-872-4607; www.du rangotrain.com; 12th St; deluxe/adult/child return from $189/89/55; ⊙departures 1:45pm, 2:30pm & 3pm; 🎭) You can buy one-way and return tickets for the brilliant Durango & Silverton

Narrow Gauge Railroad (p103) at the Silverton terminus. The Silverton Freight Yard Museum is located at the Silverton depot. The train ticket provides admission two days prior to, and two days following, your ride on the train.

★Silverton Mountain Ski Area SKIING
(☑970-387-5706; www.silvertonmountain.com; State Hwy 110; daily lift ticket $59, all-day guide & lift ticket $159) Not for newbies, this is one of the most innovative ski mountains in the US – a single lift takes advanced and expert backcountry skiers up to the summit of an area of ungroomed ski runs. Numbers are limited and the mountain designates unguided and the more exclusive guided days.

San Juan Backcountry DRIVING
(☑970-387-5565, toll-free 800-494-8687; www.sanjuanbackcountry.com; 1119 Greene St; 2hr tour adult/child $60/40; ⊙May-Oct; 🎭) 🅿 Offering both 4WD tours and rentals, the folks at San Juan Backcountry can get you out and into the brilliant San Juan Mountain wilderness areas around Silverton. The tours take visitors around in modified open-top Chevy Suburbans.

🛏 Sleeping & Eating

Inn of the Rockies at the Historic Alma House B&B $$
(☑970-387-5336, toll-free 800-267-5336; www.innoftherockies.com; 220 E 10th St; r $129-173; 🅿🌀❄) Opened by a local named Alma in 1898, this inn has nine unique rooms furnished with Victorian antiques. The hospitality is first-rate and its New Orleans–inspired breakfasts, served in a chandelier-lit dining room, merit special mention. Cheaper rates are available without breakfast. There's also a garden hot tub for soaking after a long day.

Wyman Hotel B&B $$
(☑877-504-5272; www.thewyman.com; 1371 Greene St; d from $175; ⊙closed Nov; 🌀📶) A handsome sandstone on the National Register of Historic Places, this just-revamped 1902 building offers sleek rooms with muted colors and a fine-tuned minimalist touch. It's a stylish alternative to the usual bric-a-brac approach. Check out the historic caboose alongside a gravel patio out back.

Grand Restaurant & Saloon AMERICAN $$
(☑970-387-5527; 1219 Greene St; mains $8-26; ⊙11am-3pm May-Oct, occassional dinners 5-9pm; 🎭) Stick with the burgers and club sandwiches at

this atmospheric eatery. The player piano and historic decor are a big draw. The full bar is well serviced by locals and visitors alike.

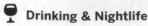

Drinking & Nightlife

★ Rum Bar   BAR
(☑970-769-8551;   www.silvertonrumbar.com;
1309 Greene St; mains $6-14; ⊘11am-2am) This
regional favorite delivers rum bliss in a
spacious minimalist bar on Greene St. On
a summer day, score a seat on the rooftop
deck. Bartenders here can talk you into anything, crafting exotic cocktails with homemade syrups and award-winning rum. Note:
low-season hours change.

ⓘ Getting There & Away

Silverton is on Hwy 550 midway between Montrose, about 60 miles to the north, and Durango,
some 48 miles to the south.

Other than private car, the only way to get to
and from Silverton is by using the **Durango and
Silverton Narrow Gauge Railroad** (p103), or
the private buses that run its return journeys.

Mesa Verde National Park

More than 700 years after its inhabitants
disappeared, **Mesa Verde** (☑970 529 4465;
www.nps.gov/meve; 7-day car/motorcycle pass Jun-
Aug $20/10, Sep-May $15/7; ☒♿☃) ☛ retains
an air of mystery. No one knows for sure why
the Ancestral Puebloans left their elaborate
cliff dwellings in the 1300s. Anthropologists
love it here: Mesa Verde is unique among
American national parks in its focus on
maintaining this civilization's cultural relics
rather than its natural treasures. It's a wonderland for adventurers of all sizes, who can
clamber up ladders to carved-out dwellings,
see rock art and delve into the mysteries of
ancient America.

Mesa Verde National Park occupies 81 sq
miles of the northernmost portion of the
mesa. Ancestral Puebloan sites are found
throughout the park's canyons and mesas,
perched on a high plateau south of Cortez
and Mancos.

The National Parks Service (NPS) strictly
enforces the Antiquities Act, which prohibits the removal or destruction of any antiquities and prohibits public access to many
of the 4000 known Ancestral Puebloan sites.

◉ Sights & Activities

If you only have time for a short visit, check
out the Chapin Mesa Museum and try a

walk through the Spruce Tree House, where
you can climb down a wooden ladder into
the cool chamber of a kiva.

Mesa Verde rewards travelers who set
aside a day or more to take the ranger-led
tours of Cliff Palace and Balcony House, explore Wetherill Mesa (the quieter side of the
canyon), linger around the museum or participate in one of the campfire programs run
at Morefield Campground.

Chapin Mesa Museum   MUSEUM
(☑970-529-4475; www.nps.gov/meve; Chapin Mesa
Rd; admission incl park entry; ⊘8am-6:30pm
Apr–mid-Oct, to 5pm mid-Oct–Apr; ☒♿) The
Chapin Mesa Museum has exhibits pertain-
ing to the park and is a good first stop. Staff
at the museum provide information on weekends when the park headquarters is closed.

Chapin Mesa   ARCHAEOLOGICAL SITE
The largest concentration of Ancestral Puebloan sites is at Chapin Mesa, where you'll see
the densely clustered **Far View Site** and the
large **Spruce Tree House**, the most accessible of sites, with a paved half-mile round-
trip path.

Wetherill Mesa   ARCHAEOLOGICAL SITE
This is the second-largest concentration of
sites. Visitors may enter stabilized surface
sites and two cliff dwellings, including the
Long House, open from late May through
August.

Aramark Mesa Verde   HIKING, TOURS
(☑970-529-4421; www.visitmesaverde.com; Mile
15, Far View Lodge; adult $42-48) The park con-
cessionaire offers varied guided private and
group tours throughout the park daily from
May to mid-October. Book online or at the
office in Far View Lodge.

⌨ Sleeping & Eating

There are plenty of accommodation options
in nearby Cortez and Mancos, and Mesa
Verde can be easily visited as a daytrip from
Durango.

Morefield Campground   CAMPGROUND $
(☑970-529-4465; www.visitmesaverde.com; Mile
4; tent/RV site $30/40; ⊘May-early Oct; ☃) ☛
The park's camping option, located 4 miles
from the entrance gate, also has 445 regular
tent sites on grassy grounds conveniently
located near Morefield Village. The village
has a general store, a gas station, a restaurant, showers and a laundry. It's managed

by Aramark. Dry RV campsites (without hookup) cost the same as tent sites.

Far View Lodge
LODGE $$
(☑970-529-4421, toll-free 800-449-2288; www.visit mesaverde.com; Mile 15; r $124-177; ⊙mid-Apr–Oct; P☺✱☎☂☀) Perched on a mesa top 15 miles inside the park entrance, this tasteful Pueblo-style lodge has 150 Southwestern-style rooms, some with kiva fireplaces. Don't miss sunset over the mesa from your private balcony. Standard rooms don't have air con (or TV) and summer daytimes can be hot.

Metate Room
MODERN AMERICAN $$$
(☑800-449-2288; www.visitmesaverde.com; Mile 15, Far View Lodge; mains $20-36; ⊙7-10am & 5:30-9:30pm Apr–mid-Oct, 5-7:30pm mid-Oct–Mar; ☑☂) ☞ With an award in culinary excellence, this upscale restaurant in the Far View Lodge offers an innovative menu inspired by Native American food and flavors. Interesting dishes include stuffed poblano chilies, prickly pear pork belly and cold smoked trout.

ⓘ Information

The Mesa Verde National Park entrance is off US 160, midway between Cortez and Mancos.

The huge **Mesa Verde Visitor & Research Center** (☑970-529-5034, 800-305-6053; www. nps.gov/meve; ⊙8am-7pm Jun–early Sep, to 5pm early Sep–mid-Oct, closed mid-Oct–May; ☎☂) has water, wi-fi and bathrooms, in addition to information desks selling tickets for tours of Cliff Palace, Balcony House or Long House. It also displays museum-quality artifacts.

Durango

An archetypal old Colorado mining town, Durango is a regional darling that's nothing short of delightful. Its graceful hotels, Victorian-era saloons and tree-lined streets of sleepy bungalows invite you to pedal around soaking up all the good vibes. There is plenty to do outdoors. Style-wise, Durango is torn between its ragtime past and a cool, cutting-edge future where townie bikes, caffeine and farmers markets rule.

⚡ Activities

★ Durango & Silverton Narrow Gauge Railroad
RAIL
(☑970-247-2733; www.durangotrain.com; 479 Main Ave; return adult/child 4-11yr from $89/55; ⊙May-Oct; ☂) Riding the Durango & Silverton Narrow Gauge Railroad is a Durango must. These vintage steam locomotives have been making the scenic 45-mile trip north to Silverton (3½ hours each way) for more than 125 years. The dazzling journey allows two hours for exploring Silverton. This trip operates only from May through October. Check online for different winter options.

Mild to Wild Rafting
RAFTING
(☑970-247-4789, toll-free 800-567-6745; www. mild2wildrafting.com; 50 Animas View Dr; trips from $59; ⊙9am-5pm; ☂) In spring and summer white-water rafting is one of the most popular sports in Durango. Mild to Wild Rafting is one of numerous companies around town offering rafting trips on the Animas River. Beginners should check out the one-hour introduction to rafting, while the more adventurous (and experienced) can run the upper Animas, which boasts Class III to V rapids.

Purgatory
SNOW SPORTS
(☑970-247-9000; www.purgatoryresort.com; 1 Skier Pl; lift tickets adult/child from $89/55; ⊙mid-Nov–Mar; ☂) Durango's winter highlight is 25 miles north on US 550. The resort offers 1200 skiable acres of varying difficulty, boasting 260in of snow per year. Two terrain parks offer plenty of opportunities for snowboarders to catch big air. Check local grocery stores and newspapers for promotions and two-for-one lift tickets and other specials before purchasing directly from the ticket window.

🛏 Sleeping

General Palmer Hotel
HOTEL $$
(☑970-247-4747, toll-free 800-523-3358; www. generalpalmer.com; 567 Main Ave; d $165-275; ✱@☎) With turn-of-the century elegance, this 1898 Victorian has a damsel's taste, with pewter four-post beds, floral prints and teddies on every bed. Rooms are small but elegant, and if you tire of TV, there's a collection of board games at the front desk. Check out the cozy library and the relaxing solarium.

★ Rochester House
HOTEL $$
(☑970-385-1920, toll-free 800-664-1920; www. rochesterhotel.com; 721 E 2nd Ave; d $169-229; ☺✱☎☀) Influenced by old Westerns (movie posters and marquee lights adorn the hallways), the Rochester is a little bit of old Hollywood in the new West. Rooms are spacious, with high ceilings. Two formal sitting rooms, where you're served cookies, and a breakfast room in an old train car, are other perks at this pet-friendly establishment.

★**Antlers on the Creek**   B&B $$$
(☑970-259-1565; www.antlersonthecreek.com; 999 Lightner Creek Rd; r from $249; P🅟🛜) Tuck yourself into this peaceful creekside setting surrounded by sprawling lawns and cottonwoods and you may never want to leave. Between the spacious main house and the carriage house there are seven tasteful rooms with jetted tubs, plush bed linens and gas fireplaces. There's also a decadent three-course breakfast and hot tub in the outdoor gazebo. It's open year-round.

✗ Eating & Drinking

★**James Ranch**   MARKET $
(☑970-385-9143; www.jamesranch.net; 33800 US Hwy 550; mains $5-18; ⊘11am-7pm Mon-Sat) 🍃 A must for those road-tripping the San Juan Skyway, the family-run James Ranch, 10 miles out of Durango, features a market and an outstanding farmstand grill featuring the farm's own organic grass-fed beef and fresh produce. Steak sandwiches and fresh cheese melts with caramelized onions rock. Kids dig the goats.

★**El Moro**   GASTROPUB $$
(☑970-259-5555; www.elmorotavern.com; 945 Main Ave; mains $10-30; ⊘11am-midnight Mon-Fri, 9am-midnight Sat & Sun) There are two reasons to come here: drinking damn good custom cocktails at the bar or dining on some innovative small plates like Korean fried cauliflower, cheeses, housemade sausages and fresh salads. It's ground zero for Durango hipsters but really aims to please all.

Ore House   STEAK $$$
(☑970-247-5707; www.orehouserestaurant.com; 147 E College Dr; mains $25-75; ⊘5-10pm; 🖐) The best steakhouse in town, with food served in casual and rustic environs. Order a hand-cut aged steak, or try the steak, crab leg and lobster combo known as the Ore House Grub-steak, easily serving two people. The meat is natural and antibiotic free and organic vegetables are the norm. There's also a large wine cellar.

★**Bookcase & the Barber**   COCKTAIL BAR
(☑970-764-4123; www.bookcaseandbarber.com; 601 E 2nd Ave, suite B; ⊘2pm-midnight) This modern speakeasy may be Durango's sexiest nightcap, hidden behind a heavy bookcase, with exquisite cocktails worth the $12 price tag and a dimly-lit allure. Enter via the barbershop, but you'll need the password (found somewhere on their Facebook page).

Try a spicy *paloma celosa* (jealous dove), a perfect tease of tequila, grapefruit and ancho chile.

★**Ska Brewing Company**   BREWERY
(☑970-247-5792; www.skabrewing.com; 225 Girard St; mains $9-15; ⊘9am-9pm Mon-Fri, 11am-9pm Sat, to 7pm Sun) Big on flavor and variety, these are the best beers in town. Although the small, friendly tasting-room bar was once mainly a production facility, over the years it's steadily climbed in the popularity charts. Today it is usually jam-packed with friends meeting for an after-work beer.

ⓘ Information

Durango Welcome Center (☑970-247-3500, toll-free 800-525-8855; www.durango.org; 802 Main Ave; ⊘9am-7pm Sun-Thu, to 9pm Fri & Sat; 🛜) An excellent information center located downtown. There is a second visitor center south of town, at the Santa Rita exit from US Hwy 550.

ⓘ Getting There & Around

Durango-La Plata County Airport (DRO; ☑970-247-8143; www.flydurango.com; 1000 Airport Rd) The regional airport is 18 miles southwest of Durango via US Hwy 160 and Hwy 172. Both United and American Airlines have direct flights to Denver; American flies to Dallas-Fort Worth and Phoenix.

Greyhound Bus Station (☑970 259 2755; www.greyhound.com; 250 E 8th Ave) Serves the region and beyond.

Durango Transit (☑970-259-5438; www.getarounddurango.com; 250 W 8th St; fares $1-2) Runs local bus routes around the city and to nearby destinations.

Great Sand Dunes National Park

For all of Colorado's striking natural sights, the surreal Great Sand Dunes National Park, a veritable sea of sand bounded by jagged peaks and scrubby plains, is a place of stirring optical illusions and where nature's magic is on full display.

🏃 Activities

Stop by the informative **Great Sand Dunes National Park Visitor Center** (☑719-378-6399; www.nps.gov/grsa; 11999 Hwy 150; ⊘8:30am-5pm Jun-Aug, 9am-4:30pm Sep-May; 🖐) before venturing out, to learn about the geology and history of the dunes or to chat with a ranger about hiking or backcountry-camping options. A free backcountry permit is required if you're planning on being adventurous, and it pays to let the ranger know where you're going.

Hiking is the main pastime in the park, but there's also mountain biking, dune sandboarding and even inner tubing in late May and early June, as the snowmelt **Medano Creek** flows down from the Sangre de Cristos and along the eastern edge of the dunes.

Hiking

There are no trails through this expansive field of sand, but it's the star attraction for hikers. Two informal hikes afford excellent panoramic views of the dunes. The first is a hike to High Dune (strangely, not the highest dune in the park), which departs from a parking area just beyond the visitor center. It's about 2.5 miles out to the peak and back, but be warned: it's not easy. If you're up for it, try pushing on to the second worthy goal: just west of High Dune is Star Dune (750ft), the tallest in the park.

From the visitor center, a short trail leads to the Mosca Picnic Area next to ankle-deep Medano Creek, which you must ford (when the creek is running) to reach the dunes. Across the road from the visitor center, the Mosca Pass Trail climbs up into the Sangre de Cristo Wilderness. Throughout summer NPS rangers lead interpretive nature walks from the visitor center and hold evening programs at the amphitheater.

🛏 Sleeping & Eating

Although there are limited supplies at the **Great Sand Dunes Oasis** (☑719-378-2222; www.greatdunes.com; 5400 Hwy 150; tent/RV sites $25/38, cabins $55, r $100; ☺Apr-Oct; P@), it's best to buy your groceries in either Alamosa or a larger town outside the San Luis Valley.

★**Zapata Falls Campground** CAMPGROUND $
(☑719-852-7074; www.fs.usda.gov; BLM Rd 5415; tent & RV sites $11; 🐾) Seven miles south of the national park, this campground offers glorious panoramas of the San Luis Valley from its 9000ft perch in the Sangre de Cristos. There are 23 first-come, first-served sites, but note that there is no water and that the 3.6-mile access road is steep and fairly washed out, making for slow going.

Zapata Ranch RANCH $$$
(☑719-378-2356; www.zranch.org; 5303 Hwy 150; d with full board $300) Ideal for horseback-riding enthusiasts, this exclusive preserve is a working cattle and bison ranch set amid

groves of cottonwood trees. Owned and operated by the Nature Conservancy, the main inn is a refurbished 19th-century log structure, with distant views of the sand dunes.

ℹ Getting There & Away

Great Sand Dunes National Park is 33 miles northeast of Alamosa.

WYOMING

You may think of Wyoming as an empty land of windswept plains and sagebrush hills baking under brooding blue skies. And, you'd be right. It is. But not all of it.

The country's least populated state is also home to some of its most dramatic mountains, most diverse wildlife, and most unique geology. From the unspoiled Snowy Range near Laramie to the granite wilderness of the Wind River Range behind Lander, the peaks only become more impressive as you travel across Wyoming toward the archetypal – and truly grand – Teton Range.

ℹ Information

Wyoming Road Conditions (☑888-996-7623; www.wyoroad.info) Up-to-date info on road conditions and closures.

Wyoming State Parks & Historic Sites (☑307-777-6323; http://wyoparks.state.wy.us; day-use $6, historic site $4, campsite $10) Wyoming has 13 state parks and 26 historic sites providing a wide range of boating, biking, hiking, fishing, climbing and camping. Campsite reservations are taken online or over the phone.

Cheyenne

Windy Cheyenne may not wow you with its looks, but like the rough-skinned cowboys you'll meet here, there's good-natured charm once you scratch the surface.

◎ Sights

Frontier Days Old West Museum MUSEUM
(☑307-778-7290; www.oldwestmuseum.org; 4610 Carey Ave; adult/child $10/free; ☺9am-5pm; 🚗) For a deep dive into Cheyenne's pioneer past and rodeo present, visit this museum year round on the Frontier Days rodeo grounds. It is chock-full of rodeo memorabilia, from saddles to trophies, displays cowboy art and photography, houses a fine collection of horse drawn buggies, and dispenses nuggets

of history – like the story of Steamboat, the un-rideable bronco who likely isn't the one depicted on Wyoming's license plates (though many will tell you he is.)

✯✯ Festivals & Events

Cheyenne Frontier Days   RODEO
(☑307-778-7222; www.cfdrodeo.com; 4610 Carey Ave; rodeo per day $17-29, concerts $20-70; ☉last full week Jul; 🖾) During the last full week in July, the world's largest outdoor rodeo and celebration of all things Wyoming features 10 days of roping, bucking, riding, singing and dancing between air shows, parades, melodramas, carnivals and chile cook-offs. There's also a lively Frontier Town, Indian village and free morning 'slack' rodeos.

🛏 Sleeping & Eating

★**Nagle Warren**
Mansion Bed & Breakfast   B&B $$
(☑307-637-3333; www.naglewarrenmansion. com; 222 E 17th St; r from $163; ❀🛜🐾) This fully-modernized historic mansion is a rare find. The 1888 house still has the original carved leather ceiling, and is decked out with late-19th-century regional antiques in 12 spacious and elegant rooms, all with private baths. The property boasts a hot tub, a reading room tucked into a turret and classic 1954 Schwinn bikes for cruising.

Tasty Bones Barbecue
& Bakery   BARBECUE $
(☑307-514-9494; www.tastybonesbarbecue.com; 1719 Central Ave; mains $8-16; ☉10am-9pm Mon-Sat, 11am-4pm Sun) Imagine that a Filipino food truck crashed into a barbecue smoker and fell in love. This mash-up of two distinct menus is the result of a husband and wife team with two very different ideas about what makes good home-cooking. Both are right. The slow-roasted brisket pairs surprisingly well with the miso ramen bowl.

🍺 Drinking & Nightlife

Accomplice Brewing
Company   MICROBREWERY
(☑307-632-2337; www.accompliecebeer.com; 115 W 15th, Depot; mains $10-15; ☉2-10pm Mon-Thu, 11am-10pm Fri-Sun; 🛜🐾) Sample as many beers as you like as often as you like at the crowded pour-it-yourself taproom in Cheyenne's latest brewery to occupy the historic Depot building. The drafts are tasty, and food options don't disappoint.

ⓘ Information

Cheyenne Visitor Center (☑307-778-3133; www.cheyenne.org; 1 Depot Sq; ☉9am-5pm Mon-Fri, to 3pm Sat, 11am-3pm Sun; 🛜)

ⓘ Getting There & Around

For a capital city, Cheyenne is hard to reach. Black Hills Stage Lines/Express Arrow stops at the **bus terminal** (☑307-635-1327; www. greyhound.com; 5401 Walker Rd, Rodeway Inn) on the north end of town with direct service to Denver ($18-33, two hours) as well as anywhere Greyhound travels. Sleepy **Cheyenne Airport** (CYS; ☑307-634-7071; www.cheyenneairport. com; 200 E 8th Ave) will get you to Denver every Thursday.

Once in town, the regular **Cheyenne Transit Program** (☑307-637-6253; 322 W Lincolnway; standard fare $1.50; ☉6am-6pm Mon-Fri, 10am-5pm Sat) will get you around while the **Cheyenne Street Railway Trolley** (☑307-778-3133; www.cheyennetrolley.com; 121 W 15th St, Depot; adult/child $12/6; ☉10am, 11:30am, 1pm, 2:30pm & 4pm May-Sep) will tour you through the most interesting bits of downtown.

Laramie

Not exactly 'in' the mountains, this prairie town definitely feels 'of' the mountains, largely thanks to Wyoming's only four-year university (University of Wyoming), which maintains a constant flow of hip and lively students who re-energize an otherwise sleepy city.

The small historic downtown, with its grid of brick buildings pressed up against the railroad tracks, can occupy an hour of window shopping, and a few museums on the pleasantly green university campus are informative ways to stretch your legs. The real reason to visit, however, is the Wyoming Territorial Prison: a well-preserved piece of frontier past.

◉ Sights

★**Wyoming Territorial Prison**   MUSEUM
(☑307-745-3733; www.wyomingterritorialprison. com; 975 Snowy Range Rd; adult/child $5/2.50; ☉8am-7pm May-Sep, 8am-5pm Apr & Oct; 🖾) See the only prison ever to hold Butch Cassidy, who was in for grand larceny from 1894–96, only to emerge a well-connected criminal who fast became one of history's greatest robbers. His story is told in thrilling detail in a back room, while the faces of other 'malicious and desperate outlaws' stare haunting-

ly at you as you explore the main cellblocks. Outside, tour the factory where convicts produced over 700 brooms a day – one of the prison's short-lived revenue-generating schemes.

Geological Museum
MUSEUM

(📞307-766-2646; www.uwyo.edu/geomuseum; SH Knight Geology Building, University of Wyoming; ⊙10am-4pm Mon-Sat) FREE The Morrison Formation – a Jurassic sedimentary rock – stretches from New Mexico to Montana and is centered in Wyoming. This layer has produced many of the world's dinosaurs fossils, an impressive collection of which are on display in this tiny university museum, including a 75ft *Apatosaurus excelsus* (formerly known as the Brontosaurus), and a *Diatryma gigantea* (a 7ft-tall carnivorous bird discovered in Wyoming). Linger at the new 'Prep Lab' and watch researchers liberate brittle fossils from solid rock. Science!

🛏 Sleeping

Find the usual suspects of chain motels along Grand Ave to the east of Laramie and I-80 to the west. Unfortunately the independent offerings near historic downtown are, for the most part, not recommendable.

Gas Lite Motel
MOTEL $

(📞307-742-6616; 960 N 3rd St; s/d $49/59; ❄️🏩🐕) The Gas Lite Motel stands out – more due to the plastic horse and rooster on the roof, and tattered plywood cowboys lounging against the banisters than the modernity of the amenities. However, the rooms are clean if dated, the owners reasonably friendly, and the price is right if variable.

Mad Carpenter Inn
B&B $$

(📞307-742-0870; www.madcarpenterinn.net; 353 N 8th St; r $95-125; 🏩) With landscaped gardens, hot breakfast, and comfy, snug wood-trimmed rooms, the Mad Carpenter Inn has warmth and class to spare. A serious game room features billiards and ping-pong while the detached 'Doll House' with its kitchenette and Jacuzzi tub is an absolute steal for a couple looking for a quiet escape.

🍴 Eating & Drinking

Having a university means Laramie has a good spread of culinary offerings. Multiple breweries, sports bars and hangouts pepper Laramie's historic downtown, many of which host local live music.

★ Sweet Melissa's
VEGETARIAN $

(📞307-742-9607; www.facebook.com/sweetmelissacafe; 213 S 1st St; mains $9-14; ⊙11am-9pm Mon-Thu, till 10pm Fri-Sat; 🏩🐕) Sweet Melissa's makes delicious vegetarian and gluten-free grub, no doubt the healthiest food for miles, like portabello fajitas or gorgonzola-leek mac 'n' cheese. The cauliflower wings are bomber, as is the service.

Coal Creek Coffee Co
CAFE

(📞307-745-7737; www.coalcreekcoffee.com; 110 E Grand Ave; mains $5-11; ⊙6am-11pm; 🏩) With superlative brews, Coal Creek Coffee is everything you want in a coffee house: modern and stylish, even borderline hipster – but not in a bad way. When the fair-trade beans and expertly prepared lattes start to feel so 10am, roll over to **Coal Creek Tap** in the west wing where you'll find over a dozen draft beers.

ℹ️ Getting There & Away

Daily **flights** (📞307-742-4164; www.laramieairport.com; 555 General Brees Rd; ⊙5am-7:30pm Mon-Fri, till 5pm Sat-Sun) connect Laramie with Denver ($87, 40 minutes), while **Greyhound** (📞307-745-7394; www.greyhound.com; 1952 N Banner Rd) buses stop at the gas station

---

WYOMING FACTS
....

Nickname Equality State

Population 586,107

Area 97,914 sq miles

Capital city Cheyenne (population 59,466)

Other cities Laramie (population 30,816), Cody (9689), Jackson (9838)

Sales tax 4%

Birthplace of Artist Jackson Pollock (1912–56)

Home of Women's suffrage, coal mining, geysers, wolves

Politics Conservative to the core (except Teton County)

Famous for Rodeo, ranches, former vice-president Dick Cheney

Tallest mountain Gannett Peak 13,809ft (4209m)

Driving distances Cheyenne to Jackson 432 miles

everyone calls the 'Diamond Shamrock,' and are a good option for regional destinations.

Lander

Nestled against the foothills of the Wind River Range, Lander has always been a frontier town. Originally established as a fort on a spur of the Oregon Trail, it was later the end of the rail line and a frequent haunt of outlaws and horse thieves. It is also the gateway to the Wind River Indian Reservation, where indigenous Eastern Shoshone share 2.2 million acres of land with displaced Northern Arapaho at the base of the state's tallest peak.

This wilderness playground landed on the radar of savvy outdoorspeople when Paul Petzoldt started the renowned National Outdoor Leadership School here in 1965. The epic climbing at Sinks Canyon and nearby Wild Iris brings climbers in droves, while expanding mountain-bike trails diversifies that crowd.

But the town's remoteness means few stay for long, leaving Lander in relative peace, retaining its mellow blend of the Old and New West.

◉ Sights & Activities

Sinks Canyon State Park　　　PARK
(☑307-332-3077; www.sinkscanyonstatepark.org; 3079 Sinks Canyon Rd; tent & RV nonresident $11; ☺visitor center 9am-6pm Jun-Sep) Beautiful Sinks Canyon State Park, 6 miles southwest of Lander on Hwy 131, centers on a curious feature of the Middle Fork of the Popo Agie River, where the rushing water suddenly turns into a small cave and disappears into the soluble Madison limestone. Although the water bubbles up a quarter-mile downstream, scientists have learned it takes nearly two hours for it to make the subterranean journey before emerging warmer and with more volume.

Fremont County Pioneer Museum　　MUSEUM
(☑307-332-3339; www.fremontcountymuseums.com/the-lander-museum; 1445 W Main St; ☺9am-4pm Mon-Sat, to 5pm summer) FREE Wyoming's first history museum has been continually updated and overhauled to share the living history of Lander, Fremont County and the state as a whole. Catch the display of Frederic Remington's engravings of frontier life for *Harper's Weekly*, before exploring the cabins and historic buildings out back.

Gannett Peak Sports　　MOUNTAIN BIKING
(351b Main St; ☺10am-6pm Mon-Fri, 9am-5pm Sat, 10am-2pm Sun) If you want to check out the single-track trails outside town, head to Gannett Peak Sports for advice, gear and equipment rentals.

🛏 Sleeping

With landscapes this beautiful you'll want to be camping, and fortunately there are a number of options up **Sinks Canyon** (sites $11-15; ☺May-Sep).

★ Outlaw Cabins　　B&B $$
(☑307-332-9655; www.outlawcabins.com; 2411 Squaw Creek Rd; cabins $125) On a working ranch are a pair of real cabins done real nice. The Lawman was built by a county sheriff over 120 years ago, but has been maintained and restored for modern sensibilities. The Outlaw is our favorite, however, on account of its more Wild West vibe. Both are beautifully appointed with quiet porches made for sittin' on.

✖ Eating & Drinking

If you're not swapping stories over a case of beer around a campfire, you should probably be at the Lander Bar. The rest of the town shuts down relatively early.

The Middle Fork　　BREAKFAST $
(☑307-335-5035; www.themiddleforklander.com; 351 Main St; mains $6-10; ☺7am-2pm Mon-Sat, 5-9pm Wed-Sat, 9am-2pm Sun; 🛜🅿) A large hall with spartan ambience leaves you free to focus on the food – which is excellent. Homemade baked goods hold court with eggs benedict and in-house corned-beef hash washed down with mimosas.

★ Cowfish　　GRILL $$
(☑307-332-8227; www.cowfishlander.com; 148 Main St; brunch $10-16, dinner $17-35; ☺8am-2pm, 5-10pm; 🛜) Spring for a candlelit dinner of brussels-sprout carbonara or coffee-rubbed rib-eye at Lander's upscale restaurant suitable for date nights. The attached brewery serves the same food in a more casual atmosphere among the mash tuns (steel brewing vessels) that churn out a rotating menu of handcrafted beer-experiments – many of which are excellent (sample a few before committing).

Lander Bar　　BAR
(☑307-332-8228; www.landerbar.com; 126 Main St; ☺11am-2am Mon-Sat, noon-10pm Sun; 🛜)

This big, wooden, barn-like watering hole is the place where local and visiting adventurers go to share notes about the day's 'sick lines' on rock or trail well into the night. There's often live music.

Get food from the attached **Gannett Grill** (307-332-8227; 128 Main St; mains $8-11; 11am-9pm).

ℹ Information

Lander Visitor Center (307-332-3892; www.landerchamber.org; 160 N 1st St; 9am-5pm Mon-Fri)

ℹ Getting There & Away

Wind River Transportation Authority (307-856-7118; www.wrtabuslines.com; Shopko; fare one-way $1) provides scheduled Monday-to-Friday services between Riverton and Lander, plus reserved service to Casper or Jackson (prices vary based on number of riders). You'll want a car, however, to access trailheads and climbing crags.

Jackson

Welcome to the other side of Wyoming. Hiding in a verdant valley between some of America's most rugged and wild mountains, Jackson looks similar to other towns in the state – false-front roof lines, covered wooden walkways, saloons on every block – but it ain't quite the same.

Here, hard-core climbers, bikers and skiers (recognizable as sunburned baristas) outnumber cowboys by a wide margin, and you're just as likely to see a celebrity as a moose wandering the urban trails.

Although Jackson being posh and popular does have its downsides for the traveler (the median house price is $1.2 million), it does mean you'll find a lively urban buzz, a refreshing variety of foods and no shortage of things to do – both in town and out.

◎ Sights & Activities

★ National Museum of Wildlife Art
MUSEUM

(307-733-5771; www.wildlifeart.org; 2820 Rungius Rd; adult/child $14/6; 9am-5pm May-Oct, from 11am Sun & closed Mon Nov-Apr;) Major works by Bierstadt, Rungius, Remington and Russell, breathe life into their subjects in impressive and inspiring ways – almost better than seeing the animals in the wild. Almost. The outdoor sculptures and building itself (inspired, oddly, by a ruined Scottish castle) are worth stopping by to see even if the museum is closed.

National Elk Refuge
WILDLIFE RESERVE

(307-733-9212; www.fws.gov/refuge/national_elk_refuge; Hwy 89; sleigh ride adult/child $21/15; 10am-4pm Dec-Apr) **FREE** This refuge protects Jackson's herd of several thousand elk, offering them a winter habitat from November to May. During summer, ask at the Jackson visitor center for the best places to see elk. An hour-long horse-drawn sleigh ride is the highlight of a winter visit; buy tickets at the visitor center.

★ Jackson Hole Mountain Resort
SNOW SPORTS

(307-733-2292; www.jacksonhole.com; adult/child day pass $140/88, summer tram $34/21; Nov-Apr & June-Sep) This mountain is larger than life. Whether tackling Jackson Hole with skis, board, boots or mountain bike, you will be humbled. With more than 4000ft of vertical rise and some of the world's most infamous slopes, Jackson Hole's 2500 acres and average 400in of snow sit at the top of every serious shredder's bucket list.

Summer months are active with a bike park, disc-golf course, climbing wall and a new high alpine *via ferrata* course (starting at $109, two hours) where you tackle mountaineering assisted by cables and ladders. The most popular activity is the scenic tram ($34, 12 minutes) which takes alpine hikers and sightseers to a network of trails at the summit of Rendezvous mountain (10,927ft). Pro-tip: climb up the 7-mile, 4139ft trail to the top, and ride the tram down for free.

Jackson Hole Paragliding
PARAGLIDING

(Jackson Hole 307-739-2626, Snow King 605-381-9358; www.jhparagliding.com; tandem flight $345; May-Oct) The only thing better than being in the Tetons is to be soaring above the Tetons. Tandem rides with experienced pilots take off from Jackson Hole Mountain Resort in the mornings, or Snow King (402 E Snow King Ave) in the afternoons.

No experience is necessary, but age and weight limits apply.

Snake River Rafting
RAFTING

(half-day adult/child from $70/50) You can't swing an oar in Jackson without hitting a rafting company eager to take you down the Snake River. Most offer a mellow 13-mile float through wetlands teeming with wildlife, from the town of Wilson to Hoback

Junction, or the more punchy Snake River canyon with its churning Class III rapids.

Only a few outfits offer trips wholly within Grand Teton National Park – if that's important to you – including Barker-Ewing and Teton Whitewater.

Trips typically include transportation and lunch.

Granite Creek Hot Springs HOT SPRINGS
(📞307-690-6323; www.fs.usda.gov/recarea/btnf/recarea/?recid=71639; Granite Creek Road, Hwy 191; adult/child $8/5; ⊙10am-6pm summer, 10am-5pm winter) Head 25 miles southeast of Jackson on Hwy 191 and turn east on gravel Granite Creek Road. Continue for 10 miles through alpine meadows and forested hills to the the natural hot springs with killer views of the surrounding peaks.

🎊 Festivals & Events

Grand Teton Music Festival MUSIC
(GTMF; 📞307-733-1128; www.gtmf.org; Walk Festival Hall, Teton Village; ⊙Jul-Aug) A near-continuous celebration of classical music in a fantastic summer venue. The Festival Orchestra plays every Friday at 8pm and Saturday at 6pm showcasing worldwide musicians and directors. The GTMF Presents program highlights noted talent on most Wednesdays. Free family concerts give you a more informal way to experience the symphony of sound.

🛏 Sleeping

Jackson has plenty of lodging, both in town and at Jackson Hole Mountain Resort (p109), but reservations are still essential in summer and winter high season. Prices, which may double during holidays or weekends, fall precipitously during the spring and fall 'slack' seasons. There are a few camping options scattered in the forest nearby, but most require a long drive, often down poor roads.

The Hostel HOSTEL $
(📞307-733-3415; www.thehostel.us; 3315 Village Dr, Teton Village; dm $34-45, r $79-139; @🛜🐕) This skier's favorite has been here so long it doesn't need a name – everybody knows the Hostel. Budget privates and cramped four-person bunk rooms are smack in the middle of everything (meaning you'll only be in them when you're sleeping). The spacious lounge, with fireplace and pool table, foosball and ski waxing station, are all chill places to socialize.

Antler Inn HOTEL $$
(📞307-733-2535; www.townsquareinns.com/antler-inn; 43 W Pearl Ave; r $100-260, ste $220-325; 🌸🛜🐕) Right in the middle of the Jackson action, this sprawling complex provides clean and comfortable rooms, some with fireplaces and bathtubs. Stepping into the cheaper 'cedar log' rooms feels like you're coming home to a cozy Wyoming cabin, mostly because you are: they were hauled here and attached to the back of the hotel.

★ **Wort Hotel** HISTORIC HOTEL $$$
(📞307-733-2190; www.worthotel.com; 50 N Glenwood St; r from $450; 🌸@🛜) A distinctly Wyoming vibe permeates this luxury historic hotel that has only gotten better with age. Knotty pine furniture and handcrafted bedspreads compliment full-size baths and Jacuzzis while the best concierge service in Jackson helps you fill out your itinerary with outdoor adventures. Even if staying here is out of your reach, swing by the antique **Silver Dollar Bar** downstairs.

🍴 Eating

Jackson is home to Wyoming's most sophisticated and diversified food scene. Look for deals dished out for happy hour at many of the bar-restaurant combos.

Persephone BAKERY $
(📞307-200-6708; www.persephonebakery.com; 145 E Broadway; mains $8-15; ⊙7am-6pm Mon-Sat, to 5pm Sun; 🛜) With rustic breads, oversized pastries and breakfast masterpieces, this tiny white-washed French bakery is worth waiting in line for (and you will). In summer the spacious patio provides more room for lingering with your coffee (though at $0.75 a refill, you might not want to linger for that long – go for a pitcher of Bloody Marys instead).

Lotus FUSION $$
(📞307-734-0882; www.theorganiclotus.com; 140 N Cache St; mains $15-26; ⊙8am-10pm; 🛜🍴) 🌿 In a region where steak and potatoes reign supreme, Lotus pushes back with things like plantain torte, vegan burgers and giant grain-and-veg bowls. There's plenty of meat, too – this is Wyoming – but it's all organic.

Gun Barrel STEAK $$
(📞307-733-3287; http://jackson.gunbarrel.com; 852 W Broadway; mains $19-36; ⊙5:30pm-late) The line stretches out the door for Jackson's best steakhouse, where the buffalo prime rib and elk chop rival the grilled bone-in

ribeye for the title of 'king cut.' For a fun game, try to match the meat with the animal watching you eat it: this place was once the wildlife and taxidermy museum, and many original tenants remain.

Mangy Moose Saloon PUB FOOD **$$**
(☑307-733-4913; www.mangymoose.com; 3295 Village Drive, Teton Village; lunch mains $9-13, dinner mains $15-32; ☺food 7am-10pm, saloon 11am-2am; ☜) For more than half a century, Mangy Moose has been the rowdy epicenter for après-ski, big-name bands, slope-side dining and general mountain mischief at Jackson Hole Mountain Resort (p109). The cavernous **pub** cranks out bowls of chile, buffalo burgers and steaks from local farms and offers a decent salad bar, while the **Rocky Moutain Oyster cafe** has your breakfast needs covered.

Thai Me Up THAI **$$**
(☑307-733-0005; www.thaijh.com; 75 E Pearl Ave; mains $15-20; ☺from 5pm; ☜) First, the beer. Meet Melvin: the IPA everyone is talking about. He has 19 friends. They're pretty good, too. So is the Thai food. And burgers. And the kung-fu movies work mesmerizingly well with the hip-hop. The reverse-curve bar is a bit cramped, but that's the point. Maybe. Did we mention the tuk-tuk out front? Just check the place out.

🍷 Drinking & Nightlife

From breweries to bars to concerts to theaters, there's no lack of things to fill your evenings in Jackson, especially during the summer and winter high seasons. Consult the Jackson Hole News & Guide (www.jhnewsandguide.com/calendar) for the latest happenings, or just head downtown and follow the sound of laughter.

★**Snake River Brewing Co** MICROBREWERY
(☑307-739-2337; www.snakeriverbrewing.com; 265 S Millward St; pints $4-5, mains $10-22; ☺food 11am-11pm, drinks till late; ☜) With an arsenal of microbrews crafted on the spot (some award-winning), it's no wonder this is a favorite among the younger, outdoor-sports-positive crowd. Food includes wood-fired pizzas, bison burgers and pasta served in a modern-industrial warehouse with two floors and plenty of (but not too many) TVs broadcasting the game.

The Rose COCKTAIL BAR
(☑307-733-1500; www.therosejh.com; 50 W Broadway; cocktails $9-14; ☺5:30pm-2am Wed-Sat,

8pm-2am Sun-Tue) Slide into a red-leather booth at this swank little lounge upstairs at the Pink Garter theater and enjoy the best craft cocktails in Jackson. Encouraged by the success of their libations, they now offer multicourse culinary adventures Thursday through Saturday from 6pm to 10pm.

ℹ Information

Jackson Hole Guest Services (☑307-739-2753, 888-333-7766; Clock Tower Bldg) Information on activities and tours, located near the tram ticket office in Teton Village.

Jackson Ranger District (☑307-739-5450; www.fs.fed.us/btnf; 25 Rosencranz Ln; ☺8am-4:30pm Mon-Fri) Side by side with the USFS Bridger-Teton National Forest Headquarters.

ℹ Getting There & Around

Alltrans (Mountain States Express; ☑307-733-3135; www.jacksonholealltrans.com) runs a shuttle to Salt Lake ($75, 5¼ hours) and Grand Targhee ski area (adult/child $114/85 includes ski-lift pass) in the winter, while **Jackson Hole Shuttle** (☑307-200-1400; www.jhshuttle.com; ☺24hr) provides regular service from the busy airport to your hotel in the town of Jackson or Teton Village.

The free **START Bus** (Southern Teton Area Rapid Transit; ☑307-733-4521; www.startbus.com) system gets you anywhere you need to go locally and to Driggs, ID ($3). A bike path runs between Jackson and Jenny Lake in Grand Teton National Park.

Cody

You have a few choices when it comes to getting into Yellowstone National Park, and approaching from the Cody side of life should be top on your list. Not just for the mesmerizing drive along the North Fork of the Shoshone – which Theodore Roosevelt once called the '50 most beautiful miles in America' – but also for the town.

Cody revels in its frontier image, a legacy that started with its founder, William 'Buffalo Bill' Cody: Chief of Scouts for the army, notorious buffalo hunter, and showman who spent years touring the world with his Wild West extravaganza. The town rallies around nightly rodeos, rowdy saloons and a world-class museum that was started by Buffalo Bill's estate and is a worthy destination all by itself.

◉ Sights

★ **Buffalo Bill Center of the West**   MUSEUM
(🖉 307-587-4771; www.centerofthewest.org; 720 Sheridan Ave; adult/child $19/12; ☺ open daily Mar-Nov, Thu-Sun Dec-Feb, hours vary; 🖫) Do not miss Wyoming's most impressive (constructed) attraction. This sprawling complex of five museums, showcases everything western: from the spectacle of Buffalo Bill's world-famous Wild West shows, to galleries featuring powerful frontier-oriented artwork, to the visually absorbing **Plains Indian Museum** to a fascinating collection of 7000 firearms. Meanwhile, the **Draper Museum of Natural History** explores the Yellowstone region's ecosystem in excruciating, yet enthralling detail. Look for Teddy Roosevelt's saddle, the busy beaver ball, and one of the world's last buffalo tepees.

🛏 Sleeping

An unusually high number of independent hotels are found along Cody's Hwy 14. They range widely in cleanliness and amenities, if not in price. Beware that eye-catching exteriors are no guarantee of comfortable rooms. Campgrounds aplenty stretch along Hwys 14, 16 and 20 between Cody and Yellowstone.

Irma Hotel   HISTORIC HOTEL $$
(🖉 307-587-4221; www.irmahotel.com; 1192 Sheridan Ave; r $147-169, ste $197; 🖫🛜) Built in 1902 by Buffalo Bill as the cornerstone of his planned city, this creaky hotel has old-fashioned charm with a few modern touches. The original high-ceiling historical suites are named after past guests (Annie Oakley, Calamity Jane), while the slightly more modern annex rooms are very similar for $20 cheaper (and still have classic pull-chain toilets).

Big Bear Motel   MOTEL $$
(🖉 307-587-3117; www.codywyomingbigbear.com; 139 W Yellowstone Ave; r $159-209; 🖫🛜🏊🐾) This friendly place on the edge of town is close (but not too close) to the Cody Nite Rodeo and offers clean rooms, a laundry, a swimming pool and a distinctly Wyoming take on 'pony rides.' Prices get out of control during high season, but are reasonable in the shoulder months.

✕ Eating

Steak, steak and more steak (and a revolving door of unforgettable Mexican restaurants) sets the tone for dining. A few creative alternatives are trying to buck the trend, and although we appreciate the variety, eating salad almost feels sacrilegious in this Wild West tribute town.

★ **The Local**   MODERN AMERICAN $$
(🖉 307-586-4262; www.thelocalcody.com; 1134 13th St; lunch $10-13, dinner $13-38; ☺ espresso from 8:30am, lunch noon-2pm, dinner 5-9pm Tue-Sat; 🖉) 🐾 When Cody's cowboy cuisine starts to weigh on your arteries, find the antidote in the Local's fresh, organic and locally sourced dishes. Think tempeh and avocado wrap for lunch, or grilled scallops and saffron risotto for dinner.

Cassie's Western Saloon   STEAK $$
(🖉 307-527-5500; www.cassies.com; 214 Yellowstone Ave; steaks $20-45; ☺ food 11am-10pm, drinks to 2am) This classic roadhouse and former house of ill repute hosts heavy swilling, swingin' country-and-western music and the occasional bar fight. Strap on the feedbag at the attached supper club and tackle tender steaks ranging in size from 8oz to 5.25lb, or the triple threat: a 2.25lb burger with five types of cheese and bacon (add a fried egg for $1).

☆ Entertainment

Cody Nite Rodeo   SPECTATOR SPORT
(www.codystampederodeo.com; 519 W Yellowstone Ave; adult/child $20/10; ☺ 8pm Jun-Aug) Experience a quintessential small-town rodeo at this summer-night Cody tradition going on 80 years old – despite the fact that animal welfare groups often criticize rodeo events as being harmful to animals. Sensitive viewers may find some events disturbing.

❶ Getting There & Away

Cody's small **airport** (COD; 🖉 307-587-5096; www.flyyra.com; 2101 Roger Sedam Drive) connects this otherwise isolated town with Salt Lake City and Denver, and you can thank Buffalo Bill Cody for the scenic byway that bears his name and connects Cody to Yellowstone – another spectacular approach to the park.

Yellowstone National Park

Teeming with moose, elk, bison, grizzlies and wolves, America's first **national park** (🖉 307-344-7381; www.nps.gov/yell; Grand Loop Rd, Mammoth, Yellowstone National Park; $30; ☺ north entrance year-round, south entrance May-Oct) also contains some of America's wildest lands just begging to be explored.

Yellowstone is home to over 60% of the world's geysers, alongside myriad Technicolor hot springs and bubbling mud pits. But while these astounding phenomena attract over 4 million people each year, it's the surrounding canyons, mountains and forests that truly astonish.

◉ Sights

Yellowstone is split into five distinct regions, each with unique attractions. Upon entering the national park you'll be given a basic map and a park newspaper detailing the excellent ranger-led talks and walks (well worth attending).

SCENIC DRIVE: THE ROOF OF THE ROCKIES

A contender for the most dramatic route into Yellowstone Park, **Beartooth Highway** (p39) connects Red Lodge to Yellowstone's northeast entrance by an incredible 68-mile journey alongside 11,000ft peaks and wildflower-sprinkled alpine tundra. It has been called both America's most scenic drive and its premier motorcycle ride. There are a dozen USFS campgrounds along the highway, four within 12 miles of Red Lodge.

◉ Geyser Country

Geothermal features litter Yellowstone (you're on top of a massive volcano, after all) but only a few places have what it takes to create geysers. The area stretching between Norris and Old Faithful – the hottest part of the park – is your best bet.

Highlights include **Old Faithful** (Upper Geyser Basin; ⊙ approx every 90min) **FREE** and the **Upper Geyser Basin**, Grand Prismatic Spring and **Norris Geyser Basin**, especially if **Steamboat Geyser** is thinking of erupting. The 1-mile hike around **Artists Paintpots** (southwest of Norris) is an uncrowded delight.

In addition to geyser gazing, the Firehole and Madison Rivers also offer superb fly-fishing and wildlife viewing.

Old Faithful Visitor Education Center   VISITOR CENTER
(☑ 307-545-2751; Old Faithful; ⊙ 8am-8pm Jun-Sep, hours vary spring & fall, 9am-5pm Dec-Mar; 🔊) 𝒫 This new, improved and environmentally friendly center is all about the thermal features at Yellowstone, exploring the differences between geysers, hot springs, fumaroles and mud pots, and explaining why there are no geysers in Mammoth. Kids will enjoy the hands-on Young Scientist displays, which include a working laboratory geyser. Available information includes standard park maps and itinerary advice, as well as predicted eruption times for a handful of the park's most notorious gushers.

Grand Prismatic Spring   SPRING
(Midway Geyser Basin) At 370ft wide and 121ft deep, Grand Prismatic Spring is the park's largest and deepest hot spring. It's also considered by many to be the most beautiful thermal feature in the park. Boardwalks lead around the multicolored mist of the gorgeous pool and its spectacularly colored rainbow rings of algae. From above, the spring looks like a giant blue eye, weeping exquisite multicolored tears. The features are linked by a 0.5-mile boardwalk; allow for 30 minutes here, after you find parking.

◉ Mammoth Country

The park's first developed area once housed US Army soldiers tasked with stopping vandalism and poaching. Success! The laundry stations have long since been removed from the majestic limestone terraces of **Mammoth Hot Springs** and herds of elk now placidly wander through the valley.

The peaks of the Gallatin Range rise to the west, towering above the area's lakes, creeks and numerous hiking trails, including beautiful Bunsen Peak (p115).

◉ Tower-Roosevelt Country

The park is rich with wildlife, and one of the best places to see much of it is in **Lamar Valley** where hundreds of buffalo roam, and the ranges of multiple wolf packs overlap. **Tower Fall** and the **Absaroka Mountains**' craggy peaks are the geographical highlights of this area, the park's most remote, scenic and undeveloped region.

◉ Canyon Country

A series of scenic overlooks linked by hiking trails explore the cliffs, precipices and waterfalls of the Grand Canyon of the Yellowstone. Here the river continues to gouge out a fault line through an ancient golden geyser

Yellowstone National Park

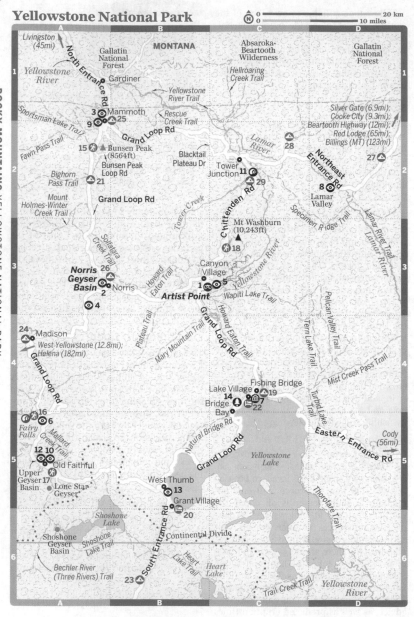

basin, most impressively at **Lower Falls**. The **South Rim Drive** leads to the canyon's most spectacular overlook at **Artist Point**, while the **North Rim Drive** accesses the daring precipices of both falls.

Grand Canyon of the Yellowstone CANYON (near Canyon Village) This is one of the park's true blockbuster sights. After its placid meanderings north from Yellowstone Lake, the Yellowstone River suddenly plummets over Upper Falls and then the much larger Lower

Yellowstone National Park

Top Sights

1	Artist Point	B3
2	Norris Geyser Basin	A3

Sights

3	Albright Visitor Center	A1
4	Artists Paintpots	A3
5	Grand Canyon of the Yellowstone	C3
6	Grand Prismatic Spring	A5
7	Lake Yellowstone Hotel	C4
8	Lamar Valley	D2
9	Mammoth Hot Springs	A2
10	Old Faithful	A5
	Old Faithful Visitor Education Center	(see 10)
11	Tower Fall	C2
12	Upper Geyser Basin	A5
13	West Thumb Geyser Basin	B5
14	Yellowstone National Park	C4

Activities, Courses & Tours

15	Bunsen Peak & Osprey Falls	A2
16	Fairy Falls Trail & Twin Buttes	A5
17	Lone Star Geyser Trail	A5
18	Mt Washburn	C3

Sleeping

19	Fishing Bridge RV Park	C4
20	Grant Village	B6
21	Indian Creek Campground	A2
22	Lake Yellowstone Hotel	C4
23	Lewis Lake Campground	B6
24	Madison Campground	A4
25	Mammoth Campground	B1
26	Norris Campground	A3
	Old Faithful Inn	(see 10)
27	Pebble Creek Campground	D2
28	Slough Creek Campground	C2
29	Tower Fall Campground	C2

Eating

	Lake House	(see 20)
	Lake Yellowstone Hotel Dining Room	(see 22)

Falls, before raging through the 300m-deep (1000ft) canyon. Scenic overlooks and a network of trails along the canyon's rims highlight its beauty from a dozen angles – South Rim Dr leads to the most spectacular overlook at Artist Point.

Lake Country

Yellowstone Lake, the region's centerpiece, is one of the world's largest alpine lakes. This watery wilderness lined with volcanic beaches is best explored by boat or sea kayak. Rising east and southeast of the lakes, the wild and snowcapped Absaroka Range hides the wildest lands in the lower 48, perfect for epic backpacking or horseback trips.

West Thumb Geyser Basin (west Yellowstone Lake) is good for a short stroll past infamous **Fishing Cone**, while colonial **Lake Yellowstone Hotel** (Lake Village) is a historic place to take an indoor break.

Activities

Hiking

Hikers can explore Yellowstone's backcountry from more than 92 trailheads that give access to over 1000 miles of hiking trails and 300 primitive campsites. Backcountry permits ($3 per person per night, up to $15) are required for overnight use, and are available at visitor centers and ranger stations up to 48 hours before your departure. Some of the backcountry sites can be reserved in advance by mail and are allotted through a lottery system.

Day hiking on any trail is free and requires no permit, but it does require proper preparation. Be sure to carry extra water, a rain jacket and bear spray on any hike.

★Bunsen Peak & Osprey Falls HIKING, MOUNTAIN BIKING

(southwest of Mammoth) Bunsen Peak (8564ft) is a popular half-day hike that you can extend to a more demanding day hike by continuing down the mountain's gentler eastern slope to the Bunsen Peak Rd and then *waaay* down (800ft) to the base of seldom-visited Osprey Falls. Better yet, bring a mountain bike and ride the two-track past the falls down to Mammoth (6.3 miles).

Lone Star Geyser Trail HIKING, CYCLING

This paved and pine-lined hike is an easy stroll along a former service road to one of the park's largest backcountry geysers. It's popular but quite a contrast to the chaotic scene around Old Faithful. Isolated Lone Star erupts every three hours for between two and 30 minutes and reaches 30ft to 45ft in height. It is definitely worth timing your visit with an eruption.

Mt Washburn HIKING, BIKING

(Tower-Roosevelt) A fairly strenuous uphill hike from Dunraven Pass trailhead to a mountaintop fire tower with 360-degree views over the park and nearby bighorn sheep (6.4 mile round-trip, moderate). Or tackle the climb on a bicycle via the dirt Chittenden Road from the north.

Fairy Falls Trail & Twin Buttes HIKING
Tucked away in the northwest corner of the Midway Geyser Basin, Fairy Falls (197ft) is a popular hike. Beyond Fairy Falls the trail continues to a hidden thermal area at the base of the Twin Buttes. The geysers are un-developed, and you're likely to have them to yourself – a stark contrast to the throngs surrounding Grand Prismatic Spring (p113) below.

Cycling

Cyclists can ride on public roads and a few designated service roads in Yellowstone, but not on the backcountry trails. Every camp-ground (except Slough Creek) has hiker/bik-er sites that rarely fill.

From mid-March to mid-April the Mam-moth–West Yellowstone park road is closed to cars but open to cyclists as plowing al-lows, offering a long and stress-free ride.

🛏 Sleeping

NPS and private campgrounds, along with cabins, lodges and hotels are all available in the park. Reservations, where possible, are essential in summer. Plentiful accommoda-tions can also be found in the gateway towns of Cody, Gardiner and West Yellowstone.

The best budget options are the seven NPS–run campgrounds in **Mammoth** (tent & RV sites $20; ⊗year-round), **Tower Fall** (Tow-er-Roosevelt, near Tower Fall; tent & small RV sites $15; ⊗mid-May–late Sep), **Indian Creek** (tents & RV sites $15; ⊗early Jun–mid-Sep), **Pebble**

Creek (off Northeast Entrance Rd; tent & RV sites $15; ⊗mid-Jun–late Sep), **Slough Creek** (Tow-er-Roosevelt; tent & small RV sites $15; ⊗mid-Jun–early Oct), Norris Campground and **Lewis Lake** (South Entrance; tent sites $15; ⊗mid-Jun–Oct), which are first come, first served.

Xanterra (☑307-344-7311, 866-439-7375; www.yellowstonenationalparklodges.com) runs five more reservable campgrounds, all with cold-water bathrooms, flush toilets and drinking water. RV sites with full hookups are available at Fishing Bridge.

⭐**Norris Campground** CAMPGROUND $
(Norris; tent & RV sites $20; ⊗mid-May–Sep) Nestled in a scenic, open, lodgepole pine for-est on a sunny hill overlooking the Gibbon River and meadows, this is one of the park's nicest campgrounds. Sites are given on a first-come basis and the few loop A riverside spots get snapped up quickly. Campfire talks are at 7:30pm and firewood is sold between 7pm and 8:30pm. Generators allowed 8am to 8pm.

Madison Campground CAMPGROUND $
(☑307-344-7311; www.yellowstonenationalpark lodges.com; Madison, W Entrance Rd; tent & RV sites $24.25; ⊗May-Oct) The nearest campground to Old Faithful and the West Entrance occu-pies a sunny, open forest in a broad mead-ow above the Madison River. Bison and the park's largest elk herd frequent the meadows to its west, making for great wildlife-watch-ing, and it's a fine base for fly-fishing the Madison. You can (and should) reserve your site in advance.

Fishing Bridge RV Park CAMPGROUND $
(www.yellowstonenationalparklodges.com; Fishing Bridge; RV sites $47.75; ⊗late May-late Sep) This is the only campground with full hookups

---

ⓘ BEAT THE CROWDS

Yellowstone's wonderland attracts up to 30,000 visitors daily in July and August and tops 4 million gatecrashers annually. Avoid the worst of the crowds with the following advice:

Visit in May or October Services may be limited, but there will be far fewer people.

Hit the trail Most (95%) of visitors never set foot on a backcountry trail; only 1% camp at a backcountry site (permit required).

Bicycle the park Most campgrounds have underutilized hiker/biker sites, and your skinny tires can slip through any traffic jam.

Mimic the wildlife Be active during the golden hours after dawn and before dusk.

Pack a lunch Eat at one of the park's many overlooked scenic picnic areas.

Bundle up Enjoy a private Old Faithful eruption during the winter months.

(water, electric, sewage) and due to heavy bear activity only allows hard-sided trailers or RVs are allowed. The 340 sites are crammed together cheek-to-jowl and have no privacy. Public facilities include a pay laundry and showers. Reservations are essential.

★ **Old Faithful Inn** HOTEL $$
(☑ 307-344-7311; www.yellowstonenationalpark lodges.com; Old Faithful; old house d with shared/private bath from $119/191, r $236-277; ☺ early May-early Oct) The historic log masterpiece of design and engineering rivals Yellowstone's natural beauty. The lobby alone is worth a visit just to sit in front of the impossibly large rhyolite fireplace and listen to the pianist upstairs. The cheapest 'Old House' rooms provide the most atmosphere with log walls and original wash basins, but bathrooms are down the hall.

Grant Village HOTEL $$
(☑ 307-344-7311; www.yellowstonenationalpark lodges.com; Grant Village; r $242; ☺ late May-Sep) The 300 condo-like boxes with standard hotel interiors at Grant Village were once dismissed by author Alston Chase as 'an inner-city project in the heart of primitive America, a wilderness ghetto.' They do happen to be the closest lodging to the Tetons for those getting an early start, and the rooms were completely updated in 2016, which helped increase their comfort (and price).

Lake Yellowstone Hotel HOTEL $$$
(☑ 866-439-7375; www.yellowstonenationalpark lodges.com; cabins $157, Sandpiper r $244, hotel r $397-452; ☺ mid-May–early Oct; @ 🐾) Commanding the northern lake shore, this buttercup-yellow colonial behemoth harks back to a bygone era – though the rooms that cost $4 in 1895 have appreciated somewhat. The spacious main-building rooms were upgraded in 2014, with new carpet and the park's only wired internet connections ($4.75 per hour). Lakeside rooms cost extra, sell out first and don't guarantee lake views.

✖ **Eating**

Lake House CAFETERIA $$
(Grant Village; mains $10-24; ☺ 6:30-10:30am & 5-9:30pm May–Sep) This quiet lakeshore spot offers casual dining with the best lakeviews in the park. Dinner includes creative items like huckleberry chicken and wild-game meatloaf.

> **SOUTH RIM TRAIL**
> ....
> Southeast of the Yellowstone Canyon's South Rim, this network of trails meanders through meadows and forests and past several small lakes. This loop links several of these and makes a nice antidote to seeing canyon views framed by the windshield of your car. It's an incredibly varied hike that combines awesome views of the Grand Canyon of the Yellowstone with a couple of lakes and even a backcountry thermal area.

Walk down from the main parking area or marina to the lakeshore. It's closed for lunch.

★ **Lake Yellowstone**
Hotel Dining Room AMERICAN $$$
(☑ 307-344-7311; www.yellowstonenationalpark lodges.com; Lake Village; mains $14-40; ☺ 6:30-10am, 11:30am-2:30pm & 5-10pm mid-May–Sep; 🖉) Save your one unwrinkled outfit (and an unwrinkled $100 bill) to feast in style at the dining room of the Lake Yellowstone Hotel. Lunch options include trout, a poached-pear salad and sandwiches. Dinner ups the ante with starters of lobster ravioli and mains of bison tenderloin, quail and rack of Montana lamb. Dinner reservations are required.

ℹ **Information**

The park is open year-round, but most roads close in winter. Park entrance permits (hiker/vehicle $15/30) are valid for seven days. For entry into both Yellowstone and Grand Teton the fee is $50.

Cell service is limited in the park, and wi-fi can only be found at Mammoth's **Albright Visitor Center** (☑ 307-344-2263; Mammoth; ☺ 8am-7pm Jun-Sep, 9am-5pm Oct-May).

ℹ **Getting There & Away**

Most visitors to Yellowstone fly into Jackson, WY, or Bozeman, MT, but it's often more affordable to choose Billings, MT. You will need a car; there is no public transportation to or within Yellowstone National Park.

Grand Teton National Park

The 12 imposing glacier-carved summits, which frame the singular Grand Teton (13,775ft), were designated a **national park**

(📞307-739-3300; www.nps.gov/grte; Teton Park Rd, Grand Teton National Park; entrance per vehicle $30) in 1929. Much of the Snake River Valley was later donated to the park by John D Rockefeller, who acquired it through secret purchases.

The scenery only gets more impressive the further into the mountains you go – make time to take a hike through the fragrant forests past glistening alpine lakes to dramatic canyons blanketed with wildflowers.

◉ Sights & Activities

With almost 250 miles of **hiking trails** you really can't go wrong in Grand Teton. Backcountry-use permits are required for overnight trips.

The Tetons are also known for excellent short-route **rock climbs** as well as classic longer routes to summits like Grant Teton, Mt Moran and Mt Owen. These are best attempted with an experienced guide.

Fishing is another draw, with several species of whitefish and cutthroat, lake and brown trout thriving in local rivers and lakes. Get a license at the **Moose Village store**, Signal Mountain Lodge (p120) or **Colter Bay Marina** (📞307-543-2811; www.gtlc.com/activities/marina; Colter Bay; ⊙8am-5pm).

Cross-country skiing and **snowshoeing** are the best ways to take advantage of park winters. Pick up a brochure detailing routes at Craig Thomas Discovery & Visitor Center.

★Craig Thomas Discovery & Visitor Center   VISITOR CENTER
(📞307-739-3399, backcountry permits 307-739-3309; Teton Park Rd, Moose; ⊙8am-7pm Jun-Aug, hours vary spring & fall, closed Nov-Feb; 🖈) FREE
Your first stop should be this incredibly well-done visitor center, if only for the sighting-lines on the floor that nail down exactly which peaks are staring back at you through the floor-to-ceiling windows. The obligatory raised-relief map helps you focus on where to go while informative kid-friendly interactive displays help you understand what you'll see. A battery of rangers are on hand to help plan your visit, and you can get backcountry permits here, too. Ranger programs include Map-chats and various guided hikes around Moose.

Mormon Row   GHOST TOWN
(Antelope Flats Rd; 🅿) Welcome to possibly the most photographed spot in the park – and for good reason. The aged wooden barns

and fence rails make a quintessential pastoral scene perfectly framed by the imposing bulk of the Tetons. The barns and houses were built by Mormon settlers in the 1890s who farmed the fertile alluvial soil irrigated via miles of hand-dug ditches.

Oxbow Bend   RIVER
(N Park Rd) One of the most famous scenic spots in Grand Teton National Park for wildlife-watching is Oxbow Bend, with the reflection of Mt Moran as a stunning backdrop. Dawn and dusk are the best times to spot moose, elk, sandhill cranes, ospreys, bald eagles, trumpeter swans, Canada geese, blue herons and white pelicans. The oxbow was created as the river's faster water eroded the outer bank while the slower inner flow deposited sediment.

★Death Canyon Trail   HIKING
Death Canyon remains one of our favorite hikes – both for the challenge and the astounding scenery. The trail ascends a mile to the Phelps Lake overlook before dropping down into the valley bottom and following Death Canyon. For a challenging add-on with impossibly beautiful views, turn right at the historic ranger cabin onto the Alaska Basin Trail and climb another 3000ft to Static Peak Divide (10,792ft) – the highest trail in Grand Teton National Park.

Garnet Canyon   HIKING, CLIMBING
Garnet Canyon is the gateway to the most popular scrambles to Middle and South Teton and the technical ascent of Grand Teton – but you need to know what you're doing and be with someone familiar with the routes. Even if you don't plan to go any higher, the 4-mile hike to the foot of the Tetons is a memorable one.

Grand Teton Multi-Use Bike Path   CYCLING
(www.nps.gov/grte/planyourvisit/bike.htm; Jackson to Jenny Lake) Starting from the excellent **Jackson Vistor Center** (📞307-733-3316; www.jacksonholechamber.com; 532 N Cache Dr; ⊙8am-7pm Jun-Sep, 9am-5pm Oct-May; 🚲) and continuing 20 miles to the **Jenny Lake Ranger Station** (📞307-739-3343; ⊙8am-6pm Jun-Aug), this new mutli-use path is an excellent way to see the park at a slower, more intimate pace. If that's too much of a commitment, rent bikes at **Dornan's** (📞307-733-2415; www.dornans.com; Moose Village; ⊙9am-6pm) in Moose for the 8-mile ride to the lake.

Grand Teton National Park

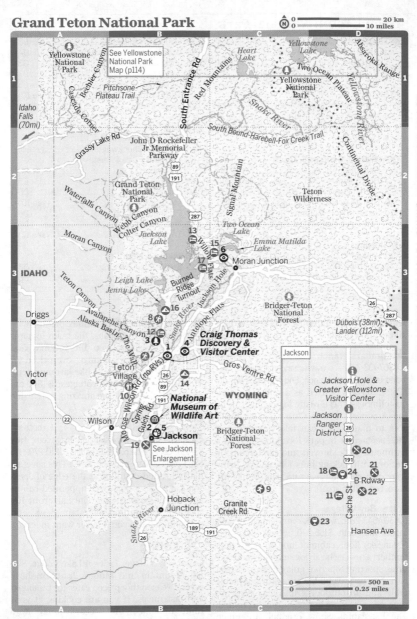

🛌 Sleeping

Demand for lodging and camping in Grand Teton is high from Memorial Day to Labor Day; book lodges well in advance. Most campsites get snatched up before 11am: **Jenny Lake** (Teton Park Rd; tent sites $28;

⊙ May–Sep) fills much earlier; **Gros Ventre** (Gros Ventre Rd; tent/RV sites $24/52; ⊙ late Apr–mid-Oct) usually stays open. **Colter Bay** (☎ 307-543-3100; www.gtlc.com; Hwy 89/191/287; tent/RV sites $30/71; ⊙ mid-May–mid-Sep) and

Grand Teton National Park

Jenny Lake have tent-only sites reserved for hikers and cyclists.

★ Climbers' Ranch   CABIN $
(☎307-733-7271; www.americanalpineclub.org/grand-teton-climbers-ranch; End Highlands Rd; dm $25; ☉Jun-Sep) Started as a refuge for serious climbers, these rustic log cabins run by the American Alpine Club are now available to hikers who can take advantage of the spectacular in-park location. There is a bathhouse with showers and sheltered cook station with locking bins for coolers. Bring your own sleeping bag and pad (bunks are bare, but still a steal).

Colter Bay Village   CABIN $$
(☎307-543-2811; www.gtlc.com; tent cabins $66, cabins with bath $155-290, without bath $85; ☉Jun-Sep) Tent cabins (June to early September) are very basic log-and-canvas structures sporting Siberian gulag charm. Expect bare bunks, a wood-burning stove, a picnic table and an outdoor grill. Bathrooms are separate and sleeping bags can be rented. The log cabins, some original, are much more comfortable and a better deal, and available late May through September.

★ Jackson Lake Lodge   LODGE $$$
(☎307-543-2811; www.gtlc.com; Jackson Lake Lodge Rd; r & cottages from $320; ☉mid-May–Sep; ☎✷☀) With soft sheets, meandering trails

for long walks and enormous picture windows framing the peaks, the main lodge is the perfect place to woo. Yet, you may find the 348 cinder-block cottages overpriced for their viewless, barracks-like arrangement. The Moose Pond View cottages ($430) are more secluded and have amazing porch-side panoramas.

Signal Mountain Lodge   LODGE $$$
(☎307-543-2831; www.signalmtnlodge.com; Hwy 89/191/287; r $253-363, cabins $210-270, ste $363-394; ☉May–mid-Oct; ☎☀) This spectacularly located complex at the edge of Jackson Lake offers cozy, well-appointed cabins and rather posh rooms. The Lakefront Retreats have stunning mountain views, and the kind of patio you'll never want to leave.

✕ Eating

Colter Bay Village, Jackson Lake Lodge, Signal Mountain and **Moose Junction** have several reasonably priced cafes for breakfast and fast meals. If you are cooking at your camp, remember this is bear country; store and dispose of food properly.

★ Dornan's Pizza & Pasta Company   PIZZA $
(☎ext 204 307-733-2415; www.dornans.com; Moose; mains $10-13, pizza $9-17; ☉11:30am-9pm; ☎) If there is a more ideal place to have pizza and a beer than sitting on Dornan's rooftop deck looking across the Snake River

and Menor's Ferry at the towering Tetons, we've yet to find it. The food is almost as good as the view here at one of the only independently owned restaurants in the park.

Blue Heron Lounge BARBECUE $
(☑ 307-543-2811; www.gtlc.com/dining; Jackson Lake Lodge; mains $11-23; ☺ 11am-midnight mid-May–Sep) An outdoor casual grill attached to an attractive corner cocktail lounge with knee-to-ceiling windows. Alcohol and appetizers are served from 11am to midnight. Occasionally you'll hit on live music.

Dornan's Chuckwagon BARBECUE $$
(☑ ext 203 307-733-2415; www.dornans.com; Moose; breakfast & lunch $7-15, dinner $21-32; ☺ 7:30am-3pm & 5-9pm Jun-Aug) At this family favorite, breakfast means sourdough pancakes and eggs off the griddle while lunchtime offers light fare and sandwiches. Come dinner, Dutch ovens are steaming. There's beef, ribs or trout, along with a bottomless salad bar. Picnic tables have unparalleled views of the Grand.

Trapper Grill CAFE $$
(☑ 307-543-2831; www.signalmountainlodge.com; Signal Mountain Lodge; mains $10-19; ☺ 7am-2:30pm & 4:30-10pm) Sandwiches, burgers and baby-back ribs are among the many choices sure to please each picky member of the family. It's the cheaper of the two restaurants at Signal Mountain Lodge, and it has the better view out over the lake. Breakfast, with sides of ham, bacon or buffalo sausage, are gut busters.

ⓘ Information

Park permits (hiker/bicycle/vehicle $24/24/30) are valid for seven days. If you are continuing on to Yellowstone, the fee is $50.

MONTANA

It's not just the sky that's big, but everything in Montana is just a little larger than life. The mountains seem just a touch taller, the valleys feel a smidge wider and the lakes are a bit longer than in other mountain states.

ⓘ Information

Visit Montana (☑ 800-847-4868; www.visitmt. com) The Office of Tourism website is well-done and informative, with maps, guides and trip suggestions.

Bozeman

Bozeman is what all those formerly-hip, now-overrun Colorado mountain towns used to be like. The laid-back, old-school rancher legacy still dominates over the New West pioneers with their mountain bikes, skis and climbing racks. But that's changing rapidly. It is now one of the fastest-growing towns in America and cost of living is on the rise, but it hasn't turned yet.

◉ Sights & Activities

★ **Museum of the Rockies** MUSEUM
(☑ 406-994-2251; www.museumoftherockies.org; 600 W Kagy Blvd; adult/child $14.50/9.50; ☺ 8am-6pm Jun-Aug, 9am-5pm Sep-May; ♠) Hands down the most entertaining museum in Montana shouldn't be missed. It has stellar dinosaur exhibits including an *Edmontosaurus* jaw with its incredible battery of teeth, the largest T-Rex skull in the world, and a new full T-Rex (with only a slightly smaller skull). Laser planetarium shows are interesting, as is the living-history outdoors section (closed in winter).

★ **Bridger Bowl Ski Area** SNOW SPORTS
(☑ 406-587-2111; www.bridgerbowl.com; 15795 Bridger Canyon Rd; lift ticket adult/child $60/22; ☺ mid-Dec–Apr) As the nation's leading nonprofit ski resort, it's all about the 'cold smoke', not cold, hard cash, at Bridger Bowl. Which means all you'll find at this small (2000 acres) community-owned hill 16 miles north of Bozeman is passionate skiers, reasonable prices, and surprisingly great skiing.

Explore Rentals OUTDOORS
(Phasmid; ☑ 406-922-0179; www.explore-rentals. com; 32 Dollar Dr; ☺ 9am-5pm Mon-Sat, 10am-4pm Sun) Imagine stepping off the plane, and there waiting for you is a car complete with luggage box, camping trailer, cook set, sleeping bags, backpacks, tent, bear spray, and full fly-fishing setup – all ready to go for your ultimate outdoor adventure. Or maybe you just forgot your stove. Explore has that and (just about) everything else for rent.

🛏 Sleeping

Most big-box chain motels are north of downtown Bozeman on 7th Ave, near I-90, with a handful of budget options east of downtown. Camping is plentiful in the Gallatin Valley toward Big Sky.

Howlers Inn
B&B $$

(☑ 406-587-2050; www.howlersinn.com; 3185 Jackson Creek Rd; r $165-170, 2-person cabin $225; ☎) Wolf-watchers will love this beautiful sanctuary 15 minutes outside of Bozeman. Rescued captive-born wolves live in enclosed natural areas on 4 acres, supported by the profits of the B&B. There are three spacious Western-style rooms in the main lodge and a two-bedroom carriage house.

The Lark
MOTEL $$$

(☑ 406-624-3070; www.larkbozeman.com; 122 W Main St; r $249-279; ❋ ☎) With a lively yellow palette and modern graphic design, this hip place is a big step up from its former life as a grungy motel. Rooms are fresh and the fine location puts it in walking distance of downtown's bars and restaurants, or hang out by the fire under the decked-out porte cochere, snacking on tacos from next door.

✖ Eating & Drinking

With seven breweries at last count (an eighth is on the way) and an active live music scene, if you're not having fun in Bozeman, you're doing it wrong. Check the Bozone (www.bozone.com) for a good music calendar.

★ Nova Cafe
CAFE $

(☑ 406-587-3973; www.thenovacafe.com; 312 E Main St; mains $8-13; ☉ 7am-2pm; ☎) ✐ A helpful map at the entrance shows you where the food you'll be eating comes from at this retro-contemporary locals' favorite. The hollandaise is a bit on the sweet side for our liking, but still excessively delicious – as is everything else.

Community Co-Op
SUPERMARKET $

(☑ 406-922-2667; www.bozo.coop; 44 E Main St; mains $7-12; ☉ 8am-8pm Mon-Fri, from 8:30am Sat, 9am-7pm Sun; ☎☑) ✐ This downtown branch of the beloved local market and deli is all about the hot bar, soups, salads and grab-and-go goodies. Fresh sandwiches and smoothies made to order. Eat in or take away.

Bozeman Taproom & Fill Station
BEER GARDEN

(☑ 406-577-2337; www.bozemantaproom.com; 101 N Rouse Ave; mains $9-13; ☉ 11am-midnight Sun-Tue, to 1am Fri & Sat) Bozeman's coolest new place to grab a pint and fill a growler has an open-air rooftop beer garden. Their 44 draft brews can be combined in as many ways as you like with the 'build your own flight' program.

Bridger Brewing
MICROBREWERY

(☑ 406-587-2124; www.bridgerbrewing.com; 1609 11th Ave; pizza $11-21; ☉ 11:30am-9pm, beer to 8pm; ☎) This well-run and friendly brewpub with central horseshoe bar draws a loyal combination of beer hounds and local MSU students. The Lee Metcalfe Pale Ale is a firm favorite and there are lots of food specials, including great pizza. The not-so-hidden upstairs deck is a great place to hang if you can find a seat.

Happy hour is from 2pm to 4pm.

❶ Information

Custer Gallatin National Forest Bozeman Ranger District (☑ 406-522-2520; www.fs.usda.gov/gallatin; 3710 Fallon, Suite C; ☉ 8:30am-4:30pm Mon-Fri) Tricky to find in the west of town, with info on campsites and cabins, plus it sells USGS topo maps.

Bozeman District Office (☑ 406-522-2520)

❶ Getting There & Away

Bozeman's **airport** (BZN; ☑ 406-388-8321; www.bozemanairport.com; 850 Gallatin Field Rd) keeps expanding to handle the increase in traffic, which also means more direct flights to more locations including LA, Seattle, Dallas and New York. **Greyhound** (Jefferson Lines; ☑ 612-499-3468; www.jeffersonlines.com; 1500 North 7th Ave, south side of Walmart; ☉ noon-5pm) buses depart daily from a nondescript bus stop on the south side of the Super Walmart near the garden center.

Gallatin & Paradise Valleys

Outdoor enthusiasts could explore the expansive beauty around the Gallatin and Paradise Valleys for days. While they now compete with the likes of the Tetons and Beartooth Pass for title of 'most dramatic approach,' cruising through the pastoral river flats flanked by the Gallatin and Abasaroka Ranges will definitely excite your passion for adventure and exploration. It's not called 'paradise' for nothing.

✖ Activities

Big Sky Resort
SNOW SPORTS

(☑ 800-548-4486; www.bigskyresort.com; 50 Big Sky Resort Rd; ski lift $129, bike lift $42) The 4th-largest ski hill in North America is actually four mountains covering 5800 acres of skiable terrain (60% advanced/expert) that get over 400in of powder a year. In short, Big

Sky is big skiing. And when the snow melts, you get over 40 miles of lift-served mountain bike and hiking trails making it a worthy summer destination as well.

Chico Hot Springs HOT SPRINGS
(☑406-333-4933; www.chicohotsprings.com; 163 Chico Road, Pray; cabins $120-135, main lodge r $71-140; ☉7am-11pm; ⛲) The unpretentious and historic Chico Hot Springs has garnered a loyal following of locals, Hollywood celebrities and return travelers. The creaking main lodge and sparkling log cabins are as much a draw as the mineral hot spring itself – which might as well be a heated swimming pool (admission for nonguests is $7.50).

Billings

It's hard to believe laid-back little Billings is Montana's largest city. The friendly oil-and-ranching center is not a must-see but makes for a decent overnight pit stop, or a point of departure for Yellowstone National Park via the breathtaking Beartooth Highway.

🛏 Sleeping

The main knot of chain motels is outside of Billings on I-90, exit 446, but there are a few standout independent options downtown – as well as a few dicey ones.

Dude Rancher Lodge MOTEL $
(☑406-545-6331; www.duderancherlodge.com; 415 N 29th St; d from $96; ❋@🛜🐾) This historic motor lodge looks a little out of place in the downtown area, but has been well maintained, with about half the rooms renovated to good effect. Western touches like tongue-and-groove walls and cattle-brand carpet give it a welcoming rustic feel.

Northern Hotel HOTEL $$
(☑406-867-6767; www.northernhotel.com; 19 N Broadway; r/ste $161/206; ❋🛜) The historic Northern was recently renovated, combining its previous elegance with fresh and modern facilities that are a solid step above generic business hotel. Breakfast or lunch is in the attached 1950s diner, and **Ten restaurant** offers one of best dinners in town.

🍴 Eating & Drinking

McCormick Cafe BREAKFAST $
(☑406-255-9555; www.mccormickcafe.com; 2419 Montana Ave; meals $8-10; ☉7am-3pm Mon-Fri, 8am-3pm Sat, 8am-2pm Sun; 🛜) For espresso, granola breakfasts, French-style crepes,

good sandwiches and a lively atmosphere, stop by this downtown favorite that started life as an internet cafe (and even still has a few Windows-XP computers – use at your own risk.)

★**Walkers Grill** MODERN AMERICAN $$
(☑406-245-9291; www.walkersgrill.com; 2700 1st Ave N; tapas $6-12, mains $15-30; ☉5-10pm) Upscale Walkers offers good grill items and fine tapas at the bar (open from 4pm) accompanied by cocktails crafted by expert mixologists. It's an elegant, large-windowed space that would be right at home in Manhattan, though maybe without the barbed-wire light fixtures – or with. You owe it to yourself to try the Korean pork fork fries.

Überbrew MICROBREWERY
(☑406-534-6960; www.facebook.com/uberbrew; 2305 Montana Ave; mains $9-11; ☉11am-9pm, beer til 8pm) The most polished of Billings' half-dozen downtown brewpubs also happens to create award-winning beers that are

---

MONTANA FACTS

Nickname Treasure State, Big Sky Country

Population 1,042,5200

Area 147,040 sq miles

Capital city Helena (population 30,581)

Other cities Billings (population 110,263), Missoula (72,364), Bozeman (45,250)

Sales tax No state sales tax

Birthplace of Movie star Gary Cooper (1901–61), motorcycle daredevil Evel Knievel (1938–2007), actress Michelle Williams (1980)

Home of Crow, Blackfeet, Chippewa, Gros Ventre and Salish Native Americans

Politics Republican ranchers and oil barons generally edge out the Democratic students and progressives of left-leaning Bozeman and Missoula

Famous for Fly-fishing, cowboys and grizzly bears

Random fact Some Montana highways didn't have a speed limit until the 1990s

Driving distances Bozeman to Denver 695 miles, Missoula to Whitefish 133 miles

a noticeable step above the rest. Their food isn't half bad either: wash down a beer-marinated bockwurst with a pint of the White Noise Hefeweizen, which outsells the other drafts three to one.

❶ Getting There & Away

Downtown Billings is just off I-90 occupying a wide valley of the Yellowstone river. The **airport** (BIL; ☑ 406-247-8609; www.flybillings.com; N 27th Street) serves major hubs (Salt Lake City, Minneapolis, Denver, Seattle, Portland, Phoenix, Los Angeles, Las Vegas and other Montana destinations) while **Jefferson Lines** (Jefferson Lines; ☑ 406-245-5116; www.jeffersonlines.com; 2502 1st Ave N; ⊙ 9am-8pm & 11pm-6am; 🕾) has service to Bozeman ($39, three hours) and Missoula ($70, seven hours) twice daily, and connects to the larger Greyhound bus system.

Helena

It's pretty easy to overlook diminutive Helena as you zip by on the interstate, but you'd be doing yourself a grave disservice. Penetrate through the drab, utilitarian commerce sprawl toward Last Chance Gulch and old Helena where imposing brick and stone buildings – all arches and angles – portray a resolute commitment to permanence.

🏃 Activities

★**The Trail Rider** HIKING, MOUNTAIN BIKING
(☑ 406-449-2107; www.bikehelena.com/trail-rider; cnr Broadway & Last Chance Gulch; ⊙ Wed-Sun late May-Sep) **FREE** During the summer months a dedicated city bus pulling a bike trailer runs mountain bikers and hikers to one of three trailheads for epic single-track journeys back to town. Destinations include the Mt Helena Ridge Trail, the Mt Ascension trails, and the Continental Divide Trail at MacDonald pass.

🛏 Sleeping & Eating

The Sanders B&B $$
(☑ 406-442-3309; www.sandersbb.com; 328 N Ewing St; r $145-165; ❄🕾) Located in the old mansion district, this historic B&B once belonged to Wilbur Sanders, a frontier lawyer and Montana's first senator. It now has seven elegant guest rooms, a wonderful old parlor and a breezy front porch. Each bedroom is unique and thoughtfully decorated, and it's run by a relative of the Ringling Brothers Circus family, with appropriate memorabilia.

Murry's CAFE $
(☑ 406-431-2886; www.murryscafe.com; 438 N Last Chance Gulch; mains $6-11; ⊙ 8am-3pm Mon-Fri, 9am-2pm Sat & Sun; 🕾🍽) From spanakopita to souffle, this little cafe on the south end of downtown offers something a little different from the regular breakfast fare. Things really go off the hook during their Saturday and Sunday brunch when the name of the game is waffles – regular, stuffed, topped or drenched.

★**General Mercantile** COFFEE
(☑ 406-442-6078; www.generalmerc.com; 413 N Last Chance Gulch; ⊙ 8am-5:30pm Mon-Fri, 9am-5pm Sat, 11am-4pm Sun; 🕾) You'll have to weave through all sorts of Montana eclectica for sale – hummingbird feeders, postcards and homemade jam – to get what is widely regarded as the best coffee in the universe. Take your espresso to a private nook where you can contemplate what you'd look like with a mermaid fin and an octopus mustache – both also available.

❶ Information

Helena Visitor Center (☑ 406-442-4120; www.helenachamber.com; 225 Cruse Ave; ⊙ 8am-5pm Mon-Fri)

❶ Getting There & Away

The **airport** (HNL; ☑ 406-442-2821; www.helenaairport.com; 2850 Mercer Loop) two miles north of downtown Helena connects to regional hubs including Salt Lake City, Seattle, Denver and Minneapolis. The **Salt Lake Express** (www.saltlakeexpress.com; 1415 N Montana Ave; ⊙ 3am-8pm) bus heads south to tie in with the Greyhound system at Butte.

Missoula

Missoulians love to get outside, and summer means an almost endless stream of farmers markets, concerts in the park, outdoor cinema and similar celebrations of community life. Patio seating is the rule not the exception, and an afternoon outing is likely to involve some human-powered activity on the miles of urban and foothills trails. The wandering Clark Fork River is popular with stand-up paddleboarders where it cuts through town, and is a fly-fishing magnet downstream. Stand on its bank for five minutes and you'll understand why the classic novella *A River Runs Through It* was set here.

The University of Montana ensures a continuous lifeblood of young energy that keeps the town vibrant and the music rocking. However, Missoula is also growing fast, which means sprawling development on the outskirts, and increasing traffic during rush hour. Stay downtown.

⊙ Sights

★**Garnet Ghost Town** GHOST TOWN
(☑ 406-329-3914; www.garnetghosttown.org; Bear Gulch Rd; adult/child $3/free; ⊙ 9:30am-4:30pm Jun-Sep; 🅿) Over a dozens buildings preserved in a state of 'arrested decay' transport you back to the gold rush days, when cities were built overnight and vanished almost as quickly. Visit the site any time roads are clear, but select structures are opened for exploration during visiting hours.

Smokejumper Visitor Center MUSEUM
(☑ 406-329-4934; www.fs.fed.us/fire/people/smokejumpers/missoula; 5765 West Broadway; ⊙ 8:30am-5pm Jun-Aug) FREE The visitor center on this active base for the heroic men and women who parachute into forests to combat raging wildfires has thought-provoking displays about an increasingly hazardous job. The real treat is touring the facility where the crew lives, trains and sews their own parachutes.

🏃 Activities

A Carousel for Missoula PLAYGROUND
(☑ 406-549-8382; www.carouselformissoula.com; 101 Carousel Drive, Caras Park; adult/child $2.25/0.75; ⊙ 11am-5:30pm Sep-May, to 7pm Jun-Aug; 🔖) Hand-carved and individually painted by local artists, every horse that gallops around the classic carousel at Caras Park has a story to tell. But the bigger story is how a community rallied around one man's dream to restore a bit of whimsy to downtown.

Mount Sentinel HIKING
(Campus Dr) A steep switchback trail from behind the University of Montana football stadium leads up to a concrete whitewashed 'M' (visible for miles around) on 5158ft Mt Sentinel. Tackle it on a warm summer's evening for glistening views of this much-loved city and its spectacular environs.

The trailhead is at Phyllis Washington Park on the east edge of campus.

🛏 Sleeping & Eating

★**Shady Spruce Hostel** HOSTEL $
(☑ 406-285-1197; www.shadysprucehostel.com; 204 E Spruce St; dm $35-40, s/ste $55/85; ❄ 🛜)

WORTH A TRIP

CUSTER'S LAST STAND

The Crow (Apsalooke) Indian Reservation is home to the **Little Bighorn Battlefield National Monument** (☑ 406-638-3224; www.nps.gov/libi; 756 Battlefield Tour Road, Hwy 212 off I-90; per car $20; ⊙ 8am-8pm). One of the USA's best-known Native American battlefields, this is where General George Custer made his famous 'last stand.' Custer, and 272 soldiers, messed one too many times with Native Americans (including Crazy Horse of the Lakota Sioux), who overwhelmed the force in a frequently painted massacre.

A visitor center tells the tale. In summer, rangers give highly entertaining dramatic lectures about every two hours (free). The entrance is a mile east of I-90 on Hwy 212, 62 miles from Billings.

We're superexcited to see the resurgence of the hostel in the US, and this clean, bright and spacious new addition to the family nails it in all the right places. Downtown is literally a block away from the converted house, but they have bikes for the walking-averse.

Goldsmith's Bed & Breakfast B&B $$
(☑ 406-728-1585; www.missoulabedandbreakfast.com; 809 E Front St; r $144-204; ❄ 🛜 🐾) Before being moved here into two massive pieces, this inviting riverside B&B was a frat house, and before that, home to the University of Montana president. The modern-Victorian rooms are all comfortable, but we're partial to the Greenough Suite with its writing table and private river-view deck.

The Catalyst CAFE $
(☑ 406-542-1337; www.thecatalystcafe.com; 111 N Higgins Ave; mains $8-13; ⊙ 8am-3pm) A local's favorite breakfast diner serves large portions of chilaquiles that you can drench in their house-made chipotle-coffee hot sauce. Don't miss the buckwheat waffles. There is usually a wait to get into this small space, but service is efficient and everyone leaves happy.

Market on Front DELI
(☑ 406-541-0246; www.marketonfront.co; 201 E Front St; ⊙ 8am-8pm, to 7pm Sun) 🍴 Order a fresh-made sandwich or overflowing breakfast bowl, or take advantage of the gourmet

grab-and-go items in the fridge. Shelves of healthy snacks, local teas, organic chocolate and local beer by the six-pack will take your picnic plans to the next level. Or dine in – with all those windows it feels like you're outside anyway.

Drinking & Nightlife

Missoula has a surprisingly high-profile music scene for a smaller town.

Top Hat Lounge · LOUNGE
(www.tophatlounge.com; 134 W Front St; ⏰11:30am-10pm Mon-Wed, to 2am Thu-Sat) Where Missoula goes to get its groove on. This dark venue features live music most weekends in a space large enough to cut a rug, but small enough to feel like the band is playing just for you.

If the headliner is too big for the Hat, you can catch them at the historic **Wilma** theater, another Logjam music venue (www.logjampresents.com).

The Old Post · BAR
(✆406-721-7399; www.facebook.com/oldpostpub; 103 W Spruce St; mains $8-12; ⏰11am-1am Mon-Thu, to 2am Fri, from 9am Sat & Sun) Great beer on tap, friendly servers, decent pub food, and a sombrero-wearing moose – what's not to love about this American Legion Forgotten Warriors Post open to all. It's a comfortable, unpretentious western bar that has a lived-in feel with well-worn booths and a cozy little patio out back.

Information

Visitor Center (✆406-532-3250; destinationmissoula.org; 101 E Main St; ⏰8am-5pm Mon-Fri) Destination Missoula has a useful website as well as a walk-in space downtown.

Getting There & Away

Though small, Missoula's **airport** (MSO; ✆406-728-4381; www.flymissoula.com; 5225 Hwy 10 W) has regular and usually affordable service to most major hubs including Salt Lake City, Denver, Phoenix, LA, Seattle and Minneapolis, while regular **Greyhound** (✆406-549-2339; www.greyhound.com; 1660 W Broadway; ⏰7:15am-noon & 6-11pm) service connects you to most regional destinations.

Flathead Lake

The largest natural freshwater lake west of the Mississippi, sitting not an hour's drive from Glacier National Park, completes western Montana's embarrassment of natural splendor. The small postcard community of **Bigfork** does its own artsy things on the north end of the lake while the southern end is anchored by the anywhere-USA town of **Polson**.

You can drive down either side of the lake, each with its own suite of campgrounds and lodges, beaches and hiking trails. Choosing is largely a matter of whether you prefer to watch the sun rise or set over the placid waters.

If you'd rather get away from the crowds, Swan Lake just to the east is a bit more primitive, while the Jewel Basin hiking area at its north draws backpackers from around the country.

Miracle of America Museum · MUSEUM
(✆406-883-6804; www.miracleofamericamuseum.org; 36094 Memory Lane, Polson; adult/child $6/3; ⏰8am-8pm Mon-Sat, reduced hours Sep-May) When Gil Mangels was a soldier on foreign soil, he became acutely aware of how America's freedom allowed for so much innovation and creativity – and he's been trying to collect every last bit of it ever since. At turns baffling and fascinating, these 5 acres are cluttered with the leftovers of American history: old motorcycles, bicycles, snow machines, steam tractors, antique quilts, coins, cast-iron skillets and countless other weird artifacts in a jumbled assortment of displays and piles.

Kwataqnuk Resort · HOTEL $$
(✆406-883-3636; www.kwataqnuk.com; 49708 Hwy 93, Polson; r from $170; ❋▣▧▨) The lakeside Kwataqnuk Resort, run by the Salish and Kootenai tribes, has a boat dock, lakeside patio with lounge chairs, indoor pool and a mellow casino-lounge. The spacious rooms were all updated in 2016, but that unfortunately didn't remove the lingering smoke smell that permeates from the casino downstairs.

★ Echo Lake Cafe · CAFE $
(✆406-837-4252; www.echolakecafe.com; 1195 Hwy 83, Bigfork; mains $9-12; ⏰6:30am-2:30pm; ▨) Go out of your way to stop by this valley favorite that serves an extensive menu of affordable breakfast and lunch creations. Try the Echo Lake crepes for a hearty take on the all-too-ubiquitous Benedict.

The **Swan Rangers** (www.swanrange.org) meet Saturday morning before heading off to clear trail. Join them for the insider scoop on area hiking.

ⓘ Information

Swan Lake Ranger District (📞406-837-7500; www.fs.usda.gov/flathead; 200 Ranger Station Rd, Bigfork; ⊗8am-4:30pm Mon-Fri) manages the forest surrounding Flathead Lake and Swan Lake to the east, including the epically scenic Jewel Basin hiking area.

Whitefish

Tiny Whitefish feels on the verge of tipping from an easy-going outdoorsy mountain town to a fur-lined playground for the glitterati. It's not quite there yet, thankfully, but there's something suspiciously refined about this charismatic and caffeinated New West town. It is home to an attractive stash of restaurants, a historic railway station and an underrated ski resort, as well as excellent biking and hiking on a rapidly growing network of trails. Whitefish is well worth a visit – just get here while it's still affordable.

🏃 Activities

**Whitefish Legacy
Partners** HIKING, MOUNTAIN BIKING
(www.whitefishlegacy.org) Whitefish is surrounded by a growing network of trails ideal for hiking and mountain biking. The driving force behind the development, Whitefish Legacy Partners rallies support for the system with things like guided walks focusing on wildflowers, bears and noxious weeds.

Whitefish Mountain Resort SKIING
(📞406-862-2900; www.skiwhitefish.com; Big Mountain Rd; ski/bike lift $76/38) Whitefish Mountain Resort at Big Mountain is a laid-back old-school ski hill with 3000 acres of varied terrain that sees 300in of snow a year. The views are unsurpassed (when it's clear).

🛏 Sleeping

★Whitefish Bike Retreat HOSTEL $
(📞406-260-0274; www.whitefishbikeretreat.com; 855 Beaver Lake Rd; dm/r $45/95; ❋🐾) Celebrating all things bicycle, this forested compound is a must-stay for two-wheel enthusiasts. The spacious polished-wood house with bunks, private rooms and a communal living area is a great place to hang when you're not hot-lapping the property trails or exploring the excellent **Whitefish Trail** that runs nearby.

The Lodge at Whitefish Lake RESORT $$$
(📞406-863-4000; www.lodgeatwhitefishlake.com; 1380 Wisconsin Ave; r from $300; ❋🐾🐾) Consistently ranked among the top luxury hotels in Montana, the Lodge exudes refinement and sophistication almost to a fault. It offers a range of rooms, from standards to fully stocked condos, on the sprawling complex. The lakefront **restaurant** and poolside tiki bar are both great places to catch the sunset.

✖ Eating & Drinking

Whitefish keeps up a lively evening scene, with a handful of bars and breweries, though the latter usually shut early due to Montana's byzantine liquor-licensing laws.

★Loula's CAFE $
(📞406-862-5614; www.whitefishrestaurant.com; 300 Second St E, downstairs; mains 9-11; ⊗7am-2pm Mon-Sun & 5-9:30pm Thu-Sun; 🐾) Downstairs in the century-old Masonic temple building, this bustling cafe has local art on the wall and culinary artists in the kitchen. The highly recommended lemon-crème-filled French toast dripping with raspberry sauce is a sinfully delicious breakfast, especially paired with the truffle eggs Benedict.

Buffalo Café CAFE $$
(📞406-862-2833; www.buffalocafewhitefish.com; 514 3rd St E; mains $12-20; ⊗7am-2pm & 5-9pm Mon-Sat, from 8am Sun) Hopping with neighborly locals, the Buffalo is what you get when a standard chain diner hires someone who actually knows how to cook. For breakfast try the original Buffalo Pie: a mountain of poached eggs and various add-ins (cheese, veggies, bacon) piled atop a wedge of hash browns. You won't leave hungry.

★Spotted Bear Spirits DISTILLERY
(📞406-730-2436; www.spottedbearspirits.com; 503 Railway St, Suite A; ⊗noon-8pm; 🐾) Award-winning spirits (vodka, gin, and agave) are paired with secret blends of herbs and spices to create unique, award-winning cocktails you won't find anywhere else. Grab a drink and head to the sofa upstairs for a relaxing break from your day.

Montana Coffee Traders COFFEE
(📞406-862-7667; www.coffeetraders.com; 110 Central Ave; ⊗7am-6pm Mon-Sat, 8am-4pm Sun; 🐾) Whitefish's home-grown microroaster runs this always-busy cafe and gift shop in the old Skyles building in the center of town. The organic, fair-trade beans are roasted in

an old farmhouse on Hwy 93 that you can tour (10am Friday by reservation).

ℹ Information

Whitefish Visitor Center (www.whitefishvisit. com; 307 Spokane Ave; ⊙9am-5pm Mon-Fri)

ℹ Getting There & Away

Glacier Park International Airport (p130), 11 miles away, has daily service to Denver, Salt Lake and Seattle, but by far the best way to get here is via **Amtrak** (⊋406-862-2268; 500 Depot St; ⊙6am-1:30pm, 4:30pm-midnight) on the Empire Builder line, which also connects to Glacier National Park via West Glacier ($7.50, 30 minutes) and East Glacier ($16, two hours).

Glacier National Park

Few places on earth are as magnificent and pristine as **Glacier** (www.nps.gov/glac). Protected in 1910 during the first flowering of the American conservationist movement, Glacier ranks with Yellowstone, Yosemite and the Grand Canyon among the United States' most astounding natural wonders.

The glacially carved remnants of an ancient thrust fault have left us a brilliant landscape of towering snowcapped pinnacles laced with plunging waterfalls and glassy turquoise lakes. The mountains are surrounded by dense forests, which host a virtually intact pre-Columbian ecosystem. Grizzly bears still roam in abundance and smart park management has kept the place accessible and authentically wild.

Glacier is renowned for its historic 'parkitecture' lodges, the spectacular Going-to-the-Sun Rd and 740 miles of hiking trails. These all put visitors within easy reach of some 1489 sq miles of the wild and astonishing landscapes found at the crown of the continent.

⊙ Sights & Activities

Visitor centers and ranger stations in Glacier National Park sell field guides and hand out hiking maps. Those at Apgar and St Mary are open daily May to October, and Logan Pass Visitor Center is open when the Going-to-the-Sun Rd is open. Many Glacier, Two Medicine and Polebridge Ranger Stations close at the end of September.

Entry to the park (hiker/vehicle $15/30) is valid for seven days.

You do not need a permit to day-hike the park's trails, but overnight backpackers do (May to October only). Half of the permits are available on a first-come-first-serve basis from the **Apgar Backcountry Office** (⊋406-888-7800; www.nps.gov/glac/planyour visit/backcountry-reservations.htm; Apgar Village; ⊙7am-5pm May–late Oct), **St Mary Visitor Center** (east end of Going-to-the-Sun Road; ⊙8am-6pm mid-Jun–mid-Aug, 8am-5pm early Jun & Sep) and the park's ranger stations. The other half can be reserved in advance online.

Logan Pass Visitor Center   VISITOR CENTER
(⊋406-888-7800; Going-to-the-Sun Rd; ⊙9am-7pm Jun-Aug, 9:30am-4pm Sep) Certainly in the most magnificent setting of all the park's visitor centers, the building has park information, interactive exhibits, and a good gift shop. The **Hidden Lakes Overlook** and Highline trails begin from here.

Check times for ranger talks and guided hikes in the area.

Bird Woman Falls   WATERFALL
(Going-to-the-Sun Rd) Standing at the artificially created Weeping Wall, look across the valley to this distant natural watery spectacle; the spectacular Bird Woman Falls drops 500ft from one of Glacier's many hanging valleys.

Sunrift Gorge   CANYON
(Going-to-the-Sun Rd) Just off the Going-to-the-Sun Rd and adjacent to a shuttle stop lies this narrow canyon carved over millennia by the gushing glacial meltwaters of Baring Creek. Look out for picturesque **Baring Bridge**, a classic example of rustic Going-to-the-Sun Rd architecture, and follow a short, tree-covered trail down to misty **Baring Falls**.

Jackson Glacier Overlook   VIEWPOINT
This popular pull-over, located a short walk from the Gunsight Pass trailhead, offers telescopic views of the park's fifth-largest glacier, which sits close to its eponymous 10,052ft peak – one of the park's highest.

Going-to-the-Sun Road   SCENIC DRIVE
(www.nps.gov/glac/planyourvisit/goingtothesun road.htm; ⊙mid-Jun–late Sep) A strong contender for the most spectacular road in America, the 50-mile Going-to-the-Sun Rd (p38) was built for the express purpose of giving park visitors a way to explore its interior without having to hike. The marvel of engineering is a national historic landmark that crosses Logan Pass (6,646ft) and is flanked by hiking trails, waterfalls and endless views.

★ **Highline Trail** HIKING
(Logan Pass) A Glacier classic, the Highline Trail contours across the face of the famous Garden Wall to **Granite Park Chalet** (☑ 406-387-5555; www.graniteparkchalet.com; 1st person US$107, extra person US$85; ⊘ Jul–mid-Sep) – one of two historic lodges only accessible by trail. The summer slopes are covered with alpine plants and wildflowers while the views are nothing short of stupendous. With only 800ft elevation gain over 7.6 miles, the treats come with minimal sweat.

From Granite Park you have four options: you can retrace your steps back to Logan Pass; continue along the continental divide to Goat Haunt (22 miles); head for Swiftcurrent Pass and the Many Glacier Valley (7 miles); or descend to the Loop (4 miles), where you can pick up a shuttle bus to all points on the Going-to-the-Sun Rd.

Avalanche Lake Trail HIKING
(north of Lake McDonald) This low-commitment introduction to Glacier hiking pays big dividends in the form of a pristine alpine lake, waterfalls and cascades. The 2.3-mile hike is relatively gentle and easily accessed by the shuttle – and therefore invariably mobbed in peak season with everyone from flip-flop-wearing families to stick-wielding seniors making boldly for the tree line.

Glacier Park Boat Co BOATING
(☑ 406-257-2426; www.glacierparkboats.com) Six historic boats – some dating back to the 1920s – ply five of Glacier's attractive mountain lakes, and some of them combine the float with a short guided hike led by interpretive, often witty, guides. For those more adventurous types, they also rent rowboats, kayaks and paddleboards ($18.30 per hour) at Lake Mary, Many Glacier, and Two Medicine.

🛏 Sleeping

There are 13 **NPS campgrounds** (☑ 518-885-3639; www.recreation.gov; tent & RV sites $10-23) and seven historic lodges in Glacier National Park, which operate between mid-May and the end of September. Lodges invariably require reservations.

Only Fish Creek, St Mary and a few sites at Many Glacier campgrounds can be booked in advance (up to five months). First-come sites fill by mid-morning, particularly in July and August.

About half the two to seven sites at each of the 65 backcountry campgrounds can be

---

> ### ℹ FREE PARK SHUTTLE
>
> See more with less stress by ditching the car and taking the park's free hop-on-hop-off **shuttle service** (www.nps.gov/glac/planyourvisit/shuttles.htm; ⊘ 9am-7pm July-Aug) 🚲 **FREE** that hits all major points along Going-to-the-Sun Rd between Apgar and St. Mary Visitor Centers. Buses run every 15 to 30 minutes depending on traffic, with the last trips down from Logan Pass leaving at 7pm.
>
> Not only does taking the shuttle reduce emissions, but it means you can actually see the scenery instead of worrying about other drivers, and actually go hiking instead of trying to find parking at the trailheads.

reserved, the rest are allotted on a first-come basis the day before you start hiking.

★ **Izaak Walton Inn** HISTORIC HOTEL **$$**
(☑ 406-888-5700; www.izaakwaltoninn.com; 290 Izaak Walton Inn Rd, Essex; r $109-179, cabins & cabooses $199-249; 🛜) Perched on a hill within snowball-throwing distance of Glacier National Park's southern boundary, this historic mock-Tudor inn was originally built in 1939 to accommodate local railway personnel. It remains a daily flag-stop (request stop) on Amtrak's *Empire Builder* route – a romantic way to arrive. Caboose cottages with kitchenettes are available, along with a historic GN441 locomotive refurbished as a luxury four-person suite ($329).

Many Glacier Hotel HISTORIC HOTEL **$$**
(☑ 303-265-7010; www.glaciernationalparklodges.com; 1 Many Glacier Rd; r $207-322, ste $476; ⊘ mid-Jun–mid-Sep; 🛜) Enjoying the most wondrous setting in the park, this massive, Swiss chalet-inspired lodge commands the northeastern shore of Swiftcurrent Lake. It was built by the Great Northern Railway in 1915, and although the comfortable, if rustic, rooms have been updated over the last 15 years, many still suffer from thin walls and antiquated plumbing.

🍴 Eating

In summer in Glacier National Park, there are grocery stores with limited camping supplies in Apgar, Lake McDonald Lodge, Rising Sun and at the Swiftcurrent Motor Inn. Most lodges have on-site restaurants. Dining options in West Glacier and St Mary offer mainly hearty hiking fare.

If cooking at a campground or picnic area, be sure to take appropriate bear safety precautions and do not leave food unattended.

★ **Serrano's Mexican Restaurant** MEXICAN $
(📞 406-226-9392; www.serranosmexican.com; 29 Dawson Ave, East Glacier Park; mains US$13-18; ⏲ 5-9pm May-Sep; 🐾) East Glacier Park's most buzzed-about restaurant serves a mean chile relleno. Renowned for its excellent iced margaritas, Serrano's also has economical burritos, enchiladas and quesadillas in the vintage Dawson house log cabin, originally built in 1909. Expect a wait.

★ **Belton Chalet Grill & Taproom** INTERNATIONAL $$$
(📞 406-888-5000; www.beltonchalet.com; 12575 US 2, West Yellowstone; mains $24-35; ⏲ 5-9pm, tap room from 3pm) 🍴 A fine option for a fine evening, West Glacier's historic chalet knows how to wine and dine. The sit-down restaurant sports tablecloths, wine glasses and a small menu with items like Montana bison meatloaf wrapped in hickory-smoked bacon.

ℹ Information

Glacier National Park Headquarters (📞 406-888-7800; www.nps.gov/glac; West Glacier; ⏲ 8am-4:30pm Mon-Fri)

ℹ Getting There & Around

Glacier Park International Airport (FCA; 📞 406-257-5994; www.iflyglacier.com; 4170 Highway 2 East, Kalispell) in Kalispell has year-round service to Salt Lake, Minneapolis, Denver, Seattle and Las Vegas, and seasonal service to Atlanta, Oakland, LA, Chicago and Portland.

The **Glacier Park Express** (📞 406-253-9192; www.bigmtncommercial.org; Whitefish Library; adult/child round-trip US$10/5; ⏲ Jul-early Sep) shuttle connects Whitefish to West Glacier.

Amtrak's *Empire Builder* stops daily (year round) at **West Glacier** (www.amtrak.com) and **East Glacier Park** (www.amtrak.com; ⏲ summer only) (April to October). Xanterra provides a shuttle ($15, 10 to 20 minutes) from West Glacier to their lodges on the west end, and Glacier Park, Inc. shuttles (from $15, one hour) connect East Glacier Park to St Mary.

Glacier National Park runs a free hop-on-hop-off **shuttle bus** (p133) from Apgar to St Mary over Going-to-the-Sun Rd during summer months, that stops at all major trailheads. Xanterra concession operates the classic guided **Red Bus Tours** (📞 303-265-7010; www.glacier

nationalparklodges.com/red-bus-tours; adult $34-100, child $17-50).

If driving a personal vehicle, be prepared for narrow winding roads, traffic jams, and limited parking at most stops along Going-to-the-Sun Rd.

IDAHO

Hiding between Montana and Oregon is a rather large chunk of land with some of the most vast and rugged mountains in the lower 48. It's called Idaho (no, not Iowa), and when the federal government was dividing the northern territories into states, it got stuck with the leftovers nobody wanted: those bothersome mountain ranges that you just can't farm in – 114 of them to be precise.

While that may have been a setback for the agriculturally deprived young state, it is a golden opportunity in the modern recreation economy. Over 60% of the state is public land, and with 3.9 million acres of Wilderness, it's the 3rd-most wild state in the union – and mountain lovers are beginning to notice. The outdoor industry now brings six times as much cash into Idaho as do its famous potatoes.

Boise

Refreshingly modern, urban and trendy are not words you usually associate with Idaho towns, but the state's capital (and largest city) isn't really into stereotypes. Boise's lively downtown scene – complete with walking streets, Parisian-style bistros and sophisticated wine bars – would fit in on the East Coast. The network of trails shooting up from town to the forested hills above rivals some of Colorado's best hiking destinations. Floating through the Greenbelt is as good as anything you'll find along Austin, Texas' beloved tubing circuit. Sample a steaming pan of paella in the Basque Block and you might as well be in Bilbao. With so much going on, you won't know what to make of Boise, but Boise will undoubtedly make a lasting impression on you.

◎ Sights & Activities

★ **Basque Block** AREA
(www.thebasqueblock.com; Grove St at 6th & Capital) Boise is home to one of the largest Basque populations outside Spain with as many as 15,000 residing here, depending on who you ask. The original émigrés arrived

in the 1910s to work as shepherds when sheep outnumbered people seven to one. Few continue that work today, but many extended families have remained, and the rich elements of their distinct culture are still very much alive – glimpses of which can be seen along Grove St between 6th St and Capitol Blvd.

Boise River Greenbelt
PARK, MUSEUM

(http://parks.cityofboise.org) The glowing emerald of Treasure Valley began as an ambitious plan in the 1960s to prevent development in the Boise River's flood-plain and provide open space in a rapidly growing city. Now, the growing collection of parks and museums along the tree-lined river-way is connected by over 30 miles of multi-use paths, and hosts an insanely popular summer floating scene. A developing $12 million whitewater park, complete with hydraulically controlled waves, promises to be the largest of its kind.

World Center for
Birds of Prey
BIRD SANCTUARY

(Peregrine Fund; 208-362-8687; www.peregrine fund.org/visit; 5668 W Flying Hawk Lane; adult/child $7/5; 10am-5pm Tue-Sun Mar-Oct, to 4pm Nov-Feb) The Peregrine Fund's worldwide raptor conservation programs have brought many species back from the brink of extinction – including the iconic California Condor, successfully bred in captivity here for release in California and the Grand Canyon. A pair of condors reside at the center, along with a dozen other impressive birds including the northern aplomado falcon, whose mating pairs work in tandem to hunt grassland sparrows. Open-air Fall Flights are a must-see (3pm, Friday to Sunday in October).

Boise Art Museum
MUSEUM

(208-345-8330; www.boiseartmuseum.org; 670 Julia Davis Dr; adult/child $6/3; 10am-5pm Tue-Sat, noon-5pm Sun) Inside 90-acre Julia Davis Park, this small but bright museum displays mostly contemporary art in all media, including the occasional Warhol, and touring exhibitions by some big names. On First Thursdays each month, admission is by donation and the museum stays open until 8pm.

Idaho State Historical Museum
MUSEUM

(208-334-2120; https://history.idaho.gov/ida ho-state-historical-museum; 610 N Julia Davis Dr, temporary: 214 Broadway; during renovation: 11am-4pm Mon-Fri) While the main building is under renovations a temporary museum

with a handful of exhibits, including the much-adored two-headed stuffed calf, are on display at 214 Broadway. The re-opening is slated for spring 2018.

Ridge to Rivers Trail System
HIKING

(208-493-2531; www.ridgetorivers.org; north-east of Boise;) Some 190 miles of hiking and mountain-biking trails meander through the foothills above town, crossing grasslands, scrub slopes and tree-lined creeks on their way to the Boise National Forest. The options are literally endless. The most convenient access is via Cottonwood Creek Trailhead east of the capitol building, or **Camel's Back Park** to the north.

Boise River Float
PARK

(www.boiseriverraftandtube.com; 4049 S Eckert Rd, Barber Park; tube rental $12, ducky $35, raft $45;) There is no better way to spend a sunny summer day in Boise than floating down the river. Rent watercraft – from tubes to six-person rafts – at Barber Park (parking $5 Monday to Thursday, $6 Friday to Sunday) where you'll put in for a self-guided 6-mile, 1½ to three-hour float downstream to Ann Morrison Park. Open June through August depending on river flows.

Sleeping

Inn at 500
HOTEL $$

(208-227-0500; www.innat500.com; 500 S Capitol; r $205-265, ste $295-315;) Finally, a luxury boutique hotel that doesn't give up at the lobby. Fine art, unique dioramas and blown glass – all from local artists – adorn the hallways and rooms, creating warm and inviting spaces a step above your standard high-quality-bed-in-a-box affair. All within walking distance of Boise's buzzing downtown.

★ Boise Guest House
GUESTHOUSE $$

(208-761-6798; www.boiseguesthouse.com; 614 North 5th St; ste $99-189;) A veritable home away from home, this appealing old house has a handful of suites with kitchenettes and living areas comfortably arranged and tastefully decorated. All rooms have access to the large grill in the relaxing backyard, red-and-white cruiser bikes and laundry.

Eating

Boise's vibrant downtown hosts a range of dining options from casual to formal. Seek out Basque specialties. The hip Hyde Park region on 13th street is even more laid-back, and a great place to grab a snack after hiking.

★**Goldy's Breakfast Bistro** BREAKFAST $
(☎208-345-4100; www.goldysbreakfastbistro.
com; 108 S Capitol Blvd; mains $6-20; ☺6:30am-
2pm Mon-Fri, 7:30am-2pm Sat & Sun) Assuming
an egg is just an egg (regardless of whether
it's sunny-side up, poached or fried) Goldy's
offers 866,320 'Create Your Own Breakfast
Combos.' Check our math – we were already
drunk on hollandaise sauce when we put
pen to napkin. Or go for the frittatas, bennies or massive breakfast burrito.

Fork MODERN AMERICAN $$
(☎207-287-1700; www.boisefork.com; 199 N
8th St; mains $15-28; ☺11:30am-10pm Mon-Fri,
9:30am-11pm Sat, 9:30am-9pm Sun; ✐) ✐ This
cavernous corner restaurant occupying the
old bank building downtown is good any-
time, but excels during weekend brunch
when things like the Dungeness crab scram-
ble pair unbelievably well with the local
favorite: asparagus fries. Try the Fork Lem-
onade for a refreshing pickup on a sunny
summer day.

🍷 Drinking & Nightlife

There is no shortage of lively and creative
drinking spots in Boise's urban center,

IDAHO FACTS

Nickname Gem State

Population 1,596,000

Area 83,570 sq miles

Capital city Boise (population 223,154)

Other cities Idaho Falls (population
60,211)

Sales tax 6%

Birthplace of Lewis and Clark guide
Sacagawea (1788–1812); politician
Sarah Palin (b 1964); poet Ezra Pound
(1885–1972)

Home of Star garnet, Sun Valley ski
resort

Politics Reliably Republican with small
pockets of Democrats, eg Sun Valley

Famous for Potatoes, Wilderness, the
world's first chairlift

North America's deepest river gorge
Idaho's Hells Canyon (7900ft deep)

Driving distances Boise to Idaho Falls
280 miles, Lewiston to Coeur d'Alene
116 miles

---

which is hopping even on a Sunday night.
The further from the city center you get, the
more generic the options become.

★**Bodovino** WINE BAR
(☎208-336-8466; www.bodovino.com; 404 S 8th
St; ☺11am-11pm, to 1am Fri-Sat, to 9pm Sun; 🛜)
Whether you're a sommelier or a swiller, the
variety of vintages on tap here is nothing
short of hazardous – especially considering
you're on your own with walls of vending
machines that decant tastes or pours from
144 different wines.

Bardenay DISTILLERY
(☎208-426-0538; www.bardenay.com; 610 Grove
St; cocktails from $7; ☺11am-late Mon-Fri, from
10am Sat & Sun) Bardenay was the USA's very
first 'distillery-pub,' and remains a one-of-
a-kind watering hole. Located on Basque
Block (p130), it makse rum in house and
has whiskey ageing for imminent release.
A dizzying array of cocktails are created
from spirits crafted in all three Idaho loca-
tions, including the dizzying Sunday Morn-
ing Paper – a lemon-vodka–Bloody Mary
experience.

ⓘ Information

Visitor Center (☎208-344-7777; www.boise.
org; 250 S 5th St, Ste 300; ☺10am-5pm Mon-
Fri, 10am-2pm Sat Jun-Aug, 9am-4pm Mon-Fri
Sep-May) Boise's tourist-info website has a
useful events calendar.

ⓘ Getting There & Around

Although small, **Boise Municipal Airport** (BOI;
☎208-383-3110; www.iflyboise.com; 3201
Airport Way, I-84 exit 53) stays busy and is well
connected, with nonstop flights to a range of
locations including Denver, Las Vegas, Phoenix,
Portland, Salt Lake City, Seattle and Chicago.
Greyhound services depart from the **bus sta-
tion** (www.greyhound.com; 1212 W Bannock
St; ☺6am-11am, 4pm-11:59pm 6am-11am,
4pm-midnight) with routes fanning out to Spo-
kane, Pendleton and Portland, Twin Falls and
Salt Lake City.

The **Green Bike** (☎208-345-7433; www.
boise.greenbike.com; per hour $5) system, is by
far the coolest way to get around downtown.

Ketchum & Sun Valley

Occupying one of Idaho's more stunning
natural locations, Sun Valley is a living piece
of ski history. It was the first purpose-built
ski resort in the US (a venture by the Un-

ion Pacific Railroad to boost ridership) and opened in 1936 to much fanfare, thanks to both its luxury showcase lodge and the world's first chairlift.

The ski area and town of Ketchum were popularized early on by celebrities like Ernest Hemingway, Clark Gable and Gary Cooper (who received free trips as a marketing ploy by Averell Harriman – politician, railroad heir and Sun Valley's founder). It has kept a steady stream of swanky Hollywood clientele ever since.

Yet it still remains a pretty and accessible place that's flush with hot springs, hiking trails, fishing, hunting and mountain biking, extending from Galena Pass down to the foothills of Hailey.

🏃 Activities

★ Galena Lodge OUTDOORS
(📞208-726-4010; www.galenalodge.com; 15187 Hwy 75; XC ski pass adult/child $17/$5; ⊗lodge 9am-4pm, kitchen 11:30am-3:30pm) Miles of mountain bike and groomed XC ski trails spiderweb out from this cool lodge that rents equipment and serves up lunch to keep you fueled for the day. If you're feeling guilty about leaving your four-legged friend at home, don't worry, they have loaner dogs (most with four legs). It's 23 miles north of Ketchum.

Sun Valley Resort SNOW SPORTS
(📞888-490-5950; www.sunvalley.com; Ketchum; winter ski ticket $89-139) Sun Valley has been synonymous with luxury skiing ever since they invented the chairlift in 1936. But while you can now sit-to-ski elsewhere, people still flock here for the fluffy powder and celebrity spotting. Two mountains – mellow **Dollar Mountain** with its extensive terrain parks to the east of town and black-and-blue **Bald Mountain** to the west – provide plenty of variety.

Wood River Trail System HIKING, CYCLING
(www.bcrd.org/wood-river-trail-summer.php) Good things happen when a community rallies behind outdoor activities. This paved urban trail system extends over 32 miles, connecting the major hubs of Sun Valley with the towns of Ketchum, Hailey and Bellevue (20 miles south) following the old Union Pacific Railroad line.

🛏 Sleeping

Ketchum's new hostel means that the free camping on Bureau of Land Management (BLM) and Forest Service lands near town is no longer the only affordable lodging option. Rates vary with the seasons, winter being most expensive.

Hot Water Inn HOSTEL $
(📞626-484-3021; www.facebook.com/thehoth2oinn; 100 Picabo St; dm $39, r $109, ste $126; 📶) Score one for the ski bums. A group of passionate locals have tricked out an old boarding school to become Ketchum's most affordable – and most chill – place to spend the weekend. The bar and stage now occupying the great room host jam sessions many an evening, and Sun Valley's Warm Springs ski lifts are just a bleary-eyed stumble away.

Tamarack Lodge HOTEL $$
(📞208-726-3344; www.tamaracksunvalley.com; 291 Walnut Ave; r from $169-179, ste $209-249; ✴📶🐾🏊) Rooms are tasteful at this aging but clean downtown lodge that exudes '1970s ski condo' vibe. Some rooms are a bit dark, but many have fireplaces and all have a balcony and use of the Jacuzzi and indoor pool.

Sun Valley Lodge HOTEL $$$
(📞208-622-2001; www.sunvalley.com; 1 Sun Valley Rd; inn from $349, lodge from $439; ✴@📶🏊) The celebrities already came in droves before the 2015 renovation that spruced up this swank 1930s-era lodge – Sun Valley's first and finest. Standard rooms have the exact same amenities as the higher end picks – including the spacious bathrooms with tub – just less floor space around the bed.

🍴 Eating & Drinking

You'll want to après-ski at **Apple's** (📞208-726-7067; www.facebook.com/applesbarandgrill; 205 Picabo St; ⊗11am-6pm summer & winter) before checking out the valley's regular live-music scene. The more swanky bars are not averse to turning out the riffraff. If you unexpectedly find yourself in that category, the **Casino Club** (📞208-726-9901; 220 N Main St; ⊗11am-2am) has a stool for you.

The Kneadery BREAKFAST $
(📞208-726-9462; www.kneadery.com; 260 N Leadville Ave; mains $8-13; ⊗8am-2pm) A solid bet for breakfast or lunch, the Kneadery is off the main drag in an old split-log cabin outfitted with large fireplace, western art and a birchbark canoe hanging from the ceiling. The ambience is almost as fine as their pancakes.

Powerhouse
PUB FOOD $

(📞 208-788-9184; www.powerhouseidaho.com; 411 N Main, Hailey; mains $9-15; ⊙ 11:30am-10pm)

🍴 We debated whether to classify this as a 'bicycle shop,' 'bar' or 'restaurant.' We don't have a category for 'awesome.' With 17 beers on tap, it's a great place to get your two-wheeler wrenched on after a hard day on Sun Valley's trails. Or just hang out and meet local dirt-jockeys. The tacos and burgers are pretty good, too.

★ Pioneer Saloon
STEAK $$$

(📞208-726-3139; www.pioneersaloon.com; 320 N Main St; mains $15-35; ⊙5-10pm, bar 4pm-late) For the best steak in Ketchum (and, some argue, Idaho) step into the former illicit gambling hall, now an unashamed Western den decorated with deer heads, antique guns (one being Hemingway's) and bullet boards. If red meat isn't your thing, they also have a range of fish options and a tasty mango-chutney and grilled-vegetable chicken kabob.

ℹ Information

Sun Valley/Ketchum Visitors Center (📞 208-726-3423; www.visitsunvalley.com; 491 Sun Valley Rd; ⊙ 6am-7pm; 🛜) Staffed only from 9am to 6pm, but you can still come in and get maps and brochures before and after hours.

ℹ Getting There & Around

Friedman Memorial Airport (SUN; 📞 208-788-4956; www.iflysun.com; 1616 Airport Circle, Hailey, ID) is located 12 miles south of Ketchum in Hailey, and has daily service to most western-states hubs (LA, San Francisco, Seattle, Salt Lake City and Denver, as well as twice-weekly flights to Portland), though it can sometimes be more economical to fly into Boise and take the three-hour **Sun Valley Express** (Caldwell Transportation; 📞 208-576-7381; www.sunvalleyexpress.com; adult/child $85/75) from there.

Mountain Rides (📞 208-788-7433; www.mountainrides.org) offers free transportation throughout Ketchum.

Stanley

Barely more than a cluster of rustic log cabins at the base of the jagged Sawtooth mountains, Stanley might be the most scenic small town in America. Its population of 60-odd is dramatically augmented in summer by an influx of white-water rafters, anglers and woodsy folk keen to lose themselves among the foreboding peaks and hidden valleys of the Sawtooths.

🏃 Activities

★ Sawtooth National Recreation Area
OUTDOORS

(www.fs.usda.gov/recarea/sawtooth/recarea/?recid=5842) You'll find rivers to boat, mountains to climb, animals to hunt, over 300 lakes to fish, and an excess of 700 miles of trails to hike or mountain bike in the dramatic Sawtooth National Recreation Area. It protects 1170 sq miles of America's public lands stretching between Stanley and Ketchum, offering unparalleled opportunities for exploration and recreation.

Middle Fork of the Salmon
RAFTING

(📞 877-444-6777; www.recreation.gov) Stanley is the jumping-off point for the legendary Middle Fork of the Salmon. Billed as the 'last wild river,' it throws over 100 rapids at boaters during the 100-mile, 3000ft run that passes through the ominously named River of No Return Wilderness. This is alpine rafting at its finest, and is accessible through a number of guiding companies.

Kirkham Creek Hot Springs
HOT SPRINGS

(Hwy 21, Lowan; ⊙ dawn-dusk) **FREE** These natural hot springs at Kirkham Campground are about 5 miles east of Lowman and 53 miles southwest of Stanley on Hwy 21. Although they can get busy on weekends (parking $5), the cascades and pools of steaming water beside the frigid Payette River are still a relaxing experience.

🛏 Sleeping & Eating

There are about half-a-dozen hotels and lodges in Stanley, and plentiful camping in the surrounding national forest. Dining is limited, even during the short summer season when a few more restaurants open up.

National Forest Campgrounds
CAMPGROUND $

(📞 877-444-6777; www.fs.usda.gov/activity/sawtooth/recreation/camping-cabins; Stanley District Office; tent & RV sites $12-18) Dozens of established campgrounds provide exceptional opportunities to sleep under the stars throughout the Sawtooth National Recreation Area; many are within an hour drive of Stanley. Some campsites are reservable online (www.recreation.gov) while others are first come, first served.

Sawtooth Hotel
HOTEL $

(☎ 208-721-2459; www.sawtoothhotel.com; 755 Ace of Diamonds St; d with/without bath $100/70; ☺ mid-May–mid-Oct; ☎) Set in a nostalgic 1931 log motel, the Sawtooth updates the slim comforts of yesteryear, but keeps the hospitality effusively Stanley-esque. Six rooms are furnished old-country style, two with private bathrooms. Don't expect TVs or speedy wi-fi, but count on excellent dining (mains $14 to $26) with vegetarian and gluten-free options and a tiny selection of drinkable wines.

★ Stanley Baking Company
BAKERY, BREAKFAST $

(www.stanleybakingco.com; 250 Wall St; mains $8-13; ☺ 7am-2pm May-Oct) Something of a legend, this middle-of-nowhere bakery and brunch spot is a must stop. Operating for five months of the year out of a small log cabin, Stanley Baking Co is the only place in town where you're likely to see a queue. The reason: off-the-ratings-scale homemade baked goods and oatmeal pancakes.

Idaho Panhandle

In many ways northern Idaho feels more like the Pacific Northwest than the Rockies. Perhaps it's the impressively large lakes speckled with sailboats giving it a nautical vibe. Or maybe it's the understated mountains, dense forests and rebounding timber industry. Or it could be as simple as sharing a timezone (the panhandle observes Pacific Standard Time) which makes those lazy days on the lake feel all the longer – encouraging you to linger.

Sandpoint reigns as the panhandle's most interesting destination, and not just because of sprawling Lake Pend Oreille (Idaho's largest) but thanks also to its neat, walkable downtown and local ski resort.

The region's largest town, Coeur d'Alene (population 46,402), is an extension of the Spokane metro area, but manages to retain a rural feel. There's a small boardwalk and a manicured park in front of the landmark resort on the north shore of Lake Coeur d'Alene.

✈ Activities

Schweitzer Mountain Resort
SNOW SPORTS

(☎ 208-263-9555; www.schweitzer.com; 10000 Schweitzer Mountain Rd, Sandpoint; ski lift $77, mountain bike lift $35) Eleven miles northwest of Sandpoint is highly rated Schweitzer Mountain Resort, lauded for its tree-skiing.

Its 2900 acres of terrain gets 300 inches of snowfall. The summer mountain-bike trails are more traditional routes, with natural features than you don't typically find in today's engineered big-drop bike parks.

Trail of the Coeur d'Alenes
CYCLING

(☎ 208-682-3814; www.parksandrecreation.idaho. gov/parks/trail-coeur-d-alenes) An excellent rails-to-trails route crosses the Idaho panhandle from Plummer to Mullan, skirting the shore of Lake Coeur d'Alene before connecting to the I-90 corridor through the mountains. The incredibly scenic 72-mile trail is completely paved with a consistent grade, making it accessible to all types of non-motorized travel – including hiking, biking and rollerblading.

🛏 Sleeping & Eating

Flamingo Motel
MOTEL $$

(☎ 208-664-2159; www.flamingomotelidaho. com; 718 E Sherman Ave, Coeur d'Alene; s/d/ste $110/120/180; ❄ ❀ ☎) Channeling the best of the 1950s car-loving, motel-staying, road-tripping culture, this retro motor inn has rooms decked out in various themes – from over-the-top 'Flamingo' to 'Irish' – but with updates like flat-screen TVs and minifridges.

★ Lodge at Sandpoint
BOUTIQUE HOTEL $$$

(☎ 208-263-2211; www.lodgeatsandpoint.com; 41 Lakeshore Dr, Sandpoint; d/ste $219/419; ❄ ☎ ☺) Stealing the best lakeside location on Lake Pend Oreille, this modern lodge raises the bar for rustic-chic. They don't skimp on amenities with a gym, two outdoor hot tubs and beach access.

★ The Garnet Cafe
BREAKFAST $

(☎ 208-667-2729; www.garnetcafe.com; 315 E Walnut Ave, Coeur d'Alene; mains $10-14; ☑) 🌿 One foolproof way to be sure your ingredients are organic and sustainably sourced is to own the farm that grows them. Enter the McLane family who personally raise the pigs, ducks and chickens that feed the satisfied customers lining up outside the Garnet Cafe's door.

❶ Getting There & Away

The closest major airport is in Spokane and several companies operate shuttles to Coeur d'Alene ($60, 45 minutes) or Sandpoint ($120, 6½ hours). **Amtrak** (SPT; www.amtrak.com; 450 Railroad Ave, Sandpoint) is another fine, if underutilized, option for getting to Sandpoint from Whitefish, MT ($30, four hours) or Spokane ($13, two hours) on the *Empire Builder* line.

Western USA's National Parks

National parks are America's big backyards. No cross-country road trip would be complete without a visit to at least one of these remarkable natural treasures, rich in unspoiled wilderness, rare wildlife and history. The nation's five dozen national parks and over 350 other protected areas are managed by the National Park Service (NPS), which celebrated its centennial in 2016.

JEFF R CLOW / GETTY IMAGES ©

PETE SEAWARD / LONELY PLANET ©

1. Towering redwoods
Experience the majesty of the world's tallest trees in Redwoods National Park (p337).

2. Mesa Arch
Take in the surreal geology of Canyonlands National Park (p207).

3. Old Faithful Geyser
Yellowstone National Park (p112) – the world's oldest national park is still one of the most spectacular.

4. Vernal Falls
Yosemite National Park (p343) is one of the planet's busiest parks for good reason.

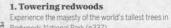

MARK COTÉ / 500PX ©

West Coast Beaches

From the wild, windswept beaches of Oregon to California's gorgeous sunkissed coast, the West Coast of the US holds some of the world's best loved and most iconic beaches. Whether you're sunning yourself on Huntington Beach, Orange County, with its perpetual sun, or surfing the amazing breaks of Rincon, Santa Barbara, you're sure to discover your perfect patch of coast.

2

COREY JENKINS / GETTY IMAGES ©

4

KRIS DAVIDSON / LONELY PLANET ©

1. Santa Monica beach
Santa Monica (p252) may be the epitome of Californian beach life.

2. La Jolla
Whether you're a surfer or a snorkeler, La Jolla is one of San Diego's (p269) most beloved beaches.

3. Hungtington Beach
Possibly Los Angeles' (p240) most iconic stretch of sand.

4. Steamer Lane
Catch a wave on one of Santa Cruz's (p297) most famous surf breaks.

3

STEVE WHISTON - FALLEN LOG PHOTOGRAPHY / GETTY IMAGES ©

Southwest

Best Places to Eat

➜ Kai Restaurant (p166)
➜ Love Apple (p229)
➜ Hell's Backbone Grill (p210)
➜ Cafe Pasqual's (p222)
➜ Red Iguana (p196)

Best Places to Sleep

➜ Washington School House (p202)
➜ Earthship Rentals (p228)
➜ La Fonda (p220)
➜ El Tovar (p181)
➜ Arizona Biltmore Resort & Spa (p164)

Why Go?

The Southwest is America's untamed playground, luring adventurous travelers with thrilling red-rock landscapes, the legends of shoot-'em-up cowboys and the kicky delights of green chile stew. Reminders of the region's Native American heritage and hardscrabble Wild West heyday dot the landscape, from enigmatic pictographs and abandoned cliff dwellings to crumbling Hispanic missions and rusty mining towns. Today, history making continues, with astronomers and rocket builders peering into star-filled skies while artists and entrepreneurs flock to urban centers and quirky mountain towns. The best part for travelers? A splendid network of scenic drives linking the most beautiful and iconic sites. But remember: it's not just iconic, larger-than-life landscapes that make a trip through the Southwest memorable. Study that saguaro up close; ask a Hopi artist about their craft; savor that green-chile stew. You may just cherish those moments the most.

When to Go
Las Vegas

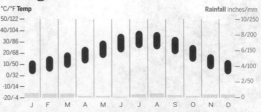

Jan Ski near Taos and Flagstaff. In Park City, hit the slopes and the Sundance Film Festival.

June–Aug High season for exploring national parks in New Mexico, Utah and northern Arizona.

Sep–Nov Hike to the bottom of the Grand Canyon or gaze at bright leaves in northern New Mexico.

History

By about AD 100, three dominant cultures were emerging in the Southwest: the Hohokam of the desert, the Mogollon of the central mountains and valleys, and the Ancestral Puebloans. Archaeologists originally called the Ancestral Puebloans the Anasazi, which comes from a Navajo term meaning 'ancient enemy' and has fallen out of favor.

Francisco Vásquez de Coronado led the first major expedition into North America in 1540. It included 300 soldiers, hundreds of Native American guides and herds of livestock. It also marked the first major violence between Spanish explorers and the native people.

In addition to armed conflict, Europeans introduced smallpox, measles and typhus, to which the Native Americans had no resistance. Pueblo populations were decimated by these diseases, shattering cultures and trade routes and proving a destructive force that far outstripped combat.

Development in the Southwest expanded rapidly during the 19th century, mainly due to railroad and geological surveys. As the US pushed west, the army forcibly removed entire tribes of Native Americans in horrifyingly brutal Indian Wars. Gold and silver mines drew fortune seekers, and the lawless mining towns of the Wild West mushroomed practically overnight. Soon the Santa Fe Railroad was luring a flood of tourists to the West.

Modern settlement is closely linked to water use. Following the Reclamation Act of 1902, huge federally funded dams were built to control rivers and irrigate the desert. Rancorous disagreements over water rights are ongoing, especially with the phenomenal boom in residential development and the extensive recent drought. The other major issue in recent years, especially in southern Arizona, has been illegal immigration across the border from Mexico.

Local Culture

Rugged individuality is the cultural idiom of the Southwest. But the reality? It's a bit more complex. The major identities of the region, centered on a trio of tribes – Anglo, Hispanic and Native American – are as vast and varied as the land that has shaped them. Whether their personal religion involves aliens, art, nuclear fission, slot machines, peyote or Joseph Smith, there's plenty of room for you in this beautiful, barely tamed chunk of America.

ℹ Getting There & Around

Las Vegas' McCarran International Airport (p156) and Phoenix's Sky Harbor International Airport (p169) are the region's busiest airports, with plenty of domestic and international connections. They're followed by those at Salt Lake City and Albuquerque.

Greyhound stops at major cities, but barely serves national parks or off-the-beaten-path

---

SOUTHWEST IN ...

One Week

Museums and a burgeoning arts scene set an inspirational tone in **Phoenix**. In the morning, follow Camelback Rd into **Scottsdale** for top-notch shopping and gallery-hopping in Old Town. Drive north to **Sedona** for spiritual recharging before pondering the immensity of the **Grand Canyon**. From here, choose either bling or buttes. For bling, detour onto **Route 66**, cross the new bridge beside **Hoover Dam** then indulge your fantasies in **Las Vegas**. For buttes, drive east from the Grand Canyon into Navajo country, cruising beneath the giant rock formations in **Monument Valley Navajo Tribal Park** then stepping back in time at stunning **Canyon de Chelly National Monument**.

Two Weeks

Start in glitzy **Las Vegas** before kicking back in funky **Flagstaff** and peering into the abyss at **Grand Canyon National Park**. Check out collegiate **Tucson** or frolic among forests of cacti at **Saguaro National Park**. Watch the gunslingers in **Tombstone** before settling into offbeat Victorian **Bisbee**. Secure your sunglasses for the blinding dunes of **White Sands National Monument** in New Mexico then sink into **Santa Fe**, a magnet for art-lovers. Explore the pueblo in **Taos** and watch the sunrise at awesome **Monument Valley Navajo Tribal Park**. Head into Utah for the red-rock national parks, **Canyonlands** and **Arches**. Do the hoodoos at **Bryce Canyon** then pay your respects at glorious **Zion**.

Southwest Highlights

1 Grand Canyon National Park (p176) Finding the rights words isn't easy: sublime, awesome, tremendous.

2 Santa Fe (p218) Lapping up the culture and diversions of this charismatic of southwest cities.

3 Angels Landing (p212) Hiking through this truly stunning slice of Utah canyonland in Zion National Park.

4 Las Vegas (p142) Finding out it's even more brash, synthetic and irresponsible than you'd hoped!

5 Sedona (p171) Rejoicing that even monetised hippy culture can't tarnish this unique red-rock city.

6 Route 66 (p188) Winding along the 'mother road' through stunning landscapes and time-capsule townships.

7 Moab (p205) Celebrating Christmas early! If you're a mountain biker. Or a hiker. Or a camper. Or …

8 Monument Valley (p185) Snapping impossibly photogenic brick-red buttes and mesas, the stars of countless Westerns.

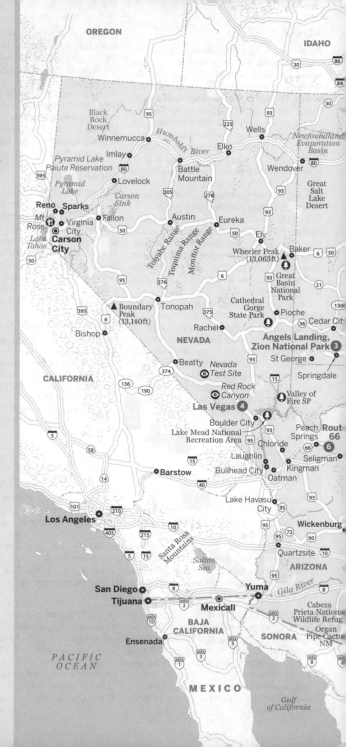

towns such as Moab. Amtrak train service is even more limited, although it too links several southwestern cities and offers bus connections to others (including Santa Fe and Phoenix). The *California Zephyr* crosses Utah and Nevada; the *Southwest Chief* stops in Arizona and New Mexico; and the *Sunset Limited* traverses southern Arizona and New Mexico.

Ultimately, this means private vehicles are often the only means to reach out-of-the-way towns, trailheads and swimming spots, and to explore the region in any depth.

NEVADA

Nevada is defined by contrasts and contradictions, juxtaposing arid plains with skyward, snow-capped mountains, while stilettos demand equal suitcase space with ski boots. Many visitors come only for the main event, Las Vegas: Nevada's twinkling desert jewel is a mecca for pleasure-seekers, and where priv-

---

NEVADA FACTS

Nickname Silver State

Population 2.84 million

Area 109,800 sq miles

Capital city Carson City (population 54,080)

Other cities Las Vegas (population 594,294), Reno (233,294)

Sales tax From 8.25%

Birthplace of Andre Agassi (b 1970), Greg LeMond (b 1961)

Home of The slot machine, Burning Man

Politics Nevada has six electoral votes – the state went for Obama in the 2012 presidential election, but it is split evenly in sending elected officials to Washington

Famous for The 1859 Comstock Lode (the country's richest known silver deposit), legalized gambling and prostitution (outlawed in certain counties), and liberal alcohol laws allowing 24-hour bars

Best Las Vegas T-Shirt 'I saw nothing at the Mob Museum.'

Driving distances Las Vegas to Reno 452 miles, Great Basin National Park to Las Vegas 313 miles

---

ilege and poverty collide and three-quarters of the state's population resides.

In this libertarian state, rural brothels coexist with Mormon churches, casinos and cowboys. Isolated ghost towns recall a pioneering past and the promise of a better life – just as Vegas riches lure punters today. But Nevada's rightful drawcard is nature, with Reno's rushing Truckee River, Lake Tahoe's crystal waters and forested peaks, the playas of the Black Rock Desert, where Burning Man's utopia was born, and the expanses of the Great Basin and the 'Loneliest Road in America.'

A place of discovery, Nevada is full of firsts, where there's something for daredevils and dreamers alike.

ℹ Information

Prostitution is illegal in Clark County (which includes Las Vegas) and Washoe County (which includes Reno), although there are legal brothels in many of the smaller counties.

Nevada is on Pacific Standard Time. **Nevada Tourism Commission** (☏ 775-687-4322; www. travelnevada.com; 401 N Carson St; ⊗ 9am-5pm Mon-Fri) Sends free books, maps and information on accommodations, campgrounds and events. **Nevada Division of State Parks** (☏ 775-684-2770; www.parks.nv.gov; 901 S Stewart St, 5th fl; ⊗ 8am-5pm Mon-Fri) Camping in state parks ($10 to $15 per night) is first come, first-served.

Las Vegas

Las Vegas remains the ultimate escape. Where else can you party in ancient Rome, get hitched at midnight, wake up in Egypt and brunch beneath the Eiffel Tower? Double down with the high rollers, browse couture or tacky souvenirs, sip a neon 3ft-high margarita or a frozen vodka martini from a bar made of ice – it's all here for the taking.

Ever notice that there are no clocks inside casinos? Vegas exists outside time, a sequence of never-ending buffets, ever-flowing drinks and adrenaline-fueled gaming tables. In this never-ending desert dreamscape of boom and bust, once-famous signs collect dust in a neon boneyard while the clang of construction echoes over the Strip. After the alarming hiccup of the 2008 recession, the city is once more back on track, attracting well over 40 million visitors per year and bursting with schemes to lure even more in future.

Las Vegas' largest casinos – each one a gigantic and baffling mélange of theme park, gambling den, shopping and dining destination, hotel and theater district – line up along the legendary Strip. Once you've explored those, head to the city's compact downtown to encounter Vegas' nostalgic beginnings, peppered with indie shops and cocktail bars where local culture thrives. Then detour further afield to find intriguing museums that investigate Vegas' gangster, atomic-fueled past.

◉ Sights

Vegas' sights are primarily concentrated along the 4.2-mile stretch of Las Vegas Blvd anchored by Mandalay Bay to the south (at Russell Rd) and the **Stratosphere** (Map p149; ✆702-380-7777; www.stratospherehotel.com; 2000 S Las Vegas Blvd; tower entry adult/child $20/10, all-day pass incl unlimited thrill rides $40; ⊘casino 24hr, tower & thrill rides 10am-1am Sun-Thu, to 2am Fri & Sat, weather permitting; ℗⊞) to the north (at Sahara Ave) and in the Downtown area around the intersection of Las Vegas Blvd (N Las Vegas Blvd at this point) and Fremont St. Note that while the street has the same name, there's an additional 2 miles between Downtown and the northern end of the Strip, with not much of interest in-between. It might look close if you decide to walk between the two, but you'll probably find yourself cursing in the desert heat if you do so. Ride-shares, the Monorail and Deuce bus services are by far the easiest ways to get around this spaced-out (in more ways than one) city.

◉ The Strip

★CityCenter   LANDMARK
(Map p149; www.citycenter.com; 3780 S Las Vegas Blvd; ℗) We've seen this symbiotic relationship before (think giant hotel anchored by a mall 'concept') but the way that this futuristic-feeling complex places a small galaxy of hypermodern, chichi hotels in orbit around the glitzy **Shops at Crystals** (www.crystal satcitycenter.com; 3720 S Las Vegas Blvd; ⊘10am-11pm Sun-Thu, to midnight Fri & Sat) is a first. The uberupscale spread includes the subdued, stylish **Vdara** (✆702-590-2111; www.vdara.com; 2600 W Harmon Ave; weekday/weekend ste from $129/189; ℗⊞✳@☎☂⊞) ⊘, the hush-hush opulent Mandarin Oriental (p151) and the dramatic architectural showpiece **Aria** (✆702-590-7111; www.aria.com; 3730 S Las Vegas Blvd; ⊘24hr; ℗), whose sophisticated casino provides a fitting backdrop to its many drop-dead-gorgeous restaurants. CityCenter's hotels have in excess of 6700 rooms!

★Cosmopolitan   CASINO
(Map p149; ✆702-698-7000; www.cosmopolitan-lasvegas.com; 3708 S Las Vegas Blvd; ⊘24hr; ℗) Hipsters who thought they were too cool for Vegas finally have a place to go where they don't need irony to endure – or enjoy – the aesthetics of the Strip. Like the new Hollywood 'It' girl, the Cosmopolitan casino looks absolutely fabulous at all times. A steady stream of ingenues and entourages parade through the lobby (with some of the coolest design elements we've seen) along with anyone else who adores cart and design.

★Bellagio   CASINO
(Map p149; ✆888-987-6667; www.bellagio.com; 3600 S Las Vegas Blvd; ⊘24hr; ℗✿) The Bellagio experience transcends its decadent casino floor with high-limit gaming tables and in excess of 2300 slot machines; locals say odds here are less than favorable. A stop on the World Poker Tour, Bellagio's tournament-worthy poker room offers kitchen-to-gaming-table delivery around-the-clock. Most, however, come for the property's stunning architecture, interiors and amenities, including the **Conservatory & Botanical Gardens** (⊘24hr; ℗⊞) FREE, **Gallery of Fine Art** (✆702-693-7871; adult/child under 12yr $18/free; ⊘10am-8pm, last entry 7:30pm; ℗⊞), unmissable **Fountains of Bellagio** (⊘shows every 30min 3-8pm Mon-Fri, noon-8pm Sat, 11am-7pm Sun, every 15min 8pm-midnight Mon-Sat, from 7pm Sun; ℗⊞) FREE and the 2000-plus hand-blown glass flowers embellishing the **hotel** lobby.

★Mandalay Bay   CASINO
(Map p149; ✆702-632-7700; www.mandalaybay.com; 3950 S Las Vegas Blvd; ⊘24hr; ℗⊞) Since opening in 1999, in place of the former '50s-era Hacienda, Mandalay Bay has anchored the southern Strip. Its theme may be tropical, but it sure ain't tacky, nor is its 135,000-sq-ft casino. Well-dressed sports fans find their way to the upscale race and sports book near the high-stakes poker room. Refusing to be pigeonholed, the Bay's standout attractions are many and include the multilevel Shark Reef Aquarium (p147), decadent day spas, oodles of signature dining and the unrivaled **Mandalay Bay Beach** (Map p149; ✆877-632-7800; www.mandalaybay.com/en/amenities/beach.html; ⊘pool 8am-5pm, Moorea Beach Club 11am-6pm; ⊞).

★LINQ Casino   CASINO
(Map p149; ✆800-634-6441; www.caesars.com/linq; 3535 S Las Vegas Blvd; ⊘24hr; ℗) With a

fresh, young and funky vibe, one of Vegas' newest casinos benefits from also being one of its smallest with just over 60 tables and around 750 slot machines. There's an airy, spacious feel to the place, tables feature high-backed, ruby-red, patent-vinyl chairs, and when you need to escape, the fun and frivolity of **LINQ Promenade** is just outside the door.

★ Paris Las Vegas

CASINO

(Map p149; ☑ 877-603-4386; www.parislasvegas. com; 3655 S Las Vegas Blvd; ⊙ 24hr; P) This mini-version of the French capital might lack the charm of the City of Light, but its efforts to emulate Paris' landmarks, including a 34-story Hotel de Ville and facades from the Opera House and Louvre, make it a fun stop for families and anyone yet to see the real thing. Its vaulted casino ceilings simulate sunny skies above myriad tables and slots, while its high-limit authentic French roulette wheels, sans 0 and 00, slightly improve your odds.

★ Caesars Palace

CASINO

(Map p149; ☑ 866-227-5938; www.caesarspalace. com; 3570 S Las Vegas Blvd; ⊙ 24hr; P) Caesars Palace claims that its smartly renovated casino floor has more million-dollar slots than anywhere in the world, but its claims to fame are far more numerous than that. Entertainment's heavyweights Celine Dion and Elton John 'own' its custom-built **Colosseum** (www.thecolosseum.com; tickets $55-500) theater, fashionistas saunter around the **Shops at Forum** (www.simon.com/mall/the-forum-shops-at-caesars-palace/stores; ⊙ 10am-11pm Sun-Thu, to midnight Fri & Sat), while Caesars group hotel guests quaff cocktails in the **Garden of the Gods Pool Oasis**. By night, megaclub **Omnia** (www.omnianightclub.com; cover female/male $20/40; ⊙ 10pm-4am Tue & Thu-Sun) is the only place to get off your face this side of Ibiza.

★ Wynn & Encore Casinos

CASINO

(Map p149; ☑ 702-770-7000; www.wynnlasvegas. com; 3131 S Las Vegas Blvd; ⊙ 24hr; P) Steve Wynn's signature casino hotel (literally - his name is emblazoned across the top) **Wynn** (weekday/weekend r from $199/259; P ✳ @ ⊚ ☲) and its younger sibling **Encore** (☑ 702-770-7100; r/ste from $199/259; P ✳ @ ⊚ ☲) are a pair of curvaceous, copper-toned twin towers, whose entrances are obscured by high fences and lush greenery. Each hotel is unique, but their sprawling subterranean casinos converge to form the Strip's second-largest and arguably most elegant gaming floor, whose popular poker rooms lure pros around the clock and labyrinth of slot machines range from a penny to $5000 per pull!

★ New York–New York

CASINO

(Map p149; ☑ 800-689-1797; www.newyork newyork.com; 3790 S Las Vegas Blvd; ⊙ 24hr; P) Opened in 1997, the mini-megalopolis of New York–New York remains a perennial hit with spring breakers. Tables in the casino's 'Party Pit' are set against a backdrop of gogo dancers and occasional live entertainers, while out front, perspective-warping replicas of the Statue of Liberty, Brooklyn Bridge, and Chrysler and Empire State buildings delight visitors from abroad. Tying it all together, the **Big Apple Arcade** (⊙ 8am-midnight; P 🚲) and **Roller Coaster** (☑ 702-740-6616; single ride/day pass $15/26; ⊙ 11am-11pm Sun-Thu, 10:30am-midnight Fri & Sat; P 🚲) are timeless hits with kids and big kids alike.

★ Lucky Dragon

CASINO

(Map p149; ☑ 702-889-8018; www.luckydragonlv. com; 300 W Sahara Ave; ⊙ 24hr) Las Vegas' newest casino hotel, Lucky Dragon opened

---

LAS VEGAS FOR KIDS

Las Vegas half-heartedly sells itself as a family destination. But because the legal gambling age is 21, many casino hotels would rather you left the kids at home. None of the mega-resorts are truly child-appropriate; even at the best places, you're still likely to expose your kids to drunk people behaving badly.

If you do land in Sin City with the kids, don't abandon hope. The **Circus Circus** (Map p149; ☑ 702-734-0410; www. circuscircus.com; 2880 S Las Vegas Blvd; weekday/weekend r from $79/95; P ✳ @ ⊚ ☲) hotel complex is all about kiddie fun, and its **Adventuredome** (Map p149; ☑ 702-794-3939; www.adven turedome.com; Circus Circus; day pass over/under 48in tall $32/18; ⊙ 10am-6pm daily, later on weekends & May-Sep; 🚲) is a 5-acre indoor theme park with rock climbing, bumper cars and, above all (literally), roller coasters. The **Carnival Midway** (11am to 11pm or later) features arcade games, animals, acrobats and magicians performing on center stage.

THRILLS & SPILLS IN LAS VEGAS

Stratosphere (Map p149; ☑ 702-383-5210; www.stratospherehotel.com/attractions/thrill-rides; Stratosphere; elevator adult $20, incl 3 thrill rides $35, all-day pass $40; ⊙ 10am-1am Sun-Thu, to 2am Fri & Sat; ⓢ Sahara) The world's highest thrill rides await, a whopping 110 stories above the Strip.

Sky Combat Ace (☑ 888-494-5850; www.skycombatace.com; 1420 Jet Stream Dr #100; experiences $249-1995) A bona-fide fighter pilot takes you through the paces of air-to-air dogfights and extreme acrobatics!

VooDoo ZipLine (Map p149; ☑ 702-388-0477; http://voodoozipline.com; Rio; $27; ⊙ 11am-midnight) If you've ever wanted to zip-line between two skyscrapers, here's your chance.

Gravady (☑ 702-843-0395; www.gravady.com; 7350 Prairie Falcon Rd #120; 1hr flight adult/child $13/10; ⊙ 9am-9pm Mon-Wed, from 3:30pm Thu, 9am-noon Fri & Sat, 11am-7pm Sun; ⓐ) Get bouncy with the kids at this high-energy trampoline park in Summerlin.

Speedvegas (☑ 702-874-8888; www.speedvegas.com; 14200 S Las Vegas Blvd; laps $39-99, experiences $395-995; ⊙ 10am-4:30pm) Burn serious rubber at the wheel of a sports car on Vegas' only custom-built track.

Richard Petty Driving Experience (☑ 800-237-3889; www.drivepetty.com; 7000 N Las Vegas Blvd, Las Vegas Motor Speedway; ride-alongs from $109, drives from $499; ⊙ hours vary) This is your chance to ride shotgun during a Nascar-style qualifying run.

its doors in December 2016. The majority of front-end staff at the city's first 'authentic' Asian casino, dining and lifestyle experience speak Mandarin or Cantonese. It's the hot ticket for inbound visitors from Asia, and lovers of Asian culture and cuisine alike.

Mirage Volcano   LANDMARK
(Map p149; ☑ 800-374-9000; www.mirage.com; Mirage; ⊙ shows 8pm & 9pm daily, also 10pm Fri & Sat) **FREE** When the Mirage's trademark artificial volcano erupts with a roar out of a 3-acre lagoon, it inevitably brings traffic on the Strip to a screeching halt. Be on the lookout for wisps of smoke escaping from the top, signaling that the fiery Polynesian-style inferno, with a soundtrack by a Grateful Dead drummer and an Indian tabla musician, is about to begin.

Shark Reef Aquarium   AQUARIUM
(Map p149; ☑ 702-632-4555; www.sharkreef.com; 3950 S Las Vegas Blvd, Mandalay Bay; adult/child $25/19; ⊙ 10am-8pm Sun-Thu, to 10pm Fri & Sat; ⓟⓐ) Mandalay Bay's (p143) unusual walk-through aquarium is home to 2000 submarine beasties, including jellyfish, moray eels, stingrays and 15 species of shark. Scuba-diver caretakers and naturalists are available to chat as you wander around. Better yet, go scuba diving yourself (from $650).

Madame Tussauds   MUSEUM
(Map p149; ☑ 866-841-3739; www.madametussauds.com/lasvegas; 3377 S Las Vegas Blvd #2001; adult/child from $30/20; ⊙ 10am-8pm Sun-Thu, to 9pm Fri & Sat; ⓐ) Outside the **Venetian** (Map p149; www.venetian.com; 3355 S Las Vegas Blvd) next to the mock Rialto Bridge is this interactive version of the wax museum many love to loathe. Strike a pose with Elvis, pretend to marry George Clooney, go '4D' with Marvel Super Heroes or don Playboy Bunny ears and sit on Hugh Hefner's lap (be sure to touch him, because Hef's made of silicone – how appropriate!).

◉ Downtown & Off the Strip

For tourists, the five-block **Fremont Street Experience** (Map p149; ☑ 702-678-5600; www.vegasexperience.com; Fremont St Mall; ⊙ shows hourly dusk-midnight or 1am; ⓠ Deuce, SDX) **FREE** is the focal point of Downtown, with its wealth of vintage casinos, where today's Vegas was born – and fear not, they're still going strong. Further south, the **18b Arts District** (www.18b.org) revolves around the **Arts Factory** (☑ 702-383-9907; www.theartsfactory.com; 107 E Charleston Blvd; ⊙ 9am-6pm; ⓠ Deuce, SDX), while heading east on Fremont St will take you to the sweetest little hodgepodge of hip bars and happening restaurants that you could possibly imagine.

★ **Mob Museum**   MUSEUM
(Map p149; ☑702-229-2734; www.themobmu
seum.org; 300 Stewart Ave; adult/child $24/14;
☺9am-9pm; P; ☐Deuce) It's hard to say
what's more impressive: the museum's physical location in a historic federal courthouse
where mobsters sat for federal hearings in
1950–51, the fact that the board of directors
is headed up by a former FBI Special Agent,
or the thoughtfully curated exhibits telling
the story of organized crime in America. In
addition to hands-on FBI equipment and
mob-related artifacts, the museum boasts a
series of multimedia exhibits featuring interviews with real-life Tony Sopranos.

★ **Neon Museum – Neon Boneyard**   MUSEUM
(☑702-387-6366; www.neonmuseum.org; 770 N
Las Vegas Blvd; 1hr tour adult/child $19/15, after
dark $26/22; ☺tours daily, schedules vary; ☐113)
This nonprofit project is doing what almost
no one else does: saving Las Vegas' history.
Book ahead for a fascinating guided walking
tour of the 'Neon Boneyard,' where irreplace-
able vintage neon signs – Las Vegas' original
art form – spend their retirement. Start exploring at the visitor center inside the salvaged La Concha Motel lobby, a mid-century
modern icon designed by African American
architect Paul Revere Williams. Tours are
usually given throughout the day, but are
most spectacular at night.

★ **Container Park**   CULTURAL CENTER
(Map p149; ☑702-359-9982; http://downtowncon
tainerpark.com; 707 Fremont St E; ☺11am-9pm
Mon-Thu, 10am-10pm Fri & Sat, to 8pm Sun) An
incubator for up-and-coming fashion designers and local artisans, the edgy Container Park stacks pop-up shops on top of one
another. Wander along the sidewalks and
catwalks while searching out handmade
jewelry, contemporary art and clothing at
a dozen or so specialty boutiques, eateries
and art installations. When the sun sets, the
container bars come to life and host regular
themed events and movie nights. It's adults
only (21-plus) after 9pm.

★ **National Atomic
Testing Museum**   MUSEUM
(Map p149; ☑702-794-5151; www.nationalatom
ictestingmuseum.org; 755 Flamingo Rd E, Desert Research Institute; adult/child $22/16; ☺10am-5pm
Mon-Sat, noon-5pm Sun; ☐202) Fascinating multimedia exhibits focus on science, technology
and the social history of the 'Atomic Age,'
which lasted from WWII until atmospheric

bomb testing was driven underground in
1961 and a worldwide ban on nuclear testing
was declared in 1992. View footage of atomic
testing and examine southern Nevada's nuclear past, present and future, from Native
American ways of life to the environmental
legacy of atomic testing. Don't miss the ticket booth (how could you?); it's a Nevada Test
Site guard-station replica.

🏃 Activities

★ **Dream Racing**   ADVENTURE SPORTS
(☑702-605-3000; www.dreamracing.com; 7000 N
Las Vegas Blvd, Las Vegas Motor Speedway; 5-lap experiences $199-599; ☺by appointment; ☻) Ever
wanted to get behind the wheel of a Porsche
911, Lamborghini, Lotus, AMG Mercedes or
McLaren and really let fly? Of course you
have. Well, now you can choose from the
largest selection of insured supercars in the
world, without having to buy one.

★ **Qua Baths & Spa**   SPA
(Map p149; ☑866-782-0655; Caesars Palace; fitness center day pass $25, incl spa facilities $50;
☺6am-8pm) Qua evokes the ancient Roman
rituals of indulgent bathing. Try a signature
'bath liqueur,' a personalized potion of herbs
and oils poured into your own private tub.
The women's side includes a tea lounge, a
herbal steam room and an Arctic ice room
where artificial snow falls. On the men's
side, there's a barber spa and big-screen
sports TVs.

Desert Adventures   KAYAKING
(☑702-293-5026; www.kayaklasvegas.com; 1647a
Nevada Hwy; full-day Colorado River kayak $179;
☺9am-6pm Apr-Oct, 10am-4pm Nov-Mar) Would-
be river rats should check in here for guided
kayaking and stand up paddle surfing (SUP)
tours on Lake Mead and the Colorado River.
Experienced paddlers can rent canoes and
kayaks for DIY trips.

🛏 Sleeping

Room rates in Las Vegas rise and fall dramatically each and every day; visiting on
weekdays is almost always cheaper than
weekends. Note that almost every Strip hotel also charges an additional 'resort fee' of
$10 to $30 per day.

🛏 The Strip

SLS   HOTEL $
(Map p149; ☑702-761-7000; www.slslasvegas.com;
2535 S Las Vegas Blvd; d from $79; P❄🛜🏊)

Las Vegas

Las Vegas

You can nab a room at Vegas' SLS (the Starwood Hotel Group's boutique brand) on the north Strip at a crazy rate compared to same-branded properties in other cities. The hotel's quirky style is infectious: you'll have fun with the acronym within minutes.

★ **Mandalay Bay** CASINO HOTEL $$
(Map p149; ☎702-632-7700; www.mandalaybay. com; 3950 S Las Vegas Blvd; weekday/weekend r from $119/229; P ❄ @ ⚛ ≋) Anchoring the south Strip, upscale Mandalay Bay's (p143) same-named hotel has a cache of classy rooms worthy of your attention in their own right, not to mention the exclusive **Four Seasons Hotel** (☎702-632-5000; www.four-seasons.com/lasvegas; weekday/weekend r from $229/289; P ❄ @ ⚛ ≋ ≋) and boutique **Delano** (☎877-632-7800; www.delanolasvegas.com; r/ste from $69/129; P ❄ @ ⚛ ≋ ≋) within its bounds and a diverse range of noteworthy attractions and amenities, not least of which is Mandalay Bay Beach (p143).

★ **NOBU Hotel** HOTEL $$
(Map p149; ☎800-727-4923; www.nobucaesarspal ace.com; 3570 S Las Vegas Blvd, Caesars Palace; d from $159) This exclusive boutique hotel within Caesars Palace (p146) is one for lovers of Japanese design from the traditional to the modern. Rooms are in high demand and suites are often the domain of celebrities.

★ **Cromwell Las Vegas** BOUTIQUE HOTEL $$
(Map p149; ☎702-777-3777; www.caesars.com/ cromwell; 3595 S Las Vegas Blvd; r/ste from $199/399; P ❄ ⚛ ≋ ≋) If you're 20- to 30-something, can hold your own with the cool kids, or you're just effortlessly stylish whatever your demographic, there are a few good reasons to choose Cromwell, the best being its location and frequently excellent rates on sassy, entry-level rooms. The others? You've got your sites set on partying at **Drai's** (☎702-777-3800; www.draislv.com; nightclub cover $20-50; ☺nightclub 10pm-5am Thu-Sun, beach club 11am-6pm Fri-Sun) or dining downstairs at **Giada** (☎855-442-3271; www. caesars.com; mains $25-58; ☺8am-11pm).

Caesars Palace CASINO HOTEL $$
(Map p149; ☎866-227-5938; www.caesarspalace. com; 3570 S Las Vegas Blvd; weekday/weekend r from $109/149; P ❄ @ ⚛ ≋ ≋) In 2016, Caesars celebrated turning 50 by (how else?) throwing a bunch of money into shaking off some gaudy and making itself look fabulous. Almost 600 rooms in its Roman Tower got a lavish makeover and the tower, a new name: Julius, of course! Augustus' guest rooms got some style too: think grey, white-gold and royal blue.

★ **Cosmopolitan** CASINO HOTEL $$$
(Map p149; ☎702-698-7575, 702-698-7000; www. cosmopolitanlasvegas.com; 3708 S Las Vegas Blvd; r/ste from $250/300; P ❄ @ ⚛ ≋ ≋; ▯Deuce) With at least eight distinctively different and equally stylish room types to choose from, Cosmo's digs are the hippest on the Strip. Ranging from oversized to decadent, about 2200 of its 2900 or so rooms have balconies (all but the entry-level category), many sport sunken Japanese tubs and all feature plush furnishings and design quirks you'll delight in uncovering.

★ **Mandarin Oriental** HOTEL $$$
(Map p149; ☎702-590-8888; www.mandarinori ental.com; 3752 S Las Vegas Blvd, CityCenter; r/ste from $239/469; ❄ ⚛ ≋ ≋) Part of the CityCenter (p143) complex, luscious oriental flavors meet the latest technology in Mandarin Oriental's 392 slick, state-of-the-art yet effortlessly elegant guest rooms and suites, undoubtedly some of the finest to be found on a Strip dripping with gold and shimmering with shiny things. Add a high ratio of courteous, attentive staff to each guest and you're on a winning streak.

🛏 Downtown & Off the Strip

★ **El Cortez** CASINO HOTEL $
(Map p149; ☎702-385-5200; www.elcortezhotelca sino.com; 651 E Ogden Ave; weekday/weekend r from $40/80; P ❄ @ ⚛) A wide range of rooms with all kinds of vibes are available at this fun, retro property close to all the action on Fremont St. Rooms are in the 1980s tower addition to the heritage-listed 1941 **El Cortez** (600 Fremont St E; ☺24hr; ▯Deuce) casino and the modern, flashier El Cortez Suites, across the street. Rates offered are generally great value, though don't expect the earth.

★ **Hard Rock** CASINO HOTEL $
(Map p149; ☎702-693-5000; www.hardrockhotel. com; 4455 Paradise Rd; weekday/weekend r from $45/89; P ❄ @ ⚛ ≋) Sexy, oversized rooms and HRH suites underwent a bunch of refurbishments in 2016 and 2017, making this party palace for music lovers a great alternative to staying on the Strip – there's even a free shuttle to take you there and bring you back.

★ **Golden Nugget** CASINO HOTEL $
(Map p149; ☎702-385-7111; www.goldennugget. com; 129 Fremont St E; weekday/weekend r from $45/85; P ❄ @ ⚛ ≋) Pretend to relive the fabulous heyday of Vegas in the 1950s at this swank Fremont St address. Rooms in the Rush Tower are the best in the house.

✖ Eating

The Strip has been studded with celebrity chefs for years. All-you-can-eat buffets and $10 steaks still exist, but today's high-rolling visitors demand ever more sophisticated dining experiences, with meals designed – although not personally prepared – by famous taste-makers.

✖ The Strip

★ Jaburrito   SUSHI $
(Map p149; ☑702-901-7375; www.jaburritos.com; LINQ Promenade; items $7-14; ☻11am-11pm Sun-Thu, to midnight Fri & Sat) It's simple: hybridize a nori (seaweed) sushi roll with a burrito. What could go wrong? Nothing actually... they're awesome!

★ Tacos El Gordo   MEXICAN $
(Map p149; ☑702-251-8226; www.tacoselgordobc. com; 3049 S Las Vegas Blvd; small plates $3-12; ☻10am-2am Sun-Thu, to 4am Fri & Sat; P♿♨; ▢Deuce, SDX) This Tijuana-style taco shop from SoCal is just the ticket when it's way late, you've got almost no money left and you're desperately craving *carne asada* (beef) or *adobada* (chile-marinated pork) tacos in hot, hand-made tortillas. Adventurous eaters order the authentic *sesos* (beef brains), *cabeza* (roasted cow's head) or tripe (intestines) variations.

Jean Philippe Patisserie   BAKERY $
(Map p149; www.jpchocolates.com; Bellagio; snacks & drinks $4-11; ☻6am-11pm Mon-Thu, to midnight Fri-Sun; ♨) As certified by the *Guinness Book of World Records,* the world's largest chocolate fountain cascades inside the front windows of this champion pastry-maker's shop, known for its fantastic sorbets, gelati, pastries and chocolate confections. Coffee and espresso are above the Strip's low-bar average.

★ Grand Wok   CHINESE $$
(Map p149; ☑702-891-7879; www.mgmgrand.com/ en/restaurants.html; MGM Grand; mains $12-28; ☻11am-10pm Sun-Thu, to 11pm Fri & Sat) Come to Grand Wok, in business for over 25 years serving some of the best pan-Asian dishes you'll find this side of the Far East. Try the garlic shrimp fried rice with dried scallops. Sensational.

★ Burger Bar   AMERICAN $$
(Map p149; ☑702-632-9364; www.burger-bar. com; Shoppes at Mandalay Place; mains $10-60; ☻11am-11pm Sun-Thu, to 1am Fri & Sat; P♿♨) Since when can a hamburger be worth $60? When it's built with Kobe beef, sautéed foie gras and truffle sauce: it's the Rossini burger, the signature sandwich of chef Hubert Keller. Most menu options are more down-to-earth – diners select their own gourmet burger toppings and pair them with skinny fries and a liquor-spiked milkshake or beer float.

★ Virgil's Real BBQ   BARBECUE $$
(Map p149; ☑702-389-7400; www.virgilsbbq. com/locations/las-vegas; LINQ Promenade; mains $10-24; ☻10am-2am) If you've never tried real-deal Southern cooking, and you're not shy of chunks of mouthwatering smoky meats, baby back ribs, cheesy grits and sugary caramelized sides, you simply must make a beeline for Virgil's and you will be converted. Hallelujah!

★ Joël Robuchon   FRENCH $$$
(Map p149; ☑702-891-7925; www.joel-robuchon. com/en; MGM Grand; tasting menus $120-425; ☻5-10pm) The acclaimed 'Chef of the Century' leads the pack in the French culinary invasion of the Strip. Adjacent to the **MGM Grand's** (Map p149; ☑877-880-0880; www. mgmgrand.com; 3799 S Las Vegas Blvd; ☻24hr; P♨) high-rollers' gaming area, Robuchon's plush dining rooms, done up in leather and velvet, feel like a dinner party at a 1930s Paris mansion. Complex seasonal tasting menus promise the meal of a lifetime – and they often deliver.

★ Morimoto   FUSION $$$
(Map p149; ☑702-891-1111; www.mgmgrand.com; MGM Grand; mains $24-75; ☻5-10pm) Iron Chef Masaharu Morimoto's latest Vegas incarnation is in his eponymous showcase restaurant, which pays homage to his Japanese roots and the cuisine of this city that has propelled him to legend status around the world. Dining here is an experience in every possible way and, we think, worth every penny.

✖ Downtown & off the Strip

★ eat.   BREAKFAST $
(Map p149; ☑702-534-1515; http://eatdtlv.com; 707 Carson Ave; mains $7-14; ☻8am-3pm Mon-Fri, to 2pm Sat & Sun; ☑) ✿ Community spirit and creative cooking provide reason enough to venture off Fremont St to find this cafe. With a concrete floor and spare decor, it can get loud as folks chow down on truffled egg sandwich-

es, cinnamon biscuits with strawberry compote, shrimp po'boy sandwiches and bowls of New Mexican green-chili chicken *posole*.

Container Park   FAST FOOD $
(Map p149; ☑702-359-9982; www.downtown containerpark.com; 707 Fremont St; items $3-12; ☺11am-11pm Mon-Thu, to 1am Fri & Sat, 10am-11pm Sun; ⚡; ☐Deuce) With food-truck-style menus, outdoor patio seating and late-night hours, food vendors inside the cutting-edge Container Park (p148) sell something to satisfy everyone's appetite. When we last stopped by, the ever-changing lineup included **Pinches Tacos** for Mexican flavors, Southern-style **Big Ern's BBQ**, raw-food and healthy vegan cuisine from **Simply Pure**, and salads and panini at **Bin 702** wine bar.

★Carson Kitchen   AMERICAN $$
(Map p149; ☑702-473-9523; www.carsonkitchen. com; 124 S 6th St; tapas & mains $8-22; ☺11:30am-11pm Thu-Sat, to 10pm Sun-Wed; ☐Deuce) This tiny eatery with an industrial theme of exposed beams, bare bulbs and chunky share tables hops with downtowners looking to escape the mayhem of Fremont St or the Strip's high prices. Excellent shared plates include rainbow cauliflower, watermelon and feta salad and decadent mac 'n' cheese, and there's a creative 'libations' menu.

★Andiamo Steakhouse   STEAK $$$
(Map p149; ☑702-388-2220; www.thed.com; 301 Fremont St E, The D; mains $24-79; ☺5-11pm; ☐Deuce, SDX) Of all the old-school steakhouses inside Downtown's carpet joints, the current front-runner is Joe Vicari's Andiamo Steakhouse. Upstairs from the casino, richly upholstered half-moon booths and impeccably polite waiters set the tone for a classic Italian steakhouse feast of surf-and-turf platters and housemade pasta, followed by a rolling dessert cart. Extensive Californian and European wine list. Reservations recommended.

La Comida   MEXICAN $$
(Map p149; ☑702-463-9900; www.lacomidalv. com; 100 6th St; mains $13-22; ☺noon-10:30pm Tue-Thu, to midnight Fri & Sat, to 11pm Sun) Meaning 'family meal,' La Comida's emphasis is on simple, culturally authentic dishes (soups, salads, tacos, enchiladas), presented in a warm, convivial environment to be shared with family. Why not throw some tequila into the mix (the restaurant has more varieties than it does seats), straight up or

in sweet and salty margaritas, and get your Downtown evening started right?

🍸 Drinking & Nightlife

🍸 The Strip

★Fireside Lounge   LOUNGE
(Map p149; ☑702-735-7635; www.peppermill laslasvegas.com; 2985 S Las Vegas Blvd, Peppermill; ☺24hr; ☐Deuce) Don't be blinded by the outlandishly bright neon outside. The Strip's most spellbinding retro hideaway awaits at the pint-sized **Peppermill** (mains $8-32; ☺24hr) casino. Courting couples adore the sunken fire pit, fake tropical foliage and 64oz goblet-sized 'Scorpion' cocktails served by waiters in black evening gowns.

★Chandelier Lounge   COCKTAIL BAR
(Map p149; ☑702-698-7979; www.cosmopolitan laslasvegas.com/lounges-bars/chandelier; Cosmopolitan; ☺24hr; ☐Deuce) Towering high in the center of Cosmopolitan (p143), this ethereal cocktail bar is inventive yet beautifully simple, with three levels connected by romantic curved staircases, all draped with glowing strands of glass beads. The second level is headquarters for molecular mixology (order a martini made with liquid nitrogen), while the third specializes in floral and fruit infusions.

★Chateau Nightclub & Gardens   BAR
(Map p149; ☑702-776-7770; www.chateaunights. com; Paris Las Vegas; ☺10pm-4am Wed, Fri & Sat) Hip-hop prevails at this rooftop venue land-scaped to look like Parisian gardens. Views over the Strip are divine from tiered outdoor terraces while, back inside, go-go dancers do their thing above a small dance floor, which can be half empty even on weekends. Sometimes on summer days, the lounge space on the open-air deck doubles as a beer garden.

🍸 Downtown & off the Strip

Want to chill out with the locals? Loads of new and interesting bars and cafes are opening along E Fremont St, making it the number-one alternative to the Strip.

★Beauty Bar   BAR
(Map p149; ☑702-598-3757; www.thebeautybar. com; 517 Fremont St E; cover free-$10; ☺9pm-4am; ☐Deuce) Swill a cocktail or just chill with the cool kids inside the salvaged innards of a 1950s New Jersey beauty salon. DJs and live

bands rotate nightly, spinning everything from tiki lounge tunes, disco and '80s hits to punk, metal, glam and indie rock. Check the website for special events like 'Karate Karaoke.' There's often no cover charge.

★ Gold Spike
BAR

(Map p149; ☑ 702-476-1082; www.goldspike.com; 217 N Las Vegas Blvd; ⊙ 24hr) Gold Spike, with its playroom, living room and backyard, is many things: bar, nightclub, performance space, work space; sometime host of roller derbies, discos, live bands or dance parties; or just somewhere to soak up the sun with a relaxed crew and escape mainstream Vegas.

☆ Entertainment

There's always plenty going on in Las Vegas, and Ticketmaster (www.ticketmaster.com) sells tickets for pretty much everything. **Tix 4 Tonight** (Map p149; ☑ 877-849-4868; www.tix4to night.com; 3200 S Las Vegas Blvd, Fashion Show Mall; ⊙ 10am-8pm) offers half-price tickets for a limited lineup of same-day shows, plus smaller discounts on 'always sold-out' shows.

Nightclubs & Live Music

Nightclubs are serious businesses in Las Vegas. Admission prices vary wildly, according to the mood of door staff, male-to-female ratio, the acts that night and how crowded the club may be. Avoid waiting in line by booking ahead with the club VIP host. Most bigger clubs have someone working the door in the late afternoon and early evening. Hotel concierges often have free passes for clubs, or can at least make reservations. Bottle service usually waives cover charges and waiting in line, but is hugely expensive.

BUFFET ALL THE WAY

Extravagant all-you-can-eat buffets are a Sin City tradition. Here are three of the best:

Bacchanal Buffet (3570 Las Vegas Blvd S, Caesars Palace; $40-58 per adult, 8am-10pm)

Wicked Spoon Buffet (3708 Las Vegas Blvd S, Cosmopolitan; $28-52 per adult, 8am-9pm)

Buffet at Bellagio (3600 Las Vegas Blvd S; Bellagio; $39-54 per adult, 7am-10pm)

Legends in Concert
LIVE MUSIC

(Map p149; ☑ 702-777-2782; www.legendsincon cert.com; Flamingo; adult/child from $58/36; ⊙ shows 4pm, 7:30pm & 9:30pm) Vegas' top pop-star impersonator show features real singing and dancing talent mimicking famous performers such as the Beatles, Elvis, Madonna, James Brown, Britney Spears, Shania Twain and many more.

★ Foundation Room
CLUB

(Map p149; ☑ 702-632-7601; www.houseofblues. com; Mandalay Bay; cover usually $30; ⊙ 5pm-2am) **House of Blues'** (☑ 702-632-7600; ⊙ box office 9am-9pm) sophisticated nightclub hosts nightly DJ parties and special events in a stylish space that's half Gothic mansion, half Hindu temple. The expansive views of the Strip are just as impressive as the decor. Look for club promoters around the casino passing out two-for-one drink and free-entry tickets. Dress code enforced.

★ XS
CLUB

(Map p149; ☑ 702-770-0097; www.xslasvegas.com; Encore; cover $20-50; ⊙ 10pm-4am Fri & Sat, from 9:30pm Sun, from 10:30pm Mon) XS is the hottest nightclub in Vegas – at least for now. Its extravagantly gold-drenched decor and over-the-top design mean you'll be waiting in line for cocktails at a bar towered over by ultra-curvaceous, larger-than-life golden statues of female torsos. Famous-name electronica DJs make the dancefloor writhe, while high rollers opt for VIP bottle service at private poolside cabanas.

★ Surrender
CLUB

(Map p149; ☑ 702-770-7300; www.surrendernight club.com; Encore; cover $20-40; ⊙ 10:30pm-4am Wed, Fri & Sat) Even the club-averse admit that this is an audaciously gorgeous place to hang out, with its saffron-colored silk walls, mustard banquettes, bright yellow patent leather entrance and a shimmering wall-art snake coiled behind the bar. Play blackjack or just hang out by the pool after dark during summer. EDM and hip-hop DJs and musicians pull huge crowds.

Production Shows

There are hundreds of shows to choose from in Vegas. Any Cirque du Soleil offering tends to be an unforgettable experience.

★ Le Rêve the Dream
THEATER

(Map p149; ☑ 702-770-9966; http://boxoffice. wynnlasvegas.com; Wynn; tickets $105-205; ⊙ shows at 7pm & 9:30pm Fri-Tue) Underwater acrobatic feats by scuba-certified performers are the centerpiece of this intimate 'aqua-in-the-round' theater, which holds a one-million-gallon swimming pool. Critics call it a less-inspiring version of Cirque's *O*, while devoted fans find the romantic underwater tango, thrilling high dives and visually spectacular adventures to be superior. Beware: the cheapest seats are in the 'splash zone.'

★ O
THEATER

(Map p149; ☑888-488-7111; www.cirquedusoleil.com; Bellagio; tickets $99-185; ⊙7pm & 9:30pm Wed-Sun) Phonetically speaking, it's the French word for water *(eau)*. With a lithe international cast performing in, on and above water, Cirque du Soleil's *O* tells the tale of theater through the ages. It's a spectacular feat of imagination and engineering, and you'll pay dearly to see it – it's one of the Strip's few shows that rarely sells discounted tickets.

★ Blue Man Group
LIVE PERFORMANCE

(Map p149; ☑702-262-4400; www.blueman.com; Luxor; tickets $80-190; ⊙shows at 7pm & 9:30pm; ⏏) Art, music and technology combine with a dash of comedy in one of Vegas' most popular, family-friendly shows at **Luxor** (☑702-262-4000; www.luxor.com; 3900 S Las Vegas Blvd; ⊙24hr; [P]).

★ Aces of Comedy
COMEDY

(Map p149; ☑702-792-7777; www.mirage.com; Mirage; tickets $40-100; ⊙schedules vary, box office 10am-10pm Thu-Mon, to 8pm Tue & Wed) You'd be hard pressed to find a better A-list collection of famous stand-up comedians than this year-round series of appearances at the **Mirage** (☑702-791-7111; 3400 S Las Vegas Blvd; ⊙24hr; [P]), which delivers the likes of Jay Leno, Kathy Griffin and Lewis Black to the Strip. Buy tickets in advance online or by phone, or go in person to the Mirage's **Cirque du Soleil** (☑877-924-7783; www.cirque dusoleil.com/las-vegas; discount tickets from $49, full-price from $69) box office.

🛍 Shopping

★ Las Vegas Premium Outlets North
MALL

(☑702-474-7500; www.premiumoutlets.com/ve gasnorth; 875 S Grand Central Pkwy; ⊙9am-9pm Mon-Sat, to 8pm Sun; ⏏; 🚌SDX) Vegas' biggest-ticket outlet mall features 120 mostly high-end names such as Armani, Brooks Brothers, Diane Von Furstenberg, Elle Tahari, Kate Spade, Michael Kors, Theory and

Tory Burch, alongside casual brands like Banana Republic and Diesel.

Retro Vegas
VINTAGE

(☑702-384-2700; www.retro-vegas.com; 1131 S Main St; ⊙11am-6pm Mon-Sat, noon-5pm Sun; 🚌108, Deuce) Near Downtown's 18b Arts District, this flamingo-pink-painted antiques shop is a primo place for picking up mid-20th-century modern and swingin' 1960s and '70s gems, from artwork to home decor.

Fashion Show
MALL

(Map p149; ☑702-369-8382; www.thefashion show.com; 3200 S Las Vegas Blvd; ⊙10am-9pm Mon-Sat, 11am-7pm Sun; ⏏) Nevada's largest shopping mall is an eye-catcher: topped off by 'the Cloud,' a silver multimedia canopy resembling a flamenco hat, Fashion Show harbors more than 250 chain shops and department stores. Hot European additions to the mainstream lineup include British clothier Topshop (and Topman for men). Live runway shows happen hourly from noon to 5pm on Friday, Saturday and Sunday.

Grand Canal Shoppes at the Venetian
MALL

(Map p149; ☑702-414-4525; www.grandcanalshop pes.com; 3377 S Las Vegas Blvd, Venetian; ⊙10am-11pm Sun-Thu, to midnight Fri & Sat) Wandering, painted minstrels, jugglers and laughable living statues perform in Piazza San Marco, while gondolas float past in the canals and mezzo-sopranos serenade shoppers. In this airy Italianate mall adorned with frescoes and cobblestone walkways, strut past Burberry, Godiva, Sephora and 85 more luxury shops.

ℹ️ Information

EMERGENCY & MEDICAL SERVICES

Police (☑911 (in emergencies) or ☑702-828-3111

Sunrise Hospital & Medical Center (☑702-731-8000; http://sunrisehospital.com; 3186 S Maryland Pkwy; ⊙24hr) Specialized children's trauma services available at a 24-hour emergency room.

University Medical Center (UMC; ☑702-383-2000; www.umcsn.com; 1800 W Charleston Blvd; ⊙24hr) Southern Nevada's most advanced trauma center has a 24-hour ER.

INTERNET ACCESS & MEDIA

Most casino hotels charge a fee of up to $15 per 24 hours (sometimes only wired access is available). Free wi-fi hot spots are more common off-Strip. Cheap internet cafes hide inside souvenir shops on the Strip and along Maryland Pkwy opposite the UNLV campus.

Newspapers & magazines *Las Vegas Review Journal* (www.reviewjournal.com), *Las Vegas Weekly* (www.lasvegasweekly.com), *Las Vegas Life* (www.lvlife.com).

Radio National Public Radio (NPR), lower end of FM dial.

TV PBS (public broadcasting); cable: CNN (news), ESPN (sports), HBO (movies), Weather Channel.

DVDs Coded for region 1 (USA and Canada) only.

POST

Post Office (Map p149; ☑702-382-5779; www.usps.com; 201 S Las Vegas Blvd; ⊙9am-5pm Mon-Fri)

TOURIST INFORMATION

Websites offering travel information and booking services include www.lasvegas.com and www.vegas.com.

Las Vegas Convention & Visitors Authority (LVCVA; Map p149; ☑702-892-7575; www.lasvegas.com; 3150 Paradise Rd; ⊙8am-5:30pm Mon-Fri; Las Vegas Convention Center)

⊙ Getting There & Around

Vegas is served by **McCarran International Airport** (LAS; Map p149; ☑702-261-5211; www.mccarran.com; 5757 Wayne Newton Blvd; ☎), near the south end of the Strip. A free, wheelchair-accessible tram links outlying gates, while free shuttle buses link Terminals 1 and 3 and serve the **McCarran Rent-a-Car Center** (☑702-261-6001; www.mccarran.com/go/rentalcars.aspx; 7135 Gillespie St; ⊙24hr).

Shuttle buses run to Strip hotels from $7 one-way, and from $9 to Downtown and off-Strip hotels. You'll pay at least $20 plus tip for a taxi to the Strip – tell your driver to use surface streets, not the I-15 Fwy airport connector tunnel ('long-hauling').

Greyhound runs long-distance buses connecting Las Vegas with Reno ($81, 9½ hours) and Salt Lake City (from $48, eight hours), as well as regular discounted services to/from Los Angeles (from $11, five to eight hours). You'll disembark at a downtown station just off the Fremont Street Experience. To reach the Strip, catch a southbound **SDX** bus (two-hour pass $6).

Day passes on the 24-hour **Deuce** and faster (though not 24-hour and not servicing all casinos) **SDX** buses are an excellent way to get around.

Around Las Vegas

Lake Mead and **Hoover Dam** are the most visited sites within the **Lake Mead National Recreation Area** (☑info desk 702-293-8906, visitor center 702-293-8990; www.nps.gov/lake; Lakeshore Scenic Dr; 7-day entry per vehicle $10; ⊙24hr; ☻), which encompasses 110-mile-long Lake Mead, 67-mile-long Lake Mohave and many miles of desert around the lakes. The excellent **Visitor Center** (Alan Bible Visitor Center; ☑702-293-8990; www.nps.gov/lake; Lakeshore Scenic Dr, off US Hwy 93; ⊙9am-4:30pm), on Hwy 93 halfway between Boulder City and Hoover Dam, has information on recreation and desert life. From there, North Shore Rd winds around the lake and makes a great scenic drive.

Straddling the Arizona–Nevada border, the graceful curve and art-deco style of the 726ft **Hoover Dam** (☑702-494-2517, 866-730-9097; www.usbr.gov/lc/hooverdam; off Hwy 93; admission visitor center incl parking $10; ⊙9am-6pm Apr-Oct, to 5pm Nov-Mar; ☻) contrasts superbly with the stark landscape. Don't miss a stroll over the **Mike O'Callaghan-Pat Tillman Memorial Bridge** (Hwy 93), which features a pedestrian walkway with perfect views upstream of Hoover Dam.

For a relaxing lunch or dinner break, head to nearby downtown Boulder City, where **Milo's** (☑702-293-9540; www.milosbouldercity.com; 534 Nevada Hwy; mains $9-14; ⊙11am-10pm Sun-Thu, to 11pm Fri & Sat) serves fresh sandwiches, salads and gourmet cheese plates at sidewalk tables outside the wine bar.

Western Nevada

The state's western corner, carved by the conifer-clad Sierra Nevada, drops off near Genoa. It's a vast treeless steppe of sagebrush, unfurling itself like a plush greengray carpet across the undulating plains of the Great Basin. From Lake Tahoe's sandy shores to the historic hamlet of Virginia City, the enduring gentility of Carson City, little Reno, Burning Man, Black Rock and beyond, Western Nevada's has plenty to entice you.

Reno

In downtown Reno you can gamble at one of two-dozen casinos in the morning then walk down the street and shoot rapids at the Truckee River Whitewater Park. That's what makes 'The Biggest Little City in the World' so interesting – it's holding tight to its gambling roots but also earning kudos as a top-notch basecamp for outdoor adventure. The Sierra Nevada Mountains and Lake Tahoe are less than an hour's drive away, the region teems with lakes, trails and ski resorts. Wedged between the I-80 and the

Truckee River, downtown's N Virginia St is casino central; south of the river it continues as S Virginia St.

◉ Sights

★ **National Automobile Museum**   MUSEUM
(☑775-333-9300; www.automuseum.org; 10 S Lake St; adult/child 6-18yr $10/4; ⊙9:30am-5:30pm Mon-Sat, 10am-4pm Sun) Stylized street scenes illustrate a century's worth of automobile history at this engaging car museum. The collection is enormous and impressive, with one-of-a-kind vehicles – including James Dean's 1949 Mercury from *Rebel Without a Cause*, a 1938 Phantom Corsair and a 24-karat gold-plated DeLorean – and rotating exhibits with all kinds of souped-up and fabulously retro rides.

★ **Atlantis**   CASINO
(☑775-825-4700; www.atlantiscasino.com; 3800 S Virginia St; ⊙24hr) Looking like it's straight out of a 1970s B-grade flick on the outside, Atlantis is all fun on the inside, modeled on the legendary underwater city, with a mirrored ceiling and tropical flourishes like indoor waterfalls and palm trees. It's one of Reno's most popular offerings, though not downtown.

★ **Discovery**   MUSEUM
(Terry Lee Wells Nevada Discovery Museum; ☑775-786-1000; www.nvdm.org; 490 S Center St; entry $10, Wed $5 after 4pm; ⊙10am-5pm Tue, Thu-Sat, to 8pm Wed, noon-5pm Sun; Pℹ) Since opening its doors in 2011 as a children's museum, the Discovery rapidly grew in popularity and expanded its focus to become a world-class, hands-on center for 'science, technology, engineering, art and math' (STEAM) learning, with 11 permanent, participatory exhibitions designed to inspire kids and young adults to have fun and develop an interest in these disciplines.

Nevada Museum of Art   MUSEUM
(☑775-329-3333; www.nevadaart.org; 160 W Liberty St; adult/child 6-12yr $10/1; ⊙10am-5pm Wed & Fri-Sun, to 8pm Thu) In a sparkling building inspired by the geological formations of the Black Rock Desert north of town, a floating staircase leads to galleries showcasing temporary exhibits and eclectic collections on the American West, labor and contemporary landscape photography. In 2016 the museum opened its $6.2-million Sky Room function area. Visitors are free to explore and enjoy the space – essentially a fabulous rooftop penthouse and patio with killer views – providing it's not in use.

VALLEY OF FIRE STATE PARK

It's about 50 miles from the Fremont Street Experience (p147) to the visitor center at the **Valley of Fire State Park** (☑702-397-2088; www.parks.nv.gov/parks/valley-of-fire; 29450 Valley of Fire Hwy, Overton; per vehicle $10; ⊙visitor center 8:30am-4:30pm, park 7am-7pm). Make this your first port of call to find out how best to tackle this masterpiece of Southwest desert scenery containing 40,000 acres of red Aztec sandstone, petrified trees and ancient Native American petroglyphs (at Atlatl Rock). Dedicated in 1935, the park was Nevada's first designated state park. Its psychedelic landscape has been carved by wind and water over thousands of years.

Silver Legacy   CASINO
(☑775-329-4777; www.silverlegacyreno.com; 407 N Virginia St; ⊙24hr) A Victorian-themed place, the Silver Legacy is easily recognized by its white landmark dome, where a giant mock mining rig periodically erupts into a fairly tame sound-and-light spectacle. The casino's hotel tower is usually lit emerald green at night and looks like something out of *The Wizard of Oz*.

Galena Creek Recreation Area   NATURE RESERVE
(☑775-849-4948; www.galenacreekvisitorcenter.org/trail-map.html; 18250 Mt Rose Hwy) Just 19 miles from downtown Reno, a complex network of scenic hiking trails beginning at this recreation area within the Humboldt-Toiyabe National Forest gets you right into the heart of the wilderness. Check in with the **Galena Creek Visitor Center** when you arrive for the latest conditions and friendly advice.

🏃 Activities

Reno is a 30- to 60-minute drive from Tahoe ski resorts, and many hotels and casinos offer special stay-and-ski packages.

Mere steps from the casinos, the Class II and III rapids at the city-run Truckee River Whitewater Park (www.reno.gov) are gentle enough for kids riding inner tubes, yet also sufficiently challenging for professional freestyle kayakers. Two courses wrap around Wingfield Park, a small river island that hosts free concerts in summertime. **Tahoe Whitewater Tours** (☑775-787-5000; www.gowhitewater.com; 400 Island Ave; 2hr kayak rental/tour from $48/68) and **Sierra Adventures** (☑866-323-8928, 775-323-8928; www.wildsierra. com; Truckee River Lane; kayak rental from $22) offer kayak trips and lessons.

🛏 Sleeping

Lodging rates vary widely, day by day. Sunday through Thursday are generally the best; Friday is more expensive and Saturday can be as much as triple the midweek rate.

In summer there's gorgeous high-altitude camping at **Mt Rose** (☑877-444-6777; www. recreation.gov; Mt Rose Hwy/Hwy 431; RV & tent sites $20-50; ⊗mid-Jun–Sep; P 🐾).

Sands Regency HOTEL $
(☑775-348-2200; www.sandsregency.com; 345 N Arlington Ave; r from $49 Sun-Thu, from $89 Fri & Sat; P 🐾🐕🛜🏊) The Sands Regency has some of the largest standard digs in town. Its rooms are decked out in a cheerful tropical palette of upbeat blues, reds and greens – a visual relief from typical motel decor. Empress Tower rooms are best. The 17th-floor gym and Jacuzzi are perfectly positioned to capture the drop-dead panoramic mountain views, and an outdoor pool opens in summer.

Peppermill CASINO HOTEL $
(☑775-826-2121; www.peppermillreno.com; 2707 S Virginia St; r from $69 Sun-Thu, from $149 Fri & Sat; P 🐾 @ 🛜🏊) 🐾 With a dash of Vegas-style opulence, the ever-popular Peppermill boasts Tuscan-themed suites in its newest 600-room tower, and plush remodeled rooms throughout the rest of the property. The two sparkling pools (one indoors) are dreamy, with a full spa on hand. Geothermal energy powers the resort's hot water and heat. The nightly resort fee is $20.

★**Whitney Peak** DESIGN HOTEL $$
(☑775-398-5400; www.whitneypeakhotel.com; 255 N Virginia St; d from $129; P 🐾🛜) 🐾 What's not to love about this independent, inventive, funky, friendly, non-smoking, non-gambling downtown hotel? Spacious guest rooms have a youthful, fun vibe celebrating the great outdoors and don't skimp on designer creature comforts. With an executive-level concierge lounge, free use of the climbing wall, a noteworthy on-site restaurant and friendly, professional staff, Whitney Peak is hard to beat.

🍴 Eating

★**Gold 'n Silver Inn** DINER $
(☑775-323-2696; www.goldnsilverreno.com; 790 W 4th St; mains $6-20; ⊗24hr) A Reno insti-

tution for over 50 years, this slightly divey but superfriendly 24-hour diner has a huge menu of homestyle American favorites such as meatloaf, plated dinners, all-day breakfasts and burgers, not to mention seriously incredible caramel milkshakes.

★**Old Granite Street Eatery** AMERICAN $$
(☑775-622-3222; www.oldgranitestreeteatery. com; 243 S Sierra St; dinner mains $12-29; ⊗11am-10pm Mon-Thu, to 11pm Fri, 10am-11pm Sat, to 3pm Sun; 🐾) A lovely well-lit place for organic and local comfort food, old-school artisanal cocktails and craft beers, this antique-strewn hot spot enchants diners with its stately wooden bar, water served in old liquor bottles and lengthy seasonal menu. Forgot to make a reservation? Check out the iconic rooster and pig murals and wait at a communal table fashioned from a barn door.

Louis' Basque Corner BASQUE $$
(☑775-323-7203; www.louisbasquecorner.com; 301 E 4th St; dinner menu $12-29; ⊗11am-9:30pm Tue-Sat, 4-9:30pm Sun & Mon) Get ready to dine on lamb, rabbit, sweetbreads and more lamb at a big table full of people you've never met before. A different set-course menu is offered every day and posted in the window.

★**Wild River Grille** GRILL $$
(☑775-847-455; www.wildrivergrille.com; 17 S Virginia St; mains lunch $11-16, dinner $21-37; ⊗11am-9pm; 🐾) At the Wild River Grille you'll love the smart-casual dining and the varied menu of creative cuisine, from the Gruyère croquettes to the lobster ravioli, but most of all the wonderful patio overlooking the lovely Truckee River: it's also the best spot in town for a drink on a balmy summer's evening and a great place to take a date.

🍷 Drinking & Nightlife

★**Pignic** BAR
(☑775-376-1948; www.renoriver.org/pignic-pub-patio; 235 Flint St; ⊗3-11pm) This awesome little place gets points for originality: occupying what was formerly a private home, the concept is simple. You bring your own food and barbecue it here, and buy your drinks at the bar. It's participatory, friendly and speaks to the importance of friends, family and community. Lots of fun.

☆ Entertainment

The free weekly *Reno News & Review* (www. newsreview.com) is your best source for listings.

Knitting Factory   LIVE MUSIC
(📞775-323-5648; http://re.knittingfactory.com; 211 N Virginia St) This midsized music venue books mainstream and indie favorites.

ℹ Information

Reno-Sparks Convention & Visitors Authority Visitor Center (📞775-682-3800; www. visitrenotahoe.com; 135 N Sierra St; ⊙9am-6pm)

ℹ Getting There & Around

About 5 miles southeast of downtown, **Reno-Tahoe International Airport** (RNO; www. renoairport.com; 🛜) is served by most major airlines, with connections throughout the US to international routes.

The **North Lake Tahoe Express** (📞866-216-5222; www.northlaketahoeexpress.com; one way $49) operates a shuttle (six to eight daily, 3:30am to midnight) to and from the airport to multiple North Shore Lake Tahoe locations. The **South Tahoe Airporter** (📞866-898-2463; www.southtahoeairporter.com; adult/child one way $29.75/16.75, round-trip $53/30.25) operates several daily shuttle buses from the airport to Stateline casinos. Casino hotels usually offer frequent free airport shuttles for their guests.

Greyhound (📞800-231-2222; www.greyhound.com) offers up to five direct buses a day to Reno from San Francisco (from $8, from five hours): book well in advance for these lowest fares.

The **Amtrak** (📞800-872-7245; www.amtrak.com) *California Zephyr* train makes one daily departure from Emeryville/San Francisco ($52, 6¾ hours) to Reno.

The local **RTC Washoe** (📞775-348-0400; www.rtcwashoe.com) RTC Ride buses blanket the city, and most routes converge at the RTC 4th St station downtown (between Lake St and Evans Ave).

Carson City

An easy drive from Reno or Lake Tahoe, this underrated town is a perfect stop for lunch and a stroll around the quiet, old-fashioned downtown.

The **Kit Carson Blue Line Trail** passes pretty historic buildings on pleasant treelined streets. Pick up a trail map at the visitor center (p142), a mile south of downtown.

The 1870 **Nevada State Capitol** (📞775-684-5670; 101 North Carson St; ⊙8am-5pm Mon-Fri) FREE anchors downtown; you might spot the governor himself chatting with a constituent. Train buffs shouldn't miss the **Nevada State Railroad Museum** (📞775-

---

ℹ **RENO AREA TRAIL INFORMATION**

For information on regional hiking and mountain-biking trails, including the Mt Rose summit trail and Tahoe-Pyramid Bikeway, download the *Truckee Meadows Trails Guide* (www.washoecounty.us/parks/trails/trail_challenge.php).

687-6953; http://nvdtca.org/nevadastaterailroadmuseumcarsoncity; 2180 S Carson St; adult/child under 18 yr $6/free; ⊙9am-5pm Thu-Mon), which displays train cars and locomotives from the 1800s to the early 1900s.

Grab lunch at fetching **Comma Coffee** (📞775-883-2662; www.commacoffee.com; 312 S Carson St; meals $7-12; ⊙7am-8pm Mon-Sat; 🛜📶) and eavesdrop on the politicians, or spend the evening in an English-style pub, the **Firkin & Fox** (📞775-883-1369; www.foxbrewpub.com; 310 S Carson St; ⊙11am-midnight Sun-Thu, to 2am Fri & Sat).

Hwy 395/Carson St is the main drag. For hiking and camping information, stop by the Nevada Division of State Parks (p142).

Virginia City

The discovery of the legendary Comstock Lode in 1859 sparked a silver bonanza in the mountains 25 miles south of Reno. During the 1860s gold rush, Virginia City was a high-flying, rip-roaring Wild West boomtown. Newspaperman Samuel Clemens, alias Mark Twain, spent time here during its heyday, and described the mining life in his book *Roughing It*.

The high-elevation town is a National Historic Landmark, with a main street of Victorian buildings, wooden sidewalks and some hokey but fun museums. To see how the mining elite lived, stop by the **Mackay Mansion** (📞775-847-0373; www.uniquitiesmackaymansion.com; 291 S D St; adult/child $5/free; ⊙10am-6pm) and the Castle (B St).

Locals agree that **Cafe del Rio** (www.cafedelriovc.com; 394 S C St; mains $11-17; ⊙11am-8pm Wed-Sat, 10am-7pm Sun) serves the town's best food – a nice blend of nuevo Mexican and good cafe meals, including breakfast. Wet your whistle at the longtime family-run **Bucket of Blood Saloon** (www.bucketofbloodsaloonvc.com; 1 S C St; ⊙10am-7pm), which serves up beer and 'bar rules' at its antique wooden bar ('If the bartender doesn't laugh, you are not funny'). The **visitor center**

(📞775-847-7500, 800-718-7587; www.visitvirginia
citynv.com; 86 S C St; ⊙9am-5pm Mon-Sat, 10am-
4pm Sun) is on the main drag, C St.

The Great Basin

A trip across Nevada's Great Basin is a serene,
almost haunting experience. Anyone seeking
the 'Great American Road Trip' will relish the
historic towns and quirky diversions tucked
away along lonely desert highways.

Along I-80

The culture of the American West is diligent-
ly cultivated in **Elko**, almost 300 miles along
I-80 northeast of Reno. Aspiring cowboys
and cowgirls should visit the **Western Folk-
life Center** (📞775-738-7508; www.westernfolk
life.org; 501 Railroad St; adult/child 6-18yr $5/1;
⊙10am-5:30pm Mon-Fri, 10am-5pm Sat), which
offers art and history exhibits, musical jams,
and dance nights, and hosts the **Cowboy
Poetry Gathering** each January. Elko also
holds a **National Basque Festival** every
July 4, with games, traditional dancing and
a 'Running of the Bulls'. If you've never sam-
pled Basque food, the best place for your in-
augural experience is the **Star Hotel** (📞775-
753-8696; www.eatdrinkandbebasque.com; 246 Silver St; lunch $8-14, dinner $16-38; ⊙11am-2pm &
5-9pm Mon-Fri, 4:30-9:30pm Sat), a family-style
supper club located in a circa-1910 boarding
house for Basque sheepherders.

Along Highway 50

The transcontinental Hwy 50 cuts across the
heart of Nevada, connecting Carson City in
the west to Great Basin National Park in the
east. Better known here by its nickname, 'The
Loneliest Road in America,' it once formed
part of the Lincoln Hwy, and follows the route
of the Overland Stagecoach, the Pony Express
and the first transcontinental telegraph line.
Towns are few, and the only sounds are the
hum of the engine or the whisper of wind.

About 25 miles southeast of Fallon, the
Sand Mountain Recreation Area (📞775-
885-6000; www.blm.gov/nv; 7-day permit $40, en-
try free Tue & Wed; ⊙24hr; 🅿) is worth a stop
for a look at its 600ft sand dune and the ruins of a Pony Express station. Just east, enjoy a juicy burger at an old stagecoach stop,
Middlegate Station (📞775-423-7134; www.
facebook.com/middlegate.station; 42500 Austin
Hwy, cnr Hwys 50 & 361; mains $6-17; ⊙6am-2am)
then toss your sneakers onto the new **Shoe
Tree** on the north side of Hwy 50 just ahead
(the old one was cut down).

A fitting reward for surviving Hwy 50
is the awesome, uncrowded **Great Basin
National Park** (📞775-234-7331; www.nps.gov/
grba; ⊙24hr) **FREE**. Near the Nevada–Utah
border, it's home to 13,063ft Wheeler Peak,
which rises abruptly from the desert. Hiking
trails near the summit take in superb country with glacial lakes, ancient bristlecone
pines and even a permanent ice field. Admission is free; in summer, you can get oriented at the **Lehman Caves Visitor Center**
(📞775-234-7331, tour reservations 775-234-7517;
www.nps.gov/grba; 5500 NV-488, Baker; adult $8-
10, child $4-5; ⊙8am-4:30pm, tours 8:30am-4pm),
just north of Baker.

Along Highways 375 & 93

Hwy 375 is dubbed the 'Extraterrestrial Hwy',
both for its huge number of UFO sightings
and because it intersects Hwy 93 near top
secret **Area 51**, part of Nellis Air Force Base,
supposedly a holding area for captured
UFOs. Some people may find Hwy 375 more
unnerving than the Loneliest Road; it's a desolate stretch of pavement where cars are few
and far between. In the tiny town of Rachel,
on Hwy 375, **Little A'Le' Inn** (📞775-729-2515;
www.littlealeinn.com; 9631 Old Mill St, Rachel; RV
sites with hookups $15, r $50-165; ⊙restaurant 8am-
10pm; ❄🛜🐾) accommodates earthlings and
aliens alike, and sells extraterrestrial souvenirs. Probings not included.

ARIZONA

Arizona is made for road trips. Yes, the state
has its showstoppers – Monument Valley, the
Grand Canyon, Cathedral Rock – but you'll
remember the long, romantic miles under
endless skies for as long as you do the icons
in between. Each drive reveals a little more of
the state's soul: for a dose of mom-and-pop
friendliness, follow Route 66 into Flagstaff; to
understand the sheer will of Arizona's mining
barons, take a twisting drive through rugged
Jerome; and American Indian history becomes contemporary as you drive past mesa-
top Hopi villages dating back 1000 years.

History

American Indian tribes and their ancestors
inhabited Arizona for millennia before Francisco Vásquez de Coronado, leading an ex-

pedition from Mexico City in 1540, became the first European to clap eyes on the Grand Canyon and Colorado River. Settlers and missionaries followed in his wake, and by the mid-19th century the US acquired Arizona from Mexico by conquest and purchase. The Indian Wars, in which the US Army battled American Indians to protect settlers and claim land for the government, officially ended in 1886 with the surrender of Apache warrior Geronimo.

Railroad and mining expansion followed and people started arriving in ever larger numbers. After President Theodore Roosevelt visited Arizona in 1903 he supported the damming of its rivers to provide year-round water for irrigation and drinking, thus paving the way to statehood: in 1912 Arizona became the last of the 48 contiguous US states to be admitted to the Union.

The state shares a 250-mile border with Mexico. Although it was traditionally a gateway for illegal immigration, far stricter controls have seen the number of people entering through the state plummet since 2005. However, after the mysterious murder of a popular rancher near the border in 2010, the legislature passed a controversial law requiring police officers to ask for identification from anyone they suspect of being in the country illegally. While the constitutionality of the request for immigration papers was upheld, key provisions of the law, known as SB 1070, were struck down by the US Supreme Court.

ℹ Information

Although Arizona is on Mountain Standard Time, it's the only western state that does not observe daylight saving time from spring to early fall – except for on the Navajo Reservation. Generally speaking, lodging rates in southern Arizona (including Phoenix, Tucson and Yuma) are much higher in winter and spring, considered to be the 'high season', so great deals can be found in the hotter areas in summer.

Arizona Office of Tourism (☏602-364-3700; www.arizonaguide.com) Free state information.

Arizona State Parks (☏877-697-2757, 602-542-4174; www.azstateparks.com) Sixteen of the state's parks have campgrounds, open to online reservations.

Public Lands Interpretative Association (www.publiclands.org) Information about USFS, NPS, Bureau of Land Management (BLM) and state lands and parks.

Phoenix

Phoenix is Arizona's indubitable cultural and economic powerhouse, a thriving desert metropolis boasting some of the best Southwestern and Mexican food you'll find anywhere. And with more than 300 days of sunshine a year, exploring the 'Valley of the Sun' is an agreeable proposition (except in the sapping heat from June to August).

Culturally, it offers an opera, a symphony, several theaters and three of the state's finest museums – the Heard, Phoenix Art and Musical Instrument Museums – while the Desert Botanical Garden is a stunning introduction to the region's flora and fauna. For sports fans, there are professional baseball, football, basketball and ice-hockey teams, and more than 200 golf courses.

⊙ Sights

Greater Phoenix consists of several distinct cities. Phoenix, the largest, combines a business-like demeanor with top-notch museums, a burgeoning cultural scene and great sports facilities. Southeast of here, lively, student-flavored Tempe (tem-pee), hugs 2-mile-long Tempe Town Lake, while suburban Mesa, further east, holds a couple of interesting museums. Two ritzy enclaves lie northeast of Phoenix – Scottsdale, known for its cutesy old town, galleries and lavish resorts, and the largely residential Paradise Valley.

⊙ Phoenix

⭐**Heard Museum** MUSEUM (Map p166; ☏602-252-8848; www.heard.org; 2301 N Central Ave; adult $18, child 6-17yr & student $7.50, senior $13.50; ☺9:30am-5pm Mon-Sat, 11am-5pm Sun; P🚸) This extraordinary museum spotlights the history, life, arts and culture of

American Indian tribes in the Southwest. Visitors will find art galleries, ethnographic displays, films, a get-creative kids exhibit and an unrivaled collection of Hopi kachinas (elaborate spirit dolls, many gifted by Presidential nominee Barry Goldwater). The Heard emphasizes quality over quantity and is one of the best museums of its kind in America.

★ **Musical Instrument Museum** MUSEUM
(☑480-478-6000; www.themim.org; 4725 E Mayo Blvd; adult/teen/child 4-12yr $20/15/10; ◷9am-5pm; P) From Uganda thumb pianos to Hawaiian ukuleles to Indonesian boat lutes, the ears have it at this lively museum that celebrates the world's musical instruments. More than 200 countries and territories are represented within five regional galleries, with wireless recordings bringing many to life as you get within 'earshot' (headsets are provided). You can also bang a drum in the Experiences Gallery and listen to Taylor Swift or Elvis Presley rock out in the Artist Gallery.

★ **Desert Botanical Garden** GARDENS
(Map p166; ☑480-941-1225; www.dbg.org; 1201 N Galvin Pkwy; adult/senior/student 13-18yr/child 3-12yr $22/20/12/10; ◷8am-8pm Oct-Apr, 7am-8pm May-Sep) Blue bells and Mexican gold poppies are just two of the colorful showstoppers blooming from March to May along the Desert Wildflower Loop Trail at this well-nurtured botanical garden, a lovely place to reconnect with nature while learning about desert plant life. Looping trails lead past a profusion of desert denizens, arranged by theme (including a Sonoran Desert nature loop and an edible desert garden). It's pretty dazzling year-round, but the flowering spring season is the busiest and most colorful.

Phoenix Art Museum MUSEUM
(Map p166; ☑602-257-1880; www.phxart.org; 1625 N Central Ave; adult/senior/student/child 6-17yr $18/15/13/9; ◷10am-5pm Tue & Thu-Sat, 10am-9pm Wed, noon-5pm Sun; P♿) Arizona's premier repository of fine art includes works by Claude Monet, Diego Rivera and Georgia O'Keeffe. Make a beeline for the Western Gallery, to see how the astonishing Arizona landscape has inspired everyone from the early pioneers to modernists. Got kids? Pick up a Kidpack at Visitor Services, examine the ingeniously crafted miniature period Thorne Rooms or visit the PhxArtKids Gallery.

◉ Scottsdale

For a list of permanent and temporary public art displays, visit www.scottsdalepublic art.org.

Old Town Scottsdale AREA
(Map p166; http://downtownscottsdale.com) Tucked among Scottsdale's malls and bistros is its Old Town, a Wild West–themed enclave filled with cutesy buildings, covered sidewalks and stores hawking mass-produced 'Indian' artifacts. There's also a museum, public sculptures, saloons, a few galleries stocking genuine American Indian art.

Taliesin West ARCHITECTURE
(☑480-860-2700; www.franklloydwright.org; 12621 N Frank Lloyd Wright Blvd; tours from $26; ◷8:30am-6pm Oct-May, shorter hours Jun-Sep, closed Tue & Wed Jun-Aug) Taliesin West was the desert home and studio of Frank Lloyd Wright, one of America's greatest 20th-century architects. A prime example of organic architecture, with buildings incorporating elements and structures found in surrounding nature, it was built between 1938 and 1940, and is still home to an architecture school. It's now a National Historical

---

ARIZONA FACTS

Nickname Grand Canyon State

Population 6.9 million

Area 113,637 sq miles

Capital city Phoenix (population 1.563,025)

Other cities Tucson (population 531,641), Flagstaff (70,320), Sedona (10,388)

Sales tax 5.6%

Birthplace of Cesar Chavez (1927–93), singer Linda Ronstadt (b 1946)

Home of The OK Corral, mining towns turned art colonies

Politics Majority vote Republican

Famous for Grand Canyon, saguaro cacti

Best souvenir Pink cactus-shaped neon lamp from roadside stall

Driving distances Phoenix to Grand Canyon Village 235 miles, Tucson to Sedona 230 miles

Monument, open to the public for informative guided tours.

◎ Tempe

Founded in 1885 and home to around 50,000 students, **Arizona State University** (ASU; Map p166; ☑ 480-965-2100; www.asu.edu) is the heart and soul of Tempe. The **Gammage Auditorium** (Map p166; ☑ box office 480-965-3434, tours 480-965-6912; www.asugammage.com; 1200 S Forest Ave, cnr Mill Ave & Apache Blvd; entry free, performances from $20; ☺ box office 10am-5pm Mon-Thu in summer, 10am-6pm Mon-Fri rest of year) was Frank Lloyd Wright's last major building. Easily accessible by light-rail from downtown Phoenix, **Mill Avenue**, Tempe's main drag, is packed with restaurants, themed bars and other collegiate hangouts. You could also check out **Tempe Town Lake** (Map p166; www.tempe.gov/lake), an artificial lake with boat rides and hiking paths.

◎ Mesa

★ Arizona Museum
of Natural History   MUSEUM
(☑ 480-644-2230; www.azmnh.org; 53 N MacDonald St; adult/child 3-12yr/student/senior $12/7/8/10; ☺ 10am-5pm Tue-Fri, 11am-5pm Sat, 1-5pm Sun; ♿) Even if you're not staying in Mesa, this museum is worth a trip, especially if your kids are into dinosaurs (and aren't they all?). In addition to the multilevel Dinosaur Mountain, there are loads of life-sized casts of the giant beasts plus a touchable apatosaurus thighbone. Other exhibits highlight the Southwest's pre-conquest past, and that of the Americas more broadly, from a prehistoric Hohokam village to an entire hall on ancient Mesoamerican cultures.

☂ Activities

Camelback Mountain   HIKING
(Map p166; ☑ 602-261-8318; www.phoenix.gov; ☺ sunrise-sunset) This 2704ft twin-humped mountain sits smack in the center of the Phoenix action. Two trails, the Cholla Trail (6131 E Cholla Lane) and the Echo Canyon Trail (4925 E McDonald Dr), climb about 1200ft to the summit. The newly renovated Echo Canyon Trail is extremely popular in spring and winter – the car park fills very early, even with 135 spots.

Salt River Recreation   WATER SPORTS
(☑ 480-984-3305; www.saltrivertubing.com; 9200 N Bush Hwy; tubes & shuttle $17; ☺ 8:30am-6pm

CATHEDRAL GORGE
....
Fifteen miles north of Caliente, just past the turn-off to Panaca, **Cathedral Gorge State Park** (☑ 775-728-4460; http://parks.nv.gov/parks/cathedral-gorge; Hwy 93, Pioche; $7; ☺ visitor center 9am-4:30pm, park 24hr; P ♿) is one of those magical out-of-the-way places that you never regret traveling all that way for. Wandering among its wind- and water-eroded shapes, you get the feeling that you've stepped into a magnificent, many-spired cathedral, albeit one whose dome is the blue sky above. Head to the **Miller Point Overlook** for sweeping views and easy hikes into narrow side canyons.

May-late Sep, hours vary after Labor Day; ♿) With Salt River Recreation you can float in an inner tube on the Lower Salt River through the stark Tonto National Forest. The launch is in northeast Mesa, about 15 miles north of Hwy 60 on Power Rd. Floats are two, three or five hours long, including the shuttle-bus ride back. Cash only.

Cactus Adventures   MOUNTAIN BIKING
(☑ 480-688-4743; www.cactusadventures.com; 8000 S Arizona Grand Pkwy; half-day rental $60; ☺ phone line 8am-8pm) Based at Arizona Grand Resort, Cactus Adventures rents bikes for use at South Mountain and offers guided hiking and biking tours at various parks. For rentals, they will meet you at the trailhead; guided tours start from $155 per person (minimum two people).

Ponderosa Stables   HORSEBACK RIDING
(☑ 602-268-1261; www.arizona-horses.com; 10215 S Central Ave; 1/2/3hr rides $40/60/80, minimum 2 riders for 3hr rides; ☺ 9am-8pm Mon-Sat; ♿) This outfitter leads breakfast, lunch, dinner and sunset rides through South Mountain Park. Reservations required for most trips. The stables are around 7 miles south of downtown Phoenix, directly down Central Ave.

☆ Festivals & Events

First Fridays   ART
(www.artlinkphoenix.com; ☺ 6-10pm first Fri of month) Up to 20,000 people hit the streets of downtown Phoenix on the first Friday of every month for this self-guided 'art walk,' held across more than 70 galleries and performance spaces. Free shuttles radiating

out from the Phoenix Art Museum ferry the cognoscenti from venue to venue.

Arizona State Fair FAIR

(☑602-252-6771; www.azstatefair.com; 1826 W McDowell Rd; adult/child 5-13yr $10/5; ☺Oct) This fair lures over a million folks to the Arizona State Fairgrounds every October, with a rodeo, rides and amusements, livestock displays, a pie-eating contest and plenty of live performances.

🛏 Sleeping

🛏 Phoenix

HI Phoenix Hostel HOSTEL $

(Map p166; ☑602-254-9803; www.phxhostel.org; 1026 N 9th St; dm/r from $24/37; ✳@🛜) Fall in love with backpacking again at this small hostel with fun owners who know Phoenix and want to enjoy it with you. The 22-bed hostel sits in an up-and-coming working-class neighborhood and has relaxing garden nooks. The 'talking table' – at which laptops and other devices are banned from 8am to 10am and 5pm to 10pm each day – is a very sociable innovation.

Maricopa Manor BOUTIQUE HOTEL $$

(Map p166; ☑602-264-9200, 800-292-6403; www.maricopamanor.com; 15 W Pasadena Ave; ste from $149; P🛜🏊) This small, Spanish-ranch-style place right near busy Central Ave has six individually appointed suites, many with French doors onto a deck overlooking the pool, garden and fountain areas. Although Maricopa Manor is central, it's well supplied with shady garden nooks, and privacy is easily achieved.

★ Arizona Biltmore Resort & Spa RESORT $$$

(Map p166; ☑800-950-0086, 602-955-6600; www.arizonabiltmore.com; 2400 E Missouri Ave; d from $480; P✳@🛜🏊🐾) With architecture inspired by Frank Lloyd Wright and past guests including Irving Berlin, Marilyn Monroe and every president from Hoover to Bush the younger, the Biltmore is perfect for connecting to the magic of yesterday. A landmark, lending its name to much in the surrounding area, it boasts over 700 beautifully appointed units, two golf courses, several pools and endless luxe touches.

Royal Palms Resort & Spa RESORT $$$

(Map p166; ☑602-840-3610; www.royalpalmshotel.com; 5200 E Camelback Rd; r/ste from $499/519; P✳🛜🏊🐾) Camelback Mountain is the photogenic backdrop for this posh and intimate resort, built as the winter retreat of New York industrialist Delos Cook in 1929. Today, it's a hushed and elegant place, dotted with Spanish Colonial villas, flower-lined walkways and palms imported from Egypt. Pets can go Pavlovian for soft beds, personalized biscuits and walking services.

Palomar Phoenix HOTEL $$$

(Map p166; ☑602-253-6633, reservations 877-488-1908; www.hotelpalomar-phoenix.com; 2 E Jefferson St; r/ste from $449/509; P✳🛜🏊🐾) Shaggy pillows, antler-shaped lamps and portraits of blue cows. Yep, the 242 rooms of the Palomar are whimsical, and we like it. Larger than average and popping with fresh, modern style, the rooms come with yoga mats, animal-print robes and Italian Frette linens. There's a nightly wine reception, and Phoenix's major baseball and basketball stadiums are just around the corner.

🛏 Scottsdale

★ Bespoke Inn, Cafe & Bicycles B&B $$$

(Map p166; ☑480-664-0730; www.bespokeinn.com; 3701 N Marshall Way; d incl brunch from $349; P✳🛜🏊🐾) A small slice of 'European' hospitality in downtown Scottsdale, this breezy B&B offers guests chocolate scones to nibble in the chic cafe, an infinity pool to loll in and Pashley city bikes to roam the neighborhood on. Rooms are plush, with handsome touches like handcrafted furniture and nickel bath fixtures. Gourmet brunch is served at the on-site restaurant Virtu. Book early.

Boulders RESORT $$$

(☑480-488-9009; www.theboulders.com; 34631 N Tom Darlington Dr, Scottsdale; casitas/villas from $239/391; P✳@🛜🏊🐾) Tensions evaporate upon arrival at this desert oasis that blends into a landscape of natural rock formations – and that's before you've put in a session at the on-site spa or settled in at one of the four pools. Basically, everything here is calculated to make life better.

★ Hotel Valley Ho BOUTIQUE HOTEL $$$

(Map p166; ☑480-376-2600; www.hotelvalleyho.com; 6850 E Main St; r/ste $409/532; P✳@🛜🏊🐾) Everything's swell at the Valley Ho, where midcentury modern gets a 21st-century twist. This jazzy joint once bedded Bing Crosby, Natalie Wood and Janet Leigh, and today it's a top pick for movie stars filming on location in Phoenix. Bebop music, upbeat staff and eye magnets like the 'ice fire-place' recapture the Rat Pack vibe, and the theme travels well to the balconied rooms.

 Tempe

Sheraton Wild Horse
Pass Resort & Spa RESORT $$$
(✆602-225-0100; www.wildhorsepassresort.com; 5594 W Wild Horse Pass Blvd, Chandler; r/ste from $339/534; P✳︎☞⊗) At sunset, scan the lonely horizon for the eponymous wild horses silhouetted against the South Mountains. Owned by the Gila River tribe and nestled on their sweeping reservation south of Tempe, this 500-room resort is a stunning alchemy of modern luxury and American Indian tradition. The domed lobby is a mural-festooned roundhouse, and rooms reflect the traditions of local tribes.

✕ Eating

✕ Phoenix

★Desoto Central Market MARKET $
(Map p166; ✆602-680-7747; http://desotocentralmarket.com; 915 N Central Ave; mains $11-15; ⊙7am-10pm Mon-Wed, 7am-midnight Thu-Sat, 8am-9pm Sun) Making great use of a sensitively restored 1920s DeSoto dealership, this indoor 'market' is really a collective of inventive kitchens, slinging their goods together under the one roof. Special mention goes to New Southern affair the Larder and the Delta, whose shrimp 'n' grits (with smoked andouille sausage and hot sauce) or chili-garlic glazed baby back ribs will leave you gasping.

★Phoenix Public Market CAFE $
(Map p166; ✆602-253-2700; www.phxpublicmarket.com; 14 E Pierce St; mains $9-10; ⊙7am-10pm; ☞) This buzzing barn of a place – the on-site cafe for Arizona's largest farmers market – attracts a dedicated clientele of Arizona State University (ASU) students, local professionals at lunch, vegetarians and food lovers of all stripes. The housemade bagels and flame-roasted chicken are fantastic, while inventive daily specials, community dinners and happy hours keep the cognoscenti coming at all hours.

Green New
American Vegetarian VEGAN, VEGETARIAN $
(Map p166; ✆602-258-1870; www.greenvegetarian.com; 2022 N 7th St; mains $8-10; ⊙11am-9pm Mon-Sat; ☞) Your expectations of vegan food

will be forever raised after dining at this hip cafe, where chef Damon Brasch stirs up savory vegan and vegetarian dishes. Made with mock meats, the burgers, po'boys and Asian-style bowls taste as good, if not better, than their carnivorous counterparts. Order at the counter then take a seat in the garage-style digs.

Barrio Café MEXICAN $$
(Map p166; ✆602-636-0240; www.barriocafe.com; 2814 N 16th St; mains $12-29; ⊙11am-10pm Tue-Sat, to 9pm Sun; ☞) Barrio's staff wear T-shirts emblazoned with *comida chingona,* which translates as 'fucking good food,' and they don't lie. This is Mexican food at its most creative: how many menus have you seen featuring guacamole spiked with pomegranate seeds, buttered corn with chipotle, aged cheese, cilantro and lime or goat's-milk-caramel-filled churros? Drinks are half price from 2pm to 5pm daily.

★Dick's Hideaway NEW MEXICAN $$$
(Map p166; ✆602-265-5886; http://richardsonsnm.com; 6008 N 16th St; breakfast $15-16, mains $25-27; ⊙8am-11pm Sun-Wed, to midnight Thu-Sat) At this pocket-sized ode to New Mexican cuisine, grab a small table beside the bar or settle in at the communal table in the side room and prepare for hearty servings of savory, chile-slathered New Mexican fare, from enchiladas to tamales to rellenos. We especially like the Hideaway for breakfast, when the Bloody Marys arrive with a shot of beer.

House of Tricks AMERICAN $$$
(Map p166; ✆480-968-1114; www.houseoftricks.com; 114 E 7th St, Tempe; lunch $12-13, dinner $27-30; ⊙11am-10pm Mon-Sat) No, they don't do magic, but Robin and Robert Trick will still wow you with their eclectic, contemporary American menu that borrows influences from the Southwest, the Med and Asia. The trellised garden patio usually buzzes with regulars and drop-ins, but the tables inside the vintage cottages are equally charming.

✕ Scottsdale

★The Mission MEXICAN $$
(Map p166; ✆480-636-5005; www.themissionaz.com; 3815 N Brown Ave; lunch $14-18, dinner $14-30; ⊙11am-3pm & 5-10pm) With its dark interior and glowing votives, we'll call this *nuevo* Latin spot sexy – although our exclamations about the food's deliciousness may ruin the sultry vibe. The Tecate-marinated steak taco with lime and avocado is superb and makes

Phoenix

for a satisfying light lunch. The guacamole is made table-side, and wins raves. Margaritas and mojitos round out the fun.

Herb Box   AMERICAN **$$**

(Map p166; ✆480-289-6160; www.theherbbox. com; 7134 E Stetson Dr; brunch $13-15, lunch $14-17, dinner $17-22; ⊙11am-9pm Mon-Thu, 11am-10pm Fri, 9am-10pm Sat, 9am-4pm Sun; 🛜✎) It's not just about sparkle and air kisses at this chi-chi bistro in the heart of Old Town Scottsdale's Southbridge. It's also about fresh regional ingredients, artful presentation and attentive service. For a light, healthy lunch,

settle in on the patio and toast your good fortune with a blackberry mojito.

🍴 Tempe

⭐ **Kai Restaurant**   AMERICAN INDIAN **$$$**

(✆602-225-0100; www.wildhorsepassresort.com; 5594 W Wild Horse Pass Blvd, Chandler; mains $48-54, tasting menus $145-$245; ⊙5:30-9pm Tue-Sat) American Indian cuisine – based on traditional crops grown along the Gila River – soars to new heights at Kai ('seed'). Expect creations such as grilled buffalo tenderloin with smoked corn puree and cholla buds, or

Taliesin West (13mi)

Camelback Mountain Echo Canyon Recreation Area

Experience Scottsdale

N Goldwater Blvd

E Lafayette Blvd

E Indian School Rd

E Osborn Rd

N Drinkwater Blvd

E McDowell Rd

Desert Botanical Garden

E Roosevelt St

Papago Park & Golf Course

E McKellips Rd

E Van Buren St

E Washington St

E Curry Rd

Red Mountain Fwy

Tempe Town Lake

W 1st St

Tempe Tourism Office

TEMPE

W 5th St

E University Dr

E 8th St

E Apache Blvd

Arizona Museum of Natural History (4.7mi); Mesa Convention & Visitors Bureau (5mi)

Headquarters, this stylish seating-only cocktail bar shakes up some serious mixes and slings some delicious food to keep drinkers upright. Particularly lip-smacking is the dragon dumpling burger – pork and beef with Sichuan pickle and dumpling sauce.

Lux Central Coffeebar CAFE
(Map p166; ☑602-327-1396; www.luxcoffee.com; 4402 N Central Ave; ⏱6am-midnight Sun-Thu, to 2am Fri & Sat; 🛜) MacBooks, tatts and hipster looks are de rigueur at this cafe-bar. The staff are adept and welcoming, the coffee is hand-roasted and the vibe is lively – everything you need to while away an hour over mid-morning coffee, dinner or a cocktail.

Four Peaks Brewing Company BREWERY
(Map p166; ☑480-303-9967; www.fourpeaks. com; 1340 E 8th St; ⏱11am-midnight Mon-Wed, 11am-1am Thu & Fri, 9am-midnight Sat & Sun; 🛜) Hipsters, families, craft-beer obsessives and the plain thirsty congregate happily in this 1890s brick brewhouse, filling growlers of Kilt Lifter or Pitchfork Pale from the tap, or just chatting over a pint or two. There's also toothsome pub grub, tasting tours ($10 per head), a gift shop, and further locations in Tempe, Scottsdale and Phoenix Sky Harbor.

☆ Entertainment

Check *Arizona Republic Calendar* (www. azcentral.com/thingstodo/events) and *Phoenix New Times* (www.phoenixnewtimes. com) for listings.

The **Phoenix Symphony** (Map p166; ☑administration 602-495-1117, box office 602-495-1999; www.phoenixsymphony.org; 75 N 2nd St) performs at **Symphony Hall** (Map p166; ☑602-262-6225; www.phoenixconventioncenter.com; 75 N 2nd St) and other local venues, while the **Arizona Opera** (Map p166; ☑602-266-7464; www.azopera.com; 75 N 2nd St) is based at an opera hall across the street from the Phoenix Art Museum (p162). The **Arizona Diamondbacks** (Map p166; ☑602-462-6500; http://arizona.diamondbacks.mlb.com; 401 E Jefferson St) play baseball at downtown's air-conditioned **Chase Field** (☑tours 602-462-6799; www. mlb.com/ari/ballpark; adult/senior/child $7/5/3; ⏱tours 9:30am, 11am, 12:30pm Mon-Sat, additional tours on game days), while the men's basketball team, the **Phoenix Suns** (Map p166; ☑602-379-7900; www.nba.com/suns; 201 E Jefferson St), and the women's team, the **Phoenix Mercury** (☑602-252-9622; www.wnba.com/mercury), are also downtown, at **Talking Stick Resort Arena**. The **Arizona Cardinals** (☑602-379-

wild scallops with mesquite-smoked caviar and tepary-bean crackling. The unobtrusive service is flawless, the wine list expertly curated and the room decorated with American Indian art.

Kai is at the Sheraton Wild Horse Pass Resort & Spa (p165) on the Gila River Indian Reservation. Book ahead and dress nicely.

🍷 Drinking & Nightlife

★ **Bitter & Twisted** COCKTAIL BAR
(Map p166; ☑602-340-1924; https://bitterandtwistedaz.com; 1 W Jefferson St; ⏱4pm-2am Tue-Sat) Housed in the former Arizona Prohibition

Phoenix

0101; www.azcardinals.com; 1 Cardinals Dr) play football in Glendale at the **University of Phoenix Stadium**.

Herberger Theater Center   THEATER
(Map p166; ☑602-252-8497; www.herbergertheater.org; 222 E Monroe St; ☉box office 10am-5pm Mon-Fri, from noon Sat & Sun & 1hr before performances) Housing several theater companies and three stages, the Herberger also plays host to visiting troupes and productions. The predominant fare is drama and musicals, but you can also catch dance, opera and exhibitions of local art here.

Char's Has the Blues   BLUES
(Map p166; ☑602-230-0205; www.charshastheblues.com; 4631 N 7th Ave; cover $3 Thu-Sun; ☉8pm-1am) Dark and intimate – but very welcoming – this shabby-fronted blues and R&B shack packs 'em in with solid acts most nights of the week, but somehow still manages to feel like a well-kept secret.

🛍 Shopping

Phoenix Public Market   MARKET
(Map p166; ☑602-625-6736; https://phxpublicmarket.com; 721 N Central Ave; ☉8am-1pm Sat Oct-Apr, 8am-noon Sat May-Sep) The largest farmers market in Arizona brings the state's best produce, both fresh and pre-made, together in one open-air jamboree of good tastes. Alongside spanking-fresh fruit and veg, you can find indigenous foods, wonderful bread, spices, paste and salsas, organic meat, BBQ trucks and plenty more to eat on the spot. Jewelry, textiles and body products also make appearances.

Heard Museum Shop & Bookstore   ARTS & CRAFTS
(Map p166; ☑602-252-8344; www.heardmuseumshop.com; 2301 N Central Ave; ☉9:30am-5pm Mon-Sat, 11am-5pm Sun; 🛜) This museum store has a top-notch collection of American Indian original arts and crafts; the variety and quality of kachina dolls alone is mind-boggling. Jewelry, pottery, American Indian books and a broad selection of fine arts can also be found, while the bookstore sells a wide array of books about the American Indian cultures of the Southwest.

Biltmore Fashion Park   MALL
(Map p166; ☑602-955-8400; www.shopbiltmore.com; 2502 E Camelback Rd; ☉10am-8pm Mon-Sat, noon-6pm Sun) Packed with high-end fashion

retailers, this exclusive mall preens from her perch on Camelback just south of the Arizona Biltmore Resort. Parking for under two hours is free, with validation.

ℹ️ Information

EMERGENCY & MEDICAL SERVICES

Police (📞 emergency 911, non-emergency 602-262-6151; http://phoenix.gov/police; 620 W Washington St)

Both **Banner – University Medical Center Phoenix** (📞602-839-2000; www.bannerhealth. com; 1111 E McDowell Rd) and **St Joseph's Hospital & Medical Center** (📞602-406-3000; www.stjosephs-phx.org; 350 W Thomas Rd) have 24-hour emergency rooms.

INTERET RESOURCES & MEDIA

KJZZ 91.5 FM (http://kjzz.org) National Public Radio (NPR).

Wi-fi is ubiquitous throughout Phoenix, or you can use the free internet at **Burton Barr Central Library** (📞602-262-4636; www.phoenixpub liclibrary.org; 1221 N Central Ave; ⊙9am-5pm Mon, Fri & Sat, 9am-9pm Tue-Thu, 1-5pm Sun; 📶); see the website for additional locations.

POST

Downtown Post Office (Map p166; 📞602-253-9648; www.usps.com; 522 N Central Ave; ⊙9am-5pm Mon-Fri) Housed in a beautiful 1930s federal building.

TOURIST INFORMATION

Downtown Phoenix Visitor Information Center (Map p166; 📞877-225-5749; www. visitphoenix.com; 125 N 2nd St, Suite 120; ⊙8am-5pm Mon-Fri) The Valley's most complete source of tourist information. Located across from the Hyatt Regency.

Experience Scottsdale (Map p166; 📞480-421-1004, 800-782-1117; www.experience scottsdale.com; 7014 E Camelback Rd; ⊙9am-6pm Mon-Sat, 10am-5pm Sun) In the Food Court of Scottsdale Fashion Square.

Mesa Convention & Visitors Bureau (📞480-827-4700, 800-283-6372; www.visitmesa.com; 120 N Center St; ⊙8am-5pm Mon-Fri)

Tempe Tourism Office (Map p166; 📞800-283-6734, 480-894-8158; www.tempetourism. com; 222 S Mill Ave, Suite 120; ⊙8:30am-5pm Mon-Fri)

ℹ️ Getting There & Away

Sky Harbor International Airport (Map p166; 📞602-273-3300; http://skyharbor.com; 3400 E Sky Harbor Blvd; 📶) is 3 miles southeast of downtown Phoenix and served by airlines including United, American, Delta and British Airways. Its three terminals (Terminals 2, 3 and 4; Terminal 1 was demolished in 1990) and the parking lots are linked by free shuttles and the **Phoenix Sky Train** (www.skyharbor.com/phxskytrain).

Greyhound (Map p166; 📞602-389-4200; www. greyhound.com; 2115 E Buckeye Rd) runs buses to Tucson ($18, two hours, six daily), Flagstaff ($25, three hours, five daily), Albuquerque ($70 to $87, 9½ hours, three daily) and Los Angeles ($46, 7½ hours, seven daily). Valley Metro's No 13 bus links the airport and the Greyhound station; tell the driver your destination is the station.

For shared rides from the airport, the citywide door-to-door shuttle service provided by **Super Shuttle** (📞602-244-9000, 800-258-3826; www.supershuttle.com) costs about $13 to downtown Phoenix, $15 to Tempe, $17 to Old Town Scottsdale and $21 to Mesa.

Valley Metro (📞602-253-5000; www.val leymetro.org) operates buses all over the Valley and a 20-mile light-rail line linking north Phoenix with downtown Phoenix, Tempe/ASU and downtown Mesa. Fares for both light-rail and bus are $2 per ride (no transfers) or $4 for a day pass. Buses run daily at intermittent times.

Central Arizona

North of Phoenix, the wooded, mountainous and much cooler Colorado Plateau is draped with scenic sites and attractions. You

PHOENIX FOR KIDS

Wet 'n' Wild Phoenix (📞623-201-2000; www.wetnwildphoenix.com; 4243 W Pinnacle Peak Rd, Glendale; over/under 42in tall $43/33, senior $33; ⊙10am-8pm Sun-Thu, to 10pm Fri & Sat Jun & Jul, shorter hours & weeks Mar-May & Aug-Oct; 📶) This water park has pools, tube slides, wave pools, waterfalls and floating rivers. It's in Glendale, 2 miles west of I-17 at exit 217.

Children's Museum of Phoenix (Map p166; 📞602-253-0501; http://childrensmuseumof phoenix.org; 215 N 7th St; entry $11; ⊙9am-4pm Tue-Sun; 📶) A tactile, climbable, paintable wonderland of interactive (and surreptitiously educational) exhibits.

Arizona Science Center (Map p166; 📞602-716-2000; www.azscience.org; 600 E Washington St; adult/child $18/13; ⊙10am-5pm; 📶) A high-tech temple of discovery; there are more than 300 hands-on exhibits and a planetarium.

ARIZONA'S BEST SCENIC DRIVES

Oak Creek Canyon A thrilling plunge past swimming holes, rockslides and crimson canyon walls on Hwy 89A between Flagstaff and Sedona.

Hwy 89/89A Wickenburg to Sedona The Old West meets the New Weston on this lazy drive past dude ranches, mining towns, art galleries and stylish wineries.

Patagonia–Sonoita Scenic Road This one's for the birds, and those who like to track them, in Arizona's southern wine country on Hwys 82 and 83.

Kayenta–Monument Valley Star in-your own Western on an iconic loop past cinematic red rocks in Navajo country.

Vermilion Cliffs Scenic Road A solitary drive on Hwy 89A through the Arizona Strip linking condor country, the North Rim and Mormon hideaways.

can channel your inner goddess at a vortex, hike through ponderosa-perfumed canyons, admire ancient Native American dwellings and delve into Old West history.

The main hub, Flagstaff, is a lively and delightful college town that's the gateway to the Grand Canyon South Rim. Summer, spring and fall are the best times to visit. On I-17, you can drive the 145 miles between Phoenix and Flagstaff in just over two hours. Opt for the more leisurely Hwy 89 and you'll be rewarded with beautiful landscapes and intriguing diversions.

Prescott

With its historic Victorian-era downtown and colorful Wild West heritage, Prescott feels like the Midwest-meets-cowboy country. Boasting more than 500 buildings on the National Register of Historic Places, it's the home of the world's oldest rodeo, while the infamous strip of old saloons known as Whiskey Row still plies its patrons with booze.

Just south of downtown, the winningly retro **Motor Lodge** (☑ 928-717-0157; www. themotorlodge.com; 503 S Montezuma St; r/ste/apt from $109/129/139; ❋ ⬆) welcomes guests with 12 snazzy bungalows arranged around a central driveway – it's indie lodging at its best. For breakfast, mosey into the friendly

Local (☑ 928-237-4724; 520 W Sheldon St; mains $11-12; ◷ 7am-2.30pm; ⬆), where home baking and a classic Southwestern breakfast can be counted on. Cajun and Southwest specialties spice up the menu at delightful **Iron Springs Cafe** (☑ 928-443-8848; www.iron springscafe.com; 1501 Iron Springs Rd; brunch & lunch $11-13, dinner $16-20; ◷ 11am-8pm Wed-Sat, 9am-2pm Sun), which sits inside an old train station 3 miles northwest of downtown.

On Whiskey Row, the **Palace** (☑ 928-541-1996; www.historicpalace.com; 120 S Montezuma St; ◷ 11am-10pm Sun-Thu, to 11pm Fri & Sat) is an atmospheric place to drink; you enter through swinging saloon doors into a big room anchored by a Brunswick bar. The **visitor center** (☑ 800-266-7534, 928-445-2000; https://prescott.org; 117 W Goodwin St; ◷ 9am-5pm Mon-Fri, 10am-2pm Sat & Sun) has tourist information, while **Arizona Shuttle** (☑ 928-226-8060, 800-888-2749; www.arizonashuttle. com) runs buses to/from Phoenix airport.

Jerome

This resurrected ghost town was known as the 'Wickedest Town in the West' during its late-1800s mining heyday, but its historic buildings have now been restored to hold galleries, restaurants, B&Bs and wine-tasting rooms.

Feeling brave? Stand on the glass platform covering the 1910ft mining shaft at **Audrey Headframe Park** (www.jeromehistoricalsocie ty.com; 55 Douglas Rd; ◷ 8am-5pm) **FREE** – it's deeper than the Empire State Building by 650ft! Just ahead, the excellent **Jerome State Historic Park** (☑ 928-634-5381; www. azstateparks.com; 100 Douglas Rd; adult/child 7-13yr $7/4; ◷ 8:30am-5pm) preserves the 1916 mansion of mining mogul Jimmy 'Rawhide' Douglas.

A community hospital in the mining era, the **Jerome Grand Hotel** (☑ 928-634-8200; www.jeromegrandhotel.com; 200 Hill St; r/ste $225/325; ❋ ⬆) plays up its past with medical relics in the hallways and an entertaining ghost tour kids will enjoy. The adjoining **Asylum Restaurant** (☑ 928-639-3197; www.asylum restaurant.com; 200 Hill St; lunch $12-14, dinner $26-28), with its sweeping views, is a breathtaking spot for a fine meal and glass of wine.

Downtown, the **Spirit Room Bar** (☑ 928-634-8809; www.spiritroom.com; 166 Main St; ◷ 11am-1am) is a lively watering hole. Step into the **Flatiron Café** (☑ 928-634-2733; www. theflatironjerome.com; 416 Main St; breakfast $8-10, lunch $11-13; ◷ 8:30am-3:30pm Wed-Mon) at the Y intersection for a gourmet breakfast or lunch; the specialty coffees are delicious. For information, call in at the **chamber of commerce** (☑928-634-2900; www.jeromechamber. com; 310 Hull Ave; ⊙11am-3pm Thu-Mon).

Sedona

Nestled amid striking red sandstone formations at the south end of the 16-mile Oak Creek Canyon, Sedona attracts spiritual seekers, artists and healers, as well as day-trippers from Phoenix trying to escape the oppressive heat. Many New Age types believe that this area is the center of vortexes (not 'vortices' here in Sedona) that radiate the earth's power, and you'll find all sorts of alternative medicines and practices on display. More tangibly, the surrounding canyons offer outstanding hiking, biking, swimming and camping.

⊙ Sights & Activities

New Agers believe Sedona's rocks, cliffs and rivers radiate Mother Earth's mojo. The four best-known vortexes are **Bell Rock** near the Village of Oak Creek east of Hwy 179; **Cathedral Rock** near Red Rock Crossing; **Airport Mesa** (Airport Rd) along Airport Rd; and **Boynton Canyon**. Airport Rd is also a great location for watching the Technicolor sunsets.

★**Red Rock State Park**   PARK
(☑928-282-6907; https://azstateparks.com/redrock; 4050 Red Rock Loop Rd; adult $7, child 7-13yr $4, 6yr & under free; ⊙8am-5pm, visitor center 9am-4:30pm; ⊞) Not to be confused with Slide Rock State Park, this 286-acre park includes an environmental education center, picnic areas and 5 miles of well-marked, interconnecting trails in a riparian environment amid gorgeous red-rock country. Trails range from flat creekside saunters to moderate climbs to scenic ridges. Ranger-led activities include nature and bird walks. Swimming in the creek is prohibited. It's 9 miles west of downtown Sedona off Hwy 89A, on the eastern edge of the 15-mile Lime Kiln Trail.

★**Slide Rock State Park**   SWIMMING
(☑928-282-3034, information line 602-542-0202; www.azstateparks.com/parks/slro; 6871 N Hwy 89A, Oak Creek Canyon; per car Jun-Sep $20, Oct-May $10; ⊙8am-7pm Jun-Aug, shorter hours rest of the year; ⊞) One of Sedona's most popular and most crowded destinations, this state park 7 miles north of town features an 80ft sandstone chute that whisks swimmers

through Oak Creek. Short trails ramble past old cabins, farming equipment and an apple orchard, but the park's biggest draw is the set of wonderful natural rock slides.

★**Pink Jeep Tours**   DRIVING
(☑800-873-3662, 928-282-5000; www.pinkjeeptours.com; 204 N Hwy 89A; ⊙6am-10pm; ⊞) It seems like this veteran of Sedona's tour industry has jeeps everywhere, buzzing around like pink flies. But once you join a tour, laughing and bumping around, you'll see why they're so popular. Pink runs 15 thrilling, bone-rattling off-road and adventure tours around Sedona, with most lasting from about two hours (adult/child from $59/54) to four hours (from $154/139).

⏨ Sleeping

Sedona and nearby Oak Creek Canyon host many beautiful B&Bs, creekside cabins, motels and full-service resorts. Dispersed camping is not permitted in Red Rock Canyon. The Forest Service runs campgrounds, without hookups, in the woods of Oak Creek Canyon, just off Hwy Alt 89. It costs $18 to camp, and you don't need a Red Rock Pass. All campgrounds except Pine Flat East accept reservations. Six miles north of town, Manzanita has 19 sites, showers and is open year round; 11.5 miles north, Cave Springs has 82 sites, and showers; Pine Flat East and Pine Flat West, 12.5 miles north, together have 58 sites, 18 of which can be reserved.

Cozy Cactus   B&B $$
(☑800-788-2082, 928-284-0082; www.cozycactus.com; 80 Canyon Circle Dr, Village of Oak Creek; d from $210; ⊞⊛) This five-room B&B, run by Carrie and Mark, works well for adventure-loving types – the Southwest-style house bumps up against Agave Trail, and is just around the bend from cyclist-friendly Bell Rock Pathway. Post-adventuring, get comfy beside the firepit on the back patio, perfect for wildlife watching and stargazing, and enjoy the three-course breakfast that awaits you the next morning.

★**El Portal**   B&B $$$
(☑928-203-9405, 800-313-0017; www.elportalsedona.com; 95 Portal Lane; d from $300; ⊛⊞) ⏀ This discreet little inn is a beautiful blend of Southwestern and Craftsman style. It's a pocket of relaxed luxury tucked away in a corner across from the galleries and restaurants of Tlaquepaque, and marvelously removed from the chaos of Sedona's tourist-heavy

downtown. The look is rustic but sophisticated, incorporating reclaimed wood, Navajo rugs, river rock and thick adobe walls.

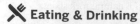 Eating & Drinking

Sedona's restaurants are clustered around Uptown and strung along Highways 89A and 179. Pick up groceries and picnic ingredients at **Whole Foods** (📞928-282-6311; 1420 W Hwy 89A; ⊙8am-9pm Mon-Sat, to 8pm Sun; 🅿) or **Bashas'** (📞928-282-5351; 160 Coffee Pot Dr; ⊙6am-11pm).

Sedona Memories   DELI $
(📞928-282-0032; 321 Jordan Rd; sandwiches $8.50; ⊙10am-2pm Mon-Fri) This tiny local spot assembles gigantic sandwiches on slabs of homemade bread. A great choice for a picnic, as they pack 'em tight to-go, so there's less mess. You can also nosh on their quiet porch. If you call in your order, they'll toss in a free cookie. Cash only.

★Elote Cafe   MEXICAN $$$
(📞928-203-0105; www.elotecafe.com; Arabella Hotel, 771 Hwy 179; mains $22-28; ⊙5-10pm Tue-Sat) Come here for some of the best, most authentic Mexican food in the region. Elote Cafe serves unusual and traditional dishes you won't find elsewhere, like the namesake *elote* (fire-roasted corn with spicy mayo, lime and cotija cheese) or smoked chicken in guajillo chiles. Reservations are not accepted and the line can be off-putting: come early, bring a book, order a margarita.

Dahl & DiLuca Ristorante   ITALIAN $$$
(📞928-282-5219; www.dahlanddiluca.com; 2321 Hwy 89A; mains $27-38; ⊙5-10pm) Though this lovely Italian place fits perfectly into the groove and color scheme of Sedona, at the same time it feels like the kind of place you'd find in a small Italian seaside town. It's a bustling, welcoming spot serving excellent, authentic Italian food. Try the pork chop and asparagus from the grill or the four-cheese ravioli in truffle cream.

ℹ Information

Red Rock Country Visitor Center (📞928-203-2900; www.redrockcountry.org; 8375 Hwy 179; ⊙9am-4:30pm) Get a Red Rock Pass here, as well as hiking guides, maps and local national forest information.

Sedona Chamber of Commerce Visitor Center (📞928-282-7722, 800-288-7336; www.visitsedona.com; 331 Forest Rd; ⊙8:30am-5pm) Located in the pedestrian center of Uptown Sedona; pick up free maps and buy a Red Rock Pass.

ℹ Getting There & Around

Ace Xpress (📞800-336-2239, 928-649-2720; www.acexshuttle.com; one-way/round-trip adult $68/109, child $35/55; ⊙office hours 7am-8pm Mon-Fri, 8am-8pm Sat & Sun) and **Arizona Shuttle** (📞800-888-2749, 928-282-2066; www.arizonashuttle.com) run shuttle services between Sedona and Phoenix's Sky Harbor International Airport.

Amtrak (📞800-872-7245; www.amtrak.com) and **Greyhound** (📞800-231-2222; www.greyhound.com) both stop in nearby Flagstaff.

Barlow Jeep Rentals (📞928-282-8700, 800-928-5337; www.barlows.us; 3009 W Hwy 89A; half-/1-/3-day jeep rental $250/350/576; ⊙8am-6pm) is great for rough-road exploring. Free maps and trail information are provided. **Bob's Taxi** (📞982-282-1234; www.bobstaxisedona.com) is a good local operator, while rental cars are available at **Enterprise** (📞928-282-2052; www.enterprise.com; 2090 W Hwy 89A; per day from $50; ⊙8am-6pm Mon-Fri, 9am-2pm Sat & Sun).

> ### RED ROCK PASS
>
> To park on National Forest land around Sedona and Oak Creek Canyon, you'll need to buy a Red Rock Pass, which is available at ranger stations, visitor centers and vending machines at most trailheads and picnic areas. Passes cost $5 per day or $15 per week and must be displayed under the windshield of your car. You don't need a pass if you're just stopping briefly for a photograph or to enjoy a viewpoint, or if you have one of the Federal Interagency Passes.

Flagstaff

Flagstaff's laid-back charms are many, from a pedestrian-friendly historic downtown crammed with eclectic vernacular architecture and vintage neon, to hiking and skiing in the country's largest ponderosa pine forest. And the locals are a happy, athletic bunch, skewing more toward granola than gunslinger: buskers play bluegrass on street corners while cycling culture flourishes. Northern Arizona University (NAU) gives Flag its college-town flavor, while its railroad history still figures firmly in the town's identity. Throw in a healthy appreciation for craft beer, freshly roasted coffee beans and

VERDE VALLEY WINE TRAIL

Vineyards, wineries and tasting rooms are increasingly thick on the ground in the well-watered valley of the Verde River. Bringing star power is Maynard James Keenan, lead singer of the band Tool and owner of Caduceus Cellars and Merkin Vineyards. His 2010 documentary *Blood into Vine* takes a no-holds-barred look at the wine industry.

In Cottonwood, drive or float to **Alcantara Vineyards** (928-649-8463; www.alcantaravineyard.com; 3445 S Grapevine Way, Cottonwood; wine tasting $10-15; 11am-5pm) on the Verde River, then stroll through Old Town where **Arizona Stronghold** (928-639-2789; www.azstronghold.com; 1023 N Main St; wine tasting $9; noon-7pm Sun-Thu, to 9pm Fri & Sat), **Merkin Vineyards Osteria** (928-639-1001; http://merkinvineyardsosteria.com; 1001 N Main St; 11am-9pm;) and **Pillsbury Wine Company** (928-639-0646; www.pillsburywine.com; 1012 N Main St; wine tasting $10-12; 11am-6pm Sun-Thu, to 9pm Fri & Sat) are three of the best wine-tasting rooms on oenophile-friendly Main St.

In Jerome, start at **Cellar 433** (928-634-7033; www.cellar433.com; 240 Hull Ave; 11am-6pm Thu-Sun, to 5pm Mon-Wed) near the visitor center. From there, stroll up to Keenan's **Caduceus Cellars** (928-639-9463; www.caduceus.org; 158 Main St; 11am-6pm Sun-Thu, to 8pm Sat), near the Connor Hotel.

Three wineries with tasting rooms hug a scrubby stretch of Page Springs Rd east of Cornville: bistro-housing **Page Springs Cellars** (928-639-3004; http://pagespringscellars.com; 1500 Page Springs Rd, Cornville; tours $10; 11am-7pm Sun-Wed, to 9pm Thu-Sat), the welcoming **Oak Creek Vineyards** (928-649-0290; www.oakcreekvineyards.net; 1555 N Page Springs Rd, Cornville; wine tasting $10; 10am-6pm) and the mellow-rock-playing **Javelina Leap Vineyard** (928-649-2681; www.javelinaleapwinery.com; 1565 Page Springs Rd, Cornville; tasting per wine $2-3; 11am-5pm Sun-Thu, to 6pm Fri & Sat).

For a wine-trail map and more details about the wineries, visit www.vvwinetrail.com.

an all-around good time and you have the makings of the perfect northern Arizonan escape.

Sights

★ **Lowell Observatory** OBSERVATORY
(main phone 928-774-3358, recorded information 928-233-3211; www.lowell.edu; 1400 W Mars Hill Rd; adult/senior/child 5-17yr $15/14/8; 10am-10pm Mon-Sat, to 5pm Sun;) Sitting atop a hill just west of downtown, this national historic landmark - famous for the first sighting of Pluto, in 1930 - was built by Percival Lowell in 1894. Weather permitting, visitors can stargaze through on-site telescopes, including the famed 1896 Clark Telescope, the impetus behind the now-accepted theory of an expanding universe. Kids will love the paved Pluto Walk, which meanders through a scale model of our solar system.

★ **Museum of Northern Arizona** MUSEUM
(928-774-5213; www.musnaz.org; 3101 N Fort Valley Rd; adult/senior/child 10-17yr $12/10/8; 10am-5pm Mon-Sat, noon-5pm Sun;) Housed in an attractive Craftsman-style stone building amid a pine grove, this small but excellent museum spotlights local American Indian archaeology, history and culture, as well as geology, biology and

the arts. Intriguing permanent collections are augmented by exhibitions on subjects such as John James Audubon's paintings of North American mammals. On the way to the Grand Canyon it makes a wonderful introduction to the human and natural history of the region.

Riordan Mansion
State Historic Park HISTORIC SITE
(928-779-4395; https://azstateparks.com/riordan-mansion; 409 W Riordan Rd; tour adult/child 7-13yr $10/5; 9:30am-5pm May-Oct, 10:30am-5pm Thu-Mon Nov-Apr) Having made a fortune from their Arizona Lumber Company, brothers Michael and Timothy Riordan built this sprawling duplex in 1904. The Craftsman-style design was the brainchild of architect Charles Whittlesey, who also designed El Tovar in Grand Canyon Village. The exterior features hand-split wooden shingles, log-slab siding and rustic stone. Filled with Edison, Stickley, Tiffany and Steinway furniture, the interior is a shrine to arts and crafts.

Activities

Absolute Bikes CYCLING
(928-779-5969; www.absolutebikes.net; 202 E Rte 66; bike rentals per day from $39; 9am-7pm

Mon-Fri, 9am-6pm Sat, 10am-4pm Sun Apr-Thanksgiving, shorter hours Dec-Mar) Visit these super-friendly gearheads for the inside track on the local mountain-biking scene, and to hire wheels for the surrounding trails.

Arizona Snowbowl SKIING
(☑928-779-1951; www.arizonasnowbowl.com; 9300 N Snowbowl Rd; lift ticket adult $75, youth 13-17yr $64, child 8-12yr $42; ⊙9am-4pm mid-Nov–mid-Apr; ⊕) About 14 miles north of downtown Flagstaff, Arizona Snowbowl is small but lofty, with eight lifts that service 40 ski runs between 9200ft and 11,500ft. The season normally runs from November to April.

🛏 Sleeping

Unlike in southern Arizona, summer is high season here.

★Motel Dubeau HOSTEL $
(☑928-774-6731; www.modubeau.com; 19 W Phoenix Ave; dm/r from $27/53; P🐾@🛜) Built in 1929 as Flagstaff's first motel, this independent hostel offers the same friendly service and clean, well-run accommodations as its sister property, Grand Canyon International Hostel. The private rooms are similar to basic, but handsome, hotel rooms, with refrigerators, cable TV and private bathrooms. On-site Nomads serves beer, wine and light snacks. There are also kitchen and laundry facilities.

Flagstaff KOA CAMPGROUND $
(☑928-526-9926, reservations 800-562-3524; www.flagstaffkoa.com; 5803 N Hwy 89; tent/RV site $33/38, cabins & tipis from $65; P🛜🐾) This big ponderosa-shaded campground lies a mile north of I-40 off exit 201, 5 miles northeast of downtown Flagstaff. A path leads from the campground to trails at Mt Elden, and it's family friendly, with banana-bike rentals, summer barrel-train rides, weekend movies and a splash park. The four one-room cabins sleep four, but bedding isn't supplied.

★Hotel Monte Vista HISTORIC HOTEL $$
(☑928-779-6971; www.hotelmontevista.com; 100 N San Francisco St; r/ste from $115/145; 🐾🛜) A huge, old-fashioned neon sign towers over this 1926 landmark hotel, hinting at what's inside: feather lampshades, vintage furniture, bold colors and eclectic decor. Rooms are named for the movie stars who stayed here, including the 'Humphrey Bogart,' with dramatic black walls, yellow ceiling and gold-satin bedding. Several resident ghosts supposedly make regular appearances.

★Inn at 410 B&B $$
(☑928-774-0088; www.inn410.com; 410 N Leroux St; r from $185; P🐾🛜) This fully renovated 1894 house offers 10 spacious, beautifully decorated and themed bedrooms, each with a fridge and bathroom, and many with four-poster beds and delightful views. A short stroll from downtown, the inn has a shady orchard-garden and a cozy dining room, where a full gourmet breakfast and afternoon snacks are served.

🍴 Eating

Flagstaff's college population and general dedication to living well translate into one of the best dining scenes in the state. Self-caterers can try **Bashas'** (☑928-774-3882; www.bashas.com; 2700 S Woodlands Village Blvd; ⊙6am-11pm), a good local chain supermarket with a respectable selection of organic foods. For healthy food, there's **Whole Foods Market** (☑928-774-5747; www.wholefoodsmarket.com; 320 S Cambridge Lane; ⊙7am-9pm; 🅿).

★Macy's CAFE $
(☑928-774-2243; www.macyscoffee.net; 14 S Beaver St; breakfast/lunch $6/7; ⊙6am-6pm; 🛜🅿) The delicious coffee at this Flagstaff institution – house roasted in the original, handsome, fire-engine-red roaster in the corner – has kept local students and caffeine devotees buzzing since the 1980s. The vegetarian menu includes many vegan choices, along with traditional cafe grub like pastries, steamed eggs, waffles, yogurt and granola, salads and veggie sandwiches.

Diablo Burger BURGERS $
(☑928-774-3274; www.diabloburger.com; 120 N Leroux St; mains $11-14; ⊙11am-9pm Sun-Wed, 11am-10pm Thu-Sat; 🛜) This locally focused gourmet-burger joint slings hefty burgers on English-muffin buns and delicious Herbes de Provence seasoned fries. The cheddar-topped Blake gives a nod to New Mexico with Hatch-chile mayo and roasted green chiles. The place is tiny, so come early or sit outside and people-watch. Beer and wine are also served.

★Criollo Latin Kitchen FUSION $$
(☑928-774-0541; www.criollolatinkitchen.com; 16 N San Francisco St; mains $17-20; ⊙11am-9pm Mon-Fri, 9am-9pm Sat & Sun) 🅿 Sister to Brix Restaurant & Wine Bar and **Proper Meats + Provisions** (☑928-774-9001; www.propermeats.com; 110 S San Francisco St; sandwiches $12-13; ⊙10am-7pm) 🅿, this on-trend Latin-fusion

restaurant gives similar encouragement to local producers, sourcing ingredients from Arizona wherever possible. Set up your day with the Haitian brunch of slow-roasted pork with over-easy eggs, pinto beans and Ti-Malice hot sauce, or come back at happy hour (3pm to 6pm Monday to Friday) for fish tacos and $4 margaritas.

★**Brix Restaurant**
& Wine Bar   INTERNATIONAL $$$
(📲 928-213-1021; www.brixflagstaff.com; 413 N San Francisco St; mains $30-32; ⏰ 5-9pm Sun & Tue-Thu, to 10pm Fri & Sat; 🖊) Brix offers seasonal, locally sourced and generally top-notch fare in a handsome room with exposed brick walls and an intimate copper bar. Sister business Proper Meats + Provisions, supplies charcuterie, free-range pork and other fundamentals of lip-smacking dishes. The wine list is well curated, and reservations are recommended.

★**Coppa Cafe**   CAFE $$$
(📲928-637-6813; www.coppacafe.net; 1300 S Milton Rd; lunch & brunch $11-15, mains $28-31; ⏰3-9pm Wed-Fri, 11am-3pm & 5-9pm Sat, 10am-3pm Sun; 🛜) Brian Konefal and Paola Fioravanti, who met at an Italian culinary school, are the husband-and-wife team behind this friendly, art-strewn bistro with egg-yolk-yellow walls. Expect ingredients foraged from nearby woods (and further afield in Arizona) in dishes such as slow-roasted top loin with wildflower butter, or clay-baked duck's egg with a 'risotto' of Sonoran wheat and wild herbs.

🍷 **Drinking & Entertainment**

For details about festivals and music programs, call the Visitor Center or check www.flagstaff365.com. On Friday and Saturday nights in summer, people gather on blankets for free music and family movies at Heritage Sq. The fun starts at 5pm.

On Thursdays pick up a free copy of *Flagstaff Live!* (www.flaglive.com) for current shows and happenings around town.

★**Hops on Birch**   PUB
(📲928-774-4011; www.hopsonbirch.com; 22 E Birch Ave; ⏰1:30pm-12:30am Mon-Thu, to 2am Fri, noon-2am Sat, noon-12.30am Sun) Simple and handsome, Hops on Birch has 34 rotating beers on tap, live music five nights a week and a friendly local-crowd vibe. In classic Flagstaff style, dogs are as welcome as humans.

WALNUT CANYON

The Sinagua cliff dwellings at **Walnut Canyon** (📲928-526-3367; www.nps.gov/waca; I-40 exit 204; adult/child under 16yr $8/free; ⏰8am-5pm Jun-Oct, 9am-5pm Nov-May, trails close 1hr earlier; 🅿) are set in the nearly vertical walls of a small limestone butte amid this stunning forested canyon. The mile-long Island Trail steeply descends 185ft (more than 200 stairs), passing 25 rooms built under the natural overhangs of the curvaceous butte. A shorter, wheelchair-accessible Rim Trail affords several views of the cliff dwelling from across the canyon.

Monte Vista Cocktail Lounge   BAR
(📲928-779-6971; www.hotelmontevista.com; 100 N San Francisco St, Hotel Monte Vista; ⏰4pm-2am Mon-Sat) With a prime corner spot in downtown Flagstaff, complete with broad windows for people-watching, this former speakeasy in the historic Hotel Monte Vista has a pressed-tin ceiling, pool table, live music three nights a week, plus a Sunday quiz, karaoke and all-day 'happy hour' on Mondays.

ℹ **Information**

USFS Flagstaff Ranger Station (📲928-526-0866; www.fs.usda.gov; 5075 N Hwy 89; ⏰8am-4pm Mon-Fri) Provides information on the Mt Elden, Humphreys Peak and O'Leary Peak areas north of Flagstaff.

Visitor Center (📲800-842-7293, 928-213-2951; www.flagstaffarizona.org; 1 E Rte 66; ⏰8am-5pm Mon-Sat, 9am-4pm Sun) Located inside the Amtrak station, the visitor center has a great Flagstaff Discovery map and tons of information on things to do.

ℹ **Getting There & Away**

Greyhound (📲928-774-4573, 800-231-2222; www.greyhound.com; 880 E Butler Ave; ⏰10am-6.30am) stops in Flagstaff en route to/from Albuquerque, Las Vegas, Los Angeles and Phoenix. **Arizona Shuttle** (p170) and **Flagstaff Shuttle & Charter** (📲888-215-3105; www.flagshuttle.com) have shuttles that run between Flagstaff, Grand Canyon National Park, Williams, Sedona and Phoenix's Sky Harbor International Airport.

Operated by **Amtrak** (📲800-872-7245, 928-774-8679; www.amtrak.com; 1 E Rte 66; ⏰3:30am-10:30pm), the *Southwest Chief* stops at Flagstaff on its daily run between Chicago and Los Angeles.

Mountain Line Transit (☑ 928-779-6624; www.mountainline.az.gov; one-way adult/child $1.25/0.60) has several fixed bus routes daily; pick up a user-friendly map at the visitor center. Buses are equipped with ramps for passengers in wheelchairs.

If you need a taxi, call **Action Cab** (☑ 928-774-4427) or **Sun Taxi** (☑ 928-774-7400; www.suntaxi andtours.com). Several major car-rental agencies operate from the airport and downtown.

Williams

Affable Williams, 60 miles south of Grand Canyon Village and 35 miles west of Flagstaff, is a gateway town with character. Classic motels and diners line Route 66, and the old-school homes and train station give a nod to simpler times.

Most tourists visit to ride the turn-of-the-20th-century **Grand Canyon Railway** (☑ reservations 800-843-8724; www.thetrain.com; 233 N Grand Canyon Blvd, Railway Depot; round-trip adult/child from $79/47) to the Canyon's South Rim, which departs Williams 9:30am and returns at 5:45pm. Even if you're not a train buff, a trip is a scenic stress-free way to visit the Grand Canyon. Characters in period costumes provide historical and regional narration, and banjo folk music sets the tone.

The **Red Garter Inn** (☑ 928-635-1484; www. redgarter.com; 137 W Railroad Ave; d from $170; ❈⑨) is an 1897 bordello turned B&B where the ladies used to hang out the windows to flag down customers. The four rooms have nice period touches and the downstairs bakery has good coffee. The funky little **Grand Canyon Hotel** (☑ 928-635-1419; www.thegrand canyonhotel.com; 145 W Route 66; dm/r from $33/87; ⊘ Mar-Nov; ❈@⑨) has small themed rooms, a six-bed dorm and no TVs. You can also sleep inside a 1929 Santa Fe caboose or a Pullman railcar at the **Canyon Motel & RV Park** (☑ 928-635-9371, 800-482-3955; www.the canyonmotel.com; 1900 E Rodeo Rd; tent/RV sites from $31/44, cottages/cabooses from $90/180; ❈⑨⚇❈), just east of downtown.

Grand Canyon National Park

No matter how much you read about the **Grand Canyon** (☑ 928-638-7888; www.nps. gov/grca; 20 South Entrance Rd; ⊘ 7-day entry per car/individual $30/15), or how many photographs you've seen, nothing really prepares you for the sight of it. The sheer immensity of the canyon grabs you first, followed by the dramatic layers of rock, which pull you in for a closer look. Next up are the artistic details – rugged plateaus, crumbly spires, maroon ridges – that flirt and catch your eye as shadows flicker across the rock.

Snaking along its floor are 277 miles of the Colorado River, which has carved the canyon over the past six million years and exposed rocks up to two billion years old – half the age of the earth. The two rims of the Grand Canyon offer quite different experiences; they lie more than 200 miles apart by road and are rarely visited on the same trip. Most visitors choose the South Rim with its easy access, wealth of services and vistas that don't disappoint. The quieter North Rim has its own charms; at 8200ft elevation (1000ft higher than the South Rim), its cooler temperatures support wildflower meadows and tall, thick stands of aspen and spruce.

June is the driest month, July and August the wettest. January has average overnight lows of 13°F (-11°C) to 20°F (-7°C) and daytime highs around 40°F (4°C). Summer temperatures inside the canyon regularly soar above 100°F (38°C). While the South Rim is open year-round, most visitors come between late May and early September. The North Rim is open from mid-May to mid-October.

❶ Information

The most developed area in the Grand Canyon National Park is **Grand Canyon Village**, 6 miles north of the South Rim Entrance Station. The North Rim has one entrance, which is 30 miles south of Jacob Lake on Hwy 67; continue another 14 miles south to the actual rim. The North and South Rims are 215 miles apart by car, 21 miles on foot through the canyon, or 10 miles as the condor flies

The park entrance ticket is valid for seven days and can be used at both rims. All overnight hikes and backcountry camping in the park require a permit. The **Backcountry Information Center** (☑ 928-638-7875; www.nps.gov/grca; Grand Canyon Village; ⊘ 8am-noon & 1-5pm, phone staffed 8am-5pm Mon-Fri; ⚇ Village) accepts applications for backpacking permits ($10, plus $8 per person per night) starting four months before the proposed month. Your chances are decent if you apply early and provide alternative hiking itineraries. Reservations are accepted in person or by mail or fax, not by phone or email. For more information see www.nps.gov/grca/ planyourvisit/backcountry-permit.htm.

If you arrive at the South Rim without a permit, head to the backcountry office, by **Maswik**

Lodge (☑888-297-2757, ext 6784, front desk & reservations within 48hr 928-638-2631; www.grandcanyonlodges.com; Grand Canyon Village; r South/North $107/205; P❄@🛜; 🖵 Village), to join the waiting list. As a conservation measure, the park no longer sells bottled water. Fill your flask at water filling stations along the rim or at **Canyon Village Market** (p181).

South Rim

If you don't mind bumping elbows with other travelers, you'll be fine on the South Rim, where you'll find an entire village worth of lodging, restaurants, bookstores, libraries, a supermarket and a deli. Museums and historic stone buildings illuminate the park's human history, and rangers lead daily programs on subjects from geology to resurgent condors. In summer, when day-trippers converge en masse, escaping the crowds can be as easy as taking a day hike below the rim or merely tramping a hundred yards away from a scenic overlook.

🏃 Activities

Driving & Hiking

A **scenic route** follows the rim on the west side of Grand Canyon Village along Hermit Rd. Closed to private vehicles March through November, the 7-mile road is serviced by free park shuttle buses; cycling is encouraged because of the relatively light traffic. Stops offer spectacular views, and interpretive signs explain canyon features.

Desert View Drive starts east of Grand Canyon Village and follows the canyon rim for 26 miles to Desert View, the east entrance of the park. Pullouts offer tremendous views.

Hiking trails along the South Rim include options for every skill level. The **Rim Trail** is the most popular, and easiest, walk in the park. It dips in and out of the scrubby pines of Kaibab National Forest to connect scenic points and historical sights over 13 miles. Portions are paved, and every viewpoint is accessed by one of the three shuttle routes. Along the **Trail of Time**, bordering the Rim Trail just west of Yavapai Geology Museum, every meter represents one million years of geologic history.

Hiking down into the canyon itself is a serious undertaking; most visitors are content with short day hikes. Bear in mind that the climb back out of the canyon is much harder than the descent into it, and do not attempt to hike all the way to the Colorado River and

WORTH A TRIP

SUNSET CRATER VOLCANO NATIONAL MONUMENT

Around AD 1064 a volcano erupted on this spot, spewing ash across 800 sq miles, spawning the Kana-A lava flow and forcing farmers to vacate lands tilled for 400 years. Now the 8029ft **Sunset Crater Volcano National Monument** (☑928-526-0502; www.nps.gov/sucr; Park Loop Rd 545; car/motorcycle/bicycle or pedestrian $20/15/10; ◷9am-5pm Nov-May, from 8am Jun-Oct) is quiet, and mile-long trails wind through the Bonito lava flow (formed c 1180), and up Lenox Crater (7024ft). More ambitious hikers and bikers can ascend O'Leary Peak (8965ft; 8 miles round-trip), or there's a gentle, 0.3-mile, wheelchair-accessible loop overlooking the petrified flow.

Sunset Crater is 19 miles northeast of Flagstaff. Access fees include entry to nearby **Wupatki National Monument** (☑928-679-2365; www.nps.gov/wupa; Park Loop Rd 545; car/motorcycle/bicycle or pedestrian $20/15/10; ◷visitor center 9am-5pm, trails sunrise-sunset; P♿), and are valid for seven days.

back in a single day. On the most popular route, the beautiful **Bright Angel Trail**, the scenic 8-mile drop to the river is punctuated with four logical turnaround spots. Summer heat can be crippling; day hikers should either turn around at one of the two resthouses (a 3- or 6-mile round-trip) or hit the trail at dawn to safely make the longer hikes to **Indian Garden** and **Plateau Point** (9.2- and 12.2-mile round-trips, respectively).

The steeper and much more exposed **South Kaibab Trail** is one of the park's prettiest routes, combining stunning scenery and unobstructed 360-degree views with every step. Hikers overnighting at **Phantom Ranch** generally descend this way, and return the next day via the Bright Angel. Summer ascents can be dangerous, and during this season rangers advise day hikers to turn around at **Cedar Ridge** (about 3 miles round-trip).

Cycling

Bright Angel Bicycles & Cafe at Mather Point CYCLING
(☑928-814-8704, 928-638-3055; www.bikegrandcanyon.com; 10 S Entrance Rd, Visitor Center Plaza; 24hr rental adult/child 16yr & under $40/30, 5hr

Grand Canyon National Park

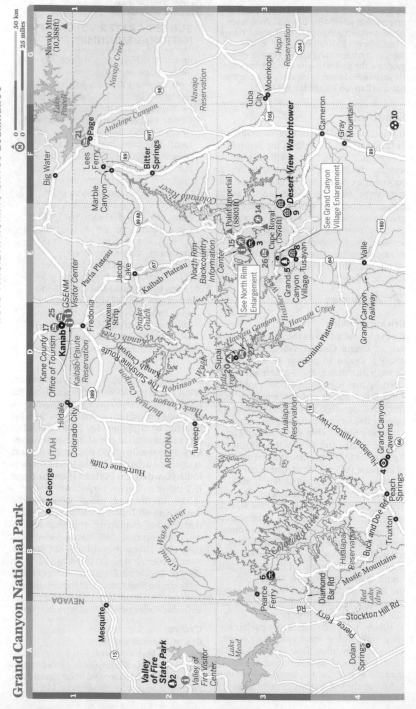

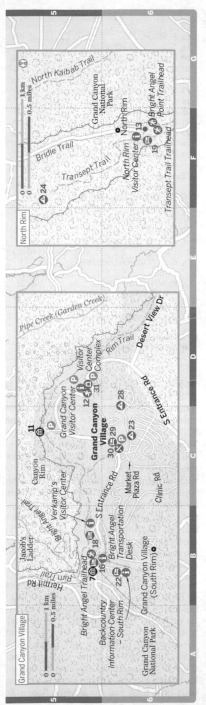

rental $30/20, wheelchair $10, s/d stroller up to 8hr $18/27; ⏱7am-5pm Mar-Oct; 🚌Village, 🚌Kaibab/ Rim) Half-or full-day bicycle rentals, with helmets and an add-on pull-along trailer option, can be reserved in advance online or by phone. With the exception of the peak stretch from July through mid-August, however, walk-ins can usually be accommodated. Hermit Rd bicycle-shuttle packages allow you to ride past overlooks going one way, and hop on one of their private shuttles the other.

👉 Tours

⭐**Canyon Vistas Mule Rides**   TOURS
(📞888-297-2757, same day/next day reservations 928-638-3283; www.grandcanyonlodges.com; Bright Angel Lodge; 3hr mule ride $135, 1-/2-night mule ride incl meals & accommodation $552/788; ⏱rides available year-round, hours vary) This outfit takes groups of up to 20 mules 4 miles along the East Rim Trail. If you want to descend into the canyon, the only option is an overnight trip to Phantom Ranch. These trips follow the Bright Angel Trail 10.5 miles (5½ hours) down, spend one or two nights at Phantom Ranch, and return 7.8 miles (five hours) along the South Kaibab Trail.

🛏 Sleeping

The South Rim's six lodges are operated by **Xanterra** (📞888-297-2757, 303-297-2757, 928-638-3283; www.grandcanyonlodges.com). Contact them to make advance reservations (essential in summer), although it's best to call Phantom Ranch, down beside the Colorado River, directly. For same-day reservations or to reach a guest, call the South Rim **switchboard** (📞928-638-2631). If you can't find accommodations in the national park, try Tusayan (at South Rim Entrance Station), Valle (31 miles south), Cameron (53 miles east), Williams (about 60 miles south) or Flagstaff (80 miles southeast). All campgrounds and lodges are open year-round except Desert View.

Phantom Ranch   CABIN $
(📞888-297-2757, same day or next-day reservations 928-638-3283; www.grandcanyonlodges.com; dm $49, cabin d $142; ❄) Bunks at this camplike complex on the canyon floor are spread across cozy private cabins sleeping up to four people and single-sex dorms for 10 people. Rates include bedding, liquid soap and towels, but meals are extra and must be reserved when booking your bunk. Phantom

Grand Canyon National Park

is only accessible by mule trip, on foot or via raft on the Colorado River.

Desert View Campground CAMPGROUND $
(www.nps.gov/grca; Desert View; campsites $12; ☺mid-Apr–mid-Oct) In a forest near the East Entrance, this first-come, first-served 50-site NPS campground is quieter than campgrounds in the Village, with a spread-out design that ensures a bit of privacy. The best time to secure a spot is mid-morning, when people are breaking camp. It usually fills by midafternoon. Facilities include toilets and drinking water, but no showers or hookups.

Trailer Village CARAVAN PARK $
(☎877-404-4611, same-day booking 928-638-1006; www.visitgrandcanyon.com; Trailer Village Rd; hookups $45; ☺year-round; ☐Village) A trailer park with RVs lined up tightly at paved pull-through sites on a rather barren patch of ground. You'll find picnic tables, barbecue grills and full hookups, but coin-operated showers and laundry are a quarter-mile away at **Mather Campground** (☎877-444-6777, late arrival 928-638-7851; www.recreation.gov; 1 Mather Campground Rd; sites $18; ☺year-round; ☎; ☐Village).

★**Bright Angel Lodge** LODGE $$
(☎888-297-2757, ext 6285, front desk & reservations within 48hr 928-638-2631; www.grandcanyonlodges.com; Village Loop Dr; r with/without bath $110/89, cabins/ste $197/426; [P]☎; ☐Village) This 1935 log-and-stone lodge on the canyon ledge delivers simple historic charm by the bucketload. Small public spaces bustle with activity, and the **transportation desk** (☎928-638-3283; Bright Angel Lodge; ☺5am-8pm summer; ☐Village) in the lobby is the central contact for hiking services, mule rides and guided trips. Though the lodges are an excellent economy option, historic cabins are brighter, airier and have tasteful Western character.

Yavapai Lodge MOTEL $$
(☎877-404-4611, reservations within 48hr 928-638-6421; www.visitgrandcanyon.com; 11 Yavapai Lodge Rd; r from $153; ☺year-round; [P]✳@☎✻; ☐Village) Basic one- and two-story motel-style lodgings cluster in the piñon and juniper forest about a mile from the rim. Air-conditioned rooms at Yavapai East sleep four to six, and offer two queen beds or a king and bunk beds. Rooms in

Yavapai West sleep up to four and do not have air-conditioning.

★ El Tovar
LODGE **$$$**

(☎ 888-297-2757, ext 6380, front desk & reservations within 48hr 928-638-2631; www.grandcanyon lodges.com; Village Loop Dr; r/ste from $187/381; ☺ year-round; P✱☎; ☐ Village) Stuffed mounts. Thick pine walls. Sturdy fireplaces. Is this the fanciest hotel on the South Rim or a backcountry hunting lodge? Despite renovations, this rambling 1905 wooden lodge hasn't lost a lick of its genteel historic patina, or its charm.

✖ Eating & Drinking

Grand Canyon Village has all the eating options you need, whether it's picking up picnic sandwiches at **Canyon Village Market** (☎ 928-638-2262; Market Plaza; ☺ 6:30am-9pm May 19–Sep 13, shorter hours rest of year; ☐ Village), an après-hike ice-cream cone at **Bright Angel Ice-Cream Fountain** (☎ 928-638-2631; www.grandcanyonlodges.com; Bright Angel Lodge; mains $4-6; ☺ 11am-6pm May-Sep, shorter hours rest of year; ♿; ☐ Village) or a sit-down celebratory dinner at El Tovar Dining Room.

Yavapai Lodge Restaurant
AMERICAN **$**

(☎ 928-638-6421; www.visitgrandcanyon.com; 11 Yavapai Lodge Rd, Yavapai Lodge; breakfast $7-9, lunch & dinner $13-16; ☺ 6am-10pm May-Sep, shorter hours rest of year; ♿; ☐ Village) The restaurant at the Yavapai Lodge serves barbecue and sandwiches as well as beer and wine. Place your order, pick up your drinks, and your number will get called when the food is ready.

★ El Tovar Dining Room & Lounge
AMERICAN **$$$**

(☎ 928-638-2631; www.grandcanyonlodges.com; National Historic Landmark District; mains $20-30; ☺ restaurant 6-10:30am, 11am-2pm & 4:30-10pm, lounge 11am-11pm; ♿; ☐ Village) Dark-wood tables are set with china and white linen, eye-catching murals spotlight American Indian tribes and huge windows frame views of the Rim Trail and canyon beyond. Breakfast options include El Tovar's pancake trio (buttermilk, blue cornmeal and buckwheat pancakes with pine-nut butter and prickly pear syrup), and blackened trout with two eggs.

Arizona Room
AMERICAN **$$$**

(☎ 928-638-2631; www.grandcanyonlodges.com; 9 Village Loop Dr, Bright Angel Lodge; lunch $13-16, dinner $22-28; ☺ 11:30am-3pm & 4:30-10pm Jan-Oct; ♿; ☐ Village) Antler chandeliers hang from the ceiling and picture windows overlook the Rim Trail and canyon beyond. Try to get on the waitlist when the doors open at 4:30pm, because by 4:40pm you may have an hour's wait – reservations are not accepted. Agave and citrus-marinated chicken, oven-roasted squash and ribs with chipotle barbecue give a Western vibe.

ⓘ Information

SOUTH RIM VISITOR CENTERS
Grand Canyon Visitor Center (☎ 928-638-7888; www.nps.gov/grca; Visitor Center Plaza, Grand Canyon Village; ☺ 9am-5pm; ☐ Village, ☐ Kaibab/Rim) Three hundred yards behind Mather Point, a large plaza holds the visitor center and the **Visitor Center Plaza Park Store** (☎ 800-858-2808; www.grandcanyon. org; Visitor Center Plaza; ☺ 8am-8pm Jun-Aug, shorter hours rest of year; ☐ Village, Kaibab/Rim). Outdoor bulletin boards display information about trails, tours, ranger programs and the weather.

National Geographic Visitor Center (☎ 928-638-2203; www.explorethecanyon.com; 450 Hwy 64; adult/child $14/11; ☺ visitor center 8am-10pm Mar-Oct, 10am-8pm Nov-Feb, theater 8:30am-8:30pm Mar-Oct, 9:30am-6:30pm Nov-Feb; ☐ Tusayan) In Tusayan, 7 miles south of Grand Canyon Village; pay your $30 vehicle entrance fee here to spare yourself a potentially long wait at the park entrance. The IMAX theater screens the terrific film *Grand Canyon – The Hidden Secrets*. In addition to the visitor centers already mentioned, information is available inside the park:

Desert View Watchtower (www.nps.gov/grca; Desert View, East Enrance; ☺ 8am-sunset mid-May–Aug, 9am-6pm Sep–mid-Oct, 9am-5pm mid-Oct–Feb, 8am-6pm Mar–mid-May)

Kolb Studio (☎ 928-638-2771; www.nps.gov/grca; National Historic Landmark District; ☺ 8am-7pm Mar-May & Sep-Nov, to 6pm Dec-Feb, to 8pm Jun-Aug; ☐ Village)

Tusayan Museum & Ruins (www.nps.gov/grca; Desert View Dr; ☺ 9am-5pm)

Verkamp's Visitor Center (☎ 928-638-7888; www.nps.gov/grca; Rim Trail; ☺ 8am-8pm Jun-Aug, shorter hrs rest of year; ☐ Village)

Yavapai Geology Museum (☎ 928-638-7890; www.nps.gov/grca; Grand Canyon Village; ☺ 8am-7pm Mar-May & Sep-Nov, to 6pm Dec-Feb, to 8pm Jun-Aug; ♿; ☐ Kaibab/Rim)

ⓘ Getting There & Around

Most people arrive at the canyon in private vehicles or on a tour. Parking can be a chore in Grand Canyon Village. Once inside the park, free park shuttles operate along three routes: around

Grand Canyon Village, west along Hermits Rest Route and east along Kaibab Trail Route. Buses typically run every 15 minutes, from one hour before sunset to one hour afterward. In summer a free shuttle from Bright Angel Lodge, the Hiker's Express, has early-morning pickups at the Backcountry Information Center and Grand Canyon Visitor Center, and then heads to the South Kaibab trailhead.

North Rim

Solitude reigns supreme on the North Rim. There are no shuttles or bus tours, no museums, shopping centers, schools or garages. In fact, there isn't much of anything here beyond a classic rimside national park lodge, a campground, a motel, a general store and miles of trails carving through sunny meadows thick with wildflowers, willowy aspen and towering ponderosa pines

The entrance to the North Rim is 24 miles south of **Jacob Lake** on Hwy 67; Grand Canyon Lodge lies another 20 miles beyond. At 8000ft, it's about 10°F (6°C) cooler here than the South Rim – even on summer evenings you'll need a sweater. All facilities on the North Rim are closed from mid-October to mid-May, although you can drive into the park and stay at the campground until snow closes the road from Jacob Lake.

🏃 Activities

The short and easy paved trail (0.5 miles) to **Bright Angel Point** (www.nps.gov; North Rim) is a canyon must. Beginning from the back porch of Grand Canyon Lodge, it goes to a narrow finger of an overlook with fabulous views.

The **North Kaibab Trail**, the North Rim's only maintained rim-to-river trail, connects with trails to the South Rim in the Phantom Ranch (p180) area. The first 4.7 miles are the steepest, dropping 3050ft to **Roaring Springs** – a popular all-day hike. If you prefer a shorter day hike below the rim, walk just 0.75 miles down to **Coconino Overlook**, or 2 miles to the **Supai Tunnel** to get a taste of steep inner-canyon hiking. The 28-mile round-trip to the Colorado River is a multiday affair.

For a short hike up on the rim, which works well for families, try the 4-mile round-trip **Cape Final Trail**, on the **Walhalla Plateau** east of Grand Canyon Lodge, which leads through ponderosa pines to sweeping views of the eastern Grand Canyon area.

Canyon Trail Rides TOURS
(🖉 435-679-8665; www.canyonrides.com; North Rim; 1hr/half-day mule ride $45/90; ⊙ schedules vary mid-May–mid-Oct) You can make reservations anytime for the upcoming year, but, unlike mule trips on the South Rim, you can usually book a trip upon your arrival at the park; just duck inside the Grand Canyon Lodge to the Mule Desk. Rides don't reach the Colorado River, but the half-day trip gives a taste of life below the rim.

🛏 Sleeping

North Rim Campground CAMPGROUND $
(🖉 877-444-6777, 928-638-7814; www.recreation. gov; tent sites $18, RV sites $18-25; ⊙ by reservation May 15-Oct 15, first-come, first-served Oct 16-31; 🐾) Operated by the National Park Service, this campground, 1.5 miles north of the Grand Canyon Lodge, offers shaded sites on level ground blanketed in pine needles. Sites 11, 14, 15, 16 and 18 overlook the Transept (a side canyon) and cost $25. There's water, a store, a snack bar, coin-operated showers and laundry facilities, but no hookups. Make reservations online.

⭐ **Grand Canyon Lodge** HISTORIC HOTEL $$
(🖉 advance reservations 877-386-4383, reservations outside USA 480-337-1320, same-day reservations 928-638-2611; www.grandcanyonlodgenorth.com; r/ cabins from $130/143; ⊙ May 15-Oct 15) 🌿 Walk through the front door of the lodge, and here, framed by picture windows, is the canyon in all its glory. Built in 1937 with wood, Kaibab limestone and glass, the lodge features a spacious rimside dining room and sun porches lined with Adirondack chairs. Guest rooms are not in the lodge itself – most accommodations are cozy log cabins nearby.

🍴 Eating

⭐ **Grand Canyon Lodge Dining Room** AMERICAN $$
(🖉 May-Oct 928-638-2611, Nov-Apr 928-645-6865; www.grandcanyonforever.com; breakfast $8-11, lunch $10-13, dinner $18-28; ⊙ 6:30-10:30am, 11:30am-2:30pm & 4:30-9:30pm May 15-Oct 15; 🖉 🕍) Although seats beside the window are wonderful, views from the dining room are so huge it really doesn't matter where you sit. While the solid dinner menu includes buffalo steak, western trout and several vegetarian options, don't expect great culinary memories – the view is the thing. Make reservations in advance of your arrival to guarantee a spot for dinner.

❶ Information

North Rim Backcountry Information Center
(☑ 928-638-7875; www.nps.gov/grca; Administrative Bldg; ☉ 8am-noon & 1-5pm May 15-Oct 15) Backcountry permits for overnight camping on and below the rim, at Tuweep Campground, or camping anytime between November 1 and May 14.

North Rim Visitor Center (☑ 928-638-7888; www.nps.gov/grca; ☉ 8am-6pm May 15-Oct 15) Beside Grand Canyon Lodge, this is the place to get information on the park, and the starting point for ranger-led nature walks.

❶ Getting There & Away

The only access road to the Grand Canyon North Rim is Hwy 67, which closes with the first snowfall and reopens in spring after the snowmelt (exact dates vary).

Although only 11 miles from the South Rim as the crow flies, it's a grueling 215-mile, four- to five-hour drive on winding desert roads between here and Grand Canyon Village. You can drive yourself or take the **Trans-Canyon Shuttle** (☑ 928-638-2820, 877-638-2820; www.trans-canyonshuttle.com; one-way rim to rim $90, one-way South Rim to Marble Canyon $80). Reserve at least two weeks in advance.

Around the Grand Canyon

Havasupai Canyon

In a hidden side canyon off the Colorado River, complete with stunning, spring-fed waterfalls and azure swimming holes, this beautiful spot is hard to reach, but the hike down and back up makes the trip unique – and an amazing adventure.

Located on the Havasupai Indian Reservation, Havasu Canyon is just 35 miles directly west of the South Rim, but it's more like 195 miles by road. The four falls lie 10 miles below the rim, accessed via a moderately challenging hiking trail that starts from Hualapai Hilltop, and is reached by following a 62-mile road that leaves Route 66 7 miles east of Peach Springs.

All trips require an overnight stay, which must be reserved in advance, and there's a $50 entrance fee for all guests.

The village of Supai, 8 miles along the trail, is home to **Supai Lodge** (☑ 928-448-2201, 928-448-2111; www.havasuwaterfalls.net; Supai; r for up to 4 people $145; ❈), where basic motel-style rooms have nothing to recom-

mend them bar the location. Check in by 5pm, when the lobby closes. A village cafe serves meals and accepts credit cards.

The **Havasu Campground** (☑ 928-448-2180, 928-448-2141, 928-448-2121, 928-443-2137; www.havasuwaterfalls.net; Havasu Canyon; sites per person per night $25), 2 miles beyond, has primitive campsites along a creek; every camper must pay an additional $10 environmental fee. Continue deeper into Havasu Canyon to reach the waterfalls and blue-green swimming holes. If you don't want to hike to Supai, call the lodge or campground to arrange for a mule or horse (one-way/round-trip to Lodge $121/242) to carry you there.

Hualapai Reservation

Run by the Hualapai Nation, around 215 driving miles west of the South Rim or 70 miles northeast of Kingman, the remote site known as Grand Canyon West is not part of Grand Canyon National Park. The rough road out here is partly unpaved, and unsuitable for RVs (though Joshua-tree forests and other scenic delights make it worth the effort).

Grand Canyon West (West Rim)   VIEWPOINT
(☑ 888-868-9378, 928-769-2636; www.grandcanyonwest.com; Hualapai Reservation; per person $44-81; ☉ 7am-7pm Apr-Sep, 8am-5pm Oct-Mar) Nowadays, the only way to visit Grand Canyon West, the section of the Grand Canyon overseen by the Hualapai Nation, is to purchase a package tour. These include a hop-on, hop-off shuttle ride, which loops to scenic points along the rim. Tours can include lunch, cowboy activities at an ersatz Western town and informal American Indian performances.

Northern & Eastern Arizona

Between the brooding buttes of Monument Valley, the blue waters of Lake Powell and the fossilized logs of the Petrified Forest National Park are photogenic lands locked in ancient history. Inhabited by Native Americans for centuries, this region is dominated by the Navajo reservation – widely known as the Navajo Nation – which spills into surrounding states. The Hopi reservation is here as well, completely surrounded by Navajo land.

Lake Powell

The country's second-largest artificial reservoir, Lake Powell, stretches north from Arizona into Utah. Set amid striking red-rock formations, sharply cut canyons and dramatic desert scenery, and part of the **Glen Canyon National Recreation Area** (☑928-608-6200; www.nps.gov/glca; 7-day pass per vehicle $25, per pedestrian or cyclist $12), it's water-sports heaven

The lake was created by the construction of Glen Canyon Dam, 2.5 miles north of what's now the region's central town, Page. The Carl Hayden Visitor Center is located beside the dam.

To visit other-worldly **Antelope Canyon**, a stunning sandstone slot canyon, you must join a Navajo-led tour. Several tour companies offer trips into **Upper Antelope Canyon**, which is easier to navigate. Expect a bumpy ride and a bit of a cattle call; try **Roger Ekis' Antelope Canyon Tours** (☑928-645-9102; www.antelopecanyon.com; 22 S Lake Powell Blvd; adult/child 5-12yr from $45/35). The more strenuous **Lower Antelope Canyon** sees much smaller crowds.

A deservedly popular hike is the 1.5 mile round-trip to **Horseshoe Bend**, where the Colorado wraps around a dramatic stone outcropping to form a perfect U on a jaw-dropping scale. The trailhead is south of Page off Hwy 89, across from mile marker 541.

Chain hotels line Page's main strip, Hwy89, but there are independent alternatives along 8th Ave. The revamped **Lake Powell Motel** (☑480-452-9895; www.lakepow ellmotel.net; 750 S Navajo Dr; ste from $99, r with kitchen from $139; ☺Apr-Oct; ❄️🐾) was originally built to house workers building the Glen Canyon Dam; four of its units have kitchens, and book up quickly, while a fifth, smaller room is usually held for walk-ins.

For breakfast in Page, the **Ranch House Grille** (☑928-645-1420; www.ranchhousegrille. com; 819 N Navajo Dr; mains $9-14; ☺6am-3pm) has good food, huge portions and fast service. If you're in need of a more substantial feed, later in the day, **Big John's Texas BBQ** (☑928-645-3300; www.bigjohnstexasbbq. com; 153 S Lake Powell Blvd; mains $13-18; ☺11am-10pm; 🐾) is an unabashed celebration of meat and smoke.

Navajo Nation

The Navajo Nation is vast: at 27,000 sq miles it's bigger than some US states, and spreads across the junction of Arizona, New Mexico, Colorado and Utah. It also contains natural beauty of staggering richness, and, of course, the living culture, language, institutions, farms and homes of the Diné (Navajo) America's largest Indian nation.

Unlike the rest of Arizona, the Navajo Nation observes mountain daylight saving time. During summer, the reservation is one hour ahead of Arizona. For details about hiking and camping, and required permits, visit www.navajonationparks.org.

CAMERON

Cameron, a historic settlement that serves as the gateway to the east entrance of the Grand Canyon's South Rim, is one of the few worthwhile stops on Hwy 89 between Flagstaff and Page. The Cameron Trading Post, just north of the Hwy 64 turnoff to the Grand Canyon, offers food, lodging, a gift shop and a post office.

NAVAJO NATIONAL MONUMENT

The sublimely well-preserved Ancestral Puebloan cliff dwellings of Betatakin and Keet Seel are protected within the **Navajo National Monument** (☑928-672-2700; www. nps.gov/nava; Hwy 564; ☺visitor center 8am-5:30pm Jun-early Sep, 9am-5pm early Sep-May) **FREE** and can only be reached on foot. This walk in the park is no walk in the park, but there's truly something magical about approaching these ancient stone villages in relative solitude, among the piñon and juniper. The National Park Service controls access to the site and maintains the visitor center, which is informative and has excellent staff.

During summer months the park observes daylight saving time.

CANYON DE CHELLY NATIONAL MONUMENT

The many-fingered Canyon De Chelly (duh-shay) contains several beautiful Ancestral Puebloan sites, including ancient cliff dwellings. For centuries, though, it has been home to Navajo farmers, who winter on the rims then move to hogans (traditional roundhouses) on the canyon floor in spring and summer. The canyon is private Navajo property administered by the NPS. Enter hogans only with a guide and don't photograph people without their permission.

The only lodging in the park is **Thunderbird Lodge** (☑928-674-5842, 800-679-2473; http://thunderbirdlodge.com; Rural Rte 7; d/ste $100/110; ❄️🐾🐾), just outside the canyon itself. It has comfortable rooms and an inexpensive cafeteria serving Navajo and American meals. The nearby Navajo-run campground has about 90 sites on a first-come, first-served basis ($10), with water but no showers.

The Canyon de Chelly **visitor center** (📞 928-674-5500; www.nps.gov/cach; ☉ 8am-5pm) is 3 miles off Rte 191, beyond the small village of Chinle, near the mouth of the canyon. Two scenic drives follow the canyon's rim, but you can only explore the canyon floor on a guided tour. Stop by the visitor center, or check the park website, for a list of tour companies. The only unguided hiking trail you can follow in the park is a short but very spectacular round-trip route that descends to the amazing **White House Ruin**.

MONUMENT VALLEY NAVAJO TRIBAL PARK

When Monument Valley rises into sight from the desert floor, you realize you've always known it. Its brick-red spindles, sheer-walled mesas and grand buttes, stars of countless films, TV commercials and magazine ads, are part of the modern consciousness. And Monument Valley's epic beauty is only heightened by the barren landscape surrounding it: one minute you're in the middle of sand, rocks and infinite sky, then suddenly you're transported to a fantasyland of crimson sandstone towers, thrusting up to 1200ft skyward.

For up-close views of the towering formations, visit the **Monument Valley Navajo Tribal Park** (📞 435-727-5870; www.navajo nationparks.org; per 4-person vehicle $20; ☉ drive 6am-7pm Apr-Sep, 8am-4:30pm Oct-Mar, visitor center 6am-8pm Apr-Sep, 8am-5pm Oct-Mar; 🅿️), where a rough and unpaved scenic driving loop covers 17 miles of stunning valley views. You can drive it yourself, or arrange a tour through one of the kiosks in the parking lot, which will take you to areas where private vehicles can't go (1½ hours $75; two-hour trail ride $98).

Inside the tribal park, the sandstone-colored **View Hotel** (📞 435-727-5555; www.monumentvalleyview.com; Indian Rte 42; r/ste from $247/349; ❄️@🛜) blends naturally with its surroundings, and most of the 96 rooms have private balconies facing the monuments. The Navajo-accented food at the adjoining restaurant (mains $11 to $15, no alcohol) aren't life-changing, but the vista makes up for all.

The peerlessly-situated **View Campground** (📞 435-727-5802; http://monument valleyview.com/campground; Indian Rte 42; tent/RV sites $20/40) is a cheaper option, while historic **Goulding's Lodge** (📞 435-727-3231; www.gouldings.com; Monument Valley, Utah; d/ste from $184/199; 🅿️❄️🛜❄️❄️), just over the road in Utah, offers basic rooms, camping and small cabins. Book early for summer. Kayenta, 20 miles south, has a handful of acceptable motels and borderline-acceptable restaurants; try the **Wetherill Inn** (📞 928-697-3231; www.wetherill-inn.com; 1000 Main St/Hwy 163; r $149; ❄️🛜❄️) if everything in Monument Valley is booked.

SOUTHWEST NORTHERN & EASTERN ARIZONA

RAFTING THE COLORADO

A boat trip down the Colorado is an epic, adrenaline-pumping adventure, which will take you beyond contact with civilization for several nights. The biggest single drop at Lava Falls plummets 37ft in just 300yd. But the true highlight is experiencing the Grand Canyon by looking up, not down from the rim. Its human history comes alive in ruins, wrecks and rock art. Commercial trips run from three days to three weeks and vary in the type of watercraft used.

Arizona Raft Adventures (📞 800-786-7238, 928-526-8200; www.azraft.com; 6-day Upper Canyon hybrid/paddle trips $2097/2197, 10-day Full Canyon motor trips $3160) This multigenerational-family-run outfit offers motor, paddle, oar and hybrid (with opportunities for both paddling and floating) trips. Music fans can join one of the folk and bluegrass trips, with professional pickers and banjo players providing background music.

Arizona River Runners (📞 602-867-4866, 800-477-7238; www.raftarizona.com; 6-day Upper Canyon oar trip $1984, 8-day Full Canyon motor trip $2772) At their game since 1970, this outfit offers oar-powered and motorized trips. Arizona River Runners specializes in family trips as well as 'Hiker's Special' trips that take place over six to 12 days in the cooler temperatures of April. The company also caters to travelers with special needs, offering departures for people with disabilities.

Petrified Forest National Park

Home not only to an extraordinary array of fossilized logs that predate the dinosaurs but also the multicolored sandscape of the Painted Desert, this **national park** (📞928-524-6228; www.nps.gov/pefo; vehicle $20, walk-in/bicycle/motorcycle $10; ⊘7am-7pm Mar-Sep, shorter hours Oct-Feb) is a compulsory spectacle. The park straddles I-40 at exit 311, 25 miles east of **Holbrook**. Its **visitor center** (📞928-524-6228; www.nps.gov; 1 Park Rd, Petrified Forest National Park; ⊘8am-5pm), just half a mile north of I-40, holds maps and information on guided tours, while the 28-mile paved park road beyond offers a splendid scenic drive. There are no campsites, but a number of short trails, ranging from less than a mile to 2 miles, pass through the stands of petrified trees and ancient Native American dwellings. Those prepared for rugged backcountry camping need to pick up a free permit at the visitor center.

Western Arizona

The Colorado River is alive with sun worshippers at Lake Havasu City, while Route 66 offers well-preserved stretches of classic highway near Kingman. Much further south, beyond I-10 towards Mexico, the wild, empty landscape is among the most barren in the West. If you're already here, there are some worthwhile sites, but there's nothing worth planning an itinerary around unless you're a Route 66 or boating fanatic.

Kingman & Around

Among Route 66 aficionados, Kingman is known as the main hub of the longest uninterrupted stretch of the historic highway, running from Topock to Seligman. Among its early-20th-century buildings is the former Methodist church at 5th and Spring Sts where Clark Gable and Carole Lombard eloped in 1939. Hometown hero Andy Devine had his Hollywood breakthrough as the perpetually befuddled driver of the eponymous *Stagecoach* in John Ford's Oscar-winning 1939 movie.

Pick up maps and brochures at the historic **Kingman Visitor Center** (📞866-427-7866, 928-753-6106; www.gokingman.com; 120 W Andy Devine Ave; ⊘8am-5pm), housed in an old powerhouse and entailing a small but engaging Route 66 museum and a display of electric cars.

A cool neon sign draws road-trippers to the **Hilltop Motel** (📞928-753-2198; www.hilltopmotelaz.com; 1901 E Andy Devine Ave; r from $44; ❄@🛜🐾) on Route 66. Rooms are basic-but-comfortable (thanks to a heritage grant) but the views, retro style and price can't be beaten. Pets (dogs only) stay for $5. There's tasty pit-smoked meats at **Floyd & Co Real Pit BBQ** (📞928-757-8227; www.redneckssouthernpitbbq.com; 420 E Beale St; mains $9-13; ⊘11am-8pm Tue-Sat; 🐾) and commendable coffee at **Beale Street Brews** (📞928-753-1404; www.bealestreetbrews.net; 510 E Beale St; ⊘6am-6pm; 🛜).

Southern Arizona

This is a land of Stetsons and spurs, where cowboy ballads are sung around the campfire under starry, black-velvet skies and thick steaks sizzle on the grill. Anchored by the bustling college town of Tucson, it's a vast region, where long, dusty highways slide past rolling vistas and steep, pointy mountain ranges. Majestic saguaro cacti, the symbol of the region, stretch out as far as the eye can see.

Tucson

A college town with a long history, Tucson (*too*-sawn) is attractive, fun-loving and one of the most culturally invigorating places in the Southwest. Set in a flat valley hemmed in by snaggletoothed mountains and swathes of saguaro, Arizona's second-largest city smoothly blends American Indian, Spanish, Mexican and Anglo traditions. Distinct neighborhoods and 19th-century buildings give a rich sense of community and history not found in the more modern, sprawling Phoenix. The eclectic shops toting vintage garb, scores of funky restaurants and dive bars don't let you forget Tucson is a college town at heart, home turf to the 40,000-strong University of Arizona.

⊙ Sights & Activities

Downtown Tucson and the historic district lie east of I-10 exit 258. The University of Arizona campus is a mile northeast of downtown; 4th Ave, the main drag here, is packed with cafes, bars and interesting shops. Many of Tucson's most fabulous treasures lie on the periphery, or even beyond town.

Presidio Historic District AREA
(www.nps.gov/nr/travel/amsw/sw7.htm) The Tucson Museum of Art (p187) is part of this low-key neighborhood, bounded by W 6th St, W Alameda St, N Stone Ave and Granada Ave, and embracing the site of the original Spanish fort and upmarket 'Snob Hollow.' This is one of the oldest continually inhabited places in North America: the Spanish **Presidio de San Agustín del Tucson** dates back to 1775, but the fort itself was built over a Hohokam site that has been dated to AD 700 to 900.

Barrio Histórico
District (Barrio Viejo) AREA
This compact neighborhood was an important business district in the late 19th century. Today it's home to funky shops and galleries in brightly painted adobe houses. The barrio is bordered by I-10, Stone Ave and Cushing and 17th Sts.

★ **Arizona-Sonora Desert Museum** MUSEUM
(🖉520-883-2702; www.desertmuseum.org; 2021 N Kinney Rd; adult/senior/child 3-12yr $20.50/18.50/8; ☉8:30am-5pm Oct-Feb, 7:30am-5pm Mar-Sep, incl 10pm Sat Jun-Aug) Home to cacti, coyotes and palm-sized hummingbirds, this 98-acre ode to the Sonoran Desert is one-part zoo, one-part botanical garden and one-part museum – a trifecta that'll entertain young and old for easily half a day. Desert denizens, from precocious coatis to playful prairie dogs, inhabit natural enclosures, the grounds are thick with desert plants, and docents give demonstrations. Strollers and wheelchairs are available, and there's a gift shop, an art gallery, a restaurant and a cafe.

Arizona State Museum MUSEUM
(🖉520-621-6302; www.statemuseum.arizona.edu; 1013 E University Blvd; adult/child 17yr & under $5/free; ☉10am-5pm Mon-Sat) To learn more about the history and culture of the region's American Indian tribes, visit the Arizona State Museum, the oldest and largest anthropology museum in the Southwest. The exhibit covering the tribes' cultural history is extensive but easy to navigate, and should appeal to newbies and history buffs alike. These galleries are complemented by much-envied collections of minerals and Navajo textiles.

Reid Park Zoo ZOO
(🖉520-791-3204; https://reidparkzoo.org; 3400 E Zoo Ct; adult/senior/child 2-14yr $11/8.50/6.50; ☉9am-4pm Oct-May, 8am-3pm Jun-Sep; 🖝) At the compact Reid Park Zoo, a global menag-

HOPI INDIAN RESERVATION

Direct descendants of the Ancestral Puebloans, the Hopi have arguably changed less in the last five centuries than any other Native American group. Their village of Old Oraibi may be the oldest continuously inhabited settlement in North America. Hopi land is surrounded on all sides by the Navajo Nation. Hwy 264 runs past the three mesas (First, Second and Third Mesa) that form the heart of the reservation.

On Second Mesa, 8 miles west of First Mesa, the **Hopi Cultural Center Restaurant & Inn** (🖉928-734-2401; www.hopiculturalcenter.com; Hwy 264, Mile 379; r $115; ☉restaurant 7am-9pm summer, to 8pm winter) is as visitor-oriented as things get on the Hopi reservation. It provides food and lodging, and holds the small **Hopi Museum** (🖉928-734-6650; Hwy 264, Mile 379; adult/child 12yr & under $3/1; ☉8am-5pm Mon-Fri, 9am-3pm Sat; 🅿), filled with historic photographs and cultural exhibits.

Photographs, sketching and recording are not allowed anywhere on the reservation.

erie, including grizzly bears, jaguars, giant anteaters and pygmy hippos, delights young and old. Cap a visit with a picnic in the surrounding park, which also has playgrounds and a pond with paddleboat rentals.

Old Tucson Studios FILM LOCATION
(🖉520-883-0100; www.oldtucson.com; 201 S Kinney Rd; adult/child 4-11yr $19/11; ☉10am-5pm daily Feb-Apr, 10am-5pm Fri-Sun May, 10am-5pm Sat & Sun Jun-early Sep; 🅿🖝) Nicknamed 'Hollywood in the Desert,' this old movie set of Tucson in the 1860s was built in 1939 for the filming of *Arizona*. Hundreds of flicks followed, bringing in movie stars from Clint Eastwood to Leonardo DiCaprio. Now a Wild West theme park, it's all about shoot-outs, stagecoach rides, stunt shows and dancing saloon girls. Closed from early September to the end of January, it does open for 'Nightfall' after-dark ghost tours in October.

Tucson Museum of Art MUSEUM
(🖉520-624-2333; www.tucsonmuseumofart.org; 140 N Main Ave; adult $12, senior & student $10, child 13-17yr $7; ☉10am-5pm Tue-Sat, noon-5pm

Sun) For a small city, Tucson boasts an impressive art museum. There's a respectable collection of American, Latin American and modern art, and the permanent exhibition of pre-Columbian artifacts will awaken your inner Indiana Jones. The special exhibits are varied and interesting, there's a superb gift shop, and the block surrounding the building holds a number of notable historic homes. The museum stays open to 8pm on the first Thursday of the month, when admission is free from 5pm.

Tucson Children's Museum MUSEUM
(☑520-792-9985; www.childrensmuseumtucson. org; 200 S 6th Ave; $8; ☺9am-5pm Tue-Fri, 10am-5pm Sat & Sun; ☀) Parents sing the praises of the Tucson Children's Museum, which has plenty of engaging, hands-on exhibits – from Dinosaur World to Wee World (as in tiny) and an aquarium.

🎉 Festivals & Events

Tucson Gem & Mineral Show CULTURAL
(☑520-332-5773; www.tgms.org; ☺Feb) The most famous event on the city's calendar, held on the second full weekend in February, this is the largest gem and mineral show in the world. An estimated 250 retail dealers who trade in minerals, crafts and fossils take over the Tucson Convention Center.

Fiesta de los Vaqueros RODEO
(Rodeo Week; ☑520-741-2233; www.tucsonrodeo. com; 4823 S 6th Ave, Tucson Rodeo Grounds; tickets $15-70; ☺last week of Feb) Held in the last week of February for nearly a century, the Fiesta de los Vaqueros brings world-famous cowboys to town and features a spectacular parade with Western-themed floats and buggies, historical horse-drawn coaches, folk dancers and marching bands.

🛏 Sleeping

Lodging prices vary considerably, with lower rates in summer and fall. To sleep under the stars and saguaros, try **Gilbert Ray Campground** (☑520-724-5000; www.pima.gov; 8451 W McCain Loop Rd; tent/RV sites $10/20; ☀) near the western district of Saguaro National Park.

★**Hotel Congress** HISTORIC HOTEL $$
(☑800-722-8848, 520-622-8848; www.hotel congress.com; 311 E Congress St; d from $109; 🅿✳🛜☀) Perhaps Tucson's most famous hotel, this is where infamous bank robber John Dillinger and his gang were captured during their 1934 stay, when a fire broke out. Built in 1919 and beautifully restored, this charismatic place feels very modern, despite period furnishings such as rotary phones and wooden radios (but no TVs). There's a popular cafe, bar and club on-site.

ROADSIDE ATTRACTIONS ON ROUTE 66

Route 66 enthusiasts will find 400 miles of America's Highway stretching across Arizona, including the longest uninterrupted portion of old road left in the country, between Seligman and Topock. The **Mother Road** (www.azrt66.com) connects the dots between gun-slinging Oatman, Kingman's mining settlements, Williams' 1940s-vintage downtown and Winslow's windblown streets, with plenty of kitschy sights, listed here from west to east, along the way.

Wild burros of Oatman Feral mules, the progeny of mining days, beg for treats in the middle of the road.

Grand Canyon Caverns & Inn (☑928-422-3223, 855-498-6969; www.grandcanyoncav erns.com; Mile 115, Rte 66; tour adult/child from $16/11; ☺8am-6pm May-Sep, call for off-season hours) A guided tour 21 stories underground loops past mummified bobcats, civil-defense supplies and an $800 motel room (or cave).

Burma Shave signs Red-and-white ads from a bygone era between Grand Canyon Caverns and Seligman.

Snow Cap Drive-In (☑928-422-3291; 301 Rte 66; mains $5-6.50; ☺10am-6pm Mar-Nov) Prankish burger and ice-cream joint open in Seligman since 1953.

Meteor Crater (☑800-289-5898, 928-289-5898; www.meteorcrater.com; Meteor Crater Rd; adult/senior/child 6-17yr $18/16/9; ☺7am-7pm Jun–mid-Sep, 8am-5pm mid-Sep–May; 🅿♿) A 550ft-deep pockmark that's nearly 1 mile across, 38 miles east of Flagstaff.

Wigwam Motel (☑928-524-3048; www.galerie-kokopelli.com/wigwam; 811 W Hopi Dr; r $56-62; ✳) Concrete wigwams with hickory logpole furniture in Holbrook.

★ **Desert Trails B&B** B&B $$
(✆520-885-7295; www.deserttrails.com; 12851 E Speedway Blvd; r/guesthouse from $140/175; ❀ 🛜 🞮) Outdoorsy types who want a personable B&B close to Saguaro National Park (Rincon Mountain District) have their answer at Desert Trails on Tucson's eastern fringe. Rooms are comfy with all the latest amenities. John Higgins, an avid backpacker, was a fireman for Saguaro National Park for six years and is glad to share his knowledge about the park's trails.

Aloft Tucson HOTEL $$
(✆520-908-6800; www.starwoodhotels.com; 1900 E Speedway Blvd; d from $145; ❀ 🛜) Tucson is surprisingly light on for stylish hotels. The new Aloft, near the university, isn't an indie property, but it is a slick operation catering to tech-minded, style-conscious travelers. Rooms and common areas pop with bright, spare, yet inviting decor, there's an on-site bar, and 24-hour grab 'n' go food is available beside the lobby.

★ **Hacienda del Sol** RANCH $$$
(✆520-299-1501; www.haciendadelsol.com; 5501 N Hacienda del Sol Rd; d/ste from $209/339; ❀ @ 🛜 🞮) An elite hilltop girls' school built in the 1920s, this relaxing refuge has artist-designed Southwest-style rooms and teems with unique touches like carved ceiling beams and louvered exterior doors to catch the courtyard breeze. The Hacienda del Sol has sheltered Spencer Tracy, Katharine Hepburn, John Wayne and other legends, so you'll be sleeping with history. Its restaurant, the Grill, is fabulous too.

✖ **Eating**

Diablo Burger BURGERS $
(✆520-882-2007; www.diabloburger.com; 312 E Congress St; burgers $10-12; ⊙11am-9pm Sun-Wed, to 10pm Thu-Sat) This satellite of Flagstaff's popular burger joint does a mean patty of open-range, locally sourced beef. Try the Big Daddy Kane, with sharp cheddar, pickles and special sauce. The herby 'Belgian-style' fries are salty, but so good.

★ **Lovin' Spoonfuls** VEGAN $
(✆520-325-7766; www.lovinspoonfuls.com; 2990 N Campbell Ave; breakfast $6-9, lunch $5.25-8, dinner $7.25-11.25; ⊙9:30am-9pm Mon-Sat, 10am-3pm Sun; 🞦) Burgers, country-fried chicken and club sandwiches – the menu reads like one at your typical diner but there's a big difference: no animal products will ever find

their way into this vegan haven. Outstandingly creative choices include the Old Pueblo bean burrito and Buddha's Delight – a gingery stir-fry of cabbage, shiitake and other goodies over brown rice.

★ **Cafe Poca Cosa** MEXICAN $$
(✆520-622-6400; www.cafepocacosatucson.com; 110 E Pennington St; lunch $13-15, dinner $20-24; ⊙11am-9pm Tue-Thu, to 10pm Fri & Sat) Chef Suzana Davila's award-winning nuevo-Mexican bistro is a must for fans of Mexican food in Tucson. A Spanish-English blackboard menu circulates between tables because dishes change twice daily – it's all freshly prepared, innovative and beautifully presented. The undecided can't go wrong by ordering the 'Plato Poca Cosa' and letting Suzana decide what's best. Great margaritas, too.

El Charro Café MEXICAN $$
(✆520-622-1922; www.elcharrocafe.com; 311 N Court Ave; lunch $10-12, dinner $16-20; ⊙10am-9pm) This rambling, buzzing hacienda has been making great Mexican food on this site since 1922. It's particularly famous for the *carne seca,* sundried lean beef that's been reconstituted, shredded and grilled with green chile and onions. The fabulous margaritas pack a burro-stunning punch, and help while away the time as you wait for your table.

🍷 **Drinking & Entertainment**

Congress St in downtown and 4th Ave near the University of Arizona are both busy party strips.

★ **Che's Lounge** BAR
(✆520-623-2088; http://cheslounge.com; 350 N 4th Ave; ⊙noon-2am) This slightly grungy but hugely popular watering hole does cheap Pabst Blue Ribbon and features a huge wraparound bar and fantastic murals by local artist (and bartender) Donovan. A popular college hangout, Che's rocks with live music most Saturday nights and on the patio on Sunday afternoons (4pm to 7pm) in the summer.

IBT's GAY
(✆520-882-3053; www.ibtstucson.com; 616 N 4th Ave; ⊙noon-2am) At Tucson's most sizzling gay fun house, the theme changes nightly – from drag shows to karaoke – plus the monthly Sunday 'Fun Day,' with karaoke, DJs and drink specials all day. Chill on the

DON'T MISS

MINI TIME MACHINE OF MUSEUM OF MINIATURES

Divided into the Enchanted Realm, Exploring the World and the History Gallery, this delightful **museum** (☑520-881-0606; www.theminitimemachine.org; 4455 E Camp Lowell Dr; adult/senior/child 4-17yr $9/8/6; ☺9am-4pm Tue-Sat, noon-4pm Sun; ⊞) of miniatures presents dioramas fantastical, historical and plain intriguing. You can also walk over a snow-globe-y Christmas village, peer into tiny homes constructed in the 1700s and 1800s, and search for the little inhabitants of a magical tree. The museum grew from a personal collection in the 1930s. Parents may find themselves having more fun than their kids.

patio, check out the bods or sweat it out on the dance floor.

Thunder Canyon Brewery   MICROBREWERY
(☑520-396-3480; www.thundercanyonbrewery. com; 220 E Broadway Blvd; ☺11am-11pm Sun-Thu, to midnight Fri & Sat) This cavernous microbrewery, within walking distance of the Hotel Congress, has more than 40 beers on tap, serving up its own creations as well as handcrafted beers from across the US. There's now a second location at 1234 N Williams St.

Club Congress   LIVE MUSIC
(☑520-622-8848; www.hotelcongress.com; 311 E Congress St; ☺live music from 7pm, club nights from 10pm) Skinny jeansters, tousled hipsters, aging folkies, dressed-up hotties – the crowd at Tucson's most happening club inside the grandly aging Hotel Congress defines the word eclectic. And so does the musical lineup, which usually features the finest local and regional talent, and DJs some nights. And for a no-fuss drink, there's the Lobby Bar for cocktails, or the Tap Room, open since 1919.

❶ Information

General information on Tucson is available from the **Tucson Visitor Center** (☑800-638-8350, 520-624-1817; www.visittucson.org; 811 N Euclid Ave; ☺9am-5pm Mon-Fri, to 4pm Sat & Sun), while specific information on access and camping in the Coronado National Forest can be found at the downtown **Coronado National Forest Supervisor's Office** (☑520-388-8300; www.fs.usda.gov/coronado; 300 W Congress St, Federal Bldg; ☺8am-4:30pm Mon-Fri).

❶ Getting There & Around

Tucson International Airport (☑520-573-8100; www.flytucson.com; 7250 S Tucson Blvd; ☎) is 15 miles south of downtown and served by six airlines, with nonstop flights to destinations including Atlanta, Denver, Las Vegas, Los Angeles and San Francisco.

Greyhound (☑520-792-3475; www.grey hound.com; 471 W Congress St) runs seven buses to Phoenix (from $10, two hours), among other destinations.

The *Sunset Limited*, operated by **Amtrak** (☑800-872-7245, 520-623-4442; www.amtrak. com; 400 N Toole Ave), comes through on its way west to Los Angeles (10 hours, three weekly) and east to New Orleans (36 hours, three weekly).

The **Ronstadt Transit Center** (215 E Congress St, at 6th Ave) is the main hub for the public buses with **Sun Tran** (☑520-792-9222; www. suntran.com) that serve the entire metro area. Single/day fares are $1.50/4 using the SunGo smart card. The same fares apply on the new streetcar line **SunLink**.

Around Tucson

All the places listed here are less than 1½ hours' drive from Tucson, and make great day trips.

Saguaro National Park

Saguaros (sah-wah-ros) are icons of the American Southwest, and an entire cactus army of these majestic, ribbed sentinels is protected in this desert **playground** (☑Rincon 520-733-5153, Tucson 520-733-5158, park information 520-733-5100; www.nps.gov/sagu; 7-day pass per vehicle/bicycle $10/5; ☺sunrise-sunset). Or, more precisely, playgrounds: the park is divided into east and west units, separated by 30 miles and Tucson itself. Both sections – the Rincon Mountain District in the east and Tucson Mountain District in the west – are filled with trails and desert flora; if you only visit one, make it the spectacular western half.

The larger section is the **Rincon Mountain District**, about 15 miles east of downtown. The **Red Hills Visitor Center** (☑520-733-5158; www.nps.gov/sagu; 2700 N Kinney Rd; ☺9am-5pm) has information on day hikes, horseback riding and backcountry camping. The camping requires a permit ($8 per site per day) and must be obtained by noon on the day of your hike. The meandering 8-mile **Cactus Forest Scenic Loop Drive**, a paved road open to cars and bicycles, provides access to picnic areas, trailheads and viewpoints.

Hikers pressed for time should follow the 1-mile round-trip **Freeman Homestead Trail** to a grove of massive saguaro. For a full-fledged desert adventure, head out on the steep and rocky Tanque Verde Ridge Trail, which climbs to the summit of Mica Mountain (8666ft) and back in 20 miles (backcountry camping permit required for overnight use). If you'd rather someone (or something) else did the hard work, family-run **Houston's Horseback Riding** (☎520-298-7450; www.tucsonhorsebackriding. com; 12801 E Speedway Blvd; per person 2hr tour $60) offers trail rides in the eastern section of the Park.

West of town, the **Tucson Mountain District** has its own branch of the Red Hills Visitor Center. The **Scenic Bajada Loop Drive** is a 6-mile graded dirt road through cactus forest that begins 1.5 miles north of the visitor center. Two quick, easy and rewarding hikes are the 0.8-mile **Valley View Overlook** (awesome at sunset) and the half-mile **Signal Hill Trail** to scores of ancient petroglyphs. For a more strenuous trek we recommend the 7-mile **King Canyon Trail**, which starts 2 miles south of the visitor center, near the Arizona-Sonora Desert Museum. The 0.5-mile informative **Desert Discovery Trail**, which is one mile northwest of the visitor center, is wheelchair accessible. Distances for all four hikes are round-trip.

As for the park's namesake cactus, don't refer to the limbs of the saguaro as branches. As park docents will quickly tell you, the mighty saguaro grows arms, not lowly branches – a distinction that makes sense when you consider their human-like features.

Saguaros grow slowly, taking about 15 years to reach a foot in height, 50 years to reach 7ft and almost a century before they begin to take on their typical many-armed appearance. The best time to visit is April, when the cacti begin blossoming with lovely white blooms – Arizona's state flower. By June and July, the flowers give way to ripe red fruit that local American Indians use for food. Their foot soldiers are the spidery ocotillo, the fluffy teddy bear cactus, the green-bean-like pencil cholla and hundreds of other plant species. It is illegal to damage or remove saguaros.

Note that trailers longer than 35ft and vehicles wider than 8ft are not permitted on the park's narrow scenic loop roads.

HOT DIGGITY DOG

The Sonoran hot dog is a local specialty, a palm-held heart attack comprising a bacon-wrapped hot dog layered with tomatillo salsa, pinto beans, shredded cheese, mayo, ketchup, mustard, chopped tomatoes and onions. They may not be for everyone, but the curious should head to where they're done best – **El Guero Canelo** (☎520-295-9005; www.elguerocanelo.com; 5201 S 12th Ave; hot dogs $3-4, mains $7-9; ⊗10am-10pm Sun-Thu, 8:30am-midnight Fri & Sat).

West of Tucson

You want wide solitude? Follow Hwy 86 west from Tuscon into some of the emptiest parts of the Sonoran Desert – except for the ubiquitous green-and-white border-patrol trucks. The lofty **Kitt Peak National Observatory** (☎520-318-8726; www.noao.edu/kpno; Hwy 86; tours adult/child $9.75/3.25; ⊗9am-4pm; ♠) **FREE**, about a 75-minute drive from Tucson, features the largest collection of optical telescopes in the world. Guided tours (adult/child $10/3.25, at 10am, 11:30am and 1:30pm) last about an hour. Book two to four weeks in advance for the worthwhile nightly observing program (adult $50; no programs from mid-July through August).

Clear, dry skies equal an awe-inspiring glimpse of the cosmos. Dress warmly, buy gas in Tucson (the nearest gas station is 30 miles from the observatory) and note that children under eight years of age are not allowed at the evening program. The picnic area draws amateur astronomers at night

If you truly want to get away from it all, you can't get much further off the grid than the huge and exotic **Organ Pipe Cactus National Monument** (☎520-387-6849; www.nps. gov/orpi; Hwy 85; per vehicle $12; ⊗visitor center 8:30am-5pm) along the Mexican border. It's a gorgeous, forbidding land that supports an astonishing number of animals and plants, including 28 species of cacti, first and foremost its namesake organ-pipe. A giant columnar cactus, it differs from the more prevalent saguaro in that its branches radiate from the base.

The 21-mile **Ajo Mountain Drive** takes you through a spectacular landscape of steep-sided, jagged cliffs and rock tinged a faintly hellish red. There are 208 first-come, first-served sites at **Twin Peaks Campground** (☑520-387-6849, ext 7302; www.nps. gov/orpi; 10 Organ Pipe Dr; tent & RV sites $16) by the visitor center.

South of Tuscon

South of Tucson, I-19 is the main route to Nogales and Mexico. Along the way are several interesting stops.

The magnificent **Mission San Xavier del Bac** (☑520-294-2624; www.patronatosanxavier. org; 1950 W San Xavier Rd; donations appreciated; ☺museum 8:30am-4:30pm, church 7am-5pm), on the San Xavier reservation 9 miles south of downtown Tucson, is Arizona's oldest Hispanic-era building still in use. Completed in 1797, it's a graceful blend of Moorish, Byzantine and late-Mexican Renaissance architecture, with an unexpectedly ornate interior.

At exit 69, 16 miles south of the mission, the **Titan Missile Museum** (☑520-625-7736; www.titanmissilemuseum.org; 1580 Duval Mine Rd, Sahuarita; adult/senior/child 7-12yr $9.50/8.50/6; ☺9:45am-5pm Sun-Fri, 8:45am-5pm Sat, last tour 3:45pm) features an underground launch site for Cold War–era intercontinental ballistic missiles. Tours are chilling, informative and should be booked ahead.

If history or shopping for crafts interest you, head 48 miles south of Tucson to the small village of Tubac (www.tubacaz.com), with more than 100 galleries, studios and shops clustered around a Spanish colonial-era Presidio.

Patagonia & the Mountain Empire

This lovely riparian region, sandwiched between the Mexican border and the Santa Rita and Patagonia Mountains, is one of the shiniest gems in Arizona's jewel box. It's a tranquil destination for bird-watching and wine tasting. Bird-watchers and nature-lovers wander the gentle trails at the **Patagonia-Sonoita Creek Preserve** (☑520-394-2400; www.nature.org/arizona; 150 Blue Heaven Rd; $6; ☺6:30am-4pm Wed-Sun Apr-Sep, 7:30am-4pm Wed-Sun Oct-Mar), an enchanting creekside willow and cottonwood forest managed by the Nature Conservancy. The peak migratory seasons are April through May, and late August to September.

For a leisurely afternoon of wine tasting, head to the villages and surrounding wineries of **Sonoita** and **Elgin**, north of Patagonia. If you're in Patagonia for dinner, try the satisfying gourmet pizzas at **Velvet Elvis** (☑520-394-2102; www.velvetelvispizza.com; 292 Naugle Ave, Patagonia; mains $8-24; ☺11:30am-8pm; ☞). Then salute the Old West and its simple charms at the **Stage Stop Inn** (☑520-394-2211; www.stagestophotelpatagonia.com; 303 McKeown Ave, Patagonia; d/ste from $99/149; ☞☱☲), where rooms surround a central courtyard and pool. The stage coach did indeed stop here on the Butterfield Trail, and a small **visitor center** (☑520-394-7750, 888-794-0060; www.patagoniaaz.com; 299 McKeown Ave, Patagonia; ☺10am-4pm daily Oct-May, Fri-Sun Jun-Sep) now provides information.

Southeastern Arizona

Chockablock with places that loom large in Wild West folklore, southern Arizona is home to the wonderfully preserved mining town of Bisbee, the OK Corral in Tombstone, and a wonderland of stone spires at Chiricahua National Monument.

Kartchner Caverns State Park

This wonderland of spires, shields, pipes, columns, soda straws and other ethereal formations has been five million years in the making, but miraculously wasn't discovered until 1974. In fact, its very location was kept secret for another 25 years in order to prepare for its opening as **Kartchner Caverns State Park** (☑information 520-586-4100, reservations 877-697-2757; http://azstateparks.com/kartchner; 2980 Hwy 90; park entrance per vehicle/bicycle $7/3, tours adult/child $23/13; ☺park 7am-6pm, visitor center 8am-6pm late Dec-May, shorter hours rest of year; ℗☝). Two tours are available, both about 90 minutes long and equally impressive.

The Big Room tour closes to the public around mid-April, when a colony of migrating female cave myotis bats starts arriving from Mexico to roost and give birth to pups in late June. Mom and baby bats hang out until mid-September before flying off to their wintering spot. While a bat nursery, the cave is closed to the public.

There's a campground (with cabins) and the entrance is 9 miles south of I-10, off Hwy 90, exit 302.

Tombstone

In Tombstone's 19th-century heyday as a booming mining town, the whiskey flowed and six-shooters blazed over disputes large and small, most famously at the OK Corral.

Now a National Historic Landmark, it attracts hordes of tourists to its old Western buildings, stagecoach rides and gunfight reenactments.

And yes, you must visit the **OK Corral** (☑520-457-3456; www.ok-corral.com; Allen St, btwn 3rd & 4th Sts; entry $10, without gunfight $6; ⊙9am-5pm), site of the legendary gunfight where the Earps and Doc Holliday took on the McLaurys and Billy Clanton on October 26, 1881. The McClaurys, Clanton and many other casualties of those violent days now rest at the **Boothill Graveyard** (☑520-457-3300; www.boothillgiftshop.com; 408 Hwy 80; adult/child 15yr & under $3/free; ⊙8am-6pm) **FREE** on Hwy 80 north of town.

Also make time for the dusty **Bird Cage Theater** (☑520-457-3421; www.tombstonebirdcage.com; 517 E Allen St; adult/senior/child 8-18yr $10/9/8; ⊙9am-6pm), a one-time dance hall, saloon and bordello crammed with historic odds and ends. And a merman. The **Visitor Center** (☑520-457-3929, 888-457-3929; www.tombstonechamber.com; 395 E Allen St, at 4th St; ⊙9am-4pm Mon-Thu, to 5pm Fri-Sun) has walking maps.

Bisbee

Oozing untidy, unforced old-world charm, Bisbee is a former copper-mining town that's now a delightful mix of aging bohemians, elegant buildings, sumptuous restaurants and charming hotels. Most businesses are in the Historic District (Old Bisbee), along Subway and Main Sts.

To burrow under the earth in a tour led by the retirees who once mined here, take the **Queen Mine Tour** (☑520-432-2071; www.queenminetour.com; 478 Dart Rd, off Hwy 80; adult/child 4-12yr $13/5.50; ⊛). The Queen Mine Building, just south of downtown, also holds the local **visitor center** (☑866-224-7233, 520-432-3554; www.discoverbisbee.com; 478 Dart Rd; ⊙8am-5pm Mon-Fri, 10am-4pm Sat & Sun), and is the obvious place to start exploring. Right outside of town, check out the **Lavender Pit**, an ugly yet impressive testament to strip mining.

Rest your head at **Shady Dell RV Park** (☑520-432-3567; www.theshadydell.com; 1 Douglas Rd, Lowell; trailers from $85; ⊙closed high summer & winter; ⊛), a deliciously retro trailer park where meticulously restored Airstream trailers are neatly fenced off and kitted out with fun furnishings. Swamp coolers provide cold air. You can sleep in a covered wagon at the quirky but fun **Bisbee Grand Hotel**

(☑520-432-5900; www.bisbeegrandhotel.com; 61 Main St; d/ste from $99/135; ⊛⊚), which brings the Old West to life with Victorian-era decor and a kick-up-your spurs saloon.

For good food, stroll up Main St and pick a restaurant – you can't go wrong. For fine American food, try stylish **Cafe Roka** (☑520-432-5153; www.caferoka.com; 35 Main St; dinner $20-30; ⊙5-9pm Thu-Sat, 3-8pm Sun), where four-course dinners include salad, soup, sorbet and a rotating choice of crowd-pleasing mains. Continue up Main St for wood-fired pizzas and punk-rock style at **Screaming Banshee** (☑520-432-1300; www.screamingbansheepizza.net; 200 Tombstone Canyon Rd; pizzas $14-16; ⊙4-9pm Tue & Wed, 11am-10pm Thu-Sat, 11am-9pm Sun). Bars cluster in the aptly-named Brewery Gulch, at the south end of Main St.

Chiricahua National Monument

The towering rock spires at remote but mesmerizing **Chiricahua National Monument** (☑520-824-3560; www.nps.gov/chir; 12856 E Rhyolite Creek Rd; ⊙visitor center 8:30am-4:30pm; ℗⊛) **FREE** in the Chiricahua Mountains sometimes rise hundreds of feet high and often look like they're on the verge of tipping over. The **Bonita Canyon Scenic Drive** takes you 8 miles to Massai Point (6870ft) where you'll see thousands of spires positioned on the slopes like some petrified army. There are numerous hiking trails,but if you're short on time, hike the **Echo Canyon Trail** at least half a mile to the Grottoes, an amazing 'cathedral' of giant boulders where you can lie still and enjoy the wind-caressed silence. The monument is 36 miles southeast of Willcox off Hwy 186/181.

UTAH

Welcome to nature's most perfect playground. From red-rock mesas to skinny slot canyons, powder-bound slopes and slick rock trails, Utah's diverse terrain will stun you. The biking, hiking and skiing are world-class. And with more than 65% of the state lands public, including 13 national parks and monuments, the access is simply superb.

Southern Utah is defined by red-rock cliffs, sorbet-colored spindles and seemingly endless sandstone desert. The pine-forested and snow-covered peaks of the Wasatch Mountains dominate northern Utah. Interspersed are old pioneer remnants, ancient rock art and ruins, and traces of dinosaurs.

Mormon-influenced rural towns can be quiet and conservative, but the rugged beauty has attracted outdoorsy progressives as well. Salt Lake City (SLC) and Park City, especially, have vibrant nightlife and dining scenes. So pull on your boots and stock up on water: Utah's wild and scenic hinterlands await.

History

Traces of the Ancestral Puebloan and Fremont peoples, this land's earliest human inhabitants, remain in the rock art and ruins they left behind. But the modern Ute, Paiute and Navajo tribes were living here when settlers of European heritage arrived in large numbers. Led by Brigham Young (second president of the Mormon church), Mormons fled to this territory to escape religious persecution starting in the late 1840s. They set out to settle every inch of their new land, no matter how inhospitable, which resulted in skirmishes with Native Americans – and more than one abandoned ghost town.

For nearly 50 years after the United States acquired the Utah Territory from Mexico, petitions for statehood were rejected due to the Mormon practice of polygamy (taking multiple wives). Tension and prosecutions grew until 1890, when Mormon leader Wilford Woodruff had a divine revelation and the church officially discontinued the practice. Utah became the 45th state in 1896. The modern Mormon church, now called the Church of Jesus Christ of Latter-Day Saints (LDS), continues to exert a strong influence.

❶ Information

Utah Office of Tourism (☑800-200-1160; www.utah.com) Publishes the free *Utah Travel Guide* and runs several visitor centers statewide. The website has links in six languages.

Utah State Parks & Recreation Department (☑801-538-7220; www.stateparks.utah.gov) Produces a great guide to the 40-plus state parks; available online and at visitor centers.

❶ Getting There & Around

International flights land in Salt Lake City. Larger cities and tourist hubs have car-rental offices.

Utah is not a large state, but it is largely rural – so unless you're staying in Salt Lake City or Park City, you'll need a car. If you're headed to the parks in southern Utah, your cheapest bet may be to fly into Las Vegas, and rent a ride there.

Salt Lake City

Sparkling Salt Lake, with its bluebird skies and powder-dusted mountains, is Utah's capital city. The only Utah city with an international airport, it still manages to emanate a small-town feel. Downtown is easy to get around and fairly quiet come evening. It's hard to grasp that 1.2 million people live in the metro area. While it's the Mormon equivalent of Vatican City, and the LDS owns a lot of land, less than half the population are church members. The university and excellent outdoor access have attracted a wide range of residents. A liberal spirit permeates the coffeehouses and yoga classes, where elaborate tattoos are the norm. Foodies find much to love among the multitude of international and organic dining options. And when the trail beckons, it's a scant 45 minutes from the Wasatch Mountains' brilliant hiking and skiing. Friendly people, great food and outdoor adventure – what could be better?

◉ Sights & Activities

Mormon Church–related sights cluster mostly near the town center point for SLC addresses: the intersection of Main and South Temple Sts. (Streets are so wide – 132ft – because they were originally built so that four oxen pulling a wagon could turn around.) The downtown hub underwent a renaissance with the development of City Creek. To the east, the University-Foothills District has most of the museums and kid-friendly attractions.

◉ Temple Square Area

Temple Square PLAZA
(www.visittemplesquare.com; cnr S Temple & N State Sts; ◷grounds 24hr, visitor centers 9am-9pm) **FREE** The city's most famous sight occupies a 10-acre block surrounded by 15ft-high walls. LDS docents give free, 30-minute tours continually, leaving from the visitor centers at the two entrances on South and North Temple Sts. Sisters, brothers and elders are stationed every 20ft or so to answer questions. (Don't worry, no one is going to try to convert you – unless you express interest.) In addition to the noteworthy sights, there are administrative buildings and two theater venues.

Museum of Church History & Art MUSEUM
(www.churchhistorymuseum.org; 45 N West Temple St; ☺9am-9pm Mon-Fri, 10am-7pm Sat & Sun)
FREE Adjoining Temple Sq, this museum has impressive exhibits of pioneer history and fine art.

Salt Lake Temple RELIGIOUS SITE
(Temple Sq) Lording over Temple Sq is the impressive 210ft-tall Salt Lake Temple. Atop the tallest spire stands a statue of the angel Moroni, who appeared to LDS founder Joseph Smith. Rumor has it that when the place was renovated, cleaners found old bullet marks in one of the gold-plated surfaces. The temple and ceremonies are private, open only to LDS members in good standing.

Tabernacle CHRISTIAN SITE
(www.mormontabernaclechoir.org; Temple Sq; ☺9am-9pm) **FREE** The domed, 1867 auditorium – with a massive 11,000-pipe organ – has incredible acoustics. A pin dropped in the front can be heard in the back, almost 200ft away. Free daily organ recitals are held at noon Monday through Saturday, and at 2pm Sunday.

Beehive House HISTORIC SITE
(☏801-240-2671; www.visittemplesquare.com; 67 E South Temple St; ☺9:30am-8:30pm Mon-Sat) **FREE** Brigham Young lived with one of his wives and families in the Beehive House during much of his tenure as governor and church president in Utah. The required tours vary; some offer historic house details over religious education, depending on the LDS docent.

⊙ Greater Downtown

Utah State Capitol HISTORIC BUILDING
(www.utahstatecapitol.utah.gov; 350 N State St; ☺7am-8pm Mon-Fri, 8am-6pm Sat & Sun, visitor center 8:30am-5pm Mon-Fri) **FREE** The grand, 1916 State Capitol is set among 500 cherry trees on a hill north of Temple Sq. Inside, colorful Works Progress Administration (WPA) murals of pioneers, trappers and missionaries adorn part of the building's dome. Free guided tours (hourly, 9am to 5pm, Monday to Friday) start at the 1st-floor visitor center; self-guided tours are available from the visitor center.

Clark Planetarium MUSEUM
(☏385-468-7827; www.clarkplanetarium.org; 110 S 400 W; adult/child $9/7; ☺10am-10pm Sun-Thu, to 11pm Fri & Sat) You'll be seeing stars at Clark Planetarium, home to the latest and greatest

3D sky shows and Utah's only IMAX theater. There are free science exhibits, too. The planetarium is on the edge of the **Gateway** (www.shopthegateway.com; 200 S to 50 N, 400 W to 500 W; ☺10am-9pm Mon-Sat, noon-6pm Sun), a combination indoor-outdoor shopping complex anchored by the old railway depot.

⊙ University-Foothill District & Beyond

★**Natural History Museum of Utah** MUSEUM
(http://nhmu.utah.edu; 301 Wakara Way; adult/child 3-12yr $15/10; ☺10am-5pm Thu-Tue, to 9pm Wed) Rio Tinto Center's stunning architecture forms a multistory indoor 'canyon' that showcases exhibits to great effect. Walk up through the layers as you explore both indigenous peoples' cultures and natural history. Past Worlds paleontological displays are the most impressive – an incredible perspective from beneath, next to and above a vast collection of dinosaur fossils offers the full breadth of prehistory.

This is the Place Heritage Park HISTORIC SITE
(www.thisistheplace.org; 2601 E Sunnyside Ave; adult/child $13/9; ☺9am-5pm Mon-Sat, 10am-5pm Sun; ▣) Dedicated to the 1847 arrival of the Mormons, this heritage park covers 450 acres. The centerpiece is a living-history village where, June through August, costumed docents depict mid-19th-century life. Admission includes a tourist-train ride and activities. The rest of the year, access is limited to varying degrees at varyingly reduced prices; you'll at least be able to wander around the exterior of the 41 buildings. Some are replicas, but some are originals, such as Brigham Young's farmhouse.

Red Butte Garden GARDENS
(www.redbuttegarden.org; 300 Wakara Way; adult/child $12/7; ☺9am-9pm May-Aug) Both landscaped and natural gardens cover a lovely 150 acres, with access to trails in the Wasatch foothills. Check online to see who's playing at the popular, outdoor summer concert series also held here. Daylight hours in low season.

⌂ Sleeping

Downtown chain properties cluster around S 200 West near 500 South and 600 South; there are more in Mid-Valley (off I-215) and near the airport. At high-end hotels rates are lowest on weekends. Parking downtown is often not included. Look for camping and alternative lodging in the Wasatch Mountains.

Wildflowers B&B
B&B $

(☑385-419-2301; http://wildflowersbb.com; 936 E 1700 S; r $90-125) Quaint to the core, this old-fashioned B&B revels in stained glass and period furnishings. Cheaper than most B&Bs in town, it's probably worth it for the breakfast alone. It sits in a characterful neighborhood of Salt Lake with plenty of shops and restaurants.

★Engen Hus
B&B $$

(☑801-450-6703; http://engenhusutah.com; 2275 6200 S; r $125-140; ☎) Ideally positioned for mountain jaunts, this lovely home features four rooms with handmade quilts on log beds and flat-screen TVs. Hosts are knowledgeable about local hiking. The cozy quotient is high, with board games, a hot-tub deck and DIY laundry. Dig the buffet breakfast with the likes of caramel French toast. Has a room that's accessible to travelers in wheelchairs.

★Inn on the Hill
INN $$

(☑801-328-1466; www.inn-on-the-hill.com; 225 N State St; r $155-240; P✳@☎) Exquisite woodwork and Maxfield Parrish Tiffany glass adorn this sprawling, 1906 Renaissance Revival mansion-turned-inn. Guest rooms are classically comfortable, not stuffy, with Jacuzzi tubs and some fireplaces and balconies. Great shared spaces include patios, a billiard room, a library and a dining room where chef-cooked breakfasts are served.

Hotel Monaco
BOUTIQUE HOTEL $$

(☑801-595-0000; www.monaco-saltlakecity.com; 15 W 200 S; r $229-279; P✳@☎☎) Subdued with a dollop of funk, rich colors and plush prints create a whimsical vibe at this boutique chain. Here, pampered-guest pets receive special treatment, and the front desk will loan you a goldfish if you need company. Evening wine receptions are free, as are cruiser bicycles; parking is extra.

Hotel RL
HOTEL $$

(☑801-521-7373; www.redlion.com/salt-lake; 161 W 600 S; r from $239; P✳@☎☎) Sleek comfort in a remodeled Red Lion hotel with almost 400 rooms, which feature black-and-white wall murals and flat-screen TVs. There's a classic diner attached, a modern-woodsy design lounge, 24-hour gym and outdoor pool and Jacuzzi. As big box hotels go, this one delivers.

✕ Eating

★Red Iguana
MEXICAN $

(www.rediguana.com; 736 W North Temple St; mains $10-18; ☯11am-10pm Mon-Thu, to 11pm Fri, 10am-11pm Sat, 10am-9pm Sun) Mexico at its most authentic, aromatic and delicious – no wonder the line is usually snaking out the door at this family run restaurant. Ask for samples of the mole to decide on one of seven chili- and chocolate-based sauces. The incredibly tender *cochinita pibil* (shredded roast pork) tastes like it's been roasting for days.

★Tosh's Ramen
RAMEN $

(☑801-466-7000; 1465 State St; mains $9-11; ☯11:30am-3pm & 5-9pm Tue-Sat) Ecstasy by the steaming oversized bowl, Tosh's ramen comes with silken broth and crunchy sprouts, topped with a poached egg if you like it that way. It couldn't get more authentic. Try to carve out some room for an order of spicy wings. Everyone is drawn to this happy place in a nondescript strip mall, so go early.

Caputo's Deli
DELI $

(☑801-486-6615; 1516 S 1500 E; mains $5-15; ☯7am-8pm Mon-Sat) Stock up on gorgeous cheeses, marinated peppers, fresh sandwiches and pastries at this deli counter and gourmet store.

UTAH FACTS

Nickname Beehive State

Population 2.9 million

Area 82,169 sq miles

Capital city Salt Lake City (population 186,440), metro area (1,153,340)

Other cities St George (population 82,318

Sales tax from 4.7%

Birthplace of Entertainers Donny (b 1957) and Marie (b 1959) Osmond, beloved bandit Butch Cassidy (1866–1908)

Home of 2002 Winter Olympic Games

Politics Mostly conservative

Famous for Mormons, red-rock canyons, polygamy

Best souvenir Wasatch Brewery T-shirt:'Polygamy Porter – Why Have Just One?'

Del Mar al Lago PERUVIAN $$

(☑801-467-2890; 310 Bugatti Ave S; mains $16-24; ☺11am-4pm & 6-9pm Mon-Thu, 11am-10pm Fri & Sat) Get ready for a treat. The Peruvian patrons tell you it's authentic. Chef Wilmer from Trujillo cooks up the country's best dishes, including ceviche (fish marinated in lime), yucca fries and whipped potato *causas* with jalapeño aioli.

Takashi JAPANESE $$

(☑801-519-9595; 18 W Market St; rolls $10-18, mains $10-19; ☺11:30am-2pm & 5:30-10pm Mon-Sat) Who wouldn't be tempted by 'sex on rice'? The best of a number of surprisingly good sushi restaurants here in landlocked Salt Lake, and often packed. Even LA restaurant snobs rave about the innovative rolls at this ever-so-chic establishment.

★**Avenues Bistro on Third** BISTRO $$$

(☑801-831-5409; http://avenuesbistroonthird.com; 564 E 3rd Ave; mains $16-37; ☺11am-10pm Wed-Fri, 9am-3pm & 5pm-close Sat & Sun) 🍷 An intimate, food-first experience. Enter the tiny house in the Avenues to a handful of tables around an open grill. The owner is seating guests and chatting up neighbors. The fare: fresh greens with Utah trout, trumpet mushrooms brushed in honey lavender and homemade fig newtons all melt in your mouth.

🍷 **Drinking & Nightlife**

Pubs and bars that also serve food are mainstays of SLC's nightlife, and no one minds if you mainly drink and nibble. A complete schedule of local bar music is available in the *City Weekly* (www.cityweekly.net).

★**Beer Bar** PUB

(www.beerbarslc.com; 161 E 200 S; ☺11am-2am Mon-Sat, 10am-2am Sun) With shared wooden tables and over 140 beers and 13 sausage styles, Beer Bar is a little slice of Bavaria in Salt Lake City. The crowd is diverse and far more casual than at Bar X next door (a linked venue). A great place to meet friends and make friends, but it gets pretty loud.

Bar X COCKTAIL BAR

(155 E 200 S; ☺4pm-2am Mon-Fri, 6pm-2am Sat, 7pm-2am Sun) So low-lit and funky, it's hard to believe you're down the street from Temple Sq (p194). Cozy up to the crowded bar with a Moscow Mule and listen to Motown or funk (or the guy at the next table saying to his date, 'Your voice is pretty').

MUSEUM OF ANCIENT LIFE

A family friendly **museum** (☑801-768-2300; www.thanksgivingpoint.org; 3003 N Thanksgiving Way, Lehi; all-attraction pass adult/child $25/20, museum adult/child $15/12; ☺10am-8pm Mon-Sat; 🚹) at Thanksgiving Point . Prehistoric life is on display with exhibits on dinosaurs and aquatic life, lots of interactive exhibits for kids and a 3D theater.

★**Jack Mormon Coffee Co** CAFE

(www.jackmormoncoffee.com; 82 E St; ☺10am-6pm Mon-Sat) Utah's finest roaster also serves mean espresso drinks. When the temps rise, locals binge on a Jack Frost.

Gracie's BAR

(www.graciesslc.com; 326 S West Temple St; ☺11am-2am Mon-Sat, 10am-2am Sun) Even with two levels and four bars, Gracie's trendy bar-restaurant still gets crowded. The two sprawling patios are the best place to kick back. Live music or DJs most nights.

☆ **Entertainment**

We wouldn't say the nightlife here is all that hot; major dance clubs change frequently and few are open more than a couple of nights a week. See the *City Weekly* (www.cityweekly.net) for listings. Classical entertainment options, especially around Temple Sq (p194), are plentiful.

Music

★**Mormon Tabernacle Choir** LIVE MUSIC

(☑801-570-0080, 801-240-4150; www.mormontabernaclechoir.org) Hearing the world-renowned Mormon Tabernacle Choir is a must-do on any SLC bucket list. A live choir broadcast goes out every Sunday at 9:30am. September through November, and January through May, attend in person at the Tabernacle (p195). Free public rehearsals are held here from 8pm to 9pm Thursday.

Theater

The Salt Lake City Arts Council provides a complete cultural events calendar on its website (www.slcgov.com/city-life/ec). Local venues include the **Gallivan Center** (www.thegallivancenter.com; 200 S, btwn State & Main Sts), **Depot** (☑801-355-5522; www.smithstix.com; 400 W South Temple St), and the **Rose Wagner Performing Arts Center**

THE BOOK OF MORMON, THE MUSICAL

Singing and dancing Mormon missionaries? You betcha...at least on Broadway. In the spring of 2011, *The Book of Mormon* musical opened to critical acclaim at the Eugene O'Neill Theatre in New York. The light-hearted satire about LDS missionaries in Uganda came out of the comic minds that also created the musical *Avenue Q* and the animated TV series *South Park*. No wonder people laughed them all the way to nine Tony Awards.

The LDS church's official response? Actually quite measured, avoiding any direct criticism – though it was made clear that their belief is that while 'the Book, the musical' can entertain you, the scriptures of the actual Book of Mormon can change your life.

(https://artsaltlake.org; 138 W 300 S); you can reserve through **ArtTix** (☏ 801-355-2787, 888-451-2787; https://artsaltlake.org).

Eccles Theatre   THEATER
(☏ 385-468-1010; www.eccles.theatersaltlakecity. com; 131 Main St) Opened in 2016, this gorgeous building has two theaters (one seating 2500 people), showing Broadway shows, concerts and other entertainment.

Sports

Utah Jazz   BASKETBALL
(☏ 801-325-2500; www.nba.com/jazz; 301 W South Temple St) Utah Jazz, the men's professional basketball team, plays at the **Vivint Smart Home Arena** (www.vivintarena.com; 301 W South Temple St), where concerts are also held.

Real Salt Lake   SOCCER
(☏ 844-732-5849; www.rsl.com; 9256 State St, Rio Tinto Stadium; ☉ Mar-Oct) Salt Lake's winning Major League Soccer team (*ree*-al) has a loyal local following and matches are fun to take in at the **Rio Tinto Stadium**.

🛍 Shopping

An interesting array of boutiques, antiques and cafes line up along Broadway Ave (300 South), between 100 and 300 East. Drawing on Utah pioneer heritage, SLC has quite a few crafty shops and galleries scattered around; a few can be found on the 300 block of W Pierpont Ave. Many participate in the one-day Craft Salt Lake expo in August.

Utah Artist Hands   ARTS & CRAFTS
(www.utahands.com; 163 E Broadway; ☉ noon-6pm Mon-Fri, to 5pm Sat) Local artists' work, all made in-state, runs the gamut from fine art and photography to scarves and pottery.

ℹ Information

EMERGENCY & MEDICAL SERVICES

Local Police (☏ 801-799-3000; 315 E 200 S)

Salt Lake Regional Medical Center (☏ 801-350-4111; www.saltlakeregional.com; 1050 E South Temple St; ☉ 24hr emergency)

University Hospital (☏ 801-581-2121; 50 N Medical Dr)

TOURIST INFORMATION

Public Lands Information Center (☏ 801-466-6411; www.publiclands.org; 3285 E 3300 S, REI Store; ☉ 10:30am-5:30pm Mon-Fri, 9am-1pm Sat) Recreation information for nearby public lands (state parks, BLM, USFS), including the Wasatch-Cache National Forest.

Visit Salt Lake (☏ 801-534-4900; www. visitsaltlake.com; 90 S West Temple St, Salt Palace Convention Center; ☉ 9am-6pm Mon-Fri, to 5pm Sat & Sun) Publishes a free visitor-guide booklet; large gift shop onsite at the visitor center.

ℹ Getting There & Around

Five miles northwest of downtown, **Salt Lake City International Airport** (SLC; ☏ 801-575-2400; www.slcairport.com; 776 N Terminal Dr; 🛜) has mostly domestic flights, though you can fly direct to Canada and Mexico. **Express Shuttle** (☏ 801-596-1600; www.xpressshuttleutah. com; to downtown $17) run shared van services to the airport.

Greyhound (☏ 800-231-2222; www.grey hound.com; 300 S 600 W; 🛜) has buses to nationwide destinations and the **Union Pacific Rail Depot** (340 S 600 W) is serviced daily by **Amtrak** (☏ 800-872-7245; www.amtrak.com) trains heading to Denver and California.

Utah Transit Authority (UTA; www.rideuta. com; one way $2.50; 🛜) runs light-rail services to the international airport and downtown area. Bus 550 travels downtown from the parking structure between Terminals 1 and 2.

Park City & Wasatch Mountains

Utah offers some of North America's most awesome skiing, with fabulous low-density, low-moisture snow – between 300in and 500in annually – and thousands of acres of high-altitude terrain. The Wasatch Mountain Range, which towers over SLC, holds numerous ski resorts, abundant hiking, camping and mountain biking – not to mention chichi Park City, with its upscale amenities and famous film festival.

Salt Lake City Resorts

Because of Great Salt Lake–affected snow patterns, these resorts receive almost twice as much snow as Park City. The four resorts east of Salt Lake City sit 30 to 45 miles from the downtown core at the end of two canyons. In summer, access the numerous hiking and biking trails that lead off from both canyons.

🏃 Activities

⭐ **Alta**   SNOW SPORTS
(☑801-359-1078, 888-782-9258; www.alta.com; Little Cottonwood Canyon; day lift-pass adult/child $96/50) Dyed-in-the-wool skiers make a pilgrimage to Alta, at the top of the valley. No snowboarders are allowed here, which keeps the snow cover from deteriorating, especially on groomers. Wide-open powder fields, gullies, chutes and glades, such as **East Greeley**, **Devil's Castle** and **High Rustler**, have helped make Alta famous. Warning: you may never want to ski anywhere else.

⭐ **Snowbird**   SNOW SPORTS
(☑800-232-9542; www.snowbird.com; Hwy 210, Little Cottonwood Canyon; day lift-ticket adult/child $116/55) The biggest and busiest of all the Salt Lake City resorts, with all-round great snow riding – think steep and deep. Numerous lift-assist summer hiking trails; aerial tramway runs year-round.

Solitude   SNOW SPORTS
(☑801-534-1400; www.skisolitude.com; 12000 Big Cottonwood Canyon Rd; day lift-ticket adult/child $83/53) Exclusive, European-style village surrounded by excellent terrain. The **Nordic Center** (http://skisolitude.com/winter-activities/nordic-skiing-nordic-center; day pass adult/child $18/free; ⏱8:30am-4:40pm Dec-Mar & Jun-Aug) has cross-country skiing in winter and nature trails in summer.

Brighton   SNOW SPORTS
(☑801-532-4731, 800-873-5512; www.brightonresort.com; Big Cottonwood Canyon Rd; day lift-ticket adult/child $79/free; 🐕) Slackers, truants and bad-ass boarders rule at Brighton. But don't be intimidated: the low-key resort where many Salt Lake residents first learned to ski remains a good first-timers' spot, especially if you want to snowboard. Thick stands of pines line sweeping groomed trails and wide boulevards, and from the top, the views are gorgeous.

Park City

With a dusting of snow, the century-old buildings on main street create a snow globe scene come to life. A one-time silver boom-and-bust town, pretty Park City is now lined

---

SALT LAKE CITY FOR KIDS

Salt Lake is a child-friendly city if ever there was one. The wonderful hands-on exhibits at the **Discovery Gateway** (www.discoverygateway.org; 444 W 100 S; $8.50; ⏱10am-6pm Mon-Thu, to 7pm Fri & Sat, noon-6pm Sun; 🐕) stimulate imaginations and senses.

Kids can help farmhands milk cows, churn butter and feed animals at **Wheeler Historic Farm** (☑385-468-1755; www.wheelerfarm.com; 6351 S 900 E, South Cottonwood Regional Park; hay ride $3, house tour adult/child $4/2; ⏱daylight hours; 🐕) FREE, which dates from 1886. There's also blacksmithing, quilting and hay rides in summer.

More than 800 animals inhabit zones such as the Asian Highlands on the landscaped 42-acre grounds at **Hogle Zoo** (www.hoglezoo.org; 2600 E Sunnyside Ave; adult/child $15/11; ⏱9am-6pm; 🐕). Daily animal encounter programs help kids learn more about their favorite species.

Tracy Aviary (www.tracyaviary.org; 589 E 1300 S; adult/child $8/5; ⏱9am-4pm; 🐕) lets little ones toss fish to the pelicans as one of its interactive programs and performances. More than 400 winged creatures from around the world call this bird park home.

With 55 acres of gardens, a full-scale working and petting farm, golf course, giant movie theater, museum, dining, shopping and ice-cream parlor, what doesn't Thanksgiving Point (p197), located in Lehi, have? The on-site Museum of Ancient Life (p160) is one of the highest-tech and most hands-on dinosaur museums in the state. Kids can dig for their own bones, dress up a dinosaur or play in a watery Silurian reef. Lehi is 28 miles south of downtown SLC; to get there take exit 287 off I-15.

CAN I GET A DRINK IN UTAH?

Absolutely. Although a few unusual liquor laws remain, in recent years they've been relaxed and private club membership bars are no more. Some rules to remember:

➡ Few restaurants have full liquor licenses: most serve beer and wine only. You have to order food to drink.

➡ Minors aren't allowed in bars.

➡ Mixed drinks and wine are available only after midday; 3.2% alcohol beer can be served starting at 10am.

➡ Mixed drinks cannot contain more than 1.5oz of a primary liquor, or 2.5oz total including secondary alcohol. Sorry, no Long Island Iced Teas or double shots.

➡ Packaged liquor can only be sold at state-run liquor stores; grocery and convenience stores can sell 3.2% alcohol beer and malt beverages. Sales are made from Monday through Saturday only.

ing, bobsledding, skeleton, Nordic combined and luge events, which continues to host national competitions. There are 10m, 20m, 40m, 64m, 90m and 120m Nordic ski-jumping hills as well as a bobsled-luge run. The US Ski Team practices here year-round – in summer, the freestyle jumpers land in a bubble-filled jetted pool, and the Nordic jumpers on a hillside covered in plastic. Call for a schedule; it's free to observe.

★ **Park City Museum** MUSEUM
(www.parkcityhistory.org; 528 Main St; adult/child $10/4; ⊙10am-7pm Mon-Sat, noon-6pm Sun) A well-staged interactive museum touches on the highlights of the town's history as a mining boomtown, hippie hangout and premier ski resort. There are fascinating exhibits on the world's first underground ski lift, a real dungeon in the basement and a 3D map of mining tunnels under the mountain.

🏃 Activities

Skiing is the big area attraction, but there are activities enough to keep you more than busy in both summer and winter. Most are based out of the three resorts: Canyons, Park City Mountain and Deer Valley.

Deer Valley SNOW SPORTS, ADVENTURE SPORTS
(☑435-649-1000, snowmobiling 435-645-7669; www.deervalley.com; Deer Valley Dr; day lift ticket adult/child $128/80, round-trip gondola ride $17; ⊙snowmobiling 9am-5pm) Want to be pampered? Deer Valley, a resort of superlatives, has thought of everything – from tissue boxes at the base of slopes to ski valets. Slalom, mogul and freestyle-aerial competitions in the 2002 Olympics were held here, but the resort is just as famous for its superb dining, white-glove service and uncrowded slopes as meticulously groomed as the gardens of Versailles.

Canyons Village at Park City SNOW SPORTS, ADVENTURE SPORTS
(☑435-649-5400; www.thecanyons.com; 4000 Canyons Resort Dr; lift ticket adult/child $134/86) Bolstered by tens of millions of dollars in improvements, and now merged with Park City Resorts, Canyons seeks novelty with the first North American 'bubble' lift (an enclosed, climate-controlled lift), expanded services, 300 new acres of advanced trails and an increased snow-making capability. The resort currently sprawls across nine aspen-covered peaks 4 miles outside of town, near the freeway.

with condos and mansions in the valleys. Utah's premier ski village boasts fabulous restaurants and cultural offerings. It recently annexed the adjacent Canyons Resort to become the largest ski resort in North America.

Park City first shot to international fame when it hosted the downhill, jumping and sledding events at the 2002 Winter Olympics. Today it's the permanent home base for the US Ski Team. There's usually snow through mid-April.

Come summer, more residents than visitors gear up for hiking and mountain biking among the nearby peaks. June to August, temperatures average in the 70s; nights are chilly. Spring and fall can be wet and boring; resort services, limited in summer compared with winter, shut down entirely between seasons.

👁 Sights

★ **Utah Olympic Park** AMUSEMENT PARK
(☑435-658-4200; www.utaholympiclegacy.com; 3419 Olympic Pkwy; museum free, activity day pass adult/child $70/45; ⊙10am-6pm, tours 11am-4pm) Visit the site of the 2002 Olympic ski jump-

Park City

Mountain Resort SNOW SPORTS, ADVENTURE SPORTS
(☑435-649-8111; www.parkcitymountainresort.
com; 1310 Lowell Ave; lift ticket adult/child $134/86;
🖳) From boarder dudes to parents with tots,
everyone skis Park City Mountain Resort,
host of the Olympic snowboarding and giant
slalom events. The awesome terrain couldn't
be more family friendly – or more accessible,
rising as it does right over downtown.

✿✧ Festivals & Events

Sundance Film Festival FILM
(☑888-285-7790; www.sundance.org/festival) Independent films and their makers, and movie stars and their fans, fill the town to bursting for 10 days in late January. Passes, ticket
packages and the few individual tickets sell
out well in advance – plan ahead.

🛏 Sleeping

Mid-December through mid-April is winter
high season, with minimum stays required;
rates rise during Christmas, New Year's and
the Sundance Film Festival. Off-season rates
drop 50% or more. For better nightlife, stay
in the old town.

Chateau Apres Lodge HOSTEL $
(☑435-649-9372; www.chateauapres.com; 1299
Norfolk Ave; dm $50, r $140-165; 🛜) The only
budget-oriented accommodation in town
is this basic, 1963 lodge – with a 1st-floor
dorm – near the town ski lift. Reserve ahead,
as it's very popular with groups and seniors.

★ **Old Town Guest House** B&B $$
(☑435-649-2642; www.oldtownguesthouse.com;
1011 Empire Ave; r $169-229; 🖳@🛜) Grab the
flannel robe, pick a paperback off the shelf
and snuggle under a quilt on your lodgepole
bed or kick back on the large deck at this
comfy in-town B&B. The host will gladly give
you the lowdown on the great outdoors, guid-
ed ski tours, mountain biking and the rest.

Park City Peaks HOTEL $$
(☑435-649-5000; www.parkcitypeaks.com; 2121
Park Ave; d/ste $219/319; 🖳@🛜🖳) Comfort-
able, contemporary rooms include access to
a heated outdoor pool, hot tub, restaurant

BEARS EARS NATIONAL MONUMENT

Protecting 1.35 million acres filled with ancient cliff dwellings, ponderosa forests, five-
thousand-year-old petroglyphs, mesas, canyons and red rock, **Bears Ears National
Monument** (www.fs.fed.us/visit/bears-ears-national-monument) is the newest addition to the
awesome collection of American parks.

Some notable landmarks within the monument include the **Bears Ears Buttes**, **Cedar
Mesa**, **White Canyon**, **San Juan River**, **Indian Creek**, **Comb Ridge** and **Valley of the
Gods**. Their treasures, described by David Roberts' *In Search of the Old Ones*, are nothing
short of exquisite.

Archaeological sites dating back 8500 years have been threatened by vandalism and destruction over recent years. The Navajo, Hopi, Zuni, Ute Mountain and Ute Indian tribes led
the Bears Ears proposal, and will have a strong stake in the management of the monument,
a status that makes this area's conservation approach unique among the Utah parks.

The designation has been plagued by controversy. Protecting this vast area goes against
energy leasing and development interests that are very strong in the state. Governor Gary
Herbert's vocal support to remove protection for the monument to promote fossil fuel development was met by the Outdoor Retailer show pulling out of holding its annual gathering
in Salt Lake City.

Patagonia's founder, Yvon Chouinard, spearheaded the boycott with an editorial letter
arguing that outdoor recreation brings $12 billion in consumer spending in Utah and sup-
ports 122,000 jobs – three times the number of positions that the fossil fuel industry offers
in Utah.

As the Trump administration rallies to increase jobs in the fossil fuel sector and ease
environmental protections on public lands, the status of Bears Ears remains precarious.
Only this designation protects Lockhart Basin bordering Canyonlands, considered Utah's
Serengeti for its pronghorn antelope and mountain lions, from future energy leasing.

No park infrastructure has been created yet, though parts of the monument feature
trails, information centers and campgrounds already. For updates on the site, its highlights
and its status, check out www.bearsearscoalition.org.

WORTH A TRIP

ANTELOPE ISLAND STATE PARK

White-sand beaches, birds and buffalo are what attract people to the pretty, 15-mile-long **Antelope Island State Park** (☏ 801-773-2941; http://stateparks. utah.gov; Antelope Dr; day use per vehicle $10, tent & RV sites without hookups $15; ⊙ 7am-10pm Jul-Sep, to 7pm Oct-Jun). That's right, the largest island in the Great Salt Lake is home to a 600-strong herd of American bison (buffalo). The November roundup, for veterinary examination, is a thrilling wildlife spectacle. Hundreds of thousands of migratory birds stop to feast on tiny brine shrimp along the Great Salt Lake's shore en route to distant lands during fall and spring migrations.

and bar. Great deals off-season. December through April, breakfast is included.

★ **Washington School House**   BOUTIQUE HOTEL $$$
(☏ 435-649-3800; www.washingtonschoolhouse. com; 543 Park Ave; r $405; ❄ 🛜 🏊) Architect Trip Bennett oversaw the restoration that turned an 1898 limestone schoolhouse on a hill into a luxurious boutique hotel with 12 suites. How did the children ever concentrate when they could gaze out at the mountains through 9ft-tall windows instead?

✗ Eating

Park City is well known for exceptional upscale eating – a reasonably priced meal is harder to find. The ski resorts have numerous eating options in season. Dinner reservations are required at all top-tier places in winter. From April through November restaurants reduce opening hours variably, and may take extended breaks, especially in May.

★ **Vessel Kitchen**   CAFE $
(☏ 435-200-8864; www.vesselkitchen.com; 1784 Uinta Way; mains $7-13; ⊙ 8am-9pm; 🚗 ♿) Locals in the know head to this gourmet cafeteria in the shopping plaza for fast value eats. With kombucha on tap, avocado toast and lovely winter salads and stews, there's something for everyone. Even kids. Breakfasts shine with skillets of *shakshuka* (poached eggs in tomato sauce) and sweet-potato hash.

Good Karma   INDIAN, FUSION $$
(www.goodkarmarestaurants.com; 1782 Prospector Ave; breakfast $8-13, mains $12-25; ⊙ 7am-10pm; 🚗) 🌱 Whenever possible, local and organic ingredients are used in the Indo-Persian meals at Good Karma. Start the day with Punjabi eggs and dine on curries and grilled meats. You'll recognize the place by the Tibetan prayer flags flapping out front.

★ **Riverhorse on Main**   AMERICAN $$$
(☏ 435-649-3536; www.riverhorseparkcity.com; 540 Main St; dinner mains $38-60; ⊙ 5-10pm Mon-Thu, to 11pm Fri & Sat, 11am-2:30pm & 5-10pm Sun; 🚗) A fine mix of the earthy and exotic, with cucumber quinoa salad, polenta fries and macadamia-crusted halibut. There's a separate menu for vegetarians. A wall-sized window and the sleek modern design creates a stylish atmosphere. Reserve ahead: this is a longtime, award-winning restaurant.

★ **J&G Grill**   AMERICAN $$$
(☏ 435-940-5760; www.jggrilldeercrest.com; 2300 Deer Valley Drive E, Deer Valley Resort; lunch mains $17-31, dinner mains $33-65; ⊙ 7am-9pm) A favorite of locals, who love the tempura onion rings and seared scallops with sweet chili sauce. The bold flavors of meat and fish star here at one of celebrity chef Jean-Georges Vongerichten's collaborative projects. The mid-mountain **St Regis** (☏ 435-940-5700; www.stregisdeervalley.com; 2300 Deer Valley Dr E; r from $446; ❄ @ 🛜 🏊) setting is spectacular.

Wahso   ASIAN $$$
(☏ 435-615-0300; www.wahso.com; 577 Main St; mains $30-56; ⊙ 5:30-10pm Wed-Sun, closed mid-Apr–mid-Jun) Park City's cognoscenti flock to this modern pan-Asian phenomenon, where fine-dining dishes may include lamb vindaloo or Malaysian snapper. The sake martinis pack a punch. Expect to see and be seen.

🍸 Drinking & Nightlife

Main St is where it's at. In winter there's action nightly; weekends are most lively off-season. For listings, see www.thisweekinparkcity. com. Several restaurants, such as **Bistro 412** (☏ 435-649-8211; www.bistro412.com; 412 Main St; mains $13-34; ⊙ 11am-2:30pm & 5pm-1am) 🌱, **Squatters** (☏ 435-649-9868; www.squatters. com; 1900 Park Ave; burgers $10-15, mains $10-23; ⊙ 8am-10pm Sun-Thu, to 11pm Fri & Sat; 🚗) and **Wasatch Brew Pub** (☏ 435-649-0900; www. wasatchbeers.com; 250 Main St; lunch & sandwiches $10-15, dinner $10-30; ⊙ 11am-10pm Mon-Fri, 10am-10pm Sat & Sun), also have good bars.

★ **High West Distillery** BAR
(☑ 435-649-8300; www.highwest.com; 703 Park Ave; ☉ 11am-9pm Sun-Thu, to 10pm Fri & Sat, tours 3pm & 4pm) This former livery and Model A–era garage is now home to Park City's most happenin' nightspot. The ski-in distillery was founded by a biochemist whose home-made rye whiskey fuels a spicy lemonade bound to kill the strongest colds.

Spur BAR
(☑ 435-615-1618; www.thespurbarandgrill.com; 350 Main St; ☉ 10am-1am) What an upscale Western bar should be: rustic walls, leather couches, roaring fire. Good grub, too. Live music on weekends in summer or daily in ski season.

ℹ Information

Visitor Information Center (☑ 435-658-9616; www.visitparkcity.com; 1794 Olympic Pkwy; ☉ 9am-6pm; 🛜) Vast visitor center with a coffee bar, a terrace and incredible views of the mountains at **Olympic Park** (p200). Visitor guides available online.

ℹ Getting There & Around

Downtown Park City is 5 miles south of I-80 exit 145, 32 miles east of Salt Lake City and 40 miles from **Salt Lake City International Airport** (p198). Hwy 190 (closed October through March) crosses over Guardsman Pass between Big Cottonwood Canyon and Park City. In addition to public buses, a number of van services go to the airport and other mountain destinations:

All Resort Express (☑ 435-649-3999; www.allresort.com; one-way $39)

Canyon Transportation (☑ 800-255-1841; www.canyontransport.com; shared van $39)

Park City Transportation (☑ 435-649-8567; www.parkcitytransportation.com; shared van $39)

Powder for the People (☑ 435-649-6648)

Utah Transit Authority (www.rideuta.com; one-way $4.50)

The excellent **public transit system** (www.parkcity.org; 558 Swede Alley; ☉ 8am-11pm winter) covers most of Park City, including the three ski resorts, and makes it easy not to need a car to get around.

Northeastern Utah

Northeastern Utah is high-wilderness terrain, much of which is more than a mile above sea level. Most travelers come to see Dinosaur National Monument, but you'll also find other dino dig sites and museums, as well as Fremont Indian rock art and ruins in the area. Up near the Wyoming border, the Uinta Mountains and Flaming Gorge attract trout fishers and wildlife lovers alike.

Vernal

As the closest town to Dinosaur National Monument, it's not surprising that Vernal welcomes you with a large pink allosaurus. The informative film, interactive exhibits, video clips and giant fossils at the **Utah Field House of Natural History State Park Museum** (☑ 435-789-3799; http://stateparks.utah.gov; 496 E Main St; ☉ 9am-7pm Apr-Aug, to 5pm low season; 🛗) FREE make a great all-round introduction to Utah's dinosaurs.

Don Hatch River Expeditions (☑ 435-789-4316, 800-342-8243; www.donhatchrivertrips.com; 221 N 400 E; one-day tour adult/child $105/85) offers rapid-riding and gentler float trips on the nearby Green and Yampa Rivers.

Chain motels are numerous along Main St, but they book up with local workers – so don't expect a price break. **Holiday Inn Express & Suites** (☑ 800-315-2621, 435-789-4654; www.holidayinn.com/vernal; 1515 W Hwy 40; r $119-176; ❋🛜🏊) and **Landmark Inn & Suites** (☑ 435-781-1800, 888-738-1800; www.landmark-inn.com; 301 E 100 S; r from $90; 🛜) offer a few upscale touches. For dinner, try the excellent pub food at **Vernal Brewing Company** (☑ 435-781-2337; www.vernalbrewingco.com; 55 S 500 E; mains $11-20; ☉ 11:30am-9pm Mon-Sat), or go Mexican at **Don Pedro's** (☑ 435-789-3402; http://klcyads.com/don-pedros; 3340 N Vernal Ave; dishes $8-15; ☉ 11am-2pm & 5-10pm).

SCENIC DRIVE: MIRROR LAKE HIGHWAY

This alpine route, also known as Hwy 150, begins about 12 miles east of Park City in **Kamas** and climbs to elevations of more than 10,000ft as it covers the 65 miles into Wyoming. The highway provides breathtaking mountain vistas, passing by scores of lakes, campgrounds and trailheads in the **Uinta-Wasatch-Cache National Forest** (www.fs.usda.gov/uwcnf). Note that sections may be closed to traffic well into spring due to heavy snowfall; check online first.

Dinosaur National Monument

Straddling the Utah-Colorado state line, **Dinosaur National Monument** (www.nps.gov/dino; off Hwy 40, Vernal; 7-day passes per vehicle $20; ☉24hr) protects a huge dinosaur fossil bed, discovered in 1909. Both states' sections are beautiful, but Utah has the bones. Don't miss the **Quarry Exhibit** (www.nps.gov/dino; per vehicle $20; ☉8am-7pm Memorial Day–Labor Day, to 4:30pm rest of year), an enclosed, partially excavated wall of rock with more than 1600 bones protruding. In summer, shuttles run to the Quarry itself, 15 miles northeast of Vernal's **Quarry Visitor Center** (☉8am-6pm mid-May–late Sep, 9am-5pm late Sep–mid-May) on Hwy 149; out of season you drive there in a ranger-led caravan. Follow the Fossil Discovery Trail from below the parking lot (2.2 miles round-trip) to see a few more giant femurs sticking out of the rock. The rangers' interpretive hikes are highly recommended.

In Colorado, the **Canyon Area** – 30 miles further east, outside Dinosaur, CO, and home to the monument's main **visitor center** (☑970-374-3000; 4545 E Hwy 40; ☉8am-5pm May-Sep, 9am-5pm Sep-May) – holds some stunning overlooks, but thanks to its higher elevation is closed by snow until late spring. Both sections have numerous hiking trails, interpretive driving tours, Green or Yampa river access and campgrounds ($18 per tent and RV site).

Flaming Gorge National Recreation Area

Named for its fiery red sandstone formations, this gorge-ous park has 375 miles of reservoir shoreline, part of the Green River system. Resort activities at **Red Canyon Lodge** (☑435-889-3759; www.redcanyonlodge.com; 790 Red Canyon Rd, Dutch John; 2-/4-person cabin from $155/165; ☎☒) include fly-fishing, rowing, rafting and horseback riding; its pleasantly rustic cabins have no TVs but there's wi-fi in the decent restaurant. **Nine Mile Bunk & Breakfast** (☑435-637-2572; http://9mileranch.com; r $70-85, cabin $50-80, campsite $15) offers themed rooms, a log cabin and campgrounds, and can organise canyon tours.

Contact the **USFS Flaming Gorge Headquarters** (☑435-784-3445; www.fs.usda.gov/ashley; 25 W Hwy 43, Manila; park day use $5; ☉8am-5pm Mon-Fri) for the public camping

lowdown. The area's 6040ft elevation ensures pleasant summers.

Moab & Southeastern Utah

Experience the earth's beauty at its most elemental in this rocky-and-rugged desert corner of the Colorado Plateau. Beyond the few pine-clad mountains, there's little vegetation to hide the impressive handiwork of time, water and wind: the thousands of red-rock spans in Arches National Park, the sheer-walled river gorges from Canyonlands to Lake Powell, and the stunning buttes and mesas of Monument Valley. The town of Moab is the best base for adventure, with as much four-wheeling, white-knuckle rafting, outfitter-guided fun as you can handle. Or you can lose the crowd while looking for Ancestral Puebloan rock art and dwellings in miles of isolated and undeveloped lands.

Green River

The 'World's Watermelon Capital,' the town of Green River offers a good base for river running on the Green and Colorado Rivers. The legendary one-armed Civil War veteran, geologist and ethnologist John Wesley Powell first explored these rivers in 1869 and 1871. Learn about his amazing travels at the **John Wesley Powell River History Museum** (☑435-564-3427; www.jwprhm.com; 885 E Main St; adult/child $6/2; ☉9am-7pm Mon-Sat, noon-5pm Sun Apr-Oct, 9am-5pm Nov-Mar), which doubles as the local visitor center.

Holiday River Expeditions (☑800-624-6323, 435-564-3273; www.holidayexpeditions.com; 10 Holiday River St; day trip $190) run one-day rafting trips in Westwater Canyon, as well as multiday excursions. Family-owned, clean and cheerful, **Robbers Roost Motel** (☑435-564-3452; www.rrmotel.com; 325 W Main St; r from $58; ☒☎☒) is a motorcourt budget-motel gem. Otherwise, there's the **Green River State Park campground** (☑800-322-3770; http://utahstateparks.reserveamerica.com; tent/RV sites $21/30, cabins $60), or numerous chain motels where W Main St (Business 70) connects with I-70.

Residents and rafters alike flock to **Ray's Tavern** (☑435-564-3511; 25 S Broadway; dishes $8-27; ☉11am-9:30pm), the local beer joint, for hamburgers and fresh-cut French fries. Green River is 182 miles southeast of Salt Lake City and 52 miles northwest of Moab, and is a stop on the daily California Zephyr train, run by **Amtrak** (☑800-872-7245; www.amtrak.com; 250 S Broadway) to Denver, CO (from $59, 10¾ hours).

Moab

Doling out hot tubs and pub grub after a dusty day on the trail, Moab is southern Utah's adventure base camp. Mobs arrive to play in Utah's recreation capital. From the hiker to the four-wheeler, the cult of recreation borders on fetishism.

The town becomes overrun from March through October. The impact of all those feet, bikes and 4WDs on the fragile desert is a serious concern. People here love the land, even if they don't always agree about how to protect it. If the traffic irritates you, just remember – you can disappear into the vast desert in no time.

🏃 Activities

★Canyonlands Field Institute   TOURS
(☑435-259-7750; www.cfimoab.org; 1320 S Hwy 191; ☺May-Oct) This nonprofit operation uses proceeds from guided tours to create youth outdoor-education programs and train local guides. It offers occasional workshops and seminars throughout the summer. Top tours include the Rock Art Tour (8am Friday to Sunday), the geology-focused Arches Sunset Tour (4pm Friday to Sunday) and customized river trips.

Moab Desert Adventures   OUTDOORS
(☑804-814-3872; www.moabdesertadventures.com; 415 N Main St; ☺7am-7pm) Top-notch climbing tours scale area towers and walls; the 140ft arch rappel is especially exciting. Canyoneering trips are also available.

Sheri Griffith Expeditions   RAFTING
(☑800-332-2439; www.griffithexp.com; 2231 S Hwy 191; ☺8am-6pm) Operating since 1971, this rafting specialist has a great selection of river trips on the Colorado, Green and San Juan Rivers – from family floats to Cataract Canyon rapids, and from a couple of hours to a couple of weeks.

★Rim Cyclery   MOUNTAIN BIKING
(☑435-259-5333; www.rimcyclery.com; 94 W 100 N; ☺8am-6pm) Moab's longest-running family owned bike shop not only does rentals and repairs, it also has a museum of mountain-bike technology, and rents cross-country skis in the winter.

DON'T MISS

ROBERT REDFORD'S SUNDANCE RESORT

Robert Redford's **ski resort** (☑reservations 801-223-4849; 8841 Alpine Loop Scenic Byway; day lift-ticket adult/child $70/43) could not be more idyllic. There are four chairlifts and a beginner area. Most terrain is intermediate and advanced, climbing 2150ft up the northeast slope of Mt Timpanogos. It hosts the independent Sundance Film Festival (p201) and the nonprofit Sundance Institute.

🛏 Sleeping

Prices drop by as much as 50% outside March to October; some smaller places close November through March. Most lodgings have hot tubs and mini-refrigerators, and motels have laundries. Cyclists should ask whether a property provides *secure* bike storage, not just an unlocked closet.

Though there's a huge number of motels, they are often booked out. Reserve as far ahead as possible. For a full lodging list, see www.discovermoab.com.

Individual **BLM campsites** (☑435-259-2100; www.blm.gov; Hwy 128; tent sites $15; ☺year-round) in the area are first-come, first-served. In peak season, check with the Moab Information Center (p206) to see which sites are full.

Kokopelli Lodge   MOTEL **$**
(☑435-259-7615; www.kokopellilodge.com; 72 S 100 E; r $79-149; ❋ 🛜 🐾) Retro styling meets with desert chic at this great-value budget motel. Amenities include a hot tub, a BBQ grill and secure bike storage.

★Cali Cochitta   B&B **$$**
(☑435-259-4961, 888-429-8112; www.moabdreaminn.com; 110 S 200 E; cottages $155-190; ❋ 🛜) Charming and central, these adjoining brick cottages offer snug rooms fitted with smart decor. A long wooden table on the patio makes a welcome setting for communal breakfasts. You can also take advantage of the porch chairs, hammock or backyard hot tub in the Zen garden.

Pack Creek Ranch   LODGE **$$**
(☑888-879-6622; www.packcreekranch.com; off La Sal Mountain Loop; cabins $175-235; 🛜 ❋) This hidden Shangri-la's log cabins are tucked beneath mature cottonwoods and

willow trees in the La Sal Mountains, 2000ft above Moab. Most feature fireplaces; all have kitchens and gas grills (bring groceries). No TV or phones. Edward Abbey is among the artists and writers who came here for inspiration. Amenities include horseback riding and an indoor hot tub and sauna.

★ Sunflower Hill Inn   INN $$$

(☑ 435-259-2974; www.sunflowerhill.com; 185 N 300 E; r $208-293; ❋ ☎ ☲) Wow! This is one of the best bets in town. A top-shelf B&B, Sunflower Hill offers 12 rooms in a quaint country setting. Grab a room in the cozier cedar-sided early-20th-century home over the annex rooms. All rooms come with quilt-piled beds and antiques – some even have jetted tubs.

Sorrel River Ranch   LODGE $$$

(☑ 877-317-8244; www.sorrelriver.com; Mile 17, Hwy 128; r from $529; ❋ @ ☲) Southeast Utah's only full-service luxury resort and gourmet restaurant was originally an 1803 homestead. The lodge and log cabins sit on 240 lush acres, with riding areas and alfalfa fields along the Colorado River. Details strive for rustic perfection, with bedroom fireplaces, handmade log beds, copper-top tables and Jacuzzi tubs.

✖ Eating

There's no shortage of places to fuel up in Moab, from backpacker coffeehouses to gourmet dining rooms. Pick up the *Moab Menu Guide* (www.moabmenuguide.com) at area lodgings. Some restaurants close or operate on variable days, from December through March.

★ Milt's   BURGERS $

(☑ 435-259-7424; 356 Mill Creek Dr; mains $4-9; ☺ 11am-8pm Mon-Sat) Meet greasy goodness. A triathlete couple bought this classic 1954 burger stand and smartly changed nothing. Heaven is one of their honest burgers made from grass-fed wagyu beef, jammed with pickles, fresh lettuce, a side of fresh-cut fries and creamy butterscotch milkshake. Be patient: the line can get long. It's near the **Slickrock Trail** (Sand Flats Recreation Area; www.discovermoab.com/sandflats.htm; car/cyclist $5/2).

Sabaku Sushi   SUSHI $$

(☑ 435-259-4455; www.sabakusushi.com; 90 E Center St; rolls $6-11; mains $13-19; ☺ 5pm-midnight Tue-Sun) The ocean is about a million miles away, but with overnight delivery from Hawaii, you still get a creative selection of fresh rolls, catches of the day and a few Utah originals at this small hole-in-the-wall sushi joint. Go for happy hour (5pm to 6pm on Wednesdays and Thursdays) for discounts on rolls.

Twisted Sistas   CAFE $$

(☑ 435-355-0088; 11 E 100 N; lunch $11-13, mains $16-30; ☺ noon-3pm & 5-9pm Fri-Tue, 5-9pm Thu; ☑) For a calm alternative to the breweries, this low-lit cafe delivers warm ambience, attentive service and tasty food inspired by global flavors. For lighter fare, try the tapas, such as stuffed piquillo peppers and lollipop chicken. There's also a full bar. Check out the rooftop patio.

★ Desert Bistro   SOUTHERN US $$$

(☑ 435-259-0756; www.desertbistro.com; 36 S 100 W; mains $20-60; ☺ 5:30-11pm Wed-Sun) Stylized preparations of game and fresh, flown-in seafood are the specialty at this welcoming white-tablecloth restaurant inside an old house. Think smoked elk in a huckleberry glaze, pepper-seared scallops and jicama salad with crisp pears. Everything is made onsite, from freshly baked bread to delicious pastries. Great wine list, too.

ⓘ Information

Moab Information Center (www.discover moab.com; 25 E Center St; ☺ 8am-7pm; ☎) Excellent source of information on area parks, trails, activities, camping and weather. Extensive bookstore and knowledgeable staff. Walk-in only.

ⓘ Getting There & Around

Moab is 235 miles southeast of Salt Lake City, 150 miles northeast of Capitol Reef National Park, and 115 miles southwest of Grand Junction, CO.

Canyonlands Airport (CNY; www.moabairport. com; off Hwy 191), 16 miles north of town, receives flights from Salt Lake City. Major car-rental agencies, such as **Enterprise** (☑ 435-259-8505; N Hwy 191, Mile 148; ☺ 8am-5pm Mon-Fri, to 2pm Sat), have representatives at the airport.

Boutique Air (☑ 855-268-8478; www.bou tiqueair.com) flies to Salt Lake City and Denver.

There are also limited bus and shuttle van services, including **Elevated Transit** (☑ 888-353-8283; www.elevatedtransit.com; Moab to Salt Lake City airport $70) and **Moab Luxury Coach** (☑ 435-940-4212; www.moabluxury coach.com; 3320 E Fairway Loop), to get you to Salt Lake City, Grand Junction, Colorado and regional destinations.

A private vehicle is pretty much a requirement to get around Moab and the parks. Vehicle traffic is heavy in high season. There's a number of bike paths in and around town; the Moab Information Center can offer a map guide.

Coyote Shuttle (☑435-259-8656; www. coyoteshuttle.com) and **Roadrunner Shuttle** (☑435-259-9402; www.roadrunnershuttle. com) travel on-demand to Canyonlands Airport and do hiker-biker and river shuttles.

Arches National Park

Stark, exposed, and unforgettably spectacular, **Arches National Park** (www.nps.gov/arch; 7-day pass per vehicle/motorcycle/bike $25/15/10; ☺9am-4pm) boasts the world's greatest concentration of sandstone arches – more than 2000, ranging from 3ft to 300ft wide at last count. Nearly one million visitors make the pilgrimage here each year; it's just 5 miles north of Moab, and small enough for you to see the rest of it within a day. Many noteworthy arches are easily reached by paved roads and relatively short hiking trails. To avoid crowds, consider a moonlight exploration, when it's cooler and the rocks feel ghostly.

Highlights along the park's main scenic drive include **Balanced Rock**, precariously perched beside the main park road, and, for hikers, the moderate-to-strenuous, 3-mile round-trip trail that ascends the slick rock to reach the unofficial state symbol, **Delicate Arch** (best photographed in the late afternoon).

Further along the road, the spectacularly narrow canyons and maze-like fins of the **Fiery Furnace** must be visited on three-hour, ranger-led hikes, for which advance reservation is usually necessary. It's not easy: be prepared to scramble up and over boulders, chimney down between rocks and navigate narrow ledges.

The scenic drive ends 19 miles from the visitor center at **Devils Garden**. The trailhead marks the start of a 2- to 7.7-mile round-trip hike that passes at least eight arches, though most hikers only go the relatively easy 1.3 miles to Landscape Arch, a gravity-defying, 290ft-long behemoth. For stays between March and October, advance reservations are a must for the **Devils Garden Campground** (☑877-444-6777; www.recreation.gov; tent & RV sites $25). No showers, no hookups.

Because of water scarcity and heat, few visitors backpack, though it is allowed with free permits (available from the visitor center).

ⓘ LOCAL PASSPORTS

Southeastern Utah national parks sell a **Southeast Utah Parks Pass** (per vehicle $50) that's good for a year's entry to Arches and Canyonlands National Parks, plus Hovenweep and Natural Bridges National Monuments. **National Park Service Passes** (www. nps.gov/findapark/passes.htm; per vehicle adult/senior $80/10), available online and at parks, allow year-long access to all federal recreation lands in Utah and beyond – and are a great way to support the Southwest's amazing parks.

Canyonlands National Park

Red-rock fins, bridges, needles, spires, craters, mesas, buttes – **Canyonlands National Park** (www.nps.gov/cany; per vehicle 7 days $25, tent & RV sites without hookups $15-20; ☺24hr) is a crumbling, decaying beauty, a vision of ancient earth. Roads and rivers make inroads into this high-desert wilderness stretching 527 sq miles, but much of it is still untamed. You can hike, raft and 4WD here but be sure that you have plenty of gas, food and water.

The canyons of the Colorado and Green Rivers divide the park into several entirely separate areas. The appropriately named **Island in the Sky** district, just over 30 miles northwest of Moab, consists of a 6000ft-high flat-topped mesa that provides astonishing long-range vistas. Starting from the **visitor center** (☑435-259-4712; www.nps.gov/ cany; Hwy 313; ☺8am-6pm Mar-Oct, 9am-4:30pm Nov-Feb), a scenic drive leads past numerous overlooks and trailheads, ending after 12 miles at **Grand View Point**, where a sinuous trail runs for a mile along the very lip of the mesa. Our favorite short hike en route is the half-mile loop to oft-photographed **Mesa Arch**, a slender, cliff-hugging span that frames a magnficent view of Washer Woman Arch. Seven miles from the visitor center, the first-come, first served, 12-site **Willow Flat Campground** (www.nps.gov/ cany/planyourvisit/islandinthesky.htm; Island in the Sky; tent & RV sites $15; ☺year-round) has vault toilets but no water, and no hookups.

Named for the spires of orange-and-white sandstone jutting skyward from the desert floor, the wild and remote **Needles** district is ideal for backpacking and off-roading. To reach the **visitor center** (☑435-259-

4711; Hwy 211; ⊙8am-6pm Mar-Oct, 9am-4:30pm Nov-Feb), follow Hwy 191 south for 40 miles from Moab, then take Hwy 211 west. This area is much more about long, challenging hikes than roadside overlooks. The awesome **Chesler Park/Joint Trail Loop** is an 11-mile route across desert grasslands, past towering red-and-white-striped pinnacles, and through deep, narrow slot canyons, at times just 2ft across. Elevation changes are moderate, but the distance makes it an advanced day hike. The first-come, first-served, 27-site **Squaw Flat Campground** (www.nps.gov/cany; Needles; tent & RV sites $15; ⊙year-round), 3 miles west of the visitor center, fills up every day, spring to fall. It has flush toilets and running water, but no showers or hookups.

In addition to normal entrance fees, advance-reservation permits from the **NPS Backcountry Permits Office** (☑ reservations 435-259-4351; https://canypermits.nps.gov/index.cfm; 2282 SW Resource Blvd, Moab; permits $10-30; ⊙ 8:30am-noon Mon-Fri) are required for backcountry camping, mountain biking, 4WD trips and river trips. Remoter areas west of the rivers, only accessible southwest of the town of Green River, include **Horseshoe Canyon**, where determined hikers are rewarded with extraordinary ancient rock art, and the **Maze**.

Dead Horse Point State Park

Tiny but stunning **Dead Horse Point State Park** (www.stateparks.utah.gov; Hwy 313; park day use per vehicle $15, tent & RV sites $35; ⊙ park 6am-10pm, visitor center 8am-6pm Mar-Oct, 9am-4pm Nov-Feb) has been the setting for numerous movies, including the climactic scenes of *Thelma & Louise*. It's not a hiking destination, but mesmerizing views merit the short detour off Hwy 313 en route to the Island in the Sky in Canyonlands National Park: look out at red-rock canyons rimmed with white cliffs, the Colorado River, Canyonlands and the distant La Sal Mountains. The excellent **visitor center** (http://stateparks.utah.gov/parks/dead-horse; ⊙ 8am-6pm mid-Mar–mid-Oct, 9am-5pm mid-Oct–mid-Mar) has exhibits, on-demand videos, books and maps, along with ranger-led walks and talks in summer. To the south, the 21-site **campground** (☑ 800-322-3770; www.stateparks.utah.gov; sites $30, yurts $90) has limited water (bring your own if possible); no showers, no hookups. Reserve ahead.

Bluff

One hundred miles south of Moab, this little community (population 320) makes a comfortable, laid-back base for exploring Utah's desolately beautiful southeastern corner. Founded by Mormon pioneers in 1880, Bluff sits surrounded by red rock and public lands near the junction of Hwys 191 and 162, along the San Juan River. Other than a trading post and a couple of places to eat or sleep, there's not much town.

For backcountry tours that access rock art and ruins, join **Far Out Expeditions** (☑ 435-672-2294; www.faroutexpeditions.com; day tours $295) on a day or multiday hike into the remote region. A rafting trip along the San Juan with **Wild Rivers Expeditions** (☑ 800-422-7654; www.riversandruins.com; half-day trip adult/child $89/69), a history and geology-minded outfitter, also includes ancient site visits. The hospitable **Recapture Lodge** (☑ 435-672-2281; www.recapturelodge.com; Hwy 191; d $98; ✿ @ 🛈 🐾 🖳) is a rustic, cozy place to stay. Owners sell maps and know the region inside and out. You might also get off-grid at **Valley of the Gods B&B** (☑ 970-749-1164; http://valleyofthegodsbandb.com; off Hwy 261; s/d $145/175, cabins $195) 🐾, one of the original ranches in the area.

Artsy **Comb Ridge Bistro** (☑ 435-485-5555; http://combridgebistro.com; 680 S Hwy 191; breakfast mains $5-7, dinner mains $10-17; ⊙ 8am-3pm & 5-9pm Tue-Sun; 🛈 🐾) serves standout single-pour coffee, blue-corn pancakes and breakfast sandwiches loaded with peppers and eggs, inside a timber and adobe cafe, while the Western-themed **Cottonwood Steakhouse** (☑ 435-672-2282; www.cottonwoodsteakhouse.com; Hwy 191, cnr Main & 4th East Sts; mains $18-27; ⊙ 5:30-9:30pm Mar-Nov) serves substantial portions of barbecued steak and beans.

Hovenweep National Monument

Beautiful, little-visited **Hovenweep** (www.nps.gov/hove; Hwy 262; tent & RV sites $10; ⊙ park dusk-dawn, visitor center 8am-6pm Jun-Sep, 9am-5pm Oct-May) **FREE**, meaning 'deserted valley' in the Ute language, showcases several neighboring Ancestral Puebloan sites, where impressive towers and granaries stand in shallow desert canyons. The Square Tower Group is accessed near the **ranger station** (☑ 970-562-4282; www.nps.gov/hove; McElmo Rte; ⊙ 8am-6pm Apr-Sep, to 5pm Oct-Mar; ♿); other sites require long hikes. The **campground** (tent & RV sites $10) has 31 basic, first-come, first-served sites (no showers, no hookups). The main access is east of Hwy 191 on Hwy 262 via Hatch Trading Post, more than 40 miles northeast of Bluff.

Natural Bridges National Monument

Fifty-five miles northwest of Bluff, the ultra-remote **Natural Bridges National Monument** (www.nps.gov/nabr; Hwy 275; 7-day pass per vehicle $10, tent & RV sites $10; ☺24hr, visitor center 8am-6pm May-Sep, 9am-5pm Oct-Apr) protects a white sandstone canyon (it's not red!) containing three impressive and easily accessible natural bridges. The oldest, **Owachomo Bridge**, spans 180ft but is only 9ft thick. The flat 9-mile Scenic Drive loop is ideal for overlooking. The campground offers 13 basic sites on a first-come, first served basis; no showers, no hookups. There is some primitive overflow camping space, but be aware that the nearest services are in Blanding, 40 miles east.

Zion & Southwestern Utah

Wonder at the deep-crimson canyons of Zion National Park; hike among the delicate pink-and-orange minarets at Bryce Canyon; drive past the swirling grey-white-and-purple mounds of Capitol Reef. Southwestern Utah is so spectacular that the vast majority of the territory has been preserved as national park or forest, state park or BLM wilderness. The whole area is ripe for outdoor exploration, with narrow slot canyons to shoulder through, pink sand dunes to scale and wave-like sandstone formations to seek out.

Capitol Reef National Park

Not as crowded as its fellow parks but equally scenic, **Capitol Reef** (☑ext 4111 435-425-3791; www.nps.gov/care; cnr Hwy 24 & Scenic Dr; admission free, 7-day scenic drive per vehicle $10, tent & RV sites $20; ☺24hr, visitor center & scenic drive 8am-6pm Apr-Oct, to 4:30pm Nov-Mar) contains much of the 100-mile Waterpocket Fold, created 65 million years ago when the earth's surface buckled up and folded, exposing a cross-section of geologic history that is painterly in its colorful intensity.

Hwy 24 cuts grandly through the park, but make sure you head south on the **Capitol Reef Scenic Drive** (7-day pass per vehicle/

person $5/3), a paved, dead-end 9-mile road that passes through orchards – a legacy of Mormon settlement. In season you can freely pick cherries, peaches and apples, as well as stop by the historic **Gifford Farmhouse** (☺8am-5pm Mar-Oct) to see an old homestead and buy fruit-filled mini-pies. Great walks en route include the **Grand Wash** and **Capitol Gorge** trails, each following the level floor of a separate slender canyon; if you're in the mood for a more demanding hike, climb the **Golden Throne Trail** instead. The shady, green **campground** (www.nps.gov/care; Scenic Dr; sites $20) has no showers, no hookups and is first-come, first served; it fills early spring through fall.

Torrey

Just 15 miles west of Capitol Reef, the small pioneer town of Torrey serves as the base for most national-park visitors. In addition to a few Old West–era buildings, there are a dozen or so restaurants and motels.

Flirting with cowboy style, **Capitol Reef Resort** (☑435-425-3761; www.capitolreefresort.com; 2600 E Hwy 24; r $139-179, cabins & tipis from $249; 🅿❄☎☒) is one of the closest to the national park of the same name. Dressed with country elegance, each airy room at the 1914 **Torrey Schoolhouse B&B** (☑435-633-4643; www.torreyschoolhouse.com; 150 N Center St; r $120-160; ☺Apr-Oct; ❄☎) has a story to tell. (Butch Cassidy may have attended a town dance here.) After consuming the gourmet breakfast, laze in the garden or the huge 1st-floor lounge.

Thanks to its outstanding, highly stylized Southwestern cooking, **Cafe Diablo** (☑435-425-3070; www.cafediablo.net; 599 W Main St; lunch $10-14, dinner mains $22-40; ☺11:30am-10pm mid-Apr–Oct; ☑) ranks highly among the finest restaurants in southern Utah.

Boulder

Though the tiny outpost of **Boulder** (www.boulderutah.com; population 222) is just 32 miles south of Torrey on Hwy 12, you have to cross Boulder Mountain to reach it. From here, the attractive **Burr Trail Rd** heads east across the northeastern corner of the Grand Staircase-Escalante National Monument, eventually winding up on a gravel road that leads either up to Capitol Reef or down to Bullfrog Marina on Lake Powell.

The small **Anasazi State Park Museum** (www.stateparks.utah.gov; Main St/Hwy 12; $5;

ⓘ ELEVATION MATTERS

Southern Utah is generally warmer than northern Utah. But before you go making any assumptions about weather, check the elevation of your destination. Places less than an hour apart may have several thousand feet of elevation – and 20°F (10°C) temperature – difference.

➡ St George (3000ft)

➡ Zion National Park – Springdale entrance (3900ft)

➡ Cedar Breaks National Monument (10,000ft)

➡ Bryce National Park Lodge (8100ft)

➡ Moab (4026ft)

➡ Salt Lake City (4226ft)

➡ Park City (7100ft)

⊙8am-6pm Mar-Oct, 9am-5pm Nov-Feb) curates artifacts and a Native American site inhabited from AD 1130 to 1175. Rooms at **Boulder Mountain Lodge** (☑435-335-7460; www.boulder-utah.com; 20 N Hwy 12; r $140-175, ste $325, apt $230; ✳@☞🐾) are plush, but it's the 15-acre wildlife sanctuary setting that's unsurpassed. An outdoor hot tub with mountain views is a soothing spot to bird-watch. The lodge's destination restaurant, **Hell's Backbone Grill** (☑435-335-7464; www.hellsbackbonegrill.com; ⊙7.30-11.30am & 5-9.30pm Mar-Nov; breakfast $10-12, lunch $9-17, dinner $17-36) serves soulful, earthy preparations of regionally inspired and sourced cuisine – book ahead – while the nearby **Burr Trail Grill & Outpost** (☑435-335-7511; cnr Hwy 12 & Burr Trail Rd; dishes $8-18; ⊙grill 11:30am-9:30pm, outpost 8:30am-6pm Mar-Oct; ☞) offers organic vegetable tarts, eclectic burgers and scrumptious homemade desserts.

Grand Staircase-Escalante National Monument

The 2656-sq-mile **Grand Staircase-Escalante National Monument** (GSENM; ☑435-826-5499; www.blm.gov; ⊙24hr) **FREE**, a waterless region so inhospitable that it was the last to be mapped in the continental US, covers more territory than Delaware and Rhode Island combined. The nearest services, and GSENM visitor centers, are in Boulder and Escalante on Hwy 12 in the north, and Kanab on US 89 in the south. Otherwise, infrastructure is minimal, leaving a vast, uninhabited

canyonland full of 4WD roads that call to adventurous travelers who have the time, equipment and knowledge to explore.

The most accessible and most used trail in the monument is the 6-mile round-trip hike to the magnificent multicolored waterfall on **Lower Calf Creek** (Hwy 12, Mile 75; day use $5; ⊙day use dawn-dusk), between Boulder and Escalante. The 14 sought-after creekside sites at **Calf Creek Campground** (www.blm.gov/ut; Hwy 12; tent & RV sites $15), just off Hwy 12, fill fast; no showers, no hookups, and no reservations taken.

Escalante

This national-monument gateway town of 800 souls is the closest thing to a metropolis for many a lonely desert mile. Thirty slow and winding miles from Boulder, and 65 from Torrey, it's a good place to base yourself before venturing into the adjacent Grand Staircase-Escalante National Monument. The **Escalante Interagency Visitor Center** (☑435-826-5499; www.ut.blm.gov/monument; 775 W Main St; ⊙8am-4:30pm daily Apr-Sep, Mon-Fri Oct-Mar) is a superb resource center with complete information on nearby monument and forest-service lands.

Escalante Outfitters (☑435-826-4266; www.escalanteoutfitters.com; 310 W Main St; natural history tours $45; ⊙7am-9pm) is a traveler's oasis: the bookstore sells maps, guides, camping supplies – and liquor(!) – while the pleasant cafe serves homemade breakfast, pizzas and salads. It also rents out tiny, rustic cabins (from $50) and mountain bikes (from $35 per day). Long-time area outfitter **Excursions of Escalante** (☑800-839-7567; www.excursionsofescalante.com; 125 E Main St; all-day canyoneering $175; ⊙8am-6pm) leads canyoneering, climbing and photo hikes.

Other fine lodgings in town include **Canyons B&B** (☑435-826-4747, 866-526-9667; www.canyonsbnb.com; 120 E Main St; d $160; ⊙Mar-Oct; ✳☞) with upscale cabin-rooms that surround a shady courtyard, and **Escalante Grand Staircase B&B** (☑435-826-4890; www.escalantebnb.com; 280 W Main St; d $142; ✳☞), where you can get a spacious room and plenty of local information.

Bryce Canyon National Park

The Grand Staircase, a series of uplifted rock layers that climb in clearly defined 'steps' north from the Grand Canyon, culminates in the Pink Cliffs formation at this deservedly popular **national park** (☎435-834-5322; www.nps.gov/brca; Hwy 63; 7-day pass per vehicle $30; ⏰24hr, visitor center 8am-8pm May-Sep, to 4:30pm Oct-Apr). Not actually a 'canyon', but an amphitheater eroded from the cliffs, it's filled with wondrous sorbet-colored pinnacles and points, steeples and spires, and totem-pole-shaped 'hoodoos'. The park is 50 miles southwest of Escalante; from Hwy 12, turn south on Hwy 63.

Rim Road Scenic Drive (8000ft) travels 18 miles, roughly following the canyon rim past the **visitor center** (☎435-834-5322; www.nps.gov/brca; Hwy 63; ⏰8am-8pm May-Sep, 8am-6pm Oct & Apr, 8am-4:30pm Nov-Mar; 🛜), the lodge, incredible overlooks – don't miss **Inspiration Point** – and trailheads, ending at **Rainbow Point** (9115ft). From early May through early October, a free shuttle bus runs (8am until at least 5:30pm) from a staging area just north of the park to as far south as **Bryce Amphitheater**.

The park has two camping areas, both of which accept some reservations through the park website. **Sunset Campground** (☎877-444-6777; www.recreation.gov; Bryce Canyon Rd; tent/RV site $20/30; ⏰Apr-Sep) is bit more wooded, but is not open year-round. Coin-op laundry and showers are available at the general store near **North Campground** (☎877-444-6777; www.recreation.gov; Bryce Canyon Rd; tent/RV sites $20/30). During summer, remaining first-come sites fill before noon.

The 1920s **Bryce Canyon Lodge** (☎877-386-4383, 435-834-8700; www.brycecanyonforever.com; Hwy 63; r & cabins $208-270; ⏰Apr-Oct; @🛜) exudes rustic mountain charm. Rooms are in modern hotel-style units, with up-to-date furnishings, and thin-walled duplex cabins with gasfire places and front porches. No TVs. The lodge **restaurant** (☎435-834-5361; Bryce Canyon Rd; breakfast & lunch $10-20, dinner $10-35; ⏰7am-10pm Apr-Oct) 🍴 is excellent, if expensive, while **Bryce Canyon Pines Restaurant** (☎435-834-5441; Hwy 12; breakfast & lunch $5-14, dinner mains $12-24; ⏰6:30am-9:30pm Apr-Oct) is a diner classic.

Just north of the park boundaries, **Ruby's Inn** (www.rubysinn.com; 1000 S Hwy 63) is a resort complex with multiple motel lodging options, plus a campground. You can also dine at several restaurants, admire Western art, wash laundry, shop for groceries, fill up with gas, and take a helicopter ride.

Eleven miles east on Hwy 12, the small-town of **Tropic** (www.brycecanyoncountry.com) has additional food and lodging.

NEWSPAPER ROCK STATE HISTORIC MONUMENT

This tiny recreation area showcases a single large sandstone rock panel packed with more than 300 petroglyphs attributed to Ute and Ancestral Puebloan groups during a 2000-year period. The many red rock figures etched out of a black 'desert varnish' surface make for great photos. It's located 50 miles south of Moab, east of Canyonlands National Park (p207) on Hwy 211.

Kanab

At the southern edge of Grand Staircase-Escalante National Monument, vast expanses of rugged desert surround remote Kanab (population 4500). Western filmmakers made dozens of movies here from the 1920s to the 1970s, and the town still has an Old West feel.

John Wayne and Gregory Peck are among Hollywood notables who slumbered at the somewhat dated **Parry Lodge** (☎888-289-1722, 435-644-2601; www.parrylodge.com; 89 E Center St; r $119-149; ❄🛜🐾🐕). The renovated, **Canyons Lodge** (☎435-644-3069, 800-644-5094; www.canyonslodge.com; 236 N 300 W; r $169-179; ❄@🛜🐾🐕) 🐾 motel has an art-house Western feel; rooms feature original artwork. Stay there, then eat downtown at **Rocking V Cafe** (☎435-644-8001; www.rockingvcafe.com; 97 W Center St; lunch $8-18, dinner $18-48; ⏰11:30am-10pm; 🍴) or the classy **Sego** (☎435-644-5680; 190 N 300 W, Canyons Boutique Hotel; mains $14-23; ⏰5-9pm Tue-Sat), where you can expect gorgeous eats such as foraged mushrooms with goat's cheese and noodles with red-crab curry.

The **Kanab GSENM Visitor Center** (☎435-644-1300; www.ut.blm.gov/monument; 745 E Hwy 89; ⏰8am-4:30pm) provides monument information; **Kane County Office of Tourism** (☎435-644-5033, 800-733-5263; www.visitsouthernutah.com; 78 S 100 E; ⏰8:30am-6pm Mon-Fri, to 4pm Sat) focuses on town and movie sites.

Zion National Park

Get ready for an overdose of awesome. **Zion National Park** (www.nps.gov/zion; Hwy 9; 7-day pass per vehicle $30; ⏰24hr, visitor center 8am-7:30pm Jun-Aug, closes earlier Sep-May) abounds in amazing experiences: gazing up at the red-and-white cliffs of **Zion Canyon**, soaring high over the **Virgin River**; peering beyond **Angels Landing** after a 1400ft ascent; or hiking downriver through the notorious **Narrows**. But it also holds more delicate beauties: weeping rocks, tiny grottoes, hanging gardens and meadows of mesa-top wildflowers. Lush vegetation and low elevation give the magnificent rock formations a far lusher feel than the barren parks in the east.

Most visitors enter the park along Zion Canyon floor; even the most challenging hikes become congested May through September (shuttle required). If you've time for only one activity, the 6-mile **Scenic Drive**, which pierces the heart of Zion Canyon, is the one. From mid-March through early-November, you have to take a free shuttle from the **visitor center** (☑ 435-586-0895; www.nps. gov/zion; Kolob Canyons Rd; ⊗ 8am-7.30pm late May-Sep, to 5pm rest of year), but you can hop off and on at any of the scenic stops and trailheads along the way.

Of the easy-to-moderate trails, the paved, mile-long **Riverside Walk** at the end of the road is a good place to start. The **Angels Landing Trail** is a much more strenuous,

5.4-mile vertigo-inducer (1400ft elevation gain, with sheer drop-offs), but the canyon views are phenomenal. Allow four hours round-trip.

The most famous backcountry route is the unforgettable **Narrows**, a 16-mile journey into skinny canyons along the Virgin River's north fork (June through October). Plan on getting wet: at least 50% of the 12-hour hike is in the river. Split the hike into two days, reserving an overnight camping spot in advance, or finish it in time to catch the last park shuttle. A trailhead shuttle is necessary for this one-way trip.

Heading eastwards, Hwy 9 climbs out of Zion Canyon in a series of six tight switchbacks to reach the 1.1-mile Zion-Mt Carmel Tunnel, a 1920s engineering marvel. It then leads quickly into dramatically different terrain – a landscape of etched multicolor slickrock, culminating at the mountainous **Checkerboard Mesa**.

Reserve far ahead and request a riverside site in the canyon's cottonwood-shaded **Watchman Campground** (☑ reservations 877-444-6777; www.recreation.gov; Hwy 9, Zion National Park; tent sites $20, RV sites with hookups $30; ⊗ year-round; 🐾); adjacent **South Campground** (☑ 435-772-3256; Hwy 9; tent & RV sites $20; ⊗ year-round; 🐾) is first-come, first-served only. Smack in the middle of the scenic drive, rustic **Zion Lodge** (☑ 435-772-7700, 888-297-2757; www.zionlodge.com; Zion Canyon Scenic Dr; cabins/r $227/217; ❋ @ 🛜) has basic motel rooms and cabins with gas fireplaces. All have wooden porches with stellar red-rock cliff views, but no TVs. The lodge's full-service dining room, **Red Rock Grill** (☑ 435-772-7760; Zion Canyon Scenic Dr, Zion Lodge; breakfast & sandwiches $6-15, dinner $16-30; ⊗ 6:30-10am, 11:30am-2:30pm & 5-9pm Mar-Oct, hours vary Nov-Feb), has similarly amazing views. Just outside the park, the town of Springdale offers many more services.

Note that you must pay the park entrance fee to drive on public Hwy 9 in the park, even if you are just passing through.

NEW MEXICO FACTS

Nickname Land of Enchantment

Population 2.1 million

Area 121,599 sq miles

Capital city Santa Fe (population 69,976)

Other cities Albuquerque (population 556,500), Las Cruces (101,643)

Sales tax 5% to 9%

Birthplace of John Denver (1943–97), Smokey Bear (1950–76)

Home of International UFO Museum & Research Center (Roswell), Julia Roberts

Politics A 'purple' state, with a more liberal north and conservative south

Famous for Ancient pueblos, the first atomic bomb (1945), where Bugs Bunny should have turned left

State question 'Red or green?' (chili sauce, that is)

Highest/Lowest points Wheeler Peak (13,161ft) / Red Bluff Reservoir (2842ft)

Driving distances Albuquerque to Santa Fe 50 miles, Santa Fe to Taos 71 miles

Springdale

Positioned at the main, south entrance to Zion National Park, Springdale is a perfect little park town. Stunning red cliffs form the backdrop to eclectic cafes, restaurants are big on organic ingredients, and galleries are interspersed with indie motels and B&Bs.

In addition to hiking trails in the national park, you can take outfitter-led climbing,

213

canyoneering, mountain biking and 4WD trips (from $140 per person, per half-day) on adjacent BLM lands. **Zion Adventure Company** (☑435-772-1001; www.zionadventures.com; 36 Lion Blvd; canyoneering day from $177; ☺8am-8pm Mar-Oct, 9am-noon & 4-7pm Nov-Feb) offers excellent excursions, Narrows outfitting, hiker-biker shuttles and river tubing, while **Zion Cycles** (☑435-772-0400; www.zioncycles.com; 868 Zion Park Blvd; half-/full-day rentals from $30/40, car racks from $15; ☺9am-7pm Feb-Nov) is the most helpful bike shop in town.

Desert Pearl Inn (☑888-828-0898, 435-772-8888; www.desertpearl.com; 707 Zion Park Blvd; r from $239; ❋@🕱🐾) offers the most stylish digs in town, while **Red Rock Inn** (☑435-772-3139; www.redrockinn.com; 998 Zion Park Blvd; cottages $199-259; ❋🕱) has five romantic country-contemporary cottages

Zion Canyon B&B (☑435-772-9466; www.zioncanyonbnb.com; 101 Kokopelli Circle; r $159-199; ❋🕱) is the most traditional local B&B, with full gourmet breakfasts and mini-spa. The owners' creative collections of art and artifacts enliven the 1930s bungalow that is **Under the Eaves Inn** (☑435-772-3457; www.undertheeaves.com; 980 Zion Park Blvd; r $109-189; ❋🕱); the morning meal is a coupon for a local restaurant.

For a coffee and *trés bonnes crepes* – both sweet and savory – make **MeMe's Cafe** (☑435-772-0114; www.memescafezion.com; 975 Zion Park Blvd; mains $10-14; ☺7am-9pm) your first stop of the day. It also serves paninis and waffles, and for dinner, beef brisket and pulled pork. In the evening, the Mexican-tiled patio with twinkly lights at **Oscar's Cafe** (www.cafeoscars.com; 948 Zion Park Blvd; mains $12-18, breakfast $6-12; ☺8am-9pm) and the rustic **Bit & Spur Restaurant & Saloon** (www.bitandspur.com; 1212 Zion Park Blvd; mains $13-28; ☺5-11pm daily Mar-Oct, 5-10pm Thu-Sat Nov-Feb; 🕱) are local-favored places to hang out, eat and drink. Resere ahead for the excellent hotel-restaurant **King's Landing** (☑435-772-7422; www.klbzion.com; 1515 Zion Park Blvd, Driftwood Lodge; mains $16-38; ☺5-9pm) 🍴.

NEW MEXICO

They call this the Land of Enchantment for a reason. Maybe it's the drama of sunlight and shadow playing out across juniper-speckled hills, or the traditional mountain villages of horse pastures and adobe homes. Maybe it's the centuries-old towns on the northern pla-

teaus, overlooked by the magnificent Sangre de Cristos, or the volcanoes, canyons and vast desert plains spread beneath an even vaster sky. The beauty casts a powerful spell. Mud-brick churches filled with sacred art, ancient Indian pueblos, real-life cowboys and legendary outlaws, chile-smothered enchiladas – all add to the pervasive sense of otherness that often makes New Mexico feel like a foreign country.

Maybe the state's all-but-indescribable charm is best expressed in the iconic paintings of Georgia O'Keeffe. The artist herself exclaimed, on her very first visit: 'Well! Well! Well!... This is wonderful! No one told me it was like this.'

But seriously, how could they?

History

Ancestral Puebloan civilization first began to flourish in the 8th century AD, and the impressive structures at Chaco Canyon were begun not long after. By the time Francisco Vasquez de Coronado got here in the 16th century, many Pueblo Indians had migrated to the Rio Grande Valley and were the dominant presence. After Santa Fe was established as the Spanish colonial capital in around 1610, Spanish settlers fanned out across northern New Mexico and Catholic missionaries began their often violent efforts to convert the Puebloans. Following the Pueblo Revolt of 1680, Native Americans occupied Santa Fe until 1692, when Don Diego de Vargas recaptured the city.

The US took control of New Mexico in 1846 during the Mexican-American War, and it became a US Territory in 1850. Native American wars with the Navajo, Apache and Comanche further transformed the region, and the arrival of the railroad in the 1870s prompted an economic boom.

Painters and writers set up art colonies in Santa Fe and Taos in the early 20th century, and New Mexico became the 47th state in 1912. A top-secret scientific community descended on Los Alamos in 1943 and developed the atomic bomb. Some say that four years later, aliens crashed outside of Roswell...

ⓘ Information

For information on the New Mexico stretch of Route 66, visit www.rt66nm.org.
New Mexico State Parks (www.emnrd.state.nm.us) Info on state parks, with a link to campsite reservations.

New Mexico Tourism (www.newmexico.org) Information on destination planning, activities and events.

Recreation.gov (www.recreation.gov) Reservations for national park and forest campsites and tours.

Albuquerque

Albuquerque: it's the pink hues of the Sandia Mountains at sunset, the Rio Grande's cottonwood bosque, Route 66 diners and the hometown of Walter White and Jesse Pinkman. It's a bustling desert crossroads and the largest city in the state, yet you can still hear the howls of coyotes when the sun goes down.

Often passed over by travelers on their way to Santa Fe, Albuquerque has plenty of understated appeal beneath its gritty urban facade. Good hiking and mountain-biking trails abound just outside of town, while the city's modern museums explore Pueblo culture, New Mexican art and space. Take the time to let your engine cool as you take a walk among the desert petroglyphs or order up a plate of red chile enchiladas and a local beer.

👁 Sights

👁 Old Town

From its foundation in 1706 until the arrival of the railroad in 1880, the plaza, centering on the diminutive 1793 **San Felipe de Neri Church** (www.sanfelipedeneri.org; Old Town Plaza; ⊙7am-5:30pm daily, museum 9:30am-5pm Mon-Sat), was the hub of Albuquerque. Today Old Town is the city's most popular tourist area.

★**American International Rattlesnake Museum**   MUSEUM
(📞505-242-6569; www.rattlesnakes.com; 202 San Felipe St NW; adult/child $5/3; ⊙10am-6pm Mon-Sat, 1-5pm Sun Jun-Aug, 11:30am-5:30pm Mon-Fri, 10am-6pm Sat, 1-5pm Sun Sep-May) Anyone charmed by snakes and all things slithery will find this museum fascinating; for ophidiophobes, it's a complete nightmare, filled with the world's largest collection of different rattlesnake species. You'll also find snake-themed beer bottles and postmarks from every town named 'Rattlesnake' in the US.

★**Albuquerque Museum of Art & History**   MUSEUM
(📞505-242-4600; www.cabq.gov/museum; 2000 Mountain Rd NW; adult/child $4/1; ⊙9am-5pm Tue-Sun) With a great Albuquerque history gallery that's imaginative, interactive and easy to digest, as well as a permanent New Mexico art collection that extends to 20th-century masterpieces from Taos, this showpiece museum should not be missed. There's free admission on Saturday afternoons and Sunday mornings, and free guided walking tours of Old Town at 11am (March to mid-December).

👁 Around Town

★**Indian Pueblo Cultural Center**   MUSEUM
(IPCC; 📞505-843-7270; www.indianpueblo.org; 2401 12th St NW; adult/child $8.40/5.40; ⊙9am-5pm) Collectively run by New Mexico's 19

ALBUQUERQUE FOR KIDS

Albuquerque has lots on offer for kids, from hands-on museums to cool hikes.

¡Explora! (📞505-224-8300; www.explora.us; 1701 Mountain Rd NW; adult/child $8/4; ⊙10am-6pm Mon-Sat, noon-6pm Sun; 👶) From the lofty high-wire bike to the mind-boggling Light, Shadow, Color area, this gung-ho museum holds a hands-on exhibit for every type of child (don't miss the elevator). Not traveling with kids? Check the website to see if you're around for the 'Adult Night.' Hosted by an acclaimed local scientist, it's one of the hottest tickets in town.

New Mexico Museum of Natural History & Science (📞505-841-2800; www.nmnaturalhistory.org; 1801 Mountain Rd NW; adult/child $8/5; ⊙9am-5pm Wed-Mon; 👶) Dinosaur-mad kids are certain to love this huge modern museum, on the northeastern fringes of Old Town. From the T Rex in the main atrium onwards, it's crammed with ferocious ancient beasts. The emphasis throughout is on New Mexico, with dramatic displays on the state's geological origins and details of the impact of climate change; there's also a planetarium and large-format 3D movie theater (both of which have additional admission fees).

Pueblos, this cultural center is an essential stop-off during even the shortest Albuquerque visit. The museum downstairs holds fascinating displays on the Pueblos' collective history and individual artistic traditions, while the galleries above offer changing temporary exhibitions. They're arrayed in a crescent around a plaza that's regularly used for dances and crafts demonstrations, and as well as the recommended **Pueblo Harvest Cafe** (☑505-724-3510; lunch $12-16, dinner $13-28; ⊙7am-9pm Mon-Sat, 7am-4pm Sun; 🖋🖨) there's also a large gift shop and retail gallery.

Petroglyph National
Monument   ARCHAEOLOGICAL SITE
(☑505-899-0205; www.nps.gov/petr; 6001 Unser Blvd NW; ⊙visitor center 8am-5pm) FREE The lava fields preserved in this large desert park, west of the Rio Grande, are adorned with more than 23,000 ancient petroglyphs (1000 BC–AD 1700). Several trails are scattered far and wide: **Boca Negra Canyon** is the busiest and most accessible (parking $1/2 weekday/weekend); **Piedras Marcadas** holds 300 petroglyphs; while **Rinconada Canyon** is a lovely desert walk (2.2 miles round-trip), but with fewer visible petroglyphs.

Sandia Peak Tramway   CABLE CAR
(☑505-856-7325; www.sandiapeak.com; 30 Tramway Rd NE; adult/youth 13-20yr/child $25/20/15, parking $2; ⊙9am-9pm Jun-Aug, 9am-8pm Wed-Mon, from 5pm Tue Sep-May) The United States' longest aerial tram climbs 2.7 miles from the desert floor in the northeast corner of the city to the summit of 10,378ft Sandia Crest. The views are spectacular at any time, though sunsets are particularly brilliant. The complex at the top holds gift shops and a **cafeteria** (☑505-243-0605; www.sandiacrest house.com; Hwy 536; mains $5.50-14; ⊙10am-5pm, weekends only winter), while hiking trails lead off through the woods, and there's also a small **ski area** (☑505-242-9052; www.sandi apeak.com; lift tickets adult/child $55/40; ⊙9am-4pm Fri-Sun mid-Dec–Mar). If you plan on hiking down (or up), a one-way ticket costs $15.

🏃 **Activities**

The omnipresent Sandia Mountains and the less-crowded Manzano Mountains offer outdoor activities, including hiking, skiing (downhill and cross-country), mountain biking, rock climbing and camping.

Cycling is the ideal way to explore Albuquerque under your own steam. In addition to cycling lanes throughout the city, moun-

---

SCENIC DRIVE: HIGHWAY 12

Arguably Utah's most diverse and stunning route, **Hwy 12 Scenic Byway** (www.scenicbyway12.com) winds through rugged canyonland on a 124-mile journey west of Bryce Canyon to near Capitol Reef. The section between Escalante and Torrey traverses a moonscape of sculpted slickrock, crosses narrow ridge backs and climbs over 11,000ft Boulder Mountain. Pretty much everything between Torrey and Panguitch is on or near Hwy 12.

---

tain bikers will dig the foothills trails east of town and the scenic **Paseo del Bosque** (⊙dawn-dusk), alongside the Rio Grande. For details of the excellent network of cycling lanes (slated to reach 50 interconnected miles in 2018), see www.bikeabq.org.

Elena Gallegos
Open Space   HIKING, MOUNTAIN BIKING
(www.cabq.gov; Simms Park Rd; weekday/weekend parking $1/2; ⊙7am-9pm Apr-Oct, closes 7pm Nov-Mar) The western foothills of the Sandias are Albuquerque's outdoor playground, and the high desert landscape here is sublime. As well as several picnic areas, this section holds trailheads for hiking, running and mountain biking; some routes are wheelchair-accessible. Come early, before the sun gets too hot, or late, to enjoy the panoramic views at sunset amid the lonesome howls of coyotes.

🎉 **Festivals & Events**

Friday's *Albuquerque Journal* (www.abq journal.com) includes exhaustive listings of festivals and activities.

Gathering of Nations Powwow   CULTURAL
(www.gatheringofnations.com; ⊙Apr) Dance competitions, displays of Native American arts and crafts, and the 'Miss Indian World' contest. Held in late April.

⭐**International Balloon Fiesta**   BALLOON
(www.balloonfiesta.com; ⊙early Oct) The largest balloon festival in the world. You simply haven't lived until you've seen a three-story-tall Tony the Tiger land in your hotel courtyard, and that's exactly the sort of thing that happens during the festival, which features mass dawn take-offs on each of its nine days, overlapping the first and second weekends in October.

🛏 Sleeping

Route 66 Hostel   HOSTEL $

(📞505-247-1813; http://route66hostel.com; 1012 Central Ave SW; dm $25, r from $30; P@🛜) This pastel-lemon hostel, in a former residence a few blocks west of downtown, holds male and female dorms plus simple private rooms, some of which share bathrooms. The beds are aging, but there's a welcoming atmosphere, with common facilities including a library and a kitchen offering free self-serve breakfasts. Voluntary chores; no check-ins between 1:30pm and 4:30pm.

★ Andaluz   BOUTIQUE HOTEL $$

(📞505-242-9090; www.hotelandaluz.com; 125 2nd St NW; r from $174; P🕸@🛜🏊) Albuquerque's finest historic hotel, built in the heart of downtown in 1939, has been comprehensively modernized while retaining period details like its stunning central atrium, where cozy arched nooks hold tables and couches. Rooms feature hypoallergenic bedding and carpets, the **Más Tapas Y Vino** (📞505-923-9080; www.hotelandaluz.com; 125 2nd St NW; tapas $6-16, mains $26-36; ⊙7am-2pm & 5-9:30pm) restaurant is notable, and there's a rooftop bar. Reserve 30 days in advance for the best rates.

Böttger Mansion   B&B $$

(📞505-243-3639; www.bottger.com; 110 San Felipe St NW; r $115-159; P🕸@🛜) The friendly proprietor gives this well-appointed B&B, built in 1912 and one minute's walk from the plaza, an edge over tough competition. Three of its seven themed, antique-furnished rooms have pressed-tin ceilings, one has a Jacuzzi tub, and sumptuous breakfasts are served in a honeysuckle-lined courtyard loved by bird-watchers. Past guests include Elvis, Janis Joplin and Machine Gun Kelly.

★ Los Poblanos   B&B $$$

(📞505-344-9297; www.lospoblanos.com; 4803 Rio Grande Blvd NW; r $230-450; P🕸@🛜🏊) This amazing 20-room B&B, on a 1930s rural ranch that's a National Historic Place, is five minutes' drive north of Old Town. Close to the Rio Grande, it's set amid 25 acres of gardens, lavender fields (blooming mid-June through July) and an organic farm. The gorgeous rooms feature kiva fireplaces, while produce from the farm is served for breakfast.

✖ Eating

★ Pop Fizz   MEXICAN $

(📞505-508-1082; www.pop-fizz.net; 1701 4th St SW, National Hispanic Cultural Center; mains $5-7.50; ⊙11am-8pm; 🛜🚼) These all-natural *paletas* (popsicles) straight-up rock: cool off with flavors such as cucumber chile lime, mango or pineapple habanero – or perhaps you'd rather splurge on a cinnamon-churro ice-cream taco? Not to be outdone by the desserts, the kitchen also whips up all sorts of messy goodness, including carne asada fries, Sonoran dogs and Frito pies.

★ Golden Crown Panaderia   BAKERY $

(📞505-243-2424; www.goldencrown.biz; 1103 Mountain Rd NW; mains $7-20; ⊙7am-8pm Tue-Sat, 10am-8pm Sun) Who doesn't love a friendly neighborhood cafe-bakery? Especially one in a cozy old adobe, with gracious staff, oven-fresh bread and pizza (with green chile or blue-corn crusts), fruity empanadas, smooth espresso coffees and cookies all round? Call ahead to reserve a loaf of quick-selling green chile bread – then eat it hot, out on the patio.

Slate Street Cafe & Wine Loft   MODERN AMERICAN $$

(📞505-243-2210; www.slatestreetcafe.com; 515 Slate St; breakfast $7.50-15, lunch $10-15, dinner $11-27; ⊙7:30am-3pm Mon-Fri, 9am-2pm Sat & Sun, 5-9pm Tue-Thu, 5-10pm Fri & Sat; 🍴) A popular downtown rendezvous, the cafe downstairs is usually packed with people enjoying imaginative comfort food, from green chile mac-and-cheese to herb-crusted pork chops, while the upstairs wine loft serves 25 wines by the glass and offers regular tasting sessions. It's off 6th St NW, just north of Lomas Blvd.

★ Artichoke Cafe   MODERN AMERICAN $$$

(📞505-243-0200; www.artichokecafe.com; 424 Central Ave SE; lunch mains $12-19, dinner mains $16-39; ⊙11am-2:30pm & 5-9pm Mon-Fri, 5-10pm Sat) Elegant and unpretentious, this popular bistro prepares creative gourmet cuisine with panache and is always high on foodies' lists of Albuquerque's best. It's on the eastern edge of downtown, between the bus station and I-40.

🍷 Drinking & Entertainment

Popejoy Hall (📞505-925-5858; www.popejoy presents.com; 203 Cornell Dr) and the historic **KiMo Theatre** (📞505-768-3544; www.cabq. gov/kimo; 423 Central Ave NW) are the primary venues for big-name national acts, local opera, symphony and theater. **Launch Pad**

(☑505-764-8887; www.launchpadrocks.com; 618 Central Ave SW) is best for local acts.

Java Joe's CAFE
(☑505-765-1514; www.downtownjavajoes.com; 906 Park Ave SW; ⊘6:30am-3:30pm; 📶🖥) Best known these days for its explosive cameo role in *Breaking Bad*, this comfy coffee shop still makes a great stop-off for a java jolt or a bowl of the hottest chile in town.

★ **Anodyne** BAR
(☑505-244-1820; 409 Central Ave NW; ⊘4pm-1:30am Mon-Sat, 7-11:30pm Sun) An excellent spot for a game of pool, Anodyne is a huge space with book-lined walls, wood ceilings, plenty of overstuffed chairs, more than 100 bottled beers and great people-watching.

★ **Marble Brewery** BREWERY
(☑505-243-2739; www.marblebrewery.com; 111 Marble Ave NW; ⊘noon-midnight Mon-Sat, to 10:30pm Sun) Popular downtown brewpub, attached to its namesake brewery, with a snug interior for winter nights and a beer garden where local bands play early-evening gigs in summer. Be sure to try its Red Ale.

ℹ **Information**

EMERGENCY & MEDICAL SERVICES
Police (☑505-242-2677; www.apdonline.com; 400 Roma Ave NW)
Presbyterian Hospital (☑505-841-1234; www.phs.org; 1100 Central Ave SE; ⊘emergency 24hr)
UNM Hospital (☑505-272-2411; 2211 Lomas Blvd NE; ⊘emergency 24hr)

POST
Post Office (☑800-275-8777; 201 5th St SW; ⊘9am-4:30pm Mon-Fri)

TOURIST INFORMATION
Old Town Information Center (☑505-243-3215; www.visitalbuquerque.org; 303 Romero Ave NW; ⊘10am-5pm Oct-May, to 6pm Jun-Sep)
UNM Welcome Center (☑505-277-1989; 2401 Redondo Dr; ⊘8am-5pm Mon-Fri)

USEFUL WEBSITES
Albuquerque Journal (www.abqjournal.com) Local news, events and sports.
City of Albuquerque (www.cabq.gov) Public transportation and area attractions.
Gil's Thrilling (And Filling) Blog (www.nmgastronome.com) Local foodie eats his way across ABQ, Santa Fe and the rest of the state.

ℹ **Getting There & Around**

AIR
New Mexico's largest airport, **Albuquerque International Sunport** (ABQ; ☑505-244-7700; www.abqsunport.com; 🛜), is 5 miles southeast of downtown and served by multiple airlines. Free shuttles connect the terminal building with the Sunport Car Rental Center at 3400 University Blvd SE, home to all the airport's car-rental facilities.

The **Sunport Shuttle** (☑505-883-4966; www.sunportshuttle.com) runs from the airport to local hotels and other destinations.

BUS
The **Alvarado Transportation Center** (100 1st St SW, cnr Central Ave) is home to **Greyhound** (☑800-231-2222, 505-243-4435; www.greyhound.com; 320 1st St SW), which serves destinations throughout the state and beyond, though not Santa Fe or Taos.

ABQ Ride (☑505-243-7433; www.cabq.gov/transit; 100 1st St SW; adult/child $1/0.35, day pass $2) is a public bus system covering most of Albuquerque on weekdays and major tourist spots daily.

TRAIN
Amtrak's *Southwest Chief* stops at Albuquerque's **Amtrak Station** (☑800-872-7245; www.amtrak.com; 320 1st St SW), which is part of the Alvarado Transportation Center. Trains head east to Chicago (from $117, 26 hours) or west to Los Angeles (from $66, 16½ hours), once daily in each direction.

A commuter light rail line, the **New Mexico Rail Runner Express** (www.nmrailrunner.com), shares the station. It makes several stops in the Albuquerque metropolitan area, but more importantly for visitors it runs all the way north to Santa Fe (one-way $10, 1¾ hours), with eight departures on weekdays and four on weekends.

Along I-40

Although you can zip between Albuquerque and Flagstaff, AZ, in less than five hours, the national monuments and pueblos along the way are well worth a visit. For a scenic loop, take Hwy 53 southwest from Grants, which leads to all the following sights except Acoma. Hwy 602 brings you north to Gallup.

Acoma Pueblo

The dramatic mesa-top 'Sky City' sits 7000ft above sea level and 367ft above the surrounding plateau. One of the oldest continuously inhabited settlements in North America, this place has been home to pottery-making

Pueblo peoples since the 11th century. Guided tours leave from the **cultural center** (☏800-747-0181; www.acomaskycity.org; Rte 38; tours adult/child $25/17; ⊗hourly tours 8:30am-3:30pm Mar-Oct, 9:30am-2:30pm Sat & Sun Nov-Feb) at the foot of the mesa and take two hours, or one hour just to tour the historic mission. From I-40, take exit 102, which is about 60 miles west of Albuquerque, then drive 12 miles south. Check ahead to make sure it's not closed for ceremonial or other reasons.

El Morro National Monument

The 200ft sandstone outcropping at the El **Morro National Monument** (☏505-783-4226; www.nps.gov/elmo; Hwy 53; ⊗9am-6pm Jun-Aug, to 5pm Sep-May) FREE, also known as 'Inscription Rock,' has been a travelers' oasis for millennia. Thousands of carvings – from petroglyphs in the pueblo at the top (c 1275) to elaborate inscriptions by Spanish conquistadors and Anglo pioneers – offer a unique historical record. It's about 38 miles southwest of Grants via Hwy 53.

Zuni Pueblo

The Zuni are known for their delicately inlaid silverwork, which is sold in stores lining Hwy 53. Check in at the **Zuni Tourism Office** (☏505-782-7238; www.zunitourism.com; 1239 Hwy 53; tours $15; ⊗8:30am-5:30pm Mon-Fri, 10:30am-4pm Sat, noon-4pm Sun) for information, photo permits and tours of the pueblo, which lead you among stone houses and beehive-shaped adobe ovens to the massive **Our Lady of Guadalupe Mission**, featuring impressive kachina (spirit) murals. The **A:shiwi A:wan Museum & Heritage Center** (☏505-782-4403; www.ashiwi-museum.org; Ojo Caliente Rd; admission by donation; ⊗9am-5pm Mon-Fri) displays early photos and other tribal artifacts.

The friendly, eight-room **Inn at Halona** (☏505-782-4547; www.halona.com; 23b Pia Mesa Rd; r from $75; 🅿🛜), decorated with local Zuni arts and crafts, is the only place to stay on the pueblo. Its breakfasts rank with the best in the state.

Santa Fe

Welcome to 'the city different,' a place that makes its own rules without ever forgetting its long and storied past. Walking through its adobe neighborhoods, or around the busy Plaza that remains its core, there's no denying that Santa Fe has a timeless, earthy soul. Indeed, its artistic inclinations are a principal attraction – there are more quality museums and galleries here than you could possibly see in just one visit.

At over 7000ft above sea level, Santa Fe is also the nation's highest state capital. Sitting at the foot of the Sangre de Cristo range, it makes a fantastic base for hiking, mountain biking, backpacking and skiing. When you come off the trails, you can indulge in chile-smothered local cuisine, buy turquoise and silver directly from Native American jewelers in the Plaza, visit remarkable churches, or simply wander along centuries-old, cottonwood-shaded lanes and daydream about one day moving here.

◉ Sights

⭐**Georgia O'Keeffe Museum**　MUSEUM
(Map p222; ☏505-946-1000; www.okeeffemuseum.org; 217 Johnson St; adult/child $12/free; ⊗10am-5pm Sat-Thu, to 7pm Fri) With 10 beautifully lit galleries in a rambling 20th-century adobe, this museum boasts the world's largest collection of O'Keeffe's work. She's best known for her luminous New Mexican landscapes, but the changing exhibitions here range through her entire career, from her early years through to her time at Ghost Ranch. Major museums worldwide own her most famous canvases, so you may not see familiar paintings, but you're sure to be bowled over by the thick brushwork and transcendent colors on show.

⭐**Meow Wolf**　MUSEUM
(☏505-395-6369; https://meowwolf.com; 1352 Rufina Circle; adult/child $18/12; ⊗10am-8pm Sun, Mon, Wed, Thu, to 10pm Fri & Sat) If you've been hankering for a trip to another dimension but have yet to find a portal, the House of Eternal Return by Meow Wolf could be the place for you. The premise here is quite ingenious: visitors get to explore a re-created Victorian house for clues related to the disappearance of a California family, following a narrative that leads deeper into fragmented bits of a multiverse (often via secret passages), all of which are unique, interactive art installations.

Wheelwright Museum of the American Indian　MUSEUM
(☏505-982-4636; www.wheelwright.org; 704 Camino Lejo; adult/child $8/free, 1st Sun of month free; ⊗10am-5pm) Mary Cabot established this museum in 1937 to showcase Nava-

CANYON ROAD GALLERIES

Originally a Pueblo Indian footpath and later the main street through a Spanish farming community, Santa Fe's most famous art avenue embarked on its current incarnation in the 1920s, when artists led by Los Cinco Pintores (five painters who fell in love with New Mexico's landscape) moved in to take advantage of the cheap rent.

Today Canyon Rd is a top attraction, holding more than a hundred of Santa Fe's 300-plus galleries. The epicenter of the city's vibrant art scene, it offers everything from rare Native American antiquities to Santa Fe School masterpieces and in-your-face modern work. If gallery-hopping seems a bit overwhelming, don't worry, just wander.

Friday nights are particularly fun: that's when the galleries put on glittering openings, starting around 5pm. Not only are these great social events, but you can also browse while nibbling on cheese, sipping Chardonnay or sparkling cider, and chatting with the artists.

The following is just a sampling of some Canyon Rd (and around) favorites. For more, pick up the handy, free *Collector's Guide* map, or check out www.santafegalleryassociation. org. More contemporary galleries around the Railyard are also worth checking out.

Adobe Gallery (Map p222; ☑505-955-0550; www.adobegallery.com; 221 Canyon Rd; ⊙10am-5pm Mon-Sat)

Economos/Hampton Galleries (Map p222; ☑505-982-6347; 500 Canyon Rd; ⊙9:30am-4pm, closed Wed & Sun)

Gerald Peters Gallery (Map p222; ☑505-954-5700; www.gpgallery.com; 1005 Paseo de Peralta; ⊙10am-5pm Mon-Sat)

GF Contemporary (☑505-983-3707; www.gfcontemporary.com; 707 Canyon Rd; ⊙10am-5pm Mon-Sat, noon-5pm Sun)

Marc Navarro Gallery (Map p222; ☑505-986-8191; 520 Canyon Rd; ⊙11am-4pm)

Morning Star Gallery (Map p222; ☑505-982-8187; www.morningstargallery.com; 513 Canyon Rd; ⊙9am-5pm Mon-Sat)

Nedra Matteucci Galleries (Map p222; ☑505-982-4631; www.matteucci.com; 1075 Paseo de Peralta; ⊙9am-5pm Mon-Sat)

jo ceremonial art, and its major strength is Navajo and Zuni jewellery, in particular silverwork. The first gallery hosts temporary exhibits, showcasing Native American art from across North America. The gift store, known as the Case Trading Post, sells museum-quality rugs, jewelry, kachinas and crafts.

🏃 Activities

The **Pecos Wilderness** and **Santa Fe National Forest**, east of town, have more than 1000 miles of hiking and biking trails, several of which lead to 12,000ft peaks. Contact the Public Lands Information Center for maps and details, and check weather reports for advance warnings of frequent summer storms.

Mellow Velo (Map p222; ☑505-995-8356; www.mellowvelo.com; 132 E Marcy St; mountain bikes per day from $40; ⊙10am-6pm Mon-Sat) rents mountain bikes and provides trail information. Operators including **New Wave Rafting Co** (☑800-984-1444; www.newwaverafting.com; adult/child from $57/51; ⊙mid-Apr–Aug) offer white-water rafting adventures through the Rio Grande Gorge, the wild Taos Box and the Rio Chama Wilderness.

Dale Ball Trails   MOUNTAIN BIKING, HIKING
(www.santafenm.gov/trails_1) Over 20 miles of shared mountain biking and hiking trails, with fabulous desert and mountain views. The 9.7-mile Outer Limits trail is a classic ride here, combining fast singletrack in the north section with the more technical central section. Hikers should check out the 4-mile round-trip trail to Picacho Peak, with a steep but accessible 1250ft elevation gain.

Ski Santa Fe   SKIING
(☑505-982-4429, snow report 505-983-9155; www.skisantafe.com; lift ticket adult/teen/child $75/60/52; ⊙9am-4pm Dec-Mar) Often overlooked for its more famous cousin outside Taos, the smaller Santa Fe ski area boasts the same dry powder (though not quite

as much), with a higher base elevation (10,350ft). It caters to families and expert skiers, who come for the glades, steep bump runs and long groomers a mere 16 miles from town.

Santa Fe School of Cooking COOKING
(Map p222; ☎505-983-4511; www.santafeschoolofcooking.com; 125 N Guadalupe St; 2/3hr class $78/98; ⏰9:30am-5:30pm Mon-Fri, 9:30am-5pm Sat, 10:30am-3:30pm Sun) Sign up for green or red chile workshops to master the basics of Southwestern cuisine, or try your hand at rellenos, tamales or more sophisticated flavors such as mustard mango habanero sauce. It also offers several popular restaurant walking tours.

Festivals & Events

★**International Folk Art Market** CULTURAL
(☎505-992-7600; www.folkartalliance.org; ⏰mid-Jul) The world's largest folk art market draws around 150 artists from 50 countries to the Folk Art Museum for a festive weekend of craft shopping and cultural events in July.

★**Santa Fe Indian Market** CULTURAL
(☎505-983-5220; www.swaia.org; ⏰Aug) Over a thousand artists from 100 tribes and Pueblos show work at this world-famous juried show, held the weekend after the third Thursday in August. Around 100,000 visitors converge on the Plaza, at open studios, gallery shows and the Native Cinema Showcase. Come Friday or Saturday to see pieces competing for the top prizes; wait until Sunday before trying to bargain.

★**Santa Fe Fiesta & Burning of Zozobra** CULTURAL
(☎505-913-1517; www.santafefiesta.org; ⏰early Sep) This 10-day celebration of the 1692 resettlement of Santa Fe following the 1680 Pueblo Revolt includes concerts, a candlelit procession and the much-loved Pet Parade. Everything kicks off with the unmissable Friday-night torching of **Zozobra** (https://burnzozobra.com) – a 50ft-tall effigy of 'Old Man Gloom' – before some 40,000 people in Fort Marcy Park.

Sleeping

Silver Saddle Motel MOTEL $
(☎505-471-7663; www.santafesilversaddlemotel.com; 2810 Cerrillos Rd; r from $62; P❄@🛜🐾) This old-fashioned, slightly kitschy Route 66 motel compound offers the best budget value in town. Some rooms have pleasant tiled kitchenettes, while all have shady wooden arcades outside and cowboy-inspired decor inside – get the Kenny Rogers or Wyatt Earp rooms if you can. It's located 3 miles southwest of the Plaza on busy Cerillos Rd.

Black Canyon Campground CAMPGROUND $
(☎877-444-6777; www.recreation.gov; Hwy 475; tent & RV sites $10; ⏰May–mid-Oct) A mere 8 miles from the Plaza is this gorgeous and secluded spot, complete with 36 sites and hiking and biking trails nearby. Water is available, but no hookups. If it's full, Hyde Memorial State Park is just up the road, while the Big Tesuque and Aspen Basin campgrounds (free, but no potable water) are closer to the ski area.

★**El Paradero** B&B $$
(Map p222; ☎505-988-1177; www.elparadero.com; 220 W Manhattan Ave; r from $155; P❄@🛜) Each room in this 200-year-old adobe B&B, south of the river, is unique and loaded with character. Two have their own bathrooms across the hall, the rest have en suites; our favorites are rooms 6 and 12. The full breakfasts satisfy, and rates also include afternoon tea. A separate casita holds two kitchenette suites that can be combined into one.

★**Santa Fe Motel & Inn** HOTEL $$
(Map p222; ☎505-982-1039; www.santafemotel.com; 510 Cerrillos Rd; r from $149, casitas from $169; P❄@🛜🐾) Even the motel rooms in this downtown option, close to the Railyard and a real bargain in low season, have the flavor of a Southwestern B&B, with colorful tiles, clay sunbursts and tin mirrors. The courtyard casitas cost a little more and come with kiva fireplaces and little patios. Rates include a full hot breakfast, served outdoors in summer.

★**La Fonda** HISTORIC HOTEL $$$
(Map p222; ☎800-523-5002; www.lafondasantafe.com; 100 E San Francisco St; r from $259; P❄@🛜🏊🐾) Long renowned as the 'Inn at the end of the Santa Fe Trail,' Santa Fe's loveliest historic hotel sprawls through an old adobe just off the Plaza. Retaining its beautiful folk-art windows and murals, it's both classy and cozy, with some wonderful top-floor luxury suites, and superb sunset views from the rooftop **Bell Tower Bar** (Map p222; 100 E San Francisco St; ⏰3pm-sunset Mon-Thu, 2pm-sunset Fri-Sun May-Oct).

DON'T MISS

THE MUSEUM OF NEW MEXICO

The Museum of New Mexico administers four excellent museums in Santa Fe. Two are at the Plaza, two are on Museum Hill, 2 miles southwest.

Palace of the Governors & New Mexico History Museum (Map p222; 505-476-5100; www.palaceofthegovernors.org; 105 W Palace Ave; adult/child $12/free; 10am-5pm, closed Mon Oct-May) The oldest public building in the US, this low-slung adobe complex started out as home to New Mexico's first Spanish governor in 1610. It was occupied by Pueblo Indians following their revolt in 1680, and after 1846 became the seat of the US Territory's earliest governors. It now holds fascinating displays on Santa Fe's multifaceted past, and some superb Hispanic religious artwork – join a free tour if possible.

New Mexico Museum of Art (Map p222; 505-476-5072; www.nmartmuseum.org; 107 W Palace Ave; adult/child $12/free; 10am-5pm Tue-Sun) Built in 1917 and a prime early example of Santa Fe's Pueblo Revival architecture, the New Mexico Museum of Art has spent a century collecting and displaying works by regional artists. A treasure trove of works by the great names who put New Mexico on the cultural map, from the Taos Society of Artists to Georgia O'Keeffe, it's also a lovely building in which to stroll around, with a cool garden courtyard. Constantly changing temporary exhibitions ensure its continuing relevance.

Museum of International Folk Art (505-827-6344; www.internationalfolkart.org; 706 Camino Lejo; adult/child $12/free; 10am-5pm, closed Mon Nov-Apr) Santa Fe's most unusual and exhilarating museum centers on the world's largest collection of folk art. Its huge main gallery displays whimsical and mind-blowing objects from more than 100 different countries. Tiny human figures go about their business in fully realized village and city scenes, while dolls, masks, toys and garments spill across the walls. Changing exhibitions in other wings explore vernacular art and culture worldwide.

Museum of Indian Arts & Culture (505-476-1250; www.indianartsandculture.org; 710 Camino Lejo; adult/child $12/free; 10am-5pm, closed Mon Sep-May) This top-quality museum sets out to trace the origins and history of the various Native American peoples of the entire Southwest, and explain and illuminate their widely differing cultural traditions. Pueblo, Navajo and Apache interviewees describe the contemporary realities each group now faces, while a truly superb collection of ceramics, modern and ancient, is complemented by stimulating temporary displays.

✗ Eating

★ La Choza   NEW MEXICAN $
(505-982-0909; www.lachozasf.com; 905 Alarid St; lunch $9-13, dinner $10.50-18; 11:30am-2pm & 5-9pm Mon-Sat; P) Blue-corn burritos, a festive interior and an extensive margarita list make La Choza a perennial (and colorful) favorite among Santa Fe's discerning diners. Of the many New Mexican restaurants in Santa Fe, this one always seems to be reliably excellent. As with the Shed, its sister restaurant, arrive early or reserve.

Tia Sophia's   NEW MEXICAN $
(Map p222; 505-983-9880; www.tiasophias.com; 210 W San Francisco St; mains $7-12; 7am-2pm Mon-Sat, 8am-1pm Sun;) Local artists and visiting celebrities outnumber tourists at this longstanding and always packed Santa Fe favorite. Breakfast is the meal of choice,

with fantastic burritos and other Southwestern dishes, but lunch is pretty damn tasty too; try the perfectly prepared *chile rellenos* (stuffed chile peppers), or the rota of daily specials. The shelf of kids' books helps little ones pass the time.

★ Jambo Cafe   AFRICAN $$
(505-473-1269; www.jambocafe.net; 2010 Cerrillos Rd; mains $9-17; 11am-9pm Mon-Sat) Hidden within a shopping center, this African-flavored cafe is hard to spot from the road; once inside, though, it's a lovely spot, always busy with locals who love its distinctive goat, chicken and lentil curries, veggie sandwiches and roti flatbreads, not to mention the reggae soundtrack.

Dr Field Goods   NEW MEXICAN $$
(505-471-0043; http://drfieldgoods.com; 2860 Cerrillos Rd, Suite A1; mains $13.50-18;

Santa Fe

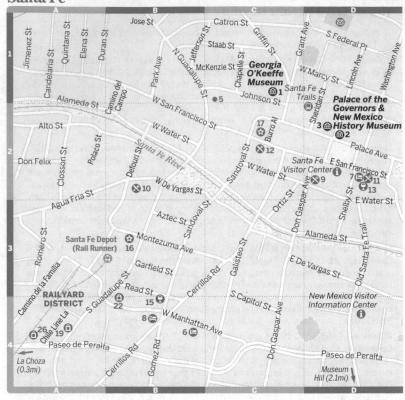

⊘11am-9pm) This locavore deli has a dedicated following, and for good reason – it's a top pick for a casual bite out on Cerillos Rd. Diners can choose between free-range buffalo enchiladas, goat tortas with honey habanero sauce, grilled fish tostadas and green chile–pulled pork sandwiches, among other delicacies. A butcher shop and bakery is a few doors down.

★Cafe Pasqual's NEW MEXICAN $$$
(Map p222; ☑505-983-9340; www.pasquals.com; 121 Don Gaspar Ave; breakfast & lunch $14-18.75, dinner $15-39; ⊘8am-3pm & 5:30-10pm; ☑🐾)
🍃 Whatever time you visit this exuberantly colorful, utterly unpretentious place, the food, most of which has a definite south-of-the-border flavor, is worth every penny of the high prices. The breakfast menu is famous for dishes such as *huevos motuleños*, made with sautéed bananas, feta cheese and

more; later on, the meat and fish mains are superb. Reservations taken for dinner only.

★La Plazuela NEW MEXICAN $$$
(Map p222; ☑505-982-5511; www.lafondasantafe. com; 100 E San Francisco St, La Fonda de Santa Fe; lunch $11-22, dinner $15-39; ⊘7am-2pm & 5-10pm Mon-Fri, 7am-3pm & 5-10pm Sat & Sun) One of Santa Fe's greatest pleasures is a meal in the Fonda's irresistible see-and-be-seen central atrium, with its excited bustle, colorful decor and high-class New Mexican food, with contemporary dishes sharing menu space with standards like fajitas and tamales.

Joseph's Culinary Pub FRENCH $$$
(Map p222; ☑505-982-1272; www.josephsofsan tafe.com; 428 Agua Fria St; mains $24-42; ⊘5:30-10pm, closed Mon Nov-Mar) This romantic old adobe, open for dinner only, is best seen as a fine-dining restaurant rather than a pub. Order from the shorter, cheaper bar menu if you'd rather, but it's worth lingering in

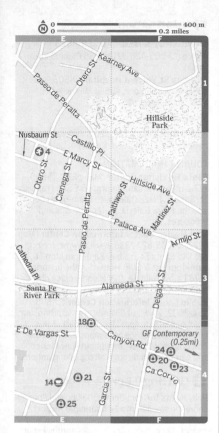

the warm-hued dining room to savor rich, hybrid French dishes with a modern twist: think campfire cassoulet with housemade sausage or sweet and spicy duck confit.

🍷 Drinking & Entertainment

★**Kakawa Chocolate House**　　CAFE
(Map p222; ☎505-982-0388; https://kakawachoc olates.com; 1050 Paseo de Peralta; ⊙10am-6pm Mon-Sat, noon-6pm Sun) Chocolate addicts simply can't miss this loving ode to the sacred bean. This isn't your mom's marshmallow-laden hot chocolate, though – these rich elixirs are based on historic recipes and divided into two categories: European (eg 17th-century France) and Meso-American (Mayan and Aztec). Bonus: it also sells sublime chocolates (prickly pear mescal) and spicy chili caramels.

★**Santa Fe Spirits**　　DISTILLERY
(Map p222; ☎505-780-5906; https://santafespir its.com; 308 Read St; ⊙3-8:30pm Mon-Thu, to 10pm Fri & Sat) The local distillery's $10 tasting flight includes an impressive amount of liquor, including shots of Colkegan single malt, Wheeler's gin and Expedition vodka. Leather chairs and exposed rafters make the in-town tasting room an intimate spot for an aperitif; fans can reserve a spot on the hourly tours of the distillery.

★**Santa Fe Opera**　　OPERA
(☎505-986-5900; www.santafeopera.org; Hwy 84/285, Tesuque; backstage tours adult/child $10/free; ⊙Jun-Aug, backstage tours 9am Mon-Fri Jun-

Aug) Many visitors flock to Santa Fe for the opera alone: the theater is a marvel, with 360-degree views of sandstone wilderness crowned with sunsets and moonrises, while at center stage the world's finest talent performs magnificent masterworks. It's still the Wild West, though; you can even wear jeans. Shuttles run to and from Santa Fe ($24) and Albuquerque ($39); reserve online.

Lensic Performing Arts Center
PERFORMING ARTS

(Map p222; ☑505-988-7050; www.lensic.com; 211 W San Francisco St) A beautifully renovated 1930 movie house, the theater hosts touring productions and classic films as well as seven different performance groups, including the Aspen Santa Fe Ballet and the Santa Fe Symphony Orchestra & Chorus.

Jean Cocteau Cinema
CINEMA

(Map p222; ☑505-466-5528; www.jeancocteau cinema.com; 418 Montezuma Ave) Revived by George RR Martin in 2013, this is the top cinema in town for indie flicks; also has book signings, occasional live concerts and an in-theater bar.

🛍 Shopping

★Santa Fe Farmers Market
MARKET

(Map p222; ☑505-983-4098; www.santafefarm ersmarket.com; Paseo de Peralta & Guadalupe St; ⊘7am-1pm Sat year-round, 7am-1pm Tue & 4-8pm Wed May-Nov; 🖪) Local produce, much of it heirloom and organic, is on sale at this spacious indoor-outdoor market, alongside homemade goodies, inexpensive food, natural body products and arts and crafts.

★Blue Rain
ART

(Map p222; ☑505-954-9902; www.blueraingallery. com; 544 S Guadalupe St; ⊘10am-6pm Mon-Sat) This large space in the Railyard district is the top gallery in town representing contemporary Native American and regional artists. There are generally several shows on at once, encompassing everything from modern pottery and sculpture to powerful landscapes and portraits.

Kowboyz
CLOTHING

(Map p222; ☑505-984-1256; www.kowboyz.com; 345 W Manhattan Ave; ⊘10am-5:30pm) Secondhand shop selling everything you need to cowboy up. Shirts are a great deal; the amazing selection of boots, however, demands top dollar. Movie costumers in search of authentic Western wear often come here.

ℹ Information

EMERGENCY & MEDICAL SERVICES
Police (☑505-428-3710; 2515 Camino Entrada)
Christus St Vincent Hospital (☑505-983-3361; www.stvin.org; 455 St Michaels Dr; ⊘24hr emergency)

POST
Post Office (Map p222; 120 S Federal Pl; ⊘8am-5:30pm Mon-Fri, 9am-4pm Sat)

TOURIST INFORMATION
Santa Fe Visitor Center (Map p222; ☑800-777-2489; www.santafe.org; 66 E San Francisco St, Suite 3, Plaza Galeria; ⊘10am-6pm) Pop into the Plaza Galeria center for maps and brochures.
New Mexico Visitor Information Center (Map p222; ☑505-827-7336; www.newmexico.org; 491 Old Santa Fe Trail; ⊘8am-5pm Mon-Fri, 8am-4pm Sat & Sun) Housed in the historic 1878 Lamy Building, this friendly place offers helpful advice and free coffee.
Public Lands Information Center (☑505-954-2002; www.publiclands.org; 301 Dinosaur Trail; ⊘8:30am-4pm Mon-Fri) Staff at this hugely helpful office have maps and information on public lands throughout New Mexico, and can talk you through all the hiking options.

ℹ Getting There & Around

Daily flights to/from Denver, Dallas, and Phoenix serve the small **Santa Fe Municipal Airport** (SAF; ☑505-955-2900; www.santafenm.gov/airport; 121 Aviation Dr), 10 miles southwest of downtown.

The **Sandia Shuttle Express** (☑888-775-5696; www.sandiashuttle.com; $30) connects Santa Fe with the Albuquerque Sunport.

North Central Regional Transit (☑505-629-4725; www.ncrtd.org) provides free shuttle bus service from downtown Santa Fe to Española on weekdays, where you can transfer to shuttles to Taos, Los Alamos, Ojo Caliente and other northern destinations. Pick-up/drop-off is by the Santa Fe Trails bus stop on Sheridan St, a block northwest of the Plaza.

On weekends, the **Taos Express** (☑866-206-0754; www.taosexpress.com; one way $5; ⊘Sat & Sun) runs north to Taos from the corner of Guadalupe and Montezuma Sts, by the Railyard.

The **Rail Runner** (www.nmrailrunner.com; adult/child $10/5) commuter train offers eight daily connections (four on weekends) with Albuquerque from its terminus in the Railyard and the South Capitol Station, a mile southwest. The trip takes about 1¾ hours. Arriving passengers can make use of the free Santa Fe Trails bus network.

Amtrak (☎800-872-7245; www.amtrak.com) serves Lamy station, 17 miles southeast, with 30-minute bus connections to Santa Fe.

If driving between Santa Fe and Albuquerque, try to take Hwy 14 (the Turquoise Trail), which passes through the old mining town (now arts colony) of Madrid, 28 miles south of Santa Fe.

Santa Fe Trails (Map p222; ☎505-955-2001; www.santafenm.gov; one way adult/child $1/free, day pass $2) operates buses from the Downtown Transit Center, with routes M, to Museum Hill, and 2, along Cerrillos Rd, being the most useful for visitors. If you need a taxi, call **Capital City Cab** (☎505-438-0000; www.capitalcitycab.com).

Around Santa Fe

Santa Fe Area Pueblos

The region north of Santa Fe remains the heartland of New Mexico's Pueblo Indian peoples. Eight miles west of Pojoaque along Hwy 502, the ancient **San Ildefonso Pueblo** (☎505-455-2273; www.sanipueblo.org; Hwy 502; per vehicle $10, camera/video/sketching permits $10/20/25; ⏲8am-5pm) was the home of Maria Martinez, who in 1919 revived a distinctive traditional black-on-black pottery style. Stop to browse the shops of the exceptional potters (including Maria's direct descendants) who work in the pueblo today.

Just north of San Ildefonso, on Hwy 30, **Santa Clara Pueblo** (☎505-753-7330) is home to the **Puyé Cliff Dwellings**, where you can visit Ancestral Puebloan cliffside and mesa-top ruins.

Las Vegas

Not to be confused with Nevada's glittery gambling megalopolis, this Las Vegas is one of the loveliest towns in New Mexico, and the largest and oldest community east of the Sangre de Cristo Mountains. Its eminently strollable downtown has a pretty Old Town Plaza and holds some 900 Southwestern and Victorian buildings listed in the National Register of Historic Places.

Built in 1882 and carefully remodeled a century later, the elegant **Plaza Hotel** (☎505-425-3591; http://plazahotellvnm.com; 230 Old Town Plaza; r $89-149; ❄@📶🐾) is Las Vegas' most celebrated lodging, as seen in the movie *No Country For Old Men*. Choose between Victorian-style, antique-filled rooms in the original building or bright, modern rooms in a newer adjoining wing. You can get your caffeine fix at **World Treasures Traveler's Cafe** (☎505-426-8638; 1814 Plaza St; salads & sandwiches $6-8.50; ⏲7am-7pm Mon-Sat; 📶), right on the plaza, and great modern American fare at **El Fidel** (☎505-425-6659; 510 Douglas Ave; sandwiches $8-13, pasta $11-14, dinner mains $16-24; ⏲11am-3pm & 5-9pm Mon-Fri, 5-9pm Sat, 11am-2pm Sun).

Los Alamos

When the top-secret Manhattan Project sprang to life in 1943, it turned the sleepy mesa-top village of Los Alamos into a busy laboratory of secluded brainiacs. Here, in the 'town that didn't exist,' the first atomic bomb was developed in almost total secrecy. Today you'll encounter a fascinating dynamic in which souvenir T-shirts emblazoned with atomic explosions and 'La Bomba' wine are sold next to books on pueblo history and wilderness hiking.

While you can't visit the **Los Alamos National Laboratory**, where classified cutting-edge research still takes place, the interactive **Bradbury Science Museum** (☎505-667-4444; www.lanl.gov/museum; 1350 Central Ave; ⏲10am-5pm Tue-Sat, 1-5pm Sun & Mon) FREE covers atomic history in fascinating detail. The small but interesting **Los Alamos Historical Museum** (☎505-662-6272; www.losalamoshistory.org; 1050 Bathtub Row; ⏲9:30am-4:30pm Mon-Fri, 11am-4pm Sat & Sun) FREE is on the nearby grounds of the former Los Alamos Ranch School – an outdoorsy school for boys that closed when the scientists arrived. Grab a bite with a boffin at the **Blue Window Bistro** (☎505-662-6305; www.labluewindowbistro.com; 813 Central Ave; lunch $10-12.50, dinner $11.25-28.50; ⏲11am-2:30pm Mon-Fri, 5-8:30pm Mon-Sat).

Bandelier National Monument

Ancestral Puebloans dwelt in the cliffsides of beautiful Frijoles Canyon, now preserved within **Bandelier** (☎505-672-3861; www.nps.gov/band; Hwy 4; per vehicle $20; ⏲dawn-dusk; 👪). The adventurous can climb ladders to reach ancient caves and kivas (chambers) used until the mid-1500s. Backcountry camping (restricted to mesa tops from July to mid-September because of flood danger) requires a free permit, or there are around 100 sites at Juniper Campground, set among the pines near the monument entrance.

Note that between 9am and 3pm, from May 14 to October 15, you have to take a shuttle bus to Bandelier from the **White Rock Visitor Center** (Hwy 4) 8.5 miles north on Hwy 4.

Abiquiu

The Hispanic village of Abiquiu (sounds like 'barbecue'), on Hwy 84 about 45 minutes' drive northwest of Santa Fe, is famous because artist Georgia O'Keeffe lived and painted here from 1949 until her death in 1986. With the Chama River flowing through farmland and spectacular rock landscape, this ethereal setting continues to attract artists. O'Keeffe's adobe house is open for limited visits, with one-hour **tours** (🖉505-685-4539; www.okeeffemuseum.org; tours $35-65; ☉ Tue-Sat mid-Mar–mid-Nov) offered at least three days per week, but often booked months in advance.

Set amid 21,000 Technicolor acres 15 miles northwest, **Ghost Ranch** (🖉505-685-1000; www.ghostranch.org; US Hwy 84; day pass adult/child $5/3; 🖷) is a retreat center where O'Keeffe stayed many times. Besides fabulous hiking trails, it holds a **dinosaur museum** and offers basic **lodging** (tent & RV sites $25, dm $69, r with/without bath from $119/109; 🌢@) plus horseback rides (from $50).

The lovely **Abiquiú Inn** (🖉505-685-4378; www.abiquiuinn.com; US Hwy 84; r from $110, casitas from $120; 🅿🛜) is a sprawling collection of shaded faux-adobes. Its spacious casitas have kitchenettes, and the menu at the onsite restaurant, **Cafe Abiquiú** (🖉505-685-4378; www.abiquiuinn.com; Abiquiú Inn; lunch $10-14, dinner $21-26; ☉7am-8pm; 🛜), includes the usual array of New Mexico specialties.

Ojo Caliente

At 140 years old, **Ojo Caliente Mineral Springs Resort & Spa** (🖉505-583-2233; www.ojospa.com; 50 Los Baños Rd; r $189, cottages $229, ste $299-399, tent & RV $40; 🌢🛜) is one of the country's oldest health resorts – and Pueblo Indians have used the springs for centuries! Fifty miles north of Santa Fe on Hwy 285, it offers 10 soaking pools with several combinations of minerals. In addition to the pleasant, if nothing special, historic hotel rooms, the resort has several plush, boldly colored suites with kiva fireplaces and private soaking tubs, and New Mexican–style cottages. Its **Artesian Restaurant** (www.ojospa.com; Hwy 285; lunch $11-16, dinner $16-32; ☉7:30am-11am, 11:30am-2:30pm &

5-9pm; 🛜🍴) 🍴 prepares organic and local ingredients with aplomb.

Taos

A magical spot even by the standards of this Land of Enchantment, Taos remains forever under the spell of the powerful landscape that surrounds it: 12,300ft snowcapped peaks rise behind town, while a sage-speckled plateau unrolls to the west before plunging 800ft straight down into the Rio Grande Gorge. The sky can be a searing sapphire blue or an ominous parade of rumbling thunderheads so big they dwarf the mountains. And then there are the sunsets...

Taos Pueblo, a marvel of adobe architecture, ranks among the oldest continuously inhabited communities in the US, and stands at the root of a long history that also extends from conquistadors to mountain men to artists. The town itself is a relaxed and eccentric place, with classic mud-brick buildings, fabulous museums, quirky cafes and excellent restaurants. Its 5700 residents include bohemians and hippies, alternative-energy aficionados and old-time Hispanic families. It's both rural and worldly, and a little bit otherworldly.

⊙ Sights

★**Millicent Rogers Museum**   MUSEUM
(🖉575-758-2462; www.millicentrogers.org; 1504 Millicent Rogers Rd; adult/child $10/2; ☉10:10am-5pm Apr-Oct, closed Mon Nov-Mar) Rooted in the private collection of model and oil heiress Millicent Rogers, who moved to Taos in 1947, this superb museum, 4 miles northwest of the Plaza, ranges from Hispanic folk art to Navajo weaving, and even modernist jewelry designed by Rogers herself. The principal focus, however, is on Native American ceramics, and especially the beautiful black-on-black pottery created during the 20th century by Maria Martínez from San Ildefonso Pueblo.

Martínez Hacienda   MUSEUM
(🖉575-758-1000; www.taoshistoricmuseums.org; 708 Hacienda Way, off Lower Ranchitos Rd; adult/child $8/4, Blumenschein Museum joint ticket $12; ☉10am-5pm Mon-Sat, noon-5pm Sun Apr-Oct, closed Wed & Thu rest of the year) Set amid the fields 2 miles southwest of the Plaza, this fortified adobe homestead was built in 1804. It served as a trading post, first for merchants venturing north from Mexico City along the Camino Real, and then west along

the Santa Fe Trail. Its 21 rooms, arranged around a double courtyard, are furnished with the few possessions that even a wealthy family of the era would have been able to afford. Cultural events are held here regularly.

Harwood Foundation Museum MUSEUM
(☑ 575-758-9826; www.harwoodmuseum.org; 238 Ledoux St; adult/child $10/free; ☉ 10am-5pm Mon-Sat, noon-5pm Sun Apr-Oct, closed Mon & Tue Nov-Mar) Attractively displayed in a gorgeous and very spacious mid-19th-century adobe compound, the paintings, drawings, prints, sculpture and photographs here are predominantly the work of northern New Mexican artists, both historical and contemporary. Founded in 1923, the Harwood is the second-oldest museum in New Mexico, and is as strong on local Hispanic traditions as it is on Taos' 20th-century school.

**Taos Art Museum
& Fechin Institute** MUSEUM
(☑ 575-758-2690; www.taosartmuseum.org; 227 Paseo del Pueblo Norte; adult/child $10/free; ☉ 10am-5pm Tue-Sun May-Oct, to 4pm Nov-Apr) Russian artist Nicolai Fechin moved to Taos in 1926, aged 46, and adorned the interior of this adobe home with his own distinctly Russian woodcarvings between 1928 and 1933. Now a museum, it displays Fechin's paintings and sketches along with his private collection and choice works by members of the Taos Society of Artists, and also hosts occasional chamber music performances in summer.

San Francisco de Asís Church CHURCH
(☑ 575-751-0518; St Francis Plaza, Ranchos de Taos; ☉ 9am-4pm Mon-Fri) Just off Hwy 68 in Ranchos de Taos, 4 miles south of Taos Plaza, this iconic church was completed in 1815. Famed for the rounded curves and stark angles of its sturdy adobe walls, it was repeatedly memorialized by Georgia O'Keeffe in paint, and Ansel Adams with his camera. Mass is celebrated at 6pm the first Saturday of the month, and usually at 7am, 9am and 11:30am every Sunday.

Blumenschein Home & Museum MUSEUM
(☑ 575-758-0505; www.taoshistoricmuseums.org; 222 Ledoux St; adult/child $8/4, Martínez Hacienda joint ticket $12; ☉ 10am-5pm Mon-Sat, noon-5pm Sun Apr-Oct, closed Wed & Thu rest of year) Wonderfully preserved adobe residence, dating originally from 1797, which provides a vivid glimpse of life in Taos' artistic community during the 1920s. Ernest L Blumenschein,

founder member of the Taos Society of Artists, lived here with his wife and daughter, Mary and Helen Greene Blumenschein, both also artists, and every room remains alive with their artworks and personal possessions.

Earthships ARCHITECTURE
(☑ 575-613-4409; www.earthship.com; US Hwy 64; self-guided tours $7; ☉ 9am-5pm Jun-Aug, 10am-4pm Sep-May) Numbering 70 Earthships, with capacity for 60 more, Taos' pioneering community was the brainchild of architect Michael Reynolds. Built with recycled materials such as used automobile tires and cans, and buried on three sides, Earthships heat and cool themselves, make their own electricity and catch their own water; dwellers grow their own food. Stay overnight (p228) if possible; the 'tour' is a little disappointing. The visitor center is 1.5 miles west of the Rio Grande Gorge Bridge on US Hwy 64.

✶ Activities

During summer, white-water rafting is popular in the Taos Box, the steep-sided cliffs that frame the Rio Grande. There are also plenty of excellent hiking and mountain biking trails. With a peak elevation of 11,819ft and a 3274ft vertical drop, **Taos Ski Valley** (☑ 866-968-7386; www.skitaos.org; lift ticket

---

CHIMAYÓ

The so-called 'Lourdes of America' – the extraordinarily beautiful two-towered adobe chapel of **El Santuario de Chimayó** (☑ 505-351-9961; www.elsantuariodechimayo.us; ☉ 9am-6pm May-Sep, to 5pm Oct-Apr) FREE – nestles amid the hills of the 'High Road' east of Hwy 84, 28 miles north of Santa Fe. It was built in 1826, on a site where the earth was said to have miraculous healing properties. Even today, the faithful come to rub the *tierra bendita* (holy dirt) from a small pit inside the church on whatever hurts. During Holy Week, about 30,000 pilgrims walk to Chimayó from Santa Fe, Albuquerque and beyond, in the largest Catholic pilgrimage in the USA. The artwork in the santuario is worth a trip on its own. Stop at **Rancho de Chimayó** (☑ 505-984-2100; www.ranchodechimayo.com; County Rd 98; mains $7-10.75, dinner $10.25-25; ☉ 11:30am-9pm, closed Mon Nov-Apr) afterward for lunch or dinner.

DON'T MISS

TAOS PUEBLO

Centered on twin five-story adobe complexes, set either side of the Río Pueblo de Taos, against the stunning backdrop of the Sangre de Cristos mountains, **Taos Pueblo** (☑575-758-1028; www.taospueblo.com; Taos Pueblo Rd; adult/child $16/free; ☺8am-4:30pm Mon-Sat, 8:30am-4:30pm Sun, closed mid-Feb–mid-Apr) are quintessential examples of ancient Pueblo architecture. They're thought to have been completed by around 1450 AD. Modern visitors are thus confronted by the same staggering spectacle as New Mexico's earliest Spanish explorers, though a small and very picturesque Catholic mission church now stands nearby.

Residents lead guided walking tours of the Pueblo (by donation) and explain some of the history. You'll also have the chance to buy fine jewelry, pottery and other arts and crafts, and sample flatbread baked in traditional beehive-shaped adobe ovens. Note that the Pueblo closes for 10 weeks around February through April, and at other times for ceremonies and events; call ahead or check the website for dates.

adult/teen/child $98/81/61; ☺9am-4pm) offers some of the most challenging skiing and boarding in the US and yet remains low-key and relaxed.

Los Rios River Runners   RAFTING
(☑575-776-8854; www.losriosriverrunners.com; 1033 Paseo del Pueblo Sur; adult/child half-day from $54/44; ☺late Apr-Aug) Half-day trips on the Racecourse – in one- and two-person kayaks if you prefer – full-day trips on the Box (minimum age 12), and multinight expeditions on the scenic Chama. On its 'Native Cultures Feast and Float' you're accompanied by a Native American guide and have lunch homemade by a local Pueblo family. Rates rise slightly at weekends.

🛌 Sleeping

Sun God Lodge   MOTEL $
(☑575-758-3162; www.sungodlodge.com; 919 Paseo del Pueblo Sur; r from $55; ▣❋🐾) The hospitable folks at this well-run two-story motel can fill you in on local history and point you to a restaurant to match your mood. Rooms

are clean – if a bit dark – and decorated with low-key Southwestern flair. The highlight is the lush-green courtyard dappled with twinkling lights, a scenic spot for a picnic or enjoying the sunset. It's 1.5 miles south of the Plaza.

★**Doña Luz Inn**   B&B $$
(☑575-758-9000; www.stayintaos.com; 114 Kit Carson Rd; r $119-209; ❋@🛜🐾) Funky and fun, this central B&B is a labor of love by owner Paul Castillo. Rooms are decorated in colorful themes from Spanish colonial to Native American, with abundant art, murals and artifacts plus adobe fireplaces, kitchenettes and hot tubs. The cozy La Luz room is the best deal in town, and there are also sumptuous larger suites.

★**Earthship Rentals**   BOUTIQUE HOTEL $$
(☑575-751-0462; www.earthship.com; US Hwy 64; earthship $185-410; 🛜🐾) 🍃 How about an off-grid night in a boutique-chic, solar-powered dwelling? Part Gaudí-esque visions, part space-age fantasy, these futuristic structures are built using recycled tires and aluminum cans, not that those components are visible. Set on a beautiful mesa across the river 14 miles northwest, they offer a unique experience, albeit rather different to staying in Taos itself. Drop-ins welcome.

★**Historic Taos Inn**   HISTORIC HOTEL $$
(☑575-758-2233; www.taosinn.com; 125 Paseo del Pueblo Norte; r from $119; ▣❋🛜) Lovely and always lively old inn, where the 45 characterful rooms have Southwest trimmings such as heavy-duty wooden furnishings and adobe fireplaces (some functioning, some for show). The famed Adobe Bar spills into the cozy central atrium, and features live music every night – for a quieter stay, opt for one of the detached separate wings – and there's also a good **restaurant** (☑575-758-1977; breakfast & lunch $7-15, dinner $15-28; ☺11am-3pm & 5-9pm Mon-Fri, 7:30am-2:30pm & 5-9pm Sat & Sun).

★**Mabel Dodge Luhan House**   INN $$
(☑505-751-9686; www.mabeldodgeluhan.com; 240 Morada Lane; r from $116; ▣) Every inch of this rambling compound, once home to Mabel Dodge Luhan, the so-called Patroness of Taos, exudes elegant-meets-earthy beauty. Sleep where Georgia O'Keeffe, Willa Cather or Dennis Hopper once laid their heads, or even use a bathroom decorated by DH Lawrence. It also runs arts, crafts, spiritual and

creative workshops. Rates include buffet breakfast. Wi-fi in public areas only.

✖ Eating

Michael's Kitchen NEW MEXICAN $
(☑ 575-758-4178; www.michaelskitchen.com; 304c Paseo del Pueblo Norte; mains $8-13.50; ☺ 7am-2:30pm Mon-Thu, to 8pm Fri-Sun; 🖐) Locals and tourists alike converge on this old favorite because the menu is long, the food's reliably good, it's an easy place for kids, and the in-house bakery produces goodies that fly out the door. Plus, it serves the best damn breakfast in town. You just may spot a Hollywood celebrity or two digging into a chile-smothered breakfast burrito.

★ Love Apple NEW MEXICAN $$$
(☑ 575-751-0050; www.theloveapple.net; 803 Paseo del Pueblo Norte; mains $17-29; ☺ 5-9pm Tue-Sun) A real 'only in New Mexico' find, from the setting in the converted 19th-century adobe Placitas Chapel, to the delicious, locally sourced and largely organic food. Everything – from the local beefburger with red chile and blue cheese, via the tamales with mole sauce, to the wild boar tenderloin – is imbued with regional flavors, and the understated rustic-sacred atmosphere enhances the experience. Reserve; cash only.

★ Lambert's MODERN AMERICAN $$$
(☑ 505-758-1009; www.lambertsoftaos.com; 123 Bent St; lunch $11-14, dinner $23-38; ☺ 11:30am-close; 🖐🖐) Consistently hailed as the 'Best of Taos,' this charming old adobe just north of the Plaza remains what it's always been – a cozy, romantic local hangout where patrons relax and enjoy sumptuous contemporary cuisine, with mains ranging from lunchtime's barbecue pork sliders to dinner dishes such as chicken mango enchiladas or Colorado rack of lamb.

☕ Drinking & Entertainment

Adobe Bar BAR
(☑ 575-758-2233; Historic Taos Inn, 125 Paseo del Pueblo Norte; ☺ 11am-11pm, music 6:30-10pm) There's something about the Adobe Bar. Everyone in Taos seems to turn up at some point each evening, to kick back in the comfy covered atrium, enjoying no-cover live music from bluegrass to jazz, and drinking the famed Cowboy Buddha margaritas. If you decide to stick around, you can always order food from the well-priced bar menu.

Caffe Tazza CAFE
(☑ 575-758-8706; 122 Kit Carson Rd; ☺ 7am-6pm) For a taste of how Taos used to be, back when hippies stalked the earth – or just to enjoy some great coffee – call in at Tazza, which now caters mostly to the crunchy-hipster-tattooed crowd. It's not everyone's cup of tea, but there's plenty of space to kick back, and most evenings see open mics or live music.

KTAOS Solar Center LIVE MUSIC
(☑ 575-758-5826; www.ktao.com; 9 Ski Valley Rd; ☺ bar 4-9pm Mon-Thu, to 11pm Fri & Sat) Taos' best live-music venue, at the start of Ski Valley Rd, shares its space with much-loved radio station KTAOS 101.9FM. Local and touring acts stop by to rock the house; when there's no show, watch the DJs in the booth at the 'world's most powerful solar radio station' while hitting happy hour at the bar.

🛍 Shopping

Taos has historically been a mecca for artists, demonstrated by the huge number of galleries and studios in and around town. Indie stores and galleries line the **John Dunn Shops** (www.johndunnshops.com) pedestrian walkway linking Bent St to Taos Plaza.

Just east of the Plaza, pop into **El Rincón Trading Post** (☑ 575-758-9188; 114 Kit Carson Rd; ☺ 10am-5pm) for classic Western memorabilia.

ℹ Information

Taos Visitor Center (☑ 575-758-3873; http://taos.org; 1139 Paseo del Pueblo Sur; ☺ 9am-5pm; 🖥) This excellent visitor center stocks information of all kinds on northern New Mexico and doles out free coffee; everything, including the comprehensive *Taos Vacation Guide*, is also available online.

ℹ Getting There & Away

From Santa Fe, take either the scenic 'High Road' along Hwys 76 and 518, with galleries, villages and sites worth exploring, or follow the lovely unfolding Rio Grande landscape on Hwy 68.

Greyhound buses do not serve Taos, but on weekdays, **North Central Regional Transit** (☑ 866-206-0754; www.ncrtd.org) provides free shuttle service to Española, where you can transfer to Santa Fe and other northern destinations; pick-up/drop-off is at the Taos County offices off Paseo del Pueblo Sur, a mile south of the Plaza.

Taos Express has shuttle service to Santa Fe on Satuday and Sunday (one-way adult/child $5/free), connecting with RailRunner trains to and from Albuquerque.

Northwestern New Mexico

New Mexico's wild northwest is home to wide-open, empty spaces. It's still dubbed Indian Country, and for good reason: huge swaths of land fall under the aegis of the Navajo, Zuni, Acoma, Apache and Laguna. This portion of New Mexico showcases remarkable ancient sites alongside modern, solitary Native American settlements. And when you've had your fill of culture, you can ride a historic narrow-gauge railroad through the mountains, hike around some trippy badlands or cast for huge trout.

Farmington & Around

The largest town in northwest New Mexico, Farmington makes a convenient base from which to explore the Four Corners area. The **visitors bureau** (☑505-326-7602; www. farmingtonnm.org; 3041 E Main St; ⊙8am-5pm Mon-Sat) has more information. **Shiprock**, a 1700ft-high volcanic plug that rises eerily over the landscape to the west, was a landmark for the Anglo pioneers and is a sacred site to the Navajo.

Fourteen miles northeast of Farmington, the 27-acre **Aztec Ruins National Monument** (☑505-334-6174; www.nps.gov/azru; 84 Ruins Rd; adult/child $5/free; ⊙8am-5pm Sep-May, to 6pm Jun-Aug) features the largest reconstructed kiva in the country, with an internal diameter of almost 50ft. A few steps away, let your imagination wander as you stoop through low doorways and dark rooms inside the West Ruin.

About 35 miles south of Farmington along Hwy 371, the undeveloped **Bisti Badlands & De-Na-Zin Wilderness** is a trippy, surreal landscape of strange, colorful rock formations, especially spectacular in the hours before sunset; desert enthusiasts shouldn't miss it. The Farmington **BLM office** (☑505-564-7600; www.blm.gov/nm; 6251 College Blvd; ⊙7:45am-4:30pm Mon-Fri) has information.

The lovely, three-room **Silver River Adobe Inn B&B** (☑505-325-8219; www.silveradobe. com; 3151 W Main St; r $115-205; ❋🛜) offers a peaceful respite among the trees along the San Juan River. Managing to be both trendy

and kid-friendly, the hippish **Three Rivers Eatery & Brewhouse** (☑505-324-2187; www. threeriversbrewery.com; 101 E Main St; mains $9-27, pizza $7.50-13.50; ⊙11am-9pm; 🛜🍴) has good steaks, pub grub and its own microbrews. It's the best restaurant in town by a mile.

Chaco Culture National Historical Park

Featuring massive Ancestral Puebloan buildings set in an isolated high-desert environment, intriguing **Chaco** (☑505-786-7014; www.nps.gov/chcu; per vehicle $20; ⊙7am-sunset) contains evidence of 5000 years of human occupation.

In its prime, the community at Chaco Canyon was a major trading and ceremonial hub for the region – and the city the Puebloan people created here was masterly in its layout and design. **Pueblo Bonito** is four stories tall and may have had 600 to 800 rooms and kivas. As well as driving the self-guided loop tour, you can hike various backcountry trails. For stargazers, there are evening astronomy presentations in summer. The park is in a remote area approximately 80 miles south of Farmington, far beyond the reach of any public transport. **Gallo Campground** (☑877-444-6777; www. recreation.gov; tent & RV sites $15) is 1 mile east of the visitor center. No RV hookups.

Northeastern New Mexico

East of Santa Fe, the lush Sangre de Cristo Mountains give way to high and vast rolling plains. Dusty grasslands stretch to infinity and beyond – or at least to Texas. Cattle and dinosaur prints dot a landscape punctuated by volcanic cones. Ranching is an economic mainstay, and on many stretches of road you'll see more cattle than cars – and quite possibly herds of bison too.

The Santa Fe Trail, along which early traders rolled in wagon trains, ran from Missouri to New Mexico. You can still see the wagon ruts in some places off I-25 between Santa Fe and Raton. For a bit of the Old West without a patina of consumer hype, this is the place.

Cimarron

Cimarron once ranked among the rowdiest of Wild West towns; its name even means 'wild' in Spanish. According to local lore, murder was such an everyday occurrence in the 1870s that peace and quiet was newsworthy, one paper going so far as to report: 'Everything is quiet in Cimarron. Nobody has been killed in three days.'

Today, the town really is quiet, luring nature-minded travelers who want to enjoy the great outdoors. Driving to or from Taos, you'll pass through gorgeous **Cimarron Canyon State Park**, a steep-walled canyon with several hiking trails, excellent trout fishing and camping.

You can stay or dine at what's reputed to be one of the most haunted hotels in the USA, the 1872 **St James** (☑575-376-2664; www.exstjames.com; 617 Collison St; r $85-135; ❋✿) – one room is so spook-filled that it's never been rented out! Many legends of the West stayed here, including Buffalo Bill, Annie Oakley, Wyatt Earp and Jesse James, and the front desk has a long list of who shot whom in the hotel bar.

Capulin Volcano National Monument

Rising 1300ft above the surrounding plains, **Capulin** (☑575-278-2201; www.nps.gov/cavo; vehicle $7; ☉8am-5pm Jun-Aug, to 4:30pm Sep-May) is the most accessible of several volcanoes in the area. A 2-mile road spirals up the mountain to a parking lot at the rim (8182ft), where trails lead around and into the crater. The entrance is 3 miles north of Capulin village, which itself is 30 miles east of Raton on Hwy 87.

Southwestern New Mexico

The Rio Grande Valley unfurls from Albuquerque down to the bubbling hot springs of funky Truth or Consequences and on toward Mexico and Texas. En route, it feeds one of New Mexico's agricultural treasures: Hatch, the so-called chile capital of the world. East of the river, the desert is so dry it's been known since Spanish times as the Jornada del Muerto, which literally translates as the 'day-long journey of the dead man.' Pretty appropriate that this area was chosen for the detonation of the first atomic bomb, at what's now Trinity Site.

Away from Las Cruces, the state's second-largest city, residents in these parts are few and far between. To the west, the rugged Gila National Forest is wild with backcoun-

try adventure, while the Mimbres Valley is rich with archaeological treasures.

Truth or Consequences & Around

An offbeat joie de vivre permeates the funky little town of Truth or Consequences ('T or C'), which was built on the site of natural hot springs in the 1880s. Originally, called, sensibly enough, Hot Springs, it changed its name in 1950, after a then-popular radio game show called, you guessed it, Truth or Consequences. Publicity these days comes courtesy of Virgin Galactic CEO Richard Branson and other space-travel visionaries driving the development of nearby **Spaceport America**, where wealthy tourists are expected to launch into orbit sometime soon.

About 60 miles north, sandhill cranes and Arctic geese winter in the 90 sq miles of fields and marshes at **Bosque del Apache National Wildlife Refuge** (www.fws.gov/refuge/bosque_del_apache; Hwy 1; per vehicle $5; ☉dawn-dusk).

🛏 Sleeping & Eating

⭐**Riverbend Hot Springs** BOUTIQUE HOTEL $$ (☑575-894-7625; www.riverbendhotsprings.com; 100 Austin St; r $97-218, RV sites $60; ❋✿✿) This delightful place, occupying a fantastic perch beside the Rio Grande, is the only T or C hotel to feature outdoor, riverside hot tubs – tiled, decked and totally irresistible. Accommodation, colorfully decorated by local artists, ranges from motel-style rooms to a three-bedroom suite. Guests can use the public pools for free, and private tubs for $10. No children under 12 years.

Blackstone Hotsprings BOUTIQUE HOTEL $$ (☑575-894-0894; www.blackstonehotsprings.com; 410 Austin St; r $85-175; 🅿❋✿) Blackstone embraces the T or C spirit with an upscale wink, decorating each of its ten rooms in the style of a classic TV show, from *The Jetsons* to *The Golden Girls* to *I Love Lucy*. Best part? Each room comes with its own oversized tub or waterfall fed from the hot springs. No children under 12.

Passion Pie Cafe CAFE $ (☑575-894-0008; www.deepwaterfarm.com; 406 Main St; breakfast & lunch mains $4.25-9.50; ☉7am-3pm; ✿) Watch T or C get its morning groove on through the windows of this espresso cafe, and set yourself up with a breakfast waffle; the Elvis (with peanut butter) or the Fat Elvis (with bacon too) should do the job. Later on there are plenty of healthy salads and sandwiches.

Las Cruces & Around

Las Cruces and her older and smaller sister city, Mesilla, sit at the edge of a broad basin beneath the fluted Organ Mountains, at the crossroads of two major highways, I-10 and I-25. An eclectic mix of old and young, Las Cruces is home to New Mexico State University (NMSU), whose 18,000 students infuse it with a healthy dose of youthful liveliness, while at the same time its 350 days of sunshine and numerous golf courses are turning it into a popular retirement destination.

◉ Sights

For many, a visit to neighboring **Mesilla** (aka Old Mesilla) is the highlight of their time in Las Cruces. Wander a few blocks off Old Mesilla's plaza to gather the essence of a mid-19th-century Southwestern town of Hispanic heritage.

★**New Mexico Farm & Ranch Heritage Museum**   MUSEUM
(☑575-522-4100; www.nmfarmandranchmuseum.org; 4100 Dripping Springs Rd; adult/child $5/3; ⊙9am-5pm Mon-Sat, noon-5pm Sun; ⊕) This terrific museum doesn't just display engaging exhibits on the state's agricultural history – it's got livestock too. Enclosures on the working farm alongside hold assorted breeds of cattle, along with horses, donkeys, sheep and goats. The taciturn cowboys who tend the animals proffer little extra information, but they add color, and you can even buy a pony if you have $450 to spare. There are daily milking demonstrations plus weekly displays of blacksmithing, spinning and weaving, and heritage cooking.

White Sands Missile Test Center Museum   MUSEUM
(☑575-678-3358; www.wsmr-history.org; ⊙8am-4pm Mon-Fri, 10am-3pm Sat) FREE Explore New Mexico's military technology history with a visit to this museum, 25 miles east of Las Cruces along Hwy 70. It represents the heart of the White Sands Missile Range, a major testing site since 1945. There's a missile garden, a real V-2 rocket and a museum with lots of defense-related artifacts. Visitors have to park outside the Test Center gate and check in at the office before walking in.

🛌 Sleeping

★**Best Western Mission Inn**   MOTEL $
(☑575-524-8591; www.bwmissioninn.com; 1765 S Main St; r from $71; ❋🐾🛜❄) A truly out-of-the-ordinary accommodation option: yes it's a roadside chain motel, but the rooms are beautifully kitted out with attractive tiling, stonework and colorful stenciled designs; they're sizable and comfortable; and the rates are great.

★**Lundeen Inn of the Arts**   B&B $$
(☑505-526-3326; www.innofthearts.com; 618 S Alameda Blvd, Las Cruces; r/ste $125/155; 🅿❋🛜❄) Each of the 20 guest rooms in this large and very lovely century-old Mexican Territorial–style inn is unique and decorated in the style of a New Mexico artist. Check out the soaring pressed-tin ceilings in the great room. Owners Linda and Jerry offer the kind of genteel hospitality you seldom find these days.

✘ Eating

★**Chala's Wood-Fired Grill**   NEW MEXICAN $
(☑575-652-4143; 2790 Ave de Mesilla, Mesilla; mains $5-10; ⊙8am-9pm Mon-Sat, to 8pm Sun) With house-smoked carnitas and turkey, housemade bacon and chile-pork sausage, plus *calabacitas* (squash and corn), quinoa salad and organic greens, this place rises well above the standard New Mexican diner fare. Located at the southern end of Mesilla, it's kick-back casual and the price is right.

Double Eagle Restaurant   STEAK $$$
(☑575-523-6700; www.double-eagle-mesilla.com; 308 Calle de Guadalupe, Mesilla; mains $24-45; ⊙11am-10pm Mon-Sat, 11am-9pm Sun) A glorious melange of Wild West opulence, all dark wood and velvet hangings, and featuring a fabulous old bar, this Plaza restaurant is on the National Register of Historic Places. The main dining room offers continental and Southwestern cuisine, especially steaks, while the less formal **Peppers** (mains $7 to $15) occupies the verdant courtyard.

❶ Information

Las Cruces Visitors Bureau (☑575-541-2444; www.lascrucescvb.org; 211 N Water St; ⊙8am-5pm Mon-Fri)

Mesilla Visitor Center (☑575-524-3262; www.oldmesilla.org; 2231 Ave de Mesilla; ⊙9:30am-4:30pm Mon-Sat, 11am-3pm Sun)

ⓘ Getting There & Away

Greyhound (☑575-523-1824; www.greyhound. com; 800 E Thorpe Rd, Chucky's Convenience Store) Buses run to all major destinations in the area, including El Paso, Albuquerque and Tucson. The bus stop is about 7 miles north of town.

Las Cruces Shuttle Service (☑575-525-1784; www.lascrucesshuttle.com) Runs eight to 10 vans daily to the El Paso International Airport ($49 one-way, $33 each additional person), and to Deming, Silver City and other destinations on request.

Silver City & Around

The spirit of the Wild West still hangs in the air in Silver City, 113 miles northwest of Las Cruces, as if Billy the Kid himself – who grew up here – might amble past at any moment. But things are changing, as the mountain-man/cowboy vibe succumbs to the charms of art galleries, coffee houses and gelato.

Silver City is also the gateway to outdoor activities in the **Gila National Forest**, which is rugged country suitable for remote cross-country skiing, backpacking, camping, and fishing. Two hours north of town, up a winding 42-mile road, is **Gila Cliff Dwellings National Monument** (☑575-536-9461; www.nps.gov/gicl; Hwy 15; adult/child $5/free; ⊗trail 9am-4pm, visitor center to 4:30pm), occupied in the 13th century by the Mogollon people. Mysterious and relatively isolated, these remarkable cliff dwellings are easily accessed from a 1-mile loop trail and look very much as they would have at the turn of the first millennium. For pictographs, stop by the **Lower Scorpion Campground** and walk a short distance along the marked trail.

Weird rounded monoliths make the **City of Rocks State Park** an intriguing playground, with great **camping** (☑575-536-2800; www.nmparks.com; Hwy 61; tent/RV sites $10/18) among the formations; there are tables and fire pits. For a rock-lined gem of a spot, check out campsite 43, the Lynx. Head 33 miles southeast of Silver City along Hwy 180 and Hwy 61.

For a smattering of Silver City's architectural history, overnight in the 22-room **Palace Hotel** (☑575-388-1811; www.silvercity palacehotel.com; 106 W Broadway; r incl breakfast $58-94; ❉🛜). Exuding a low-key, turn-of-the-19th-century charm (no air-con, older fixtures), the Palace is a great choice for those tired of cookie-cutter chains.

Downtown eating options range from the comfy, come-as-you-are **Javalina** (☑575-388-1350; 201 N Bullard St; ⊗6am-6pm Sun-Thu, to 9pm Fri & Sat; 🛜) coffee shop to the gastronomically adventurous **1zero6** (☑575-313-4418; http://1zero6-jake.blogspot.com; 106 N Texas St; mains $19-24; ⊗5pm-10pm Fri-Sun). For a taste of local culture, head 7 miles north to Pinos Altos and the atmospheric **Buckhorn Saloon** (☑575-538-9911; www.buckhorn saloonandoperahouse.com; 32 Main St, Pinos Altos; mains $11-49; ⊗4-10pm Mon-Sat), where the specialty is steak and there's live music most nights. Call for reservations.

ⓘ Information

Visitor Center (☑575-538-5555; www.silver citytourism.org; 201 N Hudson St; ⊗9am-5pm Mon-Sat, 10am-2pm Sun) This helpful office can provide everything you need to make the most of Silver City.

Gila National Forest Ranger Station (☑575-388-8201; www.fs.fed.us/r3/gila; 3005 E Camino del Bosque; ⊗8am-4pm Mon-Fri)

Southeastern New Mexico

Two extraordinary natural wonders are tucked away in New Mexico's arid southeast: the mesmerizing White Sands National Monument and the magnificent Carlsbad Caverns National Park. This region also swirls with some of the state's most enduring legends: aliens in Roswell, Billy the Kid in Lincoln, and Smokey Bear in Capitan. Most of the lowlands are covered by hot, rugged Chihuahuan Desert – once submerged under the ocean – but you can always escape to the cooler climes around the popular forest resorts of Cloudcroft or Ruidoso.

White Sands National Monument

Slide, roll and slither through brilliant, towerings and hills. Sixteen miles southwest of Alamogordo (15 miles southwest of Hwy82/70), gypsum covers 275 sq miles to create a dazzling white landscape at this crisp, stark **monument** (☑575-479-6124; www.nps.gov/whsa; adult/under 16yr $5/free; ⊗7am-9pm Jun-Aug, to sunset Sep-May). These captivating windswept dunes, which doubled as David Bowie's space-alien home planet in *The Man Who Fell To Earth*, are a highlight of any trip to New Mexico. Don't forget your sunglasses – the sand is as bright as snow!

WORTH A TRIP

PEERING INTO THE COSMIC UNKNOWN

Beyond the town of Magdalena on Hwy 60, 130 miles southwest of Albuquerque, the amazing **Very Large Array** (VLA; ☑505-835-7000; www. nrao.edu; off Hwy 52; adult/child $6/free; ☉8:30am-sunset) radio telescope consists of 27 huge antenna dishes sprouting like giant mushrooms in the high plains. Watch a short film at the visitor center, then take a self-guided walking tour with a window peek into the control building.

Spring for a $15 plastic saucer at the visitor center gift store then sled one of the backdunes. It's fun, and you can sell the disc back for $5 at day's end. Check the park calendar for sunset strolls and occasional moonlight bicycle rides (adult/child $5/2.50). Backcountry campsites, with no water or toilet facilities, are a mile from the scenic drive. Pick up a permit ($3, issued first-come, first-served) in person at the visitor center at least one hour before sunset.

Alamogordo & Around

In Alamogordo, a desert outpost famous for its space- and atomic-research programs, the four-story **New Mexico Museum of Space History** (☑575-437-2840; www.nmspacemuseum.org; 3198 Hwy 2001; adult/child $7/5; ☉10am-5pm Wed-Sat & Mon, noon-5pm Sun; 🚹) has excellent exhibits on space research and flight, and shows outstanding science-themed films in its adjoining **New Horizons Dome Theater** (adult/child $7/5).

Motels stretch along White Sands Blvd, including a decent branch of **Super 8** (☑575-434-4205; www.wyndhamhotels.com; 3204 N White Sands Blvd; r incl breakfast from $60; ✴@🛜). If you'd rather camp, hit **Oliver Lee State Park** (☑575-437-8284; www.nmparks. com; 409 Dog Canyon Rd; tent/RV sites $8/14), 12 miles south of Alamogordo. Grab some good Mexican grub at the brisk **Rizo's** (☑575-434-2607; 1480 White Sands Blvd; $8.75-15; ☉9am-9pm Tue-Sat, to 6pm Sun; 🛜).

Cloudcroft

Situated high in the mountains, little Cloudcroft provides welcome relief from the lowlands heat. With turn-of-the-19th-century buildings, it offers lots of outdoor recreation, is a good base for exploration and has a low-key feel. **High Altitude** (☑575-682-1229; 310 Burro Ave; rentals per day from $30; ☉10am-5:30pm Mon-Thu, to 6pm Fri & Sat, to 5pm Sun) rents mountain bikes and has maps of local fat-tire routes.

The **Lodge Resort & Spa** (☑800-395-6343; www.thelodgeresort.com; 601 Corona Pl; r $125-235; @🛜✴) is one of the Southwest's finest historic hotels. Rooms in the main Bavarian-style hotel are furnished with period and Victorian pieces, while the great-value **Cloudcroft Mountain Park Hostel** (☑575-682-0555; www.cloudcrofthostel.com; 1049 Hwy 82; dm $19, r with shared bath $35-60; 🛜🚹) sits on 28 wooded acres west of town. **Rebecca's** (☑575-682-3131; Lodge Resort, 601 Corona Pl; lunch $9-15, dinner $22-38; ☉7-10am, 11:30am-2pm & 5:30-9pm) offers the best food in town.

Ruidoso

Perched on the eastern slopes of Sierra Blanca Peak (11,981ft), Ruidoso is a year-round resort town that's downright bustling in the summer, attracts skiers in winter, has a lively arts scene, and is also home to a renowned racetrack. Neighboring Texans and locals escaping the summer heat of Alamogordo and Roswell are happy campers here (or more precisely, happy cabiners). The lovely Rio Ruidoso, a small creek with good fishing, runs through town.

☉ Sights & Activities

To stretch your legs, try the easily accessible forest trails on Cedar Creek Rd just west of Smokey Bear Ranger Station. Choose from the USFS Fitness Trail or the meandering paths at the Cedar Creek Picnic Area. Longer day hikes and backpacking routes abound in the White Mountain Wilderness, north of town. Always check fire restrictions around here – the forest closes during dry spells.

Hubbard Museum of the American West MUSEUM
(☑575-378-4142; www.hubbardmuseum.org; 26301 Hwy 70; adult/child $7/2; ☉9am-5pm Thu-Mon; 🚹) This town-run museum focuses on local history, with a wonderful gallery of old photos, and also displays Native American kachinas, war bonnets, weapons and pottery. Traces of its original incarnation as

the Museum of the Horse linger in various horse-related exhibits – and be sure to check out the fascinating, if completely irrelevant, history of toilets in the restrooms.

Ski Apache
SKIING

(☑575-464-3600; www.skiapache.com; 1286 Ski Run Rd; lift ticket adult/child $68/48) Unlikely as it sounds, Ski Apache, 18 miles northwest of Ruidoso on the slopes of Sierra Blanca Peak, really is owned by the Apache. Potentially it's the finest ski area south of Albuquerque, a good choice for affordability and fun. Snowfall down here can be sporadic, though – check conditions ahead.

🛏 Sleeping & Eating

Rental cabins are a big deal in Ruidoso. Most have kitchens and grills, and often fireplaces and decks. Some cabins in town are cramped, while newer ones are concentrated in the Upper Canyon. There's also free primitive camping along the forest roads on the way to the ski area; for campsite specifics, ask at the **ranger station** (☑575-257-4095; www.fs.usda.gov/lincoln; 901 Mechem Dr; ⊘8am-4pm Mon-Fri, plus Sat in summer).

Sitzmark Chalet
HOTEL $

(☑575-257-4140; www.sitzmark-chalet.com; 627 Sudderth Dr; r from $87; ❄🐾) This ski-themed chalet offers 17 simple but nice rooms. Picnic tables, grills and an eight-person hot tub are welcome perks.

Upper Canyon Inn
LODGE $$

(☑575-257-3005; www.uppercanyoninn.com; 215 Main Rd; r & cabins from $149; ❄🐾🐕) Rooms and cabins here range from simple good values to rustic-chic luxury. Bigger doesn't necessarily mean more expensive, so look at a few options. The pricier cabins have some fine interior woodwork and Jacuzzi tubs.

★ Cornerstone Bakery
CAFE $

(☑575-257-1842; www.cornerstonebakerycafe.com; 1712 Sudderth Dr; mains $5.50-11; ⊘7am-3pm Mon-Fri, to 4pm Sat & Sun; 🐾) Totally irresistible, hugely popular local bakery and cafe, where everything, from the breads, pastries and espresso to the omelets and croissant sandwiches, is just the way it should be. Stick around long enough and the Cornerstone may become your morning touchstone.

☆ Entertainment

Ruidoso Downs Racetrack
SPORTS GROUND

(☑575-378-4431; www.raceruidoso.com; 26225 Hwy 70; grandstand seats free; ⊘Fri-Mon late May-early Sep) National attention focuses on the Ruidoso Downs racetrack on Labor Day for the world's richest quarter-horse race, the All American Futurity, which has a purse of $2.4 million. The course is also home to the Racehorse Hall of Fame, and the small Billy the Kid Casino.

Flying J Ranch
LIVE MUSIC

(☑575-336-4330; www.flyingjranch.com; 1028 Hwy 48; adult/child $27/15; ⊘from 5:30pm Mon-Sat late May-early Sep, Sat only early Sep–mid-Oct; 👶) Families with little ones will love this 'Western village,' 1.5 miles north of Alto, as it delivers a full night of entertainment, with gunfights, pony rides and Western music, to go with its cowboy-style chuckwagon dinner.

❶ Information

Visitor Center (☑575-257-7395; www.ruidosonow.com; 720 Sudderth Dr; ⊘8am-5pm Mon-Fri, 9am-3pm Sat)

Lincoln & Capitan

Fans of Western history won't want to miss little Lincoln. Twelve miles east of Capitan along the **Billy the Kid National Scenic Byway** (www.billybyway.com), this is where the gun battle known as the Lincoln County War turned Billy the Kid into a legend. The whole town is beautifully preserved in close to original form, with its unspoiled main street designated as the **Lincoln Historic Site** (☑575-653-4082; www.nmmonuments.org/lincoln; adult/child $7/free; ⊘Apr-Oct).

Buy tickets to the historic town buildings at the **Anderson-Freeman Visitors Center**, where you'll also find exhibits on Buffalo soldiers, Apaches and the Lincoln County War. Make the fascinating **Courthouse Museum**, the well-marked site of Billy's most daring – and violent – escape, your last stop. For overnighters, the **Wortley Hotel** (☑575-653-4300; www.wortleyhotel.com; Hwy 380; r $110) has been a fixture since 1874.

Like Lincoln, cozy Capitan is surrounded by the beautiful mountains of Lincoln National Forest. The main reason to come is so the kids can visit **Smokey Bear Historical Park** (☑575-354-2748; 118 W Smokey Bear Blvd; adult/child $2/1; ⊘9am-4:30pm), where the original Smokey is buried.

Roswell

If you believe 'The Truth Is Out There', then the Roswell Incident is already filed away in your memory bank. In 1947 a mysterious object crashed at a nearby ranch. No one would have skipped any sleep over it, but the military made a big to-do of hushing it up, and for a lot of folks, that sealed it: the aliens had landed! International curiosity and local ingenuity have transformed the city into a quirky extraterrestrial-wannabe zone. Bulbous white heads glow atop the downtown streetlamps and busloads of tourists come to find good souvenirs.

Believers and kitsch-seekers must check out the **International UFO Museum & Research Center** (☑575-625-9495; www.roswellufomuseum.com; 114 N Main St; adult/child $5/2; ☺9am-5pm), while the annual **Roswell UFO Festival** (www.roswellufofestival.com) beams down in early July.

Ho-hum chain motels line N Main St. About 36 miles south of Roswell, the **Heritage Inn** (☑575-748-2552; www.artesiaheritageinn.com; 209 W Main St, Artesia; r incl breakfast from $99; ✴@☎) in Artesia is the nicest lodging in the area.

For simple, dependable New Mexican fare, try Martin's **Capitol Cafe** (☑575-624-2111; 110 W 4th St; mains $6-12; ☺6am-8:30pm Mon-Sat); for American eats, **Big D's Downtown Dive** (☑575-627-0776; 505 N Main St; mains $7-13; ☺11am-9pm) has the best salads, sandwiches and burgers in town.

Pick up local information at the **visitors bureau** (☑575-624-6700; www.seeroswell.com; 912 N Main St; ☺8:30am-5:30pm Mon-Fri, 10am-3pm Sat & Sun; ☎); **Greyhound** (☑575-622-2510; www.greyhound.com; 1100 N Virginia Ave) has buses to Las Cruces.

Carlsbad

Carlsbad is the closest town to Carlsbad Caverns National Park and the Guadalupe Mountains. To the northwest **Living Desert State Park** (☑575-887-5516; www.nmparks.com; 1504 Miehls Dr N, off Hwy 285; adult/child $5/3; ☺8am-5pm Jun-Aug, 9am-5pm Sep-May, last zoo entry 3:30pm) is a great place to see and learn about desert plants and wildlife. There's a good 1.3-mile trail that showcases different habitats of the Chihuahuan Desert, with live antelopes, wolves, roadrunners and more.

However, a recent boom in the oil industry means that even the most ordinary motel room in Carlsbad is liable to cost well over $200 per night, so it makes much more sense to visit on a long day-trip from, say, Roswell or Alamogordo. The best room rates, oddly enough, tend to be at the appealing **Trinity Hotel** (☑575-234-9891; www.thetrinityhotel.com; 201 S Canal St; r $149-209; ✴☎), originally the First National Bank. The sitting room of one suite is inside the old vault, and the restaurant is Carlsbad's classiest.

The perky **Blue House Bakery & Cafe** (☑575-628-0555; 609 N Canyon St; ☺6am-noon Mon-Sat) brews the best coffee in these parts, while the lip-smackin' **Red Chimney Pit Barbecue** (☑575-885-8744; www.redchimneybbq.com; 817 N Canal St; mains $6.50-16; ☺11am-2pm & 4:30-8:30pm Tue-Fri, 11am-8:30pm Sat) serves succulent Southern-style meats.

Greyhound (☑575-628-0768; www.greyhound.com; 3102 National Parks Hwy) buses depart from Food Jet South, 2 miles south of downtown. Destinations include El Paso, TX, and Las Cruces.

California

Best Places to Eat

→ Benu (p316)

→ Rich Table (p317)

→ Otium (p259)

→ Chez Panisse (p327)

→ SingleThread Farm-Restaurant-Inn (p332)

Best Places to Sleep

→ Post Ranch Inn (p293)

→ Inn of the Spanish Garden (p289)

→ Chateau Marmont (p257)

→ Jabberwock (p296)

→ Hotel del Coronado (p277)

Why Go?

With bohemian spirit and high-tech savvy, not to mention a die-hard passion for the good life – whether that means cracking open a bottle of old-vine Zinfandel, climbing a 14,000ft peak or surfing the Pacific – California soars beyond any expectations sold on Hollywood's silver screens.

More than anything, California is iconic. It was here that the hurly-burly gold rush kicked off in the mid-19th century, where poet-naturalist John Muir rhapsodized about the Sierra Nevada's 'range of light,' and where Jack Kerouac and the Beat Generation defined what it really meant to hit the road.

California's multicultural melting pot has been cookin' since this bountiful promised land was staked out by Spain and Mexico. Today, waves of immigrants from around the world still look to find their own American dream on these palm-studded Pacific shores.

Come see the future in the making here in the Golden State.

When to Go
Los Angeles

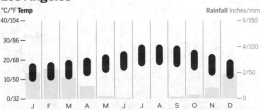

Jun–Aug Mostly sunny weather, occasional coastal fog; summer vacation crowds.

Apr–May & Sep–Oct Cooler nights, many cloudless days; travel bargains galore.

Nov–Mar Peak tourism at ski resorts and in SoCal's warm deserts.

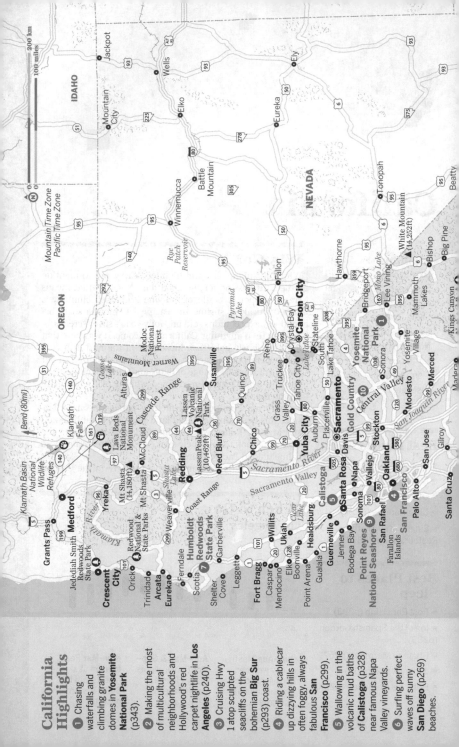

California Highlights

1. Chasing waterfalls and climbing granite domes in **Yosemite National Park** (p343).

2. Making the most of multicultural neighborhoods and Hollywood's red carpet nightlife in **Los Angeles** (p240).

3. Cruising Hwy 1 atop sculpted seacliffs on the bohemian **Big Sur** (p299) coast.

4. Riding a cablecar up dizzying hills in often foggy, always fabulous **San Francisco** (p299).

5. Wallowing in the volcanic mud baths of **Calistoga** (p328) near famous Napa Valley vineyards.

6. Surfing perfect waves off sunny **San Diego** (p269) beaches.

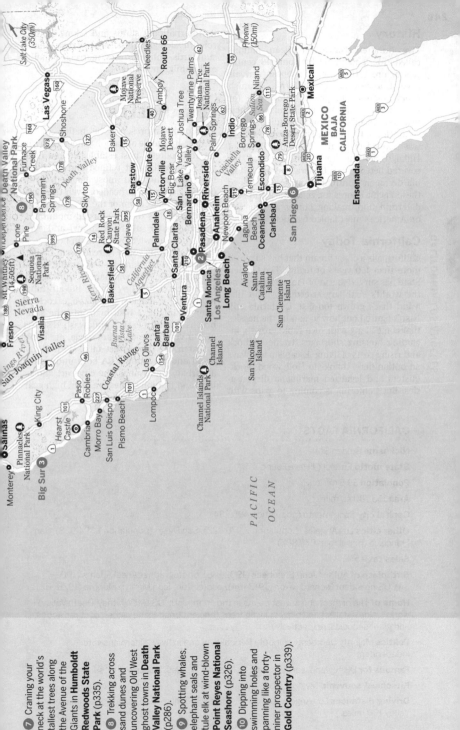

7 Craning your neck at the world's tallest trees along the Avenue of the Giants in **Humboldt Redwoods State Park** (p335).

8 Trekking across sand dunes and uncovering Old West ghost towns in **Death Valley National Park** (p286).

9 Spotting whales, elephant seals and tule elk at wind-blown **Point Reyes National Seashore** (p326).

10 Dipping into swimming holes and panning like a forty-niner prospector in **Gold Country** (p339).

History

Five hundred Native American nations called this land home for some 18 centuries before 16th-century European arrivals gave it a new name: California. Spanish conquistadors and priests came here for gold and god, but soon relinquished their flea-plagued missions and ill-equipped presidios (forts) to Mexico. The unruly territory was handed off to the US in the Treaty of Hidalgo mere months before gold was discovered here in 1848. Generations of California dreamers continue to make the trek to these Pacific shores for gold, glory and self-determination, making homes and history on America's most fabled frontier.

California Today

California is a crazy dream that has survived more than 150 years of reality. The Golden State has surged ahead of France to become the world's sixth-largest economy. But like a kid that's grown too fast, California still hasn't figured out how to handle the hassles that come along with such rapid growth, including housing shortages, traffic gridlock and rising costs of living. Escapism is always an option here, thanks to Hollywood blockbusters and legalized marijuana dispensaries. But California is coming to grips with its international status and taking leading roles in such global issues as environmental standards, online privacy, marriage equality and immigrant rights.

LOS ANGELES

LA County represents the nation in extremes. Its people are among America's richest and poorest, most established and most newly arrived, most refined and roughest, most beautiful and most botoxed, most erudite and most airheaded. Even the landscape is a microcosm of the USA: from cinematic beaches to snow-dusted mountains, skyscrapers to suburban sprawl and even wilderness prowled by mountain lions.

If you think you've already got LA figured out – celebutantes, smog, traffic, bikini babes and pop-star wannabes – think again. LA is best defined by simple life-affirming moments: a cracked-ice, jazz-age cocktail after midnight, a hike high into the sagebrush of Griffith Park, a pink-washed sunset over a Venice Beach drum circle, or simply a search for the perfect taco. With Hollywood and Downtown LA both undergoing an urban renaissance, the city's art, music, food and fashion scenes are all in high gear.

CALIFORNIA FACTS

Nickname Golden State

State motto Eureka ('I Have Found It')

Population 39.5 million

Area 155,780 sq miles

Capital city Sacramento (population 495,234)

Other cities Los Angeles (population 3,976,322), San Diego (population 1,394,928), San Francisco (population 870,887)

Sales tax 7.5%

Birthplace of Author John Steinbeck (1902–68), photographer Ansel Adams (1902–84), US president Richard Nixon (1913–94), pop-culture icon Marilyn Monroe (1926–62)

Home of The highest and lowest points in the contiguous US (Mt Whitney, Death Valley), world's oldest, tallest and biggest living trees (ancient bristlecone pines, coast redwoods and giant sequoias, respectively)

Politics Majority Democrat, minority Republican, one in five Californians vote independent

Famous for Disneyland, earthquakes, Hollywood, hippies, Silicon Valley, surfing

Kitschiest souvenir 'Mystery Spot' bumper sticker

Driving distances Los Angeles to San Francisco 380 miles, San Francisco to Yosemite Valley 190 miles

CALIFORNIA IN ...

One Week

California in a nutshell: start in beachy **Los Angeles**, detouring to **Disneyland**. Head up the breezy **Central Coast**, stopping in **Santa Barbara** and **Big Sur**, before getting a dose of big-city culture in **San Francisco**. Head inland to nature's temple, **Yosemite National Park**, then zip back to LA.

Two Weeks

Follow the one-week itinerary above, but at a saner pace. Add jaunts to NorCal's **Wine Country**; **Lake Tahoe**, perched high in the Sierra Nevada; the bodacious beaches of Orange County and laid-back **San Diego**; or **Joshua Tree National Park**, near the chic desert resort of **Palm Springs**.

One Month

Do everything described above, and more. From San Francisco, head up the foggy **North Coast**, starting in Marin County at **Point Reyes National Seashore**. Stroll Victorian-era **Mendocino** and **Eureka**, find yourself on the **Lost Coast** and ramble through fern-filled **Redwood National & State Parks**. Inland, snap a postcard-perfect photo of **Mt Shasta**, drive through **Lassen Volcanic National Park** and ramble in California's historic **Gold Country**. Trace the backbone of the **Eastern Sierra** before winding down into other-worldly **Death Valley National Park**.

Chances are, the more you explore, the more you'll love 'La-La Land.'

History

The hunter-gatherer existence of the area's Gabrielino and Chumash peoples ended with the arrival of Spanish missionaries and colonists in the late 18th century. Spain's first civilian settlement, El Pueblo de Nuestra Señora la Reina de Los Ángeles del Río de Porciúncula, remained an isolated farming outpost for decades after its founding in 1781. The city wasn't officially incorporated until 1850.

LA's population repeatedly swelled after the collapse of the California gold rush, the arrival of the transcontinental railroad, the growth of the citrus industry, the discovery of oil, the launch of the port of LA, the birth of the movie industry and the opening of the California Aqueduct. After WWII, the city's population doubled from nearly two million in 1950 to around four million today.

⊙ Sights

A dozen miles inland from the Pacific, Downtown LA combines history and high-brow arts and culture. Hip-again Hollywood awaits northwest of Downtown, while urban-designer chic and gay pride rule West Hollywood. South of WeHo, Museum Row is Mid-City's main draw. Further west are ritzy Beverly Hills, Westwood near the University of California, Los Angeles (UCLA) campus and West LA. Beach towns include kid-friendly Santa Monica, boho Venice, star-powered Malibu and busy Long Beach. Leafy Pasadena lies northeast of Downtown.

⊙ Downtown

Downtown is divided into numerous areas. Bunker Hill is home to major modern-art museums and the **Walt Disney Concert Hall**. To the east is **City Hall** and, further east still, **Little Tokyo**. Southeast of Little Tokyo lies the trendy **Arts District**. Broadway is flanked by glorious heritage buildings, while the city's oldest colonial buildings flank Olvera St, north of City Hall and the 101 freeway. Further north still is **Chinatown**.

★**Hauser & Wirth**   GALLERY
(Map p246; ☑213-943-1620; www.hauserwirth losangeles.com; 901 E 3rd St; ☺11am-6pm Wed & Fri-Sun, to 8pm Thu) **FREE** The LA outpost of internationally acclaimed gallery Hauser & Wirth has art fiends in a flurry with its museum-standard exhibits of modern and contemporary art. It's a huge space, occupying 116,000 square feet of a converted flour mill complex in the Arts District. Past exhibits have showcased the work of luminaries such as Louise Bourgeois, Eva Hesse and Jason Rhoades. The complex is also home to a superlative art bookshop.

Bradbury Building   HISTORIC BUILDING
(Map p246; www.laconservancy.org; 304 S Broadway; ☺lobby usually 9am-5pm; Ⓜ Red/Purple Lines to Pershing Sq) Debuting in 1893, the Bradbury is one of the city's undisput-ed architectural jewels. Behind its robust Romanesque facade lies a whimsical galleried atrium that wouldn't look out of place in New Orleans. Inky filigree grillwork, rickety birdcage elevators and yellow-brick walls

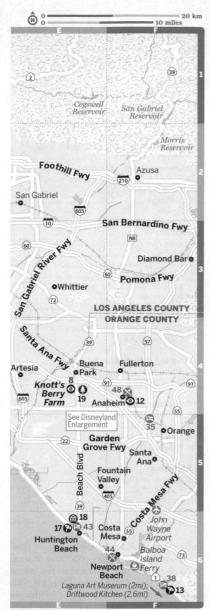

El Pueblo de Los Angeles & Around

Compact, colorful and car free, this historic district immerses you in LA's Spanish-Mexican roots. Its spine is festive **Olvera St** (Map p246; www.calleolvera.com; 🚇), where you can snap up handmade folkloric trinkets, then chomp on tacos and sugar-sprinkled churros. 'New' **Chinatown** (Map p246; www.chinatownla.com) is about a half mile north along Broadway and Hill St, crammed with dim-sum parlors, herbal apothecaries, curio shops and Chung King Rd's edgy art galleries.

LA Plaza   MUSEUM
(La Plaza de Cultura y Artes; Map p246; ☎213-542-6200; www.lapca.org; 501 N Main St; ⊙noon-5pm Mon, Wed & Thu, to 6pm Fri-Sun; 🚇) **FREE** This museum offers snapshots of the Mexican American experience in Los Angeles, from Spanish colonization in the late 18th century and the Mexican–American War (when the border crossed the original *pueblo*), to the Zoot Suit Riots, activist César Chávez and the Chicana movement. Exhibitions include a re-creation of 1920s Main St as well as rotating showcases of modern and contemporary art by LA-based Latino artists.

Avila Adobe   MUSEUM
(Map p246; ☎213-628-1274; www.elpueblo.lacity.org; 10 Olvera St; ⊙9am-4pm) **FREE** The oldest surviving house in LA was built in 1818 by wealthy ranchero and one-time LA mayor Francisco José Avila. After subsequent lives as a boarding house and restaurant, the abode was restored to offer a glimpse into domestic LA life circa 1840. Rooms are filled with period furniture and furnishings, including a handful of items that belonged to the Avila family. Among these is the sewing machine. The house is open for self-guided tours.

Union Station   NOTABLE BUILDING
(Map p246; www.amtrak.com; 800 N Alameda St; 🅿) Built on the site of LA's original Chinatown, Union Station opened in 1939 as America's last grand rail station. It's a glamorous exercise in Mission Revival style with art-deco and American Indian accents. The marble-floored main hall, with cathedral ceilings, original leather chairs and 3000-pound chandeliers, is breathtaking. The station's Traxx Bar was once the telephone room, complete with operator to place customers' calls. The LA Conservancy

glisten golden in the afternoon light, which filters through the peaked glass roof. Such striking beauty hasn't been lost on Hollywood – the building's star turn came in the cult sci-fi flick *Blade Runner*.

Greater Los Angeles

◎ Top Sights

1 Autry Museum of the American West C2
2 Battleship Iowa C5
3 Frederick R Weisman Art Foundation C2
4 Getty Center B2
5 Getty Villa B3
6 Griffith Observatory C2
7 Huntington Library, Art Collections & Botanical Gardens D2
8 Knott's Berry Farm E4
9 Museum of Latin American Art D5
10 Museum of Tolerance C3
11 Watts Towers D3

◎ Sights

12 Anaheim Packing District F4
   California Science Center .... (see 21)
   Center Street Anaheim .... (see 12)
13 Crystal Cove State Park F6
14 Disneyland Resort B5
15 Griffith Park C2
   Hammer Museum .... (see 24)
16 Hollywood Forever Cemetery C2
17 Huntington City Beach E6
18 International Surfing Museum E6
19 Knott's Soak City E4
20 Los Angeles Zoo & Botanical Gardens C2
21 Natural History Museum of Los Angeles C3
22 Norton Simon Museum D2
   Rose Garden .... (see 21)
23 Universal Studios Hollywood C2
24 Westwood Village Memorial Park Cemetery B3

◎ Activities, Courses & Tours

25 Bronson Canyon C2
26 Malibu Canyon A3
27 Malibu Creek State Park A2
28 Paramount Pictures C2
29 Runyon Canyon C2

30 Sony Pictures Studios C3
31 Topanga Canyon State Park B2
32 Warner Bros Studio Tour C2

◎ Sleeping

33 Alpine Inn B6
34 Avalon Hotel C3
35 Ayres Hotel Anaheim F5
36 Best Western Plus Stovall's Inn A6
37 Bissell House B&B D2
38 Crystal Cove Beach Cottages F6
39 Disneyland Hotel A5
40 Disney's Grand Californian Hotel & Spa A5
41 Hotel Maya D5
42 Montage C2
43 Paséa E6

◎ Eating

44 Bear Flag Fish Company F6
45 Bestia D3
46 Earl of Sandwich A5
   Fourth & Olive .... (see 9)
   Lot 579 .... (see 43)
47 Napa Rose A5
48 Pour Vida F4
   Ración .... (see 22)
49 Ralph Brennan's New Orleans Jazz Kitchen A5

◎ Drinking & Nightlife

50 Pike D5
51 Polo Lounge C2

◎ Entertainment

52 Cavern Club Theater C2
53 Dodger Stadium D2
54 Geffen Playhouse B3
55 Hollywood Bowl C2

◎ Shopping

56 Malibu Country Mart A3
   Pacific City .... (see 43)
57 Rose Bowl Flea Market D2

runs 2½-hour walking tours of the station on Saturdays at 10am (book online).

◉ Civic Center & Cultural Corridor

★ **Broad**   MUSEUM
(Map p246; ☏ 213-232-6200; www.thebroad.org; 221 S Grand Ave; ⊗ 11am-5pm Tue & Wed, to 8pm Thu & Fri, 10am-8pm Sat, to 6pm Sun; 🅿 ♿; Ⓜ Red/Purple Lines to Civic Center/Grand Park) **FREE** From the instant it opened in September 2015, the Broad (rhymes with 'road') be-

came a must-visit for contemporary-art fans. It houses the world-class collection of local philanthropist and billionaire real-estate honcho Eli Broad and his wife Edythe, with more than 2000 postwar pieces by dozens of heavy hitters, including Cindy Sherman, Jeff Koons, Andy Warhol, Roy Lichtenstein, Robert Rauschenberg, Keith Haring and Kara Walker.

★ **Walt Disney Concert Hall**   NOTABLE BUILDING
(Map p246; ☏ 323-850-2000; www.laphil.org; 111 S Grand Ave; ⊗ guided tours usually noon & 1:15pm Thu-Sat, 10am & 11am Sun; 🅿; Ⓜ Red/

Purple Lines to Civic Center/Grand Park) FREE A molten blend of steel, music and psychedelic architecture, this iconic concert venue is the home base of the Los Angeles Philharmonic, but has also hosted contemporary bands such as Phoenix and classic jazz musicians such as Sonny Rollins. Frank Gehry pulled out all the stops: the building is a gravity-defying sculpture of heaving and billowing stainless steel.

★ **MOCA Grand** MUSEUM
'(Museum of Contemporary Art; Map p246; ☑213-626-6222; www.moca.org; 250 S Grand Ave; adult/child $15/free, 5-8pm Thu free; ☉11am-6pm Mon, Wed & Fri, to 8pm Thu, to 5pm Sat & Sun) MOCA's superlative art collection focuses mainly on works created from the 1940s to the present. There's no shortage of luminaries, among them Mark Rothko, Dan Flavin, Willem de Kooning, Joseph Cornell and David Hockney. Their creations are housed in a postmodern building by award-winning Japanese architect Arata Isozaki. Galleries are below ground, yet sky-lit bright.

La Placita CHURCH
(Map p246; www.laplacita.org; 535 N Main St; ☉6am-8:30pm) Founded as la Iglesia de Nuestra Señora la Reina de Los Ángeles (Our Lady the Queen of the Angels Church) in 1781, and now affectionately known as 'Little Plaza.' Head inside for a peek at the gilded altar and painted ceiling.

◉ Little Tokyo

Little Tokyo swirls with shopping arcades, Buddhist temples, traditional gardens, authentic sushi bars and noodle shops, and a provocative branch of **MOCA** (Map p246; ☑213-625-4390; www.moca.org; 152 N Central Ave; adult/student/child under 12yr $15/8/free, 5-8pm Thu free; ☉11am-6pm Mon, Wed & Fri, to 8pm Thu, to 5pm Sat & Sun; Ⓜ Gold Line to Little Tokyo/Arts District).

**Japanese American
National Museum** MUSEUM
(Map p246; ☑213-625-0414; www.janm.org; 100 N Central Ave; adult/child $10/6, 5-8pm Thu & all day 3rd Thu of month free; ☉11am-5pm Tue, Wed & Fri-Sun, noon-8pm Thu; 🚻; Ⓜ Gold Line to Little Tokyo/Arts District) A great first stop in Little Tokyo, this is the country's first museum dedicated to the Japanese immigrant experience. The 2nd floor is home to the permanent 'Common Ground' exhibition, which explores the evolution of Japanese-American culture since the late 19th century and offers moving insight into the painful chapter of America's WWII internment camps. Afterwards relax in the tranquil garden and browse the well-stocked gift shop.

◉ South Park

South Park isn't actually a park but an emerging Downtown LA neighborhood around **LA Live** (Map p246; ☑866-548-3452, 213-763-5483; www.lalive.com; 800 W Olympic

---

LOS ANGELES IN ...

Distances are ginormous in LA, so allow extra time for traffic and don't try to pack too much into a day.

One Day

Fuel up for the day at the **Original Farmers Market**, then go star-searching on the **Hollywood Walk of Fame** along Hollywood Blvd. Up your chances of spotting actual celebs by hitting the fashion-forward boutiques on paparazzi-infested **Robertson Boulevard**, or get a dose of nature at **Griffith Park**. Then drive west to the lofty **Getty Center** or head out to the **Venice Boardwalk** to see the seaside sideshow. Catch a Pacific sunset in **Santa Monica**.

Two Days

Explore rapidly evolving **Downtown LA**. Dig up the city's roots at **El Pueblo de Los Angeles**, then catapult to the future at dramatic **Walt Disney Concert Hall** topping Grand Ave's **Cultural Corridor**. Walk off lunch ambling between Downtown's historic buildings, **Arts District** galleries and **Little Tokyo**. At South Park's glitzy **LA Live** entertainment center, romp through the multimedia **Grammy Museum**, then join real-life celebs cheering on the LA Lakers next door at the **Staples Center**. After dark, hit the dance floor at clubs in **Hollywood**.

Downtown Los Angeles

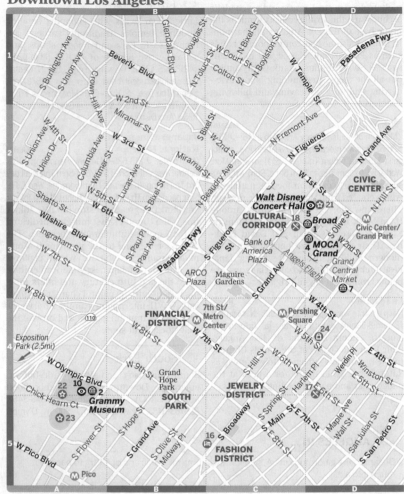

Blvd; P), a dining and entertainment hub where you'll find the Staples Center (p263) and **Microsoft Theater** (Map p246; 213-763-6020; www.microsofttheater.com; 777 Chick Hearn Ct).

★**Grammy Museum** MUSEUM
(Map p246; 213-765-6800; www.grammymuse um.org; 800 W Olympic Blvd; adult/child $13/11; 10:30am-6:30pm Mon-Fri, from 10am Sat & Sun; P) It's the highlight of LA Live (p245). Music-lovers will get lost in interactive exhibits, which define, differentiate and link musical genres. Spanning three levels, the museum's rotating exhibitions might include threads worn by the likes of Michael Jackson, Whitney Houston and Beyonce, scribbled words from the hands of Count Basie and Taylor Swift and instruments once used by world-renowned rock deities. Inspired? Interactive sound chambers allow you to try your own hand at singing, mixing and remixing.

⊙ Exposition Park & Around

Just south of the University of Southern California (USC) campus, this park has a full day's worth of kid-friendly museums.

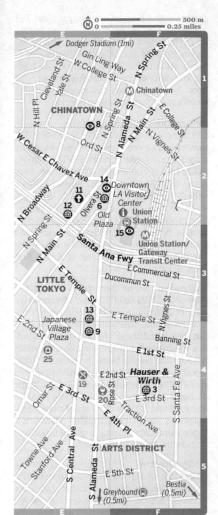

Outdoor landmarks include the **Rose Garden** (Map p242; ☎ 213-763-0114; www.laparks.org/expo/garden; 701 State Dr, Exposition Park; ⌚ 8:30am-sunset Mar 16–Dec 31; 🅿; Ⓜ Expo Line to Exposition Park/USC) **FREE** and the **Los Angeles Memorial Coliseum**, site of the 1932 and 1984 Summer Olympic Games. Parking costs around $10. From Downtown, take the Metro Expo Line or DASH minibus F.

California Science Center MUSEUM
(Map p242; ☎ film schedule 213-744-2019, info 323-724-3623; www.californiasciencecenter.org; 700 Exposition Park Dr, Exposition Park; IMAX movie adult/child $8.50/5.25; ⌚ 10am-5pm; 🖐) **FREE** Top billing at the Science Center goes to the Space Shuttle Endeavour, one of only four space shuttles nationwide, but there's plenty else to see at this large, multistory, multimedia museum filled with buttons to push, lights to switch on and knobs to pull. A simulated earthquake, baby chicks hatching and a giant techno-doll named Tess bring out the kid in everyone. Admission is free, but special exhibits, experiences and IMAX movies cost extra.

★ Watts Towers LANDMARK
(Map p242; ☎ 213-847-4646; www.wattstowers.us; 1761-1765 E 107th St, Watts; adult/child 13-17yr & senior/child under 13yr $7/3/free; ⌚ tours

11am-3pm Thu & Fri, 10:30am-3pm Sat, noon-3pm Sun; **P**; **M**Blue Line to 103rd St) The three Gothic spires of the fabulous Watts Towers rank among the world's greatest monuments of folk art. In 1921 Italian immigrant Simon Rodia set out 'to make something big' and then spent 33 years cobbling together this whimsical free-form sculpture from concrete, steel and a motley assortment of found objects: green 7Up bottles, sea shells, tiles, rocks and pottery.

**Natural History
Museum of Los Angeles** MUSEUM
(Map p242; **J**213-763-3466; www.nhm.org; 900 Exposition Blvd, Exposition Park; adult/student & senior/child $12/9/5; ⊙9:30am-5pm; **P**; **M**Expo Line to Expo/Vermont) Dinos to diamonds, bears to beetles, hissing roaches to African elephants – this museum will take you around the world and back, through millions of years in time. It's all housed in a beautiful 1913 Spanish Renaissance–style building that stood in for Columbia University in the first Toby McGuire *Spider-Man* movie – yup, this was where Peter Parker was bitten by the radioactive arachnid. There's enough to see here to fill several hours.

🅞 Hollywood

Just as aging movie stars get the occasional face-lift, so has Hollywood. While it still hasn't recaptured its mid-20th-century 'Golden Age' glamour, its contemporary seediness is disappearing. The **Hollywood Walk of Fame** (Map p249; www.walkoffame.com; Hollywood Blvd; **M**Red Line to Hollywood/Highland) honors more than 2400 celebrities with stars embedded in the sidewalk.

The Metro Red Line stops beneath **Hollywood & Highland** (Map p249; www.hollywoodandhighland.com; 6801 Hollywood Blvd; ⊙10am-10pm Mon-Sat, to 7pm Sun; **M**Red Line to Hollywood/Highland), a multistory mall with nicely framed views of the hillside Hollywood sign, erected in 1923 as an advertisement for a land development called Hollywoodland. Two-hour validated mall parking costs $2 (daily maximum $15).

⭐**Hollywood Museum** MUSEUM
(Map p249; **J**323-464-7776; www.thehollywoodmuseum.com; 1660 N Highland Ave; adult/child $15/5; ⊙10am-5pm Wed-Sun; **M**Red Line to Hollywood/Highland) For a taste of Old Hollywood, do not miss this musty temple to the stars, its four floors crammed with movie and TV costumes and props. The museum is housed inside the Max Factor Building, built in 1914 and relaunched as a glamorous beauty salon in 1935. At the helm was Polish-Jewish businessman Max Factor, Hollywood's leading authority on cosmetics. And it was right here that he worked his magic on Hollywood's most famous screen queens.

⭐**Grauman's Chinese Theatre** LANDMARK
(TCL Chinese Theatres; Map p249; **J**323-461-3331; www.tclchinesetheatres.com; 6925 Hollywood Blvd; guided tour adult/senior/child $16/13.50/8; **M**; **M**Red Line to Hollywood/Highland) Ever wondered what it's like to be in George Clooney's shoes? Just find his footprints in the forecourt of this world-famous movie palace. The exotic pagoda theater – complete with temple bells and stone heaven dogs from China – has shown movies since 1927 when Cecil B DeMille's *The King of Kings* first flickered across the screen.

Hollywood Forever Cemetery CEMETERY
(Map p242; **J**323-469-1181; www.hollywoodforever.com; 6000 Santa Monica Blvd; ⊙usually 8:30am-5pm, flower shop 9am-5pm Mon-Fri, to 4pm Sat & Sun; **P**) Paradisiacal landscaping, vainglorious tombstones and epic mausoleums set an appropriate resting place for some of Hollywood's most iconic dearly departed. Residents include Cecil B DeMille, Mickey Rooney, Jayne Mansfield, punk rockers Johnny and Dee Dee Ramone and *Golden Girls* star Estelle Getty. Valentino lies in the Cathedral Mausoleum (open from 10am to 2pm), while Judy Garland rests in the Abbey of the Psalms.

Dolby Theatre THEATER
(Map p249; **J**323-308-6300; www.dolbytheatre.com; 6801 Hollywood Blvd; tours adult/child, senior & student $23/18; ⊙10:30am-4pm; **P**; **M**Red Line to Hollywood/Highland) The Academy Awards are handed out at the Dolby Theatre, which has also hosted the *American Idol* finale, the Excellence in Sports Performance Yearly (ESPY) Awards and the Daytime Emmy Awards. The venue is home to the annual PaleyFest, the country's premier TV festival, held in March. Guided tours of the theater will have you sniffing around the auditorium, admiring a VIP room and nosing up to an Oscar statuette.

🅞 Griffith Park

America's largest urban **park** (Map p242; **J**323-644-2050; www.laparks.org; 4730 Crystal Springs Dr; ⊙5am-10pm, trails sunrise-sunset;

Hollywood

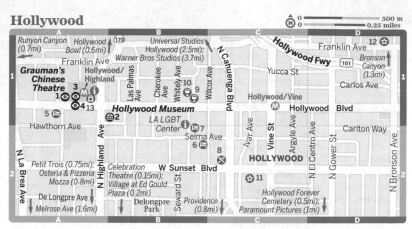

P ♿) **FREE** is five times the size of New York's Central Park, with an outdoor theater, zoo, observatory, museum, merry go-round, antique and miniature trains, children's playgrounds, golf, tennis and over 50 miles of hiking paths, including to the original Batman TV series cave.

★ **Griffith Observatory** MUSEUM
(Map p242; ☎213-473-0890; www.griffithobservatory.org; 2800 E Observatory Rd; admission free, planetarium shows adult/child $7/3; ⊙noon-10pm Tue-Fri, from 10am Sat & Sun; P ♿; ☐DASH Observatory) **FREE** LA's landmark 1935 observatory opens a window onto the universe from its perch on the southern slopes of Mt Hollywood. Its planetarium claims the world's most advanced star projector, while its astronomical touch displays explore some mind-bending topics, from the evolution of the telescope and the ultraviolet x-rays used to map our solar system to the cosmos itself. Then, of course, there are the views, which (on clear days) take in the entire LA Basin, surrounding mountains and Pacific Ocean.

★ **Autry Museum of the American West** MUSEUM
(Map p242; ☎323-667-2000; www.autrynationalcenter.org; 4700 Western Heritage Way, Griffith Park; adult/senior & student/child $14/10/6, 2nd Tue each month free; ⊙10am-4pm Tue-Fri, to 5pm Sat & Sun; P ♿) Established by singing cowboy Gene Autry, this expansive, underrated museum offers contemporary perspectives on the history and people of the American West, as well as their links to the region's contemporary culture. Permanent exhibitions explore everything from Native American traditions to the cattle drives of the 19th century and daily frontier life; look for the beautifully carved vintage saloon bar. You'll also find costumes and artifacts from famous Hollywood westerns such as *Annie Get Your Gun,* as well as rotating art exhibitions.

Los Angeles Zoo & Botanical Gardens ZOO
(Map p242; ☎323-644-4200; www.lazoo.org; 5333 Zoo Dr, Griffith Park; adult/senior/child $20/17/15; ⊙10am-5pm, closed Christmas Day; P ♿) Home

STUDIO TOURS

Did you know it takes a week to shoot a half-hour sitcom? Or that you rarely see ceilings on shows because the space is filled with lights and lamps? You'll learn these and other nuggets of information about the make-believe world of film and TV while touring a working studio. Star-sighting potential is better than average, except during 'hiatus' (May to August) when studios are deserted. Reservations are required and so is photo ID.

Paramount (Map p242; ☑323-956-1777; www.paramountstudiotour.com; 5555 Melrose Ave; tours from $55; ⊙ tours 9:30am-5pm, last tour 3pm) *Star Trek, Indiana Jones* and *Shrek* are among the blockbusters that originated at Paramount, the longest-operating movie studio and the only one still in Hollywood proper. Two-hour tours through the back lots and sound stages are available daily year-round and are led by passionate, knowledgeable guides.

Sony (Map p242; ☑310-244-8687; www.sonypicturesstudiotours.com; 10202 W Washington Blvd; tour $45; ⊙ tours usually 9:30am, 10:30am, 1:30pm & 2:30pm Mon-Fri) Running on weekdays only, this two-hour tour includes visits to the sound stages where *Men in Black, Spider-Man,* and *Charlie's Angels* were filmed. Munchkins hopped along the Yellow Brick Road in *The Wizard of Oz,* filmed when this was still the venerable MGM studio.

Warner Bros (Map p242; ☑877-492-8687, 818-972-8687; www.wbstudiotour.com; 3400 W Riverside Dr, Burbank; tours adult/child 8-12yr from $62/52; ⊙8:30am-3:30pm, extended hours Jun-Aug; ☐155, 222, 501 stop about 400yd from tour center) This tour offers the most fun and authentic look behind the scenes of a major movie studio. Consisting of a two-hour guided tour and a self-guided tour of Studio 48, the adventure kicks off with a video of WB's greatest film hits – among them *Rebel Without a Cause* and *La La Land* – before a tram whisks you to sound stages, back-lot sets and technical departments, including props, costumes and the paint shop. Tours run daily, usually every half-hour.

to 1100 finned, feathered and furry friends from more than 250 species, the LA Zoo rarely fails to enthrall the little ones. Adults who have been to bigger zoos, however, may find the place a little average. To save time, purchase tickets online. To save money, bring your own food and drinks as the offerings at the zoo are expectantly overpriced.

◉ West Hollywood & Mid-City

In WeHo, rainbow flags fly proudly over Santa Monica Blvd, while celebs keep gossip rags happy by misbehaving at clubs on the fabled Sunset Strip. Boutiques along Robertson Blvd and Melrose Ave purvey sassy and ultrachic fashions for Hollywood royalty and celebutantes. WeHo's also a hotbed of cutting-edge interior design, fashion and art, particularly in the **West Hollywood Design District** (http://westhollywooddesigndistrict. com). Further south, some of LA's best museums line Mid-City's Museum Row along Wilshire Blvd east of Fairfax Ave.

★ Los Angeles County
Museum of Art   MUSEUM
(LACMA; Map p252; ☑323-857-6000; www.lacma. org; 5905 Wilshire Blvd, Mid-City; adult/child $15/ free, 2nd Tue each month free; ⊙11am-5pm Mon, Tue & Thu, to 8pm Fri, 10am-7pm Sat & Sun; ℗; ☐Metro lines 20, 217, 720, 780 to Wilshire & Fairfax) The depth and wealth of the collection at the largest museum in the western US is stunning. LACMA holds all the major players – Rembrandt, Cézanne, Magritte, Mary Cassatt, Ansel Adams – plus millennia's worth of Chinese, Japanese, pre-Columbian and ancient Greek, Roman and Egyptian sculpture. Recent acquisitions include massive outdoor installations such as Chris Burden's *Urban Light* (a surreal selfie backdrop of hundreds of vintage LA streetlamps) and Michael Heizer's *Levitated Mass,* a surprisingly inspirational 340-ton boulder perched over a walkway.

La Brea Tar Pits & Museum   MUSEUM
(Map p252; www.tarpits.org; 5801 Wilshire Blvd, Mid-City; adult/student & senior/child $12/9/5, 1st Tue of month Sep-Jun free; ⊙9:30am-5pm; ℗◕) Mammoths, saber-toothed cats and dire wolves used to roam LA's savannah in prehistoric times. We know this because of an archaeological trove of skulls and bones unearthed here at the La Brea Tar Pits, one of the world's most fecund and famous fossil sites. A museum has been built here, where generations of young dino hunters have come to seek out fossils and learn about

paleontology from docents and demonstrations in on-site labs.

👁 Beverly Hills & the Westside

The major cultural sight here is the **Getty Center**, located in the hills of Brentwood. Westwood is home to the well-tended UCLA campus, the contemporary-art-focused **Hammer Museum** (Map p242; ☑ 310-443-7000; www.hammer.ucla.edu; 10899 Wilshire Blvd, Westwood; ⊘ 11am-8pm Tue-Fri, to 5pm Sat & Sun; **P**) **FREE** and the star-studded **Westwood Village Memorial Park Cemetery** (Map p242; ☑ 310-474-1579; 1218 Glendon Ave, Westwood; ⊘ 8am-6pm; **P**), all three of which are within walking distance of each other. Beverly Hills claims Rodeo Dr, a prime people-watching spot. Guided tours of celebrity homes depart from Hollywood.

★ Getty Center   MUSEUM
(Map p242; ☑ 310-440-7300; www.getty.edu; 1200 Getty Center Dr, off I-405 Fwy; ⊘ 10am-5:30pm Tue-Fri & Sun, to 9pm Sat; **P** 🚼; 🚌 734, 234) **FREE** In its billion-dollar, in-the-clouds perch, high above the city grit and grime, the Getty Center presents triple delights: a stellar art collection (everything from medieval triptychs to baroque sculpture and impressionist brushstrokes), Richard Meier's cutting-edge architecture, and the visual splendor of seasonally changing gardens. Admission is free, but parking is $15 ($10 after 3pm).

★ Museum of Tolerance   MUSEUM
(Map p242; ☑ reservations 310-772-2505; www.museumoftolerance.com; 9786 W Pico Blvd; adult/senior/student $15.50/12.50/11.50, Anne Frank Exhibit adult/senior/student $15.50/13.50/12.50; ⊘ 10am-5pm Sun-Wed & Fri, to 9:30pm Thu, to 3:30pm Fri Nov-Mar; **P**) Run by the Simon Wiesenthal Center, this deeply moving museum uses interactive technology to engage visitors in discussion and contemplation around racism and bigotry. Particular focus is given to the Holocaust, with a major basement exhibition that examines the social, political and economic conditions that led to the Holocaust as well as the experience of the millions persecuted. On the museum's 2nd floor, another major exhibition offers an intimate look into the life and effect of Anne Frank.

★ Frederick R Weisman
Art Foundation   MUSEUM
(Map p242; ☑ 310-277-5321; www.weismanfoundation.org; 265 N Carolwood Dr; ⊘ 90min guided tours 10:30am & 2pm Mon-Fri, by appointment only) **FREE** The late entrepreneur and philanthropist Frederick R Weisman had an insatiable passion for art, a fact confirmed when touring his former Holmby Hills home. From floor to ceiling, the mansion (and its manicured grounds) bursts with extraordinary works from visionaries such as Picasso, Kandinsky, Miró, Magritte, Rothko, Warhol, Rauschenberg and Ruscha. There's even a motorcycle painted by Keith Haring. Tours should be reserved at least a few days ahead.

👁 Malibu

The beach is king, of course, and whether you find a sliver of sand among the sandstone rock towers and topless sunbathers at El Matador or enjoy the wide loamy blonde beaches of Zuma and Westward, you'll have a special afternoon. Many A-listers have homes here and can sometimes be spotted shopping at the village-like **Malibu Country Mart** (Map p242; ☑ 310-456-7300; www.malibucountrymart.com; 3835 Cross Creek Rd, Malibu; ⊘ 10am-midnight Mon-Sat, to 10pm Sun; 🚼; 🚌 MTA line 534).

One of Malibu's natural treasures is canyon-riddled **Malibu Creek State Park** (Map p242; ☑ 818-880-0367; www.malibucreekstatepark.org; 1925 Las Virgenes Rd, Cornell; parking $12; ⊘ dawn-dusk), a popular movie and TV filming location with hiking trails galore (parking $12). A string of famous Malibu beaches include aptly named Surfrider near Malibu Pier, secretive El Matador, family fave Zuma Beach and wilder Point Dume (beach parking $3 to $12.50).

★ Getty Villa   MUSEUM
(Map p242; ☑ 310-430-7300; www.getty.edu; 17985 Pacific Coast Hwy, Pacific Palisades; ⊘ 10am-5pm Wed-Mon; **P** 🚼; 🚌 line 534 to Coastline Dr) **FREE** Stunningly perched on an ocean-view hillside, this museum in a replica 1st-century Roman villa is an exquisite, 64-acre showcase for Greek, Roman and Etruscan antiquities. Dating back 7000 years, they were amassed by oil tycoon J Paul Getty. Galleries, peristiles, courtyards and lushly landscaped gardens ensconce all manner of friezes, busts and mosaics, millennia-old cut, blown and colored glass and brain-bending geometric configurations in the Hall of Colored Marbles. Other highlights include the Pompeii fountain and Temple of Herakles.

West Hollywood & Mid-City

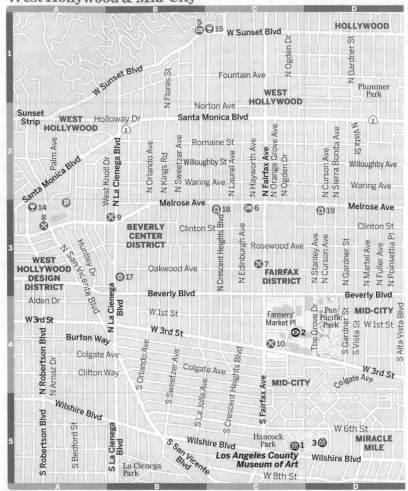

Santa Monica

The belle by the beach mixes urban cool with a laid-back vibe. Tourists, teens and street performers throng car-free, chain-store-lined Third Street Promenade. For more local flavor, shop posh **Montana Avenue** or eclectic **Main Street**, backbone of the neighborhood once nicknamed 'Dogtown,' – the birthplace of skateboard culture. There's free 90-minute parking in most public garages downtown.

★ **Santa Monica Pier**   LANDMARK
(Map p254; ☎310-458-8901; www.santamonica pier.org; ⊕) Once the very end of the mythical Route 66 and still the object of a tourist love affair, the Santa Monica Pier dates back to 1908 and is the city's most compelling landmark. There are arcades, carnival games, a vintage carousel, a Ferris wheel, a roller coaster and an aquarium, and the pier comes alive with free concerts (Twilight Dance Series) and outdoor movies in the summertime.

CALIFORNIA LOS ANGELES

a genteel escape among funky to modernist homes around the waterways that lent the neighborhood its name. For a quieter beach scene, head down the Marina Del Rey peninsula (one of America's largest pleasure-boat harbors is just inland), or head around the Ballona Wetlands to the wide open beaches of Playa del Rey.

◎ Venice

Be it beach, canal or wetlands, you're never far from water in these oceanside communities. Prepare for sensory overload on Venice's Boardwalk, a one-of-a-kind experience. Buff bodybuilders brush elbows with street performers and sellers of sunglasses, string bikinis, Mexican ponchos and medical marijuana, all while cyclists and rollerbladers whiz by on the bike path and skateboarders and graffiti artists get their own domains. A few blocks away, the Venice Canals offer

◎ Long Beach

Long Beach stretches along LA County's southern flank, harboring the world's third-busiest container port after Singapore and Hong Kong. Its industrial edge has been worn smooth downtown – Pine Ave is chockablock with restaurants and bars – and along the restyled waterfront. The Metro Blue Line connects Downtown LA with Long Beach in under an hour. **Passport** (www.lbtransit.com) minibuses shuttle around major tourist sights for free.

Santa Monica & Venice

which churned out 8000 hot meals a day during WWII.

★ **Aquarium of the Pacific**　　　AQUARIUM
(Map p242; ☑ tickets 562-590-3100; www.aquariumofpacific.org; 100 Aquarium Way, Long Beach; adult/senior/child $30/27/19; ⊙9am-6pm; 🅿🚼) Long Beach's most mesmerizing experience, the Aquarium of the Pacific is a vast, high-tech indoor ocean where sharks dart, jellyfish dance and sea lions frolic. More than 11,000 creatures inhabit four re-created habitats: the bays and lagoons of Baja California, the frigid northern Pacific, tropical coral reefs and local kelp forests.

★ **Museum of Latin American Art**　MUSEUM
(Map p242; ☑562-437-1689; www.molaa.org; 628 Alamitos Ave, Long Beach; adult/senior & student/child $10/7/free, Sun free; ⊙11am-5pm Wed, Thu, Sat & Sun, to 9pm Fri; 🅿) This gem of a museum is the only one in the US to present art created since 1945 in Latin America and in Latino communities in the US, in important temporary and traveling exhibits. Blockbuster shows have recently included Caribbean art and the works of LA's own Frank Romero.

⊙ Pasadena

Below the lofty San Gabriel Mountains, this city drips with wealth and gentility, feeling a world apart from urban LA. It's known for its early 20th-century arts-and-crafts archi-

★ **Battleship Iowa**　　MUSEUM, MEMORIAL
(Map p242; ☑877-446-9261; www.pacificbattleship.com; Berth 87, 250 S Harbor Blvd, San Pedro; adult/senior/child $20/17/12; ⊙10am-5pm, last entry 4pm; 🅿🚼; 🚇Metro Silver Line) This WWII to Cold War–era battleship is now permanently moored in San Pedro Bay and open to visitors as a museum. It's massive – 887ft long (that's 5ft longer than *Titanic*) and about as tall as an 18-story building. Step onto the gangway and download the app to take a self-guided audio tour of everything from the stateroom where FDR stayed to missile turrets and the enlisted men's galley,

tecture and the Tournament of Roses Parade on New Year's Day. Amble on foot around the shops, cafes, bars and restaurants of Old Town Pasadena, along Colorado Blvd east of Pasadena Ave. Metro Gold Line trains connect Pasadena and Downtown LA (20 minutes).

★**Huntington Library, Art Collections & Botanical Gardens**   MUSEUM, GARDEN
(Map p242; ☑626-405-2100; www.huntington. org; 1151 Oxford Rd, San Marino; adult weekday/ weekend & holidays $23/25, child $10, 1st Thu each month free; ☺10am-5pm Wed-Mon; ℗) One of the most delightful, inspirational spots in LA, the Huntington is rightly a highlight of any trip to California thanks to a world-class mix of art, literary history and over 120 acres of themed gardens (any one of which would be worth a visit on its own), all set amid stately grounds. There's so much to see and do that it's hard to know where to begin; allow three to four hours for even a basic visit.

★**Gamble House**   ARCHITECTURE
(Map p242; ☑info 626-793-3334, tickets 844-325-0712; www.gamblehouse.org; 4 Westmoreland Pl, Pasadena; tours adult/child $15/free; ☺tours 11:30am-3pm Thu & Fri, noon-3pm Sat & Sun Sep-May, 11am-3pm Thu-Sat, noon-3pm Sun Jun-Aug, bookstore 11am-2pm Tue, 10am-5pm Thu-Sun; ℗) This mansion in northwest central Pasadena has been called one of the 10 most architecturally significant homes in America, a 1908 masterpiece of California arts-and-crafts architecture built by Charles and Henry Greene for Procter & Gamble heir David Gamble. Incorporating 17 woods, art glass and subdued light, the entire home is a work of art, with its foundation, furniture and fixtures all united by a common design and theme inspired by its Southern California environs and Japanese and Chinese architecture.

Norton Simon Museum   MUSEUM
(Map p242; www.nortonsimon.org; 411 W Colorado Blvd, Pasadena; adult/child $12/free; ☺noon-5pm Mon, Wed & Thu, 11am-8pm Fri & Sat, 11am-5pm Sun; ℗) Rodin's *The Burghers of Calais* standing guard by the entrance is only a mind-teasing overture to the full symphony of art in store at this exquisite museum. Norton Simon (1907–93) was an entrepreneur with a Midas touch and a passion for art who parlayed his millions into an admirable collection of Western art and Asian sculpture. Meaty captions really help tell each piece's story.

 Activities

Despite spending a lot of time jammed on freeways, Angelenos love to get physical. Theirs is a city made for pace-quickening thrills, with spectacular mountain hikes, one of the country's largest urban nature reserves and surf-pounded beach. Add to this almost 300 days of sunshine and you'll forgive the locals for looking so, so good.

Hiking

If hiking doesn't feel like an indigenous LA activity to you, you need to reassess. This town is hemmed in and defined by two mountain ranges and countless canyons. In the **San Gabriel Mountains**, trails wind from Mt Wilson into granite peak wilderness, once the domain of the Gabrielino people and the setting for California's last grizzly-bear sighting. The Chumash roamed the **Santa Monica Mountains** (www.nps.gov/samo/index.htm), which are smaller, but still offer spectacular views of chaparral-draped peaks with stark drops into the Pacific. The **Backbone Trail** spans the range, but our favorite hike is to Sandstone Peak. Day hikes in **Topanga Canyon State Park** (Map p242; ☑310-455-2465; www.parks.ca.gov; 20828 Entrada Rd, Topanga; per vehicle $10; ☺8am-dusk), **Malibu Canyon** (Map p242; Malibu Canyon Rd, Malibu), Point Mugu and **Leo Carrillo** (☑310-457-8143; www.parks.ca.gov; 35000 W Pacific Coast Hwy, Malibu; per car $12; ☺8am-10pm; ℗♿) state parks are also recommended. If you only have an hour or two, check out **Runyon** (Map p242; www.runyoncanyonhike.com; 2000 N Fuller Ave; ☺dawn-dusk) or **Bronson** (Map p242; ☑818-243-1145; www.laparks.org; 3200 Canyon Dr; ☺5am-10:30pm) canyons in Hollywood. For more advice about trails in and around Southern California check out www.trails.com, or buy any of *Afoot and Afield: Los Angeles County: A Comprehensive Hiking Guide* (Wilderness Press; 2009), *Secret Walks: A Walking Guide to the Hidden Trails of Los Angeles* (Santa Monica Press; 2015) or *60 Hikes Within 60 Miles* (Menasha Ridge Press; 2009).

Cycling & In-line Skating

Get scenic exercise pedaling or skating along the paved **South Bay Bicycle Trail**, which parallels the beach for most of the 22 miles between Santa Monica and Pacific Palisades. Rental shops are plentiful in busy beach towns. Warning: it's crowded on weekends.

Surfing & Swimming

Top beaches for swimming are Malibu's **Leo Carrillo State Park**, **Santa Monica State Beach** and the South Bay's **Hermosa Beach**. Malibu's **Surfrider Beach** is a legendary surfing spot. Parking rates vary seasonally. 'Endless summer' is, sorry to report, a myth – much of the year you'll want a wetsuit in the Pacific. Water temperatures become tolerable by June and peak just under 70°F (21°C) in August. Water quality varies – check the 'Beach Report Card' at http://brc.healthebay.org.

Tours

★ **Esotouric**   BUS

(☎213-915-8687; www.esotouric.com; tours $58) Discover LA's lurid and fascinating underbelly on these offbeat, insightful and entertaining walking and bus tours themed around famous crime sites (Black Dahlia anyone?), literary lions (Chandler to Bukowski) and more.

★ **Los Angeles Conservancy**   WALKING

(☎213-623-2489; www.laconservancy.org; adult/child $15/10) Downtown LA's intriguing historical and architectural gems – from an art-deco penthouse to a beaux-arts ballroom and a dazzling silent-movie theater – are revealed on this nonprofit group's 2½-hour walking tours. To see some of LA's grand historic movie theaters from the inside, the conservancy also offers the Last Remaining Seats film series, screening classic movies in gilded theaters.

Dearly Departed   BUS

(☎855-600-3323; www.dearlydepartedtours.com; tours $50-85) This long-running, occasionally creepy, frequently hilarious tour will clue you in on where celebs kicked the bucket, George Michael dropped his trousers, Hugh Grant received certain services and the Charles Manson gang murdered Sharon Tate. Not for kids.

Festivals & Events

First Friday   STREET CARNIVAL

(www.abbotkinneyfirstfridays.com; ⊙5-11pm 1st Fri each month) Businesses along Abbot Kinney Blvd stay open late and the street is filled with food trucks at this monthly street fair.

Academy Awards   FILM

(www.oscars.org) Ogle your favorite film stars from the Dolby Theatre's red-carpet-adjacent bleachers. Apply in November or December for one of around 700 lucky spots. Held in late February or early March.

Rose Parade   PARADE

(www.tournamentofroses.com; ⊙Jan) This cavalcade of flower-festooned floats snakes through Pasadena on New Year's Day. Get close-ups during post-parade viewing at Victory Park. Avoid traffic and take the Metro Rail Gold Line to Memorial Park.

**West Hollywood
Halloween Carnaval**   CARNIVAL

(www.visitwesthollywood.com/halloween-carnaval) This rambunctious street fair brings 500,000 revelers – many in over-the-top and/or X-rated costumes – out for a day of dancing, dishing and flirting on Halloween. In late October.

Sleeping

For seaside life, base yourself in Santa Monica, Venice or Long Beach. Cool-hunters and party people will be happiest in Hollywood or WeHo; culture vultures should go to Downtown LA. Prices do not include lodging taxes (12% to 14%).

Downtown

Ace Hotel   HOTEL $$$

(Map p246; ☎213-623-3233; www.acehotel.com/losangeles; 929 S Broadway; lofts from $400; P❋❋❋) The ever-hip, buzzy, 182-room Ace is big on quirky details: Haas Brothers murals in the lobby and restaurant, whimsically themed cocktails at the rooftop bar and retro-inspired rooms with boxer-style robes, blank music sheets and, in many cases, record players or guitars. Small rooms can feel tight, so consider opting for a medium. Valet parking is $36 a night.

Hollywood

USA Hostels Hollywood   HOSTEL $

(Map p249; ☎800-524-6783, 323-462-3777; www.usahostels.com; 1624 Schrader Blvd; dm $38-49, r with bath from $120; ❋@❞; Ⓜ Red Line to Hollywood/Vine) This sociable hostel puts you within steps of the Hollywood party circuit. Private rooms are a bit cramped, but making new friends is easy during staff-organized barbecues, comedy nights and various walking tours. Freebies include wi-fi and a cook-your-own-pancake breakfast. It has cushy lounge seating on the front porch and free beach shuttles, too.

LA INSIDER MOVES

Classic movies on Broadway What better place to enjoy cult-status films than in one of Broadway's old movie palaces? Throughout the year, Cinespia (http://cinespia.org) runs special film screenings in historic Downtown theaters usually not open to the public. Many of the films are screened in 35mm. Check the Cinespia website for upcoming movies.

City Hall Farmers Market City Hall's South Lawn transforms into a mouthwatering farmers market on Thursday mornings. You'll find everything from organic fruit and vegetables to fresh seafood, meats, specialty food producers and ready-to-eat-food stalls. Best of all, 10% of sales goes to neighborhood nonprofit LARABA (Los Angeles River Artists and Business Association).

Run, yoga and beer If you feel like really earning your beer, join Angel City Brewery (p261) on its weekly Sunday morning exercise and beer-drinking combo ($15). The session begins with a 30-minute warm-up run through Downtown before a Vinyasa Flow yoga session (bring your own mat). Sweaty and centered, it's time for your well-deserved draft. Sign up online at www.brew-yoga.com.

★ **Mama Shelter** BOUTIQUE HOTEL $$
(Map p249; ☑ 323-785-6666; www.mamashel ter.com; 6500 Selma Ave; r from $179; ❄ @ 🛜; Ⓜ Red Line to Hollywood/Vine) Hip, affordable Mama Shelter keeps things playful with its lobby gumball machines, foosball table and live streaming of guests' selfies and videos. Standard rooms are small but cool, with quality beds and linen and subway-tiled bathrooms with decent-sized showers. Quirky in-room touches include movie scripts, masks and Apple TVs with free Netflix. The rooftop bar is one of LA's best.

★ **Hollywood Roosevelt Hotel** HISTORIC HOTEL $$$
(Map p249; ☑ 323-856-1970; www.thehollywood roosevelt.com; 7000 Hollywood Blvd; d from $282; Ⓟ❄@🛜⊠; Ⓜ Red Line to Hollywood/Highland) Roosevelt heaves with Hollywood lore: Shirley Temple learned to tap dance on the stairs off the lobby, Marilyn Monroe shot her first print ad by the pool (later decorated by David Hockney) and the ghost of actor Montgomery Clift can still be heard playing the bugle. Poolside rooms channel a modernist, Palm Springs vibe, while those in the main building mix contemporary and 1920s accents.

🛏 West Hollywood & Mid-City

★ **Palihotel** BOUTIQUE HOTEL $$
(Map p252; ☑ 323-272-4588; www.pali-hotel.com; 7950 Melrose Ave, Mid-City; r from $195; Ⓟ@🛜) We love the rustic wood-panelled exterior, the polished-concrete floor in the lobby, the elemental Thai massage spa, and the 32 contemporary rooms with two-tone paint jobs, a wall-mounted flat-screen TV, and enough room for a sofa. Some have terraces. Terrific all-around value.

★ **Chateau Marmont** HOTEL $$$
(Map p252; ☑ 323-656-1010; www.chateaumar mont.com; 8221 W Sunset Blvd, Hollywood; r $450, ste from $820; Ⓟ😊❄🛜⊠) The French-flavored indulgence may look dated, but this faux castle has long lured A-listers with its hilltop perch, five-star mystique and legendary discretion. Howard Hughes used to spy on bikini beauties from the same balcony suite that became the favorite of U2's Bono. If nothing else, it's worth stopping by for a cocktail at Bar Marmont (Map p252; ☑ 323-650-0575; www.chateaumarmont.com; 8171 Sunset Blvd, Hollywood; ⌚ 6pm-2am).

🛏 Beverly Hills

Avalon Hotel HOTEL $$$
(Map p242; ☑ 844-328-2566, 310-277-5221; www. avalon-hotel.com/beverly-hills; 9400 W Olympic Blvd, Beverly Hills; r from $289; Ⓟ❄@🛜⊠🐾) Mid-century modern gets a 21st-century spin at this fashion-crowd fave, which was Marilyn Monroe's old pad in its days as an apartment building. Funky retro rooms are all unique, but most have arched walls, marble slab desks and night stands, as well as playful art and sculpture. Perks include a sexy hourglass-shaped pool. Call it affordable glamor.

★ **Montage** HOTEL $$$
(Map p242; ☑ 888-860-0788; www.montagebev erlyhills.com; 225 N Canon Dr, Beverly Hills; r/ste from $695/1175; Ⓟ@🛜⊠) Drawing on-point eye candy and serious wealth, the 201-room Montage balances elegance with warmth

and affability. Models and moguls lunch by the gorgeous rooftop pool, while the property's sprawling five-star spa is a Moroccan-inspired marvel, with both single-sex and unisex plunge pools. Rooms are classically styled, with custom Sealy mattresses, dual marble basins, spacious showers and deep-soaking tubs.

🛏 Santa Monica

HI Los Angeles – Santa Monica   HOSTEL **$**
(Map p254; ☑310-393-9913; www.hilosangeles. org; 1436 2nd St; dm low season $27-45, May-Oct $40-55, r with shared bath $109-140, with private bath $160-230; ⊝❄@🤖; Ⓜ Expo Line to Downtown Santa Monica) Near the beach and Promenade, this hostel has an enviable location and recently modernized facilities that rival properties charging many times more. Its approximately 275 beds in single-sex dorms are clean and safe, private rooms are decorated with hipster chic and public spaces (courtyard, library, TV room, dining room, communal kitchen) let you lounge and surf.

Sea Shore Motel   MOTEL **$$**
(Map p254; ☑310-392-2787; www.seashoremo tel.com; 2637 Main St; r $125-175, ste $200-300; P❄🤖) The friendly, family-run lodgings at this comfy 25-unit motel put you just a Frisbee toss from the beach on happening Main St (quadruple-pane windows help cut street noise). The tiled, rattan-decorated rooms are basic, but 2nd-floor rooms have high ceilings and families can stretch out in the suites (basically full apartments) with kitchen and balcony a few doors down.

★Palihouse   BOUTIQUE HOTEL **$$$**
(Map p254; ☑310-394-1279; www.palihousesanta monica.com; 1001 3rd St; r/studios from $315/350; P❄@🤖📶) LA's grooviest hotel brand (not named Ace) occupies the 38 rooms, studios and one-bedroom apartments of the 1927 Spanish Colonial Embassy Hotel, with antique-meets-hipster-chic style. Each comfy room is slightly different, but look for picnic-table-style desks and wallpaper with intricate sketches of animals. Most rooms have full kitchens (and we love the coffee mugs with lifelike drawings of fish).

🛏 Long Beach

★Hotel Maya   BOUTIQUE HOTEL **$$**
(Map p242; ☑562-435-7676; www.hotelmayalong beach.com; 700 Queensway Dr, Long Beach; r from $179; P❄@🤖📶📶) West of the *Queen Mary*, this boutique property hits you with hip immediately upon entering the rusted-steel, glass and magenta-paneled lobby. The feel continues in the 199 rooms (coral tile, river-rock headboards, Mayan-icon accents), set in four 1970s-era hexagons with views of downtown Long Beach that are worth the upcharge.

🛏 Pasadena

★Bissell House B&B   B&B **$$**
(Map p242; ☑626-441-3535; www.bissellhouse. com; 201 S Orange Grove Ave, South Pasadena; r from $159; P🤖📶) Antiques, hardwood floors and a crackling fireplace make this secluded Victorian (1887) B&B on 'Millionaire's Row' a bastion of warmth and romance. The hedge-framed garden feels like a sanctuary, and there's a pool for cooling off on hot summer days. The Prince Albert room has gorgeous wallpaper and a claw-foot tub. All seven rooms have private baths.

LA FOR CHILDREN

Keeping kids happy is child's play in LA. The sprawling **Los Angeles Zoo** (p249) in family-friendly **Griffith Park** (p248) is a sure bet. Dino fans will dig the **La Brea Tar Pits** (p250) and the **Natural History Museum** (p248), while budding scientists crowd the **Griffith Observatory** (p249) and **California Science Center** (p247). For under-the-sea creatures, head to the **Aquarium of the Pacific** (p254) in Long Beach. The amusement park at **Santa Monica Pier** (p252) is fun for all ages. Activities for younger kids are more limited at tween-teen-oriented **Universal Studios Hollywood** (Map p242; ☑800-864-8377; www.universalstudioshollywood.com; 100 Universal City Plaza, Universal City; admission from $99, child under 3yr free; ☺daily, hours vary; P♿; Ⓜ Red Line to Universal City). In neighboring Orange County, **Disneyland** (p265) and **Knott's Berry Farm** (p266) are the first and last word in theme parks.

✖ Eating

Bring an appetite. A big one. LA's cross-cultural make up is reflected at its table, which is an epic global feast. And while there's no shortage of just-like-the-motherland dishes – from Cantonese *xiao long bao* to Ligurian *farinata* – it's the takes on tradition that really thrill. Ever tried Korean-Mexican tacos? Or a vegan cream-cheese donut with jam, basil and balsamic reduction? LA may be many things, but a culinary bore isn't one of them.

✖ Downtown

Cole's   SANDWICHES $
(Map p246; ☎213-622-4090; http://213hospitality. com/project/coles; 118 E 6th St; sandwiches $10-13.50; ⏰11am-midnight Sun-Wed, to 2am Thu-Sat; ☎) An atmospheric old basement tavern with vintage vinyl booths, original glass lighting and historic photos, Cole's is known for originating the French Dip sandwich way back in 1908, when those things cost a nickel. You know the drill – French bread piled with sliced lamb, beef, turkey, pork or pastrami, dipped once or twice in *au jus*.

★ Sushi Gen   JAPANESE $$$
(Map p246; ☎213-617-0552; www.sushigen.org; 422 E 2nd St; sushi $11-23; ⏰11:15am-2pm & 5:30-9:45pm Tue-Fri, 5-9:45pm Sat; ℗; Ⓜ Gold Line to Little Tokyo/Arts District) Come early to grab a table at this classic sushi spot, where bantering Japanese chefs carve thick slabs of melt-in-your-mouth salmon, buttery *toro* (tuna belly), Japanese snapper and more. At lunch, perch yourself at the sushi counter for à la carte options, or queue for a table in the dining room, where the sashimi lunch special ($17) is a steal.

★ Otium   MODERN AMERICAN $$$
(Map p246; ☎213-935-8500; http://otiumla. com; 222 S Hope St, Downtown; dishes $15-45; ⏰11:30am-2:30pm & 5:30-10pm Tue-Thu, 11:30am-2:30pm & 5:30-11pm Fri, 11am-2:30pm & 5:30-11pm Sat, 11am-2:30pm & 5:30-10pm Sun; ☎) In a modernist pavilion beside the Broad is this fun, of-the-moment hot spot helmed by chef Timothy Hollingsworth. Prime ingredients conspire in unexpected ways, from the crunch of wild rice and amaranth in an eye-candy salad of avocado, beets and pomegranate, to a twist of lime and sake in flawlessly al dente whole-wheat bucatini with Dungeness crab.

★ Bestia   ITALIAN $$$
(Map p242; ☎213-514-5724; www.bestiala.com; 2121 7th Pl; pizzas $16-19, pasta $19-29, mains $28-120; ⏰5-11pm Sun-Thu, to midnight Fri & Sat; ℗) Years on, this loud, buzzing, industrial dining space remains the most sought-after reservation in town (book at least a week ahead). The draw remains its clever, produce-driven take on Italian flavors, from charred pizzas topped with housemade 'nduja (a spicy Calabrian paste), to a sultry stinging-nettle raviolo with egg, mixed mushrooms, hazelnut and ricotta. The wine list celebrates the boutique and obscure.

✖ Hollywood & Griffith Park

Life Food Organic   VEGETARIAN $
(Map p249; ☎323-466-0927; www.lifefoodorganic.com; 1507 N Cahuenga Ave; dishes $7-14; ⏰7:30am-9pm; ☎) 🍴 If you're done with the tacos and cocktails, detox at this little health shop and eatery. Slurp on an almond-milk chocolate shake and fill up on the likes of turmeric-and-quinoa salads, veggie chili burgers and chocolate-cream pie. Some of it might sound naughty, but everything on the menu is raw, vegetarian and nutritious.

★ Petit Trois   FRENCH $$
(Map p252; ☎323-468-8916; http://petittrois. com; mains $14-36; ⏰noon-10pm Sun-Thu, to 11pm Fri & Sat; ℗) Good things come in small packages...like tiny, no-reservations Petit Trois! Owned by acclaimed TV chef Ludovic Lefebvre, its two long counters (the place is too small for tables) are where food-lovers squeeze in for smashing, honest, Gallic-inspired grub, from a ridiculously light Boursin-stuffed omelette to a showstopping double cheeseburger served with a standout foie gras–infused red-wine bordelaise.

★ Providence   MODERN AMERICAN $$$
(Map p252; ☎323-460-4170; www.providencela. com; 5955 Melrose Ave; lunch mains $40-45, tasting menus $120-250; ⏰noon-2pm & 6-10pm Mon-Fri, 5:30-10pm Sat, 5:30-9pm Sun; ℗) The top restaurant pick by preeminent LA food critic Jonathan Gold for four years running, this two-starred Michelin darling turns superlative seafood into arresting, nuanced dishes that might see abalone paired with eggplant, turnip and nori, or spiny lobster conspire decadently with macadamia nut and earthy black truffle.

CALIFORNIA LOS ANGELES

★ **Osteria & Pizzeria Mozza** ITALIAN $$$
(Map p252; ☑osteria 323-297-0100, pizzeria 323-297-0101; http://la.osteriamozza.com; 6602 Melrose Ave; pizzas $11-25, osteria mains $29-38; ⊘pizzeria noon-midnight, osteria 5:30-11pm Mon-Fri, 5-11pm Sat, 5-10pm Sun; P) Osteria Mozza crafts fine cuisine from market-fresh, seasonal ingredients, but being a Mario Batali joint, you can expect adventure – think squid-ink *chitarra freddi* with Dungeness crab, sea urchin and jalapeño – and consistent excellence. Reservations are recommended. Next door, Pizzeria Mozza is more laid-back and cheaper, its gorgeous thin-crust pies topped with combos such as squash blossoms, tomato and creamy *burrata*.

✖ West Hollywood & Mid-City

Original Farmers Market MARKET $
(Map p252; ☑323-933-9211; www.farmersmarketla.com; 6333 W 3rd St; mains $6-12; ⊘9am-9pm Mon-Fri, to 8pm Sat, 10am-7pm Sun; P⬤) The Farmers Market is a great spot for a casual meal any time of day, especially if the rug rats are tagging along. There are lots of options here, from gumbo and diner food to Singapore-style noodles and tacos, sit-down or takeout. Before or afterwards, go check out the **Grove** (Map p252; www.thegrovela.com; 189 The Grove Dr, Los Angeles; P⬤; ☐MTA lines 16, 17, 780 to Wilshire & Fairfax), next door.

Canter's DELI $$
(Map p252; ☑323-651-2030; www.cantersdeli.com; 419 N Fairfax Ave, Mid-City; ⊘24hr; P) As old-school delis go, Canter's is hard to beat. A fixture in the traditionally Jewish Fairfax district since 1931, it serves up the requisite pastrami, corned beef and matzo-ball soup with a side of sass by seen-it-all waitresses, in a rangy room with deli and bakery counters up front.

EP & LP SOUTHEAST ASIAN $$
(Map p252; ☑310-855-9955; http://eplosangeles.com; 603 N La Cienega Blvd, West Hollywood; small plates $10-18, large plates $20-34; ⊘5pm-2am Mon-Fri, from noon Sat & Sun) Louis Tikaram, Australia's Chef of the Year in 2014, has brought the creative, bold flavors of his Fijian-Chinese heritage – *kakoda* (Fijian-style ceviche), Chiang Mai larb (spiced salmon stands in for meat), and crispy chicken with black vinegar, chili and lemon – to some of LA's most enviable real estate, at the corner of Melrose and La Cienega.

★ **Catch LA** FUSION $$$
(Map p252; ☑323-347-6060; http://catchrestaurants.com/catchla; 8715 Melrose Ave, West Hollywood; shared dishes $11-31, dinner mains $28-41; ⊘11am-3pm Sat & Sun, 5pm-2am daily; P) An LA-scene extraordinaire. You may well find sidewalk paparazzi stalking celebrity guests and a doorman to check your reservation, but all that's forgotten once you're up in this 3rd-floor rooftop restaurant/bar above WeHo. The Pacific Rim–inspired menu features creative cocktails and shared dishes such as truffle sashimi and black-cod lettuce wraps.

✖ Santa Monica & Venice

★ **Santa Monica Farmers Markets** MARKET $
(Map p254; www.smgov.net/portals/farmers market; Arizona Ave, btwn 2nd & 3rd Sts; ⊘Arizona Ave 8:30am-1:30pm Wed, 8am-1pm Sat, Main St 8:30am-1:30pm Sun; ⬤) ✔ You haven't really experienced Santa Monica until you've explored one of its weekly outdoor farmers markets stocked with organic fruits, vegetables, flowers, baked goods and freshly shucked oysters. The mack daddy is the Wednesday market, around the intersection of 3rd and Arizona – it's the biggest and arguably the best for fresh produce, and often patrolled by local chefs.

★ **Gjelina** AMERICAN $$$
(Map p254; ☑310-450-1429; www.gjelina.com; 1429 Abbot Kinney Blvd, Venice; veggies, salads & pizzas $10-18, large plates $15-45; ⊘8am-midnight; ⬤; ☐Big Blue Bus line 18) If one restaurant defines the new Venice, it's this. Carve out a slip on the communal table between the hipsters and yuppies, or get your own slab of wood on the elegant stone terrace, and dine on imaginative small plates (raw yellowtail spiced with chili and mint and drenched in olive oil and blood orange) and sensational thin-crust, wood-fired pizza.

★ **Cassia** SOUTHEAST ASIAN $$$
(Map p254; ☑310-393-6699; 1314 7th St; appetizers $12-24, mains $18-77; ⊘5-10pm Sun-Thu, to 11pm Fri & Sat; P) Ever since it opened in 2015, open, airy Cassia has made about every local and national 'best' list of LA restaurants. Chef Bryant Ng draws on his Chinese-Singaporean heritage in dishes such as *kaya* toast (with coconut jam, butter and a slow-cooked egg), 'sunbathing' prawns, and the encompassing Vietnamese pot-au-feu: short-rib stew, veggies, bone marrow and delectable accompaniments.

Long Beach

★ Fourth & Olive
ALSATIAN $$
(Map p242; ☑562-269-0731; www.4thandolive.
com; 743 E 4th St, East Village, Long Beach; mains
$15-29; ⊙4:30-10pm Mon & Tue, 11am-10pm Wed,
Thu & Sun, 11am-11pm Fri & Sat) There's much
to love about this new Cal-French bistro:
farmers-market produce, small-farm-raised
beef and pork, housemade sausages, classic
dishes such as *steak frites* and *choucroute
garnie*, and low-key service, all under a
high-raftered roof with generous windows
to watch the world go by. *And* many of its
staff are disabled veterans, so you're doing
good while eating well.

Pasadena

Ración
SPANISH $$$
(Map p242; ☑626-396-3090; www.racionrestau
rant.com; 119 W Green St, Pasadena; small plates
$4-14, mains $20-58; ⊙6-10pm Mon-Thu, 11:30am-
3pm & 6-10:30pm Fri, 11:30am-3pm & 5:30-10:30pm
Sat, 5:30-10pm Sun; Ⓜ Gold Line to Memorial Park
or Del Mar) A foodie favorite, this minimalist,
Basque-inspired spot offers tapas such as
conservas (pâté), chicken croquettes and
seared prawns in salsa verde. Its house cures
yellowfin tuna in anchovy vinaigrette and
offers larger plates *(raciones)* ranging from
a wild market fish with heirloom beans to
duck breast with date jam and slow-braised
lamb belly.

🍷 Drinking & Nightlife

Whether you're after an organic Kurimi
espresso, a craft cocktail made with pea-
nut-butter-washed Campari, or a saison
brewed with Chinatown-sourced Oolong
tea, LA pours on cue. From post-industrial
coffee roasters and breweries to mid-century
lounges, classic Hollywood martini bars and
cocktail-pouring bowling alleys, LA serves
its drinks with a generous splash of wow.
So do the right thing and raise your glass to
America's finest town.

Angel City Brewery
MICROBREWERY
(Map p246; ☑213-622-1261; www.angelcitybrewery.
com; 216 S Alameda St; ⊙4pm-1am Mon-Thu, to 2am
Fri, noon-2am Sat, noon-1am Sun) Where suspen-
sion cables were once manufactured, craft
brews are now made and poured. Located
on the edge of the Arts District, it's a popular
spot to knock back an Indian pale ale or chai-
spiced Imperial stout, listen to some tunes
and chow down some food-truck tacos.

★ No Vacancy
BAR
(Map p249; ☑323-465-1902; www.novacancyla.
com; 1727 N Hudson Ave; ⊙8pm-2am; Ⓜ Red Line
to Hollywood/Vine) If you prefer your cocktail
sessions with plenty of wow factor, make
a reservation online, style up (no sports-
wear, shorts or logos) and head to this old
shingled Victorian. A vintage scene of dark
timber panels and elegant banquettes, it
has bars in nearly every corner, tended by
clever barkeeps while burlesque dancers
and a tightrope walker entertain the droves
of party people.

★ Dirty Laundry
BAR
(Map p249; ☑323-462-6531; http://dirtylaun
drybarla.com; 1725 N Hudson Ave; ⊙10pm-2am
Tue-Sat; Ⓜ Red Line to Hollywood/Vine) Under
a cotton-candy-pink apartment block of
no particular import is this funky den of
musty odor, low ceilings, exposed pipes and
good times. There's fine whiskey, funkali-
cious tunes on the turntables and plenty of
eye-candy peeps with low inhibitions. Alas,
there are also velvet-rope politics at work
here, so reserve a table to make sure you slip
through.

★ Abbey
GAY & LESBIAN
(Map p252; ☑310-289-8410; www.theabbey
weho.com; 692 N Robertson Blvd, West Hollywood;
⊙11am-2am Mon-Thu, from 10am Fri, from 9am
Sat & Sun) It's been called the best gay bar in
the world, and who are we to argue? Once
a humble coffee house, the Abbey has expanded into WeHo's bar/club/restaurant
of record.It has so many different-flavored
martinis and mojitos that you'd think they
were invented here, plus a full menu of upscale pub food (mains $14 to $21).

★ Polo Lounge
COCKTAIL BAR
(Map p242; ☑310-887-2777; www.dorchestercol
lection.com/en/los-angeles/the-beverly-hills-hotel;
Beverly Hills Hotel, 9641 Sunset Blvd, Beverly Hills;
⊙7am-1:30am) For a classic LA experience,
dress up and swill martinis in the Beverly
Hills Hotel's legendary bar. Charlie Chaplin
had a standing lunch reservation at booth
1 and it was here that HR Haldeman and
John Ehrlichman learned of the Watergate
break-in in 1972. There's a popular Sunday
jazz brunch (adult/child $75/35).

★ Basement Tavern
BAR
(Map p254; www.basementtavern.com; 2640 Main
St; ⊙5pm-2am) A creative speakeasy, housed
in the basement of the Victorian, and our

favorite well in Santa Monica. We love it for its craftsman cocktails, cozy booths, island bar and nightly live-music calendar that features blues, jazz, bluegrass and rock bands. It gets way too busy on weekends for our taste, but weeknights can be special.

★ Pike   BAR
(Map p242; ☑ 562-437-4453; www.pikelongbeach.com; 1836 E 4th St, Long Beach; ⊙11am-2am Mon-Fri, from 9am Sat & Sun; ☐ line 22) Adjacent to Retro Row, this nautical-themed dive bar, owned by Chris Reece of the band Social Distortion, brings in the cool kids for live music acts every night – with no cover, thank you – and serves beer by the pitcher or bottle and cocktails such as the Mezcarita and Greenchelada (a *michelada* with cucumber, jalapeño and lime).

☆ Entertainment

For discounted and half-price tickets, check Goldstar (www.goldstar.com) or LA StageTix (www.lastagetix.com), the latter strictly for theater.

★ Hollywood Bowl   CONCERT VENUE
(Map p242; ☑ 323-850-2000; www.hollywoodbowl.com; 2301 N Highland Ave; rehearsals free, performance costs vary; ⊙Jun-Sep) Summers in LA just wouldn't be the same without alfresco melodies under the stars at the Bowl, a huge natural amphitheater in the Hollywood Hills. Its annual season – which usually runs from June to September – includes symphonies, jazz bands and iconic acts such as Blondie, Bryan Ferry and Angélique Kidjo. Bring a sweater or blanket as it gets cool at night.

LGBTIQ LA

LA is one of the country's gayest cities and has made a number of contributions to gay culture. Your gaydar may well be pinging throughout the county, but the rainbow flag flies especially proudly in Boystown, along Santa Monica Blvd in West Hollywood, which is flanked by dozens of high-energy bars, cafes, restaurants, gyms and clubs. Most cater to gay men, although there's plenty for lesbians and mixed audiences. Thursday through Sunday nights are prime time.

Beauty reigns supreme among the buff, bronzed and styled of Boystown. Elsewhere the scene is considerably more laid back and less body conscious. The crowd in Silver Lake is more mixed age and runs from cute hipsters to leather-and-Levi's, while Downtown's burgeoning scene is an equally eclectic mix of hipsters, East LA Latinos, general counterculture types and business folk. Venice and Long Beach have the most relaxed, neighborly scenes.

If nightlife isn't your scene, there are plenty of other ways to meet, greet and engage. Outdoor options include the **Frontrunners** (www.lafrontrunners.com) running club and the **Great Outdoors** (www.greatoutdoorsla.org) hiking club. The latter runs day and night hikes, as well as neighborhood walks. For insight into LA's fascinating queer history, book a walking tour with **Out & About Tours** (www.thelavendereffect.org/tours; tours from $30).

There's gay theater all over town, but the **Celebration Theatre** (Map p252; ☑323-957-1884; www.celebrationtheatre.com; 6760 Lexington Ave, Hollywood) ranks among the nation's leading stages for LGBT plays. The **Cavern Club Theater** (Map p242; www.cavernclubtheater.com; 1920 Hyperion Ave, Silver Lake) pushes the envelope, particularly with uproarious drag performers; it's downstairs from Casita del Campo restaurant. If you're lucky enough to be in town when the **Gay Men's Chorus of Los Angeles** (www.gmcla.org) is performing, don't miss out: this amazing group has been doing it since 1979.

The **LA LGBT Center** (Map p249; ☑323-993-7400; www.lalgbtcenter.org; 1625 Schrader Blvd; ⊙9am-9pm Mon-Fri, to 1pm Sat) is a one-stop service and health agency, and its affiliated **Village at Ed Gould Plaza** (Map p252; ☑323-993-7400; https://lalgbtcenter.org; 1125 N McCadden Pl, Hollywood; ⊙6-10pm Mon-Fri, 9am-5pm Sat; ℗) offers art exhibits, theater and film screenings throughout the year.

The festival season kicks off in mid- to late May with the **Long Beach Pride Celebration** (☑562-987-9191; www.longbeachpride.com; 450 E Shoreline Dr, Long Beach; parade free, festival admission adult/child & senior $25/free; ⊙mid-May) and continues with the three-day **LA Pride** (www.lapride.org) in mid-June with a parade down Santa Monica Blvd. On Halloween (October 31), the same street brings out 500,000 outrageously costumed revelers of all persuasions.

★**Upright Citizens Brigade Theatre** COMEDY
(Map p249; ☑323-908-8702; http://franklin.ucbthe
atre.com; 5919 Franklin Ave; tickets $5-12) Origi-
ally founded in New York by *Saturday Night
Live* alums Amy Poehler and Ian Roberts
along with Matt Besser and Matt Walsh.
With nightly shows spanning anything from
stand-up comedy to improv and sketch, it's
arguably the best comedy hub in town. Valet
parking costs $7.

★**Geffen Playhouse** THEATER
(Map p242; ☑310-208-5454; www.geffenplay
house.com; 10886 Le Conte Ave, Westwood) American magnate and producer David Geffen
forked over $17 million to get his Mediter-
ranean-style playhouse back into shape.
The center's season includes both American
classics and freshly minted works, and it's
not unusual to see well-known film and TV
actors treading the boards.

Largo at the Coronet LIVE MUSIC, PERFORMING ARTS
(Map p252; ☑310-855-0530; www.largo-la.com; 366
N La Cienega Blvd, Mid-City) Ever since its early
days on Fairfax Ave, Largo has been progen-
itor of high-minded pop culture (it nurtured
Zach Galifianakis to stardom). Now part of
the Coronet Theatre complex, it features edgy
comedy, such as Sarah Silverman and Nick
Offerman, and nourishing night music such
as the Preservation Hall Jazz Band.

ArcLight Cinemas CINEMA
(Map p249; ☑323-464-1478; www.arclightcin
emas.com; 6360 W Sunset Blvd; ⓂRed Line to
Hollywood/Vine) Assigned seats, exceptional
celeb-sighting potential and a varied program that covers mainstream and art-house
movies make this 14-screen multiplex the
best around. If your taste dovetails with its
schedule, the awesome 1963 geodesic Ciner-
ama Dome is a must.

★**Los Angeles Philharmonic** CLASSICAL MUSIC
(Map p246; ☑323-850-2000; www.laphil.org; 111 S
Grand Ave) The world-class LA Phil performs
classics and cutting-edge works at the Walt
Disney Concert Hall, under the baton of
Venezuelan phenom Gustavo Dudamel.

★**Harvelle's** BLUES
(Map p254; ☑310-395-1676; www.harvelles.com;
1432 4th St; cover $5-15) This dark blues grot-
to has been packing 'em in since 1931, but
somehow still manages to feel like a well-
kept secret. There are no big-name acts here,

but the quality is usually high. Sunday's To-
ledo Show mixes soul, jazz and cabaret, and
Wednesday night brings the always-funky
House of Vibe All-Stars.

★**Dodger Stadium** BASEBALL
(Map p242; ☑866-363-4377; www.dodgers.com;
1000 Vin Scully Ave) Few clubs can match the
Dodgers when it comes to history, success
and fan loyalty. The club's newest owners
bought the organization for roughly $2 bil-
lion, an American team-sports record.

Staples Center STADIUM
(Map p246; ☑213-742-7100; www.staplescenter.
com; 1111 S Figueroa St) South Park got its first
jolt in 1999 with the opening of this sau-
cer-shaped sports and entertainment arena.
It's home court for the Los Angeles **Lakers**
(Map p246; ☑888-929-7849; www.nba.com/
lakers; tickets from $30), **Clippers** (Map p246;
☑213-204-2900; www.nba.com/clippers; tickets
from $20) and Sparks basketball teams, and
home ice for the LA Kings. Parking costs $10
to $30, depending on the event.

🔒 **Shopping**

Consider yourself a disciplined shopper?
Get back to us after your trip. LA is a pro
at luring cards out of wallets. After all, how
can you *not* bag that super-cute vintage-fab-
ric frock? Or that tongue-in-cheek tote? And
what about that mid-century-modern lamp,
the one that perfectly illuminates that rare,
signed Hollywood film script you scored?
Creativity and whimsy drive this town, right
down to its racks and shelves.

★**Raggedy Threads** VINTAGE
(Map p246; ☑213-620-1188; www.raggedythreads.
com; 330 E 2nd St; Ⓧnoon-8pm Mon-Sat, to 6pm
Sun; ⓂGold Line to Little Tokyo/Arts District) A tremendous vintage Americana store just off the
main Little Tokyo strip. There's plenty of beautifully ragged denim, with a notable collection
of pre-1950s workwear from the US, Japan
and France. You'll also find a good number of
Victorian dresses, soft T-shirts and a wonderful turquoise collection at decent prices.

★**Last Bookstore in Los Angeles** BOOKS
(Map p246; ☑213-488-0599; www.lastbookstorela.
com; 453 S Spring St; Ⓧ10am-10pm Mon-Thu, to
11pm Fri & Sat, to 9pm Sun) What started as a
one-man operation out of a Main St store-
front is now California's largest new-and-
used bookstore, spanning two levels of an
old bank building. Eye up the cabinets of

rare books before heading upstairs, home to a horror-and-crime book den, a book tunnel and a few art galleries to boot. The store also houses a terrific vinyl collection.

Melrose Avenue FASHION & ACCESSORIES
(Map p252) A popular shopping strip as famous for its epic people-watching as it is for its consumer fruits. You'll see hair (and people) of all shades and styles, and everything from Gothic jewels to custom sneakers to medical marijuana to stuffed porcupines available for a price.

★**Fred Segal** FASHION & ACCESSORIES
(Map p252; ☑323-651-4129; www.fredsegal.com; 8100 Melrose Ave, Mid-City; ◷10am-7pm Mon-Sat, noon-6pm Sun) Celebs and beautiful people circle for the very latest from Babakul, Aviator Nation and Robbi & Nikki at this warren of high-end boutiques under one impossibly chic but slightly snooty roof. The only time you'll see bargains (sort of) is during the two-week blowout sale in September.

Waraku SHOES
(Map p254; ☑310-452-5300; www.warakuusa.com; 1225 Abbot Kinney Blvd, Venice; ◷10am-7pm; ▢Big Blue Bus line 18) Waraku is a compact, Japanese-owned shop for shoe-lovers. It blends Far East couture with mainstream street brands such as Puma and Converse. Some 60% of the shoes are imported from Japan; the rest are domestic limited editions.

★**Rose Bowl Flea Market** MARKET
(Map p242; www.rgcshows.com; 1001 Rose Bowl Dr, Pasadena; admission from $9; ◷9am-4:30pm 2nd Sun each month, last entry 3pm, early admission from 5am) Every month since the 1960s, the Rose Bowl football field has hosted 'America's Marketplace of Unusual Items,' with rummaging hordes seeking the next great treasure. Over 2500 vendors and some 20,000 buyers converge here, and it's a great time.

NAVIGATING THE FASHION DISTRICT

Bargain hunters love the frantic, 100-block warren of fashion in southwestern Downtown that is the Fashion District. Deals can be amazing, but first timers are often bewildered by the district's size and immense selection. For orientation, check out www.fashion district.org.

ⓘ Information

DANGERS & ANNOYANCES

Despite its seemingly apocalyptic list of dangers – guns, violent crime, earthquakes – Los Angeles is a reasonably safe place to visit. The greatest danger is posed by car accidents (buckle up – it's the law), while the biggest annoyance is city traffic.

MEDIA

➧ **KCRW 89.9 FM** (www.kcrw.com) LA's cultural pulse, the best radio station in the city.

➧ **KPFK 90.7 FM** (www.kpfk.org) Part of the Pacifica radio network; news and progressive talk.

➧ **LA Weekly** (www.laweekly.com) Free alternative news, live music and entertainment listings.

➧ **Los Angeles Times** (www.latimes.com) Major, center-left daily newspaper.

MEDICAL SERVICES

Cedars-Sinai Medical Center (☑310-423-3277; http://cedars-sinai.edu; 8700 Beverly Blvd, West Hollywood; ◷24hr) 24-hour emergency room skirting West Hollywood.

Keck Medicine of USC (☑323-226-2622; www.keckmedicine.org; 1500 San Pablo St, Downtown; ◷24hr emergency room) 24-hour emergency department just east of Downtown.

Ronald Reagan UCLA Medical Center (☑310-825-9111; www.uclahealth.org; 757 Westwood Plaza, Westwood; ◷24hr emergency room) 24-hour emergency room on the UCLA campus.

TOURIST INFORMATION

Downtown LA Visitor Center (Map p246; www.discoverlosangeles.com; Union Station, 800 N Alameda St; ◷9am-5pm; Ⓜ Red/Purple/Gold Lines to Union Station)

Hollywood Visitor Information Center (Map p249; ☑323-467-6412; www.discoverlosange les.com; Hollywood & Highland, 6801 Hollywood Blvd; ◷8am-10pm Mon-Sat, 9am-7pm Sun; Ⓜ Red Line to Hollywood/Highland)

Santa Monica Visitor Information Center (Map p254; ☑800-544-5319; www.santamon ica.com; 2427 Main St)

ⓘ Getting There & Away

AIR

The main LA gateway is **Los Angeles International Airport** (LAX; Map p242; www.lawa.org/wel comeLAX.aspx; 1 World Way). Its nine terminals are linked by the free LAX Shuttle A, leaving from the lower (arrival) level of each terminal. Cabs and hotel and car-rental shuttles stop here as well. A free minibus for travelers with disabilities can be ordered by calling ☑310-646-6402.

Some domestic flights also arrive at **Burbank Hollywood Airport** (BUR, Bob Hope Airport;

Map p242; www.burbankairport.com; 2627 N Hollywood Way, Burbank), while to the south the small **Long Beach Airport** (Map p242; www.lgb.org; 4100 Donald Douglas Dr, Long Beach) is convenient for Disneyland.

BUS

The main bus terminal for **Greyhound** (Map p242; ☑ 213-629-8401; www.greyhound.com; 1716 E 7th St) is in an industrial part of Downtown, so try not to arrive after dark.

CAR

The usual international car-rental agencies have branches at LAX airport and throughout LA.

TRAIN

Amtrak (www.amtrak.com) trains roll into Downtown's historic **Union Station** (☑ 800-872-7245; www.amtrak.com; 800 N Alameda St). Interstate trains stopping in LA are the daily *Coast Starlight* to Seattle, the daily *Southwest Chief* to Chicago and the thrice-weekly *Sunset Limited* to New Orleans. The *Pacific Surfliner* travels numerous times daily between San Diego, Santa Barbara and San Luis Obispo via LA.

ℹ Getting Around

TO/FROM THE AIRPORT

LAX FlyAway (☑ 866-435-9529; www.lawa.org/FlyAway) runs to Union Station (Downtown), Hollywood, Van Nuys, Westwood Village near UCLA, and Long Beach. A one-way ticket costs $9.75. For scheduled bus services, catch the free shuttle bus from the airport toward parking lot C. It stops by the LAX City Bus Center hub for buses serving all of LA County.

Taxis are readily available outside the terminals. The flat rate to Downtown LA is $47. Expect to pay around $30 to $35 to Santa Monica, $40 to West Hollywood and $50 to Hollywood. These rates exclude the $4 LAX airport surcharge.

CAR & MOTORCYCLE

Driving in LA doesn't need to be a hassle, but be prepared for some of the worst traffic in the country during weekday rush hours (roughly 7am to 10am and 3pm to 7pm). Self-parking at motels is usually free; most hotels charge from $10 to $45. Valet parking at restaurants, hotels and nightspots is common, with average rates of $5 to $10.

PUBLIC TRANSPORTATION

Most public transportation is handled by **Metro** (☑323-466-3876; www.metro.net), which offers maps, schedules and trip-planning help through its website.

To ride Metro trains and buses, buy a reusable TAP card. Available from TAP vending machines at Metro stations with a $1 surcharge, the cards allow you to add a preset cash value or day passes. The regular base fare is $1.75 per boarding, or $7 for a day pass with unlimited rides. Both single-trip tickets and TAP cards loaded with a day pass are available on Metro buses (ensure you have the exact change). When using a TAP card, tap the card against the sensor at station entrances and aboard buses.

TAP cards are accepted on DASH and municipal bus services and can be reloaded at vending machines or online on the TAP website (www.taptogo.net).

TAXI

Because of LA's size and heavy traffic, getting around by cab will cost you. Metered taxis charge $2.85 at flagfall, then $2.70 per mile. Except for taxis lined up outside airports, train stations and major hotels, it's best to phone for a cab.

SOUTHERN CALIFORNIAN COAST

Disneyland & Anaheim

The mother of all West Coast theme parks, aka the 'Happiest Place on Earth,' **Disneyland** (Map p242; ☑714-781-4636; www.disneyland.com; 1313 Harbor Blvd; adult/child 3-9yr 1-day pass from $97/91, 2-day park-hopper pass $244/232; ⊙ open daily, seasonal hr vary) is a parallel world that's squeaky clean, enchanting and wacky all at once. It's an 'imagineered' hyper-reality where the employees – called 'cast members' – are always upbeat and there are parades every day of the year. More than 16 million kids, grandparents, honeymooners and international tourists stream through the front gates annually.

Disneyland opened to great fanfare in 1955 and the workaday city of Anaheim grew up around it. Today the Disneyland Resort comprises the original Disneyland Park and newer Disney California Adventure park. And Anaheim itself has developed some surprising pockets of cool that have nothing to do with the Mouse House.

◉ Sights & Activities

Spotless, wholesome **Disneyland Park** is still laid out according to Walt's original plans. It's here you'll find plenty of rides and some of the attractions most associated with the Disney name – Main Street, U.S.A., Sleeping Beauty Castle and Tomorrowland.

Disneyland Resort's larger but less crowded park, **Disney California Adventure**, celebrates the natural and cultural glories

WORTH A TRIP

KNOTT'S BERRY FARM

What, Disney's not enough for you? Find even more thrill rides and cotton candy at **Knott's Berry Farm** (Map p242; ☑714-220-5200; www.knotts.com; 8039 Beach Blvd, Buena Park; adult/child 3-11yr $75/42; ⊙ from 10am, closing hours vary 5-11pm; P). This Old West–themed amusement park teems with packs of speed-crazed adolescents testing their mettle on a line-up of rides. Gut-wrenchers include the Boomerang 'scream machine,' wooden GhostRider and 1950s-themed Xcelerator. Younger kids will enjoy tamer action at Camp Snoopy. From late September through October, the park transforms at night into Halloween-themed 'Knott's Scary Farm.'

When summer heat waves hit, jump next door to **Knott's Soak City** (Map p242; ☑714-220-5200; www.soakcityoc.com; 8039 Beach Blvd, Buena Park; adult/child 3-11yr $43/38; ⊙10am-5pm, 6pm or 7pm mid-May–mid-Sep; P) water park. Save time and money by buying print-at-home tickets for either park online. All-day parking is $18.

of the Golden State but lacks the original's density of attractions and depth of imagination. The best rides are Soarin' Around the World, a virtual hang glide, and Guardians of the Galaxy – Mission: BREAKOUT! that drops you 183ft down an elevator chute.

Going on all the rides at both theme parks requires at least two days, as queues for top attractions can be an hour or more. To minimize wait times, arrive midweek (especially during summer) before the gates open, buy print-at-home tickets online and take advantage of the parks' FASTPASS system, which preassigns boarding times at select rides and attractions. For seasonal park hours and schedules of parades, shows and fireworks, check the official website.

While of course Disneyland Resort dominates Anaheim tourism, it's worth visiting the redeveloped neighborhoods around city hall, the **Anaheim Packing District** (Map p242; www.anaheimpackingdistrict.com; S Anaheim Bl) and **Center Street** (Map p242; www.centerstreetanaheim.com; W Center St). By the latter is the Frank Gehry–designed hockey rink where the Anaheim Ducks practice; it's open to the public.

🛏 Sleeping

While the Disney resorts have their own hotels, there are a number of other worthwhile hotels just offsite or a few miles away, and every stripe of chain hotel you can imagine. Generally Anaheim's hotels are good value relative to those in the OC beach towns.

Alpine Inn
MOTEL $

(Map p242; ☑714-535-2186, 800-772-4422; www.alpineinnanaheim.com; 715 W Katella Ave; r $99-149; P) Connoisseurs of kitsch will hug their Hummels over this 42-room,

snow-covered chalet facade on an A-frame exterior and icicle-covered roofs – framed by palm trees, of course. Right on the border of Disney California Adventure, the inn also has Ferris-wheel views. It's circa 1958, and air-con rooms are well kept. Simple grab 'n' go breakfast served in the lobby.

Best Western Plus Stovall's Inn
MOTEL $$

(Map p242; ☑714-778-1880, ext 3 800-854-8175; www.bestwestern.com; 1110 W Katella Ave; r $99-175; P) Generations of guests have been coming to this 289-room motel about 15 minutes' walk to Disneyland. Around the side are two pools, two Jacuzzis, fitness center, kiddie pool and a garden of topiaries (for real). The remodeled sleek and modern design rooms sparkle; all have air-con, a microwave and minifridge. Rates include a hot breakfast and there's a guest laundry.

Ayres Hotel Anaheim
HOTEL $$

(Map p242; ☑714-634-2106; www.ayreshotels.com/anaheim; 2550 E Katella Ave; r incl breakfast $139-219; P) This well-run minichain of business hotels delivers solid-gold value. The 133 recently renovated rooms have microwaves, minifridges, safes, wet bar, pillow-top mattresses and design inspired by the Californian arts-and-crafts movement. Fourth-floor rooms have extra-high ceilings. Rates include a full breakfast and evening social hours Monday to Thursday with beer, wine and snacks.

★Disney's Grand Californian Hotel & Spa
RESORT $$$

(Map p242; ☑info 714-635-2300, reservations 714-956-6425; https://disneyland.disney.go.com/grand-californian-hotel; 1600 S Disneyland Dr; d from $360; P) Soaring timber beams rise above the cathedral-like lobby of the six-story Grand Californian, Disney's homage to the arts-and-crafts architectural movement. Cushy rooms have triple-sheeted beds, down pillows, bathrobes and all-custom furnishings. Outside there's a faux-redwood waterslide into the pool. At night, kids wind down with bedtime stories by the lobby's giant stone hearth.

✗ Eating & Drinking

From stroll-and-eat Mickey-shaped pretzels ($4) and jumbo turkey legs ($10) to deluxe, gourmet dinners (sky's the limit), there's no shortage of eating options, though mostly pretty expensive and targeted to mainstream tastes. Phone **Disney Dining** (☏714-781-3463; http://disneyland.disney.go.com/dining) to make reservations up to 60 days in advance.

If you want to steer clear of Mickey Mouse food, drive to the Anaheim Packing District (3 miles northeast), Old Towne Orange (7 miles southeast), Little Arabia (3 miles west) or Little Saigon (8 miles southwest).

★Pour Vida   MEXICAN $
(Map p242; ☏657-208-3889; www.pourvidalatin flavor.com; 185 W Center St Promenade; tacos $2-8; ⊙10am-7pm Mon, to 9pm Tue-Thu, to 10pm Fri, 9am-10pm Sat, 9am-7pm Sun) Chef Jimmy has worked in some of LA's top kitchens but returned to his Mexican roots to make some of the most gourmet tacos we've ever seen: pineapple skirt steak, tempura oyster, heirloom cauliflower...*caramba*! Even the tortillas are special, made with squid ink, spinach and a secret recipe. It's deliberately informal, all brick and concrete with chalkboard walls.

Earl of Sandwich   SANDWICHES $
(Map p242; ☏714-817-7476; www.earlofsand wichusa.com; Downtown Disney; mains $4.50-7.50; ⊙8am-11pm Sun-Thu, to midnight Fri & Sat; ➡) This counter-service chain near the **Disneyland Hotel** (Map p242; ☏714-778-6600; www.disneyland.com; 1150 Magic Way, Anaheim; r $210-395; ➲@🛜🏊) serves grilled sandwiches that are both kid- and adult-friendly. The 'original 1762' is roast beef, cheddar and horseradish, or look for chipotle chicken with avocado or holiday turkey. There are also pizza, salad and breakfast options.

Ralph Brennan's
New Orleans Jazz Kitchen   CAJUN $$
(Map p242; ☏714-776-5200; http://rbjazzkitchen. com; Downtown Disney; mains lunch/dinner $14-19/$24.50-38.50; ⊙8am-10pm Sun-Thu, to 11pm Fri & Sat; ➡) Hear live jazz combos on the week-

ends and piano weeknights at this resto-bar with NOLA-style Cajun and Creole dishes: gumbo, po-boy sandwiches, jambalaya, plus a (less adventurous) kids' menu and specialty cocktails. There's breakfast and lunch express service if you don't have time to linger.

★Napa Rose   CALIFORNIAN $$$
(Map p242; ☏714-300-7170; https://disneyland.dis ney.go.com/dining; Disney's Grand Californian Hotel & Spa; mains $38-48, 4-course prix-fixe dinner from $100; ⊙5:30-10pm; ➡) High-back arts-and-crafts-style chairs, leaded-glass windows and towering ceilings befit Disneyland Resort's top-drawer restaurant. On the plate, seasonal 'California Wine Country' (read: NorCal) cuisine is as impeccably crafted as the Sleeping Beauty Castle. Kids menu available. Reservations essential. Enter the hotel from Disney California Adventure or Downtown Disney.

ℹ Information

Disneyland's **City Hall** (Map p242; ☏714-781-4565; Main Street, U.S.A.) offers foreign-currency exchange. In Disney California Adventure, head to the guest relations lobby. Multiple ATMs are found in both theme parks and at Downtown Disney.

For information or help inside the parks, just ask any cast member or visit Disneyland's City Hall or Disney California Adventure's guest relations lobby.

ℹ Getting There & Around

Disneyland and Anaheim can be reached by car (off the I-5 Fwy) or Amtrak or Metrolink trains at Anaheim's **ARTIC** (Anaheim Regional Transportation Intermodal Center; 2150 E Katella Ave, Anaheim) transit center. From here it's a short taxi, ride share or **Anaheim Resort Transportation** (ART; ☏888-364-2787; www.rideart.org; adult/child fare $3/1, day pass $5.50/2, multiple-day passes available) shuttle to Disneyland proper. The closest airport is Orange County's **John Wayne Airport** (SNA; Map p242; www.ocair. com; 18601 Airport Way, Santa Ana).

The miniature biodiesel Disneyland Railroad chugs in a clockwise circle around Disneyland, stopping at Main Street USA, New Orleans Square, Mickey's Toontown and Tomorrowland, taking about 20 minutes to make a full loop.

Orange County Beaches

If you've seen *The OC* or *The Real Housewives*, you might imagine you already know what to expect from this giant quilt of suburbia connecting LA and San Diego, lolling beside 42 miles of glorious coastline. In

---

DON'T MISS

LAGUNA'S FESTIVAL OF ARTS

The **Festival of Arts** (www.foapom.com; 650 Laguna Canyon Rd; admission $7-10; ⊙ usually 10am-11:30pm Jul & Aug; ⛢) is a two-month celebration of original artwork in almost all its forms. About 140 exhibitors display works ranging from paintings and handcrafted furniture to scrimshaw; there are also kid-friendly art workshops and live music and entertainment daily.

---

reality, Hummer-driving hunks and Botoxed beauties mix it up with hang-loose surfers and beatnik artists to give each of Orange County's beach towns a distinct vibe.

Just across the LA–OC county line, old-fashioned **Seal Beach** is refreshingly noncommercial, with a quaint walkable downtown. Less than 10 miles further south along the Pacific Coast Hwy (Hwy 1), **Huntington Beach** – aka 'Surf City, USA' – epitomizes SoCal's surfing lifestyle. Fish tacos and happy-hour specials abound at bars and cafes along downtown HB's Main St, not far from a shortboard-sized **surfing museum** (Map p242; ☑ 714-960-3483; www.surfingmuseum.org; 411 Olive Ave; adult/child $2/1; ⊙ noon-5pm Tue-Sun).

Next up is the ritziest of the OC's beach communities: yacht-filled **Newport Beach**. Families and teens steer toward **Balboa Peninsula** for its beaches, vintage wooden pier and quaint amusement center. From near the 1906 Balboa Pavilion, **Balboa Island Ferry** (Map p242; www.balboaislandferry.com; 410 S Bay Front; adult/child $1/50¢, car incl driver $2; ⊙ 6:30am-midnight Sun-Thu, to 2am Fri & Sat) shuttles across the bay to Balboa Island for strolls past historic beach cottages and boutiques along Marine Ave.

Continuing south, Hwy 1 zooms past the wild beaches of **Crystal Cove State Park** (Map p242; ☑ 949-494-3539; www.parks.ca.gov; 8471 N Coast Hwy; per car $15; ⊙ 6am-sunset; ⛢⛢) 🌊 before winding downhill into **Laguna Beach**, the OC's most cultured seaside community. Secluded beaches, glassy waves and eucalyptus-covered hillsides create a Riviera-like feel. Art galleries dot the narrow streets of the 'village' and the coastal highway, where the **Laguna Art Museum** (☑ 949-494-8971; www.lagunaartmuseum.org; 307 Cliff Dr; adult/student & senior/child under 13yr $7/5/free, 5-9pm 1st Thu of month free; ⊙ 11am-

5pm Fri-Tue, to 9pm Thu) exhibits modern and contemporary Californian works. Soak up the natural beauty right in the center of town at **Main Beach**.

Another 10 miles south, detour inland to **Mission San Juan Capistrano** (☑ 949-234-1300; www.missionsjc.com; 26801 Ortega Hwy; adult/child $9/6; ⊙ 9am-5pm; ⛢), one of California's most beautifully restored Spanish Colonial missions, with flowering gardens, a fountain courtyard and the charming 1778 Serra Chapel.

🛏 Sleeping & Eating

★ **Crystal Cove Beach Cottages**　CABIN $$
(Map p242; ☑ reservations 800-444-7275; www.crystalcovealliance.org; 35 Crystal Cove, Crystal Cove State Park Historic District; r with shared bath $35-140, cottages $171-249; ⊙ check-in 4-9pm; ℗) Right on the beach, these two dozen preserved cottages (circa 1930s to '50s) now host guests for a one-of-a-kind stay. Each cottage is different, sleeping between two and eight people in a variety of private or dorm-style accommodations. To snag one, book on the first day of the month seven months before your intended stay – or pray for cancellations.

★ **Paséa**　RESORT $$$
(Map p242; ☑ 888-674-3634; http://meritagecollection.com/paseahotel; 21080 Pacific Coast Hwy; r from $359; ℗😊❄@🛜🌊) This hotel is slick and serene, with tons of light and air. Floors are themed for shades of blue from denim to sky and each of its 250 shimmery, minimalist, high-ceilinged rooms has an ocean-view balcony. As if the stunning pool, gym and Balinese-inspired spa weren't enough, it also connects to **Pacific City** (www.gopacificcity.com; 21010 Pacific Coast Hwy; ⊙ hours vary).

★ **Lot 579**　FOOD HALL
(Map p242; www.gopacificcity.com/lot-579; Pacific City, 21010 Pacific Coast Hwy; ⊙ hours vary; ℗🛜⛢) The food court at HB's stunning new ocean-view mall offers some unique and fun restaurants for pressed sandwiches (Burnt Crumbs – the spaghetti grilled cheese is so Instagrammable), Aussie meat pies (Pie Not), coffee (Portola) and ice cream (Han's). For best views, take your takeout to the deck, or eat at American Dream (brewpub) or Bear Flag Fish Company.

★ **Bear Flag Fish Company**　SEAFOOD $
(Map p242; ☑ 949-673-3474; www.bearflagfishco.com; 3421 Via Lido; mains $10-16; ⊙ 11am-9pm Tue-Sat, to 8pm Sun & Mon; ⛢) This is *the* place for

generously sized, grilled and *panko*-breaded fish tacos, ahi burritos, spankin' fresh ceviche and oysters. Pick out what you want from the ice-cold display cases, then grab a picnic-table seat. About the only way this seafood could be any fresher is if you caught and hauled it off the boat yourself!

★**Driftwood Kitchen**   AMERICAN $$$
(☑949-715-7700; www.driftwoodkitchen.com; 619 Sleepy Hollow Lane; mains lunch $15-36, dinner $24-39; ⊙9-10:30am & 11am-2:30pm Mon-Fri, 5-9:30pm Sun-Thu, to 10:30pm Fri & Sat, 9am-2:30pm Sat & Sun) Ocean views and ridonkulous sunsets alone ought to be enough to bring folks in, but gourmet Driftwood steps up the food with seasonal menus centered around fresh, sustainable seafood, plus options for landlubbers. Inside it's all beachy casual, whitewashed and pale woods. And the cocktails are smart and creative.

San Diego

San Diego calls itself 'America's Finest City' and its breezy confidence and sunny countenance filter down to folks you encounter every day on the street. It feels like a collection of villages each with its own personality, but it's the nation's eighth-largest city and we're hard-pressed to think of a more laid-back place.

⊙ Sights

San Diego's **Downtown** is the region's main business, financial and convention district. Whatever intense urban energy Downtown generally lacks, it makes up for in spirited shopping, dining and nightlife in the historic **Gaslamp Quarter** and the hipster havens of **East Village** and **North Park**. The waterfront **Embarcadero** is great for a stroll; in the northwestern corner of Downtown, vibrant **Little Italy** is full of good eats, and **Old Town** is the seat of local history.

The city of **Coronado**, with its landmark 1888 Hotel del Coronado (p277) and top-rated beach, sits across San Diego Bay from Downtown. At the entrance to the bay, **Point Loma** has sweeping views across sea and city from the Cabrillo National Monument (p275). **Mission Bay**, northwest of Downtown, has lagoons, parks and recreation from waterskiing to camping. The nearby coast – Ocean, Mission and Pacific Beaches – epitomizes the SoCal beach scene.

⊙ Downtown & Embarcadero

Downtown once harbored a notorious strip of saloons, gambling joints and bordellos known as Stingaree. These days, Stingaree has been beautifully restored and rechristened the **Gaslamp Quarter**, a heart-thumping playground of restaurants, bars, clubs, boutiques and galleries. At downtown's northern edge, **Little Italy** has evolved into one of the city's hippest neighborhoods to live, eat and shop in.

USS Midway Museum   MUSEUM
(Map p272; ☑619-544-9600; www.midway.org; 910 N Harbor Dr; adult/child $20/$10; ⊙10am-5pm, last admission 4pm; P♿) The giant aircraft carrier USS *Midway* was one of the navy's flagships from 1945 to 1991, last playing a combat role in the First Gulf War. On the flight deck of the hulking vessel, walk right up to some 29 restored aircraft including an F-14 Tomcat and F-4 Phantom jet fighter. Admission includes an audio tour along the narrow confines of the upper decks to the bridge, admiral's war room, brig and 'pri-fly' (primary flight control; the carrier's equivalent of a control tower). Parking costs $10.

★**Maritime Museum**   MUSEUM
(Map p272; ☑619-234-9153; www.sdmaritime.org; 1492 N Harbor Dr; adult/child $16/8; ⊙9am-9pm late May-early Sep, to 8pm early Sep-late May; ♿) This museum is easy to find: look for the 100ft-high masts of the iron-hulled square-rigger *Star of India*. Built on the Isle of Man and launched in 1863, the tall ship plied the England–India trade route, carried immigrants to New Zealand, became a trading ship based in Hawaii and, finally, ferried cargo in Alaska. It's a handsome vessel, but don't expect anything romantic or glamorous on board.

Museum of Contemporary Art   MUSEUM
(MCASD Downtown; Map p272; ☑858-454-3541; www.mcasd.org; 1001 Kettner Blvd; adult/child under 25yr/senior $10/free/$5, free 5-8pm 3rd Thu each month; ⊙11am-5pm Thu-Tue, to 8pm 3rd Thu each month) This Financial District museum has brought an ever-changing variety of innovative artwork to San Diegans since the 1960; check the website for exhibits. Tickets are valid for seven days.

⊙ Coronado

Technically a peninsula, Coronado Island is joined to the mainland by a 2.2-mile-long bridge. The peninsula's main draw is the

Greater San Diego

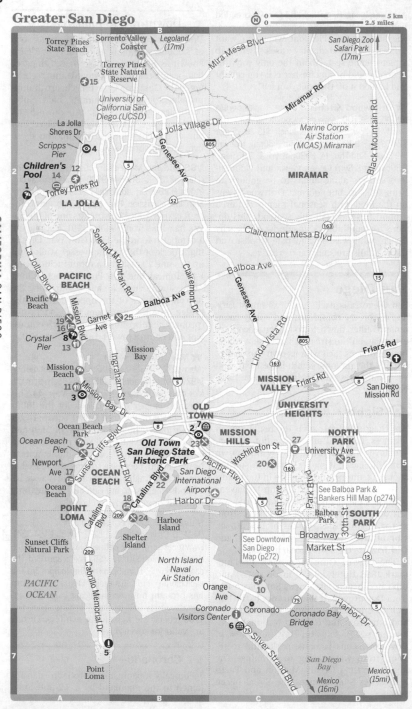

0   5 km
0   2.5 miles

Torrey Pines State Beach
Sorrento Valley Coaster
Legoland (17mi)
Mira Mesa Blvd
San Diego Zoo Safari Park (17mi)
Torrey Pines State Natural Reserve
15
University of California San Diego (UCSD)
La Jolla Village Dr
Miramar Rd
Black Mountain Rd
Marine Corps Air Station (MCAS) Miramar
MIRAMAR
La Jolla Shores Dr
Scripps Pier
4
Children's Pool
14 12
1
Torrey Pines Rd
LA JOLLA
Soledad Mountain Rd
Clairemont Mesa Blvd
163
PACIFIC BEACH
Balboa Ave
15
Pacific Beach
Balboa Ave
Clairemont Dr
Genesee Ave
19 25
16 Garnet Ave
8 13
Crystal Pier
Mission Blvd
Linda Vista Rd
805
163
Friars Rd
9
Mission Bay
MISSION VALLEY
Friars Rd
San Diego Mission Rd
8
Mission Beach
Ingraham St
5
11 Mission Bay Dr
3
OLD TOWN
UNIVERSITY HEIGHTS
Ocean Beach Park
2 7
MISSION HILLS
27
NORTH PARK
Ocean Beach Pier
21
Old Town San Diego State Historic Park
23
University Ave
26
Newport Ave
17
Sunset Cliffs Blvd
Nimitz Blvd
22
San Diego International Airport
Harbor Dr
Washington St
20
163
Park Blvd
See Balboa Park & Bankers Hill Map (p274)
Ocean Beach
OCEAN BEACH
18
Catalina Blvd
6th Ave
5
Balboa Park
SOUTH PARK
POINT LOMA
Catalina Blvd
209
24
Harbor Island
Shelter Island
See Downtown San Diego Map (p272)
30th St
Broadway
94
Market St
15
Sunset Cliffs Natural Park
209
Cabrillo Memorial Dr
North Island Naval Air Station
10
75
Harbor Dr
5
PACIFIC OCEAN
Orange Ave
Coronado
Coronado Bay Bridge
Coronado Visitors Center
6 75
5
Point Loma
San Diego Bay
Silver Strand Blvd
Mexico (16mi)
Mexico (15mi)

Greater San Diego

CALIFORNIA SAN DIEGO

Hotel del Coronado (p277), known for its seaside Victorian architecture and illustrious guestbook, which includes Thomas Edison, Babe Ruth and Marilyn Monroe (its exterior stood in for a Miami hotel in the classic flick *Some Like it Hot*).

The hourly **Coronado Ferry** (Map p272; ☏ 800-442-7847; www.flagshipsd.com; 990 N Harbor Dr; 1 way $4.75; ◷ 9am-10pm) departs from the Embarcadero's **Broadway Pier** (1050 N Harbor Dr) and from downtown's convention center. All ferries arrive on Coronado at the foot of 1st St, where **Bikes & Beyond** (Map p270; ☏ 619-435-7180; www.bikes-and-beyond. com; 1201 1st St, Coronado; per hr/day from $8/30; ◷ 9am-sunset) rents cruisers and tandems, perfect for pedaling past Coronado's white-sand beaches sprawling south along the Silver Strand.

◎ Balboa Park

Balboa Park is an urban oasis brimming with more than a dozen museums, gorgeous gardens and architecture, performance spaces and a zoo. Early 20th-century beaux arts and Spanish Colonial Revival–style buildings (the legacy of world's fairs) are grouped around plazas along east–west ElPrado promenade.

The free **Balboa Park Tram** bus makes a continuous loop around the park; however, it's most enjoyable to walk, past the 1915 **Spreckels Organ Pavilion** (Map p274; ☏ 619-702-8138; http://spreckelsorgan.org; Balboa Park)

FREE, the shops and galleries of the **Spanish Village Art Center** (Map p274; ☏ 619-233-9050; http://spanishvillageart.com; 1770 Village Place, Balboa Park; ◷ 11am-4pm) **FREE** and the international themed exhibition cottages by the **United Nations Building**.

★ **San Diego Zoo**   ZOO
(Map p274; ☏ 619-231-1515; http://zoo.sandiego. org; 2920 Zoo Dr; 1-day pass adult/child from $52/42; 2-visit pass to zoo &/or safari park adult/ child $83.25/73.25; ◷ 9am-9pm mid-Jun–early Sep, to 5pm or 6pm early Sep–mid-Jun; P ⊞) ✦ This justifiably famous zoo is one of SoCal's biggest attractions, showing more than 3000 animals representing more than 650 species in a beautifully landscaped setting, typically in enclosures that replicate their natural habitats. Its sister park is **San Diego Zoo Safari Park** (☏ 760-747-8702; www.sdzsafari park.org; 15500 San Pasqual Valley Rd, Escondido; 1-day adult/child $52/42, 2-visit pass to zoo and/or safari park adult/child $83.25/73.25; ◷ 8am-6pm, to 7pm late Jun–mid-Aug; P ⊞) in northern San Diego County.

★ **Mingei International Museum**   MUSEUM
(Map p274; ☏ 619-239-0003; www.mingei.org; 1439 El Prado; adult/youth/child $10/7/free; ◷ 10am-5pm Tue-Sun; ⊞) A diverse collection of folk art, costumes, toys, jewelry, utensils and other handmade objects of traditional cultures from around the world, plus changing exhibitions covering beads to surfboards. Check the website to find out what's on.

Downtown San Diego

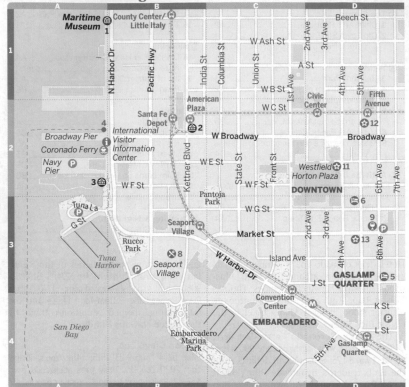

CALIFORNIA SAN DIEGO

Reuben H Fleet Science Center MUSEUM
(Map p274; ☑619-238-1233; www.rhfleet.org; 1875 El Prado; adult/child 3-12 years incl IMAX $20/17; ⊙10am-5pm Mon-Thu, to 6pm Fri-Sun; ⊕) One of Balboa Park's most popular venues, this hands-on science museum features interactive displays and a toddler room. Look out for opportunities to build gigantic structures with Keva planks and visit the **Gallery of Illusions and Perceptions**. The biggest draw is the **Giant Dome Theater**, which screens several different films each day. The hemispherical, wraparound screen and 152-speaker state-of-the-art sound system create sensations ranging from pretty cool to mind-blowing.

San Diego Natural History Museum MUSEUM
(Map p274; ☑877-946-7797; www.sdnhm.org; 1788 El Prado; adult/youth 3-17/child under 2 $19/12/free; ⊙10am-5pm; ⊕) The 'Nat' houses 7.5 million specimens, including rocks, fossils and taxidermied animals, as well as an impressive

dinosaur skeleton and a California fault-line exhibit, all in beautiful spaces. Kids love the movies about the natural world in the giant-screen cinema; the selections change frequently. Children's programs are held most weekends. Special exhibits (some with an extra charge) span pirates to King Tut. The museum also arranges field trips and nature walks in Balboa Park and further afield.

San Diego Museum of Man MUSEUM
(Map p274; ☑619-239-2001; www.museumofman. org; Plaza de California, 1350 El Prado; adult/child/teen $13/6/8; ⊙10am-5pm; ⊕) This is the county's only anthropological museum, with exhibits spanning ancient Egypt, the Mayans and local indigenous Kumeyaay people as well as human evolution and the human life cycle. Recent temporary exhibits have covered everything from cannibalism to beer. The basket and pottery collections are especially fine and the museum shop sells handicrafts from Central America and elsewhere.

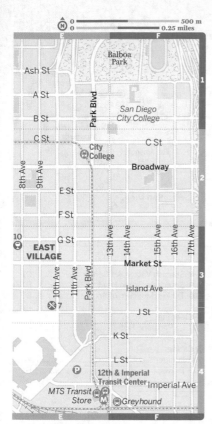

important traveling exhibits. The sculpture garden has works by Alexander Calder and Henry Moore.

San Diego Air & Space Museum MUSEUM
(Map p274; ☑619-234-8291; www.sandiegoairand-space.org; 2001 Pan American Plaza; adult/youth/child under 2 $19.75/$10.75/free; ◎10am-4:30pm; ⚑) The round building at the southern end of the plaza houses an excellent museum with extensive displays of aircraft throughout history – originals, replicas, models – plus memorabilia from legendary aviators, including Charles Lindbergh and astronaut John Glenn. Catch films in the 3D/4D theater.

◎ Old Town & Mission Valley

Mission & Pacific Beaches BEACH
(Map p270) FREE Central San Diego's best beach scene is concentrated in a narrow strip of land between the ocean and Mission Bay. There's amazing people-watching on the **Ocean Front Walk**, the boardwalk that connects the two beaches. From South Mission Jetty to Pacific Beach Point, it's crowded with joggers, in-line skaters and cyclists any time of the year. On warm summer weekends, oiled bodies, packed like

Timken Museum of Art MUSEUM
(Map p274; ☑619-239-5548; www.timkenmuseum.org; 1500 El Prado; ◎10am-4:30pm Tue-Sat, from noon Sun) FREE Don't skip the Timken, home of the Putnam collection, a small but impressive group of paintings, including works by Rembrandt, Rubens, El Greco, Cézanne and Pissarro, plus a wonderful selection of Russian icons. Built in 1965, the building stands out for *not* being in imitation-Spanish style.

San Diego Museum of Art MUSEUM
(SDMA; Map p274; ☑619-232-7931; www.sdmart.org; 1450 El Prado; adult/child $15/free; ◎10am-5pm Mon, Tue & Thu-Sat, from noon Sun) The SDMA is the city's largest art museum. The permanent collection has works by a number of European masters from the renaissance to the modernist eras (though no renowned pieces), American landscape paintings and several fantastic pieces in the Asian galleries; the museum also often has

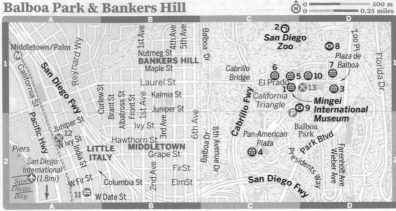

Balboa Park & Bankers Hill

sardines, cover the beach from end to end and cheer the setting sun.

★ Old Town San Diego State Historic Park   HISTORIC SITE

(Map p270; ☎619-220-5422; www.parks.ca.gov; 4002 Wallace St; ⊙visitor center & museums 10am-5pm daily; 🅿🚻) **FREE** This park has an excellent history museum in the **Robinson-Rose House** at the southern end of the plaza. You'll also find a diorama depicting the original pueblo at the park's **visitor center**, where you can pick up a copy of the *Old Town San Diego State Historic Park Tour Guide & Brief History* ($3), or a presentation tour (free) at 11am and 2pm daily.

Mission Basilica San Diego de Alcalá   CHURCH

(Map p270; ☎619-281-8449; www.missionsandiego. com; 10818 San Diego Mission Rd; adult/child/under 5 $5/2/free; ⊙9am-4:30pm; 🅿🚻) Although the site of the first California mission (1769) was on Presidio Hill by present-day Old Town, in 1774 Padre Junípero Serra moved it about 7 miles upriver, closer to water and more arable land, to what is now the Mission Basilica San Diego de Alcalá. In 1784 missionaries built a solid adobe-and-timber church, which was destroyed by an earthquake in 1803. The church was promptly rebuilt, and at least some of it still stands on a slope overlooking Mission Valley.

Junípero Serra Museum   MUSEUM

(Map p270; ☎619-232-6203; www.sandiegohis tory.org/serra_museum; 2727 Presidio Dr; by donation; ⊙10am-4pm Fri-Sun early Jun-early Sep, 10am-5pm Sat & Sun early Sep-early Jun; 🅿🚻) Located at one of the most important sites in the city, the Junípero Serra Museum stands atop Presidio Hill, the place where California first began. In 1769, the first mission, known as the Mission San Diego de Alcalá, was established here before it was moved 7 miles upriver.. The current Presidio building is Spanish Revival in style and houses a small but interesting collection of artifacts and pictures from San Diego's Mission and rancho periods.

◉ Point Loma

On maps Point Loma looks like an elephant's trunk guarding the entrance to San Diego Bay. Highlights are the **Cabrillo National Monument** (Map p270; ☑ 619-557-5450; www.nps.gov/cabr; 1800 Cabrillo Memorial Dr; per car $10; ☺ 9am-5pm; P ♿) ✈ (at the end of the trunk), the shopping and dining of **Liberty Public Market** (Map p270; ☑ 619-487-9346; http://libertypublicmarket.com; 2820 Historic Decatur Rd; ☺ 7am-10pm) (at its base) and seafood meals around **Shelter Island**.

◉ Mission Bay & Beaches

San Diego's big three beach towns all have ribbons of hedonism where armies of tanned, taut bodies frolic in the sand. West of amoeba-shaped Mission Bay, surf-friendly **Mission Beach** and its northern neighbor, **Pacific Beach** (aka 'PB'), are connected by car-free **Ocean Front Walk**, which swarms with skaters, joggers and cyclists year-round.

South of Mission Bay, bohemian **Ocean Beach** (OB) has a fishing pier, beach volleyball and good surf. Its main drag, **Newport Avenue**, is chockablock with scruffy bars, flip-flop eateries and shops selling surf gear, tattoos, vintage clothing and antiques.

Belmont Park   AMUSEMENT PARK
(Map p270; ☑ 858-228-9283; www.belmontpark.com; 3146 Mission Blvd; per ride $3-6, all-day pass adult/child $30/20; ☺ from 11am daily, closing times vary; P) This old-style family-amusement park at the southern end of Mission Beach has been here since 1925. There's a large indoor pool, known as the **Plunge**, and a classic wooden roller coaster named the **Giant Dipper**, plus adventure golf, a new escape-room game, a carousel and other classics. More modern attractions include wave machines like **Flowrider** (Map p270; ☑ 858-228-9283; www.belmontpark.com/flow/; WaveHouse Beach Club, 3125 Ocean Front Walk; wave-riding per hour $30) FREE, for simulated surfing. Even if it sits on dry land, Belmont is to San Diego what the Santa Monica Pier amusement park is to LA.

◉ La Jolla

Facing one of SoCal's loveliest sweeps of coastline, wealthy La Jolla (Spanish for 'the jewel,' pronounced la-hoy-ah) possesses shimmering beaches and an upscale downtown filled with boutiques and cafes. Oceanfront diversions include the **Children's Pool** (La Jolla seals; Map p270; 850 Coast Blvd) (no longer for swimming, it's now home to barking sea lions), kayaking, exploring sea caves at **La Jolla Cove** and snorkeling at **San Diego-La Jolla Underwater Park** (Map p270).

**Torrey Pines State
Natural Reserve**   STATE PARK
(☑ 858-755-2063; www.torreypine.org; 12600 N Torrey Pines Rd; ☺ 7:15am-sunset, visitor center 10am-4pm Oct-Apr, 9am-6pm May-Sep; P ♿) ✈ FREE Between N Torrey Pines Rd and the ocean, and from the **Torrey Pines Gliderport** (Map p270; ☑ 858-452-9858; www.flytorrey.com; 2800 Torrey Pines Scenic Dr; 20min paragliding $175, hang-gliding tandem flight per person $225) to Del Mar, this reserve preserves the last mainland stands of the Torrey pine *(Pinus torreyana),* a species adapted to sparse rainfall and sandy, stony soils. Steep sandstone gullies have eroded into wonderfully textured surfaces, and the views over the ocean and north, including whale-watching, are superb. Volunteers lead nature walks on weekends and holidays. Several trails wind through the reserve and down to the beach.

Birch Aquarium at Scripps   AQUARIUM
(Map p270; ☑ 858-534-3474; www.aquarium.ucsd.edu; 2300 Expedition Way; adult/child $18.50/14; ☺ 9am-5pm; P ♿) ✈ Marine scientists were working at the Birch Aquarium at Scripps Institution of Oceanography (SIO) as early as 1910 and, helped by donations from the ever-generous Scripps family, the institute has grown to be one of the world's largest marine research institutions. It is now a part of University of California (UC) San Diego. Off N Torrey Pines Rd, the aquarium has brilliant displays. The **Hall of Fishes** has more than 60 fish tanks, simulating marine habitats from the Pacific Northwest to tropical seas.

✦ Activities

There are plenty of hikes in San Diego, but most outdoor activities involve the ocean. These waters are a dream for surfers, paddleboarders, kayakers and boaters. Call ☑ 619-221-8824 for surf reports.

Pacific Beach Surf Shop   SURFING
(Map p270; ☑ 858-373-1138; www.pbsurfshop.com; 4150 Mission Blvd; group surfing lessons from $75; ☺ store 9am-6pm (winter), 9am-7pm (summer)) This shop provides instruction through its Pacific Beach Surf School. It has friendly

SURFING IN SAN DIEGO

A good number of residents moved to San Diego just for the surfing, and boy, is it good. Even beginners will understand why it's so popular.

Fall brings strong swells and offshore Santa Ana winds. In summer swells come from the south and southwest, and in winter from the west and northwest. Spring brings more frequent onshore winds, but the surfing can still be good. For the latest beach, weather and surf reports, call **San Diego County Lifeguard Services** (☑619-221-8824).

Beginners should head to Mission or Pacific Beach (p273), for beach breaks (soft-sand bottomed). North of Crystal Pier, **Tourmaline Surfing Park** is a crowded, but good, improvers spot for those comfortable surfing reef.

Rental rates vary depending on the quality of the equipment, but figure on soft boards from around $15/45 per hour/full day; wetsuits cost $7/28. Packages are available.

service and also rents wetsuits and both soft (foam) and hard (fiberglass) boards. Call ahead for lessons, offered hourly until 3pm in winter and 5pm in summer.

Hike, Bike, Kayak San Diego　　　ADVENTURE SPORTS
(Map p270; ☑858-551-9510; www.hikebikekayak. com; 2222 Avenida de la Playa; kayak rental from $28, tours from $50) Join a kayak tour to La Jolla's cove and caves or opt for a coastal biking tour. Rentals also available.

Flagship Cruises　　　BOATING
(Map p272; ☑619-234-4111; www.flagshipsd.com; 990 N Harbor Dr; tours adult/child from $24/12; ⊕) Harbor tours and seasonal whale-watching cruises from the Embarcadero, from one to several hours long.

🛏 Sleeping

We list high-season (summer) rates for single- or double-occupancy rooms. Prices drop significantly between September and June, but whatever time of year, ask about specials, suites and package deals. San Diego Tourism runs a **room-reservation line** (☑800-350-6205; www.sandiego.org).

🛏 Downtown & Around

⭐ **USA Hostels San Diego**　　　HOSTEL $
(Map p272; ☑800-438-8622, 619-232-3100; www. usahostels.com; 726 5th Ave; dm/r with shared bath from $32/80; ❄@🛜) Lots of charm and color at this convivial hostel in a former Victorian-era hotel with cheerful rooms, a full kitchen and a communal lounge. Rates include linens, lockers and bagels for breakfast. Surrounded by bars, it's smack-bang in the middle of Gaslamp's nightlife scene, so bring earplugs if you're a light sleeper.

⭐ **La Pensione Hotel**　　　BOUTIQUE HOTEL $$
(Map p274; ☑619-236-8000, 800-232-4683; www.lapensionehotel.com; 606 W Date St; r from $145-200; P❄🛜) Despite the name, Little Italy's La Pensione isn't a pension but an intimate, friendly, recently renovated hotel of 67 rooms with queen-size beds and private bathrooms. It's set around a frescoed courtyard and is just steps to the neighborhood's dining, cafes and galleries, and walking distance to most Downtown attractions. There's an attractive cafe downstairs, and a recently introduced spa. Parking is $20.

⭐ **Hotel Solamar**　　　BOUTIQUE HOTEL $$
(Map p272; ☑619-819-9500; www.hotelsolamar. com; 435 6th Ave; r $169-299; P❄@🛜🏊) A great compromise in the Gaslamp: hip style that needn't break the bank. A new pool bar is set to open in 2017, with cabanas, outdoor games (like corn hole) and skyscraper views. Rooms have sleek lines and nautical blue and neo-rococo accents for a touch of fun. There's a fitness center, in-room yoga kit, free loaner bikes and a nightly complimentary wine hour. Parking costs $47.

🛏 Beaches

Pearl　　　MOTEL $$
(Map p270; ☑877-732-7573, 619-226-6100; www. thepearlsd.com; 1410 Rosecrans St; r $125-199; P❄🛜🏊) The mid-century-modern Pearl feels more Palm Springs than San Diego. The 23 rooms in its 1959 shell have soothing blue hues, trippy surf motifs and fishbowls. There's a lively pool scene (including '**dive-in' movies** on Wednesday nights), or you can play Jenga or Parcheesi in the groovy, shag-carpeted lobby. Light sleepers: request a room away from busy street traffic.

Inn at Sunset Cliffs INN $$
(Map p270; ☑619-222-7901, 866-786-2453; www.
innatsunsetcliffs.com; 1370 Sunset Cliffs Blvd; r/
ste from $175/289; P ❂ ✿ @ ❄ ✿) At the south
end of Ocean Beach, wake up to the sound of
surf crashing onto the rocky shore. This low-
key 1950s charmer wraps around a flower-
bedecked courtyard with a small heated
pool. Its 24 breezy rooms are compact, but
most have attractive stone-and-tile bath-
rooms, and some suites have full kitchens.

★ **Hotel del Coronado** LUXURY HOTEL $$$
(Map p270; ☑800-468-3533, 619-435-6611; www.
hoteldel.com; 1500 Orange Ave; r from $297; P ❂
✿ @ ❄ ✿ ✿) San Diego's iconic hotel provides the essential Coronado experience:
over a century of history, a pool, full-service
spa, shops, restaurants, manicured grounds,
a white-sand beach and an ice-skating rink
during Christmas season. Even the basic
rooms have luxurious marbled bathrooms.
Note: half the accommodations are not in the
main Victorian-era hotel (368 rooms) but in
an adjacent seven-story building constructed
in the 1970s. For a sense of place, book a room
in the original hotel. Self-parking is $39.

Crystal Pier Hotel & Cottages COTTAGE $$$
(Map p270; ☑800-748-5894; www.crystalpier.
com; 4500 Ocean Blvd, Pacific Beach; d $185-525;
P ❂ ✿ ❄) Charming, wonderful and unlike
any other place in San Diego, Crystal Pier
has cottages built right on the pier above
the water. Almost all 29 cottages have full
ocean views and kitchens; most date from
the 1930s. Newer, larger cottages sleep up
to six. Book eight to 11 months in advance
for summer reservations. Minimum-stay
requirements vary by season. No air-condi-
tioning. Rates include parking.

✖ Eating

San Diego has a thriving dining culture,
with an emphasis on Mexican, Californian
and seafood.

✖ Downtown & Around

Basic PIZZA $$
(Map p272; ☑619-531-8869; www.barbasic.com;
410 10th Ave; small/large pizzas from $14/32;
⊙11:30am-2am) East Village hipsters feast on
fragrant thin-crust, brick-oven-baked pizzas
under Basic's high ceiling (it's in a former
warehouse). Small pizzas have a large footprint but are pretty light. Toppings span the
usual to the newfangled, like the mashed

pie with mozzarella, mashed potatoes and
bacon. Wash them down with beers (craft,
naturally) or one of several cocktails.

★ **Puesto at the
Headquarters** MEXICAN $$
(Map p272; ☑610-233-8880; www.eatpuesto.com;
789 W Harbor Dr, The Headquarters; mains $11-19;
⊙11am-10pm) This eatery serves Mexican
street food that knocked our *zapatos* off:
innovative takes on traditional tacos like
chicken (with hibsicus, chipotle, pineapple
and avocado) and some out-there fillings
like zucchini and cactus. Other highlights:
crab guacamole, the lime-marinated shrimp
ceviche, and the grilled Baja striped bass.

★ **Old Town Mexican Café** MEXICAN $$
(Map p270; ☑619-297-4330; www.oldtownmex
cafe.com; 2489 San Diego Ave; mains $5-17; ⊙7-
11pm weekdays, to midnight weekends; ⊕) Other restaurants come and go, but this place
has been in this busy adobe with hardwood
booths since the 1970s. While you wait to
be seated, watch the staff turn out tortillas.
Then enjoy *machaca* (shredded beef with
eggs, onions and peppers), carnitas and
Mexican ribs. For breakfast: *chilaquiles*
(tortilla chips with salsa or mole, broiled or
grilled with cheese).

★ **Juniper & Ivy** CALIFORNIAN $$$
(Map p274; ☑619-269-9036; www.juniperandivy.
com; 2228 Kettner Blvd; small plates $10-23, mains
$19-45; ⊙5-10pm Sun-Thu, to 11pm Fri & Sat) The
menu changes daily at chef Richard Blais'
highly rated San Diego restaurant, opened
in 2014. The molecular gastronomy includes
dishes in the vein of lobster congee, Hawai-
ian snapper with Valencia Pride mango, ahi
(yellowfin tuna) with creamed black trum-
pets, and pig-trotter *totelloni*. It's in a rock-
in' refurbished warehouse.

✖ Balboa Park & Around

★ **Hash House a Go Go** AMERICAN $$
(Map p270; ☑619-298-4646; www.hashhouse
agogo.com; 3628 5th Ave, Hillcrest; breakfast $10-
22, dinner mains $15-29; ⊙7.30am-2.30pm Mon,
7:30am-2pm & 5:30-9pm Tue-Thu, to 2:30pm and
9:30pm Fri-Sun; ⊕) This buzzing bungalow
makes biscuits and gravy straight outta Indiana, towering Benedicts, large-as-your-head
pancakes and – wait for it – hash seven different ways. Eat your whole breakfast, and
you won't need to eat the rest of the day. It's
worth coming back for the equally massive

burgers, sage-fried chicken and award-winning meatloaf sandwich. No wonder it's called 'twisted farm food.'

★ **Urban Solace**   CALIFORNIAN $$
(Map p270; ☑ 619-295-6464; www.urbansolace.net; 3823 30th St, North Park; mains lunch $12-22, dinner $14-27; ⊙ 11am-9pm Mon-Tue, to 9:30pm Wed-Thu, to 10:30pm Fri, 10:30am-10:30pm Sat, 9:30am-2:30pm & 4-9pm Sun) North Park's young hip gourmets revel in creative comfort food here: quinoa-veg burger; 'not your mama's' meatloaf of ground lamb, fig, pine nuts and feta; 'duckaroni' (mac 'n' cheese with duck confit); and pulled chicken and dumplings. The setting's surprisingly chill for such great eats, maybe because of the creative cocktails.

★ **Prado**   CALIFORNIAN $$$
(Map p274; ☑ 619-557-9441; www.pradobalboa.com; 1549 El Prado; lunch $8-19, dinner $8-37; ⊙ 11:30am-3pm Mon, 11am-10pm Tue-Thu, 11:30am-9:30pm Sat, 11am-9pm Sun; ☑) In one of San Diego's more beautiful dining rooms, feast on Cal-eclectic cooking by one of San Diego's most renowned chefs: bakery sandwiches, lobster bucatini, and thyme-roasted Jidori half-chicken. Go for a civilized lunch on the verandah or for afternoon cocktails and appetizers in the bar.

✗ Beaches

★ **Dirty Birds**   AMERICAN $
(Map p270; www.dirtybirdsbarandgrill.com; 4656 Mission Blvd; 5 wings for $7.50/20 for $26; ⊙ 11am-12pm Sun-Wed, 11am-2am Thu-Sat) Come to this sports bar–slash–surf hangout for its award-winning chicken wings. On the menu are 37 different flavors including classic buffalo, plus weird and wonderful concoctions like salt and vinegar, apple bourbon chipotle and chicken enchilada. Wash them down with 10 rotating draft brews.

★ **Point Loma Seafoods**   SEAFOOD $
(Map p270; ☑ 619-223-1109; www.pointlomaseafoods.com; 2805 Emerson St; mains $7-16; ⊙ 9am-7pm Mon-Sat, 10am-7pm Sun; ☑☑) For off-the-boat-fresh seafood sandwiches, salads, sashimi, fried dishes and icy-cold beer, order at the counter at this fish-market-cum-deli and grab a seat at a picnic table on the upstairs harbor-view deck. It also does great sushi and takeout dishes from ceviche to clam chowder.

★ **Hodad's**   BURGERS $
(Map p270; ☑ 619-224-4623; www.hodadies.com; 5010 Newport Ave; dishes $4-15; ⊙ 11am-10pm) Since the flower-power days of 1969, OB's legendary burger joint has served great shakes, massive baskets of onion rings and succulent hamburgers wrapped in paper. The walls are covered in license plates; grunge/surf-rock plays (loud!) and your bearded, tattooed server might sidle into your booth to take your order. No shirt, no shoes, no problem, dude.

★ **The Patio on Lamont**   AMERICAN $$
(Map p270; ☑ 858-412-4648; www.thepatioonlamont.com; 4445 Lamont St; dishes $7-26; ⊙ 9am-midnight) Popular local hangout serving beautifully prepared New American small plates and cocktails. Try the crab and ahi tower or crispy artichoke with goat's cheese in a cozy fairy-lit patio area (with outside heaters in winter). Daily happy hours on selected beers and cocktails ($5/6) run from 3pm to 6pm and 10pm to midnight.

🍷 Drinking & Nightlife

San Diego's bar scene is diverse, ranging from live-music pubs and classic American pool bars to beach bars with tiki cocktails, gay clubs offering drag shows, and even a few hidden speakeasies. It's easy to find a local craft beer in town, or you can venture out to one of the 100 breweries or vineyards in the Temecula area.

★ **Bang Bang**   BAR
(Map p272; ☑ 619-677-2264; www.bangbangsd.com; 526 Market St; cocktails $14-26; ⊙ 5-10:30pm Wed-Thu, to 2am Fri & Sat) Beneath lantern light, the Gaslamp's hottest new spot brings in local and world-renowned DJs and serves sushi and Asian small plates like dumplings and *panko*-crusted shrimp to accompany the imaginative cocktails (some in giant goblets meant for sharing with your posse). Plus, the bathrooms are shrines to Ryan Gosling and Hello Kitty: in a word, awesome.

Noble Experiment   BAR
(Map p272; ☑ 619-888-4713; http://nobleexperimentsd.com; 777 G St; ⊙ 7pm-2am Tue-Sun) This place is literally a find. Open a secret door and enter a contemporary speakeasy with miniature gold skulls on the walls, classical paintings on the ceilings and inventive cocktails on the list (from $12). The hard part: getting in. Text for a reservation, and they'll tell you if your requested time

is available and how to find the place. It's also possible to turn up to the bar upstairs, **Neighborhood** (☑ 619-446-0002; www.neighborhoodsd.com; ☺ noon-midnight), and put your name on a waiting list.

Gossip Grill   LESBIAN
(Map p270; ☑ 619-260-8023; www.thegossipgrill.com; 1220 University Ave; ☺ noon-2am Mon-Fri, 10am-2am Sat & Sun) They pour the drinks strong at San Diego's premier lesbian bar. It has a full patio, restaurant and dance floor, decorated with plants, chandeliers and two fire pits. The menu includes wings, sliders, flatbreads, soups, salads and sandwiches (mains from $9). There are often themed events, DJs and weekly drinks offers.

☆ Entertainment

Check out the San Diego *City Beat* or *UT San Diego* for the latest movies, theater, galleries and music gigs around town. **Arts Tix** (Map p272; ☑ 858-437-9850; www.sdartstix.com; 28 Horton Plaza (next to Balboa Theatre); ☺ 10am-4pm Tue-Thu, to 6pm Fri & Sat, to 2pm Sun), in a kiosk near Westfield Horton Plaza, has half-price tickets for same-day evening or next-day matinee performances; it also offers discounted tickets to other events. **Ticketmaster** (☑ 800-653-8000; www.ticketmaster.com) and **House of Blues** (Map p272; ☑ 619-299-2583; www.houseofblues.com/sandiego; 1055 5th Ave; ☺ 4-11pm) sell tickets to other gigs around the city.

Prohibition Lounge   LIVE MUSIC
(Map p272; http://prohibitionsd.com; 548 5th Avenue; ☺ 8:00pm-1:30am Wed-Sat) Find the unassuming doorway on 5th Ave with 'Eddie O'Hare's Law Office' on it, then flip the light switch on to alert the doorman, who'll guide you into a dimly lit basement serving craft cocktails, with patrons enjoying live jazz (music from 9:30pm). Come early as it gets busy fast; at weekends expect to put your name on a list.

Balboa Theatre   THEATER
(Map p272; ☑ 619-570-1100; http://sandiegotheatres.org; 868 4th Ave; from $35) Built in 1924, this building has a colorful past: in the '30s it screened films from Mexico City to San Diego's growing Latino audience. During World War II, it was turned into US Navy bachelor quarters. It was later closed, before a recent $26 million refurbishment. Since 2008, this fabled stage has hosted everything from comedy to movies and operas.

ℹ Information

MEDIA
➠ Free listings magazines *Citybeat* (http://sdcitybeat.com) and *San Diego Reader* (www.sdreader.com), cover the active music, art and theater scenes. Find them in shops and cafes.

➠ KPBS 89.5 FM (www.kpbs.org) National Public Radio station.

➠ *San Diego Magazine* (www.sandiegomagazine.com) Glossy monthly.

➠ *UT San Diego* (www.utsandiego.com) The city's major daily.

MEDICAL SERVICES
Scripps Mercy Hospital (☑ 619-294-8111; www.scripps.org; 4077 5th Ave; ☺ 24hr) has a 24-hour emergency room. There are also 24-hour drugstores around the city, including CVS stores in Pacific Beach, Gas Lamp and Adams Ave.

TOURIST INFORMATION
International Visitor Information Center (Map p272; ☑ 619-236-1242; www.sandiego.org; 1140 N Harbor Dr; ☺ 9am-5pm Jun-Sep, to 4pm Oct-May) Across from the B St Cruise Ship Terminal, helpful staff offer very detailed neighborhood maps, sell discounted tickets to attractions and maintain a hotel-reservation hotline.

Coronado Visitor Center (Map p270; ☑ 866-599-7242, 619-437-8788; www.coronadovisitorcenter.com; 1100 Orange Ave; ☺ 9am-5pm Mon-Fri, 10am-5pm Sat & Sun)

USEFUL WEBSITES
San Diego Tourism (www.sandiego.org) Search hotels, sights, dining, rental cars and more, and make reservations.

Gaslamp Quarter Association (http://gaslamp.org) Everything you need to know about the bustling Gaslamp Quarter, including parking secrets.

ℹ Getting There & Away

Most flights to **San Diego International Airport** (SAN; Map p270; ☑ 619-400-2404; www.san.org; 3325 N Harbor Dr; ☎) are domestic.

Greyhound (Map p272; ☑ 619-515-1100, 800-231-2222; www.greyhound.com; 1313 National Ave; ☺ ticket office 5am-11:59pm) serves San Diego from cities across North America from its Downtown location.

Amtrak (☑ 800-872-7245; www.amtrak.com; 1050 Kettner Blvd) runs the *Pacific Surfliner* several times daily to Anaheim (two hours), Los Angeles (2¾ hours) and Santa Barbara (6½ hours) from the historic **Union Station** (Santa Fe Depot; ☑ 800-872-7245; 1050 Kettner Blvd; ☺ 3am-11:59pm).

CALIFORNIA SAN DIEGO

All the big-name car-rental companies have desks at the airport; smaller agencies (such as **West Coast Rent a Car** (☑619-544-0606; http://westcoastrentacar.net; 834 W Grape St; ⊙9am-6pm Mon-Sat, to 5pm Sun), in Little Italy) may be cheaper.

❶ Getting Around

MTS (Metropolitan Transit System) bus 992 'The Flyer' ($2.25) runs every 10 to 15 minutes between the airport and Downtown with stops along Broadway. Airport shuttles like **Super Shuttle** (☑800-258-3826; www.supershuttle. com) charge from around $10 to downtown; book in advance. An airport taxi to downtown averages $12 to $18, plus tip.

City buses ($2.25 to $2.50) and trolleys ($2.50), including routes to the Mexico border, are operated by MTS, whose **Transit Store** (Map p272; ☑619-234-1060; www.sdmts.com; 1255 Imperial Ave; ⊙8am-5pm Mon-Fri) sells regional passes (or purchase one-day passes on board buses). Taxi fares vary, but plan on about $12 for a 3-mile journey.

PALM SPRINGS & THE DESERTS

From swanky Palm Springs to desolate Death Valley, Southern California's desert region swallows up 25% of the entire state. At first what seems harrowingly barren may eventually be transformed in your mind's eye to perfect beauty: weathered volcanic peaks, booming sand dunes, purple-tinged mountains, cactus gardens, tiny wildflowers pushing up from hard-baked soil in spring, lizards scurrying beside colossal boulders, and in the night sky, uncountable stars. California's deserts are serenely spiritual, surprisingly chic and ultimately irresistible, whether you're a bohemian artist, movie star, rock climber or 4WD adventurer.

Palm Springs

The Rat Pack is back, baby, or at least its hangout is. In the 1950s and '60s, Palm Springs, some 100 miles east of LA, was the swinging getaway of Sinatra, Elvis and other Hollywood stars. Once the Rat Pack packed it in, though, Palm Springs surrendered to golfing retirees. However, in the mid-1990s new generations discovered the city's retro-chic vibe and elegant mid-century modern structures built by famous architects. Today, retirees and snowbirds mix com-

fortably with hipsters, hikers and a sizeable LGBT community, on getaways from LA or from across the globe.

◉ Sights & Activities

Palm Springs is the principal city of the Coachella Valley, a string of desert towns ranging from ho-hum Cathedral City to glamtastic Palm Desert and Coachella, home of the star-studded music festival, all linked by Hwy 111.

★**Palm Springs Aerial Tramway**   CABLE CAR
(☑760-325-1391, 888-515-8726; www.pstramway. com; 1 Tram Way, Palm Springs; adult/child $26/17, parking $5; ⊙1st tram up 10am Mon-Fri, 8am Sat & Sun, last tram down 9:45pm daily, varies seasonally; ℙ♿) This rotating cable car climbs nearly 6000 vertical feet and covers five different vegetation zones, from the Sonoran desert floor to pine-scented Mt San Jacinto State Park, in 10 minutes during its 2.5-mile journey. From the mountain station (8561ft), which is 30°F to 40°F (up to 22°C) cooler than the desert floor, you can enjoy stupendous views, dine in two restaurants (ask about ride 'n' dine passes), explore over 50 miles of trails or visit the natural-history museum.

★**Palm Springs Art Museum**   MUSEUM
(☑760-322-4800; www.psmuseum.org; 101 Museum Dr, Palm Springs; adult/student $12.50/free, all free 4-8pm Thu; ⊙10am-5pm Sun-Tue & Sat, noon-9pm Thu & Fri; ℙ) Art fans should not miss this museum which presents changing exhibitions drawn from its stellar collection of international modern and contemporary painting, sculpture, photography and glass art. The permanent collection includes works by Henry Moore, Ed Ruscha, Mark di Suvero, Frederic Remington and many more heavy hitters. Other highlights are glass art by Dale Chihuly and William Morris and a collection of pre-Columbian figurines.

★**Sunnylands Center & Gardens**   GARDENS
(☑760-202-2222; www.sunnylands.org; 37977 Bob Hope Dr, Rancho Mirage; tours $20-45, center & gardens free; ⊙9am-4pm Thu-Sun, closed early Jun–mid-Sep; ℙ) Sunnylands is the mid-century modern winter retreat of Walter and Leonore Annenberg, one of America's 'first families.' It was here that they entertained seven US presidents, royalty, Hollywood celebrities and heads of state. The only way to get inside is on a guided 90-minute tour ($45) which must be booked far in advance via the website. No reservations are required to see the film and

exhibits at the new visitor center, surrounded by magnificent desert gardens.

★ **Living Desert Zoo & Gardens** ZOO
(☑760-346-5694; www.livingdesert.org; 47900 Portola Ave, Palm Desert; adult/child $20/10; ◷9am-5pm Oct-May, 8am-1:30pm Jun-Sep; P🚻)
🏊 This amazing animal park showcases desert plants and animals alongside exhibits on regional geology and Native American culture. Highlights include a walk-through wildlife hospital and an African-themed village with a fair-trade market and storytelling grove. Camel rides, giraffe feeding, a spin on the endangered species carousel, and a hop-on, hop-off shuttle cost extra. It's educational, fun and worth the 15-mile drive down-valley.

★ **Indian Canyons** HIKING
(☑760-323-6018; www.indian-canyons.com; 38520 S Palm Canyon Dr, Palm Springs; adult/child $9/5, 90min guided hike $3/2; ◷8am-5pm Oct-Jun, Fri-Sun only Jul-Sep) Streams flowing from the San Jacinto Mountains sustain rich plant varieties in oases around Palm Springs. Home to Native American communities for centuries, these canyons are a hiker's delight. Follow the Palm Canyon trail to the world's largest oasis of fan-palm trees, the Murray Canyon trail to a seasonal waterfall or the Andreas Canyon trail to rock formations along a year-round creek.

Smoke Tree Stables HORSEBACK RIDING
(☑760-327-1372; www.smoketreestables.com; 2500 S Toledo Ave, Palm Springs; 1/2hr guided ride $50/120; ◷1hr rides hourly 8am-3pm, 2hr rides 9am,11am&1pm; 🚻) Near the Indian Canyons, this outfit offers public one-hour guided horse rides along the base of the mountains and two-hour tours into palm-lined Murray Canyon. Both are geared toward novice riders. Reservations are not needed but call to confirm departure times. Private tours are available by arrangement.

🛏 **Sleeping**

Palm Springs and the Coachella Valley offer an astonishing variety of lodging, including fine vintage-flair boutique hotels, full-on luxury resorts and chain motels. Some places don't allow children. Campers should head to Joshua Tree National Park or into the San Jacinto Mountains (via Hwy 74).

Caliente Tropics MOTEL **$$**
(☑800-658-6034, 760-327-1391; www.caliente tropics.com; 411 E Palm Canyon Dr, Palm Springs; r $99-225; P🌣🛜🖥🍴) Elvis and the Rat Pack once frolicked poolside at this premier budget pick, a nicely spruced-up 1964 tiki-style motor lodge. Drift off to dreamland on quality mattresses in spacious rooms dressed in warm colors.

★ **Arrive Hotel** BOUTIQUE HOTEL **$$**
(☑760-507-1650; www.arrivehotels.com; 1551 N Palm Canyon Dr, Palm Springs; studio from $179; P🍴🌣🛜🖥🍴) 🏊 Ecofriendly rusted steel, wood and concrete are the main design ingredients of this new adult-only lair where the bar doubles as the reception. The 32 rooms (some with patio) tick all the requisite hipster boxes such as rain shower, Apple TV and fancy bath products. The poolside restaurant, coffee shop, ice-cream parlor and craft-beer bar score high among locals.

★ **L'Horizon** BOUTIQUE HOTEL **$$**
(☑760-323-1858; http://lhorizonpalmsprings.com; 1050 E Palm Canyon Dr, Palm Springs; r $169-249; P🌣🛜🖥🍴) The intimate William F Cody–designed retreat that saw Marilyn Monroe and Betty Grable lounging poolside has been rebooted as sleek and chic adult-only desert resort with 25 bungalows scattered across generous grounds for maximum privacy. Treat yourself to alfresco showers, a chemical-free swimming pool and private patio.

★ **El Morocco Inn & Spa** BOUTIQUE HOTEL **$$**
(☑888-288-9905, 760-288-2527; http://elmo roccoinn.com; 66810 4th St, Desert Hot Springs; r $199-219; P🍴🌣🛜🖥) Heed the call of the casbah at this drop-dead gorgeous hideaway where the scene is set for romance. Twelve exotically furnished rooms wrap around

CALIFORNIA PALM SPRINGS

WORLD'S BIGGEST DINOSAURS

West of Palm Springs, you may do a double take when you glimpse 'Dinny the Dinosaur' and 'Mr Rex' from the I-10. Claude K Bell, a sculptor for Knott's Berry Farm, spent over a decade in the 1980s crafting the concrete behemoths at **World's Biggest Dinosaurs** (☑951-922-8700; www.cabazondinosaurs.com; 50770 Seminole Dr, Cabazon; adult/child $10/9; ◷10am-4:30pm Mon-Fri, 9am-6:30pm Sat & Sun; P🚻). Today you can pan for dino fossils, climb inside Rex's mouth, marvel at dozens of dinosaur models and stock up on dino souvenirs in the gift shop.

PIONEERTOWN

Looking like an 1870s frontier town, **Pioneertown** (www.pioneertown.com; P 🚻) **FREE** was actually built in 1946 as a Hollywood Western movie set. Gene Autry and Roy Rogers were among the original investors, and more than 50 movies and several TV shows were filmed here in the 1940s and '50s. These days, it's fun to stroll around the old buildings and drop into the local honky-tonk for refreshments. Mock gunfights take place on 'Mane St' at 2:30pm every second and fourth Saturday, April to October.

Within staggering distance is the atmospheric **Pioneertown Motel** (📞 760-365-7001; www.pioneertown-motel. com; 5040 Curtis Rd, Pioneertown; r from $155; P ❄ 🛜 🐾), where yesteryear's silver-screen stars once slept during filming, and whose rooms are now filled with eccentric Western-themed memorabilia; some rooms have kitchenettes.

a pool deck where your enthusiastic hosts serve free 'Morocco-tinis' during happy hour. The on-site spa offers such tempting massages as 'Moroccan Rain' using an essential oil to purge the body of toxins.

Hacienda at Warm Sands BOUTIQUE HOTEL $$$
(📞 760-327-8111; www.thehacienda.com; 586 Warm Sands Dr, Palm Springs; r $309-439; P ❄ @ 🛜 🏊) With Indonesian teak furnishings, this 10-suite gay male resort raises the bar for luxury with its pillow menu, flawless landscaping, two pools and Jacuzzi with fireplace. The genial innkeepers are happy to customize stays with everything from in-room massages to arranging a personal shopper.

✕ Eating

A new line-up of zeitgeist-capturing restaurants has seriously elevated the level of dining in Palm Springs. The most exciting newcomers, including several with eye-catching design, flank N Palm Canyon Dr in the Uptown design district.

★**Cheeky's** CALIFORNIAN $
(📞 760-327-7595; www.cheekysps.com; 622 N Palm Canyon Dr, Palm Springs; mains $9-14; ⏰ 8am-2pm Thu-Mon, last seating 1:30pm; ❄) Waits can be long and service only so-so at this breakfast

and lunch spot, but the farm-to-table menu dazzles with witty inventiveness. The kitchen tinkers with the menu on a weekly basis but perennial faves such as custardy scrambled eggs and grass-fed burger with pesto fries keep making appearances.

Trio CALIFORNIAN $$
(📞 760-864-8746; www.triopalmsprings.com; 707 N Palm Canyon Dr, Palm Springs; mains lunch $13-16, dinner $15-30; ⏰ 11am-10pm Sun-Thu, to 11pm Fri & Sat; ❄) The winning formula in this '60s modernist space: updated American comfort food (awesome Yankee pot roast!) amid eye-catching artwork and picture windows. The $19 prix-fixe three-course dinner (served until 6pm) is a steal, and the all-day daily happy hour lures a rocking after-work crowd with bar bites and cheap drinks.

★**Workshop Kitchen + Bar** AMERICAN $$$
(📞 760-459-3451; www.workshoppalmsprings. com; 800 N Palm Canyon Dr, Palm Springs; mains $26-45; ⏰ 5-10pm Mon-Sun, 10am-2pm Sun; ❄) Hidden away in the back of the ornate 1920s El Paseo building, a large patio with olive trees leads to this starkly beautiful space centered on a lofty concrete tunnel flanked by mood-lit booths. The kitchen crafts market-driven American classics reinterpreted for the 21st century and the bar is among the most happening in town.

🍷 Drinking & Nightlife

Arenas Rd, east of Indian Canyon Dr, is gay-and-lesbian-nightlife central.

★**Bootlegger Tiki** COCKTAIL BAR
(📞 760-318-4154; www.bootleggertiki.com; 1101 N Palm Canyon Dr, Palm Springs; ⏰ 4pm-2am) Crimson light bathes even pasty-faced hipsters into a healthy glow, as do the killer crafted cocktails at this teensy speakeasy with blowfish lamps and rattan walls. The entrance is via the Ernest coffee shop.

Birba BAR
(📞 760-327 5678; www.birbaps.com; 622 N Palm Canyon Dr, Palm Springs; ⏰ 5-11pm Sun & Wed-Thu, to midnight Fri & Sat; ❄) On a balmy night, Birba's hedge-fringed patio with twinkle lights and sunken fire pit is perfect for unwinding with a glass of wine or smooth libations like the tequila-based Heated Snake. Get a plate of *cicchetti* (Italian bar snacks) to stave off the blur or order modern pizza or pasta from the full menu.

🔒 Shopping

For art galleries, modern design stores and fashion boutiques, including fabulous **Trina Turk** (☑760-416-2856; www.trinaturk.com; 891 N Palm Canyon Dr, Palm Springs; ☺10am-6pm Mon-Sat, 11am-5pm Sun), head 'Uptown' to North Palm Canyon Dr. If you're riding the retro wave, uncover treasures in thrift, vintage and consignment shops scattered around downtown and along Hwy 111. For a local version of Rodeo Dr, drive down-valley to Palm Desert's El Paseo.

ℹ Information

Palm Springs Visitor Center (☑800-347-7746, 760-778-8418; www.visitpalmsprings. com; 2901 N Palm Canyon Dr, Palm Springs; ☺9am-5pm) Well-stocked and well-staffed visitor center in a 1965 Albert Frey–designed gas station at the Palm Springs Aerial Tram turnoff, 3 miles north of downtown.

Palm Springs Historical Society (☑760-323-8297; www.pshistoricalsociety.org; 221 S Palm Canyon Dr, Palm Springs; ☺10am-4pm Mon & Wed-Sat, noon-3pm Sun) Volunteer-staffed nonprofit organization. Maintains two museums and offers guided tours focusing on local history, architecture and celebrities.

ℹ Getting There & Around

Palm Springs International Airport (PSP; ☑760-318-3800; www.palmspringsairport. com; 3400 E Tahquitz Canyon Way, Palm Springs) connects year-round to destinations throughout North America. Ask if your hotel provides free airport transfers. Otherwise, a taxi to downtown Palm Springs costs about $12 to $15, including a $2.50 airport surcharge.

The Sunset Limited operated by **Amtrak** (www.amtrak.com) comes through three times weekly on its route between New Orleans and Los Angeles.

SunLine (☑800-347-8628; www.sunline.org; ticket $1, day pass $3) alternative-fuel-powered public buses travel around the valley, albeit slowly.

Joshua Tree National Park

Taking a page from a Dr Seuss book, the whimsical Joshua trees (actually tree-sized yuccas) welcome visitors to this 794,000-acre park at the transition zone of two deserts: the low and dry Colorado and the higher, moister and slightly cooler Mojave.

Rock climbers know 'JT' as one of the best places to climb in California; hikers seek out hidden, shady, desert fan-palm oases fed by natural springs and small streams; and mountain bikers are hypnotized by the desert vistas.

👁 Sights & Activities

Dominating the north side of the **park** (☑760-367-5500; www.nps.gov/jotr; 7-day entry per car $25; ☺24hr; P♿) 🅿, the epic **Wonderland of Rocks** calls to climbers, as does **Hidden Valley**. Sunset-worthy **Keys View** overlooks the San Andreas Fault and on clear days, you can see as far as Mexico. For pioneer history, tour **Keys Ranch** (☑760-367-5500; www.nps.gov/jotr; tour adult/child $10/5; ☺tour schedules vary; P♿). Hikers seek out native desert fan-palm oases like **49 Palms Oasis** (3-mile round-trip) and **Lost Palms Oasis** (7.2-mile round-trip). Kid-friendly nature trails include **Barker Dam** (1.1-mile loop), which passes Native American petroglyphs; **SkullRock** (1.7-mile loop); and **Cholla Cactus Garden** (0.25-mile loop). For a scenic 4WD route, tackle bumpy 18-mile **Geology Tour Road**, also open to mountain bikers.

🛏 Sleeping

Of the park's eight campgrounds, only **Cottonwood** (☑760-367-5500; www.nps.gov/jotr; Pinto Basin Rd; per site $20) and **Black Rock** (☑760-367-5500, reservations 877-444-6777; www.nps.gov/jotr; Joshua Lane; per site $20; P) have potable water, flush toilets and dump stations. **Indian Cove** (☑760-367-5500, reservations 877-444-6777; www.nps.gov/jotr; Indian Cove Rd; per site $20) and Black Rock accept reservations from October through May. The others are first-come, first-served and have pit toilets, picnic tables and fire grates. None have showers, but there are some at **Coyote Corner** (☑760-366-9683; www.jtcoyotecorner. com; 6535 Park Blvd, Joshua Tree; ☺9am-6pm) in Joshua Tree. Details are available at www. nps.gov/jotr or ☑760-367-5500.

Budget and midrange motels line Hwy 62. Twentynine Palms and Yucca Valley have mostly national chain motels, while pads in Joshua Tree have plenty of charm and character.

Harmony Motel MOTEL **$**
(☑760-367-3351, 760-401-1309; www.harmonymotel.com; 71161 29 Palms Hwy/Hwy 62, Twentynine Palms; r $65-85; P☺❄🐾📶⛱) This well-kept 1950s motel, run by the charming Ash, was where U2 stayed while working on the *Joshua Tree* album. It has a small pool and seven

CALIFORNIA JOSHUA TREE NATIONAL PARK

large, cheerfully painted rooms (some with kitchenette) set around a tidy desert garden with serenely dramatic views. A light breakfast is served in the communal guest kitchen.

★ **Kate's Lazy Desert**   INN $$
(☑ 845-688-7200; www.lazymeadow.com; 58380 Botkin Rd, Landers; Airstream $175 Mon-Thu, $200 Fri & Sat; ⌷❄✳📶🏊) Owned by Kate Pierson of the B-52s, this desert camp has a coin-sized pool (May to October) and half a dozen Airstream trailers to sleep inside. Each is kitted out with matching fantasia-pop design and a double bed and kitchenette.

★ **Sacred Sands**   B&B $$$
(☑ 760-424-6407; www.sacredsands.com; 63155 Quail Springs Rd, Joshua Tree; north/west r $329/359, 2-night minimum; ⌷❄✳📶) 🍽 In an isolated, pin-drop-quiet spot, these two desert-chic suites are the ultimate romantic retreat, each with a private outdoor shower, hot tub, sundeck and sleeping terrace under the stars. There are astounding views across the desert hills and into the National Park. Owners Scott and Steve are gracious hosts and killer breakfast cooks.

✖ Eating

There's no food available inside the park itself. Nearby **Crossroads Cafe** (☑ 760-366-5414; www.crossroadscafejtree.com; 61715 29 Palms Hwy/Hwy 62, Joshua Tree; mains $6-12; ⊙ 7am-9pm Mon-Sat, to 8pm Sun; ⌷📶) is a JT institution. It's the go-to place for carb-loaded breakfast, dragged-through-the-garden salad and fresh sandwiches that make both omnivores and vegans happy.

★ **La Copine**   AMERICAN $
(www.lacopinekitchen.com; 848 Old Woman Rd, Flamingo Heights; mains $10-16; ⊙ 9am-3pm Thu-Sun; ⌷✳) It's a long road from Philadelphia to the high desert, but that's where Nikki and Claire decided to take their farm-to-table brunch cuisine from pop-up to brick and mortar. Their roadside bistro serves zeitgeist-capturing dishes such as the signature salad with smoked salmon and poached egg, homemade crumpets and gold milk turmeric tea. Expect a wait on weekends.

ℹ Information

Pick up park information at NPS visitor centers at **Joshua Tree** (www.nps.gov/jotr; 6554 Park Blvd, Joshua Tree; ⊙ 8am-5pm; 📶🚻), **Oasis** (www.nps.gov/jotr; 74485 National Park Dr, Twentynine Palms; ⊙ 8:30am-5pm; 🚻) and **Cotton-**

wood (www.nps.gov/jotr; Cottonwood Springs; ⊙ 8:30am-4pm; 🚻). There are no park facilities aside from restrooms, so bring all the drinking water and food you'll need. Get gas and stock up in the three towns linked by the Twentynine Palms Hwy (Hwy 62) along the park's northern boundary: Yucca Valley, with the most services (banks, supermarkets etc); beatnik Joshua Tree, where outdoor outfitters and shops offering internet access cluster; and Twentynine Palms.

Anza-Borrego Desert State Park

Shaped by an ancient sea and tectonic forces, Anza-Borrego is the USA's largest state park outside Alaska. Cradling the park's only commercial hub – tiny Borrego Springs (pop 3429) – are more than 600,000 acres of mountains, canyons and badlands; a fabulous variety of plants and wildlife; and intriguing historical relics of Native American tribes, Spanish explorers and gold-rush pioneers. Early spring wildflower blooms bring the biggest crowds, while in summer, Hades-like heat makes daytime exploring dangerous.

◎ Sights & Activities

Two miles west of Borrego Springs, the park **visitor center** (☑ 760-767-4205; www.parks.ca.gov; 200 Palm Canyon Dr, Borrego Springs; ⊙ 9am-5pm daily mid-Oct–mid-May, Sat, Sun & holidays only mid-May–mid-Oct) has natural-history exhibits, information handouts and updates on road conditions. Driving through the park is free, but if you camp, hike or picnic, a day-use parking fee ($5 per car) applies. You'll need a 4WD to tackle the 500 miles of backcountry dirt roads. If you're hiking, always bring extra water.

Park highlights include **Fonts Point** desert lookout, **Clark Dry Lake** for birding, the **Elephant Tree Discovery Trail** near Split Mountain's wind caves, and **Blair Valley**, with its Native American pictographs and pioneer traces. Further south, soak in concrete hot-spring pools at **Agua Caliente Regional Park** (☑ 760-765-1188; www.sdparks.org; 39555 Great Southern Overland Stage Route of 1849/County Rte S2; per car $3; ⊙ 9:30am-5pm Mon-Fri, to sunset weekends Sep-May).

🛏 Sleeping & Eating

A handful of seasonally open motels and hotels cluster in and around Borrego Springs. Otherwise, camping is the go (free backcountry camping is permitted anywhere).

SALTON SEA & SALVATION MOUNTAIN

East of Anza-Borrego and south of Joshua Tree awaits a most unexpected sight: the **Salton Sea** (☑ 760-393-3052; www.parks.ca.gov; 100-225 State Park Rd, North Shore; car $7; ☺ visitor center 10am-4pm Oct-May, Fri-Sun only Jun-Sep; P), California's largest lake in the middle of its biggest desert. After the Colorado River flooded in 1905, it took 1500 workers and half a million tons of rock to put it back on course. With no natural outlet, the artificial lake's surface is 220ft below sea level and its waters 50% saltier than the Pacific – an environmental nightmare that's yet to be cleaned up.

An even stranger sight near the lake's eastern shore is **Salvation Mountain** (www.salvationmountain.us), a 100ft-high hill of hand-mixed clay slathered in colorful acrylic paint and found objects, and inscribed with Christian messages. This creation of folk artist Leonard Knight (1931–2014) is in Niland, about 3 miles east of Hwy 111, via Main St/Beal Rd.

Borrego Palm Canyon Campground
CAMPGROUND $

(☑ 800-444-7275; www.reserveamerica.com; 200 Palm Canyon Dr, Borrego Springs; tent/RV sites $25/35; P 🐾) Near the Anza-Borrego Desert State Park visitor center, this campground has award-winning toilets, campsites that are close together and an amphitheater with ranger programs.

Palm Canyon Hotel & RV Resort
HOTEL $$

(☑ 760-767-5341; www.palmcanyonrvresort.com; 221 Palm Canyon Dr, Borrego Springs; incl tax d $128-177, RV with full hook-up $48-56, trailers $70-150; ☺ Oct-May; P 🐾🛜🏊) About a mile west of the park's visitor center, this modern property has spacious rooms, some with Jacuzzi; for a memorable experience, stay in one of the vintage Airstream trailers. Upstairs rooms have nice mountain views, and there are two pools and a restaurant-saloon. Two-night-minimum weekends September to June.

★ La Casa del Zorro
RESORT $$$

(☑ 760-767-0100; www.lacasadelzorro.com; 3845 Yaqui Pass Rd; r $224-350; P ❄🛜🏊🐾) After a top-to-bottom facelift, this venerable 1937 resort is again the region's grandest stay. The ambience exudes desert romance in 67 elegantly rustic poolside rooms and family-sized casitas sporting vaulted ceilings and marble bathtubs. A staggering 28 pools and Jacuzzi are scattered across the 42 landscaped acres, and there's a spa, five tennis courts, fun bar and gourmet restaurant.

ℹ Information

Borrego Springs has banks with ATMs, gas stations, a supermarket, a post office and a public library with free wi-fi and internet terminals, all on Palm Canyon Dr. Call the **Wildflower Hotline** (☑ 760-767-4684) for information on seasonal blooms.

Mojave National Preserve

If you're on a quest for the 'middle of nowhere,' you may find it in **Mojave National Preserve** (☑ 760-252-6100; www.nps.gov/moja; btwn I-15 & I-40) FREE a 1.6-million-acre jumble of sand dunes, Joshua trees, volcanic cinder cones and habitat for endangered desert tortoises. Warning: no gas is available here.

Southeast of Baker and the I-15 Fwy, Kelbaker Rd crosses a ghostly landscape of cinder cones before arriving at **Kelso Depot**, a 1920s Mission Revival–style railroad station. It now houses the park's main **visitor center** (☑ 760-252-6108; www.nps.gov/moja; Kelbaker Rd, Kelso; ☺ 10am-5pm), which has excellent natural-and-cultural history exhibits, and an old-fashioned lunch counter. It's another 11 miles southwest to 'singing' **Kelso Dunes**. When wind conditions are right, they emanate low-pitched vibrations caused by shifting sands – running downhill can jump-start the effect. From Kelso Depot, Kelso–Cima Rd takes off northeast. After 19 miles, Cima Rd slingshots northwest toward I-15 around **Cima Dome**, a 1500ft-high hunk of granite with lava outcroppings, the slopes of which are home to the world's largest **Joshua tree forest**. For close-ups, summit **Teutonia Peak** (3 miles round-trip); the trailhead is 6 miles northwest of Cima.

🛏 Sleeping & Eating

Camping is the only way to overnight in the preserve. Baker, on the northwestern edge along I-15, has plenty of cheap, charmless motels. Coming from the north, the casino hotels in Primm on the Nevada border offer slightly better options. If you're traveling on the I-40, Needles is the closest town to spend the night.

The only place in the park to get a bite is at the old-fashioned lunch counter in the Kelso Visitor Center. Baker is the closest town with restaurants and grocery stores.

Death Valley National Park

The very name evokes all that is harsh, hot and hellish – a punishing, barren and lifeless place of Old Testament severity. Yet closer inspection reveals that in Death Valley nature is putting on a truly spectacular show: singing sand dunes, water-sculpted canyons, boulders moving across the desert floor, extinct volcanic craters, palm-shaded oases, stark mountains rising to 11,000ft and plenty of endemic wildlife.

This is a land of superlatives, holding the US records for hottest temperature (134°F/57°C), lowest point (Badwater, 282ft below sea level) and largest national park outside Alaska (over 5000 sq miles).

◉ Sights & Activities

In summer, stick to paved roads, limit your exertions outdoors to early morning hours and night, and visit higher-elevation areas of the park. From **Furnace Creek**, the central hub of the **park** (☑760-786-3200; www.nps.gov/deva; 7-day-pass per car $25; ☺24hr; [P][♿] ♂, drive southeast up to **Zabriskie Point** for spectacular sunset views across the valley and golden badlands eroded into waves, pleats and gullies. Twenty miles southeast at **Dante's View**, you can simultaneously spot

the highest (Mt Whitney,14,505ft) and lowest (Badwater) points in the contiguous USA.

Badwater itself, a timeless landscape of crinkly salt flats, is 17 miles south of Furnace Creek. Along the way, **Golden Canyon** and **Natural Bridge** are easily explored on short hikes. A 9-mile detour along **Artists Drive** through a narrow canyon is best in late afternoon when the eroded hillsides erupt in fireworks of color.

Northwest of Furnace Creek, near Stovepipe Wells Village, trek across Saharanesque **Mesquite Flat** sand dunes – magical under a full moon – and scramble along the smooth marble walls of **Mosaic Canyon**.

About 55 miles northwest of Furnace Creek at whimsical **Scotty's Castle** (☑760-786-3200; www.nps.gov/deva; ☺closed), tour guides in historical character dress bring to life the Old West tales of con man 'Death Valley Scotty' (reservations advised). Five miles west of Grapevine junction, circumambulate volcanic **Ubehebe Crater** and its younger sibling.

🛏 Sleeping & Eating

Camping is plentiful but if you're looking for a place with a roof, in-park options are limited, pricey and often booked solid in springtime. Alternative bases are the gateway towns of Beatty (40 miles from Furnace Creek), Lone Pine (40 miles), Death Valley Junction (30 miles) and Tecopa (70 miles). Options a bit further afield include Ridgecrest (120 miles) and Las Vegas (140 miles).

**Mesquite Springs
Campground**　　　　　CAMPGROUND $
(☑760-786-3200; www.nps.gov/deva; Hwy 190; per site $14) In the northern reaches of the park, this first-come, first-served campground has only 40 spaces and is a handy base for Ubehebe Crater and Racetrack Rd. At an elevation of 1800ft, it's also a lot cooler than the desert floor. Sites come with fire pits and tables, and there's water and flush toilets.

Ranch at Furnace Creek　　　RESORT $$
(☑760-786-2345; www.furnacecreekresort.com; Hwy 190, Furnace Creek; cabin/r from $140/180; [P][♿][❄][📶][♨]) Tailor-made for families, this rambling resort with multiple, motel-style buildings has received a vigorous facelift, resulting in spiffy rooms swathed in desert colors, updated bathrooms and French doors leading to porches with comfortable patio furniture. The grounds encompass a

playground, spring-fed swimming pool, tennis courts, golf course, restaurants, shops and the Borax Museum (⊙9am-9pm Oct-May, variable summer; P ♿) FREE.

Inn at Furnace Creek HOTEL $$$
(☎760-786-2345; www.furnacecreekresort.com; Hwy 190; d from $450; ⊙mid-Oct–mid-May; P ♿ ✳@令≋) Roll out of bed and count the colors of the desert as you pull back the curtains in your room at this 1927 Spanish Mission–style hotel. After a day of sweaty touring, enjoy languid valley views while lounging by the spring-fed swimming pool, cocktail in hand. It's the classiest place in Death Valley, but rooms would benefit from updating.

Amargosa Opera House Cafe CAFE $$
(☎760-852-4432; www.amargosacafe.org; Death Valley Junction; mains $9-19, pie per slice $5; ⊙8am-3pm Mon, Fri, Sat & Sun, 6:30-9pm Sat; P ✳) *∅* This charmer in the middle of nowhere gets you ready for a day in Death Valley with hearty breakfasts or healthy sandwiches, but truly shows off its farm-to-table stripes at dinnertime on Saturdays. Combine with a tour of (or show at) the late Marta Becket's kooky opera house. Excellent coffee to boot.

ⓘ Information

Park entry permits ($25 per vehicle) are valid for seven days and available from self-service pay stations at the park's access roads and at the **Furnace Creek Visitor Center** (☎760-786-3200; www.nps.gov/deva; ⊙8am-5pm; 令 ♿). This modern visitor center has engaging exhibits on the park's ecosystem and the indigenous tribes as well as a gift shop, clean toilets, (slow) wi-fi and friendly rangers to answer questions and help you plan your day.

CENTRAL COAST

Too often forgotten or dismissed as 'flyover' country between San Francisco and LA, this fairy-tale stretch of California coast is packed with wild beaches, misty redwood forests that hide hot springs, and rolling golden hills of fertile vineyards and farm fields.

Santa Barbara

Perfect weather, beautiful buildings, excellent bars and restaurants, and activities for all tastes and budgets make Santa Barbara a great place to live (as the locals will proudly tell you) and a must-see place for visitors to Southern California. Check out the Spanish Mission church first, then just see where the day takes you.

◉ Sights

★**MOXI** MUSEUM
(Wolf Museum of Exploration + Innovation; ☎805-770-5000; www.moxi.org; 125 State St; adult/child $14/10; ⊙10am-5pm; ♿) Part of the regeneration of this neglected strip of State St, Moxi's three floors filled with hands-on displays covering science, arts and technology themes will tempt families in, even when it's not raining outside. If all that interactivity gets too much, head to the roof terrace for views across Santa Barbara and a nerve-challenging walk across a glass ceiling.

★**Santa Barbara County Courthouse** HISTORIC BUILDING
(☎805-962-6464; http://sbcourthouse.org; 1100 Anacapa St; ⊙8am-5pm Mon-Fri, 10am-5pm Sat & Sun) FREE Built in Spanish-Moorish Revival style in 1929, the courthouse features hand-painted ceilings, wrought-iron chandeliers and tiles from Tunisia and Spain. On the 2nd floor, step inside the hushed mural room depicting Spanish-colonial history, then head up to El Mirador, the 85ft clock tower, for arch-framed panoramas of the city, ocean and mountains.

★**Mission Santa Barbara** CHURCH
(☎805-682-4713; www.santabarbaramission.org; 2201 Laguna St; adult $9, child 5-17yr $4; ⊙9am-5pm, last entry 4:15pm; P ♿) California's 'Queen of the Missions' reigns above the city on a hilltop perch over a mile north of downtown. Its imposing Ionic facade, an architectural homage to an ancient Roman chapel, is topped by an unusual twin-bell tower. Inside the mission's 1820 stone church, notice the striking Chumash artwork. In the cemetery the elaborate mausoleums of early California settlers stand out, while the graves of thousands of Chumash lie largely forgotten.

Santa Barbara Maritime Museum MUSEUM
(☎805-962-8404; www.sbmm.org; 113 Harbor Way; adult $8, child 6-17yr $5; ⊙10am-5pm Thu-Tue; P ♿) On the harborfront, this jam-packed, two-story exhibition hall celebrates the town's briny history with nautical artifacts, memorabilia and hands-on exhibits, including a big-game fishing chair from which you can 'reel in' a trophy marlin. Take a virtual trip through the Santa Barbara Channel,

CHANNEL ISLANDS NATIONAL PARK

Remote, rugged **Channel Islands National Park** (☑805-658-5730; www.nps.gov/chis) 🅿 **FREE** earns the nickname 'California's Galápagos' for its unique wildlife. These islands offer superb snorkeling, scuba diving and sea kayaking. Spring, when wildflowers bloom, is a gorgeous time to visit; summer and fall are bone-dry, but the latter brings the calmest water and winds; winter can be stormy.

Anacapa, an hour's boat ride from the mainland, is the best island for day-tripping, with easy hikes and unforgettable views. **Santa Cruz**, the biggest island, is for overnight camping excursions, kayaking and hiking. Other islands require longer channel crossings and multiday trips. **San Miguel** is often shrouded in fog. Tiny **Santa Barbara** supports seabird and seal colonies. So does **Santa Rosa**, which also protects Torrey pine trees.

Boats leave from Ventura Harbor, 32 miles south of Santa Barbara on Hwy 101, where the park's **visitor center** (805-658-5730; www.nps.gov/chis; 1901 Spinnaker Dr, Ventura; 8:30am-5pm) has info and maps. The main tour-boat operator is Island Packers (805-642-1393; www.islandpackers.com; 1691 Spinnaker Dr, Ventura; 3hr cruise adult/child 3-12yr from $36/26); book ahead. Primitive island campgrounds require reservations; book through Recreation.gov and bring food and water.

stand on a surfboard or watch deep-sea-diving documentaries in the theater. There's 90 minutes of free parking in the public lot or take the **Lil' Toot** water taxi (☑805-465-6676; www.celebrationsantabarbara.com; 1-way fare adult/child $5/1; ⊙usually noon-6pm Apr-Oct, hours vary Nov-Mar; 👪) from Stearns Wharf.

🏃 Activities

Overlooking busy municipal beaches, 1872 **Stearns Wharf** (www.stearnswharf.org; ⊙open daily, hours vary; P 👪) **FREE** is the West's oldest continuously operating wooden pier, strung with touristy shops and restaurants. Outside town off Hwy 101, bigger palm-fringed **state beaches** await at Carpinteria, 12 miles east, and El Capitan and Refugio, more than 20 miles west.

Wheel Fun Rentals   CYCLING
(☑805-966-2282; http://wheelfunrentalssb.com; 23 E Cabrillo Blvd; ⊙8am-8pm; 👪) Hourly rentals of beach cruisers ($9.95), mountain bikes ($10.95) and two-/four-person surreys ($28.95/38.95), with discounted half-day and full-day rates. A second, seasonal branch is in the Fess Parker Double Tree Hotel at 633 E Cabrillo Blvd.

Santa Barbara Sailing Center   CRUISE, SAILING
(☑805-962-2826; www.sbsail.com; Marina 4, off Harbor Way; ⊙9am-6pm, to 5pm winter; 👪) Climb aboard the *Double Dolphin,* a 50ft sailing catamaran, for a two-hour coastal or sunset cruise ($35). Seasonal whale-watching trips ($40) and quick half-hour spins around the harbor to view marine life ($18)

are more kid-friendly. It also offers kayak and SUP rentals and tours.

Condor Express   CRUISE
(☑805-882-0088; www.condorcruises.com; 301 W Cabrillo Blvd; 2½/4½hr cruises adult from $50/99, child 5-12yr from $30/50; 👪) Take a whale-watching excursion aboard the high-speed catamaran *Condor Express*. Whale sightings are guaranteed, so if you miss out the first time, you'll get a free voucher for another cruise.

🛏 Sleeping

Hello, sticker shock: even basic motel rooms can command over $200 in summer. Less expensive motels line upper State St, north of downtown, and Hwy 101.

⭐ Santa Barbara
Auto Camp   CAMPGROUND $$
(☑888-405-7553; http://autocamp.com/sb; 2717 De La Vina St; d $175-215; P ❄🛜🐶) 🐾 Ramp up the retro chic and bed down with vintage style in one of five shiny metal Airstream trailers parked near upper State St, north of downtown. All five architect-designed trailers have unique perks, such as a clawfoot tub or extra twin-size beds for kiddos, as well as full kitchen and complimentary cruiser bikes to borrow.

Agave Inn   MOTEL $$
(☑805-687-6009; www.agaveinnsb.com; 3222 State St; r from $119; P 🐶❄🛜) While it's still just a motel at heart, this boutique-on-a-budget property's 'Mexican pop meets modern' motif livens things up with a color palette from a Frida Kahlo painting. Flat-screen TVs,

microwaves, minifridges and air-con make it a standout option. Family-sized rooms have a kitchenette and pullout sofa beds.

Harbor House Inn
MOTEL $$

(☑805-962-9745; www.harborhouseinn.com; 104 Bath St; r from $180; P☻❋☎) Down by the harbor, this friendly, converted motel offers brightly lit studios with hardwood floors and a beachy design scheme. Most have a full kitchen and one has a fireplace. Rates include a welcome basket of breakfast goodies (with a two-night minimum stay) and beach towels, chairs, umbrellas and three-speed bicycles to borrow.

★Inn of the Spanish Garden
BOUTIQUE HOTEL $$$

(☑805-564-4700; www.spanishgardeninn.com; 915 Garden St; r from $309; P☻❋@☎☒) At this Spanish Colonial–style inn, casual elegance, first-rate service and a romantic central courtyard will have you lording about like the don of your own private villa. Rooms have a balcony or patio, beds have luxurious linens and bathrooms have oversized tubs. The concierge service is top-notch. Chill by the small outdoor pool, or unwind with a massage in your room.

✕ Eating

★La Super-Rica Taqueria
MEXICAN $

(☑805-963-4940; 622 N Milpas St; ☺11am-9pm Thu-Mon) It's small, there's usually a line and the decor is basic, but all that's forgotten once you've tried the most authentic Mexican food in Santa Barbara. The fish tacos, tamales and other Mexican staples have been drawing locals and visitors here for decades, and were loved by TV chef and author Julia Child.

★Mesa Verde
VEGAN $$

(☑805-963-4474; http://mesaverderestaurant. com; 1919 Cliff Dr; mains $15-21; ☺11am-9pm; ♪) ✿ Perusing the menu is usually a quick job for vegetarians – but not at Mesa Verde. There are so many delicious, innovative all-vegan dishes on offer here (the tacos with jackfruit are a highlight) that meat-avoiding procrastinators will be in torment. If in doubt, pick a selection and brace yourself for flavor-packed delights. Meat-eaters welcome (and possibly converted).

★Lark
CALIFORNIAN $$$

(☑805-284-0370; www.thelarksb.com; 131 Anacapa St; shared plates $7-17, mains $19-48; ☺5-10pm Tue-Sun, bar to midnight) ✿ There's no better

place in Santa Barbara County to taste the bountiful farm and fishing goodness of this stretch of SoCal coast. Named after an antique Pullman railway car, this chef-run restaurant in the Funk Zone morphs its menu with the seasons, presenting unique flavor combinations such as crispy Brussels sprouts with dates or harissa-and-honey chicken. Make reservations.

🍷 Drinking & Nightlife

Nightlife orbits lower State St and the Funk Zone. Ramble between a dozen wine-tasting rooms along the city's Urban Wine Trail (www.urbanwinetrailsb.com). Check the free alt-weekly *Santa Barbara Independent* (www.independent.com) for an entertainment calendar.

★Figueroa Mountain Brewing Co
BAR

(☑805-694-2252; www.figmtnbrew.com; 137 Anacapa St; ☺11am-11pm Sun-Thu, to midnight Fri & Sat) Father and son brewers have brought their gold-medal-winning hoppy IPA, Danish red lager and double IPA from Santa Barbara's Wine Country to the Funk Zone. Knowledgeable staff will help you choose before you clink glasses on the taproom's open-air patio while acoustic acts play. Enter on Yanonali St.

ℹ Information

Santa Barbara Visitors Center (☑805-568-1811, 805-965-3021; www.santabarbaraca. com; 1 Garden St; ☺9am-5pm Mon-Sat, 10am-5pm Sun, closes 1hr earlier Nov-Jan) Pick up maps and brochures while consulting with the helpful but busy staff.

ℹ Getting There & Around

Amtrak (☑800-872-7245; www.amtrak.com; 209 State St) trains run south to LA ($31, 2½ hours) via Carpinteria, Ventura and Burbank's airport, and north to San Luis Obispo ($22, 2¾ hours) and Oakland ($43, 8¾ hours), with stops in Paso Robles, Salinas and San Jose.

Greyhound (☑805-965-7551; www.greyhound. com; 224 Chapala St) operates a few direct buses daily to LA ($15, three hours), Santa Cruz ($42, six hours) and San Francisco ($40, nine hours).

Local buses operated by the **Metropolitan Transit District** (MTD; ☑805-963-3366; www. sbmtd.gov) cost $1.75 per ride (exact change, cash only). Equipped with front-loading bike racks, these buses travel all over town and to adjacent communities.

Santa Barbara to San Luis Obispo

You can speed up to San Luis Obispo in less than two hours along Hwy 101, or take all day detouring to wineries, historical missions and hidden beaches.

A scenic backcountry drive north of Santa Barbara follows Hwy 154, where you can go for the grape in the **wine country** (www.sbcountywines.com) of the Santa Ynez and Santa Maria Valleys. Ride along with **Sustainable Vine** (☑805-698-3911; www.sustainablevinewinetours.com; tours from $150) ☞, or just follow the pastoral **Foxen Canyon Wine-Trail** (www.foxencanyonwinetrail.com) north to discover cult winemakers' vineyards. In the town of **Los Olivos**, where two dozen more wine-tasting rooms await, **Los Olivos Wine Merchant & Café** (☑805-688-7265; www.winemerchantcafe.com; 2879 Grand Ave; mains breakfast $9-12, lunch & dinner $13-29; ⏰11:30am-8:30pm daily, also 8-10:30am Sat & Sun) is a charming Cal-Mediterranean bistro with a wine bar.

Further south, the Danish-immigrant village of **Solvang** (www.solvangusa.com) abounds with windmills and fairy-tale bakeries. Fuel up on breakfast biscuits, buttermilk fried-chicken sandwiches and farm-fresh salads at **Succulent Café** (☑805-691-9444; www.succulentcafe.com; 1555 Mission Dr; mains breakfast & lunch $5-15, dinner $16-36; ⏰10am-3pm & 5-9pm Mon & Wed-Sun, from 8:30am Sat & Sun; ☷☷). For a picnic lunch or BBQ takeout, swing into **El Rancho Market** (☑805-688-4300; http://elranchomarket.com; 2886 Mission Dr; ⏰6am-11pm; ☷), east of Solvang's 19th-century Spanish Colonial **mission** (☑805-688-4815; www.missionsantaines.org; 1760 Mission Dr; adult $5, child under 12yr free; ⏰9am-4:30pm; ☷☷).

Follow Hwy 246 about 15 miles west of Hwy 101 to **La Purísima Mission State Historic Park** (☑805-733-3713; www.lapurisimamission.org; 2295 Purísima Rd, Lompoc; per car $6; ⏰9am-5pm, tours at 1pm Wed-Sun & public holidays Sep-Jun, daily Jul & Aug; ☷☷) ☞. Exquisitely restored, it's one of California's most evocative Spanish Colonial missions, with flowering gardens, livestock pens and adobe buildings. South of Lompoc off Hwy 1, Jalama Rd travels 14 twisting miles to windswept **Jalama Beach County Park** (☑recorded info 805-736-3616; www.countyofsb.org/parks/jalama; Jalama Beach Rd, Lompoc; per car $10). Book ahead for its crazy-popular **campground** (☑805-568-2460; www.countyofsb.org/parks/jalama.sbc; 9999 Jalama Rd, Lompoc; tent/RV

sites from $25/40, cabins $120-220; ☷☷), where simple cabins have kitchenettes.

Where Hwy 1 rejoins Hwy 101, **Pismo Beach** is a long, lazy stretch of sand with a **butterfly grove** (☑805-773-5301; www.monarchbutterfly.org; Hwy 1; ⏰sunrise-sunset; ☷) ☞ **FREE**, where migratory monarchs perch in eucalyptus trees from late October until February. Adjacent **North Beach Campground** (☑reservations 800-444-7275; www.reserveamerica.com; 399 S Dolliver St; tent & RV sites $40; ☷) offers beach access and hot showers. Dozens of motels and hotels stand by the ocean and along Hwy 101, but rooms fill quickly, especially on weekends. **Pismo Lighthouse Suites** (☑805-773-2411; www.pismolighthousesuites.com; 2411 Price St; ste from $239; ☷☷☷☷☷☷) has everything vacationing families need, including a life-sized outdoor chessboard; ask about off-season discounts. Near Pismo's seaside pier, **Old West Cinnamon Rolls** (☑805-773-1428; www.oldwestcinnamonrolls.com; 861 Dolliver St; snacks $3-6; ⏰6:30am-5:30pm; ☷) offers gooey goodness. Uphill at the **Cracked Crab** (☑805-773-2722; www.crackedcrab.com; 751 Price St; mains $16-59; ⏰11am-9pm Sun-Thu, to 10pm Fri & Sat; ☷), make sure you don a plastic bib before a fresh bucket o' seafood gets dumped on your butcher-paper-covered table.

The nearby town of **Avila Beach** has a sunny waterfront promenade, an atmospherically creaky wooden fishing pier and a historical **lighthouse** (☑guided hike reservations 805-528-8758, trolley tour reservations 805-540-5771; www.pointsanluislighthouse.org; lighthouse $5, incl trolley tour adult/child 3-12yr $20/15; ⏰guided hikes 8:45am-1pm Wed & Sat, trolley tours noon & 1pm Wed & Sat). Back toward Hwy 101, pick juicy fruit and feed the goats at **Avila Valley Barn** (☑805-595-2816; www.avilavalleybarn.com; 560 Avila Beach Dr; ⏰9am-6pm mid-Mar–late Dec, to 5pm Thu-Mon Jan–mid-Mar; ☷) farmstand, then do some stargazing from a private redwood hot tub at **Sycamore Mineral Springs** (☑805-595-7302; www.sycamoresprings.com; 1215 Avila Beach Dr; 1hr per person $15-20; ⏰8am-midnight).

San Luis Obispo

Halfway between LA and San Francisco, San Luis Obispo is normally a low-key place. Cal Poly college students inject a healthy dose of hubbub into the streets, bars and cafes, especially during the weekly **farmers market** (☑805-541-0286; www.downtownslo.com; Higuera

St; ⊙6-9pm Thu; 🚲🅿) 🍴, which turns downtown's Higuera St into a party with live music and sidewalk BBQs.

Like several other California towns, SLO grew up around a Spanish Catholic **mission** (📞805-543-6850; www.missionsan luisobispo.org; 751 Palm St; suggested donation $5; ⊙9am-5pm late Mar-Oct, to 4pm Nov–mid-Mar; 🅿), founded in 1772 by Junípero Serra. These days, SLO is just a grape's throw from thriving Edna Valley wineries (www. slowine.com), known for crisp chardonnay and subtle pinot noir.

🛏 Sleeping

Motels cluster off Hwy 101 in San Luis Obispo, especially off Monterey St northeast of downtown and around Santa Rosa St (Hwy 1).

HI Hostel Obispo
HOSTEL $

(📞805-544-4678; www.hostelobispo.com; 1617 Santa Rosa St; dm $32-39, r from $65, all with shared bath; ⊙check in 4:30-10pm; 🅿🛜) On a tree-lined street near SLO's train station, this solar-powered, avocado-colored hostel inhabits a converted Victorian, which gives it a bit of a B&B feel. Amenities include a kitchen, bike rentals (from $10 per day) and complimentary sourdough pancakes and coffee for breakfast. BYOT (bring your own towel).

Madonna Inn
HOTEL $$

(📞805-543 3000; www.madonnainn.com; 100 Madonna Rd; r $209-329; 🅿@🛜🏊) The fantastically campy Madonna Inn is a garish confection visible from Hwy 101. Japanese tourists, vacationing Midwesterners and irony-loving hipsters adore the 110 themed rooms – including Yosemite Rock, Caveman and hot-pink Floral Fantasy (check out photos online). The urinal in the men's room is a bizarre waterfall. But the best reason to stop here? Old-fashioned cookies from the storybook bakery.

🍴 Eating & Drinking

Downtown in SLO, Higuera St is littered with college-student-jammed bars, and craft-beer fans have plenty to look forward to.

Luna Red
FUSION $$

(📞805-540-5243; www.lunaredslo.com; 1023 Chorro St; shared plates $6-20, mains $20-39; ⊙11:30am-9:30pm Mon-Thu, to midnight Fri, 9am-11:30pm Sat, to 9pm Sun; 🍴) 🍴 Local bounty from the land and sea, artisan cheeses and farmers-market produce pervade the chef's Californian, Asian and Mediterranean

small-plates menu. Cocktails and glowing lanterns enhance a sophisticated ambience indoors and there is a mission-view garden patio where you can linger over brunch.

Guiseppe's Cucina Rustica
ITALIAN $$

(📞805-541-9922; www.giuseppesrestaurant.com; 849 Monterey St; pizza & sandwiches $13-16, mains $21-36; ⊙11:30am-11pm) 🍴 Visit Guiseppe's for a leisurely downtown lunch of excellent salad, pizza and antipasti, or to grab a take-out meatball or Caprese sandwich from the deli counter out the front. Out the back, the facade of the heritage Sinsheimer Brothers building looks over a shaded courtyard that's equally suited to long dinners of slow-roasted chicken and SLO County wines.

Luis Wine Bar
WINE BAR

(📞805-762-4747; www.luiswinebar.com; 1021 Higuera St; ⊙3-11pm Sun-Thu, to midnight Fri-Sat) Evincing style and sophistication, this downtown wine bar has wide-open seating, a strong craft-beer list of more than 70 brews, and small plates including cheese and charcuterie platters. Welcome to an urbane but unpretentious alternative to SLO's more raucous student-heavy bars and pubs.

ℹ Information

San Luis Obispo Visitor Center (📞805-781-2777; www.visitslo.com; 895 Monterey St; ⊙10am-5pm Sun-Wed, to 7pm Thu-Sat) Free maps and tourist brochures.

ℹ Getting There & Away

Amtrak (📞800-872-7245; www.amtrak.com; 1011 Railroad Ave) runs daily Seattle–LA *Coast Starlight* and twice-daily SLO–San Diego *Pacific Surfliner* trains. Both routes head south to Santa Barbara ($35, 2¾ hours) and Los Angeles ($57, 5½ hours). The *Coast Starlight* connects north via Paso Robles to Salinas ($28, 3 hours) and Oakland ($41, six hours). Several daily Thruway buses link to more regional trains.

San Luis Obispo Regional Transit Authority (RTA; 📞805-541-2228; www.slorta.org; single-ride fares $1.50-3, day pass $5) operates daily county-wide buses with limited weekend services. All buses are equipped with bicycle racks. Lines converge on downtown's **transit center** (cnr Palm & Osos Sts).

SLO Transit (📞805-541-2877; www.slocity.org) runs local city buses ($1.25), plus a trolley (50¢) that loops around downtown every 20 minutes between 5pm and 9pm on Thursdays year-round, on Fridays from June to early September and on Saturdays from April through October.

Morro Bay to Hearst Castle

A dozen miles northwest of San Luis Obispo via Hwy 1, Morro Bay is a sea-sprayed fishing town where **Morro Rock**, a volcanic peak jutting up from the ocean floor, is your first hint of the coast's upcoming drama. (Never mind those power-plant smokestacks obscuring the views.) Hop aboard boat cruises or rent kayaks along the **Embarcadero**, which is packed with touristy shops. A classic seafood shack, **Giovanni's** (☑877-521-4467; www.giovannisfishmarket.com; 1001 Front St; mains $5-15; ☉market 9am-6pm, restaurant from 11am; ✈) cooks killer garlic fries and fish-and-chips. Midrange motels cluster uphill off Harbor and Main Sts and along Hwy 1.

Nearby are fantastic state parks for coastal hikes and **camping** (☑reservations 800-444-7275; www.reserveamerica.com; tent & RV sites $25-50; ✈). South of the Embarcadero, **Morro Bay State Park** (☑805-772-2694; www.parks.ca.gov; 60 State Park Rd; park entry free, museum adult/child under 17yr $3/free; ☉museum 10am-5pm; P✈) has a natural-history museum for kids. Further south in Los Osos, west of Hwy 1, wilder **Montaña de Oro State Park** (☑805-528-0513; www.parks.ca.gov; 3550 Pecho Valley Rd, Los Osos; ☉6am-10pm; P✈) 🅵FREE features coastal bluffs, tide pools, sand dunes, peak hiking and mountain-biking trails. Its Spanish name (which means 'mountain of gold') comes from native California poppies that blanket the hillsides in spring.

Heading north of downtown Morro Bay along Hwy 1, surfers love the Cal-Mexican **Taco Temple** (☑805-772-4965; www.tacotemple.com; 2680 Main St; mains $10-16; ☉11am-9pm; ✈), a cash-only joint, and **Ruddell's Smokehouse** (☑805-995-5028; www.smokerjim.com; 101 D St; dishes $4-13; ☉11am-6pm; ✈✈), serving smoked-fish tacos by the beach in Cayucos. Vintage motels on Cayucos' Ocean Ave include the cute, family-run **Seaside Motel** (☑805-995-3809; www.seasidemotel.com; 42 S Ocean Ave; d $80-170; ✈). You can fall asleep to the sound of the surf at the ocean-view **Shoreline Inn on the Beach** (☑805-995-3681; www.cayucosshorelineinn.com; 1 N Ocean Ave; r $159-249; ✈).

North of Harmony (population: just 18 souls), Hwy 46 leads east into the vineyards of **Paso Robles wine country** (www.pasowine.com). Tired of wine? Off Hwy 101 in Paso Robles, **Firestone Walker Brewing Company** (☑805-225.5913; www.firestonebeer.com; 1400 Ramada Dr; ☉tasting room & restaurant 10am-9pm, tours 10:30am-3:30pm) offers brewery tours ($3; reservations recommended), or just stop by the taproom for samples.

Further north along Hwy 1, quaint **Cambria** has lodgings along unearthly-pretty Moonstone Beach, where the **Blue Dolphin Inn** (☑805-927-3300; www.cambriainns.com; 6470 Moonstone Beach Dr; r from $188; ✈✈) embraces modern rooms with romantic fireplaces. Inland, **Bridge Street Inn** (☑805-215-0724; www.bsicambria.com; 4314 Bridge St; r $50-90, vans $30; ✈) sleeps like a hostel but feels like a B&B, while the retro **Cambria Palms Motel** (☑805-927-4485; www.cambriapalmsmotel.com; 2662 Main St; r from $109; ☉check-in 3-9pm; ✈✈) has clean-lined rooms and cruiser bicycles to borrow. An artisan cheese and wine shop, **Indigo Moon** (☑805-927-2911; www.indigomooncafe.com; 1980 Main St; lunch $9-14, dinner $14-35; ☉10am-9pm; ✈) 🍴 has breezy bistro tables and market-fresh salads and sandwiches at lunch. With a sunny patio and takeout counter, **Linn's Easy as Pie Cafe** (☑805-927-0371; www.linnsfruitbin.com; 4251 Bridge St; dishes $6-12; ☉10am-7pm Mon-Thu, to 8m Fri-Sat; ✈) is famous for its olallieberry pie.

About 10 miles north of Cambria, hilltop **Hearst Castle** (☑info 805-927-2020, reservations 800-444-4445; www.hearstcastle.org; 750 Hearst Castle Rd; tours adult/child 5-12yr $25/12; ☉from 9am; P✈) is California's most famous monument to wealth and ambition. Newspaper magnate William Randolph Hearst entertained Hollywood stars and royalty at this fantasy estate dripping with European antiques, accented by shimmering pools and surrounded by flowering gardens. Try to make tour reservations in advance or show up early in the day.

Across Hwy 1, overlooking a historic whaling pier, **Sebastian's** (☑805-927-3307; www.facebook.com/SebastiansSanSimeon; 442 SLO–San Simeon Rd; mains $9-14; ☉11am-4pm Tue-Sun) sells Hearst Ranch beef burgers and giant sandwiches for impromptu beach picnics. Five miles back south along Hwy 1, past a forgettable row of budget and midrange motels in San Simeon, **Hearst San Simeon State Park** (☑reservations 800-444-7275; www.reserveamerica.com; Hwy 1; tent & RV sites $25) offers primitive and developed creekside campsites.

Heading north, Point Piedras Blancas is home to an enormous **elephant seal colony** that breeds, molts, sleeps, frolics and, occasionally, goes aggro on the beach. Keep your distance from these wild animals who move faster on the sand than you can. The sign-posted vista point, about 4.5 miles north of Hearst Castle, has interpretive panels. Seals haul out year-round, but the frenzied birthing and mating season runs from January through March. Nearby, the 1875 **Piedras Blancas Light Station** (☑805-927-7361; www.piedrasblancas.gov; off Hwy 1; tours adult/child 6-17yr $10/5; ⊙tours 9:45am Mon-Tue & Thu-Sat mid-Jun–Aug, 9:45am Tue, Thu & Sat Sep–mid-Jun) is an outstandingly scenic spot; call ahead to confirm tour schedules (no reservations) and directions to the meet-up point.

Big Sur

Much ink has been spilled extolling the raw beauty and energy of this 100-mile stretch of craggy coastline sprawling south of Monterey Bay. More a state of mind than a place you can pinpoint on a map, Big Sur has no traffic lights, banks or strip malls. When the sun goes down, the moon and stars are the only illumination – if summer fog hasn't extinguished them, that is.

Lodging, food and gas are all scarce and pricey in Big Sur. Demand for rooms is high year-round, especially on weekends, so book ahead. The free Big Sur Guide (www.bigsurcalifornia.org), an info-packed newspaper, is available at roadside businesses. The day use parking fee (per car $10) charged at Big Sur's state parks is valid for same-day entry to all except Limekiln.

It's about 25 miles from Hearst Castle to blink-and-you-miss-it Gorda, home of **Treebones Resort** (☑877-424-4787; www.treebonesresort.com; 71895 Hwy 1; campsites $95, d with shared bath from $320; ⊛🐾🎿), which offers back-to nature clifftop yurts. Basic United States Forest Service (USFS) campgrounds are just off Hwy 1 at shady **Plaskett Creek** (☑reservations 877-477-6777; www.recreation.gov; Hwy 1; tent & RV sites $35) and ocean-side **Kirk Creek** (☑reservations 877-444-6777; www.recreation.gov; Hwy 1; tent & RV sites $35).

Ten miles north of Lucia is new-agey **Esalen Institute** (☑831-667-3000; www.esalen.org; 55000 Hwy 1), famous for its esoteric workshops and ocean-view hot springs. By reservation only (call 831-667-3047 between 9am and noon daily), you can frolic nekkid in the baths from 1am to 3am nightly ($30, credit cards only). It's surreal.

Another 3 miles north, **Julia Pfeiffer Burns State Park** (☑831-667-2315; www.parks.ca.gov; Hwy 1; per car $10; ⊙30min before

PINNACLES NATIONAL PARK

A study in geological drama, **Pinnacles National Park's** (☑831-389-4486; www.nps.gov/pinn; per car $15; 🅿🚻) 🌲 craggy monoliths, sheer-walled canyons and twisting caves are the result of millions of years of erosion. Besides hiking and rock climbing, the park's biggest attractions are endangered California condors and talus caves where bats live. It's best visited during spring or fall; summer's heat is too extreme.

sunrise-30min after sunset; 🅿🚻) 🌲 hides 80ft-high McWay Falls, one of California's only coastal waterfalls.

Over 7 miles further north, the beatnik **Henry Miller Memorial Library** (☑831-667-2574; www.henrymiller.org; 48603 Hwy 1; ⊙10am-5pm & longer hours for specific events; 🔊) is the art and soul of Big Sur bohemia, with a jam-packed bookstore, live-music concerts, open-mic nights and outdoor film screenings. Opposite, food takes a backseat to dramatic panoramic views at clifftop **Nepenthe** (☑831-667-2345; www.nepenthebigsur.com; 48510 Hwy 1; mains $18-50; ⊙11:30am-4:30pm & 5-10pm; 🍴🚻), meaning 'island of no sorrow.'

Heading north, rangers at **Big Sur Station** (☑831-667-2315; www.bigsurcalifornia.org/contact.html; 47555 Hwy 1; ⊙9am-4pm) have information on area camping and hiking, including the popular 10-mile one-way hike to **Sykes Hot Springs**. On the opposite side of Hwy 1 just south, turn onto Sycamore Canyon Rd, which drops two narrow, twisting miles to crescent-shaped **Pfeiffer Beach** (☑831-667-2315; www.fs.usda.gov/lpnf; end of Sycamore Canyon Rd; per car $10; ⊙9am-8pm; 🅿🚻🐾), with a towering offshore sea arch. Strong currents make it too dangerous for swimming. Dig down into the sand – it's purple!

Next up, **Pfeiffer Big Sur State Park** (☑831-667-2315; www.parks.ca.gov; 47225 Hwy 1; per car $10; ⊙30min before sunrise-30min after sunset; 🅿🚻) 🌲 is crisscrossed by sun-dappled trails through redwood forests. Make **campground** (☑reservations 800-444-7275; www.reserveamerica.com; 47225 Hwy 1; tent & RV sites $35-50; 🅿🐾) reservations or ramp up the luxury and watch the surf break far below from your private deck at the delightful **Post Ranch Inn** (☑831-667-2200; www.postranchinn.com; 47900 Hwy 1; d from $925; 🅿⊛❄@🔊🐾).

Most of Big Sur's commercial activity is concentrated just north along Hwy 1, including private campgrounds with rustic cabins, motels, restaurants, gas stations and shops. **Glen Oaks Motel** (📞831-667-2105; www.glenoaksbigsur.com; 47080 Hwy 1; d $300-475; P 🐾 ❄ 🛜) 🐾 is a redesigned 1950s redwood-and-adobe motor lodge with romantic, woodsy cabins and cottages. Nearby, the Big Sur River Inn's **general store** (📞831-667-2700; www.bigsurriverinn.com; 46840 Hwy 1; breakfast & lunch $15-20, dinner $15-40; ⊙8am-9pm; 🛜📶) hides a burrito and fruit-smoothie bar at the back, while **Maiden Publick House** (📞831-667-2355; Village Center Shops, Hwy 1; ⊙3pm-2am Mon-Thu, from 1pm Fri & from 11am Sat-Sun) offers an encyclopedic beer menu and live-music. Back south by the post office, put together a picnic at **Big Sur Deli** (📞831-667-2225; www.bigsurdeli.com; 47520 Hwy 1; snacks $2-12; ⊙7am-8pm), attached to the laid-back **Big Sur Taphouse** (📞831-667-2225; www.bigsurtaphouse.com; 47520 Hwy 1; ⊙noon-10pm Mon-Fri, 10am-midnight Sat, to 10pm Sun; 🛜), a beer-centric bar with board games and pub grub.

Heading north again, don't skip **Andrew Molera State Park** (📞831-667-2315; www.parks.ca.gov; Hwy 1; per car $10; ⊙30min before sunrise-30min after sunset; P 📶) 🐾, a gorgeous trail-laced pastiche of grassy meadows, waterfalls, ocean bluffs and rugged beaches. Learn all about endangered California condors at the park's **Discovery Center** (📞831-624-1202; www.ventanaws.org/discovery_center; Andrew Molera State Park; ⊙10am-4pm Sat & Sun late May–early Sep; P 📶) 🐾 **FREE**. From the dirt parking lot, a 0.3-mile trail leads to a primitive, no-reservations **campground** (www.parks.ca.gov; Hwy 1; tent sites $25).

Six miles before the landmark **Bixby Creek Bridge**, you can go on a tour (includ-ing a seasonal moonlight walk) of the 1889 lighthouse at **Point Sur Historic Park** (📞831-625-4419; www.pointsur.org; off Hwy 1; adult/child 6-17yr from $12/5; ⊙tours usually at 1pm Wed, 10am Sat & Sun Oct-Mar; 10am & 2pm Wed & Sat, 10am Sun Apr-Sep, also 10am Thu Jul & Aug) **FREE**. Check online or call for tour schedules and directions to the meeting point. Arrive early since space is limited (no reservations).

Carmel

With borderline-fanatical devotion to its canine citizens, quaint Carmel has the well-manicured feel of a country club. Watch the parade of behatted ladies toting fancy-label shopping bags to lunch and dapper gents driving top-down convertibles along Ocean Ave, the village's slow-mo main drag.

◉ Sights & Activities

Escape downtown Carmel's harried shopping streets and stroll tree-lined neighborhoods on the lookout for domiciles charming and peculiar. The Hansel and Gretel houses on Torres St, between 5th and 6th Avenues, are just how you'd imagine them. Another eye-catching house in the shape of a ship, made from local river rocks and salvaged ship parts, is on Guadalupe St near 6th Ave.

★ Mission San Carlos Borromeo de Carmelo   CHURCH
(📞831-624-1271; www.carmelmission.org; 3080 Rio Rd; adult/child 7-17yr $6.50/2; ⊙9:30am-7pm; 📶) Monterey's original mission was established by Franciscan friar Junípero Serra in 1770, but poor soil and the corrupting influence of Spanish soldiers forced the move to Carmel two years later. Today this is one of California's most strikingly beautiful missions, an oasis of solemnity bathed in flowering gardens. The mission's adobe chapel was later replaced with an arched basilica made of stone quarried in the Santa Lucia Mountains. Museum exhibits are scattered throughout the meditative complex.

★ Point Lobos State Natural Reserve   STATE PARK
(📞831-624-4909; www.pointlobos.org; Hwy 1; per car $10; ⊙8am-7pm, to 5pm early Nov–mid-Mar; P 📶) 🐾 They bark, they bathe and they're fun to watch – sea lions are the stars here at Punta de los Lobos Marinos (Point of the Sea Wolves), almost 4 miles south of Carmel, where a dramatically rocky coastline offers

ℹ **DRIVING HIGHWAY 1**

Driving this narrow two-lane highway through Big Sur and beyond is very slow going. Allow about three hours to cover the distance between the Monterey Peninsula and San Luis Obispo, and much more if you want to explore the coast. Traveling after dark can be risky and, more to the point, it's futile, because you'll miss out on the seascapes. Watch out for cyclists and make use of signposted roadside pullouts to let faster-moving traffic pass.

excellent tide-pooling. The full perimeter hike is 6 miles, but shorter walks take in wild scenery too, including **Bird Island**, shady cypress groves, the historical **Whaler's Cabin** and the **Devil's Cauldron**, a whirlpool that gets splashy at high tide.

🛏 Sleeping

Shockingly overpriced boutique hotels, inns and B&Bs fill up quickly in Carmel-by-the-Sea, especially in summer. Ask the **chamber of commerce** (☎831-624-2522; www.carmelcalifornia.org; San Carlos St, btwn 5th & 6th Aves; ⊙10am-5pm) about last-minute deals. For better-value lodgings, head north to Monterey.

🍴 Eating & Drinking

Winery tasting rooms dot Carmel's compact and well-kept centre, and the best option for late-night drinks is the cool and energetic scene at **Barmel** (☎831-626-2095; www.facebook.com/BarmelByTheSea; San Carlos St, btwn Ocean & 7th Aves; ⊙2pm-2am Mon-Fri, 1pm-2am Sat-Sun).

Cultura Comida y Bebida   MEXICAN $$
(☎831-250-7005; www.culturacarmel.com; Dolores St btwn 5th & 6th Aves; mains $19-32; ⊙11:30am-midnight Thu-Sun, 5pm-midnight Mon-Tue) Located near art galleries in a brick-lined courtyard, Cultura Comida y Bebida is a relaxed bar and eatery inspired by the food of Oaxaca in Mexico. Pull up a seat at the elegant bar and sample a vertical tasting of mezcal, or partner Monterey squid tostadas and oak-roasted trout with cilantro, lime and garlic with Californian and French wines.

Mundaka   TAPAS $$
(☎831-624-7400; www.mundakacarmel.com; San Carlos St, btwn Ocean & 7th Aves; small plates $8-15; ⊙5-9pm Sun-Thu, to 10pm Fri-Sat) This stone courtyard hideaway is a svelte escape from Carmel's stuffy 'newly wed and nearly dead' crowd. Taste Spanish tapas and housemade sangria while world beats spin. Partner the garlic prawns or grilled octopus with a chilled glass of local wine.

Monterey

Working-class Monterey is all about the sea. What draws many visitors is a world-class aquarium overlooking **Monterey Bay National Marine Sanctuary**, which protects dense kelp forests and a sublime variety of marine life, including seals and sea lions, dolphins and whales. The city itself possesses the best-preserved historical evidence of California's Spanish and Mexican periods, with many restored adobe buildings. An afternoon's wander through downtown's historic quarter promises to be more edifying than time spent in the tourist ghettos of Fisherman's Wharf and Cannery Row.

◉ Sights

★**Monterey Bay Aquarium**   AQUARIUM
(☑info 831-648-4800, tickets 866-963-9645; www.montereybayaquarium.org; 886 Cannery Row; adult/child 3-12yr/youth 13-17yr $50/30/40; ⊙10am-6pm; 🚼) 🍃 Monterey's most mesmerizing experience is its enormous aquarium, built on the former site of the city's largest sardine cannery. All kinds of aquatic creatures are featured, from kid-tolerant sea stars and slimy sea slugs to animated sea otters and surprisingly nimble 800lb tuna. The aquarium is much more than an impressive collection of glass tanks – thoughtful placards underscore the bay's cultural and historical contexts.

★**Monterey State Historic Park**   HISTORIC SITE
(☑info 831-649-7118; www.parks.ca.gov) **FREE** Old Monterey is home to an extraordinary assemblage of 19th-century brick and adobe buildings, administered as Monterey State Historic Park and all found along a 2-mile self-guided walking tour portentously called the 'Path of History.' You can inspect dozens of buildings, many with charming gardens; expect some to be open while others not, according to a capricious schedule dictated by unfortunate state-park budget cutbacks.

Cannery Row   HISTORIC SITE
(🚼) John Steinbeck's novel *Cannery Row* immortalized the sardine-canning business that was Monterey's lifeblood for the first half of the 20th century. A bronze **bust** of the Pulitzer Prize–winning writer sits at the bottom of Prescott Ave, just steps from the unabashedly touristy experience that the famous row has devolved into. The historical **Cannery Workers Shacks** at the base of flowery Bruce Ariss Way provide a sobering reminder of the hard lives led by Filipino, Japanese, Spanish and other immigrant laborers.

🏃 Activities

You can spot whales off the coast of Monterey Bay year-round. The season for blue and

CALIFORNIA MONTEREY

humpback whales runs from April to early December, while gray whales pass by from mid-December through March. Tour boats depart from Fisherman's Wharf and **Moss Landing** (🖳 info 831-917-1042, tickets 888-394-7810; www.sanctuarycruises.com; 7881 Sandholdt Rd; tours $45-55; 🖳) 🖉. Reserve trips at least a day in advance; be prepared for a bumpy, cold ride.

Monterey Bay Whale Watch   BOATING
(🗹 831-375-4658; www.montereybaywhalewatch. com; 84 Fisherman's Wharf; 3hr tour adult/child 4-12yr from $44/29; 🖳) Morning and afternoon departures; young children and well-behaved dogs are welcome on board.

Adventures by the Sea   CYCLING, KAYAKING
(🗹 831-372-1807; www.adventuresbythesea.com; 299 Cannery Row; rental per day kayak or bicycle $35, SUP set $50, kayak tours from $60; ⊙ 9am-5pm, to 8pm in summer; 🖳) Beach cruisers, electric bikes and watersports gear rentals and tours available at multiple locations on Cannery Row and **downtown** (🗹 831-372-1807; www.adventuresbythesea.com; 210 Alvarado St; ⊙ 9am-5pm, to 8pm in summer; 🖳).

Monterey Bay Dive Charters   DIVING
(🗹 831-383-9276; www.mbdcscuba.com; scuba-gear rental $75, shore/boat dives from $65/85) Arrange shore or boat dives and rent a full scuba kit with wetsuit from this well-reviewed outfitter.

🛏 Sleeping

Book ahead for special events, on weekends and in summer. To avoid the tourist congestion and jacked-up prices of Cannery Row, look to Pacific Grove. Cheaper motels line Munras Ave, south of downtown, and N Fremont St, east of Hwy 1.

HI Monterey Hostel   HOSTEL $
(🗹 831-649-0375; www.montereyhostel.org; 778 Hawthorne St; dm with shared bath $30-40; ⊙ check in 4-10pm; @🛜) Four blocks from Cannery Row and the aquarium, this simple, clean hostel houses single-sex and mixed dorms, as well as private rooms accommodating up to five people. Budget backpackers stuff themselves silly with make-your-own-pancake breakfasts. Reservations strongly recommended. Take MST bus 1 from downtown's Transit Plaza.

Monterey Hotel   HISTORIC HOTEL $$
(🗹 831-375-3184; www.montereyhotel.com; 406 Alvarado St; r $131-275; 🛜) In the heart of downtown and a short walk from Fisherman's Wharf, this 1904 edifice harbors smallish but renovated rooms and suites with Victorian-styled furniture and plantation shutters. No elevator. A recently added boutique spa offers massage and beauty treatments.

★ **Jabberwock**   B&B $$$
(🗹 831-372-4777; www.jabberwockinn.com; 598 Laine St; r $249-339; @🛜) Barely visible through a shroud of foliage, this 1911 arts-and-crafts house hums a playful *Alice in Wonderland* tune through seven immaculate rooms, a few with fireplaces and Jacuzzis. Over afternoon tea and cookies or evening wine and hors d'oeuvres, ask the genial hosts about the house's many salvaged architectural elements. Weekends are more expensive and have a two-night minimum.

✖ Eating

Uphill from Monterey's Cannery Row, Lighthouse Ave features casual, budget-friendly eateries including Hawaiian barbecue and Thai flavors, through to sushi and Middle Eastern kebabs. Downtown around Alvarado St also features cafes and pub dining.

Zab Zab   NORTHERN THAI $
(🗹 831-747-2225; www.zabzabmonterey.com; 401 Lighthouse Ave; mains $11-15; ⊙ 11am-2:30pm & 5-9pm Tue-Fri, noon-9pm Sat-Sun; 🖉) Our pick of Lighthouse Ave's ethnic eateries, Zab Zab channels the robust flavors of northeast Thailand. The bijou cottage interior is perfect in cooler weather, but during summer the best spot is on the deck surrounded by a pleasantly overgrown garden. For fans of authentic Thai heat, go for the Kai Yang grilled chicken. Lunch boxes ($11 to $13) are good value.

LouLou's Griddle in the Middle   AMERICAN $$
(🗹 831-372-0568; www.loulousgriddle.com; Municipal Wharf 2; mains $8-17; ⊙ 7:30am-4pm Sun, Mon, Wed & Thu, to 6pm Fri-Sat, closed Tue; 🖳 🐾) Stroll down the municipal wharf to this zany diner, best for breakfasts of ginormous pancakes and omelettes with Mexican *pico de gallo* salsa, or fresh seafood for lunch. Breezy outdoor tables are dog-friendly, or secure a spot at the counter and chat with the friendly chefs.

Montrio Bistro   CALIFORNIAN $$$
(🗹 831-648-8880; www.montrio.com; 414 Calle Principal; shared plates $12-30, mains $25-44; ⊙ 4:30-10pm Sun-Thu, to 11pm Fri & Sat) 🖉 Inside a 1910 firehouse, Montrio combines leather walls and iron trellises, and the tables have butcher paper and crayons for kids. The ec-

lectic seasonal menu mixes local, organic fare with Californian, Asian and European flair, including tapas-style shared plates and mini desserts. Well-priced bar snacks and happy-hour prices from 4:30pm daily are a fine end-of-the-day option.

ℹ️ Information

Monterey Visitor Center (📋 831-657-6400; www.seemonterey.com; 401 Camino el Estero; ⊙9am-6pm Mon-Sat, to 5pm Sun, closes 1hr earlier Nov-Mar) Ask for a *Monterey County Literary & Film Map*. Also a handy accommodation-booking service.

ℹ️ Getting There & Away

Monterey-Salinas Transit (MST; 📋 888-678-2871; www.mst.org; Jules Simmoneau Plaza; single-ride fares $1.50-3.50, day pass $10) operates local and regional buses; routes converge on downtown's Transit Plaza (cnr Pearl & Alvarado Sts), including routes to Pacific Grove, Carmel and Big Sur. From late May until early September, MST's free trolley loops around downtown, Fisherman's Wharf and Cannery Row between 10am and 7pm or 8pm daily.

Santa Cruz

Santa Cruz is a city of madcap fun, with a vibrant but chaotic downtown. On the waterfront is the famous beach boardwalk, and in the hills redwood groves embrace the University of California Santa Cruz (UCSC) campus. Plan at least half a day here, but to appreciate the aesthetic of jangly skirts, crystal pendants and Rastafarian dreadlocks, stay longer and plunge headlong into the rich local brew of surfers, students, punks and eccentric characters.

◉ Sights & Activities

One of the best things to do in Santa Cruz is simply stroll, shop and watch the sideshow along **Pacific Ave** downtown. A 15-minute walk away is the beach and **Municipal Wharf**, where seafood restaurants, gift shops and barking sea lions compete for attention. Ocean-view **West Cliff Dr** follows the waterfront southwest of the wharf, paralleled by a paved recreational path.

★**Santa Cruz
Beach Boardwalk**   AMUSEMENT PARK
(📋 831-423-5590; www.beachboardwalk.com; 400 Beach St; per ride $4-7, all-day pass $37-82; ⊙daily Apr-early Sep, seasonal hours vary; 🅿️♿) The West Coast's oldest beachfront amusement park, this 1907 boardwalk has a glorious old-school Americana vibe. The smell of cotton candy mixes with the salt air, punctuated by the squeals of kids hanging upside down on carnival rides. Famous thrills include the **Giant Dipper**, a 1924 wooden roller coaster, and the 1911 **Looff carousel**, both National Historic Landmarks. During summer, catch free midweek movies and Friday-night concerts by rock veterans you may have thought were already dead.

★**Seymour Marine
Discovery Center**   MUSEUM
(📋831-459-3800; http://seymourcenter.ucsc.edu; 100 Shaffer Rd; adult/child 3-16yr $8/6; ⊙10am-5pm Tue-Sun; 🅿️♿) 🦕 By Natural Bridges State Beach, this kids educational center is part of UCSC's Long Marine Laboratory. Interactive natural-science exhibits include tidal touch pools and aquariums, while outside you can gawk at the world's largest blue-whale skeleton. Guided one-hour tours happen at 1pm, 2pm and 3pm daily, with a special 30-minute tour for families with younger children at 11am; sign up for tours in person an hour in advance (no reservations).

Santa Cruz Surfing Museum   MUSEUM
(📋831-420-6289; www.santacruzsurfingmuseum.org; 701 W Cliff Dr; by donation; ⊙10am-5pm Wed-Mon Jul 4-early Sep, noon-4pm Thu-Mon early Sep-Jul 3; ♿) A mile southwest of the wharf along the coast, this tiny museum inside an old lighthouse is packed with memorabilia, including vintage redwood surfboards. Fittingly, Lighthouse Point overlooks two popular surf breaks.

Natural Bridges State Beach   BEACH
(📋831-423-4609; www.parks.ca.gov; 2531 W Cliff Dr; per car $10; ⊙8am-sunset; 🅿️♿) Best for sunsets, this family favorite has lots of sand, tide pools and monarch butterflies from mid-October through mid-February. It's at the far western end of W Cliff Dr.

O'Neill Surf Shop   SURFING
(📋831-475-4151; www.oneill.com; 1115 41st Ave; wetsuit/surfboard rental from $15/25; ⊙9am-8pm Mon-Fri, from 8am Sat & Sun) Head east toward Pleasure Point to worship at this internationally renowned surfboard-maker's flagship store, with branches on the beach boardwalk and downtown.

★**Santa Cruz Food Tour**   FOOD
(📋866-736-6343; www.santacruzfoodtour.com; per person $59; ⊙2:30-6pm Fri & Sat) Combining

CALIFORNIA SANTA CRUZ

Afghan flavors, a farm-to-table bistro, vegan cupcakes and artisan ice cream, these highly recommended walking tours also come with a healthy serving of local knowledge and interesting insights into Santa Cruz history, culture and architecture. Sign up for a tour when you first arrive in town to get your bearings in the tastiest way possible.

Richard Schmidt Surf School SURFING
(☑831-423-0928; www.richardschmidt.com; 849 Almar Ave; 2hr group/1hr private lesson $90/120; ✦) Award-winning, time-tested surf school can get you out there, all equipment included. Summer surf camps hook adults and kids alike.

🛏 Sleeping

Santa Cruz does not have enough beds to satisfy demand: expect high prices at peak times for nothing-special rooms. Places near the beach boardwalk range from friendly to frightening. For a decent motel, cruise Ocean St inland or Mission St (Hwy 1). Several new hotels scheduled to open from late 2017 will improve the city's accommodations options. Contact the visitor center for details.

**California State Park
Campgrounds** CAMPGROUND $
(☑reservations 800-444-7275; www.reserveameri ca.com; tent & RV sites $35-65) Book well ahead to camp at state beaches off Hwy 1 south of Santa Cruz or up in the foggy Santa Cruz Mountains off Hwy 9. Family-friendly campgrounds include Henry Cowell Redwoods State Park in Felton and New Brighton State Beach in Capitola.

HI Santa Cruz Hostel HOSTEL $
(☑831-423-8304; www.hi-santacruz.org; 321 Main St; dm $28-31, r $85-140, all with shared bath; ☺check in 5-10pm; @🛜) Budget overnighters dig this cute hostel at the century-old Carmelita Cottages, just two blocks from the beach. Cons: midnight curfew, daytime lockout (11am to 5pm) and three-night maximum stay. Reservations essential. Street parking costs $2.

★Adobe on Green B&B B&B $$
(☑831-469-9866; www.adobeongreen.com; 103 Green St; r $179; P☺🛜) ✐ Peace and quiet are the mantras at this place, a short walk from Pacific Ave. The hosts are practically invisible, but their thoughtful touches are everywhere, from boutique-hotel amenities in spacious, solar-powered rooms to breakfast spreads from their organic gardens.

Eating

Downtown Santa Cruz is packed with casual cafes. If you're looking for seafood, wander the wharf's takeout counter joints. Mission St, near UCSC, and 41st Ave offer cheaper eats.

Akira JAPANESE $
(☑831-600-7093; www.akirasantacruz.com; 1222 Soquel Ave; sushi & sashimi $10-15; ☺11am-11pm; ✦) ✐ Head northeast of downtown Santa Cruz to Soquel Ave's restaurant strip for Akira's modern take on sushi, sashimi and other Japanese flavors. Combining sake, craft brews and a surf-town ambience, Akira's menu harnesses briny-fresh tuna, salmon, eel and shellfish for a huge variety of sushi. Bento boxes for lunch ($10 to $14) are good value, and there's a wide range of vegetarian options.

Soif BISTRO $$
(☑831-423-2020; www.soifwine.com; 105 Walnut Ave; small plates $5-17, mains $19-25; ☺5-9pm Sun-Thu, to 10pm Fri & Sat; ✦) ✐ Following a recent makeover, one of Santa Cruz's more established restaurants is now better than ever, and the chic and cosmopolitan decor showcases a stunning wine list – including tasting flights ($20.50) of local Santa Cruz varietals – and a well-curated menu with standouts like slow-roasted pork and scallops wrapped in bacon. Wine-matching suggestions are available for all dishes.

★Assembly CALIFORNIAN $$
(☑831-824-6100; www.assembly.restaurant; 1108 Pacific Ave; brunch & lunch $12-16, dinner mains $22-28; ☺11:30am-9pm Mon & Wed-Thu, to 10pm Fri, 10am-10pm Sat-Sun; ✦) ✐ Farm-to-table and proudly regional flavors feature at this excellent bistro in downtown Santa Cruz. Assembly's Californian vibe belies real culinary nous in the kitchen, and the seasonal menu could include dishes such as chicken breast with crispy pancetta or a truffle-laced asparagus risotto. Don't miss trying the Scotch olives and meatballs with a tasting flight of local craft beers.

🍷 Drinking & Nightlife

Santa Cruz's downtown overflows with bars, lounges and coffee shops. Heading west on Mission St (Hwy 1), craft breweries and wine-tasting rooms fill the raffish industrial ambience of the Smith St and Ingalls St courtyards.

Verve Coffee Roasters · CAFE
(☑831-600-7744; www.vervecoffee.com; 1540 Pacific Ave; ⊗6:30am-9pm; 🛜) To sip finely roasted artisan espresso or a cup of rich pour-over coffee, join the surfers and hipsters at this industrial-zen cafe. Single-origin brews and house blends rule. It's been so successful around their home patch that it's also opened satellite cafes in Los Angeles and Tokyo.

Lupulo Craft Beer House · CRAFT BEER
(☑831-454-8306; www.lupulosc.com; 233 Cathcart St; ⊗11:30am-10pm Sun-Thu, to 11:30pm Fri-Sat) Named after the Spanish word for hops, Lupulo Craft Beer House is an essential downtown destination for traveling beer fans. Modern decor combines with an ever-changing taplist – often including seasonal brews from local California breweries – and good bar snacks such as empanadas, tacos and charcuterie plates. Almost 400 bottled and canned beers create delicious panic for the indecisive drinker.

❶ Information

Santa Cruz Visitor Center (☑831-425-1234; www.santacruzca.org; 303 Water St; ⊗9am-noon & 1-4pm Mon-Fri, 11am-3pm Sat & Sun) Free public internet terminal, maps and brochures.

❶ Getting There & Around

Santa Cruz is 75 miles south of San Francisco via coastal Hwy 1 or Hwy 17, a nail-bitingly narrow, winding mountain road. Monterey is about an hour's drive further south via Hwy 1.
Santa Cruz Airport Shuttles (☑831-421-9883; www.santacruzshuttles.com) runs shared shuttles to/from the airports at San Jose ($50), San Francisco ($80) and Oakland ($80), with a $5 cash discount; the second passenger pays $10.
Greyhound (☑800-231-2222; www.greyhound.com; Metro Center, 920 Pacific Ave) has a few daily buses to San Francisco ($16, three hours), Salinas ($15, one hour), Santa Barbara ($53, six hours) and Los Angeles ($59, nine hours).
Santa Cruz Metro (☑831-425-8600; www.scmtd.com; 920 Pacific Ave; single-ride/day pass $2/6) operates local and countywide bus routes that converge on downtown's **Metro Center** (920 Pacific Ave). Hwy 17 express buses link Santa Cruz with San Jose's Amtrak/CalTrain station ($5, 50 minutes, once or twice hourly).

From late May through early September, the **Santa Cruz Trolley** (www.santacruztrolley.com; per ride 25¢) shuttles between downtown and the beach from 11am until 9pm daily.

SAN FRANCISCO & THE BAY AREA

San Francisco
Grab your coat and a handful of glitter, and enter the land of fog and fabulousness. So long, inhibitions; hello, San Francisco.

History
Native Californians had found gold in California long before 1849 – but it hardly seemed worth mentioning, as long as there were oysters for lunch and venison for dinner. Once word circulated, San Francisco was transformed almost overnight from bucolic trading backwater to gold-rush metropolis. Over 160 years of booms, busts, history-making high jinks and lowdown dirty dealings later, SF remains the wildest city in the west.

◉ Sights
Most major museums are downtown, though Golden Gate Park is home to the de Young Museum and the California Academy of Sciences. The city's most historic districts are the Mission, Chinatown, North Beach and the Haight. Galleries are clustered downtown and in North Beach, the Mission, Potrero Flats and Dogpatch. You'll find hilltop parks citywide, but Russian, Nob and Telegraph Hills are the highest and most panoramic.

◎ Embarcadero

★**Ferry Building** · LANDMARK
(Map p304; ☑415-983-8030; www.ferrybuildingmarketplace.com; cnr Market St & the Embarcadero; ⊗10am-7pm Mon-Fri, 8am-6pm Sat, 11am-5pm Sun; 🚼; 🚎2, 6, 9, 14, 21, 31, Ⓜ Embarcadero, Ⓑ Embarcadero) Hedonism is alive and well at this transit hub turned gourmet emporium, where foodies happily miss their ferries over Sonoma oysters and bubbly, SF craft beer and Marin-raised beef burgers, or locally roasted coffee and just-baked cupcakes. Star chefs are frequently spotted at the farmers market (p316) that wraps around the building all year.

★**Exploratorium** · MUSEUM
(Map p304; ☑415-528-4444; www.exploratorium.edu; Pier 15; adult/child $30/20, 6-10pm Thu $15; ⊗10am-5pm Tue-Sun, over 18yr only 6-10pm Thu; Ⓟ🚼; ⓂE, F) 🐾 Is there a science to

skateboarding? Do toilets really flush counterclockwise in Australia? At San Francisco's hands-on science museum, you'll find out things you wished you learned in school. Combining science with art and investigating human perception, the Exploratorium nudges you to question how you perceive the world around you. The setting is thrilling: a 9-acre, glass-walled pier jutting straight into San Francisco Bay, with large outdoor portions you can explore free of charge, 24 hours a day.

Union Square & Civic Center

Bordered by high-end department stores, **Union Square** (Map p304; btwn Geary, Powell, Post & Stockton Sts; ⛟ Powell-Mason, Powell-Hyde, Ⓜ Powell, Ⓑ Powell) was named for pro-Union Civil War rallies held here 150 years ago. People-watch with espresso from **Emporio Rulli** (Map p304; ☎ 415-433-1122; www.rulli.com; Union Sq; pastries $4-8; ⊘ 8am-7pm; ⛟; Ⓜ Powell, Ⓑ Powell) cafe.

★ Asian Art Museum   MUSEUM
(Map p304; ☎ 415-581-3500; www.asianart.org; 200 Larkin St; adult/student/child $15/10/free, 1st Sun of month free; ⊘ 10am-5pm Tue, Wed & Fri-Sun, to 9pm Thu; ⛟; Ⓜ Civic Center, Ⓑ Civic Center) Imaginations race from ancient Persian miniatures to cutting-edge Japanese minimalism across three floors spanning 6000 years of Asian art. Besides the largest collection outside Asia – 18,000 works – the museum offers excellent programs for all ages, from shadow-puppet shows and tea tastings

with star chefs to mixers with cross-cultural DJ mash-ups.

Powell St Cable Car Turnaround   LANDMARK
(Map p304; www.sfmta.com; cnr Powell & Market Sts; ⛟ Powell-Mason, Mason-Hyde, Ⓜ Powell, Ⓑ Powell) Peek through the passenger queue at Powell and Market Sts to spot cable-car operators leaping out, gripping the chassis of each trolley and slooowly turning the car atop a revolving wooden platform. Cable cars can't go in reverse, so they need to be turned around by hand here at the terminus of the Powell St lines. Riders queue up midmorning to early evening here to secure a seat, with raucous street performers and doomsday preachers on the sidelines as entertainment.

Chinatown

Since 1848, this community has survived riots, bootlegging gangsters and earthquakes.

★ Chinatown Alleyways   AREA
(Map p304; btwn Grant Ave, Stockton St, California St & Broadway; ⛟ 1, 30, 45, ⛟ Powell-Hyde, Powell-Mason, California) The 41 historic alleyways packed into Chinatown's 22 blocks have seen it all since 1849: gold rushes and revolution, incense and opium, fire and icy receptions. In clinker-brick buildings lining these narrow backstreets, temple balconies jut out over bakeries, laundries and barbers – there was nowhere to go but up in Chinatown after 1870, when laws limited Chinese immigration, employment and housing. **Chinatown**

SAN FRANCISCO IN ...

One Day
Since the Gold Rush, San Francisco adventures have started in Chinatown, where you can still find hidden fortunes – in cookies, that is. After dining on dim sum, beat it to **City Lights Bookstore** to revel in Beat poetry. Stroll past the Italian streetside cafes of **North Beach** to climb **Coit Tower** for 360-degree city and bay views. Then head to Civic Center's **Asian Art Museum**, where art transports you across centuries and oceans within an hour. Have an early dinner at the **Ferry Building** before taking a spooky night tour of **Alcatraz**. Make your escape from the island prison in time to hit the dance floor in **SoMa** clubs.

Two Days
Start your day in the **Mission** amid mural-covered garage doors lining **Balmy Alley**, then step inside meditative **Mission Dolores**. Break for burritos before hoofing it to the **Haight** for flashbacks at vintage boutiques and the Summer of Love site: **Golden Gate Park**. Glimpse bay views atop the **de Young Museum**, take a walk on the empirical side at the **California Academy of Sciences** and brave howling winds on the **Golden Gate Bridge**.

San Francisco & the Bay Area

N
0 — 20 km
0 — 10 miles

Sacramento (30mi)

Occidental
Santa Rosa
Sebastopol
Freestone
Bohemian Hwy
Glen Ellen
Yountville
Napa
SONOMA COUNTY
Sonoma Valley
Napa Valley
Silverado Trail
SOLANO COUNTY
Sonoma
Napa
Tomales
Petaluma
Petaluma River
NAPA COUNTY
Fairfield
MARIN COUNTY
American Canyon
Grizzly Bay
Inverness
Point Reyes Station
Novato
San Pablo Bay
Vallejo
Suisun Bay
Point Reyes National Seashore
Olema
Pittsburg
Drakes Bay
Point Reyes
Crockett
Benicia
Martinez
Stinson Beach
San Rafael
San Pablo
Concord
Larkspur
Richmond
Pleasant Hill
Walnut Creek
Bolinas
Mill Valley
Tiburon
Albany
Mount Diablo State Park
Sausalito
Berkeley
Danville
SAN FRANCISCO COUNTY
San Francisco
Alameda
Oakland
San Ramon
See Greater San Francisco Map (p302)
Oakland International Airport
Castro Valley
Farallon National Wildlife Refuge
Daly City
San Francisco Bay
San Lorenzo
Hayward
ALAMEDA COUNTY
Pacifica
San Bruno
San Francisco International Airport
Sunol
San Mateo
Foster City
Fremont
Montara
Moss Beach
Newark
Half Moon Bay
Redwood City
Woodside
Palo Alto
Milpitas
Mineta San José International Airport
SAN MATEO COUNTY
San Jose
San Gregorio
La Honda
Saratoga
PACIFIC OCEAN
Pescadero
Los Gatos
SANTA CLARA COUNTY
Pigeon Point
Big Basin Redwoods State Park
Boulder Creek
Año Nuevo State Reserve
SANTA CRUZ COUNTY
Davenport
Henry Cowell Redwoods State Park
Santa Cruz
Capitola
Monterey Bay

Greater San Francisco

N 0 —— 5 km
0 —— 2.5 miles

Greater San Francisco

◉ Top Sights
1 Alcatraz	C2
2 Crissy Field	C3
3 Golden Gate Bridge	C3
4 Point Bonita Lighthouse	B3

◎ Sights
5 Alamo Square Park	C3
6 Bay Area Discovery Museum	C2
7 Bay Model Visitors Center	B2
8 Marine Mammal Center	B2
9 Mt Tamalpais State Park	A1
10 Nike Missile Site SF-88	B2
11 Presidio Officers' Club	C3

⬤ Sleeping
12 Cavallo Point	C2
13 HI Marin Headlands	B2
Inn at the Presidio	(see 11)
14 Metro Hotel	C3
15 Pantoll Campground	A1
16 West Point Inn	A1

✴ Eating
17 A16	C3
18 Ichi Sushi	C4
19 Outerlands	B4
20 Warming Hut	C3

◉ Entertainment
21 Independent	C3

Alleyway Tours (Map p304; ☎415-984-1478; www.chinatownalleywaytours.org; Portsmouth Sq; adult/student $26/16; ⊘ tours 11am Sat; 🚹; ☐1, 8, 10, 12, 30, 41, 45, 🚋 California, Powell-Mason, Powell-

Hyde) and **Chinatown Heritage Walking Tours** (Map p304; ☎415-986-1822; www.cccsf. us; Chinese Culture Center, Hilton Hotel, 3rd fl, 750 Kearny St; group tour adult $25-30, student $15-20, private tour (1-4 people) $60; ⊙ tours 10am, noon & 2pm Tue-Sat; 👤; 🚌1, 8, 10, 12, 30, 41, 45, 🚃 California, Powell-Mason, Powell-Hyde) offer community-supporting, time-traveling strolls through defining moments in American history.

Chinese Historical Society of America
MUSEUM
(CHSA; Map p304; ☑415-391-1188; www.chsa.org; 965 Clay St; adult/student/child $15/10/free; ⊙11am-4pm Wed-Sun; 👤; 🚌1, 8, 30, 45, 🚃California, Powell-Mason, Powell-Hyde) **FREE** Picture what it was like to be Chinese in America during the gold rush, transcontinental railroad construction or Beat heyday in this 1932 landmark, built as Chinatown's YWCA by Julia Morgan (chief architect of Hearst Castle). CHSA historians unearth fascinating artifacts, from 1920s silk *qipao* dresses to Chinatown miniatures created by set designer Frank Wong. Exhibits reveal once-popular views of Chinatown, including the sensationalist opium-den exhibit at San Francisco's 1915 Panama-Pacific International Expo inviting fairgoers to 'Go Slumming' in Chinatown.

⊙ North Beach

★ City Lights Books
CULTURAL CENTER
(Map p304; ☑415-362-8193; www.citylights.com; 261 Columbus Ave; ⊙10am-midnight; 👤; 🚌8, 10, 12, 30, 41, 45, 🚃Powell-Mason, Powell-Hyde) Free speech and free spirits have flourished here since 1957, when City Lights founder and poet Lawrence Ferlinghetti and manager Shigeyoshi Murao won a landmark ruling defending their right to publish Allen Ginsberg's magnificent epic poem *Howl*. Celebrate your freedom to read freely in the designated Poet's Chair upstairs overlooking Jack Kerouac Alley, load up on zines on the mezzanine and entertain radical ideas downstairs in the new Pedagogies of Resistance section.

Beat Museum
MUSEUM
(Map p304; ☑800-537-6822; www.kerouac.com; 540 Broadway; adult/student $8/5, walking tours $25; ⊙museum 10am-7pm, walking tours 2-4pm Sat; 🚌8, 10, 12, 30, 41, 45, 🚃Powell-Mason) The closest you can get to the complete Beat experience without breaking a law. The 1000-plus artifacts in this museum's literary-ephemera collection include the sublime (the banned edition of Ginsberg's *Howl*, with the author's own annotations) and the ridiculous (those Kerouac bobblehead dolls are definite head-shakers). Downstairs, watch Beat-era films in ramshackle theater seats redolent with the odors of literary giants, pets and pot. Upstairs, pay your respects at shrines to individual Beat writers.

⊙ Russian Hill & Nob Hill

★ Lombard Street
STREET
(Map p304; 🚃Powell-Hyde) You've seen the eight switchbacks of Lombard St's 900 block in a thousand photographs. The tourist board has dubbed it 'the world's crookedest street,' which is factually incorrect: Vermont St in Potrero Hill deserves that award, but Lombard is much more scenic, with its redbrick pavement and lovingly tended flowerbeds. It wasn't always so bent; before the arrival of the car it lunged straight down the hill.

★ Cable Car Museum
HISTORIC SITE
(Map p304; ☑415-474-1887; www.cablecarmuseum.org; 1201 Mason St; donations appreciated; ⊙10am-6pm Apr-Sep, to 5pm Oct-Mar; 🚃Powell-Mason, Powell-Hyde) **FREE** Hear that whirring beneath the cable-car tracks? That's the sound of the cables that pull the cars, and they all connect inside the city's long-functioning cable-car barn. Grips, engines, braking mechanisms... if these warm your gearhead heart, you'll be besotted with the Cable Car Museum.

Diego Rivera Gallery
GALLERY
(Map p304; ☑415-771-7020; www.sfai.edu; 800 Chestnut St; ⊙9am-7pm; 🚌30, 🚃Powell-Mason) **FREE** Diego Rivera's 1931 *The Making of a Fresco Showing the Building of a City* is a trompe l'oeil fresco within a fresco, showing the artist himself, pausing to admire his work, as well as the work in progress that is San Francisco. The fresco covers an entire wall in the Diego Rivera Gallery at the San Francisco Art Institute.

⊙ Fisherman's Wharf

★ Maritime National Historical Park
HISTORIC SITE
(Map p304; ☑415-447-5000; www.nps.gov/safr; 499 Jefferson St, Hyde St Pier; 7-day ticket adult/child $10/free; ⊙9:30am-5pm Oct-May, to 5:30pm Jun-Sep; 👤; 🚌19, 30, 47, 🚃Powell-Hyde, Ⓜ F) Four historic ships are floating museums at this maritime national park, Fisherman's Wharf's most authentic attraction. Moored along Hyde St Pier are the 1891 schooner *Alma*, which hosts guided sailing trips in summer; 1890 steamboat *Eureka*; paddlewheel tugboat *Eppleton Hall*; and iron-hulled *Balclutha*.

CALIFORNIA SAN FRANCISCO

Downtown San Francisco

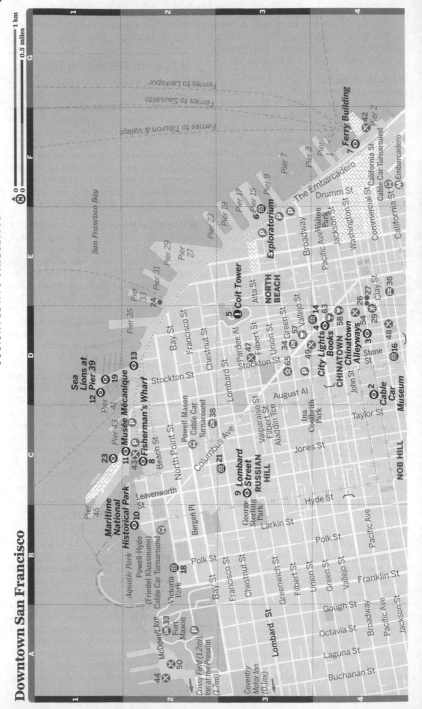

N
0   0.5 miles
0   1 km

San Francisco Bay

Ferries to Larkspur
Ferries to Sausalito
Ferries to Tiburon & Vallejo

Ferry Building

Pier 2
42

Pier 1
7

California St
Cable Car Turnaround
Commercial St
Embarcadero
California St

The Embarcadero
Drumm St
Washington St
Jackson St
Pacific Ave
Walton Park
Broadway

Pier 3
Pier 7
Pier 9
Pier 15
Pier 17
Pier 19

Exploratorium
6

Pier 23
Pier 27
Pier 29
Pier 31
Pier 33
Pier 35

24

Coit Tower
5

NORTH BEACH

Alta St
Filbert St
Union St
Green St
Vallejo St

Francisco St
Chestnut St
Lombard St
Stockton St

Pardee Al

34
65
57
49
47
14
4

City Lights Books
CHINATOWN
Chinatown Alleyways

63
58
26
27
54
29
48
36

Clay St
Stone St

16
30

John St

Cable Car Museum
2

NOB HILL

Taylor St
Jones St
Hyde St
Larkin St
Polk St

Pacific Ave
Broadway
Jackson St

Sea Lions at Pier 39
12
19

Musée Mécanique
11
13

Fisherman's Wharf
8
43

Pier 41
Pier 43
23

Beach St
North Point St
Powell-Mason Cable Car Turnaround
38

Stockton St
Columbus Ave

21

Lombard Street
9

RUSSIAN HILL

George Sterling Park
Ina Coolbrith Park
Valparaiso St
Filbert St Tce
Aladdin Tce
August Al

Pier 45

Maritime National Historical Park

Aquatic Park
Powell-Hyde Cable Car Turnaround (Friedel Klussmann)

10

Leavenworth St
Bergen Pl

Victoria Park
18

Fort Mason
33

McDowell Ave
50
44

Coventry Motor Inn (0.1m)
Cissy Field (1.2m);
Inn at the Presidio (1.7m)

Lombard St

Bay St
Francisco St
Chestnut St
Greenwich St
Filbert St
Union St
Green St
Vallejo St

Polk St
Octavia St
Gough St
Franklin St
Laguna St
Buchanan St

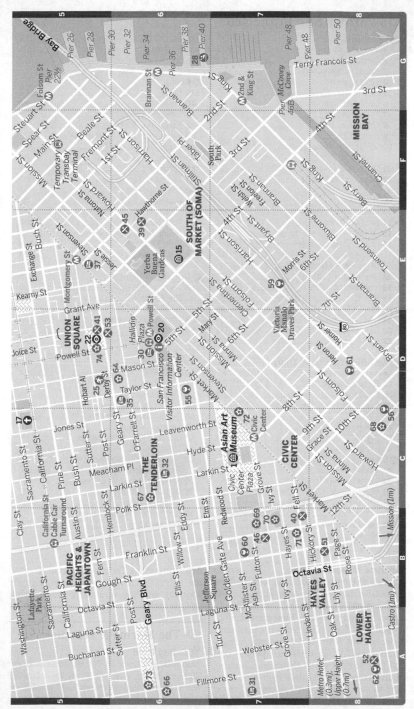

Downtown San Francisco

Maritime Museum   MUSEUM
(Aquatic Park Bathhouse; Map p304; www.maritime. org; 900 Beach St; ⊘10am-4pm; ☞; ☐19, 30, 47, ☐Powell-Hyde) FREE A monumental hint to sailors in need of a scrub, this restored, ship-shaped 1939 Streamline Moderne landmark is decked out with Works Progress Administration (WPA) art treasures: playful seal and frog sculptures by Beniamino Bufano, Hilaire Hiler's surreal underwater dreamscape murals, and recently uncovered wood reliefs by Richard Ayer. Acclaimed African American artist Sargent Johnson created the stunning carved green slate marquee doorway and the verandah's mesmerizing aquatic mosaics.

◉ The Marina & Presidio

★ **Crissy Field**   PARK
(Map p302; ☎415-561-4700; www.crissyfield.org; 1199 East Beach; ☐☞; ☐30, PresidiGo Shuttle) War is for the birds at Crissy Field, a military airstrip turned waterfront nature preserve

with knockout Golden Gate views. Where military aircraft once zoomed in for landings, bird-watchers now huddle in the silent rushes of a reclaimed tidal marsh. Joggers pound beachside trails and the only security alerts are raised by puppies suspiciously sniffing surfers. On foggy days, stop by the certified-green **Warming Hut** (☑415-561-3042; www.parksconservancy.org/visit/eat/warming-hut.html; 983 Marine Dr; items $4-9; ⊙9am-5pm; P ♿; 🚌 PresidiGo shuttle) 🍃 to browse regional-nature books and warm up with fair-trade coffee.

Presidio Officers' Club HISTORIC BUILDING
(Map p302; ☑415-561-4165; www.presidio.gov/officers-club-internal; 50 Moraga Ave; ⊙10am-6pm Tue, Wed, Sat & Sun, to 8pm Thu & Fri; 🚌PresidiGo shuttle) **FREE** The Presidio's oldest building dates to the late 1700s, and was fully renovated in 2015, revealing gorgeous Spanish-Moorish adobe architecture. The free **Heritage Gallery** shows the history of the Presidio, from Native American days to the present. Moraga Hall – the former officers'-club lounge – is a lovely spot to sit fireside and also has free wi-fi. Thursday and Friday evenings the club hosts a dynamic lineup of events and lectures; check the website.

★Musée Mécanique AMUSEMENT PARK
(Map p304; ☑415-346-2000; www.museemechanique.org; Pier 45, Shed A; ⊙10am-8pm; ♿; 🚌47, 🚋Powell-Mason, Powell-Hyde, Ⓜ E, F) A flashback to penny arcades, the Musée Mécanique houses a mind-blowing collection of vintage mechanical amusements. Sinister, freckle-faced Laughing Sal has creeped out kids for over a century, but don't let this manic mannequin deter you from the best arcade west of Coney Island. A quarter lets you start brawls in Wild West saloons, peep at belly dancers through a vintage Mutoscope and even learn a cautionary tale about smoking opium.

★Sea Lions at Pier 39 SEA LIONS
(Map p304; www.pier39.com; Pier 39, cnr Beach St & the Embarcadero; ⊙24hr; ♿; 🚌15, 37, 49, Ⓜ E, F) Beach bums took over San Francisco's most coveted waterfront real estate in 1990 and have been making a public display of themselves ever since. Naturally these unkempt squatters have become San Francisco's favorite mascots, and since California law requires boats to make way for marine mammals, yacht owners have to relinquish valuable slips to accommodate as many as 1300 sea lions. These giant mammals 'haul out' onto the docks between January and July, and whenever else they feel like sunbathing.

★Baker Beach BEACH
(Map p310; ☑10am-5pm 415-561-4323; www.nps.gov/prsf; ⊙sunrise-sunset; P; 🚌29, PresidiGo Shuttle) Picnic amid wind-sculpted pines, fish from craggy rocks or frolic nude at mile-long Baker Beach, with spectacular views of the Golden Gate. Crowds come weekends, especially on fog-free days; arrive early. For nude sunbathing (mostly straight girls and gay boys), head to the north. Families in clothing stick to the south, nearer parking. Mind the currents and the c-c-cold water.

◉ The Mission & the Castro

★Balmy Alley PUBLIC ART
(Map p308; ☑415-285-2287; www.precitaeyes.org; btwn 24th & 25th Sts; 🚌10, 12, 14, 27, 48, 🅱24th St Mission) Inspired by Diego Rivera's 1930s San Francisco murals and provoked by US foreign policy in Central America, 1970s Mission *muralistas* (muralists) led by Mia Gonzalez set out to transform the political landscape, one mural-covered garage door at a time. Today, Balmy Alley murals span three decades, from an early memorial for El Salvador activist Archbishop Óscar Romero to a homage to Frida Kahlo, Georgia O'Keeffe and other trailblazing female modern artists.

Mission Dolores CHURCH
(Misión San Francisco de Asís; Map p308; ☑415-621-8203; www.missiondolores.org; 3321 16th St; adult/child $5/3; ⊙9am-4pm Nov-Apr, to 4:30pm May-Oct; 🚌22, 33, 🅱16th St Mission, Ⓜ J) The city's oldest building and its namesake, whitewashed adobe Misión San Francisco de Asís was founded in 1776 and rebuilt from 1782 with conscripted Ohlone and Miwok labor – a graveyard memorial hut commemorates 5000 Ohlone and Miwok laborers who died in mission measles epidemics in the early 19th century. Today the modest adobe structure is overshadowed by the ornate adjoining 1913 basilica, featuring stained-glass windows depicting California's 21 missions.

★Dolores Park PARK
(Map p308; http://sfrecpark.org/destination/mission-dolores-park; Dolores St, btwn 18th & 20th Sts; ⊙6am-10pm; ♿🐕; 🚌14, 33, 49, 🅱16th St Mission, Ⓜ J) Semiprofessional tanning and taco picnics: welcome to San Francisco's sunny side. Dolores Park has something for everyone,

The Mission & The Castro

from street ball and tennis to the Mayan-pyramid playground (sorry, kids: no blood sacrifices allowed). Political protests and other favorite local sports happen year-round, and there are free movie nights and mime troupe performances in summer. Climb to the upper southwestern corner for superb views of downtown, framed by palm trees.

★**Women's Building** NOTABLE BUILDING
(Map p308; ☎415-431-1180; www.womensbuilding.org; 3543 18th St; 🚹; 🚌14, 22, 33, 49, 🚆16th St Mission, 🚇J) The nation's first women-owned-and-operated community center has quietly done good work with 170 women's organizations since 1979, but the 1994 addition of the *Maestrapeace* mural showed the Women's Building for the landmark it truly is. An all-star team of *muralistas* covered the building with images of cross-cultural goddesses and women trailblazers, including Nobel Prize winner Rigoberta Menchú, poet

Audre Lorde, artist Georgia O'Keeffe and former US Surgeon General Dr Joycelyn Elders.

⊙ The Haight & Around

★**Haight Street** STREET
(Map p310; Haight St, btwn Fillmore & Stanyan Sts; 🚌7, 22, 33, 43, 🚇N) Was it the fall of 1966 or the winter of '67? As the Haight saying goes, if you can remember the Summer of Love, dude, you probably weren't there. The fog was laced with pot, sandalwood incense and burning draft cards, entire days were spent contemplating Day-Glo Grateful Dead posters, and the corner of **Haight and Ashbury Sts** (Map p310; 🚌6, 7, 33, 37, 43) became the turning point for an entire generation.

Alamo Square Park PARK
(Map p302; www.sfparksalliance.org/our-parks/parks/alamo-square; cnr Hayes & Steiner Sts; ☉sunrise-sunset; 🚹🚸; 🚌5, 21, 22, 24) Hippie communes and Victorian bordellos, jazz

The Mission & The Castro

greats and opera stars, earthquakes and Church of Satan services: these genteel **'Painted Lady' Victorian mansions** have hosted them all since 1857, and survived elegantly intact. Pastel Postcard Row mansions along Alamo Sq's eastern side pale in comparison with the colorful characters along the northwestern end of this hilltop park. The northern side features Barbary Coast baroque mansions at their most bombastic, bedecked with fish-scale shingles and gingerbread trim dripping from peaked roofs.

⊙ Golden Gate & Around

In 1865 the city voted to turn more than 1000 acres of sand dunes into Golden Gate Park. At the park's western end is **Ocean Beach** (Map p310; ☏415-561-4323; www.parksconservancy.org; Great Hwy; ☉sunrise-sunset; 🅿🚻🐕; ⌑5, 18, 31, Ⓜ N), where **Cliff House** (Map p310; ☏415-386-3330; www.cliffhouse.com; 1090 Point Lobos Ave; ☉9am-11pm Sun-Thu, to midnight Fri & Sat; ⌑5, 18, 31, 38) 🆓 overlooks the splendid ruin of **Sutro Baths** (Map p310; www.nps.gov/goga/historyculture/sutro-baths.htm; 680 Point Lobos Ave; ☉sunrise-sunset, visitor center 9am-5pm; 🅿; ⌑5, 31, 38) 🆓. Follow the partly paved hiking trail around **Lands End** for shipwreck sightings and **Golden Gate Bridge** (Map p302; ☏toll information 877-229-8655; www.goldengatebridge.org/visitors; Hwy 101; northbound free, southbound $6.50-7.50; ⌑28, all Golden Gate Transit buses) views. On Sundays, when JFK Drive is closed to cars, rent your own wheels from **Golden Gate Park Bike & Skate** (Map p310; ☏415-668-1117; www.goldengateparkbikeandskate.com; 3038 Fulton St; skates per hour $5-6, per day $20-24, bikes per hour $3-5, per day $15-25, tandem bikes per hour/day $15/75, discs $6/25; ☉10am-6pm Mon-Fri, to 7pm Sat & Sun; 🚻; ⌑5, 21, 31, 44).

★ **Golden Gate Park** PARK
(Map p310; www.golden-gate-park.com; btwn Stanyan St & Great Hwy; 🅿🚻🐕; ⌑5, 7, 18, 21, 28, 29, 33, 44, Ⓜ N) 🆓 When San Franciscans refer to 'the park,' there's only one that gets the definite article: Golden Gate Park. Everything San Franciscans hold dear is here: free spirits, free music, redwoods, Frisbee, protests, fine art, bonsai and buffalo. Thanks to SF's mystical microclimates and natural eccentricity, the park is filled with flora from around the world and extraordinary sights, including the **de Young Museum** (☏415-750-3600; http://deyoung.famsf.org; 50 Hagiwara Tea Garden Dr; adult/child $15/free, 1st Tue of month free; ☉9:30am-5:15pm Tue-Sun, to 8:45pm Fri Apr-Nov; 🚻; ⌑5, 7, 44, Ⓜ N), California Academy of Sciences (p315), **San Francisco Botanical Garden** (Strybing Arboretum; ☏415-661-1316; www.strybing.org; 1199 9th Ave; adult/child $8/2, before 9am daily & 2nd Tue of month free; ☉7:30am-7pm Mar-Sep, to 6pm Oct–mid-Nov & Feb, to 5pm mid-Nov–Jan, last entry 1hr before closing, bookstore 10am-4pm; 🚻; ⌑6, 7, 44, Ⓜ N) 🅿, **Japanese Tea Garden** (☏415-752-1171; www.japaneseteagardensf.com; 75 Hagiwara Tea Garden Dr; adult/child $8/2, before 10am Mon, Wed & Fri free; ☉9am-6pm Mar-Oct, to 4:45pm Nov-Feb; 🅿🚻; ⌑5, 7, 44, Ⓜ N), **Conservatory of Flowers** (☏415-831-2090; www.conservatoryofflowers.org; 100 John F Kennedy Dr; adult/student/child $8/6/2, 1st Tue of month free; ☉10am-4pm Tue-Sun; 🚻; ⌑5, 7, 21, 33, Ⓜ N) and **Stow**

The Richmond, The Haight & Golden Gate Park

CALIFORNIA SAN FRANCISCO

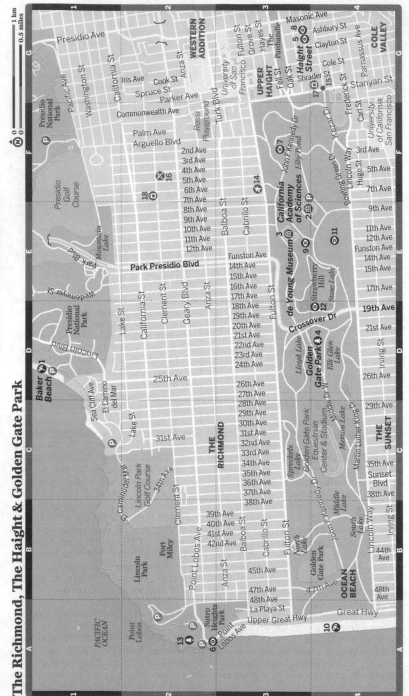

The Richmond, The Haight & Golden Gate Park

Lake (www.sfrecpark.org; ☉sunrise-sunset; 🚾; 🚌7, 44, Ⓜ N).

🏃 Activities

Blazing Saddles
CYCLING
(Map p304; ☏415-202-8888; www.blazingsaddles. com; 433 Mason St; bike hire per hour $8-15, per day $32-88, electric bikes per day $48-88; ☉8am-8pm; 🚋Powell-Hyde, Powell-Mason, Ⓑ Powell, Ⓜ Powell) Rent bicycles near Union Sq to cover downtown in a day – just mind the traffic. Reserve online for 20% off rates.

City Kayak
KAYAKING
(Map p304; ☏415-294-1050, 888-966-0953; www. citykayak.com; Pier 40, South Beach Harbor; kayak rentals per hour $35-125, 3hr lesson & rental $49, tours $59-75; ☉rentals noon-3pm, return by 5pm Thu-Mon; 🚌30, 45, Ⓜ N, T) You haven't seen San Francisco until you've seen it from the water. Newbies to kayaking can take lessons and paddle calm waters near the Bay Bridge; experienced paddlers can rent kayaks to brave currents near the Golden Gate (conditions permitting; get advice first). Sporty romantics: twilight tours past the Bay Bridge lights are ideal for proposals. Check website for details.

👉 Tours

★Precita Eyes
Mission Mural Tours
WALKING
(Map p308; ☏415-285-2287; www.precitaeyes.org; 2981 24th St; adult $15-20, child $3; 🚾; 🚌12, 14, 48, 49, Ⓑ 24th St Mission) Muralists lead weekend walking tours covering 60 to 70 Mission murals within a six- to 10-block radius of mural-bedecked Balmy Alley (p307). Tours last 90 minutes to two hours and 15 minutes (for the more in-depth Classic Mural Walk).

Proceeds fund mural upkeep at this community arts nonprofit.

Drag Me Along Tours
WALKING
(Map p304; ☏415-857-0865; www.dragmealong tours.com; Portsmouth Sq; $20; ☉tours usually 11am-1pm Sun; 🚌1, 8, 10, 12, 30, 41, 45, 🚋California, Powell-Mason, Powell-Hyde) Explore San Francisco's bawdy Barbary Coast with a bona-fide legend: gold-rush burlesque star Countess Lola Montez, reincarnated in drag by SF historian Rick Shelton. Her Highness leads you through Chinatown alleyways where Victorian ladies made and lost reputations, and past North Beach saloons where sailors were shanghaied. Barbary Coast characters gambled, loved and lived dangerously. Adult content; reservations required; cash only.

Haight-Ashbury
Flower Power Walking Tour
WALKING
(Map p310; ☏415-863-1621; www.haightashbury tour.com; adult/under 10yr $20/free; ☉10:30am Tue & Sat, 2pm Fri; 🚾; 🚌6, 7, Ⓜ N) Take a long, strange trip through 12 blocks of hippie history, following in the steps of Jimi, Jerry and Janis – if you have to ask for last names, you seriously need this tour, dude. Tours meet at the corner of Stanyan and Waller Sts and last about two hours; reservations required.

🎉 Festivals & Events

Bay to Breakers
SPORTS
(www.baytobreakers.com; race registration from $65; ☉3rd Sun May) Run costumed or in not much at all from the Embarcadero to Ocean Beach; joggers dressed as salmon run upstream.

SF Pride Celebration
LGBT
(☉Jun) A day isn't enough to do SF proud: June begins with the San Francisco LGBTQ Film Festival (www.frameline.org; tickets $10-35;

Alcatraz

A HALF-DAY TOUR

Book a ferry from Pier 33 and ride 1.5 miles across the bay to explore America's most notorious former prison. The trip itself is worth the money, providing stunning views of the city skyline. Once you've landed at the ❶ **Ferry Dock & Pier**, you begin the 580-yard walk to the top of the island and prison; if you need assistance to reach the top, there's a twice-hourly tram.

As you climb toward the ❷ **Guardhouse**, notice the island's steep slope; before it was a prison, Alcatraz was a fort. In the 1850s, the military quarried the rocky shores into near-vertical cliffs. Ships could then only dock at a single port, separated from the main buildings by a sally port (a drawbridge and moat in what became the guardhouse). Inside, peer through floor grates to see Alcatraz' original prison.

Volunteers tend the brilliant ❸ **Officer's Row Gardens** an orderly counterpoint to the overgrown rose bushes surrounding the burned-out shell of the ❹ **Warden's House**. At the top of the hill, by the front door of the ❺ **Main Cellhouse**, beautiful shots unfurl all around, including a view of the ❻ **Golden Gate Bridge**. Above the main door of the administration building, notice the ❼ **historic signs & graffiti**, before you step inside the dank, cold prison to find the ❽ **Frank Morris cell**, former home to Alcatraz' most notorious jail-breaker.

TOP TIPS

➡ Book at least one month prior for self-guided daytime visits, longer for ranger-led night tours. For info on garden tours, see www.alcatraz gardens.org.

➡ Be prepared to hike; a steep path ascends from the ferry landing to the cell block. Most people spend two to three hours on the island. You need only reserve for the outbound ferry; take any ferry back.

➡ There's no food (just water) but you can bring your own; picnicking is allowed at the ferry dock only. Dress in layers as weather changes fast and it's usually windy.

Historic Signs & Graffiti
During their 1969–71 occupation, Native Americans graffitied the water tower: 'Home of the Free Indian Land.' Above the cellhouse door, examine the eagle-and-flag crest to see how the red-and-white stripes were changed to spell 'Free.'

Warden's House
Fires destroyed the warden's house and other structures during the Indian Occupation. The government blamed the Native Americans; the Native Americans blamed agents provocateurs acting on behalf of the Nixon Administration to undermine public sympathy.

Parade Grounds

Officer's Row Gardens
In the 19th century soldiers imported topsoil to beautify the island with gardens. Well-trusted prisoners later gardened – Elliott Michener said it kept him sane. Historians, ornithologists and archaeologists choose today's plants.

Main Cellhouse

During the mid-20th century, the maximum-security prison housed the day's most notorious troublemakers, including Al Capone and Robert Stroud, the 'Birdman of Alcatraz' (who actually conducted his ornithology studies at Leavenworth).

View of Golden Gate Bridge

The Golden Gate Bridge stretches wide on the horizon. Best views are from atop the island at Eagle Plaza, near the cellhouse entrance, and at water level along the Agave Trail (September to January only).

Power House

Recreation Yard

Water Tower

Officers' Club

Guardhouse

Alcatraz' oldest building dates to 1857 and retains remnants of the original drawbridge and moat. During the Civil War the basement was transformed into a military dungeon – the genesis of Alcatraz as prison.

Lighthouse

Guard Tower

Frank Morris Cell

Peer into cell 138 on B-Block to see a recreation of the dummy's head that Frank Morris left in his bed as a decoy to aid his notorious – and successful – 1962 escape from Alcatraz.

Ferry Dock & Pier

A giant wall map helps you get your bearings. Inside nearby Bldg 64, short films and exhibits provide historical perspective on the prison and details about the Indian Occupation.

DON'T MISS

ALCATRAZ

For more than 150 years, the name **Alcatraz** (Map p302; ☑ Alcatraz Cruises 415-981-7625; www.nps.gov/alcatraz; tours adult/child 5-11yr day $37.25/23, night $44.25/26.50; ☺ call center 8am-7pm, ferries depart Pier 33 half-hourly 8:45am-3:50pm, night tours 5:55pm & 6:30pm; ♿) has given the innocent chills and the guilty cold sweats. Over the decades, it's been the nation's first military prison, a forbidding maximum-security penitentiary and disputed territory between Native American activists and the FBI. No wonder that first step you take onto 'the Rock' seems to cue ominous music: dunh-dunh-dunnnnh!

Today, first-person accounts of daily life in the Alcatraz lockup are included on the award-winning audio tour provided by **Alcatraz Cruises** (Map p304; ☑ 415-981-7625; www.alcatrazcruises.com; tours day adult/child/family $37.25/23/112.75, night adult/child $44.25/26.50; Ⓜ E, F). But take your headphones off for just a moment and notice the sound of carefree city life traveling across the water: this is the torment that made perilous escapes into riptides worth the risk. Though Alcatraz was considered escape-proof, in 1962 the Anglin brothers and Frank Morris floated away on a makeshift raft and were never seen again. Security and upkeep proved prohibitively expensive, and finally the island prison was abandoned to the birds in 1963.

☺ Jun) and goes out in style over the last weekend with Saturday's **Dyke March** (www.thedykemarch.org) to the Castro's Pink Party and the joyous, million-strong **Pride Parade** (www.sfpride.org; ☺ last Sun Jun) on Sunday.

Hardly Strictly Bluegrass   MUSIC
(www.hardlystrictlybluegrass.com; ☺ Oct) The West goes wild for free bluegrass at Golden Gate Park, with three days of concerts by 100-plus bands and seven stages of headliners.

🛏 Sleeping

Although hostels and budget hotels are cheapest, rooms are never truly cheap in SF: expect to pay $100 for a private hostel room, $200 at a budget motel and over $300 at midrange hotels. Note the hefty 15% room tax on top of quoted rates.

🛏 Embarcadero, SoMa, Union Square & Civic Center

HI San Francisco City Center   HOSTEL $
(Map p304; ☑ 415-474-5721; www.sfhostels.org; 685 Ellis St; dm $33-52, r $90-155; @ 🛜; 🚌 19, 38, 47, 49) The seven-story, 1920s Atherton Hotel was recently remodeled into a better-than-average hostel, with private baths in all rooms. All-you-can-eat pancakes or eggs cost $1 and there's an on-site bar – though dive bars and bargain eats are the main selling point of this location.

★ Axiom   BOUTIQUE HOTEL $$
(Map p304; ☑ 415-392-9466; www.axiomhotel. com; 28 Cyril Magnin St; d $189-342; @ 🛜 ☒;

🚋 Powell-Mason, Powell-Hyde, Ⓑ Powell, Ⓜ Powell) Of all the downtown SF hotels aiming for high-tech appeal, this one gets it right. The lobby is razzle-dazzle LED, marble and riveted steel, but the game room looks like a start-up HQ, with arcade games and foosball. Guest rooms have king platform beds, dedicated routers for high-speed wireless streaming to Apple/Google/Samsung devices, and Bluetooth-enabled everything.

★ Marker   BOUTIQUE HOTEL $$
(Map p304; ☑ 844-736-2753, 415-292-0100; http://themarkersanfrancisco.com; 501 Geary St; r from $209; ❀ @ 🛜 ☒; 🚌 38, 🚋 Powell-Hyde, Powell-Mason) 🍃 Snazzy Marker gets details right, with guest-room decor in bold colors – lipstick-red lacquer, navy-blue velvet and shiny purple silk – and thoughtful amenities like high-thread-count sheets, ergonomic workspaces, digital-library access, multiple electrical outlets and ample space in drawers, closets and bathroom vanities. Extras include a spa with a Jacuzzi, a small gym, evening wine reception and bragging rights to stylish downtown digs.

★ Palace Hotel   HOTEL $$$
(Map p304; ☑ 415-512-1111; www.sfpalace.com; 2 New Montgomery St; r from $300; ❀ @ 🛜 ☒; Ⓜ Montgomery, Ⓑ Montgomery) The 1906 landmark Palace remains a monument to turn-of-the-century grandeur, with 100-year-old Austrian-crystal chandeliers and Maxfield Parrish paintings. Cushy (if staid) accommodations cater to expense-account travelers, but prices drop at weekends. Even if you're not staying

here, visit the opulent Garden Court to sip tea beneath a glass ceiling. There's also a spa; kids love the big pool.

North Beach

Pacific Tradewinds Hostel
HOSTEL $

(Map p304; 415-433-7970; www.san-francis co-hostel.com; 680 Sacramento St; dm $35-45; front desk 8am–midnight; @; 1, California, Montgomery) San Francisco's smartest all-dorm hostel has a blue-and-white nautical theme, a fully equipped kitchen (free peanut butter and jelly sandwiches all day!), spotless glass-brick showers, a laundry (free sock wash!), luggage storage and no lockout time. Bunks are bolted to the wall, so there's no bed-shaking when bunkmates roll. No elevator means hauling bags up three flights – but it's worth it. Great service; fun staff.

San Remo Hotel
HOTEL $

(Map p304; 800-352-7366, 415-776-8688; www. sanremohotel.com; 2237 Mason St; r without bath $119-159; @; 30, 47, Powell-Mason) One of the city's best-value stays, the San Remo was built in 1906, right after the Great Earthquake. More than a century later, this upstanding North Beach boarding house still offers Italian *nonna* (grandma)-styled rooms with mismatched turn-of-the-century furnishings and shared bathrooms. The least expensive rooms have windows onto the corridor, not outdoors. Family suites accommodate up to five. No elevator.

★ Hotel Bohème
BOUTIQUE HOTEL $$

(Map p304; 415-433-9111; www.hotelboheme. com; 444 Columbus Ave; r $235–295; @;

10, 12, 30, 41, 45) Eclectic, historic and unabashedly poetic, this quintessential North Beach boutique hotel has jazz-era color schemes, pagoda-print upholstery and photos from the Beat years on the walls. The vintage rooms are smallish, some face noisy Columbus Ave (quieter rooms are in back) and bathrooms are teensy, but novels beg to be written here – especially after bar crawls.

Fisherman's Wharf, the Marina & Presidio

★ HI San Francisco Fisherman's Wharf
HOSTEL $

(Map p304; 415-771-7277; www.sfhostels.com; Fort Mason, Bldg 240; dm $30-53, r $116-134; @; 28, 30, 47, 49) Trading downtown convenience for a glorious park-like setting with million-dollar waterfront views, this hostel occupies a former army-hospital building, with bargain-priced private rooms and dorms (some co-ed) with four to 22 beds (avoid bunks one and two – they're by doorways). Huge kitchen. No curfew, but no heat during daytime: bring warm clothes. Limited free parking.

★ Inn at the Presidio
HOTEL $$

(Map p302; 415-800-7356; www.innatthepresid io.com; 42 Moraga Ave; r $295-380; @; 43, PresidiGo Shuttle) Built in 1903 as bachelor quarters for army officers, this three-story, redbrick building in the Presidio was transformed in 2012 into a spiffy national-park lodge, styled with leather, linen and wood. Oversized rooms are plush, including feather beds with Egyptian-cotton sheets. Suites have gas fireplaces. Nature surrounds

---

SAN FRANCISCO FOR CHILDREN

Although it has almost the fewest children per capita of any US city – there are more canines than kids in town – San Francisco is packed with family-friendly attractions, including the **California Academy of Sciences** (Map p310; 415-379-8000; www.calacademy. org; 55 Music Concourse Dr; adult/student/child $35/30/25; 9:30am-5pm Mon-Sat, from 11am Sun; ; 5, 6, 7, 21, 31, 33, 44, N) in Golden Gate Park and the waterfront **Exploratorium** (p299), **Crissy Field** (p306), **Musée Mécanique** (p307) and **Pier 39** (Map p304; 415-705-5500; www.pier39.com; cnr Beach St & the Embarcadero; ; 47, Powell-Mason, E, F), with its barking sea lions and hand-painted Italian carousel.

The **Children's Creativity Museum** (Map p304; 415-820-3320; http://creativity. org/; 221 4th St; $12; 10am-4pm Wed-Sun; ; 14, Powell, Powell) in SoMa has technology that's too cool for school: robots, live-action video games and 3D animation workshops. At the **Aquarium of the Bay** (Map p304; 415-623-5300; www.aquariumofthebay. org; Pier 39; adult/child/family $24.95/14.95/70; 9am-8pm late May-early Sep, shorter hours low season; ; 49, Powell-Mason, E, F) on Pier 39, wander through underwater glass tubes as sharks circle overhead, then let tots gently touch tide-pool critters.

you, with hiking trailheads out back, but taxis downtown cost $25. Free parking.

🛏 The Mission & the Castro

Inn San Francisco
B&B $$

(Map p308; ☑ 415-641-0188, 800-359-0913; www.innsf.com; 943 S Van Ness Ave; r $195-255, without bath $165-225, cottages $365-475; ▣⊖@◈⊛; ▣14, 49) 🖉 An elegant 1872 Italianate-Victorian mansion has become a stately Mission District inn, impeccably maintained and packed with antiques. All rooms have fresh-cut flowers and sumptuous mattresses with feather beds; some have Jacuzzis. Outside there's an English garden and a redwood hot tub open 24 hours – a rarity in SF. Limited parking; reserve. No elevator.

★ Parker Guest House
B&B $$

(Map p308; ☑ 888-520-7275, 415-621-3222; www.parkerguesthouse.com; 520 Church St; r $219-279, without bath $179-99; @◈; ▣33, Ⓜ J) The Castro's stateliest gay digs occupy two side-by-side Edwardian mansions. Details are elegant and formal, never froufrou. Rooms feel like they belong more to a swanky hotel than to a B&B, with super-comfortable beds and down duvets. The garden is ideal for a lovers' tryst – as is the steam room. No elevator.

🛏 The Haight

Metro Hotel
HOTEL $

(Map p302; ☑ 415-861-5364; www.metrohotelsf.com; 319 Divisadero St; r $107; @◈; ▣6, 24, 71) The Metro Hotel has a prime position – some rooms overlook the garden patio of top-notch Ragazza Pizzeria. Rooms are cheap and clean, if bland – if possible, get the one with the SF mural. Some have two double beds. The hotel's handy to the Haight and has 24-hour reception; no elevator.

★ Chateau Tivoli
B&B $$

(Map p304; ☑ 800-228-1647, 415-776-5462; www.chateautivoli.com; 1057 Steiner St; r $195-300, without bath $150-200; ◈; ▣5, 22) The source of neighborhood gossip since 1892, this gilded and turreted mansion once hosted Isadora Duncan, Mark Twain and (rumor has it) the ghost of a Victorian opera diva – and now you too can be Chateau Tivoli's guest. Nine antique-filled rooms and suites set the scene for romance; most have claw-foot bathtubs, though two share a bathroom. No elevator; no TVs.

✗ Eating

✗ Embarcadero & SoMa

★ Ferry Plaza Farmers Market
MARKET $

(Map p304; ☑ 415-291-3276; www.cuesa.org; cnr Market St & the Embarcadero; street food $3-12; ⊙10am-2pm Tue & Thu, from 8am Sat; 🖉🍴; ▣2, 6, 9, 14, 21, 31, Ⓜ Embarcadero, Ⓑ Embarcadero) 🖉 The pride and joy of SF foodies, the Ferry Building market showcases 50 to 100 prime purveyors of California-grown organic produce, pasture-raised meats and gourmet prepared foods at accessible prices. On Saturdays, join top chefs early for prime browsing, and stay for eclectic bayside picnics of Namu Korean tacos, RoliRoti porchetta, Dirty Girl tomatoes, Nicasio cheese samples, and Frog Hollow fruit turnovers.

★ In Situ
CALIFORNIAN, INTERNATIONAL $$

(Map p304; ☑ 415-941-6050; http://insitu.sfmoma.org; SFMOMA, 151 3rd St; mains $14-34; ⊙11am-3:30pm Mon & Tue, 11am-3:30pm & 5-9pm Thu-Sun; ▣5, 6, 7, 14, 19, 21, 31, 38, Ⓑ Montgomery, Ⓜ Montgomery) The landmark gallery of modern cuisine attached to SFMOMA also showcases avant-garde masterpieces – but these ones you'll lick clean. Chef Corey Lee collaborates with star chefs worldwide, scrupulously recreating their signature dishes with California-grown ingredients so that you can enjoy Harald Wohlfahrt's impeccable anise-marinated salmon, Hiroshi Sasaki's decadent chicken thighs and Albert Adrià's gravity-defying cocoa-bubble cake in one unforgettable sitting.

★ Benu
CALIFORNIAN, FUSION $$$

(Map p304; ☑ 415-685-4860; www.benusf.com; 22 Hawthorne St; tasting menu $285; ⊙6-9pm seatings Tue-Sat; ▣10, 12, 14, 30, 45) SF has pioneered Asian fusion cuisine for 150 years, but the pan-Pacific innovation chef-owner Corey Lee brings to the plate is gasp-inducing: foie-gras soup dumplings – what?! Dungeness crab and truffle custard pack such outsize flavor into Lee's faux–shark's fin soup, you'll swear Jaws is in there. A Benu dinner is an investment, but don't miss star sommelier Yoon Ha's ingenious pairings ($185).

✗ Union Square, Civic Center & Hayes Valley

★ Tout Sweet
BAKERY $

(Map p304; ☑ 415-385-1679; www.toutsweetsf.com; Macy's, 3rd fl, cnr Geary & Stockton Sts; baked goods $2-8; ⊘ 11am-6pm Sun-Wed, to 8pm Thu-Sat; 🛜🚻; 🚌 2, 38, 🚋 Powell-Mason, Powell-Hyde, Ⓑ Powell) Mango with Thai chili or peanut butter and jelly? Choosing your favorite California-French macaron isn't easy at Tout Sweet, where *Top Chef Just Desserts* champion Yigit Pura keeps outdoing his own inventions – he's like the love child of Julia Child and Steve Jobs. Chef Pura's sweet retreat on Macy's 3rd floor offers unbeatable views overlooking Union Sq, excellent teas and free wi-fi.

★ Rich Table   CALIFORNIAN $$

(Map p304; ☑ 415-355-9085; http://richtablesf. com; 199 Gough St; mains $17-36; ⊘ 5:30-10pm Sun-Thu, to 10:30pm Fri & Sat; 🚌 5, 6, 7, 21, 47, 49, Ⓜ Van Ness) 🥢 Impossible cravings begin at Rich Table, inventor of porcini doughnuts, miso-marrow-stuffed pasta and fried-chicken madeleines with caviar. Married co-chefs and owners Sarah and Evan Rich playfully riff on seasonal California fare, freestyling with whimsical off-menu amuse-bouches like trippy beet marshmallows or the Dirty Hippie: nutty hemp atop silky goat-buttermilk *pannacotta*, as offbeat and entrancing as Hippie Hill drum circles.

★ Cala   MEXICAN, CALIFORNIAN $$$

(Map p304; ☑ 415-660-7701; www.calarestaurant. com; 149 Fell St; ⊘ 5-10pm Mon-Wed, to 11pm Thu-Sat, 11am-3pm Sun, taco bar 11am-2pm Mon-Fri; 🚌 6, 7, 21, 47, 49, Ⓜ Van Ness) Like discovering a long-lost twin, Cala's Mexico Norte cuisine is a revelation. San Francisco's Mexican-rancher roots are deeply honored here: silky bone-marrow salsa and fragrant heritage-corn tortillas grace a sweet potato slow-cooked in ashes. Brace yourself with mezcal margaritas for the ultimate California surf and turf: sea urchin with beef tongue. Original and unforgettable, even before Mayan-chocolate gelato with amaranth brittle.

✖ Chinatown & North Beach

★ Liguria Bakery   BAKERY $

(Map p304; ☑ 415-421-3786; 1700 Stockton St; focaccia $4-6; ⊘ 8am-1pm Tue-Fri, from 7am Sat; 🥢🚻; 🚌 8, 30, 39, 41, 45, 🚋 Powell-Mason) Bleary-eyed art students and Italian grandmothers are in line by 8am for cinnamon-raisin focaccia hot out of the 100-year-old oven, leaving 9am dawdlers a choice of tomato or classic rosemary and garlic, and 11am stragglers out of luck. Take yours in waxed paper or boxed

COIT TOWER

The exclamation mark on San Francisco's skyline is **Coit Tower** (Map p304; ☑ 415-249-0995; www.sfrecpark.org; Telegraph Hill Blvd; nonresident elevator fee adult/child $8/5; ⊘ 10am-6pm Apr-Oct, to 5pm Nov-Mar; 🚌 39), with 360-degree views of downtown and wraparound 1930s Works Progress Administration (WPA) murals glorifying SF workers. Initially denounced as communist, the murals are now a national landmark. For a wild-parrot's panoramic view of San Francisco 210ft above the city, take the elevator to the tower's open-air platform. To glimpse seven recently restored murals up a hidden stairwell on the 2nd floor, join the 11am tour Wednesday or Saturday (free; donations welcome).

for picnics – but don't kid yourself that you're going to save some for later. Cash only.

★ Molinari   DELI $

(Map p304; ☑ 415-421-2337; www.molinarisalame. com; 373 Columbus Ave; sandwiches $10-13.50; ⊘ 9am-6pm Mon-Fri, to 5:30pm Sat; 🚌 8, 10, 12, 30, 39, 41, 45, 🚋 Powell-Mason) Observe quasi-religious North Beach noontime rituals: enter Molinari, and grab a number and a crusty roll. When your number's called, wisecracking staff pile your roll with heavenly fixings: milky buffalo mozzarella, tangy sun-dried tomatoes, translucent sheets of prosciutto di Parma, slabs of legendary house-cured salami, drizzles of olive oil and balsamic. Enjoy hot from the panini press at sidewalk tables.

★ Mister Jiu's   CHINESE $$

(Map p304; ☑ 415-857-9688; http://misterjius. com; 28 Waverly Pl; mains $14-45; ⊘ 5:30-10:30pm Tue-Sat; 🚌 30, 🚋 California) Ever since the gold rush, San Francisco has craved Chinese food, powerful cocktails and hyperlocal specialties – and Mister Jiu's satisfies on all counts. Build your own banquet of Chinese classics with California twists: chanterelle chow mein, Dungeness-crab rice noodles, quail and Mission-fig sticky rice. Cocktail pairings are equally inspired – try jasmine-infused-gin Happiness ($13) with tea-smoked Sonoma-duck confit.

★ Z & Y   CHINESE $$

(Map p304; ☑ 415-981-8988; www.zandyrestau rant.com; 655 Jackson St; mains $9-20;

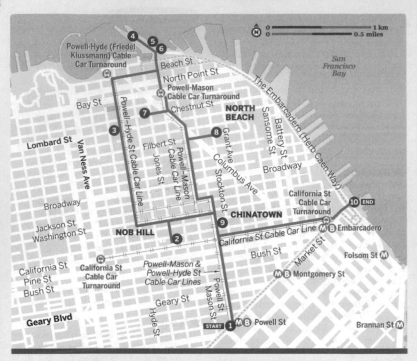

City Walk
SF by Cable Car

START POWELL ST CABLE CAR TURNAROUND
END FERRY BUILDING
LENGTH 2 MILES; 2 HOURS WITH STOPS

At the **❶Powell St Cable Car Turnaround** (p300), you'll see operators turn the car atop a revolving wooden platform and a vintage kiosk where you can buy an all-day Muni Passport for $21, instead of paying $7 per ride. Board the red-signed Powell-Hyde cable car and begin your 338ft ascent of Nob Hill.

As your cable car lurches uphill, you can imagine horses struggling up this slippery crag. Nineteenth-century city planners were skeptical of inventor Andrew Hallidie's 'wire-rope railway' – but Hallidie's cable cars even survived the 1906 earthquake and fire that destroyed 'Snob Hill' mansions, returning the faithful to the rebuilt **❷Grace Cathedral** – hop off to say hello to SF's gentle patron, St Francis.

Back on the Powell-Hyde car, enjoy Bay views as you careen past crooked, flower-lined **❸Lombard Street** (p303) toward **❹Fisherman's Wharf**. The waterfront terminus is named for Friedel Klussmann, who saved cable cars from mayoral modernization plans in 1947. She did the math: cable cars brought in more tourism dollars than they cost in upkeep. For her funeral in 1986, cable cars citywide were draped in black.

At the wharf, emerge from the submarine **❺USS Pampanito** to glimpse SF as sailors used to. Witness Western saloon brawls in vintage arcade games at the **❻Musée Mécanique** (p307) before hitching the Powell-Mason cable car to North Beach.

Hop off to see Diego Rivera's 1934 cityscape at the **❼San Francisco Art Institute**, or follow your rumbling stomach directly to **❽Liguria Bakery** (p317). Stroll through North Beach and Chinatown alleyways, or take the Powell-Mason line to time-travel through the **❾Chinese Historical Society of America** (p303). Nearby, catch a ride on the city's oldest line: the California St cable car. The terminus is near the **❿Ferry Building** (p299), where champagne-and-oyster happy hour awaits.

⊙11am-9:30pm Sun-Thu, to 11pm Fri & Sat; 🚌8, 10, 12, 30, 45, 🚋Powell-Mason, Powell-Hyde) Graduate from ho-hum sweet-and-sour and middling *mu-shu* to sensational Szechuan dishes that go down in a blaze of glory. Warm up with spicy pork dumplings and heat-blistered string beans, take on the housemade *tantan* noodles with peanut-chili sauce, and leave lips buzzing with fish poached in flaming chili oil and buried under red Szechuan chili peppers. Go early; worth the inevitable wait.

✕ Fisherman's Wharf, the Marina & Presidio

★ Off the Grid   FOOD TRUCK $

(Map p304; www.offthegridsf.com; Fort Mason Center, 2 Marina Blvd; items $6-14; ⊙5-10pm Fri Apr-Oct; 👶; 🚌22, 28) Spring through fall, some 30 food trucks circle their wagons at SF's largest mobile-gourmet hootenannies on Friday night at Fort Mason Center, and 11am to 4pm Sunday for **Picnic at the Presidio** on the Main Post lawn. Arrive early for the best selection and to minimize waits. Cash only.

Fisherman's Wharf Crab Stands   SEAFOOD $

(Map p304; Taylor St; mains $5-15; 🚋F) Brawny men stir steaming cauldrons of Dungeness crab at several side-by-side takeout crab stands at the foot of Taylor St, the epicenter of Fisherman's Wharf. Crab season typically runs winter through spring, but you'll find shrimp and other seafood year-round.

★ Greens   VEGETARIAN, CALIFORNIAN $$

(Map p304; ☑415-771-6222; www.greensrestaurant. com; Fort Mason Center, 2 Marina Blvd, Bldg A; mains lunch $16-19, dinner $20-28; ⊙11:45am-2:30pm & 5:30-9pm; 🚗👶; 🚌22, 28, 30, 43, 47, 49) 🍽 Career carnivores won't realize there's zero meat in the hearty black-bean chili, or in Greens' other flavor-packed vegetarian dishes, made using ingredients from a Zen farm in Marin. And, oh, what views! The Golden Gate rises just outside the window-lined dining room. The on-site cafe serves to-go lunches, but for sit-down meals, including Sunday brunch, reservations are essential.

★ A16   ITALIAN $$$

(Map p302; ☑415-771-2216; www.a16pizza.com; 2355 Chestnut St; pizzas $18-21, mains $22-36; ⊙lunch 11:30am-2:30pm Wed-Sun, dinner 5:30-10pm Mon-Thu, 5-11pm Fri & Sat, 5-10pm Sun; 🚌28, 30, 43) Even before A16 won a James Beard Award, it was hard to book, but persevere:

the housemade mozzarella *burrata*, blister-crusted pizzas from the wood-burning oven and 12-page Italian wine list make it worth your while. Skip the spotty desserts and instead double up on adventurous appetizers, including house-cured *salumi* platters and delectable marinated tuna.

✕ The Mission & the Castro

★ La Taqueria   MEXICAN $

(Map p308; ☑415-285-7117; 2889 Mission St; items $3-11; ⊙11am-9pm Mon-Sat, to 8pm Sun; 👶; 🚌12, 14, 48, 49, 🅱24th St Mission) SF's definitive burrito has no saffron rice, spinach tortilla or mango salsa – just perfectly grilled meats, slow-cooked beans and tomatillo or mesquite salsa wrapped in a flour tortilla. They're purists at James Beard Award–winning La Taqueria. You'll pay extra to go without beans, because they add more meat – but spicy pickles and *crema* (sour cream) bring burrito bliss. Worth the wait, always.

★ Craftsman & Wolves   BAKERY, CALIFORNIAN $

(Map p308; ☑415-913-7713; http://crafts man-wolves.com; 746 Valencia St; pastries $3-8; ⊙7am-6pm Mon-Fri, from 8am Sat & Sun; 🚌14, 22, 33, 49, 🅱16th St Mission, 🚋J) Breakfast routines are made to be broken by the infamous Rebel Within: a sausage-spiked Asiago-cheese muffin with a silken soft-boiled egg baked inside. SF's surest pick-me-up is a Highwire macchiato with *matcha* (green tea) cookies; a Thai coconut-curry scone enjoyed with pea soup and rosé is lunch perfected. Exquisite hazelnut cube-cakes and vanilla-violet cheesecakes are ideal for celebrating unbirthdays and imaginary holidays.

★ Ichi Sushi   SUSHI $$

(Map p302; ☑415-525-4750; www.ichisushi.com; 3369 Mission St; sushi $4-8; ⊙11:30am-2pm & 5:30-10pm Mon-Thu, to 11pm Fri & Sat, 5:30-9:30pm Sun; 🚌14, 24, 49, 🅱24th St Mission, 🚋J) 🍽 Alluring on the plate and positively obscene on the tongue, Ichi Sushi is a sharp cut above other seafood joints. Chef Tim Archuleta slices silky, sustainably sourced fish with a jeweler's precision, balances it atop well-packed rice, and tops it with tiny but powerfully tangy dabs of gelled *yuzu* and microscopically cut spring onion and chili daikon that make soy sauce unthinkable.

★ Al's Place   CALIFORNIAN $$

(Map p308; ☑415-416-6136; www.alsplacesf.com; 1499 Valencia St; share plates $15-19; ⊙5:30-10pm

Wed-Sun; ✐; ⌂ 12, 14, 49, Ⓜ J, Ⓑ 24th St Mission)
✐ The Golden State dazzles on Al's plates, featuring homegrown heirloom ingredients, pristine Pacific seafood, and grass-fed meat on the side. Painstaking preparation yields sun-drenched flavors and exquisite textures: crispy-skin cod with frothy preserved-lime dip, grilled peach melting into velvety foie gras. Dishes are half the size but thrice the flavor of mains elsewhere – get two or three, and you'll be California dreaming.

Commonwealth　　　　CALIFORNIAN **$$$**
(Map p308; ✐415-355-1500; www.commonwealthsf.com; 2224 Mission St; small plates $15-22; ⊙5:30-10pm Sun-Thu, to 11pm Fri & Sat; ✐; ⌂14, 22, 33, 49, Ⓑ16th St Mission) Wildly imaginative farm-to-table dining where you'd least expect it: in a converted cinder-block Mission dive. Chef Jason Fox serves adventurous dishes like *uni* and bone-marrow cream with nasturtiums, and lamb with beets and seaweed. Try the six-course tasting menu ($80) knowing that a portion benefits local charities.

✖ The Haight & Fillmore

Rosamunde Sausage Grill　　FAST FOOD **$**
(Map p304; ✐415-437-6851; http://rosamunde sausagegrill.com; 545 Haight St; sausages $8-8.50; ⊙11:30am-10pm Sun-Wed, to 11pm Thu-Sat; ⌂6, 7, 22, Ⓜ N) Impress a dinner date on the cheap: load up Coleman Farms pork Brats or free-range duck links with complimentary roasted peppers, grilled onions, whole-grain mustard and mango chutney, and enjoy with your choice of 45 seasonal draft brews at Toronado (p322) next door. To impress a local lunch date, call ahead or line up by 11:30am Tuesday for massive $6 burgers.

★ Jardinière　　　　　CALIFORNIAN **$$**
(Map p304; ✐415-861-5555; www.jardiniere.com; 300 Grove St; mains $20-36; ⊙5-9pm Sun-Thu, to 10:30pm Fri & Sat; ⌂5, 21, 47, 49, Ⓜ Van Ness) ✐ *Iron Chef* winner, *Top Chef Masters* finalist and James Beard Award–winner Traci Des Jardins champions sustainable, salacious California cuisine. She has a way with California's organic produce, sustainable meats and seafood, slathering sturgeon with buttery chanterelles and lavishing root vegetables with truffles and honey from Jardinière's rooftop hives. Mondays bring $55 three-course dinners with wine pairings.

✖ Golden Gate Park & Around

Burma Superstar　　　　　BURMESE **$$**
(Map p310; ✐415-387-2147; www.burmasuperstar.com; 309 Clement St; mains $11-28; ⊙11:30am-3:30pm & 5-9:30pm Sun-Thu, to 10pm Fri & Sat; ✐; ⌂1, 2, 33, 38, 44) Yes, there's a wait, but do you see anyone walking away? Blame it on fragrant *moh hinga* (catfish curry), tangy vegetarian *samusa* soup, and traditional Burmese green-tea salads tarted up with lime and fried garlic. Reservations aren't accepted – ask the host to call you so you can browse Burmese cookbooks at **Green Apple Books** (Map p310; ✐415-742-5833; www.greenapplebooks.com; 506 Clement St; ⊙10am-10:30pm; ⌂2, 38, 44) while you wait.

★ Outerlands　　　　　CALIFORNIAN **$$**
(Map p302; ✐415-661-6140; www.outerlandssf.com; 4001 Judah St; sandwiches & small plates $8-14, mains $15-27; ⊙9am-3pm & 5-10pm; ✐⊛; ⌂18, Ⓜ N) ✐ When windy Ocean Beach leaves you feeling shipwrecked, drift into this beach-shack bistro for organic Californian comfort food. Brunch demands Dutch pancakes in iron skillets with housemade ricotta, lunch brings cast-iron-grilled artisan cheese on house-baked levain bread with citrusy Steely Dan–themed beach cocktails; and dinner means creative coastal fare like hazelnut-dusted California salmon with black-eyed peas. Reserve.

♟ Drinking & Nightlife

For a pub crawl, start with North Beach saloons or Mission bars around Valencia and 16th Sts. The Castro has historic gay bars; SoMa adds dance clubs. Downtown and around Union Square mix dives with speakeasies. Haight bars draw mixed alternacrowds.

★ Bar Agricole　　　　　　　BAR
(Map p304; ✐415-355-9400; www.baragricole.com; 355 11th St; ⊙5-11pm Mon-Thu, 5pm-12am Fri & Sat, 10am-2pm & 6-9pm Sun; ⌂9, 12, 27, 47) ✐ Drink your way to a history degree with well-researched cocktails: Whiz Bang with house bitters, whiskey, vermouth and absinthe scores high, but El Presidente with white rum, farmhouse curaçao and California-pomegranate grenadine takes top honors. This overachiever wins James Beard Award nods for spirits and eco-savvy design, plus popular acclaim for $1 oysters and $5 aperitifs during happy hour (5pm to 6pm, Monday to Sunday).

LGBTIQ SF

Doesn't matter where you're from, who you love or who your daddy is: if you're here, and queer, welcome home. The Castro is the heart of the gay cruising scene, but South of Market (SoMa) has leather bars and thump-thump clubs. The Mission is the preferred 'hood for many women and has a diverse transgender community.

Bay Area Reporter (aka BAR; www.ebar.com) covers community news and listings. *San Francisco Bay Times* (www.sfbaytimes.com) focuses on LGBTIQ perspectives and events. Free *Gloss Magazine* (www.glossmagazine.net) locks down nightlife.

Over 1.5 million people come out for **SF Pride** (p311) parades and parties in late June. For weekly roving dance parties, check **Honey Soundsystem** (http://hnysndsystm.tumblr.com).

Blackbird (Map p308; ☑415-503-0630; www.blackbirdbar.com; 2124 Market St; �9 3pm-2am Mon-Fri, from 2pm Sat & Sun; MChurch St) Castro's first-choice lounge offers craft cocktails, billiards and everyone's favorite: a photo booth.

HiTops (Map p308; http://hitopssf.com; 2247 Market St; �9 11:30am-midnight Mon-Wed, to 2am Thu & Fri, 10am-2am Sat & Sun; MCastro St) Castro's prime-time sports bar for friendly guys, big-screen TVs, shuffleboard and pub grub.

Cafe Flore (Map p308; ☑415-621-8579; www.cafeflore.com; 2298 Market St; �9 10am-10pm Mon-Fri, 9am-10pm Sat & Sun; ☎; MCastro St) You haven't done the Castro till you've lolly-gagged on the sundrenched patio here.

Stud (Map p304; www.studsf.com; 399 9th St; $5-8; �9 noon-2am Tue, 5pm-3am Thu-Sat, 5pm-midnight Sun; ☐12, 19, 27, 47) Rocking SoMa's gay scene since 1966. Anything goes here, especially on 'Club Some Thing' Fridays.

Oasis (Map p304; ☑415-795-3180; www.sfoasis.com; 298 11th St; tickets $15-35; ☐9, 12, 14, 47, MVan Ness) SoMa drag shows so fearless and funny, you'll laugh till it hurts. Afterwards, shake it on the dance floor.

EndUp (Map p304; ☑415-646-0999; www.facebook.com/theendup; 401 6th St; $10-25; �9 11pm Fri-8am Sat, 10pm Sat-4am Mon; ☐12, 19, 27, 47) A mixed gay/straight crowd and marathon dance parties that don't end with sunrise over the 101 freeway ramp.

Aunt Charlie's Lounge (Map p304; ☑415-441-2922; www.auntcharlieslounge.com; 133 Turk St; free-$5; �9 noon-2am Mon-Fri, from 10am Sat, 10am-midnight Sun; ☐27, 31, MPowell, ⒷPowell) Tenderloin drag dive bar for fabulously seedy glamour and a vintage pulp fiction vibe.

★**Caffe Trieste**   CAFE
(Map p304; ☑415-392-6739; www.caffetrieste.com; 601 Vallejo St; �9 6:30am-10pm Sun-Thu, to 11pm Fri & Sat; ☎; ☐8, 10, 12, 30, 41, 45) Poetry on bathroom walls, opera on the jukebox, live accordion jams and sightings of Beat poet-laureate Lawrence Ferlinghetti: this is North Beach at its best, since the 1950s. Linger over espresso and scribble your screenplay under the Sardinian fishing mural just as young Francis Ford Coppola did. Perhaps you've heard of the movie: *The Godfather*. Cash only.

★**Comstock Saloon**   BAR
(Map p304; ☑415-617-0071; www.comstocksaloon.com; 155 Columbus Ave; �9 4pm-midnight Sun-Mon, to 2am Tue-Thu & Sat, noon-2am Fri; ☐8, 10, 12, 30, 45, ☐Powell-Mason) Relieving yourself in the marble trough below the bar is no longer advisable – Emperor Norton is watching from above – but otherwise this 1907 Victorian saloon brings back the Barbary Coast's glory days with authentic pisco punch and martini-precursor Martinez (gin, vermouth, bitters, maraschino liqueur). Reserve booths or back-parlor seating to hear on nights when ragtime-jazz bands play.

★**El Rio**   CLUB
(Map p308; ☑415-282-3325; www.elriosf.com; 3158 Mission St; cover free-$8; �9 1pm-2am; ☐12, 14, 27, 49, Ⓑ24th St Mission) Work it all out on the dance floor with SF's most down and funky crowd – the full rainbow spectrum of colorful characters is here to party. Calendar highlights include Salsa Sunday, free oysters from 5:30pm Friday, drag-star DJs, backyard bands and ping-pong. Expect knockout margaritas and shameless flirting on a patio that's seen it all since 1978. Cash only.

★ **%ABV** COCKTAIL BAR

(Map p308; ☑ 415-400-4748; www.abvsf.com; 3174 16th St; ☉2pm-2am; ☐14, 22, ☐16th St Mission, ⓂJ) As kindred spirits will deduce from the name (the abbreviation for 'percent alcohol by volume'), this bar is backed by cocktail crafters who know their Rittenhouse rye from their Japanese malt whisky. Top-notch hooch is served promptly and without pretension, including excellent Cali wine and beer on tap and original historically inspired cocktails.

★ **Vesuvio** BAR

(Map p304; ☑ 415-362-3370; www.vesuvio.com; 255 Columbus Ave; ☉8am-2am; ☐8, 10, 12, 30, 41, 45, ☐Powell-Mason) Guy walks into a bar, roars and leaves. Without missing a beat, the bartender says to the next customer, 'Welcome to Vesuvio, honey – what can I get you?' Jack Kerouac blew off Henry Miller to go on a bender here and, after you've joined neighborhood characters on the stained-glass mezzanine for microbrews or Kerouacs (rum, tequila and OJ), you'll see why.

★ **Smuggler's Cove** BAR

(Map p304; ☑ 415-869-1900; www.smugglerscovesf. com; 650 Gough St; ☉5pm-1:15am; ☐5, 21, 47, 49, ⓂCivic Center, ⒷCivic Center) Yo-ho-ho and a bottle of rum...wait, make that a Dead Reckoning (Nicaraguan rum, port, pineapple and bitters), unless you'll split the flaming Scorpion Bowl? Pirates are bedeviled by choice at this Barbary Coast-shipwreck tiki bar, hidden behind tinted-glass doors. With 550 rums and 70-plus cocktails gleaned from rum-running around the world – and $2 off 5pm to 6pm daily.

★ **Toronado** PUB

(Map p304; ☑ 415-863-2276; www.toronado.com; 547 Haight St; ☉11:30am-2am; ☐6, 7, 22, ⓂN) Glory hallelujah, beer-lovers: your prayers are answered. Genuflect before the chalkboard altar that lists 40-plus beers on tap and hundreds more bottled, including sensational microbrews. Bring cash for all-day happy hours and score sausages from Rosamunde (p320) to accompany ale made by Trappist monks. It sometimes gets too loud to hear your date talk, but you'll hear angels sing.

☆ **Entertainment**

At Union Square, **TIX Bay Area** (Map p304; http://tixbayarea.org; 350 Powell St; ☐Powell-Mason, Powell-Hyde, ⒷPowell, ⓂPowell) sells last minute theater tickets for half-price.

★ **San Francisco Symphony** CLASSICAL MUSIC

(Map p304; ☑ box office 415-864-6000, rush-ticket hotline 415-503-5577; www.sfsymphony.org; Grove St, btwn Franklin St & Van Ness Ave; tickets $20-150; ☐21, 45, 47, ⓂVan Ness, ⒷCivic Center) From the moment conductor Michael Tilson Thomas bounces up on his toes and raises his baton, the audience is on the edge of their seats for another thunderous performance by the Grammy-winning SF Symphony. Don't miss signature concerts of Beethoven and Mahler, live symphony performances with such films as *Star Trek*, and creative collaborations with artists from Elvis Costello to Metallica.

★ **SFJAZZ Center** JAZZ

(Map p304; ☑ 866-920-5299; www.sfjazz.org; 201 Franklin St; tickets $25-120; ⓐ; ☐5, 6, 7, 21, 47, 49, ⓂVan Ness) ⚑ Jazz legends and singular talents from Argentina to Yemen are showcased at North America's newest, largest jazz center. Hear fresh takes on classic jazz albums and poets riffing with jazz combos in the downstairs Joe Henderson Lab, and witness extraordinary main-stage collaborations ranging from Afro-Cuban All Stars to roots legends Emmylou Harris, Rosanne Cash and Lucinda Williams.

★ **San Francisco Opera** OPERA

(Map p304; ☑ 415-864-3330; www.sfopera.com; War Memorial Opera House, 301 Van Ness Ave; tickets $10-350; ☐21, 45, 47, 49, ⒷCivic Center, ⓂVan Ness) Opera was SF's gold-rush soundtrack – and SF Opera rivals the Met, with world premieres of original works ranging from Stephen King's *Dolores Claiborne* to *Girls of the Golden West*, filmmaker Peter Sellars' collaboration with composer John Adams. Expect haute couture costumes and radical sets by painter David Hockney. Score $10 same-day standing-room tickets at 10am; check website for Opera Lab pop-ups.

★ **Independent** LIVE MUSIC

(Map p302; ☑ 415-771-1421; www.theindependentsf. com; 628 Divisadero St; tickets $12-45; ☉box office 11am-6pm Mon-Fri, to 9:30pm show nights; ☐5, 6, 7, 21, 24) Bragging rights are earned with breakthrough shows at the small but mighty Independent, featuring indie dreamers (Magnetic Fields, Death Cab for Cutie), legends (Steel Pulse, Guided by Voices), alt-pop (the Killers, Imagine Dragons) and international bands (Tokyo Chaotic, Australia's Airbourne). Ventilation is poor in this max-capacity-800 venue, but the sound is stellar, drinks reasonable and bathrooms improbably clean.

⭐**American Conservatory Theater** THEATER
(ACT; Map p304; ☑415-749-2228; www.act-sf.
org; 405 Geary St; ☉box office 10am-6pm Mon, to
curtain Tue-Sun; ☐8, 30, 38, 45, ☐Powell-Mason,
Powell-Hyde, ☐Powell, ☐Powell) Breakthrough
shows launch at this turn-of-the-century
landmark, which has hosted ACT's productions of Tony Kushner's *Angels in America*
and Robert Wilson's *Black Rider*, with William S Burroughs' libretto and music by Tom
Waits. Major playwrights like Tom Stoppard,
Dustin Lance Black, Eve Ensler and David
Mamet premiere work here, while the ACT's
new **Strand Theater** (Map p304; ☑415-749-
2228; www.act-sf.org/home/box_office/strand.
html; 1127 Market St; ☐F, ☐Civic Center, ☐Civic
Center) stages experimental works.

San Francisco Ballet DANCE
(Map p304; ☑tickets 415-865-2000; www.sfballet.
org; War Memorial Opera House, 301 Van Ness Ave;
tickets $22-141; ☉ticket sales 10am-4pm Mon-Fri;
☐5, 21, 47, 49, ☐Van Ness, ☐Civic Center) The
USA's oldest ballet company is looking sharp
in more than 100 shows annually, from *The
Nutcracker* (the US premiere was here) to
modern originals. Performances are mostly
at the War Memorial Opera House from January to May, and occasionally at the Yerba
Buena Center for the Arts. Score $15-to-$20
same-day standing-room tickets at the box
office (from noon Tuesday to Friday, 10am
weekends).

⭐**Beach Blanket Babylon** CABARET
(BBB; Map p304; ☑415-421-4222; www.beach
blanketbabylon.com; 678 Green St; $25-130;
☉shows 8pm Wed, Thu & Fri, 6pm & 9pm Sat, 2pm
& 5pm Sun; ☐8, 30, 39, 41, 45, ☐Powell-Mason)
Snow White searches for Prince Charming
in San Francisco: what could possibly go
wrong? The Disney-spoof musical-comedy
cabaret has been running since 1974, but
topical jokes keep it outrageous as wigs
remain big and parade floats gasp-worthy.
Spectators must be over 21 to handle racy
humor, except at cleverly sanitized Sunday
matinees. Reservations essential; arrive one
hour early for best seats.

Fillmore Auditorium LIVE MUSIC
(Map p304; ☑415-346-6000; http://thefillmore.
com; 1805 Geary Blvd; tickets from $20; ☉box of-
fice 10am-3pm Sun, plus 30min before doors open
to 10pm show nights; ☐22, 38) Jimi Hendrix,
Janis Joplin, the Doors – they all played the
Fillmore. Now you might catch the Indigo
Girls, Willie Nelson or Tracy Chapman in the

historic 1250-capacity, standing-room-only
theater (if you're polite and lead with the
hip, you might squeeze up to the stage).
Don't miss the priceless collection of psychedelic posters in the upstairs gallery.

⭐**Great American Music Hall** LIVE MUSIC
(Map p304; ☑415-885-0750; www.gamh.com; 859
O'Farrell St; shows $20-45; ☉box office 10:30am-
6pm Mon-Fri & show nights; ☐; ☐19, 38, 47, 49)
Everyone busts out their best sets at this
opulent 1907 bordello turned all-ages venue – indie rockers like the Band Perry throw
down, international legends such as Salif
Keita grace the stage, and John Waters hosts
Christmas extravaganzas. Pay $25 extra for
dinner with prime balcony seating to watch
shows comfortably, or rock out with the
standing-room scrum downstairs.

⭐**Roxie Cinema** CINEMA
(Map p308; ☑415-863-1087; www.roxie.com; 3117
16th St; regular screening/matinee $11/8; ☐14,
22, 33, 49, ☐16th St Mission) This vintage 1909
cinema is a neighborhood nonprofit with
an international reputation for distributing
documentaries and showing controversial
films banned elsewhere. Tickets to film-
festival premieres, rare revivals and raucous
Oscars telecasts sell out – get tickets online
– but if the main show's packed, discover
riveting documentaries in teensy next-door
Little Roxie instead. No ads, plus personal
introductions to every film.

Sundance Kabuki Cinema CINEMA
(Map p304; ☑415-346-3243; www.sundancecine
mas.com; 1881 Post St; adult $11-16.50; ☐2, 3, 22,
38) ✎ Cinema-going at its best. Reserve a
stadium seat, belly up to the bar and order
wine and surprisingly good food to enjoy
during the film. A multiplex initiative by
Robert Redford's Sundance Institute, Kabuki features big-name flicks and festivals
– and it's green, with recycled-fiber seating,
reclaimed-wood decor and local chocolates
and booze (hence the 21-plus designation
most shows). Validated parking.

🛍 Shopping

⭐**Aggregate Supply** CLOTHING, HOMEWARES
(Map p308; ☑415-474-3190; www.aggregatesup
plysf.com; 806 Valencia St; ☉11am-7pm Mon-Sat,
noon-6pm Sun; ☐14, 33, 49, ☐16th St Mission)
Wild West modern is the look at Aggregate
Supply, purveyors of California-cool fashion
and home decor. Local designers and indie
makers get pride of place, including vintage

SAN FRANCISCO'S BEST SHOPPING AREAS

All those rustic-chic dens, well-stocked cupboards and fabulous outfits don't just pull themselves together – San Franciscans scoured their city for it all. Here's where to find what:

Ferry Building Local food, wine and kitchenware.

Hayes Valley Independent fashion designers, housewares, gifts.

Valencia Street Bookstores, local design collectives, art galleries, vintage whatever.

Haight Street Head shops, music, vintage, skate and surf gear.

Union Square Department stores, megabrands, discount retail, Applestore.

Russian Hill and the Marina Date outfits, urban accessories, housewares, gifts.

Grant Avenue From Chinatown souvenirs to funky North Beach boutiques.

Heath stoneware mugs, Turk+Taylor's plaid shirt-jackets, and SF artist Tauba Auerbach's 24-hour clocks. Souvenirs don't get more authentically local than Aggregate Supply's own op-art California graphic tee and NorCal-forest-scented organic soaps.

★ Amoeba Music
MUSIC

(Map p310; ☑ 415-831-1200; www.amoeba.com; 1855 Haight St; ⊙ 11am-8pm; ☐ 6, 7, 33, 43, ⓜN) Enticements are hardly necessary to lure the masses to the West Coast's most eclectic collection of new and used music and video, but Amoeba offers listening stations, free zines with uncannily accurate staff reviews, and a free concert series that recently starred the Violent Femmes, Kehlani, Billy Bragg and Mike Doughty – plus a foundation that's saved one million acres of rainforest.

Betabrand
CLOTHING

(Map p308; ☑ 415-400-9491; www.betabrand.com; 780 Valencia St; ⊙ 11am-7pm Mon-Fri, to 8pm Sat, noon-6pm Sun; ☐ 14, 22, 33, 49, Ⓑ 16th St Mission) Crowdsource fashion choices at Betabrand, where experimental designs are put to an online vote and winners are produced in limited editions. Recent approved designs include office-ready dress yoga pants, disco-ball windbreakers and sundresses with a smiling-poo-emoji print. Some styles are clunkers – including the 'chillmono,' a kimono-style down puffer jacket – but at these prices you can afford to take fashion risks.

ⓘ Information

DANGERS & ANNOYANCES
Keep your city smarts and wits about you, especially at night in the Tenderloin, South of Market (SoMa) and the Mission.

MEDICAL SERVICES
San Francisco General Hospital (Zuckerberg San Franciso General Hospital and Trauma Center; ☑ emergency 415-206-8111, main hospital 415-206-8000; www.sfdph.org; 1001 Potrero Ave; ⊙ 24hr; ☐ 9, 10, 33, 48) Best ER for serious accidents.

TOURIST INFORMATION
SF Visitor Information Center (Map p304; ☑ 415-391-2000; www.sftravel.com/visitor-information-center; lower level, Hallidie Plaza, cnr Market & Powell Sts; ⊙ 9am-5pm Mon-Fri, to 3pm Sat & Sun, closed Sun Nov-Apr; ☐ Powell-Mason, Powell-Hyde, ⓜ Powell, Ⓑ Powell) Muni Passports, activities deals, culture and event calendars.

USEFUL WEBSITES
SFGate.com (www.sfgate.com)
SFist (www.sfist.com)
7x7 (www.7x7.com)

ⓘ Getting There & Away

AIR
San Francisco International Airport (SFO; www.flysfo.com; S McDonnell Rd) is 14 miles south of downtown, off Hwy 101 and accessible by Bay Area Rapid Transit (BART). Serving primarily domestic destinations, **Oakland International Airport** (OAK; www.oaklandairport.com; 1 Airport Dr; ☎; Ⓑ Oakland International Airport) is a 40-minute BART ride across the Bay, while **Mineta San José International Airport** (SJC; ☑ 408-392-3600; www.flysanjose.com; 1701 Airport Blvd) is 45 miles south via Hwy 101.

BUS
Until the new terminal is complete in late 2017, SF's intercity hub remains the **Temporary Transbay Terminal** (Map p304; cnr Howard & Main Sts; ☐ 5,38,41,71). From here you can catch the following buses:

AC Transit (📞510-891-4777; www.actransit. org) Buses to the East Bay.

Greyhound (📞800-231-2222; www.greyhound. com) Buses leave daily for Los Angeles ($39 to $90, eight to 12 hours), Truckee near Lake Tahoe ($35 to $46, 5½ hours) and other major destinations.

Megabus (📞877-462-6342; http://us.mega bus.com) Low-cost bus service to San Francisco from Los Angeles, Sacramento and Reno.

SamTrans (📞800-660-4287; www.samtrans. com) Southbound buses to Palo Alto and the Pacific coast.

TRAIN

Caltrain (www.caltrain.com; cnr 4th & King Sts) connects San Francisco with Silicon Valley hubs and San Jose.

Amtrak (📞800-872-7245; www.amtrakcali fornia.com) serves San Francisco via stations in Oakland and Emeryville (near Oakland), with free shuttle-bus connections to San Francisco's Ferry Building and Caltrain station, and Oakland's Jack London Sq.

❶ Getting Around

TO/FROM SAN FRANCISCO INTERNATIONAL AIRPORT

From SFO's **BART** (Bay Area Rapid Transit; www. bart.gov) station, connected to the International Terminal, it's a 30-minute ride to downtown SF. A taxi to downtown SF from SFO costs $40 to $55, plus tip. Airport shuttles (one way $17 to $20 plus tip) depart from *upper-level* ticketing areas (not lower-level baggage claim); anticipate 45 minutes to most SF locations. **SuperShuttle** (📞800-258-3826; www.supershuttle.com) offers shared van rides for $17 per person.

BOAT

San Francisco Bay Ferry (📞415-705-8291; http://sanfranciscobayferry.com) Operates from both Pier 41 and the Ferry Building to Oakland/Alameda. Fares are $6.60.

CAR & MOTORCYCLE

If you can, avoid driving in San Francisco: heavy traffic is a given, street parking is harder to find than true love, and meter readers are ruthless.

PUBLIC TRANSPORTATION

When San Franciscans aren't pressed for time, most walk, bike or ride **Muni** (San Francisco Municipal Transportation Agency) instead of taking a car or cab. For Bay Area transit options, departures and arrivals, call 511 or check www.511.org. A detailed Muni Street & Transit Map is available free online.

Cable cars Frequent, slow and scenic, from 6am to 12:30am daily. Single rides cost $7; for frequent use, get a Muni Passport ($21 per day).

Muni streetcar and bus Reasonably fast, but schedules vary wildly by line; infrequent after 9pm. Fares are $2.50.

BART High-speed transit to East Bay, Mission St, SF airport and Millbrae, where it connects with Caltrain.

TAXI

Fares are about $2.75 per mile; meters start at $3.50. Hailing a cab in the street can be difficult. Download the mobile app Flywheel (http://fly wheel.com) for prompt service.

Marin County

Majestic redwoods cling to tawny coastal headlands just across the Golden Gate Bridge in laid-back Marin. The southernmost town, Sausalito (www.sausalito.org), is a tiny bayfront destination for cycling trips over the bridge (take the ferry back to San Francisco). Near the harbor, where picturesque bohemian houseboats are docked, the **Bay Model Visitors Center** (Map p302; 📞415-332-3871; www.spn.usace.army.mil/mis sions/recreation/baymodelvisitorcenter.aspx; 2100 Bridgeway Blvd; ⊙9am-4pm Tue-Sat, extended summer hours 10am-5pm Sat & Sun; 🅿🚼) **FREE** houses a giant hydraulic re-creation of the entire bay and delta.

Marin Headlands

These windswept, rugged headlands are laced with hiking trails, providing panoramic bay and city views. To find the **visitor center** (Map p302; 📞415-331-1540; www.nps. gov/goga/marin-headlands.htm; Bunker Rd, Fort Barry; ⊙9:30am-4:30pm), take the Alexander Ave exit after crossing north over the Golden Gate Bridge, turn left under the freeway and follow the signs.

Attractions west of Hwy 101 include **Point Bonita Lighthouse** (Map p302; 📞415-331-1540; www.nps.gov/goga/pobo.htm; ⊙12:30-3:30pm Sat-Mon; 🅿) **FREE**, Cold War–era **Nike Missile Site SF-88** (Map p302; 📞415-331-1540; www.nps.gov/goga/nike-missile-site.htm; Field Rd; ⊙12:30-3:30pm Sat; 🅿) **FREE** and the educational **Marine Mammal Center** (Map p302; 📞415-289-7325; www.marinemammal center.org; 2000 Bunker Rd; by donation, audio tour adult/child $9/5; ⊙10am-4pm; 🅿🚼) 🚶 uphill from **Rodeo Beach** (Map p302; www.park sconservancy.org/visit/park-sites/rodeo-beach. html; off Bunker Rd; 🅿🚼). East of Hwy 101 at Fort Baker, the interactive **Bay Area Discovery Museum** (Map p302; 📞415-339-3900;

www.baykidsmuseum.org; 557 McReynolds Rd; $14, 1st Wed each month free; ⊙9am-4pm Tue-Fri, to 5pm Sat & Sun, also 9am-4pm some Mon; P⚑) is awesome for kids.

Near the visitor center, **HI Marin Headlands Hostel** (Map p302; ☑415-331-2777; www.norcalhostels.org/marin; Fort Barry, Bldg 941; r with shared bath $105-135, dm $31-40; ⊙reception 7:30am-11:30pm; P⊖@🛜) ⌖ occupies two 1907 military buildings on a forested hill. For historical luxury, book a fireplace room with bay views at Fort Baker's LEED-certified **Cavallo Point** (Map p302; ☑415-339-4700; www.cavallopoint.com; 601 Murray Circle; r from $399; P⊖❄@🛜💻🐾) ⌖ lodge.

Mt Tamalpais State Park

Majestic Mt Tam (2572ft) is a woodsy playground for hikers and mountain bikers. **Mt Tamalpais State Park** (Map p302; ☑415-388-2070; www.parks.ca.gov; per car $8; ⊙7am-sunset; P⚑) ⌖ encompasses 6300 acres of parklands and over 200 miles of trails. Don't miss driving up to East Peak Summit lookout. Panoramic Hwy passes through the park, connecting Muir Woods with **Stinson Beach**, a coastal town with a sandy crescent-shaped beach on Hwy 1.

Park headquarters are **Pantoll Station** (Map p302; ☑415-388-2070; www.parks.ca.gov; 801 Panoramic Hwy; ⊙hours vary; 🛜), the nexus of many trails, with a first-come, first-served **campground** (Map p302; ☑info 415-388-2070; www.parks.ca.gov; Panoramic Hwy; tent sites $25; P💻). Book far ahead for a rustic cabin (no electricity or running water) or walk-in campsite at **Steep Ravine** (☑reservations 800-444-7275; www.reserveamerica.com; tent sites $25, cabins $100; ⊙Nov-Sep; P), off Hwy 1 south of Stinson Beach. Or hike in with a sleeping bag, towel and food to off-the-grid **West Point Inn** (Map p302; ☑info 415-388-9955, reservations 415-646-0702; www.westpointinn.com; 100 Old Railroad Grade, San Anselmo; r with shared bath per adult/child $50/25, linen rental $10; ⊖) ⌖; reservations required.

Point Reyes National Seashore

The windswept peninsula of **Point Reyes National Seashore** (☑415-654-5100; www.nps.gov/pore; P⚑) ⌖ FREE juts 10 miles out to sea on an entirely different tectonic plate, protecting over 100 sq miles of beaches, lagoons and forested hills. A mile west of Olema, **Bear Valley Visitor Center** (☑415-464-5100; www.nps.gov/pore; 1 Bear Valley Rd, Point Reyes Station; ⊙10am-

5pm Mon-Fri, 9am-5pm Sat & Sun; ⚑) has maps, information and natural-history displays. The 0.6-mile **Earthquake Trail**, which crosses the San Andreas Fault zone, starts nearby.

Crowning the peninsula's westernmost tip, **Point Reyes Lighthouse** (☑415-669-1534; www.nps.gov/pore; end of Sir Francis Drake Blvd; ⊙10am-4:30pm Fri-Mon, lens room 2:30-4pm Fri-Mon) is ideal for winter whale-watching. Off Pierce Point Rd, the 10-mile round-trip **Tomales Point Trail** rolls atop blustery bluffs past herds of tule elk to the peninsula's northern tip. To paddle out into Tomales Bay, **Blue Waters Kayaking** (☑415-669-2600; www.bluewaterskayaking.com; 12944 Sir Francis Drake Blvd; rentals/tours from $60/68; ⊙usually 9am-5pm, last rental 2pm; ⚑) launches from Inverness and Marshall.

Nature-lovers bunk at the only in-park lodging, **HI Point Reyes Hostel** (☑415-663-8811; www.norcalhostels.org/reyes; 1390 Limantour Spit Rd; r with shared bath $105-130, dm $29-38; ⊙reception 7:30-10:30am & 4:30-10pm; P⊖@) ⌖, 8 miles inland from the visitor center. In the coastal town of Inverness, the **Cottages at Point Reyes Seashore** (☑415-669-7250; www.cottagespointreyes.com; 13275 Sir Francis Drake Blvd; r $129-269; P⊖🛜💻🐾) is a family-friendly place tucked away in the woods. The **West Marin Chamber of Commerce** (☑415-663-9232; www.pointreyes.org) checks availability at more cozy inns, cottages and B&Bs.

Two miles north of Olema, the tiny town of **Point Reyes Station** has bakeries, cafes and restaurants. Gather a picnic lunch at **Cowgirl Creamery at Tomales Bay Foods** (☑415-663-9335; www.cowgirlcreamery.com; 80 4th St; deli items $3-10; ⊙10am-6pm Wed-Sun; 🐾⚑) ⌖ or head 10 miles north of town for an oyster feast at **Hog Island Oyster Company** (☑415-663-9218; https://hogislandoysters.com; 20215 Hwy 1, Marshall; 12 oysters $13-16, picnic per person $5; ⊙shop 9am-5pm daily, picnic area from 10am, cafe 11am-5pm Fri-Mon).

Berkeley

As the birthplace of the free-speech and disability-rights movements and the home of the hallowed halls of the University of California, Berkeley (aka 'Cal'), it is no bashful wallflower. A national hot spot of (mostly left-of-center) intellectual discourse and one of the most vocal activist populations in the country, this infamous college town has an interesting mix of graying progressives and idealistic undergrads.

◉ Sights & Activities

Leading to the campus's south gate, **Telegraph Avenue** is a youthful street carnival, packed with cheap cafes, music stores, streethawkers and buskers.

University of California, Berkeley   UNIVERSITY
(☑510-642-6000; www.berkeley.edu; **P**; **B**Downtown Berkeley) 'Cal' is one of the country's top universities, California's oldest university (1866), and home to 40,000 diverse, politically conscious students. Next to **California Memorial Stadium** (www.californiamemorial stadium.com), the **Koret Visitor Center** (☑510-642-5215; http://visit.berkeley.edu; 2227 Piedmont Ave; ⊙8:30am-4:30pm Mon-Fri, 9am-1pm Sat & Sun; 🚌AC Transit 36) has information and maps, and leads free campus walking tours (reservations required). Cal's landmark is the 1914 **Campanile** (Sather Tower; ☑510-642-6000; http://campanile.berkeley.edu; adult/child $3/2; ⊙10am-3:45pm Mon-Fri, 10am-4:45pm Sat, to 1:30pm & 3-4:45pm Sun; 🦽; **B**Downtown Berkeley), with elevator rides ($3) to the top and carillon concerts. The **Bancroft Library** (☑510-642-3781; www.lib.berkeley.edu/libraries/ bancroft-library; University Dr; ⊙archives 10am-4pm or 5pm Mon-Fri; **B**Downtown Berkeley) `FREE` displays the small gold nugget that started the California gold rush in 1848.

🛏 Sleeping

Lodging rates spike during special university events such as graduation (mid-May) and home football games. A number of older, less expensive motels along University Ave can be handy during peak demand, as can chain motels and hotels off I-80 in Emeryville or Vallejo.

Hotel Shattuck Plaza   HOTEL **$$**
(☑510-845-7300; www.hotelshattuckplaza.com; 2086 Allston Way; r from $200; **P**🅿❄@🛜; **B**Downtown Berkeley) Following a $15-million renovation and greening of this 100-year-old downtown jewel, a foyer of red Italian glass lighting, flocked Victorian-style wallpaper – and yes, a peace sign tiled into the floor – leads to comfortable rooms with down comforters and an airy, columned restaurant serving all meals.

★Claremont Resort & Spa   RESORT **$$$**
(☑510-843-3000; www.fairmont.com/clare mont-berkeley; 41 Tunnel Rd; r from $240; **P**🅿❄ @🛜🏊🎾) The East Bay's classy crème de la crème, this Fairmont-owned historic hotel is a glamorous white 1915 building with elegant restaurants, a fitness center, swimming pools, tennis courts and a full-service spa. The bayview rooms are superb. It's located at the foot of the Berkeley Hills, off Hwy 13 (Tunnel Rd) near the Oakland border. Parking is $30.

🍴 Eating & Drinking

★Chez Panisse   CALIFORNIAN **$$$**
(☑cafe 510-548-5049, restaurant 510-548-5525; www.chezpanisse.com; 1517 Shattuck Ave; cafe dinner mains $22-35, restaurant prix-fixe dinner $75-125; ⊙cafe 11:30am-2:45pm & 5-10:30pm Mon-Thu, 11:30am-3pm & 5-11:30pm Fri & Sat, restaurant seatings 5:30pm & 8pm Mon-Sat; 🅿; 🚌AC Transit 7) 🌿 Foodies come to worship here at the church of Alice Waters, inventor of California cuisine. It's in a lovely arts-and-crafts house in Berkeley's 'Gourmet Ghetto,' and you can choose to pull out all the stops with a prix-fixe meal downstairs, or go less expensive and a tad less formal in the upstairs cafe. Reservations accepted one month ahead.

Ippuku   JAPANESE **$$**
(☑510-665-1969; www.ippukuberkeley.com; 2130 Center St; shared plates $5-20; ⊙5-10pm Tue-Thu, to 11pm Fri & Sat; **B**Downtown Berkeley) Japanese expats gush that Ippuku reminds them of *izakaya* (Japanese gastropubs) back in Tokyo. Choose from a menu of yakitori (skewered meats and vegetables) and handmade soba noodles as you settle in at one of the traditional tatami tables (no shoes, please) or cozy booth perches. Order *shōchū*, a distilled alcohol usually made from rice or barley. Reservations essential.

Jupiter   PUB
(☑510-843-8277; www.jupiterbeer.com; 2181 Shattuck Ave; ⊙11:30am-12:30am Mon-Thu, to 1:30am Fri, noon-1:30am Sat, noon-11:30pm Sun; **B**Downtown Berkeley) This downtown pub has loads of regional microbrews, a beer garden, decent pizza and live bands most nights. Sit upstairs for a bird's-eye view of bustling Shattuck Ave.

☆ Entertainment

Berkeley Repertory Theatre   THEATER
(☑510-647-2949; www.berkeleyrep.org; 2025 Addison St; tickets $40-100; ⊙box office noon-7pm Tue-Sun; **B**Downtown Berkeley) This highly respected company has produced bold versions of classical and modern plays since 1968. Most shows have half-price tickets for patrons under 30.

Freight & Salvage Coffeehouse LIVE MUSIC
(☎510-644-2020; www.thefreight.org; 2020 Addison St; tickets $5-45; ☉shows daily; ♿; B Downtown Berkeley) This legendary club has almost 50 years of history and is conveniently located in the downtown arts district. It features great traditional folk, country, bluegrass and world music and welcomes all ages, with half-price tickets for patrons under 21.

❶ Getting There & Around

To get to Berkeley, catch a Richmond-bound train to one of three **BART** (Bay Area Rapid Transit; www.bart.gov) stations: Ashby, Downtown Berkeley or North Berkeley. Fares between Berkeley and San Francisco cost $4.10 to $4.40, between Berkeley and downtown Oakland $1.95.

NORTHERN CALIFORNIA

The Golden State goes wild in Northern California, with coast redwoods swirled in fog, Wine Country vineyards and hidden hot springs. Befitting this dramatic meeting of land and water is an unlikely mélange of local residents: timber barons and hippie tree huggers, dreadlocked Rastafarians and biodynamic ranchers, pot farmers and political radicals of every stripe. Come for the scenery, but stay for the top-notch wine and farm-to-fork restaurants, misty hikes among the world's tallest trees and rambling conversations that begin with 'Hey, dude!' and end hours later.

Wine Country

America's premier viticulture region has earned its reputation among the world's best. Despite hype about Wine Country style, it's from the land that all Wine Country lore springs. Rolling hills, dotted with century-old oaks, turn the color of lion's fur under the summer sun and swaths of vineyards carpet hillsides as far as the eye can see. Where they end, redwood forests follow serpentine rivers to the sea.

❶ Getting There & Around

Either Napa or Sonoma is a 90-minute drive north of San Francisco via Hwy 101 or I-80. Getting to and around the valleys by public transportation (mainly buses, perhaps in combination with BART trains or ferries) is slow and complicated, but just possible – consult http://511.org for trip planning and schedules.

Rent bicycles from **Wine Country Cyclery** (☎707-966-6800; www.winecountrycyclery.com; 262 W Napa St; bicycle rental per day $30-75; ☉10am-6pm), **Napa Valley Bike Tours** (☎707-944-2953; www.napavalleybiketours.com; 6500 Washington St, Yountville; bicycle rental per day $45-75, tours $109-124; ☉8:30am-5pm), **Calistoga Bike Shop** (☎707-942-9687; http://calistogabikeshop.com; 1318 Lincoln Ave; bicycle rental from $28, guided tours from $149; ☉10am-6pm) or **Spoke Folk Cyclery** (☎707-433-7171; www.spokefolk.com; 201 Center St; hybrid bicycle rental per hour/day from $14/38; ☉10am-6pm Mon-Fri, to 5pm Sat & Sun).

Napa Valley

More than 200 wineries crowd 30-mile-long Napa Valley along three main routes. Traffic-jammed on weekends, **Highway 29** is lined with blockbuster wineries. Running parallel, **Silverado Trail** moves faster, passing boutique winemakers, bizarre architecture and cult-hit Cabernet Sauvignon. Heading west toward Sonoma, **Carneros Highway** (Hwy 121) winds by landmark vineyards specializing in sparkling wines and Pinot Noir.

At the southern end of the valley, **Napa** – the valley's workaday hub – lacks rusticity, but has trendy restaurants and tasting rooms downtown. Stop by the **Napa Valley Welcome Center** (☎855-847-6272, 707-251-5895; www.visitnapavalley.com; 600 Main St; ☉9am-5pm; ♿) for wine-tasting passes and winery maps.

Heading north on Hwy 29, the former stagecoach stop of tiny **Yountville** has more Michelin-starred eateries per capita than San Francisco. Another 10 miles north, traffic snarls in charming **St Helena**, where there's genteel strolling and shopping – if you can find parking. At the valley's northern end, folksy **Calistoga** is home to hot-springs spas and mud-bath emporiums using volcanic ash from nearby Mt St Helena.

◉ Sights & Activities

Many Napa wineries require reservations. Plan to visit no more than a few tasting rooms each day.

★**Hess Collection** WINERY, GALLERY
(☎707-255-1144; www.hesscollection.com; 4411 Redwood Rd, Napa; museum free, tasting $25 & $35, tours free; ☉10am-5:30pm, last tasting 5pm)
✐ Art-lovers: don't miss Hess Collection, whose galleries display mixed-media and large-canvas works, including pieces by Francis Bacon and Robert Motherwell. In

the elegant stone-walled tasting room, find well-known Cabernet Sauvignon and Chardonnay, but also try the Viognier. There's garden service in the warmer months, which is lovely, as Hess overlooks the valley. Make reservations and be prepared to drive a winding road. Bottles are $30 to $100. Public tour 10:30am.

★**Frog's Leap**   WINERY
(☎707-963-4704; www.frogsleap.com; 8815 Conn Creek Rd, Rutherford; tasting $20-25, incl tour $25; ⊙10am-4pm by appointment only; P♿🐾) 🚲 Meandering paths wind through magical gardens and fruit-bearing orchards surrounding an 1884 barn and farmstead with cats and chickens. The vibe is casual and down-to-earth, with a major emphasis on *fun*. Sauvignon Blanc is its best-known wine but the Merlot merits attention. There's also a dry, restrained Cabernet, atypical of Napa.

★**Tres Sabores**   WINERY
(☎707-967-8027; www.tressabores.com; 1620 South Whitehall Lane, St Helena; tour & tasting $40; ⊙10:30am-3pm, by appointment; 🐾) 🚲 At the valley's westernmost edge, where sloping vineyards meet wooded hillsides, Tres Sabores is a portal to old Napa – no fancy tasting room, no snobbery, just great wine in a spectacular setting. Bucking the Cabernet custom, Tres Sabores crafts elegantly structured, Burgundy-style Zinfandel and spritely Sauvignon Blanc, which the *New York Times* dubbed a top 10 of its kind in California. Reservations are essential.

Castello di Amorosa   WINERY, CASTLE
(☎707-967-6272; www.castellodiamorosa.com; 4045 Hwy 29, Calistoga; entry & tasting $25-35, incl guided tour $40-85; ⊙9:30am-6pm Mar-Oct, to 5pm Nov-Feb; P♿) It took 14 years to build this perfectly replicated, 13th-century Italian castle, complete with moat, hand-cut stone walls, ceiling frescoes by Italian artisans, Roman-style cross-vault brick catacombs, and a torture chamber with period equipment. You can taste without an appointment, but this is one tour worth taking. Oh, the wine? Some respectable Italian varietals, including a velvety Tuscan blend and a Merlot that goes great with pizza. Bottles are $20 to $98.

🛏 Sleeping

Pricey and fabulous hotels are scattered throughout Napa Valley, with the most opulent stays perched in and around St Helena and Yountville. Calistoga is a bit more relaxed and affordable, and the best budget option, without question, is a yurt (or campsite) in Bothe-Napa Valley State Park.

★**El Bonita**   MOTEL $$
(☎707-963-3216, 800-541-3284; www.elbonita.com; 195 Main St; r $140-325; P♿❄@🐾🏊🐕) Book in advance to secure this sought-after motel, with up-to-date rooms (quietest are in the back), attractive grounds, a heated pool, hot tub and sauna.

Napa Valley Railway Inn   INN $$
(☎707-944-2000; www.napavalleyrailwayinn.com; 6523 Washington St; r $215-295; P♿❄@🐾🏊) Sleep in a converted railroad car, part of two short trains parked at a central platform. They've little privacy, but are moderately priced compared with the competition. Bring earplugs.

Las Alcobas   BOUTIQUE HOTEL $$$
(☎707-963-7000; www.lasalcobasnapavalley.com; 1915 Main St; r from $600-2500; ❄🐾🏊) A newcomer with a sister property in Mexico City, this boutique has already secured its place among Napa Valley's finest stays. The plush, modern rooms offer both vineyard vista and proximity to some of the region's best dining, shopping and wine tasting. That's if you attempt to pry yourself from the delicious hotel-restaurant Acacia, heated pool and relaxing spa.

🍴 Eating

The $400-per-person, 12-course meals are procured in Yountville where Thomas Keller and his French Laundry reign, and St Helena, home of equally fabulous Meadowwood. For the less indulgent, the valley has a delicious array of midrange options and country stores offering picnic items and gourmet sandwiches. At wineries, charcuterie plates and food pairings are popular; show up hungry.

★**Oxbow Public Market**   MARKET $
(☎707-226-6529; www.oxbowpublicmarket.com; 610 & 644 1st St; items from $3; ⊙9am-9pm; 🐾🏠) 🚲 Graze at this gourmet market and plug into the Northern California food scene. Standouts: **Hog Island Oyster Co**; comfort cooking at celeb-chef Todd Humphries' **Kitchen Door**; great Cal-Mexican tacos at **C Casa & Taco Lounge**; the India pale ales (IPAs) and sour beers at **Fieldwork Brewing Company**; espresso from **Ritual Coffee**; and **Three Twins** certified-organic ice cream.

CALIFORNIA WINE COUNTRY

Bouchon Bakery
BAKERY $

(☎707-944-2253; www.bouchonbakery.com; 6528 Washington St; items from $3; ⊙7am-7pm; 🖉) Bouchon makes as-good-as-in-Paris French pastries and strong coffee. There's always a line and rarely a seat: get it to go.

Gott's Roadside
AMERICAN $$

(☎707-963-3486; http://gotts.com; 933 Main St; mains $8-16; ⊙10am-10pm May-Sep, to 9pm Oct-Apr; 🖘) 🖉 Wiggle your toes in the grass and feast on quality burgers – beef, turkey, ahi or veggie – plus Cobb salads and fish tacos at this classic roadside drive-in. Avoid weekend waits by phoning ahead or ordering online. There's another at Oxbow Public Market.

★French Laundry
CALIFORNIAN $$$

(☎707-944-2380; www.thomaskeller.com/tfl; 6640 Washington St; prix-fixe dinner $310; ⊙seatings 11am-12:30pm Fri-Sun, 5-9pm daily) The pinnacle of California dining, Thomas Keller's French Laundry is epic, a high-wattage culinary experience on par with the world's best. Book one month ahead on the online app Tock, where tickets are released in groupings. This is the meal you can brag about the rest of your life.

Sonoma Valley

We have a soft spot for Sonoma's folksy ways. Unlike fancy Napa, nobody cares if you drive a clunker and vote Green. Locals call it 'Slow-noma.' Anchoring the bucolic 17-mile-long valley, the town of Sonoma makes a great jumping-off point for exploring Wine Country – it's an hour from San Francisco – and has a marvelous sense of place, with storied 19th-century historical sights surrounding the state's largest town square.

◉ Sights & Activities

Downtown Sonoma was once the capital of the short-lived Bear Flag Republic. Today Sonoma Plaza – the state's largest town square – is bordered by historic hotels, busy restaurants, chic shops and a **visitor center** (☎866-966-1090; www.sonomavalley.com; 453 1st St E; ⊙9am-5pm Mon-Sat, 10am-5pm Sun).

★Gundlach-Bundschu Winery
WINERY

(☎707-938-5277; www.gunbun.com; 2000 Denmark St, Sonoma; tasting $20-30, incl tour $30-60; ⊙11am-5:30pm May-Oct, to 4:30pm Nov-Apr; P) 🖉 California's oldest family-run winery looks like a castle but has a down-to-earth vibe. Founded in 1858 by a Bavarian immigrant, its signatures are Gewürztraminer and Pinot Noir, but 'Gun-Bun' was the first American winery to produce 100% Merlot. Down a winding lane, it's a terrific bike-to-winery with picnicking, hiking, a lake and frequent concerts, including a two-day folk-music festival in June. Tour the 1800-barrel cave by reservation only. Bottles are $20 to $50.

Bartholomew Park
PARK

(☎707-938-2244; www.bartholomewpark.org; 1000 Vineyard Lane; ⊙10am-4:30pm; P🖘) **FREE** The top near-town outdoors destination is 375-acre Bartholomew Park, off Castle Rd, where you can picnic beneath giant oaks and hike 2 miles of trails, with hilltop vistas to San Francisco. The **Palladian Villa**, at the park's entrance, is a re-creation of Count Haraszthy's original Pompeian residence, open noon to 3pm Saturdays and Sundays. There's also a good **winery**, independently operated. Last entry is at 4:30pm.

Jack London State Historic Park
PARK

(☎707-938-5216; www.jacklondonpark.com; 2400 London Ranch Rd, Glen Ellen; per car $10, cottage adult/child $4/2; ⊙9:30am-5pm; P🖘) 🖉 Napa has Robert Louis Stevenson, but Sonoma has Jack London. This 1400-acre park frames that author's last years; don't miss the excellent on-site **museum**. Miles of **hiking trails** (some open to mountain bikes) weave through oak-dotted woodlands, between 600ft and 2300ft elevations; an easy 2-mile loop meanders to **London Lake**, great for picnicking. On select summer evenings, the park transforms into a theater for 'Broadway Under the Stars.' Be alert for poison oak.

Benziger
WINERY

(☎888-490-2739, 707-935-3000; www.benziger.com; 1883 London Ranch Rd, Glen Ellen; tasting $20-40, tours $25-50; ⊙10am-5pm; P🖘) 🖉 If you're new to wine, make Benziger your first stop for Sonoma's best crash course in winemaking. The worthwhile tour (11am–3:30pm; reservations recommended) includes an open-air tram ride (weather permitting) through biodynamic vineyards and a five-wine tasting. Great picnicking, excellent for families. The large-production wine is OK (head for the reserves); the tour's the thing. Bottles are $20 to $80.

Kunde
WINERY

(☎707-833-5501; www.kunde.com; 9825 Hwy 12, Kenwood; tasting $15-50, cave tours free;

⊘10:30am-5pm; Ⓟ) 🍴 This family-owned winery on a historic ranch has vineyards that are more than a century old. It offers mountaintop tastings with impressive valley views and seasonal guided hikes (advance reservations recommended), though you can also just stop for a tasting and a tour. Elegant, 100% estate-grown wines include crisp Chardonnay and unfussy red blends, all made sustainably. Bottles $17 to $100.

Cline Cellars   WINERY
(✆707-940-4030; www.clinecellars.com; 24737 Arnold Dr, Hwy 121; tasting free-$20; ⊘tasting room 10am-6pm, museum to 4pm) 🍴 Balmy days are for pondside picnics and rainy ones for fireside tastings of old-vine Zinfandel and Mourvèdre inside an 1850s farmhouse. Stroll out back to the **California Mission Museum**, housing 1930s miniature replicas of California's original 21 Spanish Colonial missions.

🛏 Sleeping

The most sensible bases for exploring this valley are historic downtown Sonoma and lush, romantic Glen Ellen. Kenwood also has one sumptuous inn.

⭐**Windhaven Cottage**   COTTAGE $$
(✆707-938-2175, 707-483-1856; www.windhavencottage.com; 21700 Pearson Ave; cottages $165-175; ❄🐾) Great-bargain Windhaven has two units: a hideaway cottage with vaulted wooden ceilings and fireplace, and a handsome 800-sq-ft studio. We prefer the romantic cottage. Both have hot tubs. Bicycles and barbecues sweeten the deal.

Beltane Ranch   B&B $$
(✆707-833-4233; www.beltaneranch.com; 11775 Hwy 12, Glen Ellen; d $185-375; Ⓟ❄🐾) 🍴 Surrounded by horse pastures and vineyards, Beltane is a throwback to 19th-century Sonoma. The cheerful 1890s ranch house has double porches lined with swinging chairs and white wicker. Though it's technically a B&B, each country-Americana-style room and the cottage has a private entrance – nobody will make you pet the cat. No phone or TV means zero distraction from pastoral bliss.

🍴 Eating & Drinking

⭐**Fremont Diner**   AMERICAN, SOUTHERN $$
(✆707-938-7370; www.thefremontdiner.com; 2698 Fremont Dr; mains $9-22; ⊘8am-3pm Mon-Wed, to 9pm Thu-Sun; 🚐) 🍴 Lines snake out the door at peak times at this farm-to-table roadside diner. We prefer the indoor tables but will happily accept a picnic table to feast on buttermilk pancakes with homemade cinnamon-vanilla syrup, chicken and waffles, oyster po'boys, finger-licking barbecue and skillet-baked cornbread.

Fig Cafe & Winebar   FRENCH, CALIFORNIAN $$
(✆707-938-2130; www.thefigcafe.com; 13690 Arnold Dr, Glen Ellen; mains $12-24, 3-course dinner $36; ⊘10am-2:30pm Sat & Sun, 5-9pm Sun-Thu, 5-9:30pm Fri & Sat) The Fig's earthy California-Provençal comfort food includes flash-fried calamari with spicy lemon aioli, fig and arugula salad and *steak frites*. Good wine prices and weekend brunch give reason to return. No reservations; complimentary corkage.

Hopmonk Tavern   PUB FOOD $$
(✆707-935-9100; www.hopmonk.com; 691 Broadway; mains $11-23; ⊘11:30am-9pm Sun-Thu, to 10pm Fri & Sat) This happening gastropub and beer garden takes its brews seriously with over a dozen of its own and guest beers on tap, served in type-appropriate glassware. Live music Friday through Sunday, open mike on Wednesday starting at 8pm.

⭐**Cafe La Haye**   CALIFORNIAN $$$
(✆707-935-5994; www.cafelahaye.com; 140 E Napa St; mains $19-25; ⊘5:30-9pm Tue-Sat) 🍴 One of Sonoma's top tables for earthy New American cooking, La Haye only uses produce sourced from within 60 miles. Its dining room gets packed cheek-by-jowl and service can border on perfunctory, but the clean simplicity and flavor-packed cooking make it many foodies' first choice. Reserve well ahead.

Russian River Valley

Redwoods tower over small wineries in the Russian River Valley, about 75 miles northwest of San Francisco (via Hwys 101 and 116), in western Sonoma County. Famous for its apple orchards and farm tour trails, **Sebastopol** has a new-age spiritual aura, with downtown bookshops, art galleries and boutiques, and antiques stores further south. Wander around the **Barlow** (✆707-824-5600; www.thebarlow.net; cnr Sebastopol & Morris Sts; ⊘hours vary; Ⓟ🚐) 🍴, an indoor market of food producers, winemakers, coffee roasters, spirit distillers and indie chefs. Or go straight to the source by driving or cycling local farm trails (www.farmtrails.org).

Guerneville is the main river beach town, buzzing with Harleys and gay-friendly honky-tonks. Explore old-growth redwoods at **Armstrong Redwoods State Reserve** (🖄info 707-869-2015, visitor center 707-869-2958; www.parks.ca.gov; 17000 Armstrong Woods Rd; per car $8; ⊙8am-1hr after sunset; P⅏) 🍃, next to no-reservations **Bullfrog Pond Campground** (🖄707-869-2015; www.stewardscr.org; sites reserved/nonreserved $35/25; 🐾). Paddle downriver with **Burke's Canoe Trips** (🖄707-887-1222; www.burkescanoetrips.com; 8600 River Rd, Forestville; canoe/kayak rental incl shuttle $68/$45, cash only). Head southeast to sip sparkling wines at hilltop **Iron Horse Vineyards** (🖄707-887-1507; www.ironhorsevineyards.com; 9786 Ross Station Rd, off Hwy 116, Sebastopol; tasting $25, incl tour $50; ⊙10am-4:30pm, last tasting 4pm; P); reserve tours in advance.

Other excellent wineries, many known for award-winning pinot noir, scatter along rural **Westside Road**, which follows the river toward Healdsburg. Guerneville's **visitor center** (🖄707-869-9000; www.russianriver.com; 16209 1st St; ⊙10am-5pm Mon-Sat, plus to 3pm Sun May-Oct) offers winery maps and lodging info. It's worth the wait for a table at California-smart **Boon Eat + Drink** (🖄707-869-0780; http://eatatboon.com; 16248 Main St; mains lunch $15-18, dinner $15-26; ⊙11am-3pm Thu-Tue, 5-9pm Sun-Thu, to 10pm Fri & Sat; 🍃), which also manages boutique **Boon Hotel + Spa** (🖄707-869-2721; www.boonhotels.com; 14711 Armstrong Woods Rd; tents $175-225, r $225-425; P⊜⌗🛜🐾🐾) 🍃, a minimalist oasis with a saline pool.

The aptly named Bohemian Hwy winds10 miles south of the river to tiny **Occidental**, where **Howard Station Cafe** (🖄707-874-2838; www.howardstationcafe.com; 3611 Bohemian Hwy; mains $8-14; ⊙7am-2:30pm Mon-Fri, to 3pm Sat & Sun; ⅏🐾) serves hearty breakfasts like blueberry cornmeal pancakes (cash only), and **Barley & Hops Tavern** (🖄707-874-9037; www.barleynhops.com; 3688 Bohemian Hwy; ⊙4-9pm Mon-Thu, 1-9:30pm Fri-Sun) pours craft beers. It's another few miles south to Freestone, home of the phenomenal bakery **Wild Flour Bread** (🖄707-874-2938; www.wildflourbread.com; 140 Bohemian Hwy, Freestone; items from $3; ⊙8:30am-6:30pm Fri-Mon; ⅏) and invigorating cedar-enzyme baths at **Osmosis** (🖄707-823-8231; www.osmosis.com; 209 Bohemian Hwy, Freestone; packages from $219; ⊙by appointment 9am-8pm) spa.

Healdsburg & Around

More than 100 wineries dot the valleys within a 20-mile radius of Healdsburg, where upscale eateries, wine-tasting rooms and styl-

ish hotels surround a leafy plaza. For tasting passes and maps, drop by the **visitor center** (🖄800-648-9922, 707-433-6935; www.healdsburg.com; 217 Healdsburg Ave; ⊙10am-4pm Mon-Fri, to 3pm Sat & Sun). Dine with California-chic locavores at the **Shed** (🖄707-431-7433; www.healdsburgshed.com; 25 North St; dinner mains $15-30; ⊙8am-9pm Wed-Mon, to 6pm Tue; ⅏) 🍃 or **SingleThread** (🖄707-723-4646; www.singlethreadfarms.com; 131 North St; tasting menu per person $293; ⊙5:30-11pm Tue-Sun), or grab lunch near the vineyards at country-style **Dry Creek General Store** (🖄707-433-4171; www.drycreekgeneralstore1881.com; 3495 Dry Creek Rd; sandwiches $10-13; ⊙7am-5pm Mon-Fri, to 5:30 Sat & Sun). Afterward bed down at old-fashioned **L&M Motel** (🖄707-433-6528; www.landmmotel.com; 70 Healdsburg Ave; r $175-195; P⊜⌗🛜🐾🐾) or romantic **Healdsburg Modern Cottages** (🖄707-395-4684; www.healdsburgcottages.com; 425 Foss St; d $340-575; ⌗🛜🐾).

Picture-perfect farmstead wineries await discovery in Dry Creek Valley, west of Hwy 101 and Healdsburg. Pedal a bicycle out to taste citrusy Sauvignon Blanc and peppery Zinfandel at biodynamic **Preston Vineyards** (🖄707-433-3372; www.prestonvineyards.com; 9282 W Dry Creek Rd; tasting/tours $10/25; ⊙11am-4:30pm; P⅏) 🍃 and **Quivira Vineyards** (🖄707-431-8333, 800-292-8339; www.quivirawine.com; 4900 W Dry Creek Rd; tasting $15-30, incl tour $40, tour & estate tasting by reservation only; ⊙11am-4pm, 10am-4:30pm Apr-Oct; P⅏🐾) 🍃. Motor toward the Russian River and **Porter Creek Vineyards** (🖄707-433-6321; www.portercreekvineyards.com; 8735 Westside Rd; tasting $15; ⊙10:30am-4:30pm; P) 🍃 for forest-floor Pinot Noir and fruity Viognier poured at a bar made from a bowling-alley lane.

Northwest of Healdsburg off Hwy 101, follow Hwy 128 through the **Anderson Valley**, known for its fruit orchards and family-owned wineries like **Navarro** (🖄707-895-3686; www.navarrowine.com; 5601 Hwy 128, Philo; ⊙8am-6pm Mon-Fri, to 5pm Sat & Sun; P) 🆓 and **Husch** (🖄707-462-5370; www.huschvineyards.com; 4400 Hwy 128, Philo; ⊙10am-6pm, to 5pm Nov-Mar; P) 🆓. Outside Boonville, which has roadside cafes, bakeries and delis, brake for disc-golf and beer at solar-powered **Anderson Valley Brewing Company** (🖄707-895-2337; www.avbc.com; 17700 Hwy 253, Boonville; tasting from $2, tours & disc-golf course free; ⊙11am-6pm Sat-Thu, to 7pm Fri; P⅏) 🍃.

North Coast

This is not the legendary California of the Beach Boys' song – there are very few surfboards and no palm-flanked beaches. The jagged edge of the continent is wild, scenic and even slightly foreboding: spectral fog and an outsider spirit have fostered the world's tallest trees, most potent weed and a string of idiosyncratic two-stoplight towns.

Coastal Highway 1 to Mendocino

Often winding precariously atop ocean cliffs, this serpentine slice of Hwy 1 passes salty fishing harbors and hidden beaches. Use roadside pullouts to scan the Pacific horizon for migrating whales or to amble coves bounded by startling rock formations and relentlessly pounded by the surf. The 110-mile stretch from Bodega Bay to Fort Bragg takes at least three hours of nonstop driving; at night or in the fog, it takes steely nerves and much, much longer.

Bodega Bay, the first pearl in a string of sleepy fishing villages, was the setting for Hitchcock's terrifying 1963 psycho-horror flick *The Birds*. Today the skies are free from bloodthirsty gulls, but you'd best keep an eye on that picnic basket as you explore the arched rocks, blustery coves and wildflower-covered bluffs of **Sonoma Coast State Park** (www.parks.ca.gov; per car $8), with beaches rolling beyond Jenner, 10 miles north. **Bodega Bay Sportfishing Center** (☑707-875-3495; www.bodegacharters.com; 1410b Bay Flat Rd; fishing trips $135, whale-watching adult/child $50/35; ☑) runs winter whale-watching trips (adult/child $50/35). Landlubbers hike Bodega Head or saddle up at **Chanslor Ranch** (☑707-875-3333, 707-875-2721; www.horsenaroundtrailrides.com; 2660 N Hwy 1; rides from $125; ☑10am-5pm; ☑).

Where the wide, lazy Russian River meets the Pacific, you'll find **Jenner**, a cluster of shops and restaurants dotting coastal hills. Informative volunteers protect the resident colony of harbor seals at the river's mouth during pupping season, between March and August. **Water Treks Ecotours** (☑707-865-2249; www.watertreks.com; kayak rental from $30; ☑hours vary) rents kayaks on Hwy 1; reservations recommended.

Twelve miles north of Jenner, the salt-weathered structures of **Fort Ross State Historic Park** (☑707-847-3437; www.fortross.org; 19005 Hwy 1; per car $8; ☑10am-4:30pm) preserve an 1812 trading post and Russian Orthodox church. It's a quiet place, but the history is riveting: this was once the southernmost reach of Tsarist Russia's North-American trading expeditions. The small, wood-scented museum offers historical exhibits and respite from the windswept cliffs.

Several miles further north, **Salt Point State Park** (☑707-847-3221; www.parks.ca.gov; 25050 Hwy 1; per car $8; ☑park sunrise-sunset, visitor center 10am-3pm Sat & Sun Apr-Oct; ☑) abounds with hiking trails and tide pools and has two **campgrounds** (☑800-444-7275; www.reserveamerica.com; Salt Point State Park; tent/RV sites $25/35; ☑). At neighboring **Kruse Rhododendron State Natural Reserve**, pink blooms spot the misty greenwoods between April and June. Cows graze the fields on the bluffs heading north to **Sea Ranch** (www.tsra.org), where public-access hiking trails lead downhill from roadside parking lots (per car $7) to pocket beaches.

Two miles north of Point Arena town, detour to wind-battered **Point Arena Lighthouse** (☑707-882-2809; www.pointarenalighthouse.com; 45500 Lighthouse Rd; adult/child $7.50/1; ☑10am-3:30pm mid-Sep–mid-May, to 4:30pm mid-May–mid-Sep; ☑), built in 1908. Ascend 145 steps to inspect the flashing Fresnel lens and get jaw-dropping coastal views. Eight miles north of the Little River crossing at Hwy 128 is **Van Damme State Park** (☑707-937-5804; www.parks.ca.gov; 8001 N Hwy 1, Little River; per car $8; ☑8am-9pm; ☑), where the popular 5-mile round-trip **Fern Canyon Trail** passes through a lush river canyon with young redwoods, continuing another mile each way to a pygmy forest. The park's **campground** (☑800-444-7275; www.reserveamerica.com; 8001 Hwy 1, Little River; tent/RV sites $25/35; ☑☑) has coin-op hot showers.

In **Mendocino**, a historical village perched on a gorgeous headland, baby boomers stroll around New England saltbox and water-tower B&Bs, quaint shops and art galleries. Wilder paths pass berry brambles, wildflowers and cypress trees standing guard over rocky cliffs and raging surf at **Mendocino Headlands State Park** (www.parks.ca.gov). The **Ford House Museum & Visitor Center** (☑707-537-5397; www.mendoparks.org; 45035 Main St; ☑11am-4pm) is nearby.

Just south of town, paddle your way up the Big River with **Catch a Canoe & Bicycles, Too** (☑707-937-0273; www.catchacanoe.com; 44850 Comptche-Ukiah Rd, Stanford Inn by the Sea; 3hr kayak, canoe or bicycle rental adult/child $28/14; ⊙9am-5pm; 🚹). North of town, 1909 **Point Cabrillo Light Station** (☏707-937-6123; www.pointcabrillo.org; 45300 Lighthouse Rd; ⊙park sunrise-sunset, lighthouse 11am-4pm) **FREE** is a perfect winter whale-watching perch.

🛏 Sleeping

Standards are high in stylish Mendocino and so are prices; two-day minimums often crop up on weekends. Fort Bragg, 10 miles north, has cheaper lodgings. All B&B rates include breakfast; only a few places have TVs. For a range of cottages and B&Bs, contact **Mendocino Coast Reservations** (☏707-937-5033; www.mendocinovacations.com; 45084 Little Lake St; ⊙9am-5pm).

Gualala Point Regional Park   CAMPGROUND $
(☏707-567-2267; http://parks.sonomacounty. ca.gov; 42401 Hwy 1, Gualala; tent & RV sites $35; P) Shaded by a stand of redwoods and fragrant California bay laurel trees, a short trail connects this creekside campground to the windswept beach. The quality of sites, including several secluded hike-in spots, makes it the best drive-in camping on this part of the coast.

Andiron Seaside Inn & Cabins   CABIN $$
(☏707-937-1543; http://theandiron.com; 6051 N Hwy 1, Little River; d $109-299; P😊📶🐕) ✐ Styled with hip vintage decor, this cluster of 1950s roadside cottages is a refreshingly playful option amid the cabbage-rose and lace aesthetic of Mendocino. Each cabin houses two rooms with complementing themes: 'Read' has old books, comfy vintage chairs and retro eyeglasses, while the adjoining 'Write' features a huge chalkboard and a ribbon typewriter.

⭐**Alegria**   B&B $$$
(☏707-937-5150; www.oceanfrontmagic.com; 44781 Main St; r $239-299; 😊📶) A perfect romantic hideaway: beds have views over the coast, decks have ocean views and all rooms have wood-burning fireplaces; outside, a gorgeous path leads to a big, amber-gray beach. Ever-so-friendly innkeepers whip up amazing breakfasts served in the sea-view dining area. Less expensive rooms are available across the street at bright and simple **Raku House** (☏800-780-7905; www.rakuhouse. com; 998 Main St; r $109-139; P😊📶).

⭐**Mar Vista Cottages**   CABIN $$$
(☏707-884-3522; www.marvistamendocino. com; 35101 Hwy 1, Anchor Bay; cottages $190-310;

P😊📶🐕) ✐ These elegantly renovated 1930s fishing cabins offer a simple, stylish seaside escape with a vanguard commitment to sustainability. The harmonious environment is the result of pitch-perfect details: linens are line-dried over lavender, guests browse the organic vegetable garden to harvest their own dinner and chickens cluck around the grounds laying the next morning's breakfast. It often requires two-night stays.

🍴 Eating & Drinking

Even tiny coastal towns usually have a bakery, deli, natural-foods market and a couple of roadside cafes and restaurants.

Franny's Cup & Saucer   BAKERY $
(☏707-882-2500; www.frannyscupandsaucer.com; 213 Main St; cakes from $2; ⊙8am-4pm Wed-Sat) The cutest patisserie on this stretch of coast is run by Franny and her mother, Barbara (a veteran of Chez Panisse in Berkeley). The fresh berry tarts and creative housemade chocolates seem too beautiful to eat, until you take the first bite and immediately want to order another. Once a month they pull out all the stops for a farmhouse dinner ($28).

Spud Point Crab Company   SEAFOOD $
(☏707-875-9472; www.spudpointcrab.com; 1860 Westshore Rd; mains $6.75-12; ⊙9am-5pm; P🚹) In the classic tradition of dockside crab shacks, Spud Point serves salty-sweet crab sandwiches and *real* clam chowder (that consistently wins local culinary prizes). You can also buy a crab to take home if you fancy. Eat at picnic tables overlooking the marina. Take Bay Flat Rd to get here.

Mendocino Cafe   CALIFORNIAN, FUSION $$
(☏707-937-6141; www.mendocinocafe.com; 10451 Lansing St; lunch mains $12-16, dinner mains $21-33; ⊙11:30am-8pm; 📶✐) One of Mendocino's few fine dinner spots also serves lovely alfresco lunches on its ocean-view deck surrounded by roses. Try the Thai burrito or the 'Healing Bowl' of soba noodles, miso, shitake mushrooms and choice of meat or seafood. At dinner there's grilled steak and seafood.

⭐**Café Beaujolais**   CALIFORNIAN $$$
(☏707-937-5614; www.cafebeaujolais.com; 961 Ukiah St; lunch mains $10-18, dinner mains $23-38; ⊙11:30am-2:30pm Wed-Sun, dinner from 5:30pm daily; P) ✐ Mendocino's iconic, beloved country-Cal–French restaurant occupies an 1893 farmhouse restyled into a monochromatic urban-chic dining room, perfect for holding hands by candlelight. The refined,

inspired cooking draws diners from San Francisco, who make this the centerpiece of their trip. The locally sourced menu changes with the seasons, but the Petaluma duck confit is a gourmand's delight.

955 Ukiah Street
CALIFORNIAN $$$

(☑707-937-1955; www.955restaurant.com; 955 Ukiah St; mains $18-37; ⊙from 6pm Thu-Sun) One of those semi-secret institutions, the menu here changes with what's available locally. When we visited, that meant wondrous things such as a roasted cauliflower, feta and caramelized-onion appetizer. The dimly lit, bohemian setting overlooks rambling gardens. Check the website for the excellent-value, three-course meal with wine for $25 every Thursday, and other events.

Dick's Place
BAR

(☑707-937-6010; 45080 Main St; ⊙11:30am-2am) A bit out of place among the fancy-pants shops downtown, but an excellent spot to check out the *other* Mendocino and do shots with rowdy locals. And don't miss the retro experience of dropping 50¢ in the jukebox to hear that favorite tune.

🛈 Getting There & Around

The **Mendocino Transit Authority** (MTA; ☑800-696-4682, 707-462-1422; www.mendocinotransit. org; 241 Plant Rd, Ukiah; most 1-way fares $1.50-6) operates bus 65, which travels between Willits, Ukiah and Santa Rosa daily, with an afternoon return ($26.25, three hours, four daily). Bus 95 runs between Point Arena (Hwy 1) and Santa Rosa daily, via Jenner and Bodega Bay with an afternoon return ($8.25, 3¼ hours, one daily). The North Coast route 60 goes north between Navarro River junction and Albion, Little River, Mendocino and Fort Bragg, Monday to Friday ($2.25, 1½ hours, two daily). Route 75 connects Gualala with the Navarro River Junction and continues to Ukiah ($6.75 2¾ hours, daily).

Along Highway 101 to Avenue of the Giants

To get into the most remote and wild parts of the North Coast behind the 'Redwood Curtain' on the quick, eschew winding Hwy 1 for inland Hwy 101, which occasionally pauses under the traffic lights of small towns. Diversions along the way include bountiful redwood forests past Leggett and the abandoned wilds of the Lost Coast.

Although **Ukiah** is mostly a place to gas up or grab a bite downtown, it's worth a 30-minute meandering mountain drive

west to soak at clothing-optional **Orr Hot Springs** (☑707-462-6277; www.orrhotsprings. org; 13201 Orr Springs Rd; day-use adult/child $30/25; ⊙by appointment 10am-10pm).

Just north of tiny **Leggett** on Hwy 101, take a dip in the Eel River at **Standish-Hickey State Recreation Area** (☑707-925-6482; www.parks.ca.gov; 69350 Hwy 101; per car $8; 🖬), where hiking trails traipse through virgin and second-growth redwoods. South of **Garberville** on Hwy 101, **Richardson Grove State Park** (☑707-247-3318; www.parks.ca.gov; 1600 Hwy 101, Garberville; per car $8) also protects old-growth redwood forest beside the river. Both parks have developed **campgrounds** (☑reservations 800-444-7275; www.reserveamerica.com; 1600 Hwy 101; tent & RV sites $35; 🅿).

The **Lost Coast** tempts hikers with the most rugged coastal backpacking in California. It became 'lost' when the state's highway bypassed the mountains of the King Range, which rises over 4000ft within a few miles of the ocean. From Garberville, it's 23 steep, twisting miles along a paved road to **Shelter Cove**, the main supply point but little more than a seaside subdivision with a general store, cafes and none-too-cheap ocean-view lodgings.

Along Hwy 101, 82-sq-mile **Humboldt Redwoods State Park** (☑707-946-2409; www. parks.ca.gov; Hwy 101; 🅿🖬) 🌿**FREE** protects some of California's oldest redwoods, including more than half of the world's tallest 100 trees. Magnificent groves rival those in Redwood National Park, a long drive further north. If you don't have time to hike, at least drive the awe-inspiring **Avenue of the Giants**, a 31-mile, two-lane road parallel to Hwy 101. Book ahead for **campsites** (☑information 707-946-2263, reservations 800-444-7275; www. reserveamerica.com; tent & RV sites $20-35; 🅿🎇).

🛏 Sleeping & Eating

Main motel chains are well represented on Hwy 101, particularly in and around Ukiah and Clear Lake, while midrange options and some memorable B&Bs can be found in and around the Anderson Valley.

★Old West Inn
MOTEL $

(☑707-459-4201; www.theoldwestinn.com; 1221 S Main St; r $79; 🅿🌀🌐🌐) The facade looks like a mock-up of an Old West main street and each room has a theme, from the 'Stable' to the 'Barber Shop.' The decor is simple and comfy with just enough imagination to make it interesting. Besides that this is the cleanest, friendliest and most highly recommended place in town.

★ Lakeport English Inn
B&B $$

(☑707-263-4317; www.lakeportenglishinn.com; 675 N Main St, Lakeport; r $185-210, cottages $210; P ⊖ ❄ 🕾) The finest B&B at Clear Lake is an 1875 Carpenter Gothic with 10 impeccably furnished rooms, styled with a nod to the English countryside and with such quaint names as the Prince of Wales or (wait for it) Roll in the Hay. Weekends take high tea (nonguests welcome by reservation), with scones and real Devonshire cream.

★ Boonville Hotel
BOUTIQUE HOTEL $$$

(☑707-895-2210; www.boonvillehotel.com; 14050 Hwy 128, Boonville; d $295-365; P ⊖ ❄ 🕾) Decked out in a contemporary American country feel with sea-grass flooring, pastel colors and fine linens, this historic hotel's rooms and suites are safe for urbanites who refuse to abandon style just because they've gone to the country. The rooms are all different and there are agreeable extras, including hammocks and fireplaces.

Jyun Kang Vegetarian Restaurant
VEGETARIAN $

(☑707-462-0939; www.cttbusa.org; 4951 Bodhi Way; mains $8-12; ⊙11:30am-3pm Wed-Mon; 🍴) Vegetarians (and vegans) will be swooning at the superb Asian-influenced dishes at this lunchtime restaurant located at the site of the City of Ten Thousand Buddhas (☑707-462-0939; www.cttbusa.org; 4951 Bodhi Way; ⊙8am-6pm; P).

★ Saucy Ukiah
PIZZA $$

(☑707-462-7007; www.saucyukiah.com; 108 W Standley St; pizzas $14-19, mains $13-19; ⊙11:30am-9pm Mon-Thu, to 10pm Fri, noon-10pm Sat) Yes there are arty pizzas with toppings like organic fennel pollen and almond basil pesto but there are also amazing soups, salads, pastas and starters – Nana's meatballs are to die for and the 'kicking' minestrone lives up to its name. The small-town ambience is mildly chic but fun and informal at the same time.

❶ Getting There & Around

Mendocino Transit Authority (☑707-462-1422; www.mendocinotransit.org; 241 Plant Rd) operates bus 65, which travels between Willits, Ukiah and Santa Rosa daily, with an afternoon return ($26.25, three hours, four daily). Bus 75 heads north every weekday from Gualala to the Navarro River junction at Hwy 128, then runs inland through the Anderson Valley to Ukiah, returning in the afternoon ($6.75, 2½ hours, daily).

Highway 101 from Eureka to Crescent City

Past the strip malls sprawling around its edges, the heart of Eureka is Old Town, abounding with fine Victorians buildings, antique shops and restaurants. Cruise the harbor aboard the blue-and-white 1910 Madaket (Madaket Cruises; ☑707-445-1910; www.humboldtbaymaritimemuseum.com; 1st St; narrated cruises adult/child $22/18; ⊙1pm, 2:30pm & 4pm Wed-Sat, 1pm & 2:30pm Sun-Tue mid-May–mid-Oct; 🍴) – 75-minute cruises cost adults $22 and depart from the foot of C St, while sunset cocktail cruises ($10) serve from the state's smallest licensed bar. The visitor center (www.fws.gov/refuge/humboldt_bay/visit/visitor center.html; 1020 Ranch Rd, Loleta; ⊙8am-5pm) is on Hwy 101, south of downtown.

On the north side of Humboldt Bay, Arcata is a patchouli-dipped hippie haven of radical politics. Biodiesel-fueled trucks drive in for the Saturday farmers market (www.humfarm.org; 9am-2pm Apr-Nov, from 10am Dec-Mar) on the central plaza, surrounded by art galleries, shops, cafes and bars. Make reservations to soak at Finnish Country Sauna & Tubs (☑707-822-2228; http://cafe mokkaarcata.com; 495 J St; per 30min adult/child $9.75/2; ⊙noon-11pm Sun-Thu, to 1am Fri & Sat; 🍴). Northeast of downtown stands eco-conscious, socially responsible Humboldt State University (HSU; ☑707-826-3011; www.humboldt.edu; 1 Harpst Dr; P) 🍴.

Sixteen miles north of Arcata, Trinidad sits on a bluff overlooking a breathtakingly beautiful fishing harbor. Stroll sandy beaches or take short hikes around Trinidad Head after meeting tide-pool critters at the HSU Telonicher Marine Laboratory (☑707-826-3671; www.humboldt.edu/marinelab; 570 Ewing St; $1; ⊙9am-4:30pm Mon-Fri year-round, plus 10am-5pm Sat & Sun mid-Sep–mid-May; P 🍴) 🍴. Heading north of town, Patrick's Point Dr is dotted with forested campgrounds, cabins and lodges. Patrick's Point State Park (☑707-677-3570; www.parks.ca.gov; 4150 Patrick's Point Dr; per car $8; ⊙sunrise-sunset; P 🍴) 🍴 has stunning rocky headlands, beachcombing, an authentic reproduction of a Yurok village and a campground (☑information 707-677-3570, reservations 800-444-7275; www.reserveamerica.com; 4150 Patrick's Point Dr; tent/RV sites $35/45; P 🐾) with coin-op hot showers.

Heading north, Hwy 101 passes Redwood National Park's **Thomas H Kuchel Visitor Center** (☎707-465-7765; www.nps.gov/redw; Hwy 101, Orick; ◷9am-5pm Apr-Oct, to 4pm Nov-Mar; ♿). Together, the national park and three state parks – Prairie Creek, Del Norte and Jedediah Smith – are a World Heritage site containing more than 40% of the world's remaining old-growth redwood forests. The national park is free, while state parks have an $8 day-use parking fee and developed campgrounds (p335). This patchwork of state- and federally managed land stretches all the way north to the Oregon border, interspersed with several towns. Furthest south, you'll encounter **Redwood National Park**, where a 1-mile nature trail winds through Lady Bird Johnson Grove.

Six miles north of Orick, the 10-mile Newton B Drury Scenic Parkway runs parallel to Hwy 101 through **Prairie Creek Redwoods State Park**. Roosevelt elk graze in the meadow outside the **visitor center** (☎707-488-2039; www.parks.ca.gov; Newton B Drury Scenic Pkwy; ◷9am-5pm May-Sep, to 4pm Wed-Sun Oct-Apr; ♿), where sunlight-dappled hiking trails begin. Three miles back south, mostly unpaved Davison Rd heads northwest to Gold Bluffs Beach, dead-ending at the trailhead for unbelievably lush **Fern Canyon**.

North of tiny Klamath, Hwy 101 passes the **Trees of Mystery** (☎707-482-2251; www.treesofmystery.net; 15500 Hwy 101; museum free, gondola adult/child $16/8; ◷8:30am-6:30pm Jun-Aug, 9am-6pm Sep & Oct, 9:30am-4:30pm Nov-May; ♿), a kitschy roadside attraction. Next up, Del Norte Coast Redwoods State Park preserves virgin redwood groves and unspoiled coastline. The 4.5-mile round-trip **Damnation Creek Trail** careens over 1000ft downhill past redwoods to a hidden rocky beach, best visited at low tide. Find the trailhead at a parking turnout near mile-marker 16 on Hwy 101.

Backed by a fishing harbor and bay, Crescent City is drab because, after more than half the town was destroyed by a tidal wave in 1964, it was rebuilt with utilitarian architecture. When the tide's out, you can walk across to the 1856 **Battery Point Lighthouse** (☎707-467-3089; www.delnortehistory.org; South A St; adult/child $3/1; ◷10am-4pm Wed-Sun Apr-Sep) from the south end of A St.

Beyond Crescent City, **Jedediah Smith Redwoods State Park** is the northernmost park in the system. The redwood stands here are so dense that there are few trails, but

a couple of easy hikes start near riverside swimming holes along Hwy 199 and rough, unpaved Howland Hill Rd, a 10-mile scenic drive. The Redwood National & State Parks' **Crescent City Information Center** (☎707-465-7335; www.nps.gov/redw; 1111 2nd St; ◷9am-5pm Apr-Oct, to 4pm Nov-Mar) has maps and info.

🛏 Sleeping

A mixed bag of budget and midrange motels is scattered along Hwy 101, including in Eureka, Arcata and Crescent City.

Curly Redwood Lodge　MOTEL **$**
(☎707-464-2137; www.curlyredwoodlodge.com; 701 Hwy 101 S; r $79-107; 🅿🌀❄🛜) The motel is a marvel: it's entirely built and paneled from a single curly redwood tree that measured over 18ft thick in diameter. Progressively restored and polished into a gem of mid-20th-century kitsch, the inn is like stepping into a time capsule and a delight for retro junkies. Rooms are clean, large and comfortable (request one away from the road).

★ Historic Requa Inn　HISTORIC HOTEL **$$**
(☎707-482-1425; www.requainn.com; 451 Requa Rd; r $119-199; 🅿🌀🛜) 🌿 A woodsy country lodge on bluffs overlooking the mouth of the Klamath, the creaky and bright 1914 Requa Inn is a North Coast favorite and – even better – it's a carbon-neutral facility. Many of the charming, old-timey Americana rooms have mesmerizing views over the misty river, as does the dining room, which serves locally sourced, organic New American cuisine.

Carter House Inns　B&B **$$$**
(☎707-444-8062; www.carterhouse.com; 301 L St; r $184-384; 🅿🌀🛜) Constructed in period style, this aesthetically remodeled hotel is a Victorian lookalike. Rooms have all modern amenities and top-quality linens; suites have in-room Jacuzzis and marble fireplaces. The same owners operate four other sumptuously decorated lodgings: a single-level house, two honeymoon hideaway cottages and a replica of an 1880s San Francisco mansion, which the owner built himself, entirely by hand.

🍴 Eating & Drinking

Arcata has the biggest variety of dining options, from organic juice bars and vegan cafes to Californian and world-fusion bistros.

Wildberries Marketplace　MARKET, DELI **$**
(☎707-822-0095; www.wildberries.com; 747 13th St, Arcata; sandwiches $4-10; ◷7am-midnight;

P ♪) Wildberries Marketplace is Arcata's best grocery, with natural foods, a good deli, a bakery and a juice bar.

★ **Cafe Nooner**   MEDITERRANEAN $
(☏ 707-443-4663; www.cafenooner.com; 409 Opera Alley; mains $10-14; ⊙ 11am-4pm Sun-Wed, to 8pm Thu-Sat; ♠) Exuding a cozy bistro-style ambience with red-and-white checkered tablecloths, this perennially popular restaurant serves natural, organic and Med-inspired cuisine with choices that include a Greek-style *meze* platter, plus kebabs, salads and soups. There's a healthy kids menu, as well.

★ **Brick & Fire**   CALIFORNIAN $$
(☏ 707-268-8959;   www.brickandfirebistro.com; 1630 F St, Eureka; dinner mains $14-23; ⊙ 11:30am-9pm Mon & Wed-Fri, 5-9pm Sat & Sun; 🔊) Eureka's best restaurant is in an intimate, warm-hued, bohemian-tinged setting that is almost always busy. Choose from thin-crust pizzas, delicious salads (try the pear and blue cheese) and an ever-changing selection of appetizers and mains that highlight local produce and wild mushrooms. There's a weighty wine list and servers are well-versed in pairings.

★ **Six Rivers Brewery**   MICROBREWERY
(☏ 707-839-7580; www.sixriversbrewery.com; 1300 Central Ave, McKinleyville; ⊙ 11:30am-11:30pm Sun & Tue-Thu, to 12:30am Fri & Sat, from 4pm Mon) One of the first female-owned breweries in California, the 'brew with a view' kills it in every category: great beer, amazing community vibe, occasional live music and delicious hot wings. The spicy chili-pepper ale is amazing. At first glance the menu might seem like ho-hum pub grub, but portions are fresh and huge. They also make a helluva pizza.

❶ Getting There & Away

Arcata's **Greyhound** (☏ 800-231-2222; www.greyhound.com; 🔊) depot has daily buses to San Francisco ($57, seven hours) via Eureka, Garberville, Ukiah and Santa Rosa. Several daily **Redwood Transit System** (☏ 707-443-0826; www.redwoodtransit.org) buses stop in Eureka and Arcata on the Hwy 101 (Trinidad–Scotia) route ($3, 2½ hours).

Sacramento

Sacramento is a city of contrasts. It's a former cow town where state legislators' SUVs go bumper-to-bumper with farmers' muddy, half-ton pickups at rush hour. It has sprawling suburbs, but also new lofts and upscale boutiques squeezed between aging mid-century storefronts.

The people of 'Sac' are a resourceful lot that have fostered small but thriving food, art and nightlife scenes. They rightfully crow about **Second Saturday**, the monthly Midtown gallery hop that is the symbol of the city's cultural awakening. Their ubiquitous farmers markets, farm-to-fork fare and craft beers are another point of pride.

⊙ Sights

★ **Golden 1 Center**   STADIUM
(☏ 916-701-5400; www.golden1center.com; 500 David J Stern Walk; ♠) ✐ Welcome to the arena of the future. This gleaming home to the Sacramento Kings is one of the most advanced sports facilities in the country. Made to the highest sustainability standard, it's built from local materials, powered by solar and cooled by five-story airplane hangar doors that swing open to capture the Delta breeze.

★ **California Museum**   MUSEUM
(☏ 916-653-0650; www.californiamuseum.org; 1020 O St; adult/child $9/6.50; ⊙ 10am-5pm Tue-Sat, from noon Sun; ♠) This modern museum is home to the California Hall of Fame and so the only place to simultaneously encounter César Chávez, Mark Zuckerberg and Amelia Earhart. The *California Indians* exhibit is a highlight, with artifacts and oral histories of more than 10 tribes.

Crocker Art Museum   MUSEUM
(☏ 916-808-7000; https://crockerartmuseum.org; 216 O St; adult/child $10/5; ⊙ 10am-5pm Tue, Wed & Fri-Sun, to 9pm Thu) Housed in the ornate Victorian mansion of a railroad baron, this museum has an excellent collection. Works by California painters and European masters hang beside an enthusiastically curated collection of contemporary art.

★ **California State Capitol** HISTORIC BUILDING
(☏ 916-324-0333;   http://capitolmuseum.ca.gov; 1315 10th St; ⊙ 8am-5pm Mon-Fri, from 9am Sat & Sun; ♠) **FREE** The gleaming dome of the California State Capitol is Sacramento's most recognizable structure. A painting of Arnold Schwarzenegger in a suit hangs in the West Wing along with the other governors' portraits. Some will find Capitol Park, the 40 acres of gardens and memorials surrounding the building, more interesting than what's inside. Tours run hourly until 4pm.

🛏 Sleeping

Hotels cater to business travelers, so look for weekend bargains. The freeways and suburbs around the city are glutted with budget and midrange chain lodgings.

HI Sacramento Hostel   HOSTEL $
(☎916-443-1691; http://norcalhostels.org/sac; 925 H St; dm $30-33, r from $86, without bath from $58; ⊙reception 2-10:30pm; 🅿❄@🛜) In a grand Victorian mansion, this hostel offers impressive trimmings at rock-bottom prices. It's within walking distance of the capitol, Old Sac and the train station, and has a piano in the parlor and large dining room. It attracts an international crowd often open to sharing a ride to San Francisco or Lake Tahoe.

★Citizen Hotel   BOUTIQUE HOTEL $$
(☎877-829-2429, 916-442-2700; www.thecitizen hotel.com; 926 J St; r from $180; 🅿⊖❄@🛜🐾) After an elegant, ultra-hip upgrade, this long-vacant 1927 beaux-arts tower became Downtown's coolest place to stay. The details are spot-on: luxe linens, wide-striped wallpaper and a rooftop patio with a great view of the city. There's an upscale farm-to-fork **restaurant** (☎916-492-4450; www.grange sacramento.com; 926 J St; mains $19-39; ⊙6:30-10:30am, 11:30am-2pm & 5:30-10pm Mon-Thu, to 11pm Fri, 8am-2pm & 5:30-11pm Sat, to 10pm Sun; 🛜) on the ground floor.

Greens Hotel   BOUTIQUE HOTEL $$
(www.thegreenshotel.com; 1700 Del Paso Blvd.; r from $127; 🅿⊖❄@🛜🏊) This stylishly updated motel is one of Sacramento's hippest places to stay. Although the neighborhood is a bit rough around the edges, the Greens' secure parking, pool and spacious grounds make it an ideal place for families to stop en route to or from Tahoe. The chic rooms are also classy enough for a romantic getaway.

🍴 Eating & Drinking

Skip the overpriced fare in Old Sacramento or by the capitol and head Midtown or to the Tower District.

La Bonne Soupe Cafe   DELI $
(☎916-492-9506; 920 8th St; items $5-8; ⊙11am-3pm Mon-Sat) Divine soup and sandwiches assembled with such care that the line of Downtown lunchers snakes out the door. If you're in a hurry, skip it. This humble lunch counter is focused on quality that predates drive-through haste.

★Empress Tavern   NEW AMERICAN $$$
(☎916-662-7694; www.empresstavern.com; 1013 K St; mains $13-40; ⊙11:30am-9pm Mon-Thu, to 10pm Fri, 5-10pm Sat) In the catacombs under the historic Crest Theater, this gorgeous restaurant hosts a menu of creative, meat-focused dishes. The space itself is just as impressive; the arched brick ceilings and glittering bar feel like a speakeasy supper club from a bygone era.

★Fieldwork Brewing Company   BREWERY
(☎916-329-8367; www.fieldworkbrewing.com; 1805 Capitol Ave; ⊙11am-9pm Sun-Thu, to 11pm Fri & Sat) Bustling with activity, this ultra-hip brewpub has over a dozen rotating taps of excellent, fresh beer. Playful variations of hoppy IPAs are the specialty (like the peachy Hammer Pants IPA), but it does lighter seasonal brews like the Salted Watermelon Gose. It also has board games – making it an easy place to linger when the weather is sweltering.

ℹ Getting There & Around

Sacramento International Airport is one of the nearest options for those traveling to Yosemite National Park.

The regional **Yolobus** (☎530-666-2877; www. yolobus.com) route 42B costs $2 and runs hourly between the airport and downtown; it also goes to West Sacramento, Woodland and Davis. Local **Sacramento Regional Transit buses** (RT; ☎916-321-2877; www.sacrt.com; fare $2.75) run around town; RT also runs a trolley between Old Sacramento and Downtown, as well as Sacramento's light-rail system.

Sacramento is also a fantastic city to cruise around by bike; rent them from **City Bicycle Works** (www.citybicycleworks.com; 2419 K St; per hour/day from $5/20; ⊙10am-7pm Mon-Fri, to 6pm Sat, 11am-5pm Sun).

Gold Country

The miner forty-niners are gone, but a ride along Hwy 49 through sleepy hill towns, past clapboard saloons and oak-lined byways, is a journey back to the wild ride that was modern California's founding: umpteen historical markers tell tales of gold-rush violence and banditry.

Hwy 50 divides the Northern and Southern Mines. Winding Hwy 49, which connects everything, provides plenty of vistas of the famous hills. The **Gold Country Visitors Association** (www.calgold.org) has many more touring ideas.

❶ Getting There & Around

You can reach the region by train on the transcontinental line that links Sacramento and Truckee/Reno and has a stop in Auburn. Auburn is the main entry point of the area, a short hop on the I-80 from Sacramento. From Auburn pick up Hwy 49, the classic route through the Gold Country.

Northern Mines

Known as the 'Queen of the Northern Mines,' the narrow streets of Nevada City gleam with lovingly restored buildings, tiny theaters, art galleries, cafes and shops. The **visitor center** (☑530-265-2692; www.nevada citychamber.com; 132 Main St; ☺9am-5pm Mon-Fri, 11am-4pm Sat, 11am-3pm Sun) dispenses information and self-guided walking-tour maps. On Hwy 49, the **Tahoe National Forest Headquarters** (☑530-265-4531; www. fs.usda.gov/tahoe; 631 Coyote St; ☺8am-4:30pm Mon-Fri) provides camping and hiking information and wilderness permits.

Just over a mile east of utilitarian **Grass Valley** and Hwy 49, **Empire Mine State Historic Park** (☑530-273-8522; www.empire mine.org; 10791 Empire St; adult/child $7/3; ☺10am-5pm; P♿) marks the site of one of the richest mines in California. From 1850 to 1956 it produced almost 6 million ounces of gold – over $6 billion in today's market.

If it's hot, one of the best swimming holes in the area is at **Auburn State Recreation Area** (☑530-885-4527; www.parks.ca.gov; per car $10; ☺7am-sunset). It's just east of Auburn, an I-80 pit stop about 25 miles south of Grass Valley.

Coloma is where California's gold rush started. Riverside **Marshall Gold Discovery State Historic Park** (☑530-622-3470; www. parks.ca.gov; Hwy 49, Coloma; per car $8; ☺8am-8pm late May–early Sep, to 5pm early Sep–late May; P♿☺) pays tribute to James Marshall's riot-inducing discovery, with restored buildings and gold-panning opportunities.

🛏 Sleeping & Eating

Nevada City has the biggest spread of restaurants and historical B&Bs. Motels speckle Hwy 49 in Grass Valley and I-80 in Auburn.

★**Outside Inn**   INN, COTTAGE $$
(☑530-265-2233; http://outsideinn.com; 575 E Broad St; d $79-210; P♿❄🛜🏊🐕) The best option for active explorers, this is an unusually friendly and fun inn, with 12 rooms and three cottages maintained by staff who love the outdoors. Some rooms have a patio overlooking a small creek; all have nice quilts and access to BBQ grills. It's a 10-minute walk from downtown.

★**Broad Street Inn**   INN $$
(☑530-265-2239; www.broadstreetinn.com; 517 W Broad St; r $119-134; ❄🛜🐕) ✔ This six-room inn in the heart of town is a favorite because it keeps things simple. (No weird old dolls, no yellowing lace doilies.) The good-value rooms are modern, brightly but soothingly furnished and elegant. No breakfast served.

★**Argonaut Farm to Fork Cafe**   AMERICAN $
(☑530-626-7345; www.argonautcafe.com; 331 Hwy 49, Coloma; items $3-10; ☺8am-4pm; 🛜🐕♿) Truly delicious soups, sandwiches, baked goods and coffee from well-known Sacramento and local purveyors find their way to this little wooden house in Marshall Gold Discovery State Historic Park. Crowds of schoolkids waiting for gelato can slow things down.

★**New Moon Cafe**   CALIFORNIAN $$$
(☑530-265-6399; www.thenewmooncafe.com; 203 York St; dinner mains $23-38; ☺11:30am-2pm Tue-Fri, 5-8:30pm Tue-Sun) ✔ Pure elegance, Peter Selaya's organic- and local-ingredient menu changes with the seasons. If you visit during spring or summer, go for the line-caught fish or the house-made, moon-shaped fresh ravioli. The wine list is excellent.

Southern Mines

The towns of the Southern Mines – from Placerville to Sonora – receive less traffic and their dusty streets have a whiff of Wild West, today evident in the motley crew of Harley riders and gold prospectors (still!) who populate them. Some, like **Plymouth** (ol' Pokerville), **Volcano** and **Mokelumne Hill**, are virtual ghost towns, slowly crumbling into photogenic oblivion. Others, like **Sutter Creek**, **Murphys** and **Angels Camp**, are gussied-up showpieces of Victorian Americana. Get off the beaten path at family-run vineyards and subterranean caverns, where geological wonders reward those who first navigate the touristy gift shops above ground.

A short detour off Hwy 49, **Columbia State Historic Park** (☑209-588-9128; www.parks.ca.gov; Main St; ☺most businesses 10am-5pm; P♿) **FREE** preserves blocks of authentic 1850s buildings complete with shopkeepers and street musicians in period costumes. Also near Sonora, **Railtown 1897**

State Historic Park ($\square$209-984-3953; www.railtown1897.org; 10501 Reservoir Rd, Jamestown; adult/child $5/3, incl train ride $15/10; $\odot$9:30am-4:30pm Apr-Oct, 10am-3pm Nov-Mar, train rides 10:30am-3pm Sat & Sun Apr-Oct; $\boxed{P}$ ⛓) offers excursion trains through the surrounding hills where Hollywood Westerns including *High Noon* have been filmed.

🛌 Sleeping & Eating

Lacy B&Bs, cafes and ice-cream parlors are found in nearly every town. Sonora, about an hour's drive from Yosemite National Park, and Placerville have the most motels.

⭐ **Imperial Hotel**   B&B **$$**
($\square$209-267-9172; www.imperialamador.com; 14202 Hwy 49, Amador City; r $110-155, ste $125-195; ❋⛓) Built in 1879, this is one of the area's most inventive updates to the typical antique-cluttered hotel, with sleek art-deco touches accenting the warm red brick, a genteel bar and a very good, seasonally minded restaurant (dinner mains $14 to $30). On weekends and holidays, expect a two-night minimum.

Union Inn   HISTORIC HOTEL **$$**
($\square$209-296-7711; www.volcanounion.com; 21375 Consolation St; r $130-150; $\boxed{P}$⊝❋⛓) The more comfortable of the two historic hotels in Volcano: there are four lovingly updated rooms with crooked floors, two with street-facing balconies. Flat-screen TVs and modern touches are a bit incongruous in the old building, but it's a cozy place to stay. The on-site **Union Pub** ($\square$209-296-7711; www.volcanounion.com; 21375 Consolation St; mains $10-30; $\odot$5-8pm Mon & Thu, to 9pm Fri, noon-9pm Sat, noon-8pm Sun) has the best food in town and a lovely patio garden.

City Hotel   HISTORIC HOTEL **$$**
($\square$information 209-532-1479, reservations 800-444-7275; www.reserveamerica.com; 22768 Main St; r $85-115; $\boxed{P}$⊝❋⛓) Among a handful of restored Victorian hotels in the area, City Hotel is the most elegant, with rooms that overlook a shady stretch of Main St. Adjoining the on-site restaurant Christopher's at the City Hotel (mains $10 to $30), What Cheer Saloon is an atmospheric Gold Country joint with oil paintings of lusty ladies and striped wallpaper.

Farm Table Restaurant   MEDITERRANEAN **$$**
($\square$530-295-8140; https://ourfarmtable.com; 311 Main St; sandwiches from $8, mains from $14; $\odot$11am-5pm Mon, 11am-8pm Wed, 11am-9pm Thu-

Sat, 9am-5pm Sun; ✍) A lovely deli-style place dishing up well-cooked farm-fresh food with a Mediterranean feel, alongside homespun fare such as rabbit pot pie. It specializes in charcuterie and preserving, and has plenty of gluten-free and veggie options on the menu too.

California's Northern Mountains

Remote, empty and eerily beautiful, these are some of California's least visited wild lands, an endless show of geological wonders, clear lakes, rushing rivers and high desert. The major peaks – Lassen, Shasta and the Trinity Alps – have few geological features in common, but all offer backcountry camping under starry skies.

Redding to Mt Shasta

Much of the drive north of Redding is dominated by Mt Shasta, a 14,180ft snowcapped goliath at the southern end of the volcanic Cascades Range. It arises dramatically, fueling the anticipation felt by mountaineers who seek to climb its slopes.

Don't believe the tourist brochures: Redding, the region's largest city, is a snooze. The best reason to detour off I-5 is the **Sundial Bridge**, a glass-bottomed pedestrian marvel designed by Spanish neofuturist architect Santiago Calatrava. It spans the Sacramento River at **Turtle Bay Exploration Park** ($\square$800-887-8532; www.turtlebay.org; 844 Sundial Bridge Dr; adult/child $16/12, after 3:30pm $11/7; $\odot$9am-5pm Mon-Sat, from 10am Sun, closes 1hr earlier Nov–mid-Mar; ⛓), a kid-friendly science and nature center with botanical gardens. Six miles west of Redding along Hwy 299, explore a genuine gold-rush town at **Shasta State Historic Park** ($\square$520-243-8194; www.parks.ca.gov; 15312 CA 299; museum entry adult/child $3/2; $\odot$10am-5pm Thu-Sun). Two miles further west, **Whiskeytown National Recreation Area** ($\square$530-246-1225; www.nps.gov/whis; Hwy 299 at JFK Memorial Dr, Whiskeytown; $\odot$10am-4pm) harbors **Whiskeytown Lake**, with sandy beaches, waterfall hikes and watersports and camping opportunities. In sleepy **Weaverville**, another 35 miles further west, **Joss House State Historic Park** ($\square$530-623-5284; www.parks.ca.gov; 630 Main St; tour adult/child $4/2; $\odot$tours hourly 10am-4pm Thu-Sun; $\boxed{P}$) preserves an ornate 1874 Chinese immigrant temple.

North of Redding, I-5 crosses deep-blue **Shasta Lake**, California's biggest reservoir, formed by colossal **Shasta Dam** (☑530-275-4463; www.usbr.gov/mp/ncao/shasta-dam.html; 16349 Shasta Dam Blvd; ☺visitor center 8am-5pm, tours 9am, 11am, 1pm & 3pm; P🐾) **FREE** and ringed by houseboat marinas and RV campgrounds. High in the limestone megaliths on the lake's northern side are prehistoric **Lake Shasta Caverns** (☑530-238-2341, 800-795-2283; www.lakeshastacaverns.com; 20359 Shasta Caverns Rd, Lakehead; 2hr tour adult/child 3-15yr $26/15; ☺tours every 30min 9am-4pm late May-early Sep, hourly 9am-3pm Apr-late May & early-late Sep,10am, noon & 2pm Oct-Mar; P🐾), where tours include a catamaran ride.

Another 35 miles north on I-5, **Dunsmuir** is a teeny historic railroad town with vibrant art galleries inhabiting a quaint downtown district. Six miles south off I-5, **Castle Crags State Park** (☑530-235-2684; www.parks.ca.gov; per car $8; ☺sunrise-sunset) shelters forested **campsites** (☑reservations 800-444-7275; www.reserveamerica.com; tent & RV sites $15-30). Be awed by stunning views of Mt Shasta from the top of the park's hardy 5.6-mile round-trip **Crags Trail**.

Nine miles north of Dunsmuir, **Mt Shasta city** lures climbers, new-age hippies and back-to-nature types, all of whom revere the majestic mountain looming overhead. Usually open and snow-free beyond Bunny Flat from June until October, **Everitt Memorial Hwy** ascends the mountain to a perfect sunset-watching perch at almost 8000ft – simply head east from town on Lake St and keep going. For experienced mountaineers, climbing the peak above 10,000ft requires a Summit Pass ($25), available from **Mt Shasta Ranger Station** (☑530-926-4511; www.fs.usda.gov/stnf; 204 W Alma St; ☺8am-4:30pm Mon-Fri), which has weather reports and sells topgraphic maps. Stop by downtown's **Fifth Season** (☑530-926-3606; http://thefifthseason.com; 300 N Mt Shasta Blvd; ☺9am-6pm Mon-Fri, from 8am Sat, 10am-5pm Sun) outdoor-gear shop for equipment rentals. **Shasta Mountain Guides** (☑530-926-3117; http://shastaguides.com; 2-day climbs from $625 per person) offers mountaineering trips (from $550).

🛏 Sleeping

Roadside motels are abundant, including in Mt Shasta city. Redding has the most chain lodgings, clustered near major highways. Campgrounds are abundant, especially on public lands.

★ **Shasta MountInn**   B&B $$
(☑530-926-1810; www.shastamountinn.com; 203 Birch St; r $150-175; P🐾📶) Only antique on the outside, this bright Victorian 1904 farmhouse is all relaxed minimalism, bold colors and graceful decor on the inside. Each airy room has a great bed and exquisite views of the luminous mountain. Enjoy the expansive garden, wraparound deck, outdoor hot tub and sauna. Not relaxed enough yet? Chill on the perfectly placed porch swings.

★ **McCloud River Mercantile Hotel**   INN $$
(☑530-964-2330; www.mccloudmercantile.com; 241 Main St; r $129-250; P🐾📶) Stroll upstairs to the 2nd floor of McCloud's central Mercantile Hotel and try not to fall in love; it's all high ceilings, exposed brick and a perfect marriage of preservationist class and modern panache. Antique-furnished rooms have open-floor plans. Guests are greeted with fresh flowers and can drift to sleep on feather beds after soaking in claw-foot tubs.

Railroad Park Resort   INN, CAMPGROUND $$
(☑530-235-4440; www.rrpark.com; 100 Railroad Park Rd; tent/RV sites from $29/37, d $135-165; ❋📶🐾🏊) About 2 miles south of town, off I-5, visitors can stay in refitted vintage railroad cars and cabooses. The grounds are fun for kids, who can run around the engines and plunge in a centrally situated pool. The deluxe boxcars are furnished with antiques and claw-foot tubs.

🍴 Eating & Drinking

★ **Dunsmuir Brewery Works**   PUB FOOD $
(☑530-235-1900; www.dunsmuirbreweryworks.com; 5701 Dunsmuir Ave; mains $9-13; ☺11am-10pm May-Sep, to 9pm Tue-Sun Oct-Apr; 📶) It's hard to describe this little microbrew pub without veering into hyperbole. Start with the beer: the crisp ales and porter are perfectly balanced and the IPA is apparently pretty good too, because patrons are always drinking it dry. Soak it up with awesome bar food: a warm potato salad, bratwurst, or a thick Angus or perfect veggie nut burger.

Berryvale Grocery   MARKET, CAFE $
(☑530-926-1576; www.berryvale.com; 305 S Mt Shasta Blvd; cafe items from $5; ☺store 8am-8pm, cafe to 7pm; 🐾🐾) 🌿 This market sells groceries and organic produce to health-conscious eaters. The excellent cafe serves good coffee, fresh juices and an array of tasty – mostly veggie – salads, sandwiches and wraps.

★**Café Maddalena** EUROPEAN, NORTH AFRICAN **$$**
(📞530-235-2725; www.cafemaddalena.com; 5801 Sacramento Ave; mains $15-26; ☺5-9pm Thu-Sun Feb-Dec) Simple and elegant, this cafe put Dunsmuir on the foodie map. The menu was designed by chef Brett LaMott (of Trinity Cafe fame) and changes seasonally to feature dishes from southern Europe and northern Africa. Some highlights include pan-roasted king salmon with basil cream, wild mushroom soup or sautéed rabbit with carrots and morel sauce.

Seven Suns Coffee & Cafe CAFE
(1011 S Mt Shasta Blvd; ☺5:30am-7pm; 🛜) This snug little hangout serves organic, locally roasted coffee, light meals (around $10) and is consistently busy. There's live acoustic music some evenings.

ⓘ Getting There & Around

Greyhound (www.greyhound.com) buses heading north and south on I-5 stop at the depot (628 S Weed Blvd) in Weed, 8 miles north of Mt Shasta city on I-5. Services include Redding ($15, one hour and 20 minutes, three daily), Sacramento ($40, 5½ hours, three daily) and San Francisco ($50, 10½ hours, two or three times daily).

The **STAGE bus** (📞530-842-8295; www.co.siskiyou.ca.us; 914 Pine St; fares $2.50-8) includes Mt Shasta City in its local I-5 corridor route (fares $2.50 to $8, depending on distance), which also serves McCloud, Dunsmuir, Weed and Yreka several times each weekday. Other buses connect at Yreka.

Northeast Corner

Site of California's last major Native American conflict and a half-million years of volcanic destruction, **Lava Beds National Monument** (📞530-667-8113; www.nps.gov/labe; 1 Indian Well HQ, Tulelake; 7-day entry per car $15; 🅿🚻) 🏕 is a peaceful monument to centuries of turmoil. This park's got it all: lava flows, cinder and spatter cones, volcanic craters and amazing lava tubes. It was the site of the Modoc War, and ancient Native American petroglyphs are etched into rocks and pictographs painted on cave walls. Pick up info and maps at the **visitor center** (📞530-667-8113; www.nps.gov/labe; Tulelake; ☺8am-6pm late May-early Sep, to 5pm mid-Sep–mid-May), which sells basic spelunking gear (borrow flashlights for free). Nearby is the park's basic **campground** (www.nps.gov/labe/planyourvisit/campgrounds.htm; tent & RV sites $10; 🏕), where drinking water is available.

Over 20 miles northeast of the park, the dusty town of **Tulelake** off Hwy 139 has basic motels, roadside diners and gas. Comprising six separate refuges in California and Oregon, **Klamath Basin National Wildlife Refuge Complex** is a prime stopover on the Pacific Flyway and an important wintering site for bald eagles. When the spring and fall migrations peak, more than a million birds can fill the sky. The **visitor center** (📞530-667-2231; www.klamathbasinrefuges.fws.gov; 4009 Hill Rd, Tulelake; ☺8am-4:30pm Mon-Fri, 9am-4pm Sat & Sun) is off Hwy 161, about 4 miles south of the Oregon border. Self-guided 10-mile auto tours of the Lower Klamath and Tule Lake refuges provide excellent birding opportunities. Paddle the Upper Klamath refuge's 9.5-mile canoe trail by launching from **Rocky Point Resort** (📞541-356-2287; 28121 Rocky Point Rd, Klamath Falls, OR; canoe & kayak rental per hour/half-day/day $20/45/60; ☺Apr-Oct; 🅿🚻). For gas, food and lodging, drive into Klamath Falls, OR, off Hwy 97.

Quietly impressive **Lassen Volcanic National Park** (📞530-595-4480; www.nps.gov/lavo; 38050 Hwy 36 E, Mineral; 7-day entry per car mid-Apr–Nov $20, Dec–mid-Apr $10; 🅿🚻) 🏕 has hydrothermal sulfur pools, boiling mud pots and steaming pools, as glimpsed from the **Bumpass Hell** boardwalk. Tackle **Lassen Peak** (10,457ft), the world's largest plug-dome volcano, on a strenuous, but non-technical 5-mile roundtrip trail. The park has two entrances: an hour's drive east of Redding off Hwy 44, near popular **Manzanita Lake Campground** (📞reservations 877-444-6777; www.recreation.gov; tent & RV sites $15-24; 🚻); and a 40-minute drive northwest of Lake Almanor off Hwy 89, by the **Kom Yah-mah-nee Visitor Facility** (📞530-595-4480; www.nps.gov/lavo; ☺9am-5pm, closed Mon & Tue Nov-Mar; 🚻) 🏕 Hwy 89 through the park is typically snow free and open to cars from June though October.

SIERRA NEVADA

The mighty Sierra Nevada – baptized the 'Range of Light' by poet-naturalist John Muir – is California's backbone. This 400-mile phalanx of craggy peaks, chiseled and gouged by glaciers and erosion, both welcomes and challenges outdoor-sports enthusiasts. Cradling three national parks (Yosemite, Sequoia and Kings Canyon), the Sierra is a spellbinding wonderland of superlative wilderness, boasting the contiguous USA's highest peak (Mt Whitney), North America's tallest waterfall (Yosemite Falls) and the world's oldest and biggest trees.

Yosemite National Park

There's a reason why everybody's heard of it: the granite-peak heights are dizzying, the mist from thunderous waterfalls drenching, the Technicolor wildflower meadows amazing and the majestic silhouettes of El Capitan and Half Dome almost shocking against a crisp blue sky. It's a landscape of dreams, surrounding oh-so-small people on all sides.

Crowds can be an issue in summer holidays: try to go in a shoulder season, start early and walk to escape the throng.

◎ Sights

There are four main entrances to the park ($25-30 per vehicle, depending on the season): South Entrance (Hwy 41), Arch Rock (Hwy 140), Big Oak Flat (Hwy 120 W) and Tioga Pass (Hwy 120 E). Hwy 120 traverses the park as Tioga Rd, connecting Yosemite Valley with the Eastern Sierra.

◎ Yosemite Valley

From the ground up, this dramatic valley cut by the meandering Merced River is song inspiring: rippling green meadow-grass; stately pines; cool, impassive pools reflecting looming granite monoliths; and cascading ribbons of glacially-cold white water. Often overrun and traffic-choked, **Yosemite Village** is home to the park's main **visitor center** (📞 209-372-0200; 9035 Village Dr, Yosemite Village; ⊘ 9am-5pm; 📶), **museum** (www.nps.gov/yose; 9037 Village Dr, Yosemite Village; ⊘ 9am-5pm summer, 10am-4pm rest of year, often closed noon-1pm) 🆓 **FREE**, photography gallery, movie theater, general store and many more services. **Curry Village** is another valley hub, offering public showers and outdoor-equipment rental and sales, including camping gear.

Spring snowmelt turns the valley's famous waterfalls into thunderous cataracts; most are reduced to a mere trickle by late summer. **Yosemite Falls** is North America's tallest, dropping 2425ft in three tiers. A wheelchair-accessible trail leads to the bottom of this cascade or, for solitude and different perspectives, you can trek the grueling trail to the top (6.8 miles round-trip). No less impressive are other waterfalls around

the valley. A strenuous granite staircase beside **Vernal Fall** leads you, gasping, right to the waterfall's edge for a vertical view – look for rainbows in the clouds of mist.

You can't ignore the valley's monumental **El Capitan** (7569ft), an El Dorado for rock climbers. Toothed **Half Dome** (8842ft) soars above the valley as Yosemite's spiritual centerpiece. The classic panoramic photo op is at **Tunnel View** on Hwy 41 as you drive into the valley.

◎ Glacier Point

Rising over 3000ft above the valley floor, dramatic Glacier Point (7214ft) practically puts you at eye level with Half Dome. It's at least an hour's drive from Yosemite Valley up Glacier Point Rd (usually open from May into November) off Hwy 41, or a strenuous hike along the **Four Mile Trail** (actually 4.6 miles, one way) or the less-crowded, waterfall-strewn **Panorama Trail** (8.5 miles one way). To hike one way downhill from Glacier Point, reserve a seat on the **Glacier Point Hikers' Bus** (📞 888-413-8869; 1 way/return $25/49; ⊘ mid-May–Oct).

◎ Wawona

At Wawona, an hour's drive south of Yosemite Valley, is the **Pioneer Yosemite History Center** (rides adult/child $5/4; ⊘ 24hr, rides Wed-Sun Jun-Sep; 🅿 🚻), with its covered bridge, historic buildings and horsedrawn stagecoach rides. Further south the towering **Mariposa Grove** is home to the Grizzly Giant and other giant sequoia trees. Free shuttle buses usually run to the grove from spring through fall.

◎ Tuolumne Meadows

A 90-minute drive from Yosemite Valley, high-altitude Tuolumne Meadows (pronounced *twol*-uh-mee) draws hikers, backpackers and climbers to the park's northern wilderness. The Sierra Nevada's largest subalpine meadow (8600ft) is a vivid contrast to the valley, with wildflower fields, azure lakes, ragged granite peaks, polished domes and cooler temperatures. Hikers and climbers have a paradise of options, and lake swimming and picnicking are also popular. Access is via scenic Tioga Rd (Hwy 120), which is only open seasonally. West of Tuolumne Meadows and **Tenaya Lake**, stop at **Olmsted Point** for epic vistas of Half Dome.

Hetch Hetchy

A 40-mile drive northwest of Yosemite Valley, it's the site of perhaps the most controversial dam in US history. Despite not existing in its natural state, Hetch Hetchy Valley remains pretty and mostly crowd free. A 5.4-mile round-trip hike across the dam and through a tunnel to the base of **Wapama Falls** lets you get thrillingly close to an avalanche of water crashing down into the sparkling reservoir.

Activities

With more than 800 miles of varied hiking trails, you're spoiled for choice. Easy valley-floor routes can get jammed – escape the teeming masses by heading up. Other diversions include rock climbing, cycling, trail rides, swimming, rafting and cross-country skiing.

For overnight backpacking trips, wilderness permits (from $10) are required year round. A quota system limits the number of hikers leaving daily from each trailhead. Make reservations up to 26 weeks in advance, or try your luck at the **Yosemite Valley Wilderness Center** (☑209-372-0745; Yosemite Village; ⊙8am-5pm May-Oct) or another permit-issuing station, starting at 11am on the day before you aim to hike.

Yosemite Mountaineering School   CLIMBING
(☑209-372-8344; www.travelyosemite.com; Half Dome Village; ⊙Apr-Oct) Offers top-flight instruction for novice to advanced climbers, plus guided climbs, equipment rental and bouldering instruction. Operating since the 1960s.

Sleeping

Camping, even if it's car camping in a campground near busy Yosemite Village, enhances the being-out-in-nature feeling. Backcountry wilderness camping is for the prepared and adventurous. All non-camping reservations within the park are handled by **Aramark/Yosemite Hospitality** (☑888-413-8869; www.travelyosemite.com) and can be made up to 366 days in advance; reservations are critical from May to early September. Rates – and demand – drop from October to April.

Yosemite Valley Lodge   MOTEL $$$
(☑reservations 888-413-8869; www.travelyosemite.com; 9006 Yosemite Lodge Dr, Yosemite Valley; r from $260; P❄@🛜🏊) 🚲 Situated a short walk from Yosemite Falls, this large complex contains eateries, a lively bar, a big pool and handy amenities. The rooms, spread over 15 buildings, feel somewhat lodge-like, with wooden furniture and nature photography. All have cable TV, telephone, fridge and coffeemaker, and patio or balcony panoramas.

May Lake High Sierra Camp   CABIN $$$
(☑888-413-8869; www.travelyosemite.com; adult/child $175/90) Because it's the easiest of the High Sierra camps to access, May Lake is also

---

CAMPING IN YOSEMITE

From mid-March through mid-October or November, many park campgrounds accept or require reservations, which are available starting five months in advance. Campsites routinely sell out online within minutes. All campgrounds have bear-proof lockers and campfire rings; most have potable water.

In summer most campgrounds are noisy and booked to bulging, especially **North Pines** (tent & RV sites $26; ⊙Apr-Oct; 🐾), **Lower Pines** (www.nps.gov/yose; tent & RV sites $26; ⊙Apr-Oct; 🐾) and **Upper Pines** (www.nps.gov/yose; tent & RV sites $26; ⊙year-round; 🐾) in Yosemite Valley; **Tuolumne Meadows** (www.nps.gov/yose; Tioga Rd; tent & RV sites $26; ⊙Jul-Sep; 🐾) off Tioga Rd; and riverside **Wawona** (www.nps.gov/yose; Wawona; tent & RV sites $26; ⊙year-round; 🐾).

Year-round the following are all first-come, first served: **Camp 4** (www.nps.gov/yose; shared tent sites per person $6; ⊙year-round), a rock climber's hangout in the valley; **Bridalveil Creek** (www.nps.gov/yose; tent & RV sites $18; ⊙Jul-early Sep; 🐾), off Glacier Point Rd; and **White Wolf** (www.nps.gov/yose; tent & RV sites $18; ⊙Jul-early Sep; 🐾), off Tioga Rd. They often fill before noon, especially on weekends.

Looking for a quieter, more rugged adventure? Try the primitive campgrounds (no potable water) off Tioga Rd at **Tamarack Flat** (Old Big Oak Flat Rd; tent sites $12; ⊙late Jun-Sep; 🐾), **Yosemite Creek** (www.nps.gov/yose; tent sites $12; ⊙Jul-early Sep; 🐾) and **Porcupine Flat** (www.nps.gov/yose; tent & RV sites $12; ⊙Jul–mid-Oct; 🐾), all first-come, first-served.

the best for children – at least those who'll be untroubled by the mile-plus hike to get there. Views of Mt Hoffman are quite stunning. Breakfast and dinner included in rates.

★ **Majestic Yosemite Hotel** HISTORIC HOTEL $$$
(☑reservations 888-413-8869; www.travelyosemite.com; 1 Ahwahnee Dr, Yosemite Valley; r/ste from $480/590; P❖☺@⊜☀) The crème de la crème of Yosemite's lodging, this sumptuous historic property (formerly called the Ahwahnee) dazzles with soaring ceilings and atmospheric lounges with mammoth stone fireplaces. Classic rooms have inspiring views of Glacier Point and (partial) Half Dome. For high season and holidays, book a year in advance.

🛏 Outside Yosemite

Gateway towns that have a mixed bag of motels, hotels, lodges and B&Bs include Fish Camp, Oakhurst, El Portal, Midpines, Mariposa, Groveland and, in the Eastern Sierra, Lee Vining.

★ **Yosemite Bug Rustic Mountain Resort** HOSTEL, CABIN $
(☑209-966-6666; www.yosemitebug.com; 6979 Hwy 140, Midpines; dm $30, tent cabins from $65, r with/without bath from $165/95; P❖@⊜) ✿ This folksy oasis is tucked away on a forested hillside about 25 miles west of Yosemite. A wide range of accommodations types lines the narrow ridges; some require more walking from parking areas and bathrooms than others. The **June Bug Cafe** (☑206-966-6666; www.yosemitebug.com/cafe.html; Yosemite Bug Rustic Mountain Resort, 6979 Hwy 140, Midpines; mains $8-22; ☺7-10am, 11am-2pm & 6-9pm; ☑⬧) is highly recommended. Also available are yoga lessons, massages and a spa with hot tub.

ℹ TIOGA PASS

Hwy 120 is the only road connecting Yosemite National Park with the Eastern Sierra, climbing through Tioga Pass (9945ft). Most maps mark this road 'closed in winter' which, while literally true, is misleading. Tioga Rd is usually closed from the first heavy snowfall in October or November, not reopening until May or June. Call ☑209-372-0200 or check www.nps.gov/yose/planyour-visit/conditions.htm for current road conditions.

★ **Evergreen Lodge** CABIN $$$
(☑209-379-2606; www.evergreenlodge.com; 33160 Evergreen Rd, Groveland; tents $90-125, cabins $180-415; ☺usually closed Jan–mid-Feb; P❖❄@⊜☀) ✿ Outside Yosemite National Park near the entrance to Hetch Hetchy, this classic, nearly century-old resort consists of lovingly decorated and comfy cabins (each with its own cache of board games) spread among the trees. Accommodations run from rustic to deluxe, and all cabins have private porches without distracting phone or TV. Roughing-it guests can cheat with comfy, prefurnished tents.

ℹ Information

Yosemite's entrance fee is $30 per vehicle or $15 for those on a bicycle or on foot and is valid for seven consecutive days. Passes are sold (you can use cash, checks, traveler's checks or credit/debit cards) at the various entrance stations, as well as at visitor centers in Oakhurst, Groveland, Mariposa and Lee Vining.

Yosemite Valley Visitor Center (p344) Park's busiest information desk. Shares space with bookstore run by Yosemite Conservancy and part of the museum complex in the center of Yosemite Village.

ℹ Getting There & Around

Greyhound buses and **Amtrak** trains serve Merced, west of the park, where they are met by buses operated by the **Yosemite Area Regional Transportation System** (YARTS; ☑877-989-2787; www.yarts.com); you can buy Amtrak tickets that include the YARTS segment all the way into the park. One-way tickets to Yosemite Valley are $13 ($9 child and senior, three hours) from Merced and $18 ($15 child and senior, 3½ hours) from Mammoth Lakes; fares include the park-entrance fee, making them a super bargain, and drivers accept credit cards.

The free, air-conditioned **Yosemite Valley Shuttle Bus** (www.nps.gov/yose) is a comfortable and efficient way of traveling around the park. Buses operate year-round at frequent intervals and stop at 21 numbered locations, including parking lots, campgrounds, trailheads and lodges.

Bicycling is an ideal way to take in Yosemite Valley. You can rent a wide-handled cruiser (per hour/day $11.50/32) or a bike with an attached child trailer (per hour/day $19/59) at the **Yosemite Valley Lodge** or **Half Dome Village** (per hour/day $12.50/30.50; ☺9am-6pm Mar-Oct). Strollers and wheelchairs are also rented here.

Valley visitors are advised to park and take advantage of the Yosemite Valley Shuttle Bus. Even so, traffic in the valley can feel like rush hour in LA. Glacier Point and Tioga Rds are closed in winter.

Sequoia & Kings Canyon National Parks

In these neighboring parks, giant sequoia trees are bigger – up to 27 stories high! – and more numerous than anywhere else in the Sierra Nevada. Tough and fire-charred, they'd easily swallow two freeway lanes each. Giant, too, are the mountains – including Mt Whitney (14,505ft), the tallest peak in the lower 48 states. Finally, there is the deep Kings Canyon, carved out of granite by ancient glaciers and a powerful river. For quiet, solitude and close-up sightings of wildlife, including black bears, hit the trails and lose yourself in this stunning wilderness.

◉ Sights

The two **parks** (☑559-565-3341; www.nps.gov/seki; 7-day entry per car $30; P♿) ⌖, though distinct, are operated as one unit with a single admission fee; for 24-hour recorded information, including road conditions, call the number listed or visit the parks' comprehensive website. At either entrance station (Big Stump or Ash Mountain), you'll receive an NPS map and a copy of the parks' *Guide* newspaper, with information on seasonal activities, camping and special programs, including those in the surrounding national forests and the **Giant Sequoia National Monument** (www.fs.usda.gov). It's easy enough to explore sections of both parks in a single day.

◉ Sequoia National Park

We dare you to try hugging the trees in Giant Forest, a 3-sq-mile grove protecting gargantuan specimens – the world's largest is the **General Sherman Tree**. With sore arms and sticky sap fingers, lose the crowds on a network of forested hiking trails (bring a map).

Worth a detour is **Mineral King Valley**, a late-19th-century mining and logging camp ringed by craggy peaks and alpine lakes. The 25-mile one-way scenic drive – navigating almost 700 white-knuckle hairpin turns – is usually open from late May until late October.

Giant Forest Museum   MUSEUM
(☑559-565-4480; www.nps.gov/seki; cnr Generals Hwy & Crescent Meadow Rd; ⊙9am-4:30pm; P♿) ⌖ **FREE** For a primer on the intrigu-

ing ecology and history of giant sequoias, this pint-sized modern museum will entertain both kids and adults. Hands-on exhibits teach about the life stages of these big trees, which can live for over 3000 years, and the fire cycle that releases their seeds and allows them to sprout on bare soil. The museum is housed in a historic 1920s building designed by Gilbert Stanley Underwood, famed architect of the Majestic Yosemite (formerly Ahwahnee) Hotel.

Crystal Cave   CAVE
(www.explorecrystalcave.com; Crystal Cave Rd; tours adult/child/youth from $16/5/8; ⊙May-Sep; P♿) ⌖ Discovered in 1918 by two parks employees who were going fishing, this unique cave was carved by an underground river and has marble formations estimated to be 10,000 years old. Tickets for the 50-minute introductory tour are only sold online in advance or, during October and November, at the Giant Forest Museum and Foothills Visitor Center, *not* at the cave. Bring a jacket.

◉ Kings Canyon National Park & Scenic Byway

Just north of Grant Grove Village, **General Grant Grove** brims with majestic giants. Beyond, Hwy 180 begins its 30-mile descent into Kings Canyon, serpentining past chiseled rock walls laced with waterfalls. The road meets the **Kings River**, its roar ricocheting off granite cliffs soaring over 8000ft high, making this one of North America's deepest canyons.

At the bottom of the canyon, **Cedar Grove** is the last outpost before the rugged grandeur of the Sierra Nevada backcountry begins. A popular day hike climbs 4.6 miles one way to gushing **Mist Falls** from Roads End. A favorite of birders, an easy 1.5-mile nature trail loops around **Zumwalt Meadow**, just west of Roads End. Watch for lumbering black bears and springy mule deer.

The scenic byway past Hume Lake to Cedar Grove Village is usually closed from mid-November to late April.

Boyden Cavern   CAVE
(☑209-736-2708, 866-762-2837; www.caverntours.com/BoydenRt.htm; Hwy 180; tours adult/child from $17.50/9.50; ⊙late Apr–Sep; ♿) Touring the beautiful and fantastical formations here requires no advance tickets: just show up for the basic 45-minute tour, which

departs hourly from 10am to 5pm during peak summer season. Reaching the entrance requires a short walk up a steep, paved grade. The cavern was closed for much of 2016 and 2017 because of fire damage to a footbridge; check before you visit to make sure it's open.

🏃 Activities

With over 850 miles of marked trails, the parks are a backpacker's dream. Cedar Grove and Mineral King offer the best backcountry access. Trails are usually open by mid- to late May.

For overnight backcountry trips you'll need a wilderness permit (per group $15), which is subject to a quota system in summer; outside the quota season, permits are free and available by self-registration. About 75% of spaces can be reserved, while the rest are available in person on a first-come, first-served basis. Reservations can be made from March 1 until two weeks before your trip. For details, see www.nps.gov/seki/planyour visit/wilderness_permits.htm. There's also a dedicated wilderness desk at the Lodgepole Visitor Center.

All ranger stations and visitor centers carry topo maps and hiking guides. Note that you need to store your food in park-approved bear-proof canisters, which can be rented at markets and visitor centers (from $5 per trip).

🛏 Sleeping & Eating

Camping is the best and most affordable way to experience the parks, though of course sites fill up fast in high season. Sequoia National Forest and other wilderness areas that border the parks offer alternatives. Sequoia has only one official in-park lodging option: **Wuksachi Lodge** (🖉 information 866-807-3598, reservations 317-324-0753; www.visitsequoia.com; 64740 Wuksachi Way; r $215-290; 🅿️🐾🔇📶🍸). The gateway town of Three Rivers, just outside the park entrance, offers the most accommodations. Kings Canyon has lodges in Grant Grove and Cedar Grove villages.

The few park lodges – Wuksachi, **John Muir** (🖉866-807-3598; www.visitsequoia.com; Grant Grove Village; r from $225; 🅿️🐾📶) and Cedar Grove – have restaurants, as do a couple of spots in the adjoining Sequoia National Forest. Three Rivers, just south of Sequoia, is a good place to fill up.

NPS & USFS
Campgrounds ACCOMMODATION SERVICES $
(🖉877-444-6777, 518-885-3639; www.recreation. gov) Reservation service for many of the campgrounds in the parks.

DNC Parks &
Resorts ACCOMMODATION SERVICES $$
(🖉866-807-3598, 801-559-4930; www.visitse quoia.com) Delaware North is the concessionaire operating lodges and other services in Sequoia and Kings Canyon National Parks.

Cedar Grove Lodge LODGE $$
(🖉559-565-3096; www.visitsequoia.com; 86724 Hwy 180, Cedar Grove Village; r from $130; ⊙mid-May–mid-Oct; 🅿️🐾❄️📶) The only indoor sleeping option in the canyon, this riverside lodge offers 21 unexciting motel-style rooms. A recent remodel has updated some of the frumpy decor. Three ground-floor rooms with shady furnished patios have spiffy river views and kitchenettes.

★ Sequoia High Sierra Camp CABIN $$
(🖉866-654-2877; www.sequoiahighsierracamp. com; tent cabins without bath incl all meals adult/child $250/150; ⊙mid-Jun–mid-Sep) A mile's hike deep into the Sequoia National Forest, this off-the-grid, all-inclusive resort is nirvana for those who don't think luxury camping is an oxymoron. Canvas bungalows are spiffed up with pillow-top mattresses, feather pillows and cozy wool rugs. Restrooms and a shower house are shared. Reservations are required, and there's usually a two-night minimum stay.

ℹ️ Information

Lodgepole Village and Grant Grove Village are the parks' main commercial hubs. Both have visitor centers, post offices, markets, ATMs, a coin-op laundry and public showers (summer only). Expensive gas is available at Hume Lake (year-round) and Stony Creek (closed in winter) outside the parks on national-forest land.

The following visitor centres are open year-round:
Kings Canyon Visitor Center (🖉559-565-4307; Hwy 180, Grant Grove Village; ⊙9am-5pm) In the Grant Grove Village of Kings Canyon.

Lodgepole Visitor Center (🖉559-565-4436; Lodgepole Village; ⊙7am-5pm late Apr–early Oct, to 7pm peak season) Located in the heart of Sequoia.

ⓘ Getting There & Around

You can use Fresno to connect to Grant Grove in Kings Canyon with **Big Trees Transit** (☑ 800-325-7433; www.bigtreestransit.com; round-trip incl park entry fee $15; ⊘ late May-early Sep), or the **Sequoia Shuttle** (☑ 877-287-4453; www.sequoiashuttle.com; ⊘ late May-late Sep) (summer only) to get between Visalia and the Giant Forest area of Sequoia.

Sequoia and Kings Canyon are both accessible by car only from the west, via Hwy 99 from Fresno or Visalia.

Sequoia National Park has five free shuttle routes within the park; Kings Canyon has no shuttles.

Eastern Sierra

Vast, empty and majestic, here jagged peaks plummet down into the desert, a dramatic juxtaposition that creates a potent scenery cocktail. Hwy 395 runs the entire length of the eastern side of the Sierra Nevada, with turnoffs leading to pine forests, wildflower-strewn meadows, placid lakes, hot springs and glacier-gouged canyons. Hikers, backpackers, mountain bikers, fishers and skiers all find escapes here.

At **Bodie State Historic Park** (☑ 760-647-6445; www.parks.ca.gov/bodie; Hwy 270; adult/child $8/4; ⊘ 9am-6pm mid-Mar–Oct, to 4pm Nov–mid-Mar; 🅿 🚻), the weathered buildings of a gold-rush boomtown sit frozen in time on a dusty, windswept plain. To get there, head east for 13 miles (the last three unpaved) on Hwy 270, about 7 miles south of Bridgeport. Snow usually closes the access road in winter and early spring.

Further south at **Mono Lake** (www.monolake.org), unearthly tufa towers rise from the alkaline water like drip sand castles. Off Hwy 395, **Mono Basin Scenic Area Visitor Center** (☑ 760-647-3044; www.fs.usda.gov/inyo; 1 Visitor Center Dr; ⊘ generally 8am-5pm Apr-Nov; 🚻) has excellent views and educational exhibits, but the best photo ops are from the mile-long nature trail at the **South Tufa Area** (adult/child $3/free). From the nearby town of Lee Vining, Hwy 120 heads west into Yosemite National Park via seasonal Tioga Pass.

Continuing south on Hwy 395, detour along the scenic 16-mile **June Lake Loop** or push on to **Mammoth Lakes**, a popular four-seasons resort guarded by 11,053ft **Mammoth Mountain** (☑ 800-626-6684, 760-934-2571, 24hr snow report 888-766-9778; www.mammothmountain.com; adult/13-18yr/7-12yr $125/98/35; 🚻), a top-notch skiing area. The slopes morph into a mountain-bike park in summer, when scenic gondola rides run. There's also camping and day hiking around Mammoth Lakes Basin and Reds Meadow, the latter near the 60ft-high basalt columns of **Devils Postpile National Monument** (☑ 760-934-2289; www.nps.gov/depo; shuttle day pass adult/child $7/4; ⊘ late May-Oct), formed by volcanic activity. Hot-springs fans can soak in primitive pools off Benton Crossing Rd or view the geysering water at **Hot Creek Geological Site**, both off Hwy 395 southeast of town. The in-town **Mammoth Lakes Welcome Center & Ranger Station** (☑ 760-924-5500, 888-466-2666; www.visitmammoth.com; 2510 Hwy 203; ⊘ 9am-5pm) has helpful maps and information.

Further south, Hwy 395 descends into the Owens Valley. In frontier-flavored **Bishop**, **Mountain Light Gallery** (☑ 760-873-7700; www.mountainlight.com; 106 S Main St; ⊘ 10am-5pm Mon-Sat, 11am-4pm Sun) **FREE** and the historical **Laws Railroad Museum** (☑ 760-873-5950; www.lawsmuseum.org; Silver Canyon Rd; donation $5; ⊘ 10am-4pm; 🚻) are minor attractions. A gateway for packhorse trips, Bishop accesses the Eastern Sierra's best fishing and rock climbing. Budget a half-day for the thrilling drive up to the **Ancient Bristlecone Pine Forest**. These gnarled, otherworldly looking trees – the world's oldest – are found above 10,000ft on the slopes of the White Mountains. The road (closed by snow in winter and early spring) is paved to the **Schulman Grove Visitor Center** (☑ 760-873-2500; www.fs.usda.gov/inyo; White Mountain Rd; per person/car $3/6; ⊘ 10am-4pm Fri-Mon mid-May–early Nov), where hiking trails await. From Hwy 395 in Big Pine, take Hwy 168 east for 12 miles, then follow White Mountain Rd uphill for 10 miles.

Hwy 395 barrels south to **Manzanar National Historic Site** (☑ 760-878-2194; www.nps.gov/manz; 5001 Hwy 395; ⊘ 9am-5:30pm Apr–mid-Oct, 10am-4:30pm mid-Oct–Mar; 🅿 🚻) 🍴 **FREE**, which memorializes the camp where some 10,000 Japanese Americans were unjustly interned during WWII. Further south in Lone Pine, you'll finally glimpse Mt Whitney (14,505ft), the highest mountain in the lower 48 states. The heart-stopping, 12-mile scenic drive up **Whitney Portal Road** (closed in winter and early spring) is spectacular. Climbing the peak is hugely popular, but requires a permit (per person $15) awarded via annual lottery. Just south of town, the **Eastern Sierra Interagency Visitor Center** (☑760-876-6222; www.fs.fed.us/r5/inyo; cnr Hwys 395 & 136; ⊗8am-5pm) issues wilderness permits, dispenses outdoor-recreation info and sells books and maps.

West of Lone Pine, the bizarrely shaped boulders of the Alabama Hills have enchanted filmmakers of Hollywood Westerns. Peruse vintage memorabilia and movie posters back in town at the **Museum of Western Film History** (☑760-876-9909; www.museum ofwesternfilmhistory.org; 701 S Main St; adult/under 12yr $5/free; ⊗10am-6pm Mon-Wed, to 7pm Thu-Sat, to 4pm Sun Apr-Oct, 10am-5pm Mon-Sat, to 4pm Sun Nov-Mar; P♿).

🛏 Sleeping

The Eastern Sierra is freckled with campgrounds; backcountry camping requires a wilderness permit, available at ranger stations. Bishop, Lone Pine and Bridgeport have the most motels. Mammoth Lakes has a few motels and hotels and dozens of inns, B&Bs, condos and vacation rentals. Reservations are essential everywhere in summer.

★Whitney Portal Hostel & Hotel
HOSTEL, MOTEL $

(☑760-876-0030; www.whitneyportalstore.com; 238 S Main St; dm/d $25/85; ❄🎧📺) A popular launchpad for Mt Whitney trips and a locus of posthike washups (public showers are available), the Whitney has the cheapest beds in town – reserve dorms months ahead for July and August. There's no common space, just well-maintained single-sex bunk-bed rooms, though amenities include towels, TVs, in-room kitchenettes and coffeemakers.

★Inn at Benton Hot Springs
INN $$

(☑866-466-2824, 760-933-2287; www.his toricbentonhotsprings.com; Hwy 120, Benton; tent & RV sites for 2 people $40-50, d with/without bath $129/109; ❄🎧📺) Soak in your own hot-springs tub and snooze beneath the moonlight at Benton Hot Springs, a small, historic resort in a 150-year-old former silver-mining town nestled in the White Mountains. Choose from nine well-spaced camp sites with private tubs or themed, antique-filled B&B rooms with semi-private tubs. Daytime dips ($10 per person per hour) are available. Reservations essential.

Dow Hotel & Dow Villa Motel
HOTEL, MOTEL $$

(☑760-876-5521; www.dowvillamotel.com; 310 S Main St; hotel r with/without bath from $89/70, mo-

tel r $117-158; P♿❄@🎧📶📺) John Wayne and Errol Flynn are among the stars who have stayed at this venerable hotel. Built in 1922, the place has been restored but retains much of its rustic charm. The rooms in the newer motel section have air-con and are more comfortable and bright, but also more generic.

Tamarack Lodge
LODGE, CABIN $$

(☑800-626-6684, 760-934-2442; www.tamarack lodge.com; 163 Twin Lakes Rd; r with/without bath from $199/149, cabins from $169; P♿@🎧) ✔ In business since 1924, this charming year-round resort on Lower Twin Lake has a cozy fireplace lodge, a bar and excellent restaurant, 11 rustic-style rooms and 35 cabins. The cabins range from very simple to simply deluxe, and come with full kitchen, private bathroom, porch and wood-burning stove. Some can sleep up to 10 people. Daily resort fee $20.

🍴 Eating & Drinking

Alabama Hills Cafe
DINER $

(☑760-876-4675; 111 W Post St; mains $8-14; ⊗7am-2pm; 🎧📶♿) At everyone's favorite breakfast joint, the portions are big, the bread is freshly baked, and the hearty soups, sandwiches and fruit pies make lunch an attractive option too. You can also plan your drive through the **Alabama Hills** with the help of the map on the menu.

Mammoth Tavern
GASTROPUB $$

(☑760-934-3902; www.mammothtavern.com; 587 Old Mammoth Rd; mains $13-28; ⊗4-11pm Tue-Sun) Mammoth Tavern hits the spot with comfort food like shepherd's pie, oysters, fondue and garlic-turkey meatballs. Gorgeous salads too. Warm lighting, wood-paneled walls rising to a circular ceiling, and drop-dead-gorgeous views of the snow-capped Sherwin Range mean the big-screen TVs are an unnecessary distraction. Drinks include tasty house cocktails, local drafts, interesting whiskeys and over two dozen wines by the glass.

★Skadi
NORWEGIAN $$$

(☑760-914-0962; www.skadirestaurant.com; 94 Berner St; mains $30-38; ⊗5-11pm Wed-Mon) Considering its more-than-mundane location in an industrial strip, Skadi comes as a surprise. The Swiss Alps decor and innovative menu are the creation of chef Ian Algerøen, inspired by his Norwegian heritage and training in European fine-dining techniques. On the menu you'll find house-smoked trout with horseradish cream, Canadian duck breast with arctic lingonberries and pan-seared day-boat scallops. Reservations required.

★ **June Lake Brewing**   MICROBREWERY
(www.junelakebrewing.com; 131 S Crawford Ave; ⊙ 11am-8pm Wed-Mon, to 9pm Fri & Sat; 🕷️) A top regional draw, June Lake Brewing's open tasting room serves 10 drafts, including a 'SmoKin' Porter, Deer Beer Brown Ale and some awesome IPAs. Brewers swear the June Lake water makes all the difference.

Mammoth Brewing Company   BREWERY
(📞760-934-7141; www.mammothbrewingco.com; 18 Lake Mary Rd; ⊙ 10am-9:30pm Sun-Thu, to 10:30pm Fri & Sat) You be the judge whether beer is brewed best at high altitude. Boasting the highest West Coast brewery, at 8000ft, Mammoth Brewing Company offers more than a dozen brews on tap (flights $5 to $7) – including special seasonal varieties not found elsewhere. Tasty bar food's available, and you can pick up some IPA 395 or Double Nut Brown to go.

Lake Tahoe

Shimmering in myriad shades of blue and green, Lake Tahoe is the USA's second-deepest lake and, at 6255ft high, it is also one of the highest-elevation lakes in the country. Driving around the spellbinding 72-mile scenic shoreline will give you quite a workout behind the wheel. Generally, the north shore is quiet and upscale; the west shore, rugged and old-timey; the east shore, undeveloped; the south shore, busy and tacky, with aging motels and flashy casinos; and nearby Reno, the biggest little city in the region.

ℹ️ Information

Lake Tahoe Visitors Authority (📞800-288-2463; www.tahoesouth.com; 169 Hwy 50, Stateline, NV; ⊙ 9am-5pm Mon-Fri) A full range of tourist information.

North Lake Tahoe Visitors Bureaus (📞800-468-2463; www.gotahoenorth.com) Help with accommodations and outdoor-activity bookings.

ℹ️ Getting There & Around

Greyhound buses from Reno, Sacramento and San Francisco run to Truckee, and you can also get the daily Zephyr train here from the same destinations. From Truckee, take the **Truckee Transit** (📞530-587-7451; www.laketahoetransit.com; single/day pass $2.50/5) to Donner Lake, or **Tahoe Area Rapid Transit** (TART;

📞530-550-1212; www.laketahoetransit.com; 10183 Truckee Airport Rd; single/day pass $2/4) (TART) buses to the north, west and east shore of the lake.

The winter **Bay Area Ski Bus** (📞925-680-4386; www.bayareaskibus.com) connects San Francisco and Sacramento with Tahoe's slopes.

TART runs buses along the north shore as far as Incline Village, down the western shore to Ed Z'berg Sugar Pine Point State Park, and north to Squaw Valley and Truckee via Hwy 89. The main routes typically depart hourly from about 6am until 6pm daily.

South Lake Tahoe & West Shore

With retro motels and eateries lining busy Hwy 50, South Lake Tahoe gets crowded. Gambling at Stateline's casino hotels, just across the Nevada border, attracts thousands, as does the world-class ski resort of **Heavenly** (📞775-586-7000; www.skiheavenly.com; 4080 Lake Tahoe Blvd; adult/child 5-12yr/youth 13-18yr $135/79/113; ⊙ 9am-4pm Mon-Fri, from 8:30am Sat, Sun & holidays; 🕷️). In summer a trip up Heavenly's gondola (adult/child $42/20) guarantees fabulous views of the lake and the **Desolation Wilderness**, with its raw granite peaks, glacier-carved valleys and alpine lakes favored by hikers. Get maps, information and wilderness permits (per adult $5 to $10) from the **USFS Taylor Creek Visitor Center** (📞530-543-2674; www.fs.usda.gov/ltbmu; Visitor Center Rd, off Hwy 89; ⊙ 8am-5pm late May-Sep, to 4pm Oct). It's 3 miles north of the 'Y' intersection of Hwys 50/89, at **Tallac Historic Site** (www.tahoeheritage.org; Tallac Rd; optional tour adult/child $10/5; ⊙ 10am-4pm daily mid-Jun–Sep, Fri & Sat late May–mid-Jun; 🕷️) **FREE**, preserving swish early-20th-century vacation estates.

From sandy, swimmable **Zephyr Cove** (📞775-589-4901; www.zephyrcove.com; 760 Hwy 50; per car $10; 🕷️) across the Nevada border or the in-town Ski Run Marina, **Lake Tahoe Cruises** (📞800-238-2463; www.zephyrcove.com; 900 Ski Run Blvd; adult/child from $55/20; 🕷️) plies the 'Big Blue' year round. Paddle under your own power with **Kayak Tahoe** (📞530-544-2011; www.kayaktahoe.com; 3411 Lake Tahoe Blvd; kayak single/double 1hr $25/35, 1 day $65/85, lessons & tours from $40; ⊙ 9am-5pm Jun-Sep). Back on shore, boutique-chic motels include the **Alder Inn** (📞530-544-4485; www.alderinn.com; 1072 Ski Run Blvd; r $89-149; 🅿️😑🐾🛜) and the hip **Basecamp Hotel** (📞530-208-0180; www.basecamphotels.com; 4143 Cedar Ave; d $109-229, 8-person bunk room

$209-299, pet fee $40; 🛜📺) ⓟ, which has a rooftop hot tub, or pitch a tent at lakeside **Fallen Leaf Campground** (☑info 530-544-0426, reservations 877-444-6777; www.recreation.gov; 2165 Fallen Leaf Lake Rd; tent & RV sites $33-35, yurts $84; ⊙mid-May–mid-Oct; 📺). Fuel up at vegetarian-friendly **Sprouts** (www.sprouts cafetahoe.com; 3123 Harrison Ave; mains $7-10; ⊙8am-9pm; 📶🍴) natural-foods cafe, or with a peanut-butter-topped burger and garlic fries at the **Burger Lounge** (☑530-542-2010; 717 Emerald Bay Rd; dishes $4-10; ⊙10am-8pm Jun-Sep, 11am-7pm Thu-Mon Oct-May; 🍴).

Hwy 89 threads northwest along the thickly forested west shore to **Emerald Bay State Park** (☑530-541-6498; www.parks.ca.gov), where granite cliffs and pine trees frame a sparkling fjordlike inlet. A 1-mile trail leads steeply downhill to **Vikingsholm Castle** (http://vikingsholm.com; tour adult/child 7-17yr $10/8; ⊙10:30am-3:30pm or 4pm late May–Sep; ℗🍴), a 1920s Scandinavian-style mansion. From there, the **Rubicon Trail** ribbons 4.5 miles north along the lakeshore past petite coves to **DL Bliss State Park** (☑530-525-7277; www.parks.ca.gov; per car $10; ⊙late May–Sep; ℗🍴) ⓟ, offering sandy beaches. Further north, **Tahoma Meadows B&B Cottages** (☑530-525-1553; www.tahomamea dows.com; 6821 W Lake Blvd; cottages $119-239, pet fee $20; ℗⊖🛜📺) rents country cabins.

North & East Shores

A busy commercial hub, **Tahoe City** is great for grabbing food and supplies and renting outdoor-sports gear. It's not far from **Squaw Valley USA** (☑530-452-4331; www.squaw.com; 1960 Squaw Valley Rd, off Hwy 89, Olympic Valley; adult/child 5-12yr/youth 13-22yr $124/75/109; ⊙9am-4pm Mon-Fri, from 8:30am Sat, Sun & holidays; 🍴), a huge ski resort. Après-ski crowds gather at **Bridgetender Tavern & Grill** (www.tahoebridgetender.com; 65 W Lake Blvd; ⊙11am-11pm, to midnight Fri & Sat) back in town. In the morning, gobble eggs Benedict with house-smoked salmon at down-home **Fire Sign Cafe** (www.firesigncafe.com; 1785 W Lake Blvd; mains $7-13; ⊙7am-3pm; 📶🍴), 2 miles further south.

In summer, swim or kayak at **Tahoe Vista** or **Kings Beach**. Overnight at **Cedar Glen Lodge** (☑530-546-4281; www.tahoecedarglen.com; 6589 N Lake Blvd; r, ste & cottages $139-350, pet fee $30; @🛜📺📺), where rustic-themed cottages and rooms have kitchenettes, or well-kept, compact **Hostel Tahoe** (☑530-546-3266; www.hosteltahoe.com; 8931 N Lake Blvd;

dm/d/q $33/60/80; @🛜) ⓟ. East of Kings Beach's casual lakeside eateries, Hwy 28 barrels into Nevada. Catch a live-music show at a just-over-the-border casino, or for more happening bars and bistros, drive further to Incline Village.

With pristine beaches, lakes and miles of multi-use trails, **Lake Tahoe-Nevada State Park** is the east shore's biggest draw. Summer crowds splash in the turquoise waters of **Sand Harbor**. The 13-mile **Flume Trail**, a mountain biker's holy grail, ends further south at **Spooner Lake**. Back in Incline Village, **Flume Trail Bikes** (http://flumetrailtahoe.com) offers bicycle rentals and shuttles.

Truckee & Around

North of Lake Tahoe off I-80, Truckee is not in fact a truck stop but a thriving mountain town, with coffee shops, trendy boutiques and dining in downtown's historical district. Ski bums have several resorts to pick from, including glam **Northstar California** (☑530-562-1010; www.northstarcalifornia.com; 5001 Northstar Dr, off Hwy 267; adult/child 5-12yr/youth 13-18yr $130/77/107; ⊙8am-4pm; 🍴); kid-friendly **Sugar Bowl** (☑530-426-9000; www.sugarbowl.com; 629 Sugar Bowl Rd, off Donner Pass Rd, Norden; adult/child 6-12yr/youth 13-22yr $85/35/76; ⊙9am-4pm; 🍴); and **Royal Gorge** (☑530-426-3871; www.royalgorge.com; 9411 Pahatsi Rd, off I-80 exit Soda Springs/Norden, Soda Springs; adult/youth 13-22yr $32/25; ⊙9am-5pm during snow season; 🍴📺), paradise for cross-country skiers.

West of Hwy 89, **Donner Summit** is where the infamous Donner Party became trapped during the fierce winter of 1846–47. Fewer than half survived – some by cannibalizing their dead friends. The grisly tale is chronicled at the museum inside **Donner Memorial State Park** (☑530-582-7892; www.parks.ca.gov; Donner Pass Rd; per car $8; ⊙10am-5pm; ℗🍴), which offers **camping** (☑530-582-7894, reservations 800-444-7275; www.reserveamerica.com; tent & RV sites $35; ⊙late May-late Sep). Nearby **Donner Lake** is popular with swimmers and paddlers.

On the outskirts of Truckee, green-certified **Cedar House Sport Hotel** (☑530-582-5655; www.cedarhousesporthotel.com; 10918 Brockway Rd; r $170-295; ℗⊖@🛜📺) ⓟ offers stylish boutique rooms and an outstanding restaurant. Down pints of Donner Party Porter at **Fifty Fifty Brewing Co** (www.fiftyfifty brewing.com; 11197 Brockway Rd; ⊙11:30am-9pm Sun-Thu, to 9:30pm Fri & Sat).

Pacific Northwest

Best Places to Eat

➡ Ned Ludd (p392)

➡ Chow (p401)

➡ Ox (p392)

➡ Sitka & Spruce (p367)

Best Places to Sleep

➡ Timberline Lodge (p399)

➡ Crater Lake Lodge (p402)

➡ Hotel Monaco (p365)

➡ Olympic Lights B&B (p377)

➡ Historic Davenport Hotel (p381)

Why Go?

As much a state of mind as a geographical region, the northwest corner of the US is a land of subcultures and new trends, where evergreen trees frame snow-dusted volcanoes, and inspired ideas scribbled on the back of napkins become tomorrow's start-ups. You can't peel off the history in layers here, but you *can* gaze wistfully into the future in fast-moving, innovative cities such as Seattle and Portland, which are sprinkled with food carts, streetcars, microbreweries, green belts, coffee connoisseurs and weird urban sculpture.

Ever since the days of the Oregon Trail, the Northwest has had a hypnotic lure for risk-takers and dreamers; the metaphoric carrot still dangles. There's the air, so clean they ought to bottle it; the trees, older than many of Rome's Renaissance palaces; and the end-of-the-continent coastline, holding back the force of the world's largest ocean. Cowboys take note: it doesn't get much more 'wild' or 'west' than this.

When to Go
Seattle

Jan–Mar Most reliable snow cover for skiing in the Cascades and beyond.

May Festival season: Portland Rose and International Film Festival and more.

Jul–Sep The best hiking months, between the spring snowmelt and the first fall flurries.

Pacific Northwest Highlights

1 **San Juan Islands** (p377) Cycling and kayaking around the quieter corners.

2 **Oregon Coast** (p402) Exploring this gorgeous region, from scenic Astoria to balmy Port Orford.

3 **Olympic National Park** (p372) Admiring trees older than Europe's Renaissance castles.

4 **Pike Place Market** (p358) Watching the greatest outdoor show in the Pacific Northwest.

5 **Portland** (p385) Walking the green and serene neighborhoods, energized by beer, coffee and food-cart treats.

6 **Crater Lake National Park** (p402) Witnessing the impossibly deep-blue waters and scenic panoramas.

7 **Bend** (p400) Going mountain biking, rock climbing or skiing in this outdoor mecca.

8 **Walla Walla** (p384) Tasting sumptuous reds and whites in the surrounding wine regions.

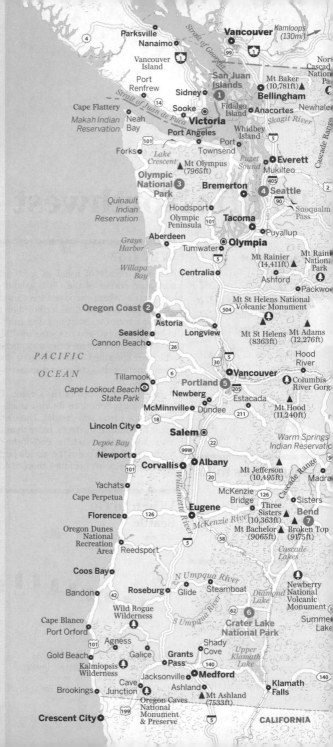

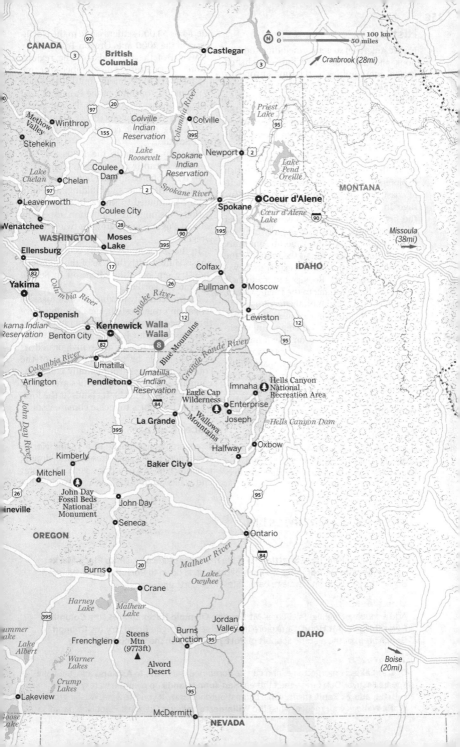

History

Native American societies, including the Chinook and the Salish, had long-established coastal communities by the time Europeans arrived in the Pacific Northwest in the 18th century. Inland, on the arid plateaus between the Cascades and the Rocky Mountains, the Spokane, Nez Percé and other tribes thrived on seasonal migration between river valleys and temperate uplands.

Three hundred years after Columbus landed in the New World, Spanish and British explorers began probing the northern Pacific coast, seeking the fabled Northwest Passage. In 1792 Captain George Vancouver was the first explorer to sail the waters of Puget Sound, claiming British sovereignty over the entire region. At the same time, an American, Captain Robert Gray, found the mouth of the Columbia River. In 1805 the explorers Lewis and Clark crossed the Rockies and made their way down the Columbia to the Pacific Ocean, extending the US claim on the territory.

In 1824 the British Hudson's Bay Company established Fort Vancouver in Washington as headquarters for the Columbia region. This opened the door to waves of settlers, but had a devastating impact on the indigenous cultures, which were assailed by European diseases and alcohol.

In 1843 settlers at Champoeg, on the Willamette River south of Portland, voted to organize a provisional government independent of the Hudson's Bay Company, thereby casting their lot with the US, which formally acquired the territory from the British by treaty in 1846. Over the next decade, some 53,000 settlers came to the Northwest via the 2000-mile Oregon Trail.

Arrival of the railroads set the region's future. Agriculture and lumber became the pillars of the economy until 1914, when WWI and the opening of the Panama Canal brought increased trade to Pacific ports. Shipyards opened along Puget Sound, and the Boeing aircraft company set up shop near Seattle.

Big dam projects in the 1930s and '40s provided cheap hydroelectricity and irrigation. WWII offered another boost for aircraft manufacturing and shipbuilding, and agriculture continued to thrive. In the postwar period, Washington's population, especially around Puget Sound, grew to twice that of Oregon.

In the 1980s and '90s, the economic emphasis shifted with the rise of the high-tech industry, embodied by Microsoft in Seattle and Intel in Portland.

Hydroelectricity production and massive irrigation projects along the Columbia have threatened the river's ecosystem in the past few decades, and logging has also left its scars. But the region has reinvigorated its eco-credentials by attracting some of the country's most environmentally conscious companies, and its major cities are among the greenest in the US. It stands at the forefront of US efforts to tackle climate issues.

Local Culture

The stereotypical image of a Pacific Northwesterner is a casually dressed latte-sipping urbanite who drives a Prius, votes Democrat and walks around with an unwavering diet

---

THE PACIFIC NORTHWEST IN ...

Four Days

Hit the ground running in **Seattle** to see the main sights, including **Pike Place Market** and the **Seattle Center**. After a couple of days, head down to **Portland**, where you can do like the locals do and cycle to bars, cafes, food carts and shops.

One Week

Add a couple of highlights such as **Mt Rainier**, **Olympic National Park**, the **Columbia River Gorge** or **Mt Hood**. Or explore the spectacular Oregon Coast (try the **Cannon Beach** area) or the historic seaport of **Port Townsend** on the Olympic Peninsula.

Two Weeks

Crater Lake is unforgettable, and can be combined with a trip to **Ashland** and its Shakespeare Festival. Don't miss the ethereal **San Juan Islands** up near the watery border with Canada, or **Bend**, the region's biggest outdoor draw. If you like wine, Washington's **Walla Walla** is your mecca, while the **Willamette Valley** is Oregon's Pinot Noir paradise.

of Nirvana-derived indie rock programmed into their iPod. But, as with most fleeting regional generalizations, the reality is far more complex.

Noted for their sophisticated cafe culture and copious microbrew pubs, the urban hubs of Seattle and Portland are the Northwest's most emblematic cities. But head east into the region's drier and less verdant interior, and the cultural affiliations become increasingly more traditional. Here, strung along the Columbia River Valley or nestled amid the arid steppes of southeastern Washington, small towns host raucous rodeos, tourist centers promote cowboy culture, and a cup of coffee is served 'straight up' with none of the chai lattes and frappés that are par for the course in the bigger cities.

In contrast to the USA's hardworking eastern seaboard, life out west is more casual and less frenetic. Ideally, Westerners would rather work to live than live to work. Indeed, with so much winter rain, the citizens of the Pacific Northwest will dredge up any excuse to shun the nine-to-five treadmill and hit the great outdoors a couple of hours (or even days) early. Witness the scene in late May and early June, when the first bright days of summer prompt a mass exodus of hikers and cyclists to make enthusiastically for the national parks and wilderness areas for which the region is justly famous.

❶ Getting There & Around

AIR
Seattle-Tacoma International Airport, aka 'Sea-Tac,' and Portland International Airport are the main airports for the region, serving many North American and several international destinations.

BOAT
Washington State Ferries (www.wsdot.wa.gov/ferries) links Seattle with Bainbridge and Vashon Islands. Other WSF routes cross from Whidbey Island to Port Townsend on the Olympic Peninsula, and from Anacortes through the San Juan Islands to Sidney, BC. Victoria Clipper (www.clippervacations.com) operates services from Seattle to Victoria, BC; ferries to Victoria also operate from Port Angeles. Alaska Marine Highway ferries (www.dot.state.ak.us/amhs) go from Bellingham, WA, to Alaska.

BUS
Greyhound (www.greyhound.com) provides service along the I-5 corridor from Bellingham in northern Washington down to Medford in southern Oregon, with connecting services across the US and Canada. East–west routes fan out toward Spokane, Yakima, the Tri-Cities (Kennewick, Pasco and Richland in Washington), Walla Walla and Pullman in Washington, and Hood River and Pendleton in Oregon. Private bus companies service most of the smaller towns and cities across the region, often connecting to Greyhound or Amtrak.

CAR
Driving your own vehicle is by far the most convenient way of touring the Pacific Northwest. Major and minor rental agencies are commonplace throughout the region. I-5 is the major north–south artery. In Washington I-90 heads east from Seattle to Spokane and into Idaho. In Oregon I-84 branches east from Portland along the Columbia River Gorge to link up with Boise in Idaho.

TRAIN
Amtrak (www.amtrak.com) runs train services north (to Vancouver, Canada) and south (to California), linking Seattle, Portland and other major urban centers with the *Cascades* and *Coast Starlight* routes. The famous *Empire Builder* heads east to Chicago from Seattle and Portland (joining up in Spokane).

WASHINGTON

Washington state is the heart of the Pacific Northwest. With that title comes everything you'd hope for, from the lush, green Olympic Peninsula to the white peaks of the Cascade Mountains and the crisp, whale-surrounded San Juan Islands. Head east and you'll see another side of the state that's more cowboy than boutique, where the world gets much of its apples and the skies go on forever. The biggest urban jolt is Seattle, but other corners such as Spokane, Bellingham and Olympia are gaining sophistication by the day.

Seattle

Combine the brains of Portland, OR, with the beauty of Vancouver, BC, and you'll get something approximating Seattle. It's hard to believe that the Pacific Northwest's largest metropolis was considered a 'secondary' US city until the 1980s, when a combination of bold innovation and unabashed individualism turned it into one of the dot-com era's biggest trendsetters, spearheaded by an unlikely alliance of coffee-sipping computer geeks and navel-gazing musicians.

WASHINGTON FACTS

Nickname Evergreen State

Population 7.3 million

Area 71,362 sq miles

Capital city Olympia (population 49,218)

Other cities Seattle (population 668,342), Spokane (population 212,052), Bellingham (population 83,365)

Sales tax 6.5%

Birthplace of Singer and actor Bing Crosby (1903–77), guitarist Jimi Hendrix (1942–70), computer geek Bill Gates (b 1955), political commentator Glen Beck (b 1964), musical icon Kurt Cobain (1967–94)

Home of Mt St Helens, Microsoft, Starbucks, Amazon.com, Evergreen State College

Politics Democrat governors since 1985

Famous for Grunge rock, coffee, Grey's Anatomy, Twilight, volcanoes, apples, wine, precipitation

State vegetable Walla Walla sweet onion

Driving distances Seattle to Portland,174 miles; Spokane to Port Angeles, 365 miles

Surprisingly elegant in places and coolly edgy in others, Seattle is notable for its strong neighborhoods, top-rated university, monstrous traffic jams and proactive city mayors who harbor green credentials. Although it has fermented its own pop culture in recent times, it has yet to create an urban mythology befitting Paris or New York, but it does have 'the Mountain.' Better known as Rainier, Seattle's unifying symbol is a 14,411ft mass of rock and ice, which acts as a perennial reminder to the city's huddled masses that raw wilderness, and potential volcanic catastrophe, are never far away.

Sights

Downtown

★**Pike Place Market**   MARKET
(Map p360; www.pikeplacemarket.org; 85 Pike St; ⊙9am-6pm Mon-Sat, to 5pm Sun; ⛆Westlake) ⏸
A cavalcade of noise, smells, personalities, banter and urban theater sprinkled liberally around a spatially challenged waterside strip, Pike Place Market is Seattle in a bottle. In operation since 1907 and still as soulful today as it was on day one, this wonderfully local experience highlights the city for what it really is: all-embracing, eclectic and proudly unique. A brand-new expansion of the market infrastructure adds vendor space, weather-protected common areas, extra parking, and housing for low-income seniors.

★**Seattle Art Museum**   MUSEUM
(SAM; Map p360; ☎206-654-3210; www.seattle artmuseum.org; 1300 1st Ave; adult/student $24.95/14.95; ⊙10am-5pm Wed & Fri-Sun, to 9pm Thu; ⛆University St) While not comparable with the big guns in New York and Chicago, Seattle Art Museum is no slouch. Always re-curating its art collection with new acquisitions and imported temporary exhibitions, it's known for its extensive Native American artifacts and work from the local Northwest school, in particular by Mark Tobey (1890–1976). Modern American art is also well represented, and the museum gets some exciting traveling exhibitions (including Yayoi Kusama's infinity mirrors).

★**Olympic Sculpture Park**   PARK, SCULPTURE
(Map p360; 2901 Western Ave; ⊙sunrise-sunset; ⛆13) **FREE** This smart urban-renewal project and outpost of the Seattle Art Museum was inaugurated in 2007 to widespread local approval. The terraced park is landscaped over railway tracks and overlooks Puget Sound with the distant Olympic Mountains winking on the horizon. Joggers and dog walkers meander daily through its zigzagging paths, enjoying over 20 pieces of modern sculpture.

◉ International District

Wing Luke Museum of the Asian Pacific American Experience   MUSEUM

(Map p360; ☑206-623-5124; www.wingluke. org; 719 S King St; adult/child $17/10; ⊙10am-5pm Tue-Sun; ☐7th & Jackson/Chinatown) The beautifully unique Wing Luke examines Asia Pacific–American culture, focusing on prickly issues such as Chinese settlement in the 1880s and Japanese internment camps during WWII. Recent temporary exhibits include 'A Day in the Life of Bruce Lee.' There are also art exhibits and a preserved immigrant apartment. Guided tours are available; the first Thursday of the month is free (with extended hours until 8pm).

◉ Seattle Center

Seattle Center   LANDMARK

(Map p360; ☑206-684-8582; www.seattlecenter. com; 400 Broad St; ☑Seattle Center) The remnants of the futuristic 1962 World's Fair hosted by Seattle and subtitled Century 21 Exposition are still visible over 50 years later at the Seattle Center. The fair was a major success, attracting 10 million visitors, running a profit (rare for the time) and inspiring a skin-crawlingly kitsch Elvis movie, *It Happened at the World's Fair* (1963). Thanks to regular upgrades, the complex has retained its luster and contains Seattle's highest concentration of A-list sights.

★Space Needle   LANDMARK

(Map p360; ☑206-905-2100; www.spaceneedle. com; 400 Broad St; adult/child $29/18; ⊙9:30am-11pm Mon-Thu, to 11:30pm Fri & Sat, 9am-11pm Sun; ☑Seattle Center) This streamlined, modern-before-its-time tower built for the 1962 World's Fair has been the city's defining symbol for over 50 years. The needle anchors the complex now called the Seattle Center and draws over one million annual visitors to its flying saucer–like observation deck and pricey rotating restaurant. Purchase a combination ticket with Chihuly Garden & Glass for $49.

★Museum of Pop Culture   MUSEUM

(Map p360; ☑206-770-2700; www.mopop.org; 325 5th Ave N; adult/child $25/16; ⊙10am-7pm Jun-Aug, to 5pm Sep-May; ☑Seattle Center) The Museum of Pop Culture (formerly EMP, the 'Experience Music Project') is an inspired marriage between super-modern architecture and legendary rock-and-roll history that sprang from the imagination (and pocket) of Microsoft co-creator Paul Allen. Inside its avant-garde frame, designed by Canadian architect Frank Gehry, you can tune into the famous sounds of Seattle (with an obvious bias toward Jimi Hendrix and grunge) or attempt to imitate the masters in the Interactive Sound Lab.

★Chihuly Garden & Glass   MUSEUM

(Map p360; ☑206-753-4940; www.chihulygarden andglass.com; 305 Harrison St; adult/child $24/14; ⊙10am-8pm Sun-Thu, to 9pm Fri & Sat; ☑Seattle Center) Opened in 2012 and reinforcing Seattle's position as the Venice of North America, this exquisite exposition of the life and work of dynamic local sculptor Dale Chihuly is possibly the finest collection of curated glass art you'll ever see. It shows off Chihuly's creative designs in a suite of interconnected dark and light rooms before depositing you in an airy glass atrium and – finally – a landscaped garden in the shadow of the Space Needle. Glassblowing demonstrations are a highlight.

◉ Capitol Hill

Millionaires mingle with goth musicians in Capitol Hill, a well-heeled but liberal neighborhood rightly renowned for its fringe theater, alternative music scene, indie coffee bars and vital gay and lesbian culture. You can take your dog for a herbal bath here, go shopping for ethnic crafts on Broadway, or blend in (or not) with the young punks and old hippies on the eclectic Pike–Pine corridor. The junction of Broadway and E John

PACIFIC NORTHWEST SEATTLE

---

❶ SEATTLE CITYPASS

If you're going to be in Seattle for a while and plan on seeing its premier attractions, consider buying a **Seattle CityPASS** (www.citypass.com/seattle; $144/97 per adult/child aged four to 12). Good for nine days, the pass gets you entry into five sights: the Space Needle, Seattle Aquarium, Argosy Cruises Seattle Harbor Tour, Museum of Pop Culture *or* Woodland Park Zoo, Pacific Science Center *or* Chihuly Garden & Glass. You wind up saving about 45% on admission costs and you never have to stand in line. You can buy one at any of the venues or online.

Seattle

500 m
0.25 miles

13th Ave E
12th Ave E
11th Ave
10th Ave

E Mercer St
E Republican St
E Harrison St
E Thomas St
E John St
E Denny Way
E Olive St
Cascina Spinasse (0.1mi)
E Howell St
E Pine St
E Union St

Capitol Hill
CAPITOL HILL
Cal Anderson Park Reflecting Pool
Nagle Pl

Broadway E
Harvard Ave E
Harvard Ave
Boylston Ave E
Boylston Ave
Belmont Ave E
Belmont Ave
Summit Ave E
Summit Ave
Bellevue Ave E
Bellevue Ave
Melrose Ave E
Melrose Ave

Broadway & Pine

E Howell St
E Pine St
E Pike St
E Union St

E Olive Way

Lake Union (0.3mi);
U District (3.5mi);
University of Washington (3.5mi)

Eastlake Ave E
Yale Ave N
Pontius Ave N
Minor Ave N
Fairview Ave N
John St
Denny Way
Yale Ave
Minor Ave
Boren Ave
Terry Ave
9th Ave
Pine St
Olive Way
8th Ave
Terry Ave
Boren Ave
Terry Ave

Quick Shuttle
Visit Seattle
Westlake Hub

Mercer St

Northwest Outdoor Center (1mi)

EASTLAKE
Lake Union Park
Terry & Mercer
Westlake & Mercer
Westlake Ave N
Westlake & Thomas
Republican St
Harrison St
Thomas St
Terry & Thomas

Westlake & 9th
Westlake & 7th
Lenora St
Virginia St
Stewart St

Westlake Center
Westlake

Fremont (2mi);
Green Lake (3mi);
Ballard (5mi)

South Lake Union Street Car

9th Ave N
8th Ave N
Dexter Ave N
Aurora Ave N
6th Ave N
Taylor Ave N
John St
Denny Park
DENNY TRIANGLE
8th Ave
7th Ave
6th Ave
5th Ave
Denny Way
Bell St
Blanchard St
Virginia St
Lenora St
3rd Ave

Roy St
Mercer St
5th Ave N
4th Ave N
Broad St

Toulouse Petit (0.1mi);
SIFF Cinema Uptown (0.2mi);
On the Boards (0.2mi)

McCaw Hall
Memorial Stadium
SEATTLE CENTER
Seattle Center
Museum of Pop Culture
Monorail
Space Needle
Chihuly Garden & Glass
Key Arena
2nd Ave N
Warren Ave N

BELLTOWN
4th St
Battery St
Vine St
Wall St
Cedar St
Clay St
Broad St
Eagle St
2nd Ave
1st Ave
Western Ave
Elliott Ave
Alaskan Way

Olympic Sculpture Park

Pier 69
Pier 67
Victoria Clipper

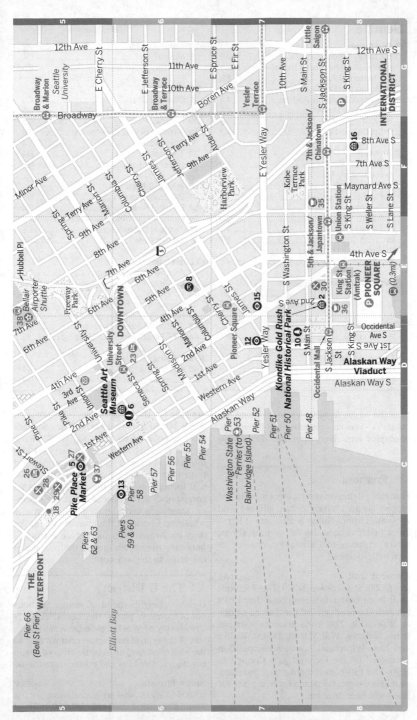

PACIFIC NORTHWEST SEATTLE

Seattle

St is the nexus from which to navigate the quarter's various restaurants, brewpubs, boutiques and dingy (but not dirty) dive bars.

◎ Fremont

Fremont pitches young hipsters among old hippies in an unlikely urban alliance and vies with Capitol Hill as Seattle's most irreverent neighborhood. It's full of junk shops, urban sculpture and a healthy sense of its own ludicrousness.

Fremont Troll   SCULPTURE
(cnr N 36th St & Troll Ave; 🚌62) The Fremont Troll is an outlandish sculpture that lurks beneath the north end of the Aurora Bridge at N 36th St. The troll's creators – artists Steve Badanes, Will Martin, Donna Walter and Ross Whitehead – won a competition sponsored by the Fremont Arts Council in 1990. The 18ft-high cement figure snacking on a Volkswagen Beetle is a favorite place for late-night beer drinking.

Waiting for the Interurban   MONUMENT
(cnr N 34th St & Fremont Ave N; 🚌62) Seattle's most popular piece of public art, *Waiting for the Interurban*, is cast in recycled aluminum and depicts six people waiting for a train that never comes. Occasionally locals will lovingly decorate the people in outfits corresponding to a special event, the weather, someone's birthday, a Mariners win – whatever. Check out the human face on the dog; it's Armen Stepanian, once Fremont's honorary mayor, who made the mistake of objecting to the sculpture.

◎ The U District

U-dub, a neighborhood of young, studious out-of-towners, places the beautiful, leafy **University of Washington** (www.washington. edu; 🚇University of Washington) campus next to the shabbier 'Ave,' an eclectic strip of cheap boutiques, dive bars and ethnic restaurants.

Burke Museum   MUSEUM
(☎206-543-5590; www.burkemuseum.org; cnr 17th Ave NE & NE 45th St; adult/child $10/7.50, 1st Thu of

month free; ⊘10am-5pm, to 8pm 1st Thu of month; 🖥70) An interesting hybrid museum covering both natural history and indigenous cultures of the Pacific Rim. On the entry-level floor is, arguably, Washington's best natural-history collection, focusing on the geology and evolution of the state. It guards an impressive stash of fossils, including a 20,000-year-old saber-toothed cat. Downstairs is the 'Pacific Voices' exhibition, with cultural artifacts amassed from around the Pacific Rim. The centerpiece is an excellent Pacific Northwest collection with some dramatic Kwakwaka'wakw masks from British Columbia.

⊙ Ballard

A former seafaring community with a strong Scandinavian heritage, Ballard still feels like a small town engulfed by a bigger city. Traditionally gritty, no-nonsense and uncommercial, it's slowly being condo-ized, but remains a good place to down a microbrew or see a live band.

★**Hiram M Chittenden Locks**   CANAL
(3015 NW 54th St; ⊘7am-9pm; 🖥40) **FREE** Seattle shimmers like an impressionist painting on sunny days at the Hiram M Chittenden Locks. Here, the freshwaters of Lake Washington and Lake Union drops 22ft into saltwater Puget Sound. You can stand inches away and watch the boats rise or sink (depending on direction). Construction of the canal and locks began in 1911; today 100,000 boats pass through them annually. You can view fish-ladder activity through underwater glass panels, stroll through botanical gardens and visit a small museum.

🏃 Activities

Cycling

Despite frequent rain and hilly terrain, cycling is still a major form of both transportation and recreation in the Seattle area.

In the city, commuter bike lanes are painted green on many streets, city trails are well maintained and the friendly and enthusiastic cycling community is happy to share the road. The wildly popular 20-mile **Burke-Gilman Trail** winds from Ballard to Log Boom Park in Kenmore on Seattle's Eastside. There, it connects with the 11-mile-long **Sammamish River Trail**, which winds past the Chateau Ste Michelle winery in Woodinville before terminating at Redmond's Marymoor Park.

Other good places to cycle are around Green Lake (congested), at Alki Beach (sublime) or, closer to downtown, through scenic Myrtle Edwards Park.

Anyone planning on cycling in Seattle should pick up a copy of the *Seattle Bicycling Guide Map*, available online and at bike shops.

For bicycle rentals and tours, try **Recycled Cycles** (🖉206-547-4491; www.recycled cycles.com; 1007 NE Boat St; rental per day from $40; ⊘10am-7pm Mon-Fri, to 8pm Thu, 10am-6pm Sat & Sun; 🖥70) or **Seattle Cycling Tours** (Map p360; 🖉206-356-5803; www.seattle-cy cling-tours.com; 714 Pike St; tours from $55; 🖥10).

Watersports

Seattle is not just on a network of cycling trails. With Venice-like proportions of downtown water, it is also strafed with kayak-friendly marine trails. The **Lakes to Locks Water Trail** links Lake Sammamish with Lake Washington, Lake Union and – via the Hiram M Chittenden Locks – Puget Sound. For launching sites and maps, check the website of the Washington Water Trails Association (www.wwta.org).

Northwest Outdoor Center   KAYAKING
(🖉206-281-9694; www.nwoc.com; 2100 Westlake Ave N; rental per hour kayak/SUP $16/18; ⊘10am-8pm Mon-Fri, 9am-6pm Sat & Sun Apr-Sep, closed Mon & Tue Oct-Mar; 🖥62) Located on the west side of Lake Union, this place rents kayaks and stand-up paddleboards (SUPs) and offers tours and instruction in sea and white-water kayaking.

👉 Tours

★**Seattle Free Walking Tours**   WALKING
(Map p360; www.seattlefreewalkingtours.org) **FREE** A nonprofit set up by a couple of world travelers and Seattle residents in 2012 who were impressed with the free walking tours offered in various European cities. An intimate two-hour walk takes in Pike Pl, the waterfront and Pioneer Square. Each tour has different starting times and meeting places; check online.

Seattle by Foot   WALKING
(🖉206-508-7017; www.seattlebyfoot.com; per person from $30) Runs a handful of tours, including the practically essential (this being Seattle) Coffee Crawl, which will ply you with caffeine while explaining the nuances of latte art and dishing the inside story of the rise (and rise) of Starbucks. The tour

costs $30 including samples; registration starts at 9:50am Thursday to Sunday at the **Hammering Man** (Map p360; 🚇University St) outside the Seattle Art Museum.

🎊 Festivals & Events

Seattle International
Film Festival   FILM
(SIFF; www.siff.net; ⏰May-Jun) Held over three weeks from mid-May to early June, this prestigious film festival uses a half-dozen cinemas to screen more than 400 movies. Major venues include the Egyptian Cinema in Capitol Hill, the **SIFF Cinema Uptown** (☎206-285-1022; 511 Queen Anne Ave N; 🚌13) in Lower Queen Anne and its own dedicated **SIFF Film Center** (Map p360; ☎206-324-9996; Northwest Rooms; Ⓢ Seattle Center) in the Seattle Center.

Seafair   FAIR
(www.seafair.com; ⏰Jun-Aug) Huge crowds attend this festival, held on the water from mid-June to mid-August, with a pirate's landing, a torchlight parade, an air show, a music marathon and even a Milk Carton Derby (look it up!).

Bumbershoot   PERFORMING ARTS
(www.bumbershoot.com; 3-day pass from $249; ⏰Sep) A fair few people – Seattleites or otherwise – would say that this is Seattle's finest festival, with major arts and cultural events at the Seattle Center on the Labor Day weekend in September. Bank on live music, comedy, theater, visual arts and dance, but also bank on crowds and hotels stuffed to capacity. Book well in advance!

🛏 Sleeping

Reserve ahead in summer, when hotels book up and prices tend to skyrocket.

City Hostel Seattle   HOSTEL $
(Map p360; ☎206-706-3255; www.hostelseattle.com; 2327 2nd Ave; dm/d from $33/99; ❀@🛜; 🚇Westlake) This well-located, boutique 'art hostel' has colorful murals painted by local artists splashed on the walls of every room. There's also a common room, hot tub, in-house movie theater and all-you-can-eat breakfast. Dorms have four or six beds and some are female only. There are also several private rooms, some with shared bathroom.

Ace Hotel   HOTEL $$
(Map p360; ☎206-448-4721; www.acehotel.com; 2423 1st Ave; r with shared/private bath from $129/239; 🅿❀❄🛜☎; 🚌13) The original locale of the highly stylized Ace Hotel chain, this place sports nouveau-industrial decor, sliding-barn-door bathrooms and Pendleton wool blankets. True to its original ethos, the hotel is economical but trendy, especially if you don't mind sharing a bathroom. Enhancing the hipster appeal, some rooms come with record players.

Hotel Five   BOUTIQUE HOTEL $$
(Map p360; ☎206-448-0924; www.hotelfiveseattle.com; 2200 5th Ave; r from $212; 🅿❀❄🛜; 🚌13) This trendy hotel mixes retro '70s furniture with sharp color accents to produce something dazzlingly modern. The ultra-comfortable beds are a valid cure for insomnia, while the large reception area invites lingering, especially when they lay out the complimentary cupcakes and coffee in the late afternoon.

SEATTLE FOR CHILDREN

Make a beeline for the Seattle Center, preferably on the monorail, where food carts, street entertainers, fountains and green spaces will make the day fly by. One essential stop is the **Pacific Science Center** (Map p360; ☎206-443-2001; www.pacificsciencecenter.org; 200 2nd Ave N; exhibits only adult/child $19.75/14.75; ⏰10am-5pm Mon-Fri, to 6pm Sat & Sun; 👶; Ⓢ Seattle Center), which entertains and educates with virtual reality exhibits, laser shows, holograms, an Imax theater and a planetarium. Parents won't be bored either.

Downtown on Pier 59, **Seattle Aquarium** (Map p360; ☎206-386-4300; www.seattleaquarium.org; 1483 Alaskan Way; adult/child $24.95/16.95; ⏰9:30am-5pm; 👶; 🚇University St) is a fun way to learn about the natural world of the Pacific Northwest. Even better is **Woodland Park Zoo** (☎206-548-2500; www.zoo.org; 5500 Phinney Ave N; adult/child May-Sep $20.95/12.95, Oct-Apr $14.95/9.95; ⏰9:30am-6pm May-Sep, to 4pm Oct-Apr; 👶; 🚌5) in the Green Lake neighborhood, one of Seattle's greatest tourist attractions and consistently rated as one of the top 10 zoos in the country.

Belltown Inn
HOTEL **$$**

(Map p360; ✆206-529-3700; www.belltown-inn. com; 2301 3rd Ave; r from $206; ☻✳@☎; ⊠Westlake) The reliable Belltown Inn is a popular midrange place to stow your suitcase – good on the basics, if a little light on embellishments. That said, there's a roof terrace, free bike rentals and some rooms have kitchenettes. Both downtown and the Seattle Center are within easy walking distance.

Moore Hotel
HOTEL **$$**

(Map p360; ✆206-448-4851; www.moorehotel. com; 1926 2nd Ave; d with shared/private bath from $99/117; ☎; ⊠Westlake) Old-world and allegedly haunted, the hip and whimsical Moore is undoubtedly central Seattle's most reliable bargain, offering fixed annual prices for its large stash of simple but cool rooms. Bonuses – aside from the dynamite location – are the cute ground-floor cafe, and zebra- and leopard-skin patterned carpets.

★Hotel Monaco
BOUTIQUE HOTEL **$$$**

(Map p360; ✆206-621-1770; www.monaco-seattle. com; 1101 4th Ave; d/ste $339/399; P@☎✳; ⊠University St) 🥢 Whimsical and with dashes of European elegance, the downtown Monaco is a classic Kimpton hotel whose rooms live up to the hints given off in the illustrious lobby. Bed down amid the bold, graphic decor and reap the perks (complimentary bikes, fitness center, free wine tasting, in-room yoga mats).

★Maxwell Hotel
BOUTIQUE HOTEL **$$$**

(Map p360; ✆206-286-0629; www.themaxwell hotel.com; 300 Roy St; r from $319; P✳@☎✲; ⊠Rapid Ride D-Line) Located in Lower Queen Anne, the Maxwell has a huge designer-chic lobby with a floor mosaic and funky furnishings that welcomes you with aplomb. Upstairs the slickness continues in 139 gorgeously modern rooms with hardwood floors and Scandinavian bedding. There's a small pool, a gym, free bike rentals and complimentary cupcakes.

Thompson Seattle
HOTEL **$$$**

(Map p360; ✆206-623-4600; www.thompson hotels.com/hotels/thompson-seattle; 110 Stewart St; d $309; bus, light rail University Street Station) The Thompson Hotel has been a hot spot among tourists and locals alike since it opened early in the summer of 2016. Designed by the famed local Olson Kundig architects, the boutique hotel is sleek and modern, and offers expansive views of Puget Sound.

LOCAL KNOWLEDGE

HIGHER THAN THE SPACE NEEDLE

Everyone rushes for the iconic Space Needle, but it's not the tallest Seattle viewpoint. That honor goes to the sleek **Columbia Center** (Map p360; ✆206-386-5564; www.skyviewobservatory.com; 701 5th Ave; adult/child $14.75/9; ⏱10am-8pm; ⊠Pioneer Sq) at 932ft high with 76 floors. An elevator in the lobby takes you up to the free-access 40th floor, where there's a Starbucks. From here you must take another elevator to the plush Sky View Observatory on the 73rd floor, from where you can look down on ferries, cars, islands, roofs and – ha, ha – the Space Needle!

🍴 Eating

The best budget meals are to be found in Pike Place Market (p358). Take your pick from fresh produce, baked goods, deli items and takeout ethnic foods.

★Salumi Artisan Cured Meats
SANDWICHES **$**

(Map p360; ✆206-621-8772; www.salumicured meats.com; 309 3rd Ave S; sandwiches $10-14; ⏱11am-1:30pm Mon for takeout only, to 3:30pm Tue-Fri; ⊠International District/Chinatown) With a shopfront as wide as a smart car and a following as large as the Seattle Mariners, Salumi is a well-known vortex of queues. But it's worth the wait for the legendary Italian-quality salami and cured-meat sandwiches (grilled lamb, pork shoulder, meatballs) that await you at the counter. Grab one and go! Fresh homemade gnocchi is available most Tuesdays.

★Piroshky Piroshky
BAKERY **$**

(Map p360; www.piroshkybakery.com; 1908 Pike Pl; snacks $3-6; ⏱8am-6pm; ⊠Westlake) Piroshky knocks out its delectable sweet and savory Russian pies and pastries in a space about the size of a walk-in closet. Get the savory smoked-salmon pâté or the sauerkraut with cabbage and onion, and follow it with the chocolate-cream hazelnut roll or a fresh rhubarb piroshki.

★Fonda la Catrina
MEXICAN **$**

(✆206-767-2787; www.fondalacatrina.com; 5905 Airport Way S; mains $9-14; ⏱11am-10pm Mon-Thu, to 11pm Fri, 10am-11pm Sat, 10am-10pm Sun;

PACIFIC NORTHWEST SEATTLE

DON'T MISS

PIONEER SQUARE

Pioneer Sq is Seattle's oldest quarter, which isn't saying much if you're visiting from Rome or London. Most of the buildings here date from just after the 1889 fire (a devastating inferno that destroyed 25 city blocks, including the entire central business district), and are referred to architecturally as Richardsonian Romanesque, a redbrick revivalist style in vogue at the time. In the early years, the neighborhood's boom-bust fortunes turned its arterial road, Yesler Way, into the original 'skid row' – an allusion to the skidding logs that were pulled downhill to Henry Yesler's pier-side mill. When the timber industry fell on hard times, the road became a haven for the homeless and its name subsequently became a byword for poverty-stricken urban enclaves countrywide. Thanks to a concerted public effort, the neighborhood avoided being laid to waste by the demolition squads in the 1960s and is now protected in the Pioneer Sq–Skid Rd Historic District.

The quarter today mixes the historic with the seedy, harboring art galleries, cafes and nightlife. Its most iconic building is the 42-story **Smith Tower** (Map p360; ☑206-622-4004; www.smithtower.com; 506 2nd Ave; observatory tickets from $12; ☺10am-10pm; ℝPioneer Sq), completed in 1914 and, until 1931, the tallest building west of the Mississippi. Other highlights include the 1909 **Pergola** (Map p360; cnr Yesler Way & James St; ℝPioneer Sq), a decorative iron shelter reminiscent of a Parisian Metro station, and **Occidental Park** (Map p360; btwn S Washington & S Main Sts; ℝOccidental Mall), containing totem poles carved by Chinook artist Duane Pasco.

The **Klondike Gold Rush National Historical Park** (Map p360; ☑206-553-3000; www.nps.gov/klse; 319 2nd Ave S; ☺10am-5pm; ℝOccidental Mall) FREE is a city-based visitor-center outpost. It shows off exhibits, photos and news clippings from the 1897 Klondike gold rush, when a Seattle-on-steroids acted as a fueling depot for prospectors bound for the Yukon in Canada.

☑124) The search to find a decent Mexican restaurant in Seattle comes to an end in Georgetown in the busy confines of Fonda la Catrina, where Day of the Dead iconography shares digs with Diego Rivera–like murals and – more importantly – fabulous food. Offering way beyond the standard taco-burrito-enchilada trilogy, this place puts soul into its Latino cooking.

The highlight? One of the best *moles poblanos* this side of the Rio Grande.

Crumpet Shop BAKERY $
(Map p360; ☑206-682-1598; www.thecrumpet shop.com; 1503 1st Ave; crumpets $3-6; ☺7am-3pm Mon, Wed & Thu, to 4pm Fri-Sun; ℝWestlake) 🍃 The treasured British crumpet has been given a distinct American twist with lavish toppings such as pesto, wild salmon or lemon curd at this casual Pike Place Market eatery, family owned and operated for 40 years. Organic ingredients make it very Pacific Northwest, though there's Marmite for homesick Brits.

★**Tavolàta** ITALIAN $$
(Map p360; ☑206-838-8008; 2323 2nd Ave; pasta dishes $17-21, mains $24-28; ☺5-11pm; ☐13) Owned by top Seattle chef Ethan Stowell, Ta-

volàta is a dinner-only, Italian-inspired eatery emphasizing homemade pasta dishes. Keeping things simple with venison-stuffed ravioli and *linguine nero* (clams with black pasta), the results are as good as those found in Italy – and there's no praise finer than that!

★**Toulouse Petit** CAJUN, CREOLE $$
(☑206-432-9069; www.toulousepetit.com; 601 Queen Anne Ave N; dinner mains $17-45; ☺9am-2am Mon-Fri, from 8am Sat & Sun; ☐13) Hailed for its generous happy hours, cheap brunches and rollicking atmosphere, this perennially busy Queen Anne eatery has the common touch. The menu is large and varied, offering choices such as blackened rib-eye steak, freshwater gulf prawns and house-made gnocchi with artichoke hearts.

Le Pichet FRENCH $$
(Map p360; ☑206-256-1499; www.lepichet seattle.com; 1933 1st Ave; dinner mains $21-24; ☺8am-midnight; ℝWestlake) Say *bonjour* to Le Pichet, just up from Pike Place Market, a cute and very French bistro with pâtés, cheeses, wine, *chocolat* and a refined Parisian feel. Dinner features delicacies such as wild-boar shoulder or foie gras with duck

eggs. The specialty is a roast chicken ($45) – just know that there's an hour's wait when you order one.

Revel KOREAN, AMERICAN **$$**
(☑206-547-2040; www.revelseattle.com; 403 N 36th St; small plates $11-18; ☻11am-2pm & 5-10pm Mon-Fri, 10am-2pm & 5-10pm Sat & Sun; ▯40) This modern Korean-American crossover restaurant (with a bit of French influence thrown in) has quickly established itself as a big name on the Seattle eating scene thanks, in part, to its simple, shareable plates. Of note are the pork-belly pancakes, the short-rib dumplings and the various seasonal hot pots, all of which go down well with a cocktail or two.

★**Sitka & Spruce** MODERN AMERICAN **$$$**
(Map p360; ☑206-324-0662; www.sitkaandspruce.com; 1531 Melrose Ave; plates $15-35; ☻11:30am-2pm & 5-10pm Mon-Fri, 10am-2pm & 5-11pm Sat, 10am-2pm & 5-9pm Sun; ▱; ▯10) The king of all locavore restaurants, Sitka & Spruce was the pilot project of celebrated Seattle chef Matt Dillon. It's since become something of an institution and a trendsetter, with its small country-kitchen decor and a constantly changing menu concocted with ingredients from Dillon's own Vashon Island farm. Sample items include housemade charcuterie, conica morels or roasted-asparagus-and-liver parfait.

Cascina Spinasse ITALIAN **$$$**
(☑206-251-7673; www.spinasse.com; 1531 14th Ave; mains $26-45; ☻5-10pm Sun-Thu, to 11pm Fri & Sat; ▯11) Successfully re-creating the feel of an Italian trattoria, Spinasse specializes in the cuisine of northern Italy's Piedmont region. This means dishes like *agnolotti* (veal-stuffed pasta pockets) in beef broth, veal in tuna sauce, and top-notch risotto (from the region famous for its arborio rice). The finely curated wine list includes the kings and queens of Piedmontese reds: Barolo and Barbaresco.

Upper Bar Ferdinand AMERICAN **$$$**
(Map p360; ☑206-693-2434; www.barferdinandseattle.com; 1424 11th Ave; mains $45; ☻4-11pm Tue-Fri, 1-11pm Sat) Homey, rustic, cozy, charming and classic all at once, Ferdinand serves locally sourced, Asian-inspired food cooked by fire and paired with a carefully curated wine selection. Located a few blocks from the original Bar Ferdinand bottle shop and wine bar, Upper Bar Ferdinand sits in Chop-house Row (p370) and offers a unique take on a wine bar with its innovative food.

🍷 Drinking & Nightlife

It's hard to complain too much about Seattle's crappy weather when the two best forms of rainy-day solace – coffee and beer – are available in such abundance. No doubt about it, Seattle's an inviting place to enjoy a drink, whatever your poison. Adding fresh flavors to an already complex brew is a new obsession with micro-distilleries and cider houses.

★**Fremont Brewing Company** BREWERY
(☑206-420-2407; www.fremontbrewing.com; 3409 Woodland Park Ave N; ☻11am-9pm; ▮▦; ▯62) ✎ This relatively new microbrewery, in keeping with current trends, sells its wares via an attached tasting room rather than a full-blown pub. Not only is the beer divine (try the seasonal bourbon barrel-aged Abominable), the industrial-chic tasting room and 'urban beer garden' are highly inclusive spaces, where pretty much everyone in the 'hood comes to hang out at communal tables.

★**Zeitgeist Coffee** CAFE
(Map p360; ☑206-583-0497; www.zeitgeistcoffee.com; 171 S Jackson St; ☻6am-7pm Mon-Fri, 7am-7pm Sat, 8am-6pm Sun; ▯; ▯Occidental Mall) Possibly Seattle's best (if also busiest) indie coffee bar, Zeitgeist brews smooth *doppio macchiatos* to go with its sweet almond croissants and other luscious baked goods. The atmosphere is trendy industrial, with brick walls and large windows for people-watching. Soups, salads and sandwiches are also on offer.

★**Blue Moon** BAR
(☑206-675-9116; www.bluemoonseattle.wordpress.com; 712 NE 45th St; ☻2pm-2am Mon-Fri, noon-2am Sat & Sun; ▯74) A legendary counterculture dive that first opened in 1934 to celebrate the repeal of Prohibition, Blue Moon makes much of its former literary patrons – including Dylan Thomas and Allen Ginsberg. The place is agreeably gritty and unpredictable, with graffiti carved into the seats and punk poets likely to stand up and start pontificating at any moment. Frequent live music.

Noble Fir BAR
(☑206-420-7425; www.thenoblefir.com; 5316 Ballard Ave NW; ☻4pm-midnight Tue-Thu, to 1am Fri &

Sat, 1-9pm Sun; ▣ 40) Almost qualifying as a travel bookstore as well as a bar, Noble Fir's highly curated, hops-heavy beer list might fill you with enough liquid courage to plan that hair-raising trip into the Amazon, or even just a trek around Ballard. The bright, laid-back bar has a nook given over to travel books and maps with packing cases on which to rest your drinks.

Elysian Brewing Company   MICROBREWERY
(Map p360; ✆206-860-1920; www.elysianbrew ing.com; 1221 E Pike St; ⊘11:30am-2am Mon-Fri, noon-2am Sat & Sun; ▣Broadway & Pine) Elysian Brewing's Immortal IPA personifies the strong, bitter 'hop-forward' beers that have become part of craft-beer folklore in the Pacific Northwest, and at 6.3% alcohol by volume, it won't take many to liberally loosen your tongue. Despite being bought out by Anheuser-Busch in January 2015, Elysian maintains several popular Seattle pubs, including this one (its 1996 original) in Capitol Hill.

Zig Zag Café   COCKTAIL BAR
(Map p360; ✆206-625-1146; www.zigzagseattle. com; 1501 Western Ave; cocktails from $10; ⊘5pm-2am; ▣University St) If you're writing a research project on Seattle's culinary history, you'll need to reserve a chapter for the Zig Zag Café. For serious cocktails, this place is legendary – this is the bar that repopularized gin-based Jazz Age cocktail 'The Last Word' in the early 2000s. The drink went viral and the Zig Zag's nattily attired mixers were rightly hailed as the city's finest alchemists.

Cloudburst Brewing   MICROBREWERY
(Map p360; ✆206-602-6061; www.cloudburst brew.com; 2116 Western Ave; ⊘2-10pm Wed-Fri, noon-10pm Sat, to 8pm Sun) The brainchild of former experimental brewer at Elysian Brewing, Steve Luke, Cloudburst Brewing has become a Seattle favorite. Replicating the success of Luke's past brewing creations, Cloudburst Brewing features hoppy beers with sassy names, and the bare-bones tasting room is always packed to the gills with beer fans who want to support craft beer in Seattle.

Panama Hotel Tea
& Coffee House   CAFE
(Map p360; ✆206-515-4000; www.panama hotel.net; 607 S Main St; tea from $5; ⊘8am-9pm; ▣5th & Jackson/Japantown) The intensely atmospheric teahouse inside the historic Panama Hotel has such a thoroughly back-in-time feel that you'll be reluctant to pull out your laptop (although there is wi-fi). It's in a National Treasure–designated 1910 building containing the only remaining Japanese bathhouse in the US, and doubles as a memorial to the neighborhood's Japanese residents forced into internment camps during WWII.

GRUNGE – PUNK'S WEST COAST NIRVANA

Synthesizing Generation X angst with a questionable approach to personal hygiene, the music popularly categorized as 'grunge' first dive-bombed onto Seattle's scene in the early 1990s like a clap of thunder on a typically wet and overcast afternoon. The anger had been fermenting for years – not purely in Seattle but also in its sprawling satellite towns and suburbs. Some said it was inspired by the weather, others cited the Northwest's geographic isolation. It didn't matter which. Armed with dissonant chords and dark, sometimes ironic lyrics, a disparate collection of bands stepped sneeringly up to the microphone to preach a new message from a city that all of the touring big-name rock acts serially chose to ignore. There were Screaming Trees from collegiate Ellensburg, the Melvins from rainy Montesano, Nirvana from the timber town of Aberdeen, and the converging members of Pearl Jam from across the nation.

What should have been grunge's high point came in October 1992, when Nirvana's second album, the hugely accomplished Nevermind, knocked Michael Jackson off the number-one spot, but the kudos ultimately killed it. After several years of railing against the mainstream, Nirvana and grunge had been incorporated into it. The media blitzed in, grunge fashion spreads appeared in Vanity Fair and half-baked singers from Seattle only had to cough to land a record contract. Many recoiled, most notably Nirvana vocalist and songwriter Kurt Cobain, whose drug abuse ended in suicide in his new Madison Park home in 1994. Other bands soldiered on, but the spark – which had burnt so brightly while it lasted – was gone. By the mid-1990s, grunge was officially dead.

☆ Entertainment

Consult *The Stranger, Seattle Weekly* or the daily papers for listings. Tickets for big events are available at TicketMaster (www.ticketmaster.com).

★ **Crocodile**   LIVE MUSIC
(Map p360; ☎ 206-441-4618; www.thecrocodile.com; 2200 2nd Ave; ▣ 13) Nearly old enough to be called a Seattle institution, the Crocodile is a clamorous 560-capacity music venue that first opened in 1991, just in time to grab the coattails of the grunge explosion. Everyone who's anyone in Seattle's alt-music scene has since played here, including a famous occasion in 1992 when Nirvana appeared unannounced, supporting Mudhoney.

★ **A Contemporary Theatre**   THEATER
(ACT; Map p360; ☎ 206-292-7676; www.acttheatre.org; 700 Union St; ▣ University St) One of the three big theater companies in the city, the ACT fills its $30-million home at Kreielsheimer Pl with performances by Seattle's best thespians and occasional big-name actors. Terraced seating surrounds a central stage and the interior has gorgeous architectural embellishments.

Big Picture   CINEMA
(Map p360; ☎ 206-256-0566; www.thebigpicture.net; 2505 1st Ave; ⊗ 2pm-midnight) It's easy to miss **Big Picture** when exploring Seattle's Belltown neighborhood. For those in the know, it's an 'underground' cinema experience with affordable tickets of first-run screenings in an intimate setting. Order a cocktail from the bar, and pay for another to be delivered mid-screening. You can also linger in the cozy bar area before or after your showing.

Neumo's   LIVE MUSIC
(Map p360; ☎ 206-709-9442; www.neumos.com; 925 E Pike St; ▣ Broadway & Pine) This punk, hip-hop and alternative-music joint is, along with the Crocodile in Belltown, one of Seattle's most revered small music venues. Its storied list of former performers is too long to include, but, if they're cool and passing through Seattle, they've probably played here. The audience space can get hot and sweaty, and even smelly, but that's rock and roll.

Tractor Tavern   LIVE MUSIC
(☎ 206-789-3599; www.tractortavern.com; 5213 Ballard Ave NW; tickets $8-20; ⊗ 8pm-2am; ▣ 40)

One of Seattle's premier venues for folk and acoustic music, the Tractor books local songwriters and regional bands, plus quality touring acts. Music runs toward country, rockabilly, folk, bluegrass and old-time. It's an intimate place with a small stage and great sound; occasional square dancing is frosting on the cake.

On the Boards   DANCE, THEATER
(☎ 206-217-9888; www.ontheboards.org; 100 W Roy St; ▣ 13) *The* place for avant-garde performance art, the nonprofit On the Boards makes its home at the intimate Behnke Center for Contemporary Performance and showcases some innovative and occasionally weird dance and music.

Intiman Theatre Festival   THEATER
(Map p360; ☎ 206-441-7178; www.intiman.org; 201 Mercer St; tickets $20-50; 🚻; Ⓢ Seattle Center) Beloved theater company based at the Cornish Playhouse in the Seattle Center. Artistic director Andrew Russell curates magnificent stagings of Shakespeare and Ibsen as well as work by emerging artists. Productions run from July to October.

Seattle Children's Theater   THEATER
(Map p360; ☎ 206-441-3322; www.sct.org; 201 Thomas St; tickets from $22; ⊗ Thu-Sun Sep-May; 🚻; Ⓢ Seattle Center) This highly esteemed theater group has two auditoriums in its Seattle Center campus. Friday and Saturday matinees and evening performances run September through May. There's also a Drama School summer season.

PACIFIC NORTHWEST SEATTLE

🛍 Shopping

The city's tour de force are its bookstores and record stores, surely some of the best in the nation. The main big-name shopping area is downtown between 3rd and 6th Aves and University and Stewart Sts. Pike Place Market is a maze of arts-and-crafts stalls, galleries and small shops. Pioneer Sq and Capitol Hill have locally owned gift and thrift shops.

★**Elliott Bay Book Company**   BOOKS
(Map p360; ☑ 206-624-6600; www.elliottbaybook. com; 1521 10th Ave; ⊙10am-10pm Mon-Thu, to 11pm Fri & Sat, to 9pm Sun; ☒ Broadway & Pine) Seattle's most beloved bookstore offers over 150,000 titles in a large, airy, wood-beamed space with cozy nooks that can inspire hours of serendipitous browsing. Bibliophiles will be further satisfied with regular book readings and signings.

Chophouse Row   FOOD & DRINKS
(Map p360; 1424 11th Ave; 6am to 11:30pm; ☒ Capitol Hill, light rail Capitol Hill) Hidden among the historical and modern architecture of Capitol Hill, Chophouse Row feels like a locals-only secret. This new-in-2016 establishment features independent shops like Niche Outside, a charming garden shop; farmstead ice cream at Kurt Farm Shop and cocktail and wine bar Upper Bar Ferdinand.

ℹ Information

EMERGENCY & MEDICAL SERVICES

Seattle Police (☑ 206-625-5011; www.seattle. gov/police)

Harborview Medical Center (☑ 206-744-3000; www.uwmedicine.org/harborview; 325 9th Ave; ☒ Broadway & Terrace) Full medical care, with emergency room.

MEDIA

KEXP 90.3 FM (stream at http://kexp.org) Legendary independent music and community station.

Seattle Times (www.seattletimes.com) The state's largest daily paper.

The Stranger (www.thestranger.com) Irreverent and intelligent free weekly, formerly edited by Dan Savage of 'Savage Love' fame.

POST

Post Office (Map p360; ☑ 206-748-5417; www. usps.com; 301 Union St; ⊙8:30am-5:30pm Mon-Fri; ☒ Westlake)

TOURIST INFORMATION

Visit Seattle (Map p360; ☑ 206-461-5800; www.visitseattle.org; Washington State Convention Center, cnr Pike St & 7th Ave; ⊙9am-5pm daily Jun-Sep, Mon-Fri Oct-May; ☒ Westlake) Information desk inside the Washington State Convention Center. You can pick up leaflets even when the desk is closed.

ℹ Getting There & Away

AIR

Sea-Tac International Airport (SEA; ☑ 206-787-5388; www.portseattle.org/sea-tac; 17801 International Blvd; 🛜) Located 13 miles south of downtown Seattle, Sea-Tac has flights all over the US and to some international destinations. Amenities include restaurants, money changers, baggage storage, car-rental agencies, a cell-phone waiting area (for drivers waiting to pick up arriving passengers) and free wi-fi.

BOAT

The **Victoria Clipper** (Map p360; ☑ 206-448-5000; www.clippervacations.com; 2701 Alaskan Way, Pier 69) ferry from Victoria, BC, docks at Pier 69 just south of the Olympic Sculpture Park in Belltown. **Washington State Ferries** (Map p360) services from Bremerton and Bainbridge Island use Pier 52.

BUS

Various inter-city coaches serve Seattle and there is more than one drop-off point – it all depends on which company you are using.

Bellair Airporter Shuttle (Map p360; ☑ 866-235-5247; www.airporter.com) Runs buses to Yakima, Bellingham and Anacortes and stops at King Street Station (for Yakima) and the Washington State Convention Center (for Bellingham and Anacortes).

Cantrail (www.cantrail.com) Amtrak's bus connector runs four daily services to Vancouver (one way $42) and picks up and drops off at King Street Station.

Greyhound (☑ 206-628-5526; www.grey hound.com; 503 S Royal Brougham Way; ☒ Stadium) Connects Seattle with cities all over the country, including Chicago (from $195 one way, two days, two daily), Spokane ($39, eight hours, three daily), San Francisco ($100, 20 hours, three daily) and Vancouver (Canada; $23, four hours, five daily). The company has its own terminal just south of King Street Station in SoDo, accessible on the Central Link light rail (stadium station).

Quick Shuttle (Map p360; ☑ 800-665-2122; www.quickcoach.com; 🛜) Fast and efficient, with five to six daily buses to Vancouver ($43). Picks up at the Best Western Executive Inn in

Taylor Ave N near the Seattle Center. Grab the monorail or walk to downtown.

TRAIN

King Street Station (206-296-0100; www.amtrak.com; 303 S Jackson St) Amtrak serves Seattle's King Street Station. Three main routes run through town: the *Amtrak Cascades* (connecting Vancouver, BC, Seattle, and Portland and Eugene in Oregon); the very scenic *Coast Starlight* (connecting Seattle to Oakland and Los Angeles in California) and the *Empire Builder* (a cross-continental to Chicago, IL).

① Getting Around

TO/FROM THE AIRPORT

There are a number of options for making the 13-mile trek from the airport to downtown Seattle. The most efficient is the light-rail service run by **Sound Transit** (www.soundtransit.org). It runs every 10 to 15 minutes between 5am and midnight; the ride between Sea-Tac Airport and downtown (Westlake Center) takes 36 minutes. There are additional stops in Pioneer Sq and the International District; the service was extended to Capitol Hill and the U District in 2016.

Shuttle Express (425-981-7000; www.shuttleexpress.com) has a pickup and drop-off point on the 3rd floor of the airport garage; it charges approximately $18 and is handy if you have a lot of luggage.

Taxis are available at the parking garage on the 3rd floor. Fares to downtown start at $39.

CAR & MOTORCYCLE

Seattle traffic is disproportionately heavy and chaotic for a city of its size, and parking is scarce and expensive. Add to that the city's bizarrely cobbled-together mishmash of skewed grids, the hilly terrain and the preponderance of one-way streets and it's easy to see why driving downtown is best avoided if at all possible.

PUBLIC TRANSPORTATION

Buses are operated by **King County Metro Transit** (206-553-3000; http://kingcounty.gov/depts/transportation/metro.aspx), part of the King County Department of Transportation. The website prints schedules and maps and has a trip planner.

To make things simple, all bus fares within Seattle city limits are a flat $2.75 at peak hours (6am to 9am and 3pm to 6pm weekdays). Off-peak rates are $2.50. Those aged six to 18 pay $1.50, kids under six are free, and seniors and travelers with disabilities pay $1. Most of the time you pay or show your transfer when you board. Your transfer ticket is valid for three hours from time of purchase. Most buses can carry two to three bikes.

Monorail (206-905-2620; www.seattlemonorail.com; ⊙7:30am-11pm Mon-Fri, 8:30am-11pm Sat & Sun) This cool futuristic train, built for the 1962 World's Fair, travels only between two stops: Seattle Center and Westlake Center. Fares are $2.25/1 per adult/child.

Seattle Streetcar (www.seattlestreetcar.org) Two lines. One runs from downtown Seattle (Westlake) to South Lake Union; the other goes from Pioneer Square via the International District, the Central District and First Hill to Capitol Hill. Stops allow connections with numerous bus routes. Trams run approximately every 15 minutes throughout the day. The fare is $2.25.

TAXI

All Seattle taxi cabs operate at the same rate, set by King County: $2.60 at meter drop, then $2.70 per mile.

Seattle Orange Cab (206-522-8800; www.orangecab.net)

Seattle Yellow Cab (206-622-6500; www.seattleyellowcab.com)

STITA Taxi (206-246-9999; www.stitataxi.com)

Olympia

Small in size but big in clout, Washington state capital Olympia is a political, musical and outdoor powerhouse that punches well above its 49,000-strong population. Look no further than the street-side buskers on 4th Ave, the smartly attired bureaucrats marching across the lawns of the resplendent state legislature or the Gore-Tex–clad outdoor fiends overnighting before rugged sorties into the Olympic Mountains. Truth is, despite its Classical Greek–sounding name, creative, out-of-the-box Olympia is anything but ordinary. Progressive Evergreen college has long lent the place an artsy turn (creator of *The Simpsons* Matt Groening studied here), while the dive bars and secondhand-guitar shops of downtown provided an original pulpit for riot-grrrl music and grunge.

◎ Sights & Activities

Washington State Capitol LANDMARK (360-902-8880; 416 Sid Snyder Ave SW; ⊙7am-5:30pm Mon-Fri, 11am-4pm Sat & Sun) FREE Olympia's capitol complex is set in a 30-acre park overlooking Capitol Lake with the Olympic Mountains glistening in the background. The campus' crowning glory is the magnificent **Legislative Building**. Completed in 1927, it's a dazzling display of craning columns and polished marble, topped by a 287ft dome that is only slightly smaller than its namesake in Washington, DC. Tours are available.

Olympia Farmers Market MARKET
(☑360-352-9096; www.olympiafarmersmarket.com; 700 N Capitol Way; ☉10am-3pm Thu-Sun Apr-Oct, Sat & Sun Nov & Dec, Sat Jan-Mar) ✔ Second only to Seattle's Pike Place in size and character, Olympia's local market is a great place to shop for organic herbs, vegetables, flowers, baked goods and the famous specialty: oysters.

🛏 Sleeping & Eating

Fertile Ground Guesthouse GUESTHOUSE $$
(☑360-352-2428; www.fertileground.org; 311 9th Ave SE; s/d $110/120; 🐾) Surrounded by a lush and leafy organic garden, this comfortable, homey guesthouse offers three lovely rooms, one en suite and two with shared bath. Breakfast is made mostly from organic and locally sourced ingredients. There's a sauna on the premises. More rooms (including a dorm) are available at other locations; check the website for details.

**Traditions Cafe
& World Folk Art** HEALTH FOOD $
(☑360-705-2819; www.traditionsfairtrade.com; 300 5th Ave SW; mains $6-12; ☉9am-6pm Mon-Fri, 10am-6pm Sat, 11am-5pm Sun; 🍴🚸) ✔ This comfortable hippie enclave at the edge of Heritage Park offers fresh salads and tasty, healthy sandwiches (lemon-tahini, smoked salmon etc), coffee drinks, herbal teas, local ice cream, beer and wine. Posters advertise community-action events, and in the corner is a 'Peace and Social Justice Lending Library.' It's attached to an eclectic folk-art store.

ⓘ Information

State Capitol Visitor Center (☑360-902-8881; http://olympiawa.gov/community/visiting-the-capitol.aspx; 103 Sid Snyder Ave SW; ☉10am-3pm Mon-Fri, 11am-3pm Sat & Sun) Offers information on the capitol campus, the Olympia area and Washington state. Note the limited opening hours.

Olympic Peninsula

Surrounded on three sides by sea and exhibiting many of the characteristics of a full-blown island, the remote Olympic Peninsula is about as 'wild' and 'west' as America gets.

What it lacks in cowboys it makes up for in rare, endangered wildlife and dense primeval forest. The peninsula's roadless interior is largely given over to the notoriously wet Olympic National Park, while the margins are the preserve of loggers, Native American reservations and a smattering of small but interesting settlements, most notably Port Townsend. Equally untamed is the western coastline, America's isolated end point, where tempestuous ocean and misty old-growth Pacific rainforest meet in aqueous harmony.

Olympic National Park

Declared a national monument in 1909 and a national park in 1938, the 1406-sq-mile **Olympic National Park** (www.nps.gov/olym; 7-day access per vehicle $25, pedestrian/cyclist $10, 1yr unlimited entry $50) shelters a unique rainforest, copious glaciated mountain peaks and a 57-mile strip of Pacific coastal wilderness that was added to the park in 1953. One of North America's great wilderness areas, most of it remains relatively untouched by human habitation. Opportunities for independent exploration in this huge backcountry region abound, be they for hiking, fishing, kayaking or skiing.

EASTERN ENTRANCES

The graveled Dosewallips River Rd follows the river from US 101 (turnoff approximately 1km north of Dosewallips State Park) for 15 miles to **Dosewallips Ranger Station**, where hiking trails begin; call 360-565-3130 for road conditions. Even hiking smaller portions of the two long-distance paths, including the 14.9 mile Dosewallips River Trail, with views of glaciated **Mt Anderson**, is reason enough to visit the valley. Another eastern entry for hikers is the **Staircase Ranger Station** (☑360-877-5569; ☉May-Oct), just inside the national-park boundary, 15 miles from Hoodsport on US 101. Two campgrounds along the eastern edge of the national park are popular: **Dosewallips State Park** (☑888-226-7688; http://parks.state.wa.us/499/dosewallips; 306996 Hwy 101; tent sites $12-35, RV sites $30-45) and **Skomomish Park Lake Cushman** (☑360-877-5760; www.skokomishpark.com; tent sites from $28, RV sites from $34; ☉late May-early Sep). Both have running water, flush toilets and some RV hookups. Reservations are accepted.

NORTHERN ENTRANCES

The park's easiest – and hence most popular – entry point is at **Hurricane Ridge**, 18 miles south of Port Angeles. At the road's end, an interpretive center gives a stupendous view of Mt Olympus (7965ft) and dozens of other peaks. The 5200ft altitude can mean you'll hit inclement weather, and the winds here (as the name suggests) can be ferocious. Aside from various summer trekking opportunities, the area maintains the small, family-friendly **Hurricane Ridge Ski & Snowboard Area** (www.hurricaneridge.com; all-lift day pass $34; ☺10am-4pm Sat & Sun mid-Dec–Mar; 🐾).

Popular for boating and fishing is **Lake Crescent**, the site of the park's oldest and most reasonably priced **lodge** (🗷888-896-3818; www.olympicnationalparks.com; 416 Lake Crescent Rd; lodge r from $123, cabins from $292; ☺May-Dec, limited availability winter; P ❄ 🔊 🏊). Sumptuous Northwestern-style food is served in the lodge's ecofriendly restaurant. From **Storm King Ranger Station** (🗷360-928-3380; 343 Barnes Point Rd; ☺May-Sep) on the lake's south shore, a 1-mile hike climbs through old-growth forest to Marymere Falls.

Along the Sol Duc River, the **Sol Duc Hot Springs Resort** (🗷360-327-3583; www.olympicnationalparks.com; 12076 Sol Duc Hot Springs Rd, Port Angeles; park entrance fee $25, tent/RV sites $20/40, cabins from $179; ☺Mar-Oct; ❄ 🏊) 🏊 has lodging, dining, massage and, of course, hot-spring pools, as well as great day hikes.

WESTERN ENTRANCES

Isolated by distance and home of one of the country's rainiest microclimates, the Pacific side of the Olympics remains the wildest. Only US 101 offers access to its noted temperate rainforests and untamed coastline. The **Hoh River Rainforest**, at the end of the 19-mile Hoh River Rd, is a Tolkienesque maze of dripping ferns and moss-draped trees. The **Hoh Rain Forest Visitor Center** (🗷360-374-6925; ☺9am-4:30pm Sep-Jun, to 6pm Jul & Aug) has information on guided walks and longer backcountry hikes. The attached **campground** (🗷360-374-6925; www.nps.gov/olym/planyourvisit/camping.htm; campsites $20) has no hookups or showers, and it's first-come, first-served.

A little to the south lies **Lake Quinault**, a beautiful glacial lake surrounded by forested peaks. It's popular for fishing, boating and swimming, and is surrounded by some of the nation's oldest trees. **Lake Quinault Lodge** (🗷360-288-2900; www.olympicnationalparks.com; 345 S Shore Rd; r $219- 450; ❄ ❄ 🔊 🏊), a luxury classic of 1920s 'parkitecture,' has a massive fireplace, a manicured cricket-pitch-quality lawn and a dignified lakeview restaurant serving upscale American cuisine. For a cheaper sleep nearby, try the ultrafriendly **Quinault River Inn** (🗷360-288-2237; www.quinaultriverinn.com; 8 River Dr; r $159; 🚬 ❄ 🔊 🏊) in Amanda Park, a favorite with anglers.

A number of short hikes begin just outside the Lake Quinault Lodge, or you cantry the longer **Enchanted Valley Trail**, a medium-grade 13-miler that begins from the Graves Creek Ranger Station at the end of South Shore Rd and climbs up to a large meadow resplendent with wildflowers and copses of alder trees.

ℹ️ Information

The park entry fee is $10/25 per person/vehicle, valid for one week and payable at park entrances. Many park visitor centers double as United States Forestry Service (USFS) ranger stations, where you can pick up permits for wilderness camping ($8).

Olympic National Park Visitor Center (🗷360-565-3100; www.nps.gov/olym; 3002 Mt Angeles Rd; ☺8am-6pm Jul & Aug, to 4pm Sep-Jun)

USFS Headquarters (🗷360-956-2402; www.fs.fed.us/r6/olympic; 1835 Black Lake Blvd SW; ☺8am-4:30pm Mon-Fri)

Forks Chamber of Commerce (🗷360-374-2531; www.forkswa.com; 1411 S Forks Ave; ☺10am-5pm Mon-Sat, 11am-4pm Sun; 🔊)

Port Townsend

Inventive eateries, elegant *fin de siècle* hotels and an unusual stash of year-round festivals make Port Townsend an Olympic Peninsula rarity: a weekend vacation that doesn't require hiking boots. Cut off from the rest of the area by eight bucolic miles of US 101, this is not the spot to base yourself for national-park exploration unless you don't mind driving a lot. Instead, settle in and enjoy one of the prettiest towns in the state.

◉ Sights

Fort Worden State Park PARK
(🗷360-344-4412; http://parks.state.wa.us/511/fort-worden; 200 Battery Way; ☺6:30am-dusk

Apr-Oct, 8am-dusk Nov-Mar) FREE This attractive park located within Port Townsend's city limits is the remains of a large fortification system constructed in the 1890s to protect the strategically important Puget Sound area from outside attack – supposedly from the Spanish during the 1898 war. Sharp-eyed film buffs might recognize the area as the backdrop for the movie *An Officer and a Gentleman*.

Visitors can arrange tours of the **Commanding Officer's Quarters** (☑360-385-1003; Fort Worden State Park, 200 Battery Way; adult/child $2/free; ⊙tours by appointment), a 12-bedroom mansion. You will also find the **Puget Sound Coast Artillery Museum** (adult/child $4/2; ⊙11am-4pm, longer weekend hours Jun-Aug), which tells the story of early Pacific coastal fortifications.

Hikes lead along the headland to **Point Wilson Lighthouse Station** and some wonderful windswept beaches. On the park's fishing pier is the **Port Townsend Marine Science Center** (www.ptmsc.org; 532 Battery Way; adult/child $5/3; ⊙noon-5pm Fri-Sun Apr-Oct), featuring four touch tanks and daily interpretive programs. There are also several camping and lodging possibilities.

🛌 Sleeping & Eating

Waterstreet Hotel HOTEL $
(☑360-385-5467; www.watersthotel.com; 635 Water St; r with shared bath $50-70, with private bath $75-175; ❋☎) Homey and friendly, the Waterstreet offers great-value rooms in a naturally aged Victorian flophouse. If you're a family or group, go for suite 5 or 15 – essentially apartments, with a loft, a full kitchen and a big back porch right on Puget Sound. Reception is in the Native American gift shop next door to the hotel.

★**Palace Hotel** HISTORIC HOTEL $$
(☑360-385-0773; www.palacehotelpt.com; 1004 Water St; r $109-159, higher on festival weekends; ☎❋) Built in 1889, this beautiful Victorian building was once a brothel run by the locally notorious Madame Marie. It's been reincarnated as an attractive, character-filled period hotel with antique furnishings (plus all the modern amenities). Pleasant common spaces; kitchenettes available. The cheapest rooms share a bathroom.

Waterfront Pizza PIZZA $$
(☑360-379-9110; 951 Water St; slices $4, large pizzas $16-28; ⊙11am-8pm Sun-Thu, to 9pm Fri & Sat) If you're craving a quick snack, grab a de-licious, crispy, thin-crust slice downstairs – just be prepared for lines in the walk-in closet-sized dining room. For more relaxed, sit-down service, climb the stairs and sample the pies, topped with treats such as Cajun sausage, feta cheese, artichoke hearts and pesto.

★**Sweet Laurette Cafe & Bistro** FRENCH $$
(www.sweetlaurette.com; 1029 Lawrence St; mains $10-20, brunch $9-15; ⊙8am-9pm, closed Tue; ☑) This French shabby-chic cafe serves breakfast, lunch and dinner in the bistro and delicious coffee and pastries between mealtimes. The food is made with sustainable and mostly local ingredients – try a breakfast *croque madame* with honey-baked ham and Gruyère on French bread for breakfast, or Whidbey Island mussels in a white-wine cream sauce or Cape Cleare king salmon for dinner.

ⓘ Information

Visitor Center (☑360-385-2722; www.ptchamber.org; 2409 Jefferson St; ⊙9am-5pm Mon-Fri) Pick up a useful walking-tour map and guide to the downtown historic district here.

ⓘ Getting There & Away

Washington State Ferries (☑206-464-6400; www.wsdot.wa.gov/ferries) operates up to 15 trips daily (depending on the season) to Coupeville on Whidbey Island from the downtown terminal (car and driver/passenger $14.05/3.30, 35 minutes).

Port Angeles

Despite the name, there's nothing Spanish or particularly angelic about Port Angeles, propped up by the lumber industry and backed by the steep-sided Olympic Mountains. Rather than visiting to see the town per se, many come here to catch a ferry for Victoria, BC, or to plot an outdoor excursion into the nearby Olympic National Park.

🏃 Activities

The **Olympic Discovery Trail** (www.olympicdiscoverytrail.com) is a 30-mile off-road hiking and cycling trail between Port Angeles and Sequim, starting at the end of Ediz Hook, the sand spit that loops around the bay. Bikes can be rented at **Sound Bikes & Kayaks** (www.soundbikeskayaks.com; 120 E Front St; bike rental per hour/day $10/45, kayak rental per day $50; ⊙10am-6pm Mon-Sat, 11am-4pm Sun).

🛏 Sleeping & Eating

Downtown Hotel HOTEL **$**
(☑ 360-565-1125; www.portangelesdowntownhotel.com; 101 E Front St; d with shared/private bath from $45/65; 😊 🛜) Nothing special on the outside but surprisingly spacious and tidy within, this no-frills, family-run place down by the ferry launch is Port Angeles' secret bargain. Bright rooms are decked out in wicker and wood, and several have water views. The cheapest rooms share a bathroom in the hallway. The soundproofing isn't great, but the location is tops.

Olympic Lodge HOTEL **$$**
(☑ 360-452-2993; www.olympiclodge.com; 140 Del Guzzi Dr; r from $139; ❄ @ 🛜 ⊠) This is the most comfortable place in town, offering gorgeous rooms, on-site bistro, swimming pool with hot tub, and complimentary cookies and soup in the afternoon. Prices vary widely depending on day and month.

Bella Italia ITALIAN **$$**
(☑ 360-457-5442; www.bellaitaliapa.com; 118 E 1st St; dinner mains $10-34; ⊙4-9pm) Bella Italia has been around a lot longer than Bella, the heroine of the *Twilight* saga, but its mention in the book as the site of Bella and Edward's first date has turned what was already a popular restaurant into an icon. Try the clam linguine or the smoked duck breast, or have what Bella ordered: mushroom ravioli.

Wash it down with an outstanding wine from a list with 500 selections.

ℹ Information

Port Angeles Visitor Center (☑ 360-452-2363; www.portangeles.org; 121 E Railroad Ave; ⊙9:30am-5:30pm Mon-Fri, 10am-5:30pm Sat, noon-3pm Sun May-Sep, 10am-5pm Mon-Sat, noon-3pm Sun Oct-Apr) Adjacent to the ferry terminal. Open later in summer if volunteers are available.

ℹ Getting There & Away

Clallam Transit (☑ 360-452-4511; www.clallamtransit.com) Buses go to Forks and Sequim, where they link up with other transit buses that circumnavigate the Olympic Peninsula.
Olympic Bus Lines (www.olympicbuslines.com; Gateway Transit Center, 123 E Front St) Runs twice daily to Seattle.
Coho Vehicle Ferry (☑ 888-993-3779; www.cohoferry.com) Runs to/from Victoria, BC (1½ hours, $128 round-trip).

Northwest Peninsula

Several Native American reservations cling to the extreme northwest corner of the continent and are welcoming to visitors. The small weather-beaten settlement of **Neah Bay** on Hwy 112 is home to the Makah Indian Reservation, whose **Makah Museum** (☑ 360-645-2711; www.makahmuseum.com; 1880 Bayview Ave; adult/child $6/5; ⊙10am-5pm) displays artifacts from one of North America's most significant archaeological finds, the 500-year-old Makah village of Ozette. Several miles beyond the museum, a short boardwalk trail leads to stunning **Cape Flattery**, a 300ft promontory that marks the most northwesterly point in the lower 48 states.

Convenient to the Hoh River Rainforest and the Olympic coastline is **Forks**, a one-horse lumber town that's now more famous for its *Twilight* paraphernalia. It's a central town for exploring Olympic National Park; a good accommodation choice is the **Miller Tree Inn** (☑ 360-374-6806; www.millertreeinn.com; 654 E Division St; r from $175; 🛜 🐾).

Northwest Washington

Wedged between Seattle, the Cascades and Canada, northwest Washington draws influences from three sides. Its urban hub is collegiate Bellingham, while its outdoor highlight is the pastoral San Juan Islands, an extensive archipelago that glimmers like a sepia-toned snapshot from another era. Anacortes is the main hub for ferries to the San Juan Islands and Victoria, BC.

Whidbey Island

While not as detached (there's a bridge connecting it to adjacent Fidalgo Island at its northernmost point) or nonconformist as the San Juans, life is almost as slow, quiet and pastoral on Whidbey Island. Having six state parks is a bonus, along with a plethora of B&Bs, two historic fishing villages (Langley and Coupeville), famously good clams and a thriving artist's community.

Deception Pass State Park (☑ 360-675-2417; 41229 N State Hwy 20) straddles the eponymous steep-sided strait that flows between Whidbey and Fidalgo Islands, and incorporates lakes, islands, campsites and 38 miles of hiking trails.

Ebey's Landing National Historical Reserve (☑ 360-678-6084; www.nps.gov/ebla; 162

Cemetery Rd) comprises 17,400 acres encompassing working farms, sheltered beaches, two state parks and the town of **Coupeville**. This small settlement is one of Washington's oldest towns and has an attractive seafront, antique stores and a number of old inns, including the **Captain Whidbey Inn** (☑ 360-678-4097; www.captainwhidbey.com; 2072 W Captain Whidbey Inn Rd; r/cabins from $103/210; 🐾), a forest-clad log-built inn dating to 1907. For the famous fresh local clams, head to **Christopher's** (☑ 360-678-5480; www.christophersonwhidbey.com; 103 NW Coveland St; lunch mains $12-16, dinner mains $16-26; ☺ 11:30am-2pm & 5pm-close, closed Tue).

❶ Getting There & Around

Regular **Washington State Ferries** (WSF; ☑ 888-808-7977; www.wsdot.wa.gov/ferries) link Clinton to Mukilteo and Coupeville to Port Townsend. Free **Island Transit** (☑ 360-678-7771; www.islandtransit.org) buses run the length of Whidbey every hour daily, except Sundays, from the Clinton ferry dock.

Bellingham

Welcome to a green, liberal and famously livable settlement that has taken the libertine, nothing-is-too-weird ethos of Oregon's 'City of Roses' and given it a peculiarly Washingtonian twist. Mild in both manners and weather, the 'city of subdued excitement,' as a local mayor once dubbed it, is an unlikely alliance of espresso-sipping students, venerable retirees, all-weather triathletes and placard-waving peaceniks. Publications such as *Outside Magazine* have consistently lauded it for its abundant outdoor opportunities.

◉ Sights & Activities

Bellingham offers outdoor sights and activities by the truckload. **Whatcom Falls Park** is a natural wild region that bisects Bellingham's eastern suburbs. The change in elevation is marked by four sets of waterfalls, including **Whirlpool Falls**, a popular summer swimming hole.

Fairhaven Bike & Mountain Sports   CYCLING
(☑ 360-733-4433; www.fairhavenbike.com; 1103 11th St; rental per 4hr $25-40; ☺ 9:30am-6pm Mon-Sat, 11am-5pm Sun) Bellingham is one of the most bike-friendly cities in the Northwest, with a well-maintained intra-urban trail going as far south as **Larrabee State Park** (www.parks.wa.gov; Chuckanut Dr; ☺ dawn-dusk; ♿). This outfit rents bikes and has maps on local routes.

San Juan Cruises   CRUISE
(☑ 360-738-8099; www.whales.com; 355 Harris Ave; cruises $39-109; ☺ 8am-6pm) Runs cruises around Bellingham Bay with beer or wine tasting, plus whale-watching around the San Juan Islands and more.

🛏 Sleeping & Eating

Larrabee State Park   CAMPGROUND $
(☑ 360-676-2093; http://parks.state.wa.us/536/larrabee; Chuckanut Dr; tent/RV sites from $12/30) Seven miles south of Bellingham, along scenic Chuckanut Dr, these campsites sit among Douglas firs and cedars with access to Chuckanut Bay and 12 miles of hiking and biking trails.

★ **Hotel Bellwether**   BOUTIQUE HOTEL $$
(☑ 360-392-3100; www.hotelbellwether.com; 1 Bellwether Way; r from $198; ❋@🐾) Bellingham's finest and most charismatic hotel lies on the waterfront and offers views of Lummi Island. Standard rooms come with Italian furnishings and Hungarian-down duvets, but the finest stay is the 900-sq-ft lighthouse suite (from $525), a converted three-story lighthouse with a wonderful private lookout. Spa and restaurant on premises.

Old Town Cafe   CAFE $
(☑ 360-671-4431; www.theoldtowncafe.com; 316 W Holly St; mains $6-10; ☺ 6:30am-3pm Mon-Sat, 8am-2pm Sun) Very popular for its casual, artsy atmosphere, this bohemian breakfast joint cooks up tasty dishes such as custom omelets, egg tortillas and whole-wheat French toast. There's also homemade granola, gluten-free hotcakes, organic tofu scrambles, garden salads and 10 kinds of sandwiches.

Mount Bakery   BREAKFAST $
(www.mountbakery.com; 308 W Champion St; brunch $6-16; ☺ 8am-3:30pm; 🐾) This is where you go on Sunday mornings with a Douglas fir–sized copy of the *New York Times* for Belgian waffles, crepes and organic eggs done any way you like. Plenty of gluten-free options. There's a second location in Fairhaven.

❶ Information

Downtown Info Center (☑ 360-671-3990; www.bellingham.org; 1306 Commercial St; ☺ 11am-3pm Tue-Sat)

❶ Getting There & Away

Bellingham is the terminal for **Alaska Marine Highway** (AMHS; ☑ 800-642-0066; www.dot.state.ak.us/amhs; 355 Harris Ave) ferries, which travel weekly up the Inside Passage to Juneau, Skagway and other southeast Alaskan ports.

The **Bellair Airporter Shuttle** (www.airporter. com; 1200 Iowa St) runs around the clock to Sea-Tac Airport (round-trip $74) and Anacortes (round-trip $35).

San Juan Islands

There are 172 landfalls in this expansive archipelago, but unless you're rich enough to charter your own yacht or seaplane, you'll be restricted to seeing the big four – San Juan, Orcas, Shaw and Lopez Islands – all served daily by Washington State Ferries. Communally, the islands are famous for their tranquility, whale-watching opportunities, sea kayaking and seditious nonconformity.

A great way to explore the San Juans is by sea kayak or bicycle. Cycling-wise, Lopez is flat and pastoral and San Juan is worthy of an easy day loop, while Orcas offers the challenge of undulating terrain and a steep 5-mile ride to the top of Mt Constitution.

ℹ Getting There & Around

Two airlines have scheduled flights from the mainland to the San Juans. **Kenmore Air** (☑ 866-435-9524; www.kenmoreair.com) flies from Lake Union and Lake Washington to Lopez, Orcas and San Juan Islands daily on three- to 10-person seaplanes. Fares start at $155 one way. **San Juan Airlines** (☑ 800-874-4434; www.sanjuanairlines.com) flies from Anacortes and Bellingham to the three main islands (one way $89).

Washington State Ferries leave Anacortes for the San Juans; some continue to Sidney, BC, near Victoria. Ferries run to Lopez Island (45 minutes), Orcas Landing (60 minutes) and Friday Harbor on San Juan Island (75 minutes). Fares vary by season; the cost of the entire round-trip is collected on westbound journeys only (except those returning from Sidney, BC).

Shuttle buses ply Orcas and San Juan Island between May and October.

San Juan Island

San Juan Island is the archipelago's unofficial capital, a harmonious mix of low forested hills and small rural farms that resonates with a dramatic and unusual 19th-century history. The only real settlement is Friday Harbor, home to the visitor center and **Chamber of Commerce** (☑ 360-378-5240; www.sanjuanisland.org; 165 1st St S, Friday Harbor; ⊙ 10am-5pm).

◉ Sights

San Juan Island
National Historical Park   HISTORIC SITE
(☑ 360-378-2240; www.nps.gov/sajh; ⊙ visitor center 8:30am-5pm Jun-Aug, to 4:30pm Sep-May) 🎫 FREE Known more for their scenery than their history, the San Juans nonetheless hide one of the 19th century's oddest political confrontations, the so-called 'Pig War' between the USA and Britain. This curious standoff is showcased in two separate historical parks at either end of the island, which once housed opposing **American** (☑ 360-378-2240; www.nps.gov/sajh; ⊙ grounds 8:30am-11pm) FREE and **English** military encampments.

Lime Kiln Point State Park   PARK
(☑ 360-902-8844; http://parks.state.wa.us/540/ lime-kiln-point; 1567 Westside Rd; ⊙ 8am-dusk) 🎫 Clinging to the island's rocky west coast, this beautiful park overlooks the deep Haro Strait and is reputedly one of the best places in the world to view whales from the shoreline. The word is out, however, so the view areas are often packed with hopeful picnickers. There's a small **interpretive center** (☑ 360-378-2044; ⊙ 11am-4pm Jun–mid-Sep) in the park, along with trails, a restored lime kiln and the landmark **Lime Kiln Lighthouse**, built in 1919.

🛏 Sleeping & Eating

There are hotels, B&Bs and resorts scattered around the island, but Friday Harbor has the highest concentration.

Wayfarer's Rest   HOSTEL **$**
(☑ 360-378-6428; www.hostelssanjuan.com; 35 Malcolm St, Friday Harbor; dm $40, r from $70, cabins from $85; 🛜 🐾) A short walk from the ferry terminal, this pleasant hostel is located in a homey house with comfortable dorms and affordable private rooms. The main kitchen overlooks the grassy backyard, and there's also a suite that sleeps six ($245). Reserve two months ahead in summer.

★ **Olympic Lights B&B**   B&B **$$**
(☑ 360-378-3186; www.olympiclights.com; 146 Starlight Way; r $165-185; 🛜) Once the centerpiece of a 320-acre estate, this splendidly restored 1895 farmhouse now hosts an equally formidable B&B that stands on an open bluff facing the snow-coated Olympic Mountains. The four rooms are imaginatively named Garden, Ra, Heart and Olympic; sunflowers adorn the garden and the

hearty breakfasts include homemade buttermilk biscuits. Two-night minimum.

Market Chef
DELI $

(☑ 360-378-4546; 225 A St, Friday Harbor; sandwiches from $9; ☺ 10am-4pm Mon-Fri) ✐ Super popular and famous for its delicious sandwiches, including its signature curried-egg salad with roasted peanuts and chutney, or roast beef and rocket. Salads are also available; local ingredients are used. If you're in town on a Saturday in summer, visit Market Chef at the San Juan Island Farmers Market (10am to 1pm).

Backdoor Kitchen
FUSION $$$

(☑ 360-378-9540; www.backdoorkitchen.com; 400 A St, Friday Harbor; mains $30-37; ☺ 11:30am-2:30pm Mon, 5-9pm Wed-Sun) One of San Juan Island's finest restaurants, Backdoor Kitchen uses fresh local ingredients to serve up creative multi-ethnic dishes such as Spanish-style pork with wild-prawn stew and East Indian spiced lentils with spinach cake. Dine in the pretty garden in summer. Reserve.

Orcas Island

More rugged than Lopez yet less crowded than San Juan, Orcas has struck a delicate balance between friendliness and frostiness, development and preservation, tourist dollars and priceless privacy – for the time being, at least. The ferry terminal is at Orcas Landing, 8 miles south of the main village, Eastsound.

On the island's eastern lobe is **Moran State Park** (☑ 360-376-6173; 3572 Olga Rd; Discover Pass required at some parking lots $10; ☺ 6:30am-dusk Apr-Sep, 8am-dusk Oct-Mar), dominated by Mt Constitution (2409ft), with 40 miles of trails and an amazing 360-degree mountaintop view. **Camping** (☑ 360-376-2326; http://moranstatepark.com; campsites from $25) is a great option here.

🛏 Sleeping

★ Golden Tree Hostel
HOSTEL $

(☑ 360-317-8693; www.goldentreehostel.com; 1159 North Beach Rd, Eastsound; dm/d with shared bath $45/115; @ 🗢 ☻) Located in an 1890s-era heritage house, this hip hostel offers cozy rooms and pleasant common spaces, along with a hot tub and sauna in the grassy garden. There's even a separate recreation building with pool, Foosball, shuffleboard

and darts. Bicycle rentals are $20. Friday pizza nights. Reserve in summer.

Doe Bay Village Resort & Retreat
HOSTEL $

(☑ 360-376-2291; www.doebay.com; 107 Doe Bay Rd, Olga; campsites from $60, cabins from $100, yurts from $80; 🗢 ☻) ✐ One of the least expensive resorts in the San Juans, Doe Bay has the atmosphere of an artists' commune combined with a hippie retreat. Accommodations include sea-view campsites and various cabins and yurts, some with views of the water.

Outlook Inn
HOTEL $$

(☑ 360-376-2200; www.outlookinn.com; 171 Main St, Eastsound; r with shared/private bath from $89/159; @ 🗢 ☻) Eastsound's oldest and most eye-catching building, the Outlook Inn (1888) is an island institution. Budget rooms are cozy and neat (try for room 30), while the luxurious suites have fireplaces, Jacuzzi tubs and stunning water views from their balconies. Excellent attached cafe.

🍴 Eating & Drinking

★ Brown Bear Baking
BAKERY $

(cnr Main St & North Beach Rd, Eastsound; pastries $7; ☺ 8am-5pm, closed Tue) No one wants to pay $7 for a pastry, but the trouble is that once you start eating the baked goods here, nothing else will do. Options include croissants *aux amandes*, quiche using fresh Orcas Island eggs and roast veggies, caramel sticky buns and fruit pie. Balance the nutritional ledger with one of the hearty soups or sandwiches.

★ Inn at Ship Bay
SEAFOOD $$$

(☑ 877-276-7296; www.innatshipbay.com; 326 Olga Rd; mains $21-30; ☺ 5:30-10pm Tue-Sat) ✐ Locals unanimously rate this place as the best fine-dining experience on the island. The chefs work overtime preparing everything from scratch using the freshest island ingredients. Seafood is the specialty and it's served in an attractive 1860s orchard house a couple of miles south of Eastsound. There's also an on-site 11-room hotel (doubles from $195).

Island Hoppin' Brewery
BREWERY

(www.islandhoppinbrewery.com; 33 Hope Lane, Eastsound; ☺ noon-9pm Tue-Sun) The location just off Mt Baker Rd near the airport makes this tiny brewery hard to find, but the locals sure know it's there – this is *the* place to go to enjoy local brews on tap. Don't come hungry – only snacks are served. Happy hour runs from 7pm to 9pm Sunday to Thursday, while a ping-pong table adds some action.

Lopez Island

If you're going to Lopez – or 'Slow-pez,' as locals prefer to call it – take a bike. With its undulating terrain and salutation-offering residents (who are famous for their three-fingered 'Lopezian wave'), this is the ideal cycling isle. A leisurely pastoral spin can be tackled in a day, with good overnight digs available next to the marina in the **Lopez Islander Resort** (☑360-468-2233; www.lopezfun.com; 2864 Fisherman Bay Rd; r from $129; 🖥️🏊). For something more upscale, try the **Edenwild Inn** (☑360-468-3238; www.eden wildinn.com; Lopez Rd, Lopez Village; r $115-225; 🖥️), a Victorian mansion set in lovely formal gardens.

If you arrive cycleless, call up **Village Cycles** (☑360-468-4013; www.villagecycles.net; 214 Lopez Rd; rental per hour $7-16), which can deliver a bicycle to the ferry terminal for you.

North Cascades

Dominated by Mt Baker and – to a lesser extent – the more remote Glacier Peak, the North Cascades is made up of a huge swath of protected forests, parks and wilderness areas that dwarf even the expansive Rainier and St Helens parks to the south. The crème de la crème is the North Cascades National Park, a primeval stash of old-growth rainforest, groaning glaciers and untainted ecosystems whose savage beauty is curiously missed by all but 2500 or so annual visitors who penetrate its rainy interior.

Mt Baker

Rising like a ghostly sentinel above the sparkling waters of upper Puget Sound, Mt Baker has been mesmerizing visitors to the Northwest for centuries. A dormant volcano that last belched smoke in the 1850s, this haunting 10,781ft peak shelters 12 glaciers, and in 1999 registered a record-breaking 95ft of snow in one season.

Well-paved Hwy 542, known as the Mt Baker Scenic Byway, climbs 5100ft to **Artist Point**, 56 miles from Bellingham. Near here you'll find the **Heather Meadows Visitor Center** (Mt Baker Hwy, Mile 56; ⊘8am-4:30pm mid-Jul–late Sep) and a plethora of varied hikes, including the 7.5-mile **Chain Lakes Loop** that leads you around a half-dozen lakes surrounded by huckleberry meadows.

Receiving more annual snow than any ski area in North America, the **Mt Baker Ski Area** (☑360-734-6771; www.mtbaker.us; lift tickets adult/child $60/40) has 38 runs, eight lifts and a vertical rise of 1500ft. The resort has gained something of a cult status among snowboarders, who have been coming here for the Legendary Baker Banked Slalom every January since 1985.

On your way up the mountain, stop for a bite at authentic honky-tonk bar and restaurant **Graham's** (☑360-599-9883; 9989 Mt Baker Hwy; mains $6-18; ⊘noon-9pm Mon-Fri, 8-11am & noon-9pm Sat & Sun) and grab trail munchies at **Wake & Bakery** (☑360-599-1658; www.get sconed.com; 6903 Bourne St, Glacier; snacks from $4; ⊘7:30am-5pm), both in the town of **Glacier**.

Leavenworth

Blink hard and rub your eyes. This isn't some strange Germanic hallucination. This is Leavenworth, a former lumber town that underwent a Bavarian makeover back in the 1960s after the re-routing of the cross-continental railway threatened to put it permanently out of business. Swapping wood for tourists, Leavenworth today has successfully reinvented itself as a traditional *Romantische Strasse* village, right down to the beer, sausages and lederhosen-loving locals (25% of whom are of German descent). The classic *Sound of Music* mountain setting helps, as does the fact that Leavenworth serves as the main activity center for sorties into the nearby Alpine Lakes Wilderness.

The **Leavenworth Chamber of Commerce** (www.leavenworth.org; 940 Hwy 2; ⊘8am-5pm Mon-Thu, 8am-6pm Fri & Sat, 10am-4pm Sun) can advise on the local outdoor activities. Highlights include the best climbing in the state at **Castle Rock** in Tumwater Canyon, about 3 miles northwest of town off US 2.

The **Devil's Gulch** is a popular off-road mountain-bike trail (25 miles, four to six hours). Local outfitters **Der Sportsmann** (☑509-548-5623; www.dersportsmann.com; 837 Front St; 1-day cross-country ski/snowshoe rentals $15/12; ⊘9am-6pm) rents mountain bikes.

🛏️ Sleeping & Eating

Hotel Pension Anna   HOTEL **$$**
(☑509-548-6273; www.pensionanna.com; 926 Commercial St; r from $179, ste from $300; 🖥️) The most authentic Bavarian hotel in town

is also spotless and incredibly friendly. Each room is kitted out in imported Austrian decor and the European-inspired breakfasts (included) may induce joyful yodels. A recommended room is the double with hand-painted furniture, but the spacious suite in the adjacent St Joseph's chapel is perfect for families.

Enzian Inn HOTEL **$$**
(☑509-548-5269; www.enzianinn.com; 590 Hwy 2; d from $140; ❄❀) At this Leavenworth classic the day starts with a blast on an alpenhorn before breakfast. If that doesn't send you running for your lederhosen, consider the free putting green (with resident grass-trimming goats), the indoor and outdoor swimming pools, and the nightly pianist pounding out requests in the Bavarian lobby.

München Haus GERMAN **$**
(☑509-548-1158; www.munchenhaus.com; 709 Front St; brats $5-7; ☉11am-9pm) The Haus is 100% alfresco, meaning that the hot German sausages and pretzels are essential stomach warmers in winter, while the Bavarian brews will cool you down in summer. The casual beer-garden atmosphere is complemented by an aggressively jaunty accordion soundtrack, laid-back staff, a kettle of cider relish and an epic mustard bar. Hours vary outside summer.

Lake Chelan

Long, slender Lake Chelan is central Washington's watery playground. The town of Chelan, at the lake's southeastern tip, is the primary base for accommodations and services, and has a **USFS Ranger Station** (☑509-682-4900; 428 W Woodin Ave).

Lake Chelan State Park (☑509-687-3710; https://washington.goingtocamp.com/lake chelanstatepark; 7544 S Lakeshore Rd; primitive/standard sites from $20/25) has 144 campsites; a number of lakeshore campgrounds are accessible only by boat. If you'd rather sleep in a real bed, try the great-value **Midtowner Motel** (☑800-572-0943; www.midtowner.com; 721 E Woodin Ave; r $45-130; ❄❀❀) or the delightful **Riverwalk Inn** (☑509-682-2627; www.riverwalkinnchelan.com; 205 E Wapato St; d $79-119, f $89-189; ❀❀), both in town.

Several wineries have also opened in the area and many have excellent restaurants. Try **Tsillan Cellars** (☑509-682-9463; www.tsillancellars.com; 3875 Hwy 97A; ☉noon-6pm) or the swanky Italian **Sorrento's Ristorante**

(☑509-682-5409; mains $22-36; ☉5pm-late Wed-Fri, noon-late Sat, 10am-late Sun).

Link Transit (☑509-662-1155; www.linktran sit.com) buses connect Chelan with Wenatchee and Leavenworth ($2.50 one way).

Beautiful **Stehekin**, on the northern tip of Lake Chelan, is accessible only by **boat** (www.ladyofthelake.com; 1418 W Woodin Ave, Chelan; round-trip $61), or a long hike across Cascade Pass, 28 miles from the lake. You'll find lots of information about hiking, campgrounds and cabin rentals at www.stehekin.com. Most facilities are open from mid-June to mid-September.

Methow Valley

The Methow's combination of powdery winter snow and abundant summer sunshine has transformed this valley into one of Washington's primary recreation areas. You can bike, hike and fish in summer, and cross-country ski on the second-biggest snow trail network in the US in winter.

The 200km of trails are maintained by the nonprofit **Methow Valley Sport Trails Association** (MVSTA; ☑509-996-3287; www.methowtrails.org; 309 Riverside Ave, Winthrop; ☉9am-3:30pm Mon-Fri) ✎, which in winter provides the most comprehensive network of hut-to-hut (and hotel-to-hotel) skiing in North America. An extra blessing is that few people seem to know about it. For classic accommodations and easy access to the skiing, hiking and cycling trails, decamp at the exquisite **Sun Mountain Lodge** (☑509-996-2211; www.sunmountainlodge.com; 604 Patterson Lake Rd, Winthrop; r from $205, cabins from $405; ❄❀❀), 10 miles west of the town of Winthrop. Winthrop is also the locus of the area's best eating: try the fine-dining **Arrowleaf Bistro** (☑509-996-3920; www.arrowleafbistro.com; 253 Riverside Ave; mains $22-28; ☉5-10pm Wed-Sun).

North Cascades National Park

Even the names of the lightly trodden, dramatic mountains in **North Cascades National Park** (www.nps.gov/noca) sound wild and untamed: Desolation Peak, Jagged Ridge, Mt Despair and Mt Terror. Not surprisingly, the region offers some of the best backcountry adventures outside of Alaska.

The **North Cascades Visitor Center** (☑206-386-4495, ext 11; 502 Newhalem St, Newhalem; ☉9am-5pm daily Jun-Sep, Sat & Sun May & Oct) ✎, in the small settlement of Newhalem on Hwy 20, is the best orientation point for visitors and is staffed by expert rangers who can enlighten you on the park's highlights.

Built in the 1930s for loggers working in the valley (which was soon to be flooded by Ross Dam), the floating cabins at the **Ross Lake Resort** (☑206-386-4437; www.rosslake resort.com; 503 Diablo St, Rockport; cabins $195-370; ☺mid-Jun–late Oct; ☻) on the eponymous lake's west side are the state's most unique accommodations. There's no road in – guests can either hike the 2-mile trail from Hwy 20 or take the resort's tugboat-taxi-and-truck shuttle from the parking area near Diablo Dam.

Northeastern Washington

Spokane

Washington's second-biggest population center is one of the state's latent surprises and a welcome break after the treeless monotony of the eastern scablands. Situated at the nexus of the Pacific Northwest's so-called 'Inland Empire,' this understated yet confident city sits on the banks of the Spokane River, close to where British fur traders founded a short-lived trading post in 1810. Though rarely touted in national tourist blurbs, Spokane hosts one of the world's largest mass-participation running events (May's annual Bloomsday).

◉ Sights

Riverfront Park   PARK
(www.spokaneriverfrontpark.com; ☒) The site of the 1974 World's Fair and Exposition, this park has numerous highlights, including a 17-point **Sculpture Walk** (Riverfront Park) and the scenic **Spokane Falls**. A short gondola ride, the **Spokane Falls SkyRide** (Riverfront Park) takes you directly above the falls, as does the equally spectacular **Monroe Street Bridge** (Monroe St), built in 1911 and still one of the largest concrete arches in the USA. An ongoing renovation project means parts of the park are inaccessible and most attractions are closed until fall 2017.

Northwest Museum
of Arts & Culture   MUSEUM
(MAC; ☑509-456-3931; www.northwestmuseum. org; 2316 W 1st Ave; adult/child $15/10; ☺10am-5pm Tue-Sun, to 8pm Wed; ☒) In a striking state-of-the-art building in the historic Browne's Addition neighborhood, this museum has – arguably – one of the finest collections of indigenous artifacts in the Northwest. Leading off a plush glass foyer overlooking the Spokane River are four galleries showcasing Spokane's history, as well as a number of roving exhibitions that change every three to four months.

🛏 Sleeping & Eating

Hotel Ruby   MOTEL $
(☑509-747-1041; www.hotelrubyspokane.com; 901 W 1st Ave; r from $78; ⓟ🕸🐾📶🐕) An arty redesign of a formerly basic motel, the Ruby has a '70s feel, with cool original art on the walls, funky light fixtures and a sleek cocktail lounge attached to the lobby. Rooms have minifridge and microwave, and you can use the gym at the nearby sister hotel, Ruby 2. It's an easy walk to bars and restaurants.

★Historic
Davenport Hotel   HISTORIC HOTEL $$
(☑800-899-1482; www.thedavenporthotel.com; 10 S Post St; r from $188; 🕸📶🐕) This historic landmark (opened in 1914) is considered one of the best hotels in the country. Even if you're not staying here, linger in the exquisite lobby or have a drink in the Peacock Lounge. The adjacent, modern Davenport Tower sports a safari-themed lobby and bar.

Mizuna   FUSION $$
(☑509-747-2004; www.mizuna.com; 214 N Howard St; dinner mains $20-36; ☺11am-10pm Mon-Sat, 4-10pm Sun; 🍽) Located in an antique brick building, the simply furnished Mizuna is well known for its specialties, such as quinoa meatloaf and pan-roasted organic chicken, as well as an extensive vegetarian menu. Wash dinner down with an exquisite wine for a memorable experience.

🍸 Drinking & Entertainment

From opera and cocktail bars to billiards and craft breweries, Spokane has the best nighttime entertainment and drinking scene east of the Cascades.

NoLi Brewhouse   BREWERY
(☑509-242-2739; www.nolibrewhouse.com; 1003 E Trent Ave; mains $12-16; ☺11am-10pm Sun-Wed, to 11pm Thu-Sat) A student hangout near Gonzaga University, Spokane's best microbrewery serves some weird and wonderful flavors, including a tart cherry ale and an imperial stout with coffee, chocolate and brown-sugar tones. Food-wise, check out the

cod and chips cooked in batter made with the brewery's own pale ale.

Mootsy's BAR
(☑509-838-1570; 406 W Sprague Ave; ⊘2pm-2am) This popular dive bar is the hub of the nightlife and alternative-music scene that hops all along this block between Stevens and Washington Sts. Cheap Pabst Blue Ribbon during happy hour keeps its customer base loyal.

Bing Crosby Theater THEATER
(☑509-227-7638; www.bingcrosbytheater.com; 901 W Sprague Ave) Yes, Bing Crosby hailed from Spokane, and now his namesake venue the 'Bing' presents concerts, plays and festivals in a fairly intimate setting.

ⓘ Information

Spokane Area Visitor Information Center
(☑888-776-5263; www.visitspokane.com; 808 W Main Ave; ⊘8am-5pm Mon-Sat, 11am-6pm Sun) Has plenty of pamphlets and maps.

ⓘ Getting There & Away

Spokane International Airport (www.spokaneairports.net) Flights to Seattle, Portland, OR, and Boise, ID.

Spokane Intermodal Center (221 W 1st Ave) Buses and trains depart from this station.

South Cascades

More rounded and less hemmed in than their saw-toothed cousins to the north, the South Cascades are nonetheless higher. Their pinnacle in more ways than one is 14,411ft Mt Rainier, the fifth-highest mountain in the lower 48 and arguably one of the most dramatic stand-alone mountains in the world. Further south, fiery Mt St Helens needs zero introduction, while unsung Adams glowers way off to the east like a sulking middle child.

Mt Rainier National Park

The USA's fifth-highest peak outside Alaska, majestic Mt Rainier is also one of its most beguiling. Encased in a 368-sq-mile national park, the mountain's snowcapped summit and forest-covered foothills boast numerous hiking trails, huge swaths of flower-carpeted meadows, and an alluring conical peak that presents a formidable challenge for aspiring climbers.

Mt Rainier National Park (www.nps.gov/mora; car $25, pedestrian & cyclist $10, under 17yr free, 1yr pass $50) has four entrances. Call 800-695-7623 for road conditions. The National Park Service (NPS) website includes downloadable maps and descriptions of dozens of park trails. The most famous is the hardcore, 93-mile-long Wonderland Trail that completely circumnavigates Mt Rainier and takes around 10 to 12 days to tackle.

Campgrounds located in the park have running water and toilets, but no showers or RV hookups. Reservations at park **campsites** (☑800-365-2267; www.nps.gov/mora; campsites $20) are strongly advised during summer and can be made up to two months in advance by phone or online. For overnight backcountry trips, you'll need a wilderness permit – check the NPS website for details.

NISQUALLY ENTRANCE

The busiest and most convenient gate to Mt Rainier National Park, Nisqually lies on Hwy 706 via Ashford, near the park's southwest corner. It's open year-round. Longmire, 7 miles inside the Nisqually entrance, has a **museum and information center** (☑360-569-6575; Hwy 706; ⊘9am-4:30pm May-Jul), a number of important trailheads, and the rustic **National Park Inn** (☑360-569-2275; Hwy 706; r with shared/private bath from $126/177; ✱), complete with an excellent restaurant.

More hikes and interpretive walks can be found 12 miles further east at loftier **Paradise**, which is served by the informative **Henry M Jackson Visitor Center** (☑360-569-6571; Paradise; ⊘10am-5pm daily May-Oct, Sat & Sun Nov-Apr), and the vintage **Paradise Inn** (☑360-569-2275; r with shared/private bath from $123/182; ⊘May-Oct; ☷☎), a historical 'parkitecture' inn constructed in 1916. Climbs to the top of Rainier leave from the inn; excellent four-day guided ascents are led by **Rainier Mountaineering Inc** (☑888-892-5462; www.rmiguides.com; 30027 Hwy 706 E, Ashford; 4-day climb $1087).

OTHER ENTRANCES

The three other entrances to Mt Rainier National Park are **Ohanapecosh**, accessed via Hwy123 and the town of Packwood, where lodging is available; **White River**, off Hwy 410, which literally takes the highroad (6400ft) to the beautiful viewpoint at the **Sunrise Lodge Cafeteria** (snacks $6-9; ⊘10am-7pm Jul & Aug); and remote **Carbon River** in the northwest corner, which gives access to the park's inland rainforest.

Mt St Helens National Volcanic Monument

What it lacks in height, Mt St Helens makes up for in fiery infamy – 57 people perished on the mountain when it erupted with a force of 1500 atomic bombs on May 18, 1980. The cataclysm began with an earthquake measuring 5.1 on the Richter scale, which sparked the biggest landslide in recorded history and buried 230 sq miles of forest under millions of tons of volcanic rock and ash. Today it's a fascinating landscape of recovering forests, new river valleys and ash-covered slopes. There's an $8 per person fee to enter the National Monument.

NORTHEASTERN ENTRANCE

From the main northeast entrance on Hwy 504, your first stop should be the **Silver Lake Visitor Center** (www.mtsthelensinfo.com/visitor_centers/silver_lake; 3029 Spirit Lake Hwy; adult/child $5/2.50; ⊗9am-5pm May-Sep, to 4pm Oct-Apr; ⏿) 🅿, which has films, exhibits and free information about the mountain (including trail maps). For a closer view of the destructive power of nature, venture to the **Johnston Ridge Observatory** (☑360-274-2140; 24000 Spirit Lake Hwy; day use $8; ⊗10am-6pm mid-May–Oct), situated at the end of Hwy 504, which looks directly into the mouth of the crater. A welcome stop in an accommodations-light area, the **Eco Park Resort** (☑360-274-7007; www.ecoparkresort.com; 14000 Spirit Lake Hwy, Toutle; campsites $25, cabins $140-150; 🛏) offers campsites and RV hookups, and basic two- or four-person cabins.

SOUTHEASTERN & EASTSIDE ENTRANCES

The southeastern entrance via the town of **Cougar** on Hwy 503 holds some serious lava terrain, including the 2-mile-long Ape Cave lava tube, which you can explore year round; be prepared for the chill as it remains a constant 41°F (5°C). Bring two light sources per adult or rent lanterns at **Apes' Headquarters** (☑360-449-7800; ⊗10am-5pm mid-Jun–early Sep) for $5 each.

The eastside entrance is the most remote, but the harder-to-reach **Windy Ridge** viewpoint on this side gives you a palpable, if eerie, sense of the destruction from the blast. It's often closed until June. A few miles down the road you can descend 600ft on the 1-mile-long Harmony Trail (hike 224) to **Spirit Lake**.

Central & Southeastern Washington

The sunny, dry, near-California-looking central and southeastern parts of Washington harbor one not-so-secret weapon: wine. The fertile land that borders the Nile-like Yakima and Columbia River Valleys is awash with enterprising new wineries producing quality grapes that now vie with the Napa and Sonoma Valleys for recognition. Yakima and its more attractive cousin Ellensburg once held the edge, but nowadays the real star is Walla Walla.

Yakima & Ellensburg

The main reason to stop in Yakima is to visit one of the numerous wineries that lie between here and Benton City; pick up a map at

---

WORTH A TRIP

GRAND COULEE DAM

While the more famous Hoover Dam (conveniently located between Las Vegas and the Grand Canyon) gets around 1.6 million visitors per year, the four-times-larger and arguably more significant **Grand Coulee Dam** FREE (inconveniently located far from everything) gets only a trickle of tourism. If you're in the area, don't miss it – it's one of the country's most spectacular displays of engineering and you'll get to enjoy it crowd-free.

The **Grand Coulee Dam Visitor Center** (☑509-633-9265; www.usbr.gov/pn/grandcoulee/visit; ⊗8:30am-11pm Jun & Jul, to 10:30pm Aug, to 9:30pm Sep, 9am-5pm Oct-May) details the history of the dam and surrounding area with movies, photos and interactive exhibits. Free guided tours run on the hour from 10am to 5pm May to September, and at 11am and 2pm the rest of the year, and involve taking a glass-walled elevator 465ft down into the Third Power Plant, where you can view the generators from an observation deck.

the **visitor center** (📞800-221-0751; www.visit yakima.com; 101 N 8th St; ⏰9am-5pm Mon-Sat, 10am-4pm Sun Jun-Aug, reduced hours Sep-May).

A better layover is Ellensburg, a diminutive settlement 36 miles to the northwest that juxtaposes the state's largest rodeo (each Labor Day) with a town center that has more coffee bars per head than anywhere else in the world (allegedly). Grab your latte at local roaster **D&M Coffee** (📞509-962-9333; www.dmcoffee.com; 323 N Pearl St; mains $5-7; ⏰7am-10pm Mon-Sat, to 8pm Sun) 🍴 and eat at the unconventional **Yellow Church Cafe** (📞509-933-2233; www.theyellow churchcafe.com; 111 S Pearl St; dinner mains $17-27; ⏰11am-9pm Mon-Thu, 8am-9pm Fri-Sun).

Greyhound services both cities, with buses to Seattle, Spokane and points in between.

Walla Walla

Walla Walla has converted itself into the hottest wine-growing region outside of California. While venerable Marcus Whitman College is the town's most obvious cultural attribute, you'll also find zany coffee bars, cool wine-tasting rooms, fine Queen Anne architecture, and one of the state's freshest and most vibrant farmers markets.

◎ Sights & Activities

You don't need to be sloshed on wine to appreciate Walla Walla's historical and cultural heritage. Its Main St has won countless historical awards, and to bring the settlement to life, the local **chamber of commerce** (📞509-525-0850; www.wallawalla.org; 29 E Sumach St; ⏰8:30am-5pm Mon-Fri) has concocted some interesting walking tours. Main St and environs are also crammed with tasting rooms. Expect tasting fees of $5 to $10.

Fort Walla Walla Museum　　MUSEUM
(📞509-525-7703; www.fwwm.org; 755 Myra Rd; adult/child $8/3; ⏰10am-5pm Mar-Oct, to 4pm Nov-Feb; 🅿) This is a pioneer village of 17 historic buildings. There are collections of farm implements, ranching tools and what could be the world's largest plastic replica of a mule team.

Waterbrook Wine　　WINE
(📞509-522-1262; www.waterbrook.com; 10518 W US 12; tastings $5-10; ⏰11am-5pm Sun-Thu, to 6pm Fri & Sat Oct-Apr, 11am-7pm May-Sep) About 10 miles west of town, this large winery has a pond-side patio that's a great place to imbibe a long selection of wines on a sunny day. Food served Thursday to Sunday.

Amavi Cellars　　WINE
(📞509-525-3541; www.amavicellars.com; 3796 Peppers Bridge Rd; ⏰10am-4pm) South of Walla Walla, amid a scenic spread of grape and apple orchards, you can sample some of the most talked about wines in the valley (try the Syrah and Cabernet Sauvignon). The classy yet comfortable patio has views of the Blue Mountains.

🛏 Sleeping & Eating

Walla Walla Garden Motel　　MOTEL $
(📞509-529-1220; www.wallawallagardenmotel. com; 2279 Isaacs Ave; r from $72; ✳🐾) A simple family-run motel halfway to the airport, the Garden Motel (formerly the Colonial) is welcoming and bike friendly, with safe bike storage and plenty of local maps.

Marcus Whitman Hotel　　HOTEL $$
(📞509-525-2200; www.marcuswhitmanhotel.com; 6 W Rose St; r from $149; 🅿✳🐾🐕) Walla Walla's best-known landmark is also the town's only tall building, impossible to miss with its distinctive rooftop turret. In keeping with the settlement's well-preserved image, the red-brick 1928 beauty has been elegantly renovated and decorated, with ample rooms in rusts and browns, embellished with Italian-crafted furniture, huge beds and great views over the nearby Blue Mountains. Its restaurant, the **Marc** (mains $15-40; ⏰from 5:30pm), is one of the town's fanciest eating joints.

Graze　　CAFE $
(📞509-522-9991; 5 S Colville St; sandwiches $8-12; ⏰10am-7:30pm Mon-Sat, to 3:30pm Sun; 🐾) Amazing sandwiches are packed for your picnic or (if you can get a table) eaten in at this simple cafe. Try the turkey and pear panini with provolone and blue cheese or the flank-steak torta with pickled jalapeños, avocado, tomato, cilantro and chipotle dressing. There are plenty of vegetarian options.

Saffron Mediterranean Kitchen　　MEDITERRANEAN $$$
(📞509-525-2112; www.saffronmediterraneankitch en.com; 125 W Alder St; mains $26-42; ⏰2-10pm Tue-Sat, to 9pm Sun May-Oct, 2-9pm Tue-Sun Nov-Apr) This place isn't about cooking, it's about alchemy: Saffron takes seasonal, local ingredients and turns them into pure gold. The Med-inspired menu lists dishes such as bison rib eye and nettle pappardelle with duck ragù. Then there are the intelligently paired wines – and beers. Reserve.

ℹ Getting There & Away

Alaska Airlines has two daily flights to Seattle-Tacoma International Airport from the **Walla Walla Regional Airport** (www.wallawallaairport.com), northeast of town off US 12.

Greyhound buses run once daily to Seattle ($47, seven hours) via Pasco, Yakima and Ellensburg; change buses in Pasco for Spokane.

OREGON

It's hard to slap a single characterization onto Oregon's geography and people. Its landscape ranges from rugged coastline and thick evergreen forests to barren, fossil-strewn deserts, volcanoes and glaciers. As for its denizens, you name it – Oregonians run the gamut from pro-logging conservatives to tree-hugging liberals. What they have in common is an independent spirit, a love of the outdoors and a fierce devotion to where they live.

It doesn't usually take long for visitors to feel a similar devotion. Who wouldn't fall in love with the spectacle of glittering Crater Lake, the breathtaking colors of the Painted Hills in John Day or the hiking trails through deep forests and over stunning mountain passes? And then there are the towns: you can eat like royalty in funky Portland, see top-notch dramatic productions in Ashland or sample an astounding number of brewpubs in Bend.

Portland

Oregon's largest city used to seem like a well-kept secret: it had all the cultural advantages of a major city but the feel and affordability of a small town. But little old Stumptown is growing up, in many ways.

Most of the changes happening in Portland are for the better. Sure, parking might be a little harder, and grubby dive bars are now pretty scarce, but on the other hand, there's a coffee roastery and a craft brewery on just about every block. And the food carts – more and better than ever.

Portland has an almost unfair abundance of natural beauty – perfect parks, leafy trees, vibrantly flowering shrubs lining pretty residential streets, the Willamette River meandering through town, and Mt Hood on the horizon. And the open-minded, appealingly off-kilter vibe of the place – that whole 'Keep

---

OREGON FACTS

Nickname Beaver State

Population 4,028,977

Area 98,466 sq miles

Capital city Salem (population 160,614)

Other cities Portland (population 632,309), Eugene (population 160,561), Bend (population 87,014)

Sales tax Oregon has no sales tax

Birthplace of Former US president Herbert Hoover (1874–1964), actor and dancer Ginger Rogers (1911–95), writer Ken Kesey (1935–2001), filmmaker Gus Van Sant (b 1952), *The Simpsons* creator Matt Groening (b 1954)

Home of Oregon Shakespeare Festival, Nike, Crater Lake

Politics Democrat governors since 1987

Famous for Forests, rain, microbrews, coffee, Death with Dignity Act

State beverage Milk (dairy's big here)

Driving You can't pump your own gas in Oregon; Portland to Eugene, 110 miles; Portland to Astoria, 96 miles

---

Portland Weird' thing – certainly hasn't changed. These days, there's just more to love.

◉ Sights

◉ Downtown

★**Tom McCall Waterfront Park** PARK
(Map p386; Naito Parkway) This popular riverside park, which lines the west bank of the Willamette River, was finished in 1978 after four years of construction. It replaced an old freeway with 1.5 miles of paved sidewalks and grassy spaces, and attracts heaps of joggers, in-line skaters, strollers and cyclists. During summer the park is perfect for hosting large outdoor events such as the Oregon Brewers Festival (p390). Walk over the Steel and Hawthorne bridges to the **Eastbank Esplanade**, making a 2.6-mile loop.

★**Pioneer Courthouse Square** LANDMARK
(Map p386; www.thesquarepdx.org; ⊠ Red, Blue, Green) The heart of downtown Portland, this brick plaza is nicknamed 'Portland's living room' and is the most-visited public

Portland

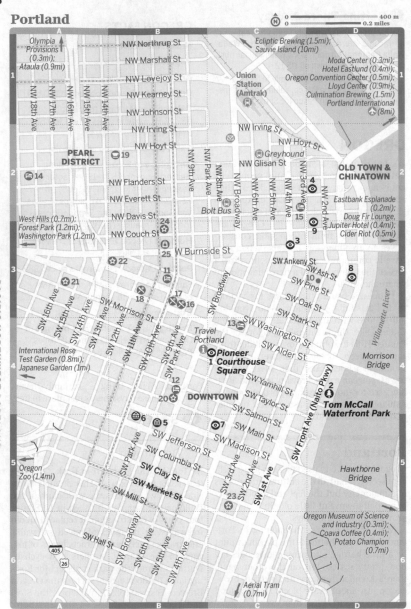

space in the city. When it isn't full of Hacky Sack players, sunbathers or office workers lunching, the square hosts concerts, festivals, rallies, farmers markets, and even summer Friday-night movies (aka 'Flicks on the Bricks').

Portland Building LANDMARK
(Map p386; cnr SW 5th Ave & SW Main St) This controversial 15-story building (1982) was designed by Michael Graves and catapulted the postmodern architect to celebrity status. But the blocky, pastel-colored edifice has

Portland

never been popular with the people who work inside it, and in recent years the city has found structural problems that mean the building will need massive reconstruction in order to stay standing. At least it's been made somewhat green: an eco-roof was installed in 2006.

Oregon Historical Society MUSEUM
(Map p386; ☑503-222-1741; www.ohs.org; 1200 SW Park Ave; adult/child $11/5; ☺10am-5pm Mon-Sat, noon-5pm Sun; 🚊Red, Blue) Along the tree-shaded **South Park Blocks** sits the state's primary history museum, which dedicates most of its space to the story of Oregon and the pioneers who featured in it. There are interesting sections on various immigrant groups, Native American tribes and the travails of the Oregon Trail. Temporary exhibits furnish the downstairs space.

Portland Art Museum MUSEUM
(Map p386; ☑503-226-2811; www.portlandartmuseum.org; 1219 SW Park Ave; adult/child $19.99/free; ☺10am-5pm Tue-Sun, to 8pm Thu & Fri; 🚌6, 38, 45, 55, 58, 68, 92, 96, 🚊NS Line, A-Loop) Alongside the South Park Blocks, the art museum's excellent exhibits include Native American carvings, Asian and American art, photography and English silver. The museum also houses the Whitsell Auditorium, a first-rate theater that frequently screens rare or international films and that is part of the Northwest Film Center and school.

⊙ **Old Town & Chinatown**

The core of rambunctious 1890s Portland, once-seedy Old Town had a reputation as the lurking ground of unsavory characters. Now it's home to some lovely historic buildings, plus Waterfront Park, Saturday Market and a few good pockets of nightlife.

Old Town is generally lumped together with the city's historic Chinatown – no longer the heart of the Chinese community (that's moved to outer Southeast) but still home to the ornate **Chinatown Gates** (Map p386; cnr W Burnside St & NW 4th Ave; 🚊Blue, Red), tranquil **Lan Su Chinese Garden** (Map p386; ☑503-228-8131; www.lansugarden.org; 239 NW Everett St; adult/child $10/7; ☺10am-7pm mid-Apr–mid-Oct, to 5pm mid-Oct–mid-Apr; 🚌4, 8, 16, 35, 44, 77, 🚊Blue, Red) and the so-called **Shanghai Tunnels** (Map p386; ☑503-622-4798; www.shanghaitunnels.info; 120 NW 3rd Ave; adult/child $13/8; 🚌12, 19, 20, 🚊Blue, Red), some of which can be toured.

Saturday Market MARKET
(Map p386; ☑503-222-6072; www.portlandsaturdaymarket.com; 2 SW Naito Parkway; ☺10am-5pm Sat, 11am-4:30pm Sun Mar-Dec; 👶; 🚌12, 16, 19, 20, 🚊Red, Blue) The best time to walk along the Portland Waterfront is on a weekend, when you can catch this famous market showcasing arts and crafts, street entertainers and food booths.

The Pearl District & Northwest

When Portlanders talk about 'Northwest,' they're usually referring to the attractive neighborhood surrounding NW 21st and 23rd Aves, north of W Burnside St. The residential heart of late-19th-century Portland, this area later became the city's upper-crust commercial strip, but it's struggled a bit in recent years as the dining-and-shopping buzz has spread eastward. Still, it's a pleasant and scenic strolling neighborhood, anchored by vintage apartment buildings and one of the city's best art-house cinemas. Parking is tough but not impossible; you can also take the streetcar (or just walk) from downtown.

Just east of Northwest, the **Pearl District** is an old industrial precinct that has been transformed into Portland's swankiest neighborhood. Warehouses have been converted to fancy lofts commanding some of the highest real-estate prices in Oregon. It's a great place to walk around and check out upscale boutiques, trendy restaurants and art galleries.

West Hills

Forest Park PARK
(📞 503-223-5449; www.forestparkconservancy. org) Abutting the more manicured Washington Park to the south (to which it is linked by various trails) is the far wilder 5100-acre Forest Park, a temperate rainforest that harbors plants and animals and hosts an avid hiking fraternity. The **Portland Audubon Society** (📞 503-292-6855; www.audubonportland.org; 5151 NW Cornell Rd; ⏱ 9am-5pm, nature store 10am-6pm Mon-Sat, to 5pm Sun; 🚌 20) **FREE** maintains a bookstore, a wildlife-rehabilitation center and 4.5 miles of trails within its Forest Park sanctuary.

Washington Park PARK
(www.washingtonparkpdx.org; 🚻; 🚇 Blue, Red) Tame and well-tended Washington Park contains several key attractions within its 400 acres of greenery. The **International Rose Test Garden** (www.rosegardenstore. org; 400 SW Kingston Ave; ⏱ 7:30am-9pm; 🚌 63) **FREE** is the centerpiece of Portland's famous rose blooms; there are 400 types on show here, plus great city views. Further uphill is the **Japanese Garden** (📞 503-223-1321; www. japanesegarden.com; 611 SW Kingston Ave; adult/child $14.95/10.45; ⏱ noon-7pm Mon, 10am-7pm Tue-Sun mid-Mar–Sep, noon-4pm Mon, 10am-4pm Tue-Sun Oct–mid-Mar; 🚌 63), another oasis of tranquility. If you have kids, the **Oregon Zoo** (📞 503-226-1561; www.oregonzoo.org; 4001 SW Canyon Rd; adult/child $14.95/9.95; ⏱ 9:30am-6pm Jun-Aug, reduced hours Sep-May; 🚻; 🚌 63, 🚇 Blue, Red) and **Portland Children's Museum** (📞 503-233-6500; www.portlandcm.org; 4015 SW Canyon Rd; $10.75, 4-7pm 1st Fri of month free; ⏱ 9am-5pm; 🚻; 🚌 63, 🚇 Red, Blue) should be on your docket.

Northeast & Southeast

Across the Willamette River from downtown is the **Lloyd Center** (📞 503-282-2511; www.lloydcenter.com; 2201 Lloyd Center; ⏱ 10am-9pm Mon-Sat, 11am-6pm Sun; 🚇 Red, Blue, Green), Oregon's largest shopping mall and where notorious ice-queen Tonya Harding first learned to skate. A few blocks to the southwest are the unmissable glass towers of the **Oregon Convention Center** (www.oregoncc. org; 777 NE Martin Luther King Jr Blvd; 🚇 Red, Blue, Green, Yellow), and nearby is the **Moda Center** (📞 503-235-8771; www.rosequarter.com/ venue/moda-center; 1 N Center Court St; 🚇 Yellow), home of professional basketball team the Trailblazers.

Further up the Willamette, **N Mississippi Ave** used to be full of run-down buildings, but is now a hot spot of trendy shops and eateries. Northeast is artsy **NE Alberta St**, a long ribbon of art galleries, boutiques and cafes (don't miss the **Last Thursday** (www. lastthursdayonalberta.com) street-art event here, taking place the last Thursday of each month). **SE Hawthorne Blvd** (near SE39th Ave) is affluent hippy territory, with gift stores, cafes, coffeeshops and two branches of Powell's bookstores. One leafy mile to the south, **SE Division St** has become a foodie destination, with plenty of excellent restaurants, bars and pubs. The same is true of **E Burnside at NE 28th Ave**, though it has a more concentrated and upscale feel.

🏃 Activities

Hiking

Portland boasts the 5000-acre Forest Park within city limits, which will keep avid hikers busy for a while. There's also a network of trails in **Hoyt Arboretum** (📞 503-865-8733; www.hoytarboretum.org; 4000 Fairview Blvd; ⏱ trails 5am-9:30pm, visitor center 9am-4pm Mon-Fri, 11am-3pm Sat & Sun; 🚇 Washington Park) **FREE**, easily reached by light rail, and more

PORTLAND FOR CHILDREN

Washington Park has the most to offer families with young kids. Here you'll find the world-class Oregon Zoo, which is set in a beautiful natural environment parents will also enjoy. Next door is the Portland Children's Museum and **World Forestry Center** (☑503-228-1367; www.worldforestry.org; 4033 SW Canyon Rd; adult/child $7/5; ☺10am-5pm, closed Tue & Wed Labor Day-Memorial Day; ⊞; ⊒63, ⊒Blue, Red), both offering fun learning activities and exhibits.

On the other side of the **Willamette River**, the **Oregon Museum of Science and Industry** (OMSI; ☑503-797-4000; www.omsi.edu; 1945 SE Water Ave; adult/child $14/9.75; ☺9:30am-5:30pm Jun-Aug, closed Mon Sep-May; ⊞; ⊒9, 17, ⊒A Loop, B Loop, ⊒Orange) is a top-notch destination with a theater, planetarium and even a submarine to explore. And finally, further south is **Oaks Amusement Park** (☑503-233-5777; www.oakspark.com; 7805 SE Oaks Park Way; ride bracelets $15-31, individual rides $3.75, skating $6.60-7.50; ☺hours vary; ⊞; ⊒35, 99), home to pint-size roller coasters, miniature golf and carnival games.

to explore at **Tryon Creek State Natural Area** (☑503-636-9886; www.oregonstateparks. org; 11321 SW Terwilliger Blvd).

If that's not enough, the hiking wonderlands of Mt Hood (p398) and the Columbia River Gorge (p397) are each less than an hour's drive away.

Cycling

Portland often tops lists of the USA's most bike-friendly cities.

Look for pleasant paths along the **Willamette River** downtown, or try the 21-mile **Springwater Corridor**, which heads out to the suburb of Boring.

Mountain bikers can head to **Leif Erikson Dr**, or for single-track and technical trails, **Hood River** and **Mt Hood** (both about an hour's drive away) have great options.

For scenic farm country, head to **Sauvie Island** (www.sauvieisland.org; Hwy 30; daily parking pass $10), 10 miles northwest of downtown Portland.

Snag a free *Portland by Bicycle* or $6 *Bike There!* map from a visitor center or a bike shop.

Everybody's Bike Rentals & Tours CYCLING (☑503-358-0152; www.pdxbikerentals.com; 305 NE Wygant St; tours per person from $69, rentals per hour $8-15; ☺10am-3pm; ⊒6) It's true that Portland is best seen by bicycle, and this company offers low-key, fun tours of the city and its surroundings – whether you're into food and farms or beer and parks. Bicycle rentals are also available.

Kayaking

Situated close to the confluence of the Columbia and Willamette Rivers, Portland has miles of navigable waterways.

Portland Kayak Company KAYAKING (☑503-459-4050; www.portlandkayak.com; 6600 SW Macadam Ave; rental per hour from $14; ☺10am-5pm; ⊒43) Kayaking rentals (minimum two hours), instruction and tours – notably a three-hour circumnavigation of Ross Island on the Willamette River ($49), available at 10am and 2pm daily and at sunset (starts 6pm) May through September.

☞ Tours

Pedal Bike Tours CYCLING (Map p386; ☑503-243-2453; www.pedalbiketours. com; 133 SW 2nd Ave; tours $59-199; ☺10am-6pm; ⊒12, 19, 20, ⊒Blue, Red) Offers all sorts of themes – history, food carts, beer – and even a Pot Tour through Portland ($69), where you spend three hours touring the city through the lens of the new retail pot industry. Learn about Oregon's history with hemp, visit dispensaries and head shops, and get the lowdown on what's legal in terms of buying and smoking. Vegan munchies available!

Portland Walking Tours WALKING (☑503-774-4522; www.portlandwalkingtours.com; tours per person $20-79) Food, chocolate, underground and even ghost-hunting tours are available daily. A new tour of 'makers and their spaces' offers a glimpse behind the scenes of Portland's indie-creative side, from crafts and woodworking to leather goods and a brewery. Each tour meets at a different location; reservations recommended.

☆ Festivals & Events

Portland Rose Festival CULTURAL (www.rosefestival.org; ☺late May–mid-Jun) Rose-covered floats, dragon-boat races, a riverfront carnival, fireworks, roaming packs of sailors and the crowning of a Rose Queen all make this Portland's biggest celebration. The evening Starlight Parade and the Grand Floral Parade (mid-June) are the highlights.

Oregon Brewers Festival BEER
(www.oregonbrewfest.com; Tom McCall Waterfront Park; admission free, tasting glass $7, per taste $1; ⊙late Jul) In the last full weekend in July you can quaff microbrews from near and far in Waterfront Park – everyone's happy and even nondrinkers have fun. There are also food stalls and other beer-focused vendors in the park.

Bite of Oregon FOOD & DRINK
(www.biteoforegon.com; tickets $6; ⊙early Sep) Bite of Oregon features all the food (and beer) you could think of consuming, much of it from great local restaurants – and some of it from Portland's famous food carts. You'll find good microbrews too. The festival benefits Special Olympics Oregon. Dates and location vary by year; check online.

🛌 Sleeping

Tariffs listed are for the summer season, when reservations are a good idea. Prices at top-end hotels are highly variable depending on occupancy and day of the week.

Hawthorne Portland Hostel HOSTEL $
(☑503-236-3380; www.portlandhostel.org; 3031 SE Hawthorne Blvd; dm $34-37, d with shared bath $74; ❄@🛜; 🚌14) 🚲 This ecofriendly hostel has a great Hawthorne location. The two private rooms are good and the dorms are spacious. There are summertime open-mike nights in the grassy backyard, and bicycle rentals (and a fix-it station) are available. The hostel composts and recycles, harvests rainwater for toilets, and has a nice eco-roof. Discounts are offered to those who are bicycle touring.

Northwest Portland Hostel HOSTEL $
(Map p386; ☑503-241-2783; www.nwportland hostel.com; 425 NW 18th Ave; dm $34-40, d with shared bath from $89; ❄@🛜; 🚌77) Perfectly located between the Pearl District and NW 21st and 23rd Aves, this friendly and clean hostel takes up four old buildings and features plenty of common areas (including a small deck) and discounted bicycle rentals. Dorms are spacious and private rooms can be as nice as those in hotels, though all share

outside bathrooms. Non-HI members pay $3 extra.

★Kennedy School HOTEL $$
(☑503-249-3983; www.mcmenamins.com/ken nedyschool; 5736 NE 33rd Ave; d from $155; 🛜; 🚌70) This former elementary school is now home to a hotel (sleep in old classrooms!), a restaurant with a great garden courtyard, several bars, a microbrewery and a movie theater. Guests can use the soaking pool for free. The whole school is decorated in the McMenamins' distinctive art style – mosaics, fantasy paintings and historical photographs.

★Ace Hotel BOUTIQUE HOTEL $$
(Map p386; ☑503-228-2277; www.acehotel. com; 1022 SW Stark St; d with shared/private bath from $175/245; 🅿❄❄@🛜❄; 🚌20) A well-established brand, the Ace fuses industrial, minimalist and retro styles to great effect. From the photo booth in its lobby to the recycled fabrics and salvaged-wood furniture in its rooms, the hotel feels very chic and very Portland. There's a Stumptown coffee shop and underground bar on-site and **Clyde Common bistro** (Map p386; ☑503-228-3333; www.clydecommon.com; 1014 SW Stark St; mains $9-29; ⊙11:30am-midnight Mon-Fri, 3pm-midnight Sat, 3-11pm Sun) adjoins the lobby. The location can't be beat.

★Society Hotel HOTEL $$
(Map p386; ☑503-445-0444; www.thesocietyho tel.com; 203 NW 3rd Ave; bunks $55, d from $129; 🛜; 🚌4, 8, 16, 35, 44, 77, 🚈Red, Blue, Green) A newcomer and the only place to stay in Old Town-Chinatown, this pretty hotel in the historic 1881 Mariners Building – originally a lodging house for sailors – has impeccable fashion sense. Options include dorms as well as private rooms. There's a lively bar and rooftop deck. Some corner rooms have huge windows designed to catch sunlight.

Jupiter Hotel MOTEL $$
(☑503-230-9200; www.jupiterhotel.com; 800 E Burnside St; d from $143; ❄❄❄; 🚌20) This slick motel is within walking distance of downtown and attached to the Doug Fir (p393), a top-notch live-music venue. Standard rooms are tiny – go for the Metro rooms instead – and ask for a pad away from the bar patio if you're not into staying up late. Bicycle rentals are available; walk-ins after midnight get a discount if there are vacancies.

PACIFIC NORTHWEST PORTLAND

Caravan BOUTIQUE HOTEL **$$**
(☑503-288-5225; www.tinyhousehotel.com; 5009 NE 11th Ave; r $165-175; 🐾; 📶72) The tiny-house trend is, ironically, huge these days. Get a taste of what it's like to live in one of these adorable minuscule dwellings (84 to 170 sq ft – smaller than most hotel rooms – complete with kitchen and bathroom) at this hotel in the artsy Alberta neighborhood. Free s'mores nightly and live music some nights. Book way ahead in summer.

Heathman Hotel HOTEL **$$$**
(Map p386; ☑503-241-4100; www.heathmanhotel.com; 1001 SW Broadway; d from $265; P❄@🐾🐾; 📶15, 17, 35, 51) A Portland institution, the Heathman has top-notch services and a newly reopened seafood restaurant run by beloved chef Vitaly Paley. Rooms are elegant, stylish and luxurious, and the location is central. It hosts high tea in the afternoons, plays jazz Wednesday to Saturday evenings and has a library stocked with 2700 signed books by authors who have stayed here.

Hotel Eastlund HOTEL **$$$**
(☑503-235-2100; www.hoteleastlund.com; 1021 NE Grand Ave; r from $249; P❄🐾; 📶6) This shiny new hotel in the Lloyd District replaced what was the Red Lion. From the lobby on up, it's all ultra-modern furniture, huge art, bright colors and open spaces. Rooms have one king or two queen beds; suites are not huge but include kitchenettes and floor-to-ceiling windows. The restaurant upstairs, **Altabira** (☑503-963-3600; www.altabira.com; 1021 NE Grand Ave; mains $17-28; ⊙11:30am-11pm), has a long beer list and a great patio.

Eating

Portland has become nationally recognized for its food scene, with dozens of young, top-notch chefs pushing the boundaries of ethnic and regional cuisines and making the most of locally sourced, sustainably raised ingredients.

Nong's Khao Man Gai FOOD TRUCK **$**
(Map p386; ☑971-255-3480; www.khaomangai.com; cnr SW 10th Ave & SW Alder St; mains from $9; ⊙10am-4pm Mon-Sat; 📶NS Line, A Loop, 🚊Red, Blue) This widely adored food cart dishes out tender poached chicken with rice in a magical sauce. That's it – and that's plenty. There are bricks-and-mortar locations at 411 SW College St and 609 SE Ankeny St, both of which have a more extensive menu.

Bing Mi! FOOD TRUCK **$**
(Map p386; www.bingmiportland.com; cnr SW 9th Ave & SW Alder St; crepes $6; ⊙7:30am-3pm Mon-Fri, 11am-4pm Sat; 🚊Red, Blue) This downtown food cart – a critics' fave – serves savory *jian bing* (grilled crepes from Northern China, stuffed with scrambled egg, pickled vegetables, fried crackers, black-bean paste and chili sauce). That's all you get, and that's all you'll need.

★Stammtisch GERMAN **$$**
(☑503-206-7983; www.stammtischpdx.com; 401 NE 28th Ave; small plates $4-9, mains $12-23; ⊙3pm-1:30am Mon-Fri, 11am-1:30am Sat & Sun; 🐾; 📶19) Dig into serious German food – with a beer list to match – at this dark and cozy neighborhood pub. Don't miss the *Maultaschen* (a gorgeous pasta pocket filled with leek fondue in a bright, lemony wine sauce), the mussels in nettle broth, or the paprika-spiced roast chicken.

PORTLAND'S FOOD CARTS

Some of Portland's most amazing food comes from humble little kitchens-on-wheels. Found all over town clumped together in parking lots or otherwise unoccupied spaces, food carts offer hungry wanderers a chance to try unusual dishes at low prices, and they often have covered seating areas if you don't like to walk while you eat. A few to try:

Holy Mole (https://www.facebook.com/holymolepdx)

Nong's Khao Man Gai

Potato Champion (☑503-683-3797; www.potatochampion.tumblr.com; 1207 SE Hawthorne Blvd; mains $3-11; ⊙11am-1am Tue-Thu & Sun, to 3am Fri & Sat; 🐾)

Bing Mi!

Viking Soul Food (☑971-506-5579; www.vikingsoulfood.com; 4255 SE Belmont St; mains $3-10; ⊙noon-8pm Sun-Thu, to 9pm Fri & Sat; 📶15)

Ken's Artisan Pizza
PIZZA $$

(☎503-517-9951; www.kensartisan.com; 304 SE 28th Ave; pizzas $13-18; ⊙5-9:30pm Mon-Thu, 5-10pm Fri, 4-10pm Sat, 4-9pm Sun; ☐20) Glorious wood-fired, thin-crust pizzas with toppings such as prosciutto, fennel sausage and green garlic. Super-cool atmosphere, with huge sliding windows that open to the street on warm nights. Expect a long wait – no reservations taken.

Olympia Provisions
FRENCH $$

(☎503-894-8136; www.olympiaprovisions.com; 1632 NW Thurman St; charcuterie $14-18, sandwiches $11-15, mains $22-35; ⊙11am-10pm Mon-Fri, 9am-10pm Sat & Sun; ☐16) French-inspired rotisserie bistro serving up charcuterie and cheese boards, gourmet sandwiches, salads and deli items, and main plates such as rotisserie chicken and steamed clams. It also does delicious eggs Benedict for brunch. There's another branch at 107 SE Washington St.

Paadee
THAI $$

(☎503-360-1453; www.paadeepdx.com; 6 SE 28th Ave; mains $12-19; ⊙11:30am-3pm & 5-10pm; ☐20) Located on a strip of 28th Ave dubbed 'Restaurant Row' is this beautiful dining room with birdcages as lampshades, inspired by the owner's childhood in Thailand. Bright, fresh flavors come alive in plates such as the steak salad or *gra prao muu grob* (crispy pork belly with basil and chili). Tasty cocktails are available, too.

People's Pig
BARBECUE $$

(☎503-282-2800; www.peoplespig.com; 3217 N Williams Ave; sandwiches $10-12, mains $14-25; ⊙11am-9pm Sun-Thu, to 10pm Fri & Sat; ☐4, 24, 44) The smoked fried-chicken sandwich at the People's Pig, with jalapeño jelly and spicy mayo, occupies the top position on many Portlanders' lists of favorite sandwiches. It comes with one side: get the collard greens. You can also have it as a plate, with extra sides – or opt for the pork shoulder, ribs, lamb or brisket. It's all good.

Tasty n Sons
AMERICAN $$

(☎503-621-1400; www.tastynsons.com; 3808 N Williams Ave; small plates $2-13, mains $12-30; ⊙9am-2:30pm & 5-10pm Sun-Thu, to 11pm Fri & Sat; ☐44) Superb small plates in a high-ceilinged, industrial-feel dining room along a suddenly wildly hip stretch of Portland's bicycle-commuter highway. Share delicacies such as bacon-wrapped dates, grilled quail with couscous or lamb souvlaki – don't skip the Burmese stew if it's available. A wait is guaranteed at brunch. Compare and contrast with its sibling, **Tasty n Alder** (Map p386; ☎503-621-9251; www.tastynalder.com; 580 SW 12th Ave; mains $16-27; ⊙9am-2pm & 5:30-10pm Sun-Thu, to 11pm Fri & Sat; ☐15, 51).

★ Ava Gene's
ITALIAN $$$

(☎971-229-0571; www.avagenes.com; 3377 SE Division St; mains $20-36; ⊙5-10pm Mon-Thu, 5-11pm Fri, 4:30-11pm Sat, 4:30-10pm Sun; ☐4) This renowned trattoria-inspired eatery – owned by Duane Sorenson, who founded Stumptown Coffee – serves rustic Italian cuisine, with exquisite pasta and vegetable dishes as highlights. Exceptional ingredients, a great wine list and cocktails, and outstanding service make it a swoon-worthy dining experience worth seeking out. Reserve.

★ Ned Ludd
AMERICAN $$$

(☎503-288-6900; www.nedluddpdx.com; 3925 NE Martin Luther King Jr Blvd; small plates $4-15, mains $25-32; ⊙5-10pm; ☐6) ⌖ Quintessentially Portland, this offbeat, upscale joint exudes thick artisan vibes, from its rustic-peasant decor to the prominent brick wood-fired oven where all dishes are cooked. The beautifully presented small plates are rotated daily. This is not a place to simply fill your tummy but one in which to sample eclectic 'American craft' delicacies.

★ Ox
STEAK $$$

(☎503-284-3366; www.oxpdx.com; 2225 NE Martin Luther King Jr Blvd; mains $13-52; ⊙5-10pm Sun-Thu, to 11pm Fri & Sat; ☐6) One of Portland's most popular restaurants is this upscale, Argentine-inspired steakhouse. Start with the smoked bone-marrow clam chowder, then go for the gusto: the grass-fed beef rib eye. If there's two of you, the *asado* (barbecue grill; $80) is a good choice, allowing you to try several different cuts. Reserve.

Ataula
SPANISH $$$

(☎503-894-8904; www.ataulapdx.com; 1818 NW 23rd Pl; tapas $8-17, paella dishes $34-40; ⊙4:30-10pm Tue-Sat; ☐15, 77) This critically acclaimed Spanish tapas restaurant offers outstanding cuisine. If these are on the menu, try the *nuestras bravas* (sliced, fried potatoes in milk aioli), *croquetas* (salt-cod fritters), *xupa-xup* (chorizo lollipop) and *ataula montadito* (salmon with mascarpone yogurt and black-truffle honey). Great cocktails, too. Be sure to reserve.

🍷 Drinking & Nightlife

Drinking, whether it's coffee or a craft brew, cider or kombucha, is practically a sport in Portland. In winter it's a reason to hunker down and escape the rain; in summer, an excuse to sit on a patio or deck and soak up the long-awaited sunshine. Whatever you like to drink, there's bound to be a hand-crafted, artisan version of it here.

★Barista   COFFEE
(Map p386; ☑503-274-1211; www.baristapdx.com; 539 NW 13th Ave; ☺6am-6pm Mon-Fri, 7am-6pm Sat & Sun; ☒4, 6, 10, 14, 15, 30, 51) One of Portland's best coffee shops, this tiny, stylish shop is owned by award-winning barista Billy Wilson. Beans are sourced from specialty roasters. Three other locations in town.

Coava Coffee   COFFEE
(☑503-894-8131; www.coavacoffee.com; 1300 SE Grand Ave; ☺6am-6pm Mon-Fri, 7am-6pm Sat & Sun; ☎; ☒6, 15, ☒B Loop) The decor takes the concept of 'neo-industrial' to extremes, but it works – and Coava delivers where it matters. The pour-over makes for a fantastic cup of java, and the espressos are exceptional, too. Also at 2631 SE Hawthorne Blvd.

Stumptown Coffee Roasters   COFFEE
(☑503-230-7702;   www.stumptowncoffee.com; 4525 SE Division St; ☺6am-7pm Mon-Fri, 7am-7pm Sat & Sun; ☎; ☒4) Stumptown was the first micro-roaster to put Portland on the coffee map and this small, narrow space is where it all started.

Breakside Brewery   BREWERY
(☑503-719-6475; www.breakside.com; 820 NE Dekum St; ☺11:30am-10pm Sun-Thu, to 11pm Fri & Sat; ☒8) Over 20 taps of some of the most experimental, tasty beer you'll ever drink, laced with fruits, vegetables and spices (try the hoppy Breakside IPA). Past beers have included a Meyer lemon kölsch, a mango IPA and a beet beer with ginger. For dessert, pray they have the salted-caramel stout. Good food and nice outdoor seating, too.

Culmination Brewing   MICROBREWERY
(www.culminationbrewing.com; 2117 NE Oregon St; plates $5-13; ☺noon-9pm Sun-Thu, to 10pm Fri & Sat; ☒12) At this comfortable tasting room in a refurbished old warehouse, you'll find some of the city's best beers (including the top-notch Phaedrus IPA plus a whole array of limited-edition seasonals) and a brief but unusually ambitious food menu. If the *pêche*

is available, try it, even if you don't normally like 'fruit' beers.

Ecliptic Brewing   BREWERY
(☑503-265-8002; www.eclipticbrewing.com; 825 N Cook St; ☺11am-10pm Sun-Thu, to 11pm Fri & Sat; ☒4) It's in kind of a chilly industrial space, but the beer speaks for itself – Ecliptic was founded by John Harris, who previously brewed for McMenamins, Deschutes and Full Sail. The brewery's astronomically named creations (such as the Craft Beer medal-winning Spica Pilsner) are ambitious and wildly successful. Food includes a roast-lamb sandwich, razor clams and sauteed kale.

Cider Riot   BREWERY
(www.ciderriot.com; 807 NE Couch St; ☺4-11pm Mon & Wed-Fri, noon-11pm Sat & Sun; ☒12, 19, 20) Portland's best cider company now has its very own pub and tasting room, so you can sample Everybody Pogo, Never Give an Inch or Plastic Paddy at the source of the goodness. Ciders here are dry and complex, made with regional apples and hyper-regional attitude.

Hopworks Urban Brewery   BREWERY
(HUB;   ☑503-232-4677;   www.hopworksbeer. com; 2944 SE Powell Blvd; ☺11am-11pm Sun-Thu, to midnight Fri & Sat; ☒; ☒9) 🚲 All-organic beers made with local ingredients, served in an ecofriendly building with bicycle frames above the bar. Try the IPA or the Survival Stout, made with Stumptown coffee. There's a good selection of food and a family-friendly atmosphere, and the back deck can't be beat on a warm day. There's another branch at 3947 N Williams Ave.

☆ Entertainment

For current guides to what's on around town, check the two local weekly papers and their websites: *Willamette Week* (www. wweek.com), which comes out on Wednesday, and the *Portland Mercury* (www.port landmercury.com), out on Thursday.

Live Music

Doug Fir Lounge   LIVE MUSIC
(☑503-231-9663; www.dougfirlounge.com; 830 E Burnside St; ☒20) Combining futuristic elements with a rustic log-cabin aesthetic, this venue has helped transform the LoBu (lower Burnside) neighborhood from seedy to slick. Doug Fir books great bands and the sound quality is usually tops. Crowds range from tattooed youth to suburban yuppies. Its

DON'T MISS

POWELL'S

One of the USA's largest independent bookstores, **Powell's City of Books** (Map p386; ☑800-878-7323; www.powells. com; 1005 W Burnside St; ⊙9am-11pm; 🔲20) has a whole city block of new and used titles and a well-attended series of readings. There's another branch at 3723 SE Hawthorne Blvd (with a Home and Garden bookstore next door), and one at the airport.

upstairs restaurant has long hours. Find it next door to the after-party-friendly Jupiter Hotel (p390).

Crystal Ballroom   LIVE MUSIC
(Map p386; ☑503-225-0047; www.mcmenamins. com; 1332 W Burnside St; 🔲20) This large, historic ballroom has hosted some major acts, including James Brown and Marvin Gaye in the early '60s. The bouncy, 'floating' dance floor makes dancing almost effortless.

Mississippi Studios   LIVE MUSIC
(☑503-288-3895; www.mississippistudios.com; 3939 N Mississippi Ave; 🔲4) This intimate bar is good for checking out budding acoustic talent along with more established musical acts. Excellent sound system, and good restaurant-bar with patio (and awesome burgers) next door. Located right on busy N Mississippi Ave.

Performing Arts

Portland Center Stage   THEATER
(Map p386; ☑503-445-3700; www.pcs.org; 128 NW 11th Ave; tickets from $25; 🔲4, 8, 44, 77) The city's main theater company now performs in the Portland Armory – a renovated Pearl District landmark with state-of-the-art features.

**Arlene Schnitzer
Concert Hall**   CLASSICAL MUSIC
(Map p386; ☑503-248-4335; www.portland5.com; 1037 SW Broadway; 🔲10, 14, 15, 35, 36, 44, 54, 56) This beautiful, if not acoustically brilliant, downtown venue, built in 1928, hosts a wide range of shows, lectures, concerts and other performances.

Artists Repertory Theatre   THEATER
(Map p386; ☑503-241-1278; www.artistsrep. org; 1515 SW Morrison St; tickets preview/ regular $25/50; 🔲15, 51) Some of Portland's

best plays, including regional premieres, are performed in two intimate theaters here.

Keller Auditorium   PERFORMING ARTS
(Map p386; ☑503-248-4335; www.portland5.com; 222 SW Clay St; 🔲38, 45, 55, 92, 96) Built in 1917 and formerly known as the Civic Auditorium, Keller hosts a wide range of performers, from big-name musicians (Sturgill Simpson) to the Portland Opera and the Oregon Ballet Theatre, along with some Broadway productions.

Shopping

Portland's downtown shopping district extends in a two-block radius from Pioneer Courthouse Sq and hosts all of the usual suspects. The Pearl District is dotted with high-end galleries, boutiques and home decor shops. On weekends, you can visit the quintessential Saturday Market by the Skidmore Fountain. For a pleasant, upscale shopping street, head to NW 23rd Ave.

Eastside has lots of trendy shopping streets that also host restaurants and cafes. SE Hawthorne Blvd is the biggest, N Mississippi Ave is the newest and NE Alberta St is the most artsy and funkiest. Down south, Sellwood is known for its antique shops.

🛈 Information

EMERGENCY & MEDICAL SERVICES

Portland Police Bureau (☑503-823-0000; www.portlandoregon.gov/police; 1111 SW 2nd Ave) Police and emergency services.

Legacy Good Samaritan Medical Center (☑503-413-7711; www.legacyhealth.org; 1015 NW 22nd Ave) Convenient to downtown.

MEDIA

KBOO 90.7 FM (www.kboo.fm) Progressive local station run by volunteers; alternative news and views.

Portland Mercury (www.portlandmercury. com) Free **local sibling of Seattle's** *The Stranger.*

Willamette Week (www.wweek.com) Free weekly covering local news and culture.

POST

Post Office (Map p386; ☑503-525-5398; www.usps.com; 715 NW Hoyt St; ⊙8am-6:30pm Mon-Fri, 8:30am-5pm Sat)

TOURIST INFORMATION

Travel Portland (Map p386; ☑503-275-8355; www.travelportland.com; 701 SW 6th Ave; ⊙8:30am-5:30pm Mon-Fri, 10am-4pm Sat Nov-Apr, plus 10am-2pm Sun May-Oct; 🔲Red,

Blue, Green, Yellow) Super-friendly volunteers staff this office in Pioneer Courthouse Sq. There's a small theater with a 12-minute film about the city, and Tri-Met bus and light-rail offices inside.

ℹ Getting There & Away

AIR

Portland International Airport (PDX; ☑ 503-460-4234; www.flypdx.com; 7000 NE Airport Way; 🚐; 🚇 red) Award-winning Portland International Airport has daily flights all over the US, as well as to several international destinations. It's situated just east of I-5 on the banks of the Columbia River (20 minutes' drive from downtown).

BUS

Greyhound (Map p386; ☑ 503-243-2361; www.greyhound.com; 550 NW 6th Ave; 🚇 green, orange, yellow) Greyhound connects Portland with cities along I-5 and I-84. Destinations beyond Oregon include Chicago, Denver, San Francisco, Seattle and Vancouver, BC.

Bolt Bus (Map p386; ☑ 877-265-8287; www.boltbus.com) Connects Portland with Seattle (from $25), Bellingham ($40), Eugene ($15) and Vancouver, BC ($50), among other cities. Buses leave from the corner of NW 8th Ave and NW Everett St.

TRAIN

Amtrak (☑ 800-872-7245; www.amtrak.com; 800 NW 6th Ave; 🚊 17, 🚇 green, yellow) Amtrak serves Chicago, Oakland, Seattle and Vancouver, BC. Departures are from Union Station.

ℹ Getting Around

TO/FROM THE AIRPORT

Tri-Met's light-rail MAX red line takes about 40 minutes to get from downtown to the airport (adult/child $2.50/1.25). If you prefer a bus, **Blue Star** (☑ 503-249-1837; www.bluestarbus.com) offers shuttle services between PDX and several downtown stops.

Taxis charge around $35-40 (not including tip) from the airport to downtown.

BICYCLE

Clever Cycles (☑ 503-334-1560; www.clevercycles.com; 900 SE Hawthorne Blvd; rentals per day $30, cargo bikes $60; ⊙ 11am-6pm Mon-Fri, to 5pm Sat & Sun; 🚊 10, 14) Rents folding, family and cargo bikes.

PUBLIC TRANSPORTATION

Portland has a good public-transportation system, which consists of local buses, streetcars and the MAX light rail. All are run by TriMet, which has an **information center** (☑ 503-238-7433, 503-725-9005; www.trimet.org; 701 SW 6th Ave; ⊙ 8:30am-5:30pm Mon-Fri; 🚇 blue, red, green, yellow) at Pioneer Courthouse Sq.

Tickets for the transportation systems are completely transferable within 2½ hours of the time of purchase. Buy tickets for local buses from fare machines as you enter; for streetcars, you can buy tickets at streetcar stations or on the streetcar itself. Tickets for the MAX must be bought from ticket machines at MAX stations (*before* you board); there is no conductor or ticket seller on board (but there *are* enforcers).

If you're a night owl, be aware that there are fewer services at night, and most stop running at 1am; check the website for details on a specific line.

CAR

Most major car-rental agencies have outlets both downtown and at Portland's airport. Many of these agencies have added hybrid vehicles to their fleets. **Car 2 Go** (www.car2go.com/en/portland; membership fee $5, rental per hour from $15) and **Zipcar** (www.zipcar.com; membership fee per month from $7, rental per hour $8-10) are two popular car-sharing options.

CHARTER SERVICE

For custom bus or van charters and tours, try **EcoShuttle** (☑ 503-548-4480; www.ecoshuttle.net). Its vehicles run on 100% biodiesel.

TAXI

Cabs are available 24 hours by phone. Downtown, you can sometimes flag them down, and some bartenders will call you a cab on request. **Broadway Cab** (☑ 503-333-3333; www.broadwaycab.com)

Radio Cab (☑ 503-227-1212; www.radiocab.net)

Willamette Valley

The Willamette Valley, a fertile 60-mile wide agricultural basin, was the Holy Grail for Oregon Trail pioneers who headed west more than 170 years ago. Today it's the state's breadbasket, producing more than 100 kinds of crops – including renowned Pinot Noir grapes. Salem, Oregon's capital, is about an hour's drive from Portland at the northern end of the valley, and most of the other attractions in the area make easy day trips as well. Toward the south is Eugene, a dynamic college town worth a day or two of exploration.

Salem

Oregon's legislative center is renowned for its cherry trees, art-deco capitol building and Willamette University.

PACIFIC NORTHWEST WILLAMETTE VALLEY

WORTH A TRIP

HOT SPRINGS

Wine isn't the only liquid indulgence to be had in the Willamette Valley – it's also known for its many natural hot springs. Three are easily accessible from Salem and Eugene.

Bagby Hot Springs (www.bagbyhotsprings.org; $5; ☉24hr) is a rustic hot spring with various wooden tubs in semi-private bathhouses. It's a couple of hours' drive east of Salem, accessible via a lovely 1.5-mile hiking trail.

Enjoy salubrious climes at **Breitenbush Hot Springs** (☎503-854-3320; www.brei tenbush.com; 53000 Breitenbush Rd, Detroit; day use per person $18-32; ☉office 9am-4pm Mon-Sat), a fancy spa with massages, yoga and the like. Day-use activities include the hot springs and sauna, yoga and meditation, massage, hiking trails, and a library; you can also stay the night here. Reservations are required, including for day use.

About 40 miles east of Eugene, **Terwilliger Hot Springs** (Cougar Hot Springs; $6) is a beautiful cluster of terraced outdoor pools framed by large rocks. The springs are rustic but well maintained, with the hottest on top. From the parking lot, walk a quarter-mile to the springs. To get here, turn south onto Aufderheide Scenic Byway from Hwy 126 and drive 7.5 miles. Clothing is optional, no alcohol is allowed and it's day use only.

The University's **Hallie Ford Museum of Art** (☎503-370-6855; www.willamette.edu/arts/hfma; 700 State St; adult/child $6/free, Tue free; ☉10am-5pm Tue-Sat, 1-5pm Sun) showcases the state's best collection of Pacific Northwest art, including an impressive Native American gallery.

The **Oregon State Capitol** (☎503-986-1388; www.oregonlegislature.gov; 900 Court St NE; ☉8am-5pm Mon-Fri) **FREE**, built in 1938, looks like a background prop from a lavish Cecil B DeMille movie; free tours are offered. Rambling 19th-century **Bush House** (☎503-363-4714; www.salemart.org; 600 Mission St SE; adult/child $6/3; ☉park 10am-5pm Tue-Fri, noon-5pm Sat & Sun, tours 1-4pm Wed-Sun Mar-Dec) is an Italianate mansion now preserved as a museum with historical accents, including original wallpapers and marble fireplaces.

You can get oriented at the **Visitors Information Center** (☎503-581-4325; www.travelsalem.com; 181 High St NE; ☉9am-5pm Mon-Fri, 10am-4pm Sat). Salem is served daily by **Greyhound** (☎503-362-2428; www.greyhound.com; 500 13th St SE) buses and **Amtrak** (☎503-588-1551; www.amtrak.com; 500 13th St SE) trains.

Eugene

'Track Town' offers a great art scene, exceptionally fine restaurants, boisterous festivals, miles of riverside paths and several lovely parks. Its location at the confluence of the Willamette and McKenzie Rivers, just west of the Cascades, means there's plenty of outdoor recreation on offer – especially around the McKenzie River region, the Three Sisters Wilderness and Willamette Pass.

☉ Sights

Alton Baker Park PARK
(100 Day Island Rd) This popular 400-acre riverside park, which provides access to the **Ruth Bascom Riverbank Trail System**, a 12-mile bikeway that flanks both sides of the Willamette, is heaven for cyclists and joggers. There's good downtown access via the DeFazio Bike Bridge.

University of Oregon UNIVERSITY
(☎541-346-1000; www.uoregon.edu; 1585 E 13th Ave) Established in 1872, the University of Oregon is the state's foremost institution of higher learning, with a focus on the arts, sciences and law. The campus is filled with historic ivy-covered buildings and includes a **Pioneer Cemetery**, with tombstones that give a vivid insight into life and death in the early settlement. Campus tours are held in summer.

🛏 Sleeping

Prices can rise sharply during key football games (September to November) and at graduation (mid-June).

Eugene Whiteaker International Hostel HOSTEL **$**
(☎541-343-3335; www.eugenehostel.org; 970 W 3rd Ave; dm from $35, r from $50; ✿@🛜) This casual hostel in an old, rambling house has an artsy vibe, nice front and back patios to hang out on, and a free simple breakfast. Towels and bedding are included in the price.

C'est La Vie Inn
B&B $$

(☑541-302-3014; www.cestlavieinn.com; 1006 Taylor St; r from $160; ❷❈@🛜) This gorgeous Victorian house, run by a friendly French woman and her American husband, is a neighborhood showstopper. Beautiful antique furniture fills the living and dining areas, while the four tastefully appointed rooms (each named for a French artist) offer comfort and luxury. Hosts provide a full breakfast, as well as afternoon port and other nice touches.

✕ Eating & Drinking

Kiva
HEALTH FOOD $

(☑541-342-8666; www.kivagrocery.com; 125 W 11th Ave; sandwiches $4-9; ⊙8am-8pm Mon-Fri, 9am-8pm Sat & Sun) An exceptional natural-food grocery store, Kiva stocks allorganic and mostly local produce. There are sandwiches and soups available too.

Papa's Soul Food Kitchen
SOUTHERN US $

(☑541-342-7500; www.papassoulfoodkitchen. com; 400 Blair Blvd; mains $9-14; ⊙noon-2pm & 5-10pm Tue-Fri, 2-10pm Sat) This popular Southern-food spot grills up awesome jerk chicken, pulled-pork sandwiches, crawfish jambalaya and fried okra. The best part is the live blues music that keeps the joint open late on Friday and Saturday nights. Nice back patio, too.

★ Beppe & Gianni's Trattoria
ITALIAN $$

(☑541-683-6661; www.beppeandgiannis.net; 1646 E 19th Ave; mains $15-26; ⊙5-9pm Sun-Thu, to 10pm Fri & Sat) One of Eugene's most beloved restaurants, Beppe & Gianni's serves up homemade pastas and excellent desserts. Expect a wait, especially on weekends.

Board
AMERICAN $$

(☑541-343-3023; www.boardrestaurant.com; 394 Blair Blvd; mains $10-19; ⊙4-11pm Tue, Thu & Sun, to 10pm Wed, to 1am Fri & Sat) The menu sounds fancy, but the atmosphere in this low-ceilinged neighborhood joint – the former home of Eugene's oldest and diviest bar, Tiny's Tavern – is comfy, soothing and completely unpretentious. Rough-hewn wood and copper accents give everything a warm glow; the cocktails don't hurt, either. The food is top notch. Try the burger (perfect), anything with lamb, or shrimp and grits.

Ninkasi Brewing Company
BREWERY

(☑541-344-2739; www.ninkasibrewing.com; 272 Van Buren St; ⊙noon-9pm Sun-Wed, to 10pm Thu-Sat) Head to this tasting room to sample some of Oregon's most distinctive and innovative microbrews at the source. There's a sweet patio with snacks available, and a rotating lineup of food carts. Brewery tours start at 4pm daily, plus 2pm Thursday to Monday and 12:30pm Saturday and Sunday.

❶ Information

Visitor Center (☑541-484-5307; www.eugene cascadescoast.org; 754 Olive St; ⊙8am-5pm Mon-Fri) This center is open weekdays. On weekends, stop by the visitor center at 3312 Gateway St in Springfield for information.

❶ Getting There & Around

Eugene Airport (☑541-682-5544; www. flyeug.com; 28801 Douglas Dr) is about 7 miles northwest of the center. **Greyhound** (☑541-344-6265; www.greyhound.com; 987 Pearl St) provides long-distance services to Salem, Corvallis, Portland, Medford, Grants Pass, Hood River, Newport and Bend.

Trains leave from the **Amtrak station** (☑541-687-1383; www.amtrak.com; 433 Willamette St) for Portland, Seattle, WA, and Vancouver, BC (among other places).

Local bus service is provided by **Lane Transit District** (☑541-687-5555; www.ltd.org). For bike rentals, head to **Paul's Bicycle Way of Life** (☑541-344-4105; www.bicycleway.com; 556 Charnelton St; rentals per day $24-48; ⊙9am-7pm Mon-Fri, 10am-5pm Sat & Sun).

Columbia River Gorge

The fourth-largest river in the US by volume, the mighty Columbia runs 1243 miles from Alberta, Canada, into the Pacific Ocean just west of Astoria. For the final 309 miles of its course, the heavily dammed waterway delineates the border between Washington and Oregon and cuts though the Cascade Mountains via the spectacular Columbia River Gorge. Sheltering numerous ecosystems, waterfalls and magnificent vistas, the land bordering the river is protected as a National Scenic Area and is a popular sporting nexus for windsurfers, cyclists, anglers and hikers.

Not far from Portland, **Multnomah Falls** is a huge tourist draw, while **Vista House** offers stupendous gorge views. And if you want to stretch your legs, the **Eagle Creek Trail** is the area's premier tromping ground – provided you don't get vertigo!

Hood River & Around

Famous for its surrounding fruit orchards and wineries, the small town of Hood River – 63 miles east of Portland on I-84 – is also a huge mecca for windsurfing and kiteboarding. Premier wineries have also taken hold in the region, providing good wine-tasting opportunities.

⊙ Sights & Activities

Mt Hood Railroad   RAIL
(☑800-872-4661; www.mthoodrr.com; 110 Railroad Ave; excursions adult/child from $35/30) Built in 1906, the railroad once transported fruit and lumber from the upper Hood River Valley to the main railhead in Hood River. The vintage trains now transport tourists beneath Mt Hood's snowy peak and past fragrant orchards. The line is about 21 miles long and ends in pretty Parkdale. See the website for schedules and fares. Reserve.

Cathedral Ridge Winery   WINE
(☑800-516-8710; www.cathedralridgewinery.com; 4200 Post Canyon Dr; tastings from $10; ⊙11am-6pm) This attractive winery in pretty farm country at the edge of town has signature red blends and a slew of awards on display. In nice weather, sit outdoors and take in the awesome view of Mt Hood. Tours and tastings at various levels are available.

Hood River Waterplay   WATER SPORTS
(☑541-386-9463; www.hoodriverwaterplay.com; I-84 exit 64; 3hr windsurfing course $119, SUP lessons per hour from $48; ⊙May-Oct) Interested in windsurfing, kayaking, SUP, catamaran sailing and so on? Contact this company, with a location right on the water.

Discover Bicycles   CYCLING
(☑541-386-4820; www.discoverbicycles.com; 210 State St; rentals per day $30-80; ⊙10am-6pm Mon-Sat, to 5pm Sun) This shop rents road, hybrid and mountain bikes and can give advice on area trails.

🛏 Sleeping & Eating

Hood River Hotel   HISTORIC HOTEL $$
(☑541-386-1900; www.hoodriverhotel.com; 102 Oak St; d from $91, ste from $169; ☯❋🛜🐾) Located right in the heart of downtown, this fine 1913 hotel offers comfortable, old-fashioned rooms with four-poster or sleigh beds, some with tiny bathrooms. The suites have the best amenities and views. Kitchen-

ettes are also available, and there's a restaurant and a sauna on the premises.

Columbia Gorge Hotel   HOTEL $$$
(☑800-345-1921; www.columbiagorgehotel.com; 4000 Westcliff Dr; r $149-329; ☯❋@🛜🐾) Hood River's most famous place to stay is this historic Spanish-style hotel, set high on a cliff above the Columbia. The atmosphere is classy and the grounds lovely, and there's a fine restaurant on the premises. Rooms have antique beds and furnishings. River-view rooms cost more but are worth it.

pFriem Tasting Room   GASTROPUB $
(☑541-321-0490; www.pfriembeer.com; 707 Portway Ave; mains $10-18; ⊙11:30am-9pm) The highly regarded beers at this brewery are matched by a meat-heavy menu that is definitely not run-of-the-mill: think mussels and *frites*, beef tongue, pork terrine, and a stew made with braised lamb and duck confit. It's located near the waterfront along a stretch of industrial-chic new development.

ℹ Information

Chamber of Commerce (☑541-386-2000; www.hoodriver.org; 720 E Port Marina Dr; ⊙9am-5pm Mon-Fri, 10am-4pm Sat & Sun Apr-Oct, 9am-5pm Mon-Fri Nov-Mar) Visitor information for Hood River and the surrounding area.

ℹ Getting There & Away

Greyhound (☑541-386-1212; www.greyhound.com; 110 Railroad Ave) Hood River is connected to Portland by daily Greyhound buses (three daily, one hour, from $15).

Oregon Cascades

The Oregon Cascades offer plenty of dramatic volcanoes that dominate the skyline for miles around. Mt Hood, overlooking the Columbia River Gorge, is the state's highest peak, and has year-round skiing plus a relatively straightforward summit ascent. Tracking south you'll pass Mt Jefferson and the Three Sisters before reaching Crater Lake, the ghost of erstwhile Mt Mazama that collapsed in on itself after blowing its top approximately 7000 years ago.

Mt Hood

The state's highest peak, 11,240ft Mt Hood pops into view over much of northern Oregon whenever there's a sunny day, exerting an almost magnetic tug on skiers, hikers and sightseers. In summer, wildflowers bloom on the mountainsides and hidden ponds shimmer in blue, making for some unforgettable hikes; in winter, downhill and cross-country skiing dominates people's minds and bodies.

Mt Hood is accessible year-round on Hwy 26 from Portland (56 miles), and from Hood River (44 miles) on Hwy 35. Together with the Columbia River Hwy, these routes comprise the Mt Hood Loop, a popular scenic drive. Government Camp, the center of business on the mountain, is at the pass over Mt Hood.

 Activities

Skiing

Hood is rightly revered for its skiing. There are six ski areas on the mountain, including Timberline, which lures snow-lovers with the only year-round skiing in the US. Closer to Portland, **Mt Hood SkiBowl** (☑503-272-3206; www.skibowl.com; Hwy 26; lift tickets $51, night skiing $37) is no slacker either. It's the nation's largest night-ski area and popular with city slickers who ride up for an evening of powder play from the metro zone. The largest ski area on the mountain is **Mt Hood Meadows** (☑503-337-2222; www.skihood.com; lift tickets adult/child $89/44), where the best conditions usually prevail.

Hiking

The Mt Hood National Forest protects an astounding 1200 miles of trails. A Northwest Forest Pass ($5 per day) is required at most trailheads.

One popular trail loops 7 miles from near the village of Zigzag to beautiful **Ramona Falls**, which tumble down mossy columnar basalt. Another heads 1.5 miles up from US 26 to **Mirror Lake**, continues 0.5 miles around the lake, then tracks 2 miles beyond to a ridge.

The 41-mile **Timberline Trail** circumnavigates Mt Hood through scenic wilderness. Noteworthy portions include the hike to McNeil Point and the short climb to Bald Mountain. From Timberline Lodge, Zigzag Canyon Overlook is a 4.5-mile round-trip.

Climbing Mt Hood should be taken seriously, as deaths do occur, though dogs have made it to the summit and the climb can be done in a long day. Contact **Timberline Mountain Guides** (☑541-312-9242; www.timberlinemtguides.com; 2-day summit per person $645) for guided climbs.

Sleeping & Eating

Most area **campsites** (☑877-444-6777; www.recreation.gov; sites $16-39) have drinking water and vault toilets. Reserve on busy weekends, though some walk-in sites are usually set aside. For more information, contact a nearby ranger station.

Huckleberry Inn   INN $$
(☑503-272-3325; www.huckleberry-inn.com; 88611 E Government Camp Loop; r $90-150, 10-bed dm $160; ☻☎) Simple and comfortably rustic rooms are available here, along with bunk rooms that sleep up to 10. It's in a great central location in Government Camp. The casual restaurant (which doubles as the hotel's reception) serves good breakfasts. Peak holiday rates are higher.

★**Timberline Lodge**   LODGE $$$
(☑800-547-1406; www.timberlinelodge.com; 27500 Timberline Rd; bunk r $145-195, d from $255; ☻☎⊛) As much a community treasure as a hotel, this gorgeous **historic lodge** (☑800-547-1406; www.timberlinelodge.com; 27500 Timberline Rd) offers a variety of rooms, from dorms that sleep up to 10 to deluxe fireplace rooms. There's a heated outdoor pool, and the **ski lifts** (☑503-272-3158; www.timberlinelodge.com; Government Camp; lift tickets adult/child $68/46) are close by. Enjoy awesome views of Mt Hood, nearby hiking trails, two bars and a good dining room. Rates vary widely.

Mt Hood Brewing Co   PUB FOOD $$
(☑503-272-3172; www.mthoodbrewing.com; 87304 E Government Camp Loop, Government Camp; mains $12-20; ⊙11am-10pm) Government Camp's only brewery-restaurant offers a friendly, family-style atmosphere and pub fare including hand-tossed pizzas, sandwiches and short ribs.

**Rendezvous Grill
& Tap Room**   AMERICAN $$
(☑503-622-6837; http://thevousgrill.com; 67149 E Hwy 26, Welches; mains $12-29; ⊙11:30am-8pm Tue-Sun, to 9pm Fri & Sat) In a league of its own is this excellent restaurant with outstanding dishes such as wild salmon with caramelized shallots and artichoke hash or chargrilled pork chop with rhubarb chutney. Lunch means gourmet sandwiches, burgers and salads on the patio. Bonus: excellent cocktails.

❶ Information

For maps, permits and information, contact regional ranger stations. If you're approaching

PACIFIC NORTHWEST OREGON CASCADES

from Hood River, visit the **Hood River Ranger Station** (☑541-352-6002; 6780 OR 35, Parkdale; ☺8am-4:30pm Mon-Fri). The **Zigzag Ranger Station** (☑503-622-3191; 70220 E Hwy 26; ☺7:45am-4:30pm Mon-Sat) is more handy for Portland arrivals. Mt Hood **Information Center** (☑503-272-3301; 88900 E Hwy 26; ☺9am-5pm) is in Government Camp. The weather changes quickly here; carry chains in winter.

ℹ Getting There & Away

From Portland, Mt Hood is one hour (56 miles) by car along Hwy 26. Alternatively, you can take the prettier and longer approach via Hwy 84 to Hood River, then Hwy 35 south (1¾ hours, 95 miles).

The **Central Oregon Breeze** (☑800-847-0157; www.cobreeze.com) shuttle between Bend and Portland stops briefly at Government Camp, 6 miles from the Timberline Lodge. **Sea to Summit** (☑503-286-9333; www.seatosummit.net; round-trip from $59) runs regular shuttles from Portland to the ski areas during the winter.

Sisters

Once a stagecoach stop and trade town for loggers and ranchers, today Sisters is a bustling tourist destination whose main street is lined with boutiques, art galleries and eateries housed in Western-facade buildings. Visitors come for the mountain scenery, spectacular hiking, fine cultural events and awesome climate – there's plenty of sun and little precipitation here.

At the southern end of Sisters, the **city park** (Creekside Campground; ☑541-323-5220; S Locust St; tent/RV sites $20/40; ☺May-Oct) has camp sites, but no showers. For ultra comfort, bag a room in the luxurious **Five Pine Lodge** (☑866-974-5900; www.fivepinelodge.com; 1021 Desperado Trail; d from $159, cabins from $179; ⊜❋@🛜🐾🐕). Or there's **Blue Spruce** (☑888-328-9644; www.bluesprucebnb.com; 444 S Spruce St; d $149-189; ⊜❋🛜), a fine B&B with fireplaces and jet-tubs in each room.

For refined French food you might not expect out here, head to **Cottonwood Cafe** (☑541-549-2699; www.intimatecottagecuisine.com; 403 E Hood Ave; breakfast $9-13, lunch mains $9-13), while **Three Creeks Brewing** (☑541-549-1963; www.threecreeksbrewing.com; 721 Desperado Ct; mains $11-21, pizzas $11-26; ☺11:30am-9pm Sun-Thu, to 10pm Fri & Sat) is the place for home brew and pub grub.

ℹ Information

Chamber of Commerce (☑541-549-0251; www.sisterscountry.com; 291 E Main Ave; ☺10am-4pm Mon-Sat)

ℹ Getting There & Away

Valley Retriever (☑541-265-2253; www.kokkola-bus.com/VRBSchedule) Buses connect Sisters with Bend, Newport, Corvallis, Salem, McMinnville and Portland; the buses stop at the corner of Cascade and Spruce Sts.

Bend

Bend is where all lovers of the outdoors should live – it's an absolute paradise. You can ski fine powder in the morning, paddle a kayak in the afternoon and play golf into the evening. Or would you rather go mountain biking, hiking, mountaineering, stand-up paddleboarding, fly-fishing or rock climbing? It's all close by and top drawer. Plus, you'll probably be enjoying it all in great weather, as the area gets nearly 300 days of sunshine each year.

◉ Sights

★**High Desert Museum**   MUSEUM
(☑541-382-4754; www.highdesertmuseum.org; 59800 Hwy 97; adult/child $12/7; ☺9am-5pm May-Oct, 10am-4pm Nov-Apr; 🚹) This excellent museum, about 3 miles south of Bend, charts the exploration and settlement of the West, using reenactments of a Native American camp, a hard-rock mine and an old Western town. The region's natural history is also explored; kids love the live snake, tortoise and trout exhibits, and watching the birds of prey and otters is always fun. Guided walks and other programs are well worth attending – don't miss the raptor presentation.

Smith Rock State Park   STATE PARK
(☑800-551-6949; www.oregonstateparks.org; 9241 NE Crooked River Dr; day use $5) Best known for its glorious rock climbing, Smith Rock State Park boasts rust-colored 800ft cliffs that tower over the pretty Crooked River. Nonclimbers have several miles of fine hiking trails, some of which involve a little simple rock scrambling. Nearby Terrebonne has a climbing store, along with some restaurants and grocery stores. There's **camping** right next to the park, or at **Skull Hollow** (no water; campsites $5), 8 miles east. The nearest motels are a few miles south in Redmond.

✦ Activities

Smith Rock
Climbing Guides Inc   CLIMBING
(☑ 541-788-6225; www.smithrockclimbingguides.com; Terrebonne; half-day per person from $65) This company offers a variety of climbing instruction (basic, lead, trad, multipitch, aid and self-rescue), along with guided climbs to famous routes at Smith Rock State Park. Gear is included. Prices depend on the number in your group. Open by appointment.

Mt Bachelor Ski Resort   SKIING
(☑ 800-829-2442; www.mtbachelor.com; lift tickets adult/child $92/52, cross-country day pass $19/12; ☉ Nov-May, depending on snowfall; 🅟) Bend hosts some of Oregon's best skiing 22 miles southwest of town at Mt Bachelor Ski Resort, famous for its 'dry' powdery snow, long season and ample terrain (it's the largest ski area in the Pacific Northwest). The resort has long advocated cross-country skiing in tandem with downhill and it maintains 35 miles of groomed trails.

Mountain Biking
Bend is a mountain-biking paradise, with hundreds of miles of awesome trails to explore. The good Bend Area Trail Map ($12; www.adventuremaps.net/shop/product/product/bend-area-trail-map) is available at the Visit Bend tourist office and elsewhere.

The king of Bend's mountain biking trails is **Phil's Trail** network, which offers a variety of excellent fast single-track forest trails just minutes from town. If you want to catch air, don't miss the **Whoops Trail**.

Cog Wild   CYCLING
(☑ 541-385-7002; www.cogwild.com; 255 SW Century Dr, Suite 201; half-day tours from $60, rentals $30-80; ☉ 9am-6pm) This adventure-oriented company offers tours and shuttles out to the best trailheads. You can also arrange to rent bikes, either directly from Cog or through other local shops.

🛏 Sleeping

There's an endless supply of cheap motels, hotels and services on 3rd St (US 97). Because of festivals and events, Bend's lodging rates head north most weekends, and booking ahead is recommended.

Mill Inn   INN $
(☑ 541-389-9198; www.millinn.com; 642 NW Colorado Ave; d $100-170; ☻ 🕾) A 10-room boutique hotel with small, classy rooms decked out with velvet drapes and comforters; four share outside bathrooms. Full breakfast and hot-tub use are included, and there are nice small patios on which to hang out.

★**McMenamins Old**
St Francis School   HOTEL $$
(☑ 541-382-5174; www.mcmenamins.com; 700 NW Bond St; r from $155; ☻ ❋ 🕾) One of McMenamins' best venues, this old schoolhouse has been remodeled into a classy 19-room hotel – two rooms even have side-by-side clawfoot tubs. A recent expansion has added 41 new rooms. The fabulous tiled saltwater Turkish bath alone is worth the stay, though nonguests can soak for $5. A restaurant-pub, three bars, a movie theater and artwork complete the picture.

★**Oxford Hotel**   BOUTIQUE HOTEL $$$
(☑ 541-382-8436; www.oxfordhotelbend.com; 10 NW Minnesota Ave; r from $249; ☻ ❋ 🕾 🅟) 🅿 Bend's premier boutique hotel is deservedly popular. The smallest rooms are still huge (470 sq ft) and are decked out with ecofriendly features such as soy-foam mattresses and cork flooring. High-tech aficionados will love the iPod docks and smart-panel desks. Suites (with kitchen and steam shower) are available, and the basement restaurant is slick.

🍴 Eating

★**Chow**   AMERICAN $
(☑ 541-728-0256; www.chowbend.com; 1110 NW Newport Ave; mains $8-15; ☉ 7am-2pm) 🅿 The signature poached-egg dishes here are spectacular and beautifully presented, coming with sides such as crab cakes, house-cured ham and cornmeal-crusted tomatoes (don't miss the house-made hot sauces). Gourmet sandwiches and salads, some with an Asian influence, are served for lunch. Much of the produce is grown in the garden, and there are good cocktails, too.

10 Barrel Brewing Co   AMERICAN $
(☑ 541-678-5228; www.10barrel.com; 1135 NW Galveston Ave; mains $11-15, pizzas $15-20; ☉ 11am-11pm Sun-Thu, to midnight Fri & Sat) Located in a charming house, this popular brewery-restaurant has a great patio for warm nights. The tasty pub-food menu includes starters such as fried brussels sprouts and steak and gorgonzola nachos, while mains run the gamut from elk burgers to coconut-lime mussels. Sports lovers should head to the bar in the back.

Sparrow Bakery
BAKERY $

(☑541-330-6321; www.thesparrowbakery.net; 50 SE Scott St; breakfasts $5-9; ⊙7am-2pm Mon-Sat, 8am-2pm Sun) This bakery is famous for its Ocean Rolls, a delicious cardamom-laced sweet pastry – but the breakfast sandwiches, including an outstanding cream cheese and lox bagel, are also great.

Victorian Café
BREAKFAST $$

(1404 NW Galveston Ave; mains $13-25; ⊙7am-2pm) One of Bend's best breakfast spots, the Victorian Café is especially awesome for its eggs Benedict (nine kinds). It's also good for sandwiches, burgers and salads. There's really nice outdoor seating in summer. Be ready to wait for a table, especially on weekends.

Zydeco
AMERICAN $$$

(☑541-312-2899; www.zydecokitchen.com; 919 NW Bond St; dinner mains $12-32; ⊙11:30am-2:30pm & 5-9pm Mon-Fri, 5-9pm Sat & Sun) Zydeco is one of Bend's most acclaimed restaurants, and with good reason. Start with the duck fries (french fries fried in duck fat) or tricolored beet salad with goat cheese, then move on to your main course: pan-roasted steelhead, crawfish jambalaya or roasted duck with mushroom gravy. Reserve.

❶ Information

Visit Bend (☑541-382-8048; www.visitbend. com; 750 NW Lava Rd; ⊙9am-5pm Mon-Fri, 10am-4pm Sat & Sun) Great information, plus maps, books and recreation passes available for purchase.

❶ Getting There & Around

Central Oregon Breeze (☑541-389-7469; www.cobreeze.com) offers transport to Portland two or more times daily ($52 one-way, reserve ahead).

High Desert Point (☑541-382-4193; http://oregon-point.com/highdesert-point) buses link Bend with Chemult, where the nearest train station is located (65 miles south). It also has bus services to Eugene, Ontario and Burns.

Cascades East Transit (☑541-385-8680; www.cascadeseasttransit.com) is the regional bus company in Bend, covering La Pine, Mt Bachelor, Sisters, Prineville and Madras. It also provides bus transport within Bend.

Newberry National Volcanic Monument

Showcasing 400,000 years of dramatic seismic activity is **Newberry National Volcanic Monument** (☑541-593-2421; Hwy 97; day use $5; ⊙May-Sep). Start your visit at the **Lava Lands Visitor Center** (☑541-593-2421; 58201 S Hwy 97; ⊙9am-5pm late May-Sep, closed Nov-May), 13 miles south of Bend. Nearby attractions include **Lava Butte**, a perfect cone rising 500ft, and **Lava River Cave**, Oregon's longest lava tube. Four miles west of the visitor center is **Benham Falls**, a good picnic spot on the Deschutes River.

Newberry Crater was once one of the most active volcanoes in North America, but after a large eruption a caldera was born. Close by are **Paulina Lake** and **East Lake**, deep bodies of water rich with trout, while looming above is 7985ft **Paulina Peak**.

Crater Lake National Park

It's no exaggeration: **Crater Lake** (☑541-594-3000; www.nps.gov/crla; 7-day vehicle pass $15) is so blue, you'll catch your breath. And if you get to see it on a calm day, the surrounding cliffs are reflected in those deep waters like a mirror. It's a stunningly beautiful sight. Crater Lake is Oregon's only national park.

The classic tour is the 33-mile rim drive (open from approximately June to mid-October), but there are also exceptional hiking and cross-country skiing opportunities. Note that because the area receives some of the highest snowfalls in North America, the rim drive and north entrance are sometimes closed up until early July.

You can stay from late May to mid-October at the **Cabins at Mazama Village** (☑888-774-2728; www.craterlakelodges.com; d $160; ⊙late May–mid-Oct; ☻) or the majestic **Crater Lake Lodge** (☑888-774-2728; www. craterlakelodges.com; r from $220; ⊙late May–mid-Oct; ☻☎), opened in 1915. Campers head to **Mazama Campground** (☑888-774-2728; www.craterlakelodges.com; tent/RV sites from $22/31; ⊙Jun–mid-Oct; ☎☻). For more information, head to **Steel Visitor Center** (☑541-594-3000; ⊙9am-5pm May-Oct, 10am-4pm Nov-Apr).

Oregon Coast

This magnificent littoral is paralleled by US 101, a scenic highway that winds its way through towns, resorts, state parks (more than 70 of them) and wilderness areas. Everyone from campers to gourmets will find a plethora of ways to enjoy this exceptional region, which is especially popular in summer (reserve accommodations in advance).

Astoria

Named after America's first millionaire, John Jacob Astor, Astoria sits at the 5-mile-wide mouth of the Columbia River and was the first US settlement west of the Mississippi. The city has a long seafaring history and has seen its old harbor, once home to poor artists and writers, attract fancy hotels and restaurants in recent years. Inland are many historical houses, including lovingly restored Victorians – a few converted into romantic B&Bs.

◉ Sights

Adding to the city's scenery is the 4.1-mile **Astoria-Megler Bridge**, the longest continuous truss bridge in North America, which crosses the Columbia River into Washington state. See it from the **Astoria Riverwalk**, which follows the trolley route. **Pier 39** is an interesting covered wharf with an informal cannery museum and a couple of places to eat.

Columbia River
Maritime Museum   MUSEUM
(✐503-325-2323; www.crmm.org; 1792 Marine Dr; adult/child $14/5; ◷9:30am-5pm; ⊕) Astoria's seafaring heritage is well interpreted at this wave-shaped museum. It's hard to miss the retired Coast Guard boat, frozen mid-rescue, through a huge outside window. Other exhibits highlight the salmon-packing industry and the Chinese immigrants who made up the bulk of its workforce; the river's commercial history; and the crucial job of the bar pilot. You get a keen sense of the treacherous conditions that define this area, known for good reason as the 'Graveyard of the Pacific.'

Flavel House   HISTORIC BUILDING
(✐503-325-2203; www.cumtux.org; 441 8th St; adult/child $6/2; ◷11am-4pm Oct-Apr, 10am-5pm May-Sep) The extravagant Flavel House was built by Captain George Flavel, one of Astoria's leading citizens during the 1880s. The Queen Anne house has been repainted in its original colors and the grounds have been returned to Victorian-era landscaping; it has great views of the Columbia River, too.

Fort Stevens State Park   PARK
(✐ext 21 503-861-3170; www.oregonstateparks.org; 100 Peter Iredale Rd, Hammond; day use $5) Ten miles west of Astoria, this park holds the historic military installation that once guarded the mouth of the Columbia River. Near the **Military Museum** (✐503-861-2000; http://visitftstevens.com; Fort Stevens State Park; day-use fee $5; ◷10am-6pm May-Sep, to 4pm Oct-Apr) [FREE] are gun batteries dug into sand dunes – interesting remnants of the fort's mostly demolished military stations (truck and walking tours available). There's a popular **beach** at the small *Peter Iredale* 1906 shipwreck, and good ocean views from parking lot C. There's also camping and 12 miles of paved **bike trails**.

🛏 Sleeping & Eating

Fort Stevens State Park   CAMPGROUND $
(✐503-861-1671; www.oregonstateparks.org; 100 Peter Iredale Rd, Hammond; tent/RV sites $22/32, yurts/cabins $46/90) About 560 sites (most for RVs) are available at this popular campground 10 miles west of Astoria. Great for families; reserve in summer. Entry off Pacific Dr.

Commodore Hotel   BOUTIQUE HOTEL $$
(✐503-325-4747; www.commodoreastoria.com; 258 14th St; d with shared/private bath from $79/154; ⊕�ই) Hip travelers should make a

---

LEWIS & CLARK: JOURNEY'S END

In November 1805 William Clark and his fellow explorer Meriwether Lewis of the Corps of Discovery staggered, with three dozen others, into a sheltered cove on the Columbia River, 2 miles west of the present-day Astoria-Megler Bridge, completing what was indisputably the greatest overland trek in American history.

After the first truly democratic ballot in US history (in which a woman and a black slave both voted), the party elected to make their bivouac 5 miles south of Astoria at Fort Clatsop, where the Corps spent a miserable winter in 1805–06. Today this site is called the **Lewis and Clark National Historical Park** (✐503-861-2471; www.nps.gov/lewi; 92343 Fort Clatsop Rd; adult/child $5/free; ◷9am-6pm mid-Jun–Aug, to 5pm Sep–mid-Jun). Here you'll find a reconstructed Fort Clatsop, along with a visitor center and historical reenactments in summer.

beeline for this stylish hotel, which offers attractive but small, minimalist rooms. Choose a room with bathroom or go Euro style (sink in room, bathroom down the hall; 'deluxe' rooms have better views). There's a lounge-style lobby with cafe, free samples of local microbrews from 5pm to 7pm, an impressive movie library and record players to borrow.

Bowpicker   SEAFOOD $
(☑ 503-791-2942; www.bowpicker.com; cnr 17th & Duane St; dishes $8-10; ⊙ 11am-6pm Wed-Sun) On just about every list of great seafood shacks is this adorable place in a converted 1932 gillnet fishing boat, serving beer-battered chunks of albacore and steak fries and that's it.

Fort George Brewery   PUB FOOD $
(☑ 503-325-7468; www.fortgeorgebrewery.com; 1483 Duane St; mains $7-16, pizzas $13-25; ⊙ 11am-11pm, noon-11pm Sun) Fort George has established itself as one of the state's best and most reliable craft brewers. Its atmospheric brewery-restaurant is in a historic building that was the original settlement site of Astoria. Apart from the excellent beer, you can get gourmet burgers, house-made sausages, salads and, upstairs, wood-fired pizza.

Astoria Coffeehouse
& Bistro   AMERICAN $$
(☑ 503-325-1787; www.astoriacoffeehouse.com; 243 11th St; dinner mains $12-25; ⊙ 7am-9pm Sun, to 10pm Mon-Thu, to 11pm Fri & Sat) ✔ Small, popular cafe with attached bistro offering an eclectic menu – things like Peruvian root-vegetable stew, wasabi wonton prawns, chili-relleno burger, fish tacos, pad Thai and mac 'n' cheese. Everything is made in-house, even the ketchup. There's sidewalk seating and excellent cocktails. Expect a wait at dinner and Sunday brunch.

❶ Getting There & Away

Northwest Point (☑ 503-484-4100; http://oregon-point.com/northwest-point) Daily buses head to Seaside, Cannon Beach and Portland; check the website for schedules.
Pacific Transit (☑ 360-642-9418; www.pacifictransit.org) Buses to Washington.

Cannon Beach

Charming Cannon Beach is one of the most popular beach towns on the Oregon coast. Several premier hotels here cater to a fancier clientele, as do the town's many boutiques and art galleries. In summer the streets are ablaze with flowers. Lodging is expensive,

and the streets are jammed: on a warm, sunny Saturday, you'll spend a good chunk of time just finding a parking spot.

◉ Sights & Activities

Photogenic **Haystack Rock**, a 295ft seastack, is the most spectacular landmark on the Oregon coast and is accessible from the beach at low tide. Birds cling to its ballast cliffs and tide pools ring its base.

The coast to the north, protected inside **Ecola State Park** (☑ 503-436-2844; www.oregonstateparks.org; day use $5), is the Oregon you may have already visited in your dreams: sea stacks, crashing surf, hidden beaches and gorgeous pristine forest. The park is 1.5 miles from town and is crisscrossed by paths, including part of the **Oregon Coast Trail**, which leads over Tillamook Head to the town of Seaside.

The Cannon Beach area is good for surfing, though not the beach itself. The best spots are **Indian Beach** in Ecola State Park, 3 miles to the north, and **Oswald West State Park**, 10 miles south. **Cleanline Surf Shop** (☑ 503-738-2061; www.cleanlinesurf.com; 171 Sunset Blvd; board/wet-suit rentals from $20/15; ⊙ 10am-6pm Sun-Fri, 9am-6pm Sat) is a friendly local shop that rents out boards and mandatory wetsuits.

⨄ Sleeping

Cannon Beach is pretty exclusive; for budget choices head 7 miles north to Seaside. For vacation rentals, check out www.visitcb.com.

★ **Ocean Lodge**   HOTEL $$$
(☑ 888-777-4047, 503-436-2241; www.theoceanlodge.com; 2864 S Pacific St; d $219-369; ⊖❄☎✿) This gorgeous place has some of Cannon Beach's most luxurious rooms, most with ocean view and all with fireplace and kitchenette. A complimentary continental breakfast, an 800-DVD library and pleasant sitting areas are available to guests. Located on the beach at the southern end of town.

✖ Eating & Drinking

Here you'll find everything from coffee shops to a coffee shop that doubles as a fine restaurant. If you're just after a warm cup of buttery clam chowder with a view, stop in at **Mo's** (www.moschowder.com).

★ **Irish Table**   IRISH $$$
(☑ 503-436-0708; 1235 S Hemlock St; mains $20-30; ⊙ 5:30-9pm Fri-Tue) ✔ Excellent restau-

rant hidden at the back of the Sleepy Monk coffee shop, serving a fusion of Irish and Pacific Northwest cuisine made with local and seasonal ingredients. The menu is small and simple, but the choices are tasty; try the vegetarian shepherd's pie, lamb-loin chops or seared Piedmontese flat-iron steak. If the curried mussels are on the menu, don't hesitate.

Sleepy Monk Coffee   COFFEE
(☑503-436-2796; www.sleepymonkcoffee.com; 1235 S Hemlock St; drinks & snacks $2-7; ☺8am-3pm Mon, Tue & Thu, to 4pm Fri-Sun) 🍴 For organic, certified-fair-trade coffee, try this little coffee shop on the main street. Sit on an Adirondack chair in the tiny front yard and enjoy the rich brews, all tasty and roasted on the premises. Good homemade pastries, too.

ⓘ Information

Chamber of Commerce (☑503-436-2623; www.cannonbeach.org; 207 N Spruce St; ☺10am-5pm) Has good local information, including tide tables.

ⓘ Getting There & Around

Northwest Point (☑541-484-4100; www.oregon-point.com/northwest-point) Twice-daily routes between Portland and the coast. Buy tickets online, at Portland's Union Station, or at the Astoria Transit Center. The one-way fare from Portland to Astoria is $18.

Cannon Beach Shuttle (☑503-861-7433; www.ridethebus.org) Buses between Cannon Beach and Astoria, plus other coastal stops. The Cannon Beach bus runs the length of Hemlock St to the end of Tolovana Beach; the schedule varies depending on day and season.

Tillamook County Transportation (The Wave; ☑503-815-8283; www.tillamookbus.com) Buses between Astoria and Newport, with stops all along the coast.

Newport

Home to Oregon's largest commercial fishing fleet, Newport is a lively tourist city with several fine beaches and a world-class aquarium. In 2011 it became the host of NOAA (the National Oceanic and Atmospheric Administration). Good restaurants – along with some tacky attractions, gift shops and barking sea lions – abound in the historic bayfront area, while bohemian Nye Beach offers art galleries and a friendly village atmosphere. The area was first explored in the 1860s by fishing crews who found oyster beds at the upper end of Yaquina Bay.

⊙ Sights

The world-class **Oregon Coast Aquarium** (☑541-867-3474; www.aquarium.org; 2820 SE Ferry Slip Rd; adult/3-12yr/13-17yr $22.95/14.95/19.95; ☺10am-6pm Jun-Aug, to 5pm Sep-May; 🚻) is an unmissable attraction, featuring a sea-otter pool, surreal jellyfish tanks and Plexiglas tunnels through a shark tank. Nearby, the **Hatfield Marine Science Center** (☑541-867-0100; www.hmsc.oregonstate.edu; 2030 SE Marine Science Dr; ☺10am-5pm Jun-Aug, to 4pm Thu-Mon Sep-May; 🚻) **FREE** is much smaller, but still worthwhile. For awesome tide-pooling and views, don't miss the **Yaquina Head Outstanding Natural Area** (☑541-574-3100; 750 NW Lighthouse Dr; vehicle fee $7; ☺8am-sunset, interpretive center 10am-6pm) **FREE**, site of the coast's tallest lighthouse and an interesting interpretive center.

🛏 Sleeping & Eating

Campers can head to large and popular **South Beach State Park** (☑541-867-4715; www.oregonstateparks.org; tent/RV sites $21/29, yurts $44; 🚻), two miles south on US101. Book-lovers can stay at the **Sylvia Beach Hotel** (☑541-265-5428; www.sylviabeachhotel.com; 267 NW Cliff St; d $135-235; ☻) and nautical and romantic types at the shipshape **Newport Belle** (☑541-867-6290; http://newportbelle.com; 2126 SE Marine Science Dr, South Beach Marina, H Dock; d $165-175; ☺Feb-Oct; ☻🛜).

For crab po'boys, pan-fried oysters and other tasty seafood, head to **Local Ocean Seafoods** (☑541-574-7959; www.localocean.net; 213 SE Bay Blvd; mains $16-28; ☺11am-9pm, to 8pm winter) – it's especially great on warm days, when the glass walls open to the port area.

ⓘ Information

Visitor Center (☑541-265-8801; www.newportchamber.org; 555 SW Coast Hwy; ☺8:30am-5pm Mon-Fri)

Yachats & Around

One of the Oregon coast's best-kept secrets is the neat and friendly little town of Yachats (ya-*hots*). Lying at the base of massive Cape Perpetua, Yachats offers the memorable scenery of a rugged and windswept land. People come here to get away from it all, which isn't hard to do along this relatively undeveloped stretch of coast.

Lining the town is the 804 Coast Trail, providing a lovely walk and access to tide pools and fabulous ocean vistas. It hooks up with the Amanda trail to the south, eventually arriving at Cape Perpetua Scenic Area.

★ **Cape Perpetua Scenic Area**   PARK
(Hwy 101; day-use fee $5) Located 3 miles south of Yachats, this volcanic remnant was sighted and named by England's Captain James Cook in 1778. Famous for dramatic rock formations and crashing surf, the area contains numerous trails that explore ancient shell middens, tide pools and old-growth forests. Views from the cape are incredible, taking in coastal promontories from Cape Foulweather to Cape Arago.

For spectacular ocean views, head up Overlook Rd to the **Cape Perpetua** day-use area.

Deep fractures in the old volcano allow waves to erode narrow channels into the headland, creating effects such as **Devil's Churn**, about a half-mile north of the visitor center. Waves race up this chasm, shooting up the 30ft inlet to explode against the narrowing sides of the channel. For an easy hike, take the paved **Captain Cook Trail** (1.2 miles round-trip) down to tide pools near **Cooks Chasm**, where at high tide the geyser-like spouting horn blasts water out of a sea cave. (There's also parking along Hwy 101 at Cooks Chasm.)

The **Giant Spruce Trail** (2 miles round-trip) leads up Cape Creek to a 500-year-old Sitka spruce with a 15ft diameter. The **Cook's Ridge–Gwynn Creek Loop Trail** (6.5 miles round-trip) heads into deep old-growth forests along Gwynn Creek; follow the Oregon Coast Trail south and turn up the Gwynn Creek Trail, which returns via Cook's Ridge. The **visitor center** (☎541-547-3289; www.fs.usda.gov/siuslaw; 2400 Hwy 101; vehicle fee $5; ☺9:30am-4:30pm Jun-Aug, 10am-4pm Sep-May) details human and natural histories, and has displays on the Alsi tribe.

Heceta Head Lighthouse   LIGHTHOUSE
(☎541-547-3416; Heceta.h.lighthouse@oregon. gov; day use $5; ☺11am-3pm, to 2pm winter) Built in 1894 and towering precipitously above the churning ocean, this lighthouse, 13 miles south of Yachats on Hwy 101, is supremely photogenic and still functioning. Tours are available; hours may be erratic, especially in winter, so call ahead. Park at Heceta Head State Park for views.

Sea Lion Caves   CAVE
(☎541-547-3111; www.sealioncaves.com; 91560 Hwy 101, Florence; adult/child $14/8; ☺9am-5pm) Fifteen miles south of Yachats is an enormous sea grotto that's home to hundreds of Steller sea lions. An elevator descends 208ft to a dark interpretive area, and an observation window lets you watch the sea lions jockeying for the best seat on the rocks. There are also outside observation areas, as usually from late September to November there are no sea lions in the cave. There are lots of interesting coastal birds to look for.

Ya'Tel Motel   MOTEL $
(☎541-547-3225; www.yatelmotel.com; cnr Hwy 101 & 6th St; d $74-119; ⊛@🖥🐾🐕) This eight-room motel has personality, along with large, clean rooms, some with kitchenette. A large room that sleeps six is also available ($119). Look for the (changeable) sign out front, which might say something like, 'Always clean, usually friendly.'

Green Salmon Coffee House   CAFE $
(☎541-547-3077; www.thegreensalmon.com; 220 Hwy 101; coffee drinks $2-5; ☺7:30am-2:30pm; 🖥) 🍴 Organic and fair trade are big words at this eclectic cafe, where locals meet for tasty breakfast items (pastries, lox bagels, homemade oatmeal). The inventive list of hot beverages ranges from regular drip coffee to organic chocolate chai latte to lavendar rosemary cocoa. Vegan menu available, plus a used-book exchange.

Oregon Dunes National Recreation Area

Stretching for 50 miles between Florence and Coos Bay, the Oregon Dunes form the largest expanse of coastal dunes in the USA. They tower up to 500ft and undulate inland as far as three miles to meet coastal forests, harboring curious ecosystems that sustain an abundance of wildlife, especially birds. The area inspired Frank Herbert to pen his epic sci-fi *Dune* novels. Hiking trails, bridle paths, and boating and swimming areas are available, but avoid the stretch south of Reedsport as noisy dune buggies dominate. Find out more at the **Oregon Dunes National Recreation Area Visitor Center** (☎541-271-6000; www.fs.usda.gov/siuslaw; 855 Hwy 101; ☺8am-4:30pm Mon-Sat Jun-Aug, Mon-Fri Sep-May) in Reedsport.

State parks with camping include popular **Jessie M Honeyman** (☎800-452-5687, 541-997-3641; www.oregonstateparks.org; 84505 Hwy 101 S; tent/RV sites $21/29, yurts $44; 🐾), 3 miles south of Florence, and pleasant, wooded **Umpqua Lighthouse** (☎541-271-4118; www.oregonstateparks.org; 460 Lighthouse Rd;

tent/RV sites $19/26, yurts/deluxe yurts $41/80; 🐾), 4 miles south of Reedsport. There's plenty of other camping in the area, too.

Port Orford

Occupying a rare natural harbor and guarding plenty of spectacular views, the scenic hamlet of Port Orford sits on a headland wedged between two magnificent state parks. **Cape Blanco State Park** (☑541-332-2973; www.oregonstateparks.org; Cape Blanco Rd) **FREE**, nine miles to the north, is the second-most-westerly point in the continental US, and the promontory is often lashed by fierce 100mph winds. As well as hiking, visitors can tour the **Cape Blanco Lighthouse** (☑541-332-2207; www.oregonstateparks. org; 91814 Cape Blanco Rd; tour adult/child $2/free; ☉10am-3:15pm Wed-Mon Apr-Oct) – built in 1870, it's the oldest and highest operational lighthouse in Oregon.

Six miles south of Port Orford, in **Humbug Mountain State Park** (☑541-332-6774), mountains and sea meet in aqueous disharmony, generating plenty of angry surf. You can climb the 1750ft peak on a 3-mile trail through old-growth cedar groves.

For an affordable stay try **Castaway-by-the-Sea Motel** (☑541-332-4502; www.castawaybythesea.com; 545 W 5th St; d $75-135, ste $115-165; ❀@🐾🐾); for a more luxurious cabin, **Wildspring Guest Habitat** (☑866-333-9453; www.wildspring.com; 92978 Cemetery Loop; d $298-328; ❀@🐾). Eating well in this fishing village means a visit to slick **Redfish** (☑541-366-2200; www.redfishportorford.com; Hawthorne Gallery, 517 Jefferson St; mains $18-34; ☉11am-9pm Mon-Fri, 10am-9pm Sat & Sun) 🍴 for the freshest seafood in town.

Southern Oregon

With a warm, sunny and dry climate that belongs in nearby California, Southern Oregon, the state's 'banana belt,' is an exciting place to visit. Rugged and remote landscapes are entwined with a number of designated 'wild and scenic' rivers, which are famous for their challenging white-water rafting, world-class fly-fishing and excellent hiking.

Ashland

This pretty city is the cultural center of Southern Oregon thanks to its internationally renowned Oregon Shakespeare Festival (OSF), which runs for nine months of the year and attracts hundreds of thousands of theatergoers from all over the world. The festival is so popular that it's Ashland's main attraction, packing it out in summer and bringing in steady cash flows for the town's many fancy hotels, upscale B&Bs and fine restaurants.

Even without the OSF, however, Ashland is still a pleasant place whose trendy downtown streets buzz with well-heeled shoppers and youthful bohemians. In late fall and early winter – those few months when the festival doesn't run – folks come to ski at nearby Mt Ashland. And wine-lovers, take note: the area has several good wineries worth seeking out.

◎ Sights & Activities

Lithia Park   PARK
(59 Winburn Way) Adjacent to Ashland's three splendid theaters lies what is arguably the loveliest city park in Oregon, the 93 acres of which wind along Ashland Creek above the center of town. Unusually, the park is in the National Register of Historic Places. It is embellished with fountains, flowers, gazebos and an ice-skating rink (winter only), plus a playground and woodsy trails.

Schneider Museum of Art   MUSEUM
(☑541-552-6245; http://sma.sou.edu; 1250 Siskiyou Blvd; suggested donation $5; ☉10am-4pm Mon-Sat) If you like contemporary art, check out this Southern Oregon University museum, where new exhibitions go up every month or so. The university also puts on theater and opera performances, along with classical concerts.

Siskiyou Cyclery   CYCLING
(☑541-482-1997; www.siskiyoucyclery.com; 1729 Siskiyou Blvd; half-/full-day rental $30/45; ☉10am-6pm Mon-Sat) Rent a bicycle and explore the countryside on Bear Creek Greenway, a 21-mile bike path between Ashland and the town of Central Point.

⌂ Sleeping

From May to October, try to arrive with reservations. Rooms are cheaper in Medford, 12 miles north of Ashland.

Ashland Hostel   HOSTEL **$**
(☑541-482-9217; www.theashlandhostel.com; 150 N Main St; dm $29, s/d from $45/55; ❀🌀@🐾) his is a central and somewhat upscale hostel (shoes off inside!) in a bungalow on the National Registry. Most private rooms share

OREGON SHAKESPEARE FESTIVAL

As a young town, Ashland was included in the Methodist Church's cultural education program. By the 1930s, one of the venues had deteriorated to a dilapidated wooden shell. Angus Bowmer, a drama professor at the local college, noted the resemblance of the roofless structure to drawings of Shakespeare's Globe Theatre. He convinced the town to sponsor two performances of Shakespeare's plays and a boxing match (the Bard would have approved) as part of its 1935 July 4 celebration. The plays proved a great success, and the **Oregon Shakespeare Festival** (OSF; ☑541-482-4331; www.osfashland.org; cnr Main & Pioneer Sts; tickets $30-136; ⊙Tue-Sun Feb-Oct) was off and running. Performances sell out quickly, but the box office sometimes has rush tickets an hour before showtime.

Check with the **OSF Welcome Center** (76 N Main St; ⊙11am-5pm Tue-Sun) for other events, including scholarly lectures, play readings, concerts and pre-show talks.

bathrooms; some can be connected to dorms. Hangout spaces include the cozy basement living room and the shady front porch. No pets, and no alcohol or smoking; call ahead, as reception times are limited.

Palm BOUTIQUE HOTEL $$
(☑541-482-2636; www.palmcottages.com; 1065 Siskiyou Blvd; d $75-249; ❋❖☎❄❄) Fabulous small motel remodeled into 16 charming garden-cottage rooms and suites (some with kitchens). It's an oasis of green on a busy avenue, complete with grassy lawns and a saltwater pool. A house nearby harbors three large suites (from $249). No breakfast, but it's right next to the popular Morning Glory cafe.

✗ Eating & Drinking

Morning Glory CAFE $
(☑541-488-8636; 1149 Siskiyou Blvd; mains $9.50-15; ⊙8am-1:30pm) This colorful, casual cafe is one of Ashland's best breakfast joints. Creative dishes include the Alaskan-crab omelet, vegetarian hash with roasted chilies, and shrimp cakes with poached eggs. For lunch there's gourmet salad and sandwiches. Go early or late to avoid a long wait.

Agave MEXICAN $
(☑541-488-1770; www.agavetaco.net; 5 Granite St; tacos $3.75-5; ⊙11am-8pm Sun-Thu, to 9pm Fri & Sat, later in summer) Tasty and creative tacos are cooked up at this popular restaurant. There's the regular stuff such as *carnitas* (little meats) and grilled chicken, but for something more exotic go for the shredded duck or sautéed lobster ($9.95). There's ceviche, salads and tamales, too.

Caldera Brewing BREWPUB $$
(☑541-482-4677; www.calderabrewing.com; 590 Clover Lane; mains $13-23; ⊙11am-10pm; ☼) This bright, airy brewery-restaurant just off I-5

has pleasant outdoor seating and views of the countryside. It's kid friendly until 10pm and serves pizza, fancy pasta, burgers and good salads. Wash it all down with one of the 40 beers on tap. Also located at 31 Water St on the river with more of a cozy pub atmosphere.

Greenleaf DINER $$
(☑541-482-2808; www.greenleafrestaurant.com; 49 N Main St; mains $10-21; ⊙8am-8pm; ☼) ☙ This casual diner, with booths as well as counter seating, focuses on sustainable ingredients in innovative combinations. There are lots of vegetarian options, and the specials board is well worth checking out, although the regular menu is so massive that you might not ever need to venture that far. There's a whole gluten-free menu, too.

Amuse FRENCH $$$
(☑541-488-9000; www.amuserestaurant.com; 15 N 1st St; mains $26-38; ⊙5:30-9pm Wed-Sun) Amuse is a fine French bistro serving dishes like Parisian gnocchi, pan-seared scallops and truffle-roasted game hen. Dessert means bittersweet chocolate-truffle cake and warm beignets with crème anglaise. Reserve.

❶ Information

Ashland Chamber of Commerce (☑541-482-3486; www.ashlandchamber.com; 110 E Main St; ⊙9am-5pm Mon-Fri)

Jacksonville

This small but endearing ex-gold-prospecting town is the oldest settlement in southern Oregon and a National Historic Landmark. The main drag is lined with well-preserved buildings dating from the 1880s, now converted into boutiques and galleries. Music lovers shouldn't miss the September **Britt Festival** (☑541-773-6077; www.brittfest.org; cnr

1st & Fir Sts; ☺ Jun-Sep), a world-class musical experience with top-name performers. Seek more enlightenment at the **Chamber of Commerce** (☑541-899-8118; www.jacksonville oregon.org; 185 N Oregon St; ☺10am-3pm daily May-Oct, to 2pm Mon-Sat Nov-Apr).

Jacksonville is full of fancy B&Bs; for budget motels head 6 miles east to Medford. The **Jacksonville Inn** (☑541-899-1900; 175 E California St; r $159-325; ☺❋🔊🐾) is the most pleasant abode, shoehorned downtown in an 1863 building with regal antique-stuffed rooms. There's a fine restaurant on-site.

North Umpqua River

This 'Wild and Scenic' river boasts world-class fly-fishing, fine hiking and serene camping. The 79-mile **North Umpqua Trail** begins near Idleyld Park, 3 miles east of Glide, and passes through Steamboat en route to the Pacific Crest Trail. A popular sideline is pretty **Umpqua Hot Springs**, east of Steamboat near Toketee Lake. Not far away, stunning, two-tiered **Toketee Falls** (113ft) flows over columnar basalt, while **Watson Falls** (272ft) is one of the highest waterfalls in Oregon. For information, stop by Glide's **Colliding Rivers Information Center** (☑541-496-3532; 18782 N Umpqua Hwy, Glide; ☺9am-5pm May-Sep). Adjacent is the **North Umpqua Ranger District** (☑541-496-3532; 18782 N Umpqua Hwy, Glide; ☺8am-4:30pm Mon-Fri).

Between Idleyld Park and Diamond Lake are dozens of riverside campgrounds; these include lovely **Susan Creek** and primitive **Boulder Flat** (no water). Area accommodations fill up quickly in summer; try the log cabin–like rooms at **Dogwood Motel** (☑541-496-3403; www.dogwoodmotel.com; 28866 N Umpqua Hwy, Idleyld Park; s/d from $60/70; ☺❋🔊🐾).

Oregon Caves National Monument & Preserve

This very popular cave (singular) lies 19 miles east of Cave Junction on Hwy 46. Three miles of passages are explored via 90-minute cave tours that include 520 rocky steps and dripping chambers running along the River Styx. Dress warmly, wear shoes with good traction and be prepared to get dripped on.

Cave Junction, 28 miles south of Grants Pass on US 199 (Redwood Hwy), provides the region's services – though one of the best accommodations in the area is **Out 'n' About Treesort** (☑541-592-2208; www.

treehouses.com; 300 Page Creek Rd, Takilma; tree houses $150-330; ☺) – super-fun treehouses in Katilma, 12 miles south. For fancy lodgings right at the cave there's the impressive **Oregon Caves Chateau** (☑541-592-3400; www.oregoncaveschateau.com; 20000 Caves Hwy; r $117-212; ☺May-Oct; ☺) – grab a milkshake at the old-fashioned soda fountain here.

Eastern Oregon

Oregon east of the Cascades bears little resemblance to its wetter western cohort, either physically or culturally. Few people live here – the biggest town, Pendleton, numbers only 17,000 – and the region holds high plateaus, painted hills, alkali lake-beds and the country's deepest river gorge.

John Day Fossil Beds National Monument

Within the soft rocks and crumbly soils of John Day country lies one of the world's greatest fossil collections, laid down between six and 50 million years ago. The national monument includes 22 sq miles at three different units: Sheep Rock Unit, Painted Hills Unit and Clarno Unit. Each has hiking trails and interpretive displays.

Visit the excellent **Thomas Condon Paleontology Center** (☑541-987-2333; www.nps.gov/joda; 32651 Hwy 19, Kimberly; ☺10am-5pm) **FREE**, 2 miles north of US 26 at the **Sheep Rock Unit**. Displays include a three-toed horse and petrified dung-beetle balls, along with many other fossils and geologic history exhibits. If you feel like walking, take the short hike up the Blue Basin Trail.

The **Painted Hills Unit**, near the town of Mitchell, consists of low-slung, colorfully banded hills formed about 30 million years ago. Ten million years older is the **Clarno Unit**, which exposes mud flows that washed over an Eocene-era forest and eroded into distinctive, sheer white cliffs topped with spires and turrets of stone.

Rafting is popular on the John Day River, the longest free-flowing river in the state. **Oregon River Experiences** (☑800-827-1358; www.oregonriver.com; 4/5/9-day trips per person $635/735/1195; ☺May-Jun) offers trips of up to five days. There's also good fishing for smallmouth bass and rainbow trout; find out more at the Oregon Department of Fish & Wildlife (www.dfw.state.or.us).

Most towns in the area have at least one hotel; these include the atmospheric **Historic Oregon Hotel** (☑541-462-3027; www.the oregonhotel.net; 104 E Main St, Mitchell; dm $20, d $50-110; 🛜) in Mitchell. The town of John Day has most of the district's services and there are several public campgrounds in the area (sites $5), including Lone Pine and Big Bend, both on Hwy 402.

Wallowa Mountains Area

The Wallowa Mountains, with their glacier-hewn peaks and crystalline lakes, are among the most beautiful natural areas in Oregon. The only drawback is the large number of visitors who flock here in summer, especially to the pretty Wallowa Lake area.

Escape them all on one of several long hikes into the nearby **Eagle Cap Wilderness**, such as the 6-mile one-way jaunt to **Aneroid Lake** or the 8-mile trek on the **Ice Lake Trail**.

Just north of the mountains, in the Wallowa Valley, **Enterprise** is a homely backcountry town with several motels – try the **Ponderosa** (☑541-426-3186; 102 E Greenwood St; s/d from $69/75; ❄🛜🐾). If you like beer and good food, don't miss the town's microbrewery, **Terminal Gravity Brewing** (☑541-426-3000; www.terminalgravitybrewing.com; 803 SE School St; mains $9-14; ⊘11am-9pm Sun, Mon & Wed, to 10pm Thu-Sat). Just 6 miles south is Enterprise's fancy cousin, the upscale town of **Joseph**. Expensive bronze galleries and artsy boutiques line the main strip, along with some good eateries.

Hells Canyon

The mighty Snake River has taken 13 million years to carve its path through the high plateaus of eastern Oregon to its present depth of 8000ft, creating Aerica's deepest gorge.

For perspective, drive 30 miles northeast from Joseph to Imnaha, where a slow-going 24-mile gravel road leads up to **Hat Point**. From here you can see the Wallowa Mountains, Idaho's Seven Devils, the Imnaha River and the wilds of the canyon itself. This road is open from late May until snowfall; give yourself two hours each way for the drive.

For white-water action and spectacular scenery, head down to **Hells Canyon Dam**, 25 miles north of the small community of Oxbow. A few miles past the dam, the road ends at the **Hells Canyon Visitors Center** (Hells Canyon Rd, Hells Canyon Dam; ⊘8am-4pm

May-Oct), which has good advice on the area's campgrounds and hiking trails. Beyond here, the Snake River drops 1300ft through wild rapids accessible only by jet boat or raft. **Hells Canyon Adventures** (☑800-422-3568; www.hellscanyonadventures.com; jet-boat tours adult/child from $75/38; ⊘May-Sep) is the main operator running raft trips and jet-boat tours (reservations required).

The area has many campgrounds and more solid lodgings. Just outside Imnaha is the beautiful **Imnaha River Inn** (☑541-577-6002; www.imnahariverinn.com; 73946 Rimrock Rd; s/d from $70/130), a B&B replete with Hemingway-esque animal trophies. For more services, head to the towns of Enterprise, Joseph and Halfway.

Steens Mountain & Alvord Desert

The highest peak in southeastern Oregon, Steens Mountain (9773ft) is part of a massive, 30-mile-long fault-block range that was formed about 15 million years ago.

Beginning in Frenchglen, the gravel 59-mile **Steens Mountain Loop Rd** is Oregon's highest road, offers the range's best sights, and has access to camping and hiking trails. You'll see sagebrush, bands of juniper and aspen forests, and finally fragile rocky tundra at the top. **Kiger Gorge Viewpoint**, 25 miles up from Frenchglen, is especially stunning. It takes about three hours all the way around if you're just driving through, but you'll want to see the sights, so give yourself much more time. You can also see the eastern side of the Steens via the **Fields-Denio Rd**, which goes through the Alvord Desert between Hwys 205 and 78. Take a full tank of gas and plenty of water, and be prepared for weather changes at any time of year.

Frenchglen, with a population of roughly 12, nonetheless supports the historic **Frenchglen Hotel** (☑541-493-2825; www. frenchglenhotel.com; 39184 Hwy 205; r with shared bath $75-82, Drovers' Inn s/d $115/135; ⊘mid-Mar–Oct; ➡❄🐾), with eight small rooms, huge meals (reserve for dinners), a small store with a seasonal gas pump and not much else. There are camping options on the Steens Mountain Loop Rd, such as the BLM's pretty **Page Springs** ($8 per vehicle, open year-round). A few other campgrounds further into the loop are very pleasant, but accessible in summer only. Water is available at all of these campgrounds. Free backcountry camping is also allowed in the Steens.

Understand Western USA

Western USA Today

Rapid growth is shaping the new West. Immigration, traffic, climate change, precarious water levels and environmental concerns consistently grab headlines. The long-term allure of the West will depend on how these issues are tackled. But the West, and California in particular, has also remained firmly progressive at a time when politics elsewhere in the US have swung conservative and increasingly insular.

Best on Film

Stagecoach (1939) Monument Valley may be the true star of this John Ford Western drama.

Butch Cassidy & The Sundance Kid (1969) Follows the adventures of two real-life outlaws who hid out in Utah.

Thelma & Louise (1991) Two gal pals run from the law and into stunning Southwest scenery.

The Hangover (2009) It's a bachelor party gone wrong – or right – in Las Vegas.

127 Hours (2010) Aron Ralston's harrowing experience in Utah's red-rock country.

Best in Print

The Grapes of Wrath (John Steinbeck; 1939) Dust Bowl migrants travel west to California.

Desert Solitaire (Edward Abbey; 1968) Essays about the Southwest and industrial tourism by no-holds-barred eco-curmudgeon.

Bean Trees (Barbara Kingsolver; 1988) Thoughtful look at motherhood and cross-cultural adoption in Tucson.

Into the Wild (Jon Krakauer; 1996) Alexander Supertramp wanders across the West in search of meaning.

Wild (Cheryl Strayed; 2013) Author hikes the Pacific Crest Trail solo after the death of her mother.

This Land is Your Land

Who-has-rights-to-what has become a hot-button topic. In 2016, one of Obama's last acts as president was to establish Bears Ears National Monument, protecting 1.35 million acres in southern Utah renowned for its sheer quantity of ancient rock carvings. In a region where tourism is central to the economy, its conservation is viewed by many as a forward-thinking investment.

Not everyone agrees. Hand-in-hand with industry, some states are eager to introduce more oil and gas development leases on public lands, with plans already in the works on the doorstep of national parks near Chaco Canyon in Arizona and Zion in Utah. Most recently, an executive order by President Trump has put all national monuments created since January 1996 under review. Could mining and gas drilling be coming to your favorite national park soon?

In the West, ranching and recreation interests have locked horns with public land-management agencies for generations. In Nevada, rancher Cliven Bundy faces federal charges after raising an armed standoff to keep federal officials from impounding his cattle (Bundy had failed to pay grazing fees and fines for using public land). In 2015, a tense 41-day takeover of the Malheur National Wildlife Refuge in southern Oregon by armed extremists (including Bundy's sons) resulted in a casualty when one participant resisted arrest. Ultimately, seven of the 26 participants were acquitted.

The issue extends into US society as increasingly intolerant policies toward immigration take hold nationwide. At the start of 2017, surprise deportations of undocumented immigrants and the promise of a 1954-mile wall along the Mexican border (estimated to cost taxpayers $21 billion) signaled difficult times for a region largely bolstered by immigrant labor and a fluid Latino identity.

Legalized Marijuana

California, Colorado, Nevada, Oregon and Washington have legalized recreational and medicinal use of marijuana. While it's still controversial in some circles, even suit-and-tie lawmakers bliss out seeing state coffers grow thanks to legalized weed.

Since Colorado legalized marijuana in 2014 it has contributed $2.4 billion to the state economy, bolstering education, infrastructure and social programs. Legalization in Washington state is expected to add $730 million in tax revenue in 2017–19.

The federal government under Obama did not challenge these state laws, which are in conflict with federal laws. Yet uncertainty comes with the current administration, which may translate to investors pulling out of the green revolution.

Fire & Water

Environmental concerns remain in the forefront. Climate change in the West affects both human and wildlife populations.

According to the Environmental Protection Authority, temperatures have increased by almost 2°F (1°C) in the last century. Coming out of a 14-year drought, major reservoirs are starting to fill up again but the pressures of a growing population and agricultural demands point to a precarious future.

Although the exact causes are unclear – climate change, residential development, government policy – the West has also been hard hit by forest fires, with numerous blazes taking lives, homes and volumes of public land at an enormous cost to the government.

In June 2017, President Trump announced plans to withdraw from the Paris Climate Accord, an agreement between 195 nations to mitigate global warming. US states and cities have rallied, most notably California, where aggressive pro-environment legislation hopes to pick up the slack.

Moving Forward

Innovation and tech development continues to fuel the region. Northern California leads with a burgeoning biotech industry and Silicon Valley, ground zero for PCs, iPods and Google. While Facebook tries to rein in fake news, it's adding Menlo Park and Seattle headquarters designed by world-renown architect Frank Gehry. Meanwhile, Apple has installed a $5 billion campus in Cupertino. Yet the mood in tech and other industries darkens as foreign-born innovators could face serious immigration restrictions under the Trump administration. Will brain drain hobble progress?

Growth does continue. In Las Vegas, Resorts World plans to open in 2019 with a replica of the Great Wall of China. Meanwhile, Colorado adds a new wind farm, expands public transportation and adds a state-of-the-art Google campus to Boulder, Colorado.

POPULATION: **324 MILLION**

AREA: **3.79 MILLION SQ MILES**

GDP: **$18.6 TRILLION**

UNEMPLOYMENT: **4.8%**

if USA were 100 people

65 would be white
15 would be Hispanic
13 would be African American
4 would be Asian American
3 would be other

belief systems
(% of population)

Protestant unaffiliated or Jewish
other

Roman Catholic Mormon Muslim

population per sq mile

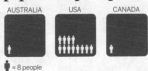

AUSTRALIA USA CANADA

≈ 8 people

History

Throughout time, the West has been a place for seekers to reinvent fortunes. Its first inhabitants crossed the Bering Strait between modern-day Russia and Alaska and moved south into diverse communities that adapted to the weather and surrounding landscapes. They were followed by the Spanish, explorers like Lewis and Clark, gold rush enthusiasts and today's immigrants and tech industries. Whatever comes next will be highly influenced by the frontier spirit of those who came before.

The First Americans

Western America's earliest inhabitants crossed the Bering Strait more than 20,000 years ago. When Europeans arrived, 2 to 18 million Native American people lived north of present-day Mexico and spoke more than 300 languages.

Pacific Northwest

Many modern Pueblo Indians object to the term 'Anasazi,' a Navajo word meaning 'enemy ancestors'; it's no longer used.

In the Pacific Northwest, early coastal inhabitants went out to sea in pursuit of whales or sea lions, or depended on catching salmon and cod and collecting shellfish. On land they hunted deer and elk while gathering berries and roots. Food was stored for the long winters, when free time could be spent on artistic, religious and cultural pursuits. The construction of ornately carved cedar canoes led to extensive trading networks that stretched along the coast.

Inland, a regional culture based on seasonal migration developed among tribes. During salmon runs, tribes gathered at rapids and waterfalls to net or harpoon fish. In the harsh landscapes of Oregon's southern desert, tribes were nomadic peoples who hunted and scavenged in the northern reaches of the Great Basin desert.

California

By AD 1500 more than 300,000 Native Americans spoke some 100 distinct languages in the California region. Central-coast fishing communities built subterranean roundhouses and saunas, where they held ceremonies, told stories and gambled for fun. Northwest hunting com-

TIMELINE	20,000–40,000 BC	7000 BC–AD 100	1300
	The first peoples to come to the Americas arrive from Central Asia by migrating over a wide land bridge between Siberia and Alaska (when sea levels were lower than today).	'Archaic period' marked by nomadic hunter-gatherer lifestyles. By the end of this period, corn, beans and squash, and permanent settlements, are well established.	The entire civilization of Ancestral Puebloans living in Mesa Verde, CO, abandons the area, possibly due to drought, leaving behind a sophisticated city of cliff dwellings.

munities constructed big houses and redwood dugout canoes, while the inhabitants of southwest California created sophisticated pottery and developed irrigation systems that made farming in the desert possible. Native Americans in California had no written language but observed oral contracts and zoning laws.

Within a century of the arrival of Spanish colonists in 1769, California's Native American population was decimated to 20,000 by European diseases, conscripted labor regimes and famine.

The Southwest & Southern Colorado

Archaeologists believe that the Southwest's first inhabitants were hunters. As the population grew, wild game became extinct, forcing hunters to augment their diets with berries, seeds, roots and fruits. After 3000 BC, contacts with farmers in what is now central Mexico led to the beginnings of agriculture in the Southwest.

By about AD 100, three dominant cultures were emerging in the Southwest: the Hohokam of the desert, the Mogollon of the central mountains and valleys, and the Ancestral Puebloans – formerly known as the Anasazi.

The Hohokam lived in the deserts of Arizona, adapting to desert life by creating an incredible river-fed irrigation system. They also developed low earthen pyramids and sunken ball courts with earthen walls. By about 1400, the Hohokam had abandoned their villages. There are many theories on this tribe's disappearance, but it most likely involves a combination of factors including drought, overhunting, conflict among groups and disease.

The Mogollon culture settled near the Mexican border from 200 BC to AD 1400. They lived in small communities, often elevated on isolated mesas or ridgetops, and built simple pit dwellings. Although they farmed, they depended more on hunting and foraging for food. By around the 13th or 14th century, the Mogollon had probably been peacefully incorporated by the Ancestral Puebloan groups from the north.

The Ancestral Puebloans inhabited the Colorado Plateau, also called the Four Corners area. This culture left the richest archaeological sites and ancient settlements that are still inhabited in the Southwest. Their descendants live in Pueblo Indian communities in New Mexico. The oldest links with the Ancestral Puebloans are found among the Hopi tribe of northern Arizona. The mesa-top village of Old Oraibi has been inhabited since the 1100s, making it the oldest continuously inhabited settlement in North America.

Cliff Dwellings

Mesa Verde National Park, NM

Bandelier National Monument, NM

Gila Cliff Dwellings National Monument, NM

Montezuma Castle National Monument, AZ

Walnut Canyon National Monument, AZ

1492	1598	c 1600	1787–91
Italian explorer Christopher Columbus 'discovers' America, eventually making three voyages to the Caribbean. He dubs the indigenous inhabitants 'Indians,' mistakenly thinking he'd reached the Indies.	A large force of Spanish explorers, led by Don Juan de Onate, stops near present-day El Paso, TX, and declares the land to the north New Mexico for Spain.	Santa Fe, America's oldest capital city, is founded. The Palace of Governors is the only 17th-century structure that survives into the 21st century; the rest of Santa Fe is destroyed by a 1914 fire.	The Constitutional Convention in Philadelphia draws up the US Constitution. The Bill of Rights is later adopted as constitutional amendments articulating citizens' rights.

The Europeans Arrive

The Spanish arrived in the Southwest in the 1540s, looking for the Seven Cities of Gold. Missions and missionaries followed in the 1700s as the Spanish staked their claim along the California coast.

Spain's Mission Impossible

Francisco Vázquez de Coronado led the first major expedition into North America in 1540. It included 300 soldiers, hundreds of Native American guides and herds of livestock. It also marked the first major violence between Spanish explorers and the native people.

The expedition's goal were the fabled immensely rich Seven Cities of Cibola. For two years, the expedition traveled through what is now Arizona, New Mexico and as far east as Kansas. Instead of gold and precious gems, the expedition found adobe pueblos, which they violently commandeered. During the Spaniards' first few years in northern New Mexico, they tried to subdue the pueblos, with much bloodshed. The Spanish established Santa Fe as the capital around 1610. The city remains the capital of New Mexico today and is the oldest capital in what is now the USA.

When 18th-century Russian and English trappers began trading valuable otter pelts from Alta California, Spain concocted a plan for colonization. For the glory of God and the tax coffers of Spain, missions would be built across the state and within 10 years these would be going concerns run by local converts.

Spain's missionizing plan was approved in 1769, and Franciscan Padre Junípero Serra secured support to set up *presidios* (military posts) alongside several missions in northern and central California in the 1770s and '80s. Clergy relied on soldiers to round up conscripts to build missions. In exchange for their labor, Native Americans were allowed one meal a day (when available) and a place in God's kingdom – which came much sooner than expected due to the smallpox the Spanish brought with them. In the Southwest, more than half of the pueblo populations were decimated by smallpox, measles and typhus.

> In 1680, during the Pueblo Revolt, the northern New Mexico Pueblos banded together to drive out the Spanish after the latter's bloody campaign to destroy Puebloan ceremonial objects. The Spanish were pushed south of the Rio Grande and the Pueblo people held Santa Fe until 1682.

Lewis & Clark

After President Thomas Jefferson bought the Louisiana Territory from Napoleon in 1803 for $15 million, he sent his personal secretary, Meriwether Lewis, west to chart North America's western regions. The goal was to find a waterway to the Pacific while exploring the newly acquired Louisiana Purchase and establish a foothold for American interests. Lewis, who had no training for exploration, convinced his good friend William Clark, an experienced frontiersman and army veteran, to tag along. In 1804, the 40-member party, called the Corps of Discovery, left St Louis.

1803	1803–06	1811	1841
Napoleon sells the Louisiana Territory to the US for $15 million, thereby extending the boundaries of the new nation from the Mississippi River to the Rocky Mountains.	President Jefferson sends Meriwether Lewis and William Clark west. Guided by Shoshone tribeswoman Sacagawea, they trailblaze from St Louis, Missouri, to the Pacific Ocean and back.	Pacific Fur Company mogul John Jacob Astor establishes Fort Astoria, the first permanent US settlement on the Pacific Coast. He later becomes the country's first millionaire.	Wagon trains follow the Oregon Trail, and by 1847 over 6500 emigrants a year are heading West, to Oregon, California and Mormon-dominated Utah.

The expedition fared relatively well, in part because of the presence of Sacagawea, a young Shoshone woman married to a French-Canadian trapper who was part of the entourage. Sacagawea proved invaluable as a guide, translator and ambassador to the area's Native Americans. York, Clark's African American servant, also softened tensions between the group and the Native Americans.

The party traveled some 8000 miles in about two years, documenting everything they came across in their journals. Meticulous notes were made about 122 animals and 178 plants, with some new discoveries along the way. In 1805 the party finally reached the mouth of the Columbia River and the Pacific Ocean at Cape Disappointment and bedded down for the winter nearby, thus establishing Fort Clatsop.

Lewis and Clark returned to a hero's welcome in St Louis in 1806.

Eureka!

Real estate speculator, lapsed Mormon and tabloid publisher Sam Brannan was looking to unload some California swampland in 1848 when he heard rumors of gold flakes found near Sutter's Mill, 120 miles from San Francisco. Figuring this news should sell some newspapers and raise real-estate values, Brannan published the rumor as fact. Initially the story didn't generate excitement. So Brannan ran another story, this time verified by Mormon employees at Sutter's Mill who had sworn him to secrecy. Brannan reportedly kept his word by running through the San Francisco streets, brandishing gold entrusted to him as tithes for the Mormon church, shouting, 'Gold on the American River!'

Other newspapers hastily published stories of 'gold mountains' near San Francisco. By 1850, the year California was fast-tracked for admission as the 31st state, its non-Native population had ballooned from 15,000 to 93,000. Most arrivals weren't Americans, but Peruvians, Australians, Chileans and Mexicans, with some Chinese, Irish, native Hawaiian and French prospectors.

Westward, Ho!

As the 19th century dawned on the young nation, optimism was the mood of the day. With the invention of the cotton gin in 1793 – followed by threshers, reapers, mowers and later combines – agriculture was industrialized, and US commerce surged. The 1803 Louisiana Purchase doubled US territory, and expansion west of the Appalachian Mountains began in earnest.

Exploiting the West's vast resources became a patriotic duty in the 1840s – a key aspect of America's belief in its Manifest Destiny. During the early territorial days, movement of goods and people from the East

The moving Boarding School Experience exhibit at the Heard Museum in Phoenix traces the forced relocation of Native American children to federally run boarding schools in the 1800s and 1900s for 'Americanization.'

You can follow the Lewis and Clark expedition on its extraordinary journey west to the Pacific and back again online at www.pbs.org/lewisand clark, featuring historical maps, photo albums and journal excerpts.

1844	1846–48	1847	1849
First telegraph line is inaugurated with the phrase 'What hath God wrought?'. In 1845, Congress approves a transcontinental railroad, completed in 1869. Together, telegraph and train open the frontier.	The battle for the West is waged with the Mexican–American War. The war ends with the 1848 Guadalupe–Hidalgo treaty that gives most of present-day Arizona and New Mexico to the USA.	Mormons fleeing religious persecution in Illinois start arriving in Salt Lake City; over the next 20 years more than 70,000 Mormons head to Utah via the Mormon Pioneer Trail.	After the 1848 discovery of gold near Sacramento, an epic cross-country gold rush sees 60,000 'forty-niners' flock to California's Mother Lode. San Francisco's population explodes to 25,000.

to the West was very slow. Horses, mule trains and stagecoaches represented state-of-the-art transportation at the time.

An estimated 400,000 people trekked west across America between 1840 and 1860, lured by tales of gold, promises of religious freedom and visions of fertile farmland. The 'Wild West' years soon followed with ranchers, cowboys, miners and entrepreneurs staking claims and raising hell. Law, order and civilization arrived, hastened by the telegraph, the transcontinental railroad and a continual flow of new arrivals who just wanted to settle down and enjoy their piece of the American pie.

One of the major routes was the Oregon Trail. Spanning six states, it sorely tested the families who embarked on this perilous trip. Their belongings were squirreled away under canvas-topped wagons, which often trailed livestock. The journey could take up to eight months, and by the time the settlers reached eastern Oregon their food supplies were running on fumes. Other major routes included the Santa Fe Trail and the Old Spanish Trail, which ran from Santa Fe into central Utah and across Nevada to Los Angeles in California. Regular stagecoach services along the Santa Fe Trail began in 1849; the Mormon Trail reached Salt Lake City in 1847.

The arrival of more people and resources via the railroad led to further land exploration and the frequent discovery of mineral deposits. Many Western mining towns were founded in the 1870s and 1880s; some, like Santa Rita, are now ghost towns while others like Tombstone and Silver City remain active.

Those Who Came Before, by Robert H and Florence C Lister (1984), is an excellent source about the prehistory of the Southwest and the archaeological sites of its national parks and monuments.

The Long Walk & Apache Conflicts

For decades, US forces pushed west across the continent, killing or forcibly moving whole tribes of Native Americans who were in their way. The most widely known incident is the forceful relocation of many Navajo in 1864. US forces, led by Kit Carson, destroyed Navajo fields, orchards and houses, and forced the people into surrendering or withdrawing into remote parts of Canyon de Chelly. Eventually, they were starved out. About 9000 Navajo were rounded up and marched 400 miles east to a camp at Bosque Redondo, near Fort Sumner in New Mexico. Hundreds of Native Americans died from sickness, starvation or gunshot wounds along the way. The Navajo call this 'The Long Walk', and it remains an important part of Navajo history.

On November 7, 1893, Colorado became the first US state – and one of the first places in the world – to grant women the right to vote.

The last serious conflicts were between US troops and the Apache. This was partly because raiding was the essential path to manhood for the Apache. As US forces and settlers moved into Apache land, they became obvious targets for the raids that were part of the Apache way of life. These continued under the leadership of Mangas Coloradas, Cochise, Victorio and, finally, Geronimo, who surrendered in 1886 after being

1861–65	1864	1881	1882
American Civil War erupts between North and South. The celebration of the war's end on April 9, 1865, is marred by President Lincoln's assassination five days later.	Kit Carson forces 9000 Navajo to walk 400 miles to a camp near Fort Sumner. Hundreds of Native Americans die from sickness, starvation and gunshot wounds along 'The Long Walk.'	Wyatt Earp, his brothers Virgil and Morgan, and Doc Holliday, kill Billy Clanton and the McLaury brothers in a blazing gunfight at the OK Corral in Tombstone, AZ.	Racist sentiment, particularly in California (where over 50,000 Chinese immigrants had arrived since 1848) leads to the Chinese Exclusion Act, the only US immigration law to exclude a specific race.

promised that he and the Apache would be imprisoned for two years and then allowed to return to their homeland. As with many promises made during these years, this one, too, was broken.

Even after the wars were over, Native Americans were treated like second-class citizens for many decades. Non–Native Americans used legal loopholes and technicalities to take over reservation land. Many children were removed from reservations and shipped off to boarding schools where they were taught in English and punished for speaking their own languages or behaving 'like Indians' – this practice continued into the 1930s.

The Wild West

Romanticized tales of gunslingers, cattle rustlers, outlaws and train robbers fuel Wild West legends. Good and bad guys were designations in flux – a tough outlaw in one state became a popular sheriff in another. Gunfights were more frequently the result of mundane political struggles in emerging towns than storied blood feuds. New mining towns mushroomed overnight, playing host to rowdy saloons and bordellos where miners would come to brawl, drink and gamble. Riders and swift horses were the backbone of the short-lived but legendary Pony Express (1860–61). They carried letters between Missouri and California in an astounding 10 days!

Legendary figures Billy the Kid and Sheriff Pat Garrett, both involved in the infamous Lincoln County War, were active in the late 1870s. Billy the Kid reputedly shot and killed more than 20 men in a brief career as a gunslinger – he himself was shot and killed by Garrett at the age of 21. In 1881, Wyatt Earp, along with his brothers Virgil and Morgan, and Doc Holliday, shot dead Billy Clanton and the McLaury brothers in a blazing gunfight at the OK Corral in Tombstone – the showdown took less than a minute. Both sides accused the other of cattle rustling, but the real story will never be known.

Among the provisions recommended for those traveling the Oregon Trail were coffee (15lb per person), bacon (25lb per person), 1lb of castile soap, citric acid to prevent scurvy and a live cow for milk and emergency meat.

Water & Western Development

For many years, the lingering image of the Great American Desert, a myth propagated by early explorers, deterred agricultural settlers and urban development. Though the western interior was not a desert, water was a limiting factor as cities such as Denver began to spring up at the base of the Front Range. With recent droughts plaguing the West, regulating water use has become a necessity.

The struggle for an adequate supply of water for the growing desert population marked the early years of the 20th century, resulting in federally funded dam projects such as the 1936 Hoover Dam and, in 1963, the Glen Canyon Dam and Lake Powell. These large-scale dams permanently

1919	1938	1945	1946
The Grand Canyon becomes the USA's 15th national park, and a dirt road to the North Rim is built from Kanab. By 2013, the park is visited by 4.5 million people annually.	Route 66 becomes the first cross-country highway to be completely paved, including more than 750 miles across Arizona and New Mexico. The Mother Road is officially decommissioned in 1984.	The first atomic bomb is detonated in the ironically named Jornada del Muerto (Journey of Death) Valley in southern New Mexico, which is now part of the White Sands Missile Range.	The opening of the glitzy Flamingo casino in Las Vegas sparks a mob-backed building spree. By the fabulous '50s, Sin City has reached its first golden peak.

altered delicate ecosystems, flooded ancient ruins and continue to prevent the migration of native fish.

Water supply remains a key challenge in this region, and one that creates regional tension, as desert states downstream of the Rockies compete for this increasingly limited resource.

Reforming the Wild West

When the great earthquake and fire hit San Francisco in 1906, it signaled change for California. With public funds for citywide water mains and fire hydrants siphoned off by corrupt bosses, there was only one functioning water source in San Francisco. When the smoke lifted, one thing was clear: it was time for the Wild West to change.

While San Francisco was rebuilt at a rate of 15 buildings per day, California's reformers set to work on city, state and national politics, one plank at a time. Californians concerned about public health and trafficking in women pushed for passage of the 1914 statewide Red Light Abatement Act. Mexico's revolution from 1910 to 1921 brought a new wave of migrants and revolutionary ideas, including ethnic pride and worker solidarity. As California's ports grew, longshoremen's unions coordinated a historic 83-day strike in 1934 along the entire West Coast that forced concessions for safer working conditions and fair pay.

At the height of the Depression in 1935, some 200,000 farming families fleeing the drought-stricken Dust Bowl in Texas and Oklahoma arrived in California, where they found scant pay and deplorable working conditions at major farming concerns. California's artists alerted middle America to the migrants' plight, and the nation rallied around Dorothea Lange's haunting documentary photos of famine-struck families and John Steinbeck's harrowing fictionalized account in his 1939 novel *The Grapes of Wrath*.

WWII & the Atomic Age

The West took on a more important economic and technological role during WWII. Scientists developed the atomic bomb in the secret city of Los Alamos. War-related industries, such as timber production and work at naval yards and airplane factories, thrived in the Pacific Northwest and California.

Los Alamos

In 1943, Los Alamos, New Mexico, then home to a boys school perched on a 7400ft mesa, was chosen as the top-secret headquarters of the Manhattan Project, the code name for the research and development of the atomic bomb. The 772-acre site, accessed by two dirt roads, had no gas or oil lines and only one wire service, and it was surrounded by forest.

The Denver Mint struck and minted its first gold and silver coins on February 1, 1906. It is the largest producer of coins in the world. The mint was robbed of $200,000 in broad daylight on 18 December, 1922.

Chinatown (1974) is the fictionalized yet surprisingly accurate account of the brutal water wars that were waged to build both Los Angeles and San Francisco.

1947	1964	1976	1980
An unidentified object falls in the desert near Roswell. The government first calls it a crashed disk, then a day later a weather balloon, and mysteriously closes off the area.	Congress passes the Civil Rights Act, outlawing discrimination on the basis of race, color, religion, sex or national origin. First proposed by Kennedy, it is one of President Johnson's crowning achievements.	Designed by Steve Wozniak, the first Apple computer is released. With 4KB of memory, it costs $666. Apple becomes integral to the identity of Silicon Valley, now home to over a quarter of a million tech workers.	Mt St Helens blows her top, killing 57 people and destroying 250 homes. Her elevation is cut from 9677ft to 8365ft, and where a peak once stood, a mile-wide crater is born.

Isolation and security marked every aspect of life on 'the hill.' Not only was resident movement restricted and mail censored, there was also no outside contact by radio or telephone. Perhaps even more unsettlingly, most residents had no idea why they were living in Los Alamos. Knowledge was on a 'need to know' basis; everyone knew only as much as their job required.

In just under two years, Los Alamos scientists successfully detonated the first atomic bomb at the Trinity site, now White Sands Missile Range.

After the US detonated the atomic bomb in Japan, the secret city of Los Alamos was exposed to the public. The city continued to be cloaked in secrecy, however, until 1957, when restrictions on visiting were lifted.

Changing Workforce & New Industries

California's workforce permanently changed in WWII, when women and African Americans were recruited for wartime industries and Mexican workers were brought in to fill labor shortages. Contracts in military communications and aviation attracted an international elite of engineers, who would launch California's high-tech industry. Within a decade after the war, California's population had grown by 40%, reaching almost 13 million.

The war also brought economic fortune to the Pacific Northwest, when the area became the nation's largest lumber producer and both Oregon's and Washington's naval yards bustled, along with William Boeing's airplane factory. The region continued to prosper through the second half of the 20th century, attracting new migrations of educated, progressively minded settlers from the nation's east and south.

After the war, industry took on new forms, with Silicon Valley's dotcom industry drawing talented entrepreneurs to the Bay area in the 1990s. The film industry still holds strong in Los Angeles, but tax incentives have drawn filmmakers to other western enclaves, particularly New Mexico.

For behind-the-scenes stories about Wild West legends, along with their photographs, pick up the monthly magazine *True West* (www.truewestmagazine.com), or visit the website to see who's in the spotlight.

Hollywood & Counterculture

In 1908, California became a convenient movie location for its consistent sunlight and versatile locations, although its role was limited to doubling for more exotic locales and providing backdrops for period-piece productions. But gradually, California began stealing the scene in movies and iconic TV shows with waving palms and sunny beaches.

Not all Californians saw themselves as extras in *Beach Blanket Bingo*, however. WWII sailors discharged for insubordination and homosexuality in San Francisco found themselves at home in North Beach's bebop jazz clubs, bohemian coffeehouses and City Lights Bookstore. San Francisco became the home of free speech and free spirits, and soon everyone

1995	1999	2000	2008
Amazon, one of the first major companies to sell products online, is launched in Seattle. Originally starting as a bookseller, it does not become annually profitable until 2003.	From November 30 to December 1, 40,000 protesters in Seattle take on economic globalization at the World Trade Organization's international trade negotiations; it's the biggest protest to date in US history.	Coloradans vote for Amendment 20 in the state election, which provides for dispensing cannabis to registered patients. A proliferation of medical marijuana clinics ensues over the next decade.	California voters pass Proposition 8, which bans gay marriage. Federal courts rule the law unconstitutional. In 2013, the US Supreme Court does not take up an appeal; same-sex marriages resume.

who was anyone was getting arrested: Beat poet Lawrence Ferlinghetti for publishing Allen Ginsberg's epic poem *Howl*, comedian Lenny Bruce for uttering the F-word onstage, and Carol Doda for going topless. When flower power faded, other Bay Area rebellions grew in its place: black power, gay pride and medical marijuana clubs.

But while Northern California had the more attention-grabbing counterculture from the 1940s to '60s, nonconformity in sunny Southern California shook America to the core. In 1947, when Senator Joseph McCarthy attempted to root out suspected communists in the movie industry, 10 writers and directors who refused to admit communist alliances or to name names were charged with contempt of Congress and barred from working in Hollywood. The Hollywood Ten's impassioned defenses of the Constitution were heard nationwide, and major Hollywood players boldly voiced dissent and hired blacklisted talent until California lawsuits put a legal end to McCarthyism in 1962.

The Oscar-winning *There Will Be Blood* (2007), adapted from Upton Sinclair's book *Oil!*, depicts a Californian oil magnate and was based on real-life SoCal tycoon Edward Doheny.

On January 28, 1969, an oil rig dumped 200,000 gallons of oil into Santa Barbara Channel, killing dolphins, seals and some 3600 shore birds. The beach community organized a highly effective protest, spurring the establishment of the Environmental Protection Agency.

Geeking Out

When California's Silicon Valley introduced the first personal computer in 1968, Hewlett-Packard's 'light' (40lb) machine cost just $4900 (about $29,000 today). Hoping to bring computer power to the people, 21-year-old Steve Jobs and Steve Wozniak introduced the Apple II at the 1977 West Coast Computer Faire with unfathomable memory (4KB of RAM) and microprocessor speed (1MHz).

In 2014 the HBO series *Silicon Valley* premiered on HBO. Co-created by Mike Judge, the comedy follows the ups and downs of an internet start-up company and its amusingly quirky founders.

By the mid-1990s, an entire dot-com industry boomed in Silicon Valley with online start-ups, and suddenly people were getting their mail, news, politics, pet food and, yes, sex online. But when dot-com profits weren't forthcoming, venture funding dried up, and fortunes in stock options disappeared on one nasty Nasdaq-plummeting day: March 10, 2000. Overnight, 26-year-old vice-presidents and Bay Area service-sector employees alike found themselves jobless. But as online users continued to look for useful information and one another in those billions of web pages, search engines and social media websites boomed. Between 2011 and 2015, social media giant Facebook jumped from 2000 employees to 6800.

Meanwhile, California biotech was making strides. In 1976, an upstart company called Genentech cloned human insulin and introduced the hepatitis B vaccine. California voters approved a $3 billion bond measure in 2004 for stem-cell research, and by 2008 California had be-

2008	2010	2012	2012
Barack Obama is elected president of the United States, the first African American to hold the office.	Arizona passes controversial legislation requiring police officers to ask for identification from anyone they suspect of being in the US without authorization. Immigration rights activists call for a boycott of the state.	New Mexico and Arizona, the 47th and 48th states to join the Union, celebrate their Centennials.	Colorado and Washington become the first states to legalize recreational marijuana for adults aged 21 and older.

come the biggest funder of stem-cell research and the focus of Nasdaq's Biotech Index.

On January 27, 2017, President Trump issued an executive order suspending entry from seven countries in the Middle East and North Africa and cutting the US refugee program. While various courts have banned implementation of the ban, it has a huge psychological impact on immigrant communities and there's speculation that it could result in a brain drain from Silicon Valley and tech industries. Companies like Google, Expedia and Amazon have spoken out against the ban.

America Turns Inward

After a highly contentious campaign season, Donald Trump staged the upset of the century and became the 45th president of the US on November 8, 2016. His platform, 'America First,' has set the stage for the next phase of US politics. With precarious relations with NATO and new terms for many international alliances, a new era has begun. The defunding of international aid campaigns and institutions like the State Department have put global issues in the back seat. This is not to say that all of America waxes nostalgic for the 'good old days.' Shortly after Trump's inauguration, half a million people stood up against the administration at the Women's March on Washington on January 21, 2017, joined by five million marchers worldwide. This initial tour-de-force of dissent was followed by subsequent marches for science and climate change.

On June 3, 2017, professional rock climber Alex Honnold became the first to climb the 3000ft rock face of Yosemite's El Capitan without ropes, in just under four hours. The daring practice of 'free-soloing' is the most extreme expression of the sport.

2015	2016	2017	2017
In a landmark five-four decision, the US Supreme Court decides that same-sex marriage is a right guaranteed by the Constitution. Thirteen states banning such unions must comply with the ruling.	A divided nation elects Donald Trump as the 45th president of the United States through a majority in the electoral college, despite Hillary Clinton having won the popular vote.	The US pulls out of the Paris Climate Accord, joining Nicaragua and Syria as the only countries not participating.	In Portland, Oregon, two men are killed and one injured for standing up to hate speech on light-rail train. The event becomes a lightning rod for larger issues of racism, religious freedom and nonviolence.

The Way of Life

If you believe the headlines, Westerners are a quirky bunch, with angry Arizonans up-in-arms about illegal immigration, hair-pulling housewives in Orange County and pot-smoking deadbeats in Colorado. And, according to *Portlandia* comedy sketches, Portland brims with bike-riding, organic-obsessed hipsters who want to put a bird on everything. Are these accurate depictions? Yes and no. The headlines may reflect some regional attitudes, but most folks are just trying to go about their lives with as little drama as possible.

Regional Identity

The cowboy has long been a symbol of the West – brave, self-reliant, and a solitary seeker of truth, justice and a straight shot of whiskey. The truth behind the myth? Those who settled the West were indeed self-reliant and brave. They had to be. In that harsh and unforgiving landscape, danger was always a few steps behind opportunity. As the dangers dissipated, however, and settlers put down roots, the cowboy stereotype became less accurate. Like the red-rock mesas that have weathered into new and varying forms over the years, the character of the populace has also evolved. Stereotypes today, accurate or not, are regionally based, and the residents of Portland, San Diego, Santa Fe and Phoenix are perceived very differently from one another.

In September 2016, approximately 70,000 euphoric souls descended upon the Nevada desert for Burning Man, an annual camping extravaganza, art festival and rave where freedom of expression, costume and libido are all encouraged.

California

Hey dude, don't stick a label on me, that's so uncool. And what's the label? According to the stereotype, Californians are laid-back, self-absorbed, health-conscious, open-minded and eco-aware. The stats behind the stereotype? According to the the National Oceanic and Atmospheric Administration (NOAA), more than 25.5 million Californians lived in a coastal shoreline county in 2010 – the highest number for any coastal state. The state's southern beaches are sunniest and most swimmable, thus Southern California's inescapable associations with surf, sun and classic prime-time TV soaps like *Baywatch* and *The OC*.

Self-help, fitness and body modification are major industries throughout California, successfully marketed since the 1970s, while exercise and good food help keep Californians among the fittest in the nation. Politically, the scene is not rosy for Republicans. In 2016, only 27.3% of registered voters in the state were Republicans while 44.8% were registered Democrats and 23.3% were considered Independent.

Environmentally, Golden Staters have zoomed ahead of the national energy-use curve in their smog-checked cars; more hybrid cars are sold here than in any other state. By the end of 2017, fully self-driving vehicles may be legal on California roads.

Pacific Northwest

And what about those folks living in Washington and Oregon? Tree-hugging hipsters with activist tendencies and a penchant for latte? That's pretty accurate, actually. Many locals are proud of their independent spirit, profess a love for nature and, yes, will separate their plastics when it's time to recycle. They're a friendly lot and, despite the common tendency to denigrate Californians, most are transplants themselves. Why did they all come here? Among other things, for the lush scenery, the good quality of life and the lack of pretension that often afflicts bigger, more popular places. Primping up and putting on airs is not a part of Northwestern everyday life, and wearing Gore-Tex outerwear to restaurants, concerts or social functions will rarely raise an eyebrow.

Rocky Mountain States

The iconic Western cowboy? You're likely to find the real deal here. Ranching is big business in these parts, and the solitary cowboy – seen riding a bucking bronco on the Wyoming license plate – is an appropriate symbol for the region. It takes a rugged individualist to scratch out a living on the lonely, windswept plains – plains that can leave big-city travelers feeling slightly unmoored.

Politically, the northern Rockies – Wyoming, Montana and Idaho – skew conservative, although you will find pockets of liberalism in the college and resort towns. Wyoming may have been the first territory to give women the right to vote, in 1869, but this nod to liberal thinking has been overshadowed by Wyoming's association with former vice-president Dick Cheney, the divisive Republican who was a six-term congressman from the state.

Colorado is the West's most recognizable swing state. For every bastion of liberalism like Boulder there's an equally entrenched conservative counterpart like Colorado Springs. Yet, a growing urban population has it leaning left: in the 2016 presidential election, Clinton garnered almost 3.5 million more votes than Trump.

Colorado averages 300 days of sun annually – if you count one hour of sunshine as being a full day. According to the no-fun but more precise National Weather Service, the Front Range averages 115 clear-sky days, 130 partly-cloudy days and 120 cloudy days.

Southwest

The Southwest has long drawn stout-hearted settlers – Mormons, cattle barons, prospectors – pursuing slightly different agendas than those of the average American. A new generation of idealistic entrepreneurs has transformed former mining towns into New Age art enclaves and Old West tourist attractions. Scientists flocked to the empty spaces to develop and test atomic bombs and soaring rockets. Astronomers built observatories on lonely hills and mountains, making the most of the dark skies and unobstructed views.

In recent years high-profile governmental efforts to stop illegal immigration have impacted the let's-coexist vibe, most vocally in the southern reaches of Arizona, though the state remains politically split between conservatives and liberals. President Trump's proposal for a border wall – with costs estimated up to $70 billion – is at its most controversial in this

EQUAL MARRIAGE RIGHTS FOR ALL

Forty thousand Californians were already registered as domestic partners when, in 2004, San Francisco Mayor Gavin Newsom issued marriage licenses to same-sex couples in defiance of a California same-sex marriage ban. Four thousand same-sex couples promptly got hitched. The state ban was nixed by California courts in June 2008, but then Proposition 8 passed in November 2008 to amend the state's constitution and prohibit same-sex marriage. Civil-rights activists challenged the constitutionality of the proposition, and federal courts eventually ruled that the law unconstitutionally violated the equal protection and due process clauses. In 2013, the US Supreme Court did not take up an appeal and same-sex marriages resumed in the Golden State. In June 2015 the US Supreme Court settled the question across the country by ruling that the Constitution guarantees a right to same-sex marriage.

region, where the public actually understands what the 1900-mile border looks like. Conservatives still hope for expansions on border patrols while others would rather see immigration reform.

Population & Multiculturalism

California, with 39 million residents, is the most populous state in the USA. California has the country's highest Asian American population, 5.6 million, and the highest Latino population at 14 million, both numbers from the 2010 census. In 2014, Latinos became the state's largest racial or ethnic group. Latino culture is deeply enmeshed with that of California, and most residents see the state as an easygoing multicultural society that gives everyone a chance to live the American Dream. The state had an estimated 2.5 million undocumented immigrants in 2014 – about 6% of the state population.

Colorado, Arizona and New Mexico all have large Native American and Latino populations. These residents take pride in maintaining their cultural identities through preserved traditions and oral history lessons.

The Tucson sector of the United States Border Patrol is one of the busiest border sectors in the nation in terms of apprehensions and drug seizures. It oversees 262 miles of borderland between Arizona and Mexico and employs 4200 agents across eight stations.

Religion

Although Californians are less churchgoing than the American mainstream, and one in five Californians professes no religion at all, it remains one of the most religiously diverse states. About a third of Californians are Catholic, due in part to the state's large Latino population, while another third are Protestants. About 1% of California's population is Muslim. LA has the third-largest Jewish community in North America behind NYC and southern Florida. About 2% of California's population identifies as Buddhist and another 2% as Hindu.

About a third of Pacific Northwesterners have no religious affiliation. Those who are religious tend to adhere to Christianity and Judaism. Asian Americans have brought Buddhism and Hinduism, and New Age spirituality isn't a stranger here.

The Southwest has its own anomalies. In Utah, 55% of the state's population identifies as Mormon. The church stresses traditional family values; drinking, smoking and premarital sex are frowned upon. Family and religion are also core values for Native Americans and Hispanics throughout the Southwest. For the Hopi, tribal dances are such sacred events that they are mostly closed to outsiders. And, although many Native Americans and Hispanics are now living in urban areas, working as professionals, large family gatherings and traditional customs are still important facets of daily life.

THE SPORTING LIFE

Westerners cherish their sports, whether they're players themselves or just watching their favorite teams. Here is a breakdown of the West's professional teams by sport.

National Football League AFC West: Denver Broncos, Oakland Raiders (moving to Las Vegas in 2019), LA Chargers; NFC West: Arizona Cardinals, San Francisco 49ers, Seattle Seahawks

National Basketball Association Western Conference Pacific: Golden State Warriors, LA Clippers, LA Lakers, Phoenix Suns, Sacramento Kings; Northwest: Denver Nuggets, Portland Trailblazers, Utah Jazz

Women's National Basketball Association LA Sparks, Phoenix Mercury, Seattle Storm

Major League Baseball American League: LA Angels, Oakland Athletics, Seattle Mariners; National League: Arizona Diamondbacks, Colorado Rockies, LA Dodgers, San Diego Padres, San Francisco Giants

Native Americans

According to the 2010 census California has the largest Native American population in the country, with Arizona and New Mexico ranking in the top 10. The Navajo tribe is the largest western tribe, second only to the Cherokee nationwide.

Culturally, tribes today grapple with questions about how to prosper in contemporary America while protecting their traditions from erosion and their lands from further exploitation, and how to lift their people from poverty while maintaining their sense of identity and the sacred.

The Tribes

Most of the major Western tribes are located in the Southwest. Well-known tribes with large reservations in Arizona include the Navajo, the Hopi and the Apache. Two smaller Arizona tribes, the Hualapai and the Havasupai, live on reservations beside the Grand Canyon. New Mexico's tribes are clustered in 19 pueblos located in the north-central region of the state.

Apache

The Southwest has three major Apache reservations: New Mexico's Jicarilla Apache Reservation and Arizona's San Carlos Apache Reservation and Fort Apache Reservation, home to the White Mountain Apache tribe. All the Apache tribes descend from Athabascans who migrated from Canada around 1400. They were nomadic hunter-gatherers who became warlike raiders, particularly of Pueblo tribes and European settlements, and they fiercely resisted relocation to reservations.

The most famous Apache is Geronimo, a Chiricahua Apache who resisted the American takeover of native lands until he was finally subdued by the US Army with the help of White Mountain Apache scouts.

For decades, traditional Navajo and Hopi have thwarted US industry efforts to strip mine sacred Big Mountain. Black Mesa Indigenous Support (www. supportblack-mesa.org) tells their story.

Havasupai

The Havasupai Reservation abuts Arizona's Grand Canyon National Park beneath the canyon's South Rim. The tribe's one village, Supai, can only be reached by an 8-mile hike or a mule or helicopter ride from road's end at Hualapai Hilltop.

Havasupai (hah-vah-*soo*-pie) means 'people of the blue-green water,' and tribal life has always been dominated by the Havasu Creek tributary of the Colorado River. Reliable water meant the ability to irrigate fields, which led to a season-based village lifestyle. The deep Havasu Canyon also protected them from others; this extremely peaceful people basically avoided Western contact until the 1800s. Today, the tribe relies on tourism, and Havasu Canyon's gorgeous waterfalls draw a steady stream of visitors. The tribe is related to the Hualapai.

Hopi

Surrounded by the Navajo Reservation in northeast Arizona, the Hopi Reservation covers more than 1.5 million acres. Most Hopi live in 12 villages at the base and on top of three mesas jutting from the main

Black Mesa; Old Oraibi, on Third Mesa, is considered (along with Acoma Pueblo) the continent's oldest continuously inhabited settlement. Like all Pueblo peoples, the Hopi are descended from the Ancestral Puebloans (formerly known as Anasazi).

Hopi (*ho*-pee) translates as 'peaceful ones' or 'peaceful person,' and perhaps no tribe is more renowned for leading such a humble, traditional and deeply spiritual lifestyle. The Hopi practice an unusual, near-miraculous technique of 'dry farming'. The soil isn't plowed, instead, seeds are planted in 'wind breaks' and natural water catchments. Their main crop has always been corn, which is central to their creation story.

Hopi ceremonial life is complex and intensely private, and extends into all aspects of daily living. Following the 'Hopi Way' is considered essential to bringing the life-giving rains, but the Hopi also believe it fosters the wellbeing of the entire human race. Each person's role is determined by their clan, which is matrilineal. Even among themselves, the Hopi keep certain traditions of their individual clans private.

The Hopi are skilled artisans; they are famous for their pottery, coiled baskets and silverwork, as well as for their ceremonial kachina (spirit) dolls.

> For a helpful introduction to Navajo culture, stop by the Explore Navajo Interactive Museum (www.explorenavajo.com) in Tuba City, on the way to Monument Valley from Grand Canyon National Park.

Hualapai

The Hualapai Reservation occupies around 1 million acres along 108 miles of the Grand Canyon's South Rim. Hualapai (*wah*-lah-pie) means 'people of the tall pines.' Because this section of the Grand Canyon was not readily arable, the Hualapai were originally seminomadic, gathering wild plants and hunting small game.

Today, forestry, cattle ranching, farming and tourism are the economic mainstays. The tribal headquarters are in Peach Springs, AZ, which was

---

ETIQUETTE

When visiting a reservation, ask about and follow any specific rules. Almost all tribes ban alcohol, and some ban pets and restrict cameras. All require permits for camping, fishing and other activities. Tribal rules may be posted at the reservation entrance, or you can visit the tribal office or check the reservation's website.

When you visit a reservation, you are visiting a unique culture with customs that may be unfamiliar. Be courteous, respectful and open-minded, and don't expect locals to share every detail of their lives.

Ask first, document later Some tribes restrict cameras and sketching entirely; others may charge a fee, or restrict them at ceremonies or in certain areas. *Always ask before taking pictures or drawing.* If you want to photograph a person, ask permission first; a tip is polite and often expected.

Pueblos are not museums The incredible adobe structures are homes. Public buildings will be signed; if a building isn't signed, assume it's private. Don't climb around. *Kivas* (sacred buildings) are nearly always off limits.

Ceremonies are not performances Treat ceremonies like church services; watch silently and respectfully, without talking, clapping or taking pictures, and wear modest clothing. Powwows are more informal, but remember: unless they're billed as theater, they are for the tribe, not you.

Privacy and communication Many Native Americans are happy to describe their tribe's general religious beliefs, but not always, or to the same degree, and details about rituals and ceremonies are often considered private. Always ask before discussing religion and respect each person's boundaries. Also, Native Americans consider it polite to listen without comment; silent listening, given and received, is another sign of respect.

the inspiration for 'Radiator Springs' in the animated movie *Cars*. Hunting, fishing, rafting and the lofty Skywalk are prime draws.

Navajo

Nationwide, there are about 300,000 Navajo, making it the USA's second-largest tribe after the Cherokee. The Navajo Reservation (www.discovernavajo.com) is by far the largest and most populous in the US. Also called the Navajo Nation and Navajoland, it covers 17.5 million acres (over 27,000 sq miles) in Arizona and parts of New Mexico and Utah.

The Navajo were feared nomads and warriors who both traded with and raided the Pueblos and who fought settlers and the US military. They also borrowed generously from other traditions: they acquired sheep and horses from the Spanish, learned pottery and weaving from the Pueblos, and picked up silversmithing from Mexico. Today, the Navajo are renowned for their woven rugs, pottery and inlaid silver jewelry, as well as for their intricate sandpainting, which is used in healing ceremonies.

Pueblo

New Mexico contains 19 Pueblo reservations. Four reservations lead west from Albuquerque: Isleta, Laguna, Acoma and Zuni. Fifteen pueblos fill the Rio Grande Valley between Albuquerque and Taos: Sandia, San Felipe, Santa Ana, Zia, Jemez, Santo Domingo, Cochiti, San Ildefonso, Pojoaque, Nambé, Tesuque, Santa Clara, Ohkay Owingeh (or San Juan), Picuris and Taos.

These tribes are as different as they are alike. Nevertheless, the term 'pueblo' (Spanish for 'village') is a convenient shorthand for what these tribes share: all are believed to be descended from the Ancestral Puebloans and to have inherited their architectural style and their agrarian, village-based life – often atop mesas.

Pueblos are unique among Native Americans. These adobe structures can have up to five levels, connected by ladders, and are built with varying combinations of mud bricks, stones, logs and plaster. In the central plaza of each pueblo is a *kiva*, an underground ceremonial chamber that connects to the spirit world. Catholic churches are prominent in the pueblos, a legacy of missionaries, and many Pueblos hold both Christian and native religious beliefs.

Arts

Native American art nearly always contains ceremonial purpose and religious significance; the patterns and symbols are woven with spiritual meaning that provides an intimate window into the heart of the people.

In addition to preserving their culture, contemporary Native American artists have used sculpture, painting, textiles, film, literature and performance art to reflect and critique modernity since the mid-20th century, especially after the civil-rights activism of the 1960s and cultural renaissance of the '70s. *Native North American Art*, by Janet Berlo and Ruth Phillips, offers a superb introduction to North America's varied indigenous art – from pre-contact to postmodernism.

By purchasing arts from Native Americans themselves, visitors have a direct, positive impact on tribal economies, which depend in part on tourist dollars. Many tribes run craft outlets and galleries, usually in the main towns of reservations. The Indian Arts & Crafts Board (www.iacb.doi.gov) lists Native American–owned galleries and shops state-by-state online – click on 'Source Directory of Businesses.'

Pottery & Basketry

Pretty much every Southwest tribe has pottery and/or basketry traditions. Originally, each tribe and even individual families maintained dis-

NATIVE AMERICANS ARTS

The Hopi Arts Trail spotlights artists and galleries on the three mesas that are the heart of the Hopi reservation. For a map, as well as a list of artists and galleries, visit www.hopiartstrail.com.

Most (78%) Native Americans live off the reservation. New York City is home to the largest population (111,700) followed by Los Angeles (54,200).

tinct styles, but modern potters and basket makers readily mix, borrow and reinterpret classic designs and methods.

Pueblo pottery is perhaps most acclaimed of all. Initially, local clay determined color, so that Zia pottery was red, Acoma white, Hopi yellow, Cochiti black and so on. Santa Clara is famous for its carved relief designs, and San Ildefonso for its black-on-black style, which was revived by world-famous potter Maria Martinez. The Navajo and Ute Mountain Utes also produce well-regarded pottery.

Pottery is nearly always synonymous with village life, while more portable baskets were often preferred by nomadic peoples. Among the tribes who stand out for their exquisite basketry are the Jicarilla Apache (whose name means basket maker), the Kaibab-Paiute, the Hualapai and the Tohono O'odham. Hopi coiled baskets, with their vivid patterns and kachina iconography, are also notable.

Navajo Weaving

Navajo legend says that Spider Woman taught humans how to weave, and she seems embodied today in the iconic sight of Navajo women patiently shuttling handspun wool on weblike looms, creating the Navajo's legendary rugs (originally blankets), so tight they hold water. Preparation of the wool, and sometimes the dyes, is still done by hand, and finishing a rug takes months (occasionally years).

Authentic Navajo rugs are expensive, ranging from hundreds to thousands of dollars. Not average souvenirs, they are artworks that will last a lifetime, whether displayed on the wall or the floor. Take time to research, even a little, so you recognize when quality matches price.

Silver & Turquoise Jewelry

Jewelry using stones and shells has always been a native tradition; silverwork did not arrive until the 1800s, along with Anglo and Mexican contact. In particular, Navajo, Hopi and Zuni became renowned for combining these materials with inlaid-turquoise silver jewelry. In addition to turquoise, jewelry often features lapis, onyx, coral, carnelian and shells.

Authentic jewelry is often stamped or marked by the artisan, and items may come with an Indian Arts & Crafts Board certificate; always ask. Price may also be an indicator: a high tab doesn't guarantee authenticity, but an absurdly low one probably signals trickery. A crash course can be had at the August Santa Fe Indian Market.

In the Pacific Theater during WWII, Navajo 'code talkers' sent and received military messages in the Navajo's Athabascan tongue, which is notoriously complex. Japan never broke the code, and the code talkers were considered essential to US victory.

N Scott Momaday's Pulitzer Prize–winning *House Made of Dawn* (1968), about a Pueblo youth, launched a wave of Native American literature.

Arts & Architecture

Art created in the American West is often marked by a striking collision of personality, attitude and landscape: the take-it-or-leave-it cow skulls in Georgia O'Keeffe paintings; the prominent shadows in an Ansel Adams' photograph of Yosemite's Half Dome; the gonzo journalism of Hunter S Thompson in the sun-baked Southwest; even Nirvana's grunge seems inseparable from its rainy Seattle roots. The landscape is a presence; beautiful yet unforgiving.

Literature

The West has a distinct literary tradition from the more structured, buttoned-up East. It's no surprise that freedom, exploration and wilderness emerge as rich regional themes. In a region that has long inspired novelists, poets and storytellers, California is the most populous state and a hub of storytelling magic.

Social Realism

Arguably the most influential author ever to emerge from California was John Steinbeck, who was born in Salinas in 1902. His masterpiece of social realism, *The Grapes of Wrath*, tells of the struggles of migrant farm workers.

Playwright Eugene O'Neill took his 1936 Nobel Prize money and transplanted himself to near San Francisco, where he wrote the autobiographical play *Long Day's Journey into Night*.

Upton Sinclair's *Oil!*, which inspired Paul Thomas Anderson's movie *There Will Be Blood*, was a muckraking work of historical fiction with socialist overtones.

Pulp Noir & Mysteries

In the 1930s, San Francisco and Los Angeles became the capitals of the pulp detective novel. Dashiell Hammett *(The Maltese Falcon)* made San Francisco's fog a sinister character. The king of hard-boiled crime writers was Raymond Chandler, who thinly disguised his hometown of Santa Monica as Bay City.

Since the 1990s, a renaissance of California crime fiction has been masterminded by James Ellroy *(LA Confidential)*, Elmore Leonard *(Jackie Brown)* and Walter Mosley *(Devil in a Blue Dress)*, whose Easy Rawlins detective novels are set in South Central LA's impoverished neighborhoods. *Heartsick*, a thriller by Chelsea Cain, is set in Portland, Oregon.

But not all detectives work in the cities. Tony Hillerman, an enormously popular author from Albuquerque, wrote *Skinwalkers*, *People of Darkness*, *Skeleton Man* and *The Sinister Pig*. His award-winning mystery novels take place on the Navajo, Hopi and Zuni Reservations.

Movers & Shakers

After the chaos of WWII, the Beat Generation brought about a provocative new style of writing: short, sharp, spontaneous and alive. Based in San Francisco, the scene revolved around Jack Kerouac *(On the Road)*,

The National Cowboy Poetry Gathering (www. westernfolklife. org) – the bronco of cowboy poetry events – is held in January in Elko, Nevada. Ropers and wranglers have waxed lyrical here for more than 30 years.

Allen Ginsberg *(Howl)* and Lawrence Ferlinghetti, the Beats' patron and publisher.

Joan Didion nailed California culture in *Slouching Towards Bethlehem*, a collection of essays that takes a caustic look at 1960s flower power and the Haight-Ashbury district. Tom Wolfe also put '60s San Francisco in perspective with *The Electric Kool-Aid Acid Test*, which follows Ken Kesey's band of Merry Pranksters.

In the 1970s, Charles Bukowski's semi-autobiographical novel *Post Office* captured down-and-out downtown LA, while Richard Vasquez's *Chicano* took a dramatic look at LA's Latino barrio.

Hunter S Thompson, who committed suicide in early 2005, wrote *Fear and Loathing in Las Vegas*, set in the temple of American excess in the desert; it's the ultimate, high-octane road-trip novel.

Eco Warriors, Social Commentators & New Voices

Edward Abbey, noted for his strong environmental and political views, created the thought-provoking and seminal works *Desert Solitaire* and *The Journey Home: Some Words in Defense of the American West*. His classic *Monkey Wrench Gang* is a comic fictional account of real people who plan to blow up Glen Canyon Dam before it floods Glen Canyon.

Rebecca Solnit snaps the reins of environmental advocacy, with fine-tuned lyric prose on politics and place, most notably her 2005 book of essays, *A Field Guide to Getting Lost*. Conservationist writer and poet Terry Tempest Williams examines our relationship with wilderness, honing in on her native Utah. Her latest is *The Hour of Land: A Personal Topography of America's National Parks*, 2015.

Former Tucsonian Barbara Kingsolver published two novels with Southwestern settings, *The Bean Trees* and *Animal Dreams*. She shares her thoughts about day-to-day life in the Southwest in a series of essays in *High Tide in Tucson*. Set on the Oregon coast, *Mink River* by Brian Doyle (2010) is a work of fiction filled with myths and storytelling.

Music

Much of the American recording industry is based in Los Angeles, and SoCal's film and TV industries have proven powerful talent incubators. Indeed, today's pop stars and *American Idol* winners are only here thanks to the tuneful revolutions of the decades of innovation that came before, from country folk to urban rap.

Rockin' Out

The first homegrown rock-and-roll talent to make it big in the 1950s was Ritchie Valens, whose 'La Bamba' was a rockified version of a Mexican folk song. When Joan Baez and Bob Dylan had their Northern California fling in the early 1960s, Dylan plugged in his guitar and played folk rock. When Janis Joplin and Big Brother and the Holding Company developed their shambling musical stylings in San Francisco, folk rock splintered into psychedelia. Meanwhile, Jim Morrison and The Doors and the Byrds blew minds on LA's famous Sunset Strip. The epicenter of LA's psychedelic rock scene was the Laurel Canyon neighborhood, just uphill from the Sunset Strip and the legendary Whisky a Go Go nightclub.

Rap & Hip Hop

Since the 1980s, LA has been a hotbed for West Coast rap and hip-hop. Eazy E, Ice Cube and Dr Dre released the seminal NWA (Niggaz With Attitude) album, *Straight Outta Compton*, in 1989. Death Row Records, co-founded by Dr Dre, has launched megawatt rap talents including Long Beach bad boy Snoop Dog and the late Tupac Shakur, who launched his

---

Cheryl Strayed's bestselling memoir *Wild* traces her long-distance solo hike on the Pacific Crest Trail after her mother's death. Reese Witherspoon, whose production company bought the movie rights, earned a Best Actress nomination in 2015 for her depiction of Strayed.

The bestselling novel *Where'd You Go, Bernadette?* by Maria Semple (2012) has fun with Seattle stereotypes while tracing the disappearance of the title character, a feisty but reclusive famous architect.

rap career in Marin County and was fatally shot in 1996 in Las Vegas in a suspected East Coast/West Coast rap feud.

Throughout the 1980s and '90s, California maintained a grass-roots hip-hop scene closer to the streets in LA and in the heart of the black-power movement in Oakland. In the late 1990s, the Bay Area birthed underground artists like E-40 and the 'hyphy movement,' a reaction against the increasing commercialization of hip-hop.

Grunge & Indie

Grunge started in the mid-1980s and was heavily influenced by cult group the Melvins. Distorted guitars, strong riffs, heavy drumming and gritty styles defined the unpolished musical style. Grunge didn't explode until the record label Sub Pop released Nirvana's *Nevermind* in 1991, skyrocketing the 'Seattle Sound' into mainstream music. True purists, however, shunned Nirvana for what they considered selling out to commercialism while overshadowing equally worthy bands like Soundgarden and Alice in Chains. The general popularity of grunge continued through the early 1990s, but the very culture of the genre took part in its downfall. Bands lived hard and fast, never really taking themselves seriously. Many eventually succumbed to internal strife and drug abuse. The final blow was in 1994, when Kurt Cobain – the heart of Nirvana – committed suicide.

A few western cities are especially connected with indie music. Seattle was the original stomping grounds for Modest Mouse, Death Cab for Cutie and The Postal Service. Olympia, WA, has been a hotbed of indie rock and riot grrls. Portland, OR, has boasted such diverse groups as folktronic hip-hop band Talkdemonic, alt-band The Decemberists and multi-genre Pink Martini, not to mention The Shins – originally from Albuquerque, NM – The Dandy Warhols, Blind Pilot and Elliot Smith. Washington-based Sleater-Kinney, with Carrie Brownstein, Corin Tucker and Janet Weiss, hit the road again in 2015 after a nearly 10-year hiatus for their latest album *No Cities to Love*.

At the Experience Music Project Museum in the Seattle Center, the 'Nirvana: Taking Punk to the Masses' exhibit traces the rise of grunge rockers Nirvana and singer/songwriter Kurt Cobain.

Film

From the moment movies – and later TV – became a dominant entertainment medium, California took center stage in the world of popular culture. In 2012, TV and film production and post-production projects generated 107,400 jobs in California, slightly more than half of all such jobs across the United States.

The Industry

The moviemaking industry grew out of the humble orchards of Hollywoodland, a residential neighborhood of Los Angeles, where entrepreneurial moviemakers, many of whom were European immigrants, established studios in the early 1900s. German-born Carl Laemmle built Universal Studios in 1915, selling lunch to curious guests coming to watch the magic of moviemaking; Polish immigrant Samuel Goldwyn joined with Cecil B DeMille to form Paramount Studios; and Jack Warner and his brothers, born to Polish parents, arrived a few years later from Canada.

LA's perpetually balmy weather meant that most outdoor scenes could be easily shot there. Fans loved early silent-film stars like Charlie Chaplin and Harold Lloyd, and the first big Hollywood wedding occurred in 1920 when Douglas Fairbanks wed Mary Pickford, becoming Hollywood's first de-facto royal couple. The silent-movie era gave way to 'talkies' after 1927's *The Jazz Singer*, a Warner Bros musical starring Al Jolson, premiered in downtown LA, ushering in Hollywood's glamorous Golden Age.

ARTS & ARCHITECTURE FILM

Hollywood & Beyond

From the 1920s, Hollywood became the industry's social and financial hub, but only one major studio, Paramount Pictures, stood in Hollywood proper. Most movies have been shot elsewhere around LA, from Culver City (at MGM, now Sony Pictures), to Studio City (at Universal Studios) and Burbank (at Warner Bros and later at Disney).

Today's high cost of filming has sent location scouts outside the state. During his two terms as governor of New Mexico (2002–10), Bill Richardson wooed production teams to the state by offering a 25% tax rebate on expenditures. His efforts helped inject more than $3 billion into the economy.

Las Vegas, NV, had a starring role in 2009's blockbuster comedy *The Hangover*, an R-rated buddy film that earned more than $467 million worldwide.

Westerns & Beyond

Though many Westerns have been shot in SoCal, a few places in Utah and Arizona have doubled as film and TV sets so often that they have come to define the American West. In addition to Utah's Monument Valley, first popularized by director John Ford in *The Stagecoach*, movie-worthy destinations include Moab for *Thelma and Louise* (1991), Dead Horse Point State Park for *Mission Impossible: 2* (2000), Lake Powell for *Planet of the Apes* (1968) and Tombstone for the eponymous *Tombstone* (1993). Scenes in *127 Hours* (2010), the film version of Aron Ralston's harrowing time trapped in Blue John Canyon in Canyonlands National Park, were shot in and around the canyon.

Joel and Ethan Coen shot the 2007 Oscar winner *No Country for Old Men* almost entirely around Las Vegas, NM (doubling for 1980s west Texas). The Coen brothers returned in 2010 to film their remake of *True Grit*, basing their production headquarters in Santa Fe and shooting on several New Mexico ranches. Reese Witherspoon earned an Academy Award nomination for best actress for *Wild* (2015) based on the Cheryl Strayed memoir and directed by Jean-Marc Vallée. It was mostly set on the Pacific Coast Trail.

Arizona drug-war movie *Sicario* (2015) was directed by Denis Villeneuve and starred Emily Blunt, Benicio del Toro and Josh Brolin. In the same year, the sexually-charged thriller *Fifty Shades of Grey*, directed by Sam Taylor-Johnson, was set in Seattle.

Small Screen

The first TV station began broadcasting in Los Angeles in 1931. Through the following decades, iconic images of LA were beamed into living rooms across America in shows such as *Dragnet* (1950s), *The Beverly Hillbillies* (1960s), *The Brady Bunch* (1970s), *LA Law* (1980s), *Baywatch*, *Melrose Place* and *The Fresh Prince of Bel-Air* (1990s), through to teen 'dramedies' *Beverly Hills 90210* (1990s) and *The OC* (2000s), the latter set in Newport Beach, Orange County. Fans of reality TV will spot Southern California starring in everything from *Top Chef* to the *Real Housewives of Orange County*.

Southern California has also been a versatile backdrop for edgy cable-TV dramas, from Showtime's *Weeds*, about a pot-growing SoCal widow, to TNT's cop show *The Closer*, about homicide detectives in LA, and FX's *The Shield*, which fictionalized the City of Angels' police corruption.

But SoCal isn't the only TV backdrop. Former *X-Files* writer Vince Gilligan brought more of his off-beat brilliance to the small screen with *Breaking Bad* (2008–13), set and shot in sun-baked Albuquerque. Its prequel, *Better Call Saul*, debuted in 2015. Portland will never be the

---

Top Film Festivals

AFI Fest (www.afi.com/afifest)

Outfest (www.outfest.org)

San Francisco International Film Festival (www.sffs.org)

Sundance Film Festival (www.sundance.org/festival)

Telluride Film Festival (www.telluridefilmfestival.com)

Seattle International Film Festival (www.siff.net)

In Albuquerque, *Breaking Bad* fans can take a self-guided tour of locations that appeared in the series. Visit www.visitalbuquerque.org/albuquerque/film-tourism for an interactive map and details about locations.

same after *Portlandia*, a sketch comedy series (2011–present) on IFC that pokes fun of the cultural quirks of young urbanites.

Architecture

Westerners have adapted imported styles to the climate and available materials, building cool, adobe-inspired houses in Tucson and fog-resistant redwood-shingle houses in Mendocino.

Southwestern Styles

Regional influences rule the Southwest. First and foremost are the ruins of the Ancestral Puebloans – most majestically their cliff communities – and Taos Pueblo. These traditional designs and examples are echoed in the Pueblo Revival style of Santa Fe's New Mexico Museum of Art and are speckled across the city and the region today.

Adobe dominates many New Mexico cityscapes and landscapes while the mission-style architecture of the 17th and 18th centuries is visible in religious and municipal buildings such as Santa Fe's State Capitol.

Master architect Frank Lloyd Wright was also a presence in the Southwest, most specifically at Taliesin West in Scottsdale, AZ. More recently, Route 66's kitschy motels and neon signs are icons of the American road trip.

Spanish Missions & Victorian Queens

The first Spanish missions were built around courtyards, using materials that Native Americans and colonists found on hand: adobe, limestone and grass. Many missions crumbled into disrepair as the church's influence waned, but the style remained practical for the climate. Early California settlers later adapted it into the rancho adobe style, as seen at El Pueblo de Los Angeles and in San Diego's Old Town.

During the mid-19th-century gold rush, California's nouveau riche imported materials to construct grand mansions matching European fashions, and raised the stakes with ornamental excess. Many millionaires favored the gilded Queen Anne style. Outrageous examples of Victorian architecture, including 'Painted Ladies' and 'gingerbread' houses, can be found in such Northern California towns as San Francisco, Ferndale and Eureka.

Arts & Crafts and Art Deco

Simplicity was the hallmark of the Arts and Crafts style. Influenced by both Japanese design principles and England's Arts and Crafts movement, its woodwork and handmade touches marked a deliberate departure from the Industrial Revolution. SoCal architects Charles and Henry Greene and Bernard Maybeck in Northern California popularized the versatile one-story bungalow, which became trendy at the turn of the 20th century. Today you'll spot them in Pasadena and Berkeley with their overhanging eaves, terraces and sleeping porches harmonizing indoors and outdoors.

In the 1920s, the international art-deco style took elements from the ancient world – Mayan glyphs, Egyptian pillars, Babylonian ziggurats – and flattened them into modern motifs to cap stark facades and outline streamlined skyscrapers, notably in LA and downtown Oakland. Streamline moderne kept decoration to a minimum and mimicked the aerodynamic look of ocean liners and airplanes, as seen at LA's Union Station.

A few years later master architect Frank Lloyd Wright was designing homes in the Romanza style, following the principle that for every indoor space there's an outdoor space, and this flowing design is best exhibited in LA's Hollyhock House, constructed for heiress Alice Barnsdale. His

---

In 1915 newspaper magnate William Randolph Hearst commissioned California's first licensed female architect, Julia Morgan, to build his Hearst Castle – a mixed blessing, since the commission would take Morgan decades and require careful diplomacy through constant changes and a delicate balancing act among Hearst's preferred Spanish, Gothic and Greek styles.

Arts in Out-of-the-Way Places

Bisbee, AZ

Jerome, AZ

Aspen, CO

Park City, UT

Bellingham, WA

Mancos, CO

part-time home and studio in Scottsdale, AZ, Taliesin West, complements and showcases the surrounding desert landscape.

Postmodern Evolutions

Architectural styles have veered away from strict high modernism, and unlikely postmodern shapes have been added to the landscape. Richard Meier made his mark on West LA with the Getty Center, a cresting white wave of a building atop a sunburned hilltop. Canadian-born Frank Gehry relocated to Santa Monica. His billowing, sculptural style for LA's Walt Disney Concert Hall winks cheekily at shipshape Californian streamline moderne. Renzo Piano's signature inside-out industrial style can be glimpsed in the sawtooth roof and red-steel veins on the Broad Contemporary Art Museum extension of the Los Angeles County Museum of Art.

San Francisco has lately championed a brand of postmodernism by Pritzker Prize–winning architects that magnifies and mimics California's great outdoors, especially in Golden Gate Park. Swiss architects Herzog & de Meuron clad the MH de Young Memorial Museum in copper, which will eventually oxidize green to match its park setting. Nearby, Renzo Piano literally raised the roof on sustainable design at the LEED platinum-certified California Academy of Sciences, capped by a living garden.

Jim Heimann's *California Crazy & Beyond: Roadside Vernacular Architecture* (1980) is a romp through the zany, whimsical world of California, where lemonade stands look like giant lemons and motels are shaped like tipis.

Visual Arts

Although the earliest European artists were trained cartographers accompanying Western explorers, their images of California as an island show more imagination than scientific rigor. This mythologizing tendency continued throughout the gold-rush era, as Western artists alternated between caricatures of Wild West debauchery and manifest-destiny propaganda urging pioneers to settle the golden West. The completion of the transcontinental railroad in 1869 brought an influx of romantic painters, who produced epic California wilderness landscapes.

In the early 1900s, homegrown colonies of California impressionist plein-air painters emerged, particularly at Laguna Beach and Carmel-by-the-Sea. In the Southwest, Georgia O'Keeffe (1887–1986) painted stark Southwestern landscapes that are exhibited in museums throughout the world.

Photographer Pirkle Jones saw expressive potential in California landscape photography after WWII, while San Francisco native Ansel Adams' sublime photographs had already started doing justice to Yosemite. Adams founded Group f/64 with Edward Weston from Carmel and Imogen Cunningham in San Francisco. Berkeley-based Dorothea Lange turned her unflinching lens on the plight of Californian migrant workers in the Great Depression and Japanese Americans forced into internment camps in WWII.

Photography buffs can plan their California trip around the top-notch SFMOMA in northern California, where the superb collection runs from early Western daguerreotypes to experimental postwar Japanese photography.

As the postwar American West became crisscrossed with freeways and divided into planned communities, Californian painters captured the abstract forms of manufactured landscapes. In San Francisco, Richard Diebenkorn and David Park became leading proponents of Bay Area Figurative Art, while San Francisco sculptor Richard Serra captured urban aesthetics in massive, rusting monoliths resembling ship prows and industrial Stonehenges.

Pop artists captured the ethos of conspicuous consumerism, through Wayne Thiebaud's gumball machines, British émigré David Hockney's LA pools and, above all, Ed Ruscha's studies of SoCal pop culture. In San Francisco, artists showed their love for rough-and-readymade 1950s Beat collage, 1960s psychedelic Fillmore posters, earthy '70s funk and beautiful-mess punk, and '80s graffiti and skate culture.

Today's contemporary-art scene brings all these influences together with muralist-led social commentary, an obsessive dedication to craft and a new-media milieu that embraces cutting-edge technology.

The Land & Wildlife

Crashing tectonic plates, mighty floods, spewing volcanoes, frigid ice fields: for millions and millions of years, the American West was an altogether unpleasant place. But from this fire and ice sprang a kaleidoscopic array of stunning landscapes bound by a common modern trait: an undeniable ability to attract explorers, naturalists, artists and outdoor adventurers. Back in the late 19th century and early 20th century, the writings of activist John Muir helped frame the wilderness preservation movement of today.

The Land

As Western novelist and essayist Wallace Stegner noted in his book *Where the Bluebird Sings to the Lemonade Springs,* the West is home to a dozen or so distinct and unique subregions. Their one commonality? In Stegner's view it's the aridity. Aridity, he writes, sharpens the brilliance of the light and heightens the clarity of the air in most of the West. It also leads to fights over water rights, a historic and ongoing concern.

California

The third-largest state after Alaska and Texas, California covers more than 155,000 sq miles.

California claims both the highest point in the contiguous US (Mt Whitney; 14,505ft) and the lowest elevation in North America (Badwater, Death Valley; 282ft below sea level) – plus they're only 90 miles apart, as the condor flies.

Geology & Earthquakes

California is a complex geologic landscape formed from fragments of rock and earth crust scraped together as the North American continent has drifted westward over hundreds of millions of years. Crumpled coast ranges, the downward-bowing Central Valley and the still-rising Sierra Nevada are evidence of gigantic forces that have been exerted as the continental and ocean plates continue to crush together.

About 25 million years ago, the ocean plates stopped colliding and instead started sliding against each other, creating the massive San Andreas Fault. Because this contact zone doesn't slide smoothly, but catches and slips irregularly, it rattles California with an ongoing succession of tremors and earthquakes.

The state's most famous earthquake in 1906 measured 7.8 on the Richter scale and demolished San Francisco, leaving more than 3000 people dead. The Bay Area made headlines again in 1989 when the Loma Prieta earthquake (7.1) caused a section of the Bay Bridge to collapse. Los Angeles' last 'big one' was in 1994, when the Northridge quake (6.7) caused parts of the Santa Monica Fwy to fall down. With $44 billion in damages, it is the most costly quake in US history – so far.

The Coast to the Central Valley

Much of California's coast is fronted by rugged coastal mountains that capture winter's water-laden storms. San Francisco divides the Coast Ranges roughly in half, with the foggy North Coast remaining sparsely populated, while the Central and Southern California coasts have a balmier climate and many more people.

In the northernmost reaches of the Coast Ranges, nutrient-rich soils and abundant moisture foster forests of giant trees. On their eastern flanks, the Coast Ranges subside into gently rolling hills that give way to the 450-mile-long Central Valley, an agricultural powerhouse producing more than 230 different types of crops, from nuts to fruits and vegetables. The region produces one third of all produce grown in the United States.

Mountain Highs

On the eastern side of the Central Valley looms the world-famous Sierra Nevada. At 400 miles long and 50 miles wide, it's one of the largest mountain ranges in the world and is home to 13 peaks over 14,000ft. The vast wilderness of the High Sierra (lying mostly above 9000ft) presents an astounding landscape of glaciers, sculpted granite peaks and remote canyons. The soaring Sierra Nevada captures storm systems and their water, with most of the precipitation over 3000ft falling as snow. These waters eventually flow into half a dozen major river systems that provide the vast majority of water for San Francisco and LA as well as farms in the Central Valley.

The Deserts & Beyond

With the west slope of the Sierra Nevada capturing the lion's share of water, all lands east of the Sierra crest are dry and desertlike, receiving less than 10in of rain a year. Surprisingly, some valleys at the eastern foot of the Sierra Nevada are well watered by creeks and support a vigorous economy of livestock and agriculture.

Areas in the northern half of California, especially on the elevated Modoc Plateau of northeastern California, are a cold desert at the western edge of the Great Basin, blanketed with hardy sagebrush shrubs and pockets of juniper trees. Temperatures increase as you head south, with a prominent transition as you descend from Mono Lake into the Owens Valley east of the Sierra Nevada. This southern hot desert (part of the Mojave Desert) includes Death Valley, one of the hottest places on earth.

The Southwest

Extremely ancient rocks (among the oldest on the planet) exposed in the deep heart of the Grand Canyon show that the region was under water two billion years ago. Younger layers of rocks in southern Utah reveal that this region was continuously or periodically under water. About 286 million years ago, near the end of the Paleozoic era, a collision of continents into a massive landmass known as Pangaea deformed the earth's crust and produced pressures that uplifted the ancestral Rocky Mountains. Though this early mountain range lay to the east, it formed rivers and sediment deposits that began to shape the Southwest.

Around 60 million years ago North America underwent a dramatic separation from Europe, sliding westward over a piece of the earth's crust known as the East Pacific Plate and leaving behind an ever-widening gulf that became the Atlantic Ocean. The East Pacific Plate collided with the North American Plate. This collision, named the Laramide Orogeny, resulted in the birth of the modern Rocky Mountains and uplifted an old basin into a highland known today as the Colorado Plateau. Fragments of the East Pacific Plate also attached themselves to the leading edge of the North American Plate, transforming the Southwest from a coastal area to an interior region increasingly detached from the ocean.

In contrast to the compression and collision that characterized earlier events, the earth's crust began stretching in an east–west direction about

On the evening of July 5, 2011, a mile-high dust storm with an estimated 100-mile width enveloped Phoenix after reaching speeds of more than 50mph. Visibility dropped to between zero and one-quarter of a mile. There were power outages and Phoenix International Airport temporarily closed.

30 million years ago. The thinner, stretched crust of New Mexico and Texas cracked along zones of weakness called faults, resulting in a rift valley where New Mexico's Rio Grande now flows. These same forces created the stepped plateaus of northern Arizona and southern Utah.

During the Pleistocene glacial period, large bodies of water accumulated throughout the Southwest. Utah's Great Salt Lake is the most famous remnant of these mighty ice-age lakes. Basins with now completely dry, salt-crusted lakebeds are especially conspicuous on a drive across Nevada.

For the past several million years the dominant force has probably been erosion. Not only do torrential rainstorms readily tear through soft sedimentary rocks, but also the rise of the Rocky Mountains generates large, powerful rivers that wind throughout the Southwest, carving mighty canyons in their wake. Nearly all of the contemporary features in the Southwest, from arches (Arches National Park has more than 2000 sandstone arches) to hoodoos, are the result of weathering and erosion.

Edward Abbey shares his desert philosophy and insights in his classic *Desert Solitaire: A Season in the Wilderness*, a must-read for desert enthusiasts and conservationists.

Geographic Makeup

The Colorado Plateau is an impressive and nearly impenetrable 130,000-sq-mile tableland lurking in the corner where Colorado, Utah, Arizona and New Mexico join. Formed in an ancient basin as a remarkably coherent body of neatly layered sedimentary rocks, the plateau has remained relatively unchanged even as the lands around it were compressed, stretched and deformed by powerful forces.

Perhaps the most powerful testament to the plateau's long-term stability are the precise layers of sedimentary rock stretching back two billion years. In fact, the science of stratigraphy – the reading of earth history through its rock layers – stemmed from work at the Grand Canyon, where an astonishing set of layers have been laid bare by the Colorado River cutting across them. Throughout the Southwest, particularly on the Colorado Plateau, layers of sedimentary rock detail a rich history of ancient oceans, coastal mudflats and arid dunes.

Landscape Features

The Southwest is jam-packed with remarkable rock formations. One reason for this is that the region's many sedimentary layers are so soft that rain and erosion readily carve them into fantastic shapes. But not any old rain; it has to be hard, fairly sporadic rain, as frequent rain would wash the formations away. Between rains there have to be long arid spells that keep the eroding landmarks intact. The range of colors derives from the unique mineral composition of each rock type.

Pages of Stone: Geology of the Grand Canyon & Plateau Country National Parks & Monuments by Halka and Lucy Chronic (1988) provides an excellent introduction to the Southwest's diverse landscape.

Geology of the Grand Canyon

Arizona's Grand Canyon is the best-known geologic feature in the Southwest and for good reason: not only is it on a scale so massive it dwarfs the human imagination, but it also records two billion years of geologic history – a huge amount of time considering the earth is just 4.6 billion years old. The canyon itself, however, is young, a mere five to six million years old.

Carved by the powerful Colorado River as the land bulged upward, the 277-mile-long canyon reflects the differing hardness of the 10-plus layers of rocks in its walls. Shales, for instance, crumble easily and form slopes, while resistant limestones and sandstones form distinctive cliffs.

The layers making up the bulk of the canyon walls were laid during the Paleozoic era, 542 to 251 million years ago. These formations perch atop a group of one- to two-billion-year-old rocks lying at the bottom of the inner gorge of the canyon. Between these two distinct sets of rock is the Great Unconformity, a several-hundred-million-year gap in the geologic record where erosion erased 12,000ft of rock and left a huge mystery.

Pacific Northwest

From 16 to 13 million years ago, eastern Oregon and Washington witnessed one of the premier episodes of volcanic activity in Earth's history. Due to shifting stresses in the earth's crust, much of interior western North America began cracking along thousands of lines and releasing enormous amounts of lava that flooded over the landscape. On multiple occasions, so much lava was produced that it filled the Columbia River channel and reached the Oregon coast, forming prominent headlands like Cape Lookout. Today, the hardened lava flows of eastern Oregon

PLANTS OF THE WEST

The presence of many large mountain ranges in the West creates a remarkable diversity of niches for plants. One way to understand the plants of this region is to understand life zones and the ways each plant thrives in its favored zone.

In the Southwest, at the lowest elevations, generally below 4000ft, high temperatures and a lack of water create a desert zone where drought-tolerant plants such as cacti, sagebrush and agave survive. Many of these species have small leaves or minimal leaf surface area to reduce water loss, or hold water like a cactus to survive long hot spells.

At mid-elevations, from 4000ft to 7000ft, conditions cool a bit and more moisture is available for woody shrubs and small trees. In much of Nevada, Utah, northern Arizona and New Mexico, piñon pines and junipers blanket vast areas of low mountain slopes and hills. Both trees are short and stout to help conserve water.

Nearly pure stands of stately, fragrant ponderosa pine are the dominant tree at 7000ft on many of the West's mountain ranges. In fact, this single tree best defines the Western landscape and many animals rely on it for food and shelter; timber companies also consider it their most profitable tree. High mountain, or boreal, forests composed of spruce, fir, quaking aspen and a few other conifers are found on the highest peaks in the Southwest. This is a land of cool, moist forests and lush meadows with brilliant wildflower displays.

Incredibly diverse flowers appear each year in the Southwest's deserts and mountains. These include desert flowers that start blooming in February, and late-summer flowers that fill mountain meadows after the snow melts or pop out after summer thunderstorms wet the soil. Some of the largest and grandest flowers belong to the Southwest's 100 or so species of cacti.

Southern California's desert areas begin their peak blooming in March, with other lowland areas of the state producing abundant wildflowers in April. As snows melt later at higher elevations in the Sierra Nevada, Yosemite National Park's Tuolumne Meadows is another prime spot for wildflower walks and photography, with peak blooms usually in late June or early July.

In the Pacific Northwest, the wet and wild west side of the Cascade Range captures most rain clouds coming in from the ocean, relieving them of their moisture and creating humid forests full of green life jostling for space. The dry, deserty east side – robbed of rains by the tall Cascades – is mostly home to sagebrush and other semiarid-loving vegetation, although there are lush pockets here and there, especially along the mountain foothills.

When it comes to trees, California is a land of superlatives: the tallest (coast redwoods approaching 380ft), the largest (giant sequoias of the Sierra Nevada over 36ft across at the base) and the oldest (bristlecone pines of the White Mountains that are almost 5000 years old). The giant sequoia, which is unique to California, survives in isolated groves scattered on the Sierra Nevada's western slopes, including in Yosemite, Sequoia and Kings Canyon National Parks.

and Washington are easily seen in spectacular rimrock cliffs and flat-top mesas.

Not to be outdone, the ice ages of the past two million years created a massive ice field from Washington to British Columbia – and virtually every mountain range in the rest of the region was blanketed by glaciers.

Wildlife

Although the staggering numbers of animals that greeted the first European settlers are now a thing of the past, it is still possible to see wildlife thriving in the West in the right places and at the right times of year.

Many of the Southwest's common flowers can be found in *Canyon Country Wildflowers* by Damian Fagan, 1998.

Reptiles & Amphibians

On a spring evening, canyons in the Southwest may fairly reverberate with the calls of canyon tree frogs or red-spotted toads. With the rising sun, these are replaced by several dozen species of lizards and snakes that roam among rocks and shrubs. Blue-bellied fence lizards are particularly abundant in the region's parks, but visitors can always hope to encounter a rarity such as the strange and venomous Gila monster. Equally fascinating are the Southwest's many colorful rattlesnakes. Quick to anger and able to deliver a painful or toxic bite, rattlesnakes are placid and retiring if left alone.

Birds

Migrations

There are so many interesting birds in the Southwest – home to 400 species – that it's the foremost reason many people travel to the region. Springtime is a particularly rewarding time for bird-watching here as songbirds arrive from their southern wintering grounds and begin singing from every nook and cranny. In the fall, sandhill cranes and snow geese travel in long skeins down the Rio Grande Valley to winter at the Bosque del Apache National Wildlife Refuge. The Great Salt Lake in Utah is one of North America's premier sites for migrating birds, including millions of ducks and grebes stopping each fall to feed before continuing south.

California lies on major migratory routes for more than 350 species of birds, which either pass through the state or linger through the winter. This is one of the top birding destinations in North America. Witness, for example, the congregation of one million ducks, geese and swans at the Klamath Basin National Wildlife Refuge Complex every November. During winter, these waterbirds head south into the refuges of the Central Valley, another area to observe huge numbers of native and migratory species.

A fully hydrated giant saguaro can store more than a ton of water. Saguaros grow slowly, taking 50 years to reach 7ft. Not only is it illegal to shoot them in Arizona, it is also dangerous. In 1982 a vandal shot the arm off a 27ft tall saguaro. The arm fell on the shooter and crushed him to death.

California Condors & Bald Eagles

With a 9ft wingspan, the California condor looks more like a prehistoric pterodactyl than any bird you've ever seen. Pushed to the brink of extinction, these unusual birds – which fed on the carcasses of mastodons and saber-toothed cats in prehistoric days – are staging a minor comeback at the Grand Canyon. After several decades in which no condors lived in the wild, a few pairs are now nesting on the canyon rim. The best bet for spotting them is Arizona's Vermilion Cliffs. In California, look skyward as you drive along the Big Sur coast or at Pinnacles National Monument.

The Pacific Northwest is a stronghold for bald eagles, which feast on the annual salmon runs and nest in old-growth forests. With a 7.5ft wingspan, these impressive birds gather in huge numbers in places like Washington's Upper Skagit Bald Eagle Area and the national wildlife refuges in the Klamath Basin region in northern California and southern Oregon. In California, bald eagles have regained a foothold on the Channel Islands, and they sometimes spend winter at Big Bear Lake near LA. At their low point, only two or three breeding pairs nested in Colorado, but that number has increased by eight or nine each year, and in 2015 there were about 125 nests there. Rebounding from pesticide threats, the nationwide bald eagle population has grown to an estimated 143,000.

Mammals

Many of the West's most charismatic wildlife species – grizzlies, buffalo, prairie dogs – were largely exterminated by the early 1900s. Fortunately, there are plenty of other mammals still wandering the forests and deserts. At the very least, if you keep your eyes open, you'll see some mule deer or a coyote. Wintertime can be a good time to spot tracks in the snow.

An estimated nine million free-tailed bats once roosted in Carlsbad Caverns. Though reduced in recent years, the evening flight is still one of the premier wildlife spectacles in North America.

Bears

The black bear is probably the most notorious animal in the Rockies. Adult males weigh from 275lb to 450lb; females weigh about 175lb to 250lb. They measure 3ft high on all fours and can be over 5ft when standing on their hind legs.

Black bears also roam the Pacific Northwest, the Southwest and California. They feed on berries, nuts, roots, grasses, insects, eggs, small mammals and fish, but can become a nuisance around campgrounds and mountain cabins where food is not stored properly.

The grizzly bear, which can be seen on California's state flag, once roamed California's beaches and grasslands in large numbers, eating everything from whale carcasses to acorns. Grizzlies were particularly abundant in the Central Valley. The grizzly was extirpated in the early 1900s after relentless persecution. Grizzlies are classified as an endangered species in Colorado, but they are almost certainly gone from the state; the last documented grizzly in Colorado was killed in 1979. In 2016, scientists estimated there were between 674 and 839 grizzlies wandering the Yellowstone National Park area. A recent study suggests that the introduction of wolves to Yellowstone may be helping the grizzly population there – wolves eat elk, leaving more berries for the grizzlies.

California's mountain forests are home to an estimated 25,000 to 30,000 black bears, whose fur actually ranges in color from black to dark brown, cinnamon and even blond.

Elk

More than 3000 elk roam across Rocky Mountain National Park, with a resident winter herd of 600 to 800. Mature elk bulls may reach 1100lb, and cows weigh up to 600lb. Both have dark necks with light tan bodies. Like bighorn sheep, elk were virtually extinct around Estes Park by 1890, wiped out by hunters. In 1913 and 1914, before the establishment of the park, people from Estes Park brought in 49 elk from Yellowstone. The population increase since the establishment of Rocky Mountain National Park is one of the National Park Service's great successes.

Among the Pacific Northwest's signature animals is the Roosevelt elk, whose eerie bugling courtship calls can be heard each September and October in forested areas throughout the region. Full-grown males may reach 1100lb and carry 5ft racks of antlers. During winter, large groups gather in lowland valleys and can be observed along the Spirit Lake Memorial Highway in Mt St Helens National Volcanic Monument. Olympic National Park is home to the largest unmanaged herd of Roosevelt elk in the Pacific Northwest.

Bighorn Sheep

Rocky Mountain National Park is a special place: 'Bighorn Crossing Zone' is a sign you're unlikely to encounter anywhere else. From late spring through summer, groups of up to 60 sheep – typically only ewes and lambs – move from the moraine ridge north of the highway across the road to Sheep Lakes in Horseshoe Park. Unlike the big under-curving horns on mature rams, ewes grow swept-back crescent-shaped horns that reach only about 10in in length. The Sheep Lakes are evaporative ponds ringed with tasty salt deposits that attract the ewes in the morning and early afternoon after lambing in May and June. In August they rejoin the rams in the Mummy Range.

Pronghorn Antelope

The open plains of eastern Oregon and Washington are the playing grounds of pronghorn antelope, curious-looking deer-like animals with two single black horns instead of antlers. Pronghorns belong to a unique antelope family and are only found in the American West, but they are more famous for being able to run up to 60mph for long stretches – they're the second-fastest land animal in the world.

Environmental Issues

Growth in the West comes with costs. In the Pacific Northwest, the production of cheap hydroelectricity and massive irrigation projects along the Columbia have led to the near-irreversible destruction of the river's ecosystem. Dams have all but eliminated most runs of native salmon and have further disrupted the lives of remaining Native Americans who depend on the river. Logging of old-growth forests has left ugly scars. Washington's Puget Sound area and Portland's extensive suburbs are groaning under the weight of rapidly growing population centers.

Ongoing controversies include arguments about the locations of nuclear power plants and the transport and disposal of nuclear waste in the Southwest, notably at Yucca Mountain, 90 miles from Las Vegas. Fracking, an aggressive practice of extracting oil and gas through hydraulic fracturing, has taken hold of much of the West, supplying economic minibooms in areas formerly depressed but also setting off environmental problems ranging from compromised water tables to a fatality from an exploding home in Colorado.

Water distribution and availability continue to be concerns throughout the region. In an arid landscape like the Southwest, many of the region's most important environmental issues revolve around water. Drought has so severely impacted the region that researchers have warned that 110-mile-long Lake Mead has a 50% chance of running dry by 2021, leaving an estimated 12 to 36 million people in cities from Las Vegas to Los Angeles and San Diego in need of water.

Construction of dams and human-made water features throughout the Southwest has radically altered the delicate balance of water that sustained life for countless millennia. Dams, for example, halt the flow of warm waters and force them to drop their rich loads of life-giving nutrients. These sediments once rebuilt floodplains, nourished myriad aquatic and riparian food chains, and sustained the life of ancient endemic fish that now flounder on the edge of extinction. In place of rich annual floods, dams now release cold waters in steady flows that favor the introduced fish and weedy plants that have overtaken the West's rivers. The plan to remove four dams on the Klamath River in Oregon and California, slated for completion by 2020, bucks this trend and may set a precedent for other rivers. As the largest river restoration in US history, it will bring back fish passage and water quality.

Read Marc Reisner's *Cadillac Desert: The American West and Its Disappearing Water* (1993) for a thorough account of how exploding populations in the West have utilized every drop of available water.

A report published by the National Academy of Sciences in 2016 states that human-caused climate change is behind the exponential increase in wildfires in the Western US. The report finds the threat to be greatest in the Northwest, including Idaho, Wyoming, Montana, eastern Oregon and eastern Washington.

Records show that regional temperatures have increased while snowpack has decreased. Rising sea levels and drier forests bring layered consequences to human activity and whole ecosystems. With the United States' exit from the Paris Climate Accord in 2017, many states (including Washington, California and Oregon) as well as cities (including LA, Seattle and Denver) are forging ahead to keep the commitments of the agreement for the sake of their own futures.

Salmon-conservation efforts include protecting populations around the entire Pacific Rim from the Russian Far East to northern California. Learn more at www.wildsalmoncenter.org.

Survival Guide

Directory A–Z

Accommodations

Western USA has lodging options for all budgets and tastes. It's advisable to book well in advance for visits during the summer months, school holiday weeks and ski-resort destinations. For the most popular national parks, it's not unusual to book a year out.

➡ **Hotels** Hotels range from the humble motel to luxury lodges – with a wide range in prices.

➡ **B&Bs** Usually in the midrange, inviting homes offer a higher level of interaction and personal attention.

➡ **Camping** From paying campgrounds with tent and RV spots and basic amenities to primitive sites, America loves its outdoor living.

Discounts

➡ Discount cards and auto-club membership may get you 10% or more off standard rates at participating hotels and motels.

➡ Look for freebie ad magazines packed with hotel and motel discount coupons at gas stations, travel centers, highway rest areas and tourist offices.

➡ Bargaining may be possible for walk-in guests without reservations, especially during off-peak times.

B&Bs

➡ In the USA, many B&Bs are high-end romantic retreats in restored historic homes that are run by personable, independent innkeepers who serve gourmet breakfasts. These B&Bs often take pains to evoke a theme – Victorian, rustic, Cape Cod – and amenities range from merely comfortable to indulgent. Rates normally top $100, and the best run $200 to $300. Some B&Bs have minimum-stay requirements, some exclude children and many exclude pets.

➡ European-style B&Bs also exist: they may be rooms in someone's home, with plainer furnishings, simpler breakfasts, shared baths and

cheaper rates. These often welcome families.

➡ B&Bs can close out of season and reservations are essential, especially for top-end places. To avoid surprises, always ask about bathrooms (whether shared or private).

Camping

FEDERAL & STATE PARKS

Most federally managed public lands and many state parks offer camping.

➡ First-come, first-served 'primitive' campsites offer no facilities; overnight fees range from free to under $12.

➡ 'Basic' sites usually provide toilets (flush or pit), drinking water, fire pits and picnic tables; they cost $5 to $16 a night, and some or all may be reserved in advance.

➡ 'Developed' campsites, usually in national or state parks, have nicer facilities and more amenities: showers, barbecue grills, RV sites with hookups etc. These run about $15 to $55 a night, and many can be reserved in advance.

Camping on most federal lands – including national parks, national forests, Bureau of Land Management (BLM) and so on – can be reserved through Recreation. gov. Camping is usually limited to 14 days and can be reserved up to six months in advance. For some state-park campgrounds, you can make bookings through ReserveAmerica (www.reserveamerica.com). Both websites let you search for campground locations and amenities, check availability and reserve a site, view maps and get driving directions online.

PRIVATE CAMPGROUNDS

➡ Private campgrounds are usually more expensive and tend to cater to RVs and families (tent sites may be few and lack atmosphere).

➡ Facilities may include playgrounds, convenience stores, wi-fi access, swimming pools and other activities.

➡ Some rent camping cabins, ranging from canvas-sided wooden platforms to log-frame structures with real beds, heating and private baths.

➡ Kampgrounds of America (www.koa.com) is a national network of private campgrounds with a full range of facilities. You can order KOA's free annual directory (shipping fees apply) or browse its comprehensive campground listings and make bookings online.

Dude Ranches

➡ Most dude-ranch visitors today are urbanites looking for an escape from a fast-paced, high-tech world. These days you can find anything from a working-ranch experience (smelly chores and 5am wake-up calls included) to lavish resorts.

➡ Typical week-long visits start at over $120 per person per day, including accommodations, meals, activities and equipment.

➡ While the centerpiece of dude-ranch vacations is horseback riding, many ranches feature swimming pools and have expanded their activity lists to include fly-fishing, hiking, mountain biking, tennis, golf, skeet-shooting and cross-country skiing.

➡ Accommodations range from rustic log cabins to cushy suites with Jacuzzis and cable TV. Meals range from family-style spaghetti dinners to four-course gourmet feasts.

➡ For information, contact the **Dude Ranchers' Association** (307-587-2339; www.duderanch.org).

Hostels

➡ In the West, hostels are mainly found in urban areas in the Pacific Northwest, California and the Southwest.

➡ In some large cities certain hostels attract itinerant workers and tend to remain full with long-term stays.

➡ **Hostelling International USA** (240-650-2100; www.hiusa.org) runs more than 50 hostels in the US; 18 of them are in California. Most have gender-segregated dorms, a few private rooms, shared baths and a communal kitchen. Overnight fees for dorm beds range from about $29 to $55. HI-USA members are entitled to small discounts. Reservations are accepted (you can book online) and advisable during high season, when there may be a three-night maximum stay.

Hotels

➡ Hotels in all categories typically include in-room phones, cable TV, alarm clocks, private baths and a simple continental breakfast.

➡ Many midrange properties provide microwaves, minifridges, hairdryers, internet access, air-conditioning and/or heating, swimming pools and writing desks.

➡ Top-end hotels add concierge services, fitness and business centers, spas, restaurants, bars and higher-end furnishings.

➡ Even if hotels advertise that children 'sleep free,' cots or rollaway beds may cost extra.

➡ Always ask about the hotel's policy for telephone calls; all charge an exorbitant amount for long-distance and international calls, but some also charge for dialing local and toll-free numbers.

Lodges

Normally situated within national parks, lodges are often rustic looking but are usually quite comfy inside. Standard rooms start around $100, but can easily be double that or more in high season. Since they represent the only option if you want to stay inside the park without camping, many are fully booked well in advance. Want a room today? Call anyway – you might be lucky and hit on a cancellation. In addition to on-site restaurants, they often offer touring services.

Motels

Luxury resorts really require a stay of several days to be appreciated and are often destinations in themselves. Start the day with a round of golf or a tennis match, then luxuriate with a massage, swimming, sunbathing and drinking. Many are kid

SLEEPING PRICE RANGES

The following price ranges do not include taxes, which average more than 10%, unless otherwise noted.

$	less than $100
$$	$100–$250
$$$	more than $250

PRACTICALITIES

Newspapers & Magazines

➡ National newspapers: *New York Times*, *Wall Street Journal*, *USA Today*

➡ Western newspapers: *Arizona Republic*, *Denver Post*, *Seattle Times*, *Los Angeles Times*, *San Francisco Chronicle*

➡ Mainstream news magazines: *Time*, *US News & World Report*

Radio & TV

➡ Radio news: National Public Radio (NPR), lower end of FM dial

➡ Broadcast TV: ABC, CBS, NBC, FOX, PBS (public broadcasting)

➡ Major cable channels: CNN (news), ESPN (sports), HBO (movies & TV), Weather Channel

Weights & Measures

➡ Weight: ounces (oz), pounds (lb), tons

➡ Liquid: ounces (oz), pints, quarts, gallons

➡ Distance: feet (ft), yards (yd), miles (mi)

Video Systems

➡ DVDs coded for Region 1 (US and Canada only)

friendly, with extensive children's programs.

Resorts

Luxury resorts really require a stay of several days to be appreciated and are often destinations in themselves. Start the day with a round of golf or a tennis match, then luxuriate with a massage, swimming, sunbathing and drinking. Many are kid friendly, with extensive children's programs.

Customs Regulations

For a complete and current list of US customs regulations, visit the official portal for US Customs and Border Protection (www.cbp.gov).

Duty-free allowance per person is typically as follows:

➡ 1L of liquor (provided you are at least 21 years old)

➡ 100 cigars and 200 cigarettes (if you are at least 18)

➡ $200 worth of gifts and purchases ($800 if a returning US citizen)

➡ If you arrive with $10,000 or more in US or foreign currency, it must be declared.

There are heavy penalties for attempting to import illegal drugs. Other forbidden items include drug paraphernalia, firearms, lottery tickets, items with fake brand names, and most goods made in Iran, Myanmar (Burma), North Korea and parts of Sudan. Any fruit, vegetables or other food or plant material must be declared (whereby you'll undergo a time-consuming search) or left in the bins in the arrival area.

Discount Cards

America the Beautiful Interagency Annual Pass (www.nps. gov/findapark/passes.htm; store. usgs.gov/pass) This $80 pass admits the driver and all passengers in a single, non-commercial vehicle, or four adults aged 16 or older to all national parks and federal recreational lands (eg USFS, BLM) for one year. Children aged 15 and younger are admitted free. The pass can be purchased online or at any national park entrance station. US citizens and permanent residents 62 years and older are eligible for a lifetime Senior Pass ($10), which grants free entry and 50% off some recreational-use fees like camping, as does the lifetime Access Pass (free to US citizens or permanent residents with a permanent disability). These passes are available in person or by mail. A free annual US Military Pass for current members of the US armed forces and their dependents is available at recreation sites with Common Access card or Military ID (Form 1173).

American Association of Retired Persons (www.aarp.org) This advocacy group for Americans 50 years and older offers member discounts on hotels (usually 10%), car rentals and more. People over the age of 65 (sometimes 55, 60 or 62) often qualify for the same discounts as students; any ID showing your birth date should suffice as proof of age.

American Automobile Association (www.aaa.com) Members of AAA and its foreign affiliates (eg CAA, AA) qualify for small discounts on Amtrak trains, car rentals, motels and hotels (usually 5% to 15%), chain restaurants, shopping, tours and theme parks.

International Student Identity Card (www.isic.org; $26) Offers savings on airline fares, travel insurance and local attractions for full-time students. For nonstudents under 31 years of age, an International Youth Travel Card ($26) grants similar benefits. Cards are issued by student unions, hosteling organizations and travel agencies.

Student Advantage Card (www. studentadvantage.com) For

international and US students, this card offers 10% savings on Amtrak and 20% on Greyhound, plus discounts at some chain shops and car rentals.

Electricity

**Type A
120V/60Hz**

Emergency	☑911
National Sexual Assault Hotline	☑800-656-4673
Directory assistance	☑411
Statewide road conditions	☑511

Etiquette

Greeting It's common for Americans to hug everyone, including strangers, but if you're in doubt, shake hands.

Smoking Don't assume you can smoke – even if you're outside. Most Americans have little tolerance for smokers and have even banned smoking from many parks, boardwalks and beaches.

Punctuality Do be on time. Many folks in the US consider it rude to be kept waiting.

Smiling Americans smile a lot; doing the same and having a cheerful attitude will help break the ice.

Gay & Lesbian Travelers

LGBTIQ travelers will find lots of places where they can be themselves without thinking twice. Beaches and big cities typically are the most gay-friendly destinations.

Hot Spots

You will have heard of San Francisco, the happiest gay city in America, and what can gays and lesbians do in Los Angeles and Las Vegas? Hmmm, just about anything. In fact, when LA or Vegas gets to be too much, flee to the desert resorts of Palm Springs.

Attitudes

Most major US cities have a visible and open LGBTIQ community.

The level of acceptance varies across the West. In some places, there is abso-

lutely no tolerance whatsoever, and in others acceptance is predicated on LGBTIQ people not 'flaunting' their sexual preference or identity. In rural areas and extremely conservative enclaves, it's unwise to be openly out, as violence and verbal abuse can sometimes occur. When in doubt, assume locals follow a 'don't ask, don't tell' policy.

After a 2015 US Supreme Court decision, same-sex marriage is now legal in all 50 states.

Resources

Advocate (www.advocate.com) Gay-oriented news website reports on business, politics, arts, entertainment and travel.

Gay Travel (www.gaytravel.com) Online guides to US destinations.

GLBT National Help Center (www.glbthotline.org) A national hotline for counseling, information and referrals.

National LGBTQ Task Force (www.thetaskforce.org) National activist group's website covers news, politics and current issues.

OutTraveler (www.outtraveler. com) Has useful online city guides and travel articles to various US and foreign destinations.

Purple Roofs (www.purpleroofs. com) Lists gay-owned and gay-friendly B&Bs and hotels nationwide.

Health

Health Insurance

The USA offers excellent health care. The problem is that, unless you have good insurance, it is prohibitively expensive. It's *essential* to purchase travel health insurance if your regular policy doesn't cover you when you're abroad. Even with insurance, you will probably have to pay out of pocket for treatment and then chase up reimbursement afterwards.

➡ Overseas visitors with travel health-insurance policies may need to

Embassies & Consulates

International travelers who want to contact their home country's embassy while in the US should visit www.embassy.org, which lists contact information for all foreign embassies in Washington, DC. On the West Coast some countries have consulates in LA; look under 'Consulates' in the yellow pages, or call local directory assistance.

Emergency & Important Numbers

To call any regular number, dial the area code, followed by the seven-digit number.

USA country code	☑1
International access code	☑011

WHAT'S THE BLM?

The Bureau of Land Management (www.blm.gov) is a Department of Energy agency that oversees more than 245 million surface acres of public land, much of it in the West. It manages its resources for a variety of uses, from energy production to cattle grazing to overseeing recreational opportunities.

What does that mean for you? Outdoor fun, as well as both developed camping and dispersed camping. Generally, when it comes to dispersed camping on BLM land, you can camp wherever you want as long as your campsite is several hundred feet from a water source used by wildlife or livestock (distance varies by region, from 300ft to 900ft). You cannot camp in one spot longer than 14 days. Pack out what you pack in and don't leave campfires unattended. Some regions may have more specific rules, so check the state's camping requirements on the BLM website and call the appropriate district office for specifics.

contact a call center for an assessment by phone before getting medical treatment.

➡ Keep all receipts and documentation for billing and insurance claims and reimbursement purposes.

➡ If you plan on doing any adventure sports (skiing, diving etc), check to make sure insurance covers this – some policies specifically exclude 'extreme' activities.

Vaccinations

There are no required vaccines to visit the United States.

Availability & Cost of Health Care

➡ Medical treatment in the USA is of the highest caliber, but the expense could kill you. Many healthcare professionals demand payment at the time of service, especially from out-of-towners or international visitors.

➡ Except for medical emergencies (call 911 or go to the nearest 24-hour hospital emergency room, or ER), phone around to find a doctor who will accept your insurance.

➡ Some health-insurance policies require you to get pre-authorization for medical treatment before seeking help.

➡ Carry any medications you may need in their original containers, clearly labeled.

Bring a signed, dated letter from your doctor describing all medical conditions and medications (including generic names).

Environmental Hazards
ALTITUDE SICKNESS

➡ Visitors from lower elevations undergo rather dramatic physiological changes as they adapt to high altitudes.

➡ Symptoms, which tend to manifest during the first day after reaching altitude, may include headache, fatigue, loss of appetite, nausea, sleeplessness, increased urination and hyperventilation due to overexertion.

➡ Symptoms normally resolve within 24 to 48 hours.

➡ The rule of thumb: don't ascend until the symptoms descend.

➡ More severe cases may display extreme disorientation, ataxia (loss of coordination and balance), breathing problems (especially a persistent cough) and vomiting. These folks should descend immediately and get to a hospital.

➡ To avoid the discomfort characterizing the milder symptoms, drink plenty of water and take it easy – at 7000ft, a pleasant walk around Santa Fe can wear

you out faster than a steep hike at sea level.

DEHYDRATION, HEAT EXHAUSTION & HEATSTROKE

➡ Take it easy as you acclimatize, especially on hot summer days and in the desert.

➡ Drink plenty of water. One gallon per person per day minimum is recommended when you're active outdoors.

➡ Dehydration (lack of water) or salt deficiency can cause heat exhaustion, often characterized by heavy sweating, pale skin, fatigue, lethargy, headaches, nausea, vomiting, dizziness, muscle cramps and rapid, shallow breathing.

➡ Long, continuous exposure to high temperatures can lead to possibly fatal heatstroke. Warning signs include altered mental status, hyperventilation and flushed, hot and dry skin (ie sweating stops). Hospitalization is essential. Meanwhile, get out of the sun, remove clothing that retains heat (cotton is OK), douse the body with water and fan continuously; ice packs can be applied to the neck, armpits and groin.

HYPOTHERMIA

➡ Skiers and hikers will find that temperatures in the mountains and desert can quickly drop below freezing, especially during winter or if you are canyoneering. Even a sudden spring shower or high winds can lower your body temperature dangerously fast.

➡ Instead of cotton, wear synthetic or woolen clothing that retains warmth even when wet. Carry waterproof layers (eg Gore-Tex jacket, plastic poncho, rain pants) and high-energy, easily digestible snacks like chocolate, nuts and dried fruit.

➡ Symptoms of hypothermia include exhaustion, numbness, shivering, stumbling, slurred speech, dizzy spells, muscle cramps and irrational or even violent behavior.

➡ To treat hypothermia, get out of bad weather and change into dry, warm clothing. Drink hot liquids (no caffeine or alcohol) and snack on high-calorie food.

➡ In advanced stages, carefully put hypothermia sufferers in a warm sleeping bag cocooned inside a wind- and waterproof outer wrapping. Do not rub victims, who must be handled gently.

Tap Water
You can drink tap water in the US.

Insurance

Getting travel insurance to cover theft, loss and medical problems is highly recommended.

➡ Some policies do not cover 'risky' activities such as scuba diving, motorcycling and skiing, so read the fine print. Make sure the policy at least covers hospital stays and an emergency flight home.

➡ Paying for your airline ticket or rental car with a credit card may provide limited travel accident insurance.

➡ If you already have private health insurance or

---

a homeowner's or renter's policy, it is critical to find out what those policies cover and get supplemental insurance. You do not want to have a medical emergency in the US and then find you are not covered – the costs for even minor treatments are often astronomical.

➡ If you have prepaid a large portion of your vacation, trip cancellation insurance may be a worthwhile expense.

➡ Worldwide travel insurance is available at www.lonelyplanet.com/travel-insurance. You can buy, extend and claim online anytime – even if you're already on the road.

Internet Access

➡ Travelers will have few problems staying connected in tech-savvy USA.

Most hotels, guesthouses, hostels and motels have wi-fi (usually free, though luxury hotels are more likely to charge for access); ask when reserving.

➡ Across the US, most cafes offer free wi-fi. Some cities have wi-fi-connected parks and plazas, and the public library is always a good standby. If you're not packing a laptop or other web-capable device, try the library – most have public terminals (though they have time limits) in addition to wi-fi.

➡ If you're not from the US, remember that you will need an AC adapter for your laptop, plus a plug adapter for US sockets; both are available at larger electronics shops, such as Best Buy.

Legal Matters

In everyday matters, if you are stopped by the police, remember that there is no system for paying traffic or other fines on the spot. Attempting to pay a fine to an officer is frowned upon at best and may result in a charge of bribery. For traffic offenses, the police officer or highway patroller will explain the options to you. There is usually a 30-day period to pay a fine. Most matters can be handled by mail.

If you are arrested, you have a legal right to an attorney and you are allowed to remain silent. There is no legal reason to speak to a police officer if you don't wish, but never walk away from an officer until given permission to do so.

Anyone who is arrested is legally allowed to make one phone call. If you can't afford a lawyer, a public defender will be appointed to you free of charge. Foreign visitors who don't have a lawyer, friend or family member to help should call their embassy; the police will provide the number upon request.

As a matter of principle, the US legal system presumes a person innocent until proven guilty. Each state has its own civil and criminal laws, and what is legal in one state may be illegal in others.

Driving

In all states, driving under the influence of alcohol (the blood-alcohol limit is 0.08%) or drugs is a serious offense, subject to stiff fines and even imprisonment.

Drugs

Recreational drugs are prohibited by federal and most state laws. Washington, Colorado, California, Nevada and Oregon all allow recreational marijuana use, but it is still illegal to smoke in public (which includes hotel rooms). As of 2017, it is legally possible to purchase marijuana in Colorado, Oregon and Washington. Note that pot use still remains illegal under the federal Controlled Substances Act.

Possession of any illicit drug, including cocaine, ecstasy, LSD, heroin and hashish – or more than an ounce of pot (outside of the states listed above) – is a felony potentially punishable by lengthy jail sentences. For foreigners, conviction of any drug offense is grounds for deportation.

Money

ATMs widely available. Credit cards normally required for hotel reservations and car rentals.

ATMs

➡ ATMs are available at most banks, shopping malls, airports and grocery and convenience stores.

➡ Expect a minimum surcharge of $2.50 per transaction, in addition to any fees charged by your home bank. Some ATMs in Las Vegas may charge more.

➡ Most ATMs are connected to international networks and offer decent foreign-exchange rates.

➡ Withdrawing cash from an ATM using a credit card usually incurs a hefty fee and high interest rates; check with your credit-card company for a PIN.

Cash

Most people do not carry large amounts of cash for everyday use, relying instead on credit cards, debit cards and smartphones. It is good

TIPS FOR SHUTTERBUGS

➡ If you have a digital camera, bring extra batteries and a charger.

➡ For print film, use 100 ASA film for all but the lowest light situations; it's the slowest film, and will enhance resolution.

➡ A zoom lens is extremely useful; most SLR cameras have one. Use it to isolate the central subject of your photos. A common composition mistake is to include too much landscape around the person or feature that's your main focus.

➡ Morning and evening are the best times to shoot. The same sandstone bluff can turn four or five different hues throughout the day, and the warmest hues will be at sunset. Underexposing the shot slightly (by a half-stop or more) can bring out richer details in red tones.

➡ When shooting red rocks, a warming filter added to an SLR lens can enhance the colors of the rocks and reduce the blues of overcast or flat-light days. Achieve the same effect on any digital camera by adjusting the white balance to the automatic 'cloudy' setting (or by reducing the color temperature).

➡ Don't shoot into the sun or include it in the frame; shoot what the sunlight is hitting. On bright days, move your subjects into shade for close-up portraits.

to have some cash on hand on road trips, as you may need it for campsites or the occasional cafe or restaurant.

Credit Cards

Major credit cards are almost universally accepted. In fact, it's almost impossible to rent a car, book a room or buy tickets over the phone without one. A credit card may also be vital in emergencies. Visa, MasterCard and American Express are the most widely accepted.

Exchange Rates

Australia	A$1	$0.74
Canada	C$1	$0.73
China	Y10	$1.45
Europe	€1	$1.09
Japan	¥100	$0.88
Mexico	MXN10	$0.53
New Zealand	NZ$1	$0.69
UK	£1	$1.29

For current exchange rates, see www.xe.com.

Moneychangers

➡ You can exchange money at major airports, some banks and all currency-exchange offices such as American Express or Travelex. Always inquire about rates and fees.

➡ Outside big cities, exchanging money may be a problem, so make sure you have a credit card and sufficient cash on hand.

Taxes

➡ Sales tax varies by state and county, with state sales taxes ranging from zero in Montana to 7.25% in California.

➡ Hotel taxes vary by city.

Tipping

Tipping is *not* optional. Only withhold tips in cases of outrageously bad service.

Airport skycaps and hotel bellhops $2 per bag, minimum $5 per cart

Bartenders 10% to 15% per round, minimum $1 per drink

Concierges Nothing for simple information, up to $20 for securing last-minute restaurant reservations, sold-out show tickets etc

Housekeeping staff $2 to $4 daily, left under the card provided; more if you're messy

Parking valets At least $2 when handed back your car keys

Restaurant staff and room service 15% to 20%, unless a gratuity is already charged

Taxi drivers 10% to 15% of metered fare, rounded up to the next dollar

Traveler's Cheques

➡ Traveler's checks have pretty much fallen out of use.

➡ Larger restaurants, hotels and department stores will often accept traveler's checks (in US dollars only), but small businesses, markets and fast-food chains may refuse them.

➡ Visa and American Express are the most widely accepted issuers of traveler's checks.

Opening Hours

Banks	8:30am-4:30pm Mon-Thu, to 5:30pm Fri (and possibly 9am-noon Sat)
Bars	5pm-midnight Sun-Thu, to 2am Fri & Sat
Nightclubs	10pm-2am Thu-Sat
Post offices	9am-5pm Mon-Fri
Shopping malls	9am-9pm
Stores	10am-6pm Mon-Sat, noon-5pm Sun
Supermarkets	8am-8pm, some open 24hr

Photography

➡ Print film can be found at specialty camera shops. Digital-camera memory cards are widely available at chain retailers such as Best Buy and Target.

➡ Some Native American tribal lands prohibit photography and video completely; when it's allowed, you may be required to purchase a permit. Always ask permission if you want to photograph someone close up; anyone who then agrees to be photographed may expect a small tip.

➡ For more advice on picture-taking, consult Lonely Planet's *Guide to Travel Photography*.

Post

➡ For 24-hour postal information, including post-office locations and hours, contact the US Postal Service (www.usps.com), which is reliable and inexpensive.

➡ For sending urgent or important letters and packages either domestically or overseas, Federal Express (www.fedex.com) and United Parcel Service (www.ups.com) offer more expensive door-to-door delivery services.

Postal Rates

At the time of writing, the postal rates for 1st-class mail within the USA were 49¢ for letters weighing up to 1oz (22¢ for each additional ounce) and 34¢ for postcards.

Sending & Receiving Mail

If you have the correct postage, you can drop mail weighing less than 13oz into any blue mailbox. To send a package weighing 13oz or more, go to a post-office desk for assistance.

Public Holidays

On the following national public holidays, banks, schools and government offices (including post offices) are closed, and transportation, museums and other services operate on a Sunday schedule. Holidays falling on a weekend are usually observed the following Monday.

New Year's Day January 1

Martin Luther King Jr Day Third Monday in January

Presidents' Day Third Monday in February

Memorial Day Last Monday in May

Independence Day July 4

Labor Day First Monday in September

Columbus Day Second Monday in October

Veterans Day November 11

Thanksgiving Fourth Thursday in November

Christmas Day December 25

During spring break (March and April), grade school and college students get a week off from school. For students of all ages, summer vacation runs from June to August.

Safe Travel

The Western US is a reasonably safe place to visit. The greatest danger is posed by car accidents. Wildlife can pose problems in national parks if you don't take proper precautions (eg improper food storage). Of the urban areas, LA has the most crime, though tourists are unlikely to run into trouble.

Telephone
Dialing Codes

➡ US phone numbers consist of a three-digit area code followed by a seven-digit local number.

➡ When dialing a number within the same area code, you generally have to dial the entire 10-digit number, but not always.

➡ If you are calling long distance, dial ☑1 plus the area code plus the phone number.

➡ Toll-free numbers begin with ☑800, 866, 877 or 888 and must be preceded by ☑1.

➡ For direct international calls, dial ☑011 plus the country code plus the area code (usually without the initial '0') plus the local phone number.

➡ For international call assistance, dial ☑00.

➡ If you're calling from abroad, the country code for the US is ☑1 (the same as Canada, but international rates apply between the two countries).

Cell Phones

GSM multiband models will work in the USA. If you have an unlocked phone, you can find prepaid SIM cards fairly easily.

SIMS & COVERAGE

➡ Expect little to no coverage in remote or mountainous areas.

➡ SIM cards are sold at telecommunications and electronics stores. These stores also sell inexpensive prepaid phones, including some airtime. Verizon and AT&T have the two largest networks in the US. Verizon tends to have better coverage in rural areas.

Payphones & Phonecards

➡ Where payphones still exist, they are usually coin-operated, although some may only accept credit cards (eg in national parks).

➡ Local calls usually cost 35¢ to 50¢ minimum.

➡ For long-distance calls, you're usually better off buying a prepaid phonecard, sold at convenience stores, supermarkets, newsstands and electronics stores.

Time

➡ Most of Colorado, Wyoming, Montana, Idaho, Utah, New Mexico and Arizona follow Mountain Standard Time (GMT/UTC minus seven hours). California, Nevada, Oregon and Washington generally follow Pacific Standard Time (GMT/UTC minus eight hours). There are some variations within a state, usually based on location or season.

➡ Daylight Saving Time pushes the clocks ahead an hour. It runs from the second Sunday in March to the first Sunday in November.

➡ Arizona does not observe daylight-saving time; during that period it's one hour behind other Southwestern states. The Navajo Reservation, which lies in Arizona, New Mexico and Utah, does use daylight-saving time. The Hopi Reservation, which is surrounded by the Navajo Reservation in Arizona, follows the rest of Arizona.

➡ The US date system is written as month/day/year. Thus, the 8th of June, 2008, becomes 6/8/08.

Toilets

Public toilets are free. If you can't find a public toilet, head to a gas station, restaurant or cafe (you may need to purchase something).

Tourist Information

➡ Most tourist offices have a website, where you can download free travel guides. They also field phone calls; some local offices maintain daily lists of hotel room availability, but few offer reservation services. All tourist offices have self-service racks of brochures and discount coupons; some also sell maps and books.

➡ State-run 'welcome centers,' usually placed along interstate highways, tend to have materials that cover wider territories, and offices are usually open longer hours, including weekends and holidays.

➡ Many cities have an official convention and visitor bureau (CVB); these sometimes double as tourist bureaus, but since their main focus is drawing the business trade, CVBs can be less useful for independent travelers.

➡ Keep in mind that, in smaller towns, when the local chamber of commerce runs the tourist bureau, their lists of hotels, restaurants and services usually mention only chamber members; the town's cheapest options may be missing.

➡ Similarly, in prime tourist destinations, some private 'tourist bureaus' are really agents who book hotel rooms and tours on commission. They may offer excellent service and deals, but you'll get what they're selling and nothing else.

Travelers with Disabilities

➡ If you have a physical disability, the USA can be an accommodating place. The Americans with Disabilities Act (ADA) requires that all public buildings, private buildings built after 1993 (including hotels, restaurants, theaters and museums) and public transit be wheelchair accessible. However, call ahead to confirm what is available. Some local tourist offices publish detailed accessibility guides.

➡ Download Lonely Planet's free Accessible Travel guide from http://lptravel.to/accessibletravel.

➡ Telephone companies offer relay operators, available via teletypewriter (TTY) numbers, for the hearing impaired. Most banks provide ATM instructions in Braille, and via earphone jacks for hearing-impaired customers. All major airlines, Greyhound buses and Amtrak trains will assist travelers with disabilities; just describe your needs when making reservations at least 48 hours in advance. Service animals (guide dogs) are allowed to accompany passengers, but bring documentation.

➡ Some car-rental agencies – such as Avis and Hertz – offer hand-controlled vehicles and vans with wheelchair lifts at no extra charge, but you must reserve them well in advance. Wheelchair Getaways (www.wheelchairgetaways.com) rents accessible vans throughout the USA. In many cities and towns, public buses are accessible to wheelchair riders; just let the driver know that you need the lift or ramp.

➡ Many national and some state parks and recreation areas have wheelchair-accessible paved, graded dirt or boardwalk trails. The website for the Rails-to-Trails Conservancy (www.traillink.com) lists wheelchair-accessible trails by state.

➡ US citizens and permanent residents with permanent disabilities are entitled to a free 'America the Beautiful' Access Pass, which gives free entry to all federal recreation lands (eg national parks).

Resources
Some helpful resources for travelers with disabilities:

Access Northern California (http://accessnca.org) Extensive links to accessible-travel resources, publications, tours and transportation, including outdoor recreation opportunities, plus a searchable lodgings database and an events calendar.

Arizona Raft Adventures (www.azraft.com) Can accommodate disabled travelers on rafting trips through the Grand Canyon.

Disabled Sports USA (☏301-217-0960; www.disabledsportsusa.org) Offers sport, adventure and recreation programs for those with disabilities. Also publishes *Challenge* magazine.

Mobility International USA (☏541-343-1284; www.miusa.org) Advises USA-bound disabled travelers on mobility issues.

Splore (☏801-484-4128; www.splore.org; 4029 Main St; ☺9am-5pm Mon-Fri) Offers accessible outdoor adventure trips in Utah.

Visas

Visitors from Canada, the UK, Australia, New Zealand, Japan and many EU countries don't need visas for less than 90-day stays. Other nations, see https://travel.state.gov.

Be warned that all visa information is highly subject to change. US entry requirements keep evolving as national security regulations change. All travelers should double-check current visa and passport regulations before coming to the USA.

The US State Department (https://travel.state.gov) maintains the most comprehensive visa information, providing downloadable forms, lists of US consulates abroad and even visa wait times calculated by country.

Visa Applications

➡ Apart from most Canadian citizens and travelers entering under the Visa Waiver Program (VWP), all foreign visitors to the US need a visa. For more details about visa requirements, visit https://travel.state.gov.

➡ Most visa applicants must schedule a personal interview, to which you must bring all your documentation and proof of fee payment. Wait times for interviews vary, but afterward, barring problems, visa issuance takes from a few days to a few weeks.

➡ You'll need a recent color photo (2in by 2in), and you must pay a nonrefundable $160 processing fee, plus in a few cases an additional visa issuance reciprocity fee. You'll also need to fill out the online DS-160 nonimmigrant visa electronic application.

➡ Depending on the type of visa requested, applicants may have to provide documentation confirming the purpose of their trip, their intent to depart the US after their trip and an ability to cover all costs related to the trip. Visit the website for more details.

Short-Term Departures & Re-entry

➡ It's temptingly easy to make trips across the border to Canada or Mexico, but upon return to the USA, non-Americans will be subject to the full immigration procedure.

➡ Always take your passport when you cross the border.

➡ If your immigration card still has plenty of time on it, you will probably be able to reenter using the same one, but if it has nearly expired, you will have to apply for a new card, and border control may want to see your onward air ticket, sufficient funds and so on.

➡ Citizens of most Western countries will not need a visa to visit Canada, so it's really not a problem at all to pass through on the way to Alaska.

➡ Travelers entering the USA by bus from Canada may be closely scrutinized. A round-trip ticket that takes you back to Canada will most likely make US immigration feel less suspicious.

➡ At the time of writing, most visitors did not need a visa for short-term travel in Mexico (under 90 to 180 days, depending on your nationality).

Women Travelers

➡ Women traveling alone or in groups should not expect to encounter any particular problems in the USA. In terms of safety issues, single women just need to practice common sense.

➡ When first meeting someone, don't advertise where you are staying, or that you are traveling alone. Americans can be eager to help and even take in solo travelers. However, don't take all offers of help at face value. If someone who seems trustworthy invites you to his or her home, let someone (eg hostel or hotel manager) know where you're going.

➡ This advice also applies if you go for a hike by yourself. If something happens and you don't return as expected, you want to know that someone will notice and know where to begin looking for you.

➡ Some women carry a whistle, mace or cayenne-pepper spray in case of assault. If you purchase a spray, contact a police station to find out about local regulations. Laws regarding sprays vary from state to state; federal law prohibits them being carried on planes.

➡ If you are assaulted, consider calling a rape-crisis hotline before calling the police, unless you are in immediate danger, in which case you should call ☎911. But be aware that not all police have as much sensitivity training or experience assisting sexual assault survivors, whereas rape-crisis-center staff will tirelessly advocate on your behalf and act as a link to other community services, including hospitals and the police. Telephone books have listings of local rape-crisis centers, or contact the 24-hour National Sexual Assault Hotline (☎800-656-4673). Alternatively, go straight to a hospital emergency room.

Transportation

GETTING THERE & AWAY

Flights, cars and tours can be booked online at www.lonely planet.com/bookings.

Entering Western USA

If you are flying into the US, the first airport where you land is where you must go through immigration and customs, even if you are continuing on the flight to another destination. Finger-prints are taken and biome-tric information is checked upon entry into the US.

Passports

➡ Under the Western Hemisphere Travel Initiative (WHTI), all travelers must have a valid machine-readable passport (MRP) when entering the USA by air, land or sea.

➡ The only exceptions are for most US citizens and some Canadian and Mexican citizens traveling by land or sea who can present other WHTI-compliant documents (eg pre-approved 'trusted traveler' cards).

➡ All foreign passports must meet current US standards and be valid for the length of your stay. Certain nationalities need passports that are valid for a minimum of six months longer than the intended stay.

Air

Airports & Airlines

INTERNATIONAL AIRPORTS

The western USA's primary international airports:

Los Angeles International Airport (LAX; www.lawa.org/welcomelax.aspx; 1 World Way) California's largest and busiest airport, 20 miles southwest of downtown LA, near the coast.

San Francisco International Airport (SFO; Map p301; www.flysfo.com; S McDonnell Rd) Northern California's major hub, 14 miles south of downtown, on San Francisco Bay.

Seattle-Tacoma International (SEA; ☏206-787-5388; www.portseattle.org/Sea-Tac; 17801 International Blvd; ☎) Known locally as 'Sea-Tac.'

Major regional airports with limited international service:

Albuquerque International Sunport (ABQ; ☏505-244-7700; www.abqsunport.com; ☎) Serving Albuquerque and all of New Mexico.

Denver International Airport (DEN; ☏303-342-2000; www.flydenver.com; ☎) Serving southern Colorado; if you rent a car in Denver, you can be in northeastern New Mexico in four hours.

LA/Ontario International Airport (ONT; ☏909-937-2700; www.flyontario.com; 2500 E Airport Dr; ☎) In Riverside County, east of LA.

CLIMATE CHANGE & TRAVEL

Every form of transport that relies on carbon-based fuel generates CO_2, the main cause of human-induced climate change. Modern travel is dependent on airplanes, which might use less fuel per mile per person than most cars but travel much greater distances. The altitude at which aircraft emit gases (including CO_2) and particles also contributes to their climate change impact. Many websites offer 'carbon calculators' that allow people to estimate the carbon emissions generated by their journey and, for those who wish to do so, to offset the impact of the greenhouse gases emitted with contributions to portfolios of climate-friendly initiatives throughout the world. Lonely Planet offsets the carbon footprint of all staff and author travel.

McCarran International Airport (LAS; Map p149;☎702-261-5211; www.mccarran.com; 5757 Wayne Newton Blvd; ⑥) Serves Las Vegas, NV, and southern Utah. Las Vegas is 290 miles from the South Rim of Grand Canyon National Park and 277 miles from the North Rim.

Mineta San Jose International Airport (SJC;☎408-392-3600; www.flysanjose.com; 1701 Airport Blvd) In San Francisco's South Bay.

Oakland International Airport (OAK; Map p301; www.oakland airport.com; 1 Airport Dr; ⑥; Ⓑ Oakland International Airport) In San Francisco's East Bay.

Palm Springs International Airport (PSP;☎760-318-3800; www.palmspringsairport.com; 3400 E Tahquitz Canyon Way, Palm Springs) In the desert, east of LA.

Portland International Airport (PDX;☎503-460-4234; www. flypdx.com; 7000 NE Airport Way; ⑥; Ⓡred) About 12 miles from downtown Portland, OR.

Salt Lake City International Airport (SLC;☎801-575-2400; www.slcairport.com; 776 N Terminal Dr; ⑥) Serving Salt Lake City and northern Utah; a good choice if you're headed to the North Rim and the Arizona Strip.

San Diego International Airport (SAN; Map p270;☎619-400-2404; www.san.org; 3325 N Harbor Dr; ⑥) Four miles northwest of downtown.

Sky Harbor International Airport (Map p166;☎602-273-3300; http://skyharbor.com; 3400 E Sky Harbor Blvd; ⑥) Serving Phoenix and the Grand Canyon, it's one of the 10 busiest airports in the country. Phoenix is 220 miles from the South Rim of Grand Canyon National Park and 335 miles from the North Rim.

Tucson International Airport (☎520-573-8100; www.flytuc son.com; 7250 S Tucson Blvd; ⑥) Serving Tucson and southern Arizona.

Vancouver International Airport (YVR;☎604-207-7077; www.yvr.ca; ⑥) Located 6 miles south of Vancouver, on Sea Island; between Vancouver and the municipality of Richmond.

GETTING TO/FROM AIRPORTS

Denver International Airport The easiest way to get from DIA to downtown is the train ($9, 35 minutes, every 15 minutes). The AB bus runs to Boulder ($9, 82 minutes, hourly). Shuttles run to all the major ski resorts.

Los Angeles International Airport Taxis cost about $47 to downtown; door-to-door shuttles from $17 for shared ride; free Shuttle G to Metro Green Line Aviation Station and free Shuttle C to the Metro Bus Center; FlyAway bus to downtown LA is $9.75.

Seattle-Tacoma International Airport Light-rail trains run regularly from the 4th floor of the parking garage to downtown ($3, 30 minutes, frequent); shuttle buses stop on the 3rd floor of the airport garage and cost from $18 one way; taxis cost from $42 to downtown (25 minutes).

SECURITY

➡ To get through airport security checkpoints (30-minute wait times are standard), you'll need a boarding pass and photo ID.

➡ Some travelers may be required to undergo a secondary screening, involving hand pat-downs and carry-on luggage searches.

➡ Airport security measures restrict many common items (eg pocket knives) from being carried on planes. Check current restrictions with the Transportation Security Administration (TSA; www. tsa.gov).

➡ Currently, TSA requires that all carry-on liquids and gels be stored in 3.4oz or smaller bottles placed inside a quart-sized clear plastic zip-top bag. Exceptions, which must be declared to checkpoint security officers, include medications.

➡ All checked luggage is screened for explosives. TSA may open your suitcase for visual confirmation, breaking the lock if necessary. Leave your bags unlocked or use a TSA-approved lock like Travel Sentry (www.travelsentry. org).

DEPARTURE TAX

Departure tax is included in the price of a ticket.

Land

Border Crossings

➡ It is relatively easy crossing from the USA into Canada or Mexico; it's crossing back into the USA that can pose problems if you haven't brought your required documents. Check the ever-changing passport and visa requirements with the US Department of State (www.state.gov/travel) beforehand. US Customs and Border Protection (www. cbp.gov) tracks current wait times at every Mexico border crossing.

➡ Some borders are open 24 hours, but most are not.

➡ Have your papers in order, be polite and don't make jokes or casual conversation with US border officials.

➡ Drug cartel violence and crime are serious dangers along the US–Mexico border.

BUS

➡ Greyhound (www. greyhound.com) has direct connections between Canada and the Northern US, but you may have to transfer to a different bus at the border. You can also book through Greyhound Canada (www.greyhound.ca).

➡ Northbound buses from Mexico can take some time to cross the US border, as US immigration may insist on checking every person on board.

CAR & MOTORCYCLE

➡ If you're driving into the USA from Canada or Mexico, bring your vehicle's

CROSSING THE MEXICAN BORDER

The issue of crime-related violence in Mexico has been front and center in the international press for a number of years now. Nogales, AZ, for example, is safe for travelers, but Nogales, Mexico, is a major locus for the drug trade and its associated violence. We cannot safely recommend crossing the border for an extended period until the security situation changes. You're fine for day trips, but anything past that may be risky.

The State Department (https://travel.state.gov) recommends that travelers visit its website before traveling to Mexico. Here you can check for travel updates and warnings and confirm the latest border-crossing requirements. Before leaving, US citizens can sign up for the Smart Traveler Enrollment Program (step.state.gov/step) to receive email updates.

US and Canadian citizens entering the US from Mexico at airports must present a valid passport. To enter by land or sea, US and Canadian citizens are required to present a valid WHTI-compliant document, such as a passport, US passport card, enhanced driver's license or trusted traveler card (NEXUS, SENTRI, Global Entry or FAST). Check the latest requirements as this may change.

US and Canadian children under age 16 can also enter using a birth certificate, a consular report of birth abroad, naturalization certificate or Canadian citizenship card. All other nationals must carry a passport and, if needed, visa for entering Mexico and reentering the US. Regulations change frequently, so get the latest scoop at www.cbp.gov.

registration papers, liability insurance and driver's license; an international driving permit (IDP) is a good supplement, but not required.

➡ If you're renting a car or motorcycle, ask if the agency allows its vehicles to be taken across the Mexican or Canadian border; chances are it doesn't.

To & From Canada

➡ Canadian auto insurance is typically valid in the USA, and vice versa.

➡ If your papers are in order, taking your own car across the US–Canada border is usually quick and easy.

➡ On weekends and holidays, especially in summer, border-crossing traffic can be heavy and waits long.

➡ Occasionally the authorities of either country decide to search a car *thoroughly*. Remain calm and be polite.

To & From Mexico

➡ Very few car-rental companies will let you take a car from the US into Mexico.

➡ Unless you're planning an extended stay in Tijuana, taking a car across the

Mexican border is more trouble than it's worth. Instead take the trolley from San Diego or leave your car on the US side and walk across.

➡ US auto insurance is not valid in Mexico, so even a short trip into Mexico's border region requires you to buy Mexican car insurance, available for around $25 per day at most border crossings, as well as from the American Automobile Association (www.aaa.com).

➡ For a longer driving trip into Mexico beyond the border zone or Baja California, you'll need a Mexican *permiso de importación temporal de vehículos* from Banjercito (temporary vehicle import permit; www.banjercito.com. mx).

➡ Expect long border-crossing waits, as security has tightened.

➡ See Lonely Planet's *Mexico* guide for further details.

Train

➡ Amtrak (www. amtrakcascades.com) operates the daily *Cascades* rail service between Eugene, OR, and Vancouver, Canada, with connecting bus services

to destinations not served by train.

➡ **VIA Rail** (☏888-842-7245; www.viarail.ca) also serves Vancouver, BC, with routes running north and east across Canada.

➡ US/Canadian customs and immigration inspections happen at the border, not upon boarding.

➡ Currently, no train service connects Arizona or California with Mexico.

Sea

If you're interested in taking a cruise ship to America – as well as to other interesting ports of call – a good specialized travel agency is Cruise Web (www.cruiseweb.com).

You can also travel to and from the USA on a freighter, though it will be much slower and less cushy than a cruise. Nevertheless, freighters aren't spartan (some advertise cruise ship–level amenities) and they are much cheaper (sometimes by half). Trips range from a week to two months; stops at interim ports are usually quick.

For more information, try Cruise & Freighter Travel Association (www.travltips.

com), which has listings for freighter cruises and other boat travel.

GETTING AROUND

Car The best option for travelers who leave urban areas to explore national parks and more remote areas. Drive on the right.

Train Amtrak can be slow due to frequent delays, but trains are a convenient option for travel along the Pacific Coast. Cross-country routes to Chicago run from the San Francisco area and Los Angeles.

Bus Cheaper and slower than trains; can be a good option for travel to cities not serviced by Amtrak.

Air

The domestic air system is extensive and reliable, with a number of competing airlines, hundreds of airports and thousands of flights daily. Flying is usually more expensive than traveling by bus, train or car, but it's the best option if you're in a hurry.

To/From Western USA's Major Airports

Denver International Airport The easiest way to get from DIA to downtown is the train ($9, 35 minutes, every 15 minutes). The AB bus runs to Boulder ($9, 82 minutes, hourly). Shuttles run to all the major ski resorts.

Los Angeles International Airport Taxis cost about $47 to downtown; door-to-door shuttles from $17 for shared ride; free Shuttle G to Metro Green Line Aviation Station and free Shuttle C to the Metro Bus Center; FlyAway bus to downtown LA is $9.75.

Seattle-Tacoma International Airport Light-rail trains run regularly from the 4th floor of the parking garage to downtown ($3, 30 minutes, frequent); shuttle buses stop on the 3rd floor of the airport garage and cost from $18 one way; taxis cost from $42 to downtown (25 minutes).

Airlines in Western USA

Overall, air travel in the USA is very safe (much safer than driving on the nation's highways); for comprehensive details by carrier, check out www.airsafe.com.

The main domestic carriers in the West:

Alaska Airlines (☏800-252-7522; www.alaskaair.com) Serves Alaska and the Western US, with flights to the East Coast and Hawaii.

American Airlines (☏800-433-7300; www.aa.com) Nationwide service.

Delta (☏800-221-1212; www.delta.com) Nationwide service.

Frontier Airlines (☏801-401-9000; www.flyfrontier.com) Denver-based airline with service across the continental US.

JetBlue Airways (☏800-538-2583; www.jetblue.com) Nonstop connections between Eastern and Western US cities, plus Florida, New Orleans and Texas.

Southwest Airlines (☏800-435-9792; www.southwest.com) Service across the continental USA.

Spirit Airlines (☏801-401-2222; www.spirit.com) Florida-based airline; serves many US gateway cities.

United Airlines (☏800-864-8331; www.united.com) Nationwide service.

Virgin America (☏877-359-8474; www.virginamerica.com) Flights between East and West Coast cities plus Las Vegas, Austin and Dallas.

Bicycle

Regional bicycle touring is popular. It means coasting over winding back roads (because bicycles are often not permitted on freeways) and calculating progress in miles per day, not miles per hour. Cyclists must follow the same rules of the road as automobiles, but don't expect drivers to respect your right of way. Wearing a helmet is mandatory for riders under 18 years of age in California and many Western cities.

Some helpful resources for cyclists:

Adventure Cycling Association (www.adventurecycling.org) Excellent online resource for purchasing bicycle-friendly maps and long-distance route guides.

Better World Club (www.betterworldclub.com) Annual membership ($40, plus $12 enrollment fee) entitles you to two 24-hour emergency roadside pickups with transportation to the nearest bike-repair shop within a 30-mile radius.

Bikepacking (www.bikepacking.com) Info on multiday mountain-biking trips through the backcountry.

Rental & Purchase

➡ You can rent bikes by the hour, the day or the week in most cities and major towns.

➡ Rentals start from around $20 per day for beach cruisers, and from $39 or more for basic mountain bikes; ask about multiday and weekly discounts.

➡ Most rental companies require a credit-card security deposit of several hundred dollars.

➡ Buy new models from specialty bike shops, sporting-goods stores and discount-warehouse stores, or used bicycles from notice boards at hostels, cafes and universities.

➡ To buy or sell used bikes, check online bulletin boards like Craigslist (www.craigslist.com).

Transporting Bicycles

➡ If you tire of pedaling, some local buses and trains are equipped with bicycle racks.

➡ Greyhound transports bicycles as luggage (surcharge $30 to $40), which must be packed in wood, canvas or a substantial container, and properly secured.

➜ Most of Amtrak's *Cascades*, *Pacific Surfliner*, *Capital Corridor* and *San Joaquin* trains feature onboard racks where you can secure your bike unboxed; try to reserve a spot when making your ticket reservation (surcharge up to $10).

➜ On Amtrak trains without racks, bikes must be put in a box ($15) and checked as luggage (fee $10). Not all stations or trains offer checked-baggage service.

➜ Before flying, you'll need to disassemble your bike and box it as checked baggage; contact the airline directly for details, including applicable surcharges (typically $150 to $200). There may be no surcharge for lighter and smaller bikes (under 50lb and 62 linear inches).

Boat

There is no river or canal public transportation system in the West, but there are many smaller, often state-run, coastal ferry services. Most larger ferries will transport private cars, motorcycles and bicycles.

Off the coast of Washington, ferries reach the scenic San Juan Islands. Several of California's Channel Islands are accessible by boat, as is Catalina Island, offshore from Los Angeles. On San Francisco Bay, regular ferries operate between San Francisco and Sausalito, Larkspur, Tiburon, Angel Island, Oakland, Alameda and Vallejo.

Bus

➜ Greyhound (www.greyhound.com) is the major long-distance bus company, with routes throughout the USA and Canada. Greyhound has stopped service to many small towns; routes generally trace major highways and stop at larger population

centers. To reach country towns on rural roads, you may need to transfer to local or county bus systems; Greyhound can usually provide their contact information.

➜ Most baggage has to be checked in; label it loudly and clearly to avoid it getting lost. Larger items, including skis, surfboards and bicycles, can be transported, but there may be an extra charge. Call to check.

➜ Greyhound often has excellent online fares – web-only deals will net you substantial discounts over buying at a ticket counter.

➜ The frequency of bus services varies widely. Despite the elimination of many tiny destinations, nonexpress Greyhound buses still stop every 50 to 100 miles to pick up passengers. Long-distance buses stop for meal breaks and driver changes.

➜ Greyhound buses are usually clean, comfortable and reliable. The best seats are typically near the front away from the bathroom. Limited onboard amenities include freezing air-con (bring a sweater) and slightly reclining seats; select buses have electrical outlets and wi-fi. Smoking on board is prohibited.

➜ Many bus stations are clean and safe, but some are in dodgy areas.

Costs

➜ Fares vary depending on when you're traveling and how much flexibility you need; online rates are the best and often very competitive.

➜ Discounts (on unrestricted fares only) are available for veterans (10%), for students (10%), seniors (5%) and children (varies).

➜ Special promotional discounts are often available on the Greyhound website, though they may come with

restrictions or blackout periods.

Reservations

➜ Greyhound bus tickets can be bought over the phone or online. You can print tickets at home or pick them up at the terminal using 'Will Call' service (bring photo ID).

➜ Seating is normally first-come, first-served. Greyhound recommends arriving an hour before departure to get a seat.

➜ Travelers with disabilities who need special assistance should call 800-752-4841 (TDD/TTY 800-345-3109) at least 48 hours before traveling; there are limited spaces for those in wheelchairs, although wheelchairs are also accepted as checked baggage. Service animals, such as guide dogs, are allowed on board.

Car & Motorcycle

A car allows maximum flexibility and convenience, and is essentially the only way to explore the Western interior and its wide-open spaces.

Automobile Associations

For 24-hour emergency roadside assistance, free maps and discounts on lodging, attractions, entertainment, car rentals and more:

American Automobile Association (www.aaa.com)

Better World Club (www.betterworldclub.com)

Car Rental

➜ To rent your own wheels, you'll typically need to be at least 25 years old, hold a valid driver's license and have a major credit card, not a check or debit card. Companies may rent to drivers under 25 but over 21 for a surcharge (around $25 to $30 per day). If you don't have a credit card, you may occasionally be able to make a large cash deposit instead.

➜ With advance reservations, you can often get an economy-sized vehicle with unlimited mileage from around $20 per day, plus insurance, taxes and fees. Airport locations may have cheaper rates but higher fees; if you get a fly-drive package, local taxes may be extra when you pick up the car. City-center branches may offer free pick-ups and drop-offs.

➜ Rates generally include unlimited mileage (check the mileage cap), but expect surcharges for additional drivers and one-way rentals. Some rental companies let you pay for your last tank of gas upfront; this is rarely a good deal.

➜ You might get a better deal by booking through discount-travel websites like Priceline (www.priceline.com) or Hotwire (www.hotwire.com), or by using online travel-booking sites, such as Expedia (www.expedia.com), Orbitz (www.orbitz.com) or Travelocity (www.travelocity.com). You can also compare rates across travel sites at Kayak (www.kayak.com).

➜ A few major car-rental companies (including Avis, Budget, Enterprise, and Hertz) offer 'green' fleets of hybrid, clean diesel or electric rental cars, but they're in short supply. Reserve well in advance. Also try **Simply RAC** (☑323-653-0022; www.simplyrac.com) ✪ in Los Angeles, which offers free delivery and pick-up from some locations; or **Zipcar** (☑866-494-7227; www.zipcar.com), which is available in California (Los Angeles, San Diego and the San Francisco Bay area) and Denver, Portland and Seattle. This car-sharing club charges usage fees (per hour or daily), and includes free gas, insurance (damage fee of up to $1000 may apply) and limited mileage. Apply online. Monthly memberships run from $7 to $50 and higher, and the application fee is $25. Drivers from outside the US will need to present passport, driver's license and accident history prior to rental.

➜ To compare independent car-rental companies, try Car Rental Express (www.carrentalexpress.com), which is especially useful for finding cheaper long-term rentals.

➜ If you are under 25 and in LA, check out Super Cheap Car Rental (www.supercheapcar.com), which has no surcharge for drivers aged 21 to 24; daily fee applies for drivers aged 18 to 21.

Driver's Licence

➜ Foreign visitors can legally drive a car in some states using their home driver's license, but other states may require an additional international driving permit (IDP); for info see www.usa.gov/visitors-driving.

➜ An IDP will also have more credibility with US traffic police, especially if your home license doesn't have a photo or isn't in English. Your automobile association at home can issue an IDP, valid for one year, for a small fee. Always carry your home license together with the IDP.

➜ To drive a motorcycle in the USA, you will need a valid motorcycle license. International visitors need a drivers' permit from their home country, or an IDP specially endorsed for motorcycles.

ROAD DISTANCES (MILES)

	Denver	Grand Canyon National Park (South Rim)	Las Vegas	Los Angeles	Phoenix	Portland	San Francisco	Santa Fe	Seattle
Grand Canyon National Park (South Rim)	68								
Las Vegas	750	270							
Los Angeles	1020	485	270						
Phoenix	825	215	285	375					
Portland	1260	1330	1020	965	1335				
San Francisco	1270	790	570	380	750	635			
Santa Fe	395	455	635	850	530	1450	1145		
Seattle	1330	1365	1165	1135	1500	175	810	1545	
Yellowstone National Park	530	810	670	950	920	795	1000	820	875

Insurance

➡ Liability insurance covers people and property you might hit.

➡ For a rental vehicle, a collision damage waiver (CDW) is available for about $30 per day. Before renting a car, check your auto-insurance policy to see if you're already covered. Your policy probably includes liability protection but check anyway.

➡ Some credit cards offer reimbursement coverage for collision damages when you use the card to rent a car. There may be exceptions for rentals of more than 15 days or for exotic models, Jeeps, vans and 4WD vehicles. If there's an accident, you may have to pay the rental-car company first and then seek reimbursement from the credit-card company. Check your credit card's policies carefully before renting.

➡ Many rental agencies stipulate that damage a car suffers while being driven on unpaved roads is not covered by the insurance they offer. Check with the agent when you make your reservation.

Motorcycle & Recreational Vehicle (RV) Rental

If you dream of cruising across America on a Harley, EagleRider (www.eaglerider.com) has offices in major cities nationwide and rents other kinds of adventure vehicles, too. Motorcycle rental and insurance are expensive.

Companies specializing in RV and pop-up camper rentals:

➡ **Adventures on Wheels** (www.adventuresonwheels.com)

➡ **Cruise America** (www.cruiseamerica.com)

➡ **Happy Travel Campers** (☑310-929-5666; www.camperusa.com)

➡ **Jucy Rentals** (☑800-650-4180; www.jucyrentals.com)

Road Conditions & Hazards

➡ Road hazards include potholes, city commuter traffic, wandering wildlife, and distracted and enraged drivers.

➡ Where winter driving is an issue, some cars are fitted with snow tires; snow chains are sometimes required in mountain areas. Driving off-road, or on dirt roads, is often forbidden by rental-car companies, and it can be very dangerous in wet weather.

➡ In deserts and range country, livestock sometimes grazes next to unfenced roads. These areas are signed as 'Open Range' or with the silhouette of a steer. Where deer, elk and other wild animals frequently appear roadside, you'll see signs with the silhouette of a leaping deer. Take these signs seriously, particularly at night.

For nationwide traffic and road-closure information, visit www.fhwa.dot.gov/trafficinfo.

For current road conditions within a state, call 511. From outside a state, try the following:

Arizona (888-411-7623; www.az511.com)

California (800-427-7623; www.dot.ca.gov)

Colorado (303-639-1111; www.cotrip.org)

Idaho (888-432-7623; 511.idaho.gov)

Montana (800-226-7623; www.mdt.mt.gov/travinfo)

Nevada (877-687-6237; www.nvroads.com)

New Mexico (800-432-4269; nmroads.com)

Oregon (503-588-2941; www.tripcheck.com)

Utah (866-511-8824; www.udot.utah.gov)

Washington (800-695-7623; www.wsdot.wa.gov)

Wyoming (888-996-7623; www.wyoroad.info)

Road Rules

➡ Cars drive on the right-hand side of the road.

➡ The use of seat belts and child safety seats is required in every state. Most car-rental agencies rent child safety seats for around $13 per day, but you must reserve them when booking.

➡ In some states, motorcyclists are required to wear helmets.

➡ On interstate highways, the speed limit is sometimes raised to 80mph. Unless otherwise posted, the speed limit is generally 55mph or 65mph on highways, 25mph to 35mph in cities and towns and as low as 15mph in school zones (strictly enforced during school hours). It's forbidden to pass a school bus when its lights are flashing.

➡ When emergency vehicles (ie police, fire or ambulance) approach from either direction, pull over safely and get out of the way. In an increasing number of states, it is illegal to talk on a handheld cell (mobile) phone or text while driving; use a hands-free device or pull over for a call.

➡ The maximum legal blood-alcohol concentration for drivers is 0.08%. Penalties are very severe for 'DUI' – driving under the influence of alcohol and/or drugs. Police can give roadside sobriety checks to assess if you've been drinking or using drugs. If you fail, they'll require you to take a breath test, urine test or blood test to determine the level of alcohol or drugs in your body. Refusing to be tested is treated the same as if you'd taken the test and failed.

➡ In some states it is illegal to carry 'open containers' of alcohol in a vehicle, even if they are empty.

Fueling Up

Many gas stations in the West have fuel pumps with automated credit-card pay screens. Most machines ask for your zip code. For foreign travelers, or those with cards issued outside the US, you'll have to pay inside before pumping gas. Tell the clerk how much money you'd like to put on the card. If there's still credit left, go back inside and have the difference refunded to the card.

You cannot pump your own gas in Oregon except at rural gas stations.

Local Transportation

Except in cities, public transport is rarely the most convenient option. Coverage to outlying towns and suburbs can be sparse. However, it is usually cheap, safe and reliable.

Airport Shuttles

Shuttle buses provide inexpensive and convenient transport to/from airports in most cities. Most are 12-seat vans; some have regular routes and stops (which include the main hotels), and some pick up and deliver passengers 'door to door' in their service area. Average costs run from $15 to $22 per person.

Bicycle

Some cities are more amenable to bicycles than others, but most have at least a few dedicated bike lanes and paths. Bikes can usually be carried on public transportation.

Bus

Most cities and larger towns have dependable local bus systems, though they are often designed for commuters and provide limited service in the evening and on weekends. Costs average about $2 per ride. Limited routes in tourist areas may be free.

Subway & Train

The largest systems are in Los Angeles and the San Francisco Bay Area. Other cities may have small, one- or two-line rail systems that mainly serve downtown.

Taxi

➡ Taxis are metered, with average flagfall fees of $2.50 to $3.50, plus $2 to $3 per mile. Credit cards may be accepted.

➡ Taxis may charge extra for baggage and/or airport pick-ups.

➡ Drivers expect a 10% to 15% tip, rounded up to the next dollar.

➡ Ride-sharing companies such as Uber (www.uber. com) and Lyft (www.lyft. com) are a very popular alternative to taxis.

Train

A fairly extensive rail system throughout the USA is operated by Amtrak. Fares vary according to the type of train and seating (eg reserved or unreserved coach seats, business class, sleeping compartments). Trains are comfortable, if a bit slow, and are equipped with dining and lounge cars on long-distance routes.

Amtrak routes in the West:

California Zephyr Daily service between Chicago and Emeryville (from $170, 52 hours), near San Francisco, via Denver, Salt Lake City, Reno and Sacramento.

Coast Starlight Travels the West Coast daily from Seattle to LA (from $121, 35½ hours) via Portland, Sacramento, Oakland and Santa Barbara; wi-fi may be available.

Southwest Chief Daily departures between Chicago and LA (from $176, 43¼ hours) via Kansas City, Albuquerque, Flagstaff and Barstow.

Sunset Limited Thrice-weekly service between New Orleans and LA (from $170, 46½ hours)

via Houston, San Antonio, El Paso, Tucson and Palm Springs.

Costs

➡ Purchase tickets at train stations, by phone or online. Fares depend on the day of travel, the route, the type of seating etc. Fares may be slightly higher during peak travel times such as summer.

➡ Usually seniors over 61 and veterans with a Veterans Advantage Card receive a 15% discount, while students with an ISIC or Student Advantage Card receive a 10% discount. AAA members and US military personnel and families also save 10%. Up to two children aged two to 12 who are accompanied by an adult get 50% off. Special promotions can become available anytime, so check the website or ask.

Reservations

Reservations can be made from 11 months in advance up to the day of departure. Space on most trains is limited and certain routes can be crowded, especially during summer and holiday periods, so it's a good idea to book as far in advance as you can.

Train Passes

➡ Amtrak's USA Rail Pass (www.amtrak.com) is valid for coach-class travel for 15 ($459), 30 ($689) or 45 ($899) days; children aged two to 12 pay half-price. Actual travel is limited to eight, 12 or 18 one-way 'segments,' respectively. A segment is *not* the same as a one-way trip; if reaching your destination requires riding more than one train, you'll use multiple pass segments.

➡ Purchase rail passes online; make advance reservations for each travel segment.

➡ For travel within California, consider the seven-day California Rail Pass (adult/ child $159/$79.50), which must be used within 21 consecutive days.

Behind the Scenes

SEND US YOUR FEEDBACK

We love to hear from travelers – your comments keep us on our toes and help make our books better. Our well-traveled team reads every word on what you loved or loathed about this book. Although we cannot reply individually to your submissions, we always guarantee that your feedback goes straight to the appropriate authors, in time for the next edition. Each person who sends us information is thanked in the next edition – the most useful submissions are rewarded with a selection of digital PDF chapters.

Visit **lonelyplanet.com/contact** to submit your updates and suggestions or to ask for help. Our award-winning website also features inspirational travel stories, news and discussions.

Note: We may edit, reproduce and incorporate your comments in Lonely Planet products such as guidebooks, websites and digital products, so let us know if you don't want your comments reproduced or your name acknowledged. For a copy of our privacy policy visit lonelyplanet.com/privacy.

WRITER THANKS

Hugh McNaughtan

Many thanks to Kate, Hannah, Ross and all who I worked with on this title. And to Tas, Maise and Willa, for their patience and support.

Brett Atkinson

Thanks to everyone who made my exploration of California's Central Coast so enjoyable, especially Christina Glynn in Santa Cruz. Thanks also to Margaret Leonard for travel inspiration beyond the borders of Monterey Bay. The staff at the region's visitor centers were all uniformly helpful, and at Lonely Planet, huge thanks to Cliff Wilkinson for the opportunity to return to Big Sur. Across the vast South Pacific in Auckland, thanks to Carol and my family for their support.

Loren Bell

To all of my family and friends on the way who provided hot tips, cold beer and warm support: thank you – your friendships make this all worthwhile. To Kari: I don't know how you put up with me during these projects, but your patience must be deeper than Grand Prismatic Spring – your beauty certainly is. Finally, to Hawkeye: I know you can't read, but having you by my side was the highlight of the trip. You're a good boy.

Greg Benchwick

This book wouldn't be possible without the support and love of my family. First and foremost, there's little Violeta 'Monkey Face' Benchwick, who continues to research the world with her wayward daddy. Thanks too to Sarah for making the trip to Estes and beyond, and to the lovely editors, writers and big thinkers at Lonely Planet.

Andrew Bender

Thanks to Denise Lengyeltoti, Christie Bacock, Melissa Perez, Jackie Alvarez, Jennifer Tong, Erin Ramsauer, Michael Ramirez, Jenny Wedge, Ashley Johnson and the many information center, hotel and restaurant staffers who gave me way more of their time than I deserved. In house, thanks especially to Clifton Wilkinson, Sarah Stocking, Anita Isalska, Judith Bamber and Kathryn Rowan.

Alison Bing

Thanks to Cliff Wilkinson, Sarah Sung, Lisa Park, DeeAnn Budney, PT Tenenbaum and, above all, Marco Flavio Marinucci, for making a Muni bus ride into the adventure of a lifetime.

Cristian Bonetto

A heartfelt thank you to the many Angelenos (and New Yorkers) who shared their LA secrets and insights with me, especially John-Mark Horton, Michael Amato, Andy Bender, Norge Yip, Calvin Yeung, Douglas Levine, Daphne Barahona, Nicholas Maricich, David Singleman, William J Brockschmidt, Richard Dragisic and Andy Walker. Thanks also to fellow Aussies in

SoCal, Mary-ann Gardner and Natalie Yanoulis. At Lonely Planet, much gratitude to Cliff Wilkinson.

Celeste Brash

Thanks to my Aunt Kem and Uncle Ken for Susanville roots, Gerad in Mt Shasta City for great beer and info, countless friends and family for tips and suggestions, and my husband and kids for being the best people to come home to. Last but not least, big love to the glorious state of California, where my heart will always live.

Jade Bremner

Thanks to editor Clifton Wilkinson for his support and endless knowledge about Lonely Planet guidebooks, plus everyone working their socks off behind the scenes – Cheree Broughton, Dianne Schallmainer, Jane Grisman, Neill Coen, Evan Godt and Helen Elfer. Last, but not least, thanks to the friendly staff at Fig Tree Cafe for making those marvelous egg Bennies, which often set me up for the day.

Nate Cavalieri

Many thanks to my partner Florence, who is always game for a last-minute road trip to Bakersfield. Thanks to Cliff, Daniel, Jane, Dianne and the staff Lonely Planet for all the support and to my colleague Alison Bing, who inspired me to get back in the travel writing game after a long and ill-advised hiatus.

Michael Grosberg

Thanks especially to Carly, Rosie and Booney for keeping the home fires burning; and Carly especially for sharing her experiences as a forest ranger in Mammoth Lakes and Mono Lake all those years ago. Thanks also to Peter Bartelme of Yosemite Conservancy; Lisa Cesaro from Aramark; Joe Juszkiewicz at Rush Creek Lodge; Lauren Burke in Mammoth; Tawni Thompson in Bishop; and Julie Wright for help in Sequoia.

Ashley Harrell

Thanks to: my coauthors and editors for their diligence and support; the kind people all over Wine Country for their time and recommendations; David Roth and Andy Wright (dumb people) for the endless amusement; Amy Benziger for letting me trash her apartment; Shane Henegan for his glorious Airstream; Paul Stockamore for David Applebaum; Adele Fox for being the best Gumpy; Anne Murphy for sharing her ranch and wise and hilarious opinions; and Andy Lavender for his innumerable contributions and unrelenting care.

Carolyn McCarthy

Many thanks to the fine people of southern Colorado whose help and hospitality in mud season is highly appreciated. My gratitude goes out to Dave and Lyn in Telluride, Angela and Jim in Ouray, and Katie in Durango. *Gracias* to Sandra for her contributions to the hiking portion of the trip. *Hasta la próxima*, Colorado!

Becky Ohlsen

Thanks to dad for being the greatest research assistant thus far, and to all the various park rangers and campground officials who talked about the weather and gave reassurances about road conditions, Paul Bracke for over-the-top intel on Spokane, the previous authors of this chapter, and ace editor Alex Howard.

Christopher Pitts

Huge thanks to Debbie Lew for her Summit County connections, Melissa Wisenbaker in Aspen, Sara Stookey in Snowmass, and Sally Gunter in Vail. Also big thanks to the rest of the Colorado team for input, ideas and updates.

Liza Prado

Sincere thanks to the extraordinary Lonely Planet team, especially Alex Howard and my coauthors. Special thanks to my Coloradan friends Meghan Howes, Alexia Eslan, Samantha Lentz, Kate McGoldrick, Paisley Johnson, Darin Pitts and Rob Roberts for the inside scoop on some of your favorite places. *Mil gracias* to Mom, Dad, Joe, Elyse and Susan for your loving help with the kids. Big thanks to Eva and Leo for waiting so patiently for family movie night. And to Gary: thank you for your boundless love and support – you make my world turn.

Josephine Quintero

Thanks to Cliff Wilkinson for the opportunity of researching this fabulous region of California. Also to my road trip buddy, Robin Chapman and my good local resident pals who invaluably assisted me: Janice Crowe and Linda Sinclair. Also thanks to the helpful folk in the various visitor centers and, last but not least, those, at the SPP help desk when I had a serious technical glitch!

Andrea Schulte-Peevers

Big heartfelt thankyous go to the following people for their invaluable tips, insights and hospitality (in no particular order): Valerie Summers, Kristin Schmidt, Joyce Kiehl, Andrew Bender, Abigail Wines, Bruce Moore, Susan Witty, Brandy Marino and Mona Spicer.

Helena Smith

Many thanks to everyone who offered warm hospitality in the Gold Country and Lake Tahoe, most especially Naomi Terry for keeping us company, and Anna and her family for hospitality and local expertise. King was a great road-trip buddy, and so was Art Terry, who drove and DJed me round California, and made every exploration a joy.

John A Vlahides

Thanks to commissioning editor Clifton Wilkinson and my coauthor Alison Bing, with whom it's always lovely to work. And most of all, thanks to you, dear reader – you make my life so joyful and I'm grateful for the honor of being your guide through the cool gray city of love.

Benedict Walker

First and foremost, I'm forever grateful to Alex Howard, my destination editor on the other side of the planet, who found a space for me on this gig, knowing I loved the mountains, and who dealt with some weird challenges I threw at him with an air of calm and an absence of judgement that few of today's young men could muster. Thanks to Brad, my beautiful friend from Missoula, who reminded me that while many men wage wars, some put out fires, and some paint pictures with words. And thanks to the aliens of Nevada and Colorado for pushing me out of my comfort zone. It's a beautiful world out there, whatever we choose to focus on. And there is always more...

Clifton Wilkinson

Thanks to the Santa Barbara County tourism people (Karna, Danielle, Chrisie) who provided excellent recommendations, including my favorite meal of the whole update. Thanks too to all the inhouse LP team, especially colleagues who listened patiently to all my pre-trip plans. And final thanks to the weather, which mostly played along with my research – except for all the mud on Santa Cruz Channel Island (if anyone finds some sunglasses, they might be the ones I lost falling over).

ACKNOWLEDGEMENTS

Climate map data adapted from Peel MC, Finlayson BL & McMahon TA (2007) 'Updated World Map of the Köppen-Geiger Climate Classification', Hydrology and Earth System Sciences, 11, 163344.

Illustration pp312-13 by Michael Weldon.

Cover photograph: Grand Prismatic Spring, Yellowstone National Park; Yun Gao/500px.

BEHIND THE SCENES

THIS BOOK

This 4th edition of Lonely Planet's *Western USA* guidebook was researched and written by Hugh McNaughtan, Brett Atkinson, Loren Bell, Greg Benchwick, Andrew Bender, Sara Benson, Alison Bing, Cristian Bonetto, Celeste Brash, Jade Bremner, Nate Cavalieri, Michael Grosberg, Ashley Harrell, Carolyn McCarthy, Becky Ohlsen, Christopher Pitts, Liza Prado, Josephine Quintero, Andrea Schulte-Peevers, Helena Smith, John A Vlahides, Benedict Walker and Clifton Wilkinson. The previous edition was written by Amy C Balfour along with Sandra Bao, Sara Benson, Becky Ohlsen and Greg Ward. This guidebook was produced by the following:

Destination Editors Alexander Howard, Sarah Stocking, Clifton Wilkinson

Product Editors Kate Mathews, Ross Taylor

Senior Cartographer Alison Lyall

Book Designer Nicholas Colicchia

Assisting Editors Sarah Bailey, Hannah Cartmel, Andrew Bain, James Bainbridge, Judith Bamber, Imogen Bannister, Michelle Bennett, Nigel Chin, Melanie Dankel, Andrea Dobbin, Carly Hall, Victoria Harrison, Kellie Langdon, Ali Lemer, Jodie Martire, Rosie Nicholson, Monique Perrin, Sarah Reid, Saralinda Turner, Maja Vatric, Simon Williamson

Assisting Cartographer Valentina Kremenchutskaya

Cover Researcher Marika Mercer

Thanks to Grace Dobell, Anne Mason, Martine Power, Rachel Rawling, Valerie Stimac, Greg Thilmont, Tony Wheeler

Index

Map Legend

Sights

- Beach
- Bird Sanctuary
- Buddhist
- Castle/Palace
- Christian
- Confucian
- Hindu
- Islamic
- Jain
- Jewish
- Monument
- Museum/Gallery/Historic Building
- Ruin
- Shinto
- Sikh
- Taoist
- Winery/Vineyard
- Zoo/Wildlife Sanctuary
- Other Sight

Activities, Courses & Tours

- Bodysurfing
- Diving
- Canoeing/Kayaking
- Course/Tour
- Sento Hot Baths/Onsen
- Skiing
- Snorkeling
- Surfing
- Swimming/Pool
- Walking
- Windsurfing
- Other Activity

Sleeping

- Sleeping
- Camping

Eating

- Eating

Drinking & Nightlife

- Drinking & Nightlife
- Cafe

Entertainment

- Entertainment

Shopping

- Shopping

Information

- Bank
- Embassy/Consulate
- Hospital/Medical
- Internet
- Police
- Post Office
- Telephone
- Toilet
- Tourist Information
- Other Information

Geographic

- Beach
- Gate
- Hut/Shelter
- Lighthouse
- Lookout
- Mountain/Volcano
- Oasis
- Park
- Pass
- Picnic Area
- Waterfall

Population

- Capital (National)
- Capital (State/Province)
- City/Large Town
- Town/Village

Transport

- Airport
- BART station
- Border crossing
- Boston T station
- Bus
- Cable car/Funicular
- Cycling
- Ferry
- Metro/Muni station
- Monorail
- Parking
- Petrol station
- Subway/SkyTrain station
- Taxi
- Train station/Railway
- Tram
- Underground station
- Other Transport

Note: Not all symbols displayed above appear on the maps in this book

Routes

- Tollway
- Freeway
- Primary
- Secondary
- Tertiary
- Lane
- Unsealed road
- Road under construction
- Plaza/Mall
- Steps
- Tunnel
- Pedestrian overpass
- Walking Tour
- Walking Tour detour
- Path/Walking Trail

Boundaries

- International
- State/Province
- Disputed
- Regional/Suburb
- Marine Park
- Cliff
- Wall

Hydrography

- River, Creek
- Intermittent River
- Canal
- Water
- Dry/Salt/Intermittent Lake
- Reef

Areas

- Airport/Runway
- Beach/Desert
- Cemetery (Christian)
- Cemetery (Other)
- Glacier
- Mudflat
- Park/Forest
- Sight (Building)
- Sportsground
- Swamp/Mangrove

Becky Ohlsen
Pacific Northwest Becky is a freelance writer, editor and critic based in Portland, Oregon. She writes guidebooks and travel stories about Scandinavia, Portland and elsewhere for Lonely Planet. When she's not covering ground for Lonely Planet, Becky is working on a book about motorcycles and the paradoxical appeal of risk.

Christopher Pitts
Central Colorado, New Mexico Chris's first expedition in life ended in failure when he tried to dig from Pennsylvania to China at the age of six. He went on to study Chinese in university, living for several years in China. He spent more than a decade in Paris with his wife and two children before the lure of Colorado's sunny skies and outdoor adventure proved too great to resist·

Liza Prado
Colorado, Liza has been a travel writer since 2003, when she made a move from corporate lawyering to travel writing. She's written dozens of guidebooks and articles to destinations throughout the Americas. She lives very happily in Denver, Colorado, with her husband and fellow writer, Gary Chandler, and their two kids.

Josephine Quintero
California's North Coast & Redwoods Josephine first got her taste of not-so-serious travel when she slung a guitar on her back and traveled in Europe in the early '70s, along the way working on a kibbutz in Israel and meeting her husband. She primarily covers Spain and Italy for Lonely Planet.

Andrea Schulte-Peevers
The Deserts Born and raised in Germany and educated in London and at UCLA, Andrea has traveled the distance to the moon and back in her visits to some 75 countries. She has earned her living as a professional travel writer for more than two decades and authored or contributed to nearly 100 Lonely Planet titles.

Helena Smith
Lake Tahoe, Gold Country Helena is an award-winning writer and photographer covering travel, outdoors and food. Helena is from Scotland but was partly brought up in Malawi, so Africa always feels like home. She also enjoys living in multicultural Hackney and wrote, photographed and published *Inside Hackney*.

John A Vlahides
San Francisco John has been a cook in a Parisian bordello, luxury-hotel concierge, television host, safety monitor in a sex club, French–English interpreter, and is one of Lonely Planet's most experienced guidebook authors. When not talking travel, John sings with the San Francisco Symphony, and spends free time in the Sierra Nevada.

Benedict Walker
Nevada Berlin-based Ben grew up in the 'burbs of Australia, spending weekends and long summers by the beach, and while he's magnetically drawn to big mountains, beach life is in his blood. Ben thinks that the best thing about travel isn't as much about where you go as who you meet: living vicariously through the stories of kind strangers really adds to one's own experience.

Clifton Wilkinson
Santa Barbara County Clifton has been in love with California since first visiting in 1995. Christmases spent near Sacramento, bike rides across the Golden Gate Bridge and hiking in Yosemite National Park have all reinforced Clifton's opinion that the Golden State is the best state in the whole US, and Santa Barbara is one of its most beautiful corners. Having worked for Lonely Planet for more than 11 years, he's now based in the London office, but hoping for the call back to CA's *Sideways* country and the chance to show that Merlot isn't all that bad.

Sara Benson
Marin County & the Bay Area, Coastal California The author of more than 70 travel and non-fiction books, Sara's writing has featured in national and international newspapers and magazines, including numerous Lonely Planet titles, CNN and *National Geographic Adventure*, as well as on popular travel websites such as Jetsetter.

Alison Bing
San Francisco Over 10 guidebooks and 20 years in San Francisco, author Alison Bing has spent more time on Alcatraz than some inmates, become an aficionado of drag and burritos, and willfully ignored Muni signs warning that safety requires avoiding unnecessary conversation.

Cristian Bonetto
Los Angeles, Southern California Cristian has contributed to more than 30 Lonely Planet guides, while his musings on travel, food, culture and design appear in numerous publications around the world. When not on the road, you'll find the reformed playwright and TV scriptwriter slurping espresso in his beloved hometown, Melbourne.

Celeste Brash
California's Northern Mountains Celeste has been writing guidebooks for Lonely Planet since 2005 and her travel articles have appeared in publications from BBC Travel to *National Geographic*. She's currently writing a book about her five years on a remote pearl farm in the Tuamotu.

Jade Bremner
San Diego Jade has been a journalist for more than a decade, and has edited travel magazines and sections for Time Out and Radio Times, and worked as a correspondent for *The Times*, CNN and *The Independent*. She feels privileged to share tales from this wonderful planet we call home and is always looking for the next adventure.

Nate Cavalieri
Sacramento A writer and musician based in California, Nate has authored over a dozen titles for Lonely Planet, including *Epic Bike Rides of the World*. He's cycled across China and Southern Africa as a guide with Tour d'Afrique and played third chair percussion in an Orlando theme park.

Michael Grosberg
Yosemite & the Sierra Nevada A prolific Lonely Planet author, Michael's other international work prior to his freelance writing career included development on the island of Rota in the western Pacific; investigating and writing about political violence in South Africa; and teaching in Ecuador. He has a Masters in Comparative Literature, and has taught literature and writing as an adjunct professor.

Ashley Harrell
Napa & Sonoma Wine Country, Northern California After studying journalism and working as a reporter, Ashley traveled widely and moved often, from a tiny NYC apartment to a vast California ranch to a jungle cabin in Costa Rica, where she started writing for Lonely Planet. From there her travels have only become more exotic.

Carolyn McCarthy
Colorado Specializing in travel, culture and adventure in the Americas, Carolyn has has contributed to forty guidebooks and anthologies for Lonely Planet, and written or *National Geographic*, *Outside*, *BBC Magazine*, *Sierra Magazine*, *Boston Globe* and other publications.

OUR STORY

A beat-up old car, a few dollars in the pocket and a sense of adventure. In 1972 that's all Tony and Maureen Wheeler needed for the trip of a lifetime – across Europe and Asia overland to Australia. It took several months, and at the end – broke but inspired – they sat at their kitchen table writing and stapling together their first travel guide, *Across Asia on the Cheap*. Within a week they'd sold 1500 copies. Lonely Planet was born.

Today, Lonely Planet has offices in Franklin, London, Melbourne, Oakland, Dublin, Beijing and Delhi, with more than 600 staff and writers. We share Tony's belief that 'a great guidebook should do three things: inform, educate and amuse'.

OUR WRITERS

Hugh McNaughtan

Curator, Arizona A former English lecturer, Hugh swapped grant applications for visa applications and turned his love of travel into a full-time thing. He's never happier than when on the road with his two daughters. Except perhaps on the cricket field...

Brett Atkinson

California's Central Coast Based in New Zealand, but frequently on the road for Lonely Planet, Brett's a full-time travel and food writer specialising in adventure travel, unusual destinations, and surprising angles on more well-known destinations. Craft beer and street food are Brett's favorite reasons to explore places.

Loren Bell

Rocky Mountains, Idaho, Montana, Wyoming When Loren first backpacked through Europe, he was in the backpack. That memorable experience corrupted his six-month-old brain, ensuring he would never be happy sitting still. When he's not demystifying destinations for Lonely Planet, Loren writes about science and conservation news.

Greg Benchwick

Northern Colorado A long-time Lonely Planet travel writer, Greg has rumbled in the jungles of Bolivia, trekked across Spain on the Camino de Santiago, interviewed presidents and grammy-award winners, dodged flying salmon in Alaska and climbed mountains (big and small) in between.

Andrew Bender

Los Angeles; Disneyland & Orange County Award-winning travel and food writer Andrew Bender has written three-dozen Lonely Planet guidebooks (from Amsterdam to Los Angeles, Germany to Taiwan and more than a dozen titles about Japan), plus numerous articles for lonelyplanet.com.

OVER PAGE | MORE WRITERS

Published by Lonely Planet Global Limited
CRN 554153
4th edition – April 2018
ISBN 978 1 78657 461 9
© Lonely Planet 2018   Photographs © as indicated 2018
10 9 8 7 6 5 4 3 2 1
Printed in China